W9-BXD-825

Harper's Encyclopedia of Religious Education

Harper's Encyclopedia of Religious Education

General Editors

Iris V. Cully
Kendig Brubaker Cully

1817

Harper & Row, Publishers, San Francisco

New York, Grand Rapids, Philadelphia, St. Louis
London, Singapore, Sydney, Tokyo, Toronto

Credits continue on p. 717 and are considered a continuation of this copyright page.

FIRST EDITION

Library of Congress Cataloging-in-Publication Data

Harper's encyclopedia of religious education/general editors, Iris V. Cully,
  Kendig Brubaker Cully.
    p. cm.
  ISBN 0–00–606165–6 :
  1. Christian education—Dictionaries. I. Cully, Iris V. II. Cully, Kendig
Brubaker. III. Title: Encyclopedia of religious education.
BV1461.H37 1990
268'.03—dc20   89-45392
                                                    CIP

---

90 91 92 93 94 HAD 10 9 8 7 6 5 4 3 2 1

This edition is printed on acid-free paper which meets the American National Standards Institute Z39.48 Standard.

For all those who are called to the
ministry of religious education

Editorial Board

Randolph Crump Miller, Ph.D.
Horace Bushnell Professor of Christian Nurture, Emeritus
The Yale Divinity School
The Yale University
New Haven, Connecticut

David Ng, M.Div.
Professor of Christian Education
San Francisco Theological Seminary
San Anselmo, California

Grant S. Shockley, Ed.D.
Professor Emeritus of Christian Education
The Divinity School
Duke University
Durham, North Carolina

Margaret Webster, Ph.D.
Principal and Professor of Christian Education, Emerita
Ewart College
Toronto, Ontario, Canada

Contributors

Gordon L. Anderson, Ph.D.
  Secretary General
  Professors World Peace Academy
  New York, New York

Tosh Arai, S.T.M.
  Secretary for Lay and Study Centers
  World Council of Churches
  Geneva, Switzerland

Helen A. Archibald, Ph.D.
  Associate Professor of Educational Ministry
  United Theological Seminary of the Twin
    Cities
  New Brighton, Minnesota

Isa Aron, Ph.D.
  Associate Professor of Jewish Education
  Hebrew Union College–Jewish Institute of
    Religion
  Los Angeles, California

Joseph D. Ban, Ph.D.
  Professor of Christian Ministry
  Divinity College
  McMaster University
  Hamilton, Ontario, Canada

Glenn Q. Bannerman, M.R.E.
  Professor of Recreation and Outdoor
    Education
  Presbyterian School of Christian Education
  Richmond, Virginia

Lucie W. Barber, Ed.D.
  Vice-President
  Personality Research Services
  Schenectady, New York

William R. Barr, Ph.D.
  Professor of Theology
  Lexington Theological Seminary
  Lexington, Kentucky

William E. Barrick, Ed.D.
  Professor of Religion
  McMurry College
  Abilene, Texas

Howard B. Basler, M.A.
  Director of Social Action
  Roman Catholic Diocese of Brooklyn
  Monsignor
  St. Andrew the Apostle Church
  Brooklyn, New York

Ross T. Bender, Ph.D.
  Professor of Christian Education
  Goshen Biblical Seminary
  Elkhart, Indiana

John C. Bennett, S.T.M.
  President Emeritus and Reinhold Niebuhr
    Professor of Social Ethics, Emeritus
  Union Theological Seminary
  New York, New York

Warren S. Benson, Ph.D.
  Vice-President, Academic Administration
  Trinity Evangelical Divinity School
  Deerfield, Illinois

Jerome W. Berryman, J.D.
  Canon Educator
  Christ Church Cathedral
  Houston, Texas

Leonard J. Biallas, S.T.D.
  Professor and Chair, Department of
    Theology and Religious Studies
  Quincy College
  Quincy, Illinois

Christine Eaton Blair, Ph.D.
  Assistant Professor in Church Ministry and
    Director of the Doctor of Ministry and
    Continuing Education Program
  Austin Presbyterian Theological Seminary
  Austin, Texas

Donald G. Bloesch, Ph.D.
  Professor of Theology
  University of Dubuque Theological
    Seminary
  Dubuque, Iowa

Sherry H. Blumberg, M.A.
Instructor in Jewish Education
Hebrew Union College–Jewish Institute of
Religion
New York, New York

Roger S. Boraas, Ph.D.
Professor of Religion
Upsala College
East Orange, New Jersey

Doris Cox Borchert, M.R.E.
Assistant Professor of Christian Education
The Southern Baptist Theological Seminary
Louisville, Kentucky

Locke E. Bowman, Jr., M.Div.
Professor of Christian Education and
Pastoral Theology
Virginia Theological Seminary
Alexandria, Virginia

Mary C. Boys, S.N.J.M., Ed.D.
Associate Professor of Theology and
Religious Education
Boston College
Chestnut Hill, Massachusetts

Jean Bozeman, M.A.
Professor of Educational Ministry and Dean
of Students
Lutheran School of Theology at Chicago
Chicago, Illinois

Ritamary Bradley, Ph.D.
Professor Emerita of English
St. Ambrose University
Davenport, Iowa

Georgia W. Brandstadter-Palmer, Ph.D.
Director, Forensic In-Jail Treatment
Program
Pinellas County Jail
Pinellas County Sheriff's Department
North Clearwater, Florida

Anne Hall Brautigam, Ed.D.
Former Director
Good Shepherd Day School
Lexington, Kentucky

Richard K. Brautigam, Ph.D.
Associate Professor
College of Social Work
University of Kentucky
Lexington, Kentucky

Evelyn H. Broadbent, M.A.
Consultant
Dance in Religion
Claremont, California

Loren Broadus, B.D.
Professor of the Practice of Ministry
Lexington Theological Seminary
Lexington, Kentucky

George Brown, Jr., Ph.D.
Dean of Faculty and Adjunct Professor of
Christian Education
Western Theological Seminary
Holland, Missouri

Marion E. Brown, Ph.D.
Former Professor of Practical Theology and
Christian Education
Saint Paul School of Theology
Kansas City, Missouri

Robert L. Browning, Ph.D.
Professor Emeritus of Christian Education
The Methodist Theological School in Ohio
Delaware, Ohio

Mary Charles Bryce, O.S.B., Ph.D.
Vocations Office
Archdiocese of Oklahoma City
Oklahoma City, Oklahoma

Francis J. Buckley, S.J., S.T.D.
Professor and Chairman of the Department
of Theology and Religious Studies
University of San Francisco
San Francisco, California

Harold W. Burgess, Ph.D.
Dean of Leadership Ministries
Asbury Theological Seminary
Wilmore, Kentucky

Jane Burton, B.A.
Director, Media and Interpretation
Church Women United
New York, New York

John C. Bush, D.Min.
Executive Director
Kentucky Council of Churches
Lexington, Kentucky

Richard C. Bush, Ph.D.
  Dean and Professor Emeritus
  School of Religion
  Oklahoma City University
  Oklahoma City, Oklahoma

Russell A. Butkus, Ph.D.
  Director, Program in Christian Religious
    Education and Pastoral Studies
  University of Portland
  Portland, Oregon

James A. Carr, D.Min.
  Associate Pastor
  Laurel Heights United Methodist Church
  San Antonio, Texas

Howard Clinebell, Ph.D.
  Professor Emeritus of Pastoral Psychology
    and Counseling
  School of Theology at Claremont
  Claremont, California

George W. Coats, Ph.D.
  Professor of Old Testament
  Lexington Theological Seminary
  Lexington, Kentucky

Burton I. Cohen, Ph.D.
  Assistant Professor of Jewish Education
  Jewish Theological Seminary of America
  New York, New York

Regina Coll, C.S.J., Ed.D.
  Director of Field Education
  University of Notre Dame
  South Bend, Indiana

Robert L. Conrad, Ph.D.
  Professor of Educational Ministry
  Lutheran School of Theology at Chicago
  Chicago, Illinois

John W. Cook, Ph.D.
  Professor of Religion and the Arts
  Yale University
  New Haven, Connecticut

Ronald H. Cram, Ph.D.
  Associate Professor of Christian Education
    and Director of Continuing Education
  Presbyterian School of Christian Education
  Richmond, Virginia

Paul A. Crow, Jr., Ph.D.
  President, Council on Christian Unity
  Christian Church (Disciples of Christ)
  Indianapolis, Indiana

Iris V. Cully, Ph.D.
  Professor of Christian Education
  Lexington Theological Seminary
  Lexington, Kentucky

Kendig Brubaker Cully, Ph.D.
  Rector/Dean Emeritus
  Episcopal Theological Seminary in Kentucky
  Lexington, Kentucky

William Cutter, Ph.D.
  Professor of Education and Hebrew
    Language and Literature
  Hebrew Union College–Jewish Institute of
    Religion
  Los Angeles, California

Eleanor A. Daniel, Ph.D.
  Professor of Christian Education
  Cincinnati Bible College and Seminary
  Cincinnati, Ohio

Boyd L. Daniels, Ph.D.
  Former Executive Secretary of Library
    Services
  American Bible Society
  New York, New York

Linda-Marie Delloff, Ph.D.
  Former Managing Editor
  The Christian Century
  Chicago, Illinois

Bruce J. Deverell, D.Min.
  Minister
  St. Andrew's Church
  Suva, Fiji

Dennis H. Dirks, Ph.D.
  Associate Dean and Associate Professor of
    Christian Education
  Talbot School of Theology
  La Mirada, California

Edward G. Dobson, Ed.D.
  Senior Minister
  Calvary Church
  Grand Rapids, Michigan

Catherine Dooley, O.P., Ph.D.
Associate Professor
School of Religious Studies
Catholic University of America
Washington, District of Columbia

David C. Duncombe, Ph.D.
Executive Director
Landberg Center for Health and Ministry
University of California, San Francisco
San Francisco, California

Gloria Durka, Ph.D.
Professor of Religious Education
Graduate School of Religion and Religious
Education
Fordham University
Bronx, New York

Craig R. Dykstra, Ph.D.
Vice-President, Religion
Lilly Endowment, Inc.
Indianapolis, Indiana

David L. Edwards, M.Div.
Minister
First Christian Church (Disciples of Christ)
Lynchburg, Virginia

John L. Elias, Ed.D.
Professor of Adult Religious Education
Fordham University
Bronx, New York

Paul Elmen, Ph.D.
Professor Emeritus of Moral Theology
Seabury-Western Theological Seminary
Evanston, Illinois

Donald G. Emler, Ed.D.
Dean and Professor of Christian Education
Wimberly School of Religion
Oklahoma City University
Oklahoma City, Oklahoma

Jerome M. Epstein, Ed.D.
Executive Vice-President
United Synagogue of America
New York, New York

Toinette M. Eugene, Ph.D.
Associate Professor of Practical Theology
and Culture
Chicago Theological Seminary
Chicago, Illinois

Til Evans
Professor of Religious Education
Star King School for the Ministry
Berkeley, California

Burton Everist, S.T.M.
Pastor
Grace Lutheran Church
East Dubuque, Illinois

Norma Cook Everist, Ph.D.
Associate Professor of Educational Ministry
Wartburg Theological Seminary
Dubuque, Iowa

Gabriel Fackre, Ph.D.
Abbot Professor of Christian Theology
Andover Newton Theological School
Newton Centre, Massachusetts

Eva Fogelman, Ph.D.
Director, Jewish Foundation for Christian
Rescuers
Anti-Defamation League of B'nai B'rith
New York, New York

William E. Foreman, M.Div.
Executive Associate Pastor
First Presbyterian Church
Orlando, Florida

Gerald E. Forshey, Ph.D.
Professor of Humanities
Malcolm X College
City Colleges of Chicago
Chicago, Illinois

Charles R. Foster, Ed.D.
Professor of Christian Education
Garrett-Evangelical Theological Seminary
Evanston, Illinois

Newton B. Fowler, Jr., Ph.D.
Professor of Ethics and Society
Lexington Theological Seminary
Lexington, Kentucky

Thomas A. Francoeur, Ed.D.
Professor, Faculty of Education
McGill University
Montreal, Quebec, Canada

Reginald H. Fuller, S.T.D.
Professor Emeritus of New Testament
Protestant Episcopal Theological Seminary
in Virginia
Alexandria, Virginia

Dorothy Jean Furnish, Ph.D.
    Professor Emerita of Christian Education
    Garrett-Evangelical Theological Seminary
    Evanston, Illinois

Thomas G. Gallagher, P.D.Ed.
    Secretary for Education
    U.S. Catholic Conference
    Washington, District of Columbia

Chamindaji P. Gamage, Ph.D.
    Department of the History and Literature
        of Religions
    Northwestern University
    Evanston, Illinois

Kenneth O. Gangel, Ph.D.
    Professor and Chairman, Department of
        Christian Education
    Dallas Theological Seminary
    Dallas, Texas

Freda A. Gardner, M.R.E.
    Professor of Christian Education
    Princeton Theological Seminary
    Princeton, New Jersey

Elizabeth Steele Genné, M.A.
    Past President
    Young Women's Christian Association of
        the U.S.A.
    Claremont, California

William H. Gentz, M.Th.
    Author and Editor
    New York, New York

Emily V. Gibbes, M.R.E.
    Former Associate General Secretary
    National Council of the Churches of Christ
        in the U.S.A.
    Former Professor of Religious Education
    New York Theological Seminary
    New York, New York

Loretta E. Girzaitis, M.A.
    Director of Adult Education
    Archdiocese of St. Paul and Minneapolis
    St. Paul, Minnesota

Robert F. Glover, M.Div.
    Executive for Christian Education
    Division of Homeland Ministries
    Christian Church (Disciples of Christ)
    Indianapolis, Indiana

Nahum Dov Goldberg, M.Phil.
    Doctoral Candidate
    Jewish Theological Seminary of America
    New York, New York

Millie S. Goodson, Ph.D.
    Former Associate Professor of Christian
        Education
    Scarritt Graduate School
    Nashville, Tennessee

Julie A. Gorman, D.Min.
    Assistant Professor of Christian Formation
        and Discipleship
    Fuller Theological Seminary
    Pasadena, California

Ronald W. Graham, Ph.D.
    Professor Emeritus of New Testament
    Lexington Theological Seminary
    Lexington, Kentucky

Denham Grierson, D.Rel.
    Lecturer in Education
    United Faculty of Theology, Melbourne
    Kilda, Victoria, Australia

Donald L. Griggs, D.Min.
    Griggs Educational Service
    Livermore, California
    Adjunct Professor
    Pacific School of Religion
    Berkeley, California

Patricia Griggs
    Griggs Educational Service
    Livermore, California

Thomas H. Groome, Ed.D.
    Associate Professor of Theology and
        Religious Education
    Boston College
    Chestnut Hill, Massachusetts

Mim Hanson, M.A.
    Curriculum Editor
    Harper & Row, Publishers, Inc.
    Minneapolis, Minnesota

John Harrell, M.Div.
    Author and Producer
    Berkeley, California

Walter Harrelson, Th.D.
Distinguished Professor of Hebrew Bible
The Divinity School
Vanderbilt University
Nashville, Tennessee

Mark Harris, M.Div.
Coordinator for Overseas Personnel
Episcopal Church Center
New York, New York

Richard L. Harrison, Jr., Ph.D.
Associate Professor of Church History
The Divinity School
Vanderbilt University
Nashville, Tennessee

Warren J. Hartman, M.Div.
Former Executive Secretary, Office of
Research
Board of Discipleship
United Methodist Church
Nashville, Tennessee

Maynard F. Hatch, II, Ph.D.
Professor of Religious Education
Central Baptist Theological Seminary
Kansas City, Kansas

Richard E. Hayes, M.Div.
Deputy for Congregational Life
Episcopal Diocese of Southwestern Virginia
Roanoke, Virginia

Shirley J. Heckman, Ph.D.
Former Staff for Education
General Board
Church of the Brethren
Elgin, Illinois

Rachel Henderlite, Ph.D.
Former Professor of Christian Education
Austin Presbyterian Theological Seminary
Austin, Texas

Homer Dimon Henderson, D.Min.
Senior Pastor
Claremont United Church of Christ
Claremont, California

John D. Hendrix, Ed.D.
Basil Manly Jr. Professor of Christian
Education
The Southern Baptist Theological Seminary
Louisville, Kentucky

Grace H. Henley, Esq., LL.D.
President
Helps Ministry–Alpha House
Mount Vernon, New York

Marina A. Herrera, Ph.D.
Lecturer, Consultant, and Writer
Washington Theological Union
Silver Spring, Maryland

E. Glenn Hinson, D.Phil.
David T. Porter Professor of Church
History
The Southern Baptist Theological Seminary
Louisville, Kentucky

David R. Hunter, Ed.D.
Former Deputy General Secretary
National Council of the Churches of Christ
in the U.S.A.
New York, New York

John A. Hutchison, Ph.D.
Professor Emeritus of Philosophy of
Religion
The Claremont Graduate School
The Claremont Colleges
Claremont, California

Carol Rose Ikeler, M.Div.
Director, Office of Family Ministries
Presbyterian Church (U.S.A.)
Louisville, Kentucky

Paul B. Irwin, Ed.D.
Professor Emeritus of Christian Education
School of Theology at Claremont
Claremont, California

Jonathan Jackson, Th.D.
Professor of Christian Education and Area
Chairperson
Interdenominational Theological Seminary
Atlanta, Georgia

Steve F. Jackson
Director of Television Ministry
First United Methodist Church
Pasadena, California
Former Professor of Communications
School of Theology at Claremont
Claremont, California

Walter Jacob, D.H.L.
Senior Rabbi
Rodef Shalom Congregation
Pittsburgh, Pennsylvania

Steven L. Jacobs, D.H.L.
Rabbi
Temple Emanu-El
Birmingham, Alabama

E. Alfred Jenkins, Ph.D.
Director of Doctoral Studies and Professor
of Education and Ministry
Northern Baptist Theological Seminary
Lombard, Illinois

Wendell G. Johnston, Th.D.
Vice-President for Planning and Research
Dallas Theological Seminary
Dallas, Texas

Alan W. Jones, Ph.D.
Dean
Grace Cathedral
San Francisco, California

Donald M. Joy, Ph.D.
Professor of Human Development
Ray and Mary Jo West Chair of Christian
Education
Asbury Theological Seminary
Wilmore, Kentucky

Earl Kaplan, M.A.H.L.
Rabbi
Temple Beth Israel
Pomona, California

Boardman W. Kathan, M.Div.
Former Executive Secretary
Religious Education Association of the
United States and Canada
New Haven, Connecticut
Associate Pastor
First Congregational Church
Cheshire, Connecticut

Richard E. Keady, Ph.D.
Professor of Religious Studies
San Jose State University
San Jose, California

Larry Keefauver, D.Min.
Senior Minister
First Christian Church
Lubbock, Texas

William Bean Kennedy, Ph.D.
Skinner and McAlpin Professor of Practical
Theology
Union Theological Seminary
New York, New York

Abdullah M. Khouj, Ph.D.
Director
The Islamic Center
Washington, District of Columbia

Ima Jean Kidd, M.A.
Director, Special Learning Needs
Outdoor Ministries
National Council of the Churches of Christ
in the U.S.A.
New York, New York

Chan-Hie Kim, Ph.D.
Associate Professor of New Testament and
Korean Studies
School of Theology at Claremont
Claremont, California

William Klempa, Ph.D.
Principal
The Presbyterian College
Faculty Lecturer in Theology
McGill University
Montreal, Quebec, Canada

Gerald E. Knoff, Ph.D.
Former Associate General Secretary
National Council of the Churches of Christ
in the U.S.A.
New York, New York

Ian Knox, Ph.D.
Special Lecturer
University of St. Michael's College
Toronto, Ontario, Canada

Charles E. S. Kraemer, D.D.
Former President
Presbyterian School of Christian Education
Richmond, Virginia

Manfred Kwiran, D. Theol.
Director
Religious Education Center
Braunschweig, West Germany

Erik F. Larson, B.A.
Executive Director
Boys Club of Buena Park
Buena Park, California

James Michael Lee, Ph.D.
Professor of Education
University of Alabama at Birmingham
Birmingham, Alabama

Sara S. Lee, M.A.
  Director
  Rhea Hirsch School of Education
  Hebrew Union College–Jewish Institute of
    Religion
  Los Angeles, California

William J. Leffler, II
  Former Rabbi
  Temple Adath Israel
  Lexington, Kentucky

Sara P. Little, Ph.D.
  Critz Professor Emerita of Christian
    Education
  Union Theological Seminary in Virginia
  Richmond, Virginia

James E. Loder, Ph.D.
  Professor of Christian Education
  Princeton Theological Seminary
  Princeton, New Jersey

Charles Henry Long, S.T.M.
  Director
  Forward Movement Publications
  Cincinnati, Ohio

Alan B. Loux, B.A.
  Assistant to the President
  Inter-Varsity Christian Fellowship
  Madison, Wisconsin

Mary A. Love, M.R.E.
  Editor of Church School Literature
  African Methodist Episcopal Zion Church
  Charlotte, North Carolina

Nancy Grieg Ludwig, M.M.
  Associate Organist
  The Cathedral of the Incarnation
  Garden City, New York

Robert Ludwig, M.M.
  Organist and Master of the Choirs
  The Cathedral of the Incarnation
  Garden City, New York

Joseph S. Lukinsky, Ed.D.
  Professor of Education
  Jewish Theological Seminary of America
  Teachers College, Columbia University
  New York, New York

Bruno V. Manno, Ph.D.
  Chief of Staff
  Office of Educational Research and
    Improvement
  U.S. Department of Education
  Washington, District of Columbia

Jeffrey K. Marheine
  Group Leader
  Boy Scouts of America
  Hermosa Beach, California

Berard L. Marthaler, Ph.D.
  Professor of Religion and Religious
    Education
  Catholic University of America
  Washington, District of Columbia

Steele W. Martin, S.T.M.
  Priest-in-Charge
  St. Stephen's Episcopal Church
  Providence, Rhode Island

Martin E. Marty, Ph.D.
  Fairfax M. Cone Distinguished Service
    Professor
  University of Chicago
  Chicago, Illinois

Sondra Higgins Matthaei, Ph.D.
  Assistant Professor of Christian Religious
    Education
  Saint Paul School of Theology
  Kansas City, Missouri

Lester G. McAllister, Th.D.
  Professor Emeritus of Church History
  Christian Theological Seminary
  Indianapolis, Indiana

J. Bardarah McCandless, Ph.D.
  Professor of Religion and Chair of the
    Department of Religion and Philosophy
  Westminster College
  New Wilmington, Pennsylvania

Taylor McConnell, Th.D.
  Professor of Christian Education
  Garrett-Evangelical Theological Seminary
  Evanston, Illinois

Ruth McDowell, M.S.
  Curriculum Resource
  United Methodist Publishing House
  Nashville, Tennessee

Edward N. McNulty, M.Div.
Pastor
First Presbyterian Church
Westfield, New York

Bernard E. Michel, M.Div.
Former Director of Publications
Moravian Church
Bethlehem, Pennsylvania

Donald E. Miller, Ph.D.
General Secretary
Church of the Brethren
Elgin, Illinois

Harriet L. Miller, Ph.D.
Professor Emeritus of Christian Education
United Theological Seminary
Dayton, Ohio

Randolph Crump Miller, Ph.D.
Horace Bushnell Professor of Christian
Nurture, Emeritus
The Divinity School
Yale University
New Haven, Connecticut

Leonel L. Mitchell, Th.D.
Professor of Liturgics
Seabury-Western Theological Seminary
Evanston, Illinois

Joseph Monti, Ph.D.
Associate Professor of Christian Ethics
The School of Theology
The University of the South
Sewanee, Tennessee

Allen J. Moore, Ph.D.
Dean and E. Stanley Jones Professor of
Missions and Education
School of Theology at Claremont
Claremont, California

Mary Elizabeth Moore, Ph.D.
Professor of Theology and Christian
Education
School of Theology at Claremont
Claremont, California

Gabriel Moran, Ph.D.
Director, Program of Religious Education
New York University
New York, New York

Nelle Morton, M.A.
Former Professor of Religious Education
Theological School
Drew University
Madison, New Jersey

Melissa Cully Mueller, M.A.
Doctoral Candidate
University of Toledo
Toledo, Ohio

John M. Mulder, Ph.D.
President and Professor of Historical
Theology
Louisville Presbyterian Theological Seminary
Louisville, Kentucky

Lewis A. Myers, Ph.D.
Professor
The Westminster Schools
Atlanta, Georgia

Marie Augusta Neal, S.N.D., Ph.D.
Professor of Sociology
Emmanuel College
Boston, Massachusetts

C. Ellis Nelson, Ph.D.
Visiting Professor of Christian Education
Austin Presbyterian Theological Seminary
Austin, Texas

David Ng, M.Div.
Professor of Christian Education
San Francisco Theological Seminary
San Anselmo, California

Greer Anne Ng, Ph.D.
Assistant Professor of Educational
Ministries and Director of Lay Education
Vancouver School of Theology
Vancouver, British Columbia, Canada

Kathleen A. O'Gorman, Ed.D.
Assistant Professor of Religious Education
and Religious Studies
Loyola University
New Orleans, Louisiana

Robert T. O'Gorman, Ph.D.
Lecturer in Christian Education
The Divinity School
Vanderbilt University
Nashville, Tennessee

Dan D. Rhoades, Ph.D.
  Professor of Ethics
  School of Theology at Claremont
  Claremont, California

Michael J. Roffina, M.Div.
  Associate Pastor
  Immanuel Presbyterian Church
  Los Angeles, California

Wayne R. Rood, Th.D.
  Former Professor of Religious Education
  Pacific School of Religion
  Berkeley, California

Lucy A. Rose, D.Min.
  Assistant Professor of Worship and
    Preaching
  Columbia Theological Seminary
  Decatur, Georgia

B. Keith Rowe, S.T.D.
  Former Principal
  Trinity Methodist Theological College
  Auckland, New Zealand

J. Cy Rowell, Ph.D.
  Associate Professor of Religious Education
  Brite Divinity School
  Texas Christian University
  Fort Worth, Texas

John S. Ruef, Th.D.
  Chaplain and Dean of Instruction
  Chatham Hall
  Chatham, Virginia

Beatrice Price Russell, B.S.
  Spanish Trails Council
  Girl Scouts of America
  Claremont, California

Letty M. Russell, Th.D.
  Professor of Theology
  The Divinity School
  Yale University
  New Haven, Connecticut

Don E. Saliers, Ph.D.
  Professor of Theology and Worship
  Emory University
  Atlanta, Georgia

Marianne Sawicki, Ph.D.
  Former Professor of Religious Education
  Lexington Theological Seminary
  Lexington, Kentucky

Margaret M. Sawin, Ed.D.
  Visiting Professor
  Family Life Education
  The Philippines

William J. Schmidt, Ph.D.
  Professor of Theology
  St. Peter's College
  Jersey City, New Jersey

Ruby J. Schroeder, M.Div.
  Associate Professor of Christian Education
  Eden Theological Seminary
  Webster Groves, Missouri

Delbert Schulz, M.A.
  Director, Lutheran School Services
  Visiting Professor in Education
  California Lutheran University
  Thousand Oaks, California

Lois C. Seifert, B.A.
  Diaconal Minister
  United Methodist Church
  Claremont, California

Jack L. Seymour, Ph.D.
  Professor of Religious Education
  Garrett-Evangelical Theological Seminary
  Evanston, Illinois

Margaret L. Shafer, M.A.
  Staff Associate
  National Council of the Churches of Christ
    in the U.S.A.
  New York, New York

Grant S. Shockley, Ed.D.
  Professor Emeritus of Christian Education
  The Divinity School
  Duke University
  Durham, North Carolina

Henry C. Simmons, Ph.D.
  Professor of Religion and Aging
  Presbyterian School of Christian Education
  Richmond, Virginia

Peter W. Sipple, Ph.D.
  Headmaster
  Salisbury School
  Salisbury, Connecticut

Gerald H. Slusser, Ph.D.
Professor Emeritus of Theology and
Education
Eden Theological Seminary
St. Louis, Missouri

Gregory A. Smith, Ph.D.
Research Scientist
Wisconsin Center for Educational Research
Madison, Wisconsin

Joanmarie C. Smith, Ph.D.
Professor of Christian Education
Methodist Theological School in Ohio
Delaware, Ohio

W. Alan Smith, D.Min.
Assistant Professor of Religion
Florida Southern College
Lakeland, Florida

Clarence H. Snelling, Jr., Ph.D.
Professor of Christian Education
Iliff School of Theology
Denver, Colorado

Jesse J. Sowell, Jr., Ph.D.
Chair, Department of Religion
Texas Wesleyan College
Fort Worth, Texas

John J. Spangler, D.Min.
Consultant for Special Ministries
Presbytery of Georgia
Atlanta, Georgia

Carolyn Wolf Spanier, M.A.
Doctoral Candidate
School of Theology at Claremont
Claremont, California

G. Temp Sparkman, Ed.D.
Professor of Religious Education
Midwestern Baptist Theological Seminary
Kansas City, Missouri

Janet Spector
Editorial Assistant
Young Women's Christian Association of
the U.S.A.
Chicago, Illinois

Glen H. Stassen, Ph.D.
Professor of Christian Ethics
The Southern Baptist Theological Seminary
Louisville, Kentucky

Robert W. Steffer, Ph.D.
Executive Minister
Christian Church (Disciples of Christ) in
Canada
Guelph, Ontario, Canada

Sonja M. Stewart, Ph.D.
Professor of Christian Education
Western Theological Seminary
Holland, Michigan

Kenneth Stokes, Ph.D.
Director of Adult Faith Resources and
Adjunct Professor
St. Paul Seminary School of Divinity
College of St. Thomas
Minneapolis, Minnesota

Jerry H. Stone, Ph.D.
McFee Professor of Religion
Illinois Wesleyan University
Bloomington, Illinois

Catherine Stonehouse, Ph.D.
Associate Professor of Christian Education
Asbury Theological Seminary
Wilmore, Kentucky

John N. Strout, Th.D.
Former Minister of Christian Education
United Methodist Church
Claremont, California

John P. Stump, M.Div.
Former Associate Secretary, Board of
Theological Education
Lutheran Church in America
New York, New York
Pastor
Lutheran Church of the Resurrection
Canoga Park, California

Marjorie Hewitt Suchocki, Ph.D.
Academic Dean
Wesley Theological Seminary
Washington, District of Columbia

Ralph R. Sundquist, Ph.D.
Sundquist Consultations
Bloomfield, Connecticut

William Tabbernee, Ph.D.
Principal
Churches of Christ Theological College
Mulgrave, Victoria, Australia

Constance Taraser
Lecturer in Religious Education
St. Vladimir's Orthodox Theological
Seminary
Crestwood, New York

Betty A. Thompson, B.A.
Director of Public Relations
United Methodist Board of Global
Ministries
New York, New York

Norma H. Thompson, Ph.D.
Professor Emerita of Religious Education
Program in Religious Education
New York University
New York, New York

Margaret Timmerman, M.H.S.H., M.A.
Director, Resource Department
Motherhouse of Mission Helpers of the
Sacred Heart
Baltimore, Maryland

Rosa Sofia Toledo, M.H.S.H., M.A.
Coordinator
Diocesan Catechetical Office
Caracas, Venezuela

Neil E. Topliffe, M.Div.
Executive Director of Communication
Services
Office of Communication
Christian Church (Disciples of Christ)
Indianapolis, Indiana

Suzanne C. Toton, Ed.D.
Associate Professor of Religious Education
Villanova University
Villanova, Pennsylvania

Herman Tull, Ph.D.
Assistant Professor of Religion
Rutgers University
New Brunswick, New Jersey

Arthur O. Van Eck, Ed.D.
Associate General Secretary, Division of
Education and Ministry
National Council of the Churches of Christ
in the U.S.A.
New York, New York

Kenneth Van Wyk, Ph.D.
Director, Theological Education Agency
Reformed Church in America
Orange, California
Ecclesiastical Professor
Fuller Theological Seminary
Pasadena, California

Barbara B. Varenhorst, Ph.D.
Consulting Psychologist
Portola Valley, California

Jack C. Verheyden, Ph.D.
Professor of Theology
School of Theology at Claremont
Claremont, California

Linda J. Vogel, Ph.D.
Associate Professor of Christian Education
Garrett-Evangelical Theological Seminary
Evanston, Illinois

Thomas P. Walters, Ph.D.
Associate Professor of Religious Education
St. Meinrad Seminary
St. Meinrad, Indiana

Keith Watkins, Th.D.
Professor of Worship
Christian Theological Seminary
Indianapolis, Indiana

Kenneth R. Watson, Ph.D.
Associate Regional Minister
Christian Church (Disciples of Christ),
Mid-America
Jefferson City, Missouri

David Allan Weadon, M.Mus.
Director of Music and Organist
Princeton Theological Seminary
Princeton, New Jersey

Hans-Ruedi Weber, D.Th.
Former Director for Biblical Studies
World Council of Churches
Geneva, Switzerland

Margaret Webster, Ph.D.
Principal and Professor of Christian
Education, Emerita
Ewart College
Toronto, Ontario, Canada

Louis Weeks, Ph.D.
 Dean of the Seminary and Paul Tudor
  Jones Professor of Church History
 Louisville Presbyterian Theological Seminary
 Louisville, Kentucky

Carol Swain Weir, M.A.
 Professor of Evangelism and Mission
 San Francisco Theological Seminary
 San Anselmo, California

John H. Westerhoff, III, Ed.D.
 Professor of Theology and Education
 The Divinity School
 Duke University
 Durham, North Carolina

William J. Whalen, M.S.J.
 Director of Publications and University
  Editor
 Director of the Purdue University Press
 Associate Professor of Communication
 Purdue University
 West Lafayette, Indiana

Susan J. White, Ph.D.
 Visiting Assistant Professor of Liturgics
 The School of Theology
 The University of the South
 Sewanee, Tennessee

William H. Willimon, Ph.D.
 Dean of the Chapel and Professor of
  Christian Ministry
 Duke University
 Durham, North Carolina

Vincent L. Wimbush, Ph.D.
 Associate Professor of New Testament
 School of Theology at Claremont
 Claremont, California

Douglas E. Wingeier, Ph.D.
 Professor of Practical Theology
 Garrett-Evangelical Theological Seminary
 Evanston, Illinois

Lincoln B. Wirt, B.D.
 Retired Minister
 United Church of Christ
 Claremont, California

F. Franklyn Wise, Ph.D.
 Professor Emeritus of Christian Education
 Olivet Nazarene University
 Kankakee, Illinois

Dorothea K. Wolcott, Ph.D.
 Professor Emerita of Christian Education
 Saint Paul School of Theology
 Kansas City, Missouri

Donald A. Wright, D.Min.
 Pastor
 Tustin Presbyterian Church
 Tustin, California

D. Campbell Wyckoff, Ph.D.
 Former Professor of Christian Education
 Princeton Theological Seminary
 Princeton, New Jersey

John B. Youngberg, Ed.D.
 Professor and Chair of the Department of
  Religious Education and Educational
  Foundations
 Andrews University
 Berrien Springs, Michigan

Michael Zeldin, Ph.D.
 Associate Professor of Jewish Education
 Hebrew Union College–Jewish Institute of
  Religion
 Los Angeles, California

Robert L. Zondervan, M.D.
 Psychiatrist
 Claremont, California

Preface

People engaged in the practice of religious education are always aware of the need for resource materials. A general volume that covers a wide range of materials has not often been available. This *Encyclopedia of Religious Education* is designed to fill the need.

The purpose of the book is to give both background and practical information. The 270 writers represented are scholars in the fields of Bible, theology, history, psychology, and religious education. They come from many religious traditions. They have practiced their disciplines in colleges and theological schools, churches and synagogues, and in the varied national and judicatory offices that are supportive of this work. Nearly 600 articles are offered here to enrich the work of those who read.

Many articles deal with basic biblical and theological ideas. Others deal with aspects of worship and celebration. History is developed both in extensive treatments and in small biographies of persons whose work has contributed to the field of religious education. One category of articles gives information about educational theory and practice in the context of religious education. Psychological development in its many aspects is the subject of a number of articles.

The intent of the book, however, goes beyond the imparting of information to offering readers ways of using this information in the teaching of religious education. This becomes apparent in a number of articles on specific methods and also in the inclusion of suggestions as to how biblical and theological insights can be related to the work of religious education. Charts and other illustrations further enhance the practical usefulness of the book.

For this reason, the book will become a major resource for lay and professionals who are teaching religious education classes in schools, churches, and synagogues. Clergy will find it a quick reference, supplementing other resources with specific information on educational matters. It can be used as text and resource for general courses in religious education in colleges and theological schools.

Many people in Claremont have provided supplementary information in their scholarly fields simply because a neighbor phoned and asked. All the reference librarians in town have been helpful, and I am particularly grateful to Jean Cobb at the School of Theology at Claremont, who patiently and cheerfully answered innumerable calls during the past two years. I have learned to appreciate computer networks.

An editorial board of ten people offered suggestions for content and writers in the early stages of the project. John B. Shopp, senior editor, and Kandace Hawkinson, associate editor at Harper & Row, were graciously sustaining to me in the lengthy work of completing the project.

This book was dreamed of and planned by my husband, Kendig Brubaker Cully, as the crowning achievement of more than thirty-five years of writing and editorial work. To complete this work has been my final gift for him, and his memorial.

Iris V. Cully

Harper's
Encyclopedia of
Religious Education

Action-Reflection

Since the introduction of Scholastic philosophy, Christian education has strongly emphasized the use of the mind as the route to knowledge of God's will. Today that limited and static view of education is broadly under attack around the world. Most Christian education in the Third World takes place with few library resources to expand the mind, but with much loving concern for the poor who are immediately present. Liberation theologians have labeled this process of education through active involvement as action-reflection learning. They claim that the basis of Christian education is active involvement with real people here and now and that theology as well as Christian education is done as one reflects on that activity. This action-reflection learning process is also known as praxis education. Action-reflection learning as a methodology for Christian education is very closely linked with education for social justice and for peace.

BEGINNING WITH ACTION

This process provides a counterpoint to the tendency of many North American educators to provide just the opposite—a reflection-action process of Christian education. Action-reflection education shifts the focus of the educational process from "content" to "context." We begin with our own and shared experience. It requires that we do not begin, deductively, with what our ancestors in the faith formulated. We begin with the actions and relationships in which our Christian life is grounded now.

In this approach to learning, Christian education is understood as evoking the church's growth as a liberating community and encouraging the development of its critical consciousness. It is the deliberate and sustained effort to communicate the gospel so that persons can accept or reject it. Thus, action-reflection education is centered in personal conversion as well as social transformation. The initial concern of action-reflection education should be centered on making justice and peace a constitutive dimension in every aspect of our curriculum and our programs.

Justice, from a Christian perspective, is realized when the truth is done in love. Justice is not achieved simply by knowing about the truth or love, but by doing the one in the other. In other words, if Christian education is to promote justice and peace through action-reflection, then it must invite people to decision, action, and commitment on behalf of justice and not simply to a body of new ideas. Such an invitation to praxis must be a deliberate and intentional part of the educational process and not merely implied, assumed, or left to chance.

This "invitation to decision" principle arises from the conviction that education for justice must arise from our own historical context, as well as be informed and empowered by the faith handed down by the Christian community. In light of this, not only should the action-reflection process of education invite decision, but, where possible and appropriate, the educational enterprise should provide opportunities for overt activities that will actually be a doing of the truth in love.

NAMING AND REFLECTING ON REALITY

A second tenet involved in action-reflection education entails inviting participants to express their own situation, to name their own reality. If only the teacher does the naming, then the learners are brought to the teacher's "knowing" rather than to their own. To fulfill this tenet of naming, the educational process must be one of dialogue and mutuality between all of the participants in the learning context. Of necessity, there must be a group of people who are "with" each other in dialogue as co-learners.

A third principle for action-reflection learning engages the component of critical reflection. Having named reality, the participants must be brought to reflect critically upon what they have named out of their own experience. Without critical reflection, reality as it appears is easily taken for granted instead of actively re-created toward the values of the gospel and the reign of God.

Critical reflection invites the activities of critical reason, analytical memory, and creative imagination. With critical reason learners can move beyond the appearances of reality and distinguish between what is and what ought to be. Analytical memory invites people to look beneath the surface of their own social activity, to see the interests, assumptions, and ideologies that undergird their present way of operating. Creative imagination invites people to create an alternative future, rather than allowing the future to be determined by what is "given" in the present.

CONNECTING WITH THE WIDER CHRISTIAN COMMUNITY

In the context of Christian education that involves action-reflection, a final principle requires that the "knowing" that comes to us from the "faith handed down" through the broader Christian community must also be made attractively accessible to the learning group. A characteristic technique employed to make accessible the faith of our ancestors in Scripture and in our own familial and social experience is that of storytelling that links us with our roots.

The faith of the Christian community is the story of how God has been with our ancestors in the past and of how our own people have responded to God's activity and intentions. Those intentions are the vision that arises from the story to call us forward to God's reign. As such, the story and the vision both console and confront us. To the extent that we see that past as our past, it provides us with the power to change in terms of how we view ourselves as people shaped by God's justice and peace and in terms of how we act according to God's intentions.

In the process of storytelling as part of action-reflection learning, whatever is made accessible from Scripture and tradition must be directed at promoting and empowering the quest for justice and peace. If our Christian education does not promote justice and peace through this process then it is unfaithful to the "faith handed down."

This last aspect of action-reflection learning means, then, that the educational process must promote a dialectic between what the participants have named and reflected upon (their own experiences and visions) and what is made accessible as the faith of the broader Christian community. The stories and visions of the learners and of their ancestors in the faith must become mutual sources of truth, correction, and creativity for each other.

Action-reflection learning within Christian education is an attempt to promote a "knowing" in the biblical sense, i.e., understanding that arises not by standing back from in order to look at, but by active and intentional engagement in lived experience. As a consequence, in the Judeo-Christian Scriptures, knowledge is possessed only in its exercise or actualization.

Action-reflection learning is a relational, reflective, and experiential way of knowing in which by critical reflection on lived experience people discover and name their own story and vision and, in a Christian education context, the story and vision of the faith community. It thus combines the knowing that arises from present lived experience with what was known by Christians here before us. Since this kind of praxis learning always has the purpose of promoting further understanding, the knowing that arises from a reflective, experiential engagement with the Christian story and vision seems likely to promote a deepened

Christian faith and thus lessen the gap between the faith we claim and how we live. *See also* Knowledge, Theories of; Liberation Theology; Narrative Theology; Peace, Education for; Praxis; Social Action; Social Justice, Education for; Storytelling; Teaching Theory; Theology and Education.

T. M. Eugene

Addiction

In a survey of public opinion, addiction would likely be described as a state of physical and/or psychological dependency on various chemicals, particularly alcohol and drugs. A few people might identify additional addictive substances—coffee, tobacco, chocolate, or junk food—or different forms of addiction—compulsive gambling, jogging, cleaning, or watching television. But these are only the more obvious tip of the iceberg rather than its hidden mass. In order to deal with the problem effectively we must examine the nature of addiction and what gives rise to it in the first place.

For some, addiction represents a lack of willpower and is considered a moral problem; others believe it to be a physiological condition requiring medical intervention; still others see addiction as a personality disorder best treated in a therapeutic setting. Though these viewpoints converge in an acknowledgment that addiction is problematic and involves some kind of compulsive behavior, there is little agreement about the nature of the problem or how it is best resolved.

Through the work of interdisciplinary scholars, however, a broad and systematic interpretation of addiction has been formulated that offers us insight. These scholars—most notably Gregory Bateson—regard addiction as the process of adaptation gone sour. They maintain that all life systems are both constituted and driven by processes we call change. When confronted by a stimulus to change, a life system summons a variety of resources in order to effect the required adaptation. If the agent or resource facilitates a reordering of the life of the system, adaptation is successful. Addiction is the condition of dependency which results when adaptation fails to occur. When this happens, the creature becomes dependent on the continuing presence and effect of an external substance or stimulus to regain temporary equilibrium. Addiction to tobacco is an example. When confronted by the external stimulus of increasing pressure at work some persons turn to cigarettes in order to achieve a restoration of equilibrium. The tobacco, however, merely makes the person feel better; it does nothing to enable the smoker to adapt in a healthy, holistic manner. Instead of being enabled to achieve a new equilibrium in response to pressure, the smoker becomes dependent on the continued and increased use of tobacco to cope with the stress.

Dependence on the maladaptive substance results from the temporary nature of the effects it produces within the system. As the system grows accustomed to the substance, it requires ever greater amounts to achieve a feeling of equilibrium. In sum, the substance functions as short-term and often countereffective relief for a symptom rather than as a valid response to the cause of the disorder. Instead of facilitating the process of adaptation, the addictive substance undermines the capacity of the system to regenerate itself in the wake of stimuli to change, to adapt.

Given this broad theoretical framework, at least four clues to the nature of addiction can be identified. First, addiction is more common than is ordinarily assumed. Any system within any form of life can respond to change stimuli in ways that are maladaptive; addiction is not restricted to human beings. Second, addiction can take many forms within the human species. Many addictions are not recognized or identified in our society and, consequently, remain unconscious and unexamined. Third, the consequences of addiction vary considerably, ranging from minimal negative effects to serious impairment or even death. Fourth, individual experiences of addiction must be related to social and structural addictions. To view addiction as an individual problem is to overlook how it can be socially organized and structurally induced. Individuals would not become addicted to drugs if drugs were not socially accepted, readily available options for relieving, however ineffectively, the anxiety of disequilibrium.

Those who look deeply into the social fabric of our lives point out political, economic, and cultural addictions to power, wealth, success, competition, and immediate gratification. Ideologies and religions can be used addictively and influence our behavior as individuals and as a society. The existence of these social addictions raise questions related to the chicken-and-egg debate ("Which came first?") as well as questions about freedom and determinism. But students of individual addictions believe the individual addictions cannot adequately be addressed without confronting the larger systemic contexts.

This expansive interpretation of addiction has implications for the practice of religious education. If we believe that religious education points ultimately to liberation, the forms that addiction takes in the lives of our students need to be identified and examined in light of the transforming vision that we work to make accessible to them. If we believe that religious education takes the experience of students seriously—that it perhaps even begins there—an issue such as addiction, in its personal and social dimensions, becomes relevant and important to the life of faith. If we believe that religious education makes a unique and life-giving tradition accessible to students, then we must help them to see all that stands in the way of appropriating this tradition. If we believe that religious education nurtures the life of faith and fosters holistic development, then those who practice it need to provide both the incentive and the means for transcending obstacles to this development.

More concretely, we can provide occasions for students to examine their addictions, to discern what gives rise to them, and to search for alternatives that are truly adaptive. We can help students to appreciate the constancy of change in their lives and understand that addictive responses to change threaten or impede their growth and development. We can help them to see the complexity of addiction rather than to form conclusions about the tips of the icebergs that are based on uninformed judgments.

FOR FURTHER REFERENCE

Bateson, Gregory. *Steps to an Ecology of Mind.* New York: Ballantine, 1972.

Peele, Stanton. *The Meaning of Addiction.* Lexington, MA: Lexington Books, 1985.

K. A. O'Gorman

Administration

See Management.

Adolescence

Adolescence is the name given to the period of life between the ages of twelve and twenty-two years. Because of the gradual, though noticeable, changes that occur over this span, it has been convenient to identify adolescence according to ages: early (twelve to fifteen years), middle (fifteen to eighteen years), and late (eighteen to twenty-two years).

Adolescence has been described as the sore thumb of developmental periods, sticking out, hurting, somehow dramatically different from the other periods of life. As vivid as this image may be to parents and other adults, it is negatively misleading. Nor does it match with what we are beginning to discover about youth in this period of their lives. Over the past decade much more study and research has been done about adolescence, especially of the period of early adolescence, a developmental period that has virtually been neglected until recently. We now know that adolescence *is* a critical period of life where the changes, exposures, and influences a person experiences set the framework for the man or woman he or she will be as an adult. Particularly, early adolescence is a major turning point in the life cycle because of the important physical, emotional, social, and cognitive growth that occurs at this period.

Around the turn of the century it was recognized that as our society became highly industrialized, young people needed a period of life between childhood and adulthood to learn social roles and achieve the skills necessary to function independently as adults. Parents, teachers, the media, church, government, and industry jointly agreed and supported this need for time, support, and guidance before final assumption of adult responsibilities and decision making.

To understand the significance of why this period of time was and is needed, it is helpful to examine the changes that occur, the developmental tasks that should be completed, and the kinds of support and guidance an adolescent requires to emerge at the other end as a fully functioning adult. Since adolescence is also a pivotal point in a person's religious and spiritual development, it is important to examine what influences this kind of growth as well.

THE WORK NATURE ACCOMPLISHES

Two facets of an adult are "born" during adolescence at the discretion and time schedule of nature: physical-sexual maturity and formal cognitive or abstract reasoning. Although when each of these maturations occurs varies widely across adolescents, they will occur, irrespective of anything that is done to or for them. However, the reactions to these changes, by both the person and others, significantly affects the emotional, social, and spiritual development of the adolescent.

Physical Change

Four types of change occur during puberty: a spurt in physical growth, maturation of reproductive organs, changes in the endocrine system, and the development of secondary sex characteristics. Overall, girls tend to develop about two years earlier than boys. As these changes occur, the reactions and assumptions from peers, parents, and significant others is altered. The adolescent is viewed and treated differently, and new expectations emerge in what a girl or boy experiences. These reactions and a daily reassessment of self dramatically affect a young person's self-esteem, social competence, self-consciousness, and interest in and relationship with others.

Starting in the fifth grade the frequency of thinking and talking about sex increases with each grade level, as does the interest in the opposite sex. With these developments, the choice of friends becomes more selective, now based on attributes, qualities, and status, and the reality of peer influence and peer pressure become an issue for the adolescent and his or her family. Also, beginning in early adolescence, young people begin to experience peer shock—through cliques, rejection, betrayal, and disillusionment.

U.S. pregnancy rates per every 1,000 girls, ages fifteen to nineteen, jumped from 94 in 1972 to 109 in 1984. In a comprehensive study conducted by Search Institute of Minneapolis involving over 8,000 early adolescents and over 10,000 of their parents, when eighth and ninth graders were asked about their experiences with sexual intercourse, nearly one in five reported having had that experience at least once. These statistics have raised serious questions about what is influencing this behavior and about the sexual education and guidance of adolescents.

It is revealing to note that in surveying the results of sex education programs in this country, those that do not deal with values or emotions were shown not to affect adolescent sexual behavior. Also, according to the Search study, adolescents involved in sexual intercourse tend to place less emphasis on church and religion, to have lower achievement motivation, and to receive less nurturance and support from parents (Benson et al., *The Quicksilver Years*, p. 52).

Search Institute, a research institute intended to help human service professionals and service institutes promote the welfare of adolescents and adults, has developed a human sexuality program called *Values and Choices*. This program has been piloted and experimentally researched and is now being used in public schools and churches to specifically teach both human and spiritual values that relate to this behavior. This program includes an educational component for parents and utilizes video to present the basic content information about sex and related issues. The program has been shown to have a significant effect on the reduction of teenage sexual activity.

Formal Operational Thinking

The physical changes during adolescence often mask what may be more dramatic changes occurring in children's thinking. In adolescence, one develops the ability to think on a higher level and to think in a new way. With these new thinking abilities, young people see themselves, others, and the world in general in a totally revolutionary way. This in turn affects how youth adjust to the rapid biological changes they are experiencing, as well as their appearances.

The significance of this new level of reasoning is that they are now able to deal with possibilities, with what might be rather than with what is; to go beyond the here and now, to think about consequences; and to comprehend abstract subjects. This opens up the world of the ideal and of perfection. For the first time adolescents can imagine a world of peace and harmony, a perfect church, and a perfect family. The criticalness of parents that emerges in adolescence is derived, in part, from this new ability to imagine ideal parents against whom the adolescent's real parents suffer by comparison.

These cognitive changes may occur earlier than physical changes and begin to create problems for parents who are not aware of the behaviors that result. Both parents and other adults may also fail to recognize the needs that these changes require in terms of modified instruction, communication, and relationships. Also, when a young person's physical development is ahead of his or her cognitive development, the adolescent may be viewed as being "older" than he or she can cognitively manage, which can create serious problems.

Clues to the unfolding of this new level of thinking come in different ways. One is an increased level of argumentativeness. As teenagers have the ability to marshal facts and ideas to make a case, they will no longer settle for simple dictates. Rather, they want to know the reasons why they should or should not do something. They argue for the sake of arguing because they are motivated to use and practice their new mental abilities. They need help, however, in distinguishing between arguments based on principles versus emotional issues. It is a principle that one should do required homework, despite how unfair or incompetent the teacher is accused of being.

5

Adolescents begin to think about thinking and as they do, they become aware of the perspectives of other people. As this happens, adolescents become aware of two selves within them—the public self that they exhibit for feedback from significant others and the private self with whom they interact in introspection and self-examination.

This awareness of the perspective of others creates the "imaginary audience" and the "personal fable" David Elkind describes (*All Grown Up and No Place to Go*, pp. 33–36). The imaginary audience is based on adolescents' assumption that everyone is looking at them and thinking about them in the same positive or critical way as they see themselves. This creates the self-centeredness that is so characteristic of adolescence and the conformity to fads and behaviors during this period. The imaginary audience concept helps to explain the puzzling change in teenagers that shows them going from being totally unconcerned about their appearance to spending long hours in front of the mirror. Also, this helps to explain some of an adolescent's sensitivity to criticism and public exposure.

Just as teenagers believe that everyone is looking at them, they can also create a fable about how special and unique they are. Typical examples of personal fables are: "Other people will grow old and die, but I won't"; "Other kids will get pregnant, but I won't"; "I am more lonely than others"; and "I have more problems than anyone else." Most adolescents grow out of these phases of thinking, but helpful in counteracting this kind of thinking, bringing it more into balance with reality, are group experiences where young people are able to share feelings, attitudes, and experiences in their lives.

Formal operations opens the door to new topics in young persons' lives and an expansion of thought. With this development they begin to talk about what they "believe" and "value" and about "faith" and "motives." This is a fruitful time to discuss religion, God, death, eternal life, and other theological issues, as long as such discussions are geared to the appropriate cognitive level, the early stages of formal operations. Too often the religious education adolescents receive jumps to complex abstract material only properly arrived at after personally working through some of the more basic concepts and doctrines. Those who determine the content of religious education as well as the age-level scheduling will be more successful if they take into account the reasoning capabilities of their students.

THE DEVELOPMENTAL TASKS

Unlike sexual and cognitive development, social, emotional, and spiritual growth do not happen naturally. Rather, they are a function of how well an adolescent accomplishes certain developmental tasks. In attempting to do this, young people are heavily dependent on guidance and support from parents and adults in learning to master the skills required to assume adult roles.

Establishing a Sense of Achievement

As young people move toward adulthood they want to learn how to get along with others and how to contribute to the world around them. This involves exploring a purpose in life, a reason for living, and a vocation. To do this, they need chances to experiment with their own strengths and values and opportunities to participate as citizens, members of households, workers, and responsible people in society. In addition they need instruction in attitudes toward work, service to others, and a philosophy of life, as well as in the relative values of different kinds of achievements.

In the Search study, adolescents were given a list of twenty-four values and asked to rank them according to importance for their lives. The four top values after a "happy

family life" were: (1) "to get a good job when I am older"; (2) "to do something important with my life"; (3) "to do well in school"; and (4) "to make my parents pro of me." Clearly the desire to achieve is a strong motivation, but to actualize achieve requires testing abilities in a variety of ways and the development of values, characte and the will and hope to feel achievement is possible.

An adequate answer to the pursuit of a purpose in life and a reason for living sh include a theological as well as a secular, humanistic perspective. Although young people are consistently exposed to what society views as success and a reason for liv many are being denied the religious answer to these questions. The high rate of teen, suicide seems to indicate that this aspect of the adolescent's religious education is be neglected.

Separation from Family

Adolescence is the time when young people seek to create and maintain lasting, meaningful, healthy relationships with others, particularly peers, extending their social base beyond the family. It is a difficult task for both adolescent and parents. It involve developing social competencies such as learning to share feelings, being empathetic, a learning to make friends.

Accomplishing this task is often hindered by the reactions of parents, due in part a fear associated with peer pressure. Some parents react by turning over complete freedom to the child, misreading the continuing need of young people for adults to set limits. Others react by clamping down with inappropriate controls. Data reveal that wl young persons experience low parental nurturance, high authoritarian control, high coercive punishment, and low family closeness, they often become socially alienated. Parents often need help in learning how to let their children expand their relationships gradually, while equipping them to establish meaningful social networks that can be helpful in acquiring important life-affirming values.

The interest in and ability to make friends seems to differ for boys and girls. Girls are more concerned than boys about establishing friendships and seem to develop more social competency in doing so. Boys, who are less concerned about having friends, also show less skill in interpersonal relationships. As a result, boys do not cope as well in combatting feelings of loneliness, being misunderstood, or being ridiculed. Clearly, soci competence is an important goal that tends to be underdeveloped among young adolescent boys.

Although achieving social competency is primarily a matter of skill development, attitudes and values also are critical to establishing meaningful relationships. Because adolescent peer relationships are so important to youth, they need to learn the values of honesty, promise keeping, respect, social justice, equality, and loyalty, as well as the attitudes of compassion, forgiveness, interest, and concern for others. Instruction and discussion about the importance of these values and attitudes should perhaps be the prime focus of religious education during adolescence.

Acquiring Autonomy

Another task of growing up is to gain the ability to act independently and to make decisions for oneself. The process involves parents gradually letting go of control and helping children learn responsibility for themselves. The desire for increased independence grows rapidly during early adolescence, but contrary to a common belief, autonomy does not have to be achieved through rebellion.

The parent's task is to avoid a smothering, rule-oriented, overcontrolling approach that actually results in a child continuing a dependent relationship or creates a rebellious

response. Rather, what is needed is basic instruction in decision making and progressive opportunities to exercise these skills with assigned responsibilities.

The process involves deciding which decisions are now appropriate for an adolescent; guiding the adolescent to evaluate the pros and cons; genuinely listening to his or her point of view; explaining the parental position; and letting the adolescent make the decision, even if one is made contrary to what the parent considers best. For this type of instruction to be effective, the adolescent must experience the consequences of the decision made, even when they may be painful. Turning over the responsibility for getting to school on time may initially result in a teenager being tardy and angry at a parent for not getting him or her up. Soon, however, the teenager realizes the need for and acquires self-reliance in this area of life.

Considerable evidence indicates that when independence training begins early in a child's life and is valued by parents rather than resisted, becoming independent as an adolescent is not as new or as harsh as it is frequently depicted. Increasing resistance to authority at this time is often the result of a child's changing reactions to parental roles. Not only do most parents encourage independence during early adolescence, but those adolescents who feel and are most independent report the most positive relationships with parents. Achieving autonomy is related more to respect for parents and continued affection for them, than to rebellious and oppositional behavior.

Identity Formation

Adolescence is also the period when young people construct a sense of a personal identity—one's self-definition and uniqueness as a person. This cannot be done until an adolescent has acquired the necessary ingredients to do so. It involves a reassessment of who one is based on biological and sexual maturation, the acquisition of new thinking processes that allow adolescents to reflect on how they are seen by others, and the exercise of their autonomy to acquire experiences of self. David Elkind believes that young people who have a consistent sense of their sex role, their success as students, their work habits, and their relations to adults and to the peer group find that constructing a personal identity is a challenge and a rewarding task. The ingredients are all there—they just need to be put together once the requisite mental operations are attained (*The Hurried Child*, p. 117).

Young people who are unclear about any of these roles or relationships or who lack the competencies they need to be successful socially or independently may lack a clear self-definition. These youth construct a sense of self by copying the feelings, thoughts, and beliefs of others, which Elkind claims amounts to a "patchwork" self. Not having a clear definition of the deeper core of the self, they are easily swayed and influenced by others. Some of these youth may adopt a negative identity by defining themselves in terms of what their parents are not and value least, not realizing that by defining themselves in this way, they are as tied to parents as if their identities were based on what their parents are or profess to be, because no real exploration of the self has occurred.

For some youth, identity formation comes too early due to certain early accomplishments or outstanding attributes that close off further exploration of self in terms of peer relationships, intellectual pursuits, or varied interests that contribute to a well-rounded, healthy personality. Erik Erickson refers to this as identity foreclosure. It frequently occurs with youth who experience early recognition for outstanding athletic ability, performing arts, or academic achievements. Identity foreclosure also tends to happen to early maturing boys who as a result of their physical development receive

8

much social attention and prestige. As a result, some cease the process of exploring who they can become.

In Elkind's discussion of identity formation he indicates that teenagers very much need a religious element in their identity. When teenagers have a religious faith, even if they do not practice it, it becomes a known quantity, a fixed ingredient to integrate into their developing definition of self. Yet religion is largely ignored in most books on adolescent development. It is a dimension few research psychologists consider when they study the adolescent, and therefore little has been known about the importance of a religious faith in adolescent behavior and development.

A 1980 Gallup poll revealed that 74 percent of thirteen- to fifteen-year-old youth say that religion is the most important or one of the most important influences in their lives; and 83 percent of American adults say they would want a child of theirs to receive religious instruction. Search Institute asked parents and youth: "How important is religion in your life?" The overwhelming majority affirm that "it is the most" or at least "one of the most important influences in my life." However, further data from this study indicate that religion is almost a taboo subject in the home. When asked, "How often does your family sit down together and talk about God, the Bible, or other religious things?" 42 percent of adolescents said this never happens; 32 percent said this topic is discussed once or twice a month; and 13 percent said it is discussed once a week (*Religion in America, 1979–80*).

Perhaps a large majority of parents believe that religious education is the work of the institutional church. However, the primary work of religious education must be done in the home, starting in childhood, preparing for the exploration and questioning that occurs during adolescence. Lawrence Richards states that the real task of parents is to link the Word with the *life* of a child so that he or she sees life from God's point of view ("The Teacher as Interpreter of the Bible"). Religion provides a perspective beyond ourselves and our world that helps young people realize their significance and place in the universe, and it is part of the responsibility of parents to open this part of life to their children, preparing them to make their own decisions about their faith and beliefs.

As adolescents develop new levels of thinking, they begin to distinguish between institutional religion and a personal religion. Accompanying this discovery is often an emergence of religious doubt. For both boys and girls the percentage who are unsure of what they believe about God increases with each grade level during early adolescence. Some adolescents actively reject religion during this period, feeling it is no longer relevant to their lives; some reject it as an act of rebellion against parents and religious authority. Some only become critical, pointing out the inconsistencies and hypocrisies they observe in adults and the church.

It is helpful to recognize that criticism, rejection, and doubt may be a normal, healthy, and even necessary process to be able eventually to establish a firm, personal faith. The kind of reaction a young person receives when he or she expresses this doubt or questioning may determine the future quality and kind of faith practiced or experienced as an adult.

Elkind believes that if children have been well grounded in a religious orientation, it may be appropriate during adolescence to allow youth a period of time free of institutional religion. "At this time, both the religious institution and parents should move away from religious instruction and provide opportunities for the social interaction and discussion of values, beliefs, and actions that young people need to discover who and what they really are. Such a sabbatical from institutional religion prepares the way for a later integration or personal and formal religious beliefs and values" (*All Grown Up and No Place to Go*, p. 43).

The tragic problems adolescents are increasingly experiencing, such as teenage suicide, drug and alcohol addiction, and teenage pregnancy and crime, as well as the concern about the appearance of these problems at an increasingly earlier age indicates that we no longer are a child-centered society. Nor are we giving youth a pressure-free time to develop their full potentials, learn their roles as contributing members of society, or develop a religious foundation that will be a resource in coping with the complexities and competition of present-day society. Some elements of our society cannot be changed. We will not return to a nontechnological society, nor will women return in large numbers to being full-time mothers and homemakers. But other elements can be changed, and parents, adults, and the church need to reevaluate the decisions made and the quality of the guidance, support, instruction, and time we are providing youth in their transition between childhood and maturity. If we don't, we will be denying adolescents a place in society and the adolescence they need in order to have a future. *See also* Child Development; Cognitive Development; Doubt; Peer Ministry; Psychosocial Development; Sexuality; Sexuality Education; Values; Youth Ministry; Youth Service and Training Organizations.

FOR FURTHER REFERENCE

Benson, P. and D. Williams. *Early Adolescents and Their Parents.* Minneapolis, MN: Search Institute, 1984.
Benson P., D. Williams, and A. Johnson. *The Quicksilver Years.* San Francisco: Harper & Row, 1987.
Elkind, D. *All Grown Up and No Place to Go.* Reading, MA: Addison-Wesley, 1984.
_____. *The Hurried Child.* Reading, MA: Addison-Wesley, 1981.
Religion in America, 1979–80. Princeton, NJ: Princeton Religious Research Center, 1980.
Richards, Lawrence. "The Teacher as Interpreter of the Bible." *Religious Education 77*, no. 5 (September–October 1982): 515–16.
Strommen, M. P., and A. I. Strommen. *Five Cries of Parents.* San Francisco: Harper & Row, 1985.

B. B. Varenhorst

Adult Development

Although the age at which a person is considered an adult varies from culture to culture and within a culture for different functions (marrying, voting, etc.), in most societies adults are those who have finished the childhood/adolescent period of development, now have a degree of autonomy and responsibility, and form the bulk of the population. In many cultures the attainment of "adulthood" is marked by a rite of passage.

In Western society adulthood is usually thought of as beginning in the early twenties and ending at death and until recently was not considered a period within which there were identifiable patterns of change and growth, at least not compared to the dramatic and visible changes in earlier periods. But longer life spans and increased attention to the life experiences of adults have prompted interest in how people develop through the adult years. And while there is no one universally established or even generally accepted set of stages for adult development, the proposed models are illuminating. Religious educators involved in adult education need to be aware of the existence of and the possible patterns of adult development to be effective.

ADULT LIFE CYCLE DEVELOPMENT

Early work done in developmental psychology in this century concentrated on the developmental aspects of the young. Relatively predictable patterns of development could be identified for childhood and adolescence, but the increasing complexity and diversity of adult patterns of behavior, plus the comparative length of adult life in contrast to the more compact chronological subdivisions of childhood and adolescent years, inhibited the study of the adult years until the middle of the century.

The research and writings of Robert Havighurst and Erik Erikson in the 1940s and 1950s provided the first comprehensive understanding of the developmental nature of adulthood within the context of the total life cycle. Although approaching the topic from different perspectives, both Havighurst and Erikson suggested that there are predictable physical, psychological, and social patterns that affect most, if not all, adults as they move through life.

Before reviewing the work of these and other pioneers in the field of adult developmental theory, we should remind ourselves again that all stage theories are oversimplified models of general patterns of behavior and must always be tempered with that most significant human characteristic: individuality. An overzealous tendency to categorize people, particularly adults, into stages in a culture dominated by rapid change and mobility is counterproductive to the values of understanding adult development in general through a study of stage theory.

Six developmentalists are noted as representatives of a rapidly growing body of social scientists whose focus is on or includes the adult years. Although outside the mainstream of religious research and theory building, their work is still quite relevant for religious education. Havighurst and Erikson were early pioneers in the field; the concepts of Daniel Levinson, Carol Gilligan, Anita Spencer, and Gail Sheehy emerged a generation later.

Robert Havighurst's most significant contribution is the concept of the developmental task and its educational corollary, the teachable moment. According to Havighurst, human development takes place as the individual successfully engages and completes one after another in a never-ending series of "tasks" that are fundamental to physical, psychological, and social growth. The developmental tasks of childhood emphasize physical and intellectual development (learning to walk, developing fundamental skills in reading, writing, etc.), while those of adolescence emphasize tasks of social development (learning an appropriate masculine or feminine social role, achieving emotional independence of parents, etc.).

Havighurst suggested forty-six developmental tasks throughout the entire life span, of which twenty-one occur in the adult years. Adult tasks include selecting a mate and getting started in an occupation in early adulthood, accepting physiological changes and adjusting to aging parents in middle age, and adjusting to retirement and to the death of one's spouse in later maturity.

Many of the specific tasks defined by Havighurst, particularly those related to adulthood, seem dated now and there are omissions. For example, the treatment of early adulthood has no reference to singleness or alternative life-styles; the discussion of middle age makes no mention of single-parent families or the emerging concept of the mid-life crisis; and the tasks of later maturity seem strangely simplistic in an era of extended life and the increasing ethical dilemmas related to death and dying. What is important is not so much the specific tasks as the concept underlying them: that there are relatively uniform developmental tasks that most, if not all, persons must deal with in adulthood. The tasks are not limited to a specific chronological time, but occur throughout life, each with its primary focus during certain periods of adulthood.

STAGES OF THE ADULT LIFE
(as Suggested by Daniel Levinson)

Age	Transitional Periods	Stable Periods
17–22	Early adult transition	—
22–28	—	Entering the adult world
28–33	Age 30 transition	—
33–40	—	Settling down
40–45	Mid-life transition	—
45–50	—	Entering middle adulthood
50–55	Age 50 transition	—
55–60	—	Culmination of middle adulthood
60–65	Late adult transition	—

A contemporary of Havighurst's, Erik Erikson, built upon Havighurst's model to develop a theory of personality development far more sophisticated and widely recognized. In each of Erikson's eight stages a person confronts a developmental task. In attempting to perform the task, a conflict or tension arises between two alternative attitudes. Whether the tension is resolved in a favorable (leading to psychosocial health) or unfavorable way depends upon which attitude prevails. The stages relating to adulthood and their psychosocial tensions are:

- Early Adulthood (intimacy/isolation)

- Middle Adulthood (generativity/stagnation)

- Late Adulthood (ego integrity/despair)

These concepts have become fundamental to much of the research in adult developmental psychology in the last generation. Whereas Havighurst focuses on specific tasks, Erikson sees a broad range of dynamics ever in flux that give a fullness of dimension to, in particular, adult life.

Daniel Levinson's research on males in the 1970s provided an even more specific stage theory of (male) adult development. Based on in-depth interviews with forty men and extensive reading of the biographies of men through the centuries, Levinson suggested that the adult life structure (for males, at least) evolves through a relatively ordered sequence of alternating stable (structure-building) and transitional (structure-changing) periods. The stable period is characterized by firm choices, rebuilding one's life structure, and enhancing one's life within it. The transitional period is a time of questioning and exploring possibilities for change and new directions for one's life structure. This alternation may be visualized in the table entitled Stages of the Adult Life (as Suggested by Daniel Levinson).

Levinson stated that these periods overlap, connect, and interpenetrate. While the current period is predominant, the others are present in it, as the life cycle is an organic whole and each period contains all the others. Thus the person works chiefly on the tasks of the current period, but also on the tasks of other periods that are unfinished or anticipated.

Levinson's work has been criticized for its sole focus on the male and a seeming tendency to extrapolate the data to include women. To be fair, Levinson's purpose was to study the developmental patterns of *men*. It is the casual reader and interpreter who too often erroneously suggests broader implications for both sexes based on the Levinson findings. Although as of this writing no similar definitive study of women has been published, some are in process. The writings of Carol Gilligan and Anita Spencer, in particular, if not parallel in format to Levinson's study, do address the developmental patterns of women.

Based on several studies of males and females, Gilligan emphasizes the woman's unique place in society with her special emphasis on relationships as a predominant female characteristic. She addresses the changing role of women and makes a strong case for clarity in the identity of the female role in our culture.

Spencer translates Levinson's periods into the female focus, using the images of spring (17–28), summer (28–39), autumn (39–65), and winter (65–) to suggest the similarities and differences for women in relation to Levinson's masculine orientation. She writes out of her own experience and insights and captures with sensitivity the "distaff side" of Levinson's theories.

Levinson's research and his scholarly formulation of a comprehensive stage theory based upon it has made this theory of (male) adult development one of central importance in contemporary developmental thought. Gilligan and Spencer (and, of course, many others) provide the important complementary insights that broaden the focus to include both female and male perspectives.

Any contemporary statement about stages of adult development cannot overlook Gail Sheehy's *Passages*. Although writing more as a journalist than as a scholar, Sheehy has made a most significant contribution to the field by her ability to translate the basic understandings of adult development into concepts with which average readers can easily identify.

Sheehy uses salty prose and sensitive, humorous imagery to capture vividly the human experience of being in one's twenties, thirties, and forties. Much of the popular interest in adult development generated during the 1970s and 1980s can be attributed to her book. Written more for the public than for the scholars, *Passages* was a best-seller for over two years in the late 1970s.

The authors cited above are but the tip of the iceberg of countless studies, theories, concepts, and designs that can help educators better understand the ways we grow, develop, and mature as adults.

MORAL AND FAITH DEVELOPMENT

Although social scientists have explored the physical, social, and psychological dynamics of adult development, most have tended to skirt the more elusive and difficult issue of faith and the degree to which it might be developmental. In our Western tradition, faith has traditionally been perceived as given, an "absolute" of human experience. Although some creative theologians have ventured to explore elements of change in faith perceptions, most religions have held that faith does not change—it is the individual who must change his or her life-style and attitudes to conform with the expectations of faith. For many, this has resulted in conversion and acceptance of a particular faith stance. For others, however, it has led to a rejection or at least to an ignoring of any affirmation of faith.

In the past generation, however, the concepts of moral development and faith development have increasingly become foci of research and theoretical inquiry. The major figure in the field of moral development is Harvard psychologist Lawrence Kohlberg, whose research utilized responses to a series of moral dilemmas. Kohlberg found a definite progression of moral reasoning, which he classified by stages or levels. Building upon the cognitive theory concepts of Jean Piaget, Kohlberg projected a series of six stages of moral development that apply to the entire life span. He further recognized the parallels between moral development and faith development, and his work was in many ways a major catalyst in the development of the latter field.

John Westerhoff posed a relatively simple yet appealing series of stages of faith development in the mid-1970s. Using the image of growth rings of a tree (increasingly larger concentric circles), he suggested that individual faith grows in similar ways from the center outward through increasingly complex and meaningful stages of experienced faith, affiliative faith, searching faith, and owned faith.

Since Westerhoff was less interested in stage theory than in exploring the meaning of the faith journey for religious education, he did not develop this schema into a fully formed construct. However, it does provide a logical and useful pattern of developmental theory that speaks to the needs of many.

The most comprehensive stage theory of faith development is that created by James Fowler in the 1970s. Based on over ten years of research and interviews with more than five hundred persons and influenced markedly by Kohlberg's concept of moral development, Fowler's was the first major organization of theological concepts within the framework of the human life cycle. Fowler sees faith as active, likening it to a "verb," so to speak, rather than a noun. Faith is not something that one has or does not have—a thing—but rather a process of becoming. This process involves continual growth through stages that are hierarchical (increasingly complex and qualitative), sequential (they appear one after the other in the life span), and invariant (they follow the same order for all persons). Fowler has crafted a carefully defined and complex stage structure that draws from both developmental psychology and religious nurture.

The six stages of faith development, according to Fowler, are:

- Intuitive-projective faith, where fantasy is part of the images of faith
- Mythic-literal faith, where faith becomes concrete
- Synthetic-conventional faith, where faith conforms to traditional modes and expressions
- Individuative-reflective faith, a critically developed faith
- Conjunctive faith, faith with an openness to other dimensions of faith
- Universalizing faith, identification with a universal community

Although these stages are not closely tied to specific ages of the life span, there is a general pattern. The first two are found almost wholly among children. Synthetic-conventional faith begins in the early teens and usually extends into and often throughout adulthood. The final three stages are found almost entirely among adults.

Fowler's theory of faith development is the most comprehensive research-based exploration of this emerging field. Some scholars and practitioners are uncomfortable with the hierarchical nature of Fowler's stages, which seems to imply that "higher is better." They suggest that his theory favors persons who conceptualize, verbalize, and personalize their faith experiences and does not adequately affirm those whose faith is more simplistic in those qualities of obedience and trust. This may be a fair criticism, but

Fowler has provided a research-based and carefully developed model that views faith not as an absolute given, but as a dimension of the experience of every human being, a dimension capable of growth and development within the framework of that person's life experiences. It has opened the door to a relatively unexplored field of developmental study and has served as the springboard for a broad spectrum of related research studies.

THE INTERFACE

Relatively little has been done as yet to provide an interface between the literature of the adult life cycle and that of moral and faith development, with a few exceptions. Evelyn and James Whitehead explored the ramifications of Erikson's psychosocial crises of adulthood for the faith community in *Christian Life Patterns* (1979). They see adult growth involving crises that are predictable; these patterns and crises have religious dimensions and faith implications that must be recognized. They help the religious practitioner see the profound implications of developmental theory for ministry and provide a framework for those pastors, educators, and counselors who seek to take it seriously.

A major effort of the interface is the *Faith Development in the Adult Life Cycle Project* sponsored by the Religious Education Association and twenty-one other national and regional denominations and religious organizations during the period 1981–1986. The project was directed by this writer and its purpose was to effect a dialogue between the social sciences (adult development theory) and religion (faith development theory).

By means of two significantly different research modules, data were collected that provide important insight into people's self-understanding of the relationship between the physical, psychological, and social changes of adulthood and the maturing of their faith. The project found that faith development in adults seems to be most active in young adulthood, when men and women are establishing adult life structures, and again in mid-life, when these structures are being reviewed within the context of the "mid-life crisis." Other than at these times, there are no clearly definable patterns of faith development *related solely to age*. Social factors such as cultural change and personal crises such as divorce and vocational change influence a person's faith development far more than does a person's age per se. Further, the study corroborated that there is a strong positive correlation between psychosocial health (Erikson measure) and faith development (Fowler stage theory).

Probably no single adult develops exactly according to any given pattern of stages. However, the constructs of stage theory do help us better understand the basic patterns that underlie adult development. It is a topic of interest to academic and practitioner, to laity and clergy alike—one in which significant further research is anticipated. For religious educators, this is fundamental to providing the fertile soil and nurture for growth in faith. *See also* Adult Education; Cognitive Development; Developmental Tasks; Faith Development; Moral Development; Psychosocial Development; Young Adults.

FOR FURTHER REFERENCE

Erikson, Erik. *Childhood and Society*. New York: Norton, 1950.
Fowler, James. *Stages of Faith*. San Francisco: Harper & Row, 1981.
_____. *Becoming Adult, Becoming Christian*. San Francisco: Harper & Row, 1984.
Gilligan, Carol. *In a Different Voice*. Cambridge, MA: Harvard University Press, 1982.
Havighurst, Robert J. *Developmental Tasks and Education*. New York: David McKay, 1972.
Levinson, Daniel J. *The Seasons of a Man's Life*. New York: Knopf, 1978.
Spencer, Anita Louise. *Seasons*. Mahwah, NJ: Paulist, 1982.
Stokes, Kenneth, ed. *Faith Development in the Adult Life Cycle*. New York: Sadlier, 1982.

_____. "Report of the Faith Development in the Adult Life Cycle Project." Unpublished; secure from project headquarters: 9709 Rich Road, Minneapolis, MN 55437.

Whitehead, Evelyn and James. *Christian Life Patterns.* New York: Doubleday, 1979.

K. Stokes

Adult Education

Adult education as a popular movement had its beginnings in England in the late eighteenth century, when the industrial revolution was beginning to radically affect the lives of working people. It spread to the United States early in the nineteenth century and had a greater impact in the latter half of the century. The Scandinavian countries during that period pioneered in the development of residential folk high schools for young adults.

Perhaps the best known theorist in the field of adult education today is Malcolm Knowles, who advocates a greater emphasis on educating adults and in his writings has popularized the term "andragogy" for adult education as distinct from the general term "pedagogy," which in etymology refers to the teaching of children. This primary focus on education for adults is reflected in Third World countries where the education of adults seems almost more important than that of children when budgetary priorities have to be established. Knowles at one point refers to the adult learner as "a neglected species."

Adult general education has served many needs. People have been enabled to overcome inadequate elementary education and receive secondary education, to gain literacy, to increase working skills and learn new skills, to develop as persons and enrich their lives through study. Such education may be accomplished through late day and evening sessions at high schools and colleges, but it is also found in lyceums, lecture series, and in the United States in the Chautauqua program.

Churches and synagogues have long had a concern for ameliorative general educational programs for adults. The first such work, begun in nineteenth-century England, was conducted under church auspices. Today church and synagogue facilities are offered to recognized sponsors providing basic literacy, skill training, or voter registration information. These are found primarily in economically deprived neighborhoods. Churches may also sponsor such programs and their members become volunteer helpers.

Adult religious education in the church and synagogue has a long history. In the Jewish community, the study of Torah has always been considered a lifelong task as well as a privilege, demanding in time and devotion. And in the Christian community, catechetical instruction for adult dates back centuries. Present adult religious education programs, which are the focus of the remainder of this article, stem more directly from the Sunday school movement. The Uniform Lessons Series, established more than a century ago, provides for adult Bible study. In recent decades a broad spectrum of studies has developed, including biblical and theological study, ethics, social justice, religious development, and spiritual growth. Catholic parishes entered the field after Vatican II and, unhampered by tradition, have developed a broad range of options beyond the catechetical and marriage preparation programs already being offered.

It should be noted that not only study classes but all church and synagogue programs in which adults participate have educational functions. People accrue learning experiences by participating in committees, stewardship campaigns, and governing boards or as delegates to judicatory and national meetings. These programs are based in the congregation, but they are encouraged through help from judicatory and national departments for adult education, stronger in some denominations than in others.

PURPOSES AND METHODS

Adult religious education provides an opportunity for ongoing development that enables adults to examine their relationship with God and so understand their humanity. It enables them to become aware of God's activity in their lives, enhances their use of the gift of life, and leads them to strive for deeper maturity and to minister to self, others, society, and world.

The education of adults within a church or synagogue context does not mean that learning focuses only on religious topics. Opportunities can be provided that will touch all areas of life. Since one's faith colors values, attitudes, behavior, and interaction with others, it needs to become a deeper positive influence.

Care in choosing methods will attract adult learners and sustain their interest. For example, when programs provide primarily experts who simply supply information without acknowledging and utilizing the experience and expertise of participants, planners have failed to respect learners. Lecturers are "pouring into" listeners material that will soon be forgotten rather than "drawing out" their insights. Opportunities to discuss and ask questions stimulate responses to lecture presentations, but following certain key principles can aid in fostering the kind of learning climate in which adults continue the search for knowledge.

Adults desire learning opportunities that respond to their needs. These may be related to developmental stages (deciding vocation in young adulthood, reaching out to community in middle adulthood), to life tasks (parenting, work, facing up to illness), to coping with ethical dilemmas in work or community, or to satisfying spiritual yearnings.

They require an environment conducive to their adult status. Usually there can be a more relaxed interchange if chairs are in curved rows or concentric semicircles or if participants are seated at tables. They need freedom to move around. Well-lighted and temperature-controlled rooms are a practical asset for attention.

Presenter (or lecturer) and student are both teacher and learner. Interaction in discussion and an easy exchange of ideas is essential. Questions may be posed for clarification or in order to understand more deeply the import of either the presentation or a listener's response.

A variety of learning approaches and processes are needed. These include lecture, reflection, analysis, discussion, journaling, case studies, and role playing, among others. The arts could be more widely used: short story, drama, poetry, music, and the graphic arts. Videotape resources are extensive and tend to supplant the use of small-screen film. Taping of current programs for study is increasing. Rental libraries are extensive.

A climate for developing fellowship and support is essential. Adults do not always attend programs for information; they also attend for socializing and interaction. What they talk about among themselves before and after a session may be at least as important to them as what they hear and say in the formal session. Supportive bonds are formed here.

The total community is the classroom, so educational settings may be found anywhere. People meet in shopping malls, banks, and supermarkets, on buses, trains, and planes. Some of these meetings are material for later reflection. Picnics or cookouts can be informal settings through which a group becomes acquainted. Meetings can be held in the social rooms of apartments and condos, learning centers, and homes, or in meeting rooms of the local library, where materials for study are easily accessible. People meet through shared reading of newspapers, books, or magazines and through viewing television. This happens when experiences are shared in families and with neighbors during crisis periods as well as joyous anniversaries.

PROGRAMS FOR RELIGIOUS EDUCATION

The spiritual dimensions of adult religious education apply to all adults. These include relationship to God, prayer, search for meaning in life, response to social injustices and other ethical issues, and viewing human interrelationships in a divine perspective. Specifically these suggest programs in Bible study, prayer, and worship; the traditions, liturgies, and history of each particular faith; and ethics and moral decision making. Other topics include examining the inequalities, oppressions, and injustices in economic and social systems and issues of peace and war, hunger, and ecology. Renewal programs deepen relationships with God. Other programs enrich human interrelationships between spouses, parents and children, friends, neighbors, and communities.

Such a wide range of programs would have varying appeals. Sometimes they can be offered more effectively on an ecumenical, community, or area basis.

Crisis programs must not be forgotten. Found within every religious community are the alienated; divorced, separated, or widowed; newly married and single; people with differing vocations—professionals, office workers, factory workers; the elderly, the poor, the handicapped. Others are hurting: alcoholics, drug addicts, the grieving, the lonely. Needs of parents differ with the age level of their children (or their own parents) and their status (stepparent, single parent, adoptive or foster parent, etc.). The gay and lesbian communities have special needs. Everywhere men and women are struggling with changing roles. Such a catalogue may seem diffuse, but it is also specific. Not all will be found in any one congregation, but the variety can alert planners of adult programs to the breadth of the potential constituency.

Ameliorative programs were mentioned earlier. The mission of the religious community is not complete unless money, expertise, and volunteer energy is mobilized to make opportunities for the economically deprived. They need programs to become literate and politically and economically educated. They need to learn about child care and health issues. In some communities refugees and migrants are waiting for help. Their special educational and spiritual concerns cannot be ignored.

Adequate programming opens the heart, expands the mind, and challenges the will. It broadens horizons and deepens understanding. Knowledge is enhanced by wisdom. Participants, strengthened by the Spirit, willingly share experience for the benefit of all. *See also* Adult Development; Aging; Andragogy; Chautauqua; Conference; Cursillo; Family Life Education; Group Dynamics; Leadership Development; Marriage Enrichment; Parenting; Psychosocial Development; Retreat; Workshop; Young Adults.

L. E. Girzaitis

Advent

Advent is the season of the church year that begins on the fourth Sunday before Christmas and ends on Christmas Eve. Its name is derived from the Latin *adventus*, which means "coming." It is a time of solemn preparation for Christmas, celebrating the coming of Jesus Christ, both his coming in history to Bethlehem as the son of Mary and his coming in glory at the end of time "to judge the living and the dead."

Advent is a season of expectation. "The King shall come!" and "Rejoice!" are its watchwords. The great Advent figures who dominate the traditional Scripture readings are Isaiah, John the Baptist, and the Virgin Mary.

The traditional liturgical color for Advent is violet or blue. The season is traditionally marked by the lighting of an Advent wreath of evergreen. One additional candle is lighted for each of the four weeks of Advent. This is done both in churches and in homes. Often a fifth candle in the middle of the wreath, the Christ candle, is lighted on Christmas and throughout the twelve days of Christmas.

Advent originated in Spain and Gaul in the fifth century. It began in mid-November and was called Saint Martin's Lent. (Saint Martin's day is November 11.) Its original purpose appears to have been the preparation of candidates for baptism at Epiphany. *See also* Church Year.

L. L. Mitchell

Aesthetics

While aesthetics is a branch of philosophy dealing with the nature of beauty, art, and taste and criteria for their judgment, it is perhaps more useful for the purposes of religious education to speak of it as the intelligent explanation of the sensibilities. "Aesthetic," then, is a term describing a perception characterized by reasoned feeling or feeling reason, and the aesthetic perspective is one that is concerned with human experience at its deepest and widest. It is never content with regarding experience abstractly but is always intent on its concrete disclosure to us of what it means and what it feels like to be human in a world that is both the origin and setting for human existence with its distinctive qualities and capacities.

The aesthetic quality of experience is the affectional and emotional hues that pervade an interaction and constitute it an experience. While this quality is always aesthetic in the broad sense because it constructs wholeness, it can be aesthetic in the more traditional sense when the experience of wholeness is consummatory. For John Dewey the explicitly aesthetic quality is characterized by a wholeness that is final and that arouses no search for other experience (*Quest for Certainty*, 1929).

Aesthetic religious education addresses the whole person, that is, on a feeling level as well as on a rational level. This is not to say that such religious education excludes the cognitive dimensions of human experience. To reduce the human personality entirely to emotion or intuition is as erroneous and unbalanced as the various forms of naive rationalism that stress the intellect and the role of reason and logic but exclude the more affective dimensions of the human person. Many claim that religious education, by mirroring general education and reflecting the culture's dominant concern for the intellect, has neglected the intuitional mode of consciousness; these two modes of consciousness have been artificially separated and the intellect overemphasized.

RELATED RESEARCH

For more than thirty years neurobiologists have been conducting research into the physiology of the brain. They seem to have discovered in each person two distinctly different consciousnesses. The left hemisphere of the brain was found consistently to be our rational lobe. It takes in information bit by bit, processes it in linear, rational, logical fashion, and carries on verbal and mathematical reasoning. It is verbal and uses language to communicate with the outside world. The right hemisphere never speaks. It perceives images holistically in gestalts. It thinks concretely, processes information in a spatial and intuitive way, and seems to be the locus of our creative and artistic capabilities and our appreciation for forms and music. Research also seems to indicate that there may be critical periods for the development of different talents and potentials. Music and a foreign language can be learned very readily at an early age, but later in life they become increasingly difficult to acquire mastery in. If there are critical periods for the development of the left hemisphere's mechanical ingenuity, for example, there may be similar periods for maximal development of the aesthetic sensitivities. It may then be necessary to educate people at that stage or lose forever the possibility of realizing their full potential.

Recent findings identify four distinct modes of cyclical-metaphoric (right-lobe) thought. The *symbolic metaphoric mode* exists when a symbol is substituted for an object, process, or condition. The symbol can be visual (a picture) or abstract (letters, numbers, written words, etc.). The *synergic comparative mode* exists when two or more objects, processes, or conditions are compared in such a way that both are synthesized into a greater whole as a result of comparison. Unlike rational comparisons in which the mental processes act to separate and specify, the synergic comparative mode synthesizes and extends. In this mode there are the roots of cyclical thought that in effect link all things in the universe together. It is a vital component of creativity, in that the creative mind sees unity in diversity. The *integrative metaphoric mode* occurs when the physical and psychic qualities of the person involved are extended into direct experience with objects, processes, or conditions outside the self. This mode is reintroduction of the total self in the process of experiencing during learning. Remarkably, this mode dominates in children at exactly the time that observers cite the most profound development in learning. Children in Piaget's preoperational stage acquire speech and language simultaneously while learning to cope with walking upright. Unfortunately, this mode is largely abandoned once adolescence and adulthood are reached. The *inventive metaphoric mode* obtains any time a person creates a new level of awareness or knowing as the result of self-initiated exploration of objects, processes, or conditions. Invention is personal in this mode and is the result of creatively engaging a multiplicity of variables (Samples, "Mind Cycles and Learning").

Researchers have made the amazing discovery that students from age four on and at any grade level have the capacity to perform effectively in each of the metaphoric modes. It is clear to them that the capacity to perform in all the metaphoric modes is uniform throughout the rational stages of development. However, it is also clear that in terms of school experience there is a diminishing utilization of the metaphoric modes, except symbolic abstract, as one goes through the cognitive stages. Although the capacity for expressing metaphoric knowing persists at all stages of cognitive maturity, in terms of prevailing teaching strategies and curriculum materials, appropriateness of its use is diminished throughout the school experience.

IMPLICATIONS FOR RELIGIOUS EDUCATION

A religious education curriculum that is designed to meet variation in experience and life-style means that different people need different things at any given time. Yet, although children probably have greater need for affective learning than do adults, many religious education settings, both in and out of schools, are not designed to promote affective learning. For many theorists religious education is a field where the religious intersects with education. The aesthetic is a dimension of both. Religion, with its ties to creativity and feeling, has always been the vehicle through which peoples have expressed their relationship to the divine. Education, with its focus on the intentional reconstruction of experience, has relied strongly on the creation of conceptual form but is in need of the perceptible form more proper to art. Thus, the field can only be enhanced by inclusion of the aesthetic. The aesthetic dimension of religious experience can be nurtured by providing experiences of *enrichment* that involve sight, sound, and tactile sensations, including the creation of artworks; promoting experiences of *interpretation* through exposure to a broad spectrum of artworks; and planning lessons according to four phases of *art forming*: objectifying (using the senses), reflecting (using the emotions), interpreting (using the intellect), and decision making (using the will). An example of art-forming a Scripture message might look like this:

Objective: What images struck you?

Reflective: What do you think this Scripture passage might be saying to us today?

Interpretive: Have you ever experienced anything like this in your own life?

Decisional: How do you want to be different as a result of hearing this passage?

Art forming can be used in a variety of teaching situations: lectures, readings, songs, movies, role playing, classroom decor, and paraliturgical celebrations, to mention but a few.

Of course, all of this is not to say that the cure for present difficulties in religious education is simply to attend to the right-lobe functions of the brain. Rather, it is to suggest that the implications drawn from this research show that religious educators can take the initiative in uniting the linear-logical and cyclical-metaphoric modes. There will always be a need for solid, conceptually grounded education. Religious education that overlooks the basic needs people have for conceptual frameworks on which to situate their diffuse range of feelings, questions, and peak experiences lacks true relevance. The danger that confronts religious education, then, is not that we have been too intellectually abstract and that we may become more so in the future, but rather that we have too often failed to see the necessity of educating to both sides of experience.

Religion and art make life richer and finer. All education that is aesthetic in its approach enables us to see that life can be beautiful and can be lived beautifully. Such education, like art, may not be necessary, but it is certainly human. And many propose that it is religious. *See also* Affective Development; Art in Religious Education; Child Development; Cognitive Development; Crafts; Creative Activities; Creativity; Dance; Drama; Learning Theory; Methodology; Poetry; Symbolism.

FOR FURTHER REFERENCE

Apostolos-Cappadona, Diane, ed. *Art, Creativity, and the Sacred.* New York: Crossroad, 1984.
Durka, Gloria, and Joanmarie Smith, eds. *Aes-

thetic Dimensions of Religious Education. New York: Paulist, 1979.

Harris, Maria. Teaching and the Religious Imagination. San Francisco: Harper & Row, 1987.

Samples, B. "Mind Cycles and Learning." Phi Delta Kappa (May 1977): 688–692.

G. Durka

Affective Development

Affective development refers to the thesis that the affections develop in ways analogous to the ways our bodies and minds develop, that is, according to universal and observable patterns.

Two problems about this thesis dominate writing on the subject. There is, first, no agreement about what exactly is meant by the affective. The term must include feelings, but, for example, is every feeling an emotion? The discussion also extends to the question of whether or not to include drives or instincts in the notion of affect. Moreover, there is no consensus about locating the will. Some authors include it under affect; others describe will as some third entity that is neither cognitive nor affective.

The second problem has to do with the relationship between the affective and cognitive. If we have learned nothing else from using the polygraph, or lie detector, we have learned that the cognitive and affective domains are not separate domains. Every so-called cognitive statement made by a person can be tracked as an emotional response. The cognitive and affective are like height and weight. They never exist separately. Everything that has weight also has some height; everything that has height weighs something. Yet, the distinction helps us measure them differently and work with them separately.

The dualism of Greek philosophers, especially Plato, gave rise to the radical separation of mind and body that has plagued education in the West. The mind was to preside over the affections as superior being over lesser being.

Although dualistic thinking about the affective and cognitive no longer prevails, little concentrated attention has been paid to the role of the affections in education and hardly more to the education of the affections. A number of reasons explain this situation.

First, the measurement, evaluation, and grading of affections or emotions is considered a difficult to impossible task. Like pain, the data with which one must work appears to depend on introspection or the subject's personal account of private experience. The ideal of objectivity that evaluators claim to bring to events of behavior or problem solving is not available to the student of the affective domain.

Second, addressing affections as an objective of teaching conjures up possibilities of manipulation. Even infants seem to recognize that the way to a person's decision-making faculty is through the "heart" or affections. While we tolerate the machinations of infants and small children who wrap us around their little fingers, nightmares like the Jonestown massacre, where over nine hundred adults took their own lives as the result of the manipulation of a charismatic leader, make us chary of the effects of working with affect.

Third, more than anything, educating emotions involves shaping desire or teaching values. Since the secularization of public schooling, that area of the educational enterprise has been considered very sensitive if not off-limits for teachers.

But, if secular education has steered clear of affective development for all the reasons cited above, religious educators cannot afford such avoidance. Religious educators work more than anything else toward fostering a love affair between their students and God, between their students and all humankind, between their students and all kind. Unlike their public-school counterparts who ostensibly commandeer the emotions to achieve cognitive objectives, religious educators use cognitive objectives to achieve attitudinal changes.

Although most developmental theorists consider the affective to some degree in their work, only two systematic developmental theorists have devoted extensive attention to the subject of the emotions: Sigmund Freud, whose work has been expanded by Erik Erikson, and Jean Piaget. Freud and Erikson coordinate emotional and social growth. Piaget coordinates emotional and cognitive growth.

Erikson's scheme of development is the better known. He determined that a person has to pass through eight stages, each of which is characterized by an emotional conflict. (See table entitled Erikson's Stages of Development). When one fails to cope successfully with the conflict, development is arrested.

Piaget is most associated with the cognitive schemes he plotted during his long career. Yet he did address the affective development of the child in a number of works (Play, Dreams and Imitation in Childhood, 1962; Six Psychological Studies, 1967; and The Psychology of the Child, 1969). But his major treatment of the affections, a course that he gave at the Sorbonne in 1954, was not published in English until 1981.

In this work, Intelligence and Affectivity: Their Relationship During Child Development, Piaget defends the thesis that affectivity plays the role of an energy source on which the functioning but not the structures of intelligence depend. "It would be like gasoline, which activates the motor of an automobile but does not modify its structure." The stages of affective development that Pi-

ERIKSON'S STAGES OF DEVELOPMENT

Development Period	Basic Conflicts
Oral Sensory	Trust vs. Mistrust
Muscular-Anal	Autonomy vs. Shame and Doubt
Locomotor-Genital	Initiative vs. Guilt
Latency	Industry vs. Inferiority
Puberty and Adolescence	Indentity vs. Role Diffusion
Young Adulthood	Intimacy vs. Isolation
Adulthood	Generativity vs. Stagnation
Maturity	Integrity vs. Disgust, Despair

aget outlined correspond roughly to his stages of cognitive development.

1. Preoperational: hereditary organization; instinctual drives and all other inborn affective development

2. Concrete operational: first acquired feelings; the joys, sorrows, pleasantness, and unpleasantness linked to perceptions as well as differentiated feelings of contentment and disappointment linked to action

3. Early formal operational: affects regulating intentional behavior; the feelings linked to the activation and retardation of action along with termination reactions such as feelings of success or failure

4. Formal operations-dichotomizing: Intuitive affects; elementary interpersonal feelings and the beginnings of moral feelings

5. Formal operations-dialectical: Normative affects; autonomous moral feelings with intervention of the will

6. Formal operations-synthetic: Idealistic feelings for other people are overlaid by feelings for collective ideals

Perhaps no one has done more than the team of David R. Krathwohl, Benjamin S. Bloom, and Bertram B. Masia to date to plot affective development for teachers. They constructed a taxonomy of educational objectives for both the cognitive and affective domains. A taxonomy is an ordered classification of anything (in this case of desirable outcomes of learning) according to an organizing principle. The principle of complexity was the major ordering basis for the cognitive domain. The principle of interiorization ordered their classification of the affective domain. The five categories with their subdivisions are intended to be hierar-

chically arranged along a continuum of internalization from lowest to highest.

1.0 Receiving
  1.1 Awareness: a neutral attending to something
  1.2 Willingness to receive: continues to attend (as opposed to avoiding what has been noticed)
  1.3 Controlled or selected attention: selects and attends to the favored stimulus despite competing and distracting stimuli

2.0 Responding
  2.1 Acquiescence: complies with the directive to respond
  2.2 Willingness: voluntarily responds
  2.3 Satisfaction: enjoys responding

3.0 Valuing
  3.1 Acceptance of a value: ascribes worth to a phenomenon, behavior, object, etc.
  3.2 Preference: pursues, seeks out, wants the value
  3.3 Commitment: takes action to further value

4.0 Organization
  4.1 Conceptualization of a value: sees how the value relates to those already held or new ones coming to be held
  4.2 Organization of a value system: brings a complex of values, possibly disparate ones, into an ordered system

5.0 Characterization by a value or value complex
  5.1 Generalized set: an internal consistency to the system of attitudes and values at a particular moment; a persistent and consistent response to a family of related situations or objects
  5.2 Characterization: value system or philosophy of life characterizes and pervades all behavior

21

Theorists in the field of affective development have shaped the way in which general educators understand feelings, emotions, and will. Religious educators, concerned about the shaping of attitudes, will need to probe a spiritual dimension at which these researchers only hint. *See also* Aesthetics; Cognitive Development; Confluent Education; Creative Activities; Creativity; Education, Theories of; Learning Theory; Role Playing; Taxonomy; Values.

J. C. Smith

Africa

Africa is a vast continent divided roughly into two cultural areas: North Africa, a Mediterranean culture, and sub-Saharan Africa, whose nations are black (with white minorities in several countries). Of the total African population of 340 million in 1985, roughly 46 percent were Christian, 42 percent Muslim, and 12 percent practiced tribal and traditional religions. North Africa is primarily Muslim; sub-Saharan Africa has a long history of various tribal and traditional religions, but currently both Christianity and Islam are rapidly gaining converts in sub-Saharan Africa. The balance of this article focuses primarily on religious education among sub-Saharan Christians.

Christianity, introduced by missionaries from Europe and North America, received its first encouragement from colonial governments. For example, they introduced both the English language and the Anglican church in Nigeria; in Zaire, the French language and Roman Catholicism. This article discusses the agencies for religious education as seen primarily in the mainline Protestant denominations. The basic units can be paralleled in Catholic institutions, sometimes with different names. Christianity is represented in Africa today also by indigenous groups, sometimes charismatic or gathered around a charismatic leader, that seek their own interpretation of the faith independent of its European roots.

A changed and changing scene is the background against which Christian education must be understood in Africa into the twenty-first century. Despite the political independence of all but two or three of its nations, Africa faces neocolonialism and the herculean task of building nations and developing human and natural resources. Immediately, however, Africa is in a crisis best described as one of struggle and hope. The struggle is with poverty and hunger, coups and countercoups, economic underdevelopment, and the possibility of resurgent tribalism. The hope is for a continent freed from the tyranny of any minority regime dominating a majority under duress and for every nation's taking its place in the family of nations with equal advantage to develop its resources and contribute to the commonwealth of the international community. The role of Christian education in this struggle and toward these hopes is that of providing a basic theology, a complementary ethic, and an overall educational strategy.

SUNDAY SCHOOLS

Christian education programs in Africa received their initial impulse from four basic missionary objectives: evangelization, literacy, education, and healing. In most instances, Sunday schools came into being to enable youth and adults to read the Bible in the vernacular and to write. A typical program consisted of learning to read and write the alphabet, listening to Bible stories, memorizing verses, and receiving instruction in the catechism. Students were not usually grouped or graded according to age or ability; they were simply divided into classes. Annual examinations were given by missionaries or others to determine readiness for promotion. Teachers for these Sunday schools were often secured randomly from among converts who could read and write. Many of black Africa's Christian leaders came from these Sunday schools.

In the past, Sunday schools were quite highly regarded, but with the coming of independence some new African nations did not continue their Sunday schools. They abdicated religious instruction to the rising state systems of education. In most cases, however, this proved unsatisfactory. Secular day schools regarded religious instruction as optional. Religion was often poorly taught by non-Christians or not offered at all. More recently there has been a renewal of interest in the Sunday school as a necessary setting for Christian education. The meaning of the term "Sunday school" has been enlarged to include many activities and learning opportunities; indigenous curriculum materials have been developed; leadership education has been introduced for teachers in Sunday schools; and Christians have become involved with social concerns. The work in three countries will be illustrative. In Zambia, where four million of the 5.8 million population are Christians, Sunday schools and youth groups are found in most churches. The major problem is the lack of trained teachers; classes and groups are often too large and unmanageable.

In Malawi about half of the more than five million population are Christians. Approximately two-thirds of that number are Protestants. Each parish (or district) in the Protestant church in Zambia (Church of Central Africa) has Sunday schools. If it is understood that parishes contain a dozen or more churches, one could say that about a quarter of all Protestant churches in Malawi have Sunday schools.

Tanzania, with a population of at least twenty million, four million of whom are Christians, has experienced a dramatic growth in the number of Sunday schools. The churches there seem to be enthusiastic about the "revival" of Sunday schools, especially since introduction of the relatively new Swahili edition of the Africa Sunday School Curriculum.

CURRICULUM DEVELOPMENT

Probably the most significant event in Christian education in Africa in the last twenty-five years was the development and production of the Africa Sunday School Curriculum. This breakthrough was highly instrumental in restoring the vitality of the declining Sunday school movement. The demand for indigenous curriculum materials had been growing since early in the 1950s, when four regional Christian education conferences held in 1955–56 unanimously endorsed this first indigenous curriculum project. A conference of representatives from fifteen African nations agreed on a common outline.

The Africa Sunday School Curriculum provides for five grades: beginners, primary, junior, youth, and adults. Materials for grades 1–4 are issued in annual volumes of forty-eight undated lessons following the church year. The adult material is published in a pamphlet series supplemented by handbooks.

This all-African Christian education curriculum project was initiated, guided, and partially funded by the then World Council of Christian Education and Sunday School Association. One of its concerns was that faith "must be understood in terms of Christian responsibility in areas immediately relevant to everyday life."

LEADERSHIP EDUCATION

The most serious problem confronting Christian education in Africa is that of finding and training leaders, lay and professional. Teacher education is needed in several areas: modern methods and techniques of teaching; development of church educational program; communication arts; instructional media use; and basic Christian beliefs and public witness.

Several leadership training patterns have been developed. Short-term intensive courses have proved effective and popular across the continent; longer courses are also provided. Some of these are held at the well-known Mindolo Ecumenical Training Center at Kitwe, Zambia. Originally directed by missionaries, Mindolo, organized in 1958, has become the largest lay training facility on the subcontinent and one of Africa's best-known international centers.

FORMAL EDUCATION: DAY SCHOOLS

Formal education in sub-Saharan Africa originated in mission stations; its objective was education for Christian formation. Since independence most African nations have claimed a national and secular objective for education, and this view poses new challenges to the churches and their schools. Church members are challenged as national citizens to support the state schools and challenged as church members to make a deeper commitment to Christian education. The changes also afford new opportunities for Christian groups and other religious groups to cooperate more closely with one another to maximize their relatively meager and declining resources. Another area for church-state cooperation in Africa is in meeting the school needs of disabled students.

HIGHER EDUCATION

Independence required rethinking of the purpose, objectives, and strategy for higher education. Free nations urgently needed general and universal education as soon as possible. The new social, political, and economic problems they faced demanded leadership—academic, scientific, and technical.

The role of the churches in Africa shifted significantly with this new state of affairs. The Salisbury Conference in 1962 called for a new Christian philosophy of education. It was made clear that while there was a critical need for the churches to view education in the "context" of government planning it was equally if not more important for them to see the "role of education in the total ministry of the Church to the people of Africa."

This landmark statement had clear implications for higher education under church and mission sponsorship. Christian higher education is challenged to do several things: to help people understand and practice Christian family values; to help people in the community understand the Christian aspects of any work as God's calling; to sensitize students to their responsibility for dealing with the conditions in blighted urban areas that create human misery; and to offer assistance to national governments in establishing colleges and universities *without* church control, where they do not exist or where they are needed.

THEOLOGICAL EDUCATION

Recent surveys of theological education in Africa indicate that there are about ten thousand ministerial students in more than a hundred theological colleges, schools, or Bible institutes. These institutions offer a myriad of programs, including theological studies for secondary school graduates and beyond and Bible study with pastoral training for others. Several institutional models accommodate these programs: seminaries, study centers, theological education extension centers, ministerial training institutes, and workshops. More than five hundred teaching faculty and staff personnel are involved in these programs.

Several common problems are found among these schools: impoverished pre-theological education; a grossly insufficient number of qualified students for the seminaries; the problem of constantly revising the curriculum toward a "post-independence" relevance; acquiring and maintaining an adequate theological library; recruiting faculty, especially African, for an increasingly indigenous course of study; providing a contemporaneous continuing education program; and securing adequate funding. *See also* Black Theology; Christianity; Islam.

FOR FURTHER REFERENCE

All Africa Church Conference. *Christian Education in Africa*. London: Oxford University Press, 1963.
Allen, Yorke, Jr. *A Seminary Survey*. New York: Harper, 1960.
Beaver, R. Pierce. *Christianity and African Education*. Grand Rapids, MI: Eerdmans, 1966.
Knoff, Gerald E. *The World Sunday School Movement*. New York: Seabury, 1979.
Lumen Vitae Studies: Religious Education in Africa. Brussels: Lumen Vitae Press, 1956.
World Christian Education (Quarterly). The World Council of Christian Education and Sunday School Association. 475 Riverside Drive, New York, NY 10027.

G. S. Shockley

After-school Center

An after-school center is an informal learning environment provided by a religious institution for children and youth. It has several purposes. One is to offer additional religious education beyond that given on Saturday or Sunday. Roman Catholic parishes use after-school centers to give instruction to children not enrolled in the parochial day school.

In some communities, after-school centers offer remedial school work for children and tutorial programs to undergird the work of the public schools, in particular because there may not be a quiet study environment at home. For families where adults are at work during the day, the after-school center offers a safe place for children to play and to engage in enrichment activities as well as to do homework.

Several decisions need to be made when organizing an after-school center: determining the ages (in relation to developmental stages) of the children to be served; meeting the needs of children and the expectations of families in relation to the time span during which care is needed and the ability of the parents to contribute financially; determining resources available from the sponsoring agency including budget, people, materials, and facilities; establishing charges and hours of operation; and viewing the relationship of the after-school center to the total religious education program.

Several program arrangements are possible. Two consecutive learning periods with a snack, games, and music in between could be held. Or one group could be in a learning center while another has singing (perhaps choir). One-on-one tutoring is needed for those seeking help with schoolwork. Storytelling and resting could be available for younger children, while recreation and crafts were offered to older children.

Active hands-on experiences along with the use of games, crafts, music, drama, dance, and computers all will enhance the interest and excitement of the children.

There are several steps in planning an after-school center. First, the purpose needs to be defined. This could be child care for parents who work, tutoring and enrichment for school children, or an opportunity for additional religious education (including choir). Second, the facility and the resources need to be considered: the possibilities and limitations of the building; other activities going on at the same time; finding qualified people to help and deciding on the proportion of paid staff to volunteer workers; checking to be sure that insurance needs will be met; planning for supplies and equipment; and setting up the budget and determining sources for funding.

The next step is to divide the responsibilities. Levels of responsibility and awareness of the accountability structure of the institution are important. Helping with the center becomes a learning experience for the high-school students and adults involved. The more persons involved, the wider the investment in the program, contributing to its success.

Finally, an ongoing evaluation should be part of the planning process. Get input from supervisors, workers, parents, and children. It is especially helpful to informally chat with workers at the end of each session for immediate feedback. Your after-school center will successfully meet the needs intended through careful planning and dedication to its purpose. *See also* Childhood Education; Time Arrangements.

S. H. Matthaei

Aging

Aging is the gradual process of change that begins at birth and ends at death. Although the process of aging spans the lifetime, those in the latter portion of the adult years form a special group whose educational needs require the attention of religious educators no less than those who are beginning life's journey. Specific programs addressing the simplification of life, health and economic concerns, and religious questions connected with the end of life need to be based on sympathetic concern and an understanding of the process of aging itself. Understanding the aging process requires seeing the relationships between chronological age (years lived), how the body changes as people grow older (biological aging), how they cope with changes in their environment as they grow older (psychological aging), and how social institutions interact with persons as they age (sociological aging).

Functional age is a term characterized by the adage, "You are only as old as you act (or feel)." When we measure the way persons function in given physical, psychological, intellectual, and social arenas against an accepted norm, we are dealing with functional age. For example, a seventy-year-old swimmer might have a functional age of fifty when measuring heart rate, respiration, and endurance.

Aging processes occur at different rates within a given individual and individuals age differently. It has been shown that, in general, biological maturity is reached first (in early adulthood) and begins to decline before persons achieve psychological maturity; social maturity may be reached even later and may show the least decline in later life. Biological aging is not a single process; for example, our lungs and kidneys age at a greater rate than our hearts. There are changes in physical appearance, including wrinkling and stooping. Sensory losses such as vision and hearing may contribute to social and psychological stress.

Psychological aging is studied by assessing how persons solve problems and how they adapt to change. An examination of personality types and self-image provides keys for understanding older adults and the aging process. Memory, learning, intelligence, and creativity are tasks that contribute to our understanding of psychological aging.

Sociological aging focuses on how aging persons interact in a social context as well as on how social institutions (e.g., family, world of work, government, educational institutions, medical systems, church, and synagogue) interact with the old. In many ways, role differentiation and adult socialization become increasingly less focused as persons age. The roles older persons have (e.g., parent, grandparent, divorced or widowed single, retiree, church member, part-time employee, etc.) often call for conflicting loyalties and actions. Sociological aging involves these interactions and how they contribute to and are caused by the aging process.

Older adults (those in the last third of the life cycle) generally pass certain milestones or marker events (last child leaves home, retirement with increased leisure and/or a loss of status and income, time to pursue deferred goals, loss of health, loss

of spouse) and accomplish certain predictable developmental tasks. A psychosocial approach to aging that seeks to understand a person's biological traits and personality within the context of the physical and social world can inform persons who are seeking to work with aging persons in religious education.

"You can't teach an old dog new tricks" is a widely held misconception in our culture. There are barriers to learning at every age (e.g., young children have short attention spans; adolescents want to be able to see direct and immediate applications; older people require more time to encode data). Older adults are able to grow and learn. Learning for older adults must encompass the cognitive (intellectual, rational acquisition of knowledge), the affective (emotional aspects of one's life), and the creative (flexibility and an ability to use divergent thinking).

Aging persons must first satisfy their coping needs. These include physical and economic needs. How does one cope with the loss of job or spouse or income or mobility or health? Or the attendant emotional issues of living with disabilities, facing decreasing independence and fear of dependency, and needing reassurance of self-worth? Expressive needs (sharing what one is and has), contributive needs (giving and being needed), and influence needs (making a difference) must also be met.

Finally, the need for transcendence becomes vitally important in old age as persons seek to make meaning of life and death. Enabling persons to do this is a primary task of religious education with older adults, although religious questions of suffering, death, eternal life, and continuing faith in God are well considered in an intergenerational context, for these are concerns of all adults.

As persons age, they generally engage in a process of life review and evaluation, often becoming more inner-directed. Growth toward human maturity occurs when persons can accept themselves as they are. Psychologist Erik Erikson maintains that persons in old age face and deal with issues relating to questions of integrity and transcendence. If these questions are not satisfactorily resolved, persons experience self-negation and despair.

Aging, then, is a universal process. Because we live in a society that idolizes youth and seeks to deny aging, there is a great need for aging education across the age span that helps persons see all stages of life as significant—each with its own gains and losses. See also Adult Development; Death; Maturation; Psychosocial Development.

FOR FURTHER REFERENCE

Clements, William M. Ministry with the Aging. San Francisco: Harper & Row, 1981.
Clingan, Donald F. Aging Persons in the Community of Faith. Rev. ed. St. Louis, MO: Christian Board of Publication, 1980.

LeFevre, Carol, and Perry LeFevre. *Aging and the Human Spirit*. Chicago: Exploration Press, 1981.

Vogel, Linda Jane. *The Religious Education of Our Older Adults*. Birmingham, AL: Religious Education Press, 1984.

L. J. Vogel

Agnosticism

Agnosticism is the belief that only material phenomena can be the subject of real knowledge, and consequently it is impossible to know God or the essential nature of things. It is noteworthy that the agnostic is not an atheist, denying the existence of God, but is rather a person who says one cannot be sure, since all our certain knowledge is limited to experience. The term was coined by T. H. Huxley in 1870. A philosophic agnostic claims that the evidence is not sufficient to affirm or to deny the existence of absolutes. A religious agnostic might claim that God is an incomprehensible mystery and so cannot be known by human effort, though some room may be left for revelation. Today the term is often used loosely to identify those who do not wish to be called atheists yet do not welcome the title of true believers. In popular usage this term is used for all forms of skepticism. The religious educator accepts this as a valid viewpoint from which a person may seek deeper understanding. The agnostic brings a questioning perspective to a teaching situation that challenges others to explore their own questions as well as their certainties. *See also* Atheism; Doubt.

P. Elmen

AIDS

AIDS stands for the medical term Acquired Immune Deficiency Syndrome. It is caused by a retrovirus called Human Immune Deficiency Virus or HIV. The virus itself does not cause death, but by suppressing resistance to other infections it makes an infected person susceptible to other life-threatening infections.

Persons who test positive for HIV may or may not have AIDS or even AIDS Related Complex, or ARC. Not all persons testing HIV positive develop full-blown AIDS. The incubation period between the initial infection and the development of symptoms may be brief or as long as fifteen years.

AIDS is not a "gay disease." Many gay people have AIDS, but anyone is susceptible who has sexual contact with an infected person, who comes in contact with contaminated blood or blood products, or who injects drugs with contaminated needles.

AIDS is *not* spread through everyday contact or even through sneezing. The general public needs to be continually reminded of that through a variety of educational methods. (In 1986 the Surgeon General of the U.S. Public Health Service made a very clear and forthright statement on AIDS, how it is transmitted, the relative risks of infection, and how to prevent it. Copies of this report and other information may be obtained from the local Red Cross office, or from the U.S. Public Affairs Office, Humphrey Building, Room 725-H, 200 Independence Ave., S.W., Washington, D.C. 20201.)

Without necessarily condoning or condemning, churches and synagogues must respond to the isolation, suffering, grief, and loss of persons with AIDS (called PWAs), their families, and their caregivers. The irrational fear of contracting AIDS through casual contact often results in the isolation of the PWAs and those who love or care for them. All these persons need pastoral care, to be reminded that God loves them during life, and to be assisted in experiencing a dignified death. The religious community can train special persons to provide this love and care.

Some religious groups and some families have difficulty talking about AIDS, but young people need to know the facts about AIDS and about high-risk behavior. This teaching can be a part of sexuality education or a drug abuse prevention program or a single topic, beginning as young as twelve or thirteen. Responsibility for both oneself and others needs to be taught. Parents need guidance in talking with their youth about AIDS and related issues. Younger children need to have their fears concerning AIDS dealt with and be given basic facts.

Printed resources as well as current videos are available through denominational centers, the National Council of the Churches of Christ, and the Red Cross. An excellent booklet, *AIDS and the Education of Our Children*, is available from the U.S. Department of Education. Speakers may be from medical and public health fields or specialists from the denomination. Use these in adult study groups, parent and religious education teacher meetings, as well as with young people's groups.

The church and synagogue can educate adults in the work for justice in civil rights, medical care, social services, and insurance and other benefit programs that affect people with AIDS and their families. They can also call on the government and other agencies for additional funds for research, personnel, and facilities for treatment and hospice care.

While some drugs have been found to prolong life, at this point there is no known cure for AIDS. It is a medical mystery with death as its silent partner. AIDS reminds each of us of our mortality, a subject about which most persons avoid talking or thinking. This offers additional opportunities for education and ministry. *See also* Death; Eternal Life; Ministry; Sexuality Education.

L. C. Seifert

Aims

See Goals.

Akiba ben Joseph

Akiba ben Joseph (A.D. 50–135), famous rabbi and martyr, was one of the first Jewish scholars to systematize Jewish oral law, eventually leading to the compilation of the Mishnah under Judah Hanasi. The Mishnah forms part of the Talmud, which is the basic authoritative document for all later Jewish education.

Akiba was born in Judea to a poor family and sought no formal education till mid-life. He studied at Yavneh and subsequently established his own academy in B'nai B'rak. He emphasized systematic learning and developed his own system of biblical exegesis and hermeneutics, which claimed that each word and minor textual irregularity possessed significance. He influenced one of his students, Aquila, to make a Greek translation of the Bible in accordance with his own exegesis.

Akiba sympathized with and participated in the revolt by Bar Kokhba against Rome (A.D. 132). He violated Hadrian's decrees against teaching Judaism and was tortured to death. *See also* Hermeneutic; Jewish Education; Rabbi as Educator.

W. Jacob

Alcuin

In the transition from the Dark Ages to the founding of the great universities, no one was more influential than Alcuin (ca. 732–804) in keeping alive what he called the "flower of learning." Born in Yorkshire in what is now England, Alcuin was educated at the Cathedral School of York. Shaped by Celtic humanism, York schooled Alcuin in the liberal arts as the way to Christian wisdom and virtue. A deacon, Alcuin became headmaster and librarian of York in 778.

In 781, the emperor Charlemagne invited Alcuin to the Palace School at Aachen, Germany. There his learning and Socratic style of teaching made him the most influential educator in the Carolingian renaissance of learning. As trusted ad-

viser to Charlemagne, Alcuin encouraged church reform in discipline and liturgy, himself reconstructing the lectionary and sacramentary. He guided Charlemagne's efforts to revive learning through the establishment of schools and developed the Caroline minuscule, the most perfected book script of the time. Alcuin's commitment to copying ancient manuscripts helped to ensure later access to the writings of the Greek philosophers and church fathers, crucial resources for later scholastics.

In 794 Charlemagne made Alcuin abbot of St. Martin of Tours, where he died in 804. *See also* History of Christian Education; Rabanus Maurus; Socratic Method.

T. H. Groome

Alternative Education

See Progressive Education; Teaching Styles.

Anabaptist Education

The first Anabaptists were a group of disciples of the Reformer Ulrich Zwingli in Zurich who broke with him in the 1520s over the issue of adult (believers') baptism. The Mennonites and the Hutterites are their modern-day heirs.

The movement was founded by Franz Manz and Conrad Grebel, son of Jacob Grebel, a member of the Zurich city council. Prior to his conversion, Conrad Grebel had studied at the universities of Basel, Vienna, and Paris, and before the break with their mentor Zwingli, Conrad Grebel and Franz Manz had been intended to teach

Greek and Hebrew at the theological school Zwingli was planning.

Grebel, Manz, and their colleagues developed their distinctive theological views through group Bible study, drawing on their knowledge of the Latin and the Greek and Hebrew texts of Scripture. They repudiated their own infant baptism and were rebaptized by immersion as adult believers, an unlawful act at that time. They also came to believe that the church should be a separated community, leading most of their followers to oppose the conduct of war and to refuse to take civic oaths.

Their movement attracted many adherents throughout central Europe. Eventually the Zurich city council ordered them to cease holding their Bible study groups, which were seen as subversive of Zwingli's efforts to establish a new theological consensus. The persecution that followed their refusal led to the imprisonment and execution of Conrad and Jacob Grebel and Franz Manz. Over the next few years, thousands of their followers were persecuted, tortured, and executed in a number of cities in central Europe.

Though the movement continued to spread, it was some time before its well-educated leadership could be replaced. In 1536 a Dutch priest, Menno Simons, left the priesthood; he provided organizational and theological direction to the movement for several decades. In these early years, this persecuted minority, always on the move, was unable to set up a formal education program as Luther had done in Germany and Calvin in Geneva.

The exception was the Hutterian brethren, named for Jacob Hutter, communitarian Anabaptists who found a relatively hospitable climate in Moravia. Not only were they able to set up a program to educate their children; they were fortunate to have educational theorists among them in the persons of Peter Riedemann and Peter Walpot. An important educational concept was that of instilling in the children a spirit of *Gelassenheit*, that is, "yieldedness," both a willingness to submit to the will of God and a willingness to accept the authority of the community of faith and its designated leaders. Other values to be inculcated were that of community ownership of goods rather than private holding of property and avoidance of an individualistic, self-seeking attitude.

While other Anabaptist groups did not share the idea of a common purse, the ideal of life in community is one shared by all. This ideal was expressed by them in the practice of mutual aid in the event of illness, accident, death, or other circumstances creating special need. An early illustration is the financial assistance provided by the Dutch Mennonites to their Swiss and German brothers and sisters who migrated to America beginning in the seventeenth century.

The word *community* will be found in most discussions of educational theory among Anabaptist groups even at the present time. The goal of education is not so much individual self-realization (though certainly the development of each person's full potential, i.e. is, God-given gifts, is emphasized) as it is the development of skills to function responsibly in community. This includes attention to the history of the community, its values, its sense of purpose (worship and service), its sociology, and its belief system. In recent years, there has been a growing emphasis in the curriculum upon developing relational and communication skills.

The family continues to be the primary community in which Christian faith is nurtured. The basic responsibility for nurturing faith in children rests not with the school or the church but with the families of the church. The role of the school and the church is a complementary one, supporting the efforts of parents. It is, of course, recognized that the parents do not stand alone in carrying out their responsibility. Living in community is strongly emphasized as is the idea that the congregation is a family of families. Anabaptist church groups have been fortunate in maintaining a strong sense of family solidarity. However, as America has become increasingly urbanized, secularization and individualism have begun to erode the sense of community, making family life vulnerable. For this reason, the past decade has seen the development of a variety of family life education programs designed to strengthen family life and to counteract the incidence of family breakup.

To avoid the dangers of being primarily an inward-looking, ethnic group, some Anabaptists have placed a strong emphasis on mission and service in the most recent past. The Mennonites are today present in at least sixty countries around the world, speaking a hundred languages. This growing internationalism has called for an international perspective in the curriculum, particularly on the collegiate and seminary levels. Many Mennonite college students spend a year or at least a semester outside North America studying a culture from within and finding ways to be of service, if possible. Mennonite collegians, for example, were among the first to enter mainland China in the 1980s to serve as teachers of English and learn about Chinese society and culture.

SCHOOL EDUCATION

The Dutch Mennonites were the first Anabaptists to set up a program of graduate theological education. Ministerial students now attend graduate level seminaries operated by several historically Anabaptist-related denominations.

Theological education is also available (especially in Canada) on the undergraduate level in Bible colleges and Bible institutes. Most church-related liberal arts colleges began with the stated purpose of training ministers and other church workers. All continue to offer biblical and religious studies within a liberal arts framework. They also attempt to teach the liberal arts from an avowedly Christian perspective.

There are over twenty Mennonite secondary schools in the United States and Canada. Like the colleges, they attempt to teach the various subjects from a Christian point of view and to encourage their students to enter church and service vocations. Students are strongly encouraged to adopt Christian values such as service and simplicity of life, and an awareness of the poverty, hunger, and suffering in the world, along with the responsibility to alleviate it, is fostered.

On the elementary level, there are at least a hundred schools, approximately half in the state of Pennsylvania. Forty of these schools have been established since 1980, indicating that this is still a growing movement.

No sketch of Anabaptist school education, however brief, would be complete without reference to Christopher Dock. Dock was a schoolteacher in eastern Pennsylvania north of Germantown, the site of the first Mennonite settlement in the New World, founded in 1683. In 1770, his brief treatise *School Management* was published by Christopher Saur of Germantown; it is one of the first books on pedagogy to be printed in the United States. It is said that Dock prayed for his pupils each morning before they arrived and each evening after they left. He was found dead on his knees in the posture of prayer in the fall of 1771. Dock is still held up as an example for Mennonite teachers today, though his pedagogical methods may be out of date, for teaching is seen as more than a profession: it is a high and holy calling, indeed, a ministry.

CONGREGATIONAL EDUCATION

Another level of education is that of the Christian education program in the local congregation. The first permanent Mennonite Sunday school was set up in West Liberty, Ohio, in 1863. The current Sunday school curriculum of several major Anabaptist denominations is a Mennonite-produced one known as the Foundation Series. The title refers to Menno Simons's favorite Bible verse, 1 Corinthians 3:11, "For no other foundation can any one lay than that which is laid, which is Jesus Christ." A serious effort is made by the editors and writers to focus on Jesus Christ and to interpret the Scriptures christologically. That verse appears on the title page of each teacher's guide and pupil book.

The Foundation Series for youth is organized into a four-year cycle. Each quarter is divided into two units of seven and six sessions each. Unit A focuses on the study of a biblical text; Unit B deals primarily with current issues facing youth but also includes some historical studies. Examples of current issues (always studied within the framework of relevant biblical texts) are making choices, speaking the truth in love, the church's service in the world, peacemaking, family life, social issues, encountering other faiths, expressing affection, and vocational decision making.

The Foundation Series for adults consists of a series of eight quarterly studies on biblical, historical, and contemporary themes. These themes include God's call to faith and peoplehood, family (both the congregation and the home), the kingdom of God, peacemaking, evangelism, and stewardship. All these themes are basic to the life of faith as understood by those in the Anabaptist tradition. This series is seen as complementary to the Uniform Lessons Series and is not intended to displace them. *See also* Communes, Religious.

R. T. Bender

Andragogy

Andragogy is a theory of adult learning fully developed by Malcolm S. Knowles in *The Modern Practice of Adult Education: From Pedagogy to Andragogy* (1970). Knowles argued that the traditional assumptions about learning are relevant only when the learner is a child. He popularized the new word "andragogy" (from the Greek stem *andr*, for "man" or "adult") as the term to describe a learning theory appropriate to adults. The andragogical model sees the learner as one in the process of moving from dependency to increased self-direction, having experiences that provide resources for self-learning, and as one who learns readily when the relationship is clear between a need to be met and the material to be learned. Adult learners are described as those who set their own goals, develop their own timetables for learning, evaluate their own progress, and learn best in small informal groups using a variety of interpersonal techniques. These insights have been influencing religious educators to seek distinctive and diversified programs for adults at various age levels and with varying interests. *See also* Adult Development; Adult Education.

H. A. Archibald

Anglican Education

The Anglican communion is a worldwide family of national and regional churches linked by a common faith, by ties of history and tradition, by a common book of prayers, and by a living fellowship with the See of Canterbury, England. In the United States it is called the Episcopal church, in England the Church of England, and elsewhere the Anglican church of that particular region. Christians of diverse ages, colors, races, languages, values, and experiences are both the teachers and learners. Conducted in a variety of circumstances and involving widely diverse peoples, Anglican education takes many forms, yet it has some unifying and distinctive characteristics.

CONTEXT

The church, the body of Christ, is the context of Anglican education. It is the local liturgical community that celebrates the resurrection of Jesus Christ on the first day of each week. It presupposes that what Anglicans believe about Christ is found in the Scriptures and summed up in the creeds. It is in the parish liturgy that the Scriptures are read and taught and the creeds learned and recited. The meaning and vitality of education grow within the parish—the worshiping, believing, and serving community of faith. To mature as an Anglican Christian is to be formed in the baptismal life as it is expressed in the liturgy and the total life of the parish. Each parish utilizes its own resources and gives its own unique combination of spiritual, moral, and material gifts to support regular, continuing education.

Anglican education, then, takes place within the 30,000 parishes, the 64,000 congregations, and the 417 dioceses in 164 different countries, which constitute 27 self-governing churches—a diversity that is seen as positive. Each particular church has its own needs and identity to be respected. Each governs itself according to its own policies and procedures. The responsibility for education in any place belongs primarily to the church in that location. Anglican education sees the local church community as the ultimate educator, called, gifted, and graced to shape its own life under the lordship of Christ. The development of God's indigenous people, in all they do corporately and individually, is the Anglican educational aim. The worldwide Anglican communion needs the witness the particular churches give, so each congregation strives to be conscious of and responsive to the revelation of God found in its own daily life and work. The patterns, methods, activities, programs, resources, and educational responses to these revelations are expected to be varied and a sign that Christ's revelation is inexhaustible. We can always learn more.

Though the response to God's revelation and love varies according to one's culture and circumstances, the very word "Anglican" symbolizes the fundamental unity within the communion: a common descent from and an essential continuity with the one, holy, catholic, and apostolic church that flourished in England from the earliest times and throughout the Middle Ages.

CONTENT

The content of Anglican education contains no essential doctrine and teaching that was not already held by the ancient apostolic and medieval church. Indeed, Anglican education is regarded ecumenically as a "nonconfessional" type of church education (one not based on any explicitly doctrinal confession of what must be taught and believed in order to belong).

It has been the tradition of Anglican education to contain within one body elements of both the Protestant and Catholic traditions, drawing upon each and building bridges to both, while teaching the following fundamentals: (1) the Holy Scriptures of the Old and New Testament are the revealed word of God; (2) the Nicene Creed is the sufficient statement of Christian faith; (3) the two sacraments, baptism and the Lord's Supper, are ministered with unfailing use of Christ's words of institution and of the elements ordained by him; and (4) the historic episcopate is locally adapted in the methods of its administration to the varying needs of the nations and peoples called of God into the unity of God's church.

Anglican education is grounded in these ancient fundamentals as it seeks for a balance, guarding against narrow fundamentalism, rigid traditionalism, and naive rationalism. It emphasizes Scripture, the source of Christian revelation; tradition, the unfolding of it; and reason, the ultimate test of it within the Christian community.

In the mind of an Anglican, this emphasis is an attempt to be comprehensive rather than compromising. It is not a sophisticated way of saying "anything goes," nor does it bargain one truth for another. Rather it implies that the apprehension of truth is a growing, relational dynamic. We only gradually progress in "knowing the truth." To learn the truth is to grow; to grow is to change. Anglican education is, therefore, a lifelong process of change. It invites individuals to an ongoing search and growth in spirit and faith since it is intended to help people reflect on the continuing flow and movement of God in their own experience.

Our ultimate ally is God, who, to paraphrase Augustine, has patterned into the very heart of humanity a longing that God alone can satisfy. The yearning for God is right at the center of the educational enterprise, and we need not doubt that God shares in our earnest attempts to learn and to discern the divine life intertwined with our own. It is only by the grace of God that anyone comes to know God in this world. In fact, this honest and humble search for God in creation, in the faith community, and in the structures and events of our lives provides another good definition of the purpose of Anglican education.

ORGANIZATIONS

Specific organizations for education range from graduate school to parish church. Preparation for ordained ministry is undertaken in graduate theological seminaries, but in England this includes degrees from the university colleges. The Anglican church has established colleges for higher education not only in England, where the colleges of Oxford and Cambridge were originally church foundations, but also in countries once colonial mission fields. In the United States there are several church-related colleges, although the establishment of schools was not considered a mission of the westward expansion as it was in some denominations.

Some scholastically distinguished preparatory schools in the eastern United States are or were founded under Episcopal church auspices. Preparatory schools, colleges, and theological seminaries are related to the national offices of the church through boards that exist primarily for purposes of networking. They do not set required standards or give financial support.

Elementary school education is provided through an increasing number of parish schools, which set standards of scholastic excellence and limit their enrollment. They usually strive for a diversified student body and provide some scholarship aid.

Basic parish religious education is given through the Sunday school. The morale building and educational support provided by diocesan and national boards has varied across the years. The period 1948–1968 is considered a high point during which there was a large staff in the national office and a denominational curriculum was launched. The period ended with financial cutbacks and a revising of priorities. New initiatives are only in the planning stage. For the most part, parishes are "on their own," and choose their curricular materials guided by a handbook for parish educators. Professionally trained religious education leaders are few. In parish religious education, the emphasis is on the liturgy as the basic educational experience. See also Great Britain and Northern Ireland; History of Christian Education; Private Schools and Religion.

R. E. Hayes

Anthropology, Theological

See Theological Anthropology.

Aquinas, Thomas

See Thomas Aquinas.

Archaeology, Biblical

Biblical archaeology applies the results of archaeology to biblical study. Sometimes this is direct and helpful to illuminate a biblical text, as when the carved reliefs from an Assyrian palace show the king's assault on the biblical city of Lachish in 701 B.C. (2 Chron. 32:9). At other times excavation data reveal and correct seeming errors in the biblical text, as when the described siege and capture of Ai by Joshua may have taken place further up the valley at Bethel, given the absence of a substantial early Iron Age defense system at Ai (Josh. 8:3–9).

The task of applying the results of archaeological exploration and excavation is properly the work of biblical scholars and historians. Archaeology as such is a neutral enterprise, being concerned mainly with accurate recovery of the physical remains of an earlier society and the accurate description of the life of that society. Biblical archaeologists apply this to the particulars of life in biblical times and places in order to illumine the biblical texts and understand their meanings more accurately.

The biblical world in which excavation evidence is most pertinent covers the entire Mediterranean Sea basin, the lands east of it to modern Iran's eastern border, and from modern Turkey south to Sudan. The main focus lies on sites in Syria-Palestine. The focus broadens for New Testament interests to include Turkey and points west to Italy because of the political domination of ancient Rome. The chronological focus of biblical archaeology is from about 2,500 B.C. through A.D. 150.

The main types of archaeological data of interest in such study include the following: Settlement types and plans range from nomadic camp sites to major cities like Corinth, Athens, and Jerusalem. Public structures are of primary interest—palaces, temples, markets, theaters, forums, and the art decorating such facilities. The chief items among private structures and equipment are the houses people used, storage facilities (including caves and cisterns), household goods (pottery, furniture, and utensils), and toys and tools (both for agriculture and crafts). Burial sites are important.

Found at major sites primarily, defense systems include city walls, gates through the walls, ramparts, and moats. For all sites they include hideaways, escape facilities, and personal and military weaponry (both defensive and offensive). The scarcity of sufficient fresh water throughout most of the biblical world required some extraordinary provisions to assure survival. Water systems include wells, cisterns, tunnels, aqueducts, reservoirs, and sometimes elaborate facilities at springs or dependable rivers.

Of obvious interest are religious structures and equipment—public temples (already mentioned) or shrine sites, whether in the open (as Canaanite shrines tended to be) or hidden partly underground (as the Mithraeum was normally built for initiation of new devotees). The recovery of the temples at Jerusalem suffers major limits from prior destructions except for the surviving western wall of Herod's Temple (which Jesus would have known). Equipment and symbols used in worship include bowls and knives for animal and other sacrifices or offerings, statues or paintings of the gods of the shrines, and representations of rituals appropriate to their worship.

Texts and inscriptions are of major interest because they allow movement from nonliterate to literate historical evidence. The most famous finds relating to biblical studies have been the Canaanite archive at Ras Shamra (ancient Ugarit), the Dead Sea Scrolls from Qumran (Jewish biblical and other manuscripts going back to the second century B.C.), and more recently the royal archive at Ebla, the biblical significance of which is still in debate.

Current archaeological trends focus on locating the biblical communities more precisely in their historical settings. This involves the study of surrounding contemporary cultures with which the biblical people had contact or from which they drew influence.

There is also new effort in getting more accurate environmental data for all the periods under review. This includes climate cycles, land topography, soil types, plant varieties, animal species, pollen changes, and rainfall or other water resource data.

Realizing the benefit of more precise anthropological data, scholars have focused on family and village patterns, migration habits, the interplay between village and nomadic life, the social stratification of ancient communities, and where the biblical people functioned in such societies.

Ever increasing is use of high technology in recovering field information. For the biblical archaeologist the aim is always better understanding of the biblical texts. It will continue to be an increasingly demanding discipline for the foreseeable future.

The use of this material in religious education is possible for all age groups from preschool through adult classes. In preschool classes the focus will necessarily be on objects: drawings, pictures, replicas, or other representations. Such items as the lamps, bowls, coins, or toys of the biblical period can illustrate stories told from both Old and New Testaments. For older students, the illustrations and articles in Bible dictionaries, encyclopedias, and student course books can bring the background of the Bible to life. Models of a stratigraphic cut can be made as class projects. Samples of archaeologist's tools (handpicks, trowels, cameras, drawings) can be brought to class and demonstrated. For adults, trips to local museum displays as well as the numerous audiovisual materials can make the discipline and its results vivid. The particular archaeological problems of some biblical sites may be discussed as well. *See also* Bible Study.

R. S. Boraas

Aristotle

Aristotle (ca. 384–322 B.C.) was a Greek teacher and philosopher. He studied in Plato's Academy, remaining there nearly twenty years. After leaving the Academy he became tutor to Alexander, son of Philip of Macedon, for eight years. In 335 B.C. Aristotle returned to Athens to found his own philosophical school, the Lyceum, creating at the same time one of the first great libraries. He made many basic discoveries in natural science, but his greatest achievements were in the field of philosophy. Taking Platonic thought in new directions, he formulated the principles of realistic philosophy. His most important writings include *Ethics*, *Physics*, *Metaphysics*, *Politics*, and *De Anima* (*On Human Nature*).

At the death of Alexander the Great in 323 B.C., in a wave of anti-Macedonian feeling and threatened with prosecution, Aristotle fled Athens to Chalcis on the island of Euboea, where he died a year later.

Aristotle greatly influenced Thomas Aquinas. Through him realism became basic to Western Catholic educational thought and to a "classic" approach to general education. Religious education that stresses basic knowledge of Scripture and doctrine has its roots, through medieval educational theory, in Aristotle's thought. *See also* Roman Catholic Education; Thomas Aquinas.

L. G. McAllister

Art in Religious Education

Christ upon the celestial globe; apse mosaic, San Vitale, Ravenna, Italy, mid-sixth century.

Art is a natural and necessary part of every religious tradition. A study of the religions of the world reveals that works of art emerge naturally as humans respond to values and experiences of the transcendent or divinity. Religious practice necessarily houses worshipers, creates symbols, and serves ritual needs; therefore art and architecture emerge. Art in some form is a language of all religions regardless of their teachings concerning idols or austerity. Even religions that include severe restrictions on the mode or place of the arts, such as some forms of Judaism, Islam, and Christianity, inevitably appropriate artistic and architectural elements for their function and identity. From hermit monks and simple Puritans to Byzantine processionals and "high church" ritual splendor, the language of the arts has always been at the heart of religious sensibilities. Art is one among many human responses to religious revelation and truth and is a natural part of religious expression and religious education.

Religious uses of the arts are, among other things, highly educational. The artistic expression of religion informs and shapes observers. Various kinds of knowledge come through the arts, and religious educators have at hand highly charged and enhanced tools for religious education when the arts are appropriated. While all forms of art are included in the range of human responses to religion, including music, dance, and theater, this article is primarily concerned with the visual arts, namely, painting, sculpture, architecture, photography, cinema, and video. In the following will be discussed ways in which the arts provide programmatic opportunities for religious educators, have been understood historically as religious education, and may be theologically viewed by educators.

PROGRAMMATIC OPPORTUNITIES FOR RELIGIOUS EDUCATORS

The six ways in which the arts facilitate religious education, described here, illustrate the rich variety of educational opportunities available in and through the uses of the arts.

Illustration

A basic role that art can play in any educational setting is to illustrate the stories, lessons, and truths of a religious tradition. Normally religious texts are illustrated and/or narratively rendered in prints, filmstrips, photographs, film, or electronic media. These illustrative works of art serve texts and thereby teach their content and moral lessons in a

The dance of Shiva; bronze figure from southern India, ca. thirteenth century, now in the Museum of Asiatic Art, Amsterdam.

visual medium. For the most part, in this category the work of art is secondary in the educational goal as it points beyond itself to illustrate a story, an event, an identification, or a moral point.

Instruction

Art that is used to instruct seeks to lead the observer to personal response, participation, and action. The role of art in this category is beyond the straightforward task of illustration in that attitudes or behavior of the observer may be affected or the observer may be instructed about how to achieve a goal. For instance, a video or deprived human conditions may lead to specific action, or a series of illustrations may teach CPR (cardiopulmonary resuscitation). Instruction through the arts can also dispense information that builds, over a period of time, a storehouse of knowledge for individuals and groups. Out of the history of early Christianity, Gregory the Great wrote a letter in A.D. 600 in which he stressed that art should be used in religious education, especially for those who could *not* read. He wrote, "Pictures are above all for the instruction of the people" (*Epistulae* II.13).

Inspiration

To be inspired is to be enriched, built up, and strengthened. The arts in religious education can inspire by adding beauty, a sense of mystery, vision, surprise, new perspectives, and different dimensions of time and space. The arts can introduce different rhythms and foci to a basically verbal and linear pedagogical method. Attention to beauty as well as to truth and a healthy respect for the role of the aesthetic dimension in religious education can lead to inspiration and, thereby, a more complete educational goal.

Seven-branched candlestick made of nickel, silver, and steel by artist Seymour Lipton in 1954; located in Temple Israel, Tulsa, Oklahoma.

Participation

Artistic human response through various media to religious truths and insights is an educational process as well as an end in itself. Learning involves acting and reacting, and individuals as well as traditions make artistic responses. Expressing oneself and forming interpretations through one's own art making provide ways of knowing through reflection and the process of creating. Artistic self-expression in religious education need not be restricted to children and youth. Depths of religious insight are to be gained and religious goals served through participation in and through artistic expression on the part of those of all ages. In the twentieth century, modes of psychological insight and forms of therapeutic activity have been identified through art making in the studies of Sigmund Freud and C. G. Jung among others. Misuses of participatory possibilities need to be avoided. For instance, merely filling children's time with craft activities, that is, with unstructured periods that take neither their work nor their attitudes seriously, is detrimental. Participation through art making can be an authentic religious response as well as an educational process.

Contemplation

Little encouragement is given in regularly structured educational sessions for open-ended contemplative time. Contemplation of works of art in religious education forms attitudes and responses not otherwise available and, again, are natural to religious practice. Unfortunately, little in formal educational practice happens in silence; however, contemplation of a work of art in silence can not only change the rhythm of verbal presentations and dialogue, but can open an increased depth of religious response between image and observer. Contemplation of a work of art has been central to some religious practice in the past. In the early church, great mosaic panels were placed before the worshiping community as a central focal point for contemplation. Altarpieces were erected as forms of visual instruction (for instance, those painted by El Greco in the early seventeenth century in Spain or those of carved wooden figures by

Egyptian hieroglyph depicting the judging of the dead; a portion of the Papyrus of Ani, ca. 1250 B.C., now in the British Museum, London.

Riemenschneider in the early sixteenth century in southern Germany). In modern times a large tapestry with a Christ figure designed by Graham Sutherland in Coventry Cathedral in England and the color field canvases without subject matter by Mark Rothko in the Rothko Chapel, Houston, Texas, inspire silent contemplation for religious purposes. Hinduism encourages contemplation of the dance of Shiva and Buddhism contemplation of the various attitudes of Buddha figures.

While these examples may refer to works of art in worship spaces rather than classrooms, they illustrate how education and spiritual formation take place in various settings.

Contextual and Subliminal Considerations

Education takes place and is shaped by environments, settings, symbols, and visual clues. Beside the possibilities listed above, a range of responses takes place in reaction to spatial location and arrangements, light sources and manipulation, color relationships, furnishings, and silent visual indicators. Religious educators increase the possibilities for total response and heightened involvement when the physical and visual environment is reflected upon and integrated so as to become one of the tools of the educator.

When Cyril of Jerusalem (ca. 315–386) gave his famous catechetical lectures to the pilgrims in the fourth century, he chose to teach the religious facts of Jesus's death and resurrection in the building that enshrined the actual tomb.

The role of symbols in religious education is illustrated in the ongoing power in society generally of a seven-branched candlestick, a cross, a hammer and sickle, or a flag. Symbols seldom simply instruct; they powerfully remind people of truths that are claimed and celebrated. The presence of living symbols can charge an environment, encourage memory, and foster religious formation.

HISTORICAL PERSPECTIVES

Religious education in and through the arts happened long before the beginning of the Sunday school movement or the introduction of Hebrew schools in synagogues. Generally speaking, all artistic production from prehistoric and ancient civilizations is

Athena Parthenos; a marble replica (called the Athena Varvakeion) of the chryselephantine statue completed in 438 B.C. by Pheidias, formerly in the Parthenon, now in the National Museum, Athens.

related to religious sensibilities. For instance, cave drawings of animals invoked a mysterious power to aid in the hunt. Artistic production, as seen in paintings and bone carvings, predates recorded language and illustrates the significance of image making as a natural human response. Images precede language.

Ancient civilizations formed symbol systems for verbal language out of their earlier expressions in art. Ancient Egypt's written language was a sophisticated system of artistically rendered symbols from nature. Hieroglyphs embodied the Egyptians' religious beliefs, and art and architecture served their pantheon of the gods. In ancient Greece, the arts directly narrated the hierarchy of deities, mythology, and ritual practice. The arts presented the religious consciousness of the culture. The extraordinary art of classical Greece, especially that of Periclean Athens, in a multifaceted and broad sense educated (informed and inspired) the public concerning its own identity and destiny. In the ancient Near East, the Assyrian and Mycenean arts suggest magical ritual activities and hierarchies of divinities with mysterious powers.

Among the Semitic cultures, the Hebrews formulated proscriptions for the arts that served the worship activities of the people while protecting their sense of the holy. Hebrew Scripture forbids some kinds of artistic activity, on the one hand (see Exod. 20:4), while there is, on the other, a long and rich tradition of Jewish art and architecture. Between the time of the splendid frescos of the early third-century synagogue at Dura-Europos in Syria, where the tradition is presented in visual form, to the twentieth-century stained glass windows by Marc Chagall in Jerusalem, with their interpretation of the twelve tribes of Israel, Jewish art has been a formative educational agent in the Jewish tradition.

Art instructs in a variety of settings. The broadly educational aspect of religious art appears in books, classroom presentations, wall hangings, sanctuary structures, liturgical

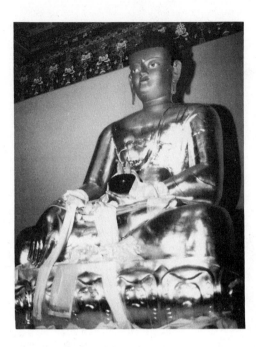

Buddha in a "touching the earth" posture; temple sculpture, ca. 1100–1300, Thailand.

furnishings, movie theaters, and communication media. Twentieth-century society is immersed in media and, within the vast array of messages that constantly shape culture, religious content is included. The various levels at which learning takes place depend on the medium and the tradition. For instance, a Hindu worshiper who repeatedly and ceremoniously circles around an image of Shiva in a temple in southern India is religiously formed in some fashion by the sculpture and architecture in that place. In a similar fashion, a faithful Muslim who quietly contemplates the meticulous calligraphy of a Qur'an text experiences the sacred word of that tradition through an artistic representation. Buddhists who meditate before an image of the seated Buddha in a "touching the earth" position are religiously educated as they recall through an art form the spirit and the teachings of the Buddha.

Christianity has educated the faithful in different kinds of settings through multiple art forms throughout history. In the early church, Scripture was illuminated with paintings and drawings for illustrative and meditative purposes. Vessels and objects such as glasses, plates, and textiles were adorned with symbols and figures representing Christian teachings and persons. Funerary art illustrated liturgical texts about deliverance and resurrection. Symbols (such as the cross and the fish) emerged in artistic form as powerful reminders. The earliest Christian art educated its followers and the public about its stories and beliefs and provided a means of communication and self-identity for the group. The walls of the baptistery room of the early third-century house-church at Dura Europos were covered with artwork that illumined the rite of baptism.

Medieval Christianity sheathed its walls with art and its liturgical vessels with jewels. Festivals of the church year and medieval drama cycles brought the annual seasons as well as the scriptural narratives, especially the episodes of the life of Christ as related in the Gospels, to the public in artistic form. Medieval Christianity in the West permeated its culture with artistic expressions of its religion, thereby educating generations through constant exposure to the traditions of the church. Religious formation took place within

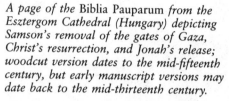

A page of the Biblia Pauparum *from the Esztergom Cathedral (Hungary) depicting Samson's removal of the gates of Gaza, Christ's resurrection, and Jonah's release; woodcut version dates to the mid-fifteenth century, but early manuscript versions may date back to the mid-thirteenth century.*

the cultural context. The arts played an unusually sensitive role in religious education in the Middle Ages because in some areas of Europe it was believed that some forms of art gave an observer direct contact with God. This was described in the twelfth century as an "anagogical" function for art. The dissemination of the *Biblia Pauparum* (*Bible of the Poor*), with its hundreds of illustrations, demonstrated an explicit use of the arts to instruct the faithful on the content of Scripture as well as the relationship of Old Testament to the New Testament.

Eastern Christian traditions incorporate artistic expression into the sacramental life of the church. The Byzantine icon, for instance, is a vehicle for spiritual awareness and response. The tradition does not worship its artworks, but rather venerates them as special images through which one communes with the spirit of the figure or episode represented. The arts therefore serve as necessary aspects of spiritual insight and formation.

During the Renaissance in the West, sacramental and anagogical uses of the arts in a broadly educational manner were superseded by an interest in naturalism, realism, and uses of classical norms. During the fourteenth and fifteenth centuries, religious subject matter was rendered realistically and with the use of perspective as natural human events. That tradition of narrative illustration continues to shape religious art used for education in the twentieth century.

The Protestant Reformation reacted strongly against all uses of the arts in a religious context because excessive uses seemed "papist" and appeared to represent the Roman Catholic church. Simultaneously, a renewed interest in preaching and hearing the word of the gospel led Protestants to a more verbal than visual religious focus. Nevertheless, the arts were used extensively by various groups of Protestants for religious education. The invention of the printing press and the ability to reproduce woodcuts and engravings brought religious propaganda to the masses in the form of pictures, and Martin Luther encouraged the artist Lucas Cranach and Cranach's son to paint altarpieces and panels to educate the public concerning Scripture and theology.

Icon of "Christ Eleemon"; mosaic from Constantinople, 1100–1150, now in the Staatliche Museum, Berlin.

The Catholic Reformation in the sixteenth century used the arts intentionally for its worship and theology and decreed in the Council of Trent that the arts should serve the church. The period of art known as the Baroque was fostered by the renewed interests of the Roman Catholic church to attract the public to its worship centers and to embody in the arts its sacramental and pedagogical goals. The grand scale and dramatic environments created by the church in the Baroque style educated masses of people and shaped the piety of generations around the world.

In the eighteenth century in the West, interest in personal experience and rational responses affected the arts in religious education. Emphasis on heightened aesthetic experience, coupled with personal insight, directed the world of religion toward modern views that value individuality and intelligence. In the process, emphasis on the artist, on the one hand, and the pedagogical force of visual illustration, on the other, pressed the arts to work in culture in two ways, to demonstrate individual artistic genius and to disseminate facts. Religious education has in the twentieth century tended to limit the role of the arts to that of a vehicle for facts. A broad view of the history of religions and of the arts suggests that the twentieth century has exercised a more limited range of possibilities than most earlier periods. In spite of the expanded communications opportunities and the state of electronic media, religious education tends to limit its uses of images to illustration.

In the modern period, art making has been viewed as psychologically significant. First Freud and later Jung established ways in which the arts work therapeutically and suggested that the arts can indicate various psychological conditions. Freud wrote of "pathography" and Jung sought archetypes in the arts. Beyond the role of the arts to illustrate texts and truths or, in a more modern guise, to indicate psychological states, there is a larger place for art in religious education that forms a person's understanding and insights through beauty, symbols, environments, and silent reminders.

THEOLOGICAL CONCERNS

In the Christian tradition, two approaches to the arts dominate. From the Catholic church, Scholastic teaching shaped in the Middle Ages by Thomas Aquinas stressed God's truth through nature and therefore through art. Neo-Scholastic thought, represented by scholars like Jacques Maritain and Etienne Gilson in the twentieth century, stresses the role of beauty in religion and the agency of the genius-artist. In this context, the French Dominican father M. A. Couturier in the 1940s and 1950s emphasized an appreciation for spiritual qualities in artistic form and the need for religious art created by society's greatest artists. In this approach, the quality and inherent value of a great work of art in itself is a source of spiritual truth.

From the Protestant tradition, a strong emphasis on the artist's expressive abilities and the insight gained in the production of art coupled with the observer's reaction to the work has religious import. Theologians like Paul Tillich emphasize the impact of highly expressive works. From his point of view, style shapes content and can determine the level of meaning. An experiential emphasis is placed on the analysis of art for religious purposes from this Protestant perspective.

There remains to be formulated a single theological position concerning the arts of popular culture and the media. The pervasive quality of these images and their symbolic character suggest that the popular arts of contemporary culture provide significant resources for religious education. Authentic religious attitudes are embodied in avant-garde expression, and religious subcultures are formed by the impact of religious media.

Throughout history, religious images have had meaning within their setting or context. In the modern world, broadcasting technology, electronic media, satellite communications, and laser transmission make images ubiquitous and negate distinctions between religious and nonreligious images or sacred and secular entities. Today's religious educators have vastly improved possibilities for integrating the arts in various media into a teaching/learning situation. At the same time, their task is vastly more complicated than in previous generations because discernment and knowledgeable choices from multiple options must be made. Ethical and moral decisions are called for.

While each religious tradition seeks to educate its followers, religious education at the end of the twentieth century necessarily views its world as global and international and looks at each tradition within the context of many traditions. Art builds bridges between individuals and God as well as between nations and between traditions. As a natural and necessary aspect of all religions, art in the service of religious education can further religious efforts to create a better world. *See also* Aesthetics; Affective Development; Crafts; Creative Activities; Creativity; History of Christian Education; Media; Symbolism; Visual Methods.

J. W. Cook

Asia

Asia covers a vast area and has a population of about three billion. Although the Christian population is estimated at about 3 percent, the church's educational ministry reaches far beyond the small number of Christians. The approaches, methodology, theological bases, and levels of development in religious education vary in different subregions; they also vary according to differences in non-Christian religious background as well as differences in churches' historical backgrounds. There is a great gap between the educationally advanced northeast (Japan, Korea, and Taiwan) and the south (the Indian subcontinent and Indonesia), where the literacy rate is very low. School systems also differ. The role of religion in public schools and the social pressure for or resistance to Christian education vary among Asian countries.

A rising tide of Asian consciousness among church leadership has not produced an "Asian religious education" to complement Asian theology. Christian religious education is not coordinated for all of Asia though some attempt at this has been made by the Christian Conference of Asia, a cooperative agency of 110 churches and national councils from sixteen Asian countries. Sunday school or other Christian school curricula are usually developed at national or denominational levels. Until recently Western models strongly influenced philosophy, methodology, and content of religious education, but now most of the Asian churches are using indigenous curricula and materials. The exceptions are among the conservative evangelical churches.

National councils of churches or Christian school unions have begun to include in their curricula an emphasis on understanding Asian neighbors and their faiths. ACUCA (Association of Christian Universities and Colleges in Asia) and a federation of Christian kindergartens for East Asia are the principal organizations of Christian schools. There is no coordinating association for Sunday schools or primary and secondary schools. There is a fellowship of Christian adult education centers (ACISCA) and an Asian Alliance of YMCAs.

SUNDAY SCHOOLS

Sunday school is still the main institution of education for most Asian churches. In many churches a majority of pupils are recruited from non-Christian homes—often by encouragement of their non-Christian parents due to the quality of education and the prestige of private schools. Many churches therefore consider Sunday school an important instrument for outreach. During the past twenty years, church membership in South Korea, for example, grew tenfold, and among the new members 33.2 percent joined their churches through Sunday school.

Producing Sunday school materials is difficult where Christians are a minority, and if churches are divided it becomes even more difficult. Even in a country where the technology is sufficient, educational materials will not be marketable unless there are enough Sunday schools and pupils. Moreover, in countries like Burma paper is rationed and audiovisual aids are restricted, thus making production of teaching materials difficult. Nevertheless, some materials are available. Lutheran churches in Southeast Asian countries are producing common textbooks in Chinese and English. The Hong Kong Christian Literature Council produces Chinese Sunday school materials for overseas Chinese in Southeast Asia. The United Church of Christ in Japan produces curriculum and related materials used by many other churches in Japan. In addition, there are audiovisual resource centers at local and national levels in most Asian countries.

PUBLIC AND PRIVATE SCHOOLS

Governments in Asia (except Japan and communist countries) encourage moral or religious education in the public schools. In the Philippines, Christian education is part of the curriculum, but the National Council of Churches is opposing it because of its possible violation of freedom of belief. In Sri Lanka, Indonesia, and Bangladesh, Christian education is given to Christian children alongside Buddhist, Hindu, or Islamic studies for other children. In Hong Kong and Singapore Christian subjects are included in secondary school examinations. In Pakistan, Malaysia, and Thailand, Islamic or Buddhist ethics are taught at public schools. Christians in Japan strongly object to any attempt by the government to revive moral education in public schools since such courses have been used historically to teach nationalism rather than broader moral values.

There are at least twenty thousand Christian schools in Asia. This figure does not include kindergartens and nursery schools. There was an almost equal number of Christian schools in China alone before the Communists nationalized them. In most countries of the Indian subcontinent also many Christian schools were nationalized. In South Korea many students without an interest in Christianity attend Christian schools at the secondary level. These schools were established with different purposes, but all provide some religious education in their programs. Some schools were built in areas where illiteracy was high, and others were built for cultivating Christian or civil leadership. Others were built for vocational training. Churches pioneered education for girls in Asia, where the status of women was low. Today among 289 Protestant schools in Japan 55 are still girls' schools even after many of them became coeducational. Among 301 Roman Catholic schools, 68.7 percent are girls' schools.

Most of the institutions for education and training of people with disabilities were created by Christians and often are still maintained by the churches. Christian education in Asia should not be measured only by regular religious course offerings or extracurricular activities like Bible classes, chapel services, or school retreats. According to a sociological survey of value concepts of graduates of International Christian University in Tokyo, many non-Christian students are strongly influenced by the Christian way of thinking and way of life during the four years of their campus life.

There is little open persecution of Christian education in the countries of Asia. (One exception is Nepal.) Nationalization of schools is no longer a problem. However, it will be difficult to start a new Christian school in many countries (e.g., Christians trying to start Genting Heights Christian College in Malaysia gave up the plan). There is a shortage of qualified Christian teachers. In an age of self-support Christian schools have had to give up support from foreign mission societies, but often this means schools must change their policy and cater to rich people's children or seek government subsidies or help from secular foundations. These new sponsors often attach ideological stipulations.

Partly for this reason, Christian schools are featuring English language education in many countries as well as moral or personal education and are attracting non-Christian students. In other countries, Christian schools are regarded as schools for the elite. Christian schools today must fight against secularization.

OTHER RELIGIOUS EDUCATION PROGRAMS

Christian adult education and lay training are carried out at many YMCAs, YWCAs, student centers, and Christian academies in Asia. Lay training centers experiment with new methodologies in Bible studies, application of group dynamics to church programs, and other new educational approaches. Although there are many Bible camps in Asia, camping as religious education is not well developed in Asia, largely because of economic conditions. Peace education in Christian schools is encouraged, but in many countries teaching "disarmament" is prohibited. *See also* Asian Americans; Buddhism; Confucianism, Hinduism; Taoism.

T. Arai

Asian Americans

When we use the term "Asian American," it is necessary to define what we mean. Asian Americans come from various Asian ethnic groups. They represent people from the Asian continent—east Asians like Japanese, Koreans, and Chinese; southeast Asians like Filipinos, Vietnamese, Indonesians, Malaysians, and Thais; and southern Asians like Indians and Pakistanis. Of course, there are many other Asian groups in the United States. For our purpose in this article we will focus on four of the largest and most religiously active Asian American groups—those whose background is Chinese (about 800,000 in the United States), Filipino (775,000), Japanese (700,000), or Korean (360,000).

It is interesting to note that among these four groups Chinese and Japanese Americans include a noticeable number of Buddhists along with Chris-

tians. Because there are no reliable statistics on their religious preferences it is hard to say what percentage of those populations are Buddhists. However, just as in the Philippines the majority of people are members of the Roman Catholic church, it is estimated that at least 90 percent of Filipino Americans are members of that church. In Korea only about 25 percent of the population are Christians, but it is estimated that 65 percent of Korean Americans are members of various Protestant churches and about 10 percent are Catholics. Buddhism and Christianity are the religions most active in Asian-American communities.

Generally speaking, the Asian-American Christian communities are not much different from those in ancestral lands. (This is particularly true among first-generation congregations.) Moreover, the goals and practices of religious education in the Asian-American churches are not much different from those in American Christian denominations. The reason is simply that the formation and development of Christian communities in Asia have been very much influenced by American churches since the turn of the century. Theory and praxis of religious education in America is quite visible in those countries as well as in Asian-American religious communities.

There are at least two phenomena peculiar to Asian-American religious education. The first is a legacy of the nineteenth-century American Protestant churches' understanding of Christian education as a means of evangelism. The Sunday school, as it is still called in most Asian-American churches today, is the strategic focal point for evangelistic endeavor. Pastors and church leaders concentrate their efforts on establishing high-quality educational programs right from the beginning of a new congregation. They do so because a good Sunday school can attract people. Influenced by the Confucian virtue of high admiration for learning, Asian Americans are eager to give their children the best available education, religious or secular. Consequently a good educational program in a local church can draw many concerned parents to the congregation. Of course, the Sunday school is not used solely as a means of attracting people; it is also regarded as an institution for teaching Christian heritage. Bible study is the major focus of religious education, though the concern for Christian nurture and growth is not lacking.

The second unique phenomenon is the integration of religious education with language instruction, so that religious education is in fact cultural orientation. Some congregations sponsor a separate language school alongside the Sunday school. But whatever arrangement they may have, religious education in the Asian-American churches and Buddhist temples has a very strong cultural component in its design and intention. There is among Asian Americans a sincere desire to teach their children their cultural values and heritage through Asian language instruction and other means. These values include respect for parents, the importance of keeping close family ties, and hard work; included also is the observance of their festivals. Asian Americans believe that cultural identity is one of their most important guarantees of survival in American society. *See also* Language, Inclusive; Liberation Theology; Multicultural Education.

C. Kim

Association of Professors and Researchers in Religious Education

See Professional Societies.

Athearn, Walter Scott ▬▬▬▬

Walter Scott Athearn (1872–1934) exerted a significant influence on American Protestant religious education for about a quarter of the twentieth century, beginning in the decade of the teens. He dreamed of integrating religious and public education on a national scale and based his hope upon research and upon a model of weekday religious education that he developed in the schools of Malden, Massachusetts. His findings were widely disseminated through the "Malden Leaflets"; his more comprehensive proposals were made in *A National System of Education* (1920).

Athearn hoped that more children could be reached for religious education and more quality time be available for such teaching if there were weekday religion classes and children were released from school for one period a week to go to these classes at nearby churches. This project was to be interdenominationally sponsored and funded. He hoped for a staggered release of classes (each class released at a different period) so that professional religious teachers could be employed full-time by the churches. Alternatively, he hoped for one period a week, for example, the last period on Wednesday afternoon, when all classes in one age group, say grades 3–6, would be released.

This never became a national movement, although variations on the form flourished for a time (and continue in some cases today) in parts of the Midwest and the South as well as in New England. *See also* Church-State Relations; Public Schools and Religion.

H. W. Burgess

Atheism

Atheists believe that God does not exist, so they maintain all claims of knowledge about God are illusory. A theoretical belief in God's existence but an indifference to God's will is known as practical atheism. The avowed atheist makes a conscious, explicit denial of transcendence. An atheist should not be confused with an agnostic, who says that we cannot be sure if God does or does not exist, or an infidel, who does not believe in some specific system about God, be it Muslim or Christian, or a skeptic, who doubts some particular accepted doctrine, whether religious or philosophical.

Atheists are a varied group. An extreme personal idealism, for example in the writings of John McTaggart (1860–1925), dismisses completely the idea of an absolute God. Marxist thought is hostile to religion, which it regards as elaborate superstition designed to keep workers in subjection. Jean-Paul Sartre gives existentialism an atheistic dimension, defining God as "the useless passion." *See also* Agnosticism.

P. Elmen

Atonement

See Redemption.

Attendance

Religious groups vary in the emphasis given to attendance at gatherings for religious education. Those who put the greatest emphasis on knowledge of the content of one's faith view attendance at such gatherings as necessary for the instruction in the faith. Others view attendance as a sign of one's interest in and faithfulness to one's religion. Yet others stress the living of one's faith in the world and put more emphasis on personal responsibility than attendance.

Most religious groups keep records of attendance at religious education functions, primarily Sunday school, CCD, or synagogue classes, and use these as indicators at least in part of their success. For most, the period immediately following World War II was a time of high levels of attendance, while the decades of the 1960s and 1970s were periods of decline. The 1980s have shown some signs of increase in attendance in many groups, especially evangelical Protestants, though there is still uncertainty as to whether this is a temporary reversal or whether all (or even most) groups will experience this reversal. One's attendance at religious education events may not guarantee one being educated, but lack of attendance usually means lack of quality religious education or is a sign of lack of interest in religion.

Among some religious groups, attendance at educational events is considered a responsibility. Members of other groups expect such events to meet personal needs for psychological strengthening or spiritual growth. Where the latter is the case, any efforts to increase attendance will involve seeking consonance between the goals of the institution and those of the learners (or their parents where children are involved), leader development so that teachers can make classes more interesting, adequate rooms, equipment, and supplies, and a variety of times for educational experiences.

The fact that some people view Saturday and Sunday as days for family travel or recreation will be a factor limiting growth in weekend church programs. Development of midweek programs, summer events, and family day or weekend events may avoid this problem. This expresses the idea that the quality of the event is more significant than the quantity of hours and that an experience concentrated in time may be as useful as one spread over many weeks.

Some groups have attempted to increase attendance through promotional efforts, notably contests in which rewards are won for meeting attendance goals. This has brought temporary increases more often than permanent ones. It also penalizes those who have serious reasons for being absent, while rewarding others who might better be absent: someone with a viral infection or the resistant child who expresses frustration in the class.

Low attendance needs to be regarded as one sign that a program may be lacking in effectiveness and become a spur to reexamination and change. It can also be a reflection of conflicting needs within the community for which events are planned. *See also* Awards; Planning; Record Keeping.

J. J. Sowell

Attitude Formation

An attitude is a descriptive characteristic of an individual that indicates the consciousness by which activities are determined, either actual or possible, in the social context. These are known as sets, prejudices, motivations, or suggestions. Although sociologists, anthropologists, educators, and psychologists have explored the nature and the formation of attitudes, the study is now considered a primary field in social psychology. In 1935 Gordon Allport gathered most previous research and focused further study with this definition: "An attitude is a mental and neural state of readiness, organized through experience, exerting a directive or dynamic influence upon the individual's response to all objects and situations with which it is related." The studies first examined the "set" or task attitude of a person, which allows one to be "ready" to perform some task.

Understanding the factors involved in attitude formation is of particular interest to religious educators in presenting material at variance with the practice of the group or in efforts to modify attitudes, for example, toward people who seem "different" or unfamiliar.

CATEGORIES OF RESEARCH

Recent research might be categorized within two major types, learning-behavioral theory and cognitive theory. Arthur W. Staats, Carl I. Hovland, Daryl J. Bem, Anthony G. Greenwald, and others have carried out extensive studies in various forms of behavioral processes. Classical and operant conditioning experiments have provided insight into human motivations. The Yale studies directed by Hovland shifted the emphasis to human communication, attitude change, and models of persuasion. Leon Festinger, Sharon Brehm, Milton Rokeach, Charles Sarnoff, Timothy Brock, Carolyn and Muzafer Sherif, and others have carried out even more studies in various forms of cognitive processes. The studies centering on cognitive consistency and cognitive dissonance became quite helpful in understanding the mechanisms of prejudice in human intergroup relations. The social judgment studies have provided refinements of instruments, measures, and an understanding of cultural differences in human attitudes. The field of social psychology is still heavily involved in such research, the results of which will continue to be useful to educators in general and to religious educators in particular because of their primary interest in human motivation, cultural understanding, and personal and intergroup relations.

RESEARCH FINDINGS

The Yale studies in communication and persuasion by Hovland and others provided educators with a clearer understanding of the mechanism of attitude formation and change. The communicator provided a persuasive message or opinion. The subject was found to "rehearse" the new opinion, perhaps comparing it with a prior opinion. This aspect of attitude change involving rehearsal or practice by the learner suggests that the heavy use of memory work in religious education may not have been inappropriate as a tool in the formation of particular religiously approved attitudes. In addition, these studies introduced the concept of "incentive" as an important variable in attitude change. Practice may help a person learn a new attitude, but it is not sufficient as a mode of bringing about an acceptance of that attitude. Three incentives were found to be of major importance:

1. The characteristics of the communicator or teacher (if the source of the opinion or information were to be trusted, the content might be trusted as well)

2. The setting or context in which the communication occurs (even the reception of the com-

munication by others in the social setting will influence the tendency toward acceptance or nonacceptance)

3. The content of the communication itself (arguments, facts, reasons, appeals, and other material with which the learner might tend to agree or at least understand and therefore become convinced)

Other experiments in this series dealt with threat as a means of persuasion; organization of material, such as saving best arguments for final position; the merits of balanced arguments, in which reasons are shared from the opposition as well as one's own views; the influence of a group setting, including the function of conformity as a variable in attitude formation; and, finally, the relationship between personality and persuasibility, that is, the tendency for those who had aggressive motives toward others, who preferred isolation, or who exhibited symptoms of psychoneurotic behavior to resist persuasion or attitude change. All of these factors might be useful to the educator in presenting material that is intended to form or intensify certain values or motives.

Festinger's research into cognitive dissonance offered religious leaders an understanding of "failed prophesy" and the function of reinterpretation in religious movements. Rokeach's study, *The Open and Closed Mind*, provided an understanding of bias, prejudice, and the relationships between personality, ideology, and cognitive functioning. The seminal work by Theodor Adorno and others on the authoritarian personality offered a method of measuring tendencies toward fascist attitudes and an understanding of the dynamics of prejudice.

Religious educators who take the insights from these social psychologists seriously will be able to more effectively intervene in the attitude formation process, as that is a part of their instruction, and will understand the dynamics of dogmatism and prejudice as they hinder the formation of certain religious values. *See also* Behavior; Behaviorism; Cognitive Dissonance; Indoctrination; Learning Theory; Motivation; Prejudice; Social Sciences; Values.

FOR FURTHER REFERENCE

Adorno, T. W., et al. *The Authoritarian Personality*. New York: Harper & Row, 1950.
Greenwald, A. G., et al. *Psychological Foundations of Attitudes*. New York: Academic Press, 1968.
Kiesler, Charles A., et al. *Attitude Change*. New York: John Wiley, 1969.
Rokeach, M. *The Open and Closed Mind*. New York: Basic Books, 1960.

C. H. Snelling

Audial Methods

In this television generation the accent is on the eye: color, shapes, motion. Graphics are highlighted in books whose text is sparse. On broadcast television the loss of the picture during a commercial usually means a 70 percent credit to the advertiser; the loss of sound receives only a 30 percent credit. But sound—hearing—still permeates our culture and receives careful attention in religious education.

In addition to face-to-face (or ear-to-ear) sound our society employs the telephone, radio, and sound recordings to communicate the sounds of the human voice, musical instruments, machinery, and nature.

Martin Luther once said "The Church is a mouth-house, not a pen-house." He was railing against the misuse of that new medium, print. He was contending that the nature of religious life is best nourished by person-to-person contact.

Audial methods in religious education begin with ways of learning to listen to people, of enabling the religious community to speak and to hear clearly what each is saying to the other—and what the world is saying to the religious community.

Preaching and teaching are the earliest ways that Jews and Christians employed to establish, nourish, and guide their life together. Public speaking skills that enable speakers to express themselves clearly are basic to the audial process of religious education. These include the basic techniques of composition (establishing the purpose of a speech, noting its central thought, outlining, and, perhaps, writing). They also include posture, gesture, and other visual elements, but articulation, inflection, and volume are still the primary elements that require attention. The resources of public education are available to help teach and hone these skills, so Christian education programs generally do not establish their own public speaking courses.

Religious educators concentrate on helping those who preach and teach focus on the *meaning* of what is to be said and on the *process* of communicating with a group. They are concerned that those who wish to be heard learn to listen as well, because they accent the *community* in communication. They want to be certain that this audial channel is not used only as a one-way information mode.

USE OF RECORDED MATERIALS

The use of recorded materials began early, with records used primarily for learning music or to enrich a class with plays and readings, particularly from the Bible. Later, publishing houses began to insert thin special-purpose records into curriculum packages.

The development of audiocassettes expanded

use of recorded material substantially. The content of these recordings broadened as well, to include lectures on the Bible, theology, ethics, education—in fact, the whole gamut of Christian education.

At first prerecorded materials were listened to in their entirety, much as one would listen to a lecture. Some educators, however, broke free from this one-way approach and began to adapt prerecorded materials for their own purposes. They would play only a selected portion of the lecture as either a discussion starter or enrichment for the discussion. When an entire lecture was used they would encourage participants in the group to ask that the tape be stopped when they wished to raise a question or make a comment. In this way they took control of their material and moved the participants beyond a consumer mode.

Continuing education of clergy and resources for lay education have been offered through subscription series such as *Catalyst* (a tape-print journal), *Thesis*, and *Resource*.

Many educators have seen process benefits in audio recording and have involved their communities in creating their own material for their own learning. Intergenerational learning has benefited as young people have interviewed the elderly members of a congregation. Church anniversaries have been turned into educational opportunities as histories have been logged on tape, later to be transferred to print and/or to be placed in the church library.

Young people have found audio recording especially attractive and have created radio-style biblical and historical dramas. These have sometimes employed *You Are There*, talk-show, and even entertainment formats. The process of creating these recordings affords multiple opportunities for learning: the initial reading of the story, discussion of its meaning, writing of a script, rehearsal of the recording of the drama, and debriefing afterward.

USE OF TELEPHONES, RADIOS, AND AUDIO AMPLIFIERS

The telephone has been used by adult education groups also, often in connection with audiocassette programs or printed curricula. The original speaker or author is contracted to be at a telephone to answer questions asked by a study group over a conference telephone that allows them to hear the resource person's answer.

Educators are less likely to consider the use of radio in teaching, although audiocassette tapes are similar. It is not easy to keep up with programming, because local newspapers give only limited coverage of their schedules. Yet there is music on such programs that might well be taped for use. Selections from a performance by an adult or children's choir could be a model for a local group. Orchestral or organ music could be back-ground for listening. An interview with a significant person or a current events program could be the basis for a discussion. A well-told children's story could be used to demonstrate storytelling to teachers. A children's story could be taped and learned for retelling to an informal group. Excerpts from a human interest talk show could form the basis for a group discussion of what is of personal concern to people who seek help through this medium.

We sometimes forget how widespread is the use of radio: people listen while they drive, while they work at a desk or in the kitchen; they listen to enliven postmidnight hours when sleep will not come. There are resources here to be tapped, but more thought needs to be given to the possibilities.

A discussion of audial methods would not be complete without a note concerning the use of amplification in education. Audio amplifiers are a (sad) necessity for large group sessions. Their use should be limited, and when they are working at their best they should not be noticed. When responses or questions are sought, the audience participants should be provided access to microphones so that their questions or comments can be easily heard.

Any use of electronic equipment requires careful planning and attention to setup of the equipment, as well as monitoring of it during use. Failure to attend to these needs can lead to disappointment if the equipment's use is central to the educational event. It is well to have backup arrangements planned ahead, such as other discussion resources available or a means to rearrange large groups to facilitate hearing or interchange.

Clues to Creativity, volumes 1, 2, and 3, by M. Franklin Dotts and Maryann J. Dotts (New York: Friendship Press, 1974), include help for discussion and interviewing, as well as some suggestions about dramatization (some of which may be noted under drama or video). Ed McNulty's series on audiovisual aids in the church published by *Your Church* magazine is also a useful resource. *See also* Communication Theory; Radio.

B. Everist

Augustine

Aurelius Augustinus (A.D. 354–430) was one of the great theologians of the Christian church and a concerned teacher of teachers. He received his early Christian training from his mother, Monica, a zealous Christian. While searching for "truth" in his late teens, he experienced a kind of conversion away from his childhood faith to philosophy. After spending a portion of his twenties teaching rhetoric, Augustine traveled to Milan, Italy, where he was influenced by the preaching of Ambrose. He converted back to Christianity and was baptized by Ambrose in 387. Abandoning his profession, he returned to Africa where, in A.D. 395, he was consecrated bishop of Hippo. From this small Numidian city of thirty thousand, Augustine became one of the most important figures in history.

Although Augustine is often thought of as a theologian, a number of his works played a role in shaping the way the church educates its young and its converts. *The Teacher* (A.D. 389) addresses the problem of how the learner learns, and *First Catechetical Instruction* (ca. A.D. 400) is a practical statement of Augustine's method for teaching new converts. In summary, Augustine argued that the effective teacher must know the topic, know the learner, vary the method according to circumstances, and engage the student's response. *See also* History of Christian Education.

H. W. Burgess

Australia

Religious education in Australia is best understood by reference to the two systems that define and shape its expression—the school system and the parish system. We will explore each system separately. This exploration takes place against a federal-state relationship in which, although the states of Australia exercise autonomy in the development of educational philosophy and practice, significant federal government involvement occurs at the level of finance and policy. The churches also operate with national and state reference,

thus complicating the religious education scene across Australia.

There are two main streams within the school system, the state-organized schools and the private or independent schools. Within this latter category a further division needs to be made between the Catholic school system and independent Christian, mainly Protestant, schools.

THE STATE SCHOOL SYSTEM

The decade 1970–1980 saw a major review of the role of religion in Australian state schools. Ministerial Committees of Inquiry took place in six states and in the Australian Capital Territory. Their reports indicate that a majority of Australians want some form of religious education for their children in government schools. There was no agreement on the form that education should take.

Although the states vary considerably in the way they address the teaching of religion in state schools, the practice of allowing volunteers to enter schools for denominationally based religious instruction has been widespread. Parental right to withdraw children from religious education sessions is universally recognized. In the state of Victoria at the level of secondary schooling (grades 7–12), chaplains are operating in a significant number of schools, paid for in the main by money raised by parents of children in the school. They assume responsibility for religious education programs, as well as making the link between home and school. A comprehensive religious education program, Religion in Life, is commonly used as a basis for classroom activity in primary schools (grades 1–6). Students at grade 12 may take a variety of approved academic subjects in religious studies.

In South Australia a religious education project team prepares resource material for the use of teachers; the material includes a broad definition of religion, as well as a study of meaning and belief.

In Tasmania a religious studies syllabus operates at the senior levels of secondary school and at the highest level religious studies can be taken as an academic subject for credit for university entrance.

The state of Western Australia appointed a curriculum officer for religious studies in 1978, and the dimension of religious experience and faith response was integrated into subjects such as English and social studies.

Queensland in 1975 appointed staff to form a Religious Education Curriculum Project within the state Department of Education. The result was a syllabus covering grades 1–12 supported by extensive in-service courses in religious education for teachers throughout the state and production of resource materials. In 1980 an academic program,

The Study of Religion, for grades 11–12 was initiated and was taken up by a small number of government and nongovernment schools.

PRIVATE, INDEPENDENT SCHOOLS

Catholic schools throughout Australia, like other independent schools, receive educational grants from federal and state governments. Comprehensive religious education programs within Catholic schools provide teacher education, in-service training events, and resources. Daily prayers and regular worship in school are common. Most schools are related to a parish church. Religious education coordinators oversee curriculum development and work with teachers, administration, and parish priests.

Institutes of Catholic education operate in states to monitor the quality of teacher education. As the number of religious teaching in schools has declined, lay teachers have been trained to take over the tasks of religious education. Postgraduate diplomas in religious education are offered at Catholic teachers' colleges in order to encourage continuing professional growth in the field. Dioceses set guidelines for the teaching of religious education and the practice of religious education in Catholic schools is often supported by consultants from diocesan education offices and religious orders.

Most private non-Catholic schools in Australia have a chaplain who is a regular member of the teaching staff and responsible for worship in the school chapel and at school assemblies. Such schools vary in kind from the well-endowed, well-established large Protestant schools to small, locally based interdenominational schools and from schools that have religious education coordinators to others without coordinators where teachers undertake religious education within the normal teaching schedule across all subjects.

Jewish schools' various styles may be identified as modern "community," progressive, modern Orthodox, national secular, Yiddish secular, European Hasidic, and Hungarian forms of yeshiva schools. It is common in such schools for two or more hours to be devoted to Jewish studies, with prayer, ritual, and worship occupying further time.

The Australian Association of Religious Education, a voluntary professional association that has branches within the states, is largely supported by and representative of the interests of chaplains and staff of the nongovernment school system.

PARISH EDUCATION

Because of the small population of Australia and the corresponding limited economic resources of the churches, most churches do not have professional directors of religious education. Parish programs are staffed by volunteers who are supported in their work by state or regional denominational agencies that provide help with curriculum resources and leadership/teacher education programs.

The cooperative curriculum developed by the Joint Board of Christian Education (see below) is widely used, and a parish Sunday school usually offers classes from early childhood through youth, as well as classes for adults. Attendance tends to lessen beginning with junior high school age. Sunday morning adult classes are few. Adult religious education is more often a weekday Bible study group and is particularly emphasized during Lent; specially prepared materials are used and meetings are frequently arranged on an ecumenical basis. Sunday evening youth groups afford study and social opportunities for bonding within the church community. There are also summer youth conferences.

THEOLOGICAL EDUCATION

In the state of Victoria theological students and others earning a theological degree for educational purposes are able to take a major in religious education in their primary degree. Through the Melbourne College of Divinity (MCD) a submajor in religious education is offered in the postgraduate Bachelor of Divinity. In addition master's and doctoral degrees in the field of religious education are available to candidates for MCD degrees. Colleges of divinity in other states also provide opportunities for tertiary work in religious education.

NATIONAL AGENCIES

Various national agencies offer resources for religious educators. The National Pastoral Institute, a Catholic center established in Melbourne, offers a year of concentrated study in the fields of pastoral and religious education, with the opportunity to pursue an area of personal interest as the focus of the year's work. The Joint Board of Christian Education is an educational agency that serves a variety of churches in Australia and New Zealand. Its curriculum resources are also sold in other countries. The board, which is a major publisher of resources for religious education, produces material for both school and parish use, covering a wide range of juvenile and adult materials. In addition the board undertakes significant biannual training events for state and regional staff and offers consultative, research, and training support for professionals and volunteers. The General Board of Religious Education (GBRE) is a national Anglican education agency offering subjects in religious education that can be taken for credit for the degrees of the Australian College of Theology, an Anglican body. Scripture Union also operates at national and state levels, with significant penetration into parachurch groups as well as the established denominations. Scripture Union provides curriculum materials, runs in-service and training events, and provides support for ongoing educational ventures such as camping and beach missions.

There are encouraging signs throughout Australia that increased attention and resources are being made available to support ventures in religious education. After a long period of relative inactivity, the cause of religious education in Australia seems to be entering a new, more open and productive phase, not only within the churches but also in the wider culture. *See also* New Zealand.

D. Grierson

Autonomy

Etymologically, autonomy means self-rule (Gk. *autos* + *nomos*). Applicable both to persons and institutions, the word suggests the presence of or capacity for self-determination and freedom from coercion. Its opposite is heteronomy: rule by external forces.

Autonomy is an important issue in philosophical and theological ethics, in psychology, and in political theory. In relation to these fields of study, its significance for religious education becomes apparent.

In much contemporary ethics, the category of autonomy is basic both to the articulation of moral principles and to the description of the human self. Especially in the tradition that follows Immanuel Kant (1724–1804), principles used to guide right moral action are principles that affirm and protect the rights of all persons to exercise freedom of thought, choice, and action. As a description of the person, autonomy refers to one's capacity to exercise self-rule. The ethically ideal society, from this perspective, would be one in which all persons are capable of autonomy and exercise it in such a way as to respect and protect the autonomy of all others.

Because the capacity for self-rule is not a given in the human person, autonomy becomes an important psychological category. Key questions concern how persons develop internal freedom and self-control. Various schools of psychology approach the issue from different perspectives, but the basic themes have to do with the development and maintenance of a sense of identity, self-esteem, and ego integrity as well as capacities in cognitive operation and social role-taking. Lawrence Kohlberg explicitly relates ethical and psychological conceptions of autonomy to one another in his theory of moral development (in which autonomy is key to the attainment of moral maturity).

Autonomy is often less central in theological accounts of morality and human selfhood in which persons are recognized to be finite and fallen, prone to evil and dependent upon God. The actual capacities of human beings for self-determination, as well as its promise for good, are often questioned by theologians. Nonetheless, sheer heteronomy rarely appears as a positive alternative. Freedom of persons from external determination is usually a high religious value, especially in the Jewish and Christian traditions. Hence, theologians often search for some alternative to both autonomy and heteronomy. An example is Paul Tillich's articulation of the concept of theonomy, that is, putting the self under the law of God.

In religious education, important issues in relation to autonomy continually surface. One set of issues has to do with whether autonomy (as both moral and psychological characteristics of persons) ought to be fostered and, if so, how. A second set has to do with the ethical dimensions of religious education itself. Education is always a form of influence and thus exercises power in relation to other persons. How can this power be exercised in a way that maintains respect for people's freedom and integrity while still being effective in shaping what they know and who they become?

Finally, since autonomy can be ascribed to institutions as well as to persons, the concept is important in political theory and religious social ethics. The significance of this dimension of autonomy for religious education is seen in debates about such issues as religious studies and rituals in public schools, the relationship of the state to religiously sponsored private and parochial schools, and the appropriateness of political and social issues as subject matter in religious education carried out by religious communities.

The ways in which all of these issues are posed and answered depend heavily upon the ethical, psychological, political, and theological intellectual resources brought to bear on them. *See also* Ethics; Freedom; Moral Development.

C. R. Dykstra

Awana

Awana is a church-sponsored weekday club for children aged three through the twelfth grade. The primary emphasis is that of reaching boys and girls for Christ through Scripture memorization. The suggested program consists of three major elements, Bible Counsel Time, Game Time, and Handbook Time, and includes an award incentive element based upon accomplishments. Organizationally there are six divisions, each encompassing two to three age levels. The Awana organization publishes curricula for the club meetings and a magazine for participants. Some 4200 churches in the United States and 400 in Canada include Awana clubs in their ministries. In addition Awana is represented in 45 foreign countries. They are presently headquartered in Streamwood, Illinois. *See also* Pioneer Clubs; Youth Ministry.

J. A. Gorman

Awards

Teachers have traditionally marked students' achievements or diligence by the granting of awards. Whether it be a gold star given to a kindergartner or an honorary doctorate given to a distinguished citizen, schools of all kinds have used awards both to recognize and to stimulate achievement.

The traditional wording of a diploma suggests that degrees themselves (B.A., M.A., Ph.D., etc.) are honors giving the graduate rights and privileges once highly defined but now understood only in an honorific sense. High achievement in college is marked by being placed on an honor roll (or dean's list) or by eligibility for honors programs.

However, while these traditional practices remain, contemporary educational practice has moved away from a once heavy reliance upon awards as a stimulus to learning. Since the early part of the twentieth century the giving of awards to mark pupil progress especially at the early stages of learning has been criticized. Educational progressives argued that the best reward was the student's satisfaction in solving real problems or acquiring new insight. They argued that all rewards should be eliminated save the intrinsic reward that learning itself brings.

This criticism was especially pertinent to practices in the Sunday schools, which throughout the nineteenth century made elaborate use of awards. Asa Bullard in *Fifty Years with the Sabbath Schools* (1876) noted an 1822 practice that gave a pupil a ticket of such trifling monetary value that, if always punctual, the child might at the end of two years accumulate enough tickets to equal one cent! Mark Twain in *The Adventures of Tom Sawyer* (1876) ridiculed an equally elaborate system of giving tickets for memorizing Bible verses.

Awards for attendance were the most widespread early in the twentieth century. They took the form of buttons, certificates, or pins with wreaths and bars that could mark perfect attendance for up to sixty years. This "cross and crown" system is still available. Religious educators influenced by the progressive movement sought to eliminate all such practices from Sunday schools or church schools, substituting in their stead religious experiences that met the deepest needs of the child far more readily than any ticket, gift, or button. However, the impact of reinforcement theory after World War II raised in a new way the issue of motivation of students and the validity of rewarding students for desirable behaviors. For instance, during the 1960s many inner city schools struggling with the problem of how to motivate students even experimented with paying students who raised their test scores.

Local churches have as yet made little creative use of reinforcement theory. This is the concept that motivation is strengthened and desired learning (of material or behavior) is more likely to become habitual if the learner connects the process with a pleasant experience. Churches that give awards tend to follow nineteenth-century patterns, and some churches that have abandoned awards of all kinds have frequently lost sight of that feeling of satisfaction in achievement that is the intrinsic reward. Few churches are responding to contemporary learning theory and the possibilities it holds for new ways of stimulating and recognizing student achievement.

A warm relationship between teacher and pupils encourages a feeling of being rewarded. A pleasant, well-equipped room and sufficient choices of activity to engage the special gifts of each child rewards creativity in a way that requiring all to accomplish tasks in the same way does not. Reinforcement can be encouraged when the difficulty of a task is faced in advance and an agreed-upon reward follows: reading a special book, going outdoors for a game, or watching a desired videotape. A class party or outing may be the concluding reward for a year's work well done.

Professional religious educators need to do careful research and critical thinking in the area of learning theory to guide the churches. Neither the practices of the nineteenth-century Sunday school or the reforms of the early twentieth-century progressives seem adequate responses in the late twentieth century. *See also* Conditioning; Learning Theory.

H. A. Archibald

B

Baptism

Baptism is the church's sacrament or rite of initiation. Through this act persons are given their identities as Christians. In baptism the church declares who Christians are and to whom they belong—"You are a chosen race, a royal priesthood, a holy nation, God's own people" (1 Pet. 2:9).

In baptism two major themes of the Christian life are dramatized—the gift of God's grace and the individual's response to the call of God. Traditionally the different practices of infant baptism and believer's (or adult) baptism have placed primary emphasis on one or the other of the themes. In infant baptism the grace theme is dominant, and in believer's baptism the personal response is stressed. In both cases, the second theme is accented in other rites. When older children or youth are confirmed, the response of the individual is highlighted, and when infants are dedicated, or presented for blessing, the focus is on thanksgiving for the grace of God in the gift of new life.

There are three ways of baptizing. One is to immerse the whole person in a tank of water and then raise the individual up immediately while the minister repeats the words, "I baptize you in the name of the Father, and of the Son, and of the Holy Spirit. Amen." This symbolizes going down into death with Christ and being raised with him into eternal life. A second way is to pour water from a shell-shaped scoop over the head of the person leaning over the baptismal font, which is a scooped-out receptacle that may be either shallow or deep. This retains the symbolism of flowing water (as biblically in the River Jordan) without immersion. The third way is to sprinkle water from the font on the head of the person to be baptized to symbolize the use of water. These forms, too, are accompanied by the trinitarian formula.

However baptism is practiced, it is the sacrament or ordinance (along with the Lord's Supper) that is foundational to the church's self-understanding. Likewise, baptism is a central focus for Christian education. Its task is to help persons both to grasp the biblical/theological meanings of baptism and to act on those meanings in their daily lives.

How then does one relate the practice of baptism as a liturgical event to the work of Christian education? In recent years a fresh vision of the interrelatedness of liturgy or worship and Christian education has emerged. It is now clear that the words and symbolic actions of worship, as in a baptism, are teaching experiences. Religious rituals affect persons' understandings, faith, and life. Some church educators even claim that a church's ritual life is more influential than formal instruction in shaping understandings and values. At the same time we know that a congregation's worship is enriched by the biblical learnings, theological insights, and faith experience persons bring to that event. Education, therefore, is essential for preparation for worship and participation in the sacraments.

BAPTISM AS EDUCATION

A baptism is a dramatic liturgical act. There are the symbolic gestures and actions of the minister; candidates and their families are actively involved; the congregation participates in the litanies and prayers; and pertinent biblical texts are read. Because the typical congregation normally baptizes persons only on selected Sundays, a baptism is a uniquely celebrative event.

Liturgy, and baptism in particular, has the power to enhance persons' sense of identification with the church. When a baptism is conducted with drama and dignity (in contrast to its being an additional, rushed element of a worship service), worshipers are reminded again of their own baptismal vows and the congregation's identity as the baptized people of God is reinforced. For this to happen, the baptismal ritual has to be conducted in such a way that there is something to be seen and heard by the baptismal candidates (or parents, in the case of infants), family, and congregation. When the baptismal water can be seen and its splashing heard, when families gather around the font or baptistry, when baptismal hymns are sung, and the congregation is actively participating, then a baptism is a lively drama molding the life of the Christian community.

EDUCATION ABOUT BAPTISM

Traditionally Christian education provides instruction about baptism primarily for older children and early adolescents. In the believer's baptism churches this instruction is part of a Pastor's Class for persons preparing to make a profession of faith and be baptized. (In some cases the instruction immediately follows baptism.) In the infant baptism churches, the instruction about baptism and its meaning is a part of the confirmation process.

There is opportunity for education focused

on baptism at other times and with other groups. Classes and retreats for parents expecting the birth or adoption of a child, especially their first one, are unique occasions for dealing with the meaning of infant baptism or baby dedication. This is also an appropriate time to help expecting parents review what baptism means for them as adults. Another group that can benefit from a study of baptism are prospective or new adult members. With denominational loyalty apparently becoming less influential as a factor in mobile adults' selection of a congregation (with the exception of those from more conservative heritages), it is not unusual to find a diversity of baptismal experiences and views within the membership of an urban congregation. A study of baptism can be a unifying experience for such groups.

A useful resource in planning baptismal education is the recent research on faith development. This research suggests that persons experience specific stages in their faith journey. The faith stage of older children or early adolescents is characterized by a sense of belonging and by claiming the stories and practices of a particular group. In this stage meaning comes from one's relationships with peers, and religion of the heart (the affective dimension) is more influential than is religious thinking. The next stage is characterized by a sense of searching rather than belonging, of sorting out one's own identity and articulating one's own beliefs and commitments as a result of intentional reflection.

These insights into the faith of older children and young adolescents raise two issues for baptismal education. The first and probably more important one is the purpose and style of the educational program for the usual sixth-grade group. A highly experiential and interpersonal educational style is appropriate to the faith stage typical of this group. The focus is on how the baptized Christian lives one's daily life. Interviews with older Christians, community service projects, a study of religious symbols, and reflection on one's human and sexual identity are relevant activities. This approach contrasts with the standard curriculum resources that stress denominational history and doctrines and congregational structure and practices.

The second issue suggested by the study of faith stages is related to the proper age debate. When is a person old enough to be baptized as a believer or be confirmed? Confirmation or believer's baptism, so the argument goes, needs to be done at the time when an individual is able to determine rationally what one believes and to make decisions with some autonomy or distance from peer pressure and the interpersonal relations of group experience. Therefore, confirmation and believer's baptism are more appropriately young adult events. This argument, influenced by studies in human development, is supported by the growing ecumenical scholarly consensus that believer's baptism (regardless of mode) is normatively an adult experience. Pastorally this alternative to traditional baptismal practices leaves a program void in the older children/early youth years. A liturgical option for those persons is an adolescent rite of belonging or responsibility. *See also* Catechumenate; Confirmation; Faith Development; Liturgy; Sacraments.

FOR FURTHER REFERENCE

Browning, Robert L., and Roy A. Reed. *The Sacraments in Religious Education and Liturgy.* Birmingham, AL: Religious Education Press, 1985.

Westerhoff, John H., and William H. Willimon. *Liturgy and Learning Through the Life Cycle.* New York: Seabury, 1980.

J. C. Rowell

Baptist Education

Baptists emerged from the Separatist movement in England in the seventeenth century. The tolerance of varied expressions of belief derives from the leader of the first Baptist congregation on English soil (1612), Thomas Helwys (ca. 1556–1616). Common to all Baptists have been the principle of voluntary participation and the vesting of church authority in the particular congregation. While Baptists are now found worldwide, the largest concentration is in the United States and Canada, where the Southern Baptist Convention has 14 million members, followed by the National Baptists, Inc., 6.3 million, the National Baptists (unincorporated), 3.5 million, and the American Baptists, 1.6 million. There are also a number of independent Baptist congregations, some with large memberships.

HISTORY

Religious education for Baptists has centered upon the Bible and its use, with a strong emphasis upon personal evangelism. Support for missionary outreach overseas and at home have accompanied Baptist educational efforts. The emphasis upon adult believers as the norm for church membership did not lessen awareness of the need to educate children. John Bunyan (1628–88) in *Pilgrim's Progress* (1678; part 2, 1684) and his *A Book for Boys and Girls* (1686) provided a substitute for a catechism in Baptist homes in Britain and its American colonies.

Baptist educational institutions generally were organized before national denominational structures developed. In Britain, Baptist and nonconforming pastors established academies in their homes in order to provide the education denied by the legislation of 1662 that barred nonconformists from admission to Oxford and Cambridge. In such dissenting academies, learned pastors boarded twenty or more students, preparing them for vocations in medicine, law, or theology. Many such enterprises became public through the support of a society or trustees. The earliest Baptist academy in the American colonies was established in Hopewell, New Jersey, in 1756 by Isaac Eaton (1726–72) under the auspices of the Philadelphia Baptist Association, formed in 1707. In 1825, Furman Academy and Theological Institute, the first academy in the South, was formed in South Carolina. In 1850 it became Furman University. Horton Academy was founded in Nova Scotia in 1828.

Baptist churches on the frontiers in the late 1700s and early 1800s were often used as schoolhouses. Baptist education societies, formed on state lines, provided encouragement to cooperative efforts that often led to establishment of educational institutions.

Baptists in Britain and its colonies felt the need for pastors equipped to interpret the Scriptures and to encourage the spiritual growth of members. This urgent need for leadership led to the founding of Baptist colleges, the earliest in Bristol, England (1720). Its graduates supported the missionary undertaking of William Carey (1761–1834), many personally joining the pioneer missioner in Serampore, India. Bristol graduates had an important role in establishing Baptist colleges in Britain and its American colonies, including the university chartered in 1764 by the General Assembly of Rhode Island, known after 1804 as Brown University. The charter placed control in Baptist hands but permitted persons of other denominations to serve as trustees and teachers. The Baptists of Massachusetts established Newton Theological Institution in 1825.

Membership and churches increased in the newly formed United States. Baptists came to number a million members by 1861. They established twenty-five permanent colleges between 1820 and 1861. Support for the mission in Burma of Ann (1789–1826) and Adoniram Judson (1778–1850) led many Baptist congregations to organize educational programs and cooperative ventures. Support of Baptist missions involved interpretation and instruction. *The Analytical Repository* was published in Georgia in 1801. The first issue of the *Massachusetts Baptist Missionary Magazine* appeared in May 1806. Many such journals were mailed to Baptist homes across the growing nation to provide education and information as well as to create a significant denominational consciousness.

Until 1845 Baptists in all the states cooperated in the work of the national societies for foreign missions, founded in 1814, and home missions, organized in 1832. Baptists in the southern states withdrew from both national societies in 1845 over the slavery issue. They continued their cooperation in the American Baptist Publication and Sunday School Society, which in 1840 expanded the work of the Baptist General Tract Society, founded in 1824.

Black Baptist congregations were first formed in the United States in the eighteenth century. The National Baptist Convention of the U.S.A., Inc., the oldest black Baptist denomination, was established in 1880; the National Baptist Convention of America (unincorporated) split from this parent group in 1915. The Progressive National Baptist Convention was formed in 1961. There are also some smaller denominational groups and a number of independent congregations.

Government educational efforts among blacks began after the Civil War with the assistance of the Freeman's Bureau in order to combat widespread illiteracy. The Northern (now American) Baptist Convention helped in the establishment of some of the first black colleges, including Shaw College, Raleigh, North Carolina, (1865), whose graduates by 1880 were establishing secondary schools. The black Baptist denominations themselves operate and/or support several colleges and seminaries.

Religious education in black Baptists congregations as in other Baptist congregations is done through the Sunday school, which includes large adult Bible classes and regular teacher training programs, usually led by the pastor on the weekly Bible lesson. Some black Baptist denominations have national boards for Christian education and publication boards to develop curricular materials and publish periodicals.

SUNDAY SCHOOLS AND OTHER EFFORTS

Baptists established Sunday schools as early as the 1790s in Boston, Rhode Island, New York, Philadelphia, and Baltimore. Churches made use of the Sunday schools for both evangelistic and educational purposes, preparing children for conversion and faith-commitment and providing Bible instruction.

In 1884, the American Baptist Publication Society first recognized that "each natural grade" in the Sunday school should have its appropriate teaching materials and introduced the Keystone International Graded Series in 1909. Judson Press is the trade name for American Baptist publications. The trade name of the publishing house of the Sunday School Board of the Southern Baptist Convention—Broadman Press—honors two pioneer advocates of Baptist education, Basil Manly, Jr. (1825–1892), and John A. Broadus (1827–1895).

Laypersons have played a major role in the Sunday school movement. Benjamin F. Jacobs (1834–1902), a Baptist businessman from Chicago, helped to organize the nation's Sunday schools. This voluntary movement became the International Sunday School Association. Jacobs, with a Methodist minister, John H. Vincent, urged the acceptance of the Uniform Lesson system. Helen Barrett Montgomery (1861–1934) advocated both missions and Christian education. In Rochester, New York, she taught a Bible class and helped to organize a dental clinic, an open-air school for tubercular children, and the first factory school in the nation. Her translation of the New Testament from the Greek text was published by Judson Press as *The New Testament in Modern English* in 1924. William Rainey Harper (1856–1906), best known as an innovative president of the University of Chicago, initiated reforms in the church school curriculum by developing graded lessons and using biblical scholarship. Harper was influential in the formation of the Religious Education Association in 1903.

Though Southern Baptists were late in forming a national organization for church education, they rapidly developed effective approaches. They voted in 1891 to establish a Sunday School Board in Nashville, Tennessee. By 1908 the Sunday School Board had established a "standard of excellence" that required congregational sponsorship of Sunday schools, the Bible as textbook, and Southern Baptist literature as helps for Bible study. The national board joined with state organizations to employ field workers to promote the organization of Sunday schools. Specific age groups in the local community were targeted for outreach. Organization and the training of leaders were stressed. National campaigns coordinated the efforts of local congregations, associations, and state conventions, resulting in significant growth in membership. While Southern Baptists tended to develop indigenous organizations rather than cooperate in interdenominational ventures, they were active in the Cooperative Curriculum Project (1960–1965), a series of work consultations involving sixteen denominations. Vacation Bible or church schools are popular with congregations as ministries to children in a community.

American Baptists support the Baptist Assembly at Green Lake, Wisconsin, as a national conference center. Southern Baptists maintain conference centers at Ridgecrest, North Carolina, and Glorieta, New Mexico. American Baptists publish resource materials in English and Spanish; Southern Baptists print educational matter in English, Spanish, Korean, Laotian, and Vietnamese. French-language congregations in Canada import available texts from France.

Baptists today continue to wrestle with the question of what it means to be a congregation of mature believers in the contemporary context and, especially, how children may best relate to such a fellowship. Theological and educational conferences on the subject have called upon the family and the congregation to foster the nurture of the child within the family of God. Baptists share with all Christians a desire to encourage the acceptance of the Uniform Lesson system.

faith development and social compassion of persons at every stage of life.

Education among Baptists began in small congregations. Today, Baptists in the United States benefit from large, effective organizations. Southern Baptists represent the dominant educational force in the Baptist World Alliance.

Education among Baptists in Canada shows some marked differences from that in the States, tending to be more loosely organized and somewhat more ecumenically involved. Canadian Baptists published church school curricula in cooperation with the United Church of Canada from 1937 to 1965, but now depend upon U.S. sources. The various Baptist conventions sponsor numerous summer camps and provide extensive programs for all ages. They support two accredited divinity colleges at Acadia University in Wolfville, Nova Scotia, and McMaster University in Hamilton, Ontario. Both offer programs leading to the Master of Religious Education degree. Baptist participation in such interdenominational enterprises as Canadian Girls in Training and the Canadian Council of Churches varies among the provinces. *See also* Anabaptist Education; Sunday School; Sunday School Movement; University.

FOR FURTHER REFERENCE

Fitts, Leroy. *A History of Black Baptists.* Nashville: Broadman, 1985.

Ingle, Clifford, ed. *Children and Conversion.* Nashville, Broadman, 1970.

Parker, Dorothy. *Dissenting Academies in England.* New York: Octagon, 1969.

Sparkman, G. Temp. *The Salvation and Nurture of the Child of God.* Valley Forge, PA: Judson, 1983.

"Sunday Schools in Southern Baptist History." In *Baptist History and Heritage* 18/1 (January 1983).

J. D. Ban

Bar/Bas Mitzvah

The term "bar/bas mitzvah" translates, literally, the "son" (*bar*) or "daughter" (*bas*) of the religious "commandment/obligation" (*mitzvah*) and is understood by Jews to be the coming of age of a Jewish young person at age thirteen for males and twelve years plus one day for females, according to "historical" Jewish tradition, although the bas mitzvah is not recognized in all traditions. Representing a significant Jewish educational milestone in the life of the learner, as well as family and friends, the bar mitzvah provides the young male with the opportunity to demonstrate a reasonable mastery of the Hebrew language, the occasion to lead one's congregation in a portion of the worship service, and the additional opportunity to share with those in attendance an appropriate age-related degree of intellectual maturity in the delivery of remarks most often dealing with the weekly scriptural selection or some other facet of Jewish education or learning. Coinciding as it does with the onset of puberty in the vast majority of cases, it is also the recognition, psychologically speaking, of the fact the young male is now entering the adult world of Jewish responsibilities and obligations. (Among the more traditional segments of the Jewish people, a *bar mitzvah* is now counted in the *minyan*, the required ten Jewish males necessary for a public Jewish worship service.)

HISTORY

To the best of our knowledge, the actual ceremony of bar mitzvah is, at most, approximately five hundred years old, though the concept of the coming of age of a Jewish male at age thirteen is much older, going back to Talmudic times and possibly earlier. Already in the second century B.C., age thirteen was considered the age of majority as regards both the taking of legal oaths and being counted in the *minyan*, the quorum needed for the Jewish worship service. The celebration of this coming of age in a religious context, primarily being called to offer the appropriate blessings before and after the Torah reading and/or actually reading from the Torah itself, came much later.

Bas mitzvah was originally celebrated in France and Italy and first made its appearance in the United States in 1922, when the late Rabbi Mordecai Kaplan, the founder of Reconstructionist Judaism, an offshoot of Conservative Judaism, celebrated the bas mitzvah of his own daughter, Judith Kaplan Eisenstein. Today, this celebration is becoming more universally accepted among both Reform and Conservative Jews and has even found its way into some "liberal" Orthodox Jewish congregations, though with significant variations, to be sure.

PRACTICE

While not, strictly speaking, required in any branch of the Jewish people, the ceremony of bar mitzvah for males is assumed to be almost the equivalent of a requirement within both Orthodox and Conservative Judaism, but continues to be an option within Reform/liberal/progressive Judaism. Increasingly, however, more and more liberal Jewish families are electing this option for their sons.

Bas mitzvah, however, is a different story. Because of the strict separation of males and females in Orthodox Judaism, there is no such thing as the bas mitzvah equivalent in terms of the individual female's conduct of the worship service and/or reading of Scripture in the presence of the male members of the congregation. Some innovative and creative Orthodox Jewish congrega-

tions have chosen, however, to create a type of graduation ceremony for females—at a time other than that normatively assigned for worship—and thus allow them the opportunity to give public evidence of their own commitment to Jewish life and learning. It is, however, usually a group rather than an individual ceremony and has no historical basis or precedent.

Conservative Judaism, which, in fact, introduced bas mitzvah celebration and ceremony, remains divided on the nature of the celebration of the female's coming of age. Some Conservative congregations do not have such ceremonies at all; some restrict the females to participation in the Friday evening worship service only (with readings from the prophetic portions of Scripture rather than the Mosaic texts); some draw no distinction whatever between male and female candidates in terms of either requirements or religious obligations. Such matters are up to the discretion of both the individual rabbi and congregation in Conservatism.

The Reform movement, committed as it is to the full and total equality between males and females, draws no qualitative distinctions whatsoever. Each candidate, male or female, is assigned those ceremonial and educational responsibilities consistent with his or her capabilities and aptitudes. So committed was the Reform movement to this concept of equality, that as early as 1810 (1846 in the United States) it "threw out" the bar mitzvah in favor of a group ceremony for both males and females called confirmation and held on the Jewish holiday of Shavuot (Weeks) in the spring of the year. This major holy day of the Jewish calendar historically and traditionally associates itself with Moses' return to the people of Israel with the Ten Commandments and was thus seen by the early Reform Jews as the natural occasion for thirteen year olds to make a "profession of faith," as it were. With the introduction of the bas mitzvah by Conservative Judaism, the bar mitzvah returned to Reform Judaism with greater significance, bas mitzvah became yet another option, and confirmation became the norm for both Reform and Conservative Judaism.

While the young person is expected to conduct a portion of the worship service, usually associated with the Sabbath on either Friday evening or Saturday morning, the heart of the celebration for both bar mitzvah and bas mitzvah still remains the reading of selected verses of Scripture, first a passage from the Torah, the Five Books of Moses, and then an additional selection (*Haftarah*) usually taken from prophetic literature and thematically related to the Torah portion. Because Scripture is also read at worship services on Monday, Thursdays, first days of the month, and holidays and festivals over the course of the year, other opportunities have presented themselves for the celebration of both bar mitzvah and bas mitzvah. For the student of limited educational ability, these programs, such as the Bethel Bible Program and the Kerygma Program, have drawn many adults into focused Bible study for the first time in their lives. Ongoing Bible classes that follow up such programs are now being developed largely at the congregational level. *See also* Adult Education; Bible Study; Curriculum.

F. A. Gardner

Bible College

A Bible college is a college-level educational institution with the distinctive function of preparing students for Christian ministries or church vocations through a program of biblical, general, and professional studies. The Bible college has been described as occupying an intermediary position between the Bible institute and the Christian liberal arts college. The quality of the Bible college has grown significantly and many colleges have achieved regional accreditation.

The Bible college is essentially a twentieth-century phenomenon. Its roots can be traced to the Bible institute movement in North America in 1882 with the founding of the New York Missionary Training College for Home Missionaries and Evangelists (now called Nyack College). Four years later the Moody Bible Institute was established in Chicago. The Bible institute was formed primarily to provide a biblical education for lay workers in the church. The curriculum consisted mainly of biblical studies with a major emphasis in practical Christian service. Evangelism, missions, and godly life-style characterized these institutions.

Soon many of the established Bible institutes began to upgrade their curricular offerings. Between 1920 and 1930 increased academic requirements extended the course of study from two to three years. As the curriculum was strengthened, efforts were made to improve the academic quality of the faculties and provide better physical facilities for students.

The Bible college was the logical outcome of the expanded development in the Bible institute. Bible colleges adopted a four-year curriculum, obtained authority to grant baccalaureate degrees, established admission requirements comparable to liberal arts colleges, and hired faculty with recognized academic credentials. One of the most significant events in the Bible college movement was the formation in 1947 of an accrediting association (now called the American Association of Bible Colleges). Later Dr. S. A. Witmer was employed as the first full-time executive director. The association is recognized by the U.S. Department of Education as a national institutional accrediting agency and is a member of the Council on Postsecondary Accreditation.

Early in the 1980s Bible colleges reached record enrollment. According to the statistics published by the American Association of Bible Colleges in 1986 over 500 Bible colleges operate in the United States and Canada. There are 87 accredited colleges with a combined enrollment of 32,000 students.

The uniqueness of the Bible college centers around three crucial aspects of the curriculum. Every baccalaureate degree course includes a mandatory thirty hours in biblical studies. Students are required to participate in practical Christian service. Special emphasis is placed on godly living and a Christian life-style that accords with the teachings of Scripture. The most important potential offered by the combination of these three aspects is the capability of integrating the Bible into all academic subjects. The biblical orientation of the Bible college makes this concept more viable there than in other kinds of colleges.

One of the attractive features of the Bible college movement has been the continuing education courses designed to offer formal biblical education to Christians in urban areas. These classes are normally held in the evening and often at off-campus locations.

Many factors led to the establishment of the Bible college. Since the middle of the nineteenth century little attention has been given to traditional Christian values as an integral part of higher education in the United States. The teaching of evolution led to the exclusion of the biblical view of creation. Liberal theology denied the inspiration and inerrancy of the Bible in most private colleges, and secularism swept the state universities. The desire for academic freedom and intellectual stimulation ruled out propositional truth set forth in the Bible. These trends fueled reactions among Christians who held to the cardinal doctrines of the Christian faith; out of this emerged the Bible college.

The growth of the Bible college is attributed to a number of elements. The population of college-aged people increased and in recent years older adults have pursued additional education. Veterans' benefits made it possible for many servicemen and -women to attend college after World War II. A number of these people who had observed the need for evangelism overseas had a desire for a biblical education that would prepare them for missionary service. The growth of the evangelical church and greater affluence among Christians supported the emerging Bible colleges. Qualified faculty in areas other than Bible and theology became available. The complexity of society called for a more educated minister. Added to all these things was the plethora of new churches being established and the need for pastors and Christian leaders. The tremendous growth of parachurch ministries also increased the demand for Bible college graduates. The upgrading and broadening of the Bible college curriculum along with accreditation made it easier for students to transfer credits to other institutions. These factors played a significant role in bringing the Bible college movement to maturity. *See also* Colleges and Universities, Church-Related; Higher Education, Religion in; Mission, Education for; Theological Education.

FOR FURTHER REFERENCE

Eagen, John L. *The Bible College in American Higher Education.* Fayetteville, AK: American Association of Bible Colleges, 1981.

Ringenberg, William C. *The Christian College.* Grand Rapids, MI: Christian University Press and Eerdmans, 1984.

Witmer, S. A. *The Bible College Story.* Manhasset, NY: Channel Press, 1962.

W. G. Johnston

The Bible in Religious Education

Both for the sake of its message and its ways of communication, the Bible remains for Christians central to religious education at all age levels. This article will not deal with which specific Bible teachings should be included in religious education for different age groups; other articles and tables address that matter. Rather, the primary question for the following comments is a more general and more fundamental one: what can the Bible teach us about the subject matter and the didactics of religious education?

Message and method must of course never be separated, but they can be distinguished. Those who emphasize primarily teaching methods and tools have to be reminded of the fact that in religious education there definitely is a cognitive and emotive message to be communicated and appropriated. Its content comes from beyond our personal experience, even from beyond this world and time. Conversely, those who emphasize only the content of what is to be taught and learned must realize that the content is always shaped by the ways in which it is transmitted. To say that "the medium is the message" exaggerates, but the medium definitely functions as a message, either facilitating or blocking the transmission.

The medium can be congenial to the message and thus incarnate it. Too often, however, the medium contradicts and falsifies the content. The Bible thus teaches us not only *what* is to be learned, but also *how* this learning is to happen. Religious educators must be sensitive to both the biblical message and method.

THE BIBLICAL CONTENT

Religious education aims at helping people grow in their knowledge of God, and Christians believe that the primary source for knowing God is the Bible.

Knowledge must be understood in the profound way in which it is characterized by the Hebrew verb *jada'*: it means to know, recognize, acknowledge God, to experience God's presence in such a way that an intimate loving community grows between God and the believer as well as among the believers themselves. Religious education invites the learning community to begin and continue an adventurous journey that lasts a whole lifetime. In this learning experience the Bible functions as a compass rather than a blueprint. It does not provide us with fixed laws and certainties but draws us into an ongoing dialogue and search for the way ahead.

This is well expressed in the intriguing conversation between God and Moses at Sinai (Exod. 33:12–23). Moses wanted to gain definite knowledge of God. He desired to see God's face and glory. The only thing given to him, however, was the assurance that God knows him, that God's favor and presence accompany him on the journey where

THE BIBLE IN RELIGIOUS EDUCATION:
Suggestions for Use with Different Age Groups

Age Level	Biblical Material	Methods of Use or Presentation
Preschool	Stories of God's love and care (i.e., the story of creation in Genesis 1, the story of Jesus and the children in Mark 10:13–16); verses of assurance and thanksgiving (i.e., Psalms 56:3; 145:10)	Storytelling or reading by the teacher, sometimes using tapes, flannelgraph, or other illustrations
Grades 1–3	Stories of people (i.e., Joseph in Genesis 37, David in 1 Samuel 16:1–23, the calling of the disciples in Mark 1:16–20, and Lydia in Acts 16:11–15); passages of assurance and thanksgiving (i.e., Psalms 100; 121)	Storytelling and reading by the teacher; use of tapes, drawings, puppets, and video equipment; children can begin to read the text themselves and answer questions about it
Grades 4–6	Continued stories (i.e., those of Moses and the people of Israel, or stories from the life of Jesus); more of the Psalms (i.e., Psalms 136, 150)	Children can read the text for themselves, discuss it, dramatize it, and further research it using time lines, maps, and various reference books
Grades 7–8	Some prophetic material (i.e., Isaiah 6; Jeremiah 36); all of the Gospels and Acts; all of the Psalms	Children can read the text for themselves and discuss both its original meaning and its meaning for us today
High School	Passages relating to matters of biblical thought and themes (i.e., the theme of covenant in Deuteronomy 5–6, the concept of gospel in Luke, and the concept of church in Philippians and Philemon)	The text can be read and discusses, and most available resource material can be used
Adult	The whole of the Bible, including all wisdom literature (such as Proverbs), the Prophets, the Letters, and apocalyptic literature (such as Daniel and Revelation)	Texts can be read and discussed, and any available resource materials can be used

here and there he will receive glimpses of God's glory. Such a reversal of roles is also described at the end of Paul's famous hymn to love (1 Cor. 13:12).

This gradual or sudden awareness of God's presence with us is at the heart of religious education. We set out to teach and learn how to know and love God, how to participate in divine action. In the course of this endeavor we discover that God already knows and loves *us*, drawing us into the covenant community. It is within and through this community that God lets us participate in the drama of divine creation, salvation, and perfection. These three actions of God shape the content of religious education. The various biblical traditions of faith are much too rich and diverse and the acts of God far too mysterious to be summed up in a few paragraphs. Looking at the content of religious education from the point of view of God's creative, saving, and perfecting activity is only one among many possible ways to sum up the biblical message.

Creator

God is confessed in the Bible to be the creator of the universe, a creative activity with which Jesus Christ is intimately associated (Gen. 1–2; Col. 1:15–17). Both the animate and inanimate world are works of God's hand. All human beings, from whatever race or social class, Christians and people of other faiths or no faith, all are created in God's image. This image was distorted but can now be restored in Jesus Christ (Gen. 1:27; Col. 3:9–11).

Biblical theology (our speaking and learning about God in response to God's speaking to us) opens up a wide horizon, including the whole universe, the world of nations and all realms of life. Religious education curricula can therefore not only include narrowly "religious" themes. One cannot adore the creator and ignore the creation. Our faith is tested by the way in which we assume our guardianship over God's creation as Psalm 8 and the Sabbath and Jubilee Year legislation in Leviticus 25 show. Our destiny depends on whether we can or cannot discern God's image in the people we meet (Gen. 9:6), whether or not we become responsible stewards of entrusted earthly possessions (Matt. 25:14–30), and on the way in which we relate to our most vulnerable fellow human beings (Matt. 25:31–46). Therefore the teaching of the Bible leads to the exploration of an ecologically responsible style of life, the development of peace education that counteracts the education for violence and war, and the search for economically responsible structures of society.

In the churches' educational work two trends are often separated or even opposed to each other. They carry various labels, for example, "Christian education" versus "development education." The one centers on the teaching of the articles of faith and on participation in worship, fellowship, and evangelistic and diaconal activities of the gathered church. The other insists on the training for a Christian presence in the "secular" realm of life, for the struggles of faith in families and neighborhoods, in the arenas of work and citizenship. The biblical message about God the creator challenges such a dichotomy. Worship and work, faith and action, life within the Christian fellowship and a Christian presence within the structures of society must be held together. Obviously not everything can be included in a Sunday school curriculum, an adult Christian education program, a biblical correspondence course, or a weekend lay training seminar. However, elements of both of the above-mentioned trends must be considered in religious education.

Savior

God is in the Bible also confessed to be the Savior of this world. According to a theological summary of the Exodus story (Exod. 6:6–8), salvation has a horizontal and a calculators and computers the memory must be trained for growing in the knowledge of God. Only what has been truly heard, what again and again can be remembered, and what has thus been internally appropriated leads to understanding and growth in knowledge. It is not true that only what is understood should be memorized. One has to live a long time with the deepest truths, recalling them in different life situations, before one begins to understand them. For such constant recalling the modern medium of audiocassettes is helpful. To record with one's own voice a gospel story and to listen to it many times is a first step toward appropriation and understanding. Only when a message from God and about God does in such a way shape and change us from within can we become true witnesses and teachers of this message.

Oral communication has a predilection for proverbs and stories, parables and poetry, chanting and songs. However, the hearing leads also to the seeing. It calls forth images, symbols, and tangible tokens. In the whole New Testament one finds no single abstract definition of what the Christian community is, but there are almost one hundred New Testament word-images for the church. The book of Revelation teaches a visual theology. During the desert journey the pillar of fire, the tent of meeting, and the ark symbolized God's presence (Exod. 14:24; 33:7–11; Num. 10:35–36). As a token and witness for the renewal of the covenant Joshua set up a great stone (Josh. 24:25–27). Similarly in his teaching Jesus often used tangible tokens and gestures. These do not simply illustrate the sayings; rather they are the primary medium of communication that Jesus then commented upon by his words. Embracing a child and putting it in the midst of his ambitious disciples, entering Jerusalem on a donkey, turning over the tables of money-changers in the Temple court, and washing the feet of his disciples are only a few instances of Jesus' visual communication. Such prophetic acts imprint themselves on the mind and memory much more strongly than the spoken words. No wonder the four New Testament accounts of the institution of the Lord's Supper give an almost identical description of the elements used and the gestures made, while they differ considerably with regard to the words spoken.

Again, religious educators have still much to learn from Jesus in the field of making the word visible through tangible tokens and gestures. Especially in a time when too many images are passively consumed as they bombard us, religious education must help children and adults to learn how to see, how to discover symbols and tangible tokens for God's presence. Jesus walked through villages and fields noticing persons in need and discerning parables of God's kingdom in everyday events. Stimulating this kind of active seeing, imaging, and empathizing is an important part of religious education. The meditation of art work and fantasy journeys, the use of the photo-language method, and the age-old medium of copying a biblical text by our own handwriting and drawing (not only by children but also by adults!) are good instruments to train the eye and the imagination. This can lead to the rediscovery of the Bible as God's great picture book. It also may help us to discern the restored image of God at first in Christ and then also in those whom we meet and in ourselves. Thus we are transfigured into God's "icon" and reflect as in a mirror something of the glory of God (2 Cor. 3:18).

Both oral communication and visualization lead to what throughout the centuries has been the way of learning most congenial to the biblical message: participation in the liturgical drama. Except for the training given to princes and scribes at the royal courts, there were no schools or formal religious education programs among the Jews almost up to the time of Jesus. How did the Israelites learn to grow in their knowledge of God? Much teaching went on within the families, where the children learned as they lived, prayed, and worked with their parents. The whole of daily life and work was indeed centered on God's commandments and promises. Twice a day every believing Jew recites the Shema (Deut. 6:4–9; 11:13–21; Num. 15:37–41), which so graphically relates prayer to work and words to symbols. This daily learning through prayer was augmented by the great feasts: Passover, which marked the beginning of the barley harvest and commemorates the liberation from slavery; Pentecost, celebrated when the wheat was harvested and recalling the giving of God's Torah; the festival of Tabernacles, at the end of the grape harvest when the living conditions during the desert journey were reenacted. Each of these festivals thus linked the daily work with the remembrance of God's great acts. Symbolic rites aroused the curiosity and questions of the children. Special psalms were sung, stories told, and prayers recited. Generation after generation the Israelites became contemporaries of the Exodus out of Egypt and the covenanting at Sinai: "The Lord our God made a covenant with us at Horeb. Not with our fathers did the Lord make this covenant, but with us, who are all of us here alive this day" (Deut. 5:2–3; Exod. 13:8). Especially after the centralization of worship by King Josiah's reform (622 B.C.), the great feasts brought many thousands of pilgrims to Jerusalem, singing on their journey hymns of ascent (Ps. 120–134) and participating in liturgies (reflected, for example, in Ps. 24).

It is by no means certain that a synagogue school existed in Nazareth when Jesus was a boy. Like Jewish boys generations before him, his learning to obey and trust God began in the midst of a God-centered daily life and work and especially by participating in the pilgrimages to Jerusalem for the Jewish festivals (Luke 2:41–52). Later he took his disciples into the same "school." Just as Jesus himself learned to know God in the first place by participating in worship, so did the early Christians. No wonder that so many parts of the Bible have arisen out of worship or were originally composed for worship. This is of crucial importance for religious educators today. In a time when the lives of children and adults are so dangerously fragmented by the multiplicity of contradictory messages, images, and idols, our greatest need is to learn again the concentration of worship. As we are worshiping the one God with our whole mind and heart and body we will learn to discover in our lives the ongoing creative, saving, and perfecting action of God. *See also* Bible Societies; Bible Study; Biblical Criticism; Biblical Translation; Communication Theory; Creation; Exegesis; Hermeneutic; Inductive Bible Study; Revelation; Salvation.

FOR FURTHER REFERENCE

Brueggemann, Walter. *The Creative Word: Canon as a Model for Biblical Education*. Philadelphia: Fortress, 1982.
Furnish, Dorothy Jean. *Living the Bible with Children*. Nashville, TN: Abingdon, 1982.
Weber, Hans-Ruedi. *Experiments with Bible Study*. Philadelphia: Westminster, 1982.

H. Weber

Bible Societies

Bible societies, nonprofit organizations supported by individual and church contributions for the purpose of printing copies of the Bible and distributing them widely, were first established after the Protestant Reformation. The invention of printing with movable type in the middle of the fifteenth century made possible for the first time the widespread dissemination of the Bible. Until then all copies had been produced by hand, a costly and time-consuming enterprise. The intellectual fervor that swept through Europe at about this same time resulted in a growing interest in having the Bible in vernacular languages. By the year 1500, the complete Bible had already been printed in six different languages and some parts of it in six others; a century later the number had more than tripled and included all the major languages of Europe.

Initially, Bibles were produced and distributed by commercial printers. In the eighteenth century, however, some of the newly formed missionary agencies began to include Scripture distribution among their aims, although it was never their primary purpose.

The first organization with a sole concern to publish and distribute the Scriptures was the Canstein Bible Institution, established in Halle in 1710 by German Pietists "to provide a more abundant supply of the Word of God for our people" and named for a young nobleman, Carl Hildebrand von Canstein, who supported the endeavor generously. More than three million inexpensive Bibles and New Testaments, in several languages, were distributed in Germany and eastern Europe during the eighteenth century. The Canstein Bible Institution was in a sense the first Bible society.

It was the establishment of the British and Foreign Bible Society (BFBS) in 1804, however, that brought the modern Bible society movement into being. A need for Welsh language Scriptures provided the immediate impetus for its creation; the rapidly expanding world missionary enterprise, with its need for an increased supply of low-cost Scriptures, made it necessary; and the dramatic changes taking place in technology made such a movement feasible. From the beginning BFBS was committed to printing the Scriptures without note or comment and to distributing them worldwide. The society grew very rapidly, and auxiliaries were organized in a number of cities both in the British Isles and in British North America to assist in securing support. BFBS took very seriously the "foreign" dimension implied in its name, disseminating Scriptures throughout Africa, the Near East, India, and China. Financial support was also given to several translation projects, including the first Chinese Bible.

Within the next few years several other Bible societies were established in Europe on the BFBS model, including the Netherlands, Danish, Swedish, Icelandic, Norwegian, Finnish, and Russian Bible societies. Many of these received financial support from BFBS.

In the United States, Bible societies first developed at the local level, and by 1816 more than 130 were in existence, scattered over 24 states and territories. The limited effectiveness of these local societies in distribution and the overlapping of their efforts pointed to the need for a central organization. Prominent American church leaders,

both lay and clergy, therefore urged establishment of a national association, and as a result delegates from the existing societies and the churches assembled in New York on 8 May 1816 to found the American Bible Society (ABS).

The Bible society movement in the nineteenth and early twentieth centuries was characterized by two differing philosophies. BFBS, ABS, the Netherlands Bible Society, and the National Bible Society of Scotland (NBSS) felt it was their mission to supply the needs of the churches worldwide; the other societies were more nationally oriented and did little Scripture distribution outside their own countries or regions. The "missionary" societies generally operated quite independently of one another and therefore on occasion overlapped in their efforts or even came into conflict. In 1919 an "Association of National Bible Societies" was proposed as a means of avoiding these problems and, although the suggestion proved to be premature, the stage was set for future discussions. In 1932 leaders of ABS, BFBS, and NBSS met in London to plan cooperative work in Asia and the Middle East. Seven years later a conference of the major Bible societies in Amsterdam adopted a proposal for a "Council of Bible Societies," but the outbreak of World War II made implementation impossible. Finally, in May 1946, the concept was made a reality when delegates of twelve European bible societies and ABS, at a conference in Haywards Heath, England, formally established the United Bible Societies (UBS). Since that date, Bible society work has increasingly been coordinated through this worldwide agency. The number of member societies and national offices now exceeds one hundred, most of which have come into existence since the end of World War II as former agencies of the four missionary Bible societies have become independent.

UBS has sponsored "common language" translations in more than 150 languages, and shared in development of interconfessional translations in more than 300 languages. It has also pioneered the publication of "New Reader" Scriptures, simplified versions that are widely used with children and adults who are newly literate.

The International Bible Society (formerly the New York International Bible Society), founded in 1809, translates, produces, and distributes Bibles in various portions, editions, and formats. It is also an evangelistic missionary organization employing missionaries and chaplains in special evangelical outreach concerns.

In 1985, 12,616,084 Bibles and 12,098,659 New Testaments in over 500 languages were circulated in more than 180 countries and territories. Total distribution of Bibles, Testaments, portions, selections, and New Reader Scriptures was nearly 550 million copies.

The American Bible Society may be contacted at 1865 Broadway, New York, NY 10023, and the United Bible Societies at P.O. Box 810340,

7000 Stuttgart 80, West Germany. *See also* Biblical Translation.

B. L. Daniels

Bible Study

In the Jewish and Christian traditions, religious education might be regarded as a continuous commentary on Scripture. The centrality of the biblical word to each suggests common commitments in the educational enterprise; disagreements over the canon and appropriate interpretation of texts hint at some of the differences between Jewish and Christian educators, as well as among Christian educators across the denominational and theological spectrum.

In both Judaism and Christianity, education begins with a careful hearing of the word of revelation. "Listen," Israel is commanded (Deut. 6:4–5): love the one God with all your being and teach this command with diligence to the next generation. "Faith," Paul exhorts in Romans (10:17), "comes from what is heard." Moreover, even those being instructed in the word are teachers; the one being instructed in the word, the catechumen (Gk. *katēchoúmenos*, whence "catechesis" and "catechism"), should share all good things with the teacher (Gal. 6:6).

But those who are confronted with this word differ in their presuppositions. The varying standpoints from which they begin their study shape their conclusions; hence, study of biblical texts results in differing interpretations. For instance, in the first century A.D., those grounded in Pharisaic (later, rabbinic) traditions interpreted the Hebrew Scriptures in ways different from the sectarians at Qumran (whose interpretations are extant in the Dead Sea Scrolls) and from the writers of the New Testament. Despite shared exegetical methods, distinct presuppositions shaped the way each group interpreted the same scriptural heritage. The "Followers of the Way" (later called Christians) saw the Hebrew Scriptures in light of Jesus, whom they called Christ. Other Jews did not agree that their Scriptures testified to the Christ.

Accordingly, Jews and Christians went in different directions. Over the years, Jews have read God's activity in the Hebrew Scriptures through the lens of rabbinic commentary in the Talmud and Midrash, whereas Christians have done so through the lens of the New Testament and ecclesial commentary. Yet for both, religious education involves entering into the dynamics of the interpretative process.

THE DYNAMICS OF INTERPRETATION

Scholars steeped in the biblical languages and history provide educators with a most important knowledge: what the text meant to the people among whom it originated. In their attentiveness to text and context, they give the community a disciplined way of understanding ancient works. Since the nineteenth century, biblical scholarship has involved the "historical-critical" study of texts. This methodology encompasses a range of tools—textual, philological, archaeological, literary, historical, sociological—to determine the original meanings of texts. Usage of historical criticism has engendered lively controversy, although today it is widely accepted, except among fundamentalists, who regard it as a humanistic relativizing of God's absolute truth revealed in the Bible.

Study of the Bible, however, is reflected not simply in scholarly exegesis, but also in the lives of the communities for whom it is a sacred and normative work. A community's rendering of a text may be found in sermons, lectionaries, cathedral windows, mystery plays, synagogue poems, paintings, and canticles. Worship is a particularly important mode of study, its depth dimension. This is reflected especially in the monastic tradition of *lectio divina*—a prayerful reading of Scripture—and in the cabalistic texts of Jewish mystics.

A number of significant issues are of mutual concern to modern biblical scholars and religious educators, including literary criticism, the social sciences, and feminist theory.

While literary criticism has long been important in probing the forms and rhetoric of biblical texts, it has assumed new significance with increased attention to narrative and with the advent of structuralism. Study of the "Bible as literature" has opened the possibility of biblical study in religiously neutral settings; it has also contributed new insights to the process of reading texts.

Psychology is likewise making an impact on biblical study. To date, developmental studies have dominated, directed especially to debating children's readiness to study the Bible. More recently, biblical scholars have been influenced by Jungian psychology in their exegesis. Not unrelated is the contribution made by sociology and anthropology, which have opened up broader horizons on the world of the Bible.

Similarly, scholars are drawing upon feminist theory for insights into the patriarchal world out of which the Bible came. The perspective they bring to study has provided a fresh reading of Scripture and opened new questions about its liberating power.

INDIVIDUAL AND GROUP METHODS

Bible study can be an individual enterprise, with a person structuring time to read and think about the text in conjunction with books that will help to interpret. For laypeople, a one-volume commentary or a commentary series specifically designed for the nonexpert is needed.

A group enterprise for Bible study can be a large group that gathers for lecture, questions, and discussion or smaller groups formed to study and share insights. Commentaries, Bible dictionaries, and atlases provide background information and alternate interpretations to stimulate thinking, and the use of several versions of the Bible shows subtle differences in translation.

Because of the wide variety of types of literary material in the Bible—narratives, parables, psalms, prophecy, poetry, history, ritual law, and homilies, to name a few—it is not always possible or even advisable to simply begin with Genesis and continue on through Revelation. In general, newcomers to the Bible and younger students benefit from the more narrative works: the patriarchal narratives in Genesis and the stories of the life of Jesus in the first three Gospels, followed perhaps by the Exodus and wilderness narratives and some of the Old Testament stories of Joshua, Solomon, and David. Also fairly accessible are selected psalms, the briefer prophets (Amos, Hosea, and Micah), and some of the New Testament Letters (1 and 2 Corinthians, Philemon, Ephesians, and Galatians). John's Gospel and some of Paul's closely reasoned theological arguments, as in Romans, require extra attention, and special care needs to be taken with examples of wisdom literature (e.g., Job), complex prophecy (Isaiah, Jeremiah, and Ezekiel), and apocalyptic (Revelation).

Study of the Bible has been enormously important in the process of handing on the faith. Yet the field of religious education also contributes to the study of the Bible by offering: (1) a concern for how that study impinges upon the religious dimension of life; (2) a predilection for analysis and synthesis, rather than for discovery and detailed examination of data; (3) an awareness of the educational demands of the material in light of particular situations; and (4) a commitment to move beyond historical criticism so as to deepen faith. Study of the Bible and religious education are inextricably linked. *See also* Bible Class; Bible in Religious Education, The; Biblical Criticism; Biblical Translation; Christianity; Exegesis; Hermeneutic; Inductive Bible Study; Judaism; Torah as Teaching; Torah, Study and Teaching of.

FOR FURTHER REFERENCE

Achtemeier, Paul J., ed. *Harper's Bible Dictionary*. San Francisco: Harper & Row, 1985.

Boadt, Lawrence, ed. *Biblical Studies: Meeting Ground for Jews and Christians*. New York: Paulist, 1981.

Grant, Robert M., and David Tracy. *A Short History of the Interpretation of the Bible*, 2d ed. Philadelphia: Fortress, 1984.

Holtz, Barry W., ed. *Reading the Classic Jewish Texts*. New York: Summit, 1984.

Little, Sara. *The Role of the Bible in Contemporary Christian Education*. Richmond, VA: John Knox, 1961.

Mays, James L., ed. *Harper's Bible Commentary*. San Francisco: Harper & Row, 1988.

M. C. Boys

Biblical Authority

Many theories of the Bible's authority have been developed through the centuries. Already in the period during which the Bible was being written there were debates over the authority of those who spoke in God's name. The notion of "false prophecy" has had a centuries-long history and is still a lively issue today.

A distinction should be drawn between theories of the Bible's authority and the actually perceived authority that the biblical literature and ideas have had in the life of the religious communities. Religious communities find that the biblical literature and thought cast illumination upon their experience in relation to God. The biblical stories have undeniable power to disclose God's way of dealing with the world and with its peoples. It might be difficult to explain the precise nature of that power, but the power is undeniable.

Some religious communities depend almost exclusively upon their reading of the Bible as the authoritative key to God's demands upon the community. The authority of the Bible for communities that do not depend so exclusively upon the biblical message is quite different. The authority of the Hebrew Bible for Jews is viewed in distinctive ways by the different communities—Orthodox, Conservative, Reform, and Reconstructionist. None of the Jewish communities, however, depends upon the biblical record exclusively, and most treat the oral law with reverence equal to that given what Christians call the Old Testament. Mishnah and Gemara, which together comprise the Talmud, rank equally or nearly equally with the Hebrew Bible. For Roman Catholics, Scripture and tradition, as interpreted authoritatively by the church's magisterium, the teaching office of the church, belong together and complement one another. For Orthodox Christian communities, the Bible is authoritative along with the great ecumenical councils of the early centuries.

The Reformation principle "Scripture alone" gave authority to the Bible that had never been claimed for it in earlier epochs. Coming at the time when printing was creating a revolution in the way in which writing was promulgated, the Reformation led some groups to place such authority upon the Bible that there developed new understandings of how the Bible came to be written and how its message had been kept safe from error or corruption through the centuries. Plenary inspiration was a term used to stress the completeness of the biblical revelation. Biblical literalism developed during the nineteenth and early twentieth centuries, a view that all that was declared in the Bible was to be accepted as literally true, without any error whatsoever on any subject with which the Bible dealt. Such a view had to be modified to allow for errors in the manuscripts that had been copied throughout the centuries by fallible human beings.

Another view is that the Bible is without error on those subjects which it deals with authoritatively. This lets the Bible be not a book of science or history or sociology, but a religious book, displaying the central religious affirmations of the Jewish and Christian communities and doing so in such a way as to lead readers and hearers to an understanding of the message the deity intends to convey through the Bible.

The religious communities first heard the biblical message, first committed it to memory, first recorded it, first edited it, and first declared it to be authoritative for the community's faith. Church and synagogue were created by the biblical message, but they also were the creators of the Bible. The authority of one should not be played off against the other.

Biblical authority, at its heart, means the power of the biblical message to enter the lives of people—individuals and groups—and claim those lives for the truth of faith. The Bible has that authority, an authority that countless individuals and groups have testified to with their lives through the centuries. The Bible, given opportunity, displays its own authority; it takes care of itself—under the authority of the God who called both it and the religious communities into being. *See also* Biblical Criticism; Biblical Translation; Exegesis; Fundamentalism; Hermeneutic; History of Christian Education; Magisterium; Revelation; Torah as Teaching; Torah, Study and Teaching of.

W. Harrelson

Biblical Criticism

Scholarly work explaining the shape and origin of particular biblical texts and attempting to show the meaning of those texts, both in their original setting and in the current world, carries the label of biblical criticism. The practice of biblical criticism is not a task that seeks to tear down the biblical text in order to criticize its ancient dress. To the contrary, it is a task that seeks to enter the world of the biblical text, to explore its shape and beauty, and to make public its aesthetic as well as its theological value. That kind of criticism is already apparent in Martin Luther's commentary on Genesis.

Biblical criticism has changed across the years as the approaches, emphases, and foci have var-

ied. The work of modern biblical criticism begins, however, with the incisive critique of the Old Testament by Julius Wellhausen. His approach, set forth in his *Prolegomena to the History of Israel* (1905), uses the techniques of literary criticism to undergird his primary goal, a reconstruction of the history of Israel. By means of his literary criticism, Wellhausen sought to show what parts of the Old Testament story were the oldest segments of tradition and what parts were added by later generations. Wellhausen and his students hypothesized that the stories about Israel's early history in the Hexateuch (the first six books of the Bible) were given their present form by editors from two or three different sources. When the analysis uncovered the distinct character of the book of Deuteronomy, the Wellhausen school suggested that two early sources, now labeled J and E, were combined by an editor. A later source, now labeled the P source, expanded the JE documents, not only by adding the legal corpus, but also by imposing its own form of the narrative into the stream of the tradition. The move from early to late sources then enabled the critic to reconstruct the historical setting that produced the story and to reconstruct the history of Israel in greater detail.

In contrast to the fragmentation of the Hexateuch into several distinct sources, the work of Hermann Gunkel (1862–1932) sought to show the form, or structure, of any given piece of biblical text, thus emphasizing unity for the major sections of the Hexateuch. He also sought to show the place of any particular text in a system of classifications, or genres, for the various texts of the Old Testament. The classifications, or genre groupings, would prove valuable in exegesis by showing similar characteristics in structure and typical functions for each genre.

Closely related to the work of the form critics is the work of those who would explore the history of particular traditions, the unique content in the pericope defined by the form critics. This pursuit, closely identified with the work of Gerhard von Rad (1901–1971) and Martin Noth (1902–1968) in Germany and Sigmund Mowinckel (1884–1965) in Norway, would ask whether any particular example of a tradition carried by some particular genre might be early or late in the story of the tradition's development. For example, when the pericope in Exodus 17:1–7 shows the people who sought water at the oasis at Meribah as rebels, it represents a later reconstruction of the story. The early form of the story represented the people who asked for water at Meribah as faithful, obedient followers of Moses and of his God (Ps. 81:7).

Closely related to the work of the form critics and the critics of tradition history is the work of the structuralists. Heavily influenced by the methods of Claude Lévi-Strauss, the structuralists examine the texts of the Bible in order to uncover "deep" structures in the literature that match "deep" structures in society. The literature reflects the function of the structure in society.

A new stage in the development of biblical criticism shows critics asking not only about the origins of tradition and the shape and genre of individual pericopes but also about the significance of the larger whole and the process that brought the whole to its present construction. What, for example, is the significance of the unit of tradition that shows the J source and the P source combined into a single unity? An examination of the shape of the received text asks not only about the history of the tradition that produced the received text, the final stage in the criticism of tradition history, but also about the significance of that final shape for the life of the community of faith. Canon criticism, developed particularly by James Sanders (1984) and Brevard Childs (1984), explores the character of the canonical text as an entity that now functions with authority for church and synagogue.

A survey of biblical criticism might mention other significant methods of criticism, such as the work of rhetorical criticism, sociological approaches to interpretation of biblical texts, and especially the distinct role of historical criticism. Moreover, the work of so-called lower criticism, the critical evaluation of the Hebrew or Greek text itself, belongs in the survey. In all of these areas, biblical criticism has served a fascinating role in bringing the Bible as a whole to communities of faith. From its earliest stages, which tended to atomize the text into numerous pieces, it has returned to a significant, critical appreciation of the beauty and theological power of the whole. It suggests, moreover, that the critical issue in the evaluation of the Bible is not simply the historical accuracy of the various texts, but the texts themselves, with their own very significant contribution to truth and beauty. *See also* Bible Study; Biblical Translation; Exegesis; Hermeneutic; Structuralism.

FOR FURTHER REFERENCE

Alter, Robert. *The Art of Biblical Narrative.* New York: Basic, 1981.

Alter, Robert, and Frank Kermode. *The Literary Guide to the Bible.* Cambridge, MA: Harvard University Press, 1987.

Berlin, Adele. *The Dynamics of Biblical Parallelism.* Bloomington, IN: Indiana University Press, 1985.

Patte, Daniel and Aline. *Structural Exegesis: From Theory to Practice.* Philadelphia: Fortress, 1978.

Sternberg, Meir. *The Poetics of Biblical Narrative.* Bloomington, IN: Indiana University Press, 1985.

G. W. Coats

Biblical Theology

Biblical theology is a movement in biblical interpretation that developed after World War II and flourished for the next two decades. It has by no means suffered demise, as seen by the international periodical *Horizons in Biblical Theology*, begun in 1979. It had a parallel in theology in the movement known as neoorthodoxy. Both were in some respects a reaction to "liberal" theology, which was perceived to be naturalistic and atomistic and lacking in theological depth.

It was anticipated in biblical theology that the movement would furnish a substantive core of Christian truth, recover fervor in preaching, and further the union of churches by transcending traditions that were divisive because not biblically based.

Among the features of the biblical theology movement was a contrast between Hebrew and Greek thought, with emphasis on the Hebrew. The Old Testament was seen as informed by the distinctive Hebrew way of thinking and the New Testament, though written in Greek, was seen as best understood in Hebrew categories.

Another feature was a distaste for dogmatic theology, which was thought to have been too deeply influenced by a church that early became much more Gentile (Hellenistic) than Jewish.

Theologians in this movement also placed an emphasis on the distinctiveness of the Bible. Israel's culture and religion and the religion of Christians were seen as radically different from those of others. The distinctiveness of the Bible was one thing that constituted its unity.

They also stressed revelation in history. "The God who acts in history" was a common theme in the movement, together with the assumption that among Greeks and others beyond Israel there was little in the way of a revelation of God in history. It is this revelation, which the Scriptures bear witness to, that comprises their unity.

A final aspect was an emphasis on word studies. Many were the books that consisted of word studies, most notably Gerhart Kittel's nine-volume *Theological Word Book of the New Testament.* (However, not all the studies in this monumental work took the positions identified with biblical theology.)

These positions met with critical comment. Some scholars maintained that biblical theology paid greater attention to earlier Hebrew thought, especially what is enshrined in the Pentateuch, and too little to the Judaism that developed between the Testaments. It is that Judaism that brought the Hebrew Scriptures to final shape and provided the matrix for a Jesus and a Paul.

Scholars have also maintained that biblical theology needs to give greater heed to apocalyptic thought. Apocalyptic is marginal in the Old Testament but is thought to be pivotal for our understanding of the New.

Diversity as much as unity characterizes today's understanding of what the Bible is all about. An important work by James D. G. Dunn, *Unity and Diversity in the New Testament* (1977), underscores that Testament's unity, to be sure, but spends more time on its diversity.

It is also difficult to make clear-cut distinctions between Hebrew and Greek ways of thinking, especially since Judaism had been under Hellenistic influence for three centuries before the time of Jesus. Moreover, Jesus came from the more hellenized part of Palestine and Paul was a native of the Greco-Roman city of Tarsus.

The biblical theology movement has also been criticized for its emphasis on God's revelatory acts in history, therein setting Christianity apart from other "religions" (following Karl Barth's definition of religion as a human construct). On the one hand, the migration of peoples in their hundreds of thousands to England, the United States, and Western Europe and the rise of a militant Islam has brought the issue of world religions to the fore again; and on the other, it has become increasingly clear that it is not at all easy to move directly from revelation to relevance, from what was meant then (in some action of God in the distant past) to what it means now. There is a very significant involvement by us in the determination of just what did happen then as well as in what that happening might or should mean for us today. And that opens up the possibility for differences, relativity, and fallibility. *See also* Kerygma; Neoorthodoxy; Theology and Education.

FOR FURTHER REFERENCE

Barr, J. "Biblical Theology." Suppl. vol., pp. 104–111. Betz, O. "Biblical Theology, History of." Vols. A–D, pp. 432–437. Stendahl, K. "Biblical Theology, Contemporary." Vols. A–D, pp. 418–432. In *Interpreter's Dictionary of the Bible*. New York: Abingdon, 1962, 1976.

R. W. Graham

Biblical Translation

Biblical translation has to do with the translation of the Scriptures into languages other than the original. The Old Testament was written in Hebrew and the New Testament in Greek, although what Jesus spoke mostly was Aramaic, a Northwest Semitic language that flourished for a thousand years until the seventh century. Translations of the Bible became necessary either when the original languages were no longer understood by the people, or when Judaism and Christianity spread into lands where languages other than Hebrew or Aramaic were spoken.

THE HISTORY OF BIBLICAL TRANSLATION

In the twelfth century B.C., the Assyrians began a policy of removing conquered peoples to some other part of their empire to break their national spirit. The Jews were among such peoples deported from their homeland, especially in the eighth and sixth centuries B.C. In time, many became unfamiliar with the Hebrew of the Scriptures and there arose the practice of making first an oral, later a written, paraphrase into Aramaic of the reading in the synagogue service.

As it had been the lack of knowledge of Hebrew that called forth these Targums, as they were called, so in time Aramaic shared the same fate and the Hebrew Bible was translated into Greek. This was done in Egypt beginning in the first half of the third century B.C. and this translation is known as the Septuagint (LXX).

Although Jesus might also have spoken Greek and classical Hebrew, his native tongue was Aramaic, and a few Aramaic words are preserved in the Gospels. But the Gospels as we now have them were written in Greek, as were the other books that constitute the New Testament.

The earliest translations of the Bible into a language other than Greek were made as a result of the church's missionary activity, especially into areas northeast of Palestine, where Syriac was the common language, and the Roman colonies of north Africa, where Latin was the standard tongue. So the Gospels were translated into Syriac by the middle of the second century and the Bible into Latin by the middle of the third. In short time, the Latin version held the field in the West.

Christianity apparently entered Britain in the third century. However, the first English version of the complete Bible was not made until that by Wycliffe in 1380–1382 (although parts such as the Ten Commandments and the Lord's Prayer were put into Anglo-Saxon by the seventh century). The sixteenth century saw an outburst of translations into English, culminating in the Protestant King James Version of 1611 and the Catholic Douay (Douai) Version of 1582–1610.

The Protestant Reformation brought translations into other European languages, beginning with Luther's German translation in 1534. The Hebrew Bible was translated into the German dialect that later became Yiddish in 1421, and the first complete translation into High German was made by Gotthold Salomon in 1837. English translations were made by individuals until that of the Jewish Publication Society of America in 1917.

Some of the more recent English versions include the Revised Standard Version (1945/1952), the Jerusalem Bible (1966), the New English Bible (1961/1970), the New American Bible (1970), Today's English Version (1966/1976), the New International Version (1970/1978), and the New Jerusalem Bible (1985). The Jewish Publication Society completed a new translation of the Hebrew Bible in 1982, and a revision of the Revised Standard Version is scheduled to be published in 1990.

The Christian missionary movement brought a concern for translation of the Scriptures into vernacular languages as early as the seventeenth century in Asia. The nineteenth-century explosion of evangelism by Protestants into Asia and Africa brought increased activity. In many African lands and the Pacific Islands, oral cultures became literate as missionaries developed alphabets and vocabularies. Today the United Bible Societies (UBS), representing more than fifty national Bible societies, coordinates translation work under four areas: Asia/Pacific, the Americas, Europe, and Africa. The Wycliffe Translation Society is an independent group specializing in pioneer work with cultures that have as yet no written language. They develop alphabets, words, and grammar to form a written language and often work in cooperation with the UBS.

THE JUSTIFICATION FOR NEW TRANSLATIONS

The demand for a translation of the Bible arises, in the first instance, from the need for the Scriptures to be "understood by the people." This was a primary reason for the translation of Jesus' words into Greek and for the various Protestant translations at the time of the Reformation. It is a basic reason for the recent Catholic versions in English.

The second justification for a new translation stems from the fact that Scripture deserves the best version possible, though "best" is not something that can be achieved once and for all. There are three chief reasons why newer translations continue to be necessary. One is that our knowledge of the original texts of the Scriptures is continually growing. An example is Konstantin von Tischendorf's discovery in 1859 of a valuable fourth-century Greek manuscript of parts of the Bible, now called Codex Sinaiticus, in St. Catherine's Convent on Mount Sinai. A second is that our knowledge of the language and vocabulary the biblical writers used is constantly improving. Important was the late nineteenth-century realization that the Greek of the New Testament is not "Holy Ghost Greek" but the common language of ordinary people. A third is that English, for example, is a living language that is ceaselessly changing, so that the words used by earlier translators often do not today convey the meanings the translators (and likewise the authors of Scripture) intended.

Biblical translation always involves a certain degree of interpretation, though the best translations do not reflect the idiosyncrasies of individual translators. Some Greek words do not have exact English equivalents (as Aramaic did not always have an exact Greek counterpart). In any case, the truest translation calls for the English idiom that is most like the Greek idiom, leaving the door open for even greater inexactitude and differences of opinion.

It is not to be wondered at, therefore, that the Scriptures continue to be translated into new highly regarded versions wherever the Bible is respected and loved. *See also* Bible Societies; Bible Study; Biblical Criticism; Exegesis; Hermeneutic; History of Christian Education.

FOR FURTHER REFERENCE

Hann, Robert R. *The Bible: An Owner's Manual.* New York: Paulist, 1983.

R. W. Graham

Biography

Biography, the writing of life stories, is, first of all, a literary genre, but it is also a very old enterprise. The concern for "origins," which always has animated a people eager to pass on its heritage to oncoming generations, may lie behind this. Strong characters who helped mold a people can be remembered only if those persons are kept before each new generation as vividly as possible. Families by themselves may do the same, although few memorable familial biographies have been produced and retained unless they have been adopted by a wider reading audience.

Autobiography is the writing of one's own life and is therefore a part of the total biographical genre. Some autobiographies are printed because they are subsidized by the writer or an organization. Others are written in tandem with another writer ("as told to") because of popular interest in a well-known person. Still other autobiographies, coming from the depths of the writer's being, become such classic statements of a powerful life that they will continue to endure for centuries. Journals that chart an inward or spiritual journey often covering the greater portion of a lifetime are also a form of autobiography.

Preceding written biography there was probably only the oral rendition of heroes' lives in the public square or around the evening fire. Only some kings were able to have the achievements of their reigns recorded after the dawn of writing, and then with the aid of servants who served as secretaries. It is probable that scores of interesting and important persons who influenced their respective cultures in their day have been forgotten because no written records were produced or survived. Even with regard to written materials, many of those too have been lost. But usually, when a civilization has reached the literary stage, time becomes the filter through which the worthy are separated from the less worthy, the memorable from the ephemeral.

In earlier years biographers often used biography as a mold into which to press a personality; for example, Plutarch praised certain Aristotelian moral qualities by incorporating them into the characters whose lives he wrote. Some Victorian biographers-for-hire tended to do similar things—finely bedecking the subject and cleaning up the loose ends and question marks in the life to produce a more perfect picture. The biographer Lytton Strachey once commented that this was like the final work of the undertaker. This is not to say, though, that a biographer may not have a point of view about the character whose life he or she is relating or a style that evokes a certain rapport with the readership. But in valuable biography the perspective and the style are used to deal honestly with the subject and facts are not denied or underestimated.

It is not only distinctively religious personalities that should constitute the biographical interest of teachers and curriculum writers. Religion permeates personalities, and sometimes the best "illustration" of a religious dimension is someone whose work, for example, is decidedly secular. On the other hand, the religious community has the obligation, just as does the civic body, to pass on its own heroes and heroines of faith, and the saints, in that broad, inclusive sense, are vast in number. Every generation produces a small avalanche of good and great souls whose stories need to be gathered and told and retold on into the distant, unforeseeable future. Think for a moment of persons whose twentieth-century religious attainments will certainly be kept in mind for centuries to come: Albert Schweitzer, Wilfred Grenfell, Dietrich Bonhoeffer, Toyohiko Kagawa, Pope John XXIII, Karl Barth, Martin Luther King, Jr., and Mother Teresa, to mention just several who come to mind. And even as we live and breathe, new saints are emerging who will become exhibits in the household of faith.

Biography is a form of storytelling. From the Bible to significant religious persons of today, there is material for teaching at every age level. One incident from a life can be chosen or a condensation of the full story given; a life story can be retold in sections over a period of weeks. Biographies or specific incidents in them can be dramatized informally. A specific biography can be the basis for study in a series of sessions for an adult class. In understanding the person in his or her setting and probing the significance of a life and work for that time and our time there are thoughtful questions for discussion.

For use in religious education, the following criteria for choosing a biography for study are suggested:

1. The style should be characterized by interesting quality, appropriateness to the subject, and literary merit.

2. The biographical content should be faithful to the character as he or she really was; the interpretation should be based on the fact.

3. The biographical content should portray the inward motives of the subject; we should see the principles stood for and the issues met through such typical avenues as love, ambition, illness, health, jealousy, spite, belief in the future (immortality), experience of God, success, and failure.

4. The biographical content should show how the subject was related to the social milieu in which the life took place.

5. The ulterior motives of the author should not obtrude upon the veracity of the portrayal.

See also Books, Religious; Journal Writing; Narrative Theology; Storytelling.

K. B. Cully

Black Experience and Religious Education

The adventures of persons of African descent who exist in a white-dominated society facing rejection and injustice because of skin color and physical features is defined as the black experience. It is living in a constant tension between hope and despair, success and failure, justice and injustice, poverty and plenty. Africans were brought to America, stripped of their native culture, enslaved, and disregarded as persons of worth. However, the struggle grew from slavery to emancipation, to reconstruction, to segregation, to integration, and on to the partial achievement of freedom and equal rights. Amidst this, black people retained the innate drive for self-determination, which provided the momentum to strive for a better day and a brighter future.

PAST AND PRESENT

Religion has played a vital role in the pursuit of this new day and is closely intertwined in all of life. The introduction of religion began as a means of indoctrinating slaves by slave owners, moving to evangelism, and eventually to providing the basic elements for educating persons, plus granting hope, survival skills, community, and a thrust for liberation. Hearing the stories of the Israelites' deliverance from Egypt gave African Americans hope that the same loving God would and could deliver them. Thus, hope was born and strength received to bear the oppressive conditions thrust upon them. The war was on, and a people deprived of their native culture were forced to create a new life in a strange and unfriendly country that viewed them as property to be disposed of at will.

Sunday church schools were often the first and only source of training, since it was illegal to teach a black person to read and write in some places. The oral tradition became an effective nurturing tool, as the black preacher evolved and became the one to assume leadership responsibility. Consequently, learning occurred; adjustments and achievements were made that resulted in new denominations, businesses, schools, colleges, and other organizations for nurturing the dispossessed and meeting needs.

Religious education in the black church began with a basic focus on the spiritual dimensions of life. Little effort has been directed toward a holistic educational ministry to individuals at every stage along the life span. Too much attention has been placed on resolving crisis situations rather than nurturing for prevention. Predominantly black denominations have struggled to develop and produce resources to meet the needs, but they are always forced to work under conditions of insufficient resources and personnel. Therefore, many religious educators have had to master the art of adaptation using their creative ingenuity to meet the challenging educational needs with whatever was available.

For religious educators to be effective with persons of African descent, they must be conscious of the equality God provides to all persons and refuse to allow the subtle ways in which racist ideas are perpetuated. A loving and caring environment must exist that exhibits God's love for all persons, builds integrity and self-esteem, fosters bonding in community, and works toward the goal of liberation and equality. In this process, the heritage and traditions must not be lost or degraded; rather they should be repeated, interpreted, and built upon. It is important to know African-American history and tradition to appreciate accomplishments and provide the motivation for the journey ahead.

Religious education is carried on through Sunday schools with materials usually provided by the denomination, although some congregations use other curricula. Frequently the Uniform Lessons Series, based on a common Scripture passage used at all age levels, forms the biblical material from which each denomination writes its material. In some Baptist churches, the pastor conducts a weekly training class primarily for teachers explaining the passage for that lesson, and teachers are encouraged to consider its application to their pupils.

Congregational worship is an important form of nurture, where hymn, prayer, and sermon, strongly biblical, teach the people both biblical interpretation and the meanings of their faith for life.

Black colleges, the first of which (Lincoln University in Pennsylvania) was established in 1854, continue to flourish. Interdenominational Theological Seminary, Atlanta, a coalition of four denominational seminaries, preserves the black tradition in ministerial training while maintaining links with nearby predominantly white theological schools. The Howard School of Religion, Washington, D.C., is another black graduate school of theological education.

SUGGESTIONS FOR THE FUTURE

To eradicate some of the problems facing those who nurture in the African-American community and provide a basis for renewal, the following suggestions are given:

Religious educators must practice what they teach or preach and have a genuine commitment to God.

More training must be provided to enable workers to be more effective in using modern technological advances and techniques in the church settings for nurturing.

Opportunities for creative expression of one's religious heritage and cultural tendencies must be allowed.

Negativism should not be associated with the word "black" and the use of more favorable terms employed.

Personal worth and self-esteem must be lifted up for all persons. The use of the "put-down syndrome" and discrimination toward anyone who is different is not compatible with true Christianity.

Christians must fight the negative and destructive images portrayed through media. Persons must be enabled to distinguish between fantasy, commercial hype, and the effects of suggestive advertising in contrast to solid Christian morals and priorities as they struggle to make ethical decisions.

More time ought to be put into the nurturing process by and for parents and leaders on every level, including educational experiences on parenting and related subjects.

Religious educators must insist that the true message of the gospel be revealed through daily living.

The visual images used in religious literature must become more inclusive of all races and groups or use more symbolic language that does not favor a particular segment of society. (This issue can be compared to the current concerns regarding sexist language.)

Every effort should be made to empower persons for ministry using the talents within a congregation to expand the scope of ministry provided.

Educational focus within the black community should embody the process of impacting society for positive change in the social, economic, and political realms. A sense of hope must perpetuate the process, replacing feelings of apathy, selfishness, and powerlessness.

Nonblack persons must search for ways to work with African-Americans rather than flee from close encounters. Minority concerns deserve understanding with a commitment that goes beyond tokenism and toleration.

Innovation must be encouraged, removing the tendency to duplicate what is dominant in society and thinking through every possible angle for ministry and problem resolution in new and more compatible ways.

More sharing and development of programs must occur across denominational and racial lines. There is strength in uniting and pooling resources.

Methodology used must employ usage of both hemispheres of the brain, removing the imbalance existing in twentieth-century educational practices. This will promote participatory learning and render a means to transport what is learned to application in daily living.

Attention must be given to nurturing the family in each of its modern configurations, thus promoting a more caring environment and resources to cope with the pressures bombarding family structures.

Planning and programming must be completed on the basis of the needs of the people rather than on traditions and prior experiences.

Alternative scheduled nurturing opportunities would provide possibilities for more involvement, efficiency, and effectiveness, plus make greater use of leisure time.

Religious education must provide more training for persons to provide nurture within the African-American community and encourage it as a viable vocation and needed ministry.

Consequently, the task of nurturing persons of African descent presents a challenge to the world and requires the application of the principle of love and self-respect to every situation. Without this, efforts to nurture will fail, problems will not be solved, and the situations that gave birth to the black experience and the unique problems of injustice will continue to exist with a space-age dimension. Nevertheless, the ministry beckons and demands commitment, loyalty, justice, and love. *See also* Black Theology; Colleges, Black; Language, Inclusive; Multicultural Education; Prejudice; Social Justice, Education for; Uniform Lessons Series.

FOR FURTHER REFERENCE

Adebonojo, Mary. *Free to Choose: Youth Resources from the Black Perspective.* Valley Forge, PA: Judson, 1980.

Foster, Charles R., Ethel R. Johnson, and Grant S. Shockley. *Christian Education Journey of Black Americans.* Nashville, TN: Discipleship Resources, 1985.

Jones, Nathan. *Sharing the Old, Old Story: Educational Ministry in the Black Community.* Winona, MN: St. Mary's Press, 1982.

Smith, Wallace Charles. *The Church in the Life of the Black Family.* Valley Forge, PA: Judson, 1985.

Williams, Williard A. *Educational Ministry in the Black Community.* Nashville, TN: Board of Education, United Methodist Church, 1972.

M. A. Love

Black Theology

Black theology is a revolutionary change movement that arose in the black church in the late 1960s. The term was probably first used in the conversations surrounding the organization in 1966 of the National Committee of Negro Churchmen (now the National Conference of Black Churchmen) and its theological commission. Its first formal use and articulation as a concept occurs in *Black Theology and Black Power* by James H. Cone (1969). Black theology may be described (not defined) as an action-reflection engagement process in the black church as it seeks to understand the relevance of the Christian faith to the black experience and to the condition of oppression experienced by black people in America.

ORIGINS

Black theology originated in the midst of the black struggle for liberation. Its unique objective was to do theology from a black perspective rather than to invent a new theology based on bankrupt European-American paradigms. It found its data for this direction from three sources: the civil rights struggle, Joseph R. Washington's then highly controversial book *Black Religion* (1964), and the black power movement.

The civil rights struggle identified the need for the black church to address past black grievances, correct injustices, and empower black people to walk, live, and participate as equals and with dignity in the mainstream of American national life. Its crusade provided the arena for black theology to articulate its case for a God who recognizes and casts his lot with the poor, the oppressed, and the persecuted. The civil rights struggle gave the black church a new mission.

J. R. Washington's *Black Religion* helped black Christians to understand that black religion had a unique individuality and that this raised fundamental questions about the nature, purpose, and form of black religion. Washington also observed the lack of a foundational theology in black religion for the task it had set for itself.

The black power movement made several significant contributions to black theology. It motivated reflection on a common black past and strengthened black identity and self-esteem. It pointed up the need to differentiate the essential gospel from later expressions, and it forged a covenant of care and responsibility between the black church and the oppressed wherever they are found.

DEVELOPMENT

Black theology has had a three-phase historical development. In its generative years, 1966–1970, it was both the prophetic and critical voice of the traditional black church challenging it to once again become the leader of the black community. In this same period it was the theological foundation for the landmark "Black Power Statement" of 1966, the powerful document on the church and the urban crisis of 1967 dissenting from a National Council of the Churches of Christ position, the basic "Urban Mission in a Time of Crisis" statement of 1968, the black church caucus movement of the late 1960s, and the earliest writings of black theologians such as James H. Cone, J. Deotis Roberts, Jr., Gayraud S. Wilmore, and others.

During its second phase of development, 1970–1976, black theology gave birth to a large number of additional books, monographs, and articles on the subject, established a Society for the Study of Black Religion (1970), and occasioned the initiation of a new theological discipline in theological education. Its third phase, about 1975, witnessed a renewed emphasis on the need for black theology to be preached and practiced in local black congregations. Evidence for this is found in Cecil Cone's work, *The Identity Crisis in Black Theology* (1975), the initiation of the black theology and unity statement of the National Committee of Black Churchmen, and the important black theology conference in Atlanta in 1977, which again addressed the issue of the black church in relation to the black community in the nation.

An equally significant development in the black theology movement has been the Theology in the Americas Project, which sponsored inter-ethnic dialogues "between" and "among" Asian, black, Hispanic, and Native American theologians in the United States and overseas. Such conferences, addressing a wide range of issues from liberation theology to Africanization classism, racism, sexism, and Marxism were held beginning in 1969.

Several trends in the black theology movement should be noted. There has been a noticeable shift from a somewhat exclusive preoccupation with racism in the United States to an understanding of oppression experienced by ethnic and racial groups across all of the nation and in the Third World. Recently, more attention is being devoted by black scholars to basic theological categories in black theology such as theodicy. Cultural indigenization as well as sexism issues are receiving attention in both study and research.

BLACK THEOLOGIES AND THEOLOGIANS

The civil rights movement, anti–civil rights intransigence, and white church reluctance to move beyond rhetoric and the safe confines of pious liberal pronouncements to basic reform forced black people to reconsider, redefine, and reconstruct their worldview and religious faith. The result of this new mood in the secular sphere was the cry for black power. In the religious domain it was black theology.

James H. Cone, in his pivotal volume *Black Theology and Black Power*, outlined the direction of this new departure in American theological thought, the first ever to challenge its dominance from a social perspective. He made several definitive assertions: theology can be done independently of any previous paradigm and it can be done from a black perspective; black theology is and ought to be a theology of and for the oppressed; black theology originated in the struggle of the black church on behalf of the black masses; and black theology is a valid explication of the role that God has always played in the history of his people.

Cone's "theology of black power" for black liberation became the major voice in the black theology movement. There were and are other positions, however. Albert Cleage in his *Black Messiah* (1968) provided a thoroughly black nationalist interpretation of both black religion and the black church. J. Deotis Roberts in his *Liberation and Reconciliation: A Black Theology* (1971), while not denying the importance of liberation, insists that it must be preceded by reconciliation.

Major J. Jones, a theologian from a "theology of hope" position, in his *Black Awareness: A Theology of Hope* (1971) believes that black theology is valid as it moves the black church toward the new community beyond racism of any kind. Charles H. Long in key articles (1971, 1975) questions the very legitimacy of black theology if based on Western rather than African theological thought. Gayraud S. Wilmore, basically agreeing with Long and still adhering to James Cone's black theology tradition, contends in his *Black Religion and Black Radicalism* (1972) that black radicalism can best be validated in a black theology based on black religion rather than on a "black" version of white theology based on black power.

Cecil W. Cone, the brother of James H. Cone, adds a significant statement to the black theology discussion with his position that black theology grows out of African Christian, black religious, and black church roots. Yet another voice is heard on the black theology issue. William Jones in *Is God a White Racist?* (1973) introduces the problem of suffering into the black theology discussion. He holds the position, from a black humanistic perspective, that black theology is an anomaly since it cannot be empirically demonstrated that God either exists or has ever really delivered black people from oppression. *See also* Action-Reflection; Black Experience and Religious Education; Liberation Theology.

FOR FURTHER REFERENCE

Bruce, Calvin E., and William R. Jones, eds. *Black Theology II: Essays on Formation and Outreach of Contemporary Black Theology.* Lewisburg, PA: Bucknell University Press, 1978.

Cone, James H. *Black Theology and Black Power.* New York: Seabury, 1969.

Roberts, J. Deotis. *Liberation and Reconciliation.* Philadelphia: Westminster, 1971.

Wilmore, Gayraud S. *Black Religion and Black Radicalism.* Garden City, NY: Doubleday, Anchor Press, 1972.

G. S. Shockley

Body Language

"Body language" usually refers to the unconscious clues we give to others by our gestures, mannerisms, and the position of our body. For example, leaning toward a person who is speaking communicates our eagerness to hear what is being said. However, a hostile facial expression coupled with the leaning would communicate a threatening attitude.

The study of body language is called kinesics. There is evidence that as much as 90 percent of communication takes place nonverbally. Studies indicate that body language, like spoken and written language, is learned and varies from culture to culture.

Educators can enhance the clarity of what they are communicating as well as get and give feedback through attention to body language. The use of ritual in most religions, which includes prescribed gestures and other movements, is a recognition of the power of body language. *See also* Communication Theory; Conversation; Feedback.

J. C. Smith

Books, Children's

Books have long been a rich resource for entertainment, delight, information, and values for children; religiously oriented books for children provide, in addition, an aid in communicating faith stories, values, and traditions. Books have the happy facility for getting inside a concept as well as a person to enhance, enliven, and evoke religious qualities. To do so, religious books must address the full possibilities for and needs of the growing child.

The years of childhood comprise that period of life span in the evolving person when the compelling lifelong need to find meaning first emerges. Foundational to that process is human development; attitudes, knowledge, values, skills, gender roles, and spiritual foundations in varying stages of maturation are in process. To the extent that carefully selected books at home and in the church or synagogue are integral components of the child's environment, they can aid in the formation of persons growing toward wholeness.

Central to the nurturance and stimulation of growing children is knowing their needs. Children have a need to be physically safe and secure; they need both to love and be loved as valued beings; they need to belong to a family and community that accepts and cares for them; they need to feel competent in facing life's tasks and terrors; and they need to have information. But more, the life of the spirit must be nurtured and stimulated as well. Children need to be introduced to the possibility of change through imaginative adventures and through lighthearted stories of fun and delight, romance and fantasy. Books that provide a variety of aesthetic experiences, that interpret the arts, that bring order out of chaos through the recreation of life situations and questions will enable life to be seen whole and clear, filled with meaning and possibility beyond simple factual data.

AGE-RELATED GUIDELINES FOR SELECTION

In order to select books for children wisely, educators and parents need to know about the moral, cognitive, and spiritual stages of children. At different stages of growth children see and perceive the world very differently from adults. Through the sensory and motor reflexes, the infant explores and learns; experience is taken at face value and as part of the environment. Only gradually does the infant become aware of the self as separate and unique. With the achievement of speech, a child is able to think with words and symbols. Permanency of objects needs continued reinforcement for learning that things exist out of sight. Picture storybooks with bright illustrations and repetitive sounds inform and reinforce the learning process.

In the preschool years, children see mainly the details of a situation. Because a preschool child can deal with only one facet of a problem at a time, thinking may be fragmentary and illogical. Hence, there is in these early years a need for a variety of simple books, books with stories that have repetitive elements, selected nursery rhymes, alphabet and counting books, concept books, and picture storybooks to be read aloud. These books provide cognitive learning skills, pleasure, and social growth through the shared reading experience.

Moral values and qualities too are rooted in the early years of life. As the child emerges from the amoral phase of toddler autonomy, a beginning understanding of what is good emerges; children soon learn to conform for the rewards of

CHILDREN'S BOOKS

Representative Recommendations for Different Age Levels

Age Level	Recommended Books
Preschool	*Who Has Seen the Wind?* by Marion Conger Illustrated by Susan Pere Abingdon, 1959 *Where Can I Find God?* by Helen Doss Illustrated by Frank Aloise Abingdon, 1968 *Peter's Chair* by Ezra Jack Keats Illustrated by Ezra Jack Keats Harper, 1967 *Friday Night is Papa Night* by Ruth Sonneborn Illustrated by Emily McNully Viking, 1970
Early Elementary	*Stories about Christian Heroes* (a series) Winston, 1978–1983. *No Good in Art* by Miriam Cohen Illustrated by Lillian Hoban Greenwillow, 1980 *Annie and the Old One* by Miska Miles Illustrated by Peter Parnall Little, Brown, 1971 *Building Blocks* by Cynthia Voigt Atheneum, 1984
Middle Elementary	*The Dark is Rising* by Susan Cooper Illustrated by Alan E. Cober Atheneum, 1973 *The Kite Song* by Margery Evernden· Illustrated by Cindy Wheeler Lothrop, Lee, Shepherd, 1984 *Ladder of Angels* by Madeleine L'Engle Illustrated by children Seabury, 1979 *Unclaimed Treasures* by Patricia MacLachlan Harper & Row, 1984
Late Elementary	*Miss Hickory* by Carolyn Sherwin Bailey Illustrated by Ruth Gannett Viking, 1946 *Are You There God? It's Me, Margaret* by Judy Blume Bradbury, 1970 *Unclaimed Treasures* by Patricia MacLachlan Harper & Row, 1984 *The Borrowers* by Mary Norton Illustrated by Beth and Joe Krush Harcourt Brace Jovanovich, 1952

approval. This involves little understanding of why certain actions are good or bad. Through stories children are able to understand that others too have feelings and rights; they begin to grow in the development of conscience and moral responsibility.

But it is in spiritual development that special possibilities are present for religious education. Children in the early years possess a sense of wonder and awe, of joy and enthusiasm, of openness and trust. In the immediacy of wonder or trust, spoken prayer is only a breath away. Books that stress the wonder and delight of the world around us, that evoke caring and trusting responses to all persons and creation build the foundations for spiritual maturation.

During the early elementary years, a new way of perceiving the world emerges. Now perception is facilitated through seeing life in whole views, though limited to concrete objects that can be seen with the five senses. Tangible objects and historical persons and events fascinate and compel attention to details. Later, the ability to think in terms of ideas and of relationships to objects will herald the emergence of adult cognitive maturation. Similarly, moral development will move to understanding the difference between rules as concrete to rules as general principles. Now a wide, diverse number of books is called for. To find meaning in the wondrous phenomena of nature, to understand the mysterious ways of human action, to experience the wide range of emotions—books can aid the process of making meaning.

The categories of books include folk tales, fables, epics, legends, poetry, realistic stories, historical fiction, biographies, informational books, biblical narratives, parables, and biographies of heroes and heroines of the faith. Chosen wisely, selected carefully, subjected to critical standards, books can build relationships, support family values, provide religious models, relate the faith stories, and enable spiritual growth.

OTHER GUIDELINES FOR SELECTION

At this point, the thrust of this work moves to provide guidelines for the choice of books for children based on the general needs for cognitive, moral, and spiritual development. We need always, however, to be alert and sensitive to the specific needs of the child. Given a wide selection of choices, a child can be trusted in the choice of particular stories. A specific fairy tale, for example, with its dramatic portrayal of good and evil, of power and powerlessness, may be requested endlessly until the child is satisfied or the inner need is resolved.

The following guidelines for choosing books provide criteria for making wise selections by parents and religious educators. A children's book needs, first of all, to meet the criteria of basic elements of all good literature. Is the theme or main idea clearly presented? Do the characters grow? What is the plot? Is it enjoyable?

From the perspective of religious education, does it tell the faith story with power? Is it written in the light of the best scholarship of the Bible so that the story can be understood faithfully? Will the story evoke further interest in the traditions and narratives of the faith?

Illustrations are powerful conveyors of attitudes and values, aesthetics, and reality. Do the illustrations reflect the mood of the story? Do they enhance the text? Are they tastefully and artistically done? Are females pictured as often as males? Do the illustrations depict both single- and two-parent families?

Language is a critical factor in the formation of identity, gender roles, self-esteem, and societal realities. Is the language inclusive? Are professions identified by function rather than gender? Are pronouns for males and females used equally? Are there words that demean children or women or men?

Societal values and worldviews are communicated subtly and overtly in a variety of ways to children. Is violence or force used to solve problems? Are there racial or economic stereotypes? How are minorities portrayed? How is fairness achieved in groups? What is the attitude about peace and justice?

Religious education can provide an environment both at home and the church or synagogue to aid children in discovering and claiming transformative faith. Do books present only a patriarchal worldview? Are metaphors that express religious insights couched in both male and female orientations? Are all modes of ministry equally possible for males and females?

Do books nurture a sense of awe and wonder? Do they teach through trust and responsibility? Is life valued and celebrated? Is there concern for the well-being of all persons and creation?

If specific books meet these criteria, informed by religious faith and heritage and by our hope and visions, then growing persons will discover that books are enlivening and enhancing aids that can evoke faithful meaning in life. *See also* Affective Development; Child Development; Cognitive Development; Faith Development; Moral Development; Storytelling.

R. J. Schroeder

Books, Religious

Christianity, like its counterpart, Judaism, is a religion of "the Book." The writings collected to be the Scriptures are the centerpiece of all that is said and done in the name of Yahweh, the God of Abraham, Isaac, and Jacob, or in the name of Jesus Christ.

Beyond Holy Scriptures, books are a necessary part of the worship, teaching, and communal life of the religious community. They give people an understanding of the faith, interpretation of the Bible, and help for spiritual development. They are an essential resource for religious education—for use by students and teachers.

HISTORY OF RELIGIOUS PUBLISHING

The earliest books were religious: liturgical materials, myths, and epics. Egyptian papyri (scrolls) were the first form of written books (used also by Greeks and Romans). The parchment codex, a paged book, was first used by Christians to put gospel books together. During the Greco-Roman period secular as well as religious books were written, but during the Middle Ages, the religious books again became paramount and these were copied, some of them beautifully illustrated, in monasteries.

The invention of printing in the fifteenth century made possible a wider availability of books, with the Bible being the first book printed by Johannes Gutenberg, the inventor of movable type in the West. Inexpensive books for the newly literate first appeared in Venice early in the sixteenth century. William Caxton was the first printer to publish in English.

The publishing of secular books, revived during the Renaissance, continued through succeeding centuries. Religious publishing became one area among many.

The Bible, translated from Latin into vernacular languages, became a best-seller, particularly as literacy increased. Portions of Scripture, psalmbooks, and hymnals were published as well as scholarly books on Scripture and theology. Some such books published in Massachusetts date back to the seventeenth century.

Religious book publishers today operate from large general publishing houses, denominational houses, and independent religious publishing houses. Bibles continue to be the mainstay of religious publishing, but other books published include popular writing for biblical study, theological understanding, inspiration, spirituality, and "how-to" books for church leaders—both lay and clerical—in many fields. Some books deal with the psychology, sociology, and history of religion. Similar books are published in a scholarly vein primarily for use among professionals. Religious fiction also has experienced a new popularity as talented writers have appeared on the scene, providing light reading with a religious background.

Religious education publishing may be said to have begun with catechisms to teach the distinctive forms of Western Christian faith as defined by the Protestant Reformation and the Council of Trent. The hornbooks, staples of seventeenth-century New England education, were reading books with a Protestant orientation. The expansion of religious education publishing began with the spread of the U.S. Sunday school into the expanding settlements of the middle and far West in mid-nineteenth century, as missionaries arrived with tracts and other educational materials. From that point Sunday school publishing became prolific, first through the interdenominational American (later named International) Sunday School Union and later through denominational agencies.

Books both for parents and for Sunday school teachers were published. *Christian Nurture* (1847) by Connecticut clergyman Horace Bushnell, is a classic. The influence of secular education on religious education was earliest evidenced in the writings of George Albert Coe early in the twentieth century.

Books on religious education are divided into two general categories: theory and practice. Material on theory includes theological, biblical, educational, psychological, and sociological foundations and is designed primarily for professionals and seriously interested laypeople. Practical works include methods and materials designed for lay teachers with little background in the field. There is a growing market as well for textbooks for religiously-sponsored elementary and high schools and for college and university classes in religious subjects. Publishers of both theoretical and practical works include denominational houses (some of whose books are expressly designed for teachers in their tradition), independent religious publishers, and the religion departments of some general publishers.

RECENT GROWTH OF RELIGIOUS PUBLISHING

The making of religious books has become a vast industry with an annual commercial sales in the United States estimated at more than $500 million and production at more than 130 million volumes (Book Industries Study Group, 1985). This represents more than a third of the total commercial book market, according to megatrends analyst John Nesbitt.

A number of factors are responsible for this growth in religious book publishing: rising religious interest over several decades, better and more sophisticated marketing by the publishers and stores, and a more appealing quality of religious books turned out by a growing number of church-sponsored as well as independent publishers.

Improvement in the quality of religious books is due partly to improved writing. More than sixty training workshops or seminars for religious writers are conducted annually with an estimated total attendance of more than 7,000. A number of books for the training of writers are available. And at least three national organizations for religious writers exist and produce correspondence courses for the training of writers.

Correspondingly, the payment for writing religious books has increased in the past few decades; many book contracts for religious titles now call for substantial advances and royalties sufficient to attract more accomplished writers to these markets.

Part of the upgrading of the religious book publishing industry can also be traced to increased competition for religious manuscripts. Like all of the book publishing industry, religious publishing is a fluid business with new companies appearing and old companies being merged with others or going out of business. This activity and change has broadened the scope of religious publishing.

Many publishers also have broadened their line so that more than one theological or biblical viewpoint may be noted in their lists. Readers, too, are less committed to particular types of publishers and range across biblical and theological interpretations. Less denominational allegiance makes it possible for planners to view a wider range of options.

Roman Catholic publishing in the United States was done in earlier days almost exclusively by firms owned and operated by individuals and families. Most of these houses have been merged with other publishers or have become departments of secular houses. Some Catholic publishing has been done and is still being carried out under the sponsorship of orders within the church. Catholic publishing has broadened its approach a great deal in recent years, especially after the changes in the church brought about by the Second Vatican Council. Most Catholic houses or departments now publish for a wider, across-the-board audience and also attract authors of this nature. The exclusively Catholic bookstore has all but disappeared from the picture.

Three national associations help to coordinate the work of Christian religious publishing—especially book publishing—today. The Christian Booksellers Association (established 1950) is primarily an organization of religious bookstores and distributors, but it also has 125 associate members who are publishers of religious books. Its national conference each year is attended by thousands who come to see and to buy the new materials on display as well as to learn more about running their business. Protestant church houses are bound together in the Protestant Church-Owned Publishers Association, with a membership of thirty-six publishers of religious books in the United States and Canada. A newer organization with fifty-three U.S. members—most of them independent houses with a religiously conservative emphasis—is the Evangelical Christian Publishers Association, based in California. Each of these associations sponsors exhibits at the large annual International Book Fair in Frankfurt, Germany, and some have been represented at smaller fairs in other countries. Through these means religious books from the United States are reaching many other countries and books from those countries are being translated and distributed in North America. The three national associations are currently in the process of a study and analysis of the history and development of religious book publishing in the United States under the direction of the Center for Book Research at the University of Scranton in Scranton, Pennsylvania.

Simultaneously with the development of Christian book publishing, there has also been a growth in books published for the Jewish market. Some of these books are being produced by Jewish publishing societies, but others come from independent houses specializing in books for this market or from houses formerly devoted only to Christian publishing. The Jewish market has been stimulated by the activities of the Jewish Book Council, based in New York, which sponsors an annual Jewish Book Month as well as competition for the best Jewish books of the year in several categories.

The growth of interest in religious books in general has led to the compiling and printing of "best-seller" lists of religious titles. These statistics show that often such books have far outsold those on general best-seller lists. The religious lists are being carried by some of the large daily newspapers as well as occasionally by *Publishers Weekly*, the industry's main trade journal. *Publishers Weekly* also devotes two whole issues each year to religious titles and carries a column on these books at other times.

Another stimulus to the reading and distribution of religious books has been the development of local church and synagogue libraries encouraged by both denominational and interfaith organizations. It is now conservatively estimated that there are at least 60,000 such libraries in existence with many of them containing thousands of volumes and with large weekly circulations. Work sponsored by Southern Baptists, Lutherans, and Methodists has been especially noteworthy. Ecumenical and interfaith associations are represented by the Church and Synagogue Library Association, the Evangelical Church Library Association, and the Association of Jewish Libraries.

Religious books are alive and well and reaching an ever-expanding market. They continue to be at the center of the life and work of the church and synagogue and of those who claim either Christianity or Judaism as their faith. *See also* Books, Children's; Devotional Literature; History of Christian Education; Periodicals, Religious.

W. H. Gentz

Bower, William Clayton

A Christian Church (Disciples of Christ) minister, William Clayton Bower (1878–1982) was one of the primary progressive leaders in religious education during the first half of the twentieth century. After serving churches in Indiana, New York, and California, he taught at the College of the Bible at Transylvania College (now Lexington Theological Seminary), the University of Chicago Divinity School, and in retirement at the University of Kentucky. Throughout his career, Bower sought to clarify the importance of religion in culture and education's responsibility in the process of cultural formation of people. He also described the relationship between the church's religious education and public education. In addition to his work in churches and through denominational agencies, Bower served on the Lexington Kentucky board of education, an advisory committee for the Chicago public schools, and the White House Conference of Children in a Democracy and developed a program in moral and spiritual values for Kentucky public schools. *See also* Public Schools and Religion.

J. L. Seymour

Boy Scouts

Boy Scouts, an international organization dedicated to helping boys develop mentally, morally, and physically through outdoor activities, citizenship, and community service, was brought to the United States from England by William Boyce in 1910 and established in Canada by an act of Parliament in 1914. The U.S. organization, Boy Scouts of America, is divided into six regions, a number of areas, local councils of about six thousand members, and troops of from ten to thirty-five. Troops meet in schools, churches, or other community locations under local leadership. Age groupings are Tiger Cub (grade 1), Cub (grades 2–3), Webelow (grades 4–5), Boy Scout (grades 6–8), and Explorer Scout (open to both boys and girls grades 9–12). Present enrollment stands at about four and a half million.

Duty to God has always been an important principle of the Boy Scouting program. Throughout its seventy-year existence, Scouting has constantly stressed the importance and necessity of a Scout's spiritual life as well as the dependence on God as Supreme Being. The religious emphasis is fully represented in the bylaws of the Boy Scouts of America. Article IX, section 1, clause 1 states: "The Boy Scouts of America maintains that no youth can grow into the best kind of citizen without recognizing his obligation to God. In the first part of the Scout Oath or Promise the member declares, 'On my honor, I will do my best, to do my duty, to God and my Country . . .' The recognition of God as the ruling and leading power in the universe and the grateful acknowledgement of His favors and blessings are necessary to the best type of citizenship and are wholesome precepts in the education of the growing members."

In order for a Scout to grow and develop within a chosen faith, Scouting has developed, through partnership with several religious bodies, the Religious Emblem Program. The fundamental aim of this program is to recognize those who demonstrate faith, recognize creeds or principles, and render service to a religious institution, all in accordance with the precepts of spiritual education maintained by each separate religious body.

Since the spiritual aims of Scouting are traditionally nonsectarian, the programs that have been developed complement the ideals and tenets of each separate religious body. Each religious institution that participates in the program develops its own guidelines and requirements and awards the emblem to Scouts who are members of that particular faith. Through the Religious Emblem Program, a Scout can reinforce what he has learned about his own faith by working toward that emblem awarded by his faith.

The Religious Emblem Program was begun over fifty years ago when the Boy Scouts and the Catholic church entered into a plan of cooperation that is still in effect today. The Catholic church recognized the educational and character-building aspects of the Scouting program, while the Boy Scouts realized the strong spiritual support provided by the church. The outcome of this plan of cooperation was the inception of the first religious emblem, the Ad Altare Dei.

The Ad Altare Dei program became a basis and guide to other religious institutions as they developed their own programs. While each award differs in respect to the concepts of spiritual education, several general characteristics can be observed. Each religious institution develops the requirements for its emblem for those members who are enrolled in Scouting. Instruction in an emblem program is carried out by the designated religious counselor of that faith. Presentation of the award is done in the context of a religious service. The Boy Scouts of America recognizes a Scout's achievement by allowing the display of the religious emblem on the official uniform of the Boy Scouts of America.

Since the Catholic church introduced the Ad Altare Dei program, some thirty other religious institutions have come up with programs for their respective faiths. The following is a summary of these awards.

- Ararat (Armenian Church of America)
- Metta (Buddhist)
- Sangha (Buddhist)
- Light Is Life (Eastern Rite Catholic)
- Ad Altare Dei (Roman Catholic)
- Pope Pius XII (Eastern Rite Catholic)

- Parvuli Dei (Roman Catholic)
- God and Country (Baptist)
- God and Church (General Protestant)
- God and Life (General Protestant)
- God and Family (General Protestant)
- Chi Rho (Eastern Orthodox)
- Alpha Omega (Eastern Orthodox)
- God and Life (Episcopal)
- God and Family (Episcopal)
- God and Church (Episcopal)
- Ner Tamid (Jewish)
- Aleph (Jewish)
- God and Family (Lutheran)
- Pro Deo et Patria (Lutheran)
- Bog I Ojczyzna (Polish National Catholic)
- World Community (Reorganized Church of Jesus Christ of Latter Day Saints)
- Religion in Life (Unitarian-Universalist)
- In the Name of God (Islamic)
- Faith in God (Church of Jesus Christ of Latter-day Saints)
- On My Honor (Church of Jesus Christ of Latter-day Saints)
- God and Country (Salvation Army)
- God and Life (Salvation Army)
- Silver Crest (Salvation Army)
- Universal Religious Emblem (all denominations)

Beside the awards available to youth members of the Boy Scouts of America, there are now awards for the adult leaders involved with Scouting. Programs such as the God and Service Recognition Program for Adults and the Scouter Development Program educate adult leaders, helping them to better relate their religion to the Scouting program.

The requirements for each award vary and information on the specific requirements can be obtained by contacting the Religious Relationships Service, Boy Scouts of America (1325 Walnut Hill Lane, Irving, TX 75038-3096), or the governing body of each specific religious organization. See also Girl Scouts; Outdoor Ministries; Youth Ministry.

J. K. Marheine

Boys and Girls Clubs of America

Boys and Girls Clubs of America serve approximately 1.4 million boys and girls ages eight through fourteen throughout the United States.

Some clubs are for boys only; others include boys and girls. About 40 percent of the children are girls. Concentrating on the needs of children in economically and culturally deprived situations, the clubs' primary concern is for children who come home after school to an empty house, children from single-parent families or with working or unemployed parents. There is no substitute for wise parental guidance, but where this is lacking or unavailable, the clubs strive to bridge the gap and provide safe, adult-supervised activities in a firm, enjoyable, and fair guidance atmosphere. Character education is emphasized and children are encouraged to become good citizens and members of the community and to participate in their religious communities.

With a varied program that includes social recreation, physical education, cultural arts, and leadership training, the clubs offer boys and girls a choice of many opportunities for active participation. While some thoroughly enjoy sports, others prefer quiet activity or special interest group clubs. Still others want to learn a new craft, discover a way to participate in community service, or simply have a concerned youth leader listen to them. Children need to develop responsibility and confidence in themselves and club programs work toward developing a sense of purpose.

Children involved in Boys and Girls Clubs must learn to respect authority, because so many never have behavioral limits set for them. The new-member orientation explains the rules of conduct and gives each new member a chance to ask questions before formal membership begins. This procedure eliminates many difficulties that could result later on because children know what behavior is expected. Children can learn about cooking or personal safety, participate in loosely organized sports, or enjoy a new game during program hours. They can also receive positive recognition, meet new friends, receive help with school work, or just visit with an adult "friend" who has their best interests in mind.

FINANCING AND LEADERSHIP

Program hours vary, but most are after school until dusk during the school year and late mornings and afternoons during vacations and holidays. The clubs receive no tax subsidy; rather, they are supported by a local volunteer board of directors, local and national foundations, civic and service organizations, and board-sponsored special events. Clubs in some areas receive support from the community's annual United Way campaign.

Boys and Girls Clubs are governed at the local level by a volunteer board of directors composed of interested, knowledgeable men and women. Members are recruited according to the needs of the agency and skills they can contribute. For example, professionals are needed with financial experience, so bankers, financial planners, and emphasis on the influence of family for religious education and on the gradualness of religious development. A graduate of Yale, Bushnell moved immediately into his only pastorate, North Church, Hartford, Connecticut. In 1847 he published the first portion of *Christian Nurture* (1861). His theme was that parents are the primary influence on their children's religious development. He believed that children should grow up as Christians and never know themselves as anything else. Children should worship with their parents in a service that has special interest for them. He criticized the churches for their treat-

ment of children and was opposed to revivalism. In 1859 he resigned his parish because of ill health and spent the rest of his life writing in the field of theology. Influenced by Samuel Taylor Coleridge, Victor Cousin, and Jonathan Edwards, he developed views of religious knowledge and religious language concerning intuition and "the sense of the heart" that contributed to his theological method and beliefs. *See also* Education, Theories of; History of Christian Education.

R. C. Miller

C

Calvin, John

John Calvin (1509–1564), Christian humanist, Reformer, and educator, was the chief intellectual organizer of Reformed theology during its formative period. Chief among his many writings is *Institutes of the Christian Religion*. He was born in Noyon, France, and educated in the humanities, law, and classics at leading universities. He came to Protestant convictions and was forced to flee France. In 1536 he found refuge in Geneva as a minister. There he wrote, among other things, his *Catechism* of 1537.

In April 1538 he was banished from Geneva and went to Strasbourg, where he served the French congregation and taught in the *gymnasium* organized by Johann Sturm. In October 1542 he was called back to Geneva and returned on his own terms, namely, that the catechism and the discipline be upheld. At once he busied himself at many tasks, among them writing a new *Catechism* and leading a committee in drafting *Ecclesiastical Ordinances* for the city.

The new *Catechism* was still long and somewhat difficult for children, but the questions were briefer and more simple than those of 1537. The *Ordinances* included provision for required catechesis for children each Sunday at noon and for the establishment of a "college" (school). The Sunday classes reflected Calvin's sober disposition and conservative methods: they adhered to "a definite formulary" and required that the children listen to lectures, be interrogated, and recite a summary of the *Catechism*.

The college was intended to provide instruction of the faithful in true doctrine and to prepare

both ministers and magistrates. It offered instruction in languages and the humanities, for Calvin recognized that theological lectures for children would be unprofitable without them. His proposal could not be executed immediately, but in 1558, after revisiting Sturm's school, he renewed efforts to set up the college. A successful drive for public subscriptions made possible the formal opening on 5 June 1559. Theodore Beza became rector. The school, emulating Sturm's *gymnasium*, was meant to serve both the children of Geneva and theological students from abroad. It consisted of a *schola privata* and a *schola publica*.

The *schola privata* compressed into seven approximately annual grades a curriculum needing eight or even ten years elsewhere. In grades 7–5 (the lower ones) children studied writing, Latin, and French. In grade 4 they added Cicero, Ovid, and beginning Greek. Grades 3–1 brought work on classical authors, grammar, history, and dialectic. In 1564, at Calvin's death, two hundred students were enrolled.

The *schola publica* was not graded; students worked at their own individual levels. It soon attained international renown in the teaching of Hebrew, Greek, philosophy, law, and theology, the last taught by Beza and Calvin himself. In 1564 the enrollment was three hundred students.

Calvin held high educational hopes and standards. His "third use of the law" gives a clue to his feeling about education: the law is no longer judge, but teacher—guiding, wise, and disciplining with love (*Institutes* 2.7.12; *Catechism* of 1537). It followed, then, that instruction was publicly supported and free and that teachers were held in honor as one of the four orders of office in the church; they were regarded as divinely appointed and equal to pastors, sharing with them the church's teaching function (*Ordinances*; *Institutes* 4.1.1; 4.3.1, 4–6). *See also* History of Christian Education; Reformed Education.

R. R. *Sundquist*

Camp Meeting

Camp meetings were religious revivals held outdoors particularly on the Southern frontier during the nineteenth century. They attracted the "plain folk" and were organized so that ritual and symbol contributed to religious conversions and prescribed moral behavior. James McGready, a Presbyterian pastor, is credited with organizing the first camp meeting, which was held at Gasper River, Kentucky, in 1800. Presbyterians, Methodists, and Baptists jointly sponsored camp meetings, which usually lasted four days in late summer. Hundreds of people coming from isolated areas camped together to hear evangelical preaching, sing revival songs, and engage in the religious fervor of the meetings, which often developed into uncontrollable jerking, rolling, laughing, and dancing. Tents encircled an open-air "auditorium," which consisted of benches and a pulpit. Such camp meetings lost their function as a religious and social institution when an increase in the frontier population allowed for the establishment of local churches.

In the late nineteenth century, permanent camp or conference grounds were developed, usually within a denominational context but with an independent board of trustees. People could own or rent houses on the land, and religious and cultural events were held during the summer months. Some permanent camp grounds continue to exist.

The modern equivalent of the camp meeting is the revival meeting—usually a week of inspirational and evangelistic services with a guest preacher. These generally are sponsored by congregations during the spring or fall, and are held either in a church building or outdoors.

S. M. *Stewart*

Campfire

Campfire is an organization founded in 1910 to serve boys and girls up to the age of twenty-one. The specific purpose is to help them realize individual potential and function effectively as self-directed and responsible persons in society. As an organization, Campfire seeks to improve societal conditions as these affect youth. Five hundred thousand boys and girls are enrolled nationally.

The programs are informal, provided in small groups led by skilled volunteer adults. The focus is on learning through activities so that boys and girls may both develop an individual positive self-image and learn to work with and care for others.

Camping programs have been one aspect of Campfire. These include day camp experiences of outdoor living in a neighborhood setting and residential camping in the summer at camps maintained by an area council. There are also specialty camps for interests such as computer learning or sailing.

Campfire is organized into 275 community-oriented councils with oversight of neighborhood groups in a broad geographical area, guided by a professional staff. These groups comprise about 15 to 20 boys and girls.

Response programs form another aspect of Campfire. These are developed to meet specific needs in an immediate situation. One course helps children of working parents develop basic living skills to cope with emergencies. Another brings a constructive approach to child abuse and its prevention. A special group in an agricultural area deals with the problems and needs of the children of migrant workers. A special outreach summer day camp program is designed for children and teenage volunteer counselors from low-income minority neighborhoods.

Campfire also sets up programs in schools with an emphasis on the development of reading, language, and citizenship skills.

Through these three programs, small group clubs, camping, and flexible response programs, Campfire seeks to meet multiple needs for children and youth. *See also* Outdoor Ministries; Youth Ministry.

I. V. Cully

Camping

See Campfire; Outdoor Ministries.

Campus Crusade for Christ International

Campus Crusade for Christ International is an interdenominational Christian ministry. Founded by Bill and Vonette Bright in 1951 on the campus of the University of California, Los Angeles, it has two emphases: discipleship and evangelism.

College work consists primarily of groups that engage in Bible study and leadership training as well as sponsor special events. Members share their faith with other students and invite them to meetings. Currently there are 4,000 staff members worldwide. In any given week approximately 127,000 students on 180 U.S. campuses are present at some Campus Crusade event.

Athletes in Action is a Campus Crusade program represented by national sports teams, the most widely known being in basketball. Where possible, the team shares its message during halftime.

Campus Crusade for Christ carries on more than forty subministries, including work with families (usually weekend conferences for engaged or married couples). It conducts Bible study and leadership training for high-school groups, in parishes, in prisons, and at breakfast or luncheon meetings for businesspeople. Campus Crusade has also sponsored widely promoted outreach programs such as the "Here's Life" program in the United States in 1975–1977 and similar programs overseas. It is currently planning "New Life 2000," a worldwide evangelistic effort. *See also* Evangelism; Higher Education, Religion in.

I. V. Cully

Cana Conference

See Marriage Enrichment.

Canada

Canada has a total population today of 25.6 million people; 46 percent are Roman Catholic, and 41 percent are Protestant. The religious education of these people is linked historically to that of their general education.

HISTORICAL BACKGROUND

Early efforts to provide education in Canada were largely church sponsored. During the French and English colonial periods of the seventeenth and eighteenth centuries schools were either provided by the churches (as in the French-speaking Roman Catholic schools of Quebec or the English-speaking Protestant parish schools of the Atlantic and Ontario regions) or through the efforts of the churches (largely Anglican, Methodist, and Presbyterian) to encourage the establishment of private grammar schools. Because of this history, religious perspectives permeated most early educational endeavors. The nineteenth century marked a transition toward public control of education, yet even then schools were viewed as sources of religious and moral teaching: spelling and reading books were likely to include prayers, catechism questions, and ethical exhortations.

The later formation of universities followed a similar pattern. Denominational institutions were often the nuclei from which universities began. During the first half of the nineteenth century, the Anglican, Baptist, Methodist, Presbyterian, and Roman Catholic churches all established colleges of higher learning, often with a view toward providing advanced education for their clergy. During the second half of the century, many of these colleges became government-supported universities, sometimes with affiliated denominational theological colleges.

Meanwhile the seeds of parish religious education in Protestant denominations were taking root in the Sunday school movement. Canadian Sunday schools from the beginning focused chiefly on religious instruction. Initiative was taken largely by the laity, who during the nineteenth century also formed Sunday school unions to provide leadership support.

The twentieth century brought together the two trends toward public control of education and the growth of local church religious education. With increased immigration and subsequent pluralism, religious influence and religious instruction began to disappear from much of public education. Denominations and local churches began to assume more responsibility for the religious education of their constituencies. The Roman Catholic church elected, in many parts of Canada, to support separate Catholic schools in which religion would permeate the whole curriculum. Protestants supported a government-administered school system.

Though most Sunday schools had been held in churches, Protestant denominations did not develop other programs until the beginning of the twentieth century: adult Bible classes, women's organizations, and young people's societies. Denominations began to sponsor the development of curriculum resources and teacher training events.

For a number of years the major Protestant denominations undertook some of their educational work cooperatively through such organizations as National Boys' and Girls' Work Boards (begun in 1914 and 1915 respectively) and the Religious Education Council of Canada (1917), which later became the Department of Christian Education (1947–1967) of the Canadian Council of Churches. More recently this cooperation within Canada has disappeared; denominations have tended to establish links with such American-based organizations as the Religious Education Association of the United States and Canada; the Division of Christian Education of the National Council of Churches of Christ, U.S.A.; and Joint Educational Development. However, from the earlier Canadian cooperative effort two interdenominational programs have continued as officially recognized programs of the Baptists, Churches of Christ (Disciples), Presbyterians, and United Churches: Explorers (girls and boys nine to eleven) and Canadian Girls in Training (CGIT; girls twelve to seventeen).

PRESENT PRACTICE IN SCHOOLS

Within Canada general education is a provincial responsibility; policies and practices in the ten provinces and two territories are diverse. Newfoundland has a denominational education system administered by three Christian Councils: Roman Catholic, Integrated (Anglican, Moravian, Presbyterian, Salvation Army, and United), and Pentecostal. Religious instruction is an integral part of the curriculum. Quebec has a dual system with Protestant and Roman Catholic school boards; religious instruction is required in all schools. Ontario and Alberta have both public schools and Roman Catholic separate schools; local boards may permit religious instruction, although this provision is seldom utilized in public schools. The remaining six provinces have completely "secular and nonsectarian" schools with almost no religious instruction courses. Even in these provinces, however, some schools begin the day with the reading of Scripture and recitation of the Lord's Prayer, with provision made for exemption of students by parental request.

In many provinces moral education courses are included in the curricula for both elementary and secondary schools. In some secondary schools religion courses may be taught from a strictly academic point of view. A number of private schools are sponsored by denominations; examples are Christian Reformed Church and Hebrew day schools.

PRESENT PRACTICE IN CHURCHES AND SYNAGOGUES

Religious education policies and practices differ from one religious group to another. However almost all groups provide program resources and leadership support for educational activities at the congregational level.

Jewish religious education normally takes place through supplementary afternoon or day schools and through synagogue-based adult classes.

The Roman Catholic church, in addition to its major thrust in many parts of Canada toward separate Catholic elementary and secondary schools, has increasing numbers of parish educational programs. For the religious education of children in either schools or parishes, a revision of a Canadian catechetical series is being produced. The aim of this program is to nourish the total faith life of the child. The approach is Scripture-inspired but begins with lived experience; the process calls for a partnership of home, parish, and school. To assist parents in this partnership a Home Religion program adapts catechism material for family use. In response to a growing concern for strengthening adult religious education, the Canadian Conference of Catholic Bishops in 1986 published *Adult Faith, Adult Church*, a report containing the recommendations of the National Advisory Committee on Adult Education. Recently dioceses and parishes have begun to employ religious education personnel.

In Protestant denominations the one-hour Sunday or weekday church school is the most common avenue for Christian education of children and youth. The United Church produces its own curriculum resources for its church schools. Other denominations utilize curriculum resources produced by comparable denominations in the United States or by independent publishers. Some denominations (e.g., Pentecostal) also have children's church.

Youth programs in local churches include CGIT, Girl Guides, Boy Scouts, Boys' Brigade, Crusaders (Pentecostal), and denominational young people's organizations.

In recent years, while mainline denominations report declining participation, the more evangelical churches have seen considerable growth in Christian education programs. Programs in these churches frequently have a strong mission emphasis.

Present developments in many Protestant churches include a new emphasis on intergenerational learning opportunities, increased recognition of the role of parents in the religious education of children and youth, and attempts at greater integration of children and youth in the total life of the congregation. Most denominations express a need for increased emphasis on adult

Christian education. Both the Presbyterian Church in Canada and the United Church of Canada have, during the eighties, undertaken to reexamine the theological and educational presuppositions that underlie their Christian education endeavors.

All denominations provide for the education of their professional religious educators—through colleges of Christian education, through Bible colleges, or by providing Master of Religious Education degrees in denominational seminaries. Theological colleges currently need to include greater emphasis on educational ministry in the preparation of the clergy. Much leadership in religious education, however, is given by laypersons; most denominations offer leadership courses, resources, and support for lay leadership development. See also Canadian Girls in Training.

M. Webster

Canadian Girls in Training

Canadian Girls in Training, popularly known by its initials, CGIT, is a church-sponsored organization for girls from twelve to seventeen years of age. The aim of the organization, as stated in the basic handbook, is "to provide opportunities for teenage girls and their leaders to grow together in Christian community as persons realizing their self-worth in relationship with God, discovering life's meaning through Jesus Christ's life and teachings, learning to be open and trusting in relationships, and responding with love to the needs of others."

The CGIT movement was begun in 1915 as a cooperative attempt by the major Canadian Protestant churches and the Young Women's Christian Association to meet the needs of Canadian girls during their teen years. It is still an officially recognized youth program of the Baptist Federation of Canada, the Christian Church (Disciples of Christ), the Presbyterian Church in Canada, and the United Church of Canada.

Although the national organization is interdenominational, each local group is an integral part of the Christian education program of an individual congregation. CGIT groups consist of eight to twelve members with an adult leader. When there is more than one group in a congregation, separate groups are usually provided for intermediates (twelve to fourteen years) and seniors (fifteen to seventeen years).

Projects undertaken during a year normally include Bible study, mission education, study of a current issue, and a service project for the local church and/or community. Frequently groups build their year's program around the various parts of the CGIT purpose.

Because of its strong emphasis on participation of members in all aspects of group life, cooperation in group program planning, and responsible sharing in the life of a congregation, CGIT has been credited with providing experience in decision making and development of leadership skills for many of the women who have filled key positions in Canadian church and community life. See also Youth Ministry.

M. Webster

Case Study

Case study involves students and teachers in disciplined examination of actual human experience, usually employing discussion methods and written accounts of that experience.

Case study has been a vital part of Christian education throughout the common era. Related pedagogically to the use of parables, stories, and other illustrative techniques, cases proved significant in classic Christian casuistry, in apprenticeship models for both male and female religious, and in situationalist ethics that have flourished periodically.

Recently, case study has also evolved in theological education and church school classes through application of inductive patterns of instruction borrowed from other professional instruction. The use of the verbatim has come from training in psychology and social work; the "brief case" from law opinions and legal instruction; and the open-ended, complex, decision-oriented case from business education.

In 1971, the Case-Study Institute (CSI) in Cambridge, Massachusetts, helped open to theological educators and others involved in religious instruction the models of case study used throughout this century at the Harvard Business School. Under the auspices of the Association of Theological Schools and funded through the Sealantic Fund, this institute provided summer workshops, short-term instruction among seminary consortia, and a clearinghouse for the dissemination of theological cases.

Through the CSI and subsequent offerings by Fuller, Southeastern, and Garrett-Evangelical seminaries more than five hundred seminary faculty members have received elementary instruction in the use of case study. Educators among the various denominations have also attended various workshops, as have several publishers of church school curricula. An Association for Case Teaching began in 1978, and it holds meetings concurrently with other components of the American Association for Religion.

In CSI patterns, cases range in length from one to fifty pages, and some use simple language while others involve considerable technical data.

The style and the selection of data relate to the learning objectives envisioned. Cases are generally written from one person's perspective and not from an "omniscient" point of view.

Typically, a case itself contains four major parts:

1. Hook: an introductory statement that names the particular problem and hints at ways it can be addressed

2. Background: historical material pertinent to the situation and sometimes profiles of the significant characters and institutions

3. Exposition: dialogue, if appropriate, and exploration of issues and alternatives

4. Coda: careful restatement of precisely the same point in time as named in the introduction and if appropriate a declaration of the dilemma of the protagonist

For certain learning objectives, inclusion of one or more exhibits follows the case text. Data from institutions, correspondence, historic confessions of the church, maps, etc., may lend perspective and aid learning. A few case teachers have begun using audiovisuals also as exhibits.

Human experience seldom follows academic disciplines, and thus cases bridge the traditional departments in theological education. Even when cases are written for courses in administration, for example, they may serve nicely in teaching ethics, history, or evangelism. Moreover, cases from the life of congregations help students anticipate ministry in various arenas.

The instruction generally remains inductive, beginning with careful analysis of a specific occasion and moving from cases and accompanying readings toward generalizations. Naturally all Christian education, as all seminary instruction, cannot be inductive in nature. The "givens" of revelation, as perceived variously in different religious communions, do not yield readily to case study—in areas of biblical study, for example, and theology. Even there, however, cases can help in presenting situations for application of principles and authoritative norms.

As with the human situations they represent, cases have no "one right outcome." People using case study over a period of time can develop a sense of "adequate," "fair," and "realistic" responses. Study also helps most students evaluate the contributions of others, ask good questions, and seek appropriate help for coping in ministry.

The role of the teacher in case study depends again on the learning goals. However, the teacher usually superintends a case discussion, adding information and asking questions as judged necessary for learning.

Case discussions take many forms, but one elementary way to discuss cases begins with identification of the characters, moves to the naming of significant issues involved, then considers alternative ways of resolving the situation. Evaluation of the various solutions, discussions of traditional theological topics, and consideration of insights that occurred in discussion can also follow. Class sessions can also mix teaching methods, such as asking for small group preparation, embodiment of particular characters, and written responses for evaluation.

Several denominational and independent presses have begun to offer casebooks for church school and other study in congregations. *See also* Interdisciplinary Studies; Professional Study; Teaching Styles; Theological Education.

FOR FURTHER REFERENCE

Evans, Robert A., and Alice Evans. *Human Rights: A Dialogue Between the First and Third Worlds.* Maryknoll, NY: Orbis, 1983.

Lewis, Douglass G. *Resolving Church Conflicts: A Case Study Approach for Local Congregations.* San Francisco: Harper & Row, 1981.

Weeks, Louis, Carolyn Weeks, Robert Evans, and Alice Evans. *Casebook for Christian Living.* Atlanta, GA: John Knox, 1977.

White, Ronald C., Louis Weeks, and Garth M. Rosell. *American Christianity: A Case Approach.* Grand Rapids, MI: Eerdmans, 1986.

L. Weeks

Catechesis

"Catechesis" is derived from a late and rarely used Greek term the literal translation of which in its verb form means "to echo," or "to sound from above," as a speaker at a podium addresses the listeners. In another setting it was used to describe the information a professional, a well-informed expert communicated to one not so knowledgeable. An illustration might be a physician informing (catechizing) a patient about the nature of the latter's malady. That there is a noun form, "catechesis," as well as a verb form, "to catechize," tells us that both the message and its communication are alternately involved in reaching an understanding of the word itself.

EARLY CATECHESIS

The term and the concept appear twelve times in the New Testament—always in the verb form. In Acts 21:21 James informs Paul that among the Jewish Christians in Jerusalem there is a rumor concerning him: "they have been told [catechized] about you that you teach [catechize] all the Jews who are among the Gentiles . . ." It is Paul, however, who employs the term most frequently and exclusively in the sense of giving instructions or informing his listeners concerning the content of faith (see Rom. 2:18; 1 Cor. 12:28; 1 Cor. 14:19; Gal. 6:6; Eph. 4:11; Col. 2:7). He seems to have deliberately adopted the term and the concept to emphasize the distinctiveness of Christianity in that early period. Due to the fact that oral instruction was the normal means of communicating knowledge about Christ, the basic element of his "good news" seemed to lend itself to the innovative employment of the less used but clearly descriptive term. Actually in the course of time the term adopted by the early Christians came to be associated somewhat exclusively with them, especially in its reference to those who were anticipating baptism. The latter came to be called "catechumens."

Another dimension of catechesis in the early centuries of Christianity is that it was essentially an adult enterprise. Catechesis was for those believers seeking admission into the Christian community as well as those already baptized. The First Letter of Peter is considered catechesis in that in it baptized readers are reminded of what it means to be a Christian and how, ideally speaking, the transparency of their lives should testify to their commitment.

The earliest Christian catechesis appears to have developed in two general forms, each dependent on the setting and the people being addressed. The catecheses of Peter, Paul, and James were addressed to Judaic converts. This form relied on the foundation of the Old Testament covenant and emphasized adherence to the word of God. According to Paul, "God has qualified us to be ministers of a new covenant, not in a written code but in the Spirit" (2 Cor. 3:6). Paul explains further that the (new) law, which came "fourhundred and thirty years afterward, does not annul a covenant previously ratified by God, so as to make the promise void. . . . The law was our custodian until Christ came, . . . but now we are no longer under a custodian; for in Christ Jesus you are all sons of God, through faith" (Gal. 3:17, 24–26). The Sermon on the Mount offers both a clear, descriptive picture of the Christian ideal and a winning catechesis (Matt. 5–7; Luke 6:20–49). That corpus became the nucleus for Christian catechesis in the early period.

With the expansion of Christianity to Syria, Asia Minor, and Greece a second but somewhat different approach appeared directed to inquirers totally unaware of Judaic ideals and practices. The converts-to-be were introduced to prayer in the Psalms and to the virtues common to both Judaic and Hellenistic codes. Models of catecheses in that period can be found in the *Didache* and the *Letter of Barnabas*, both of which use the image of the two ways: of life and death or of light and darkness. Other models of early catecheses can be found in the works of Irenaeus of Lyon (d. ca. 202), Cyril of Jerusalem (315–386; his catechetical lectures are entitled *instructions for Those*

About to Be Illumined), and Gregory of Nyssa (*Great Catechetical Discourse*, 385).

Outstanding among the early catechetical works is that of Augustine of Hippo (354–430), *De catechizandis rudibus* written between 398 and 405. The work was a response to a deacon in Carthage who had implored Augustine to write some guidelines to assist him, the deacon, in instructing candidates for the catechumenate. The work is pedagogical in a classic sense. In it he instructs the deacon on how to be patient, how to deal with the half-educated, the weary, and the bored. But as an apostle of divine love, Augustine clearly placed his emphasis on the history of God's saving deeds as perfectly summarized in love of God and neighbor.

As time went on catechesis developed a more formal character. Church leaders and scholars like Ambrose, bishop of Milan (339–397; *De sacramentis* and *De mysteriis*) and Theodore of Mopsuestia (350–428; *Catechesis*) made memorable contributions to its development.

LATER DEVELOPMENTS

In the course of time increased emphasis on the need for schooling and the education of children and youth made its impression on catechesis, which began to be associated exclusively with the younger generation. Two events played major roles in this shift. One was the invention of the printing press by Johannes Gutenberg in 1450. From that press emerged the first printed Bible. But it began to produce numerous other pieces of literature as well, some of which were of increased service to children learning to read. Now catechesis was no longer oral but written content to be memorized. The second was Martin Luther's *Small Catechism* (1529), also promoted advantageously by Gutenberg's invention. That little manual, with its threefold division of "creed," "code"—a unique emphasis on the Ten Commandments—and "cult" (liturgy, worship), is still circulated today. With that innovation the popular concept of a small handbook written for children was initiated. From that time until the present "catechesis" is frequently but unfortunately identified with a small question-and-answer manual called a "catechism" and linked exclusively with the education-formation of the young.

Three major contributions followed that of Luther's work. The first was the publication of the three-volume set by Peter Canisius (1521–1597), a Dutch Jesuit who published *Summa doctrinae christianae* (1555), *Catechismus minimus* (1556), and *Catechismus minor seu parvus* (1558). They were written in question-answer form, but retained much of the spirit and language of Scripture and the church fathers.

The second of the three major catechetical endeavors of that era was the *Catechismus romanus* (1566) commissioned by the Council of Trent and intended to be a reference volume for pastors and a norm for subsequent texts.

The third of the three major works of this period was that of Robert Bellarmine (1542–1621). His *Dottrina cristiana breve* (1597) is a short summary of Christian doctrine. The work, while not as comprehensive as that of Canisius, is commendable for its doctrinal clarity and psychological insights. The latter are due, no doubt, to Bellarmine's extended experience as a teacher.

The use of a written question-and-answer document as the form of catechesis was accepted in the Reformation traditions. In addition to Luther's catechism were similar writings by Calvin, Zwingli, and the framers of the English *Book of Common Prayer*. In America, the New England Puritans used a catechism beginning in the seventeenth century. As late as 1868 the Methodist church in the United States compiled a manual by order of the conference held in London that same year. In the American Catholic church, the *Baltimore Catechism* of 1885 became the norm. These continued in use until the twentieth century, when additional methods of instruction became more popular.

Because the term "catechesis" referred from the first century onward to the teaching of the uninstructed in the Christian faith (i.e. children and converts), any method of teaching religion would, in effect, be catechesis. A basic Protestant term was "religious instruction." In recent decades, "religious education" or "Christian education" have become preferred terms by both Catholic and Protestant educators. Now there is an effort among some religious educators to renew the use of the term "catechesis," because it links present practice with the long history of Christian education, emphasizing a continuity that has seemed lacking within Protestant religious education, rooted as it is in the nineteenth-century Sunday school and the Reformation catechisms.

Although the word "catechetics" is sometimes heard, the traditional and technical term is "catechesis." When the term continues to be used in a technical sense, the emphasis is not on the use of questions to be memorized and repeated by learners but a process through which the learners' questions are the starting point and the answers reflect the way in which the Christian faith speaks to the contexts of everyday life. No longer confined to answers that define theological doctrine, this kind of catechesis applies doctrine to life. This is the thrust of *A New Catechism: Catholic Faith for Adults* (1967), first published in Holland.

In addition to the reconsideration of the concept of catechesis that recognizes that it cannot be confined to children, the printed page, or prepackaged questions and answers is the realization that it is not solely the responsibility of church leaders. Responsible too are the Christian communities who make up the respective denominational congregations as well as the entire Christian body—each member of which always had need to grow in perception and understanding of the truths of Christ's life and message. *See also* Catechism; Catechumenate; History of Christian Education; Kerygma.

FOR FURTHER REFERENCE

Grassi, Joseph A. *The Teacher in the Primitive Church and the Teacher Today*. Santa Clara, CA: University of Santa Clara Press, 1973.

Marthaler, Berard L. *Catechetics in Context*. Huntington, IN: Our Sunday Visitor Press, 1973.

Sloyan, Gerard S. *Shaping the Christian Message*. New York: Macmillan, 1958.

M. C. Bryce

Catechetical School

"Catechetical school" is the term used to designate the *didaskaleion* in Alexandria, Egypt, and sometimes, inaccurately, the school of advanced study founded by Origen at the beginning of the third century A.D.

According to Eusebius, writing in the fourth century, "a school of sacred learning, which continues to our day, was established in ancient times" (*Ecclesiastical History* 5:10). Although Eusebius states that the school was headed by Pantaenus, who in turn was succeeded by Clement late in the second century, more critical historians regard these men as teaching in a private capacity without ecclesiastical appointment. Pantaenus and Clement were philosophers who expounded a Christian view of the world, much as Justin and Tatian had done earlier in Rome. After the manner of the day, anyone seeking wisdom could follow their lectures and discourses. Origen seems to have followed in the tradition of these philosopher-teachers, expounding the Christian religion to Christians and pagans alike.

The catechetical school of Alexandria probably had its formal beginning about A.D. 215 when Bishop Demetrius put Origen in charge of the instruction of the catechumens. (It seems unlikely that this occurred, as Eusebius would have it, in 203 when Origen was a lad of seventeen.) Sometime afterward, perhaps about A.D. 220, Origen turned his attention to teaching more advanced students, introducing them to a systematic study of the Scriptures and exegesis of the books of the Bible. The responsibility for teaching the beginners in the faith fell to his friend Heraclas (who became bishop of Alexandria in 232).

The circle of advanced students and educated persons who gathered about Origen must be regarded more properly as a theological rather than a catechetical school. It laid the groundwork for the so-called Alexandrian tradition, characterized by its manner of drawing neo-Platonism into theology, a predilection for allegory in doing biblical exegesis, and bold speculation on the means—the divine Logos—and meaning of revelation. Origen had to defend himself against the accusation that he attributed too much importance to profane learning and philosophy, but friends and students supported him enthusiastically and his reputation as a teacher spread throughout the Mediterranean world.

Origen's penchant for speculation or his popularity, or perhaps a combination of the two, seems to have been at the basis of a rift with Bishop Demetrius that caused him to quit Alexandria in 231 for Caesarea in Palestine. With the backing of the Palestinian bishops, Origen continued the theological enterprise he had begun in Egypt. St. Gregory Thaumaturgus (d. 270), who spent five years at Caesarea under the tutelage of Origen, has left in a striking panegyric a résumé of the content, manner, and spirit of Origen's efforts to develop a Christian philosophy.

The nearest parallel today to the ancient catechetical school can be found in schools of theology and the religion departments of colleges and universities. *See also* Bible College; Colleges and Universities, Church-Related; History of Christian Education; Origen; Professional Study; Religious Studies; Theological Education.

B. L. Marthaler

Catechism

According to English and German usage, the catechism is a concise summary of Christian doctrine. In Romance languages "catechism" also signifies the act of catechizing and instruction, especially of children (e.g., French *catéchisme*, Italian *catechismo*). The proliferation and spread of catechisms in the sixteenth century was made possible by the advent of the printing press. They generally fell into two categories: small or short catechisms, for the unlettered and children, and large catechisms, which present a systematic statement of doctrine for use by teachers and preachers. The former, designed for instructional purposes, are commonly in the form of questions and answers; the latter, expository in form, came in many cases to serve as standards of orthodoxy for particular traditions.

From the sixteenth century to recent years the catechism provided the principal text for Christian education in most churches. Many hundred catechisms embodying diverse church traditions and varied educational philosophies were produced in this period, but in the paragraphs that follow only those select catechisms that are most representative and seem to have exercised the greatest influence are cited.

HUMANIST WORKS

Humanists like Jakob Wimpheling, Erasmus, and Johann Agricola were strong advocates of better religious instruction. In England John Colet drew up a manual under the title *Catechyzon* (ca. 1510), which was used to instruct the boys at St. Paul's School in London, and Erasmus, following the fixed canon of medieval catechesis based on the creed, commandments, and the Lord's Prayer, published an adult catechism, *Dilucida et pia explanatio symboli . . . decalogi praeceptorum, et dominicae praecationis* (1533). The Erasmian-humanist tradition produced many instructional works characterized by ample references to the New Testament and their emphasis on the ideals of Christian moral virtue. Two well-known examples of this kind of work are the catechisms by the Spaniard Juan de Valdes: the *Dialogue on Christian Doctrine* (1529) and his brief *Christian Instruction for Children* (1549).

PROTESTANT CATECHISMS

There were similar works by other humanists and Reformers, but it was Martin Luther more than any other single individual who established the catechism genre as the vehicle for religious instruction among Protestants and Catholics alike. In 1529 he published the *German Catechism* (the title "Large Catechism" is not Luther's), based on his own catechetical sermons and intended to illustrate how pastors and preachers might apply the catechism to the needs of the people. Illustrated with woodcuts by Cranach, it was noteworthy for several innovations, principally its placement of the explanation of the Decalogue before that of the Apostles' Creed and its emphasis on the trinitarian structure of the creed by organizing the material under the headings of Father, Son, and Spirit. Almost immediately Luther published the *Small Catechism*, characterized by brevity and clarity and intended as a popular work to be used by the lower clergy and general public. In the course of time both catechisms were edited and enlarged, first by Luther himself, and then by his disciples and the church.

Luther did not foresee that his catechisms would become "confessional books" as they did fifty years later when incorporated into the *Book of Concord* (1580).

Other Protestant catechisms that were to exert widespread influence and serve as confessional statements in their respective traditions were the *Heidelberg Catechism* (1563) and the Westminster catechisms (1647).

The *Heidelberg Catechism*, compiled by Zacharias Ursinus and Caspar Olevianus of the theological faculty at Heidelberg, fixed the canon of Reformed teaching. The Elector Fredrich III formally authorized its use in the Palatinate; it soon found acceptance in all countries where the Reformed faith prevailed and continues in regular use in churches of this tradition in Europe, the United States, and elsewhere. Based on earlier catechisms of Leo Jud at Zurich (1534, 1535), the Strasbourg catechisms of Martin Bucer (1534, 1537), John Calvin's Genevan catechism (1542), Henry Bullinger's exposition of the Decalogue, creed, Lord's Prayer, and sacraments (1556), and other catechisms produced in Switzerland and the Upper Rhine, the *Heidelberg Catechism* set the lines of Reformed theology apart from that of Roman Catholics as well as that of Lutherans.

A century would pass before the appearance of the Westminster catechisms in England. In the meantime, Thomas Cranmer had translated Andreas Osiander's *Kinderpredigten*, which incorporated the text of Luther's *Small Catechism*. Cranmer, moreover, prepared another short catechism, which he incorporated into the *Book of Common Prayer* (1549) in connection with the rite of confirmation. It is a brief exposition of the creed, Lord's Prayer, and the Ten Commandments, for, by medieval custom, children could not be confirmed until they had learned these traditional formulas. In the time of King James I (1604), at the insistence of the Puritan party, the prayer book catechism was enlarged to include a section on baptism and Communion adapted from the earlier catechism of Alexander Nowell (1572).

The larger and shorter Westminster catechisms, principally the work of the Puritan divine Anthony Tuckney, represent popular presentations of the Westminster Confession (1646). The Westminster Confession, strongly Calvinist in spirit and content, became the definitive statement of Presbyterian doctrine first in Scotland (1647) and then in the English-speaking world. The *Shorter Westminster Catechism* was particularly important in the dissemination of this doctrine not only among Presbyterians but Congregationalists, Baptists, and other adherents of Calvinist theology. The effectiveness of the *Shorter Catechism* is in part due to a didactic method that begins with a question and then incorporates the question into the answer, forming a complete sentence often with a stately cadence that lends itself to easy memorization.

CATHOLIC CATECHISMS

Catholic authors attempting to offset the influence of Protestant catechisms adapted the genre for their own purposes. The catechism of Johann Dietenberger (ca. 1530), for example, copied passages verbatim from Luther's work. The Catholic catechisms that had the most lasting influence, however, were the Roman catechism commissioned by the Council of Trent and those by the Jesuits Peter Canisius and Robert Bellarmine.

In its closing days (session 24) the Council of Trent commissioned a compendium of Catholic doctrine for the use of the clergy in preaching and instructing the faithful. Popularly known as

the *Catechismus romanus*, the four-hundred-page work published by authority of Pope Pius V (1566), is divided into four parts treating the Apostles' Creed in twelve articles, the seven sacraments, the Ten Commandments, and prayer, with a commentary on the Our Father. Many editions add a syllabus suggesting how various parts of the catechism can be coordinated with the Sunday readings and integrated into the sermon. The preface acknowledges the need to adapt the contents of the catechism to needs of the learners according to their age, capacity, manners, and social condition.

In its way the Tridentine catechism was a confessional document summarizing Catholic teachings, a resource for preachers rather than a manual to be used by catechists and teachers. Catholic catechisms for popular use were almost entirely the work of individual authors, often members of the newly founded Jesuit order. Peter Canisius, for example, wrote three catechisms. After publishing his *Summa doctrinae christianae* (1555), a compendium of Christian doctrine for use by college and university students, he published an abridged edition, the so-called *Catechismus minimus*, for use by the illiterate (1556). Later he produced an intermediate version, the *Catechismus minor seu parvus* (1558). It was this last, sometimes simply called the Catholic catechism, composed of 122 questions and answers, that became normative especially in German-speaking countries. Laurence Vaux translated and adapted Canisius for an English-speaking audience under the title *A Catechisme of Christian Doctrine for Children and Ignorante People* (1567).

In Italy, however, the most popular catechism was Robert Bellarmine's *Dottrina cristiana breve* (1597). A year later he produced a more ample exposition of Catholic doctrine in which the student asks questions and the master answers them at some length. This latter work follows the tripartite structure of Augustine's *Enchiridion*, namely, faith, hope, and love.

In Spain the most popular catechetical works also had Jesuit authors: Jerome Martinez de Ripalda (1591) and Caspar Astete (1599). In France, on the other hand, it was not uncommon for a diocese to have its own catechism, often written by the bishop. The proliferation of catechisms prompted Emperor Napoleon I to commission an "imperial catechism" for use in all the dioceses of France (1806).

A similar proliferation of catechisms in the United States in the nineteenth century caused the American bishops to mandate a single, small catechism for use in the American dioceses. Compiled by Bishop John Lancaster Spalding with the assistance of Gennaro de Concilio (who later translated it into Italian), the *Catechism of the Third Plenary Council of Baltimore* (1885) became the standard catechetical text in the United

States. Its original version consisted of 421 questions and answers and, much like the *Shorter Westminster Catechism*, it incorporated the questions in the answers. For the next seventy-five years the *Baltimore Catechism*, when it was not simply memorized verbatim, provided a syllabus for catechetical programs and textbooks under Catholic auspices.

TWENTIETH-CENTURY CATECHISMS

From Luther into the nineteenth century the catechism was the focus of Christian education in the United States among Protestants as well as Roman Catholics. With the rise of the Sunday school movement and its efforts to deemphasize denominational differences, the Bible replaced the catechism as the focal point of Protestant religious education. Thus the number of revisions and new versions of the traditional catechism genre abated among Protestants as it had among Roman Catholics after the publication of the *Baltimore Catechism*. Nonetheless, the latter half of the twentieth century witnessed the publication of several catechisms of more than parochial interest.

The Common Catechism (1975), a translation of the German *Neues Glaubensbuch* (1973), conceived in an ecumenical spirit, is a statement of Christian beliefs produced jointly by theologians from the Calvinist, Lutheran, and Catholic traditions. Matters still in dispute among the churches are treated separately in part five. The 1979 edition of the *Book of Common Prayer* presents a thoroughly revised catechism that it calls "An Outline of the Faith." It appears toward the end of the prayer book, no longer connected to the rite of confirmation. In Roman Catholic circles, the "Dutch Catechism," which appeared in English as *A New Catechism: Catholic Faith for Adults* (1967), received an enthusiastic reception but was criticized in conservative circles and by the Vatican for its interpretation and negligence of traditional doctrines. Other Catholic catechisms in the years after the Second Vatican Council were criticized for similar reasons, and thus the action taken by the Extraordinary Assembly of the Synod of Bishops meeting in Rome in 1985 is seen as a preventative measure. The synod called for "a catechism or compendium of all Catholic doctrine" that will become "a point of reference" for national and regional catechisms.

There is some interest today in using a catechism in confirmation classes for young people and adults. Books that try to restate classic doctrines in contemporary form, as indicated above, are becoming the basis for adult study and discussion groups. Creative methods that link sections of the catechism to the life situation of young people are being explored as ways of introducing them to these collective statements of the Christian faith. When the term "catechism" can be separated from long-held feelings about rote memorization or unthinking acceptance, there may be opportunities for using these succinct statements of doctrine in fresh ways. *See also* Calvin, John; Catechesis; Doctrine/Dogma; History of Christian Education; Luther, Martin; Lutheran Education.

FOR FURTHER REFERENCE

Bryce, M. C. "Evolution of Catechesis from the Catholic Reformation to the Present." In Edwards, O. C., and J. H. Westerhoff, eds. *A Faithful Church*, 204–35. Wilton, CT: Morehouse-Barlow, 1981.

B. L. Marthaler

Catechumenate

The catechumenate is an organized period of preparation of adult believers for baptism. It is an ecclesial institution, rather than private instruction in the faith. While roots for the catechumenate can be traced to the earlier religious communities of Judaism, as a formal institution it came into being around the year 180 and continued to develop throughout the second and third centuries to become the most suitable means of preparing converts (*catechumens, audiens, electi, competentes, noviciol*). The *Didache* and selected writings of Justin Martyr (Rome, 100–165) and Tertullian (Carthage, ca. 160–240) speak of the instructional preparation in doctrine and morals, as well as the required praying, fasting, and all-night vigils that were a part of being admitted to baptism.

According to Hippolytus (Rome, ca. 215), the period of preparation normally lasted about three years and the candidates were involved in a two-part catechumenal process. First, there was a long-term period of preparation focusing on Christian doctrine and morals—"hearing the word" and putting it into practice. At the end of this period candidates were judged on three criteria: sorrow for sins, faith in the church as the teacher of truth, and transformation of life. This had to be attested to by a Christian witness. If the candidate was judged worthy of election, he or she entered a short period of daily exorcism, fasting, and prayer. Exorcism freed the candidate from the control of Satan (sin) to become subject to Christ. Two days before Easter the candidates kept an all-night vigil consisting of reading Scripture and instruction. The catechumenate ended with baptism on Easter morning.

Popular writings of that time indicate that in the third century, the most vital period for the catechumenate, catechumenal practice everywhere followed the same basic structure. There was a preliminary period where evangelization was stressed, followed by the catechumenal period of approximately three years, though this could be accelerated because of a person's growth in faith and morals, and then baptism on Easter or Pentecost.

DECLINE OF THE CATECHUMENATE

The Peace of Constantine in 313 signaled the decline of the catechumenate. Church membership moved from illegal religion to "privileged liberty." As a result some people entered the church for the wrong motive—marriage or civil advancement— and large numbers postponed baptism because all that was necessary to be recognized as a Christian was to be a catechumen. By the end of the fourth century the catechumenate proper had become ineffective and there were no longer serious examinations for admittance.

In an attempt to safeguard the admission requirements, the church developed Lent as a time of intense formation for baptism. There was an inscription ceremony at the beginning of Lent and a Lenten retreat. Following the baptism on Easter, the neophyte returned each day of the following week for a commentary on the sacrament he or she had just received. There are appeals in the Lenten sermons of Augustine (354–430), Cyril of Jerusalem (315–386), and John Chrysostom (347–407) challenging the catechumens to moral conversion, an appeal that would not have been required a hundred years earlier.

In addition, the spread of infant baptism, which began to take root in the third century, contributed to the disappearance of the catechumenate. During the barbarian invasions, infant baptism gained popularity as a way to maintain family solidarity and to preserve control over a growing institutional church. As infant baptism grew, so grew the need to divide baptism into parts. This eventually led to three distinct sacraments of initiation: baptism, confirmation, and Eucharist. From this period on, the catechumenate for all practical purposes disappeared. It is only in the present day that it has experienced a revival.

RENEWAL OF THE CATECHUMENATE

Until very recently, the common practice of becoming a member of the Roman Catholic community and the major traditions of the Reformation (Lutheran, Reformed, and Anglican) was a two-stage rite of initiation. The two stages were baptism in infancy (with later admission to Communion) and then an even later public confirmation rite. The rediscovery of the laity and the elaboration of a theology of ministry at Vatican II (1962–1965) as well as the need to safeguard the traditional spirit of a serious and progressive formation in faith paved the way for a renewal of the catechumenate in the Roman Catholic church.

In 1972 the *Rite of Christian Initiation of Adults* (RCIA), published by the Sacred Congregation for Divine Worship, restored the catechumenate in the Roman Catholic church. It speaks of four periods in the prospective convert's spiritual journey: the time of evangelization or precatechumenate, the awakening of faith; the time of the catechumenate, education in the faith; the time of purification or baptismal retreat; and the time of postbaptismal catechesis (mystagogia). In an effort to emphasize the fact that one is not born a Christian but must become one and that this formation takes time, the U.S. bishops in 1986 stated that the RCIA process should take at least one full year.

The renewal of the catechumenate captured in the RCIA, which is primarily experiential and encourages prayer, discipline, mission, celebrating beliefs, and mutual support and encouragement— as opposed to being simply instructional—is judged by many religious educators and ministers to be a very good educational model for facilitating the process of ongoing conversion on deepening levels for adult Christians. RCIA has not been introduced into Protestant or Anglican churches, but these have programs of various lengths for adult preparation.

Adult catechumenate programs are long and carefully prepared in some overseas countries, notably in African ones where the churches cope with large numbers seeking baptism and may require up to three years of preparation for the rite. *See also* Baptism; Catechesis; Didache; Easter; History of Christian Education; Lay Ministry; Lent; Vatican II.

FOR FURTHER REFERENCE

Dunning, James B. "The Rite of Christian Initiation of Adults: Model of Adult Growth." *Worship* 52/3 (March 1979):142–56.

Dujarier, Michel. *A History of the Catechumenate: The First to the Sixth Centuries.* Translated and edited by Edward J. Hassl. New York: Sadlier, 1979.

———. *The Rites of Christian Initiation: Historical and Pastoral Reflections.* Translated and edited by Kevin Hart. New York: Sadlier, 1979.

Kavanagh, Aiden. *The Shape of Baptism: The Rite of Christian Initiation.* New York: Pueblo, 1979.

Made, Not Born: New Perspectives on Christian Initiation and the Catechumenate. Notre Dame, IN: University of Notre Dame Press, 1976. Symposium papers from the Murphy Center for Liturgical Research.

T. P. Walters

Censorship

Censorship is the examination of material with the intent to excise objectionable portions, to prohibit its publication or broadcast by prior restraint, or to restrict its dissemination by sanctions or ratings after publication.

The ethos of traditional societies presumed the beneficent authority of rulers to prevent the dissemination of evil. So censorship has existed in all societies throughout history and has been justified by the need to protect the populace from impiety, heresy, sedition, treason, and immorality. The methods of censorship have ranged from judicial hearing (Socrates) to an executive judgment relying heavily upon informers (the Roman Empire). With the emergence of the secular nation-state and the invention of the printing press, popular challenges to the legitimacy of censorship raised the fundamental issue of freedom and authority. A free press followed from the presumption of the public's competence to know and judge for themselves. Of course, there are limits. One of the most generally recognized is that the authorities may legitimately censor material in emergencies where there is "a clear and present danger" (L. D. Brandeis, *Whitney* v. *California*, the U.S. Supreme Court, 1927).

Postpublication restrictions on dissemination of material by unofficial sanctions and ratings have long been practiced by religious, social, and political groups in an effort to establish standards of societal acceptability with respect to obscenity, violence, or prejudicial material. The result has often been some degree of self-regulation, or rating, that tries to restrict material to consenting adults.

Most Americans today probably think of censorship in relation to pornography and obscenity. This is partially the result of judicial decisions that have argued that a work must be considered as a whole with respect to its literary and social value. Furthermore a work can be considered legally obscene only if it has *no* redeeming social value. Obscenity equates with worthlessness.

In response to materials that ignore or challenge societal standards of acceptability, unofficial censorship has increased. In some cases, the latter have been based on a response that reflects social taboos more than conscientious reasoning and have led to paradoxical results.

However, most groups would seek to set standards of social acceptability higher than the legal minimum and elevate these standards where possible. Nor does unofficial censorship involve the same danger as censorship by law, so long as it does not involve a political effort for official censorship, for countervailing groups will tend to have their own influence. But the church's responsibility to uphold public morality should be exercised within the limits of the fundamental constitutional guarantee of freedom of speech. *See also* Cinema; Heresy; Prejudice.

D. D. Rhoades

Central America

See Latin America.

Chaplain

A chaplain is a member of the clergy or occasionally a layperson who provides for the religious needs of those related to public, private, or religious institutions or organizations.

Both "chaplain" and "chapel" are derived from the Latin *capella*, meaning "cloak." The *capella* of St. Martin of Tours (ca. 316–397) was revered as a holy relic by the French monarchy and military and by the church. It was eventually kept by the French monarch's clergy in a private church; the private church came to be called the chapel and the clergy chaplains. The word "chapel" has since come to refer to any private or institutional place set apart for the celebration of the Eucharist and prayer and "chaplains" for clergy ministering there.

Present-day chaplains serve in universities and colleges, schools, religious organizations, the armed forces, prisons, hospitals and mental institutions, and in industrial and other settings. Most chaplains are ordained. There are some lay or peer chaplains commissioned by churches and religious agencies to minister in particular settings. While most chaplains are full-time, some hold positions on a part-time basis. Chaplains in the armed forces and most prisons, health care facilities, and schools are employed by their institutions. Chaplains in universities and colleges are often employed by their denominations or by ecumenical church agencies.

Institutions and denominations vary in their procedures for accreditation and endorsement of persons in chaplaincy. Chaplains in federally run institutions (armed forces, federal prisons, veterans' hospitals, etc.) require endorsement by the denomination at its most central level of authority. Hospitals typically require some form of accreditation, usually from an association of pastoral counselors. Endorsement by a church body is almost universally required or assumed in all forms of chaplaincy. Associations, both ecumenical and denominational, exist to provide continuing education for chaplains, peer support, and means of accreditation.

Chaplains usually have some responsibility for religious education in their institutions. Because those ministered to in a pluralistic society are of many denominations and faiths, chaplains must be especially sensitive to ecumenical and interfaith issues in religious education. They are often called upon to support the value of religious belief rather than the values of a specific theology. The educational efforts of chaplains must always balance the needs to respect all persons in the institution and to affirm deeply held beliefs as a believing minister of a particular religious community.

Chaplaincies exist primarily to serve the needs of two constituencies: the staff of the institution and those within it. Some institutions involve voluntary association (monastic orders, universities, etc.), others involuntary association (prisons, drafted members of the armed forces, some patients in mental institutions, etc.). For almost all members, though, institutional settings differ greatly from previous experience. As a result religious education in institutional settings must address concerns for religious belief as a source of support and nurture in an alien environment.

In the United States the first full-time positions in chaplaincy were in religiously affiliated educational institutions and in the armed forces. As religiously affiliated hospitals were established they provided for chaplains, and chaplains in health care institutions derive from that beginning.

In higher education, the effort to minister to students and faculty in unaffiliated institutions grew out of the establishment of the YMCA and YWCA movements and evangelistic conferences in the 1880s and 1890s. The beginnings of this effort involved student ministers and quite soon thereafter ordained persons appointed by denominations to serve in universities. Since 1900 chaplaincies have been formed in the large majority of universities and four-year colleges. In the post-World War II period ecumenically supported ministries have been established to meet the growing needs of community colleges and urban nonresidential universities.

Chaplaincy in ministry in higher education has often required a great sensitivity to the brokenness of the Christian body and the global character of the issues confronting concerned Christians. As a result there has been a strong global and ecumenical component in this ministry. The World Student Christian Federation, the Student Christian Movement, and the work of such extra-denominational bodies as Inter-Varsity and the YMCA and YWCA have historically contributed a great deal to this work. Chaplains plan seminars, discussions, conferences, and short-term noncredit courses in such areas as Scripture, theology, ethics, and the various religious traditions.

Some persons ministering in higher education institutions are called chaplains, but others may be called campus ministers or campus pastors. Some denominations reserve the word "chaplain" for ministers who are employed by the institution.

Chaplains in medical institutions have helped health-care specialists examine moral issues and have provided new ways to minister to those who suffer life-threatening illnesses. They hold seminars and conferences for staff, as well as counsel individuals dealing with ethical dilemmas. They listen and respond to patients as needed and can provide reading or taped materials. To families they offer help in dealing with crises.

Prison chaplains have contributed greatly to the ongoing issues of prison reform. They organize study groups and may even arrange credit programs with a nearby college or theological school.

Chaplains provide important educational connections between the institutions they serve and the churches. Concerns for social justice, ethical practice, and intellectual searching are raised by these institutions and can be shared by the churches. The effort to provide an environment of support and affirmation is central to the work of chaplains. Armed forces chaplains must affirm the worth of persons in alien and often dangerous situations. Chaplains in higher education have an important role in the interpretation of the faith in academia and of the world of ideas in the church. *See also* Colleges and Universities, Church-Related; Military Services; Prisoners.

M. Harris

Character Development

The notion of character and character development has been and continues to be an issue of longstanding interest and reflection in a variety of fields of study including philosophy, psychology, sociology, and education. Generally, character can be understood as a pattern of acts that persists through time and "characterizes" or "defines" a human person. Character indicates the persistent traits or habits of an individual. Specifically, character is commonly used to indicate a person's moral behavior as it refers to a pattern of acts that intend to do good or ill to other people. In this case character means a persistent pattern of moral conduct, including a person's moral judgments, attitudes, and actions that identify or "mark" one's moral character. In this context moral virtues such as honesty, selflessness, compassion are important in the process of character formation.

The notion of development refers to the process whereby a person's moral character is formed, acquired, or attained. The specific meaning of development depends on one's disciplinary perspective. For example, in the field of psychology development refers to the levels, periods, or stages of psychological maturation from childhood to adulthood. In the field of sociology, however, development refers to the process of socialization whereby a person internalizes the values, norms, and roles of one's social environment. In either case the formation of moral character is understood as a process of psychological and/or social development. The notion of character development, therefore, suggests that one's moral character is formed through a process of development that can be understood psychologically or sociologically.

A PSYCHOLOGICAL PERSPECTIVE

Psychology has long been interested in the process of character development. Sigmund Freud, the great pioneer of psychoanalysis, understood character as a function of the personality, both ego and superego, which develops through the stages of psychosexual development. More recent psychological perspectives also maintain a lively interest in character formation.

For example, Robert F. Peck and Robert J. Havighurst (1960) devote an entire study to the process of character development. They are convinced that such a thing as individual character does exist, which they understand as a persistent pattern of attitudes and motives resulting in a predictable type and quality of moral behavior. Like Freud, Peck and Havighurst regard character as a component of the personality and a special function of certain personality characteristics such as ego strength, superego strength, self-concept, attitudes toward others, and the cognitive system. They propose four developmental periods of character formation with five corresponding character "types." Their paradigm appears like this:

Developmental Period	Character Type
Infancy	Amoral
Early Childhood	Expedient
Later Childhood	Conforming/Irrational-Conscientious
Adolescence/Adulthood	Rational-Altruistic

Their research indicates that the family context, especially the relationship between child and parents, is the most important influence in shaping one's moral character. They also suggest that religious and/or church affiliation is no guarantee of a well-developed or high-quality character.

Perhaps the most important and influential study of moral character development in the field of psychology has been the pioneering work of Lawrence Kohlberg. Kohlberg rejects and departs from the traditional "bag of virtues" (understood of character traits) approach to building character. Consequently Kohlberg does not focus on moral conduct per se but on the rationale for making moral judgments and decisions. In other words, as a structural developmentalist in the tradition of Jean Piaget, Kohlberg claims that the core of moral character development is the cognitive structural dimension of the human person. Character development occurs as individuals pass through an ascending series of increasingly adequate cognitive moral stages. Kohlberg proposes three levels and six stages of moral development. The first level is "preconventional," which contains stages one and two. Stage one is the punishment/obedience orientation, which indicates that the physical consequences of action (reward and punishment) determine its goodness or badness. Stage two is the instrumental relativist orientation, whereby the satisfaction of one's own needs determines right action.

The second level is what Kohlberg calls "conventional"; it incorporates stages three and four. Stage three is the interpersonal concordance of "good boy" orientation; in it good behavior is what helps and pleases others and is approved by them. Stage four is the law-and-order orientation,

whereby right conduct means following authority and fixed rules. Kohlberg's third level is the principled "postconventional" level, which consists of stages five and six. Stage five is the social-contract/legalistic orientation, whereby individual rights determine good conduct. Finally, stage six is the universal ethical principle orientation. At this stage, right conduct is determined by decisions of conscience in accordance with personally appropriated ethical principles of which justice is Kohlberg's primary example.

In Kohlberg's model of moral character, development stage is defined as a "structural whole" that identifies total ways of thinking. Furthermore he claims that these stages and movement through them are sequential, invariant, and culturally universal. The axis of development is the person's interaction with one's social environment, the heart of which is conflict resolution resulting in the tendency to "move up" to more adequate stages of moral judgment.

There is little question that Kohlberg has made an important contribution to our understanding of character development; however, religious educators have tended to utilize his theory uncritically. Religious educators must remember that serious critiques of Kohlberg's theory of moral character development do exist and ought to be consulted; one is Donald Cochrane et al., *The Domain of Moral Education* (1979). In another critique, Edmund Sullivan strongly argues that Kohlberg's theory of moral development is ideologically biased. Focusing, in part, on Kohlberg's notion of justice and his stage six as the "model of moral man," Sullivan claims that it is "parochial rather than universal in character" because it is grounded in Western liberal theory. Sullivan contends "that the liberal position represents a blatantly distorted conception of man when considered as a totality" (Sullivan, "A Study of Kohlberg's Structural Theory of Moral Development," p. 361).

Religious educators should also be aware of Carol Gilligan's critique of Kohlberg's theory, which to some degree confirms Sullivan's position. Gilligan also critiques Kohlberg's notion of justice but from the perspective of gender. In her book *In a Different Voice* (1982), Gilligan shows that women are more likely to use a different language than justice to describe their moral realities. Such language as "care," "concern," and "healing" indicates the relational quality of justice that is often ignored by the more abstract "rights" perspective. Gilligan's research shows that women are more apt to consider the relational and personal dimension of moral decision making than are men.

A SOCIOLOGICAL PERSPECTIVE

Another way of looking at character development is through a sociological perspective. The sociologist attempts to explain character development and conduct as a fulfillment of social function within a well-established network of social relations. This hardened pattern or network of social relations can be understood as institutions composed of social roles that are filled by human persons and their typified patterns of behavior. For example, family is a social institution composed of such roles as mother, father, grandparent, son, and/or daughter. Character, therefore, is the stable integration of a person's psychic structure linked with the social roles of the individual. Character is formed or develops by a particular combination of social roles the person internalizes through the process of socialization. In other words, character is formed by internalizing roles and the role-specific behavior expected within any given institution. Within the sociological perspective the most important context for character development is primary socialization, whereby social roles and role-specific conduct are mediated by the "significant others," such as parents, and internaled by children. Teachers and other similar adults are also important "role models," especially in secondary processes of socialization such as schools, Girl Scouts, and Little League. Unfortunately the sociological view of character development does not provide us with a detailed understanding of the dynamics of development, primarily because its focus is the social context and not the individual.

Insights from both psychology and sociology strongly suggest that the family context is primary in the development of moral character. This indicates is is vitally important that religious educators focus on adult education and provide parents and adults with the support and tools to undertake the important task of developing character. Also if a significant part of character development is internalizing role-specific conduct, then the religious educator can assist this process by providing opportunities for moral activity. For example, if compassion is an important "character trait," then learners ought to have the chance to experience, learn, and practice compassion. Perhaps this is best done by providing experiences that allow learners to grow sensitive to those who suffer.

Other "tools" for assisting in character development with children/adolescents include such things as creating a community environment in the home and/or classroom where participants interact with respect and trust; providing children with the opportunity to participate in making classroom or household rules; providing opportunities for peer group work and other interactive experiences; and providing opportunities for roleplaying exercises that "act out" typical experiences from everyday life. Role-playing parables or other Bible stories could be particularly effective in a religious education context. See also Attitude Formation; Behavior; Child Development; Cognitive Development; Moral Development; Psychosocial Development; Role Model; Values.

FOR FURTHER REFERENCE

Cochrane, Donald B., Cornel M. Hamm, and Anastasios C. Kazepides, eds. The Domain of Moral Education. New York: Paulist, 1979.

Duska, Ronald, and Mariellen Whelan. Moral Development: A Guide to Piaget and Kohlberg. New York: Paulist, 1975.

Gerth, Hans, and C. Wright Mills. Character and Social Structure. New York: Harcourt, Brace and World, 1953.

Gilligan, Carol. In a Different Voice. Cambridge, MA: Harvard University Press, 1983.

Peck, Robert F., and Robert J. Havighurst. The Psychology of Character Development. New York: Wiley, 1960.

Sullivan, Edmund V. "A Study of Kohlberg's Structural Theory of Moral Development: A Critique of Liberal Social Science Ideology." Human Development 20 (1977):352–76.

R. A. Butkus

Chautauqua

Chautauqua Institution, located at Lake Chautauqua in New York, is a summer meeting place for thousands of people wishing continuing education in religion, the arts, and sciences. Chautauqua was founded in 1874 by Bishop John H. Vincent, head of the Methodist Episcopal Sunday School Union and chairperson of the International Uniform Sunday Lessons Committee, and Lewis Miller, an inventor and architect of the Akron design for Sunday school buildings. Founded as an institute for training Sunday school teachers, it soon offered three types of educational opportunities: a public program of lectures and concerts; a summer school; and correspondence courses that included the Chautauqua Literary and Scientific Circle (1878). During the nineteenth century Chautauqua was a leading center for the popular education of adults. World-famous persons went to Chautauqua because it provided a platform for the discussion of current events and the promotion of social reforms, combined with a pleasant vacation.

Today Chautauqua continues to be a thriving community and institution; its nineteenth-century buildings now have landmark status and new ones continue to be built. Fourth-generation families spend summers there. Hundreds of other people come for part or all of a summer to enjoy courses, lectures, special worship services and preaching, and other cultural events. See also Adult Education.

S. M. Stewart

Chave, Ernest John

Ernest John Chave (1886–1961) is perhaps best known for his contributions to the theory of religious education that are laid out in his major work, *A Functional Approach to Religious Education* (1947). Chave was a consistent and courageous liberal thinker who followed his tenets to their logical conclusion. He argued that religious education could not look to traditional theological sources for its message, its method, or its incentives. Humankind must, in his view, assume primary responsibility for its own collective salvation and for the aims and processes of religious education. A key assumption in Chave's theory, then, is that religion itself arises from primary adjustments to life.

The absence of traditional theological categories in Chave's thought effectively relegates religion to the "routines" of human existence. Chave's "functional approach" accordingly concerns itself with assembling these routines into "functional" categories for understanding the aims of religious education and with hypothesizing about the processes by which religion, thus understood, might be inculcated in succeeding generations. *See also* Methodology.

H. W. Burgess

Child Abuse

Violence against children has been a pervasive practice since the beginning of civilizations as evidenced by early Greek infanticide, African clitoridectomies, Chinese footbinding, and universal childhood prostitution.

INCIDENCE

Since 1976 all 50 states have had laws requiring that child abuse be reported, and based on reports from state agencies nationwide an estimated 750,000 to 1 million children are hit, bitten, burned, kicked, raped, sodomized, and otherwise traumatized each year in the United States. One out of every four girls and one of seven boys experience sexual abuse. Actual cases exceed these estimates because of the secrecy surrounding child abuse. Most victims are under six years of age. Most perpetrators are parents, family members, or caretakers. Approximately 5,000 children are killed by their parents each year in this country.

Child abuse can be divided into two major categories, physical assault and sexual assault, and may be distinguished from child neglect in that neglect reflects omissions in basic care for health and welfare (e.g., inadequate food, shelter, clothing, medical care, supervision) so as to endanger the child's physical well-being. Perpetrators attempt to explain away the more visible signs of physical abuse; sexual abuse can be more easily denied by the adults involved. Mistreatment of children occurs most often in families with rigid paternalistic structures and few outside connections. Race, economic status, and educational level of the parents appear to have little bearing on the presence of child abuse in the family. Alcohol or drug use or the perpetrator's own childhood abuse may be factors.

PHYSICAL ABUSE

Physical abuse means physical injuries intentionally inflicted on a child by another person. The consequences to the child of physical abuse are, first, the physical injuries, which are not always treated and can lead to lifelong physical problems. Psychological damage can continue through life as well, unless treated. The child's self-esteem and self-confidence are eroded since the child concludes that he or she must be bad beyond forgiveness for the battering to happen. A pervasive distrust and anger at those in authority develop, although these feelings may be hidden from others and even repressed by the child in order to survive. Depression replaces the natural zest for living and the sense of the future is foreshortened because of the unpredictability of the present. Socially, battering teaches that "might makes right" and the stage is set for child abuse in the next generation.

The child's statement about abuse, about physical fighting between parents, or about having to make frequent trips to the emergency room of the hospital may be the first symptom. Children rarely lie about abuse except to deny it in order to protect the family. Frequently there are visible bodily symptoms: round burns; burns that are worse at the bottom than the top; broken bones or teeth; patches of hair missing; bruises that are long and narrow, especially on the backs of legs, or in a small half moon, the result of pinching and twisting; black eyes; and abrasions on the neck.

SEXUAL ABUSE

Child sexual abuse means an adult's using the child as a sexual object through fondling breasts or genitals, vaginal penetration by penis or object, masturbation of victim or perpetrator, oral copulation, voyeurism, or exhibitionism; it can also include explicit or suggestive talk and exposure to or participation in pornographic movies or photography.

Approximately 95 percent of child sexual abuse is initiated by an adult male family member. Most victims are younger than seven years. Perpetrators threaten harm or death to the child or the mother or siblings if the abuse is mentioned.

The child victim of sexual assault suffers from physical damage to delicate tissues of vagina, anus, or mouth. Exposure to venereal diseases occurs. Adult survivors report long-term conditions such as migraine headaches, pelvic pain, obesity, anorexia, and infertility. Psychologically, the child learns to distrust others and deny and distrust his or her own feelings. The secrecy that surrounds the sexual assault prevents the child from validating his or her own experience with anyone. Since the perpetrator acts as if nothing has happened, the child comes to doubt the reality of his or her own experience, resulting in vulnerability to other people's judgment and decisions. Intimate relationships are problematic because the original trust was betrayed.

The child's telling of abuse stands as the most important symptom. Believing the child is the most important step toward recovery. Other symptoms are irritation of vagina or anal tissues, excessive public masturbation, presence of venereal disease, precocious knowledge of sexual matters, excessive shyness, overly compliant behavior, inappropriate sex play with other children or toys, seductive behavior with adult males, withdrawal, depression, poor peer relationships, running away from home, and sleep disturbances.

FOR THE EDUCATOR

Teaching children about the sanctity of their own bodies can be a first line in prevention. Modeling respect of people is one way to achieve this. Helping children practice saying no to those who make them feel uncomfortable, including trusted relatives, may teach them that they have a right to say no. Teaching them to keep telling until someone believes them could pave the way for help. If a child should be a victim, then telling the child that he or she is not at fault and that you are sorry such a thing has happened can begin the process of healing.

Abused children may show learning problems or be prone to daydreaming. They may have trouble concentrating. Teachers will want to deal gently with the child, not requiring complete attention and giving help where needed for concentrating on the task at hand.

FOR FURTHER REFERENCE

Bass, Ellen, and Laura Davis. *The Courage to Heal*. New York: Harper & Row, 1988.

Daugherty, Lynn B. *Why Me? Help for Victims of Child Sexual Abuse (Even If They Are Adults Now)*. Racine, WI: Mother Courage Press, 1984.

Miller, Alice. *For Your Own Good*. New York: Farrar, Straus & Giroux, 1983.

Sanford, Linda Tcshirhart. *The Silent Children*. New York: McGraw-Hill, 1980.

Sweet, Phyllis E. *Something Happened to Me*. Racine, WI: Mother Courage Press, 1981.

J. Overturf

Child Development

Any discussion of child development must begin with a definition of each term. But what is development? Psychologists since the 1950s have talked about "progressive change in an organism," taking their cue from the biological sciences. They have shown how persons develop cognitively and affectively as well as physically. People can even develop in interpersonal skills, decision making, and ego strength. But the higher one goes in the order of human faculties, the more complex charting development becomes; indeed the question remains if the developmental model applies at all.

Of course religious educators are interested in and benefit from the work done in the areas of cognitive, affective, and physical development, but beyond the human organism, they are interested in faith, hope, and love. Religious educators are interested in conversions, transformations, and grace. Developing organisms develop toward maturity. Religiously educated persons develop beyond adult maturity. Religious development for believers has no end point; it can continue beyond the grave. This distinction between psychologists and religious educators must be held in mind as the discussion proceeds.

Now we come to development during childhood. What does childhood include? Many childhood experts define childhood as the years from age six through twelve, the years spent in elementary school. Other experts include the years from birth through twelve, while still others also include adolescence.

Another way of describing childhood is to talk about the period in an individual's life before maturity and/or autonomy is reached. Children are dependent, either irresponsible or aresponsible, and immature in interpersonal skills. Adults are independent, responsible, and able to function socially. There is a high correlation between age and maturity. There is some reason to believe that graduation from high school or college results in a mature adult. Since this is not the case for many so-called postadolescents, educational failures are apparent. Religious educators are prone to give up on Sunday school beyond twelfth grade. Many twelfth graders are still children. For that matter, many adults are still children from a developmental point of view.

Thus we return to development. When religious educators recognize that age level is only a clue to development (and no more than that) and when they realize that development is a better criterion for an educational focus, then the task of religious education can make more sense. The term "child development" is misleading because:

1. Childhood is too often thought of in terms of years in an individual's life ending at a specific year denoting adulthood.
2. Development does not end at such a specific year denoting adulthood.
3. Religious development never ends.

However, if religious educators understand the caveats outlined above, we can proceed by treating development during childhood as a stage or stages of development during the beginning years of life. As a stage or stages of development during the beginning years of life, no end point of maturity is envisioned. The cutoff in discussing the beginning years of life will be only vaguely related to adulthood and the relationship will be empirically based. Quite simply, in discussing developmental theories, stages will be omitted where no children have been found by researchers. Furthermore, readers must be reminded that in the following outlines of developmental theories, where there are ages attached, the ages are only clues to developmental level, no more. It is worth repeating that developmental level is our primary concern: age tells us very little about development for individual children; developmental level tells us a great deal more about our learners.

This long introduction to child development has been necessary not only because of the misuse of developmental theories in the past, but also because the future use of developmental theories requires caution. Psychologists now realize this. Religious educators should realize the cautions even more, because the development of the human organism (the psychologist's domain) is not the same as the development of the soul (the religious domain).

THEORIES ABOUT DEVELOPMENT DURING CHILDHOOD

Religious educators today have a great many theories to choose from in order to better understand learners. Therefore let us look at what some of these theories can mean to religious educators.

Psychosocial Development

In the middle of this century, Erik Erikson (1902–), basing his work on that of Freud and Jung, espoused a psychosocial (or psychodynamic) theory of life cycle development that attracted many religious educators. His stages are:

Stage	Average age
Trust vs. Mistrust	birth–2
Autonomy vs. Shame and Doubt	2–3
Initiative vs. Guilt	3–6
Industry vs. Inferiority	6–12
Identity vs. Role Diffusion	13–20

The names of the stages denote the prevailing attitudes that are in tension and must be resolved by the child in each stage. For example, if in stage one an infant's physical and emotional needs are met in a consistent, caring way, an attitude of trust will prevail over that of mistrust. The successful establishment of a general attitude of trust toward people and the environment results in relative psychosocial health and a surer foundation for progress in the next psychosocial stage. Yet the resolution of conflict in each stage is never 100 percent in favor of one side or the other. Each individual forms his or her own unique pattern of the interrelationship of the two, and deficiencies may affect aspects of development in later stages.

Cognitive Development

In contrast to Erikson's psychosocial approach is the structural developmental approach of Jean Piaget (1896–1980). Stages represent structures or patterns for organizing experience. Each stage incorporates previous stages but is a new structure in itself. Each successive stage provides the structure for adapting to more experiences in the environment. Piaget's stages in cognitive development include:

Stage	Age
Sensorimotor	birth to 18 months/2 years
Preoperational	2 to 7/8 years
Concrete operational	7/8 to 11/12 years
Formal operational	11/12 to 14/15 years

The babies feel their way into intelligence (through their senses). Children two to seven or eight years of age lack structure; they are intuitive and arational. Older children structure thinking concretely, while adolescents begin to deal with abstract thinking.

Ronald Goldman, a psychologist in England, found Piagetian stages in his study of religious thinking and introduced Piaget to North American religious educators. Goldman named his stages in religious thinking: prereligious (up to seven years of age), subreligious (the concrete operational stage), and religious (when abstract reasoning is attained). John Peatling confirmed the stages in religious thinking in a large sample in the United States. Other religious educators became interested in Piaget and cognitive development.

The choice of the terms "prereligious" and "subreligious" was unfortunate because it allowed excuses to be made to ignore religious education until adolescence. For those with a true comprehension of Piaget's theory, however, this is not the case. To understand development is to understand the learner. Understanding the learner is having a grasp of the readiness of the learner, the potential of the learner, and the needs of the learner. Thus the grand title "child-centered religious education" came into being in the 1960s and 1970s. "Prereligious" and "subreligious" are not useful terms; the focus should be on the developing child.

However, many professional religious educators were not satisfied with limiting the focus to cognition. A new developmental theory was on hand in the late 1960s that looked appealing to religious educators—a theory of moral development. Morals—right and wrong—might be closer to religion than just thinking religiously.

Moral Development

Kohlberg's theory of moral development is another structural developmental theory based on Piaget's. It builds toward a sense of justice, which is seen as one thing rather than a bag of virtues. As with cognitive theory stages are sequential (one after another), invariant (stages cannot be skipped), and universal (everyone goes through the same stages). The stages during childhood are:

Stage	Age
Level I: Preconventional level	
Stage 1: Obedience and punishment orientation	6–7 years
Stage 2: Naively egoistic orientation	8–9 years
Level II: Conventional level	
Stage 3: Good-boy orientation	10 years
Stage 4: Authority-and-social-order-maintaining orientation	adolescence

(Level III, the Postconventional level, contains stages five and six. But very few teenagers attain even stage five much less stage six. For that matter, few adults climb above stage four.)

The educational method used in helping learners progress in moral development is to first ascertain learners' stage(s) and then stimulate learners (usually through discussions) to think at the next higher stage. Some religious educators pointed out that this was yet another cognitive theory—the focus remained thinking morally, not behaving morally. There are also serious difficulties in assessing the stage of the learners. Problematic also are differences between males and females in moral development, although these differences do not seem to show up until learners are in their twenties.

Nonetheless, moral development theory can be a help to religious educators. Knowledge of the stages can help teachers understand the children they work with. For example, an early elementary-school child can understand that it is nice to find a coin or a sheep that is lost. But the child does not understand that one small coin is important to the housewife or one small lamb is important to the shepherd. Big is better to the child. Bible stories can only be understood at the child's level of cognitive development.

Cognitive-based theories have not been enough for religious educators. Now we move on to two other theories, one on interpersonal development, the other on ego development.

Interpersonal Development

Robert Selman, of Harvard University, uses child experiences on video, role playing, and open-ended questions to evoke responses to interpersonal situations. These can be helpful to religious educators. Here is an outline of Selman's stages:

Stage	Description	Age
Egocentric	Difficulty in distinguishing self and others	3–6
Social informational	Main focus on self; one other's perspective	6–8
Self-reflective	Sequential role taking; taking turns	8–10
Mutual	Beginning of mutual role taking	10–12
Social and conventional role taking	Awareness, greater depth, abstract and simultaneous perceptions	12–15

These stages indicate that interpersonal development is a long, hard process. Teachers of preschool children should not make social demands beyond the maturity of the child. Role taking and understanding others probably does not begin until elementary school. Good social perceptions only begin in adolescence.

Ego Development

Jane Loevinger comes out of the psychoanalytic tradition in her exploration of the self. Her theory of ego development has Freudian background similar to Erik Erikson's theory. Yet Loevinger transcends psychoanalysis and includes character development, moral development, socialization, and cognitive development. Her stage titles are Presocial, Symbiotic, Impulsive, Self-Protective, Conformist, Conscientious, Autonomous, and Integrated. Elementary-school children are not found beyond the Conformist stage. Teenagers are not found beyond the Conscientious stage. For each stage Loevinger provides descriptions of characteristics in four areas: impulse control and/or character development, interpersonal style, conscious preoccupations, and cognitive style. Loevinger sees ego as a master trait that coordinates, chooses, selects, and directs a person's activities. The higher the stage the more adequately a person makes decisions; that is, the individual takes in more aspects, has greater tolerance for complexity, and selects from a greater variety of possible actions.

Although Loevinger's theory is fairly complex, the more educators know about ego development, the better they can teach our children. But the fact remains that the goal of religious education is not solely the development of a mature personality; it is the nurture of the person of faith who continues to grow religiously. Hence we turn to the last example of a developmental theory, James Fowler's theory of faith development.

Faith Development

The six stages in James Fowler's theory of faith development, in addition to an initial "prestage" for infants called Undifferentiated faith, are Intuitive-projective, Mythic-literal, Synthetic-conventional, Individuative-reflective, Conjunctive, and Universalizing. The first stage, Intuitive-projective, corresponds to Piaget's preoperational stage in that it is preconceptual and meaning is formed in terms of images and vague internal representations. Although a child may not "understand" religious objects, symbols, or activities at this time, important images are being formed that may have an effect on later religious development. In the Mythic-literal stage, with the ability to follow logical relationships between concrete things and to tell fact from fantasy, children can form narratives of their own experience and appreciate stories that are part of the faith tradition, although symbols are still understood in a very concrete, literal way. Abstract thinking and the ability to take the perspective of other individuals and groups usually allows persons to move to the Synthetic-conventional stage of faith, where meaning is determined by the norms and conventions of the faith community with which persons identify. The last three stages pertain to adults.

Fowler's beginnings were from the life-cycle approach of Erik Erikson. He has been heavily influenced by Kohlberg, and his theory is based on Piaget's categories. The structuring he talks about is the structuring of faith, or making meaning out of experience. Like Kohlberg's, Fowler's prestage and the first three stages (those found in childhood) are empirically based. Also like Kohlberg's the last two stages are more philosophically based.

Fowler's faith development theory draws together the other theories and is also the newest and least tested. Efforts to use the theory for educational purposes are only just beginning and its benefits for religious education remain to be seen.

Current Work in Developmental Theory

Other psychologists' work may also be of interest to religious educators. Kurt W. Fischer and associates continue Piaget's work in cognitive development. Robert Selman's work continues in interpersonal development. Henry Dupont's work in affective development is new. Carol Gilligan's studies in moral development in women continue to intrigue.

Among religious educators, John Peatling continues his empirically based studies in moral development. Also, Peatling's model of integrated personality may prove important in the future. Two others acquainted with developmental theory but critical of it are Gabriel Moran and James Loder. There is a good deal happening in the 1980s that bears watching and understanding.

CONCLUSION

There have been times in the past when the armies of religious educators and social scientists were enemy camps each on its own side of the river. The river still exists today, but it is only a stream with a great deal of traffic back and forth. Psychologists want to know more about religion. Religious educators want help from the child developmentalists.

Yet the stream is important. There is a difference between psychology and religion. The stream may be called the grace of God, the Holy Spirit, transformations, whatever. Or we may refer to the goal of psychologists as wanting to understand the person from birth to death, while the goal of religious education is helping the person from birth to God. The difference is important.

However, as creatures lower than angels we can only seek to do God's will with our imperfect understanding, with our human abilities, and with the best we find on earth. Here is the crucial question. Do we believe that God is going to jump in and save us as we try blindly to educate our children religiously? Or do we believe that attending to psychologists' developmental theories can help us understand child development and better educate our children?

Some things religious educators may deduce without specific help from psychologists, for example, that the wiggle threshold of a small child during worship depends on physical development. But we can learn from cognitive development that children are not miniature people who think like adults but in smaller doses. Children's thoughts are completely different from adults'. Another example comes from interpersonal development. We can learn that preschool children are unable to empathize. There is much we can learn if we will sustain the effort and commitment to become educated by child developmentalists and it will enhance the teaching of our children.

Religious teachers certainly must model God's love to children. But beyond that they must understand where in development each child is. They must know their learners' needs and what each child is ready to learn. Another way to show God's love is being able to adjust educational goals so that unrealistic expectations are not held. Knowledge of child development helps teachers understand learners. So often understanding precedes love. Religious education needs understanding and love. Child developmentalists can be invaluable allies. See also Adolescence; Affective Development; Character Development; Childhood Education; Cognitive Development; Faith Development; Infancy; Interdisciplinary Studies; Kindergarten; Middle Childhood; Moral Development; Nursery Education; Preschool Children; Psychosocial Development.

FOR FURTHER REFERENCE

Barber, Lucie W. *Teaching Christian Values*. Birmingham, AL: Religious Education Press, 1984.

Cully, Iris V. *Christian Child Development*. San Francisco: Harper & Row, 1979.

Fowler, James W. *Stages of Faith: The Psychology of Human Development and the Quest for Meaning*. San Francisco: Harper & Row, 1981.

Moran, Gabriel. *Religious Education Development: Images for the Future*. Minneapolis, MN: Winston, 1983.

L. W. Barber

Child Evangelism

Are children born within the saving grace of God and later, perhaps at the age of accountability, confronted with personal responsibility for life and faith response? Or are children born lost and therefore the immediate objects of salvation concern by the faith community? The variety of responses to these questions have led to positions that can be labeled "covenant community," "infant damnation," and "infant salvation." All faith communities ask themselves what they will do with children and whether children need only nurture or both evangelism and nurture.

"Covenant communities" stress the solidarity of the family, some even to the "birthright membership" position of the Quakers. More commonly the covenantal community extends infant baptism to the child as a way of showing that God's grace is inclusive and that it is administered by the faith community. Individual conversion tends not to be stressed in these covenantal groups, but rather the corporate life of faith. Since fellowship and obedience are in community, so also grace is bestowed by the authorized liturgies of the community.

Those espousing "infant damnation" see all children as outside of God's saving grace and in need of personal conversion. This emphasis tends to appear in faith communities that stress individual conversion, high cognitive or at least verbal assent to belief, and believer's baptism. In the agencies that target children, this emphasis tends to seek to evangelize the child of three or four years on the thesis that the child will otherwise be damned, it is easier for a child to believe than an adult, and once a child is saved, this salvation will be irrevocable through adult life. It is not always clear how the "believer's baptism" of a preschool child differs from "infant baptism" to which this tradition is quite opposed.

Representing this viewpoint is the Child Evangelism Fellowship, begun in 1937 for the specific purpose of encouraging the evangelization and conversion of young children. Today Child Evangelism Fellowships are in ninety-two countries worldwide, enrolling 1,480,340 people in the United States alone. Believing that young children are most open to conversion, they form Good News Clubs for ages four through twelve, which usually meet in neighborhood homes under lay leaders and in weeklong summer programs. Training programs encourage teenagers to become junior teachers. Home leaders are enrolled in weekly or biweekly training programs meeting at area centers. The national office in Warrenton, Missouri, provides curricular materials and area offices publish monthly newsletters.

"Infant salvation" assumes that all children are saved, objects of God's unmerited grace, until they make an affirmation of that grace or a negative or rebellious response to God as an autonomous person, typically in adolescence or early adulthood. In such a tradition children are baptized as infants, admitted to Holy Communion, admitted to celebrations of prayer, praise, and worship, and are taken seriously as participants in the community of faith. In many cases an informal rite of passage is observed as they are confirmed at an age roughly corresponding to the popular idea of an age of accountability. One denomination offers a two-stage membership, with personal affirmation of the baptismal covenant made public at age sixteen. Traditional secular "accountability" to legal responsibility is at age eighteen or twenty-one. *See also* Bus Ministry; Evangelism.

FOR FURTHER REFERENCE

Cully, Iris V. *Christian Child Development.* San Francisco: Harper & Row, 1979.

Ingle, Clifford. *Children and Conversion.* Nashville, TN: Broadman, 1970.

Joy, Donald. "Why Teach Children." In Zuck, Roy, and Robert Clark, eds. *Childhood Education in the Church.* 2d ed. Chicago: Moody, 1985.

Russell, Gene. *Let the Children Come In: A Manual of Child Evangelism for a Local Baptist Church.* Nashville, TN: Church Growth Press, 1974.

Soderholm, Marjorie. *Explaining Salvation to Children.* Grand Rapids, MI: Beacon, 1962.

Yoder, Gideon. *The Nurture and Evangelism of Children.* Scottdale, PA: Herald, 1959.

D. M. Joy

Childhood Education

Childhood education focuses on the religious nurture, training, and development of children ages six through eleven, usually grades 1–6. It involves teaching the word of God in such a way that children discover the person and presence of God (for Christian children, in Jesus Christ) and begin to respond to him. Childhood education encompasses all facets of this process including intensive study of the child and how a child learns.

A HISTORICAL PERSPECTIVE

The earliest records of childhood education are found in the Hebrew Bible, called by Christians the Old Testament, which contains commands to parents and caretakers to teach and to inculcate knowledge of biblical history and godly principles as values in those of the next generation. While parents are identified as the primary educators, in actuality the whole life of God's people was organized to teach. This included celebrations and festivals, the patterns set up for worship and for work, and the laws God established for his people. Although nothing is specifically noted in the New Testament regarding what or how children are to be taught, there is evidence of their value and their presence when Christian teachings were shared. By the time of Jesus, Jewish society had developed schools for the memorization of Torah. But parents were still left with the major responsibility for training their own children; additional impact came from the godly living of the community to which the family belonged.

Accompanying a seeming lack of importance placed on children during the succeeding centuries is an absence of emphasis on the instruction of children. However, the Reformation in the sixteenth century brought renewed awareness of the place of children and the need for passing on to them the truths of the faith. The greatest impetus for this came in the mid-seventeenth century when John Amos Comenius supported providing a thoroughly Christian education for all children.

Several centuries later in England, Robert Raikes (1735–1811), a philanthropist who was involved in prison reform, established the first Sunday schools. These were developed primarily to promote literacy and reduce crime among uneducated, working-class children. The Scriptures were involved in achieving this purpose of reforming society. Raikes's project was so successful that at the time of his death there were reported some half million children enrolled in his Sunday schools. The arrival of this movement in America was accompanied by a greater emphasis on presentation of the gospel and by 1810 the Sunday school was permitted within the churches. In its beginning stages it existed in two forms: the mission school for the poor and the frontier children and the church school for church members' children. The Sunday school was the primary agency for childhood religious education, although the succeeding years introduced such extrachurch movements such as Scouts and Child Evangelism Fellowship. The major thrust of the Sunday school became Bible teaching and evangelism.

The twentieth century has seen an explosion in research and knowledge about the personality development and learning abilities of children. It has also provided a wealth of insight in how to communicate and an accompanying plethora of techniques and materials. Capitalizing on this impetus and outcome of research, the church has given increasing importance and effort in the direction of educating its young in matters of faith and character. In the early twentieth century division developed between the fundamentalists and modernists. The former insisted that the Bible remain the primary focus of all educational efforts and emphasized conversion, while the latter accented the religious needs of children. Today childhood education is a multifaceted discipline

encompassing numerous fields of endeavor and involving hundreds of thousands of personnel. At the heart of specialized study of this area are theories of child development reflecting research on the child's cognitive potential, social relationships, moral development, and growth in stages of faith.

DEVELOPMENTAL INSIGHTS FOR EDUCATORS

During the years from six to eleven, a child grows dramatically, offering challenging implications for teaching and learning. Cognitively children are in the concrete operational period. Logical thought can take place when related to concrete things. It is during this period that children become logically aware of classification, seriation (arrangement in series), hierarchical arrangement, and the schema of reversibility (that is, can return thoughts to their origin). Their reasoning, however, is based on involvement with physical actions or objects that then can be internalized. Thus abstraction in any form is difficult for children of this age to grasp and requires special consideration from those who would seek to help them grow conceptually. Six to eleven year olds must work at understanding abstract words. The actions of justice, goodness, mercy, and love may not be foreign to them, but the classification of those acts into the above abstract terms is. Likewise there is difficulty in grasping generalizations such as "God is everywhere" or "Love your neighbor as yourself." The children fail to see the general law that overarches many specific perceptions. They relate to particular instances rather than thinking of a general rule. Young children in this age bracket have been observed pocketing a "found object" that belonged to another after having been "taught" that stealing is wrong. Their compartmentalized, concrete conceptualization allowed them to see one act as wrong and another as okay because of their difficulty in grasping the overall rule. Another realm impacted by this struggle with abstraction is symbolism—the substitution of a literal object for an abstract idea. The use of numbers for a specific set of objects, the positioning of hands on a clock to represent the abstract of time, the understanding of proverbs and puns, the use of objects to represent ideas—all of these present learning challenges to the literal mind of growing children. Thus they often jump to wrong conclusions when hearing "I Am the Bread of Life" or "This Little Light of Mine."

How can teachers communicate to this age level so that understanding is achieved? Teaching must be more than verbal—it must be accompanied by numerous concrete situations and meaningful activities to form clear concepts growing out of hard evidence. The learner must be actively involved in the learning, being able to work with the physical in order to develop the image of the meaning. Teachers of this age level do not take for granted that verbal presentation has been understood. Rather they question, encourage conversation, or suggest retelling in the learner's own words. They give opportunity to express concepts and applications in concrete ways by drawing, acting out, or rewriting ideas. They utilize sensory learning and explain terms and ideas in a variety of ways. They seek to build bridges between what is seen to what is unseen, what is physically represented to what is represented abstractly in the mind.

Socially this age span is marked by diminishing relationships with adults and flourishing relationships with peers as the children seek to avoid loneliness and boredom. Such loneliness is occasioned by an increasing withdrawal from adults in a growing desire to gain independence. It results in a corresponding drawing to those of like age. This is a period of intense friendships and "secrets." It is also known for being a time of high criticism of adults. Increasingly members of each sex identify with their like counterparts and boundaries are closely drawn between the two sexes, each disdaining the other. This identification is accompanied by name-calling, definite division of interests, skills, and activities, and a commitment to "not being caught dead" crossing the boundaries of these sex-identified roles.

During this period there is a growing demand for personal privacy. There is also an increasing importance of and preoccupation with rules. These children are gaining control over impulses, learning to deny themselves present gratification for future benefits and gaining in emotional control, being able to channel frustrations into more socially acceptable actions. The teacher of this elementary age will want to evaluate responses and plan activities with the child's growing need for independence in mind. Utilization of peer groups and teams affirm social needs.

Children at this age are in the preconventional morality stage in moral thinking. Most children under age seven or eight determine moral judgment on the basis of punishment or reward. At this time there is unquestioned deference to all superior authorities who decide right and wrong and who enforce authority with punishment or reward. As insight and experience are integrated the child moves from thinking that the rule is sacred, unchangeable, and outside of self to realizing that rules can be changed based on mutual consent.

The child's thinking evolves from the punishment/reward mode to an instrumental-relativist one in which "right" is what satisfies personal needs. In this self-centered mode children obey rules in order to get the best deal possible—they do good if they see profit in it for themselves. One of the reasons children order their moral thinking the way they do is the difficulty a person under ten has in taking the perspective of another and in understanding that another person can take his or her perspective. Thinking for children under ten moves from realizing that other persons have perspectives different from theirs to understanding that their own perspective is not the only right and valid one. They become aware that when others observe and evaluate their acts, others may come to different conclusions.

Beyond the age of ten, children grasp the dual nature of understanding another's point of view and of being understood by another who takes their perspective. However, knowing what others want is not enough to cause children to believe they should behave in that way. Progress in moral thinking is not necessarily accompanied by progress in moral behavior. It is important for teachers of this age level to teach not only the content of moral behavior but also to help the child think through why she acts the way she does.

Awareness of the child's development affects how a teacher or parent attempts to build values and selects discipline methods for effectiveness with different levels, e.g., punishment and reward from an authority are positive in helping the younger child comply with what is right. It also means that a teacher will realize how children at different levels of moral thinking will have different understandings of the same principle such as the Golden Rule. While a child at the older end of this age level can put herself in the shoes of another and decide what another would want, a younger child would interpret this rule as "Do to others what they do to you."

Childhood education faces a child in many phases of transition. Those who work with this age span must be aware of development and growth in order to communicate religious truths and values to the growing person at each stage. They will be concerned for the internalizing of concepts, for exploration of the process the child uses to bring coherence and purpose to his world, and for adapting methodologies and content to the way the child learns best. *See also* Affective Development; Child Abuse; Child Development; Cognitive Development; Faith Development; Middle Childhood; Moral Development; Object Lesson; Psychosocial Development; Sunday School.

J. A. Gorman

Children's Books

See Books, Children's.

Children's Choir

See Choir, Children's.

Children's Church

The gathering of children with each other for worship at the same time adults are worshiping is called children's church. This gathering takes several different forms. Most predominantly children's church is a worship service modeled after adult worship where children serve as ushers, greeters, and liturgists in a service strictly for children up to age twelve. Usually adult laity serve as coordinators of the service. The sermon in children's church may sometimes be an object lesson by a layperson or special guest. This form of children's church seeks to teach children the rituals of adult worship and to familiarize them with creeds, hymns, and customs of their congregation while at the same time presenting the gospel in a more simplified format.

A second form of children's church occurs within the adult worship service. At a given time in the service all children are asked to come to the chancel area to hear a story, an object lesson, or the sermon in abbreviated form. This time is led by the pastor or a layperson who has experience with children. Often children are encouraged to participate verbally in the presentation. This form of children's church is also called the "children's sermon."

A third form of children's church occurs at the time of the sermon during adult worship services. Children participate in the adult worship experience until they are called to leave the sanctuary before the sermon. During this time there are usually refreshments, a Bible story, an activity, and perhaps recreation.

The children's service held parallel to that of the adult service is viewed by some as a way of structuring worship in terms understood by children and giving them leadership roles they would not have in the adult service. Others view this as shutting children away from the main service of worship, removing the opportunity for them to learn by participation and identification with adults.

The minister's presentation for children within the main service is seen as a way both to get acquainted and for children to hear a sermon within their understanding. Others say the congregation is watching children "perform" as they participate in answers and the content may "talk down" to children.

When the children leave just before the sermon, they have had an opportunity to worship with adults and to have instruction at their age level without being the focus of adult spectators. It is also an admission that sermons need to be structured differently for different age levels to accomplish the spiritual edification that is their task.

A definition of children's church used less frequently is literally an entire church dedicated to ministry with children. This church may grow out of a mission project with children sponsored by a parent church. *See also* Sermons, Children's; Worship; Worship, Children's.

M. S. Goodson

Children's Day

In recognition and celebration of children, Children's Day was begun by the American Sunday School Union in 1917 as a week's observance to include both community events and events in local churches. Still observed by Protestant churches in many places, usually on the second Sunday in June, Children's Day activities might include special programs presented by children for a congregation or activities and festivals designed for children. The day can be filled with joyous events—all the children of a congregation may march in a parade or procession in a worship service, children's various achievements may be recognized, or a service of blessing the children may be held. Children's Day is sometimes used as a day for remembering children across the world and collecting offerings for children's ministries. It is a festive day with special songs and prayers.

M. S. Goodson

Children's Sermons

See Sermons, Children's.

Children's Worship

See Worship, Children's.

Choir

A choir is an organized group of singers who assist with liturgy in church services; a group of singers performing at secular functions is usually called a chorus. The term "choir" is also used in architecture to denote that part of a church with chairs or fixed stalls for clergy or singers. In organology the choir is defined as one possible division of pipes located behind the organist's seat. Often American and British organ builders designate the bottommost keyboard the "choir" on an organ of three or more manuals. The remainder of this article deals with the choir as a group of singers.

The Judeo-Christian history of choirs and choir music certainly extends back to ancient Israel, with numerous references found in the historical books of the Old Testament. While the early Christian church approved of music in services, limited finances and facilities resulted in a focus upon congregational singing rather than specially trained professional ensembles as their inheritance of an elaborate and rich Jewish musical tradition might have suggested. The development of such groups came as early as the fourth century, when Christianity became recognized as a legitimate religion. Gregory I, pope from 590 to 604, was a great reformer of church music and liturgy. His reorganization of the *schola cantorum* (singing school) and the exportation of its ideals led to unprecedented consistency and quality of musical training and performances throughout the Christian world.

Until the sixth century, in some locales, women alternated with men in the singing of psalms. Throughout the Middle Ages, however, the choirs of churches and monasteries were made up of either men or men and boys. Only in convents were women permitted to sing. In the fifteenth century, church choirs began singing polyphonic music—music with more than one line sounding simultaneously—in addition to the monophonic chants. The continuing history of church choirs throughout subsequent centuries is a story of gradually expanding size and sonority: the number of singers increases, as does the richness of sound, much like the growth of the orchestra and the symphonic sound. Major choirs in the Middle Ages had as few as fourteen singers, while choirs of the Renaissance increased in size to thirty or more choristers. In the eighteenth and early nineteenth centuries festival choirs dramatically increased in size, so that choirs of hundreds and even thousands of singers came into being.

While the standard American church choir of today could be characterized as a moderately sized choir of men and women volunteers, other traditions still survive and thrive. World-famous church choirs of men and boys, following in the centuries-old tradition, exist in New York, Washington, D.C., Cambridge, Copenhagen, Leipzig, and Vienna.

The choir is an important educational organization in the parish. Members learn church music spanning many centuries and containing words and thoughts of theological and biblical significance. Choirs provide an opportunity for service, and members learn responsibility both for regular attendance at rehearsal and worship and careful concentration on a task. *See also* Choir, Children's; Choir School; Hymnody, Christian; Music in the Church.

R. Ludwig, N. G. Ludwig

Choir, Children's

A group of children who have rehearsed and prepared musical compositions to sing in a church service may be called a children's choir. Children's choirs range from groups of preschoolers who memorize simple tunes to major American, English, and Continental boy choirs, some of which are among the finest choirs in the world.

The history of choir music in Christian churches is largely a history of children's singing, since the standard choir consisted of men and boys until the nineteenth century. While a tradition of women's liturgical singing has long flourished in convents, the use of women's and men's voices simultaneously in church services first receives occasional mention in the eighteenth century and does not become commonplace until the following century. Gifted boys between the ages of eight and thirteen are able to achieve a purity of tone that has been cherished throughout the church's history. Choirboys for cathedrals and royal or collegiate chapels have traditionally been trained in choir schools established at such churches since the fourth century. Though this type of establishment is not as commonplace today as in the Middle Ages, many of the world's principal church choirs are organized in this fashion, choirs at the Sistine Chapel; St. Thomas Church, New York; Washington Cathedral; St. Paul's Cathedral, London; York Minster; Dresden Cross Choir; Hofburg (Vienna Boys Choir); and St. Thomas Church, Leipzig.

Sometime around the turn of the twentieth century, some American churches began the development of graded children's choir programs. While the traditional boy choir involved a limited number of carefully auditioned boys in a rigorous training and performance schedule, graded choirs offered more modest amounts of musical education and performance possibilities to all parish children. Some large and distinguished church programs now have a dozen or more choirs involving many hundreds of singers. Recognizing the need for musical involvement of girls as well as boys, many churches with established choirs of men and boys have developed fine and accomplished girls' choirs. Some churches with graded choir programs have likewise recognized that there are virtues, with both music and discipline, in having children's choirs organized by gender. Whatever type of children's music program is considered, the finest American examples are testimony to the fact that children are capable of singing and understanding church music of the highest quality. The experience of contributing through music to the life of a church can have a profoundly lasting and meaningful effect on a child. Many outstanding lay and professional church leaders had crucial religious experiences as a part of childhood singing in church.

Two nonprofit organizations vitally interested in high standards for children's choirs are Choristers Guild (2834 W. Kingsley Road, Garland, TX 75041) and the Royal School of Church Music (Addington Palace, Croydon, CR9 5AD stantine, who had allied himself with the Christians. Henceforward, Christianity was closely related to the state, with profound consequences. By the end of the fourth century Christianity was the official religion of Rome, and non-Christians were subject to persecution.

During this same period, Christianity began to make serious headway beyond the borders of Rome. The church penetrated into Ethiopia, India, and northern Europe.

This spread of Christianity contributed to increasing diversity of practice. This was enhanced by the deterioration of Rome's control over the Mediterranean world. Difficulty in travel and communication allowed local customs to become entrenched in ritual and organization.

Several church councils have been held from 325 (Nicaea) to the twentieth century. However, with each council taking a position on various issues, those who have not agreed with the decisions of the councils have often gone their own way. A number of these dissident groups have survived to the present.

With the collapse of the Roman Empire in the West, Christianity found itself to be one of the few surviving institutions that could provide structure and some sense of security for the peoples of the area. Thus the church grew in strength but also became an institution to be controlled by those who wanted political and military power. For the next thousand years Western Christianity was characterized by a struggle between church and state. The eastern half of the Roman Empire continued until 1453, and there the church was more dependent upon the state. Eastern (more than Western) Christians had to deal with the challenge of Islam during the seventh and eighth centuries, followed by centuries of tension and occasional armed conflict.

A major factor in both the spread and survival of Christianity after the fall of Rome was the development of monasticism. Christianity had had a tendency from the very beginning to encourage people to dedicate themselves to a life of prayer and devotion. By the sixth century, a new form of monasticism, largely inspired by Benedict of Nursia, developed self-contained, self-supporting communities of monks and nuns. They soon became centers of learning, discipline, and stability. The monasteries provided most of the missionaries for the next several centuries.

Tensions between Eastern Christians, now generally called Orthodox, and Western Christians, by now called Roman Catholic (due to the authority given to the pope, the bishop of Rome), resulted in a formal division of the two major branches of Christianity in 1054.

RENAISSANCE, REFORMATION, AND ENLIGHTENMENT

Western Christianity experienced a rebirth of learning and creativity in the twelfth and thirteenth centuries, only to experience a rapid decline, in part due to plague and economic disaster. But a vigorous recovery called the Renaissance spread over Western Europe during the fifteenth and sixteenth centuries. All areas of society were affected. The new idealism of the period led to much criticism of the church. Conflict and calls for reform reached a climax in the encounter between a German priest, Martin Luther, and the popes. This resulted in the Protestant Reformation, a shattering of the unity of the church in the West. Division bred division, and the church took many forms, each of which claimed spiritual superiority over other groups.

Western society continued to evolve, and a period of rational thought called the Enlightenment brought new challenges to the church. The Enlightenment is the basis for the modern scientific way of interpreting the universe, and its conclusions and ways of thinking were quickly found to be in opposition to traditional Christian modes of understanding. From the seventeenth through the twentieth centuries the church has found itself having to reinterpret its role and its view of reality in light of modern thought.

The Reformation and the Enlightenment coincided with the period of exploration and colonization by Western states. As traders and conquerors spread from western Europe over the rest of the globe, Christian missionaries also moved into areas that had either been non-Christian or had non-Catholic Christian traditions. Many converts were made, but Christians also found themselves having to think about other faiths as they came to know people and practices that varied from their own.

THE CURRENT SITUATION

Meanwhile, changes in national governments and economic systems have forced the church to relate to cultures and societies in new ways. The combination of a modern scientific worldview and the changed sociopolitical situation has contributed to a decline in the power of the church in Western society. Some Christians have reacted by trying to recapture the supposed purity of an earlier age or claim absolute authority for certain beliefs and practices, including a literal interpretation of Scripture.

Other Christians have responded by seeking ways for Christians to live and work together toward unity. The unity, or ecumenical, movement has been characterized by the formation of various councils of churches and church unions, as well as cooperation in ministry and service.

The current situation of Christianity is characterized by enormous diversity, general internal stability, and basic respect for non-Christian religions. In parts of the world Christians have to deal with governments and social systems that are intentionally materialistic and antireligious. Worship practices are more eclectic than ever, and new ideas reflect the various ways Christians interpret the meaning of the universe from a religious perspective. *See also* Church Year; Creed; Gospel; History of Christian Education; Jesus Christ; Reign of God; Sociology of Religion; Trinity.

FOR FURTHER REFERENCE

Cross, F. L., and E. A. Livingston, eds. *Oxford Dictionary of the Christian Church*. Oxford: Oxford University Press, 1974.
Latourette, Kenneth Scott. *A History of Christianity*. San Francisco: Harper & Row, 1953.

R. L. Harrison

Christmas

Christmas, observed on December 25, is the festival of the birth of Christ. It celebrates the incarnation of the Divine Word (John 1:1–14); the name "Christ Mass" refers to the Eucharist celebrated on that day in honor of Christ's birth. It is the second most important holy day in the Christian calendar.

The liturgical Christmas season lasts twelve days, from the Feast of the Nativity on December 25 until Epiphany on January 6. The season also includes the traditional festivals of Saint Stephen the first martyr (December 26), Saint John the Apostle (December 27), the Holy Innocents murdered by Herod in his search for the Christ child (December 28), and the Circumcision of Christ (January 1). The Circumcision has been renamed the Holy Name of Jesus by Episcopalians, Lutherans, and those who use the Common Lectionary. Among Roman Catholics it has become the Solemnity of Mary, Mother of God. The liturgical color for the Christmas season is white.

Several theological themes are connected with the Christmas season. The Nativity of Our Lord is the liturgical designation of the day, indicating that the infant Jesus was a special person from birth. The Incarnation refers to the Christian understanding that in a unique way God lived among people in the person of Jesus of Nazareth, thereby identifying with the particularity of human need (John 1:14, "The Word became flesh and dwelt among us"). Emmanuel, from the Hebrew "God is with us," is frequently found in Christmas carols, referring to the presence of God revealed in the life of Jesus.

With widespread observance, Christmas has become a community and family event, and many customs have accrued from the cultures into which the Christian faith has spread. These customs have become part of the observance of the season in families, parishes, and religious education classes. Knowing something of the background can enrich the practices.

The celebration of Christmas on December 25 began in Rome about the beginning of the fourth century. It was a Christian response to a pagan festival on that date connected with the winter solstice, the Birthday of the Unconquered Sun. The birth of Christ, the Sun of Righteousness, was observed in its place. The celebration spread from Rome to the rest of the Christian world. Some scholars have suggested an alternative explanation, deriving the date from March 25, which was believed to be the actual date of the annunciation to Mary (and of the crucifixion), with the birth following on December 25.

The winter solstice festival was observed in northern Europe where Christianity spread during its first millennium. The lights of Christmas reflect the joy that people felt when the sun began to return for a longer period each day. Yule logs, torches, and candles all speak of light, warmth, and cheer. Veneration of a sacred tree was transmuted into the symbolism of the evergreen as sign of eternal life. Similarly, other evergreens became part of the celebration: mistletoe, holly (with the Passion symbolism of thorns and red berries), and ivy.

Tradition says that Francis of Assisi introduced the use of the figures that form the manger scene, using a neighborhood barn as locale. Today, simple figures may be placed in home or church, or a community may reenact the events, complete with animals and people.

Saint Nicholas, a fourth-century bishop of Myra (Turkey), noted for good deeds done secretly for needy people, was commemorated on December 6. In northern Europe he became Father Christmas, and in Holland, Santa Claus. From Holland this figure who gave gifts to children was brought to New Amsterdam. Gift-giving became an important family activity on Christmas Eve or Christmas Day and has remained so, even in places where the religious meaning of the day is not significant.

The merrymaking of Christmas, with special foods that vary from one culture to another, is an expression of the joy and good feeling that abound with any celebration.

Christmas carols are one form of the music of the season. The word refers to a round dance or a joyous song. The carol may speak to the religious significance of the season but usually includes the dimension of popular celebration. The custom of people going from place to place caroling has become part of the celebration. Though carols are used in the liturgical celebration, they are distinct in music and words from other liturgical music, including hymns. The Christmas celebration has evoked response from many composers, whose anthems, cantatas, and oratorios have enriched the celebration.

The Christmas pageant of today is a descendant of the nativity plays in the medieval mystery cycles that retold the whole biblical story. The pageant is an interweaving of Scripture, song, and action or tableau. In some churches, this is the children's special contribution to the celebration, but in others pageants include people of all ages. Dance is another way of retelling the nativity story.

The particular customs observed reflect the ethnic and national backgrounds of churches and families. Each develops its own traditions, and all are enriched through the diversity. *See also* Church Year.

I. V. Cully, L. L. Mitchell

Church-State Relations

The relation of religion to publicly supported education has developed in response to interpretations by the courts of the First Amendment to the Constitution. The first part of that amendment is as follows: "Congress shall make no law respecting an establishment of religion, or prohibiting the free exercise thereof." The two clauses, the one about "establishment" and the one about "free exercise," at times come in conflict. It is sometimes recognized that free exercise may involve procedures that are a limited form of the establishment of religion. Note that the amendment begins by referring to action by Congress.

SUPPORT FOR PAROCHIAL SCHOOLS

The First Amendment was not applied to the states until this century and then it was by way of the application of the Fourteenth Amendment (1868), which says: "Nor shall any state deprive any person of life, liberty, or property, without due process of law." One aspect of liberty related to our subject was that citizens should be free from having their taxes used to support religious teaching in which they do not believe. The most important early application of the amendment to the states that was a more obvious case of free exercise was the Supreme Court's outlawing of an Oregon law that required all students to attend public rather than parochial schools for a number of years (*Pierce* v. *Society of Sisters*, 1925).

There was another leap in the interpretation of the First Amendment in 1947. There had been much support for the idea that the establishment clause ruled out only preferential support of one or more forms of religion but in *Everson* v. *Board of Education* the court ruled that the federal government or a state must not pass laws "which aid one religion, aid all religions or prefer one religion to another." That statement has determined most constitutional thinking about religion and public education ever since. It makes impossible the teaching of a common core of religious thought, which some religious educators and other religious leaders had advocated. However, it does not rule out fringe benefits for the students of private

schools, benefits such as transportation to and from school, some health services, lunches, or even books that are the same as those used in the public schools. It is possible to go quite far in aiding students rather than the schools as such on the basis of the "child benefit" principle even though the schools benefit.

Direct aid to parochial schools is clearly ruled out in spite of the argument that those who support parochial schools save money for the state by carrying a considerable part of the cost of general education acceptable to the state and not only religious education. Roman Catholics, among others who have parochial schools, regard this situation as unjust. Five years after the Everson decision, another decision (*Zorach* v. *Clausen*) written by Justice Douglas made room for limited cooperation between the schools and religious bodies in these words: "it follows the best in our traditions" to adjust "the schedule of public events to sectarian needs." The court went on to say that "we are a religious people whose institutions presuppose a Supreme Being." The court seemed to go out of its way to counteract the impression that it was indifferent or unfriendly to religion.

Current debates about tax credit for tuition for private, including religious, schools and vouchers provided by the state to pay part of such tuition receive much attention. The Reagan administration gave support to both procedures. The present Supreme Court would probably block them both. That they would surely encourage a vast increase of the number of religious schools should call them into question because there would be a self-defeating scattering of the resources for public education, quite apart from issues of church and state. The idea of aid by the state to religious schools for the teaching of secular subjects may take some form in the future that may be regarded as constitutional. One reason for raising it is the national need to have both competent teachers and adequate equipment for the teaching of some sciences made available to students in all schools.

RELIGION IN PUBLIC SCHOOLS

There has long been a strong conviction in the churches that neutrality between religion and nonreligion and the fear of offending any one of many religious groups encourage silence about religion in the public schools and that this implies that religion is untrue or unimportant. This lends itself to the substitution for religion of secular absolutes, even nationalist absolutes that, unintentionally as far as the law is concerned, are given religious value. This remains the great unsolved problem in relating religious education to the First Amendment.

Efforts to solve this problem have been the system of "released time" with religious classes taught under church auspices in school buildings, which was declared unconstitutional (*McCollum v. Board of Education*, 1948), and "dismissed time" (sometimes also referred to as "released time"), which involved classes taught in churches during school time. The latter was declared constitutional though in recent years it has not been widely used (*Zorach* v. *Clausen*, 1952).

In higher education a very important way of dealing with this problem is teaching *about* religion in courses about the history of religion, the philosophy of religion, the sociology of religion, about religion in literature and art, and about the role of religion in general history and culture. "Religious studies" in public higher education have become an important part of the teaching of humanities in many institutions. The Supreme Court has recognized this as constitutional and there is no legal bar to teaching about religion in the public schools. Systematic attempts to include such teaching are few and new experiments are needed. There is here an open door.

Another issue raised in this context is the attempt supported by a few legislatures to require teaching about the "creationist" view of the origin and development of life as well as about evolutionary theories. The chief difficulty about this is the insistence that creationism be taught as a scientific theory and not an interpretation dependent on one view of the Christian revelation. This is rejected as unsound religious teaching by most of the religious community and as unsound scientific teaching by most of the scientific community.

Few issues are more discussed than prayer in the public schools. The Supreme Court has outlawed spoken prayer (*Engel* v. *Vitale*, 1962). A major argument against it is that it would undermine the religious liberty of those who on principle oppose prayer or the words used in spoken prayer. If it is voluntary and such opponents absent themselves, they might suffer taunts or discrimination. It is difficult to come up with any way of determining who should compose spoken prayers. A moment of silence with no one announced purpose could be used for voluntary prayer. Thought that may prove to be permissible, it would be no significant contribution to a solution of the problem already mentioned, that silence about religion in the intellectual life of the schools suggests that religion is untrue or unimportant.

The free exercise clause should give citizens the right to seek alternatives, old or new, to the religious vacuum in public schools that results in the misrepresentation of religion. They should never forget the witness that has dominated courts in this century against allowing the free exercise of some to repress the liberty of others. That last is a major purpose of the establishment clause. *See also* History of Christian Education; Private Schools and Religion; Public Schools and Religion.

FOR FURTHER REFERENCE

Pfeffer, Leo. *God, Caesar, and the Constitution.* Boston: Beacon, 1975.
Stokes, Anson Phelps, and Leo Pfeffer. *Church and State in the United States.* New York: Harper & Row, 1964.
Tussman, Joseph. *The Supreme Court on Church and State.* New York: Oxford University Press, 1962.

J. C. Bennett

Church Women United

Church Women United (CWU) is the national ecumenical movement that brings nearly half a million Protestant, Roman Catholic, Orthodox, and other Christian women together into one community of prayer, advocacy, and service. It represents a broad spectrum of religious tradition, race, age, economic status, and ethnic background and functions through a national unit, 52 state units (including Greater Washington, D.C., and Puerto Rico) and 1,800 local units throughout the United States. Unified by a common faith in Christ and committed to the empowerment of women, Church Women United works for global peace and economic and racial justice.

CWU has a national office staff at 475 Riverside Drive (Room 812) in New York City (10115), a United Nations office at 777 United Nations Plaza, New York City (10017), and a Washington office at 110 Maryland Avenue N.E., (Room 108), Washington, D.C. (20002).

Stated goals of the movement are to grow and expand the vision of what it means to be Christian women of faith in today's world, to develop a visible, ecumenical community, to work actively for a just, peaceful, and caring society, and to use responsibly our combined intelligence, time, energy, and money to fulfill these goals.

Church Women United was founded in Atlantic City, New Jersey, in 1941 when three interdenominational women's groups, the Council of Women for Home Missions, the Committee on Women's Work of the Foreign Mission Conference, and the National Council of Federated Church Women, joined to form the United Council of Church Women. In 1949 it became one of the founding agencies of the National Council of Churches of Christ in the U.S.A. as the General Department of United Church Women. From 1960 to 1966, "Assignment: Race" was a major program emphasis. In 1966 it declared itself a "movement" and became Church Women United. Separation from the National Council of Churches was finalized in 1970 and enabled greater participation by Roman Catholic, Orthodox, and other Christian women. In the 1970s CWU developed "The People's Platform for a

Global Society," ten basic issues that shape the movement's agenda for action. In 1986 it adopted as its imperative for the next five years the mobilization of its constituency to address the "pauperization" and "marginalization" of women and children and to deal with the root causes of poverty.

Church Women United's national program includes sponsorship and production of resources for three annual celebration days, World Day of Prayer, May Fellowship Day, and World Community Day; funding of intercontinental grants for missions; and periodic ecumenical assemblies, Christian Causeways, and leadership training workshops. Its two regular periodicals are *The Church Woman*, a quarterly magazine, and *Lead Time*, a bimonthly newsletter.

CWU is open to all women who wish to participate and support its purpose and program. *See also* Feminist Movement; Peace, Education for; Social Justice, Education for; Women's Organizations.

J. Burton

Church Year

The church year, also known as the Christian year or the liturgical year, is the ordered sequence of liturgical feasts and seasons traditionally observed in the Christian church. It is composed of two cycles: a temporal or seasonal cycle, celebrating the great events in the life of Christ, and a sanctoral cycle of fixed holy days commemorating the saints. Within the temporal cycle itself there are two halves, one based upon the date of Easter and the other upon Christmas.

Some see the church year as nothing more than a superb lesson plan for encouraging Christians to model their lives on that of Christ as it is set before them season by season. Yet it is also sacramental, or more properly mystological, allowing worshipers to experience the full sweep of God's plan for the redemption of the world made present and active in the celebration of the festivals; in each festival the entire mystery of redemption is encountered, but each festival offers a different perspective on it.

STRUCTURE

The church year begins on the first Sunday in Advent, the fourth Sunday before Christmas. It celebrates the coming of Christ, both in glory at the end of time and in humility at Bethlehem. The Eastern churches do not observe Advent and begin their year on September 1, the original New Year's Day of Constantinople. They celebrate the two Sundays before Christmas as the Sunday of the Holy Ancestor of Christ and the Sunday

of the Genealogy of Christ, honoring the saints of the Old Testament.

Christmas, the celebration of the birth of Jesus Christ, is of course the fixed date December 25. The Christmas season lasts twelve days and includes a number of traditional holy days. January 1 is observed in many churches as a major festival, although there is no agreement as to what is celebrated. Roman Catholics keep it as the Solemnity of Mary, Mother of God; Episcopalians and Lutherans, as the Holy Name of Jesus; and others as the Circumcision of Christ.

Epiphany, January 6, concludes "the twelve days of Christmas" and celebrates the visit of the Magi, or Wise Men. The Eastern churches celebrate the baptism of Christ on Epiphany, although that is now celebrated on the Sunday following by Roman Catholics and most other Christians.

The season after Epiphany is called "ordinary time" by Roman Catholics. It is sometimes seen as celebrating the many manifestations of Christ: to the Magi, at the baptism, in the changing of water into wine at the wedding at Cana, and in other mighty acts. Lutherans, Episcopalians, and those who follow the Common Lectionary keep the Transfiguration of Christ on the last Sunday after Epiphany and before Ash Wednesday.

Lent is a penitential season of forty days before Easter. In the Western churches it usually begins on Ash Wednesday, the fortieth weekday before Easter. It is a season of fasting and preparation for the joy of Easter, particularly for the preparation of catechumens for baptism at the Easter Vigil. The forty days are derived from the fast of Jesus in the wilderness after his baptism (Matt. 4:1–11). Until the reforms of the church year made in the middle of this century, the three Sundays before Lent, called Septuagesima, Sexagesima, and Quinquagesima, constituted a season of Pre-Lent. This has now been generally abolished. The last week in Lent is called Holy Week. It begins with Palm Sunday, which commemorates Jesus' triumphal entry into Jerusalem, and includes Maundy Thursday (called Holy Thursday by Roman Catholics), commemorating the Last Supper, Good Friday, commemorating the crucifixion, and Holy Saturday. Its climax is the celebration of the resurrection of Christ on Easter.

Easter is traditionally observed on the Sunday following the first full moon of spring, although differences in calendars and computations have frequently caused Eastern and Western Christians to observe different dates.

Easter is the principal festival of the church year and celebrates the resurrection of Christ. It inaugurates a festal season of fifty days originally called the Pentecost but known for many centuries now as Eastertide. It celebrates Jesus Christ's passing over from death to life, his triumph, and the participation of Christians in it. Its distinctive mark is the frequent singing or saying of "Alleluia." Ascension Day is the fortieth day after Easter (Acts 1:3), and Pentecost, or Whitsunday, is the fiftieth.

Pentecost, the Old Testament Feast of Weeks, is a week of weeks (forty-nine days) following Easter. The name "Pentecost" means fiftieth. Whitsunday, the English name for the day, is White Sunday. On this day the newly baptized were present in church in their white baptismal robes. Pentecost is the conclusion of Eastertide and the festival of the Holy Spirit, whose descent upon the apostles is described as taking place on this day (Acts 2:1–4).

The season after Pentecost was called the Trinity season in some churches, numbering the Sundays from Trinity Sunday, the first Sunday after Pentecost. The Roman Catholic church today calls this period "ordinary time," like the season after Epiphany. It lasts until the beginning of Advent. It is the season of Christian history, the time between the descent of the Holy Spirit, celebrated on Pentecost, and the second coming of Christ at the end of time, celebrated in Advent. The last Sunday after Pentecost and before Advent is observed in many churches as the Feast of Christ the King and forms a bridge to the celebration of Christ's coming in glory in Advent.

Other festivals of Christ celebrated on fixed dates include Presentation (or Purification), popularly called Candlemas from the medieval custom of blessing candles on that day, on February 2; Annunciation (once popularly called Lady Day in honor of Mary) on March 25; and Transfiguration on August 6.

The most widely observed festival of the sanctoral cycle is All Saints on November 1. Other well-known festivals of the saints include: Saint John the Baptist (June 24), Saint Peter and Saint Paul (June 29), Saint Mary the Virgin, also called the Dormition and the Assumption (August 15), and Saint Michael and All Angels, popularly called Michaelmas (September 29).

The church year is made complex by the interaction of the two halves as the date of Easter varies from March 22 to April 25, lengthening and shortening the seasons after Epiphany and Pentecost, and as it is overlaid by the festivals occurring on fixed dates. Rules called Tables of Precedence have been established to determine what to do when a conflict occurs between a festival falling on a fixed date and one determined by the date of Easter; e.g., when Annunciation might fall on Good Friday.

HISTORY

The church year does not belong to the earliest stratum of Christian history. Easter and Pentecost derive from the Jewish festivals of Passover and Pentecost (Shavuot), but they were probably not generally observed until the second century. The celebration of Easter undoubtedly arose as a Christian response to the celebration of Passover

by Jews. The Day of Preparation was observed as a solemn fast commemorating the crucifixion (John 19:31), with the celebration of the Eucharist after sundown proclaiming the Lord's death, resurrection, and triumph. The Council of Nicaea (A.D. 325) fixed the date as the Sunday following the first full moon of spring.

Lent began to be observed sometime before the Council of Nicaea (its documents assume everyone knows what it is). Although there is universal agreement that Lent is forty days in length, churches have counted the days differently at various times. Pre-Lent, extending the season back an additional two and a half weeks, was kept for many centuries by most churches as a remnant of an earlier method of counting the days.

Holy Week developed in Jerusalem in the fourth century in response to the influx of pilgrims to the holy places the week before Easter and was exported by the pilgrims to their own churches.

Christmas apparently began in Rome at the beginning of the fourth century and spread from there throughout the church. The date was that of the birthday of the Unconquered Sun on the Roman calendar, and it was observed by Christians as the birthday of the true Sun of Righteousness. Epiphany, however, was an Eastern celebration believed to have originated in Egypt at the end of the second century and then been adopted universally. Its original content was both the incarnation and the baptism of Christ.

Advent originated in Spain and Gaul (France) in the fifth century as a preparation for Epiphany and was once known as Saint Martin's Lent. It is not celebrated by Eastern Christians, and American Protestants often conflate its observance with the Christmas season, considered as beginning on Thanksgiving Day.

The deaths of the martyrs in the great persecutions of the third century provided the impetus for the inclusion of the "birthday in eternity" of saints in the calendar. Polycarp of Smyrna, who was martyred about A.D. 155, is the first saint we know to have been so commemorated. Local martyrs were the first saint's days; New Testament saints were later additions.

FOR FURTHER REFERENCE

Adam, Adolf. *The Liturgical Year.* New York: Pueblo, 1981.

McArthur, A. Allen. *The Evolution of the Church Year.* London: SCM, 1953.

Porter, H. Boone. *Keeping the Church Year.* New York: Seabury, 1977.

L. L. Mitchell

Cinema

Traditionally, cinema has been divided into three functions—production, distribution, and exhibition. In addition, there has been a critical function, the evaluation of cinema and its suitability for society. In each of these four functions, the religious community has been active.

CRITICISM

The first concern about film was its influence on the populace. In the early twentieth century, clergy expressed dismay over the "movies" because of their influence on the working class, the segment of society most supportive of the fledgling industry. By 1920 there were several censor boards, many of them dominated by Protestant laypeople and supported by the major mainline Protestant denominations. Up until the 1950s, most fundamentalist churches banned watching movies, but following the wide dissemination of movies by television most of them quietly dropped their opposition.

Roman Catholics started by cooperating with the movie industry and participated significantly in developing the Motion Picture Production Code, the council the studios developed to police the industry. The Production Code's failure to improve motion pictures led to the Legion of Decency, which rated each film and exerted pressure at the box office through the Catholic press and churches.

After the failure of the Production Code in the early 1950s, there was a period of critical reevaluation in the Christian community, prompted in part by the religious and biblical spectaculars (*The Robe*, *The Ten Commandments*). Leading Protestants associated with the National Council of the Churches of Christ (NCCC) and Catholics participated in developing the rating system (G, PG, R, X), which classified each film according to language, nudity, and acceptability to community mores.

PRODUCTION

From the beginning, movies have tried to interpret the religious experience. One of the first films ever made was a recording of the Passion play in 1897, and there has been a steady stream of films about the Old Testament, Christ, the disciples, the clergy, and the religious life ever since.

Following World War II, many churches obtained projectors, and production companies began to make films available in 16mm format. Most of these films were provided by industry and athletic teams for use during church family nights and with men's and women's groups, but soon the religious community began to produce films.

Jewish affiliated groups produced quasi-secular moral tales. Some of the major Protestant denominations produced training programs and historical films (*Luther*, *John Wesley*) or small-scale biblical tales (*Day of Triumph*, *Gospel Road*). Later, some entrepreneurs for the more

conservative Protestant groups began producing films for the faithful.

Roman Catholics have had a variety of responses, with religious orders producing films and subsidiaries making others and distributing them through churches and secular organizations. Internationally, the Catholic church has kept offices of communication supporting indigenous filmmaking in the Third World through technical assistance and mission personnel.

DISTRIBUTION

Overall, religious films are distributed through a wide system of libraries ranging from Christian bookstores (e.g., Moody bookstores for evangelicals) to Catholic orders (Order of St. Paul) and media libraries by Protestant denominations. The collections tend to be diverse, derived in part from their function of serving their clientele. This means that many films from secular producers find their way into the libraries, as well as films from other denominations. They might include Bible study, interpersonal relations, spirituality materials, task-oriented training functions (e.g., membership recruitment), seasonal interpretations, as well as story programs and social issues. Jewish social materials have often been distributed by ancillary organizations like B'nai Brith.

Worldwide, Roman Catholics have made materials available to the national film offices, while in some areas of northern Europe the church participates in national cinema by helping promote secular films made in that country. In the 1960s the NCCC made available an audiovisual guide, and in the 1980s several groups pooled their resources to form a library called Ecufilm.

EXHIBITION

The exhibition of these films has been done primarily for various congregational study and fellowship groups and for task-oriented organizations within the churches.

In the 1950s, however, with the large biblical and religious spectaculars, an audience of people developed who wanted to discuss what they went to see. This led to an interest in the more liberal Protestant and Catholic churches in discussing the secular implications of the films that came to the movie theaters. In the early 1960s, the Faith and Life community at the University of Texas began using the arts to teach theology. Some of their results are reflected in William Jones's book *Sunday Night at the Movies*. Jones developed a program with Films, Inc. (a large 16mm distributor) to rent feature films and accompanying discussion guides to churches.

Soon other authors in both Roman Catholicism and mainline Protestantism were exploring other dimensions of how faith and life met. Christian film societies were begun, denominational offices of communications concerned with interpreting films were developed, and critical reviews in national denominational magazines were printed with the goal of helping faithful viewers do their own interpretation. Other programs were developed for nonfeature fictional films and documentaries, and an independent magazine, *Mass Media Ministries*, offered short reviews of these films for the Christian community. In the mid-1970s and early 1980s, most of these efforts went out of existence, but a large number of religious people continue to use the methods developed in this earlier period.

PRESENT STATUS

Churches remain interested in feature films, but the use of videotape equipment increases the possibilities for production, distribution, and exhibition. Much of what is available in 16mm film format is being simultaneously produced on videocassette. This allows a wider and less expensive distribution of film. At the same time, many churches are getting together in small groups to rent and watch feature films and then discuss them.

Much of the concern in the churches these days remains with social control of films and media. The mainline Protestant bodies have joined with conservative Christians and feminists to attempt to suppress the growing pornographic market. The NCCC completed a study on media violence, an area of concern to member denominations. There is increasing use of media to examine the social problems of Third World liberation, alcohol and drug abuse, and sexual mores particularly among teenagers. At the same time, personal stories of faith, aids in biblical study, and recordings of famous Christian thinkers have found their way to film and video.

Academically, the two main polarities in feature films center around artistic interpretation and popular culture studies. Whether films are primarily the vision of an artist and how to interpret that vision finds its corollary in the "director as author" school of secular criticism. There are a variety of popular culture approaches, which tend to look for formulas and conventional patterns to interpret what concerns audiences are expressing through their support of films. There is also an attempt to find and look at thematic material (e.g., success, apocalypticism) that the films analyze. Whatever the academics find, one suspects that it will soon make its way into the churches, where the interest remains as strong as ever. *See also* Media; Television; Visual Methods.

FOR FURTHER REFERENCE

Butler, Ivan. *Religion in the Cinema.* New York: Barnes, 1969.

G. E. Forshey

Class Meeting

A small, weekly gathering in early Methodism that served to cultivate spirituality, discipline, and stewardship was called a class meeting.

In eighteenth-century England, John Wesley and his colleagues brought a religious awakening to an established church mired in formalism and a society suffering a decline in morality and a rise in the twin evils of poverty and ignorance. After his own renewal, this Anglican priest preached to the needy and evangelized sinners, bringing new Christians into what he called societies.

Wesleyan societies were divided into small gatherings, or class meetings, quite different from the so-called band meeting. Class meetings included persons in search of salvation whose faithfulness in the class meeting determined their continuing in the overall society. Band meetings, segregated by gender, were composed of saved souls who sought Christian perfection. In all of this, one could mark Wesley's evangelistic fervor and administrative genius.

Class meetings emerged spontaneously in 1742 when individuals who had requested prayer and counsel found Wesley's answer in a supervised weekly gathering. Ten or twelve persons would assemble with a class leader in a private residence. Meetings fostered worship, instruction, fellowship, and moral discipline—this last being inherent in Wesley's disposition. The order of service often included singing, prayer, scripture, and a set topic, with counsel or exhortation from the leader, who regularly inquired into the spiritual life of the members. With such a dynamic, the class meeting produced churchly vitality and Christian vigor.

Infrequently, the group had a class steward, but it always functioned under a class leader who was appointed by the preacher. Having a measure of maturity and religious experience, the leader, who was a layman, provided spiritual care within and without the class meeting, often visiting the sick and delinquent. The leader possessed the ability to teach, advise, and discipline, elements that would constitute part of the connectional system of the future Methodist church.

Methodism came to the American colonies as a religious society, not as a church. The deployment of lay preachers and revivalism augmented its spread until it became a denomination in 1784. Circuit riders followed the movement of the frontier and gathered people into classes. Class leaders tended to oversee the work in the circuit rider's absence. Employing the careful planning and organization Methodists were known for, Bishop Francis Asbury helped form the denomination in America, and in both America and England, the importance of the class meeting gradually declined, although it consistently contributed to church life and maturity. Today, the only vestige remaining is the position of lay leader. But a parallel to the class meeting might be found today in groups that gather for mutual confession, intercession, and strengthening.

W. J. Schmidt

Classroom Management

See Discipline.

Clement of Alexandria

Clement of Alexandria (ca. A.D. 150?–215), a convert to and apologist for Christianity, was born in the latter half of the second century, probably in Athens. Learned in Greek philosophy, Clement gained a reputation as a teacher in Alexandria (Egypt), but modern scholars doubt that he headed the catechetical school there and that Origen was his disciple. His writings include the *Protrepticus*, an apologia for Christianity; the *Paedagogus*, a work on Christian ethics that portrays Christ as the supreme teacher; and the *Stromata*, the most important of his writings, which opposes "false *gnosis*" ("false knowledge") with the truth of Christian *gnosis*. Clement took a generally positive attitude toward Greek philosophy; for him knowledge and contemplation were the goals of the spiritual life. He exercised a lasting influence on Greco-Christian spirituality by affirming the essential goodness of the body, marriage, and cultural values. Clement fled Alexandria for Cappadocia during the persecution of Septimius Severus (202–203) and died there

about A.D. 215. *See also* History of Christian Education.

B. L. Marthaler

Clergy as Educators

The clergy's role in the church's educational ministry has its impetus in the New Testament. Jesus set the example. The writer of Matthew in the preface to the Sermon on the Mount observes that Jesus sat among the people and began teaching (5:1–2). The people acknowledged the authority of his teaching by calling him rabbi. His teachings were gathered into books that continue to instruct and inform people today.

Paul extended the example. He was known as both prophet and teacher. His visits to the new and struggling churches around the Mediterranean were marked by times of teaching. His Letters are filled with advice and instruction. Paul, moreover, identifies teaching as one of the gifts of the Spirit crucial to the work of building up the body of Christ (Eph. 4:11–12).

By the Middle Ages the role of clergy included several distinctive educational responsibilities. In the Mass the priest reenacted and dramatized the story of Calvary. In the sacrament of penance the priest examined the faith and morals of parishioners. The priest gathered people into the unfolding drama of salvation through the rituals of the church year. In *The Pastoral Rule*, Gregory the Great (pope 590–604) counseled clergy to adapt the word of God to the condition of the people through their preaching.

During the Reformation the educational role of clergy centered on the exposition of Scripture and doctrine. The primary activity of Reform-minded clergy was preaching, but the primary mode of preaching was teaching. John Calvin, for example, compared the church to a school and all Reformers agreed that the road to the Christian life involved continuing instruction in the word of God. Their concern for correct doctrine is evident in the involvement of Lutheran clergy in the instruction of the young prior to their first Communion, in Martin Bucer's proposal that young people could join small fellowships of Christians in the churches of Strasbourg only after a period of instruction, and in the regular supervision by clergy of the catechism.

It is during the nineteenth century that the educational role of clergy becomes increasingly diffuse. For Protestants the Sunday school and related programs became the primary agencies for the church's education. It was a lay movement and clergy were relegated primarily to a supporting or supervisory role. Although many prominent clergy—including Lyman Beecher, Stephen Tyng, and Henry Ward Beecher—actively promoted and sometimes participated in the Sunday school, others ignored and even opposed the new institution.

A new pattern was emerging. Religious education was increasingly seen as a lay responsibility; preaching, pastoral care, and administration were clergy responsibilities. By the time of his study of Protestant clergy during the 1950s, Samuel Blizzard discovered that they ranked teaching as the fourth most important of pastoral functions and that they spent no more than 5 percent of their professional time in activities related to teaching. Perhaps it is not surprising that James Smart would decry the lack of clergy involvement in educational ministries in his book *The Rebirth of Ministry* (1960). Although numerous denominations have developed program emphases to encourage clergy participation in church education, Blizzard's findings continue to be relevant.

Among Roman Catholics many of the most significant innovations and movements of the nineteenth century were instigated by clergy. Bishops and parish priests attempted to broaden the base of the emerging public schools to encompass Catholic values. When that effort failed, they led the movement to establish weekday schools in every parish. Bishops approved a new catechism for use in American churches in 1884. Clergy gave overall supervision to this burgeoning educational enterprise in the parish. The actual administration and teaching in parish religious education programs, however, was initially assumed by religious societies and more recently by laity. The active educational role of clergy became identified with the sacramental life of the parish. This distinction continues to be maintained in parish programs of catechesis usually supervised by clergy and of religious education usually administered by professionally trained educators.

REPRESENTING TEACHINGS

Over the centuries clergy have assumed responsibility for education in the church in at least three ways. In the first, clergy represent the teaching of the church. George Herbert, writing in *A Priest to the Temple: Or the Country Parson* in 1630, reflects this view when he observes that "A Pastor is the Deputy of Christ for the reducing of Man to the Obedience of God." Through the pastoral office clergy serve as agents of Christ's ministry and sacrifice into the present lived moment. That office establishes the framework and sanctions the content of both the formal teaching and the processes of socialization in a congregation or parish. It may lead clergy to sponsor or advocate specific educational programs as well as to limit or censor others. They may teach classes. Their role as educators, however, is located not so much in these educational activities as in the symbolic power and content of their office in mediating God's grace and truth. It is a sacramental view of education.

PRESENTING TEACHINGS

In the second way, clergy educate through deliberate acts of teaching in a wide variety of pastoral, liturgical, administrative, and educational settings. It is this view of clergy engaged in the direct instruction of laity and the explicit interpretation of the doctrines and traditions of the church for contemporary living that the Protestant Reformers espoused. This view of the educational role of clergy is central to the work of James Smart, Wesner Fallaw, G. Stanley Glen, and others since World War II who have sought to recover the Reformation commitment to the interdependence of preaching and teaching. Fallaw, for example, called for pastor-educators who would regularly take their place as teachers of children, youth, and adults. Smart and Glen envisioned clergy reclaiming the responsibility for introducing laity to the exegetical and interpretive skills basic to biblical and theological study. A more recent pattern of clergy teaching involves reclaiming the priestly role of instructing persons for participation in the liturgical and sacramental life of the church. The concern underlying this trend is to prepare people for baptism, Communion, confirmation, marriage, or some specific liturgical event. In whatever way clergy emphasize their role as teachers, they reveal their commitment to the collective historical character of the church. They self-consciously transmit the faith received from previous generations and interpret it for contemporary circumstances.

ADMINISTRATION

A third approach to the role of clergy in the church's education is also the most recent. It involves clergy in the administrative tasks of planning, supervising, and evaluating a congregational or parish education program. It seeks to provide ways to respond to the learning interests and needs of people of all ages. It emphasizes the responsibility of clergy in identifying and exploring with laity the theological and ethical issues to be found in committee and governing board decisions. It reinforces the role of clergy as public advocates of the church's educational ministry. This approach reflects the increasing administrative character of the work of clergy while affirming at the same time the responsibility of clergy for the overall supervision of the quality of religious education in the parish or congregation. It is a managerial approach to the role of clergy as educators.

All three perspectives on the role of clergy in congregational or parish education have historical validity. The general lack of involvement of clergy in contemporary church education, however, indicates the increasing variety of demands on clergy time and commitments and highlights a dilemma for the future of the church. Both the maintenance and vitality of any community—including that of congregation or denomination—

are dependent upon the effectiveness of its education. The extension of congregational life into the future requires handing on traditions and skills inherited from the past and instruction in its life-style and values. The relevance of congregational life calls for reinterpreting that which has been received from the past for present circumstances and events. Tradition, training, and situation point to the value of clergy participation in these tasks. It is not yet clear, however, what general direction clergy will take in reclaiming in any significant way the role of educator in the parish or congregation. *See also* Calvin, John; History of Christian Education; Luther, Martin; Private Religious Schools; Private Schools and Religion; Smart, James D.

C. R. Foster

Clowning

The word "clown" is derived from the word "clod," meaning "lowly" or "down to earth." A clown is a servant willing to do even the most menial tasks for others. Clown ministry in church or synagogue seeks to reflect this quality of servanthood.

Throughout history clowns have served as those who help persons not take themselves so seriously, the ones who bring the balance of humor to life. The uniqueness of clown ministry is that it values every person while helping people see themselves more clearly. While circus clowns sometimes play tricks on unsuspecting members of their audience, clowns in ministry seek to bring joy to persons they meet. The clown minister witnesses to God's grace through unconditional love; these clowns are friend to everyone. In worship, clowns tell the story of faith as though it were seen through the eyes of a child; they bring wonder and feeling into worship through their interaction with participants and they open new avenues of understanding the faith story. Life is relished as joyful, a gift to be celebrated.

Clown ministry can involve persons of all ages in celebration of the meaning of life, but it requires careful preparation. The elements of clown ministry are content, clown character, and reverence for life.

The story is the *content* of clown ministry. The parables are one good source for the story. They are particularly appropriate for clowning because of the "surprise" in them. The process of preparing the clown skit starts when a class hears the parable from several versions of the Bible and talks about what it means.

Research how the parable was understood by the people Jesus addressed. The reason the parable was a surprise to them provides a place to begin with the clown skit. Talk about how persons in the parable felt and how they would act. Divide the story into parts and plan how to act them out. The purpose is to help those who see the skit become aware of new meanings.

It is possible to involve persons of all ages in clown ministry. Understanding the nature of clowning as ministry is an important foundation for a *clown character*. In addition, future clowns need to have some knowledge of themselves, their personality, and their talents. Makeup, costumes, and props along with special skills like music, juggling, tumbling, mime, puppetry, and dance can be used. Ways to involve the audience so that they feel valued and happy should also be considered.

The clown as servant brings God's love to others. The unique quality of servant clowning is *reverence for life.* Clown ministry takes place in worship, in nursing homes and hospitals, in youth shelters, on college campuses, in counseling settings, and with the homeless. One of the ways value for life is expressed is by planning for the special needs of the audience for clown ministry.

People who do clowning, puppetry, mime, tumbling, and music are good resources. For written and audiovisual resources about the "how-to" of clowning and mime as ministry, consult *Contemporary Drama Resources* catalog (Contemporary Drama, Box 7710-S4, Colorado Springs, CO 80933). The movies *Mark of a Clown* (Will Vinton, 1977) and *A Clown Is Born* (Faith and Fantasy Inc., 1979) will also help develop an understanding of clown ministry. *See also* Dramatization.

S. H. Matthaei

Coe, George Albert ━━━━━━━━

George Albert Coe (1862–1951), may have been the most influential theorist in religious education in the first half of the twentieth century. His teaching at Union Theological Seminary (New York) and Columbia Teachers College reached many leaders. His books, especially *A Social Theory of Religious Education* (1917), formulated a new way of thinking similar to John Dewey's. Coe was a significant influence in the Religious Education Association from its founding in 1903. He saw religion as a normal process of adjustment by which human beings could be remade so as to bring in a new world. He provided a useful psychology for making religious education effective and made explicit the social implications of the gospel. Always he insisted that teaching have specific purposes, from which will come a democracy of God on earth. Christian education, for him, was a critical reconstruction of personal relations based on Jesus' insight that persons are of infinite worth, with God as the valuer of persons. *See also* Dewey, John; Education, Theories of; History of

Christian Education; Religious Education Association; Social Gospel.

R. C. Miller

Cognitive Development

Cognitive development is the lifelong process by which people appropriate knowledge through thinking, discussing, and expressing ideas. The traditional resource in this area is the work of Swiss psychologist Jean Piaget (1896–1980).

STAGES OF DEVELOPMENT

Piaget believed that cognitive development was composed of several stages that are understood to be processes in nature as well as progressive in movement. The stages include the sensorimotor, from birth to age two, in which the child develops the ability to walk, focus the eyes, and relate to people. The preoperational stage lasts from age two to seven. The child learns through the activities of play, through imitation, imagination, and interaction, and responses are intuitive and arational; learning is by doing. During the concrete operational stage, from seven to eleven, the child can perform logical functions in relation to concrete things; through the basic skills of reading, writing, and mathematics information in many areas can be gathered and used. The formal operational stage begins around the age of twelve and continues throughout life. At this point, brain development makes it possible for a person to think abstractly and therefore to reason.

Religious educators who teach children will immediately sense the importance for them of Piaget's work while teachers of youth and adults may tend to avoid these learnings, taking it for granted that if a stage was supposedly reached at the age of twelve, they need not be concerned further. Such a decision is misguided. Many people never progress to the formal operational stage in their religious thinking; some people remain religiously in the preoperational stage. They are content simply to be engaged in the forms of religion such as attending worship regularly. Some people remain at the concrete operational stage. They view religion only in concrete terms and do not explore the meanings of faith. For them it is enough to say "I believe" without exploring either the roots or meanings of belief. Formal operational development is based upon the learner's ability for abstract thinking and many people have never been challenged to work in that area with reference to their religious education. Neither in classes nor in youth groups do they read and discuss theological understandings about God or the purpose of life. They do not study the Bible seriously. A large number of adults also come into the life of the religious community without having had formal religious education classes. And for this reason as well they may be, religiously, in a concrete operational stage.

THE PROCESS OF ADAPTATION

Perhaps the most significant insight from Piaget for all teachers has to do with adaptation, a name given by Piaget to the process whereby both assimilation and accommodation are used to deal with new learnings. In simple terms, this has to do with the ability of a person both to incorporate and to adapt to new learning. In this way people can learn to modify their beliefs or behavior and to recognize the consonance or dissonance between them. Many people know a great deal about faith, but the challenge is to discover a process by which change can occur in living because of what an individual believes.

One of the methods used to help children adapt is that of the learning center, because this provides opportunities for experiencing in addition to being shown or told about something. Teachers of youth and adults might consider the learning center as well. It has been found helpful for confirmation classes; students can learn at an individual rate and come to the teacher personally as needed. It has also been used as an effective form of intergenerational learning. Children and adults learn comfortably together when the theme is of interest to both.

In the early years of life, cognitive development is experienced through the senses. As the child grows, preconceptual images and internal representations give way to the use of filters formed from the child's concrete understanding of life to interpret incoming data. At this point, children often display skill at committing to memory much "cognitive" material, but to identify this ability alone as "cognitive development" is erroneous. Memorization, skill at gathering data, and an appreciation of logical relationships between concrete things are examples of functions newly appropriate to the concrete operational level, but they are not a good measure of "cognitive development" itself. As we have previously stressed, cognitive development hinges on the process of adaptation. The early adolescent years signal the arrival of abstract reasoning; knowledge now may take on the shape of concepts or ideas.

In conversations with children at different ages, psychologist David Elkind asked how they thought about God. The five year old replied, "God is in heaven." The eight year old said, "God is all around." The eleven year old smiled somewhat uncomfortably and said, "I'm not sure," realizing that she might have been expected to give a more positive answer. These responses indicate that learning does not result solely from material taught by the family or in religious education classes. There is a developmental factor as children grow from the ability to think concretely into abstract thinking.

Asked about prayer, the five year old did not have any answers as to how prayers reached God. The eight year old thought a sound wave might be the vehicle (a concrete understanding). The eleven year old, no longer satisfied by that kind of ingenious answer, replied again that she really didn't know. On the edge of abstract operational thinking, she would not make a concrete reply but could not make a theological or philosophical one. It would be a few years before she could put together a synthesis. In the process she would become a believer, a nonbeliever, or still be questing. This process can continue throughout life as experiences bring changes in the human response to religious questions.

THE ROLE OF RELIGIOUS EDUCATION

This understanding of the process of cognitive development has led to differing conclusions regarding the proper role of religious education. Some people have concluded that there is no need to be concerned about apparent misunderstandings of theological and biblical questions in children. They will "outgrow" these in the process of cognitive development. They can be told the "correct" answer and can memorize it, but they probably will not understand it fully until their own thought processes and experiences along with the example and teaching of adults have made them ready. They can be encouraged to think and explore. They can ask or be asked "why" and "how" questions that assure them it is possible to grow and learn in religious terms.

This conclusion differs from that of an earlier researcher in the field, Ronald Goldman, whose work with children in England (1959) showing similar results led him to advise that young children should not study biblical or theological material with symbolic meaning that they would misinterpret and need to unlearn. Better to concentrate on relationships to God and other people and deal with abstract materials after the age of eleven. This represents a particular view of theology and Bible as well as a psychological approach.

While the concerns and issues stemming from cognitive development theory are many, our primary focus in this entry is on the struggle of religious educators to discern and teach what people need to "know" so that their lifestyles can demonstrate a body of information critical to the propagation of their faith. Obviously this will differ from group to group, but there are some common categories of information shared by many, if not all, religious groups. And the information in these categories generally is the heart of religious instruction.

The first is information regarding a Higher Power (God in Christianity and Judaism) that re-flects the ultimate in life. Second may be information about a personal representative of that Higher Power (Jesus Christ in Christianity) come to share the good news of the Higher Power's creative and redemptive power or a spiritual representative (in Christianity the Holy Spirit) that is an ever-present source of help and guidance.

A third category of information concerns a representative body (the congregation) of those who share common beliefs and find strength and faith in coming together and fulfillment in some form of acting out in the world. The fourth is the body of sacred writings or Scriptures of the faith. A fifth is information about the self, the individual on earth as well as in the afterlife. And finally there is information about others outside the faith.

This information has traditionally been passed on by means of the "Big Jug, Little Mug" teaching approach, wherein teachers simply transmit facts and data to students, requiring primarily that the students memorize the information transmitted. This requires teaching sessions to be arranged so as to provide the maximum opportunity for the presenting of information and the regurgitation of that information back to the teacher by the learners. To move beyond this method may require the application of focused knowledge to the larger scene, and the resulting knowledge may demand attention and action. To move from mere accumulation of data to evaluation based on faith in action represents a challenge to religious educators and institutions.

ISSUES AND LIMITATIONS

Although religious education recognizes the vital importance of cognitive development, its limitations must also be acknowledged. It is easy to work under the assumption that lessons are being taught instead of recognizing that people are being taught. The pressure may be there, particularly if adequate preparation time is not allowed, to just give the facts. When working with adults, the class itself may pressure the leader to just give facts because they prefer not to be bothered by the application of their knowledge to the world around them.

Then, too, to some extent there is an ability factor; some people are more comfortable thinking abstractly than others, particularly in the area of religion where, in some traditions, questioning and differing from an accepted norm are not encouraged. Sometimes the cultural content of a community, including all forms of education, has not encouraged abstract thinking. The work some people do and for which they are trained, the interests and concerns of their community are concrete. Others live and work in communities where abstract thinking is needed and valued. Their choices in reading, television, discussion, and education will have a component of idea-oriented and controversial material.

These same preferences will be reflected in religious education programs for adults. Some groups will want courses on the content of the Bible and its life application, while others will want in addition to explore critical questions of composition and meaning. Some will want to learn about the content of faith, others to ask why they so believe. Some will be concerned primarily about personal religious living; others envision more societal responsibility. Neither is *the* way: both are components in the religious life.

What one "knows" about faith as a child will reflect the understanding gleaned from family, media, and experiential learning opportunities in various environments. What one "knows" about faith as an adolescent will reflect the times being experienced during the process of maturation. What one "knows" about faith as an adult will interact with experiences from all of life.

The task of the religious educator is to manage cognitive conflict in such a way that growth and change are experienced in the belief and behavior of individuals as well as the institution within which one functions. *See also* Adolescence; Affective Development; Child Development; Childhood Education; Cognitive Dissonance; Education, Theories of; Faith Development; Learning Center; Learning Theory; Middle Childhood; Piaget, Jean; Reasoning; Taxonomy.

FOR FURTHER REFERENCE

Elkind, David. *The Child's Reality.* Hilldale, NJ: Lawrence Earlbaum, 1978.
Goldman, Ronald. *Religious Thinking from Childhood to Adolescence.* London: Routledge and Kegan Paul, 1964.

M. F. Hatch

Cognitive Dissonance

Cognitive dissonance, a term introduced in 1957 by Leon Festinger, refers to the psychological conflict that arises when one's beliefs or ideas clash with each other or with one's behavior. The subject reduces the dissonance by changing either the cognition or the behavior. An example pertaining to religious education might be when a student from a fundamentalist background enrolls in a religious education course at college. The student's beliefs and behavior are challenged by a pluralistic society. The student must change either behavior or beliefs in order to reduce cognitive dissonance.

Although the term is a useful one, it has been superseded in psychology by Jean Piaget's more general term "adaptation." One rarely hears of cognitive dissonance today. Close approximations are found in Lawrence Kolhberg's moral education, in James Loder's "transformations," and in Craig Dykstra's "conversions," to mention but a few reinterpretations of Festinger's original theory. *See also* Attitude Formation; Behavior; Moral Development.

L. W. Barber

Colleges and Universities, Church-related

Church-related colleges and universities have historically played a significant role in the education of leadership for church and society and continue to do so today.

HISTORY

The oldest institution for higher learning is Al Azhar, the Islamic college founded at Cairo in 970. The first European institution, the Sorbonne in Paris, established in 1257, received recognition from the pope in 1259. Scholars not accepted at the Sorbonne made their way to England to establish Oxford University, which was recognized by the pope in 1214. Cambridge University was established by King John in 1209 and Peterhouse, its first college, in 1284. The university was recognized by the pope in 1318.

The first university in the Western hemisphere was the University of Mexico, 1551. In Canada, the first institution for higher education was the Seminaire de Quebec, 1663. Kings College, Nova Scotia, followed in 1789. Usually the earliest foundations were for the education of clergy.

Because education has been a major form of outreach in the Christian missionary enterprise, churches have established colleges in every mission land and many of these still flourish. In China, they have now become state institutions; for example, Yenching University is today Beijing University.

In the United States from the founding of Harvard College in 1636 until well into the nineteenth century, the churches and pious clergy and laity established schools, colleges, and seminaries in the desire to provide an educated and faithful leadership for church and society. With the establishment of the land-grant colleges and the rise of the modern university in the latter half of the nineteenth century, the church-related colleges no longer dominated the scene. But, broadening the traditional liberal arts curriculum to include expanded study in the sciences, they persisted in the task they had begun. Additionally, established church-related colleges and new ones founded by individual Christians, churches, and both denominational and interdenominational mission societies provided new leadership in this era as pioneers in the education of women, newly emancipated black Americans, and the increasing waves of immigrants from Europe.

During the early years of the twentieth century, the mainline white and historically black Protestant denominations founded few colleges, concentrating their energies instead on strengthening existing institutions and establishing campus ministries at public institutions of higher education. Roman Catholic religious orders and evangelical churches, however, were actively engaged in founding new institutions in this period, adding significantly to the diversity of church-related higher education that exists today.

As a result of these endeavors, there are in the United States approximately six hundred church-related colleges and universities and about a hundred independent Christian colleges and universities; together they comprise nearly half of the independent colleges and universities and more than one-fifth of all institutions of higher education in this country. Related to more than forty denominations and numerous religious orders, these colleges and universities enroll an estimated 8 to 10 percent of the twelve million women and men now studying in institutions of higher learning in the United States.

IMAGES AND ISSUES

Until quite recently, the popular image of the church-related college was that of a comprehensive liberal arts institution that embodied certain specific characteristics—among them required chapel, required courses in Bible, rules regulating moral behavior, trustees appointed by the church, and a president of the same denomination. While a number of these were (and continue to be) characteristic of some colleges, they were never normative for all. Then too, colleges, like other dynamic institutions, are constantly changing and redefining the ways in which their mission is best expressed. What is deemed to be an essential mark of faithfulness in one time does not necessarily hold for all time. But insofar as the purportedly "ideal" characteristics of the church-related college held sway and comparisons among colleges of various traditions were based upon them, some were surmised to be more church-related than others (thus truer to their mission) and many were judged to be moving along the path toward secularization (thus indifferent or hostile to their heritage and relationship to the church).

During the past decade a serious reappraisal of what it means to be a church-related college has been going on in both church and college circles. First, based upon an increasing understanding of differences in history, denominational polity, and institutional purposes, there is a growing recognition of a legitimate diversity of church-related colleges—both within and among denominations.

Second, the development of nonpejorative, broad-based criteria for assessing the strength of church-related colleges and the vitality of the church-college connection has brought new perspective to the discussion. The understanding, for example, that church-relatedness inheres more in the intentionality with which college and church seek to maintain a continuing relationship and in the measure of congruent understanding about the nature of the institution that exists among constituent groups has brought the focus of attention back to the dynamic interaction of colleges and their supporting churches.

Third, the necessity of defining their mission and market more clearly in a time of growing competition for students and resources has led many church-related colleges both to place greater emphasis on the religious dimensions of their life and to cultivate their partnership with the church with renewed seriousness. In this regard, the question of what each partner (church and college) needs and ought to be able to receive from the other in the way of tangible and moral support is receiving greater attention.

Like other institutions of higher education (especially independent ones), church-related colleges today confront enormous obstacles and challenges in carrying out their mission. Rising costs and decreasing student aid dollars, a declining pool of eighteen year olds (particularly in the Midwest and Northeast), student preoccupation with career preparation and job security, and an increasingly complex and interdependent world for which students must be prepared are all issues with which higher education must contend. While many church-related colleges suffer from inadequate endowments, overextended faculties, and remoteness from major centers of population, as a group they possess many of the strengths essential for responding to the aforementioned challenges.

A growing partnership between the churches and colleges in interpretation and recruitment of students from church constituencies has helped church-related colleges maintain enrollments, in part, in the face of a declining pool of eligible students. A continuing commitment to the educational mission of the church and its historic ties to churches and universities around the world has made it possible for the church-related college to maintain a leadership role in global education and to prepare its students for participation in world society. And its religious commitment (to be a place where the practice and exploration of Christian faith are supported and encouraged and where questions of meaning, purpose, and vocation pervade the curriculum) continues to provide counterpoint and challenge to the fragmentation of knowledge, capitulation to vocationalism, and general narrowness of vision that characterize much of higher education today. *See also* Bible College; Higher Education, Religion in; University.

R. R. *Parsonage*

Colleges, Black

Historically "black colleges" are undergraduate, graduate, and professional institutions of higher education in the United States whose clientele are predominantly black. Except in a few instances, they are found primarily in the South. Established originally to provide educational opportunities for black ex-slaves, they have continued as indispensable providers of collegiate education to black youth who are unable to enter the higher educational mainstream or who wish an educational experience where they are in the majority. In 1986, just over one million of the 58 million total college population was black, and there were 104 predominantly black colleges. Black colleges will probably continue. They offer assistance to black students overcoming cumulative educational deficits or unable financially to attend other institutions.

EVOLUTION OF BLACK COLLEGES

Christian black colleges in America came into existence through black initiative and philanthropic interest. Immediately following the Civil War, benevolent societies, church denominations, including black church denominations, and the U.S. government's Freedman's Bureau worked cooperatively to mitigate the benighted and destitute condition of the ex-slaves. Hundreds of Christian teachers, evangelists, and missionaries, principally from the North, founded and maintained "schools" to offer blacks literacy, health, and civic skills. Many Northerners were eager to demonstrate that blacks had educational potential, while many Southerners were anxious to minimize the presence of the Northerners by teaching Southern blacks themselves. Earlier efforts to help ex-slaves and free blacks in the North included the founding of Lincoln University, Pennsylvania, in 1854 (Presbyterian), the first college in the United States having as its purpose the higher education of blacks, and Wilberforce University, Ohio, in 1856 (African Methodist Episcopal Church), the first college established by black people in America.

The educational mission of the Northern churches in the South began at the conclusion of the Civil War. Baptists founded Shaw University in Raleigh, North Carolina, in 1865 and Morehouse College in Atlanta in 1867, while the Methodist Episcopal church began Walden University in Nashville, Tennessee, in 1865. Atlanta University and Fisk University were both founded in Atlanta in 1865 by the Congregational church, and St. Augustine's College in Raleigh, North Carolina, in 1867 by the Protestant Episcopal church. The Presbyterians were responsible for Barber-Scotia College in Concord and Johnson C. Smith University in Charlotte, North Carolina, in 1867. In three decades, 1865–1895, principally North-

ern churches had organized more than two dozen colleges, including the renowned Howard University in Washington, D.C., in 1866.

SEPARATE BUT EQUAL

Several trends in the years from 1896 to 1954 negatively impacted the higher education of blacks in America. Foremost was the institutionalization of racial segregation under the "separate but equal" principle, which won sanction from the U.S. Supreme Court in the now infamous *Plessy* v. *Ferguson* case (1896). Schools run under this doctrine were grossly unequal in curricular offerings, teacher preparation, buildings, and support.

Another trend was the phasing out of white faculty and administrators and the phasing in of black faculty and administrators in situations where black students were in predominance. This pointed out the need for graduate professional education for black faculty and raised the question of access to this training at still socially exclusive graduate and professional schools. This chain of events resulted in the initiation of a long legal struggle by blacks around the issue of the legality of segregation in the schools.

The role of white churches during this controversy was equivocal. Though they had initiated and were largely sustaining whatever higher education blacks received, especially in the South, they consistently failed to engage the larger issues of segregation in public education and discrimination in their denominational schools and colleges or in the general society.

Mid-century still found American higher education basically segregated by race. In the South, blacks perforce attended black colleges. Significant numbers of blacks did not attend white institutions until the 1950s.

DESEGREGATION

The critical phase of the struggle to obtain equal educational opportunity for blacks in America climaxed in the epochal *Brown* v. *Topeka* decision of the U.S. Supreme Court rendered in May 1954, desegregating public schools across the nation on the basis of the legal finding that separate is inherently unequal.

The impact of this legislation for nonpublic and church institutions was not felt immediately. Later the Supreme Court ruled that the *Brown* v. *Topeka* decision applied to public higher education. Still later, the Civil Rights Act of 1964 directed compliance with the nondiscrimination clause as a basis for qualifying for any federal funding. This condition was a powerful incentive toward the desegregation of church-related higher education.

The desegregation of education in the public sector reintroduces several issues that constitute a challenge to Christian higher education: the continuing existence of colleges with only token integration, the inadequate and unequal funding of church-related colleges, and the lack of significant endowments at practically all black church-related colleges. *See also* Black Experience and Religious Education; Colleges and Universities, Church-Related; Multicultural Education.

G. S. Shockley

Comenius, John Amos

Committed to a student-centered process of life-long learning as the way to universal peace, John Amos Comenius (1592–1670) ranks as a founder of modern education. Born in Moravia (present-day Czechoslovakia), Comenius belonged to the Moravian Brethren, a radical group of reformed Christians who traced their roots to John Huss. Having studied theology at Herborn and Heidelberg, Comenius was eventually ordained and made a Brethren bishop. It was as an educator, however, that he had his lasting influence.

Forced to flee his homeland by the outbreak of the Thirty Years War (1618–1648), in which the Brethren had the protection of neither side, Comenius became a wandering scholar for the rest of his life. He devoted most of his efforts to writing a pansophy, an integration of human knowledge into one all-embracing unity, confident that common knowledge was a key to universal peace.

Comenius developed an inductive process of pedagogy based on student experience and observation, contending that such is the "natural" way to learn. He stated the purpose of *The Great Didactic*, his best known work, as "that the entire youth of both sexes, none being excluded, shall quickly, pleasantly and thoroughly become learned in the sciences, pure in morals, trained in piety" by "an easy and sure method." Correctly labeled a utopian, Comenius nonetheless helped

lay the foundation for the participative and democratic education of the modern era. *See also* History of Christian Education; Moravian Education.

T. H. Groome

Commitment

Commitment is often used as a synonym for faith, trust, pledge, confidence, obedience, or devotion. In religious language, it is a response to a discernment or disclosure. It is more than loyalty to a particular group or church, and ultimately it is a total commitment to the whole universe. The commitment is to God, not to any set of ideals or concepts, and it leads to action. When we give ourselves to God in trust, we are assured a covenant exists that promises preservation from ultimate evil.

Commitment provides a deeper certainty than our beliefs. Our beliefs are always tentative, because our testing of our concepts depends on our interpretation of the data. If our knowledge of God is always tentative, commitment provides a trusting relationship that makes us sure in religion while we remain open to new revelations.

When we make a decision to commit ourselves to an affirmative response to the will and laws of God, we are making a choice in loyalties that may cost many earthly values. It takes courage to make this commitment, and only as we are willing to take all the consequences is it a total commitment. There is risk, because there is freedom from human laws; and there is no assurance of victory, only that we are on the right side. Through such commitment we may discover the best in each situation; without such commitment, we are limited to a prosaic and noncreative existence.

Such commitment leads to confidence, and this can make a difference in any borderline situation. Philosopher William James (1842–1910) describes how such faith can make all the difference when one is faced with a crisis in which confident action can lead to a satisfactory solution.

There are two levels of commitment. In the first, religious persons are committed to the reality of God before they know who or what it is. Thus they give themselves to the reality of the mysterious creativity and not to their ideas about it. This is the element of risk in all acts of faith. Whatever sustains and transforms the life that has been created is worthy of our absolute devotion, for it is the source of all human good.

But this does not justify stupidity, ignorance, or superstition. In a second level of commitment one seeks whatever evidence can come from human experience and intelligence about the nature of deity and the grace that results. This commitment has an openness and tentativeness about it, because all the evidence is never in and human error distorts what we do know. So our commitment is to the transforming power active in our life and only secondarily to the processes by which we seek better understanding. *See also* Belief; Faith; Knowledge, Theories of; Praxis; Social Action.

R. C. Miller

Communes, Religious

Throughout history, in both the East and the West, groups of people have chosen to live apart from the rest of society in a community bound by shared religious beliefs and practices and usually holding property in common. Since these communes were founded on religious principles, the members sought to impart these beliefs to both adults and children.

In one sense the monasteries and convents of the Roman Catholic, Eastern Orthodox, and Anglican churches are religious communes. The members take vows of poverty, chastity, and obedience. But when we think of religious communes we do not usually think of monasteries as groups of men and women, married or celibate, who have chosen to live as communards. Yet we cannot ignore the contributions of the great monasteries of Europe, which preserved the knowledge of Western civilization and operated for many centuries the only schools on the Continent.

In the United States most of the religious communes have been established by Protestants or dissenters from Protestant orthodoxy, although there are some exceptions, such as the Hare Krishna and Catholic Worker communes.

The religious communes in the West with the longest history and the greatest stability have been those of the Hutterites. They date their founding as a movement to 1528 when Jacob Hutter joined a small band of Anabaptists in Tyrol; Hutter was later burned at the stake for heresy. The remnant of Hutterites migrated from Russia, where they had located after Hutter's death, to North America in 1874. Today the estimated 20,000 Hutterites live in about 170 colonies in North America; a third of them are in Minnesota, North and South Dakota, Montana, and Washington and the rest are in Canada.

As with all religious communards, the proper education of children in the faith is a prime concern of the Hutterites and they have many pupils; the average completed Hutterite family includes nine or ten children. The children attend public school until the age of fourteen, but none is encouraged to attend high school or college. The Hutterite children also attend their own German schools in the communes, where they learn the language of the sect and its doctrines. All members become trilingual. They speak English in the public school, High German in church, and a German dialect in the community.

The conviction that formal education should end during the early teens is characteristic of most Protestant communes, as well as of the Amish, who share some customs with the communes but maintain separate family units. An adequate education is seen to be one that gives the child a basic knowledge of the language of the church, the commune, and the outside world; enough arithmetic to solve farm problems; and a grounding in the Bible and church history. More than that would subject the child to the temptations of the secular world.

Beside the Hutterites, other religious communes in the United States survived for many decades but have now vanished. The Rappites, begun in New Harmony, Indiana, in 1814, continued for ninety-eight years; the Zoarites, coming to Ohio in 1817, lasted for eighty-three. The Amana colonies, begun in Iowa in 1855, exist today, but in a much adapted way. A few elderly members are the only survivors of the Shaker communities, which once numbered more than five thousand men, women, and children. Formally known as the United Society of Believers, the Shakers established fifty-eight communes in the Eastern and Midwestern states. Since the sect preached celibacy for all, no children were born in the Shaker communities, but the groups accepted orphans and others as apprentices and taught them Shaker ways.

Followers of John Humphrey Noyes formed a religious commune at Oneida, New York, and practiced what Noyes called a system of "complex marriage" and what critics called free love. The Oneida community was organized in 1847 and dissolved in 1880. Today the name "Oneida" is known mainly for its silverware just as the name "Amana" has come to identify a make of refrigerator rather than the religious band that descended from a seventeenth-century German Pietist sect and settled in parts of Iowa.

In his classic study Charles Nordhoff described the typical school day in an Amana commune. The day began at 7:00 A.M. and the children studied and recited their lessons until 9:30. From then until 11:00 they knit such things as gloves and stockings and then had lunch. Back at 1:00 P.M., the children resumed their lessons until 4:30, when both the boys and the girls returned to their knitting. The curriculum provided elementary instruction in the three Rs along with intensive Bible and catechism drills. Regarding the lack of any continuing education for older youths, one elder explained: "Why should we let our youth study? We need no lawyers or preachers; we have already three doctors. What they need is to live holy lives, to learn God's commandments out of the Bible, to learn submission to his will, and to love him" (*The Communistic Societies of the United States*, 1875).

In modern times the estimated three thousand Hare Krishnas in this country have set up boarding schools for the youngsters born to parents of this Hindu sect. Currently a few communities have been formed intentionally out of an evangelical concern, such as the Sojourners' group in Washington, D.C., under the leadership of Jim Wallis. The periodical for which the group is named is their principal occupation. Their concern is for peace and justice.

Communes that have been built on a religious basis have had longer histories than secular communes, but eventually most of them have dissolved. Beside the Hutterites, the United States is home to more than a dozen smaller religious communes. Taken together these groups have never totaled more than a small fraction of 1 percent of the religiously oriented population of the country. *See also* Religious Orders.

W. J. Whalen

Communication Theory

Communication may be generally defined as the process of transmission (by the sender) and reception (by the receiver) that inherently assumes message and response. Communication theory, then, may be defined as a broad area of scholarly investigation that deals in many different, yet systematic ways with sender/receiver dynamics. A limited number of examples may help to clarify the diversity of foci within the general area of communication theory.

Some communication theory centers on the general nature of the communication situation of senders and receivers. In religious education, Paulo Freire is representative of this general approach. He contends that dialogue (denoting communication and intercommunication) is loving, humble, and trusting. Antidialogue (denoting one-way communiqués), however, is arrogant and mistrustful. The latter is viewed as educationally counterproductive, while the former is viewed as educationally sound and liberating (*Education for Critical Consciousness*, 1973).

Other communication theory addresses the manner in which organizations communicate within their unique bureaucratic structures and how they communicate to the public at large. Often such theory distinguishes between reactive and proactive communication within groups of persons. Simply, reactive communication refers to an audience's inability to precisely figure out causes and motivations for management decisions (almost always ending in despair), while proactive communication requires the "why" of decisions to be overtly specified by management. This seemingly simple distinction is almost always ignored by producers of centralized religious education curriculum materials. The result is often a feeling at the local level of being left out of the process. This feeling may result in loss of denominational support insofar as the purchase of centrally produced, denominationally specific curricula is concerned.

Still another field of communication centers on the way in which the sender seeks to influence receiver response in the media. Recognizing that within the U.S. context communications has become a business within a capitalistic framework, some communication theorists have begun to analyze the ways in which knowledge is communicated to the wider public and what values are inherent in such communication. Jean Umiker-Sebeok of the Research Center for Language and Semiotic Studies at the University of Indiana, for example, has analyzed the way in which women are portrayed in American magazine advertisements. She concludes that from infancy to old age, women are portrayed in ways that are socially plausible prescriptions of the ways they ought to act out their roles. *Growing with Television, Television Awareness Training*, various pieces from Franciscan Communications, and *Cultural Information Service* are examples of resources for the local religious educational setting that help students analyze media values.

In addition, some communication theory uses language analysis to help understand why communication does or does not take place. Educator and linguist M. A. K. Halliday (*Language as Social Semiotic*, 1978) has convincingly argued, for example, that communication can only be understood if language is interpreted within its own sociocultural context. Thus, metaphors, dialect, and linguistic register are not to be viewed as haphazard or random urges, but as powerful cultural devices that inform and legitimate particular forms of social reality. Educator C. Ellis Nelson began to deal with certain of these themes from a faith perspective in his 1967 classic *Where Faith Begins*. For Nelson, "faith is communicated by a community of believers and . . . the meaning of faith is developed by its members out of their history, by their interaction with each other, and in relation to the events that take place in their lives" (p. 10). To date, Nelson's pioneering thesis has not been mined and remains a crucial area for future scholarly research in religious education. Dwayne Huebner and Maria Harris are perceptive and sensitive current voices regarding the nature of religious metaphors in education for contemporary religious education.

One avenue for cross-cultural communication theory research is nonverbal communication, namely, gestures, body language, smells, dress, and spatial arrangements. Some figures in the history of religious education have explored the relationship of nonverbal communication to education through liturgy. Others (e.g., Maria Montessori, Sofia Cavalletti) reflectively engage all the child's senses to enrich religious experience. Nonverbal communication is an area of needed research.

It may be concluded that communication theory is a dynamic area of inquiry with significant implications for the theory and practice of religious education. On the whole, however, it must be admitted that communication theory has not been taken seriously by most religious education curriculum publishers, most scholars in religious education, or by most local practitioners. Religious education without direct critical reflection on communication theory isolates itself from understanding powerful social dynamics to its own peril. *See also* Body Language; Dialogue; Language Analysis; Language, Inclusive; Media; Metaphor; Public Relations; Semiotics; Symbolism.

FOR FURTHER REFERENCE

Brussat, Frederic, ed. *Cultural Information Service.* Box 786, Madison Square Station, New York, NY 10159.
Franciscan Communications, 1229 South Santee Street, Los Angeles, CA 90015.
Friere, Paulo. *Education for Critical Consciousness.* New York: Continuum, 1973.
Halliday, M. A. K. *Language as Social Semiotic.* University Park, MD: Univ. of Maryland, 1978.
Logan, Ben, and Kate Moody, eds. *Television Awareness Training, Second Edition.* New York: Media Action Research Center, 1979.
Martin, Mary. *Growing with Television: A Study of Biblical Values and the TV Experience.* New York: Media Action Research Center, 1980.
Nelson, C. Ellis. *Where Faith Begins.* Richmond: John Knox Press, 1967.

R. H. Cram, H. C. Simmons

Competency-based Education

Competency-based education, sometimes also known as performance-based education, is an approach to education that emphasizes demonstrated mastery of particular definable skills at specified levels of attainment at various points in the educational sequence. Before students may progress to a next stage, they must demonstrate certain minimal achievements in their present stage.

Since demonstrated competence is the aim in this educational approach, greater emphasis is placed on what a student leaves being able to do than on what he or she was able to do at the beginning or along the way. The amount of time it takes to achieve competence and the ways in which that competence is gained may vary greatly among students. Therefore, such programs tend to promote individualized instruction and require continued practice until skills are learned. Instructional modules designed to teach quite specified skills tend to be the preferred form of curriculum. Clear articulations of what competence consists of (usually stated in the form of behavioral objectives) are required. Testing also plays a key role, since appropriate methods of measuring whether competence has been demonstrated must be found.

In religious education competency-based education can be used if specific goals for either content learning or behavior are previously established. If learning biblical content is a goal for grades 1–6 and biblical interpretation for grades 7–8, then what constitutes competency in each area can be established and methods created for learners to meet the goals according to their individual capabilities. If certain behaviors are considered expressions of religious living, those behaviors can be discussed and set as goals; encouragement can be given through teacher guidance and the behavior assessed at the end of the year. The behaviors to be practiced will depend on age level; an example might be taking turns or sharing toys for five year olds. *See also* Evaluation; Goals; Learning Theory; Measurement; Methodology; Skill Training.

C. R. Dykstra

Computers

Electronic computers, used widely in scientific, educational, and business communities for more than thirty years, have only been reasonably accessible to church educators since the introduction of the first personal computers around 1975. Since 1980 the cost of the equipment and the necessary computer programs has decreased dramatically. Virtually any congregation or church organization can afford some minimal computer capabilities. While there is still a significant lack of educationally sound programs on the market, educators are nevertheless finding increasing uses for this new resource.

USES

Uses of computers may be divided into two primary categories: administrative and instructional. Administrative uses are represented by such traditional office tasks as word processing, information management, and financial record keeping and analysis. In many cases, these uses represent an automating of manual systems that have been used for many years, adding a degree of efficiency and accuracy not possible before. In other cases, the power and capacity of even small desktop groups, regarded the believer's spiritual experience as the important matter and gave up confirmation in any form, though in later generations at least a "right hand of fellowship" would seem to have been a liturgical echo of the previous centuries of elaborate ceremonial. John Wesley did not include confirmation in his prayerbook for American Methodists.

Recent discussions on confirmation (and there have been many after a dearth for many decades) tend to look at the surrounding culture in which the church lives, the general mores that both inform and compete with the religious tradition, and the light thrown upon the meaning of life stages by contemporary psychology. Cues that might inform the next phases of theory and practice of confirmation may only now be emerging from these newer preoccupations. *See also* Adolescence; Baptism; Faith Development; Sacraments; Young Adults.

FOR FURTHER REFERENCE

Stevick, Daniel B. "The Liturgics of Confirmation." In Cully, Kendig Brubaker, ed. *Confirmation Reexamined*. Wilton, CT: Morehouse-Barlow, 1982.

K. B. Cully

Conflict Management

Conflict management is the creative act of implementing the process in which people deal with their differences while accomplishing a goal. Conflict is energy and interest searching for a solution; conflict management uses that energy and interest to effect reconciliation. The challenge is not to prevent conflict, but to use it instead of being abused by it. Conflict is a situation with opposing wants and wishes, a normal condition for many groups of people.

RESPONSES TO CONFLICT

A poll of several thousand people disclosed that personal rejection is the "greatest fear" of many people in the United States. This fear may explain why many people dash for cover when conflict occurs in the church. They are afraid of being criticized and confronted, rejected and roughed-up emotionally. It is little wonder that most congregations have the unspoken code of conduct "peace at all cost." The unspoken assumption is that conflict is evil, and "Love your neighbor (friend and enemy)" means "Don't hurt anyone's feelings even if to do so would feed the hungry, liberate the oppressed, heal the sick, etc."

So the most common response to conflict is to flee, to avoid the situation and people who are in conflict. Often the fleeing flock become inactive members or join another congregation and almost always talk only to people who agree with them.

A second response to conflict is to fight. When fighting, people are usually interested in one thing—getting their way. Winning the battle often becomes more important than the cause championed. The methods used to win are multiple: generalizing about people and issues ("They aren't interested in the church. They just want to tell everyone what to do"); threatening ("If we change the chancel, Mrs. Jones will leave the church"); gossiping; collecting prejudicial information and distorting facts; blaming others; and attacking the character of opponents.

A third response to conflict is to negotiate. To negotiate is to seek to understand all sides of an issue with the intent of satisfying as many people and needs as possible. Ideally, in negotiation people attempt to stimulate a win/win attitude in which all people involved receive some satisfaction from solutions. Though some compromise may be necessary at times, when too much compromise occurs, everyone feels the loss and nobody is satisfied. In such cases, interest and energy are sapped and solutions feel sterile. To negotiate is to do business while taking persons and their concerns seriously.

GOALS OF CONFLICT MANAGEMENT

The first goal of conflict management is to clarify issues, both primary and secondary. Because many people have difficulty fighting fairly, the obvious issues often get mingled with old ideas and fuzzy ideals. Old hurts spawn new causes and use them to defeat old enemies. Effective conflict management assists people in identifying and dealing with one issue at a time. Resistance to remodeling the church school room may have as much to do with Mrs. Smith's memorial desk as it does with educational philosophy. The conflict over the congregation's resolution to ban nuclear weapons may not be primarily over national defense, communism, or separation of church and state. The conflict may be fueled by a secondary issue—twenty church families who work at the nuclear energy plant. The families cannot fight on the grounds of their personal needs versus the total destruction of the earth and its inhabitants, as their opponents would describe the issue. These families need a big cause to justify their position. Conflict management helps people identify and deal with all issues contributing to the conflict.

The second goal of conflict management is to increase understanding between persons and of others' positions on issues. Because of the tendency to project onto others who disagree with us the image of an opponent (enemy), people need help remembering that those who oppose them have the same needs as they do. When in conflict, people must have the following needs met for them to feel secure enough to hear and to understand others' opinions and positions: they need to tell their side of the story, to be listened to, to believe that their ideas and wants are taken seriously, to receive attention, to feel appreciated, to effect decisions (have power to influence), to have others believe as they do, and to have structures in which decisions are made. Managers of conflict implement methods in which these needs are met.

The third goal of conflict management is to establish agreed-upon procedures for seeking solutions. Whenever possible, the structure for managing conflict should be established before it is needed. If the structure (committee, board, commission, etc.) is established after people polarize over an issue, some people will perceive the "conflict committee" as representing the other side. With established structures, little differences are managed as they occur, which prevents the stockpiling of "hurts" to be used later. People receive attention when they need it most—when they feel the need to address an issue.

The fourth goal of conflict management is to increase acceptance of others as persons. This difficult task is to enable people to appreciate others' opinions and differences while affirming their own. Acceptance does not imply agreement; it does involve respect, truth, forgiveness, and integrity. Conflict management strives for confrontation characterized by people empathizing with each other while presenting their positions on issues and their enthusiasm for causes.

The fifth goal of conflict management is to channel aggression into constructive methods of expression—to help people affirm what they believe without attacking others and denigrating their ideas. Procedures are needed to help people perceive all opinions and ideas as belonging to everyone instead of one special-interest group.

The sixth goal of conflict management is to involve passive participants in the formal decision-making process. Those afraid of conflict need ways to get their ideas into the process. This may require special methods in which these people write or tell a few friends what they think without having to take a public personal stand.

The seventh goal of conflict management is to assist people in working through conflict to reconciliation. Reconciliation is the basic purpose of conflict management. Conflict offers the opportunity for people to work through the characteristics that cause alienation from people and God. Reconciliation is not "peace at all cost"—being nice to others while pretending all is well with the world. Reconciliation is overcoming estrangement—the conflicts within persons, between people, and between people and God. Reconciliation overcomes estrangement from God, which changes people so that they can be reconciled to each other. Ideally, through confrontation, people develop a relationship characterized by truth, trust, acceptance, forgiveness, and a love that re-

fuses to settle for superficial solutions to the gospel's challenge of justice, peace, and love for all.

When reconciliation does not occur, methods are introduced to cause closure—some way in which people are helped to cease expending energy and emotions on irreconcilable issues. They are assisted in redirecting their lives to another cause or moving to a new arena to champion their cause. *See also* Congregational Life; Management; Problem Solving; Reconciliation.

FOR FURTHER REFERENCE

Bossart, Donald E. *Creative Conflict in Religious Education and Church Administration.* Birmingham, AL: Religious Education Press, 1980.
Lewis, G. Douglass. *Resolving Church Conflicts.* San Francisco: Harper & Row, 1981.

L. Broadus

Confluent Education

Confluence means coming or flowing together. In confluent education, the aim is to integrate cognitive and affective dimensions in learning, to bring them together rather than to allow them to remain separate from one another. Affective elements are those that have to do with a person's emotions and feelings. Cognitive refers to intellectual functioning, the activity of the mind in coming to know.

The term "confluent education" arose in the late 1960s and early 1970s in the context of a humanistic critique of patterns of schooling in the United States. Schools were criticized for carrying out teaching strategies and using curricula that so overemphasized the cognitive dimensions that learning became one-sided, boring, and irrelevant. This, some argued, was what was primarily responsible for student dissatisfaction with school, high dropout rates, and even violence in the schools. Schools were failing to educate "the whole person" and therefore were failing really to educate.

Confluent education proponents admitted that there is no such thing as cognition without some sort of feeling, or feelings without some element of cognition. The problem was that traditional forms of education paid no attention to what feelings were being experienced, made no use of them in the educational process, and thereby devalued them. Some argued further that patterns of socialization and education prominent in our culture lead to a "deadening" of our emotions, a denial of feelings, and ultimately an inability even to be aware of what we really do feel.

In some of its forms, confluent education proposed primarily the addition of "affective teaching techniques" to the teacher's repertoire. Often borrowed from Gestalt therapy and sensitivity training, these techniques were used to help students "get in touch with" and "express" their feelings. It was perhaps too often assumed that once this happened, integration or confluence would occur automatically. In more sophisticated forms, attempts have been made to relate the two domains much more carefully. Exercises designed to instruct learners in ways to identify and express feelings and emotions are still involved, but usually in quite concrete relationship to particular subjects being studied.

Confluent education is difficult to carry out well. It requires especially confident, creative, and discerning teachers who are personally comfortable with and skilled in affective approaches as well as in their subject areas. Since the emergence of the ideal of confluent education, attention to the affective domain has been heightened, not only in general education but also in religious education. Techniques and strategies continue to be developed, and some curriculum material as well.

However, this is only a beginning. The closest use may be in efforts to help learners "feel into" a biblical situation in such a way as to both understand (cognitive dimension) and identify with (affective dimension) decisions made. This is an effort to locate biblical people in their own time and also to see their common humanity for any time in their response to God's call, in involvement in the process of sin, repentance, forgiveness, and restoration, and in their joy and dependence felt in the presence of God. *See also* Affective Development; Cognitive Development; Methodology; Teaching Styles; Teaching Theory.

C. R. Dykstra

Confraternity of Christian Doctrine

The Confraternity of Christian Doctrine (CCD) is the official Roman Catholic organization for religious education outside the Catholic school. Confraternities are officially sanctioned organizations of clergy and laity established to carry out specific apostolates.

HISTORY

First proposed in 1560, the CCD was established to counter widespread ignorance of Catholic belief and practice by Pope Pius V in 1571. Although it prospered under dynamic post-Reformation Catholic leaders like Charles Borromeo, cardinal-archbishop of Milan, and Francis de Sales in Geneva, the movement declined and received little emphasis until the beginning of the twentieth century.

In 1905, Pope Pius X issued an encyclical, *Acerbo Nimis*, calling for catechetical renewal and the CCD in every parish. Pius X added the re-

quirement of CCD in the parish to the code of canon law in 1918.

The growth of the CCD in the United States followed the varied ecclesiastical career of Edwin V. O'Hara (1881–1956), who became archbishop of Kansas City, Missouri, in 1939. An educator, social activist, and sociologist, O'Hara conducted a survey that revealed widespread neglect of the religious instruction of Catholics in rural America. The organized movement toward the CCD in the United States began when O'Hara, on the basis of his survey, persuaded the National Catholic Rural Life Bureau (NCRLB) to add Religious Vacation Schools, modeled after Lutheran summer schools, to its complete program of services. Religious Vacation Schools prospered under NCRLB auspices long after CCD broke off on its own.

CCD was established as an independent apostolate in the United States in October 1933 by the appointment of Dom Francis Augustin Walsh as national director, with offices at the Catholic University of America. In 1934, it became a bureau of the National Catholic Welfare Conference, the forerunner of the National Conference of Catholic Bishops/United States Catholic Conference (NCCB/USCC).

In 1935, the Catechetical Office of the Congregation of the Council, the Vatican overseer of religious education, delineated the work of CCD as follows: "religious training of Catholic elementary school children not attending Catholic schools, by instruction classes during the school year and in vacation schools; religious instruction of Catholic youth of high-school age not attending Catholic schools, in study clubs and by other methods; religious discussion clubs for adult groups; religious education by parents in the home; instruction of non-Catholics in the teaching of the Catholic faith."

The newly established office took on this formidable task with a staff of only two persons but considerable ingenuity and enthusiasm. Annual national congresses were organized and run until interrupted by World War II in 1941. In 1946, they were reestablished on a five-year schedule. The national office assembled a catechetical library. It commissioned training manuals and curriculum materials and arranged for St. Anthony Guild, Paterson, New Jersey, to be the official CCD publisher. By 1956, CCD listed 146 publications under 8 general headings with translations of key titles into Spanish and French. The bishops authorized a new translation of the Bible and a revision of the *Baltimore Catechism* and entrusted both projects to the CCD.

CHARACTERISTICS

The origin and early history of the CCD in this country explain three major characteristics of the organization's history over the thirty-five years when the national center of CCD was a major influence of Roman Catholic religious education in the United States. First, CCD was tied closely to the hierarchy for support and control. The national center was part of the bishops' administrative structure a generation before the expanded network of agencies that make up the present NCCB/USCC.

Second, despite such official recognition and support, CCD always was administratively understaffed. As a result, decentralization and voluntarism were practical necessities. Although CCD's lay initiative and delegated leadership have been applauded as prophetic in the light of future pastoral trends in the Roman Catholic church, they were in fact evidence of internal weakness.

Finally, CCD never lost the informality, even hominess, of its rural origins. O'Hara had advocated a lay, service-orientated apostolate designed to meet the specific needs of rural America. CCD's programs and materials were designed exclusively for the practical levels of parish life, implementing catechetical theory of the day but not promoting academic study or research.

CCD's plan directed diocesan bishops to appoint a director, originally always a priest, with a chancery level position. These diocesan directors guided the appointment of parish priest moderators. The priest moderator formed a committee of representatives of each of the CCD areas of concern—preschool, elementary school, high school, adult discussion groups, apostolate of good will (convert classes), parent educators, and others. This committee or board established parish policy and practice, while administrators on each level recruited teachers, clerical help, and those who would reach out for students and participants, known in the manuals as "fishers." The parish program was funded by an annual Sunday collection that offered contributors an associate membership in the Confraternity, with the assurance of the prayers of the worldwide membership.

The national center saw itself as a service agency to what from a catechetical point of view was a totally volunteer, nonprofessional network. Diocesan directors and priest moderators, while theologically educated, usually had little formal training in religious education. It organized committees of teaching brothers and sisters and later lay committees to assist in its task but always emphasized the need for local adaptation and initiative.

CHANGES AND DECLINE

The late 1940s through the mid-1960s saw CCD leadership groups established in Catholic colleges and universities. Newman Clubs in secular colleges and junior Newman Clubs in public high schools gathered Catholic students for informal programs. Street preaching and a radio apostolate sought to move religious issues into the marketplace. These efforts, promoted under CCD aus-

pices and generally the responsibility of the diocesan CCD director, show how CCD became more of an umbrella for all Roman Catholic religious education outside Catholic schools, rather than a tightly knit apostolate.

Released time for religious education, which drew strong Roman Catholic support in states with established Catholic school systems, further revealed the diversity and adaptability of CCD. When Catholic schools adjusted their schedules to release their students for the one hour when public school students were released for religious education or observance, the Catholic school faculty became a resource of professional teachers for the CCD program. This became the exclusive structure for CCD elementary school programs in large Eastern dioceses, with the CCD committee structure and lay participation the exception rather than the rule.

The influence of the national center and CCD as a specific ecclesiastical structure declined quickly in the late 1960s. The last national congress was held in Miami in 1971. At the same time, the national center for CCD was reduced to a desk in the United States Catholic Conference's Department of Education (1972). Later, administration of the catechetical apostolates in and outside Catholic schools was blended into a single position (1976).

CCD has been affected both by its strengths and its weaknesses. The strength lay in its "grassroots" nature: it filled a pastoral and parish need. Parents and pastors wanted religious education for children and in particular preparation for First Communion and confirmation. It attracted as teachers and parish administrators both volunteers and professionally trained people who preferred working in a less institutionalized structure than were most of those in the church. It had a total curriculum that tried to meet the needs both of day schools and after-school classes.

The weaknesses stemmed from the strengths. By its grass-roots nature, it resisted institutionalization and did not develop a structure strong enough to give total support: it remained decentralized, functioning basically on a parish level. The curriculum was overextended; there needed to be a curriculum specifically designed for after-school use.

Today, CCD is basically a proper name given to parish religious education. The administrative strength it lacked has been provided by the professionalism of the director of religious education as a full-time Roman Catholic ministry and renewed church awareness of the importance of religious education. It has attracted Catholic sisters and brothers awakened to new vistas of church life by Vatican II and eager to work full-time in pastoral religious education, aided by the support provided by courses and institutes now being offered by colleges and universities. But to the degree that CCD defined its mission in terms of total need, willingly undertook religious education in any available setting, and trusted local initiative, a diffuse but welcome light has faded from the American Roman Catholic horizon. *See also* Roman Catholic Education.

H. B. Basler

Confucianism

Confucius is still regarded as China's greatest teacher, in spite of several campaigns to criticize him in that country in the 1960s and 1970s. The vast majority of Chinese, from scholars to those with only a rudimentary knowledge of the man and his teachings, would object stoutly to speaking of him as a teacher of religion, and undoubtedly would think it strange to include an article on Confucius in a book on religious education. Nevertheless a brief look at his life, his teaching, and the way he did his teaching will show that there are profoundly religious dimensions in his life and thought and in his contribution to the Chinese way of life.

The name Confucius is a Latinized form of K'ung Fu-tzu, which means "K'ung, the honored philosopher." He lived from 551 to 479 B.C., spending most of his years in the state of Lu, roughly the modern province of Shantung. Left fatherless at the age of three, Confucius was reared by his mother in conditions just above poverty. He was married by family arrangement at nineteen, had one son, and then held a series of government positions: supervisor of grain stores and later of public lands, then prime minister of the state of Lu at the end of the sixth century.

It was after the ruler of the state began to neglect public affairs that Confucius realized that he could not implement his ideas in government service and set forth with a band of disciples whom he taught along the way. The last three years of his life were spent back in his native place, still teaching and also engaging in literary studies.

Did he teach his own ideas or those of some earlier thinkers and teachers? It is rather amazing that several "Classics," already highly revered, were read and followed by the time of Confucius, who proceeded to study and teach what he found in these texts. The *Classic* or *Book of Changes*, a divination text, so awed him that he said he could not understand it. He also knew at least parts of the *Classic of History*, the *Classic of Poetry*, the *Record of Rites*, and the *Annals of Spring and Autumn*. The *Classic of Poetry* and parts of the *Book of Changes* come from the tenth century B.C.; the *Annals of Spring and Autumn* was compiled during the years immediately preceding Confucius' life and work. The others were written in the centuries between.

Confucius saw his role as that of a transmitter of the ideas and way of life that he found in the Five Classics, disclaiming any originality or innovation. It was his conviction that if the people of his time, particularly rulers and officials, would follow the ways of the ancients, the great rulers Yao and Shun of a mythical antiquity, then all would be well in his own age and in any time. The key to the fulfillment of this vision of the past in the present depended on rulers and officials being men of virtue, setting an example of those of lesser rank. What then are the virtues or values that lead to government of a high order and thus to a good society?

Basic to this literature, and to Chinese culture from the earliest times to the present, is filial piety, the respect and obedience given to elders while they are alive *and* the veneration or devotion to their spirits after death. Ancestral rites are foremost in the rituals and ceremony that Confucius loved so much, both because of their inherent beauty and dignity and for the way in which ritual motivated people to follow moral standards. Righteousness itself was another of the major values stressed by Confucius, who saw it as issuing from moral character more than from following rules.

Loyalty in human relationships, a "centering of the heart" on the state or family, is basic to this value system, but along with it goes reciprocity, the mutual give-and-take caught up in the Golden Rule. Confucius said that the meeting and mutual interaction of loyalty and reciprocity makes us fully human, the humanness that prevails when two human beings relate to each other. One who lives according to all of these values, plus sincerity, "straight speech" (honesty in speaking), and wisdom (emphasized by a later disciple named Mencius), is a princely or superior person.

MORAL SYSTEM AND RELIGION

All this may appear to be a rather noble moral system that produces upright and moral human beings, not a religion, but one should recall that filial piety and ritual involve a world of the spirits and participation in the meeting of heaven and earth. The Way of Heaven, Earth, and Ancestors impinges on the world of human beings and society and thus the meeting of this world and a transcendent world. Confucius' remark "Worship the spirits but keep them at a distance" may mean that he did not believe in spirits, but it can mean as well that he respected the spirit world and therefore could not respond casually to manifestations of it. When one of his disciples lay dying, he exclaimed that Heaven, which includes the dimension of deity, was destroying him. In reply to a question about prayer he said, "My prayer has been for a long time." He did not expound doctrines about deity, salvation, and the afterlife, but a total worldview rooted in the transcendent is inescapable in his thought.

It is very clear that Confucius was a deeply religious man. He choose not to talk much about religion but to concentrate on the problems of society that concerned him most. He affirmed the earlier religious practices of his people, emphasizing the ritual along with the ethical. If Jesus of Nazareth and Gautama the Buddha were religious teachers, so was Confucius.

CONFUCIAN EDUCATION

How did he teach? Once again, like those of Gautama and Jesus, his method appears to be dialogic, but as was the case with the other two disciples did not come up with many of the answers. The disciples ask questions or comment on the situation; Confucius answers or adds his own interpretation. His sayings are collected in a small book called the *Analects* (*Lunyü*), which is regarded as being faithful to the basic character of his teaching. *The Book of Mencius*, the *Doctrine of the Mean*, and the *Great Learning* continue the Master's teaching but were written during the two centuries following his death.

Confucius is credited with taking a major step in the direction of more broadly based education. Instead of limiting his teaching to young men of the higher classes, he accepted any student who paid the modest tuition of dried meat. Tradition has it that he thought of his students as his sons but insisted on a high degree of discipline. The focus, as indicated, was on moral character; therefore, he emphasized students' following the moral life as well as listening to Confucius talking about it. Thus when they were eventually appointed to government posts, they would exemplify high moral values that would influence for good the people in the communities around them.

As the Confucian system of education developed after his death, with the beginning of an examination system based on Confucian ethics in the second century B.C. and a much more structured system of civil service exams in the twelfth century A.D., those who took the exams had to know Confucian philosophy, along with a great deal about poetry and history. There was no "practical" training, with the result that government officials lacked skills that had to be learned through experience, but the humanities-oriented education provided China through the centuries with a scholarly elite that for most of its history served the country well.

The learning process in which Confucius and his disciples engaged involved the study of classical texts and discussion based on that reading. One may also find, however, references to knowledge or wisdom in a total sense that comes with an intuitive grasp or vision of the whole. The "Great Unity," as it was called, is not an abstract concept but is the continuing reality made concrete in particular ways, which for Confucius harks back to the golden age of the past.

Students must be eager to learn and must be aware that learning involves the cultivation of moral character. They also must deal with questions about themselves and attempt to gain the personal knowledge that leads to true selfhood as mind and heart are nurtured and purified in study and moral endeavor.

Confucian education, therefore, focuses on what it means to be human, on a goodness to be realized here and now. This humaneness is taught in the texts and is realized by following the example of a teacher imbued with Chinese culture and concerned that society be built and continued on the values of that culture.

Although Confucius did expand education, at least his own teaching, beyond the upper classes, it was still a limited group who could study with him. The developing examination system, which so challenged the young men of later generations because it was the route to government service, produced an educated elite. It was an impossible path, however, for the peasant masses, as well as for women, for whom education was a closed door in China until the twentieth century.

For twenty-five hundred years the Confucian tradition has provided a systematic and orderly framework for Chinese belief and practice in what may be called the Chinese religious realm. The system has been and may well continue to be a model for religious education for whatever groups may be concerned to educate youth of the present in such a way as to preserve at least some of the values of the past for a more humane present and future.

Although Marxism and Confucianism seem, to external observation, utterly incompatible, nonetheless in contemporary China these value systems appear to be mixing to a significant degree, especially in the years since the so-called Cultural Revolution (1967–77).

R. C. Bush

Congregational Life

The congregation is a group of like-minded people who through their worship, work, and interaction provide the context for religious instruction and discussion of religious issues.

The word "congregation" in biblical usage refers to an assembly of all of the people of Israel (Exod. 12:3, 6, 19; 16:1–2). The same idea is used for the establishment of the New Testament church (Acts 2). In each case the whole community of the faithful constituted the congregation. But in time as the faithful scattered or converts were made in various locations, the word "congregation" or "church" came to mean a particular group of believers. It is important to note that from a biblical view congregations are people who come together in response to what God has done. It is not a collection of people gathered to satisfy personal or social needs. Rather, the apostle Paul described the church as the "body of Christ." Christ is the head. Members have different functions; but, if all look to the head for guidance, the body will grow in love (1 Cor. 12; Eph. 4:1–16).

From biblical times congregations have been the center for religious life. The center of congregational life is worship, and worship is our way of responding to God for God's creation of us and grace toward us. From worship—with its liturgy of prayers, hymns, Scripture, sermon, and sacraments—the congregation is inspired and instructed to behave as "a colony from heaven" to educate the young and each other, to serve the community, and to share their faith with others. The high points of congregational life come when persons are baptized, for they have made a commitment to the community, and when the Lord's Supper is celebrated, for that reenacts the story of salvation. When one adds weddings, funerals, church-night suppers, study groups, committee meetings about congregational affairs, and other occasions at which members join together for common concerns, one can see that congregations are different from the society in which they are located.

This difference comes about because of the fact that congregations are in the world owning property, employing ministers, and so on, but they try not to be "of the world." As admonished all through Scripture, congregations attempt to focus attention on God's will for the world (John 15:9; Rom. 12:1; 2 Cor. 4:1–12). To the extent that they are able to be loyal to God they are unique communities. From this self-conscious religious goal come a special educational environment and characteristics of learning that are related to the congregation's situation and its interpretation of its purpose.

CHARACTERISTICS AND PURPOSE

The situation of a given congregation is known when one considers its size, location, and buildings, racial and age composition, history, outlook on the future, financial resources, and other factors that give it a corporate personality. In a small rural congregation served by a part-time minister a very close bond between members is often created because these few people must take charge of the church school and all other activities. A large congregation in a metropolitan center is different in that the members cannot know each other very well; their lives interact infrequently and often superficially. These different situations raise different ways of planning the church's work and decision-making processes. In the small church much is done by face-to-face consultation and common understanding of those able and willing to lead. The larger church must depend on

formal committee meetings, phone calls, and paid staff to keep the organization running.

A congregation's interpretation of its purpose is the other major element in the formation of its ethos. One congregation may be evangelistic; another may be concerned mainly with social issues; another might consider its pastoral role to people in trouble to be its goal; or a church located beside a university might give its money and energy to serve the special needs of students.

Each particular congregation, therefore, has an ethos—that is, a certain way of work and worship, determined by the elements in its situation and its interpretation of purpose. An individual who joins that particular congregation accepts what that congregation is and proclaims. The new member has entered a human interactional process that is educational in the most dynamic sense of that term. The interactional process conveys the mood of the people, the politics by which they govern themselves, the issues they address, and the issues they rule out of order. This latter matter, in educational terms "the null curriculum," is often overlooked. For example, some congregations never discuss in sermon or study classes racial issues that are upsetting the community. Such avoidance teaches church members that racial issues are not within the religious realm: they are assigned to the secular arena.

The ethos or corporate personality of a particular congregation permeates its whole life. Unless contested or modified by strong persistent pressure from a group of people, the ethos will influence every aspect of the life and work of the congregation. People interacting with each other in the congregation are, therefore, the dynamic educational process; and what this interaction produces is the beliefs, values, and patterns of behavior that characterize those people. In practical terms we may trace this dynamic educational process through four channels, the homes of members, the officers of the congregation, church policy, and the educational program.

LEADERSHIP, POLICIES, AND EDUCATION

The congregation is formed and controlled by adults. They provide the interest, time, leadership, and money necessary for a stable organization. This means that the beliefs and values that are shared, exalted in worship, and talked about informally influence how adults function in the home, where they have considerable authority. Children are instructed in these beliefs when they ask questions about death, the existence of God and God's relation to individuals, what is right and wrong behavior, and why such behavior is so classified. Children are influenced indirectly in countless ways about how to act in specific situations and about the appropriate attitude toward people and things as they participate with their families in congregational life.

The congregation's corporate personality is also expressed organizationally through the selection of certain adults to be its officers. In electing its officers, the congregation tends to select those persons who best personify their beliefs and attitudes. Officers thus selected tend to solidify and magnify those characteristics. If, for example, a congregation has a self-image of being "foreign-mission minded," they will select officers who reflect this concern in their decisions. Officers formalize and make operational the rather general feeling and attitude of the people who make up the congregation.

Policy decisions in which the whole congregation participates, such as financial campaigns to buy an organ or enlarge a building, are determined politically by voting or economically by pledging. But back of the voter pledge is a mental image of what adults think the church should be. This visible vote is motivated by beliefs that are formed and sometimes transformed by association of members with each other in the congregation.

With few exceptions congregations depend on laypeople to teach Sunday school classes and lead youth and adult groups. Lacking formal study of theology or Bible, these laypeople have two sources of help: printed curriculum materials and their own beliefs. Most lay teachers use the printed curriculum, but they do so within the framework of their beliefs. People who volunteer for this service do so out of loyalty to the congregation and because they have an urgency about communicating their beliefs. These emotional factors in the self-selection of teachers make for a situation whereby the lay teachers use their beliefs as the interpretive schema regardless of what the printed curriculum material proposes.

This situation is often cited as a weakness of church-sponsored education. It can, however, be considered a strength, for it means that instruction in faith is done within the context of beliefs. That is, teachers share their life experiences, thus relating beliefs to human events rather than to systematic theology. For example, teachers who relate the nature of God to prayer about life situations are trying to form or stabilize belief in God, for that is what the congregation considers to be the most important result of religious education. It becomes a worshiping congregation and so fulfills its function as the center for religious life. *See also* Belief; Goals; Koinonia; Leadership Development; Ministry; Organization in Religious Education; Public Relations; Systems Theory.

FOR FURTHER REFERENCE

Cully, Iris V. *Education for Spiritual Growth*. San Francisco: Harper & Row, 1984.

Nelson, C. Ellis. *Where Faith Begins*. Atlanta, GA: Knox, 1967.

Roozen, David A., William McKinney, and Jackson W. Carroll. *Varieties of Religious Presence*. New York: Pilgrim, 1984.

Westerhoff, John H. *Living the Faith Community*. Minneapolis, MN: Winston, 1985.

Whitehead, Evelyn, and James D. Whitehead. *Community of Faith*. New York: Seabury, 1982.

C. E. Nelson

Conscience

Conscience is the inner sense that produces feelings of guilt and shame when one does what is considered wrong or fails to do what is considered right. In the Christian tradition conscience is "the mind making moral judgments" (Thomas Aquinas).

The first definition is descriptive and applies to everyone regardless of religious beliefs. It assumes that conscience develops as a child becomes self-conscious. It comes about as parents set feeding schedules, restrain the child from danger, and punish undesirable behavior. The inventory of things to be done a certain way or not to be done becomes the action about which guilty feelings emerge. Parents also do happy and playful things with their children. This group of experiences bonds children to their parents so that if the children should not live up to expectations, the children feel shame or remorse. Although conscience is rather well formed by age five or six, it is not fully developed until well into adolescent years, for parents and other caregivers, including teachers, continue to coach children on what is desirable or undesirable behavior. Since conscience formation is rooted in personal relations and reflects community moral standards, it is no wonder that individuals differ widely on what is right or wrong.

The second definition does not contradict the first but assumes a biblical understanding of conscience in which there is emphasis on one's accountability to God for one's life and influence. Conscience is not a biblical word. It is not found in the Old Testament and does not appear in the New Testament until the apostle Paul deals with it in the Corinthian church (1 Cor. 8; 10). The biblical word for this part of oneself is "heart." In biblical usage, "heart" conveys feelings of guilt and shame in terms of accountability to God, as illustrated in the story of David's selfish use of Bathsheba (2 Sam. 12). The biblical term "heart" also indicates what persons should love, respect, and live for (Pss. 24; 73). "Heart" is a broad term that means "the self I am responsible for," of which feelings of guilt and shame are only a part.

Conscience in the biblical sense of one's accountability to God for one's conduct should be obeyed, but this does not mean that conscience is always right. Conscience can make wrong judgments because of self-interest, it can be incorrectly informed, or it can be unaware of the consequences of its judgments and thus cause a person to act unwisely. Moreover, early moral training may not easily be changed even if one has had a dramatic conversion experience, as shown in the life of Peter (Acts 10). For these reasons a Christian's conscience needs to be educated and brought into maturity in relation to Christ (Phil. 2:1–11). This is normally done through the work and worship of a congregation, prayer, study groups, and careful consideration of ethical issues that affect the quality of life of all people. *See also* Ethics; Moral Development; Values.

C. E. Nelson

Conscientization

Conscientization is learning to perceive contradictions between the way we experience social reality and the way it has been interpreted and taking steps with others to change these contradictions. This process of growth in understanding and changing consciousness is a crucial part of human development. The word "conscientization" was coined in Latin America and is widely used by liberation theologians as a description of the process of consciousness-raising among oppressed groups of people. Paulo Freire is particularly well known for his liberating pedagogy based on a literacy program that enables peasants to name their own reality and to begin to take steps to change those things that keep them in a position of poverty. Freire's best-known work is a philosophy of education based on this process of conscientization (*Pedagogy of the Oppressed*, 1970).

Freire describes the process of conscientization as the development of historical awareness and action in four overlapping stages. It begins with *doxa* (mere opinion or belief) as persons become aware of the world around them, observing and admiring it. This naive perception of reality gives way to critical awareness of the world described by Freire as *logos* (thinking). Here the subject begins to view the world as an object to be examined critically and to be analyzed in a new way. Third, critical analysis leads to *praxis* or action-reflection as human beings begin to change their world. The energy to continue this process of action and reflection comes from a realistic vision of a "good place," or *utopia*, in which human wholeness is possible. This educational process is an important basis for any group working for liberation.

Conscientization is descriptive of the same phenomenon as consciousness-raising, because it emphasizes an intentional action education process in which persons come to understand their own history and culture and learn to demystify the accepted answers and myths that they have

been taught. But it has an additional and important element often overlooked when the focus of consciousness-raising is on helping persons change their minds without providing new avenues of action and behavior. Conscientization is a continuing process that includes both action and reflection (*praxis*). Action is a key element in this continuing educational process because the reflection keeps deepening as each new action raises new questions that call for further reflection together with others.

Conscientization has become a method in the religious education of adults. Reading and study precedes the activity (action)—work on a serious problem or project. Essential to the process is the reflection period, in which the group recalls its activity, evaluates it, celebrates the good, and determines next steps. *See also* Action-Reflection; Consciousness-raising; Liberation Theology; Praxis.

L. M. Russell

Consciousness-raising

Consciousness-raising is a mutual process of learning to perceive contradictions between the way persons have experienced social reality and the way it has been interpreted to them through their culture. Intentional groups for consciousness-raising were particularly popular in the women's liberation movement of the 1970s in the United States. Women began gathering together in small groups and sharing their stories. Listening to one another in these ways helped women understand themselves and their world more clearly. They found out that what they considered deficiencies in their own lives were common in the lives of other women and were a result of social discrimination. They developed a new sense of self-esteem because others listened to them and valued their experiences and insights. Lastly, they formed continuing networks of support that enabled them to begin to take charge of their lives.

Consciousness-raising is not unique to the women's liberation movement. It is a process similar to conscientization, which is used in education with oppressed groups not only in Latin America but also around the world. In the women's movement, however, its focus was on coming to a new awareness of the force of sexism in society, rather than on actions the groups could take together toward social change. Nevertheless, as people discover that their history is changeable and needs to be changed, they begin to act according to their new perception so that they themselves change. They become more conscious of themselves as human beings capable of shaping their destiny along with others for the common good.

Such radical reorientation has been experienced, for instance, by many U.S. citizens as a result of the Vietnam War and the reports of U.S. support of terrorism, torture, and murder in Latin America. People move from "unquestioning patriotism" to "patriotic rage" at their own government and finally toward "new patriotism" in working with others to end U.S. aggression. Change in perception and action has been experienced by almost every marginal group in our society. Many have moved from acceptance of their marginal position as "happy slaves" into an attempt to emulate the dominant persons and their roles in society. Discovering that emulation is seldom successful in oppressive social systems, they move to rage and emotional rejection of social systems that turn them into the "losers" through racism, sexism, or classism. With the help of group support, they often then turn to a search for new identity and continue the process of group and self-development that will enable them to begin to cooperate with others in common action for change.

When religious educators are willing to go beneath the surface of cognitive knowledge and permit learners to view their situation in a fresh perspective, consciousness-raising is a valuable method. This needs to be a concern where there are minority group members and among the women in any congregation. This technique can assist a congregation in examining presuppositions about their task and in considering where restructuring may be needed. *See also* Conscientization; Feminist Movement; Liberation Theology; Social Action; Social Justice, Education for.

L. M. Russell

Constructive Activities

Constructive activities are procedures that facilitate learning, improvement, and development through firsthand experience. Constructive activities may be in-class, structured events or less formal extracurricular recreational activities designed by the teacher with particular learning goals in mind. They may also flow spontaneously from other planned or unplanned events in the learning environment.

Learning theorist Jean Piaget (1896–1980) identified direct experience as one of the four necessary causes of development (the other three are heredity and maturation, social interaction, and equilibration). He viewed the learner as actively constructing his or her understandings from those direct experiences and interactions with others.

Socrates' statement "To know is to do" has often been interpreted to mean "If one knows, one will do," but perhaps he really intended to say that to fully know one must do. All aspects of learning are enhanced by doing, experiencing. By

doing, understanding grows. Affective learning flows from the activities in which learners are involved. And doing is a way of expressing both what we know and what we feel about that knowledge. Direct experience is critical to learning.

Learning through experience is of particular importance to those with certain learning styles. Many people most easily perceive through concrete experience and find it very difficult to learn from abstract presentations. Though some learners enjoy reflecting on information received either through experience or from reasoning, many others must process such data through active experimentation. They need to do something with the information to test it, understand it, and make it their own. Constructive activities are essential for those whose learning style calls for the concrete and the active.

The physical needs of young children also call for constructive activities. Preschoolers need to be physically active. They find it difficult to sit for long periods of time. Ample opportunity to move around and actively participate in learning must be scheduled into the learning time.

Teachers set up learning environments and plan learning events. Key planning questions are: how can students experience directly what I want them to learn? What experiences will contribute to their improvement and development? What constructive activities can I plan to help learners toward the knowledge goals?

But teacher-designed activities are not the only events that can constructively contribute to learning. As students interact and respond to one another, they spontaneously become involved in activities rich in learning potential. An observant teacher with a clear focus on the goals of religious education will be alert for these "teachable moments," psychologist Robert Havinghurst's term for those moments of increased receptivity to the learning of a particular truth or idea (*Human Development and Education*, 1953). The teacher's role is to come alongside the students and, as appropriate, talk with them about the experience, how they felt, and what they learned.

What are some of the constructive activities that can be built into the religious education setting? Children enjoy active involvement in factual learning. Games can be designed to make factual review fun. Students get acquainted with the structure of the Bible as they use it. By searching out information in resource materials they expand their knowledge of the data and how to learn. Constructing a map, a model of the tabernacle, or a scroll enables students to visualize and more adequately understand a distant reality.

Creative activities are constructive. Understandings, perspectives, and feelings can be expressed through drawing or modeling clay. In drama students experience the story and the feelings of the characters. Role playing and dramatic play for young children provide opportunities to try on a variety of roles.

A person's sense of worth and responsibility can be built through constructive activities in the religious education setting. A necessary game rule is that each person will be respected and safe from ridicule. Some may not experience respect elsewhere. Students can be given age-appropriate responsibilities to carry out. They may be simple cleanup tasks in the preschool room, responsibility for the safety of each other as trail family members on a backpacking trip, or any number of responsibilities in between. Team work on constructive activities also teaches interdependence, responsibility, and the value of dependability.

Spiritual realities must be experienced to be understood. Prayer and worship can be experienced before they can be defined. As teachers love and forgive, students see and feel these attributes in action. The realities in the human relationships open the heart for experiencing the love and forgiveness of God.

And religious educators must not be content with either showing how or teaching definitions. True learning calls for and students need to be involved in doing acts of kindness and service, being patient, and rubbing shoulders with people in need. "Kindness," "service," "patience," "needy" are words that can come alive with meaning through experience. *See also* Cognitive Development; Crafts; Creative Activities; Experience; Learning Theory; Teaching Styles.

C. Stonehouse

Conversation

Conversation is the oral exchange of sentiments, observations, opinions, or ideas. The exchange is usually informal in nature and involves only two persons or a small group.

Conversation is two-way communication. It calls for listening as well as oral expression. The content of a conversation may deal with the simple exchange of information and observations. Or ideas, opinions, attitudes, judgments, and feelings may be shared that reveal persons to one another at deep levels.

Talking together is a natural part of human experience. Though some may not have thought of natural dialogue as a teaching method, the teaching/learning process can be greatly enhanced through the use of quality conversation. Two basic skills must be developed to maximize the value of this exchange so natural to human beings—listening and communication.

Effective listening begins with valuing what the other person has to say. Persons often enter into conversation with the sole purpose of telling another what they have on their mind. They may give the other person time to speak simply to be polite, but they are not really listening to understand. They are manipulating the conversation to deliver their content.

The teacher who uses conversation constructively will want to know where students are in their thinking, what they value, and what they understand. Listening is highly valued by such a teacher.

Good listeners do not assume they understand what the other person is thinking. Check to be sure you are getting the intended message. Restate what you thought you heard and give the other person opportunity to confirm the understanding or to clarify his or her perspective. Try to understand the rationale behind comments. Ask "why" questions and encourage the speaker to expand on ideas to reveal more of the thinking process and rationale.

Body language is also important. Standing or sitting before a person with arms folded across the chest communicates resistance to what might be said. But sitting in a relaxed position with hands in the lap communicates an openness to listen and an invitation to share without the threat of intimidation. Free-flowing conversation calls for a relaxed body position.

Real listening builds trust and a desire to communicate. In our rapidly paced, impersonal society, few people take the time to listen and concentrate on hearing with understanding. The teacher who develops the skill of listening can become a valued confidant to many and may influence lives significantly.

The other side of conversation is communication. Effective communicators use a vocabulary with which the hearers are comfortable. Through listening to students teachers can discover the vocabulary that is appropriate.

Communication in conversation is also enhanced through the use of illustrations and metaphors. Listening to students and observing them will provide a wealth of material to illustrate concepts and enhance communication.

Clearly stating what one intends to say does not assure that the hearer has received the intended message. Effective communication calls for periodic checkups. "What do you hear me saying?" or "Does that make sense to you?" are questions to help check up on the clarity of communication.

What can happen through conversation in the religious education setting? Relationships can be established and strengthened as teacher and students talk together. Through conversation teachers can communicate a genuine interest in students and come to know them. Knowing the students and being viewed as interested in their lives are critical to facilitating their learning.

Informal conversation helps set the stage for study. Students come to class with many things on their minds and interesting information they want to share. A time of friendly conversation as students arrive allows these issues to surface and be discussed. This then frees the students to be able to focus on other issues.

Through conversation teachers can discover where students are in their thinking on issues. This knowledge gives the needed clues as to the appropriate point at which to begin discussing the issue. What is learned through conversation may even indicate that students are not ready for thinking about certain topics.

With young children conversation is the main form of discussion teachers will use. Informal conversation with a child in the midst of an activity or after a story can enhance learning.

Conversation can facilitate the personal application of truth. One-on-one dialogue between teacher and student provides for the exploring of personal needs and how God's word speaks uniquely to those needs.

In the process of moral and spiritual development persons come to points of questioning and struggle. They discover inadequate perspectives and understandings that must be released if they are to grow. Through conversation teachers can become aware of these struggles in the lives of their students who need someone to listen, to help them sort through their questions, and point them toward new questions and ideas in which they can find new and more adequate understandings and answers. Conversation is a means by which we can help one another grow. *See also* Body Language; Communication Theory; Dialogue.

C. Stonehouse

Conversion

The experience of conversion, or coming to believe, has been a central feature of the Christian faith, although the phenomenon of conversion is common to all religions. Despite its centrality in the Christian tradition, conversion experiences have been marked by an extraordinary variety. This diversity has been shaped by the differences in human personalities, theological traditions, sociological factors, and historical settings. The centrality as well as the mystery of conversion are captured in the encounter of Jesus Christ with Nicodemus in John 3. Christ tells Nicodemus that he must be "born anew," and when Nicodemus inquires how this could happen, Jesus finally replies, "The wind blows where it wills, and you hear the sound of it, but you do not know whence it comes or whither it goes; so it is with every one who is born of the Spirit" (John 3:8).

The term "conversion" literally means "to turn" or "to turn around"—to move in a new direction. The turn may be physical, spiritual, emotional, intellectual, and/or moral. Yet inherent in the concept of conversion is a transformation that involves both the physical and the spiritual.

BIBLICAL UNDERSTANDINGS

The Hebrew and Greek words for conversion are rarely used in the text of the Bible. Instead, the Bible contains a number of images and metaphors capturing the meaning of conversion—the experience of turning. In the Old Testament, a frequent image is the call of the prophets to the people of Israel to return to the true worship of God. Afflicted with sin, suffering, and guilt, the psalmists longed for an experience of conversion and implored God to turn toward them to restore them to health and salvation.

In the New Testament, the preaching of Jesus in the Gospels is a summons to a new life based on the good news he proclaimed. As Christ began his ministry, he declared, "The time is fulfilled, and the kingdom of God is at hand; repent, and believe in the gospel" (Mark 1:15). Repentance—turning away from a former life to a new life—represented the beginning of following Christ.

In striking contrast to the contemporary fascination with the nature of conversion today, the New Testament is remarkably cryptic in describing the details of the conversion experiences of the early Christians. The best known of these is the conversion of the apostle Paul, but the experience is described only by Luke in three passages in the book of Acts (9:1–19; 22:1–21; 26:1–23). There is no extended account in any of the Pauline Letters, and in 2 Corinthians 12 Paul even seems to suggest that overconfidence in one's religious experiences contradicts sinful humanity's dependence upon salvation by grace through faith in Jesus Christ.

The drama of Paul's conversion is complemented in the New Testament by the more gradual and subtle changes in people like Zaccheus (Luke 19:1–10), Matthew (Matt. 9:9; Mark 2:13; Luke 5:27), Lydia (Acts 16:14), and Timothy (Acts 16).

Twentieth-century Christians are most familiar with conversion as a "born-again" or "born-anew" experience (John 3:3), but the New Testament also uses a variety of other images: moving from darkness to light or from impurity to purity, turning from Satan to God, shedding an old humanity and taking on a new one, dying to self and rising again in Christ, etc. Inherent in each image is the idea of turning away from a life characterized by sin and alienation from God to a new life of meaning and purpose through God's love and forgiveness in Jesus Christ.

THEOLOGICAL ISSUES

The mystery of conversion has been the occasion for many disputes—both within the Christian church and among scholars who study religious experience and religious movements. Important theological issues arise in any discussion of conversion: is it God who takes the initiative in making individuals aware of their sin and then turns them toward divine grace and redemption? Or is the will of individuals a critical factor in "deciding" for Christ? Should the church be composed only of members who can testify to an experience of conversion? Or should the church include those who cannot describe a conversion but who confess their faith in Jesus Christ?

For religious educators, a central debate has been waged over the question of whether it is possible to make people Christians by nurture and education, rather than by radical, life-changing experiences. This problem was posed in classic ways in nineteenth-century American Protestantism. Horace Bushnell, often described as the father of the modern Christian education movement, declared that children should grow up never knowing themselves as being anything other than Christian, while his revivalist contemporaries insisted that people should have a datable experience of knowing when they had been saved by God.

In those churches that view radical conversion as a necessary experience, most education—particularly the education of children up to the age of eight or nine—is conducted both in content and method toward this end. The individual is drawn toward a sense of guilt for sin, a feeling of repentance, and a resultant feeling of assurance of acceptance by God through Christ. Those who hold to gradual conversion do not expect a "turning around" at any given point; conversion may even be so gradual as to be imperceptible. Their religious education programs do not have conversion as an objective.

Psychologists have also argued over personality differences influencing the experience of conversion. William James in *The Varieties of Religious Experience* (1902) contrasted the "once born" and the "twice born." The former are people whose lives are not characterized by radical breaks or deep crises; rather, they seem to go "from strength to strength." "Twice-born" personalities' lives are marked by decisive moments or determinative shifts of direction. Psychologists have also developed theories that attempt to explain conversion in terms of the crisis of adolescent identity, illness and deprivation, or the therapeutic need for acceptance.

Sociologists, in turn, have pointed to various factors that seem to make conversions more likely at a particular point in history or in a particular setting. The dislocations and trauma of rapid social change, war, famine, disease, and other historical forces have frequently contributed to the outbreak of conversions on a large scale. Similarly, sociologists have cited the dynamics of mass meetings as a factor in the conversions associated with revivals.

Historians know relatively little about the nature of conversion during the early and medieval periods of Christianity. Literacy was rare, and consequently few conversion accounts exist for this period. It is also clear that millions of people were "converted" to Christianity first by the power of the sword and by governmental decree and only later through the Christian church's ministry and witness.

Beginning with the Reformation and especially after the development of the printing press and the rise of literacy, conversion accounts appeared in greater numbers, and by the nineteenth century they became a distinctive form of Christian literature. Their popularity is due in part to their use as tools of evangelism and the persistent fascination with the mystery of conversion. They become ways of answering the question posed to Paul by his jailer: "What must I do to be saved?" (Acts 16:30).

TYPES OF CONVERSION

There are some "types" or categories that can be used to explore the variety of conversion experiences represented in the history of Christianity. Conversions may be dramatic, gradual, aesthetic, intellectual, or ethical/moral.

The obvious example of the *dramatic conversion* is that of the apostle Paul, but in more recent Christian history the experience of John Wesley is also well known. People who experience a dramatic conversion are able to describe the place, the time, what they were doing, what they thought, and how they felt. For Wesley, it was in Aldersgate in London on 24 May 1738. He was attending a Bible study where someone was reading from Luther's commentary on Romans. Wesley wrote, "About a quarter before nine, while he was describing the change which God works in the heart through faith in Christ, I felt my heart strangely warmed." Dramatic conversions appear most often in print, largely because of their drama, but they are not the only or even the most common type of conversion experiences.

Gradual conversion is perhaps the most common in the history of Christianity but also the most difficult to describe. Individuals who experience conversion gradually generally cannot point to a single, life-changing experience but usually describe a series of confrontations with God and moments of insight and new understanding. In this type, conversion is seen as an extended process, sometimes lasting an entire lifetime. One of the classic examples of the model of gradual conversion comes in the writing of John Bunyan—metaphorically in *Pilgrim's Progress* and autobiographically in *Grace Abounding to the Chief of Sinners*. For Bunyan, the Christian life—and even his own life—was a journey in faith. In *Pilgrim's Progress*, the central character, Christian, negotiates his way through peaks and valleys and frequently falls from the way. Yet in dependence upon God, Christian returns to the path and ultimately reaches the Celestial City. Bunyan's imagery of Christian experience as walking with God was obviously drawn from the Bible itself, and the idea of the pilgrimage continues to characterize the conversion experiences of many.

In *aesthetic conversion*, individuals describe an overwhelming sense of the beauty and majesty of God's love and power, often through nature, music, or art. They are less apt to emphasize a feeling of guilt or sin that is forgiven; instead, they experience a heightened sense of God's holiness and beauty that transforms their understanding of themselves and God. Jonathan Edwards's account of his conversion suggests the aesthetic dimension of a conversion experience in his description of his awareness of the power and beauty of God as he saw it in nature.

Some conversions tend to emphasize an intellectual struggle about the truth of the Christian religion. In the *intellectual conversion*, individuals describe an experience of doubt being resolved by faith and new assurance about the central claims of Christian doctrine. C. S. Lewis's conversion account reflects certain aspects of this category of Christian conversion. He recounts how he struggled with his doubts and one day took a trip in a car to the seashore. When he arrived, he said that he realized he believed in God. Later he came to accept Christianity.

Every conversion has moral or ethical consequences, but when the experience of "turning" involves a radical rejection of one set of values or life-style for another, one the converts see as more fully embodying the ethical claims of the Christian faith, we categorize it as a *ethical/moral conversion*. Albert Schweitzer's decision to leave behind a promising medical and musical career in Europe to pursue a lifetime of medical missionary work in Africa might be used as an example of this type of conversion as ethical or moral transformation.

These categories do not explain or exhaust the rich variety of conversion experiences, nor does a single conversion experience belong in only one category. Most experiences will reflect characteristics of all these types and perhaps even more.

Richard Baxter, a prominent seventeenth-century English minister, described his own conversion in his famous *Autobiography*. Baxter lived in an age of intense religious, political, and military conflict in which people contended for truth with certainty and ferocity. Baxter himself recognized the shades of truth in many different persuasions, and he is sometimes described as the founder of the ecumenical movement in England. As Baxter looked back on his life, he reflected on the nature of conversion with a wisdom and insight that suggests both the centrality and mystery of the experience of God's grace:

"I afterward perceived that education is God's ordinary way for the conveyance of his grace, and ought no more to be set in opposition to the Spirit than the preaching of the Word; and that it was the great mercy of God to begin with me so soon. . . .

"I understood at last that God breaketh not all [human] hearts alike." *See also* Child Evangelism; Evangelism; Personality, Theories of; Psychology of Religion; Sociology of Religion.

FOR FURTHER REFERENCE

Conn, Walter E., ed. *Conversion: Perspectives on Personal and Social Transformation.* New York: Alba House, 1978.

Gaventa, Beverly Ross. *From Darkness to Light: Aspects of Conversion in the New Testament.* Philadelphia: Fortress, 1986.

James, William. *The Varieties of Religious Experience.* New York: Modern Library, 1936.

Kerr, Hugh T., and John M. Mulder, eds. *Conversions: The Christian Experience.* Grand Rapids, MI: Eerdmans, 1983.

J. M. Mulder

Coordinator

See Director of Religious Education; Management.

Cope, Henry Frederick ━━━━

Henry Frederick Cope (1870–1923), general secretary of the Religious Education Association, led the organization in raising educational standards in religious programs and in keeping the ideal of religious education before the public. Born in London, England, he was educated in publicly supported schools. Cope came to the United States in 1891, attended the Southern Baptist Theological Seminary, Louisville, Kentucky, and later graduated from Ripon College in Wisconsin. He was ordained a Baptist minister in 1893 and over the next ten years served congregations in New York, Illinois, and Montana. After leading a series of successful Sunday school leadership classes in the Chicago area, in 1905 he was asked to join the staff of the newly organized Religious Education Association and in 1906 became the founding editor of its journal, *Religious Education*. From 1907 until his death in 1923 he served both as editor and as general secretary of the Religious Education Association. *See also* Religious Education Association.

L. G. McAllister

Councils of Churches

Councils of churches are agencies for interchurch cooperation, study, and action giving visibility to the quest for Christian unity, peace, and social justice. They exist at world, national or regional, state or provincial, and metropolitan area or city levels. They are most numerous at the local level in the United States, Britain, and New Zealand. Each is autonomous. Membership is held by denominational bodies or local congregations.

The stream of cooperative Christianity now expressed through councils of churches had its origins in the Sunday school movement and subsequent endeavors for religious education. The earliest convention of Sunday school workers in the United States was held in 1824, under the sponsorship of the American Sunday School Union. The first national convention took place at Philadelphia in 1832. The work prepared the ground for the emergence of numerous state and city church federations or councils. For example, the Kentucky Council of Churches was organized in 1947 but traces its earliest roots to the Kentucky Sabbath School Union, which was organized in 1865.

The World Council of Churches (WCC) was organized at Amsterdam on 20 August 1948, following a period of formation that began at Utrecht in 1938 but was interrupted by World War II. The WCC brought together "Life and Work" with "Faith and Order" groups. In 1961 the International Missionary Council united with the WCC. Today, the WCC consists of 330 member churches from seven continents, including Protestant, Orthodox, and Old Catholic churches. A variety of working relationships link the WCC

with the Vatican, but the Roman Catholic church is not a member. The council is based at Geneva, Switzerland, and maintains a small office in New York. It carries out various programs and functions in the interest of Christian unity and social justice and maintains active dialogue with other faith groups as well.

National and regional councils exist in about 130 areas of the world, and about 40 of these have official Roman Catholic participation. A pioneer in this movement was the Federal Council of the Churches of Christ in America (1908), which evolved into the National Council of the Churches of Christ in the U.S.A. through a merger with such other bodies as the International Council of Religious Education, the National Protestant Council of Higher Education, the Missionary Education Movement, and the United Council of Church Women at Cleveland in 1950.

The Canadian Council of Churches was formed in 1944; the British Council in 1942; the New Zealand Council in 1941, growing out of a Council of Religious Education (1921); the Australian Council in 1946. The All African Conference of Churches came into being in 1963, and the Caribbean Conference of Churches was formed in 1973.

Local councils, sometimes also called federations, associations, or conferences of churches, existed long before the national or world bodies came into being. The first such entity in the United States was the Federation of Churches and Christian Workers of New York City, organized in 1895. The Interdenominational Commission of Maine, the first statewide body, dates from 1891. By 1917 there were about 65 such local federations, most of them having grown out of Sunday school associations. The movement toward state councils of churches gained momentum around 1922, and two years later three (Ohio, Massachusetts, and Connecticut) had full-time staff and two others (California and Pennsylvania) had part-time staff. Today, there are about 46 state councils and more than 200 metropolitan or city agencies with employed staff. Several hundred more operate with volunteers only.

In Canada, there are one provincial, one interprovincial, and thirty-six local councils. Three of the groups identify themselves as interfaith bodies.

A current trend is toward interfaith councils in major metropolitan places and in a few states (such as Arkansas and in the District of Columbia). These councils include Jewish, Buddhist, Muslim, and other religious groups along with various Christian bodies.

Another innovation is the development of community ministries within metropolitan neighborhoods. While usually choosing not to identify themselves as "councils of churches," these groups provide a similar forum for interchurch cooperation at the neighborhood level.

A further development is the increasing frequency with which evangelical and conservative churches are involved in local councils, though they ordinarily avoid official ties with some national and world bodies. *See also* Ecumenical Education; National Council of the Churches of Christ in the U.S.A.; Sunday School Movement; World Council of Churches.

J. C. Bush

Counseling

Counseling is a helping service that uses dialogue to guide a person in dealing with a problem of self, situation, or both. Most counselors are members of teaching, psychological, medical, religious, legal, or social work professions. A brief and general term for someone seeking such help is "client." Dialogue may be one-to-one or in a group.

Problems addressed in counseling range from objective to subjective concerns. For example, legal counsel may impart impersonal information, while family counseling deals with intimate feelings. A mixture of the objective and subjective, the personal and impersonal, can be volatile.

Personalities of clients and counselors similarly run the gamut.

Ideally, dialogue in counseling is candid, trustful conversation about decisions that affect the course of a life. After the brave decision to face one's predicament and seek help, and after some initial embarrassment and relief, one begins to explore and discover. Counseling becomes a vivid series of learnings about self, change, and coping with change. It is a dynamic process. Protestations may alternate with quiet reflection. Ideas, feelings, and attitudes move rapidly in changing patterns with too many levels of meaning for words to capture fully in the passing moment.

TRADITIONAL COUNSELING

Ancient priests and rulers issued authoritative advice or counsel. Lawyers and physicians still do. Clients seek out these professionals for the information they can provide about their area of expertise, and dialogue is often a "one-way street."

Socrates used dialogue for great teaching and finally for comforting his mourners as he was dying. Job's friends came to console him in his suffering, concerned for his salvation. Their dialogue became a debate on divine justice. In all eras, people have poured out grief and complaints to God and representative figures.

People often need help today coping with the many forms of loss: of persons, home, work, community, self-esteem. Grief counseling today encourages full expression of sorrow and its many connected emotions. Family, friends, and clergy bear one another's burdens, as anger, fear, and grief are poured out. Both those who grieve and those who listen can be sustained in faith through such encounters.

Of all the traditional resources for personal renewal, none is so powerful as the way of repentance, confession, and forgiveness. Often neglected because it is hard to reach, forgiveness unlocks the chains of past error and blame, releasing new energies for good. Resentment may be held against a person or a group and may be justified or the result of misunderstanding. The counselor helps a person acknowledge and view the resentment in the perspective of possible causes, present effects, and the positive results of healing. Families, friends, and communities, including religious communities, can be reunited and strengthened. Counseling can expose and remove barriers to forgiveness.

THE EXPANDING SCOPE OF COUNSELING

Vast new information has come out of human research in the past hundred years. The inner self has been explored like a new continent, and counselors have had to incorporate tentative views of personality that were rapidly expanding and often competing. Practice and research are still trying to plumb the human depths. Complexities of human thinking, feeling, and acting have led to specializations.

There is no uniform system for classifying current specializations in counseling fields. Educational and vocational counseling use tests and other means to fit persons and situations together. Psychotherapy uses dialogue, free association, and numerous other techniques as well as medications to reduce disabling symptoms. Family, drug and alcohol, sex, grief, delinquency, and welfare counseling get their labels from their problem areas. Pastoral counseling deals with many such problems, and particularly with ethical issues and spiritual growth. For "well" people who want self-fulfillment, many counselors offer growth counseling. Some approaches, named by method, are rational-emotive, cognitive, behavioral, Gestalt, and transactional analysis.

Within these overlapping and patchwork fields, there are similarities in basic skills of helping people that are useful to nonprofessionals.

COUNSELING SKILLS AND PRINCIPLES

Many people are adept at conversational courtesies, showing respect to others and encouraging their strengths. After brief training, clinics have used such persons and found them highly effective. In religious circles, laypersons often perform humane services beyond the reach of clergy. These are widely useful counseling skills:

Listening is first, using all senses so actively that one invites further telling. Any urge to give a quick solution risks interference with hearing the real problem or giving the other person a chance to develop abilities to solve problems.

The counselor's side of the dialogue should be put in *clear language*, with concrete examples and in terms the other person can understand. This sets a good example and paves the way to understanding.

Entering into someone's life is like entering that person's home, public areas first, then private. The counselor is honored as a visitor who, in turn, respects the host. While listening and responding, the counselor enters into the feelings, thoughts, and outlook of the client while maintaining objectivity. This is called *empathy*, which says, "I know how you feel." Sympathy would say, "I feel the same as you." Through empathy the counselor can be a human bridge for the client to cross over from fruitless struggle to greater competence.

An early *working agreement* avoids wasted effort. How personal or situational is the predicament? What will each participant take responsibility to do? At regular intervals, summing up and redefining will advance the process. What is going on just now and right here? What are the snags? What are the assets, the creative abilities and interests, the ultimate hopes?

Finding *further resources* is a skill for gaining versatility. Good counselors seek help and refer. Public libraries and church or pastoral libraries contain literature on counseling, but cramming experience into textbook formulas can cripple. To avoid pitfalls, nonprofessionals should consult with professionals. Most clergy have had training for counseling and referring.

In new territory one needs both practical methods and guiding principles. Counseling at its best honors these:

1. Persons are valued for their intrinsic worth in the sight of God.

2. Counseling is a quest for what is true, real, and honest. "Behold, thou desirest truth in the inward being; therefore teach me wisdom in my secret heart" (Ps. 51:6).

3. Counseling seeks wholeness, which comes through integrity within the self and with others.

4. One's well-being is linked with increasing freedom to make choices and to be responsible for decisions.

5. In ways sometimes untraceable, the ethical values of the counselor influence clients.

6. Human achievement in counseling is only a modest part of God's participation.

RELIGIOUS EDUCATORS AS COUNSELORS

Religious educators are not technically counselors and will need to sense early in a conversation if a referral is in order; if one is not sure, consulting the pastor in general terms that do not violate confidence may aid in the decision. Parents will come to talk about a child. Other teachers have a problem with a class. Young people will share with a youth leader situations that might not be shared with peers or parents. Children may reveal more of a home situation than a teacher would wish to hear. Members of an adult class may share with the teacher a personal or work-related problem. Empathy and the willingness to listen are key factors. In listening, religious educators are helping people to learn through their personal expression of concern. *See also* Communication Theory; Conversation; Dialogue; Empathy; Ministry; Peer Ministry; Psychotherapy; Social Work; Spiritual Direction.

R. A. Preston

Covenant

A covenant is an agreement made between two or more persons or groups in which each agrees to perform certain acts with reciprocal response from the other. Faithfulness is expected as a measure of the integrity of each party and the mutual trust between them.

In the Old Testament, the primary covenant is the bond that secures the relationship between God and Israel. Its form is similar to that of the suzerain-vassal treaties of the ancient Near East, examples of which come from the archives of the princes of the so-called New Empire of the Hittites. These political treaties begin with a prologue describing the suzerain's deeds on behalf of the vassal and list stipulations the vassal must fulfill. The implication of the form is that the vassal should remain loyal to the suzerain by obeying the terms of the treaty because the vassal has received the benefits of the suzerain's acts. Then the treaty is affirmed in the presence of witnesses. In the Pentateuch, the mighty act of God in the Exodus sets the stage for the delivery of the covenantal law at Sinai (Exod. 1–17). The law is presented in detail (Exod. 18–Deut. 32). And finally the witness bonds the relationship as effective (Deut. 33).

The Old Testament also uses the term "covenant" to describe another type of relationship, the promises given by God to Abraham (Gen. 15) and David (2 Sam. 7). These covenants do not follow the form of the Sinai covenant in that Abraham and David do not have to perform a specific set of stipulations or laws (except perhaps continued faithfulness to the God of Israel) to receive what God has promised them.

The idea of covenant continues as a key concept throughout the Bible. Not only is the history of Israel in the Old Testament seen in light of the Sinai covenant, but so are the story of Jesus and the development of the apostolic church in the New Testament. New Testament writers speak of the "new covenant" in Jesus Christ.

Covenant is frequently used as a theme around which the religious education curriculum is structured. Young children can be introduced to the idea of covenant through the story of the rainbow as God's promise to Noah (Gen. 9:12–17), and elementary students can learn about Abraham and the story of the Exodus culminating in the giving of the Ten Commandments to Moses on Mount Sinai. But it should be noted that a fuller grasp of the nature of promise and responsibility is not usually possible until children reach the approximate age of ten. The more complex issues connected with covenant, for example faithfulness, accountability, and freedom, are important topics for adult study both as they concern biblical history and contemporary life. The concept of the "new covenant" as it relates to the Eucharist, usually reserved for adults, helps individuals discover greater meaning and fuller participation in the liturgy. *See also* Child Development; Commitment; Faith; Freedom; Moral Development; Ten Commandments.

G. W. Coats

Crafts

Crafts refers to the use of materials in the creation of an object. Crafts evolved from skills learned out of necessity and became an outlet for the need to express a person's creative energies; thus, a person made an earthen bowl for utilitarian purposes and was moved to decorate it with a variety of designs. Structures were built to serve the basic need for shelter, and builders were moved to construct temples embellished with woodcarvings, paintings, and stained glass, their own expressions of awe and adoration for a higher being.

In religious education, crafts become a means of reflecting the image of God in each person. Individuals are given the opportunity to take creation and reshape it. In so doing, students discover that each person, as a child of God, has creative abilities; find a concept reinforced in a learning activity; and participate, in certain settings, in the recognition and appreciation of the abilities of others in the community.

A teacher in religious education might use crafts for a variety of reasons, for example, for the *stimulation of ideas*. Students are given a piece of clay and asked to show the meaning of a word or concept such as community, resurrection, love, or hate by molding the clay in any way that

expresses each individual's own interpretation. Crafts facilitate the *input of factual data*. Students are given opportunity to stitch with yarn on fabric a biblical passage or set of facts such as the Ten Commandments. *A concept or data can be reinforced*. A student might choose to create a mobile of religious symbols using coat hangers, string, paper, and crayons or markers.

Crafts are also used for *the intentional building of a positive concept of self in students*. The building up of persons as valuable children of God uses the "I can do it" principle—anything the student creates and finds meaningful is acceptable. In so doing, motivation for crafts becomes the joy of expression that is not hampered by a preconceived idea of what is worthy and unworthy, as often happens in the giving of awards for levels of achievement or expecting that each project look the same when finished.

Finally, crafts can *build community*. Before projects are chosen, the teacher can build a sense of cooperation and shared effort among students, as well as shared appreciation for the creativity of other persons. In a class where the skills of making stained glass are taught, students given the choice of creating individual pieces feel a sense of community from shared learning of skills as well as shared joy upon the completion of objects of beauty. Or the teacher might choose to involve the class in a project in which each person contributes a part to the final project, thereby creating a sense of community accomplishment.

When considering crafts within the context of religious education, teachers can think of the many artistic ways in which faith has been expressed through sign and symbol. The Bible provides many examples of this. The book of Jeremiah describes the workings of the potter at the wheel. And the New Testament records God's choice of Joseph, a craftsman, to provide the nurture for his Son.

While use of certain craft materials are more appropriate than others at times and while monitoring of craft sessions is necessary (particularly when working with very young children as shown by the table accompanying this article), the use of crafts in religious education is often overly restricted. Three year olds can use clay, as can adult artists. Small children use finger paints, and adults use them for making gift wrappings. When learners are free to explore a medium, they will find their own possibilities. Only when teachers have a specific idea in mind can a craft become too easy or too difficult for learners. Unfortunately, although crafts are widely enjoyed by adults, too little use has been made of this teaching method. This is an area for exploration. *See also* Aesthetics; Constructive Activities; Creative Activities; Creativity; Finger Painting; Project.

G. Q. Bannerman

CRAFTS

Age Level	General Guidelines	Suitable Activities and Materials
Preschool (Ages 3–5)	Close supervision is necessary at all times; clothing and carpeting should be protected from spills; craft time should be left unstructured periodically to encourage creativity; projects should be easily completed in 10–15 minutes.	Pictures and posters to illustrate stories can be made with crayons, poster and finger paints, colored paper, paste, and blunt scissors; people and objects can be molded from playdough and plasticene clay; hand puppets can be made with crayons and paper bags; rhythm instruments (drums, rattles, tambourines) can be made from discarded cardboard containers and aluminum tins, buttons, bottle tops, sticks, and stones.
Grades 1–8	Supervision can be gradually diminished, and help given only when needed; craft time should be left unstructured periodically; work on projects can continue for 15–30 at a time and projects may take several weeks to complete; some projects should require children to work together in groups.	Stories, songs, and Scripture verses can be illustrated using pens, pencils, paints, crayons, felt-tipped markers, construction paper, and scissors; older children can make models of historical scenes and events using cardboard, papier-mache, and other materials; paper, felt, cloth, and yarn can be used to make a variety of puppets and costumes for dramatizations; videotapes, films, and slide shows can also be created.
High School and Adult	Art and craft sessions should generally focus on teaching new skills and encouraging creativity; the majority of time spent on crafts should be unstructured; specific projects may be enjoyed from time to time and are best planned and agreed to by everyone.	Materials and tools can be used as needed.

Creation

Few biblical doctrines are as important as that of creation. The Hebrew Bible claims and the New Testament also affirms that God is the Creator of all that has being in the entire universe. Often the import of this claim can be missed. The doctrine of creation asserts that there is no being in the universe that is not a creation of God—thus all the powers of the universe owe their very existence to God.

God, accordingly, has no divine rivals. All powers that may seek to oppose the will of God are finally unable to do so. God as Creator may allow opposition to the divine will, but the Creator has no uncreated independent entities with which to deal.

Today the doctrine of creation requires very careful statement so that it does not support a picture of God as despotic power, insensitive to the character of created reality, insistent upon its own way, and bent upon justice irrespective of the creation's need for compassion. God's determination to be peacemaker, savior, friend, and compassionate one must be stressed. In this way creation is not viewed only as an act of power, but also an act of tenderness, love, and compassion. One fine symbol of this dimension of creation is found in Proverbs 8:22–31, where wisdom is said to have been present with God, taking delight in the wonders of God's creation and joining happily in the joy of it all.

From these basic understandings of God flow two specific applications for religious education. From their earliest years, children need to be taught to cultivate a sense of wonder at and delight in the natural world and be thankful to God for beauty. They also need to realize that there are natural forces stemming from creation that can bring disasters such as earthquakes and storms and against which human beings can only take precautions.

The doctrine of creation has also brought an emphasis on ecology and our responsibility to protect and cherish God's good creation. Teaching about care of the earth and practice of that teaching, both personally and communally, are expressions of this concern. *See also* Bible in Religious Education, The; Ecology; God, Understandings of.

W. Harrelson

Creative Activities

Creative activities are a frequently misunderstood aspect of the teaching/learning process. Some teaching strategies are called creative activities when in fact they should be named differently. And some teachers and leaders have doubts regarding the instructional value of creative activities.

Creative activities are those instructional strategies that invite participants to respond to some aspect of the subject matter by choosing from among a variety of available media. Participants utilize those media in original ways to express their own ideas, feelings, perspectives, or beliefs in order to communicate to others what is important to them. If one of the goals of instruction is to move from remembering essential information to integrating that information in one's thinking, believing, and acting, then creative activities are a necessary step toward achieving that goal.

Let us consider an illustration of one way creative activities may be employed in a typical class session. A class is studying God's call of Moses in the Midian desert. The narrative from Exodus 3 is presented through reading Scripture, viewing a filmstrip, and discussing appropriate questions. After dealing with the narrative objectively and analytically, the participants are invited to respond by choosing from among three or more options as a means to express what they personally think, feel, or believe.

The participants bring with them to the study of Moses their own memories, values, experiences, interests, and needs. They respond to the narrative of God's call of Moses with all that they bring and with the available resources to produce something personal, original, and meaningful that has never been seen or heard before. One participant produces a set of six drawings that express visually God's call of Moses. A second participant writes an entry in Moses' journal to reflect in a simulated way the impact of that event upon Moses' life. And still another participant works with a small group to choreograph a dramatic movement that captures the feelings of Moses at the time of his call by God. Following the sharing of these activities with the whole class the teacher engages the learners in a time of discussion in which they reflect on the meanings of the biblical narrative and seek to identify with that event in personal ways that connect with their own life experiences.

The above illustration represents several general, essential principles relevant to the use of creative activities as part of a teaching strategy.

1. The teacher's own session plan is in itself a creative activity.

2. Careful study of a subject precedes the use of creative activities; it provides a frame of reference from which to respond creatively.

3. Several alternative creative activities are offered, each appealing to different senses, interests, or abilities of the learners.

4. The activities invite the learners to employ their own experiences, ideas, feelings, and in-

terpretations as they respond personally to the subject.

5. The activities are presented to the rest of the class not as exhibits to be judged, but as gifts to be shared.

6. Elements of both the cognitive and the affective domains are being utilized.

7. The teacher builds upon the creative activities of all the participants by engaging them in meaningful conversation and reflection.

Many teachers and much of the curriculum resources they use include other kinds of activities that are not to be confused with creative activities. Students' workbooks contain many suggestions that can best be described as reinforcement activities—"fill-in-the-blank" activities, crossword puzzles, matching exercises, finding the words or verses, deciphering the code, and other similar activities that require the remembering of the information in order to be successful. Although these reinforcement activities usually take a lot of time, are enjoyed by many learners, and are useful in helping the learners to recall important information, they do nothing to invite the learners to express themselves creatively.

Another type of teaching activity usually mistakenly identified as creative activity is what teachers often refer to as "crafts." Many teachers' manuals and learners' workbooks (especially for children's classes) include an abundance of craft suggestions. This type of activity usually has a definite pattern to follow, a series of specific steps to take to complete the task, and a clear indication of how the finished product should appear. Learners may enjoy doing these activities and teachers may have a sense of satisfaction that something has been accomplished, but activities of this type do very little to encourage the learners to respond to the subject matter in significant ways that enable them to express their own insights, learnings, or interpretations. Crafts and reinforcement activities have their place within the varied repertoire of teaching, but they should not be confused with or take the place of creative activities. See also Affective Development; Crafts; Creativity; Methodology; Teaching Styles.

D. L. Griggs, P. Griggs

Creativity

An understanding of the nature of creativity begins with an affirmation of God as the Creator of all that exists. Scripture speaks of a Creator God and declares that God has created human beings in God's own image. Being created in the image of God suggests that every individual has both the potential and the responsibility to participate with God in a partnership that works to bring fulfillment to God's creation.

It is common to hear teachers and others in the church say, "I am not creative," and it is true that most of us are not artists in the classical sense. However, if creativity is seen as the innate, God-given ability all people have to be able to perceive their world and to express themselves in unique, meaningful ways, then no one should ever accept the status of "not being creative."

Teachers and leaders in religious education settings are creative when they use their own skills, ideas, and experiences to communicate with others. They are creative when they adapt and relate curriculum and other resources to the particular needs, interests, and abilities of the persons they teach or lead. They also act in creative ways when they relate to others in personal, sensitive, and helpful ways, responding to them as individuals who are also endowed with special gifts. When other persons are enabled to express themselves in creative ways as a result of a teacher's or leader's guidance and encouragement, that teacher's or leader's creativity is fulfilled to a significant degree.

A number of factors encourage and enhance creativity and some hinder it. Creativity is inhibited when there is preoccupation with structure and order at the expense of trying new forms and looking at the world from different perspectives. Competition to produce the best, the prettiest, the most acceptable expression, where some receive recognition and praise and others feel judged and devalued, will inhibit many from ever attempting to express themselves creatively. The "filling-in-the-blank" approach of many religious education resources and processes, with its emphasis on producing the "right answer," is a hindrance to thinking and expressing oneself in unique, meaningful ways. Creativity is also frustrated when persons are expected to produce something worthwhile in a limited amount of time, with limited resources, or without sufficient motivation.

On the other hand, many factors contribute to people's ability to express themselves creatively. What people see, hear, smell, and feel when walking into a room often affects their willingness to participate. It is important to give careful attention to the physical environment in which any class, group, or committee meets. The arrangement of furniture, the visual displays on the walls, the lighting and temperature, as well as the ease of movement and accessibility of resources can suggest an open, inviting, and safe place in which to work.

The emotional environment is as important as the physical environment. When teachers and leaders are accepting and respectful of others' expressions, even if they do not agree with them, there is increased willingness on the part of the participants to offer their own insights and proposals. Teachers and leaders can communicate in verbal as well as nonverbal ways that in their group participants will be listened to, accepted, respected, and trusted. Such acceptance contributes significantly to a creative process of mutual exploring and sharing.

Creativity is prompted by a desire to seek solutions to problems, to explore unknown realms of reality, to follow one's curiosity in searching for new insights, and to express oneself in personally fulfilling ways. When people are provided opportunities to experiment and practice with the resources at hand, they are more likely to be creative than if they are expected to produce finished products or have correct answers the first time around.

A wide variety of viable options from which to make choices also encourages creativity. When questions invite reflection and interpretation rather than just recall of information, people are stimulated to think and respond creatively. When a variety of materials or resources are provided or when two or more alternative activities are offered, the participants will be able to express themselves more creatively than if there are few resources and options.

Teachers and leaders in religious education programs are influential in fostering a climate and processes for enabling others to express themselves creatively. To do so they must first work at acting creatively themselves. *See also* Affective Development; Crafts; Creation; Creative Activities; Curiosity; Methodology; Teaching Styles.

D. L. Griggs, P. Griggs

Creed

A creed is a concise, formal, authorized statement of faith; the Apostles' and Nicene creeds are classical expressions of the faith that is fundamental to becoming and being a Christian.

The church's earliest baptismal confession was "Jesus is Lord." Gradually, following Matthew 28:19, a trinitarian creedal confession emerged. By the fourth century these various confessions evolved in the West into what is known as the Creed of the Apostles; it soon became the Western church's agreed-upon baptismal creed. In the Eastern church, by the fourth century a conciliar creed promulgated with the authority of a council emerged to define the faith upon which community life was to be founded. This creed, known as the Nicene Creed, while an expression of the Council of Nicaea in 325, was actually the product of the later Council of Constantinople in 381. In the East this creed became the church's baptismal creed; in the West it became associated with the celebration of the Eucharist. Together the Apostles' and Nicene creeds are examples of the church's faith throughout the ages and the normative recital of God's saving activity characteristic of all biblical and liturgical worship.

PURPOSE AND USAGE

While those whose roots are in the Radical Reformation (the Anabaptists) have not used the creeds as the standard for Christian faith and life or the body of distinctive Christian teaching upon which foundational or dogmatic theology is founded, the Orthodox, Roman Catholic, Anglican, and classical Reformation churches have. Even those Protestant communions who have made a point of affirming that the Holy Scriptures contain all that is necessary for salvation have also asserted that the Apostles' and Nicene creeds represent essential summaries of Christian theology. Further, while some attempt in the modern period has been made to write contemporary creedal expressions, such as the United Church of Christ's "Statement of Faith" and the United Church of Canada's "Affirmation of Faith," authorized for use by United Methodists, still the vast majority of Western Christians use the Apostles' Creed as their baptismal creed and the Nicene Creed as their eucharistic creed.

Some Christians interpret the creeds literally; others see them as symbols of faith or signs pointing to what is most surely believed among us but what is at the same time open to a variety of interpretations. Traditionally these creeds are understood as pledges of allegiance. The language of the creeds is performative; that is, it is deemed effective in that it does what it says: the creeds aim to set our hearts (*credo*) upon a particular perception of life and our lives and by so doing shape our consciousness, convictions, and commitments. A creed, therefore, is not so much an intellectual assertion that certain doctrinal propositions are true, as it is a symbolic proposition to which we freely give our loyalty; that is, it represents first of all an act of commitment, an act of the will in which heart and mind are involved and about which we suspend judgment until we discover its truth in our experience of living it.

Over the years, the creeds have served many purposes: an outline of that rule of faith into which Christians are to be formed; a standard of orthodoxy and a safeguard against false teaching; and the foundational content of the church's catechetical ministry.

The primary context for the use of the creeds in the early church was unquestionably baptismal catechesis and the rite of baptism. At the climax of the catechumen's baptismal preparation, the creed was "handed over" and interpreted to the "elect" so that they might "give it back" in the presence of the community at their baptism on the Vigil of Easter. Baptism represented a deliberate distinctive change in a person's faith and a dramatic change in her or his character: the creed encompassed the essential characteristics of this new way of faith and life. As such, its motive and purpose were doxology and witness. In both their catechetical and liturgical uses, the creeds summarize those essential affections, convictions, and commitments that are foundational to becoming and being Christian. In succeeding centuries of the Middle Ages, as Christianity became the religion of Europe, the creeds continued to be used regularly as affirmations of faith at baptism and the Eucharist, but without the early emphasis on change and witness.

During the period of the church's sixteenth-century Reformation the creeds assumed once again an important place in the church's worship and teaching as the test of orthodoxy; so it is that we find the Apostles' Creed at the heart of the confessions and catechisms of the Reformed churches. For the succeeding three centuries, after the boundaries between Catholic and Protestant nations became clearer, the creeds became predominantly an affirmation of the historic bases for the faith among those Christian groups that regularly or occasionally included them in the liturgy.

Today as baptism, baptismal renewal, and eucharistic worship assume renewed importance in Christian churches, the Apostles' and Nicene creeds once again become essential and important elements in Christian formation and education.

Among Roman Catholics, Lutherans, and Anglicans, the creed has regularly been an important element in the preparation for confirmation. This class is usually taught by the priest or pastor or some specifically designated person such as a deacon or deaconess. The age range for confirmation is nine through fourteen (older in some European countries). Younger children may be introduced to the opening sentence of each of the three basic affirmations (belief in God, belief in Jesus Christ, and belief in the Holy Spirit) in Sunday school or earlier. The creed is also used for adult study courses and is part of the Rite of Christian Initiation for Adults (RCIA) presently being encouraged for use in Roman Catholic parishes. See also Baptism; Catechesis; Catechism; Catechumenate; Commitment; Confirmation; Doctrine/Dogma; Eucharist; History of Christian Education.

J. H. Westerhoff

Cultic Religious Movements

A cult or a sect is a religious group that differs markedly from socially dominant, organized religions, in Western societies those related to the Judeo-Christian tradition. Although there is no universal agreement on the exact definitions of "cult" and "sect" and which groups may be placed in these categories, the terms are helpful in distinguishing religious organizations from a sociological perspective.

DISTINCTIONS FROM THE MAINSTREAM

How cult and sect groups differ from the mainstream religious organizations is a matter of continuing analysis and debate within the field of sociology. Among the various efforts to describe the differences there has emerged the awareness that the differences are more than religious beliefs and practices. A key point of difference is the relationship of the cult or sect to dominant culture and society. Mainstream religious organizations, often called church type, are in general accepting of dominant culture and society. Mainstream religious organizations tend to accommodate to their social setting and accept the prevailing economic and political systems. Church-type religious organizations generally support the socially accepted approaches to education, law, and medicine. Members of church-type religious organizations participate in leisure-time pursuits characteristic of their social class. Such accommodation by church-type groups does not rule out points of conflict and tension with the dominant society, but the overall posture of these groups toward society is positive.

Cult and sect groups, on the other hand, are not so positively disposed toward the dominant society and culture. The posture of these religious groups toward society and culture ranges from indifference to hostility to withdrawal. The common feature is a certain disdain of or intransigence toward society and culture. Specific groups work out different behavior patterns toward their social setting. Some groups, for instance, may accept the economic system while rejecting participation in the political system. Other groups may accept both economic and political systems while rejecting standard medical practice. Still other groups, rejecting virtually all dominant social institutions, geographically withdraw to isolated areas in order to establish a society they favor.

On deeper inspection, cult and sect groups differ from mainstream religious organizations at two other related points. The first is what is taken for granted about reality itself. What is really real? What is really real about human nature or the universe? Cult and sect groups answer these questions in various forms and differ not only among themselves, but also from the dominant society; they inhabit different landscapes of reality. These groups also differ on the ways of knowing. How does one know what is really real? Again, cult and sect groups have their own answers to this question. Church-type religious bodies, on the other hand, tend to accept the prevailing definitions of reality and ways of knowing. Such accommodation is not without tension and may be of long duration in resolution. Church-type religious organizations, at least in Western cultural settings, are relatively open to all aspects of socially sanctioned learning, including science.

DISTINCTIONS BETWEEN CULTS AND SECTS

Although cult and sect groups have some similar characteristics, there are significant differences between them. The religious sect group, although disdaining the prevalent society and culture and its religious organizations, maintains a connection with the historic religious tradition of the society. In Western cultural contexts, religious sect groups are those that continue to define themselves in terms of the Judeo-Christian tradition. Such groups may claim to be the correct or pristine form of the original religious faith and assess the mainstream religious institutions as apostate or corrupted by the world. The religious sect has a propensity for looking to the past for direction in terms of its definitions of religious experience, beliefs, ritual, and conduct. The religious sect tends to be restorationist in character. The original purity of the religious tradition has been compromised or lost, and the sect attempts to restore or reconstitute what is thought by the group to be the original religious tradition.

Religious sects, however, differ among themselves. There have been numerous attempts to place religious sects into different categories based on factors such as styles of organization and leadership, behavior patterns toward dominant social institutions and cultural values, social classes from which constituents come, and means of salvation. Most of the investigations of religious sect movements have been carried out in Western cultural settings and much of the findings reflect a Judeo-Christian orientation.

Cult groups, on the other hand, while sharing with sect groups a disdain for mainstream religious institutions, may not necessarily maintain any connection with the historic religious tradition of the society. The characteristics of a religious cult as a particular form of organization are the most difficult to find agreement on among sociologists. There is some consensus that cultic religious movements claim new disclosures of truth or new revelations of reality that are markedly different from the generally accepted knowledge of the dominant society. When a religious cult turns to the past for direction in terms of its definitions of religious experience, beliefs, ritual, and conduct, it is not bound by any historic religious tradition. The cult may claim to have truth from various religious traditions, such as Eastern or African religions. Cult groups tend to be syncretisms in which selected elements from various religious faiths are combined into a pattern or program. Elements from the Judeo-Christian tradition may be appropriated and harmonized with aspects taken from other religions of the world. It must be said, however, that the concept of cult is ambiguous and has received no unanimous definition within either social science or theology.

Religious sect and cult groups provide alternative ways of viewing the meaning of life and the nature of reality and for coping with crisis. These alternative religions offer resolution to some sense of loss experienced by individuals or by groups who share common perceptions of deprivation. Such experiences of deprivation cover a range of conditions from the loss of economic sustenance, social status, or health and bodily function to the loss of psychological equilibrium. The appeal of religious sect and cult groups is particularly felt at times of stress associated with transitional stages in human growth and development. Puberty, adolescence, mid-life, retirement, and old age mark transitional stages in the human life cycle. Such conditions are normal to human experience. When the socially accepted and traditional ways of coping fail to provide relief, alternative ways are explored. The number and persistence of religious cult and sect groups provide a new dimension to religious pluralism. *See also* Sociology of Religion.

FOR FURTHER REFERENCE

Melton, J. Gordon, and Robert L. Moore. *The Cult Experience: Responding to the New Religious Pluralism*. New York: Pilgrim, 1982.

N. B. Fowler

Culture

While the term "culture" has several meanings, in reference to human beings culture describes the characteristics of a group or society—the customs, ideas, behavior, and values that form its way of life—characteristics that are transmitted by learning processes rather than by genetics. The smaller the group, the more likely it is that the behavior and moral values of the persons in the group are uniform. The larger the group becomes, the more diverse its behavior and moral values become. Yet in both groups there is an overarching set of ideals that influences the outlook and worldview of the persons who are participants in the society.

In smaller, homogeneous, nonindustrial societies, as existed in ages past and still exist in some parts of the world today (the Bedouin in the Middle East, the tribes of sub-Saharan Africa), cultural identity is maintained primarily through allegiance to family, clan, and/or tribe. Local leaders are the arbiters of laws and religious customs and the family is the main transmitter of cultural expectations.

Larger, pluralistic societies like the United States or Canada are made up of many different ethnic, religious, economic, and geographical subgroups. Each subgroup accepts the principles of the dominant, overarching culture—as expressed through the country's laws, language, and other national social, economic, and political institutions—but each may define their implications for its life in its own way, maintaining certain other customs and traditions peculiar to the subgroup itself. Culture, whether of a particular subgroup or the pluralistic society in general, thus describes the blending of all the composite, generally held, valued ideals of a group sharing a common identity.

How is culture transmitted? The most important avenue of transmission is language. Language is the principle means by which the behavioral expectations, individual needs, desires, and reactions to others' behavior are communicated among persons. Since words are the symbols of what persons experience and value, language is a basic transmitter and shaper of culture.

Culture is also transmitted by social institutions. The basic institution in all cultures is the family. Family groupings generally are described as either nuclear or extended. In the nuclear family the traditional pattern is that the children live and are reared under the influence of the father and mother. This type is more prevalent in Western industrialized cultures. In agricultural and nonindustrialized societies the family unit includes grandparents and relatives. Whatever the family structure may be, it shapes the values and expectations of the children. The adults teach the children approved and unapproved behavior. The group's social and religious heritage and rituals are taught to each generation.

In pluralistic cultures, schools provide a major source of learning. Initially, children learn the principles of reading, writing, and mathematics. As they progress, they study increasingly specialized phases of life—art, music, science, or vocational training. They are taught the history of the nation and world.

Religious institutions are also vehicles of cultural transmission. Sects and denominations form formal groups to serve the spiritual needs of their followers and train their children in their respective religious heritage. They employ their own forms of worship and educational methods to transmit their religious faith. Religious education occurs as children participate in the life of the faith community and as they receive any formal classroom teaching the group may provide.

Political structures and processes are also a significant part of culture. Some leaders inherit their office; others are elected. The political structure, whether a democracy, dictatorship, or kingship, also establishes ways to enforce its regulations about marriage, inheritance, property rights, protection of human life, and permissible avenues for sexual expressions. The government also determines the freedoms its citizens enjoy or are denied and how dissenters from its mores and violators of its laws will be punished.

As one looks at a small tribe or large nation, one gets a composite view of its total life. One comes to know its culture—its total ideals and values. *See also* Enculturation; Ethnicity; Multicultural Education; Sociology of Religion; Tradition; Transmission.

F. F. Wise

Curiosity

Curiosity is a strong desire to know, investigate, or find out about something. Aroused curiosity leads to "teachable moments," psychologist Robert Havinghurst's term for those moments of increased receptivity to learning, and shows readiness to learn. The Old Testament indicates that religious rituals (Exod. 13:14), a life-style of obedience to God's commands (Deut. 6:20), and symbols (Josh. 4:6) will make children curious. They will then ask questions about the meaning of religious observances and adults can share their story and their faith.

The methods of religious education today should arouse curiosity. The young can be involved in rituals of the faith, helped to see the lifestyle of the parent and teacher, and introduced to appropriate symbols. Questions will come from the learners when they are ready to explore them.

Using stories containing suspense and formulating well-phrased questions can stimulate curiosity. Such material will touch the felt needs of the learners and cause them to want to know if God has answers for those needs.

Appreciation should be expressed for questions, and curiosity should be encouraged. Students should also see the teacher's deep desire to know, the teacher's own curiosity about the things of God. *See also* Creativity; Questions.

C. Stonehouse

Curriculum

Curriculum is the Latin word for "racecourse" and, alternatively, "career" or the "course of one's life." Theorists in religious education have emphasized curriculum as a dynamic course of growth guided by a standard of maturity comprising all the experiences (worship, service, study, and fellowship) a person may have in many settings (midweek and Sunday, camp and retreat, social action and mission). Most commonly, however, curriculum refers to the written materials guiding formal study.

EARLY HISTORY

While curriculum in the last sense is a modern phenomenon, throughout the centuries communities of faith have provided materials and institutions that nurtured religious growth. Ancient Israel found guidance for life in the command-

---

GUIDELINES FOR SELECTING CURRICULUM

---

1. Know your goals for religious education.
   To what extent are these reflected in the curriculum being evaluated?

2. Reflect on the basic biblical and theological understandings of your religious tradition.
   Are these similar to the ones reflected in the curriculum being evaluated?

3. Know the basic approach to education that your parents and teachers expect (the relation, for example, of content to experiential learning).
   What basic educational theories are used in the construction of the curriculum being evaluated?

4. Understand the characteristics of learners at each age level and as you intend to group them.
   How will the curriculum fit the needs of your learners as you intend to group them?

5. Look at the content of the curriculum.
   Will the whole story of the Bible be told over a span of years?
   Will basic theological understandings be learned at appropriate age levels?
   Will learners become well acquainted with their own tradition in history, practice, and worship?
   Will the material foster ecumenical understanding?
   Does it address itself to the specific life situation of the learners and adequately relate faith to life, both in personal experience and social responsibility?

6. Look at the format of the curriculum.
   Is the teacher's book attractively printed and are directions easy to follow?
   Are the pupils' books attractively illustrated and is the printed material appropriate to the age level?
   If there are activity materials or workbooks, will they stimulate various forms of learning?

---

ments and stories of the Torah, even as the need to give educational guidance to the church led to the formation of the New Testament. The Torah combined with the Prophets and the Writings remain the core of Jewish education, and these supplemented and interpreted through the Christian Scriptures remain central to Christian education.

The influence of Augustine of Hippo (A.D. 354–430) ensured that the pagan legacy of the liberal arts bequeathed to Rome from Greece would become integrated with Scripture in Christian education. The subjects of the school curriculum of the late Roman period and Middle Ages were the trivium (grammar, logic, and rhetoric) and the quadrivium (arithmetic, music, geometry, and astronomy). The Renaissance enriched the teaching of the trivium as universities developed and the Protestant Reformation gave new centrality to the Bible and hastened the development of instruction in the vernacular for the lower levels of schooling, but neither dislodged the liberal arts, which were fused with the Christian legacy of Scripture, doctrine, and theology. In the eighteenth century an emphasis upon the autonomy of human reason and the substitution of the nation-state for the church as sponsor in education split the former unity of the curriculum and gave rise to religious education as an activity distinct from education itself.

EMPHASIS OF THE BIBLE AND/OR LIFE

While the Protestant Reformation gave new vigor to an old pedagogical device, the catechism, the rapidly growing Sunday school movement in nine-teenth-century America found the Bible a more ec-umenical base for instruction than the doctrinally based catechisms. The adoption of the Uniform Lessons Series in 1872 enabled all ages in Sunday School, regardless of denominational affiliation, to study the same Bible text on a given Sunday and to complete a survey of the Bible every six years. Biblical texts for Uniform Lessons are still selected by a committee of the National Council of the Churches of Christ and still undergird some de-nominational curricula.

By 1900 Protestant Sunday school teachers were familiar with curriculum as a published se-ries of lessons based upon a biblical text and structured on a teaching method (preparation, presentation, association, and application) made popular by disciples of German educator Johann Friedrich Herbart (1776–1841).

At this same time progressive educational the-ory began to influence religious educators in the United States who saw the need to develop new teaching models responsive to the portrait drawn of children and youth in research studies, the com-plexity of urban industrial culture, and the results of the historical-critical study of the Bible. The new psychology undercut rationalist concepts of thinking and located the stimulus for learning in problem solving. When the predominantly Prot-estant religious education movement was orga-nized as the Religious Education Association in 1903, it included in its fellowship Catholic and Jewish educators equally responsive to these new opportunities.

George Albert Coe (1862–1951) defined cur-riculum for many of these reformers in *A Social Theory of Religious Education* (1917) not pri-marily as a systematic set of ideas, but as a pro-gressive order of motives actually at work here and now. The elements in this progressive order were "to help the pupil to experience growing communion with God in and through growing hu-man fellowships in the family, the church, and elsewhere, [through] fellowship in the act of wor-ship with the help of music and the other arts, and in constructive and remedial social activities, which include the missionary enterprise but ex-pand it." These all required constant and growing discrimination, foresight, and deliberation, which called for "illumination from Scripture, history, doctrines, science, current events, and the crea-tions of imagination." His definition of curricu-lum pushed the boundaries of teaching and learning beyond the study of the Bible alone and beyond the methodologies of memorization and a simple adaptation of text to life.

Despite the creative work of curriculum de-signers who sought to interpret the connections that lie between the life of the learner and the life out of which the biblical text arose, the reformers may inadvertently have contributed to a perceived dichotomy between Bible and life. Discussion of curriculum in many a local church still finds ad-vocates of Bible-centered curriculum opposed to those who advocate life-centered curriculum. However, even conservative publishers make con-nections between Bible and life. Then and now the discussion of the relationship between biblical content and life was and is sharpened by the dif-fering conceptions of the Bible held by the dis-putants. On the one side is a Bible received from tradition and on the other side a Bible the com-position of which has been uncovered by textual and historical investigation.

The appearance in 1947 of Christian Faith and Life, a curriculum published by the Presby-terian Church (U.S.A.), advanced the discussion to a new level, since the curriculum recognized the results of biblical scholarship while giving a re-newed emphasis to traditional orthodoxy. The strength of this curriculum led many other de-nominations to embrace the biblical story of sal-vation as the key to organizing their curriculum. Mary C. Boys has recounted this effort to which Roman Catholic educators gave great emphasis in the period after Vatican II in *Biblical Interpreta-tion in Religious Education* (1980).

CONFESSIONAL AND ECUMENICAL EFFORTS

In the expansive period of church growth in the 1950s many denominations developed curricula growing out of their distinctive traditions, the most ambitious and creative of which was the Episcopal church's Seabury Series. By the end of the decade, a new ecumenical effort drew sixteen Protestant denominations into the Cooperative Curriculum Project of the National Council of the Churches of Christ. These denominations adopted the following as an overarching objective to give direction to both the churches' total educational ministry and the development of curriculum. The objective of Christian education, as stated in *The Church's Educational Ministry: A Curriculum Plan* (1965), is "that all persons be aware of God through his self-disclosure, especially his redeem-ing love as revealed in Jesus Christ, and that they respond in faith and love to the end that they may know who they are and what their human situ-ation means, grow as sons of God rooted in the Christian community, live in the Spirit of God in every relationship, fulfill their common disciple-ship in the world, and abide in the Christian hope." This volume outlined topics for curriculum development growing out of this objective, even as *Sharing the Light of Faith: National Catecheti-cal Directory for Catholics of the United States* (1979) described the scope of Catholic religious education.

The recognition that the disciplines of the-ology, philosophy, history, psychology, sociology, and communications theory all contribute to the development of a sound curriculum theory made those responsible for curriculum development in the individual denominations eager to continue to work cooperatively, especially as the complexity of curriculum development was matched by rising production costs.

The Joint Education Development (JED) project of twelve denominations, which published curricula jointly from 1978 to 1988, recognized differing educational needs in local churches and the existence of theological diversity by offering its members four curricular choices: Knowing, Interpreting, Living, and Doing the Word.

When the ten-year covenant to produce curricula together ended, JED agreed to continue the publishing partnership in a limited way, but clearly there was signaled a return to a confessional emphasis by the engagement of the Presbyterian and Reformed denominations to publish curricula together.

OTHER INFLUENCES

Throughout the twentieth century the goal or objective informing curriculum shifted as developments within theology and psychology offered different standards. Theologians gave new definitions to regeneration, which led to new visions of Christian maturity and vocation. Psychology provided new understandings of the dynamics of personality formation and offered its own definitions of psychological maturity. Research into cognitive development gave a new stimulus to tracing moral and faith development, which guided and enriched curriculum development but did not simplify or unify it. Currently renewed emphasis upon sacraments and rites and the cycle of the church year are shaping curriculum in denominations previously lacking such an emphasis.

RENEWED SIMPLICITY

The Protestant experience with curricular reform in the twentieth century has led to paradoxical outcomes. The reformers' ideal of a curriculum closely tied to the developmental needs of persons yielded before the persistent need of small churches to group children and youth together across a wide age range. The reformers who stressed the challenge of urban industrial culture to Christian life-style in the first half of the century found their heirs faltering before the challenge of inner-city culture to Christian life-style in the second half. Reformers who sought to base religious education upon scientific studies of child and adolescent life found that they inadvertently addressed the needs of white suburban youth and not the needs of black, Hispanic, Native American, and other minority youth. Reformers who sought to make the evangelical Sunday school of the nineteenth century more like a modern school with a carefully crafted curriculum found they minimized the enculturating power of faith communities. Reformers who criticized Uniform Lessons as too restrictive were replaced by reformers who sought to base curriculum design upon the common lectionary so that worship, preaching, and teaching could be unified. Reformers who sought a comprehensive blueprint to guide the educational plan of a whole denomination or group of denominations were met by reformers who stressed spontaneity and local church options in curriculum design. The conclusion to be drawn from these shifts is not that reform was illusionary or misplaced, but that in a complicated world educators are now framing curriculum with a renewed simplicity born out of much experience and reflection.

It becomes clear that choosing from among curricular options is a serious task, both for publishers constructing materials, judicatories recommending them, and parishes selecting them. Involved people such as religious education committees, teachers, parents, clergy, and youth and adult learners need to become participants in the quest. Only after charting the congregation's theological and biblical assumptions, educational philosophy, goals, cultural situation, parish size, age levels for classes, and resources (both in leadership and materials) can decisions be made. Careful preparation of this sort will help parents and teachers endorse the materials chosen and cooperate in their use. *See also* Catechesis; Catechism; Catechumenate; Engagement; Goals; History of Christian Education; Problem Solving; Sunday School; Systems Theory; Theology and Education; Uniform Lessons Series.

FOR FURTHER REFERENCE

Cully, Iris V. "Changing Patterns of Protestant Curriculum." In Marvin J. Taylor, ed., *Changing Patterns of Religious Education*. Nashville, TN: Abingdon Press, 1984.

Dewey, John. *The School and Society*. 1900. *The Child and the Curriculum*. 1902. Reprint. Introduction by Leonard Carmichael. Chicago: University of Chicago, 1963.

Westerhoff, John H., and William H. Willimon. *Liturgy and Learning Through the Life Cycle*. New York: Seabury, 1980.

Wyckoff, D. Campbell. *Theory and Design of Christian Education Curriculum*. Philadelphia: Westminster, 1961.

H. A. Archibald

Cursillo

The cursillo, "little course," is the descriptive title of a contemporary movement among Roman Catholic Spanish-speaking laypeople. The first cursillo was held in Spain in 1949. The original objective was that of Christianizing the whole world through the apostolic action of its committed members. Cursillos soon spread to other Spanish-speaking people, particularly in the southwestern areas in the United States (first in Texas, 1957); from there it spread to centers on the East and West coasts and areas in between.

Ideally the cursillo is an intensive community experience by those who voluntarily gather together to explore, experience, and better comprehend the ideal of their commitment to a life in Christ. The committee and faithful members are often called *cursillistas*. Usually numbering about forty men and women including some priests, the cursillistas come together on a Thursday evening and terminate their gathering on Sunday evening. During that time the priest members give five meditations and five talks that are referred to as "drills." Certain lay members of the group give additional "drills" in which they apply the theological content of the previous presentations to the realistic level of the participants' lives. The central action of each of the cursillos is the celebration of the community Mass. The schedule also provides time for private devotions of the individual participants—praying the rosary, meditations, and other personal prayers.

Throughout, attempts are made to create an atmosphere of friendship and conviviality. There are sessions of singing together, of exchanging stories, jokes, and experiences—all of which assist in developing a sense of unity and mutual acceptance.

The follow-up program, called postcursillo, includes small weekly reunions, of three to five members, and larger group reunions, in which participants share experiences and insights about their prayer life, study, and apostolic action. The movement operates within the framework of diocesan and parish pastoral plans and functions autonomously in each diocese under the direction of the local bishop.

Members of the cursillos attest to their gratitude for the movement by pointing out their personal benefits from the experiences. One specified realization expressed is their new insight into what a Christian community with Christ at its center should be. Simultaneously they point out that Christianity without community is a contradiction in terms. Such evaluations and insights emerge out of experienced periods, weekends, and other spontaneous gatherings in which the participants disclose their own assessments of the cursillo experience. The National Cursillo Center in the United States is located in Dallas, Texas. *See also* Adult Education; Hispanic Americans; Lay Ministry; Spiritual Direction; Spirituality.

M. C. Bryce

Cyril of Jerusalem

Cyril (ca. 315–386?), bishop of Jerusalem from about 350 to 386, lived during the time when the Arian controversy was a central issue in the history of Christianity. Cyril never wavered in his adherence to orthodoxy, steadfastly refusing all complicity with Arianism or its adherents' heretical doctrines, one of which denied the divinity of Christ.

Cyril is best known for his outstanding and highly esteemed prebaptismal catechetical lectures entitled "Instruction for Those About to Be Illumined." The instructions were originally given daily during the Lenten season at that part of the ceremony when the Scripture lessons were read and explained to the assembled congregation. The catecheses were directly addressed to those "inquirers" who hoped to be baptized at the Easter celebration.

Cyril was simple and clear in his teaching, avoiding as much as possible theological terms that might confuse his listeners. One of his biographers observed that "Cyril resembled Christ in his fusion of dogmatic and moral elements when he (Christ) presented the gospel." Cyril's objective was to impart revealed doctrine, which in turn would contribute to the candidates' growth in faith, understanding, and appreciation. *See also* Catechumenate; History of Christian Education.

M. C. Bryce

D

Dance

Dance is a natural expression of the human spirit using rhythmic movements with or without music. In ancient times dance was worship for all aspects of life: birth, puberty, courtship, celebration, survival, death.

In the Bible dance expresses joy and thanksgiving. Miriam led the women in dancing after crossing the Red Sea (Exod. 15:20). David danced before the ark of the Lord (2 Sam. 6:14). The psalmist exhorts one to praise the Lord in dance (Pss. 149:3; 150:4).

In later years Justin Martyr (ca. 100–165) and Hippolytus (ca. 170–235) tell of dancing as a part of Christian liturgy. Churches in Spain developed dance as an independent art form long after it had been removed from other European churches.

Dance as an expression of religious values has had a renewal in the twentieth century. The emergence of modern dance as an art form has freed dancers to explore biblical and theological themes. Across the United States, since the 1930s dance has been introduced into churches by groups labeled variously as "rhythmic choirs," "motion choirs," "symbolic movement," "worship in movement," "liturgical dance," and recently as "sacred dance choirs." Margaret Taylor, in the 1970s, was the first to write about the history of liturgical dance giving practical suggestions on the use of dance in churches. Her books include *A Time to Dance* (1980), *Look Up and Live* (1980), *Dramatic Dance with Children in Worship and Education* (1977), and *Hymns in Action for Everyone* (1985).

Dance can be a vital part in the life of churches. It can enhance the Christmas season with interpretations of carols included as special selections in the morning service of worship, or as part of a Christmas pageant, or as an expression of worship in church school classes. The Easter season also offers hymns, poetry, scriptures, and anthems that can be expressed in movement. A number of churches have dance choirs who meet regularly in the same manner as vocal choirs. They build up a repertoire of interpretations to be used throughout the year.

Just as one views and enjoys painting and sculpture, liturgical dance brings an aesthetic element to worship involving the worshiper in a heightened sense of the presence and activity of God.

In the church school dance can be an experience of learning. Children learn through activity, and dance involves the entire being. It combines spiritual, social, and physical responses that help Bible stories and lesson material come alive. For example, it is much easier to memorize Psalm 23 if movements interpret the words. This can be done through the spoken word, a hymn ("The Lord Is My Shepherd"), or by an anthem such as "God Is My Shepherd" by Dvorak. A hymnbook is a helpful resource for useful material.

Dance is an effective way to help children who have learning disabilities. A basic 3/4 or 4/4 rhythm gives children a vehicle of expression. Rhythm sticks or a drum will keep children with short attention spans engaged. Since dance provides interaction with other children, it can help to release tensions that block learning. Children or older adults who have difficulty expressing themselves verbally welcome a chance to express themselves bodily. Those who have physical handicaps, making it impossible to move their lower limbs, will not feel excluded when they can share the interpretation using their arms and hands. These actions allow worship to be experienced on a deeper level.

Senior citizens' groups have found this expression of worship most meaningful. They are already acquainted with the Scriptures and hymns.

Teachers do not need formal dance training to make use of the benefits of dance in the educational program. However, attendance at dance workshops is a valuable aid. Certainly a love of music, poetry, and the Scripture provides a foundation for the expression of religious values in worship.

In 1958 the Sacred Dance Guild of America was incorporated to be a source of help and inspiration to dancers, teachers, choreographers, clergy, and laity. Membership is open to all faiths and is now international. A listing of resources on religious dance, names of guild members listed by states, as well as names of professional dancers and dance groups may be obtained by writing to the Sacred Dance Guild, P.O. Box 177, Peterborough, NH.

Margaret Taylor's books and other books on liturgical dance are available from the Sharing Company, P.O. Box 2224, Austin, TX 78767. *See also* Aesthetics; Dramatization; Pageantry; Worship.

E. H. Broadbent

Day-care Center

Day care is any out-of-home care for young children lasting fewer than twenty-four hours a day. Often this care is provided in a church or synagogue setting since these typically have unused space during the week. Top-quality affordable day care is a scarce commodity, so some children are cared for in less than desirable settings. Many churches and synagogues have considered it part of their mission to respond to this societal need.

HISTORY

The first day-care centers were instituted in settlement houses to care for the children of immigrants and to help them become socialized into American life. It was still considered a mother's responsibility to raise her children, but the day-care centers were willing to help out where there were deficiencies. The modern day-care center has outlived the stigma attached to these early institutions. Day care has become more respectable as middle-class and professional parents have demanded safe, reliable, convenient, and stimulating environments for their children.

The historical distinction between day-care centers and nursery schools has virtually disappeared since both now may offer the same curriculum. Most children are enrolled in some form of group educational experience prior to entering public school kindergarten. Whether this experience is day care or some other form of preschool now depends to a large extent on whether or not the mother is employed outside of the home. In 1987 over 53 percent of mothers with children under six were in the labor force. These families, whether professionals or single parents, needed good child care. At the same time as the demand was growing, however, the supply of women willing to care for young children in their homes diminished as these women also took outside jobs where they could earn more.

As day care became more common, universities and colleges responded to the need for professionalization by offering education designed to equip day-care teachers with a knowledge of child development and with appropriate skills. No longer was it considered enough for a child-care worker to be "good with children." Now teachers also needed specific training. Various forms of accreditation for personnel were inaugurated, including the Child Development Associate credential awarded for demonstrated competence.

Research has been unable to determine whether day care is advantageous or detrimental for children. It seems to have both advantages and disadvantages depending on factors such as the age of the child, the circumstances of the family, and the quality of the care. When it became apparent that day care was not going to go away, researchers changed the questions they had been asking. They are no longer asking whether day care is good for children, but rather what kind of day care should be available for them.

CHARACTERISTICS OF A GOOD DAY-CARE CENTER

A good day-care center is characterized by wholesome interactions among staff and children. The sound of the center is generally pleasant with a busy hum of children involved in activities largely of their own choice. The curriculum caters to the developmental needs of children without trying to force them all into the same mold. Staff are aware that parents are their children's first teachers and must be supported. There is frequent communication between teachers and parents both in formal newsletters and in informal get-togethers. Some centers provide parents with daily written summaries of their children's napping, eating, and toileting experiences in the form of a quickly prepared checklist. The physical environment, both inside and outside the building, is conducive to large muscle activities since it is hard for little people to sit still. Health, safety, and nutrition are major considerations. In addition to hiring well-qualified staff, the good day-care center provides for training and nonthreatening evaluation for all personnel. To help centers determine where they are in compliance with generally recognized standards of excellence, the National Association for the Education of Young Children has made available materials for self-study and accreditation.

All states require a license for opening a day-care center but they vary in their requirements. The staff/child ratio, space considerations, and numbers of children in the various groups are major considerations. Some centers, like the typical public school, group children by ages. Others consider that family grouping with children of different ages together is better since children learn so much from each other.

CONSIDERATIONS IN OPENING AND OPERATING A DAY-CARE CENTER

Children typically come to the center at different hours of the day according to their parents' work schedules, so a day-care center must be open long hours. This can cause problems with staffing patterns. There must be a teacher available both early in the morning and until the last child goes home so there may be a period in the middle of the day (frequently naptime) when, unless flexible scheduling can be arranged, more staff are present than needed.

A major problem faced by all day-care centers is "burnout" and thus frequent turnover of staff. Day-care personnel are paid lower than most professional groups. Their hours are long and benefits few. Unlike public schools, the typical center is open all year long. There is little prestige associated with the job so workers often feel unappreciated. It is essential that staff receive some sort of recognition by the board of directors and parents to help compensate for the frustrations that may build up.

Some of the problems that a church or synagogue might encounter when developing a day-care center are peculiar to the use of shared space since often the classrooms are used by Sunday school children or other groups as well. It is important for the director of religious education to serve on the board of directors of the day-care center to help defuse some of these problems. It helps for the day-care director to attend meetings of the religious education school teachers. There should be an understanding of which materials are to be used by which group and there needs to be adequate storage for those materials not for joint use.

Religious institutions ought to give careful thought to their enrollment policy. Will their own parishioners have priority over the general public? Will a scholarship fund be instituted to enable low-income parishioners to enroll their children? Does the institution want the day-care center to care for children with handicaps? Top-quality affordable centers typically soon have waiting lists and some thought should be given to how spaces should be allocated.

Along with admission policies, day-care centers should have written job descriptions for all staff. There should be a grievance policy and a well-understood chain of command, so that personnel know to whom they will be responsible. It should be determined whether or not it is important for staff to be members of the denomination sponsoring the center.

All day-care centers need to prepare a written philosophy that can be distributed to prospective parents. In addition, the day-care center affiliated with a church or synagogue must be sure that it is fulfilling the mission of the religious institution of which it is a part. The philosophy should be distributed to the congregation since some members may still disagree about whether or not day care, especially for infants, is in the best interests of children. It is not unusual for some parishioners to resent "their" building being used in this way, since there will be undeniable wear and tear on the physical facilities.

Another aspect peculiar to a church- or synagogue-related center is how much religious education will be provided for the children. Most centers will include a short grace before meals and snacks. Others will also have a daily Bible story or a short service in the sanctuary for all the children. Sometimes this is under the auspices of the religious education department of the institution, but sometimes it is left to the individual teachers. The latter situation can lead to difficulties if all teachers are not members of the sponsoring church or synagogue. In any event, since children will probably come from different religious backgrounds, it is important to spell out the educational policies so parents will know what they can expect in this area as in all others. Whether the curriculum contains specific religious instruction or not, it is generally hoped that the warm, loving feelings children associate with a high-quality center will have an enduring impact on their spiritual development. Many day-care centers believe that their mission is to help children experience the security necessary to enable them to "grow in wisdom and stature" and that, for young children, this is more effective than teaching religious concepts that may be beyond their understanding. *See also* Child Abuse; Child Development; Infancy; Nursery Education; Preschool Children.

FOR FURTHER REFERENCE

National Association for the Education of Young Children. *Guide to Accreditation.* Washington, DC, 1985.
National Council of the Churches of Christ in the U.S.A. *Helping Churches Mind the Children.* New York, 1984.

A. H. Brautigam

Death

The sensitive and emotionally overladen topic of death according to the religious traditions of both Judaism and Christianity may be viewed through two lenses: the philosophical-theological response and the pragmatic-practical response developed over the course of the centuries. We begin with the latter.

PRAGMATIC-PRACTICAL RESPONSE

Following the pattern already established in biblical times, it was the primary responsibility of the family to prepare and bury its own dead. The necessities of nomadic and desert existence mandated burial as quickly as possible, the day of death or the day after. Embalming was therefore unnecessary, and aboveground burial in any kind of mausoleum-like structure was initially understood to be contrary to Israelite practice.

Postbiblically, in the rabbinic period and later, Jewish mourning and burial practices became more and more standardized as communities found themselves outside the land of Israel (especially after A.D. 70, the destruction of the Temple in Jerusalem by the Romans), without political autonomy, and forced to communicate with one another either in writing or through messengers. Many contemporary Jewish burial and mourning practices such as the extended mourning period, the evolution of the "rending of garments," and the daily service may, therefore, be traced to rabbinic rather than biblical Judaism.

With the advent of Christianity, its separation from its Jewish beginnings, and its tolerance within the empire as extended by Constantine in 313, we see in the burial and mourning practices of the new and emerging faith evidences of its Jewish roots coupled with both Greek and Roman influences. Aboveground burial, more elaborate funeral processions, and the significant inclusion of the life, death, and resurrection of Jesus Christ in the liturgy associated with death tended to further sever the Christian community from its Jewish roots.

Though both Pharisaic Judaism and nascent Christianity stressed belief in the divine power to resurrect the dead, Jews saw this at some future time, while Christians continued to reinvigorate their faith by reference to the example of Christ's life and, thus, such a possibility for all believers.

Worked out over many generations, the structuring of both the Jewish and Christian responses to death, burial, and mourning have now assumed an almost universal pattern. Within the Jewish world, those structures are governed by both a recognition of the reality of death (without necessarily including an appeal to the life hereafter) and an overriding simplicity with regard to the actual funeral, burial, and mourning practices themselves. Within the Christian world, while those same principles may also apply, there is a stronger emphasis on the life hereafter as well as traditions not associated with the starker simplicity of Jewish customs. For example, preburial visitation and elaborate floral arrangements are unknown in historic Jewish tradition, but common among various denominational groupings within Christianity.

Additionally, Jewish religious tradition, with variations to be sure, has expended its energies in dealing with the process the living go through to cope with death through such ritual acts and observances as *avelut*, mourning, *aninut*, the period from the moment of death to the funeral, *shivah*, the seven days of mourning following the funeral, *shloshim*, the first thirty-day period of mourning, and *yahrzeit*, the anniversary of a death. The various forms of Christianity, on the other hand, have not occupied themselves as a general rule with postburial practices.

We may summarize the pragmatic-practical response of the Jewish and Christian traditions with the psychological insight that their primary purpose is to aid the individual, family, and community in, first, confronting the loss through death and, second, in helping them to return to a state of normalcy and psychological and spiritual health and well-being. The working through of grief and mourning in both Judaism and Christianity is specially and consciously designed to take mourners through that dark and shadowy valley into light.

PHILOSOPHICAL-THEOLOGICAL RESPONSE

The philosophical-theological responses of both religious communities are predicated upon an acceptance of individual human death as part of the divine plan, whether stemming from the mortality and sinfulness of an Adam, according to ancient traditions, or not. Whether directly created by God, the Creator of all, or not, death must ultimately be viewed positively and accepted as such. Thus, in the normal ordering of the world, the death that comes at the end of a life well lived and religiously inspired, while sad, is not tragic. A reversal of this natural ordering, specifically the death of one's child, *is* tragic, but still within that world of possibility though its meaning and purpose may escape our understanding. Mass death (e.g., the Holocaust, the slaughter in Cambodia, etc.) is not part of any divine plan and is all the more horrifying because it is the result of human doing and a conscious rejection of God in the world. Natural disasters (e.g., tornadoes, hurricanes, etc.) are not included in this latter category, but are, likewise, understood to exist within the created possibilities of a divinely structured world.

TEACHING ABOUT DEATH

Children from the age of three grasp the fact of death and know the difference between sleep and death, between breathing and not breathing. Usually they witness the death of an animal before there are painful family experiences. Explanations need to be factual. Children are realists and are not looking for philosophical responses. Only when a child asks, "Why did this happen?" (probably by the age of five or six) is it time for an empathetic response that reflects the adult's understanding in relation to the child's need. Some religious traditions have more specific answers than do others. Evasive answers are quickly perceived as shallow by children.

Older children may raise the question of justice, "Why did God let this happen?" Again, the religious tradition offers answers. For some, the response is that humans have the freedom to choose to do good or evil and need to look for understanding to the loving-kindness of God. For others, it is a mystery.

Teachers in religious education may find an unwillingness on the part of school-age children to talk about a death, particularly that of a child the class has known. This is where school counselors help. The teacher can stand by in loving understanding of the children's need for silence. For these children, death is not an objective fact, but an existential reality.

Very ill children are usually aware of their own dying before adults are willing to admit it to them. Instead of silence, they need help to live through anger, despair, hope, and acceptance. Frequently the pictures they draw and the ways in which they play with toys express their feelings. Usually counselors are available to them and their families.

Adolescents experience the death of friends, perhaps from accidents, drugs, or suicide, as a close reality. The first response of teachers, again, needs to be support, an understanding silence, and the willingness to listen. This is not a time for teaching about death or philosophical discussions of death; later, past experiences of reflection and faith can be drawn upon.

Young adults are preoccupied with the promise of life. Middle adulthood is a time when death is thought of as a possible but real interruption, but their main concern is with health. Older adults are more accepting of mortality and have the developmental task of reflecting on their life to find it good. This is where the teaching group becomes a support group as people ponder the meaning of a life.

Real learning occurs only when people are in the presence of death. Then the pastoral and teaching tasks become one. Families and friends learn because they are asking deeply felt questions out of their need to know and come to terms with their grief. *See also* Eternal Life; Theodicy.

I. V. Cully, S. L. Jacobs

Debate

Debate is a method of teaching designed to explicate an issue. Two people or two teams present arguments in turn for or against an issue. After time for consideration, each side presents a rebuttal of the other's and a reaffirmation of its own viewpoint. A panel of judges, considering the cogency of the arguments and the clarity of presentation, decides which side wins.

The usefulness of debate as a teaching technique lies in the careful preparation it entails. A debate is not a simple discussion of viewpoints. It requires research, historical background, recourse to authorities, clear outlines, careful reasoning, and a view to the consequences of the position. The time allotted for presentation varies but must be of sufficient length so that preparatory work can be adequately developed. Too lengthy a report loses the attention of judges and audience. The rebuttal period, always shorter, is an opportunity for participants to indicate how well they can follow an opposing argument in relation to their own, remember points of agreement and disagreement, and reformulate their own position in a brief amount of time. There is no place for fuzzy thinking in a debate because it will be quickly observed by opponents, judges, and audience.

A drawback of debate lies in the necessity of seeing an issue in polar and absolute terms. One position is "right" and one "wrong" morally or intellectually. Only one solution to an issue is possible. The "loser" may seem to have been "wrong" when, in fact, the arguments may have been weak or at least not as boldly presented as those of the opposition. Debate as a teaching method trains people to pursue a viewpoint ab-

solutely, which may prevent development of the ability to mediate, arbitrate, or compromise—ways by which most issues are settled in real situations. It feeds on tensions and the arousal of negative feelings. However, the skillful debater never confuses the opponent personally with the issue. Being objective is one key to winning because it promotes clarity of thinking and presentation.

Debate has use in religious education because it helps learners perceive both sides of an issue. The Bible and the historical religious traditions present one side as "good," but learners can only fully understand why this is so (if in fact it is so) when they can view each side. All people harbor conflicting viewpoints, a fact debate helps both participants and audience to acknowledge. Although couched in absolute terms, the format indicates that there are indeed questions to which there are no right or wrong responses.

This method is usable with young people who have entered the stage of abstract operational thinking, that is, they can think conceptually and organize thought in that manner. Twelve year olds can do so in a simple way, but the method is more frequently used at the high-school and adult levels. *See also* Discussion; Teaching Styles.

I. V. Cully

Demonstration

A demonstration is an activity or process that illustrates how a task, project, or method is accomplished so that others can repeat it. It is a method of passing on learning from one person to another and is particularly helpful when learners need to see the actual workings of a technique rather than only being told about it, yet it is most efficient and economical to have one person do the process (or it is too complicated for learners to do yet, as in some science demonstrations).

The demonstrator is a knowledgeable, skilled person who can answer questions about the process. But the demonstrator is also a learner, gaining new ideas in interaction with the audience. The audience participates in the demonstration by asking questions or by taking part as directed by the demonstrator, e.g., the magician's volunteer.

The steps in a demonstration are:

1. Determining the purpose or desired outcome (e.g., making parchment paper like the kind used in biblical times)

2. Assembling the ingredients or elements needed (newspaper and water)

3. Gathering other resources (a blender, two screens, lots of patience)

4. Doing the demonstration (mixing paper and water in the blender, pouring mixture onto screen for partial drying, ironing dry)

5. Putting on the finishing touches (writing Scripture verses on the parchment)

6. Sharing and evaluating the results

See also Instruction; Project.

S. H. Matthaei

Departments, Sunday School

Sunday school departments are administrative structures for the Sunday school whereby pupils and classes are divided, usually according to age-level groupings. Since the Sunday school focuses upon study it is most appropriate that grouping of students be related primarily to conceptual abilities, so that persons of nearly the same level of development are grouped together. This grouping usually approximates the academic groupings in general education. In the smaller Sunday school, classes and departments may be identical (if they are distinguished), but in larger schools, for administrative and curricular purposes, proximate age-level classes may be grouped in departments.

Formal grading and departmental grouping were the products of graded curricular development in the early years of this century. In the earliest days of the Sunday school movement, a century earlier, Sunday school "studies" concentrated on memorization of many Scripture passages. What groupings there were were probably related to pupils' ability to recite portions of the Bible and to the number whose recitations could be accommodated in the allotted class time. Though memorization was still strongly emphasized, more systematic Bible study followed as "selected lessons," along with study helps for the teacher, were developed after 1825. A proliferation of such study plans, some denominational, others independently produced, appeared in the next half-century. The resulting confusion and competition led to the adoption in 1872, by the American Sunday School Union, of the Uniform Lesson Series, designed to provide a single set of lessons for universal use. None of these plans, however, took into account age-level differences. Age-level groupings (classes and departments) did appear as a matter of practical necessity, but little general formal structuring or curricula for them was developed.

Age-level gradation by this time had been widely adopted in public education, and Sunday school teachers were demanding graded curricular materials for their classes. Finally several such series were developed, culminating in the International Sunday School Association's issuing a closely graded (one for each grade) series in 1908. These were changed to group graded (six levels of materials) in 1924.

The combinations of grades for which each set of group-graded lessons are developed usually constitute the departments in a local Sunday school. For purposes of administration, teacher training, cooperative lesson preparation, contiguous physical location of classes, etc., it is convenient for schools to structure themselves in this way. Early designations for such groupings were: beginners (usually four and five year olds; younger children were not normally brought to Sunday school); primary (grades 1–3); junior (grades 4–6); intermediate (grades 7–8/9), senior (grades 9/10–12); and adult. A nursery department has long since become an indispensable part of most Sunday schools, and the term "junior high" has generally supplanted the earlier "intermediate." The structure of the local public school system may also determine how a church defines and designates its departments, especially at the latter level, where "middle school" and "junior high school" may be varying titles and involve varying grades from fifth through ninth. At one time larger churches may have had an "older youth" department for those of post-high-school age. But following World War II, with its conscription of young men of this age and the subsequent granting of the vote to 18 year olds, "older youth" have generally been granted "young adult" status.

The size of a Sunday school may help determine how classes and departments may be organized. The very small church may structure its school on a "broadly graded" basis, with a spread of as many as eight years (below adult level) in one group. A typical arrangement of classes (not really departments) in a small church might be:

- Nursery (through three years of age)
- Younger children (ages four–seven)
- Older children (ages eight–eleven)
- Youth (junior- and senior-high age)
- Adults

An interesting variation on the broadly graded structure, applicable to larger as well as smaller churches, is that of the Covenant Life Curriculum, introduced by some of the churches in the Reformed tradition in the 1960s. This emphasizes not just age but modes of communication at four developmental levels of belief: (1) the nonverbal, operating through relationships (the little child or the nonbeliever); (2) the verbal (the older child, the seeker); (3) commitment (usually the teenager or other person ready to make a public confession); and (4) witness to faith (the adult; the mature Christian).

When a two-grade plan (cycle grading) for curricular materials is in use, the structure at the elementary level may be:

- Younger elementary (grades 1–2)
- Middle elementary (grades 3–4)
- Older elementary (grades 5–6)

Adaptation of any of the above configurations may need to be made to accord with local circumstances—the age at which children enter school (which is not identical nationwide), the membership composition of the local Sunday school, and other such factors.

Departments themselves may, for administrative purposes, be grouped into larger segments, sometimes called "divisions," which are in accord with broader normal social groupings. The usual divisions are:

- Children (which may be structured into two programmatically distinctive sections: younger children [preschool] and older children [elementary-age])

- Youth (junior- and senior-high school; such a "division" often bears administrative responsibility for a church's total youth program, not just Sunday morning classes)

- Adult (including age-level groups such as college-career, young adults [which may be more inclusive than college-career], middle, and older adults, and other adult study groups [short-term, interest-focused studies, etc.])

The size of a Sunday school and the nature of its program will probably determine how divisions and departments are to be administered—whether by committees or councils (which may include teachers and other workers involved in the area), by individual "superintendents" of the respective divisions or departments, or by a general or other "broader" superintendent or director. Supervision includes such things as organization and coordination, cooperative program planning, leadership education and guidance, and evaluation of both program and workers. Important in supervision is the creating of an awareness among teachers and other workers that they are not alone in their efforts, but together they constitute a genuine fellowship of Christian educators. *See also* Adolescence; Adult Education; Childhood Education; Cognitive Development; Grouping; Kindergarten; Nursery Education; Sunday School; Sunday School Movement; Superintendent, Sunday School; Young Adults.

J. N. Strout

Deschooling

Deschooling is a social and educational movement that originated in the early 1970s with the writings of Ivan Illich (*Deschooling Society*, 1970), the director of the Center for Intercultural Documentation in Cuernavaca, Mexico (CIDOC). This utopian movement, with anarchist and socialist leanings, contends that schooling in advanced industrial societies has deteriorated to such a point that the harmful side effects of schooling for individuals and society outweigh its beneficial effects. Schools are seen as institutions that foster adherence to the capitalist values of production and consumption, destroy the individuality and autonomy of individuals, and assign students to slots in industrial society. Through deschooling, schools would be replaced with face-to-face learning encounters, learning exchanges, and learning networks. Perhaps the religious educator most influenced by this movement is John Westerhoff III (*Will Our Children Have Faith*, 1976) who calls for a deschooling of church education or the elimination of the Sunday *school* in favor of family, liturgical, and community forms of education. *See also* Action-Reflection; Progressive Education.

J. L. Elias

Development

See Adolescence; Adult Development; Affective Development; Aging; Attitude Formation; Behavior; Character Development; Child Development; Childhood Education; Cognitive Development; Developmental Tasks; Education, Theories of; Faith Development; Grouping; Learning Theory; Maturation; Middle Childhood; Moral Development; Nursery Education; Preschool Children; Psychosocial Development; Young Adults.

Developmental Tasks

The development of the person through childhood, youth, and adulthood is marked by many physical, cognitive, affective, and social transitions. Developmental tasks are those activities or abilities that must be successfully performed or acquired to make transition from one level to the next possible. The physical developmental task of learning to walk must be accomplished by very young children before they can participate in the running games of somewhat older children.

The corollary is that expecting persons to function at a higher level of development than what they are capable of is either ineffective (as a teaching method) or counterproductive (actually negatively affecting either the developing structures themselves or the persons' emotional response). Writing and precise drawing or coloring should not be a part of the preschool experience until small muscle control is available. Abstractions are not understood by younger children, so most theological terms should not be used until early adolescence. Youth deal with personal identity issues; thus role clarity is important in their experience. Parallel play precedes interactive play;

185

nursery and preschool teachers should be prepared for children at each social level.

The religious education of the developing person is most effective when educators keep in mind the developmental tasks of their age group. *See also* Adolescence; Adult Development; Affective Development; Child Development; Cognitive Development; Psychosocial Development.

FOR FURTHER REFERENCE

Havighurst, Robert J. *Developmental Tasks and Education.* New York: Longmans, Green, 1950.
Jersild, A. T. *Child Development and the Curriculum.* Charlotte, NC: Darby, 1982.
Kagan, Jerome. *The Nature of the Child.* New York: Basic, 1984.

C. H. Snelling

Devotional Literature

Devotional literature, available in many forms, is an aid to the spiritual life. The long experience of those who have consciously cultivated the devotional life and shared their journey in writing assists others in enlarging and deepening their spiritual lives. This fact has convinced countless people through many generations to include in their daily devotions a time to live with the insights made available through these writings as a way of enlarging their own perspectives in the life of prayer.

SOURCES

The Bible itself is a primary source of devotional writing. Many psalms are individual laments, addressing God with a plea for help. Other psalms express confidence and reassurance or thanksgiving and praise. The needs expressed reflect the basic human condition, making the psalms the preeminent compilation of devotional literature to nourish the lives of believers.

The *Confessions* of Aurelius Augustine (fourth century) traces Augustine's spiritual pilgrimage from unbelief to faith. The rise of the mystical tradition in the Middle Ages marks the beginning of consciously compiled devotional literature, and writings on the development of monastic life, including *The Rule* of Benedict of Nursia, contribute to an understanding of the spiritual life. Devotional writers of the Middle Ages who still speak to moderns include Bernard of Clairvaux, Francis of Assisi, Hildegard of Bingham, Meister Eckhart, Johannes Tauler, Juliana of Norwich, and Thomas à Kempis (to whom is attributed *The Imitation of Christ*).

The *Spiritual Exercises* of Ignatius of Loyola (sixteenth century) suggest a method of meditative reflection in which one pictures oneself in a biblical situation that is being found helpful by people today. Two other Spanish mystics of that century are Teresa of Avila, who reformed the Carmelite order and wrote on prayer for the instruction of her nuns, and John of the Cross, from whom comes the well-known phrase "the dark night of the soul," denoting a feeling of the absence of God. Anglican piety is represented in *The Private Devotions* of Lancelot Andrews and the poetry of John Donne.

Blaise Pascal's *Thoughts*, from the seventeenth century, emphasizes the affective, in contrast to the rational, approach to faith. The writings of George Fox represent the earliest literature of the Quakers, who wait quietly upon God's gift of the Inner Light. The rise of the Methodist movement under John Wesley became a source for devotional literature. Among nineteenth-century writings are those by Danish theologian Søren Kierkegaard, the British Catholic theologian John Henry Newman, and in the United States Walter Rauschenbusch (*Prayers of the Social Awakening*). Twentieth-century writers include Anglican Evelyn Underhill, Quaker Rufus M. Jones, and Lutheran Rudolf Otto.

The Hasidic tradition, represented by the *Cabala*, or mystic writings, began in Catalonia and Provence in the thirteenth century. The modern Hasidic tradition dates from Israel ben Eliezar, the Ba'al Shem Tov, who lived in Poland in the eighteenth century, and today brings the writings of Martin Buber and Abraham Joshua Heschel.

Almost as close at hand as the Bible is the hymnal. The words do not need tunes in order to assist readers in meditating upon God. Some traditions, notably the Jewish and Anglican, have a prayerbook that is a treasury of prayers and other liturgical materials.

Today devotional guides are also available, primarily from denominational sources. These booklets, issued on a three-month, seasonal, or annual basis, usually present for each day a brief biblical verse or passage, a meditation on the theme, and a simple closing prayer. Perhaps the most widely used is *The Upper Room*, published by the Upper Room Press in Nashville, Tennessee. Specific devotional guides may be issued for one or both of the penitential seasons of the church year, Advent and Lent.

EDUCATIONAL USES

Devotional literature has been a neglected aspect of religious education. Even the psalms have been studied more for their style or meaning than for deepening the spiritual life. Yet devotional writings are an aid to spiritual growth and their value lies less in the cognitive than in the affective domain. Just as the practice of quiet listening to God can be introduced even to young children, so the use of brief Scripture passages can focus thought and feeling.

Children in religious education classes can be introduced to the psalms through simple verses of praise and assurance, so that they will feel confident in the loving presence of God and so they will be assisted as they learn to pray. Teachers can make a practice of beginning or ending a session with a Bible verse, giving students time to reflect on it, and then closing with a prayer that echoes the meaning of the verse. Some curricular materials include a brief unit on the psalms and the devotional life; infrequently a guidebook is published for children's use at home. Where a prayerbook is regularly used in the liturgy, children learn how to use it during attendance at worship, in education classes, and at home. Some denominations issue devotional guides for young people and also for families similar to the ones designed for adults that include a Scripture verse, meditation, and prayer.

These efforts at enriching the devotional life through the use of written materials can help persons develop a pattern that can grow through the years. While materials for children and youth are slim, it is encouraging to note that renewal of interest in the cultivation of the spiritual life among Jews and Christians is finding expression in new publications of spiritual classics. *See also* Books, Children's; Books, Religious; Meditation; Periodicals, Religious; Spirituality.

I. V. Cully

other person. Born in Vermont, he was a professor of philosophy and education at the University of Michigan, the University of Chicago, and at Columbia University. His position on instrumentalism and pragmatism, similar to that of William James, led to an emphasis on ideas that work.

Dewey's influence on progressive education was widespread. In *Democracy and Education* (1916) and *Experience and Education* (1938), he developed a philosophy of education centered on the quality of experience as the basis of a coherent theory that affords direction to the selection and organization of subject matter. Method is correlated with the process of thinking that originates in experience; it provides a problem, seeks information, examines options, and tests the conclusions. This life-centered approach was widely used in both secular and religious education, especially as recommended by George Albert Coe.

In 1934, Dewey published *A Common Faith*, in which he made the distinction between *religion* and the *religious* attitude. God is to be found in the relation between the ideal and the actual, which provides a religious attitude based on values. *See also* Education, Theories of; Experience; Learning Theory; Pragmatism; Progressive Education; Teaching Theory.

R. C. Miller

Dewey, John

John Dewey (1859–1952) was an American philosopher whose ways of thinking have penetrated the American mind as thoroughly as those of any

Diaconate

The diaconate is the office of deacon or a body of deacons in the Christian church. The New Testament mentions the office of deacon ("server," both men and women; Rom 16:1; Phil. 1:1; 1 Tim. 3:8–13) along with that of bishops ("overseers") and presbyters ("elders"). Clearly the office of deacon is a position set apart for some special ministerial service to the congregation, but it is not known for sure exactly which duties belonged to this office (indeed the duties of each office may have been different in different early congregations).

Likewise today there are variations in the office of deacon. In the permanent diaconate retained by the Eastern churches and restored among Roman Catholics in 1967, deacons are married men, ordained to serve evangelistic, liturgical, and social ministries while continuing their secular occupations. Among Protestants the modern diaconate has been, since the nineteenth century, primarily a community of women who serve in diverse capacities: nurses, parish deaconesses, teachers, directors of Christian education, ordained pastors, seminary professors, and also in totally secular occupations. They are set apart at a service of consecration and sustain their community by common prayer and regional, national, and international gatherings. In some Protestant congregations deacons and deaconesses are ordained and in others they are laity elected to various church responsibilities for limited time periods.

Although the original identification of deacons was with service—and this is the focus of the board of deacons in Presbyterian and Reformed churches and one function in Congregational, United Church of Christ, and Baptist churches—there has also developed a teaching function. Preparation for confirmation is a task of deaconesses in Germany. Some people in the United Methodist church choose ordination to the diaconate specifically for teaching ministry and become ministers of education in parishes. *See also* Diakonia; Teaching Mission.

B. Everist

Diakonia

Diakonia is a Greek word, usually translated into English as "service," "servanthood," "ministry," or "diaconate." Acts 6:1–6 describes a deacon as a "waiter on tables," someone who is subordinate, inconspicuous, ready to give a hand as needed. Although *diakonia* has been used in the tradition as a technical term for church ordination to the diaconate or ministry, the New Testament indicates that it is a key description of the lifestyle of all Christians. Baptized into Christ's ministry and empowered by the Holy Spirit to serve their neighbors, Christians are called to *diakonia*, or service, in the name of the one who came to be among them as a servant (Mark 10:45; Luke 4:18–19). Paul uses the word once in Philippians 1:1 in reference to the work of bishops and deacons on the collection for the Jerusalem church. Aside from that, deacons (both women and men) are his helpers and co-workers in evangelism. *See also* Diaconate; Ministry.

L. M. Russell

Dialectic(s)

From the Greek *dia* + *legein*, meaning "discourse," dialectics first emerged in classical Greek thinking as the art of debate based on logical argumentation. Aristotle credits Zeno of Elea (ca. 490–430 B.C.) as its first great exponent.

For Plato, dialectics had a number of meanings but was primarily the science of recognizing first principles that are the highest, surest, and most ultimate form of knowledge. For Aristotle, dialectics was a more inductive process that moves from commonly accepted opinions through logical

reasoning to more reliable principles to guide further inquiry. Educationally, dialectics was initially recognized as the art of teaching through discussion, epitomized in the Socratic dialogues of Plato, that moves through constant questioning to sure knowledge.

Thereafter, and up to the late Middle Ages, dialectics was listed as one of the trivium, the arts of discourse, the others being rhetoric and grammar, with dialectics being seen as the discipline of formal logic. In the work of Friedrich Hegel (1770–1831), however, dialectics shifted away from being understood as a particular art of discourse and took a new twist of meaning, one more akin to what is commonly intended when the word "dialectic" is used today.

For Hegel, dialectic is the distinguishing characteristic of speculative thought by which an idea passes over into its own negation because of contradictions inherent within it and then passes on to subsume the insights of both the first moment and the moment of negation into a new synthesis of understanding. For Hegel, then, there are three moments in the dialectical process of thought, commonly referred to as thesis, antithesis, and synthesis, but more accurately understood as the three moments of (1) affirming or accepting, (2) negating or refusing, and (3) moving beyond or sublating the truth of the first two moments into a new point of understanding. That synthesis, in turn, becomes the first moment in a new dialectical sequence.

Karl Marx (1818–1883) accepted Hegel's threefold understanding of the dialectic but applied it to his interpretation not of ideas, but of economic and social processes. Since he contended that all reality is reducible to matter and all ideas reflect the material conditions of life, his system is known as dialectical materialism. Today dialectic is typically used as a philosophical concept that describes, with its threefold dynamic, the evolutionary process of thought, nature, history, and society.

In contemporary political and liberation theologies, dialectic is often used to refer to the relationship between theory and praxis, meaning that the two are to exist in a mutually correcting relationship much akin to Hegel's threefold moments of affirming, questioning, and moving beyond. In religious education, dialectic is often used to refer to the type of hermeneutics (interpretation) that is to exist between "the faith handed down" and present, lived experience. A dialectical hermeneutic means that learners are to come to see for themselves how the tradition affirms, questions, and calls one beyond present faith practice, even as the tradition is itself reinterpreted in light of contemporary experience. *See also* Liberation Theology; Naturalism; Praxis; Teaching Theory.

T. H. Groome

Dialogue

Dialogue, broadly interpreted, refers both to a literary form and to a verbal engagement in which two or more persons exchange ideas or opinions. As a literary form, dialogue has an ancient and distinguished history, including poetry (Greek verse mimes, as early as the third century B.C.), fiction, drama, and, of primary significance for education, the dialectical exposition of philosophic ideas in conversational form. Probably best known are Plato's *Dialogues*, a form perfected by 400 B.C.; major philosophic and educational tenets are set forth in the series. In the conversational arena, dialogue is sometimes used as the equivalent of discussion, although more appropriately it refers not to a "method" of teaching, but to that form of communication where two or more persons of any age are present to each other, aware of each other's thinking and feeling, in an exchange of meaning. The interpretation of the "I-thou" relationship by the Jewish philosopher-educator Martin Buber (1878–1965) is at the heart of the concept of dialogue as it has made an impact on religious education in the twentieth century.

In the classroom setting, dialogue, in contrast to lecture, gives a teacher the opportunity to hear how the student is receiving information. The student in turn has the opportunity to respond with questions and reactions. The process of dialogue brings clarification for both. *See also* Buber, Martin; Communication Theory; Conversation; Discussion.

S. P. Little

Didache

Didache is that part of the gospel teaching directed toward ethical instruction and guidance in Christian practices, such as spiritual disciplines, rituals, organization, and practical problems. *Didache* is also the title of one of the earliest church documents, designed to prepare gentile Christians for membership in the church. In its context, it is a kind of exemplar of the role didache gradually began to assume in the life of the young church.

Consider first the New Testament. In addition to the narrative accounts of the life, death, and resurrection of Jesus Christ and the growth of the early church, there are the interpretation of the meaning of those events and instructions to act in certain ways. Distinction is often made between two forms taking their titles from Greek terms: *kerygma*, or "proclamation," and *didache*, or "teaching." Biblical scholars sometimes see the two as distinct entities. For example, C. H. Dodd, in his 1936 *Apostolic Preaching and Its Devel-*

opments, made the distinction between preaching and teaching, calling for a return to apostolic preaching of the kerygma. Some scholars recognize the two content emphases, citing exhortatory passages in Paul's writings. The pastoral Letters, 1 and 2 Timothy and Titus, are filled with instructions for proper pastoral care of congregations. James is the "instructional" Letter frequently judged inadequate because of its strong concentration on "works," or right behavior, in contrast to the theological themes held to be the essence of the gospel. More recently, there seems to be a trend toward affirmation of the New Testament connection between kerygma and didache. Jesus was most frequently called "Rabbi," that is, "Teacher," and he clearly linked his witness to God with his expectations that his followers' inner commitment would express itself in a way of life. His teachings, therefore—as in the Sermon on the Mount—were aids to that "way of life."

Many of the early church fathers, Clement of Alexandria, Polycarp of Smyrna, the Shepherd of Hermas, and others, responded to the needs of young churches to deal with internal matters, practical in nature, that would help shape their struggling communities. Moral teachings of the early Latin fathers, as in Tertullian and Cyprian, brought into high visibility concern for right living. In fact, the stream of ethical instruction has its roots deep in the Jewish tradition, is integral to Jesus' teachings, the work of Paul, and other New Testament leaders, and rose to a position of prominence in the early church.

Didache, subtitled *Teaching of the Twelve Apostles* or *Teaching of the Lord Through the Twelve Apostles to the Gentiles*, is one of the oldest surviving Christian church documents, considered by some to be the oldest, now generally viewed as dating from the late first to early second century. It was a part of the oral tradition, quoted by later writings, and viewed by some as a part of the canon. Evidently compiled over a number of years, a Greek manuscript of the *Didache* was discovered by P. Babryennios at Constantinople in 1873 and published by him in 1883. Other small fragments have been discovered since that time. To the degree that the document exemplifies the meaning of didache, it is informative to note that it begins with setting forth the two ways of life and death in the first six chapters. Chapters 7–15 deal with concerns relating to baptism and the Eucharist, prayer and fasting, and organizational matters relating to the appointment of bishops and deacons. It even deals with ways of recognizing and responding to visiting apostles and bishops. The final chapter has to do with signs of the Second Coming of the Lord. Persons preparing themselves for membership in the church would find in it a kind of manual for the moral life clearly linked with gospel interpretation of the Great Commandments, the Sermon on the Mount, and other passages giving guidance for the way of life as opposed to the way of death. Having studied the pattern for the way of life and now ready for baptism, the new Christian has received guidance from the church for rituals and personal disciplines. The effort to achieve some degree of uniform practice in scattered Christian communities was given impetus by the compilation of the *Didache* and at least portions of other similar documents.

Is ethical instruction to be the prime content of Christian education today? The answer is clearly no, according to most educators and theologians. James Smart, in *The Teaching Ministry of the Church* (1954), offers a critique of Dodd's separation of New Testament kerygma and didache. As in Acts 5:42, Smart says, the content of teaching and preaching is the same—Jesus Christ. Ethical instruction is no more than legalism if it is not rooted in kerygma, guiding the believer to explore the shape of the Christian life. Even church practices must have meaning and be rooted in some perception of the gospel. Doctrine must be elucidated and related to the obligations and situations of the learner. Too often Christian education, with its penchant for manuals, procedures, and relevance, has indeed seemed to concentrate on ethical instruction and regulations. But a study of didache and its meaning and role in the New Testament and the developing church offers a perspective from which Christian education can develop an appropriate contemporary didache. *See also* Catechesis; Ethics; History of Christian Education; Kerygma.

S. P. Little

Director of Religious Education

A director of religious education (DRE) is usually a layperson responsible for the overall administration and supervision of the religious education program of a local church or synagogue, serving as part of the pastoral team. Many denominations substitute the title "director of Christian education" (DEC). And the exact title may vary in other ways as well. The term "director" is traditionally reserved for those with a master's degree in religious or Christian education. The title "minister of religious education" or "minister of Christian education" is normally used to designate those who have been ordained or consecrated. The title "associate in education" or "educational assistant" usually refers to people with an undergraduate degree in the field. And the term "coordinator" may also be used. Despite differences in title, responsibilities are often similar.

The scope of the program supervised by the director is generally much broader than the Sunday school. In addition to Sunday school, the re-

ligious education program often includes vacation church schools, weekday classes, camping activities, family life emphases, laboratory schools, teacher training events, sexuality workshops, outreach to the community, use of the arts in religious education, and witness for social action and justice issues. Furthermore, the scope of religious education includes a wide range of ages from the newly born, who with their parents are ministered to through home-related programs, to older adults whose participation in activities outside the home may be limited, and all ages in between.

RESPONSIBILITIES

The director of religious education in many places is the only professionally trained educator on the staff, necessitating the ability to work skillfully with lay volunteers in such a way that they can together maintain a quality program of religious education for the church or synagogue. Directors as professional staff members are responsible for the total program of religious education, working closely with the pastor and a religious education committee. They often prefer a shared leadership style rather than a hierarchical one that depends on rigid lines of authority and accountability.

The responsibilities of the director of religious education vary from situation to situation, determined by the needs of the church or synagogue and by the interests and abilities of the director. While the unique talents of the director often provide a refreshingly creative approach to the task, there are, nevertheless, three areas of responsibility for which the director is almost always accountable:

1. The improvement of the quality of teaching and other lay leadership

2. Administration of the total program of religious education

3. Long-range planning

Most directors are quite clear that the major focus of their work is the quality of the teaching/learning experiences that occur throughout the church or synagogue. This involves curriculum planning, selection and recruitment of teachers and leaders, and training and supervision.

Crucial for the quality of teaching is curriculum planning and the selection of curriculum resources. At times, when it is automatically assumed that the curriculum plan of the denomination will be used, the director serves as interpreter and guide, helping teachers adapt the materials for their specific locale. At other times, when study topics are assigned to age groups and resources must be selected, the director guides this process of decision making. Increasingly directors find themselves called upon to create curriculum resources for special occasions and unique local circumstances.

It has been substantiated by both experience and research that the most influential person in the religious education program is the one who interacts most directly with the learners—the teacher or group leader. Therefore, a primary responsibility of the director is the development of effective procedures for the selection and recruitment of volunteers who possess the most potential for providing quality leadership. While selection and recruitment are done in conjunction with the religious education committee, skill development and supervision are usually the sole responsibility of the director. This occurs through classroom observation, personal consultation, regular teachers' meetings, and participation in local and regional workshops in which the director often provides leadership. One of the most significant contributions a director makes is as the "resident religious educator" who is always present and who can be counted on by lay volunteers for moral support.

The second major focus of the work of the director is administration. This is the "glue" that makes the religious education program a cohesive whole. It supports the quality of teaching by assuring accurate records, adequate supplies, appropriate space and equipment, a well-chosen library of print and audiovisual resources, and financial resources. As administrator the director is also concerned with publicity and public relations, effectively functioning committees, and the coordination of the religious education program with the other activities of the church and community. The function of administration is largely one of maintaining and improving the existing program.

The third major focus of the work of the director is long-range planning. The temptation of many busy congregations is to be comfortable with maintaining an adequate program of religious education. It is the director's role to introduce a creative discomfort by keeping before the congregation a vision of future needs and possibilities. Knowledge of community and world needs, recent biblical scholarship, current theological perspectives, regional and national churchwide planning, and contemporary insights in religious education are all necessary for long-range planning.

HISTORY OF THE PROFESSION

Historically the profession of the DRE is a twentieth-century U.S. phenomenon, unknown prior to 1907 when the Religious Education Association (REA) through the April issue of its journal asked, "What Schools now employ and pay salaries to their Directors or Superintendents? . . . For the good of all Schools write us what you know of any trying this plan." In 1910 the REA sponsored the first meeting of directors; in 1912 there were ten persons present. Recent estimates report a profession totaling over 10,000 members.

Although most of the early directors were men, by 1920 a national survey by Norman Richardson showed that of 131 known directors, almost 25 percent were women. By 1926 Paul Vieth's survey showed that almost half of the 395 directors reporting were women. During the depression years of the 1930s women held most of the positions. The post–World War II years saw a return of many men to the profession, typically as ministers of religious education. *See also* Curriculum; Evaluation; Leadership Development; Long-range Planning; Management; Ministry; Organization in Religious Education; Professional Societies; Professional Study; Religious Education Association; Religious Education Committee; Supervision; Theological Education; Theology and Education; Volunteer Principle.

FOR FURTHER REFERENCE

Furnish, Dorothy Jean. *DRE/DEC: The History of a Profession.* Nashville, TN: Christian Educators Fellowship, The United Methodist Church, 1976.
Harris, Maria, ed. *Parish Religious Education: The People, The Place, The Profession.* New York: Paulist, 1978.
Taylor, Marvin J., ed. *Changing Patterns of Religious Education.* Nashville, TN: Abingdon, 1984.

D. J. Furnish

Disabilities

See Exceptional Persons.

Discipline

Discipline, or correction, understood in diverse ways, is generally of importance for religious groups.

Punitive discipline may use either physical or psychological means to enforce an adult's will on a child, sometimes masked as an attempt to "heal the child's sins" and restore right order. Physical violence is widely condemned and probably equally widely practiced. It may often be related to an adult's frustration or inability to conceive other means of controlling the child. Psychological discipline (denying or taking away privileges, removing love from the child, creating guilt for "hurting the parent," or ultimately making the child oppress him- or herself) is not far from physical discipline in trying to protect the parent from the child or provide the teacher with a comfortably ordered world. In religious education, such forms of discipline are likely to result in fear of physical punishment (in this life or the next) and/or fear of displeasing teacher, parent, or God. Punitive discipline is not appropriate for any age.

METHODS FOR CLASSROOM MANAGEMENT

Age Level	Likely Situations	Suggestions for Classroom Management
Birth to one year	Children's curiosity is growing, as is their ability to explore	Keep precious or dangerous materials out of reach; deflect the child's attention when curiosity and explorations get out of hand; say and mean "no."
2 years	Children insist on doing as they will	Give children options when possible; set limits positively.
	Tantrums occur	Say and mean "no"; remove child from the scene if necessary and possible.
3 years	Children have difficulty sharing during group play	Reason first (i.e., "It's her turn now."); try to deflect the child's attention (i.e., "Let's see what other toys we have.").
4–6 years	Fights occur during wider group play	Restate rules (i.e., "You must not hit people."); deflect anger if possible (i.e., "I understand how you feel but . . . "); separate fighters and remove from scene if necessary and possible.
	Disruptive actions	Offer approval or some reward for changes in behavior.
7–11 years	Disruptive actions	Remove child to work alone as long as necessary.
	Disruptive words	Give more challenging work if boredom seems to be the proble; isolate briefly if the words were intended to be attention-getting.
	Quiet/shy individuals	Encourage with words and approving looks; encourage simple initial responses.
12–18 years	Self-identity problems	Seek to be/provide good mentors and role models; encourage burgeoning initiative and automony, but continue to set and enforce limits; appeal to reason when specific problems arise.
Adult	Restlessness, inattention, and absences	Offer alternatives to the group as a whole and to individuals; make sessions participatory.

The following three forms of discipline may or may not be appropriate at any age depending on the congregation's understanding of the child.

Laissez-faire discipline, or permissiveness, allows the child to develop without interference from the parent or teacher (except when the child is likely to do major harm to self or other). This may be chosen for therapeutic reasons (as in the Summerhill School experiment), or from a philosophical conviction about the inherent goodness of the child and the natural flowering of the child's potential, or from an unwillingness to get involved, often simply because it is "too much trouble" for the adult. Discipline is difficult work, and the adult who lives by the pleasure principle is unlikely to choose to engage in the process. Where this leads to lack of control in the child, the child may be ostracized by others in a learning situation and learn little.

Person-centered discipline is marked by reality-based interaction. Its principle of operation is dialogue that respects both child and adult. At its best it forms healthy, relational human beings with appropriate self-control and power. R. Dreikurs and V. Soltz (*Children: The Challenge,* 1964) base discipline on teaching children the consequences of their actions. T. Gordon (*Parent Effectiveness Training,* 1970) stresses the need for active listening on the part of parents. Person-centered discipline almost always requires some training of parents and teachers, as few have learned these skills from their own experience.

Discipline based on behavior modification is used widely in general education and in church school settings. Rewards are sometimes given for good behavior (positive reinforcement on a random schedule). More often, regrettably, this method is only used for the best students (that is, those who are academically strong or whose behavior is particularly good for the teacher); for weaker or more docile students negative reinforcement is more widely used, with the typical result of further undermining the students' confidence.

To speak of discipline in a generic way in a "typical" religious education context is quite impossible. What is possible is to observe and recognize the patterns of discipline already in effect in the classroom and to provide options that may begin to break negative cycles and to take more seriously the needs of the child. The educative task is to move from unrecognized assumptions to critical understanding—an activity of the disciplined mind. Community-accepted patterns of childrearing will normally prevail in spite of developmental insight. Indeed, even casual observation of child-parent and child-teacher interaction indicates that patterns of discipline are replicated from one's own childhood with little regard for their long-term deleterious effects.

The question is not whether the religious education teacher is disciplining children in the classroom. The question is how. For example, when a child demonstrates verbally antisocial behavior, instead of saying "I'm going to staple your lips together if you don't stop it" (punitive discipline), an alternative would be to actively listen to the child to determine the child's hurt and to say clearly to the child, "I hear what you are saying but your screaming is making me upset" (person-centered discipline). While the punitive approach may be efficient in silencing the child, the long-term effects of the person-centered approach will more likely result both in better classroom management and in the growth of the child.

It has been widely noted that what adults recall as harmful in their educational experience is harsh discipline (of many sorts) while what adults tend to remember as most beneficial in that experience is a personal relationship with a caring teacher. In this light, the link between discipline and its root "disciple" denotes a positive, person-centered approach. Discipline is, then, a matter for the education of the whole congregation, for discipline embodies basically unrecognized assumptions about gender, power, authority, age, and self-concept. *See also* Behavior; Child Abuse; Learning Theory; Parent-Teacher Relations.

H. C. Simmons, R. H. Cram

Discovery Learning

Discovery learning is an approach to teaching in which students are assisted in acquiring knowledge by being encouraged to explore subject matter and make discoveries. Related to inductive teaching, experiential education, and inquiry teaching, it has several distinguishing characteristics in common with them.

The teacher is less in control of the subject matter and at the same time more concerned about the process involving the learners. The learners are invited to utilize all their senses and to become more responsible for their own learning. The subject matter becomes material for exploration rather than being just a body of knowledge to be presented or remembered. A wide variety of teaching strategies are used to appeal to the diverse abilities, interests, and needs of the learners.

Much learning takes place as a result of the process of discovery. Discovery may happen by accident, or it may happen because a teacher has provided carefully selected resources for the learner to use to explore a subject that will lead to the achievement of identified objectives.

A child may accidentally put a paint brush with yellow paint into a cup of blue paint and discover that yellow and blue make green. An adult may read Psalm 22 and remember the words of Jesus on the cross, discovering for the first time the source of Jesus' words. A teenager may take part in a simple dramatization of Paul's conversion and discover what it means to encounter the presence of the risen Christ.

When the phrase "discovery learning" is used in the context of religious education, it usually describes a particular attitude and approach of the teacher. The teacher provides learners with an abundance of resources and motivation to use those resources. Learners are given directions for exploring the subject matter and for responding to that information in personal, creative ways. The teacher relies on the resourcefulness of the learners and the quality of the resources to enable the discoveries to occur. Learners are encouraged to share their discoveries with one another, and through sharing still more discoveries take place.

While it may appear the burden for learning is on the learner, it is important to recognize the significant responsibility of the teacher. The teacher must become familiar with the subject matter as well as a large number of resources and must carefully plan activities to involve the learners with those resources. The exciting thing about this approach is the large number of discoveries made that were never anticipated by the teacher.

It is important to remember that regardless of the teaching strategies used by the teacher, learning takes place when discoveries are made. Discoveries can be made when listening to a lecture, when searching the Scriptures, when participating in a discussion, as well as when following the directions of a learning center. *See also* Constructive Activities; Experience; Learning Center; Learning Theory; Methodology; Teaching Styles; Teaching Theory.

P. Griggs

Discussion

A discussion is an exchange of views about a subject in order to arrive at a conclusion or at some new understanding to be explored further. Such a definition excludes some casual, popular uses of the term, as, for example, reference to informal conversation or to an open forum where the audience asks questions of the speaker. Sometimes discussion is viewed as debate, sometimes as a conference exploring various facets of a topic. More technically, discussion may be viewed as problem solving, drawing primarily on John Dewey's theory and his "how we think" steps. Or it may be viewed as a teaching strategy involving a sequence of human interaction activities moving from a delineation of the question or task, through an orderly investigation of clearly stated alternatives, to analytical evaluation, and finally to conclusions or tentative working hypotheses.

Discussion continues to be one of the most

valuable assets to both learning and teaching. For example, in a youth or adult class, a teacher may offer a quotation, ask for agreement or disagreement, and the reason for the viewpoint expressed. Participants compare and contrast their views, explore reasons, and in the process come not only to clarification but to positions to be developed and explored later. Or the teacher may ask a class to paraphrase a biblical passage, read paraphrases aloud, compare them, and then discuss the meaning of the passage. In response to a lecture or the reading of a selection from a creed, students may be asked to list questions and affirmations; then the group explores the correlation between the two through discussion. After a presentation, a "circular response" allows each person the privilege of stating agreement or disagreement, with no interruption until every person has spoken. At that point, a teacher may sort out different positions and lead the group through a series of questions designed to probe divergent views.

Variations of discussions are limited only by lack of imagination. Illustrations given suggest that a grouping of ten to eighteen youth or adults would be a working-sized group. Even where larger numbers are present, it is possible to arrange a room to facilitate discussions. Circles of six may be set up and each circle assigned a quotation or a question or a paraphrase, the avenues to facilitate rapidly paced small-group discussion. Or a teacher may present a lecture, stopping periodically for conversation by twos in a large group. What happens with the large group–small group combination in discussion is engagement of people with ideas and involvement in the process. Hard, analytical thinking and a deliberate move toward consensus or resolution of ideas are more characteristic of the basic small group or class.

The same general pattern is possible with children, although for younger children in particular the activity may be nearer conversation than discussion. The format might be to start a story and ask a group to complete it, then talk about it. Looking at a picture with a group of children, asking them to describe what they see, and then asking questions can facilitate conversation. They can imagine stories about the picture. Or they can compare the picture with their own friends and experiences. With older children, the problem-solving approach is applicable. They can work in small groups with specific tasks or committee assignments. Reports can then be the basis for general discussion.

Teachers have the role of introducing concepts or tasks, guiding interaction, summarizing periodically, and relating what is said to the original focus or problem. They have the responsibility of being prepared in a broad scope of knowledge related to the subject being explored, of knowing when to bring in information as needed, and of being alert not to preempt the thinking process of participants in the discussion.

Parents may employ discussion techniques in the home. A family council that formulates a problem precisely, explores and evaluates alternatives, and agrees on working principles to be tested in action benefits participants in this problem-solving approach. Listening, reflecting on what others say, taking turns, checking on likely results if certain behaviors were approved, summarizing conclusions—all such activities are as useful and appropriate in the home as in the classroom.

Around the 1950s, social scientists began focusing on the development of interpersonal and cognitive skills in T-groups, laboratories built around group dynamics concepts; the democratic process was viewed as making individual resources available for the group or society. Similarly, in the last decades of the twentieth century, extensive use of the many forms of discussion has value for both individuals and groups. The individual who strengthens thinking and relating abilities through discussion becomes the member who, with others in a group, seeks to use that discussion process for contribution to the public good. *See also* Conference; Conversation; Debate; Engagement; Methodology; Problem Solving; Socratic Method; Teaching Theory.

S. P. Little

Disputation

The disputation is a formalized process of analysis and synthesis through structured questioning. In the early centuries of the church, learning was thought to occur most effectively through a rather stylized form of the lecture: a textual reading, then a commentary, followed by an application of the text. The teacher was active, the learner passive. With the raising of consciousness in the Middle Ages, there was a need for a more holistic methodology for dealing with and responding to the Christian message as truth. During that period of history, a capacity to call truth into question seems to have developed quite spontaneously. Accordingly the teaching/learning methods that were spawned typically entailed raising arguments for and against (pro and con) a particular facet of "truth."

The heart of one such teaching/learning process was the disputation. It was designed to ensure that a particular inquiry (or class) did not degenerate into mere argument for the sake of argument. The methodological intent was not to overwhelm an opponent but to explore a question as completely as possible. This was to be accomplished in a spirit of inquiry while using the powerful, and potentially divisive, tools of dialectic, logic, and systematic doubt. The goal of the process was a clearer and more dynamic perception and understanding of truth.

Thomas Aquinas and the Dominican order of which he was a member have often been identified with the disputation both as a method of inquiry and as a method of teaching. Aquinas's *Quaestiones disputatae* is the best known, most complete, and probably finest example of the disputation employed as an academic exercise. Although seldom used and little known today, the disputation affords a healthy tension between faith and reason and offers a certain power to deal with and to rethink significant issues in a spirit of balanced earnestness and tolerance. *See also* Dialectic(s); Questions; Thomas Aquinas.

H. W. Burgess

Divorce

It is estimated that nearly one out of every two marriages today ends in divorce. Many reasons have been given for the current trend, but actual causes of any single divorce are often unclear and may not be related at all to the following suggestions.

Some point to the breakdown of societal mores that used to sustain marriages. Families are more mobile and do not put down long-term roots in any one community, so there is no effective community (including religious community) support and encouragement for family stability. Some have felt that middle-class parenting practices of the 1950s encouraged the kind of permissiveness in children that led to self-centeredness, although the goal was to help children develop creative talents by minimizing behavioral limits. In a similar vein, others have decried what they view as an increase in narcissism, in which people are concerned with their own self-fulfillment even if this can be achieved only at the expense of others.

The media present many types of family arrangements, but the variety itself prevents any focus on what might be or lead to healthy marital patterns to sustain families. Increased opportunities for women and changing roles for both men and women have caused some confusion and stress for both husbands and wives. Lengthened life spans have brought another factor into marriage; with a potentially larger number of years for a marriage, more strains can possibly develop.

Although the current incidence of divorce is a late twentieth-century phenomenon, the themes of sudden and premature termination of marriage by death, natural catastrophes, war, and exile fill the pages of Scripture and of history, as do the stories of victims, often children, who confront these events with fear, anger, despair, and hope. Religious education teachers are presented with a unique opportunity to address divorce both within the paradigm of the nature of the religious community and as individuals.

195

Church and synagogue function in healthy families to promote maturity in family members, provide a community for the individual and the family, and provide role models through Scripture and community members. During separation and divorce, families are given support, comfort, and hope, through word and worship. Communities encourage reintegration and growth of single-parent and stepparent families and provide the context for members to reach out and minister to troubled and reintegrating families.

The teacher is often the first line of defense for members of separating families, both adults and children. He or she serves as a stable, consistent, and trustworthy adult during a time when important adults in a child or adolescent's life are suddenly absent, hostile, or have very little energy to devote to parenting due to their own distress. The teacher functions to keep the child and parents involved in parish life and offer from Scripture and recent experience stories that hold up supportive behavior and hope.

Religious education teachers and other leaders are frequently called upon to be an expert in many things in which they have had little experience. The following information may be helpful as they try to keep in touch with a situation.

Children, even at an early age, are likely to react to the separation of parents by being upset and needing comfort. They should be kept informed without overwhelming them with information they cannot assimilate. Informal conversation with a child, special attention, and sensitivity as to when they need to become involved in class activities and when they need to work alone will be helpful.

Teachers will want to know what family arrangements are in place. Children need to retain as many regions of safety in their lives as possible, so a self-confident parent or head of the household is a most important source of security. Ordinarily, it is helpful if there is still contact with the non-custodial parent.

Children who fail to resume normal development within a year of the separation may need special attention. This suggests a need for continuity in leadership and reciprocal sharing of information among teachers. It will also be noted that children's recovery from a family division will be enhanced as the parents establish satisfactory new life situations. It is hoped that children will neither be held back in their development by overprotection during this period or become prematurely mature because of the emotional responsibilities thrust upon them.

Religious education teachers need to view carefully units of study that deal with the family, because such materials, whether biblical or experiential, tend to portray the happily integrated family. This is contrary to fact for many children who need to be assured that security is to be found in all kinds of families. Similarly, leaders of adolescent groups need to review carefully units of study on marriage and family to be sure that young peoples' experiences of divorce are incorporated as part of their understanding of marriage.

Adult groups will want to review the factors contributory to divorce outlined earlier as they study the subject within the religious contexts of commitment and the resulting conflicts and estrangements. Adults can also form support groups, both for those adjusting to the immediacy of divorce and those trying to bring stability to their children in a one-parent household. *See also* Family Life Education; Marriage Enrichment; Singles.

FOR FURTHER REFERENCE

Sweiss, Robert. *Marital Separation.* New York: Basic Books, 1975.

R. L. Zondervan

Doctrine/Dogma

The term "doctrine" refers to what the church believes, teaches, and confesses. It is the English equivalent of the Latin word *doctrina* (from *docere*), which translates the Greek word *didaskalia*, referring both to the act of teaching and the content of what is taught (see Matt. 15:8; 1 Tim. 1:10; 4:13; Titus 2:1). Broadly speaking it refers to those ideas all Christians hold in common, but the term can also indicate the distinctive beliefs and teachings of various traditions or denominations (e.g., "Protestant doctrine" or "Lutheran doctrine"). In both senses the term is applied to particular aspects of Christian teaching (e.g., the doctrines of God, Christ, the Holy Spirit, salvation, justification by faith, etc.).

FORMULATION AND USAGE

Doctrines are not created "out of nothing." What the church believes, teaches, and confesses is based ultimately on the revelatory activity of God. For Protestants this usually implies a close link with the Bible as the word of God. This link between revelation and Scripture, however, should not be taken to imply that God dictated truths in propositional form that need to be extracted from Scripture and systematized as doctrine.

Revelation is much more personal and dynamic: it is God acting in history. Scripture is not to be equated with revelation; it records God's revelatory activity and reports how Israel and the early church perceived this activity. Because of the specific historical contexts in which revelation was originally experienced, the inevitable ambiguous nature of revelation, and the variety of literary genres by which revelation was recorded, the church has always had to interpret Scripture to clarify what Christians believe about God and about the various aspects of God's relationship to the world and to humankind. Doctrines are the result of this ongoing process of interpretation and clarification.

Catholic theologians, while not denying the close link between Scripture and revelation, point out that God's revelatory activity cannot be confined to what is contained in Scripture and that the process of interpreting Christian faith commenced even before the canon of Scripture was finalized. In fact, the church's delineation of the canon was determined by and then, in turn, limited what may be considered as doctrine. Christian tradition, therefore, is both a product of and a source for the church's attempt at clarifying what it believes, teaches, and confesses. While the relative importance of each may be debated, it is now generally recognized by Catholics and Protestants alike that both Scripture and tradition convey the faith of the Christian community. Consequently, both have been and continue to be interdependent sources for Christian doctrine. There is less agreement about other possible sources for doctrine, such as reason, experience, or the accumulated wisdom of culture.

The formulation of Christian doctrine has rarely been a purely academic exercise. Often it was forced upon the church by persecution or heresy. People needed to be clear about that for which martyrs were prepared to die or to define orthodox belief when internal division threatened to split the church. Having sorted out its beliefs, the church articulated its findings through apologetics, creeds, and in particular dogmas.

The English word "dogma" comes from the identical Greek word. Dogma literally meant "opinion" and was applied to the teaching or underlying principle of the various philosophical schools. This principle was taken to be axiomatic by the adherents of the particular school. Dogma also denoted authoritative statements. In this sense it is used in Luke 2:1 and Acts 17:7 for imperial decrees and in Acts 16:4 for the resolutions of the Jerusalem council. The church later combined the original and derived senses of dogma to refer to official doctrinal formulations promulgated by ecclesiastical authorities, especially church councils. Dogma, therefore, indicates the official doctrinal teaching of the church.

In Catholic theology dogma has come to have three distinguishing characteristics: a dogma is based on revelation; it is proclaimed as a dogma by the church; and it is binding on the faithful (i.e., denial of a dogma is heresy). The words "dogma" and "doctrine," therefore, are not interchangeable. While all dogmas are doctrines, not all doctrines have received or ever will receive the status of dogma. Some doctrines, although held to be true by the Catholic church, may not be based directly on revelation or, because of other reasons, may not have been proclaimed as dogmas. Some

of these doctrines, held unanimously to be true, may be referred to as "nondefined dogmas."

Protestants have been reluctant to speak of dogmas other than in a historical sense. Recognizing that the great ecumenical councils held during the first five Christian centuries and the authoritative bodies of the various Christian traditions since then have promulgated dogmas, Protestants have studied the history of dogma and used historical dogmas to clarify their own doctrines. Authoritative declarations of these doctrines, however, have normally been referred to as "confessions" rather than as dogmas.

Christian doctrines, even officially declared doctrines such as dogmas, are not static. Formulated in particular historical settings, they are influenced by the cultural and linguistic norms of their time. New times demand new formulations. That Christ is "of the same substance (Gk. *homoousios*)" as God the Father may have been an appropriate way to express the reality of the divinity of Christ for fourth-century orthodoxy, but today's Christians need to find a modern way to express this tenet of belief. Moreover, because many ancient formulations were more explicit in spelling out what was heretical than in spelling out what was orthodox, contemporary theologians need to expound and articulate the content of Christian faith in addition to restating dogmas or doctrines in current terms.

While engaging in the process of defining, classifying, and articulating what Christians believe, teach, and confess, it is important to remember that doctrines and dogmas are not ends in themselves. They have meaning only because they point beyond themselves to the God whose revelatory activity they seek to describe.

TEACHING METHODS

Because doctrine is a conceptual way of thinking, it cannot be appropriately taught until children are eleven or twelve years old. They experience the reality of a doctrine earlier, for example, repentance and forgiveness—they know what it is to be saved in various situations—but the cognitive articulation of the experience is best approached in later childhood.

Confirmation classes in some Christian traditions are doctrinally oriented, including interpretation of the Apostles' and/or Nicene creeds. Creative teachers find ways of helping children relate the affirmations to their experience and emphasize the dynamic quality. These are confessions of faith: "I believe in . . ." Although each denomination has prepared confirmation materials, the teacher's ability to adapt these to a specific group of children is important. Catechisms are less used than in the past, but inventive teachers can find ways to make them live. Preparation for baptism in those traditions that practice believers' baptism follows similar patterns.

Adolescence is the time for questioning and for thinking. It is a good time to explore the depths of doctrines through simple and lively presentations, discussions, informal writing, and sharing of experiences.

Adults need to be challenged to think theologically and to explore the basic doctrines of faith. Adult classes are frequently led by a theologically prepared person, but it is important that such a teacher be able to speak in terms laity can understand rather than the technical language of the field. Reading about doctrines can be encouraged: excerpts from theological writings and study books prepared for adult classes by the denominations. Discussion groups are important as a response either to a speaker or to reading. *See also* Catechism; Creed; Heresy; Indoctrination; Jewish Theological Concepts; Magisterium; Revelation; Tradition; Vatican II.

FOR FURTHER REFERENCE

Hodgson, Peter C., and Robert H. King. *Christian Theology: An Introduction to Its Traditions and Tasks*, 2d ed. Philadelphia: Fortress, 1985.

Lindbeck, George A. *The Nature of Doctrine.* Philadelphia: Westminster, 1984.

Lochman, Jan M. *The Faith We Confess: An Ecumenical Dogmatics.* Philadelphia: Fortress, 1984.

Pelikan, Jaroslav. *The Christian Tradition: A History of the Development of Doctrine,* 5 vols. Chicago/London: University of Chicago Press, 1971–.

Schmaus, Michael. *Dogma,* 6 vols. Kansas City/London: Sheed & Ward, 1968–1977. Reprint, Westminster: Christian Classics, 1984.

W. Tabbernee

Doubt

The twentieth-century theologian Paul Tillich often commented that doubt was a prelude to faith. Far from being evidence of an uncertain or tenuous faith, doubt can be an affirmation that an individual's relationship with God is so secure that he or she is free to explore the boundaries of that relationship through questioning and doubt. To doubt is to ask the question "Why?" or "Is this true?" Scripture is replete with accounts of men and women who rage at God, question the justice of the divine working, and ask, "Why?" Jesus himself, while hanging on the cross, seems to have had his own bouts with uncertainty. He quotes from Psalm 22 in asking, "My God, my God, why hast thou forsaken me?"

DOUBT AND CHRISTIAN FAITH

Christian educators therefore learn to regard a person's doubt as a positive opportunity for growth and strengthening of faith. When someone asks "Why?" or loses his or her once-certain grip upon the truth, that person is able to begin a process of exploration, questioning, and searching that is at the very heart of the educational process. To deny or to suppress our doubts can lead to a retarded faith, a faith that is unable to grow with the changing demands and predictable crises of life. This is not to deny that doubt can often be painful. Each of us must live in life with enough certainty, enough coherence in our worldview to enable us to function in the world. Doubt is sometimes evidence that our worldview is coming apart at the seams, that we are moving through a period of disequilibrium and disorganization in our belief structure. While the Christian faith in no way romanticizes the experience of doubt, neither does it condemn doubt. Doubt is a normal, recurring, quite expected part of the life of faith, the space between the faith once affirmed and the faith yet to be received.

Some Christians feel that the rational exploration of one's beliefs, the invitation to question one's assertions, and to explore the complexities of faith are an invitation to skepticism and ultimately rejection of the gospel. By this line of reasoning, honesty about one's doubts inevitably leads to more doubts and to less faith. Is faith undermined by our intellectual questions? Sometimes it may be. But more often, for most of us, faith is undermined through the normal process of living. Belief is a simple matter for those who never encounter tragedy, injustice, or the gap between the way things ought to be and the way they really are. Because few people are able to live life without encountering these confusing obstacles to faith, few people are immune from the experience of doubt.

When the risen Christ is confronted by the doubts of Thomas (John 20:26–29), Jesus does not rebuke Thomas for his doubt. He does praise "Those who have not seen and yet believed"— which includes most latter-day believers. Jesus reaches out to Thomas in compassion and gives his doubting disciple what he needs in order to believe. If Thomas needs tangible, physical reassurance, that is what Jesus offers him. "Put out your hand, and place it in my side; do not be faithless, but believing" (John 20:27). The foundational assertion of church life is that God graciously gives believers what we need in order to overcome our doubts. Our doubt is not rebuked, but rather ministered to by the community of faith.

DOUBT AND CHRISTIAN EDUCATION

A primary way in which the church ministers to the doubts of Christians is through the teaching office of the church. The major goal of Christian education is to give believers the cognitive structure, the concepts, the skills and understandings they need to be able to live their faith amidst a world that does not recognize the Savior of the church. A church's attitude toward doubt will help to determine the goals and the form of that church's Christian education. Where doubt is judged to be evidence of the failure of faith, doubt will be rebuked and Christian education will be indoctrination into the unquestioning acceptance of that church's official dogma. The church will seek to insulate its members from those social and personal circumstances that might lead to doubt. Such attempts may be successful, provided that the church is able to provide its members a totally protected environment where the corrosive acids of modernity and secularism, the claims of other religions, and the everyday stresses and crises of life itself are either avoided or else fully explained by reference to the accepted dogma.

On the other hand, in a church in which doubt is viewed as a normal part of the pilgrimage of faith, Christian education will be a process of being honest about one's doubts and seeking to reorganize one's belief system so that new insights are gained whereby doubt might be overcome. The task of this education will not be simply the inculcation of the approved answers but rather the acquisition of key skills, insights, and values that will enable the growing believer to deal with life's challenges to faith without being overwhelmed by them. The danger of this style of education is that doubt might be idealized—it may be seen not simply as an expected hazard of a faithful life, but as a sign of "deep honesty and intellectual ability"; in other words doubt becomes the goal rather than faith. The modern world tends to relativize all values, denying the ultimate validity of any statement of faith. Great value is placed upon a person's adaptability and toleration of all points of view. In such a climate, the presence of doubt may signal little more than an intellectual failure of nerve, a slothful inability to wrestle with one's doubts in order to gain a more sure faith.

With Jesus as our model, the church must learn neither to rebuke nor to romanticize doubt, but to minister to it, to understand more fully the factors that give rise to the undermining of a person's faith, and to minister to that person in the name of the Lord who was determined that we be not faithless, but believing. *See also* Belief; Faith; Faith Development; Indoctrination; Questions.

W. H. Willimon

Drama

Drama is an art form that tells a story by means of action and dialogue. Its principal elements of expression are movement and speech that flow from the impulse to express a thought or a feeling. While this is so in everyday life as well, acting allows a purging of a wide range of emotions. Drama is also a meeting place of all the arts. It often includes other media such as dancing, painting, sculpture, music, writing, and singing. Drama encourages the transferring of ideas from one art form to another, thereby opening new perspectives and relationships to the participants and audience.

Creative dramatics includes improvised group drama under the guidance of a leader in which extemporaneous action and dialogue are featured. Since each performance is slightly different, creative drama can be especially nurturing of the imagination. The range of creative dramatics is wide and varied. It begins with imaginative play and can include imitative and original pantomimes, story dramatizations, creative plays based on original ideas, literature, dramatizations of current events, creative work with puppets, shadow plays, and the like. While some preparation is made in advance, detailed action and dialogue are left to the spontaneous interplay of the participants. The emphasis is on the creative activity itself, rather than the disciplines of stage drama such as fixed roles, memorized actions and lines, audience reaction, sets, costumes, or makeup. Creative dramatics includes frequent interchange of roles, spontaneous dialogue and action, and group evaluation. Personal development rather than satisfaction of an audience is the goal. For young children creative dramatics offers a way of communicating through bodily movement when linguistic abilities are limited. For all ages creative dramatics offers the opportunity to give outward form to imaginative ideas.

One rich possibility for dramatization is the word of God. The Scriptures are rich in stories, events, and characters that lend themselves to dramatic presentation. To dramatize the Scriptures is to embody them, to make them part of the texture of our very being. When used in liturgical settings, scriptural drama can be a powerful event for all involved. There are two basic ways to use the Scripture texts directly. The first involves giving each person a character from the story and having the passage acted out either in the sanctuary or in a main gathering space. This can be done right during the liturgy. Another approach is to have several readers read the text—the readers are the voices—and other persons mime or role-play the action. Having young children under the age of twelve do the action works especially well because of their limited ability to read well.

The dramatic element of worship is built into every service with the colors of the seasons, the stories of faith, and the very settings of the church buildings. The dramatic is part of how we worship, drawing us into the mystery of God's saving activity. The dramatic forms of ritual help us experience a story by living it, encounter a mystery by entering it, and meeting people by remembering them. By being a part of the telling, the perspectives shift and those involved in the drama have a stake in what is happening. The senses become more alert, emotional energy is released, and the actor becomes alive to the eternal moment. And this vitality is shared by all participants in the ritual as the body channels spirit, mystery, and new life. Religious ritual is the dramatic encounter of the whole person with ultimate reality.

To summarize, drama provides opportunities for nurturing the religious imaginations of individuals and communities, allowing persons to participate in the recreative process especially as it allows for acting out our responses to God and to each other, creating situations and settings that lure participants in reflecting, interpreting, and judging their own experiences in the light of a community's values, assisting participants in the development of decision-making skills and in seeing creative alternatives in moral situations, and celebrating life in the past, the present, and the future. *See also* Dance; Dramatization; Liturgy; Pageantry; Role Playing; Simulation; Sociodrama; Worship.

FOR FURTHER REFERENCE

Pierini, Mary Paul Frances. *Creative Dramatics: A Guide for Educators.* New York: Seabury, 1971.

Waddy, Laurence. *The Bible as Drama.* New York: Paulist, 1975.

G. Durka

Dramatization

Dramatization is the acting out of a story, real-life situation, event, feeling, or idea. There are many forms of dramatization, such as plays, puppet theater, radio theater, pantomime, pageants, processionals, parades, clowning, dance, skits, role plays, simulations, interviews, dialogue sermons, monologues, etc. The purpose of a dramatization is to enable the participants to experience, understand, and communicate, in a new and exciting manner, what is being dramatized.

HISTORY

The urge to dramatize is as old as humankind. Dramatization is an essential part of religious rituals in every culture. The great dramas of the Greeks, known to us through authors such as Homer, Aeschylus, and Aristophanes, emerged from religious rites. For the ancient Hebrews, too, drama played a role in religion. The Bible exhibits literature in dramatic form.

The Christian church has been both a source of drama and an inhibitor of it. The medieval church produced mystery plays (reenactments of biblical stories) and morality plays (allegorical dramas having to do with moral issues in Chris-

tian living). These were later banned from the church. Certain strains of Protestantism, such as the Puritans and the Quakers, disapproved of drama in or out of the church.

Dramatizations are found in Christianity in worship rites such as the Lord's Supper. Most churches also have some form of Christmas pageant, Easter sunrise dramatization, or youth musical. In Judaism, the observances of religious holidays and High Holy Days, such as Passover, Yom Kippur, and Rosh Hashanah, are also centered on dramatizations.

IMPORTANCE

Dramatization is important for psychological, sociological, and educational reasons. Developmental psychologists such as Jean Piaget and Erik Erikson have demonstrated that children naturally learn and grow through imitation, play, and drama. In play, children imitate adult behavior, rehearse adult roles, express their feelings, gain empathy for others, and learn some control in changing reality. As they grow older, drama helps them to understand more abstract concepts, to gain competence in adult behavior, to develop a cognitive understanding of others, and to fit themselves into the historical community of which they are a part. Adolescent interest in heroes, which helps the learning of appropriate adult roles and behavior, is facilitated through dramatization.

Anthropologists have observed that dramatic rituals teach individuals the history of the community and help them experience identity with the community. The most important of these are "rites of passage," which occur at key periods in an individual's life such as at puberty, marriage, birth, and death. Many religious educators believe that religious institutions must become more aware of the rites of passage occurring in the individual and corporate lives of members. The educational opportunities inherent at these times could be enhanced through the use of dramatizations and other rituals.

Dramatization is an extremely effective educational process. It is participatory, involving both teacher and learners working cooperatively. It is exploratory, inviting discovery. Students learn because they are doing rather than observing. In dramatization, each person's feelings, ideas, and contributions are accepted as valid and unique.

Dramatization is also an effective way of learning religious content, whether history, stories, ideas, attitudes, or values. Through dramatizations, students learn the facts of the ancient situations as they experience that situation. They are able to identify with earlier members of their faith community and draw connections with their own life. Through dramatizations, students can also express deep feelings and anxieties. They can be helped to find meaning for their lives through the search for meaning of their dramatic characters.

EFFECTIVE USE

Dramatization can be used in almost any setting at any time, in worship, education, and recreation. To be effective, it must be well planned and appropriate to the different cognitive levels of the students. At different ages, either different stories, ideas, and situations will be chosen, or the same stories, ideas, and situations will be expressed at different levels of complexity. Appropriateness is also guided by the life experiences of the learners and their ability to relate to the characters being dramatized.

Effectiveness is increased with the additional factors of time, commitment, flexibility, and training. A flexible, movable, physical environment is essential. With time and commitment, especially when a formal play is involved, amateurs will discover hidden talents and abilities. They will produce work of which they can be proud. Training will give teachers and leaders skills and confidence to use a variety of dramatization forms in their classes. Psychological flexibility is necessary, for what is produced in dramatizations is often not quite what was expected. The results can be creative and moving.

It is more interesting to use a wide variety of dramatizations. Mime and movement are simple ways to begin. Clowning is popular, especially with teenagers (although clowns can frighten very small children). Simulation games can be helpful with all ages over six. These must be carefully planned, with plenty of time allowed for debriefing. Role plays are helpful in many religious education situations, from studying historical stories of the faith, to dealing with current events or with an individual's fears. Monologues, dialogues, skits, and plays can be historical or contemporary, bringing the feelings and events of a situation alive for all the participants. Dramatizations can be done once, informally, or practiced repeatedly and performed. Performances can also become part of the worship ritual. *See also* Creative Activities; Drama; Pageantry; Role Playing; Simulation; Sociodrama; Worship.

FOR FURTHER REFERENCE

Bennett, Gordon C. *Acting out Faith*. St. Louis, MO: CBP Press, 1986.
Contemporary Drama Service. *Catalog of Hard-to-Find Christian Participation Resources*. Colorado Springs, CO: Meriwether, published three times annually.

C. E. Blair

Dreams

Dreams are psychic phenomena taking place during the REM (rapid eye movement) stages of sleep marked by a flow of imagery arising from the unconscious. All people dream, although not all remember dreaming. Dreaming has been found to be essential to both physical and psychic health.

It is possible to encourage the remembering of dreams by recording a dream in detail as soon as possible upon awakening. Placing a notebook and pen at the bedside may stimulate remembering. This provides a concrete form that then can be used for further study and amplification.

Throughout history dreams and dreaming have been an important part of culture. Dreams have been viewed as the vehicle for communication with the divine and for healing. The Bible is full of such instances, although the terms "dream" and "vision" are used interchangeably. Dream material is found throughout the Bible, from Genesis to Revelation. Jacob's dream of a ladder with angels ascending and descending (Gen. 28:10–17) and Joseph's dreams and their interpretations (Gen. 37:5–11) are perhaps the most familiar Old Testament examples. New Testament examples show Joseph encouraged in a dream to marry the pregnant Mary and later warned in a dream to flee to Egypt, thus preserving the life of the infant Jesus (Matt. 2:19–20).

Dreams have been regarded as a source of guidance and also of healing both in ancient and modern cultures. Ancient Greek religion generally accepted dreams as a common means of revelation and the temple of Askelepios was the site where one sought a dream specifically for healing. In certain tribal cultures the dream is a tool for healing used by the shaman, or medicine man or woman. A dream or vision of power also serves as an initiation experience or call to the vocation of shaman, much as the calls of the Old Testament prophets were visionary in character.

For modern, scientifically oriented people, the field of depth psychology, with the pioneering work of Freud and Jung, has validated and legitimated the phenomenon of dreaming as an important expression of our unconscious psychic life. Speaking in the language of symbol by means of images, only the dreamer can unlock the personal meaning of a dream. The use of dream interpretation with the concomitant study of the language of myth and symbol, both personal and archetypal, has again become a tool of healing and a source of personal growth and spiritual development.

The Talmud says that an unexamined dream is like an unopened letter. Through the added findings of depth psychology, modern people are becoming open to accepting dreams and their interpretations as a legitimate path to God within and as a source of guidance and wholeness.

Children sometimes tell their dreams during a religious education class, possibly evoked by stories of biblical dreams, but teachers will want to respond on a simple sharing level.

The positive attitude toward religion found in Jungian psychology has encouraged its study by pastors for their counseling work and finds educational expression in adult study classes. Although limited in number, there are adult study courses based on a Jungian approach that include the interpretation of dreams. Such groups also use the writings of Morton Kelsey, who encourages people to search their dreams for religious meaning. *See also* Jungian Influences; Psychotherapy; Spirituality; Symbolism.

FOR FURTHER REFERENCE

Kelsey, Morton T. *God, Dreams and Revelation: A Christian Interpretation of Dreams.* Minneapolis, MN: Augsburg, 1974.

Sanford, John A. *Dreams, God's Forgotten Language.* New York: Crossroads, 1982.

Savery, Louis M., et al. *Dreams and Spiritual Growth: A Christian Approach to Dream Work.* Mahwah, NJ: Paulist, 1984.

M. F. Purcell

Drugs

See Addiction.

E

Easter

Easter is the name among English-speaking Christians of the major festival of the church year. In other European languages this important day carries a name derived from the Hebrew word *pascha*, which is commonly translated *passover*. In the northern hemisphere Easter comes in the spring, between March 22 and April 25. In folk custom the day is a happy festival inspired by the return of warmth to the world.

The traditional Christian festival gives dramatic expression to the theme of every Sunday in the classical liturgical tradition: the joyful celebration of salvation through Jesus' death on the cross and resurrection on the third day. This celebration is influenced by the close association of the Christian Easter with the Jewish Passover. Jesus' crucifixion (in the sequence reported in the Gospel of John) took place at the same hour that the passover lamb was sacrificed. The solemn remembrance of sin and the thankful praise for deliverance from Egyptian bondage combined to make this ancient festival a strong part of Jewish life. These associations were adapted and assigned to Jesus, "lamb of God who takes away the sin of the world."

After the church became distinct from Judaism, its Easter tradition continued to develop. The date of Easter continued to be determined by the Jewish lunar calendar instead of the Roman solar calendar. Its ritual structure centered directly upon the Friday of crucifixion and the third day of resurrection.

This holy period came to be the time when inquirers, who were called catechumens, reached the climax of their instruction and nurture in the faith. In dramatic ceremonies on Easter Eve they were taught the creed and the Lord's Prayer. They then were baptized, "buried with Christ in a death like his," and "raised with Christ in a new life like his." Shortly after midnight the first Easter celebration of the Eucharist took place, in a church filled with light and incense and resounding with hymns of gladness.

In the northern hemisphere, Easter comes during spring, and folk customs were generated by this juxtaposition of religious and natural celebration. Easter bunnies, colored eggs, and Easter lilies have parallels in antiquity, but seem to have originated in medieval Europe. The earlier meanings of these symbols are so attenuated, however, that there is virtually no value in these customs for the educational and liturgical life of church. Even the possible origin of the wearing of new clothes in the receiving of new garments at baptism is of little symbolic value.

More useful are efforts to recover long-standing ways of celebrating the central stories of this season. First, Easter's joy is necessarily tied to the despair of Christ's death as a sacrifice for sin. The service on the Sunday before Easter emphasizes the Passion of Christ, and the services in Holy Week give more specific attention to the final events in Jesus' life.

Second, the celebration of Easter itself appropriately combines participation in the mystery of Christ's resurrection, the celebration of baptism and the Eucharist, and the enjoyment of Christian friendship. The traditional Protestant form of the Easter liturgies begins with the sunrise service, often out of doors, perhaps at a cemetery. The people gather in the predawn light, sometimes around a large fire. As the light strengthens, trumpets call the people to attention. With singing and prayer, they recite the stories of Christ's resurrection and proclaim the joy of the Christian life. Other celebrations follow, which could include an Easter egg hunt for children and a joyful breakfast for all. Later in the morning come the regular Easter services, with music, flowers, and the celebration of baptism, culminating in the Easter eucharistic celebration.

A more ancient alternative is the Easter Vigil on Holy Saturday night. Congregants gather at the church. A small fire is lighted outside to represent the new fire of Christ, and from this fire a large paschal candle and small candles for worshipers are lighted. The congregation forms a procession into the church, where a cycle of scripture lessons is read rehearsing the whole drama of salvation. Late in the evening, new converts profess their faith in Christ and are "buried with Christ" by baptism into a death like his. They rise to walk in newness of life. Then, in a church emblazoned with light, the congregation celebrates the first Eucharist of Easter. A middle-of-the-night breakfast may follow. Later in the morning the services of Easter Day are celebrated.

Easter as a cultural festival has diminished in recent generations, while Christmas has become more prominent. In many churches, however, the central purpose of Easter—to celebrate new life in Jesus Christ—has grown stronger as the celebration of Easter as the folk festival of spring has diminished.

The special liturgies of this season, and especially the Easter Vigil, provide the most concentrated portrayal of the drama of salvation in the entire year. The story of sin and salvation is recited; Christ's redeeming work is celebrated; and our sacramental incorporation into God's new age is transacted. All of this happens in a highly charged environment that intensifies the experience of the gospel. Although liturgy is not conducted for the purpose of education, few events in the church's life do more teaching than the liturgies of Easter. See also Church Year.

FOR FURTHER REFERENCE

Ellebracht, Mary P. *Easter Passage: The RCIA Experience.* Minneapolis, MN: Winston, 1983.

Hickman, Hoyt L., Don E. Saliers, Laurence Hull Stookey, and James F. White. *Handbook of the Christian Year.* Nashville, TN: Abingdon, 1986.

Watts, Alan W. *Easter, Its Story and Meaning.* New York: Abelard-Schuman, 1959.

K. Watkins

Ecology

Ecology is the study of or concern about the environment that supports human and other organic life. Since the 1960s, ecology has become a widely used term referring to the earth as a life-supporting system in which human beings share with all other life forms. Increasing awareness of the misuse or destruction of the natural world has led to popular and scientific interest in the preservation of the delicate balance of the life-sustaining relationships within the ecosystem. The knowledge that life forms are interdependent has raised ethical questions and concern about the effects of human activity (industrial, technological, and commercial) upon the environment.

Ecology finds resonant themes in the Judeo-Christian tradition, as well as in other religious traditions that view the earth as created by God. In both Hebrew and Christian Scriptures, the earth is known as the creation of God and continues to be the object of divine love and redemption. The Genesis accounts of creation (Gen. 1–3) portray God's creating of a universe and an earth intended as the dwelling for human and other life forms. Of ethical note is the charge to the human creature to care for, or "have dominion over," the earth. Implied in dominion is stewardship, or the careful use of the world, which has been entrusted to the human creature. Dominion is not domination, the right to abuse the earth for one's own purposes that go beyond sustenance and enjoyment.

The Psalms carry the theme of the earth as creation. "The earth is the Lord's and the fulness thereof" (Ps. 24:1). Also, contemplation of the earth gives rise to human praise of the Creator (Ps. 8). The creation itself is pictured as acknowledging and giving praise to God (Pss. 96:11–13; 98:7–9).

In the Gospels, Jesus' teachings are often illustrated from the natural world. The parable of the sower (Matt. 13:1–9; Luke 8:4–8) uses everyday elements (rocks, briars, birds) to describe the various responses to God's Word. Jesus warns against anxiety by pointing to the example of the birds of the air and the flowers of the field (Matt. 6:25–33). The creation, therefore, has an instructive function for human beings.

New Testament apocalyptic language speaks of both the heavens and the earth as objects of divine redemption (2 Pet. 3:13; Rev. 21:1). The earth waits and longs for God's salvation along with human beings (Rom. 8:18–25). Even in apocalyptic theology, then, the earth is not destroyed but made new and transformed along with its people.

Ecology is taught in religious education classes beginning with preschoolers. The creation story is found in all curricula and there are many stories about God's world for young children as well as verses from the Psalms and hymns that tell of God's care. Taking care of plants and pets teaches children about responsibility for living things. Walks introduce them to nature. Teaching children how to keep the environment neat encourages care for the things around them.

School-age children are learning about a wider world, so stories and discussion for them might relate to the balance of life on land, in the water, and in the air. Television informs them of the dangers to the ecology. They learn from the Bible that people are caretakers in God's world. Simple conservation projects teach them about recycling and ways to care for land.

Adolescents learn in school about the interacting factors in earth's ecology from science classes and bring this knowledge to religious education classes. They should be encouraged to explore the relationship of religious commitment to the biblical meaning of being stewards of earth's resources and find ways of expressing this commitment in conservation efforts in their community.

Adult study can concern itself with the politics of conservation and ask the question of the relationship of biblical ethics to business and community activities. There are many videotapes available for use with adolescents and adults. They can explore how conservation begins in their homes, communities, and even with church property. *See also* Creation; Stewardship.

D. L. Edwards

Ecumenical Education

Any definition of ecumenical education begins with an exegesis of the ancient Greek word *oikoumene*, from which come the various English terms "ecumenical," "ecumenical movement," and "ecumenism." In its root form *oikoumene* means "the whole inhabited earth." As the Christian church lived out its faith down through the centuries in differing situations and cultures, its use of "ecumenical" became more focused. When meeting at Rolle, Switzerland, in 1951 the central committee of the World Council of Churches referred to ecumenical as "everything that relates to the whole task of the whole church to bring the gospel to the whole world." In this sense the ecumenical movement or ecumenism is "the hope that all Christians the world over might be brought into the unity of love which has been the dream from the beginning of the faith and that into this unity all [hu]mankind would ultimately be drawn" (Kenneth Scott Latourette).

From this perspective of what it means to be ecumenical, we can propose a working definition: ecumenical education is the process of teaching, learning, and sharing through which persons and

churches experience the wholeness of God's reconciling love and participate in the fullness of the church's liberating unity as a sign and foretaste of the unity of human community. Such education equips all Christians to participate in the one liberating and witnessing church in the midst of a divided, fragmented world. This education is personal and communal and involves both a theological vision and praxis in daily life.

THE QUEST FOR CHRISTIAN UNITY

As ecumenical education is defined more precisely, four elements can be identified. First, it calls for active participation in the quest among the different traditions and denominations for visible Christian unity. From Jesus' high-priestly prayer (John 17) to the Epistles written to the earliest Christians (e.g., 1 and 2 Corinthians, Ephesians), the biblical message is that God in Jesus Christ has given a unity to the church and to the world. To break down the walls of division and to manifest this unity visibly to the world is central to the church's proclamation and mission. Telling this story is teaching the gospel; participating in this unity is living what is essential to discipleship.

A profound ecumenical implication is grasped when Christian unity is understood in the context of a divided world. In this perspective unity is not merely bringing churches together for their own fellowship, however important. Rather the unity of the church is a sign and foretaste of the reconciling love and renewal God intends for the whole of humanity. The church is the community rooted in the triune God that overcomes all hostilities dividing the human race and embraces all the diversities of people, cultures, and nations. So teaching, the church prepares Christians to participate in a new, common humanity.

UNIVERSAL IMPLICATIONS OF THE GOSPEL

Second, ecumenical education leads persons to understand the universal implications of the gospel. A universal faith challenges parochialism, sectarianism, and all limited views of God's love. It teaches a global mission. It helps Christians who live in a small circle of caring and responsibility to recognize their insular life and to become conscious of God's presence in other places and peoples. A church bound by a particular nationality, culture, denomination, or political system is tragically less than the church God created.

Claiming universality means Christians realize they belong to a community that is truly global and truly catholic. In this sense global involves an awareness of the worldwide, interconnected system of life—economic, political, communicative, and ethical—that binds humanity together. Our lives are intertwined for good or evil. Global awareness also involves embracing, living in communion with, people of many nationalities, races,

TEACHING ECUMENISM

Age Level	Understandings	Teaching Goals, Methods, and Resources
Preschool	Children gradually realize there are people other than themselves, and they begin to learn how to relate to others; they are too young to understand concepts of difference and similarity, particularly in regard to religion.	Adults should model acceptance of and concern for others; demonstrate and teach cooperation and constructive methods of conflict resolution; include children in religious celebrations whenever possible to engender a sense of religious community as community.
Grades 1–8	Children gradually realize differences between themselves and others, including differences in religious belief and practice; they can increasingly participate in and understand their own religious community.	Tell stories of children with different religious beliefs and practices; encourage children to talk of such differences and similarities as they experience them (perhaps on the occasion of various religious holidays or events such as baptism, first Communion, and bar/bas mitzvah); encourage children's increasing participation in the religious community locally and on a global basis (joining together with others for worship, praying for others, helping to support missions); Scripture references regarding God's care for all people should be discussed.
High School	Differences and similarities between varied religious beliefs and practices can be better understood; they are increasingly aware of the interconnectedness of life on national and global levels; they can begin to understand the universal implications of their own faith.	Study of other people and other faiths should be encouraged; youth groups can visit other religious groups and services; youth of different faiths can participate together in community activities and service projects; Scripture references regarding the nature of the church and its mission in the world should be studied; further experience of and participation in the universal faith community should be encouraged.
Adult	Concepts of faith, community, and unity will be increasingly understood through action and reflection.	Active and ongoing participation in ecumenical activities and service projects should be encouraged, as should reflection and action on all issues of peace and justice; seek and demonstrate Christian unity.

languages, and cultures. No boundaries are allowed to separate or marginalize others from God's salvation or from the community of the redeemed. At the same time the universal gospel calls us into a catholic community, i.e., one that bears witness to the one tradition while recognizing the spiritual gifts of differing churches or traditions and shares the same faith, mission, sacraments, and ministry, even though the forms and practices may differ. Education toward such a community enables people to accept the richness and perspectives of other traditions and cultures and to claim a common destiny with all of God's people.

SOLIDARITY WITH THOSE WHO SUFFER

Third, ecumenical education accentuates solidarity, sharing life, with those who suffer poverty, rejection, and injustice. God's redemptive word is always "good news" for those who suffer. The teaching of this good news, therefore, seeks to free the people of one country, ethnic group, political or economic system, or race so they may become sensitive and responsive to the spiritual and human needs of those of other countries, ethnic groups, and socioeconomic conditions. In short, we are talking about preparing Christians to participate in the struggle for peace and justice—whether local or global.

Education in this context creates a full knowledge of the human injustices and social problems that distort life and dignity in different parts of the world. Poverty, the denial of human rights, racism, sexism, the arms race, and greed become personal stories that threaten our lives as well as the life of this planet earth. The poor, the dispossessed, and the exploited become our sisters and brothers. This sort of education—which comes painfully to powerful people and nations—teaches that Christian witness is the intersection between spiritual giving and human need.

SPIRITUALITY

A fourth dimension of ecumenical education is spirituality. The goal is to help people experience the unity of the church and of humankind and to participate in the service of God's people through prayer, worship, eucharistic celebration, and learning experiences of suffering love. Liturgy is always a carrier of a vision of the church. Learning about and participating in God's *oikoumene*, therefore, takes place when Christians regularly pray for other churches and people and for the unity God gives them and the world. So too, when members of one church share in the liturgy and eucharistic celebrations of other traditions, they rediscover the common spiritual heritage that binds all Christians in one fellowship. Ultimately a spirituality brings persons to commitment, to decisive actions that affirm one church and one world of justice and peace. When we *do* the truth,

we are made free and one. When it is authentic, ecumenical education leads men, women, and children to commit themselves to the whole church of Christ living for the sake of the whole world. Such learning offers hope for a belief in God's good future for all humankind as given in Jesus Christ.

The methods for ecumenical education are many and varied. Study of the Scriptures; critical reflection and dialogue about the church's identity and mission in the world; participation in the lives of people in differing churches, cultures, and countries; decisive involvement in situations of cross-cultural life, of unity and social justice, of peacemaking and affirming of human dignity; all these convey the unity of God's people and the interrelatedness of the whole creation.

Ecumenical education has implications for all Christian living and learning, for laypeople and ordained ministers. Its goal is to free every Christian, congregation, and church structure from isolation or the narrow confines of one group, nation, or tribe, and so free them to live the universal faith in company with all God's people. *See also* Ecumenical Institutes; Multicultural Education; Peace, Education for; Social Justice, Education for.

P. A. Crow

Ecumenical Institutes

Ecumenical institutes are centers for interfaith dialogue and research. Founded by various groups, they belong to the surge of ecumenical interest in this century, especially since World War II.

Probably the best known is the Ecumenical Institute of the World Council of Churches at Bossey, outside Geneva, Switzerland. From its earliest days the council realized it needed a center where the separated communions, now officially linked, could send their leaders and students for ecumenical research, study, and conversation. The institute developed programs generally of two kinds: an academic term in the winter for a group of up to fifty students from churches around the world and short-term conferences focusing on particular themes and gathering experts and interested persons from member churches and other organizations.

The winter academic term is linked with the University of Geneva. Participants come from all over the world and represent many languages, cultures, and Christian communions. There they become acquainted with one another and with their various religious and cultural traditions. They are introduced to the major developments in the World Council of Churches and organize their studies and research around a yearly theme; an example of a theme might be "The Unity and the Mission of the Church."

Short-term conferences focus on such topics as Orthodox Theology and Spirituality, Models of Renewed Community, Convergence in Eucharistic Theology, Gospel and Culture in an Asian Context, and Ecumenism for Mission, to give some examples. Such themes are typical of those in other institutes as well.

Other such institutes have developed in many parts of the world. One early pioneering effort was the Ecumenical Institute in Chicago, established in 1956, which today gathers a community of committed persons into study and action programs in over one hundred countries around the world. Many others, whether using the name "ecumenical institute" or not, have developed for a similar reason: the desire for Christians and other religious persons to work seriously together to deepen their understanding of their faith and its traditions and to build consensus and common action on issues important to human beings and the created world. Such institutes have also stimulated ecumenical programs of study and research in many other academic and research centers; both the ecumenical institutes themselves and the programs generated are responding to the same general need of committed religious people to dialogue and study together beyond narrow confessional bounds. *See also* Ecumenical Education; World Council of Churches.

W. B. Kennedy

Education, Theories of

A theory of education is a comprehensive statement of principles intended to be used as guides to educational practice. Principles, in turn, are statements that act as guides to particular aspects of practice. When principles are organized within a comprehensive framework of categories, a theory is the result.

CATEGORIES OF THEORY

Many theorists determine their categories intuitively by selecting the topics or questions that most concern or interest them. Sacrificing comprehensiveness for the sake of specificity, they focus on particular points they wish to argue or develop. For instance, H. Shelton Smith argued, in *Faith and Nurture* (1942), for priority for more traditional doctrines of the kingdom of God, human nature, salvation, and the church against the then prevalent tendencies toward child-centeredness and social experimentation in religious education. More recently, John H. Westerhoff III developed a series on topics such as social concern, the family as the context for religious education, socialization, and liturgy and education as timely foci for religious education reform. And Michael Warren, in *Youth, Gospel, Liberation* (1987), argues for youth politicization using liberation themes.

Other theorists, concerned with the overall guidance of the educational enterprise, take a systematic approach to the determination of their categories for theory. What they do, in effect, is to try to determine the essential, irreducible questions with which the educational and religious educational enterprises must deal. Since educational practice encompasses method, curriculum, and administration and is given orientation and direction by educational aims, goals, and objectives, the principles that constitute theory are often organized within these categories.

A canvass of educational questions and concerns may, however, reveal another level of categories from which directives on method, curriculum, and administration, as well as aims, goals, and objectives derive. To canvass these questions and concerns and then reduce them to their most economical elements produces a set of seven categories of educational theory: *purpose*, scope, context, process, transactors, time, and timbre (or tone).

While the ways of dealing with the *purpose*, or "why," of education have lacked standard terminology, there has been no lack of attention to the question itself. At present there is general agreement that it is to be treated on three levels. The aims of education provide overall statements of educational policy and direction. Goals are more specific statements used in connection with such large segments as age levels or courses. Objectives are even more specific statements used to guide units and sessions within courses.

The *scope* of the educational enterprise is the answer to the question, "What is to be taught and learned?" Drawing from all human endeavors, it establishes the contours and boundaries of both the subject matter and the experience to be included.

The question of the *context* of the educational enterprise is the "where" of education. How and to what extent is education a matter for the home and family, the school, the church, the community, or for special nonschool institutions and agencies? How does any given educational program determine its necessary setting or settings? How does the nature of the context or setting contribute to the dynamics of the program? In a given context, what instrumentalities (more specific agencies) are implied?

Who are the partners to the educational transaction, the *transactors*? How do they relate to one another? Fundamentally, there are the learners and the teachers. But the teachers are themselves basically learners. In religious education, God is assumed to be actively involved. What does that do to the role of the teacher? What roles are to be assumed by parents, peers, the congregation, and the community?

The *timing* of religious education takes into account a number of factors: the learner's readiness and developmental processes; the movement of the seasons; significant developments in the world around, sometimes unexpectedly and abruptly demanding; and the timing implied in the working out of God's will for contemporary life. How is it to coordinate all of these in terms of chronological time? How are timeliness, sequence (when you begin, proceed, and bring to culmination), frequency (how often), duration (for how long), and rhythm to be determined?

What is the *process*—how do teaching and learning take place? All aspects of method are caught up in answering this question, which investigates in depth the nature and conditions of teaching and learning. Part of the answer lies in the context of education (the church as a community of faith incorporates educational dynamics that include but go beyond schooling), part in the concept of transactors (when God is seen as teacher, roles shift dramatically), and part in timing (to bypass the delicate demands of timing can undermine otherwise sound decisions on method and result in fruitless confusion).

Another word for the category of *timbre* is "tone." Here affective factors, which have been implicit in other categories, come to the fore. In what ways does religious education practice "ring true"? What is its genuine "feeling tone"? What constitutes its basic sense of authenticity? In what ways does it touch the depths of the human spirit at the points where Holy Spirit and human spirit meet? How does it express the depths of that meeting in ways that may be described as rich and beautiful?

A number of theorists have probed the nature and dynamics of religious education using such a system of categories, among them James R. Schaefer, in *Program Planning for Adult Christian Education* (1972), and Thomas H. Groome, in *Christian Religious Education, Sharing Our Story and Vision* (1980).

PHILOSOPHY AND THEOLOGY

In the history of education, theories of education and philosophies of education have been relatively indistinguishable. Plato used his most fully developed work, *The Republic*, to lay out his views on education. Identifying the necessary functions to be performed in the ideal state, his educational plans elaborated the ways in which persons were to be selected and trained to perform those functions. Aristotle's methods for scientific understanding of nature and humankind implied an education that enabled persons and the state to fulfill their ends in harmony with their surroundings. The practical Sophists, whose livelihood depended on the education of young men for positions of leadership, worked with tools that gave their pupils the keys to leadership—the trivium (grammar, logic, and rhetoric) and the quadrivium (arithmetic, geometry, astronomy, and music), which together constituted the liberal arts. The liberal arts became the basis for the founding and growth of the universities in the medieval period, and to them were added theology, law, and medicine for professional training.

Modern theories of education have stemmed in the main from the thought of John Amos Comenius (1592–1670), the British empiricists, and the romantic movement. Comenius, a Moravian bishop at the time of the Thirty Years' War, insisted upon the use of sense data (pictures and objects) in education, over against the prevailing stress on the idea or form of the thing instead of the thing itself. The British empiricists, and in particular John Locke (1632–1704), saw the mind as *tabula rasa*, a blank slate, that grows by virtue of the sense data written upon it, resulting in percepts and the ideas, or concepts, that are built out of those percepts. The romantic movement had its first major educational interpreter in Jean-Jacques Rousseau (1712–1778), whose *Emile* portrayed the education of youth as a process of natural development, unfettered by society's artificialities.

The ideas of such theorists as Comenius, Locke, and Rousseau provided a stimulus for educational experiments and further expansion of theory by Johann Heinrich Pestalozzi (1746–1827), Johann Friedrich Herbart (1776–1841), and Friedrich Froebel (1782–1852). During the Napoleonic Wars, Pestalozzi gathered his first group of Swiss children in Stans, motivated by their plight as orphans of war. The group became a school almost by accident. Here and in subsequent schools, Pestalozzi made concrete his ideal of education as nurture within the community of love. Herbart, Kant's successor in the chair of philosophy at the University of Königsberg, like Plato before him and John Dewey afterwards, saw education as the central problem of philosophy. He is remembered particularly for his culture epoch theory, by which the periods in the developmental history of the individual are thought to recapitulate the historical periods in the development of the human race, and by his identification of formal steps in the instructional process: preparation, presentation, association (of the new data with ideas already in the mind), systematization, and application. Froebel, whose great achievement was the establishment of the kindergarten movement, saw play as the child's work and made use of the senses, primarily in an aesthetic and spiritual context.

Pestalozzi, Herbart, and Froebel were greatly influential in the growth and reform of American education. Teacher education followed closely the ideas of the former two, and childhood education and the child study movement were guided by followers of Froebel. They were the precursors of the views by which John Dewey (1859–1952) has influenced education in the twentieth century. Dewey's position has been given a number of revealing names: instrumentalism, both for the idea that the mind is to be seen as an instrument designed for the systematic discernment of truth and the expansion of knowledge and for ideas as instruments for change; experimentalism, for the scientific method that the mind uses to get at knowledge and thus to learn; pragmatism, for the practical tests that knowledge must meet if it is to be considered to be true; and reconstructionism, for the process of reconstruction of knowledge and for social reconstruction in the light of reliable knowledge. Since education is a science, the learning process follows the steps in the scientific discovery of reliable knowledge: discernment of a problem (in actual living), analysis of the problem and its situation into its essential elements; development of a hypothesis for the solution of the problem; data gathering and experimentation to test the hypothesis; and its acceptance or rejection according to the findings. Dewey saw the building of a curriculum unit as the systematic use of these steps in connection with any given life problem and assumed that in the process new problems would be identified as foci for new units.

J. Donald Butler, following Herman Harrell Horne (1874–1946), an educator at New York University, used four philosophies as basically determining educational theory and practice: naturalism, realism, idealism, and pragmatism. For each one he worked out systematically its implications for education and religion. Later he added existentialism and linguistic analysis to his list. Subsequent work has been done by J. Gordon Chamberlin to get at the educational implications of phenomenology for religious educators.

Theologians have also contributed to educational theory, although usually not too thoroughly and certainly with less impact. Both Augustine and Thomas Aquinas wrote treatises on education. Augustine leaned heavily on his background as a teacher of rhetoric and on his responsibilities for the guidance of catechists. Aquinas reflected the broader views of the thirteenth century's rediscovery of the thought of Aristotle. Reformers, both Protestant and Roman Catholic, spurred by the need for educational guidance of the people who became their responsibility, wrote fairly extensively on problems of education and conducted educational experiments and institutions. Outstanding among them were Martin Luther, John Calvin, the Jesuits, Jean-Baptiste de la Salle, Nikolaus Ludwig von Zinzendorf, and John Wesley.

While modern religious education has tended to follow general educational trends, there have been theologians who have attempted serious studies of religious education. Horace Bushnell (1802–1876), in opposition to those who conceived of the church's approach to children as radical evangelism, maintained that "the child is to grow up a Christian and never know himself to be otherwise." George Albert Coe (1862–1951), building on the insights of the social gospel movement and the then new science of psychology of religion, saw religious education as an instrument for religiously motivated personal transformation and social reconstruction, undergirded by the principle of "the infinite worth of persons." Emil Brunner (1889–1966) concluded that religious education must look to Socrates (education for self-fulfillment), to Johann Heinrich Pestalozzi (for guidance on Christian nurture), and to Søren Kierkegaard (for guidance on the appropriation of revelation). Nels F. S. Ferré (1908–1971) developed a theology of education centering on his concepts of God as teacher and learning from God. Lawrence O. Richards, building on biblical imperatives, interprets teachers as servant leaders whose task is to "build the body" (the church as a renewing community) and whose method is that of modeling Christ to those with whom they work. Gabriel Moran, who began as a theological interpreter of the "new catechetics," has now turned to penetrating theological critique of current ideas, trends, and movements in the field. Maria Harris has done outstanding work in women's contributions to theological thought in religious education and in the educational implications of theology and imagination. Mary Elizabeth Moore advocates a position she calls "traditioning," combining close attention to the religious tradition with a process of contemporary tradition building by working creatively at urgent present-day problems. Thomas H. Groome bases his "shared Christian praxis" on a thorough critical theological and historical analysis.

When curriculum reform was being given priority in the decades between 1940 and 1970, various theologians made substantive contributions. James D. Smart represented neoorthodox theology and biblical scholarship. Roger Shinn sought to bridge the gap between theologians and educators. David Hunter centered upon existential engagement. L. Harold DeWolf brought liberal theological insights into the picture. Randolph Crump Miller investigated the contributions of process theology.

THEORY BUILDING

Religious education theory has paid close attention to philosophy and theology, on the one hand, and to developments in educational practice, on the other hand. This has led to a broadening of the foundation disciplines from which it seeks to draw insight. At a basic level, it seeks guidance from theology and from the church's life and work (as practiced in the churches and as distilled in the discipline of practical theology).

At a second level, it looks to the behavioral sciences, philosophy, and history. Among the behavioral sciences, its attention was given, at one time, almost exclusively to psychology. In particular, it attended to educational psychology (personality, learning, motivation) and to developmental psychology. But as other related disciplines came into being, religious educators found themselves studying and listening to sociology, anthropology, social psychology, and communications. In time, the subdisciplines of educational sociology, educational anthropology, and social psychology of education appeared.

In recent years, philosophy of education, in spite of some interest in existentialism, analytic philosophy, and phenomenology, has been somewhat stagnant, so far as religious education has been concerned. History of education, however, has taken on new life as it has lost its preoccupation with the history of schooling in favor of a broader conception of educational dynamics and institutions in the wider community.

At a third level, increased importance has recently been accorded to the arts, the aesthetic disciplines. Religious educators have regained a sense of the significance of affective experience in the formation of attitudes, values, and commitments. They recognized themselves and their work in *The Taxonomy of Educational Objectives: The Affective Domain*, developed by David Krathwohl and his associates. Thus, more attention has been given to literature, music, drama, painting, and the other arts, both in terms of the appreciative use of artists and works of art and in terms of the learner's own use of the creative arts.

At a fourth level, religious educators have paid closer attention to the wisdom of their own personal and professional experience as foundational. Evidence for this is to be found in a growing literature in which such experience is shared, the spectacular increase in idiosyncratic curricula, and in the steady growth of professional associations.

How do religious educators, then, build upon these foundations? Theory building proceeds through four steps, so far as the use of foundational insights is concerned. First, religious education theorists immerse themselves in the several disciplines that appear to them to have the greatest promise for their thought and work. They may do this, in some cases, using the thought of a particular scholar or research person. This work is done with directives like these:

- Know the content and method well enough to feel confident in working with the discipline.
- Get the context and the focus of the discipline or of the particular scholar.
- Investigate the material analytically and structurally.
- Do whatever comparative work is called for.
- Do the first steps of critique, to the point of being able to make a decision on whether or not it has promise of importance for religious education.

Second, they do a preliminary check of the categories of Christian education theory (purpose, scope, context, transactors, timing, and timbre) to see where major and minor contributions from the discipline (or the thought of the particular scholar or research) may be expected.

Third, they do a thorough analysis of the material, assembling it in the categories of religious education theory and in the process reordering the categories if necessary so as to reflect the inner logic of the material and avoid misconstruction and distortion. The result should be a statement of the contributions of the material to religious education theory.

Fourth, they do as thorough a critique of the resultant material as necessary in terms of its own inner integrity and authenticity; the larger scholarship of its field; its constructive possibilities for and its challenges to religious education thought; and its implications for religious education practice.

Theorists determine the focus of their investigation, select the appropriate foundation disciplines, and work from there. For instance, the focus of Rachel Henderlite's work was the theological reorientation of Christian education; the foundations with which she worked were theology, ethics, and educational theory and research. Lewis Joseph Sherrill's focus was comprehensive and informed guidance for Christian education thought and practice; his foundations were neoorthodox theology, developmental psychology, depth psychology, communications, and personal and professional experience. Ronald Goldman's focus was the practice of religious education in the public sector; his foundations were biblical criticism, Piaget's epistemology and developmental psychology, empirical research, and professional experience. Locke Bowman's focus is the improvement of teaching; the foundations with which he works are professional experience, the educational disciplines, and educational technology. Sophie Koloumzin's focus was creative socialization into a living church tradition; her foundations were the liturgy of the church and the mission of the church within the specific Orthodox culture, and developmental psychology. Hubertus Halbfas's focus is classroom methods and curriculum resources; his foundations are existentialist theology, "the new hermeneutic," language theory, and professional experience.

TESTS OF A THEORY

Responsible critiques of religious education theories are singularly missing. Constructive work in theory has been the mark of the religious education scholar, but little attention has been given to the serious critique of the resultant theories. The situation may be remedied, however, with attention to three areas of analysis. First, in looking at any particular theory, is its focus or intended coverage clearly indicated?

Second, with regard to the categories used in constructing the theory, are they stated as questions and/or symbols? Are they appropriate to the indicated focus or intended coverage? Are they comprehensive, in terms of focus or intention? Are they sufficiently brief to be manageable? Do they clearly lend themselves to the formulation of principles? Do they invite appropriate use of the foundations of religious education?

Third, are the principles of which the theory consists clearly and adequately stated? Are they supported by personal and professional experience and by appropriate material from the foundation disciplines? Are they logically developed? Do they give promise of effective practicality?

SPECIAL THEORIES

Some religious education theories have been especially thoroughly developed and tested or have attracted special attention. George Albert Coe, for instance, wrote extensively in the first four decades of this century. His work maintains its position as precursor of the century's well-developed theories. In *Education in Religion and Morals* (1904), *A Social Theory of Religious Education* (1917), and *What Is Christian Education?* (1929), he worked out a comprehensive theory for a socially dynamic religious education for responsible social action.

Ernest Ligon's Character Research Project, an outgrowth of the character education movement of the 1920s, was based on traits of Christian character derived from the Beatitudes. Its object was to set up educational ways and means by which these traits might be developed in children and youth. Its method was rigorous research in curriculum and method, including scientifically controlled field testing. A spin-off was a concern for the improvement and dissemination of research in the broad religious education field.

James Michael Lee's "social science approach" to religious education is developed in three massive volumes, *The Shape of Religious Instruction* (1971), *The Flow of Religious Instruction* (1973), and *The Content of Religious Instruction* (1985). Since, in his opinion, the hegemony of theologians in religious education has been relatively fruitless and in fact seriously detrimental, he offers a social science approach as a more promising alternative. He advocates deliberate instruction in religion as the focus for theory and as the indicator of social science as the basis for explaining and generating the activities involved.

In terms of influence, C. Ellis Nelson's *Where Faith Begins* (1967) ranks high among contemporary theories. Drawing discriminatingly from biblical studies, theology, social psychology, and communications, it provides a basis for religious education rooted in a critical socialization within the community of faith, setting a foundation for curricula that stress the educational power of the total life of the congregation.

Jerome Berryman has become the foremost interpreter of Maria Montessori's educational views among North American religious educators. Working closely with Sofia Cavaletti, his European counterpart, he has perfected techniques of storytelling and worship that he has himself used in the parish and in his work with terminally ill children. He and Sonja M. Stewart have further experimented with his theory in a worship-based program of religious education in the parish.

James W. Fowler's research in faith development has rapidly become the most popular basis for the religious education theory. While Ronald Goldman's research in Great Britain used the theories and methods of Jean Piaget directly in the investigation of religious instruction in biblical knowledge, Fowler's research derives from Piaget by way of Lawrence Kohlberg's investigations in moral thinking and moral decision making. Using generic concepts of faith, Fowler has discerned a series of stages and transitions in personal faith development that have been of interest both to scholars and to persons responsible for curriculum development. His research methods and findings and their implications have been the subject of unusual interest and critique in the field, one especially well-designed and penetrating study being that edited by Craig Dykstra and Sharon Parks, *Faith Development and Fowler* (1986), in which the critiques of Fowler and the analyses of the implications of his work were submitted to him for his systematic response.

Theory is the basis for practical developments and the effects will be observed at a later time in curriculum building and methods. *See also* Affective Development; Cognitive Development; Faith Development; Goals; History of Christian Education; Interdisciplinary Studies; Learning Theory; Methodology; Moral Development; Progressive Education; Social Sciences; Taxonomy; Teaching Theory.

FOR FURTHER REFERENCE

Cully, Kendig Brubaker. *The Search for a Christian Education—Since 1940.* Philadelphia: Westminster, 1955.

O'Hare, Padraic, ed. *Foundations of Religious Education.* New York: Paulist, 1978.

Roloff, Marvin L. *Education for Christian Living.* Minneapolis, MN: Augsburg, 1987.

Rood, Wayne R. *Understanding Christian Education.* Nashville, TN: Abingdon, 1970.

Seymour, Jack L., and Donald E. Miller. *Contemporary Approaches to Christian Education.* Nashville, TN: Abingdon, 1982.

D. C. Wyckoff

Eichstätt Conference

The Eichstätt Conference (1960), one of a series of international study weeks, brought together at Eichstätt, West Germany, more than two hundred Roman Catholic missionaries from all parts of the globe in order to reform missionary activity in line with the pastoral renewal of the liturgy and catechesis brought on by the developments of kerygmatic theology spearheaded by Josef Jungmann in the 1930s. It was coordinated by Jungmann's disciple Johannes Hofinger of the East Asian Pastoral Institute of Manila.

Jungmann's approach aimed to restore the power of the *kerygma* of the early church (the proclamation of the historical fact that God has intervened in human history by the lordship of Christ) amid all the complexities of dogmatic theology that dominated the catechesis of the church. For Jungmann, Christian teaching had to lead not to mere handing on of a static concept of the past but to religious formation.

The Eichstätt study week focused a deeper understanding of the content of the kerygma as well as developed methodology for its proclamation. It introduced the language of the "four signs" by which the kerygma is revealed: the Bible, liturgy, witness, and doctrine.

Eichstätt marked the turning point for religious education in that the basic framework became that of pastoral ministry rather than education. Kerygmatic catechesis took religious education from being simply one activity of the church, primarily concerned with children and youth, to the forefront of the church's mission. *See also* Catechesis; Hofinger, Johannes; Jungmann, Josef A.; Kerygma.

R. T. O'Gorman

Elliott, Harrison S. ━━━━━━━━

Harrison Sackett Elliott (1882–1951) was a staunch defender of a pragmatic innovative approach to religious education based on the liberal Protestant theology of the early twentieth century. He was concerned that a shift toward neoorthodoxy would be followed by a return to more formal methods of teaching. This is developed in his book *Can Religious Education Be Christian?* (1940).

Elliott graduated from Ohio Wesleyan University, studied at Drew University, Teachers College, Columbia University, and Oxford. After receiving a Ph.D. from Yale University he was ordained to the Methodist ministry. Elliott served two years as secretary to the Methodist bishop in China (1906–1908) and worked for a number of years with the International Committee of the YMCA. He was instructor of religious psychology at Drew University (1921–1923). He began teaching at Union Theological Seminary, New York City, in 1923 and was professor of practical theology and head of the department of religious education and psychology until retirement. Among his chief writings are *How Jesus Met Life Questions* (1924), *The Bearing of Psychology upon Religion* (1927), *The Process of Group Thinking* (1928), and *Group Discussion in Religious Education* (1930). *See also* Liberalism; Neoorthodoxy.

L. G. McAllister

Emotionally Disturbed Children

Emotionally disturbed children are those whose ways of dealing with other people and events of daily living are maladaptive. They may have problems in appropriately expressing feelings or in behaving as expected for their age. Religious education teachers need to know the possibilities in order to help individuals and maintain a stable classroom situation.

Emotionally disturbed behavior in children is seen along several continuums—of origin (genetic, environmental, or interactions of both), of severity, or of duration of symptoms. For example, it can be temporary and situationally based, such as a preschooler's regression to infantile behavior upon the arrival of a newborn sibling. It can be of several years' duration, such as emotional problems that are secondary to an academic learning difficulty. It can be as longstanding as predelinquent behavior in a ten year old who has grown up in a chaotic home under economically adverse conditions. And emotionally disturbed behavior can be as chronic and unusual as that of the autistic child.

The classification of emotional difficulties in children (and adults) used by most mental health workers in the United States today is found in the *Diagnostic and Statistical Manual of Mental Disorders* (third edition, revised) published by the American Psychiatric Association in 1987. Over forty-five disorders appearing in infancy, childhood, or adolescence are listed. The major categories are mental retardation of varying severities, pervasive developmental disorders (in which many areas of the child's functioning are atypical), various types of learning disorders (academic, language and speech, and motor skills), disruptive behavior disorders, anxiety disorders, eating disorders, gender identity disorders, tic disorders, elimination disorders, other speech disorders, and some problems that do not fall into the aforementioned categories. In addition, children may be diagnosed under some categories used for adults, for example, schizophrenia.

Emotional problems can be diagnosed by pediatricians, psychiatrists, social workers, or psychologists, with parents and teachers providing valuable anecdotal information. Therapy varies according to the diagnosis. The most common therapies are psychotherapy (individual, family, group), parent counseling, behavior modification, and medication. In all but the most severe situations, treatment is usually on an outpatient basis. Psychiatric hospitalization or milieu treatment in a residential setting is also available for children in some locales.

What is the responsibility of the church or synagogue to emotionally disturbed children? It is the same as toward any children—to provide them with religious instruction and nurture in a meaningful and developmentally appropriate fashion. In addition, there is the responsibility of showing acceptance to children who might in some ways be different from their peers—and who might be difficult to have around because of behavioral peculiarities. The most obvious way to show this acceptance is to enroll these children in religious education classes commensurate with their developmental levels. While there is some controversy in the education literature about the benefits of mainstreaming exceptional children—including emotionally disturbed children—it is the law that children must be educated in the "least restrictive environment" in public schools, and separate educational programs are warranted only when proven better than integrated programs. In practice, few religious education programs are large enough to have "special" classes, so separation of disturbed children is not generally an issue. Children's social-emotional skills improve when they are around normal models, and church and synagogue offer a wonderful opportunity for disturbed children to be with nonhandicapped peers.

In attempting to meet the religious community's responsibility toward any particular emotionally disturbed child, educators need to first confer with that child's parents. They are probably well informed about their child's needs and about the best management techniques. Rarely would the religious educator be the first person to identify an emotional problem, except perhaps in a nursery or preschool situation. If the child is on a particular behavioral program, the parents might be grateful to have the child be maintained on that program in the religious education group. For example, some children are on a behavior modification program: success in certain specific tasks leads to some kind of reward (stickers, points to save up for a prize, a privilege, a food treat, etc.). A child given to temper tantrums might be on a program of "time out"—waiting in a sheltered location with an adult nearby until the child has calmed down enough to join the group. If the child is going to require some one-to-one attention, it would be wise to provide an assistant teacher or aide who can either keep the class moving for the other children when the disturbed child is in crisis or who can tend to the disturbed child. Providing a peer buddy for the disturbed child can work well. Perhaps one of the child's parents would be willing to attend class with the child for a few sessions. This enables modeling of management techniques for the teacher and demonstrates to the child that the parent feels positively toward the school and the teacher. *See also* Child Abuse; Exceptional Persons; Psychosocial Development.

M. C. Mueller

Empathy

Empathy is imaginatively entering into the inner world of another person's thoughts, feelings, and outlook while retaining one's own inner world and objectivity. It enables a teacher or counselor to understand another person's present experience and to assist that person to change through learning and personal growth.

The words "empathy" and "sympathy" contain the same Greek root for "suffering" or "experiencing." Empathy is "experiencing into," and sympathy is "experiencing with." One who empathizes understands how an angry person feels the anger, while a sympathizer shares the anger, perhaps enough to want to retaliate. Sympathy can change into empathy when the sympathizer sees the angry person in the larger perspective of a total life situation.

Native capacities for empathy differ widely. Through experience and formal training one may refine one's sensitivity to other persons, develop one's imagination, and monitor one's intuitive qualities. By focusing these abilities through listening and observation, one can perceive more fully how another person uses words, tones, facial expressions, gestures, and body language to convey ideas and feelings—or to hide them. Actors project thought and mood as a polished art. Others present cues knowingly or with lesser degrees of awareness. Skillful interpretation requires practice.

Empathy is the counselor's best way to initiate a trusting relationship. A bond of trust is a powerful healing force. Empathy is supportive, not simply toward a person's present condition but toward a potentially better condition. It is an expression of caring enough to want the very best for the client. It participates in self-criticism when a client says, "I feel like kicking myself!"—not to punish but as a challenge to change. A counselor's empathy helps a client to become a good self-counselor.

In all the arts and fields of knowledge one may be enticed into empathy and make lifelong heroes of discoverers, doers, and thinkers. Listeners to Bach's devotionally charged rendering of the *St. Matthew Passion* in music through recitative, aria, and chorale feel an emotional response that enriches the stark words of the gospel. The power of Chagall's *Crucifixion* is in linking an event two millennia past to the pogroms through which such helpless suffering is continued. This stretches the empathy of viewers to encompass a whole people. The practice of empathy, cultivated in the learning of favorite things, may be used to assist intentional learning and enliven formal education.

When a learner becomes a teacher, the teacher's own empathy invites the participation of students in a field of learning. As the teacher empathizes with students, subject matter is translated into their world.

When religious educators and biblical scholars empathize richly with pioneers of faith, students are shown the meaning of trust in God both in the lives of these heroes and heroines and in the lives of teachers and scholars themselves. With love and hope, as with trust, there is empathic transmittal of personal religious commitment. *See also* Conversation; Counseling.

R. A. Preston

Empiricism

Perhaps no other theory has had a more profound effect on religious education in the modern period than empiricism. In its most general sense, the theory of empiricism points to experience, rather than reason, as the source of knowledge. In this way, empiricism provides a basic alternative to rationalism. While empiricism had its roots in Greek antiquity (notably in Epicurus) and has seen various schools and modes of development through the centuries, it was through the writings of John Locke (1632–1704), an English philosopher, that Protestant English and American religious education was introduced to the theoretical and practical implications of empiricism. Locke's assertion that persons were not born with innate ideas but that all ideas originated from sense experience (*Concerning Human Understanding*, 1690; *Thoughts Concerning Education*, 1693) first caught the imagination of the Protestant English Sunday school leadership in the eighteenth century. It accepted and popularized the empiricist notion that children could become civilized and respectable by means of education. This was based on Locke's assumption of a *tabula rasa*, or mental blank slate present at birth, that was capable of receiving, and thus being informed by, sense experience as the basis of knowledge. Stated baldly, within this general framework one needed to change the environment (thus controlling sense experience options) in order to mold the child. Through the years, generally speaking, Protestant English and American Sunday schools accepted Locke's understanding of empiricism. Some currently used "teaching through the senses" curriculums are reminders of Locke's early influence.

In the twentieth century, the question of empiricism for religious educators in academic circles has been cast almost entirely in terms of empirical scientific research. This linking of science and empiricism has taken diverse forms, but perhaps two of the most influential figures in religious education representing this approach are John Peatling (recently of the Character Research Project) and James Michael Lee (social scientific approach). Their convincing work, however, is by no means universally welcomed by religious educators. The reasons are legion, but two basic issues seem to be at stake. First, in order to understand or conduct scientific/empirical research, one needs a wide background in empirical research methods, including advanced mathematics—something that is not generally the background of most religious educators. Second, the relationship between quantitative and what might be referred to as qualitative research is a blurred one. The latter is popularly viewed as "soft" and unscientific by the former, and the former as "hard" and reductionistic by the latter. While no one resolution of such matters has appeared thus far, it is clear that the role of empiricism in religious education is likely to remain a center of lively inquiry for theorists beyond the twentieth century. *See also* Experience; Idealism; Knowledge, Theories of; Pragmatism; Social Sciences; Sunday School Movement.

R. H. Cram, H. C. Simmons

Enculturation

Enculturation refers to the processes by which persons acquire a culture (their people's learned, shared understandings and way of life). It describes the means by which a culture is transmitted to persons and they internalize its characteristic ways of perceiving life and their personal lives, its terminal and instrumental values, and its dispositions to behave in particular ways.

"Enculturation" was coined by the anthropologist Melville Jean Herskovits in 1948 as an alternative to the term "socialization," coined by psychologists and sociologists in the 1930s to describe the processes and means by which persons are integrated into their social group. While numerous definitions and uses for both words exist, Margaret Mead suggested "socialization" be used as the term to describe abstract characteristics of learning (conscious and unconscious, formal and informal) as a universal process, and that enculturation be used as the concrete process of learning within a particular culture or subcultural grouping.

Underlying enculturation theory are three fundamental assumptions. First, all perceptions and behaviors are learned in a social context, through interaction of persons with family, kin, peers, and significant others, and through participation in a community or ethnic group—that is, a group bearing a more or less distinctive culture. Second, the existence and vitality, over time, of a society or a group within a society depends upon consensus among its members as to an understanding of life and appropriate ways of thinking, feeling, and acting. Third, every people transmits its way of life from one generation to another, through formal and informal, conscious and unconscious, spontaneous and planned means.

Enculturation needs to be distinguished from acculturation, assimilation, and biculturalization. Enculturation refers to the learning of a particular culture; acculturation is the learning and adopting of appropriate behavior in a second culture while remaining fully enculturated in one's primary culture; assimilation is learning a new culture and thereby losing or leaving behind one's original culture; and biculturalization is the blending of two cultures, keeping some learned characteristics of each and in time giving birth to a new cultural expression.

All behavior (cognitive, affective, and volitional) can be classified as either instinctual or learned. Behavioral sciences define instinctual behavior as inherited patterns of behavior that are found in all humans and appear full-blown without training. There is some evidence that human ability to use language may be instinctual but most human behavior, including the adoption of a particular language, is learned. When persons are born they are uncultured. Soon, however, they become aware that they need to acquire and internalize a particular set of understandings and ways of life if they are to be functioning members of their social group.

The results of this process are somewhat indeterminate. There are individual variabilities insofar as a person's inherited traits and characteristics affect how he or she reacts to the enculturation process. There are subcultural variabilities insofar as we all are enculturated into not only a large social group—the nation, for example—but into subcultural groups that can be distinctive from the culture at large and on occasion even have opposite expectations or conceptualizations. And there are temporal variabilities insofar as all cultures over time change; what is acceptable to one generation may not be to another.

Nevertheless, the enculturation process begins at birth and continues until death. Sometimes this process is intentional and sometimes unintentional, sometimes it is formal and sometimes informal. A fetus is being enculturated in its mother's womb. During early childhood child-rearing practices by significant adults and the environment in which young children are placed influence them. As children grow older, their range of experience broadens and through the processes of identification, observation, imitation, communication, and inference, children are enculturated further. As this process continues, language plays an increasingly important role. Words are labels for categories of experience. The culture's vocabulary defines what is important to it. The grammatical and semantic systems of a language imply a way of looking at the world.

While enculturation occurs through all interactive, relational experiences with persons and groups and within one's environment and its social structures, there are three foci of particular significance: the rites and rituals in which persons participate; the experiences persons have with significant others and within their primary communities; and the role models established by the community as well as the actions of persons and groups encouraged and supported by one's primary community. Nevertheless throughout our lifetime rituals provide a primary context for enculturation.

The name used by the church for intentional socialization or enculturation is formation. As such, formation and education comprise the two dimensions of catechesis. *See also* Behavior; Culture; Ethnicity; Multicultural Education; Prejudice; Tradition; Transmission.

J. H. Westerhoff

Engagement

The word "engagement" refers to the act of meeting, of knowing (as distinct from knowing about), of responding to or ignoring, of loving or hating. The act of hating or ignoring can lead to a high degree of disengagement or detachment, but even these reflect different levels and kinds of engagement.

The concept of engagement in the field of Christian education is associated with the educational program that was developed within the Episcopal church in the United States and used from the early 1950s through the late 1960s. The entire program is generally known by the title of the church school curriculum, the Seabury Series. However, the engagement concept was determinative within the total program, including the approach to leadership training and educational work with adults and young persons in many different settings. Engagement *now* with religious issues became the organizing principle and starting point of every program.

In the life of the church, in fact throughout all existence, the most basic fact of our common experience, consciously perceived or not, is that the God of creation is still active in the whole of creation. His action is a constant and continuing twofold one of making demands and offering the gift of love, without which we are not likely to be able to respond significantly to his demands. Engagement is the moment when God acts in or upon the life of an individual or a society and the individual or society faces the obligation to respond.

Once this action of God is accepted as universal and primary, operative in the life of children, youth, adults, communities, and nations everywhere, the action provides educational programs with an organizing principle that relates to religious issues active in the lives of those who are being educated.

The signs of these religious issues are the joys and sorrows, the doubts and convictions, the reconciliations and separations, the satisfactions and frustrations, the prejudices and passions, and the never-ending succession of points of view that characterize our everyday living. Such experiences are by no means exclusively adult in character. They manifest themselves in their own unique way from the cradle to the grave.

Consequently an educational program in a religious communion that knows God to be active in all of life should be under some constraint to maintain a program centered on immediate engagement, using the rich history and tradition of past engagement primarily as a means to this end.

In practical terms, engagement takes place whenever learners and teachers become so involved in what is being learned that the learning ceases to be only a cognitive experience, and the learners feel some identification with the persons, event, or situation being studied. In biblical study, a class can become part of the Exodus people forging a life beyond Sinai and understand more deeply how Torah shaped them into a nation. In studying the book of Acts, students see the all-too-human nature of quarrels within a community (as Corinth) or between communities (Jerusalem and Antioch) and realize the human nature of the church. Involvement in a contemporary problem through role playing can help a class view it from several perspectives while seeking possible solutions. *See also* Curriculum; Identification; Theology and Education.

D. R. Hunter

Enrollment

See Attendance.

Epiphany

Epiphany, celebrated on January 6, is the church festival celebrating the manifestation of Christ. It marks the close of the twelve days of Christmas and is observed in many churches on the first Sunday in January. The term "Epiphany" is used more broadly at times to designate the liturgical season extending from January 6 to Ash Wednesday and including between four and nine Sundays. The various "epiphanies" of Christ serve as themes for the different Sundays.

The festival itself probably originated in Egypt in the late second century, where January 6 was the date of a festival in which water was drawn from the Nile. It spread throughout the East as the unified celebration of the birth and baptism of Christ and by the middle of the fourth century was ranked with Easter and Pentecost as one of the three great feasts. In the late fourth century, the celebration of Christ's birth was separated from that of the baptism and assigned to December 25.

Since that time in Eastern churches Epiphany still celebrates primarily the baptism of Christ, while in Western churches it has primarily celebrated the coming of the Wise Men, or Magi, and is called the Manifestation of Christ to the Gentiles. The Western association of the Magi with Epiphany probably stems from the use of the Matthean nativity story as an Epiphany Gospel lesson. The present calendar used by most American

Christians follows the lead of the revised Roman Catholic calendar and commemorates the baptism separately on the Sunday after Epiphany. The miracle of changing water to wine at the wedding feast in Cana is a secondary theme. A medieval antiphon for Epiphany expounds its full Western meaning: "Today the church is united to Christ, her heavenly bridegroom, for he has washed away her sins in the Jordan; the Magi hasten with their gifts to this royal wedding, where the guests are gladdened with the water made wine. Alleluia."

Epiphany is called Three Kings Day in some countries in honor of the Magi, although the New Testament does not call the Magi kings or say how many there were; it only says that they presented three gifts (Matt. 2:1–12). It is also known as the Feast of Lights, celebrating Christ as the Light of the world (John 1:5, 9). In many countries gifts are exchanged on Epiphany, following the example of the Magi. Among Eastern Christians water is solemnly blessed, often with colorful and popular ceremonies, including diving into the water to recover a golden cross. See also Church Year.

L. L. Mitchell

Episcopal Education

See Anglican Education.

Epistemology

"Epistemology" comes from the Greek episteme, meaning "knowledge," and logos, meaning "theory." Epistemology is a theory of knowledge and constitutes one of the three main branches of speculative philosophy along with ontology, a theory of being, and axiology, a theory of good conduct or ethics. Epistemology addresses four main questions, which, taken together, constitute the scope of this branch of philosophical study: What can be known? What is the process of knowing? Who is the knower? What is the criterion for distinguishing truth from error?

The answer to the first question, "What can be known?" sets the borderline between ontology and epistemology. This is to say the answer to the question of what is will exercise some influence on what can be known, although the relative priority of epistemology versus ontology varies from one philosophical system to another. For illustration, compare two contrasting positions. Classical philosophical idealism believes that ideas are the ultimate reality, and given proper direction the mind could move beyond all appearances and come to know them. Experimentalism, holding an ontology of experience, believes that experience itself is the ultimate reality, and given proper guid-

ance the student of this position can come to know the continuity of transactions between the person and his or her environment that make experience definitive. For idealism, the ontology of ideas holds priority over how they are known; for experimentalism, how things are known, i.e., through experience, determines what is.

The process of knowing, the second question, is governed in part by what can be known. Thus, in idealism, the ontological priority of ideas means that the process of knowing must be mental and guided by a right use of reason. The highest form of reason in Platonic thought is dialectic, or the Socratic type of dialogue, which proceeds by rational inquiry to draw out from sensory experience and appearances the essential or universal truth about a given topic such as justice or virtue. The aim is an intellectual grasp of the idea in its purest form unmixed with experiential contingencies. Experimentalism, however, sees in this a splitting of idea and reality, and it affirms instead a formalization of experience in the pattern of scientific inquiry. This includes the following:

1. A sense of a problem in experience
2. Intellectual formulation of the problem
3. Exploration of hypotheses for solution to the problem
4. Selection of the most likely hypotheses on the basis of anticipated outcome
5. Subjection of the most likely hypotheses to an empirical or pragmatic test

This formalization of thinking along the lines of scientific inquiry is simply the refinement of how we think in any context; in effect, it is how we come to know anything, whether it is pursued systematically or not.

The answer to "Who is the knower?" is already partially presupposed by the answers to the first two questions. In Platonic idealism, the knower is an immortal soul that for this life exists in a body, but at birth the body obscures in forgetfulness the otherwise pure knowledge of heavenly ideas stored in the soul. Thus, the process of knowing can be called "anamnesis" because of the nature of the knower. Experimentalism assumes that the knower is an irreducible part of his or her social context, and through transactions within that context and between that context and its environment, the knower in effect becomes the creation of his or her own experiences.

The question of a criterion for distinguishing between truth and error is answered by Platonic idealism in terms of the right use of pure reason, stressing scientific inquiry and induction from experience in a social context. Thus, the pragmatic criterion of workability supersedes rational analysis.

Educationally, idealism is literally concerned with the leading out (as in Lat. e-duco) of innate but forgotten knowledge of pure ideas through the dialectical use of reason. Experimentalism is intrinsically educational in its experiential focus on the transactional formation of persons and society. Thus, John Dewey said, "Philosophy is to be defined as a general theory of education."

The scope of epistemological inquiry is also covered variously by Christian theology. For example, the self-revelation of God in Jesus Christ is what can be known through the process of grace working through faith. The knower is one redeemed from sin by that gracious faith and a member of the body of Christ, the church. The criterion for such a claim is Scripture, variously interpreted and supplemented by different traditions.

In Christian education, the epistemology of faith has been supplemented by various philosophical theories of knowledge. Thus, idealism has made faith education more a matter of grasping right ideas, images, and idealized persons in a process that stresses not only Plato, but also heirs of the idealistic tradition, particularly Immanuel Kant, Friedrich Froebel, and Friedrich Hegel. The key historical figures here in Christian education are Herman Horne and Donald Butler. Experimentalism has made faith education more a matter of communal interaction and social reconstruction. The key figure here is George Albert Coe. Thus, epistemology in Christian education has always been a mixture of more than one theory of knowledge, but the key questions addressed above provide the essential scope of any answer to the epistemological question. *See also* Empiricism; Essentialism; Experience; Idealism; Knowledge, Theories of; Pragmatism.

J. E. Loder

ego perceptual processes. His theory allows that ego ideals and religious attitudes are important for the development of a healthy personality, countering the Freudian view that religion is a neurosis. His account of psychosocial development has been very influential for many religious educators as well as many social scientists. *See also* Adult Development; Affective Development; Child Development; Faith Development; Maturation; Psychosocial Development.

D. E. Miller

Equipment

See Facilities.

Erikson, Erik H.

Erik H. Erikson (1902–) is best known for his psychosocial theory of emotional development. Trained in Vienna as a psychoanalyst, he became interested in relating psychoanalytic theory to social and cultural patterns. He carried out this project in his book *Childhood and Society* (1950), in which he proposed that each of the psychosexual stages in Freudian theory has a corresponding psychosocial modality. For example, the first twelve months of infancy are not only the time when the pattern of oral impulse control is established, but also the corresponding social modality of trust versus mistrust. Erikson thereby significantly contributed to the psychoanalytic theory of

Eschatology

Eschatology is the study of "the last (Gk. *eschatos*) things." Originally used to describe doctrines associated with the end of the world, including the second coming of Christ, the resurrection of the dead, the final judgment, and the establishment of a new heaven and a new earth, the term is broadened to include the present implications of the kingdom or reign of God.

A HISTORY OF APPROACHES

Eschatology became very popular during the nineteenth century, when, on the basis of a literal interpretation of apocalyptic biblical literature, various theories were developed to describe exactly what would happen at the end of human history. One of these theories, premillennialism, argued that, following certain signs, Christ will return (the Parousia). All faithful Christians, including the dead in Christ who are raised for the purpose, will reign with Christ on earth for a thousand years (millennium) while Satan is bound and sealed in a pit. At the end of this period Satan will be released, only to be defeated and judged by God soon afterward along with the whole of humanity. This will be followed by the creation of a new heaven and a new earth. Postmillennialism, conversely, argued that the return of Christ will occur after the millennium, which is interpreted as a kind of golden age. Both theories have links with dispensationalism, which teaches that human history may be divided into a number of periods ("dispensations") from Adam to the end of time. To the extent that they have predictive elements these theories also have parallels in adventism.

A major problem with these and similar theories (e.g., chiliasm, the doctrine that Christ will return to earth and establish his millennial reign) is that they interpret all apocalyptic language to refer to actual future events. The exegetical difficulties inherent in this were recognized as early as the mid-nineteenth century by amillennialists ("nonmillennialists"), who argued that the period of a thousand years mentioned in Revelation 20:1–6 is to be taken symbolically.

A completely different approach to eschatology, arrived at quite independently from apocalyptic eschatology, is Albert Schweitzer's "consistent eschatology." Schweitzer argued that, in order to understand the ministry of Jesus, one must consistently and in a thoroughgoing way take seriously Jesus' eschatology—even if it leads to unexpected conclusions. Schweitzer portrayed Jesus as greatly influenced by the apocalyptic views of his day, expecting the reign of God to come in his own lifetime through his own ministry. When this did not happen, he went to his death in a final attempt to force its establishment. The early church subsequently reinterpreted Jesus' apocalyptic predictions to develop a Christian eschatology. Although his thesis has been criticized strongly, Schweitzer has made one enduring contribution to the study of eschatology. He has broadened the term by liberating it from too close an identification with the apocalyptic concepts of Jesus' own time.

In the 1930s, C. H. Dodd took the study of eschatology one step further by introducing the idea of "realized Eschatology." Reacting in part to Schweitzer, he pointed to the many statements, including the parables, in which Jesus stressed that the kingdom had already come. According to him, Acts, the Pauline Letters, and certain Johannine passages all confirm that the early church believed that the end time had already occurred in the life, death, and resurrection of Jesus. The "future," therefore, has already been "realized." At first Dodd almost totally disregarded any future dimensions. Later, he conceded that it is more accurate to speak of "an eschatology that is in the process of realization." Others prefer the term "inaugurated eschatology."

Dodd shifted the focus of eschatology from the future to the present. This radical shift not only further broadened the term, it also redefined it. No longer can eschatology be discussed in purely chronological terms. It also applies to existential categories, as seen by the great emphasis placed on the reign of God as an existential-eschatological reality in contemporary theology. If the reign has already been inaugurated, even if incomplete, Christians need to discover what this means for everyday life. Rudolf Bultmann, in particular, has been very influential in interpreting eschatological themes as existential questions.

Not all modern theologians, however, are prepared to minimize the futuristic aspects of eschatology. The major criticism of Dodd and Bultmann is that they do not take sufficiently seriously the nature of history and that they concentrate on the individual rather than on the corporate entity. Wolfhart Pannenberg, for example, while agreeing that through the resurrection of Christ the end of history has already occurred, points out that the whole of history is not yet in harmony with the will of God. The revelatory act of the resurrection promises a Parousia, when the ultimate revelation of God in Christ will be confirmed. Similarly, Jürgen Moltmann speaks of Jesus as "the eschatological person" who enables the church to live in the tension between remembrance and hope. Both Pannenberg and Moltmann retain the important contemporary insight that eschatology is not only about the future, but they stress that eschatology is not only about the present either.

IN RELIGIOUS EDUCATION

Eschatology is not easily taught, even to adults, partly because the prevalent worldview sees the world as changing, even improving, but unending. Conservative religious groups hold and teach one of the interpretations of eschatology (premillennialism, millennialism, or postmillennialism) acceptable to their tradition. This teaching becomes incorporated into the religious education curriculum beginning at children's levels. It is taught through biblical stories (such as the books of Daniel and Revelation) and interpreted for a particular age level. Children in other traditions need to be taught that history and the future are in God's keeping and God's promises can be trusted.

Other traditions may allude to the eschatological aspects of the gospel through teaching the parables of the reign of God, the ten girls (Matt. 25:1–13), or the final judgment (Matt. 25:31–46). Such passages would probably be used with adolescent and adult groups. In a study of the book of Revelation for young people and adults, the interpretations used will vary with the theological understandings of the congregation. Apocalyptic passages in the books of Daniel, Ezekiel, and Zechariah are further materials for the study of eschatology.

The "mainstream" traditions have shown a hesitancy to approach this subject educationally, although this is part of the biblical worldview and is the theme for the first Sunday in Advent. This hesitancy needs rethinking at a time when many people fear some kind of apocalyptic world ending through ecological or atomic disaster. *See also* Reign of God.

W. Tabbernee

Essentialism

Essentialism is the science (knowledge) that distinguishes rational being from actual being. It is best understood by thinking of it in comparison with its better-known, complementary term, existentialism. Basically it is concerned with essence, which it understands as a concept capable of being grasped by mind and expressed in words, while existentialism is interested only in things that occupy a concrete place and time and can be recognized by the senses. Essentialism, then, can be defined as a study of cognitive, a priori experience, nontemporal and nonspatial, in contrast with the empirical study of fact. Essentialists look for truth, which they think is embedded in objective and transcendental reality, existing independently of human knowledge of it.

A homely illustration can make the simplicity appear. One may have an essentialist idea of owning a ten-dollar bill and reflect on the pleasure of having it, its origin and influence, and many other aspects. This can be done whether or not such a bill actually exists in your pocket, since existence or absence adds nothing crucial to one's thoughts about it. Existentialists are concerned with what is considered from that position the only fruitful question—whether or not such a bill actually is to be found in your pocket or pocketbook. They will not grant the omnipotence of thought but choose rather the experience of actual living.

HISTORY

Essentialism, the province of thought, has been part of our heritage since the earliest known human reflection. Parmenides (fifth century B.C.), for example, made the crucial remark: "Where there is being, there is also the logos of being," meaning that without thought and words nothing can exist. The Christian expression would be, "Wherever God is, there is also his Logos." In classical Greek *logos* signifies both "word" and "reason," and in the biblical sense it signifies the divine reason manifested in the universe as well as the Christ who enfleshed it. The best-known Greek essentialist was Plato, who established general ideas by induction, moving from ordinary concrete reality to the independent realm of ideas. Since these ideas were the form or archetype of all things in existence, Plato granted them an essential priority.

The medieval Scholastic world grappled with the problem, distinguishing between *essentia* (what a thing is known to be) and *existentia* (what a thing actually is). So the key essentialist word is *what*, the *quid est*, and the operative existentialist word is *that*, the *quod est*. A series of arguments were devised purporting to prove the existence of God, but they were persuasive only if one blurred the distinction between idea and actuality. The arguments were shown to be fraudulent when one recognized two distinct truths, truth as logical process and truth as nonreflective existence in place and time.

Baruch Spinoza (1632–1677) achieved prominence in the seventeenth century when he insisted on the essentialist ontological unity of all being, since everything that is must be a manifestation of the divine substance. This was an unembarrassed pantheism, each separate thing an aspect of the one divine substance, God. Only the infinite could be called truly and simply substantive, and in God alone there was an identity of knowing subject and object known.

But the primary philosophic essentialist was Georg Wilhelm Friedrich Hegel (1770–1831). He reached an absolute idealism, arguing that the world-soul was developed out of, and known through, dialectical logic. The whole of reality, whether essential or existential, was absorbed in the reality of "pure thought." What seemed to be violations of that unity, positive and negative forces confronting each other in the estranged world, were on closer analysis manifestations of the same hidden unity. Thesis, for example, carried that within it which drove toward its opposite, antithesis. And both together were reconciled in the basic synthesis. It has been said that in Hegel's bold rationalism the estranged world, ravished by opposing particularities, came together in a great panlogism. In a way the world came to an end, enfolded in an embracing essentialism.

PRESENT UNDERSTANDINGS

Any effort to identify reality or being as reality-as-known, the object of reason or thought, must be called essentialist, even though it serves an existentialist analysis. All scientists begin their work with the assumption that there is a truth about the world and research will help discover it, even though most modern theory seeks to model reality rather than to give a final account of it.

The present style, however, favors antiessentialist positions, furthered by rebellion in Europe in the 1840s and 1850s stressing *esse* and historic rationality. All existentialists are convinced that reason is inadequate to solve the enigmas of the universe, and all turn to some form of personal experience as our only hope of coherence. Friedrich Schelling rebelled against Hegelianism, as did also Karl Marx, Friedrich Nietzsche, Henri Bergson, Ludwig Feuerbach, and a great many others. The effect was to make dubious the authority of dogma and of morality and moral rules, all of which were in the end thought to be meaningless. Today's deconstructionism in philosophy and literary criticism follows suit, denying that there can be found behind appearances a primary truth and defying logocentrism.

Nevertheless, the association of essentialism with rational truth never dies. The assumption dominating Western thought since Plato, despite periodic protest, is that there is a basic rationality in the universe, a coherent principle regulating the objects of the natural world (stars and suns), the animate world (oak trees and bears), and conscious human beings. Nonhuman entities follow this logos by instinct, while humans are conscious of it as well as the necessity of obeying it. Essentialist reason or cosmic purpose, endowing each separate thing with specific function, seems destined to survive.

Essentialism is the basis for classical education, where the purpose is for students to learn essential knowledge and develop the basic attitudes of their culture. In religious education, this means a grounding in Scripture and interpretation and a knowledge of basic doctrines. This is in contrast to a religious education theory that begins with the experience of the learner and uses biblical and theological information as resources. Essentialism is the educational philosophy in clearly defined, religiously sponsored schools and in religious education classes, frequently in conservative religious groups, that value grounding in the tradition as the essential element of religious education. See also Existentialism; Idealism; Teaching Styles.

FOR FURTHER REFERENCE

Kafka, Franz. The Trial. Translated by Willa and Edwin Muir. New York: Knopf, 1956. A novel strongly opposing essentialism.
Kant, Immanuel. Ethical Philosophy. Translated by James E. Ellington. Indianapolis, IN: Hackett, 1983.
Tillich, Paul. Perspectives on Nineteenth and Twentieth Century Protestant Theology. Edited by Carl E. Braaten. New York: Harper & Row, 1967.

P. Elmen

Eternal Life

Eternal life has very different meanings, but in most cultures it is pictured as a life free from the pain, suffering, and limitations that beset human life and particularly as freedom from death.

THE OLD TESTAMENT AND JUDAISM

The earlier Old Testament writings show no idea of life after death (Ps. 115:17). For the Hebrew mind true life consists in relationship to God. Death ends that relationship, and although the dead go down to Sheol, it is only a shadowy existence.

Gradually however the Hebrews realized that if God was faithful to his covenant, this relationship could not be destroyed by death; hence there developed hope for a life beyond the grave (Ps. 49:15). But this did not mean a belief in the intrinsic immortality of the soul as in Platonism; it meant a resurrection of the whole person as a psychosomatic unity. Also, it was a hope not just for the individual, but for the whole people of God (or the righteous members thereof) at the end of history. Originally, "resurrection" was a metaphor for the historical restoration of Israel after the Exile (Ezek. 37:1–14). Later, especially in apocalyptic writings, the notion of resurrection was applied to the restoration of Israel in a new heaven and a new earth at the end of history. This life was to be entirely different from human existence as we know it—the resurrected would shine like stars in heaven (Dan. 12:2–3).

Hellenistic (i.e., Greek-speaking) Judaism adopted the Platonic concept of immortality of the soul. But immortality was not thought of as an intrinsic human property; it was still a gift from God and involved relationship with him (Wisd. of Sol. 3:1–9).

THE HISTORICAL JESUS

Jesus announced the coming of the kingdom (reign) of God. This kingdom was already operative in his own words and works (Mark 12:28 and parallels) yet soon to be consummated at the end of history (Mark 9:1). Sometimes Jesus uses "eternal life" (i.e., the life of the age to come) as an equivalent for the kingdom of God, especially in sayings about entering into eternal life (Mark 9:43, 45; 10:30). He offered no original teaching about the nature of eternal life but accepted the apocalyptic notion that it would be a life quite different from this life: there would be no marriage and the resurrected would be like angels (Mark 12:25). But eternal life was tied to the acceptance of Jesus' message here and now (Mark 8:38; Luke 12:8 and parallels). This is where his originality lies.

THE EARLIEST COMMUNITY

The Easter event made a decisive difference to the disciples' hope for eternal life. It was no longer merely a future hope, for One had already entered into eternal life. The resurrection of the believers would follow from his resurrection. He was the first-fruits of those who had fallen asleep (1 Cor. 15:20) and all would be resurrected in him at the end of time (verse 23).

THE PAULINE WRITINGS

The Pauline writings include works written by Paul himself (1 Thessalonians, Galatians, 1 and 2 Corinthians, Romans, Philippians, and Philemon) and those written in his name but attributed by many scholars today to his disciples after his death (2 Thessalonians, Colossians, Ephesians, 1 and 2 Timothy, and Titus). From Paul's own Letters we learn that Paul originally expected Christ to return within everyone's lifetime. The death of some of the Christians at Thessalonica created a problem Paul answered by differentiating between the fate of those who were still alive, who would be caught up to meet the Lord in the air (the rapture), and of those already dead, who would be raised to join the others (1 Thess. 4:14–18). This should not be taken literally. It assures the faithful that "whether we live or whether we die, we are the Lord's" (Rom. 14:8) and that at the end all will be with the Lord (1 Thess. 4:17).

Like the apocalypticists and Jesus, Paul regards the resurrection life as wholly different from present existence. He speaks of a "spiritual body" free from corruption and from weakness of the flesh (1 Cor. 15:35–50; 2 Cor. 5:1–10). But the picture of how this is to happen varies. In 1 Corinthians 15:51–57 resurrection involves a "change" from the earthly body to the spiritual body (cf. Phil. 3:21), whereas 2 Corinthians 5:1–10 expects the faithful to be stripped of their earthly bodies, possibly spending an interval "unclothed," and then to assume the glorious body awaiting them in heaven. What is common to all these pictures is, first, that eternal life means being with the Lord and seeing him face to face (1 Cor. 13:12) and, second, that eternal life is a promise not just for the individual at death but for the whole body of the faithful and indeed for the whole cosmos (Rom. 8:18–25).

Paul does not deal directly with the fate of those who are not "in Christ." All will be judged according to their works at the end, and those who have behaved well will be given "eternal life" (Rom. 2:6–7). This seems to contradict what Paul says elsewhere of eternal life as a gift through Christ alone. But perhaps Paul believes that the grace of Christ is available in some measure even outside of the gospel. In any case for these, as for the believers, eternal life is still God's gift, not an intrinsic human property.

Did Paul believe that all would be finally saved? Or will the unrighteous go to eternal perdition? Texts can be cited for either view. The New Testament as a whole affirms that eternal damnation is always a real possibility and also that the cause of God will ultimately triumph. This is a paradox that will not be resolved until the end.

For Paul eternal life is not only a future hope. The gift of the Spirit is an advance installment or downpayment of eternal life (2 Cor. 1:22; 5:5; Rom. 8:13). The believers are already being "changed from one degree of glory to another" (2 Cor. 3:18). However, this downpayment is never an assured possession. In Romans 6:3–11 all the references to resurrection imply that it is something that will not be fully realized until the end or something we have to work at in the present.

The Letters of Paul's disciples shift the emphasis somewhat. For them the believers are raised with Christ (Col. 3:1) and even seated with him in the heavenly places (Eph. 1:20; 2:6). But the new life still has to be implemented through ethical obedience and awaits final realization at the end (Col. 3:1–4; Eph. 4:13).

THE JOHANNINE SCHOOL

The Johannine school (the Gospel of John, 1, 2, and 3 John) goes further than the later writings of the Pauline school in accentuating the present realization of eternal life. In the discourses of the Fourth Gospel Jesus acts largely as the mouthpiece of the community's theology. Yet these discourses include core sayings that form the bases of meditations in Johannine language. Such a core saying occurs in John 12:25, which like the synoptic sayings makes eternal life contingent upon present discipleship. The Johannine Christ however announces that the believers already have eternal life (e.g., John 3:15, 16, 36). This is still not an intrinsic property of humanity but the gift of the Father through the Son (John 10:28; 17:2; 1 John 5:11). The Son confers eternal life through his words, i.e., his revelation (John 6:68). In the last analysis the content of the revelation is the person of the Son himself. This is made clear by the "I am" sayings (John 6:35, 48; 11:25; 14:6; "life" is equivalent to eternal life). The believers have already passed from death to life (John 5:24; 1 John 3:14; "passed over" suggests baptism) and that life is sustained through eating the flesh and drinking the blood of the Son of man (John 6:54). Yet even the Johannine school has not forgotten that eternal life is not fully realized until the end (e.g., John 6:39; 1 John 3:2).

Eternal life means "knowing" the Father and the Son. This sounds gnostic, but to know God means to keep his commandments and love all Christians, not just the gnostic elite (1 John 3:14).

In the prologue of the Gospel (John 1:1–18), eternal life is already present in the preincarnate Word. The Word was the agent of creation, general revelation, and the special relation to Israel.

THE REVELATION OF JOHN

The book of Revelation often echoes the Johannine language about eternal life, but uses it differently, reverting to the earlier view that eternal life is entirely future. The triumphant martyrs will enjoy the water of life and be nourished by the

224

SYMBOLISM

The Eucharist, as the dominant symbol for Christian bodies, is held together by a logic that is metaphorical rather than discursive. The key to its system of ideas is the fact that its main ritual act is a simplified meal. Because eating and drinking are such primary human actions, they can become the carriers of secondary meanings, such as thanksgiving for life and sustenance, exultation in victory, and pleading for divine mercy.

Thanksgiving naturally arises because from early times eating and drinking have connected people to the mysterious powers of the universe. The annual cycle of heat and cold, the pattern of precipitation and drought, and the varied productivity of soils are uncontrollable and only partially understood by those dependent on them for livelihood. People who depend on animals, whether domestic or wild, are made aware of life and death as well as of violence and danger and the seasonal variations in the cycle of the food supply. This precariousness leads to several human responses. When the harvest or hunt is successful, people feast and rejoice. When the cycle is depleted, they grieve. There is a strong tendency to identify these variations as signs of divine favor or disapproval, so that abundance is the reason to give thanks and famine is the reason to plead for mercy.

This first level of symbolic action based on meals can take on a second level, as illustrated by the Passover, the high point of Jewish liturgical life and one of the forerunners of the Christian Eucharist. This event was grounded in the harvest cycle of rejoicing, but was later overlaid with a second level of meaning—the political festival of liberation from Egyptian slavery. Although this political dimension is muted in the Eucharist, some theologians, especially Third World writers, argue that the early Eucharist was also a liberation rite and that it needs to express this theme more prominently today too.

In Jewish life meal ceremonies became highly stylized and included ritual sacrifices in which grain and animals were offered to God. These actions were the basic structure for confessing national and personal sins and for receiving promises of divine forgiveness. A similar idea was carried over in the Christian Eucharist. Jesus used explicitly sacrificial language and the church used explicitly Passover language in talk about Jesus' work as Redeemer.

Meals provide both nourishment and companionship. When meals are ceremonial in nature, nourishment and companionship take on divine as well as human dimensions. The God of the Jews does not need the food offered (see Isa. 1:11), yet sacrifices of incense, grain, birds, and animals ascend to heaven and are pleasing to God. Implied is a spiritualized mode of activity whereby God's own life is nourished by these gifts.

Nourishment also takes place on the human level. Certain sacrifices were to be shared with the priests to provide their needs for sustenance. And the people who offered the gifts received both physical and spiritual nourishment.

These ideas come to a high level of development in the eucharistic language attributed to Jesus in the Gospel of John (especially chapter 6). He calls himself the Bread of Life and asserts that by eating and drinking his flesh and blood his followers will have eternal life.

Closely related is the idea of companionship. As we eat and drink, we are bound up closely with those sharing the meal with us. The Eucharist also contains the idea of communion with Christ. The prayer offered as part of the Eucharist asks that the Holy Spirit bless bread, wine, and congregation, that the people may be united with Jesus Christ. Thus, the eating of the bread and the drinking of the wine become the means of communion with the One who died on the cross and is now seated with God in heavenly splendor.

When described this way, the meanings clustered around eucharistic eating and drinking seem abstract. But when the service actually takes place among people of faith, these several meanings come together powerfully. The Eucharist then demonstrates its ability to link our most elemental emotions with some of society's most elevated sentiments—of peace and justice, of forgiveness and mercy, of the union of humanity and divinity. *See also* Baptism; Liturgy; Sacraments; Symbolism.

FOR FURTHER REFERENCE

Avila, Rafael. *Worship and Politics*. Maryknoll, NY: Orbis, 1982.

The Book of Common Prayer. New York: Seabury, 1979.

The Lutheran Book of Worship. Minneapolis, MN: Augsburg, 1978.

Smolarski, Dennis C. *Eucharistia: A Study of the Eucharistic Prayer*. New York: Paulist, 1982.

K. Watkins

Europe

The countries of Europe demonstrate a variety of theoretical approaches to the legal status of religious education, the relationship between churches and schools, and the response to political changes—all within specific cultural and historical settings. Churches in each country adhere to specific theological concepts, and have specific aims and educational methods. For example, in East Germany church and school are strictly separated; in West Germany religion is a confessionally based subject within the required public school curriculum; and in Holland decisions regarding religious education are made by the local school board, teaching staff, or parents' association. In some countries religious educational approaches may differ from one jurisdiction to another, even though the content is a regular school subject. This article can only show by example how different the approaches are.

WEST GERMANY

The "people church" (*Volkskirche*) in West Germany is supported financially and by membership by 90 percent of the population, who are either evangelical (i.e., Protestant, either Lutheran or Reformed) or Roman Catholic. The Christian faith still helps determine the self-understanding, values, and traditions of most of the population.

Religious education is provided for in the Federal Constitution of West Germany (1949), restating paragraphs of the constitution of 1919. Religious instruction must be offered in schools. The federal government is required to finance this religious instruction, providing official syllabuses, training, and salaries and other benefits of teachers (who may be teaching religion in addition to another subject). The churches, however, are responsible for confessional content; federal laws guarantee the freedom of churches in this regard. Religious education is to be given in accordance with the principles of the religious community—that is, Protestant and Roman Catholic churches, the emphasis differing according to whether a region is more Lutheran or Reformed. Freedom of conscience allows children to drop the subject if their beliefs differ from those being taught. Children under fourteen may do so upon parental request. At age fourteen they may do so on their own. However, starting with grade 5, the subject "values and norms" is required as a substitute for religious education. Most children take religious education courses, and many parents consider it helpful to their children for moral decision making. Teachers have the right not to teach religion for reasons of conscience. Most religious education occurs in the public school classes either two hours each week (Protestant) or three hours (Roman Catholic). The public school is expected to remain otherwise secular and open to all children regardless of religious background.

There are only a few schools run by churches attempting to provide a Christian school atmosphere. These schools must meet the academic standard of public schools. Parishes do provide other forms of Christian nurture, however: children's worship, preconfirmation and confirmation classes, seminars, youth services, adult education, and retreats. The so-called free churches (those other than Lutheran, Reformed, or Catholic churches) may participate in the public school religious education program or may offer their own instruction if they can gather at least twelve children in a school. Most, however, allow their children to participate in the religious education the schools provide and offer additional Christian education on the parish level.

During the Nazi regime, religious education was endangered by this system, even though most textbooks had been published during the Weimar Republic. After World War II most churches were convinced that confessional religion could not be taught "objectively"; pupils needed to be confronted with the witness of the living God and be closely related to the active congregation. Teachers were to view religious education as Christian nurture. Bible stories and their message today and biblical history became the center of instruction. Children learned Bible verses, hymns, and the importance of the church year and were introduced to the life of the congregation; in upper grades they studied church history. In the fifties these emphases were criticized, and a more thorough study of the Bible and other religious literature was encouraged, including study of the original situation in which the text was formulated and the intention and message for those authors and their readers.

By 1968 religious educators had become convinced that the real interests and needs of pupils had not been met either by the Christian nurture approach or by the literary-critical approach to the texts. In an essay, "Must the Bible be in the Center of Religious Education?" (1968), the religious educator Hans Bernhard Kaufmann challenged the practices up to that time and advocated more attention to the pupil. The real needs and interests of the pupils have become most important in developing curriculum, which now includes Christian traditions, biblical studies, ethical issues, and problem-oriented topics for decision making.

West Germany's is an integrative approach; with their own distinctive emphases, most European countries have developed religious education along similar lines. Religion's status as by law a confessional subject does not encourage a dogmatic approach; rather, from this position, religious education opts for an open approach, taking seriously the situation of pupils and teachers in a world developing a global consciousness.

AUSTRIA AND EAST GERMANY

Exceptions to this integrative approach will be found in countries (like Austria) where the emphasis is mostly on biblical studies or on religious education as "teachings of the Christians." Another approach is that taken in East Germany, where Christian nurture is provided outside the schools in church buildings. Here, as in most eastern European countries, the constitution does not permit religion as a subject in public schools. But by contrast with Russia, where already in the 1920s religious instruction had been completely abolished, (and has only now begun to be recognized as important), Christian religious education under the auspices of the church has gained importance, mostly without direct interference from the state. The intent is to provide children and youth, as active partners in the educational process, with knowledge, insight, and awareness of the relevance of the gospel for present-day existence and with basic help for living responsibly.

SCANDINAVIA

What all Scandinavian countries have in common is the history of a state church and, in the past, a common faith or ethos. Even though many changes have occurred, secularization and an increase in awareness of the world have also provided the chance to understand and respect other belief systems than one's own. The separation between church and state has not changed their historical link. The states are not totally nonreligious, as they are in some eastern European countries. In Norway and Finland more of the former national unity of faith and ethos survives than in Sweden, where it has given way to secularization. Religious education in schools in Norway, Finland, and Denmark generally follows the guidance of churches. In Norway and Denmark, such religious education is generally "confessional" and Lutheran. In Finland, religious education is open to different denominations and to so-called nonbelief organizations; denominational instruction must be provided when at least eight pupils of a given confession are present.

Sweden is a country with a deep Lutheran heritage, but it is also one of the countries where religious education in the schools focuses on teaching *about* religions. Sweden has few private or church schools, and up until the reform of the school system early in the twentieth century, religious education consisted in teaching Luther's *Small Catechism*. The impetus for reform came from secularism and from the free churches with no Lutheran heritage, but particularly from the practice of teaching a catechism no longer related to real life. In 1919, after debates for many years, the breakthrough occurred. Religious education was no longer to be dominantly Lutheran but rather a teaching *about* religion. Christianity was taught in a historical and informative way, and the Bible replaced the catechism. The history of Christianity and ethical questions, rather than questions of dogma, became important. Whatever was taught about other religions was related to Christian missionary work.

After 1969 the curriculum of the comprehensive schools required that religion be taught as religious knowledge, a regular school subject comparable to philosophy or history. Other religions are taught as having equal standing with Christianity, although more time is still spent on Christianity. In contrast to Germany, Sweden has no law requiring teachers to be Christians or members of the church. Although the new laws allow children to study religion on a denominational basis, this option is seldom used.

HOLLAND

The school system of the Netherlands is complex: one-third of the schools are state run, one-third are Roman Catholic schools, and one-third are Protestant schools. There are no national guidelines for religious education. In the state schools, none is offered. The state itself is neutral and formally offers no public religious education; churches and other religious organizations are allowed to provide it to children on a voluntary basis. Because the Netherlands has become a more pluralistic and multicultural society, since 1985, new subjects have been required for all schools as an attempt to ensure that pupils will be confronted with the different life perspectives and religious convictions in their country and the world. In approach, they are similar to Sweden's teaching *about* religion or to Germany's focus on ethics.

In the confessional schools, a board of education is responsible for the organization and content of religious education; school life is expected to have a Christian identity, and religion is integrated into all aspects of life. Religion as a subject among other subjects is taught only in these confessional schools. Here pastors do the instruction, as well as teachers who must subscribe to the commitment and aims of the Christian school. Recently some in this setting have come to believe that even here religious education should provide knowledge and information about the religion(s), not church catechetics or Christian socialization.

The financial framework of the Dutch school system is radically different from that of most other European countries. The state provides equal support and financial backing for all schools, regardless of whether or not they are state operated. This total subsidy of schools (since 1920) accepts all religious and ideological educational perspectives as being in themselves legitimate.

During the past years some of the Christian schools have opened their doors to children of other faiths of immigrant parents. These so-called open Christian schools welcome Muslim and Hindu children. Having a choice, Muslim parents often prefer the Christian schools to the state schools because they have a religious atmosphere. The teachers of religion have their own Christian commitment but also respect in their teaching the commitment of others. This multifaith approach is still predominantly Christian and calls for great sensitivity on the part of school boards and especially teachers.

Beyond religious education in the schools, churches provide their own Christian nurture on the parish level, even though not as comprehensively developed as in those countries where religious education is by law not allowed in the public schools.

POLAND

As in East Germany and other eastern European countries, religious education in Poland, a predominantly Catholic country, has not been part of the public school curriculum (since 1961) but is primarily the responsibility of the local parish. Even though the state allows religious education on the premises of the churches, it also requires that *only* such instruction take place and nothing dealing with culture and ethics that might cause conflicts for the children with the political system. There are a few private schools (about seven for girls and two for boys) where two hours of religious instruction are allowed during the school week. Religious education was helped during the fifties when catechetical instruction was developed on a parish level. Two hours of religious instruction per week are provided for children in grades 1–7 and one hour for all others. The instruction is given by sisters, priests, and qualified laypersons of the congregation. The amount of instruction offered depends largely on the active participation of the local parish.

OTHER COUNTRIES

In Switzerland, Protestant and Catholic churches are supported by taxes, and religious education classes are held in the public schools. Each canton (like a state or province) makes its own educational regulations. In predominantly Catholic cantons, religious instruction in the schools will generally be taught by Catholic teachers and will be Catholic in orientation (including such things as preparation for Confirmation). Non-Catholic parents generally may request a Protestant teacher if there are enough children to make up a class. In predominantly Protestant cantons, time is released from other subjects for the study of religion within the school, but the teachers are from outside. The subject matter is generally biblical and historical; the syllabus is agreed upon by the Protestant groups involved, and preparatory courses and manuals are provided for teachers. Parish religious education in Switzerland generally takes place on Sundays. Sunday school is more prevalent among Protestant than Catholic churches. Parishes also have pre-school groups and youth groups. Theological faculties, both Protestant and Catholic, are to be found in some Swiss universities.

In France—a predominantly Catholic country—the question of the separation of church and state arose at the time of the French Revolution in 1789 but was not resolved until the 1880s when the state assumed control of the educational system and sectarian religion was no longer permitted to be taught in the schools. Today religious education is the responsibility of the churches.

There are Catholic private schools at each level, but religious education is largely a matter of parish religious education.

Through the Lateran pacts of 1929 Italian schools became state-sponsored. There is religious instruction in the elementary and secondary schools, but students may be excused upon parental request.

JEWISH RELIGIOUS EDUCATION

Religious education among Jews in most European countries has been the task of the local synagogue and the rabbi. Under Germany's Weimar Republic (1918–33) Jewish education was recognized on an equal basis with Christian religious education. Even though the educational system as a whole was based on the Christian heritage, constitutional provisions gave new freedoms to Jews (Article 137). Had they formerly been united only as synagogues for Jewish education, they could now establish associations in support of schools. While Jewish children could attend any public school, they could also have private schools. Rabbis, as representatives of a religious body, also had the right to institute and control the nature, content, and method of Jewish religious instruction. Throughout Germany, Jewish representation on local school authorities was the rule if the number of Jewish pupils warranted it. Since most of the schools were set up on a Christian basis, Jews did not serve in the position of state inspector.

Where Jewish students constituted only a small minority, the synagogue congregation was responsible for their religious education. (This was also the practice for small Protestant or Evangelical minorities). In Prussia, if Jewish students numbered twelve at a public school, the local school authorities could choose either to provide the instruction or to pay an appropriate subsidy to the synagogue that carried on the religious education.

All this changed when Hitler came to power in 1933. As chancellor he took over the educational system. Already in December 1933 Jewish teachers were dismissed from their duties, and rabbis were removed from local school boards in Prussia. In spite of the many hardships, an effective Jewish educational system was being developed in the years 1935–38, and it is estimated that in 1938 there were sixty-eight public and seventy-two private primary Jewish schools. But with the segregation of Jewish children came also the elimination of Jewish religious instruction in the public schools. In 1938, Jewish children were forbidden to attend German public schools. In 1939 the segregation of Jews into a separate school system under the responsibility of the Jewish community was decreed, and the subsequent anti-Semitic measures were the first step toward the closing of all Jewish schools on June 30, 1942.

The Holocaust destroyed all that had been de-boldly to people "from every nation" (Acts 2:5–13). Their message is told in Peter's speech to the bystanders (Acts 2:14–40; 3:12–26). Facing the bad news of human sin that separates people from God, the good news announces a gracious deed done in the life, death, and resurrection of Christ to reconcile the world to God. This had been the divine purpose from the very beginning of creation, through the covenant with Israel and the hopes of its prophets. Now God has acted in Christ to overcome the alienation and has given a new community the signs of the Spirit. This good news also points toward the final reconciliation of the world with God. So declared, the evangel is the story of God's holy love, its struggle and victory. When the message hits home, people do make a turn and join the Way (Acts 2:37–42; 4:14).

IN WORD AND DEED

Evangelism in the book of Acts is accomplished not only in words but through deeds: Acts focuses on exactly that—the *acts* of the apostles, not simply their talks. A "good deed" done to a broken body (Acts 3:7–8; 4:9) and a confrontation with the power structures of the day (Acts 4:1–3, 9) accompany the proclamation. Actions of caring and justice for those in need (Acts 2:44–45; 4:34–35) follow it. An evangelism in accord with New Testament practice, therefore, will include a reorientation to the neighbor in need along with the about-face toward Christ and into the church. Sometimes this is called "word in (the context of) deed" evangelization.

Although proclamation of the gospel is directed to those outside the Christian community, the book of Acts also tells how it is connected with nurturing the life of the church through teaching, preaching, fellowship, prayer, and worship (Acts 2:42, 46–47; 4:31). Outreach is inseparable from inreach.

Taking into account the wider and deeper aspects found in the Acts narrative, evangelism is empowerment by the Holy Spirit of the community of faith to share the full gospel in word and deed that turns persons to Christ, into the church, and out toward the neighbor in need.

Issues that have arisen in Christian history around evangelism have tended to focus on one or another of the elements found in the book of Acts. Church practice in the West in recent centuries (including its missionary movements) has been shaped by Continental Pietism, Wesleyanism, the Great Awakenings in North America, revivalism, and modern evangelicalism. It has tended to stress the individual experience of reorientation, as in "born-again" Christian believers. Others, including many from mainline Protestant denominations concerned about membership decline, interpret evangelism primarily as "church growth." Still others, attuned to contemporary crises—social, economic, and political—stress the healing actions of Jesus and the apostles, viewing evangelization as "liberation." Yet others, troubled about a perceived lack of understanding of the gospel, emphasize that theological renewal within the churches must precede evangelism. Some see it primarily as defending the faith ("apologetics"). And some devote their efforts to strengthening the inner life of the church—its worship, preaching, supportive life together, spirituality, or ethical authenticity; they believe that a "Christian presence" is the best witness to those outside.

While varying situations will bring one or another of these aspects of evangelism to the fore, the New Testament pattern finds a significant place for each element and regularly recalls the proclamation both in word and deed. Growing conversation and relationships between "evangelicals" and "ecumenicals" have fostered this kind of evangelism, which resists reduction to partial perspectives. World evangelical and ecumenical bodies, and Protestant, Roman Catholic, and Eastern Orthodox consultations, have struck similar notes on the partnership of word and deed. Billy Graham, best-known modern evangelist, has moved increasingly from an understanding that almost exclusively focuses on revivalism and personal conversion to one that includes elements of social witness, churchly commitment, congregational upbuilding, and ecumenical relationship. While mass evangelism continues to have its following and television evangelists make their impact felt, more and more the congregation is seen as the chief agent of the New Testament mission.

IN DIALOGUE WITH OTHER RELIGIONS

A pressing issue for advocates of evangelism today is the relationship of Christian mission to growing awareness of world religions and to the developing attraction of "pluralism." Some are asking, "Isn't evangelism a self-centered triumphalism? Doesn't the call to believe the gospel and join the church deny that truth can be found in other religions or people of good will?" Responses to this challenge have ranged from denial of any value in other worldviews or religions, on the one hand, to a quick acceptance of modern pluralism that abandons evangelism, believing that Christianity is adequate for those brought up in it, but not necessary for others.

Supporters of evangelism today in ecumenical and evangelical Christianity, unsatisfied with these options, are struggling to maintain both their particular claims to truth, with salvation in biblical faith, and the universal themes in the gospel that modern circumstances have lifted into view. In this perspective the impetus to evangelism is seen to be, first, the inner compulsion to share what we have found to be true for ourselves and, second, the conviction that those who do not know the good news of what God offers in Christ will be the poorer for it in this world and the next, however much truth, goodness, and beauty is accessible to them by God's "common grace" in all high religions and people of good will. This view encourages dialogue with other religions with the expectancy of enrichment of Christian understanding from it, together with an eagerness to share the gospel in word and deed with a world that needs and awaits it. *See also* Action-Reflection; Bus Ministry; Child Evangelism; Conversion; Evangelicalism; Gospel; Liberation Theology; Mission Education; Social Justice, Education for; Sunday School Movement.

FOR FURTHER REFERENCE

Anderson, Gerald H., and Thomas Stransky, eds. *Mission Trends*. Vol. 2: *Evangelization*. New York: Paulist Press; Grand Rapids, MI: Eerdmans, 1975.

Costas, Orlando E. *Christ Outside the Gate*. Maryknoll, NY: Orbis, 1982.

Fackre, Gabriel. *Word in Deed: Theological Themes in Evangelism*. Grand Rapids, MI: Eerdmans, 1975.

Green, Michael. *Evangelism in the Early Church*. Grand Rapids, MI: Eerdmans, 1970.

Sweazey, George E. *The Church as Evangelist*. New York: Harper & Row, 1978.

G. Fackre

Exceptional Persons

An exceptional person is one who, by societal standards, does not perform as others do, according to the norm, either because of advanced or impaired abilities. Exceptional persons include the gifted, the emotionally disturbed, and the physically or mentally disabled; they may have, for example, intellectual or musical capabilities beyond their years or they may have health problems, learning difficulties, speech disorders, or other handicapping conditions. The handicapped may have more than one disability, and any particular handicap may lead to other needs. One out of ten persons is affected by a disability, either individually or through someone in the family. About forty million persons in the United States and Canada live with some kind of handicapping condition. Worldwide an estimated five hundred million people live with disabilities, many of them in developing countries.

The term "exceptional" is in relation to a norm determined by society. Throughout history people who were "different" have often been excluded from community activities and opportunities, even religious ones, by physical barriers, prejudice, and misunderstanding. In modern society, people are relentlessly measured, catego-

rized, and graded, and those on either end of the scale still suffer much discrimination. (Problems with testing are becoming more apparent. It was once thought that IQ tests measured intelligence, when in fact they may have merely measured adherence to language concepts of the dominant culture group.) Religious education is a part of and influenced by the culture, but it need not be determined by it. Biblically, all people were created as individuals and as part of the community of God's people. Each person is a unique creation of a gracious, empowering God, yet all, including the differently gifted, were fashioned for interdependence. No one is to be excluded.

CHANGING TERMINOLOGY, ATTITUDES AND ACTIONS

In the past twenty-five years, society has changed in attitude and action, giving more attention to the needs of exceptional persons. Whereas only a few years ago those with physical handicaps were kept isolated, legislation has increased public access for those using wheelchairs. "Mainstreaming" has helped those with physical restrictions or learning disabilities become part of the normal course of life in school and workplace. Training in special education has provided teachers equipped to understand and help exceptional persons use their gifts and talents to develop fully.

Changes in terminology attempt to eliminate stereotypes and model positive human values. Terms with negative connotations, like "retarded" or "crippled," are falling into disuse. New phrases include "persons with handicapping or disabling conditions," "persons who are differently able," "persons with physical or mental challenges," "persons who are differently gifted," and "exceptional persons." Programs are identified as special education and ministries with persons with disabilities. The people, not their differences, are the focus. The idea is now no longer what must be done for persons with disabilities, but what all people can do together for one another.

The National Council of the Churches of Christ (NCCC), with thirty-two member denominations in the United States, has been a leader in the movement among churches to recognize the needs of exceptional persons through its Commission on Christian Education for Exceptional Persons, organized in 1958. A basic leadership guide, *The Church and the Exceptional Person*, was developed to guide church leaders in understanding the characteristics and special needs of persons with disabilities and in ways of involving them in religious programs. Major programs were begun in the 1960s to develop and support curriculum resources involving mentally handicapped persons, including the series "Adventures in Christian Living and Learning" and "Exploring Life." Socialization groups, preschool programs, camping and retreat events, confirmation and church membership classes, vacation church schools, and many other groups opened up for persons with disabilities.

In a major 1975 statement, "The Handicapped and the Wholeness of the Family of God," the World Council of Churches affirmed equality and mutuality, human worth, and personal dignity and called on churches to do everything possible to integrate persons with disabilities fully into the life of the church at every level. In 1977–1978 three major religious bodies in the United States adopted statements advocating the inclusion of persons with disabilities: the Commission on Social Action of Reform Judaism (Union of American Hebrew Congregations), the U.S. Catholic Bishops, and the governing board of the NCCC. The U.S. Catholic Conference has established the National Catholic Office for Persons with Disabilities.

GUIDELINES FOR TEACHERS

There are creative possibilities in religious education among exceptional people. Religious educators need to know about the agencies and materials available to them.

Acceptance of handicapped persons by the teacher is prerequisite to acceptance by other pupils in the class. Teachers need to relate to these pupils as persons who have special needs. When such learners feel accepted, they will try to meet the teacher's expectations. All pupils need to be included in all activities. The exceptional person need not be sheltered but encouraged to participate.

It helps when teachers are constant in teaching style and modify patterns slowly so that pupils have time to adapt. They need to be unhurried, repeat where needed, provide individual instruction for any student as needed, and use a variety of teaching techniques. It may be helpful to have a "buddy" system in classes to encourage participation by exceptional learners. Behavior problems may arise from boredom where a task is too difficult in some way. Rewarding acceptable behavior reinforces it.

Parents and day-school teachers can be helpful in suggesting ways of adapting the class situation. Although exceptional learners want to be with their age group, many have special educational needs and a helping teacher may be needed.

There are also specific needs. The visually handicapped appreciate a consistent room arrangement, the use of touch, music, role playing, tapes, large print, and repeating information as needed. Those with limited hearing are helped by a visual approach.

In the past, religious education classes sometimes measured a learner's readiness for religious rites by the ability to read or memorize Bible verses, standards not imposed in the historic initiation of such rites. An emphasis on reading aloud or answering questions based on content discourages those with learning disabilities. In the religious community, faith is not measured by the amount of facts or exact skills acquired. One learns and grows by being part of that community.

Understanding exceptionality means looking for the gifts. Teachers discover that a clinically retarded person has profound wisdom in conversations about God's love. A blind woman, with Braille tools, reads a lesson about the healing of a deaf person, and the worshiping community receives insight on the nature of mercy that no one else in the community reading that passage could have given. In a Bible class of elderly women, instead of taking turns reading the passages, one reads all the time, the one who is profoundly hard of hearing. They use her gift of speaking rather than dwelling on her inability to hear. The "hyperactive child" receives one-on-one instruction in the faith and is later in the hour again able to be part of the larger class.

When religious education classes are set up in learning centers, so that there is a choice of methods and materials, the variety of learning opportunities makes it possible for people to learn in many ways. Team teaching or a classroom aide increases the availability of one-on-one instruction.

Regular teaching materials will need to be adapted. In addition to the NCCC, some denominational religious education departments have materials or a person available to help.

Religious education teachers can be trained for including exceptional learners through one-day conferences, weekend or longer laboratory schools, and other forms of training events. Simulation experiences in which they try to feel what it is like to be unable to see, hear, learn easily, or move quickly encourage empathy and provide opportunity for teachers to explore various methods of teaching. Vignettes, in anecdotal or visual form, place them emotionally in a situation different from their own. *See also* Emotionally Disturbed Children; Gifted Children; Psychological Testing.

FOR FURTHER REFERENCE

Feigenson, Emily H., ed. *Compass: New Directions in Jewish Education.* Vol. 8, no. 3 (Winter 1986). A special issue on "New Directions for Special Needs Learners" published by Union of American Hebrew Congregations.

Opening Doors: Ministry with Persons with Disabilities. 2 vols. National Catholic Office for Persons with Disabilities, 1987 (PO Box 39111, Washington, DC 20017).

Schmidt, Carolyn. *Tips for Congregations Working with Disabled Persons.* Chicago: Evangelical Lutheran Church of America, 1986.

Special Education Leadership. Nashville, TN: Southern Baptist Sunday School Board. A quarterly magazine.

Toews, Jane Willems. *Including Persons with Handicaps: A Sunday School Teacher's Guide*. Newton, KS: Faith and Life Press, 1984.

N. C. Everist, I. J. Kidd

Exegesis

Exegesis is the discipline whereby one determines the meaning that a particular text had for its author in order to interpret and explain it for readers. Because the Bible forms the basic teaching material for religious education, it is important for teachers to learn how interpretations are arrived at.

A number of different subdisciplines can be brought to bear on this enterprise. First of all, because prior to the end of the fifteenth century books were copied letter by letter by scribes, there crept into the various copies of any given work a number of instances in which what was copied was not what the author had, in fact, written. Included in this nonoriginal material are errors, mistakes in copying, as well as glosses, intentional changes or insertions made for the purposes of explaining an obscure text. By comparing the various manuscripts of any given work, giving preference as a rule to those that were written earlier, it is possible to arrange the manuscripts into "families" (those that show the same kind of variants in the text) and by a comparison of the earliest exemplars of the various families arrive at a text most probably closest to the original, or autograph.

Having arrived at an approximation of the original, exegesis then proceeds to examine the language of the text in order adequately to render into a modern language the original sense of the text as intended by the author. Naturally, this subdivision takes advantage of the many parallels and comparisons that can be made between, for example, what one finds written in the Greek of the New Testament as compared with the Greek of nonreligious documents contemporary with it.

Having established, upon the basis of vocabulary, grammar, and syntax, the sense of the text, one must then go on to give the necessary historical background to assist in defining any terms of cultural significance. One must explain any possible allusions to such matters as religions politics, economics, geography, warfare, and general social customs of the period. What was the general worldview of the time and how does it differ from our own? Factors that help contemporary readers understand the way of thinking of the writers and their audience must be brought to bear.

In the twentieth-century study of the New Testament, for example, it has become a widely held hypothesis that, within the works as we now have them, there may well be smaller, identifiable units of material that first circulated separately or in other collections of material, probably by word of mouth. It has become part of the work of exegesis to identify these forms within the larger work and to attempt to identify as well the community need or function they seem to have fulfilled. The exegete attempts by this means to "look behind," so to speak, the text as we now have it to catch a glimpse of the formative period in the oral stage of transmission.

More recently, biblical exegesis has turned its attention to a study of the works of the writers themselves. In connection with this task there has been a recognition that writers put their work in a form (such as a letter) that would have been appropriate to the purpose of the work. Study of the particular forms as they appear in other literature of the period has greatly facilitated this task.

During the period when the smaller forms within the larger work were being thoroughly and for the first time investigated, the writers of such things as the Gospels appeared to have been mere arrangers or editors of the material. More recent study, concentrating on the works as wholes, has purported to show that the authors not only arranged their material, but shaped and reformed it in such a way as to express a particular point of view.

Exegesis is a tool for teaching. Asking what a Bible passage means solely to an individual reader is important, but not sufficient for appropriating the wealth of meaning found in the Bible. The seriousness of the biblical message makes it essential that teachers and students take advantage of the tools, methods, and findings of exegesis. Reference works (Bible dictionaries, atlases, commentaries, and several translations), attention to form (letters, chronicles, parables, poetry, narrative, etc.) and background (history and culture of the biblical period), and consideration of a variety of interpretations all enrich teaching and study of the Bible. *See also* Bible in Religious Education, The; Bible Study; Biblical Criticism; Biblical Translation; Hermeneutic.

FOR FURTHER REFERENCE

Hayes, John H. and Carl R. Holladay, eds. *Biblical Exegesis: A Beginner's Handbook*. Philadelphia: Fortress, 1982.

Rylaarsdam, J. Coert, Gene Tucker, and Dan O. Via, Jr., eds. *Guides to Biblical Scholarship*. 14 vols. to date. Philadelphia: Fortress, 1971– .

J. S. Ruef

Exhibit

An exhibit is a display that represents or clarifies a theme for the education of the public. The purpose of an exhibit might be to show what a class has studied, to pique others' interest in a topic, or to create a forum where persons of all ages can share what they know.

An example of a museum exhibit provides some clues about what is needed for a creative, colorful, and interesting exhibit. Decisions must be made about the theme, about what to communicate in relation to who will see the exhibit and the space where it will be displayed. Background material about the culture or the social context of the theme could be provided in a written paragraph, photographs, or particular cultural items. Who were the people involved? Photographs or models of persons could be included. What is happening? How can the exhibit be arranged to capture the viewer's own knowledge and imagination? *See also* Visual Methods.

S. H. Matthaei

Existentialism

"Existentialism" derives from the Latin *existare*, "to emerge," or, more basically, *exsto*, "to stand forth" or "to be." In general usage, existence is defined in contradistinction to essence: essence answers the question of *what* something is, but existence answers the question of *whether* something is.

As a philosophical position, existentialism has placed its emphasis on individual being. To paraphrase Hamlet's famous line, to be or not to be, that is the question existentialism addresses. The distinctiveness of existentialism lies in its claim that individual existence precedes essence and thus gives to being, especially individual being, a position of ontological priority. This sets existentialism over against idealism, which asserts that essence, usually meaning idea, concept, or rational construct, has a transcendent status, as in Plato. It also sets existentialism against realism, which asserts the metaphysical and logical priority of the essence of things, even though essence is always found in things as their form, giving them actuality, as in Aristotle. Further, it distinguishes existentialism from experimentalism, although the latter also is opposed to any essentialism, idealist or realist. Experimentalism was first the creation of John Dewey (1859–1952) and in contrast to existentialism stresses not the authentic being of the individual but the effective functioning of the individual in his or her corporate context. Such socially constructed effectiveness is, in fact, often taken as the target of existentialism, since it tends to obscure the boundaries of human existence and submerge the person in a social consciousness.

CHARACTERISTICS

Four outstanding characteristics of existentialism can be cited. The first is the stress upon individual freedom of choice. Whether to be or not to be is not a given but a choice, and the power to choose is the irrevocable and irreducible prerogative of each person. The second characteristic is the definitive nature of extreme or limit situations. Human life is not to be understood from the mainstream outward to the limits of despair, anxiety, and death, but from those limits inward. Thus, mainstream experience tends to be characterized as boredom, illusion, or inauthenticity until it is seen in light of the extremities it tends to conceal. The third characteristic is to claim that existence is open-ended and that the future is actually created by the choices one makes in confrontation with the extremities of his or her situation. These first three characteristics are all dramatically portrayed in contemporary literature in Walker Percy's writings. The fourth concerns the interpersonal aspect of existentialism represented by the dialogical stance of Martin Buber or the Christian existentialism of John Macquarrie. The significance of corporate reality for the existentialist must be found—if it is to be found at all—in religious or theological reality, as in Buber's "I-Thou" relationship. Any other socialized or encultured form of corporate life is seen as aggravating and obscuring the alienation that is presumably endemic to human existence. Thus, atheistic existentialism, such as that of John Paul Sartre, views corporate existence as intrinsically hostile and mutually destructive to all concerned. Thus, his notorious dictum from *No Exit*, "Hell is other people." Buber, on the other hand, says the "I-Thou" relationship is the primary word of human existence.

EXISTENTIALISM AND CHRISTIAN EDUCATION

Educationally, existentialism is primarily critical of any socialization or enculturation approach, but it is not without some educational paradigms. Education must stress the four characteristics described above and usually does so in an open-ended confrontation with the extremities of the learner's individual existence, in the face of which he or she must make choices. One example is Summerhill School, which was once widely discussed as an open-ended learn-when-you're-ready and learn-what-you-want educational context for young people, who were largely dropouts from the mainstream of British society. It often proved effective as a place where learners discovered the legitimacy and significance of creating their own education and, through that, the significance of shaping their own existence. That the school eventually failed as an institution is not in itself existentially significant, but it may serve to illustrate the fundamental tension that will always pertain between existentialism and education in any conventional sense.

Theologically, existentialism begins with Søren Kierkegaard (1813–1855), whose vivid portrayals of human extremity dramatized the ultimate alienation of human existence from God. Kierkegaard's trenchant grasp of human existence was so accurate and persuasive that his thought has had a definitive influence on figures as diverse as Jean-Paul Sartre and Karl Barth, Martin Heidegger and Niels Bohr, Ludwig Binswanger and Paul Tillich. However, for theological existentialism, existence cannot be defined phenomenologically, psychologically, or scientifically; it must be understood in its brokenness over against the gift of God's grace, which in turn restores the individual through faith in Jesus Christ. Only by this radical intervention of God's action in Jesus Christ can the abyss that separates humanity from the wholly other God be bridged. Here the human extremity of sin is met by the greater extremity of God's grace such that faith can mean nothing less than a radical alteration of one's total existence.

Existentialism, then, continually challenges Christian education to bring the learner into confrontation with the existential dichotomies of human life for the sake of Christian conviction. Self versus other, male versus female, good versus evil, death versus life, God versus humanity, time versus eternity, love versus justice all provide the context in which the fuller significance of Jesus Christ may be recognized. He becomes the One who first convicts by driving superficial human dilemmas to their depths in alienation from God, and then at the point of uttermost alienation he redeems the individual with a grace that transforms all human distortions into expressions of his reconciling nature. See also Buber, Martin; Essentialism; Idealism; Kierkegaard, Søren; Realism.

J. E. Loder

Experience

When we speak of experience we are placing an emphasis, philosophically, upon the grounding of one's understanding of self, others, and the universe on direct, personal participation in the process of living rather than on categories of thought one might bring to the interpretation of the meaning of experience. It cannot be said that we have had experience with something unless we have had direct, firsthand engagement with the things or persons involved. It is also implied that our judgments will be less than accurate if we have not had direct contact with the life situation under analysis.

ITS ROLE IN LEARNING

The experiential nature of learning is based on the belief that the human organism lives not only in a particular environment but by means of it. Learning is much more than digesting the ideas and practices presented in books or curricular materials. It is profoundly enhanced when it is in direct interaction with the world of things and persons in the actual life situations in which persons find themselves. For centuries, as a people, we have said that human beings learn from experience. Theoreticians have helped us see that we learn much better from experience if we reflect deeply upon it, test it, and relate our findings to ongoing efforts to build theories that can help us deal with subsequent issues.

John Dewey (1859–1952), a major figure in experimentalism (along with Charles S. Peirce and William James), underscored the central importance of experience for learning. In his books, especially *Experience and Nature* (1925) and *Experience and Education* (1938), he lifted up the organic nature of human life in the evolutionary process, the importance of the identification of real needs and problems of individuals and society, and the use of the scientific method in the solving of these problems and meeting human needs. Education, then, had to be person-centered, experimental, innovative, holistic, organic, and clearly value-oriented. The values to be taught were those that stimulated the learners to extend themselves to discover ways of living that would most provide opportunity for the growth of every other person and for the well-being of all aspects of life in a democratic society. No value was to be promulgated unless it actually solved human problems and freed human intelligence to work on the emerging needs of persons. This process of self-giving and devotion to the common good was seen as the product of a common faith and was, in itself, a religious quality of life. The artistic and aesthetic dimensions of life were symbolic of the human capacity to transcend concern only for self and to sacrifice vicariously for the good of others. Values were to be measured by their consequences and not primarily in relation to the persons or institutions advocating them. In his book *Democracy and Education* (1916), Dewey saw education as the reconstruction of experience that, in itself, adds to the meaningfulness of human life and increases our ability to give creative direction to the development of subsequent experience. Dewey and his colleague William Kilpatrick (*Foundations of Method*, 1926) sought to define and make operational for education the steps in the complete act of thought in direct relation to experience.

The five steps were:

1. A learner experiences a felt difficulty or interruption of ongoing life.

2. The difficulty or problem is located in order to analyze the nature of it and make it into an "intellectual problem."

3. The learner makes inferences about what needs to be done, anticipating the consequences of the inferences and designing ways to test the adequacy of the proposed solution or solutions.

4. The learner, then, begins to develop bearings concerning the potential of a particular, favored inference or hypothesis, engaging in back and forth reasoning from the hypothesis to what is observable in the actual life experience out of which the problem arose.

5. The learner then tests or tries out the solution in a simulated situation or in the actual situation, gets feedback, and is prepared to make corrections until the difficulty is resolved or not resolved, always being prepared to start the process all over again if the answer is negative.

Such assumptions have been found wanting by optional interpretations of experience and learning and have been challenged in respect to the basic understanding of human nature and the universe, about how learning takes place, and what the assumptions about ultimate reality are. However, this pattern of experiential learning has had profound influence upon both general education and religious education.

Some of the many other sources emphasizing the experiential dimension to learning are: depth psychology, humanistic psychology, human development studies, group dynamics, action research, existentialism, phenomenology, organizational development, theology, and anthropological studies of religious practices and assumptions.

ITS ROLE IN RELIGIOUS EDUCATION

The pioneering work of Horace Bushnell (1802–1876) in his book *Christian Nurture* (1861) set the stage for a strong emphasis on the power of a direct experience within the family and other human relationships to be channels of love and grace to the child. Through the nurturing love and care of parents and others within the faith community, the child would experience Christian love and truth and increasingly be able to symbolize such meaning in words. Bushnell was followed by many twentieth-century religious educators (from Dewey's contemporary George Albert Coe on) who have emphasized the crucial nature of experience. Most major denominations and faith groups have developed curricula that are life-situational, person-centered, action-reflection in style, and dialogical between the actual life issues of the learners in society and the biblical and theological understandings of the faith. Ecumenical curricular designs have also included a strong awareness of the need for experiential religious education. The Cooperative Curriculum Project, with sixteen major denominations participating in basic theoretical and theological work on the purposes and processes of Christian education (*The Church's Education Ministry: A Curriculum Plan*, 1965), affirmed the principle of intersection (which emphasizes the importance of finding key points where the real needs of persons in their total field of relationships intersected with the gospel). More recently, in the curricula designed by Joint Educational Development teams representing fifteen denominations, two of the four major designs published in the 1970s and 1980s are *Living the Word* and *Doing the Word*. Both organize Christian learning clearly around actual problems and issues in personal and corporate life.

Methods of learning that have been generated by experiential assumptions are: creative activities using art, drama, and music, projects, the resolution of problem situations, role-playing and other simulations, feedback and other evaluation procedures, internships and other clinical experiences, laboratory patterns, learning centers, discovery-oriented methods, on-the-job training, outdoor education, mentoring programs in the workplace, self-instruction and other self-motivated patterns of learning (called andragogy in adult education), practicums, and patterns of instant communications made possible by new electronic media. *See also* Empiricism; Humanism; Knowledge, Theories of; Pragmatism; Progressive Education.

R. L. Browning

Experimentalism

See Progressive Education.

Facilities

Much of education takes place in a physical environment that includes buildings, furnishings, and equipment and that is known collectively as facilities. Educators have found that the quality of a learning experience is determined, in part, by the environment in which the experience occurs. When thoughtfully designed and effectively utilized, facilities contribute a great deal to the learning process. This suggests that concern for adequate facilities is consistent with concern for such things as learning methodologies, curriculum, and so forth.

STEWARDSHIP OF RESOURCES

Balance must be found between facilities that are a suitable expression of a congregation's honor and love for an infinite God, on the one hand, yet do not cause unnecessary financial hardship, on the other. Solomon reminds us of the importance of the former when he says, "The house which I am to build will be great, for our God is greater than all gods" (2 Chron. 2:5). Still, a church should not become so indebted for facilities as to be unable to provide adequately for local ministry, missions, and other services that are primary in the work of the church. Precisely where the point of balance is to be found will vary from church to church. However, consideration of issues such as these can prevent erecting buildings as mere monuments to human pride.

Facilities tend to influence the philosophy and practice of religious education. For example, a classroom with fixed seating and a raised platform tends to favor teacher-dominated, one-way communication. Effective facilities grow out of a carefully defined philosophy of religious education. What we believe about effective learning, teaching, and mutual ministry must influence the design of facilities. Even with facilities built many years ago, physical environment cannot dictate practice. Opportunity should be given for creative learning experiences that require larger amounts of space than needed for mere sitting and listening.

Good stewardship demands educational space that is flexible and multifunctional. Large, open classrooms offer advantages of flexibility and lower construction costs. However, space can be so flexible that it is actually difficult to use for more than a few select activities, as is the case with gymnasiums. Generally, rooms are considered flexible when they can be used for at least two or three different kinds of functions. Flexibility of large areas can be enhanced by use of portable barriers or dividers, acoustical ceilings, and perhaps electronic sound masking to acoustically isolate groups in proximity to each other. One key to flexible space is storage. It is recommended that 10 percent of the total room space be provided for storage, an amount that should be more than doubled when two or more programs use the same room.

Noise and clutter are frequent learning distractions that can be minimized, even in existing buildings. Carpeting, draperies, wall insulation, and sound-absorbing wall coverings aid in noise reduction, while visual distractions can be removed or minimized by use of sight barriers. Establishing procedures for periodic disposal of unneeded materials helps prevent clutter distractions.

ACCOMMODATING THE LEARNER

It is important to view facilities through the eyes of learners. Does the room draw students in? Is it neat, comfortable, and attractive? Are pictures, charts, and other displays at learners' eye level? Are learners encouraged to become involved in learning activities or relationships? Have the rooms been recently painted? Are furnishings in good repair and appropriate to the size of the learners? Is there sufficient space for active learning without feeling cramped?

Equipment and space can contribute to the development of children's social skills necessary for later healthy fellowship with and ministry to others. Studies show that providing adequate quantities of equipment tends to limit children's aggression and stress behaviors measurably. It has also been found that young children prefer large indoor activity areas that allow much social participation rather than being placed in small partitioned areas. Consideration should also be given to providing playground equipment, particularly if children are present for long periods of time.

Age-level needs should be accounted for in other ways, such as adequate square footage (early childhood, 35 square feet per child; grades 1–6, 30 square feet; youth, 25 square feet; adults, 15 square feet), equipment and furniture appropriate to the age, and wall-mounted fixtures such as bulletin boards and chalkboards placed at learner eye level.

Preschoolers require space adequate for a variety of active learning experiences involving movement from one activity to another. Separate facilities are needed for crib babies, toddlers, and twos through fives. Rooms for babies need carpeted space for crawling and careful attention to sanitation and safety. Toddler rooms need space for crawling, walking, and playing. Washable, durable, nontoxic materials free of sharp edges should be provided. Since learning by doing is particularly helpful for twos through fives, clearly defined centers for learning activities are important. Preferably, each room should have a sink, and restroom facilities should be in the same room or in proximity. It is recommended that windows be placed low enough for children to see out easily.

Similar considerations regarding sinks, windows, and proximity of restrooms should be given grades 1–6. Walls covered with foambacked carpet or vinyl-covered cork provide flexibility for displaying pictures and student work while cutting noise. Subdued colors, particularly on walls, prevent overstimulation.

As with preschool and children's rooms, youth and adult rooms should reflect the church's philosophy of learning. A variety of small- and large-group learning activities can be accommodated by movable seating. It is often helpful to locate classrooms for adults with small children near children's classrooms.

Semidirect lighting in all rooms is preferred. Electrical outlets should be three-prong, grounded type and positioned so that there is at least one outlet on each wall. Floor coverings may be vinyl tile or carpet. However, carpet appears to be most economical in upkeep while providing extra advantages of sound control, warmth, and a relaxed environment. If children's rooms are carpeted, an area of vinyl tile should be provided for painting and other art activities. Adequate ventilation and heating should be provided so room temperature can be kept around 68–70 degrees.

While it is true that physical arrangement does not teach, it does contribute student "expectancies" for learning. For example, a circle of chairs suggests and encourages interaction, while rows imply one-way communication. Furnishings contribute similar expectancies. Round tables, for example, encourage interactive, cooperative learning. Teachers and leaders are likewise influenced by physical arrangement and will tend to conform teaching styles to the environment. It is an important challenge to assist teachers in using creative methodology despite room limitations that may be present.

Occasionally, churches are faced with crowded facilities. A number of alternative solutions may be considered. The church narthex or ends of hallways not required for traffic flow may be utilized with portable dividers. Duplicate Sunday school sessions at different successive hours may be considered. Classes for certain ages may be offered during one hour while offering other ages the alternative hour. These options have the advantage of doubling capacity without expenditures for additional buildings. Prefabricated classrooms can be rented or purchased and placed on church property, or houses nearby can be purchased. Some churches have effectively shared facilities with other churches, scheduling programs to avoid conflicts.

The importance of well-maintained facilities cannot be overstated. Rooms that are well kept communicate much to visitors and members alike. It is helpful to establish maintenance procedures that clearly identify frequency of cleaning as well as which responsibilities belong to custodians and which belong to teachers/leaders.

In all facilities, whether old or new, adequate attention must be given to the needs of the handicapped and elderly. "Barrier free" designs should be the goal. See also Finance; Kindergarten; Learning Center; Management; Nursery Education; Resources and Resource Centers.

D. H. Dirks

Fahs, Sophia Lyon

Sophia Lyon Fahs (1876–1978) was an outstanding liberal educator of the twentieth century. Born of Presbyterian missionary parents, she moved steadily toward liberalism during her career, becoming editor of the Beacon Series Curriculum (Unitarian) when she was sixty and an ordained Unitarian minister at eighty-two.

A creative teacher, she taught in the first experimental school for children located in a seminary, the Union School of Religion in New York City. She was the author of Jesus, the Carpenter's Son (1945), which tells the story of Jesus for the junior-high age group with a full appreciation of the results of biblical scholarship, and The Old Story of Salvation (1955), which contrasts the biblical story as interpreted by evangelical Christianity with the biblical narrative as reconstructed by historical-critical investigation. Her most enduring legacy may be the Martin and Judy texts for preschoolers, which explore the beginnings of religious life in children. See also Unitarian Universalist Education.

H. A. Archibald

Faith

Faith is an indispensable word in the lexicon of religion because it is a central reality in the religious life. But it refuses to be defined simply—there is no one meaning of faith. How the meaning of faith is understood has a significant impact on religious education theory and practice. Different understandings of the term can lead to quite different approaches, as the history of religious education clearly shows.

FAITH AND BELIEF

Faith is deeply related to belief. Faith also connotes profound trust, confidence, and loyalty. It is an affair of the heart as well as of the mind. Commitment and action are also dimensions of faith. Faith has to do with a person's fundamental orientation in life. It is related to seeing, discernment, understanding, and freedom from bondage. In various ways, faith involves relationship. We are related to something in faith. What that something is, or can be, makes considerable difference in a person's faith and even in what faith is understood to mean.

Some analyses of the meaning of faith start with general human phenomena such as believing, trusting, committing, and orienting life. When one begins here, it is possible to say that faith is a human universal. Faith is a dimension of every human life because belief about and belief in, trust and confidence in, and orientation to something are inherent in being human at all. In this general phenomenological approach to faith, emphasis is placed on faith as a human activity, on the ways people carry out the project of creating or discovering an overarching framework of meaning and value in life.

Others argue that the appropriate starting point is with faith's object. This approach tends to be more theological and is usually an attempt to articulate the nature of faith in terms of a particular religious tradition's normative experience of it. Thus, faith becomes belief and trust in, commitment, and fundamental life orientation to *God* as known in and revealed through the tradition's historic experience, communal life, and writings. Ultimate relationship to anyone or anything else than God is considered to be idolatry rather than faith. The very meaning of faith is understood in terms of right relationship to the one true God. In this approach, the notion of faith as a human activity is not denied, but greater emphasis is placed on faith as a gift made possible only through the activity of the God who gives it. And in receiving the gift of faith from God, we find our own believing, trusting, and committing transformed.

The relationship between faith and belief is complex. The distinction between belief *that* something is the case and belief *in* someone or something is helpful. In some cases, faith has been virtually identified with "belief that." This has been, for example, a rather strong tendency in much traditional Roman Catholic theology, where faith has often meant giving assent to divinely revealed truths of which the church is custodian and interpreter. In most cases, such truths, though not grounded in reason, are understood to be credible to the discerning mind. Therefore, intellectual inquiry is regarded as an aid to faith and is valued and fostered educationally.

Faith and belief are related in a different way when the connotation is "belief in," implying trust, confidence, and perhaps also loyalty and commitment. This connection between faith and belief has been the classical Protestant emphasis, but also characterizes much of contemporary Roman Catholicism as well as Judaism. When the emphasis is placed here, "belief that" does not become irrelevant. Rather, the two senses are reciprocally related. We have beliefs about what we believe in. Still, "belief in" is usually taken to be fundamental to "belief that." Thus, the belief, for example, that God exists means little unless one believes in, trusts, and is committed to God.

Still one other dimension of the relation between faith and belief is important. Some of our believing (in both senses) is fairly peripheral and can be given up without affecting a person's basic identity and life orientation much. But some of our believing is more central to us. This "core" believing is close to the heart of a person and thus tends to be more readily identified with faith understood in terms of trust and confidence. Given this understanding of faith, religious education tends to be oriented toward a sense of personal (though not necessarily individualistic) relationship to and encounter with God, usually understood to be mediated at least in part through experience in the ways of life and tradition (especially the Scriptures) of the religious community. Beliefs are to be appropriated personally and deeply as dimensions of a profound and heartfelt "believing in."

FAITH AND ACTION

Faith is also closely tied to action. What we most profoundly believe and believe in calls for our fidelity, our loyalty, our commitment. The test of these is not just in what we say, but in what we do. Faith and faithfulness may be distinguished, perhaps, but they are fundamentally related. Thus faith involves obedience, especially when the object of faith is deemed to be personal in the sense of being able to will something of or have expectations of the faithful. Faith is found in doing God's will and avoiding idolatry. Faith as obedience is often understood in terms of adherence to moral rules or moral law as expressions of God's will. This is, in fact, involved, but the object of faith is not the moral law, but God. Thus, faith as obedience is more adequately understood as a response of gratitude and love to a gracious and loving God in whom one believes and trusts and to whom one is committed. Faith as obedience involves both the love of God and the love of God's whole creation. Obedience therefore takes two basic forms: worship of God and care for the world. Care for the world, both natural and human, has political as well as personal dimensions. This is the basis for the relationships between faith and social action.

Another dimension of faith as action, faithfulness, or obedience is illuminated by the connection between faith and perseverance or patient endurance. Often the faithful are conceived of as a people on the way, involved in a pilgrimage or adventure on which God is leading them. Faith in this context means to hold firm, keep faith, press on in confidence and hope. This sense becomes especially powerful when obstacles are faced and suffering (perhaps even persecution) is encountered.

Religious education that takes account of the action dimension of faith will often emphasize the actual engagement in action as an educational strategy. To this is related education that attempts to raise learners' consciousness of the personal and social needs of the world, and to develop the attitudes, capacities, and skills necessary in moral decision making and appropriate action. Too often, perhaps, education for action emphasizes either action for the care of the world *or* for the praise of God in worship, but not both. Many religious educators are working hard to bring these together where they belong, however, and to place both in a context of belief and trust.

FAITH, TRUTH, AND FREEDOM

Still another dimension of faith relates it to seeing, discernment, and understanding. To have faith is in one sense to see what there is to be seen, to see beneath the surface of things, and even to see beyond what there is to see. Faith is often contrasted with spiritual blindness. In spiritual blindness, our perception is distorted by our own egocentric needs and desires. We see what we want to see and, often out of fear and anxiety, refuse even to look at things we would rather not attend to. Faith is the capacity to penetrate the haze, to face honestly what is there, both in the world and in ourselves. In this dimension, there is a deep con-

nection between faith, truth, and freedom. In the Gospel of John, for example, Jesus is regarded as the Light of the World who makes sight possible. In him, John says, "you will know the truth, and the truth will make you free" (8:32).

The bondage we are to be freed from is the bondage of sin. Thus faith is also related to freedom from sin. In faith, a confrontation with evil, despair, destruction, and even death takes place so that new life may emerge. Indeed, faith may be characterized as the experience of new life in the midst of a world largely but not ultimately governed by structures and forces of evil and death.

All of these various dimensions and meanings of faith are very much interrelated. Obedience not only results from belief and trust; it also forms and molds belief and trust. Believing shapes seeing and seeing shapes believing. Discernment and understanding of truth and freedom from bondage make possible forms of action that are otherwise impossible. In biblical understandings of faith, all of this is directly related to the gracious, merciful, and loving activity of God who, in faith, is praised and thanked for all these good gifts.

FAITH AND RELIGIOUS EDUCATION

Faith is often thought of as the goal or objective of religious education, and there is much talk about faith development. It is surely true that "faith comes from hearing," as Paul puts it (Rom. 10:17, TEV), and that education and the activities of the larger community life have a highly significant impact on the faith of persons. As Calvin put it in reference to Christian faith, "God, who could in a moment perfect his own, nevertheless desires them to grow up onto (maturity) solely under the education of the church." Nevertheless, faith is not simply the result of good religious education. Faith is also the presupposition and ground of religious education. Faith builds upon faith. Without faith, there can be no religious education. *See also* Belief; Commitment; Faith Development; Freedom; God, Understandings of; Justification; Social Action; Worship.

C. R. Dykstra

Faith Development

The term "faith development" is used in a wide variety of ways in contemporary theology. Broadly speaking, it refers to the ongoing growth that takes place in a person's religious life across the course of the life span. Certain theorists, like James Fowler, use the term in a more technical manner (*Stages of Faith*, 1981). While Fowler's work will be explored later, there are two reasons why it is important to begin with a more general understanding of this topic.

First, the recent discussion of faith development has drawn on a wide range of psychological theories to describe lifelong human development. This has given rise to a variety of ways of understanding how faith develops across the life span. Second, the Christian tradition offers a number of very different perspectives on growth in the Christian life, typically under the doctrine of sanctification. Some of the most important and divisive controversies in church history have been over this issue. Faith development, thus, must not be confined to a particular position or theory but refers to a general area understood in a variety of ways across the Christian tradition.

To gain insight into how this topic is addressed in different ways, this essay is divided into three parts: an examination of sanctification as it pertains to this topic; an examination of faith development in contemporary thought, with special emphasis on the work of James Fowler; and an examination of the critical issues that have emerged in the recent discussion of faith development.

HISTORICAL CHRISTIAN APPROACHES

The theme of growth in the religious life appears in the Christian tradition as early as the writings of Paul. In Ephesians 4:15, for example, he admonishes the members of the early church "to grow up in every way into him who is the head, into Christ." Throughout the New Testament, this emphasis on growth in the Christian life is related to the idea of holiness or sanctification. Quoting Leviticus 11:44–45, 1 Peter 1:16 summarizes the heart of this theme: "You shall be holy, for I am holy." There is common agreement among all the churches with the New Testament idea that the holiness of the church and its members is dependent on the holiness of God.

In large part, the differences between the churches grow out of the very different ways that God's reconciling action in Christ (justification) is seen as related to the church and its members' holiness (sanctification). In Martin Luther and John Calvin, justification refers to the unmerited, atoning work of Christ by which forgiveness of sins and the possibility of a right relationship with God is effected. It refers to our status as forgiven sinners, an objective status that is the exclusive result of God's finished work in Christ. Sanctification refers to the acknowledgment and actualization of this status.

Luther and Calvin are always careful to point out that all holiness in the Christian life is the work of God. As Christ grants Christians the forgiveness of sins, he simultaneously claims them for himself, placing them under his care and providing them with the gifts to carry out his ministry in the world. Sanctification, however, in no way contributes to Christians' status as forgiven sinners. That is something which God and God alone can effect. Although they differ somewhat in the emphasis they place on sanctification, both Luther and Calvin are extremely wary of any signs of moralism or works righteousness in the religious life that might undermine Christians' exclusive reliance upon the grace of God for their salvation. Indeed, in their perspective, it may be something of a contradiction to view faith, viewed as a relationship of trust in God, as something that develops.

The Roman Catholic tradition conceptualizes faith development in a very different manner. This tradition is quite diverse in the ways that it addresses this topic, and only one of its perspectives can be described in this essay. An important difference with Reformed theology is the Roman Catholic church's belief that humans retain certain good capacities that were given in creation, even after the Fall. Humans may do good within the limits of their natural state and know God through natural reason. God's salvific action in Christ is presented as building on and perfecting these natural capacities, and humans are seen as cooperating with God's grace in an unfolding process that passes through various stages. This has great implications for the way justification and sanctification are understood in this tradition.

In a sense, justification refers to the infusion of supernatural grace that takes place when persons are baptized into the church and, thereby, restored to a right relationship with God. Sanctification refers to the ongoing process by which persons cooperate with the grace of God over the course of their lives and begin to partake of the holiness of God. This ongoing faith development can only be sustained through participation in the sacramental life of the church. In an important sense, however, justification means more than the initial reception of grace upon entry into the church; it refers to the entire process by which persons work out their salvation in the church and gain merit before God.

Certain differences between this position and that of the Reformers are obvious. Here, faith development is an inherent part of the religious life. Indeed, justification and sanctification cannot be clearly separated. Christians are justified fully only as they cooperate with grace as mediated through the church and enter into full communion with God. Moreover, the Roman Catholic tradition places far greater emphasis on the contribution humans make to this process. Capacities given in creation allow people to cooperate with the divine activity. Development in the religious life builds on and perfects natural, human development.

Certain of the Christian churches have attempted to formulate a position that mediates the perspectives of the Reformers and the Roman Catholics. John Wesley's theology, which informs the United Methodist church, is an important case in point. Wesley retains the belief of Luther and Calvin that justification is based solely on faith, which is a gift of God, while formulating an understanding of sanctification as an unfolding process that is closer to Roman Catholicism. Far more than that of either Luther or Calvin, Wesley's whole conception of the religious life is based on an understanding of faith development.

While assuming a doctrine of original sin, Wesley affirms an equally strong doctrine of prevenient grace: the belief that God's grace works universally in all persons, attempting to prompt them to recognize their sin and turn toward God. When persons do so, they are justified, granted forgiveness of their sins. On this basis, they are now able to participate in a process of sanctification. Hence, prevenient grace, repentance, justification, and sanctification are related sequentially, with one building on and following the other. Moreover, faith and good works are not set over against one another; faith is seen as working through love. Indeed, Wesley believes that Christians are to move toward perfection in this lifetime, achieving "entire sanctification" (perfection in love of God and neighbor), if possible. Without faith development, the religious life will not reach fruition.

Faith development, in the broad sense in which we are using it, is an important part of the Christian tradition. As we have seen, however, there are important differences between the Christian churches as to how this topic is conceived. The responses of the different churches to the recent work in faith development reflect these historic, theological underpinnings.

CONTEMPORARY FAITH DEVELOPMENT

To a large extent, the recent discussion of faith development has been sparked by advances in developmental psychology. Two different schools of developmental theory have been important in that regard: the life cycle and the structural developmental. Life cycle theorists, like Erik Erikson (*Childhood and Society*, 1950) and Daniel Levinson (*The Seasons of a Man's Life*, 1978), focus on the entire course of human life, setting forth the various stages people pass through as a result of biological maturation, intellectual development, and alterations in social roles and statuses that correspond to these changes. Broadly speaking, they focus on the predictable issues that confront individuals at different points in their lives.

A number of persons in pastoral care and Christian education have attempted to draw on insights from this school of developmental psychology to chart the impact of movement through the life cycle on the development of faith. Over twenty-five years ago, Lewis Joseph Sherrill, in *The Struggle of the Soul* (1953) argued that the various stages of the life cycle present persons with a choice: they can either move forward and "enter upon some new level of responsibility and recompense" in their faith or they can "shrink back," losing the possibility of a fuller religious life.

In a more recent work, *Christian Life Patterns* (1979), Evelyn Eaton Whitehead and James Whitehead draw on Erikson's work to chart the possibilities for faith development during each stage of life. Drawing on a Roman Catholic theological framework, they view grace as working within and transforming natural, human development. Grace is presented as expanding the patterns of human growth, enabling persons to deepen their relationship to God and their neighbor as they move through the life cycle.

A second, extremely influential understanding of faith development has emerged from the structural developmental school of developmental psychology. This understanding of faith development is found in the work of James Fowler and those who have drawn on his work—Sharon Parks, Romney Moseley, Robert Kegan, and the author. Before describing Fowler's work, a few comments of introduction to the structural developmental tradition are in order.

The structural developmental tradition builds on a fundamental insight that has dominated philosophy since Kant: human understanding does not merely copy the external world but shapes it according to internal categories of knowing. Jean Piaget, the originator of this approach to psychology, argues that there is a developmental history to the acquisition of these internal categories (*The Psychology of the Child*, 1969). The term "structural developmental" refers to the fact that people are viewed as passing through various stages in the way that they structure experience. Unlike life cycle theorists, the structural developmentalists describe a series of stages that persons may or may not move through. A stage is not so much a predictable set of life issues as a distinctive style of organizing experience.

Drawing on Piaget, James Fowler describes six stages of faith development, plus a seventh "prestage." Before describing these stages, we must first grasp what Fowler means by the term "faith," drawing our attention to those persons beside Piaget who have informed his thought, Erik Erikson and H. Richard Niebuhr.

From Erikson's ego psychology, Fowler gains a broader understanding of the subject of development, allowing him to expand Piaget's narrow focus on cognition (intellectual development) to a more complex understanding of the self. It is Niebuhr (*Radical Monotheism and Western Culture*, 1960), however, who is the most decisive influence on Fowler's work. Fowler wrote his dissertation and first book on Niebuhr and has been deeply influenced by him in three fundamental ways.

First, he adopts Niebuhr's understanding of faith as a human universal. By faith, both writers refer to something much broader than our religious beliefs or trust in God. All persons are seen as having faith, whether they participate in organized religion or not. All people form centers of value and meaning to which they give their trust and loyalty. Second, Fowler takes over a transformational understanding of grace from Niebuhr. Faith as a human universal inevitably focuses on centers of value and meaning that are not worthy of persons' ultimate trust and loyalty. When it does, it is idolatrous and must be transformed by the power of God's grace. Hence, it is proper to speak of the transformation of human faith toward Christian faith. Third, Fowler's portrayal of the endpoint of faith development is deeply influenced by Niebuhr's concept of radically monotheistic faith. By this concept, both men describe a style of faith that has moved beyond a narrow allegiance to penultimate or tribal gods and finds its identity in a universal community that is grounded in God's love for all that is. The final stage of Fowler's theory, universalizing faith, describes persons who apprehend the possibility of an "inclusive commonwealth of being" and who strive to actualize these universalizing apprehensions.

In drawing on Piaget, Erikson, and Niebuhr, Fowler has formulated a complex theory of stages that chart the self's structuring of centers of value and meaning. These can be described briefly as follows:

While *undifferentiated faith* represents a "prestage" in Fowler's theory, it is seen as influencing faith at later stages. During the earliest part of infancy, the child does not differentiate between self and the surrounding world. Only gradually, on the basis of biological maturation and cognitive development, does the infant become aware of others as separate. As this begins to take place, understandings are formed of primal others who communicate a sense that life is basically trustworthy and good or something to be feared.

Intuitive-projective faith (stage one) corresponds with Piaget's preoperational stage in which children do not yet have the capacity to use concrete forms of reason to order their experience. This makes it difficult for them to sort out fact and fantasy, for they do not yet have the ability to follow causal explanations. Nonetheless, they are composing centers of value and meaning in terms of images—vague, internal representations. While fantasy-filled, these images continue to exert a tremendous influence at later stages, and if a person is raised in a theistic environment, he or she frequently forms some of his or her most important images of God during this stage.

Mythic-literal faith (stage two) is closely related to the child's acquisition of the ability to order concrete experience along rational lines (what Piaget calls concrete operations), allowing him or her to do several things: to differentiate the "real" world from the world of fantasy; to order experience in a temporal sequence; and to construct the perspective of other individuals in a simple fashion. These cognitive advances serve as the basis of the most important characteristic of this stage: the ability to narratize experience. Children now can remember and spontaneously generate stories to form their centers of value and meaning. Children who are brought up as members of a religious community can draw on the stories of that community to compose their own narratives of the divine. The symbols that are a part of these stories are understood in a literal fashion; hence, the title of this stage.

Synthetic-conventional faith (stage three) is closely related to the acquisition of early formal operations in Piaget's theory: the ability to reason abstractly and hypothetically. This cognitive advance, which frequently occurs during early adolescence, brings about a revolution in persons' ability to take the perspective of other individuals and groups, a key characteristic of this stage. Simply put, they now become attuned to the internal evaluations of significant others and the norms of the groups with which they identify. To a large extent, this stage is characterized by conformity to the conventional definitions of life's meaning and purpose held by these persons and groups. These conventions are tacitly held; that is, they are internalized without explicit, critical examination. Hence, people in this stage employ a style of faith in which they are highly dependent on the values and beliefs of the conventional ethos with which they identify.

Many people in our culture do not reach the stage of *individuative-reflective faith (stage four)* or the ones that follow. Individuative-reflective faith is characterized by a fuller use of formal operations than is found at the previous stage. In this stage, people form a systematic, explicit set of values and beliefs that are critically self-chosen and compared with other possibilities. Values and beliefs tacitly held at the previous stage now become conscious and are subject to critical scrutiny. Persons in this stage, thus, are engaging in a process of individuation: defining who they are and the nature of those ideas they hold to be true. Typically, they employ a dichotomizing style of reasoning by which they compare systems of thought in an either/or fashion. Hence, they define themselves over against other persons or groups who are caricatured in significant ways.

Assuming the individuation of the previous stage, people in the stage of *conjunctive faith (stage five)* now recognize the limitations of the system of values and beliefs they have constructed. They are not best described as relativistic, however, but as employing a healthy perspectivalism—the awareness that all truth, especially ultimate truth, is apprehended from a limited, finite perspective. Instead of defining themselves over against others, these persons now possess a newfound openness, especially to people and groups who do not fit neatly into the clear-cut categories formed at earlier stages. The title of this stage refers to the tendency to join together multiple perspectives, even to the point of living with paradoxical formulations. This stage of faith recovers the role of symbols in expressing multiple truths simultaneously in ways that go beyond the tendency to reduce symbols to their conceptual meanings.

Universalizing faith (stage six) is extremely rare. Building on the perspectivalism of the previous stage, universalizing faith now apprehends a transcendent source in which these multiple perspectives are grounded. It recognizes the One beyond the many. All that is is based on this transcendent ground, including all people and groups. Universalizing apprehensions give rise to an identification with a universal community. Persons in this stage move beyond the ability to hold in tension multiple perspectives and truths to a position in which they are willing to spend themselves on behalf of a universal community. They are especially sensitive to social structures that exclude or oppress members of this universal community, denying them their worth. People in this stage, thus, are frequently at odds with the powers that be, articulating and enacting a vision of the universal community that is not present in life as it is.

CRITICAL ISSUES

In this final section, we will briefly examine two critical questions that have been raised about the recent discussion of faith development in light of the way this topic has been understood in theology. Once more, special emphasis will be placed on James Fowler's work, since he remains the single most important contemporary theorist in this area.

The first critical question asks whether a developmental pattern per se is adequate to describe the Christian life. This question largely has come from representatives of the Lutheran and Reformed churches and grows out of their belief that notions of moral progress or growth in grace have an inherent tendency toward works righteousness. They also argue that a developmental perspective that is grounded in psychology seems to make natural patterns of human growth the presupposition of grace, while, in fact, God's grace breaks into human life from beyond, justifying and sanctifying a fallen humanity. Roman Catholics and United Methodists, in contrast, have frequently seen affinities between a developmental paradigm, as presented by those like Fowler, and their understandings of growth in the religious life.

There is no simple way of resolving these deeply rooted theological differences. Alternatives to a developmental paradigm have their own problems. For example, some, like James Loder, James Smart, and H. Shelton Smith, have argued that a crisis pattern is more adequate to describe the Christian life, a pattern in which grace is portrayed as intersecting human life in a series of transforming moments. This approach tends toward "occasionalism," however, a position in which God's relationship to human life and historical existence is viewed so exclusively as an event that little acknowledgment is made of the ways that God relates to these things in an ongoing fashion.

It is important to note that each of the Christian churches at some point takes into account the very real differences that characterize persons across the life span and in different structural stages. Even conservative members of the Lutheran and Reformed traditions recognize that proclamation of the gospel to children and youth is somewhat different than to adults. Their theological framework, however, leads them to appropriate the recent discussion of faith development at the level of pastoral or educational strategy, which is clearly differentiated from the activity by which persons are justified and sanctified.

A second criticism focuses specifically on Fowler's work, arguing that his use of structuralism to describe human faith distorts this phenomenon, for faith can only be described in terms of its object: God. This criticism focuses on Piaget's influence on Fowler, calling attention to the way that Fowler has accepted Piaget's distinction between structure (the underlying style of faith knowing) and content (the substantive beliefs and values that are being structured).

This criticism overlooks the Niebuhrian influence on Fowler and the ways that he has taken over Niebuhr's understanding of generic, human faith. Theologically speaking, Fowler can argue that all persons are created for relationship with God and, as such, inevitably form centers of value and meaning to which they offer their trust and loyalty. This argument is valid as far as it goes.

However, Fowler has not yet offered a full-scale examination of human sin, something that Niebuhr always included in his descriptions of natural, human faith. This omission is exacerbated by the fact that Fowler's stages of faith appear to amalgamate natural faith and sanctification, items which are clearly distinguished in Calvin and Niebuhr. Qualities of the self that are morally and religiously desirable—qualities that are properly described under the rubric of sanctification—are presented as the upper stages of a developmental sequence of natural faith.

Clearly, more theological clarification is needed on this matter. Indeed, within the confines of this brief article, it has become apparent that a wide range of important theological issues has been raised by the recent discussion of faith development. Even as they make use of the important insights that faith development research has begun to generate for Christian education and pastoral care, the different churches would do well to reflect on the difficult theological issues their own tradition raises with regard to this important area in the Christian life. *See also* Adult Development; Cognitive Development; Interdisciplinary Studies; Life Map; Moral Development; Psychosocial Development.

FOR FURTHER REFERENCE

Fowler, James. *Becoming Adult, Becoming Christian*. San Francisco: Harper & Row, 1984.
———. *To See the Kingdom: The Theological Vision of H. Richard Niebuhr*. Nashville, TN: Abingdon, 1974.
Gilligan, Carol. *In a Different Voice*. Cambridge, MA: Harvard University Press, 1982.
Kegan, Robert. *The Evolving Self*. Cambridge, MA: Harvard University Press, 1982.
Loevinger, Jane. *Ego Development*. San Francisco: Jossey-Bass, 1976.

R. R. Osmer

Family Cluster

A family cluster is a group of four or five family units that contract to meet together periodically for shared educational experiences related to their living in relationship within their families. A cluster provides mutual support, training in skills that facilitate living in the family relationship, and celebration of their life and beliefs together. An outgrowth of marriage enrichment and parent/child enrichment, the model of the family cluster was developed in 1970 at the First Baptist Church, Rochester, New York, under the leadership of Margaret Sawin as an approach to strengthening the family as an interacting, human system. Families participating in a cluster may include the traditional nuclear family, a one-parent family, a family with stepparents or stepchildren, or an extended family. Single persons can also be integrated into the family cluster.

The undergirding theoretical foundations of the model are found in a number of disciplines. Family systems theory is the base. Individuals in families are part of the learning process, as well as the system as a whole. This is the dynamic that has the greatest impact on individuals and also strengthens their living as a human unit. Group dynamics theory is the means. Families of all kinds meet in the cluster group and share their common concerns and joys as relational units. The dynamics of the intermingling of many subgroups is used.

Growth and development theory is the end result. Families are pointed toward better functioning so they can learn to live together in deeper relationship. Experiential learning theory is the tool. The techniques of experiential education that use an action-reflection mode are tapped to educate all ages as well as each system as a whole. Relational theology is the philosophical base. Family relationships provide the deepest meaning for living as well as the training ground for values and moral education. Therefore, relational theology is utilized at its most meaningful level.

Training for leaders of family clusters has been held since 1972 through thousands of thirty-hour training workshops and one-week residential laboratories. Thus, many people have learned to lead family clusters in variously sized churches of many denominations and faiths. The model has also been used in mental health and social work agencies, public and parochial schools, camps and retreat centers, as well as with families of military and clergy groups. It has been utilized in urbanized countries around the world, as family life undergoes vast changes in technological societies. *See also* Action-Reflection; Family Life Education; Group Dynamics; Parenting; Systems Theory.

FOR FURTHER REFERENCE

Sawin, Margaret M. *Family Enrichment with Family Clusters.* Valley Forge, PA: Judson, 1979.

Sawin, Margaret M., ed. *Hope for Families.* New York: Sadlier, 1982.

M. M. *Sawin*

Family Life Education

Family life education is geared toward promoting the development of the family as a unit or system. A family is a group of people who consider themselves bound to each other by enduring ties and responsible for each other's well-being. So, for example, such a unit could be a nuclear family, a one-parent family, or a family with no children.

Family systems theory is based on the belief that the family is a natural social grouping. Every individual functions within some larger ecological unit, and for most people it is the family. A system is a complex pattern of various parts working together for the existence and survival of some greater whole. A family system is the complex of patterns of behavior and ways of functioning with each other that family members believe necessary in order for the family to survive and perform its tasks.

The family can be directly described then as a system of interdependent relationships engaged in change and adaptation and geared to the growth and support of each member. The experience of family gives us our first sense of who we are and of how we relate to others; it is the basis of our understanding and interaction. It is also the foundation of our experience of God.

For more than a decade, researchers have argued that the family mediates between the child's genetic and cultural endowments. For the very young, the family is the central arena of education. Although for older children the focus shifts to school and for adults to occupations, what transpires in the family still has a considerable effect on the behavior and inner psychic process of the individual; the family as the basic social system directly affects religious values as well as moral and human values.

It follows then that any attempt at educational models for family ministry must be ecological in nature, that is, they must address the family as a unit. This is difficult in a society in which the individual is celebrated and in the professions the preparation for which emphasizes service for individuals. The notion of family as a unit and system is relatively new, and many working today in the helping professions have not been prepared to deal with families in this way. But there is growing awareness that if education is conceived of as a lifelong process, then what is needed to engage in family life education is not only a fuller understanding of the processes of education within the family, but also to see familial education in the context of multiple and ever-changing relationships within the family.

FAMILY LIFE EDUCATION

Age Level	Teaching Goals	Methods
Preschool	As children begin to differentiate between self and others, teach them to value both; begin to teach positive relational attitudes (i.e., trust) and skills (i.e., problem solving).	Adults must meet the basic needs of children, provide them with love, care, and security, and model positive relational attitudes and skills; as they grow, children should be given chances to develop and practice relational skills; play areas might include a miniature "home-living center" to encourage children to play "family"; even very young children should be included in family activities.
Grades 1–3	Children begin to grasp the concept of family and the various roles of people in the family (parent, child, etc.).	Stories of families can be told; children can be encouraged to share their own experiences and feelings in words, pictures, and role plays; varieties of families and family roles can begin to be discussed; intergenerational family events can be planned (i.e., mother/daughter days).
Grades 4–8	Children continue to learn how family members can best settle their differences and help each other.	Stories, discussions, and role plays can focus on specific situations.

(continued)

Family life education focuses on helping all the members of a family system to engage in educational experiences together in order to nurture specific behaviors. Because what happens in the life of one member has impact on all members of the family unit, family education cannot be education for the adults or for the children only; it must deal with all members of the family together. The teaching process in families includes: a clear idea of what is to be taught, the awareness that parents have of what they are modeling, knowledge of how to interest others in following that model, and communication to make it work.

One form of family education is the family cluster. This is a group of four or five family units (or living units) that agree to meet together periodically for shared learning experiences related to the concerns, questions, and problems of their family lives. Meetings provide feedback on modeling techniques and the opportunity to practice new ones.

Intergenerational events in church or synagogue provide occasions for two or three generations to meet together. These could begin with a meal. Film or video are ways of presenting a subject of interest to families. Informal role playing portrays family situations and takes on added dimension when adults and children or adolescents switch roles.

Family understanding and enjoyment are enhanced through a storyteller or puppet performance, which interests even the youngest family members. Projects such as involving families in a spring clean-up of buildings or grounds builds community. Making seasonal home decorations such as an Advent wreath interests all ages. Worship together is both an expression of the family in the presence of God and a model for family worship.

Parent meetings provide opportunities for adults to focus in depth on concerns of family life together, including the religious development of children and of families. Resource speakers make available specialized knowledge and give time for

Age Level	Teaching Goals	Methods
High School	Issues of autonomy and independence are important and must be addressed directly; encourage a broader definition of family as concepts of relationship, interdependence, and community are better understood.	Areas of conflict and tension between family members should be discussed, as should possible ways of identifying with the family rather than withdrawing from it; role plays continue to be useful.
Adults	Establishing family life and enriching it over time and through change is a key focus; balancing and interweaving family, community, and career concerns is also key.	Specific marriage and family concerns can be addressed in classes and workshops; resource collections and support groups might be established to meet specific needs; cooperation both within and between families should be encouraged.
Inter-generational	Family life is best learned and enriched through intergenerational relationships and activities.	Specific intergenerational activities include family cluster meetings, family and community worship, shared meals and celebrations, joint projects for social justice and other causes, recreational activities and entertainment gatherings, and classes and workshops.

answering questions. Meetings of parents and religious education teachers deal with the specific roles of each in the religious education of children.

Family camping provides several days of relaxed time when families share both with their own members and with other families the pleasure of being together. Events similar to those suggested earlier address concerns, but games and other entertainment and times for worship are other components of a weekend.

To summarize, family life education is a program of learning experiences planned and guided to develop the potential of individuals in their present and future roles as family members. Its central concept is that of relationships through which personality develops, about which individuals make decisions to which they are committed, and in which they gain conviction of self-worth. In religious education circles, with the growing awareness of churches of the realities and problems facing families and with the establishment of structures designed to enable and facilitate marriage and family life, family life education promises to become more widespread in the years to come. See also Family Cluster; Parenting; Systems Theory; Worship, Family.

FOR FURTHER REFERENCE

Napier, Augustus Y., with Carl A. Whitaker. The Family Crucible. New York: Harper & Row, 1978.

Satir, Virginia. Peoplemaking. Palo Alto, CA: Science and Behavior Books, 1972.

Sawin, Margaret M. Family Enrichment with Family Clusters. Valley Forge, PA: Judson, 1979.

G. Durka

Family Worship

See Worship, Family.

Feedback

A reciprocal or reflexive moment in an act of communication in which the sender of the original message receives information concerning the way that message has been received by the other party or parties is termed feedback. This information may take the form of a direct message offered by the other party in the conversation or the form of an indirect response (gestures, facial expressions, or other nonverbal signals). The effect of feedback is to indicate to the original sender that the message has been received and the nature of the receiver's evaluation of that message. This information then becomes part of the sender's formation of further messages, thus enhancing the process of communication.

Religious educators need to be aware of feedback and ways in which they can learn how their efforts at communication are being received by recipients. In this way they can modify the approach for more effective teaching. Committee members need to be aware of the responses each is making so that effective communication can take place. Sometimes a person (perhaps a helping teacher) or a committee is designated as process observer to monitor the feedback and share impressions later with the leader or group. Feedback, as popularly used, means reactions, opinions, and ideas solicited from a group by the leader(s) in order that their responses may be used for evaluation and further planning. See also Body Language; Communication Theory; Conversation; Evaluation; Process Observer.

W. A. Smith

Feminist Movement

The feminist movement is a way by which women have sought together to develop self-awareness and self-assurance, to participate in existing power structures and to influence these power structures in their behalf, and to change cultural attitudes toward women. It seeks alternatives to the patriarchal system. Patriarchy is a method of viewing the world in terms of one person (or group) having power over another. The feminist movement seeks to change this perspective to one of "power shared."

Recent historical research has discovered in many countries and many centuries groups of women who bonded together to combat patriarchy. Because history generally has been written by those in control, the records of many of these efforts have been destroyed, lost, or in one way or another made invisible. Not until means of communication and travel extended all over the world did feminists in various countries become known to one another. The beginning of feminism as a movement has been likened to the spores of mushrooms sprouting in the darkness and rising simultaneously around the world. The movement has since stimulated research and analysis to investigate the connection between patriarchy and such ancient and modern ills as racism, war, poverty, ageism, and anti-Semitism.

IMPACT ON RELIGIOUS EDUCATION

Leaders in religious education became aware early on that the church perpetuated patriarchy and its more recent form, sexism, through such things as the power of imagery in story and picture. A task force of the United Methodist Board of Social Concerns presented a documented analysis of certain nursery materials that exposed previously unexamined patriarchal symbols and images that implied that "God made it to be this way." Mothers were pictured wearing an apron, carrying a broom, cooking. Little girls were stereotyped as weak and inactive, watching while little boys fished, climbed trees, and went swimming.

Those who made the study drew up guidelines and recommended that the entire curriculum at every age level receive the same scrutiny. The response was far from positive—indeed, in some quarters, there was adamant opposition to any such study. On the other hand, it came as a great shock to many leaders when they realized that religious education was encouraging a form of idolatry in children and adults. For so long as God is portrayed as a man in the sky ruling over all, then both men and women give power to the male to rule and control on earth. It is increasingly accepted that sexism in the life of the church is one of the most powerful theological issues the church has yet to deal with.

The first theological school to develop a course on the theological dimension of feminism (Drew University Theological School) did so out of its religious education division, examining the language the church habitually employs in its mission and liturgy.

The National Council of the Churches of Christ in the U.S.A. appointed an interdenominational committee to produce guidelines for choosing and creating language that would be inclusive of all people related to the church. In the process, they discovered that such a language would also eliminate the elements of idolatry commonly found in liturgy. The struggle for change of language continues to be much resisted within the church itself, since far too many symbols are held onto for nostalgic rather than redemptive reasons.

Florence Howe of the Feminist Press pointed out in the late 1970s how curriculum in higher education began to change radically—both in content and method—once women's studies were introduced into university and college curricula. The same has happened in churches where feminism has been allowed to challenge the worship and education life of the church toward respect for all people. One change in method is the recognition of the power of presence. Abstract teaching is giving way to learning to be present to one another: telling one's own story with its hurts, disappointments, good feelings, and joys. Asking forgiveness and expressing love and gratefulness to one another takes the place of "God loves everybody"—everybody is never met, never comes, nor can be imagined. Telling one's own story leads from my story to your story, and in time to feeling "we are all a part of a long, long story."

Religious education has already begun to reject the theory/practice paradigm only to find its reverse action/reflection paradigm rearranging the same old pieces. The search for a dynamic union of the two is still in process. The use of case studies and simulation games appeared to provide an answer, but all the techniques in the world cannot guarantee we will hear one another, or develop sensitive and loving relationships with one another. According to the feminist movement, so long as we are under the spell of dualism and a "power-over" perception of this world, we shall seek for magic methods of teaching. Members of the church are too often baptized into a dogma instead of into the life and death of a living, vital community that extends into dusty streets and hungry homes.

Since that first study of sexism in children's stories and pictures, increasing attention has been given to good stories and the place of *good* art in the life of the church. Authentic stories and art speak for themselves. They do not require moralizing. They speak of reality and eternal values.

Strange as it may seem, the feminist movement has begun to open to men the vocation of teaching children. Those who have experimented with this report that both teachers and children experience a new sense of community and a new vision of a liturgy that would include men, women, and children together playing out what their lives mean when they experience the divine together.

The religious feminist movement has also affected religious education by stressing a ministry of the laity. Once adults gain the courage to think theologically fewer "outside experts" are called in to do their theological work, and more men and women and youth begin exploring for themselves the depths of their own life's questions, thus teaching one another. At last we turn to the effort of becoming more human and less playing at being God. It is given us to *be human* not to be God, not to be Satan. Nothing on earth is more powerful than a truly human community through which the Spirit lives and works. *See also* Conscientization; Consciousness-raising; Language, Inclusive; Liberation Theology; Social Action; Social Justice, Education for.

N. Morton

Field Trip

A field trip is an activity involving a visit to some location other than the usual classroom or meeting place. It apparently developed as a designation for trips away from the laboratory or the study to the field for observation and contact with objects of study in their natural environment, as in botany, zoology, and other sciences. It has been adopted by social scientists as they make trips to the field—to social agencies, clinics, ethnic groups, and to various cultures as in anthropological studies. In education the field trip has come to denote a visit for educational purposes to any site away from the classroom or school. It is a trip with definite purpose and plan, and it should be related to the curriculum under study.

In religious education the field trip has been used not only to increase knowledge of biblical materials, other religions, church history, religious approaches to social problems and moral questions, and matters of worship and liturgy, but it has increasingly become an important means for expanding the experience of teachers and students in relation to the community in which religious education takes place, making people aware of others and raising consciousness of problems. The sites for field trips range from the more obvious churches, synagogues, temples, and other places of worship, through public schools, hospitals, government agencies, police and fire headquarters, and cultural centers, on to such controversial locations as abortion clinics, nuclear power plants, and military installations. Perhaps because the term "field trip" has connotations of entertainment instead of being regarded as an integral part of a curriculum that focuses on the whole person, the term appears not to be used as much in religious educational literature as in previous periods. Instead, one is likely to find such an expression as "changing the setting for teaching."

Regardless of what the session is called, a successful field trip demands careful planning and preparation. Practical suggestions for preparation and carrying out the field trip include:

1. Allow students to participate to the extent possible in deciding on, planning for, and carrying out field experiences.

2. Plan carefully.

3. Make certain the learners understand the purpose of the trip and its relevance to the ongoing curriculum.

4. Arrange for adequate assistants.

5. Give thorough instructions to assistants, both staff and volunteers.

6. Familiarize yourself with background information on the field to be visited.

7. Help participants to sort out the features of the experience most relevant to the curriculum goals.

8. Evaluate the experience afterward both personally and with the group.

A field trip should add a dimension to the group learning experience that cannot be gained in the usual setting.

N. H. Thompson

Finance

Adequate financing is important in achieving the religious education goals of the congregation or parish. In most cases, financing will be a part of the regular budget building processes of the congregation. The board or committee responsible for religious education will need to be aware of the budgeting process and time line in order to do effective financial planning.

The group responsible for education will want to give primary attention to the needs of leaders and participants in all of the programs under its care. These may include the Sunday church school, fellowships for children and youth, the church library and media center, summer camps and conferences, scouting and other youth service programs, children's and youth choirs, special adult education programs, vacation church or Bible schools, family education programs, programs for single persons and other special constituencies, and leader training programs. Provision of the resources needed by leaders and learners of the educational programs is a significant ministry of the board or committee.

Having identified all of the educational programs for which resources are to be provided, the next step in budget building is to develop goals for each one. Goals describe the achievements that the groups and the board or committee hope for in a given period of time. Leaders and participants of groups are involved in this process by setting their own goals and referring them to the board or committee. If changes need to be made, the committee does this in consultation with the group. This makes goal setting a collegial process.

With educational goals in hand, the board or committee turns its attention to the specific items requiring financial undergirding. In most cases, the following will comprise a complete budget.

Sufficient copies of the basic *curriculum materials* for each teacher or leader and each student or group member need to be provided. There may also be a need for supplementary resources such as books, magazines, maps, films, videotapes, music, displays, and learning centers. These permanent resources may be available in the library for use by several groups. When resources are purchased for a particular group, it is good steward-

ship after they are used to place them in the library or media center.

Learning experiences are enhanced by activities requiring a variety of *expendable supplies* for arts and crafts, writing, creating posters and displays, drawing, and model construction. Keeping a central supply of these materials ensures their availability to teachers without having to spend valuable preparation time in shopping.

Equipment for effective education ranges from easels to VCRs, monitors, and personal computers. For expensive, permanent equipment, a careful study of the total needs of all groups is good economy and stewardship. The needs of programs in the congregation other than religious education also need to be taken into account. The board or committee for education may be given the responsibility for providing and maintaining such equipment for the whole church.

In many congregations the education board or committee may be assigned responsibility for *special events* at festive seasons and other occasions. These may include plays, pageants, family nights, and picnics. The financial requirements of such events are sometimes overlooked and consequently place a strain on the education budget.

Many congregations look to the education board or committee to provide and oversee the *library and media center* for the entire church. For this large task, a subcommittee is often formed. Funds for purchases of new books and audiovisual resources, repairs and maintenance need to be carefully assessed.

Repair and replacement of equipment is another concern. It is important to keep equipment and resources in good working order and to know when it is most cost-effective to discard items and purchase new ones. A regular budget item for these purposes will lessen the possibility that "emergencies" may cut into the regular education budget.

There is no higher budget priority than providing *leader support and training*. Teachers and leaders need to feel comfortable and competent in their tasks. Such support may include regular resources such as periodicals and leadership training experiences within and beyond the congregation. Adequate funds need to be provided for ongoing programs in the congregation and scholarship assistance for attending events in other locations.

The religious education budget may be supplemented by class offerings, special gifts, and memorial funds, especially for large items. Here, as well as in regular budgeting, the financial undergirding of education needs to be seen in the context of the stewardship and financing of the total church budget. The religious education program belongs to and is the responsibility of the whole church. A key way of symbolizing and actualizing this wholeness is through faithful and responsible financing. *See also* Facilities; Goals;

Leadership Development; Management; Planning; Religious Education Committee.

R. F. Glover

Finger Painting

Finger painting has proven to be an effective means of self-expression in religious education as elsewhere. Direct contact with materials using fingers, fists, knuckles, thumbs, palms, wrists, forearms, and elbows provides satisfying results with little skill. The soothing texture encourages relaxation, the bright colors are inviting, and the smell is refreshing. The sounds add interest as the hands swish, pat, and plop across the surface. And finger painting with pudding adds the experience of taste.

Preschoolers use finger painting for self-expression. Older children create murals and realistic scenes using a variety of colors and textures; for example, adding coffee grounds produces a good material for depicting the earth. Even adults use the technique for making original gift wraps.

Painting may be done on shiny paper, oilcloth, heavy plastic, or on tables with enamel, formica, or plastic tops. The paints may be homemade (liquid starch and dry tempera) or purchased. Smocks for children and a well-covered floor area are advisable. Cleanup is usually simple with warm soapy water and sponge. *See also* Art in Religious Education; Crafts; Visual Methods.

D. C. Borchert

Flannelgraph

Flannelgraph, one of many visual media for the illustration of stories within church and mission settings, can be used effectively with preschool through early primary grades. Flannelgraph provisions include figures made of sturdy paper and backed with materials that will adhere to flannel backgrounds. Simple handmade or commercially produced backgrounds may enhance a story.

In order to be employed effectively the use of flannelgraph materials takes preparation and practice. Figures must be strategically placed in order to be easily accessible to the teacher. Practice will ensure that the story action flows smoothly. Children may be encouraged to participate by placing figures on the background as the teacher tells the story. Primary-aged children may retell the story as they put the figures in place.

The use of flannelgraph provides more action and drama than flat pictures but does not require expensive projection equipment. It has the potential of bringing greater comprehension to children concerning biblical settings and other aspects of a story that may be unfamiliar to them. *See also* Preschool Children; Visual Methods.

D. C. Borchert

Francke, August Hermann

August Hermann Francke (1663–1727), Lutheran pastor and professor of theology, was a pioneer in the field of the education of the poor and in child welfare. Deeply influenced by the German Pietist Philipp Jakob Spener, he established at Glaucha (1692) an elementary school for the poor, using university students as tutors. A Latin school for wealthy youth followed at Halle. The work expanded by 1698 into the Francke Foundations, which included an orphanage school, a teacher training school, a dispensary, and a paper mill and printing shop.

Spener's emphasis on personal piety at the expense of dogma was thus extended by Francke with practical expressions of concern for and service to those in need. To this work he brought theological concern, broad practical vision, and considerable administrative ability. Attacks mainly originated with those who saw his practical pietism as threatening the fabric of Lutheranism by draining off religious interest, energy, talent, and resources into "good works." *See also* History of Christian Education.

D. C. Wyckoff

Freedom

The theme of freedom has been basic in Jewish and Christian teaching. A central event in the Hebrew Bible is the release of the Israelites from bondage to the Egyptian pharaohs. In the New Testament the apostle Paul speaks of being freed to Christ from bondage to death. To be enslaved to Christ is to be freed from the bondage of sin. To be redeemed is to have the price paid by which one's freedom is given. The Gospel of John says that in following Jesus we will know the truth, and the truth shall make us free (8:32). Religious educators see their task as helping learners understand what freedom means, to desire it, to will to have it, and to experience it.

HISTORICAL UNDERSTANDINGS

In the ancient world a significant question was whether freedom came primarily through knowledge or will. The Socratic tradition represented by Plato and Aristotle taught that knowledge of the truth makes one free. Augustine, however, taught that intellectual knowledge of the truth is not enough. One must *will* to know the truth. Only then does that truth make one free. Only as people confess their sins and accept God's forgiveness do they gain both freedom and understanding. This particular issue is important for modern theories of religious education. The Socratic tradition suggests that one can learn to be free, but the Augustinian tradition holds that freedom comes by a change of will prior to new understanding.

The Roman Catholic tradition balanced both the Socratic and Augustinian approaches to freedom, but the Protestant Reformation brought a renewal of the Augustinian doctrine. Luther taught that the person who is enslaved to Christ is the freest of all persons and that it is not necessary to participate in the sacraments to be free. Rather, one's freedom is a gift of God. Each person may freely address God in the confidence that God in Christ hears and accepts. Teaching and preaching became important to Luther because they keep people from misunderstanding freedom and thus from falling back into some form of enslavement. Freedom is God's gift to humanity in Christ, but it needs constantly to be properly proclaimed and taught. Calvin's doctrine located freedom in God's eternal election prior to human experience. Those whom God chooses are called to embody the kingdom of God.

For both Roman Catholic and Protestant doctrines of freedom the problem of error became paramount. In the medieval church the conscience represented the natural human understanding of goodness, but the conscience could err in many ways. The courts of conscience were for the sake of correcting the erroneous conscience. Protestant churches generally looked to the secular rulers to enforce the church's decision. However, the Anabaptists taught that members of the church should correct one another (but without the use of the sword). Out of the centuries of struggle over error came the modern doctrine of the freedom of conscience.

The Enlightenment of the eighteenth century raised the question of whether certain rights such as life, liberty, and happiness belong to all human life. Liberty was then interpreted in terms of freedom of religious belief, speech, and association. The nineteenth century raised the question of whether economic freedoms may not be as basic as political freedoms.

MODERN UNDERSTANDINGS

Modern understandings of freedom have been influenced by Immanuel Kant, John Stuart Mill, and Sigmund Freud. In Kant's view freedom comes in conforming to the moral principles that govern human life. Not to conform is to be propelled by unreasonable and ultimately destructive impulses. In Mill's view freedom is to be able to do whatever does not limit the freedom of another. In Freud freedom is restricted by inner psychological forces in which the conscious self is frequently in conflict with impulses of the unconscious self.

A contemporary theological doctrine of freedom must begin with God's grace in Jesus Christ to those who are responsive to him. To be free a person must be responsive to conscience and to God, but this can easily fall into a conformism or false understanding. Freedom is a constant aspiration to be led by the truth, accompanied by a willingness to be corrected. It is an interaction of thought and act carried out in gratitude for God's freeing grace. Freedom is to follow one's conscience in dialogue with other persons, as these are being shaped by God's will.

The range of freedom depends in part upon one's maturity. The child is free when able to respond to life in play, while youth are free when able to respond to life with questions of meaning. Each can be devotion to God.

The range in freedom also depends on a variety of other realities. Religious freedom is basic to political and economic freedom. The modern doctrine of freedom needs to keep the inner sense of God's grace joined to outward embodiment in political and economic realities. Educators can seek to keep faith from falling into slavery to anything except the love of Christ. But questions of health, politics, economics, and social maturity are also closely related to the religious doctrine of freedom and are therefore of concern to educators.

TEACHING ABOUT FREEDOM

Teachers and parents teach about freedom by giving freedom. They offer children concrete experiences like making choices and responding to life in play. Elementary age children learn, in addition, through hearing and talking about examples in biblical history, later religious history, and contemporary life. Adolescents need the opportunity to discuss experiences and the risk of choice and to respond to life with questions of meaning. Adults talk and act upon the notion of freedom within the context of contemporary questions and policies. *See also* Aristotle; Augustine; Faith; Grace; History of Christian Education.

D. E. Miller

Freudian Influences

The work of Sigmund Freud (1856–1939), physician, neurologist, and founder of psychoanalysis, has been a significant influence in psychology, education, and religious education. Freud was born in Freiberg, Moravia, of middle-class Jewish parents, lived and worked in Vienna, Austria, and died in exile in London. His sixty-three years of work produced more than six hundred papers and books, the best known of which deal with the clinical theory of psychoanalysis, including psychopathology and psychosexual development. Freud developed systematic propositions about human behavior and motivation and supplied the foundational concepts for modern psychotherapy and what may be referred to loosely as psychodynamics.

For the purposes of religious education, Freud's work in five major areas is of particular importance: development, the unconscious, sexuality, defenses, and religion. Freud emphasized overall attention to *development*, to the events of early life for the main features of character and for an understanding of personality and psychopathology. Freud's complex doctrine of the *unconscious* in mental life, including the general notion that only a small segment of the whole self is either present or accessible to the conscious self, is the center of his system (*The Interpretation of Dreams*, 1900). According to this, the conscious self is moved by the unconscious in ways it neither knows nor understands. The unconscious uses symbols that are shared by many persons to cloak magical logic and wishfulness—a seeking for immediate gratification of crude sexual and aggressive impulses. The unconscious is accessible through psychoanalysis, which interprets dreams using specific and scientifically verifiable procedures.

Freud stressed the importance of *sexuality* (defined broadly to include oral, anal, and other bodily pleasures, as well as genital sexuality) as a key area of human conduct (*Three Essays on the Theory of Sexuality*, 1905). Freud is also well known for his articulation of the Oedipus complex, which is defined as the inevitable but taboo incestuous attraction in families. Freud described *defenses* (structured ways of controlling impulse, such as repression, reaction formation, projection, etc.) and their use in the resolution of conflict and the lowering of anxiety (*Inhibitions, Symptoms and Anxiety*, 1925). Freud, an atheist passionately interested in *religion*, saw functional religion as illusory. His principal contribution in the area of religion was to structure the religious question in terms of the spontaneous wishes and requests addressed to God (*Beyond the Pleasure Principle*, 1920; *The Future of an Illusion*, 1927).

Some influential Protestant religious educators (e.g., Paul Vieth, Harrison Elliott, Otis Rice, Wayne Oates, and others) were well read in Freud by the mid-1940s. The Roman Catholic church was generally defensive toward Freud's discoveries until the early 1950s, although some insights of authors like Gregory Zilboorg, Louis Beirnaert, and Charles Odier (among others) reached the world of religious education in the United States, through, for example, a series of articles in *Cross Currents* from 1950 to 1960 (later collected as *Cross Currents of Psychiatry and Religion*). By the 1960s, Antoine Vergote (Catholic University of Louvain) and Andre Godin (Lumen Vitae, Brussels) were engaged in systematic attempts to consider the implications of a Freudian psychodynamics for religious education. A rare attempt to deal explicitly with Freud and religious education was R. S. Lee's *Your Growing Child and Religion*, published in the United Kingdom in 1963. Recently, James Loder (*The Transforming Moment*, 1981) has reinterpreted certain key notions of Freud, and Antoine Vergote (in a variety of writings) and Andre Godin (*The Psychological Dynamics of Religious Experience*, 1985) continue to produce works that take Freud seriously. Clinical pastoral education continues to use some of Freud's insights directly (especially transference and the sexual nature of life) for the education of religious professionals. But it is fair to say that Freud is less often footnoted in religious education texts than one might legitimately assume from his general influence and that Freud is yet to be taken seriously by the majority of religious educators.

The indirect influence of Freud on religious education has been considerable at least to the extent that most religious education texts have some sensitivity to psychodynamics. Overall, though, Freud's influence on the therapeutic dimensions of pastoral care has been far more marked than his influence on religious education. This may reflect a sense that to take seriously the central place of the unconscious in human life would somehow impair the work of religious education. The indirect influence of Freud on religious education is twofold: first, a general sensitivity to psychodynamics marked curriculum reform from the mid-1940s onward. Many Protestant denominations in the early years of the century, influenced by the pragmatism of John Dewey, by a philosophy of consciousness, and by an urgent need to construct a more human society, had seen the task of education, secular and religious, as social construction. While they did not abandon this perspective entirely, there was a widespread attempt after World War II to use the insights of psychodynamics to rethink such notions as growth, personality, guilt, self-esteem, sex morals, and anger. For some, the influence of psychiatry was openly acknowledged, e.g., among the Episcopalians and the National Council of the Churches of Christ. In other denominations the influence was less directly acknowledged, although by the mid-1950s most Protestant curricula would reflect changes sensitive to some of the insights of Freud and those who came after him. The second indirect influence of Freud on religious education occurred through his influence on other writers, most notably Carl Jung (who has had some influence on Roman Catholic religious education in the United States and who may be known in the Protestant world through the *Centerquest* curriculum) and Erik Erikson (whose developmental schema is widely accepted as a useful psychosocial basis for religious education). *See also* Dreams; Jungian Influences; Psychology of Religion; Psychosocial Development; Psychotherapy.

H. C. Simmons, R. H. Cram

Froebel, Friedrich

Friedrich Wilhelm August Froebel (1782–1852), one of the German pioneers of early childhood education, worked with Johann Pestalozzi at Yverdon, Switzerland, 1808–1810. His first independent educational venture, with several friends and their wives, was a school for boys, designed like Pestalozzi's as an educational community. *The Education of Man* (1826) summarized his early educational philosophy. His permanent legacy is the establishment of the kindergarten (1840).

In the kindergarten children engaged in various forms of self-activity and cooperative activities (games, songs, fingerplay, painting, clay and bead work, as well as circle activities), while the teacher encouraged their self-development. Froebel believed infant education was a vital first step toward comprehensive educational and social reform. By 1850 he had established a kindergarten training school.

Throughout Froebel's life, however, allegations of radicalism had interfered with his work, creating instability for him and his projects, and in 1851 the kindergarten movement was banned as subversive by the Prussian government. But enthusiasm for the kindergarten continued and his followers took it to other countries, particularly England and the United States.

A deep strain of mysticism, traced to the influence of Jakob Boehme, permeated his thought. Particularly in the "gifts" (blocks in the forms of cubes, cylinders, and spheres) the child was thought to intuit the divine unity. These were "gifts" because the teacher held and handed each one to the child (or threw the sphere like a ball), who then returned it. They were intuitions of divine unity because of their shapes: the sphere is a symbol of wholeness, the cube of order. Blocks can be matched or used in constructive ways, even as order is created in the universe. Thus simple objects used in play became symbolic of deeper meanings. *See also* History of Christian Education; Kindergarten; Pestalozzi, Johann Heinrich; Preschool Children.

D. C. Wyckoff

Fundamentalism

The fundamentalist movement was a reaction against the secularization of American society at the end of the nineteenth century. During that era the American Protestant church was struggling with three major philosophical issues. These issues became the focal point that precipitated the fundamentalist movement. First, Charles Darwin (1809–1882), an English naturalist, shocked the nineteenth-century world with the theory of evolution. Liberal theologians, in their attempt to modernize Christianity, advocated broadening the Christian view of the origin of life to include evolution. Conservative theologians denounced the theory as a rejection of the biblical account of creation.

The second major problem facing the Protestant church was that of biblical criticism. For example, scholars studying the Bible with literary tools rejected Mosaic authorship of the Pentateuch and theorized that the first five books of the Bible were the synthesis of various documents collected over an extended period of time and edited into one volume by a redactor. The liberal element of the Protestant church accepted the conclusions of these critics, but conservatives rejected this biblical criticism as an attack on the inerrancy and authority of scripture.

The third major philosophical problem was that of antisupernaturalism. The emerging influence of the scientific method generated an academic atmosphere that questioned faith and embraced reason. Liberal theologians began to reject the miracles of the Bible as contradictory to scientific fact. Conservatives declared their faith in the miracles of Scripture and rejected the antisupernatural mentality of the liberals.

The influence of Darwinism, higher criticism, and antisupernaturalism forced a major division in both the mainline Protestant denominations and their colleges and seminaries. The liberals advocated a Christianity based upon the moral teachings of Jesus and deemphasized doctrinal absolutes. On the other hand, the conservatives maintained their belief in the Bible as the final inerrant authority in all matters of faith and practice.

FOUNDATIONS

The fundamentalist movement received its name and impetus in 1909 from the publication of *The Fundamentals*. This collection of articles by a wide range of American and European conservatives set the doctrinal tone of the movement. Edited by R. A. Torrey (1865–1928), the articles defended five basic doctrines:

- The inspiration and infallibility of scripture

- The deity of Christ (including his virgin birth)

- The substitutionary atonement of Christ's death

- The literal resurrection of Christ from the dead

- The literal return of Christ in the Second Advent

These five doctrines were identified as the "fundamentals of the Christian faith" and it was argued that to deny these was to deny the essential nature of Christianity.

Between 1909 and 1930, fundamentalists waged a war against liberalism in the Protestant church. Fundamentalists were engaged in a furious battle to control the denominations and the wider culture. This battle climaxed in 1925 at the Scopes trial in Dayton, Tennessee. The trial captured great public attention and pitted Clarence Darrow, a brilliant criminal lawyer, against William Jennings Bryan, an articulate spokesman for the fundamentalist cause. The trial ended in public embarrassment and national disgrace for the fundamentalist cause. As a result, the fundamentalists began to withdraw from the mainstream of American religious and social life. During the 1920s, established denominations experienced a major decline in their numbers. Meanwhile, fundamentalists were involved in building new churches, organizations, colleges, and fellowships.

DIVISION FROM EVANGELICALISM

The formation of two very important organizations, the American Council of Christian Churches (ACCC) and the National Association of Evangelicals (NAE), gave birth to the separation between fundamentalism and evangelicalism in the early 1940s. In September 1941, the ACCC was organized to combat the influence of the Federal Council of Churches. The NAE, founded in 1942, developed out of dissatisfaction with the liberal dogma of the Federal Council of Churches and the negativism of the fundamentalist ACCC.

The division between evangelicalism and fundamentalism was further accented in the 1950s in a confrontation over the cooperative evangelism of Billy Graham. In 1957, Graham was issued an invitation from two separate groups of ministers to hold a crusade in New York City. The first group was conservative and insisted that all cooperating clergy sign a fundamentalist doctrinal statement. The second included mainline liberal clergy who would not assent to those basic doctrines. Graham accepted the invitation of the latter group and thereby angered the fundamentalist movement. After 1957, evangelicals were united in their defense of Graham and fundamentalists were united in their condemnation of Graham.

During the late 1960s and early 1970s fundamentalism and evangelicalism reacted differently to social upheaval of the student revolution and the hippie movement. Fundamentalists resisted the upheaval and demanded separation from it. Evangelicalism, on the other hand, responded to the culture with a spirit of accommodation.

FUNDAMENTALIST RELIGIOUS EDUCATION

Sunday schools are a primary vehicle for transmitting the biblical faith. Many show steady enrollments, and others are growing, with large enrollments from the youngest children through adults at every age level and a dedicated group of teachers. The difference seems to lie in a sense of purpose. Effective Sunday schools have a strong outreach program to bring in new members.

There is a growing sense among curriculum editors and teachers of the importance of developmental studies for effective religious education. No longer is biblical material selected on some general basis of simplicity for particular age groups. The material is selected with reference to what is generally accepted as the "teachable moment" of social and psychological readiness.

There are also changes in religious education curriculum for adults. The use of the Uniform Lessons Series is still strong, but some classes are forming their own objectives and writing or selecting their own curriculum materials. Some use topically oriented courses of study based on biblical materials. They are looking for applications of the Bible to life experience. Some use study guides to particular books of the Bible in preference to already constructed interpretations.

Conservatively oriented bookstores fill a need for materials because religious books are seen as a form of education and evangelism. Christian day schools, some high schools, and a number of colleges form important links in the total educational process. *See also* Biblical Authority; Evangelicalism; Secularism.

E. G. Dobson

Futures Projections

See Long-range Planning.

G

Gaebelein, Frank E.

Frank E. Gaebelein (1899–1984), who viewed himself as a Christian humanist in the Renaissance sense, was a lucid proponent of evangelical religious education. He organized the Stony Brook (New York) Preparatory School in 1921 and remained its head until 1963, maintaining high educational standards in a curriculum taught from an evangelical Christian perspective.

He chaired a committee of the National Association of Evangelicals in 1946 to draw up a statement on the philosophy and practice of Christian education, published as *Christian Education in a Democracy* (1951). His own philosophical statement on education is in *The Pattern of God's Truth* (1954). All truth is God's truth, he states, and the most complete education is the integration of human truth with God's truth, found in nature and Scripture by reason and faith. Jesus Christ is central to education and is revealed in the Bible. Christian schools must incorporate these insights in order to provide a Christian education.

Gaebelein was co-editor of *Christianity Today*, an influential evangelical periodical, from 1963 to 1966, editor of the twelve-volume Expositor's Bible Commentary (Zondervan), and literary consultant for the New International Version of the Bible.

I. V. Cully

Gerson, Jean de

A scholar, renowned theologian, and chancellor of the University of Paris, Jean de Gerson (1363–1429) lived during the turbulent period of the "Western Schism" (1378–1417); his attempts to end the schism and reunite the church merited him the title "friend of peace and union." The eldest of twelve children, he was born in the French hamlet of Gerson in 1363. He attended nearby schools and at the age of fourteen began his collegiate studies in Paris. He earned the equivalent of a bachelor's degree, was ordained a priest, and continued his education through 1394 when he completed his doctoral studies in theology.

Gerson's unwavering concern for the promulgation of Christian truth through study and a devout life manifested itself in his careful scholarship, teaching, and writing. He emphatically rejected the concept of theological research separated from a committed spiritual life and accessible only to the theologically elite. He exemplified those convictions in his own life.

While living in Lyons he regularly surrounded himself with children, teaching them the elements of Christian doctrine on their level. From that experience he wrote his two well-known treatises, *The ABCs for Ordinary Folk* and *On Drawing the Little Ones to Christ*. Those works verified and illustrated the significance of his principles. Gerson died in Lyons at the age of sixty-six. After the introduction of printing his works were published in Cologne (1483) and Paris (1606). *See also* History of Christian Education.

M. C. Bryce

Gestalt

Gestalt is a German word referring to "shape," "form," or "pattern." As applied to a theory of perception, Gestalt psychology refers to the ways persons organize phenomena into a single, unified shape, form, or pattern.

The central belief of this school of psychology is that the whole of any phenomenon is greater than the sum of its parts. One's perception of a phenomenon is not identical with the physical sensation (stimulus) and the person's reaction to it (response). "Gestalt psychology" contends that perception is an interaction between the stimulus, one's own internal organization of many stimuli into a unity, and the context within which the stimuli occur.

Gestalt theory claims that perception is organized according to several laws. The "Law of Figure-Ground Relationships" contends that one perceives "figures" against a "background" composed of the rest of the perceptual field. The "Law of Pragnanz" (or the "Law of Good Figure") claims that perception tends to organize stimuli into the best possible figure. Four other laws further explain the "Law of Pragnanz." The "Law of Similarity" states that things tend to be organized into patterns if they are similar in some way. The "Law of Contiguity" suggests persons see patterns that allow a thing to continue in the same form until new data arises to convince one to change that form. The "Law of Proximity" claims that stimuli are organized according to the nearness, or proximity, of the parts. Finally, the "Law of Closure" states that persons tend to perceive incomplete figures as complete.

Although Gestalt theory was originally developed as an explanation of perception by Max Wertheimer, Kurt Koffka, and Wolfgang Köhler in post–World War I Germany, the implications for educational theory are numerous. Gestalt theory assumes that learning occurs through central cognitive processes, not a mechanistic stimulus-response relationship. Further, learning is seen to result from the interaction of each stimulus with "memory traces" within the person. Learning is accomplished through "insight," which Gestalt theory understands to be the acquisition of new concepts and the retention and transfer of these concepts from one situation to another. Finally, Gestalt theory assumes that learning takes place through problem solving, not through either the application of universal principles to specific situations (formal logic) or through simple trial and error.

The teaching method reflecting Gestalt theory would provide a wide variety of stimuli or resources from which the learner would be encouraged to organize the data into a unity. Such a method would not have a single, fixed goal for every learner in the class; instead, the teacher would desire each learner to use the resources available according to his or her own patterns of organization to produce an insight that is uniquely the learner's own. *See also* Behaviorism; Knowledge, Theories of; Learning Theory.

W. A. Smith

Gifted Children

A gifted child is one with exceptional abilities. Since that loose definition includes everything from genius to idiot savant, educators have gravitated toward defining the gifted child as one who is "intellectually" superior. This can be explained by the public acclamation of Lewis M. Terman's study of giftedness as intelligence in the 1920s. In his original study of around 1500 children, giftedness was defined as an IQ of 140 or above—a cutoff based on intelligence tests. Longitudinal follow-up results appeared in 1959. The public learned that gifted children by and large became quite normal young adults in terms of personal and social adjustment.

Religious educators cannot equate giftedness solely with intelligence, however. Other areas in which children may show exceptional ability include, for example, art, music, writing, drama, dance, or athletics. Finally, a holistic approach is being taken by the Social Science Research Council in New York. Findings from biology, brain research, epistemology, and even literature are considered, along with psychology, in seeking more information about giftedness. This new approach deserves attention from religious educators.

In the Bible Paul describes various kinds of gifts (1 Cor. 12:4–11; Rom. 12:6–8) and points out that Christians form the body of Christ. The body has many members, each with its own function. One person's special ability does not make that individual more important; all must use their God-given abilities together to do God's will. Thus religious educators have a special responsibility to encourage each learner to develop God-given gifts, whether they are intellectual, emotional, social, artistic, or physical.

Assisting each learner in developing his or her special potential is often not easy in groups where abilities differ widely. Some solutions tried in general education may prove useful for adaptation to the religious education setting.

Grouping learners particularly able in some subjects and giving them advanced instruction is one possibility. This would require a helping teacher to whom learners could go for additional more advanced work after completing work with the whole class. Alternatively, learners from several grades might gather in a separate space for work either individually or together.

Some students can be accelerated to a higher grade level. This solves the question of grouping by ability but could result in requests from parents desiring their children's learning to be accelerated when this is not warranted. The enrichment program described above might be tactically a better solution.

Programs can be tailor-made to match a child's special interests and competencies by adapting the course of study with additional materials through a careful selection of resources. This method is useful in a learning center approach, where several areas in turn engage the interests of children who may work individually or in small groups.

Special after-school clubs held outside the regular religious education class provide the freedom to experiment with specially designed programs, methods, and resources to invite the curiosity and special abilities of children in research, exploration, and discovery. Parents need to make room for club hours in the schedule.

An individual sponsor program involves an ongoing relationship for several weeks or months between a learner and a member of the congregation with specific shared skills and interests. The two might go on field trips, share books, and/or attend special programs that they could discuss.

Although correspondence courses have long been in use in general education for American children overseas, they have not usually been considered a religious education option. They could, however, be useful for children in isolated areas or be designed for gifted children who needed a special program. The limited number of children requiring such a program, however, indicates that it would need to be denominationally funded.

With independent study learners would have an individually designed program of reading, visual resources, and study. This is a possibility for the isolated learner and can also be part of an established religious education program where resources are available for use at home. The results could be shared with the rest of the class or the person doing independent study could meet with a teacher (tutor) for reflection to develop deeper understandings.

In order to develop God-given gifts, a religious education program must have available, interested, and able people; resources; a desire among parents, children, and other learners to further this goal; funds to implement it; and finally imagination and initiative on the part of leaders. *See also* Exceptional Persons; Grouping; Intergenerational Approach; Learning Center; Time Arrangements.

L. W. Barber

Girl Scouts

Girl Scouts, an organization in which girls grow in character development and leadership skills through recreation and community service, was founded by Juliette Gordon Low (1860–1927) in Savannah, Georgia, in 1912. While previously in England, Low had become enthusiastic about the Girl Guide program begun there in 1909 as an offshoot of the popular Boy Scout movement. She had formed her own Girl Guide company and was able to see firsthand the girls' eagerness and enthusiasm for the program, one in which their abilities in citizenship and self-reliance were being developed through outdoor programs. That positive response supported her determination to carry the idea home to America, where it caught on and became as popular as it had been in England.

Originally begun as Girl Guides, the name was soon changed to Girl Scouts, to make the program more identifiable for American girls. In 1913, the first Girl Scout handbook was published, entitled "How Girls Can Help Their Country," and a national headquarters was established in Washington, D.C., though the headquarters later were moved to New York City, where they are today.

In 1915, the organization was incorporated and at the first annual convention Juliette Gordon Low was elected president, a position she held until 1920 when she retired with the honorary title of founder. The U.S. Congress issued a charter to Girl Scouts in 1950.

The purpose of the program as stated in the constitution of the Girl Scouts of the U.S.A. is to "inspire girls with the highest ideals of character, conduct, patriotism, and service that they may become happy and resourceful citizens." The motivating force in Girl Scouting is a spiritual one, and membership is open to all girls and adults who accept the Girl Scout promise and law.

The promise is:

On my honor, I will try:

To serve God and my country,

To help people at all times,

And to live by the Girl Scout Law.

The law is:

I will do my best:

to be honest

to be fair

to help where I am needed

to be cheerful

to be friendly and considerate

to be a sister to every Girl Scout

to respect authority

to use resources wisely

to protect and improve the world around me

to show respect for myself and others through my works and actions

The Girl Scout emblem, a trefoil that represents the three parts of the promise, has the profile of three young women on the face of it. All Girl Scouts wear a pin with the emblem on it. The Girl Scout motto is "Be Prepared."

The program for girls aged five to seventeen has five levels: Daisy Girl Scouts (ages five–six), Brownie Girl Scouts (seven–eight), Junior Girl Scouts (nine–eleven), Cadette Girl Scouts (twelve–fourteen), and Senior Girl Scouts (fourteen–seventeen). Scouting is open to all girls regardless of race, color, creed, origin, or physical disability, and girls may enter at the level appropriate to their age.

The program at all levels is based on the promise and law and focuses on five areas of interest: people, the arts, well-being, today and tomorrow, and the out-of-doors. Each level is geared to the age and experience of the girls participating and progresses as girls become comfortable and more proficient. The goal is for each girl to develop her own self-awareness, to develop a set of values, to learn to get along with others, and to learn how to contribute to society.

While the overall program does not include specific focus on the area of religion, a project with such a focus may be designed and added to the program by religious groups. Such projects usually include a study of faith and service within the religious community. A certificate, pendant, or pin is awarded on completion of the project.

Adult volunteers supervise all Girl Scout activities, serving in a number of capacities such as leaders, advisers, troop committee members, and as council or national board or committee members.

The program Low began with just a few girls has grown to almost 3 million girls and 500,000 adults in the United States. Girl Scouts of the U.S.A. is a member of the World Association of Girl Guides and Girl Scouts, forming a sisterhood of over 8 million girls and adults that reaches into 108 countries in the free world. In Canada there are around 250,000 Girl Guides and 27,000 adult members. The world association's purpose is to give girls opportunities for individual development, responsible citizenship, and service to their communities. In addition, it is active in international programs and opportunities that encourage experience and learning exchanges for girls and adults.

Since its inception, Girl Scouting has tried to stay abreast of and, whenever possible, ahead of educational and philosophical trends affecting the growth and development of girls. Activities have changed, uniforms and pins have changed, but over the years the movement and its basic beliefs and principles have remained true to those espoused by the founder Juliette Gordon Low. *See also* Boy Scouts; Outdoor Ministries; Youth Ministry.

B. P. Russell

Goals

Goals in education are statements of what is intended to happen or what is intended to have happened. As something that is intended to happen a goal is the same as an aim or a purpose. As something that is intended to have happened, it is an intended outcome, an end, or an objective. Other similar terms, such as criterion or standard, denote a statement by which a judgment may be reached as to the degree to which what has happened measures up to what is intended to have happened.

Educational terminology on the matter has never been standardized. At one point (in the 1960s) Christian education was using the term "objective" to mean an overall policy statement and the term "goal" as a more specific statement intended to guide a course, unit, lesson, or activity. At exactly the same time in public education the terms were used in the opposite way. It is understandable that there has been a great deal of confusion in the field as to which terms mean what.

Furthermore, the debate as to whether education is an art or a science has clouded the situation, since those who hold it to be an art are loathe to deal with specific intentions, while those who hold it to be a science insist on very precise statements of intention. Even those who hold a scientific point of view are not of one mind on the nature and function of educational goals. John Dewey (1859–1952), for instance, maintained that standard aims were irrelevant to the educational process, because the only aims that were powerful were those set and held by the learners themselves. In this view, the goal of education is to help learners set their own goals.

In view of the lack of standardization of terminology, "goal" may be said for all practical purposes to be interchangeable with aim, purpose, intended outcome, end, and objective. The only way to identify any nuance of meaning is to note carefully how the term happens to be used in a particular context.

RELIGIOUS EDUCATION GOALS

Steps for Setting Goals:

1. Establish a task force representing all concerned people. Teachers, religious education professionals, clergy, church or synagogue board members, parents, and young people may all be included, depending upon the issues at hand.

2. "Brainstorm" together, sharing information and ideas freely and compiling a written list of everything discussed.

3. Group the items on the written list into categories for possible goal setting.

4. Define what is meant by the term "goals" and decide what types of goals will be set. Are the goals actually purposes that you hope to accomplish? Do they involve desired behavioral changes that can be measured or learning material to be mastered?

5. With your definition of "goals" in mind, choose the basic areas for which goals now will be set.

6. Discuss these areas and the ideas for each area further if needed and do any research or information gathering that seems necessary.

7. Jointly determine and write down a specific goal statement or set of goals for each of these areas.

8. Share these written goals with all concerned people and invite their response.

9. Refer to these goals when choosing curriculum materials and planning all religious education activities.

10. Review these goals periodically to determine if they need revision.

Suggested Areas for Setting Goals:

- Individual and community understanding of and response to God as known through Scripture and through the world

- Knowledge of the content of Scripture, including an understanding of both its meaning when written and its meaning for individuals and the world today

- Knowledge of the religious community, including its history, theology, worship, organization, goals and endeavors, and the life-style it suggests and/or requires of its members

- Growth in faith leading to full commitment to God through the worshiping community

- Recognition of self-worth based on the affirmation of being created, redeemed, and sustained by God

- Ability to relate positively beyond the self to family, friends, community, nation, and world, with particular concern for the ecumenical religious community

- Concern for the whole of earth as God's creation and understanding of the responsibility of human beings as God's stewards

Concern with goals in American educational theory and practice arose as public education became universal and as the "Americanization" of new populations became an assigned task of the schools. The setting of goals was usually the task of various national committees independent of the government. Since firm policy decisions were in the hands of local boards of education, the findings of the national committees were advisory.

One of the agencies active in formulating and suggesting aims has been the National Education Association. Of particular interest to Christian educators was the work of its Educational Policies Commission, *Moral and Spiritual Values in the Public Schools* (1951). It identified as moral and spiritual values not only appropriate but mandatory for the public schools the following: moral responsibility, institutions as the servants of humankind, common consent, devotion to truth, respect for excellence, moral equality, brotherhood, the pursuit of happiness, and spiritual enrichment. The report was quite specific about religion in the public schools: public schools should be friendly toward the religious beliefs of their students, guard religious freedom and tolerance, and teach about religion. On reflection, there was little doubt about what the report meant by moral values, but the meaning of spiritual values remained vague. It seemed to be summed up in the term "spiritual enrichment" and connoted the kinds of experience usually associated with the arts and the humanities.

IN CATHOLIC AND PROTESTANT THOUGHT

The question of goals has not concerned Roman Catholic educators as much as it has Protestants. While major theories have shifted from catechetical instruction in the mode of the *Baltimore Catechism*, through "the new catechetics" with its orientation to biblical theology on the one hand and psychological and developmental needs on the other, to a focus on issues of peace and human justice, the official educational position of the church has been stated fairly briefly and generally in documents like *To Teach as Jesus Did* (United States Catholic Conference, 1973). Both the work of the parochial schools and the less formally oriented work of the Confraternity of Christian Doctrine (CCD) have been for the most part aligned with the church's official position.

Protestant thought on goals has, however, been continuous, intense, and varied. The variety that it has displayed has probably been due to the fact that Protestant educational theory has shown great variety as it has responded to the different theological positions that have characteristically emerged. Thus, Protestant educational goals have run the gamut from individual salvation to social reconstruction, from biblical knowledge to faith development, and from individual self-fulfillment to responsible discipleship.

In the late 1920s, in connection with the development of the International Curriculum of Religious Education (curtailed in 1929 by the Great Depression), two committees of the International Council of Religious Education held quite different views on objectives. The research committee, headed by W. W. Charters, saw the Christian life as a matter of vocation requiring specific skills and thus calling for hundreds of precise, systematized objectives. The curriculum committee, headed by William Clayton Bower (1878–1982), followed Dewey's position in eschewing such objectives and insisting on a more creative, learner-centered process of the development of objectives. Serving as staff executive for both committees, Paul H. Vieth (1895–1978) did his own research on objectives and published *Objectives in Religious Education* (1930), which set the pattern for thinking about objectives for more than two decades. He formulated the objectives of Christian education as follows:

- To foster in growing persons a consciousness of God as a reality in human experience, and a sense of personal relationship to him

- To lead growing persons into an understanding and appreciation of the personality, life, and teaching of Jesus Christ

- To foster in growing persons a progressive and continuous development of Christlike character

- To develop in growing persons the ability and disposition to participate in and contribute constructively to the building of a social order embodying the ideal of the fatherhood of God and the brotherhood of man

- To lead growing persons to build a life philosophy on the basis of a Christian interpretation of life and the universe

- To develop in growing persons the ability and disposition to participate in the organized society of Christians—the church

- To effect in growing persons the assimilation of the best religious experience of the race, as effective guidance to present experience

Analysis shows that these objectives, far milder in tone than subsequent statements, are in fact areas of curricular concern and that what makes them into objectives are the preambles, "To foster in (lead, develop in, effect in) growing persons . . ."

During the 1950s and 1960s the development of Protestant thought on goals was set in the context of curriculum development and was influenced by the work of such curriculum theorists as Ralph W. Tyler. The prototypical statement of goals for the period was produced by the National Council of Churches' Committee on Senior-High Objectives (1958): "The objective of Christian education is to help persons to be aware of God's self-disclosure and seeking love in Jesus Christ and to respond in faith and love—to the end that they may know who they are and what their human situation means, grow as sons of God rooted in the Christian community, live in the Spirit of God in every relationship, fulfill their common discipleship in the world, and abide in the Christian hope." Three things about this statement are noteworthy. It is a single-policy statement and does not contain a list of curriculum areas. The first part of the statement is in the form of an aim, since it begins, "To help persons . . ." This is followed, introduced by "to the end that . . . ," by a set of clauses in the form of goals.

The committee also worked out a set of "learning tasks" to deal with the question of basic method. A later committee devised a set of curriculum areas to indicate how the question of curricular substance was to be handled.

Probably the most thoroughgoing study and statement of objectives of Christian education has been done in connection with the long-range program of the boards of education of what is now the Evangelical Lutheran Church in America. In *The Objectives of Christian Education* (1957) the general objectives were introduced by the statement: "Inasmuch as the Church, as the Body of Christ, seeks to become more effectively that community of believers in which the Holy Spirit calls, gathers, enlightens, and sanctifies individuals in their relationships with God and their fellow men, the church's central objective, therefore, shall be—To assist the individual in his [or her] response and witness to the eternal and incarnate Word of God as he [or she] grows within this community of the church toward greater maturity in [the] Christian life through ever-deepening understandings, more wholesome attitudes, and more responsible patterns of action." This was further elaborated in a grid, one axis of which was the learner's relationship with God (Father, Son, and Holy Spirit), with the Christian church, to the Bible, with fellow humans, to the physical world, and with him- or herself. The other axis was understandings, attitudes, and responsible patterns of action.

The Age Group Objectives of Christian Education followed in 1958. Here, using the same grid, detailed objectives were spelled out for the Christian parent of the child in the first year of life, for the preschool child, for each age from one to seventeen, for older youth, the young adult, the middle adult, and the older adult.

The Functional Objectives of Christian Education (1959) was built on the pattern of the intersection of continual life involvements and continual Christian learnings and spelled these out for the church and its educational agencies—the Christian family, the Sunday church schools, the weekday agencies of the congregation, and leadership education.

RECENT ISSUES

More recently, controversy has broken out over the matter of "behavioral objectives." Introduced by general educators of a scientific bent, the behavioral objectives concept is intended to clarify not only the aim of an educational act (it must be stated in terms of something very specific to be done and accomplished), but also to facilitate evaluation. Since behavior may be observed and assessed, the degree to which the objective has been accomplished may be precisely determined. Those who regard education as an art or who see education as oriented to theological realities do not believe that it is possible to state Christian education's goals with such precision and fear that to do so will severely truncate Christian educational experience.

Benjamin Bloom, who is widely known in Christian education for his work on taxonomies of educational objectives, has also introduced the concept of "mastery learning." His thesis is that it is possible for everyone to reach a level of complete mastery of the goals of education. The educator need not be content any more with partial achievement of goals. The dynamics involved are improved methods and flexible timing. Several Christian educators, Glenn Heck in particular, have begun the process of introducing mastery learning into the field of Christian education. *See also* Curriculum; Long-range Planning; Planning; Progressive Education; Taxonomy.

FOR FURTHER REFERENCE

Heck, Glenn, and Marshall Shelley. *What Every Sunday School Worker Should Know About How Children Learn.* Elgin, IL: Cook, 1979.

D. C. Wyckoff

God, Understandings of

In biblical religion "God" is a proper noun, the personal name (Yahweh, Kyrios, Theos) of the ultimate One with whom we have to do. The response to Moses' query about the divine name (Exod. 3:13–14)—"I am who I am" or "I will be who I will be"—reminds us of the mystery of God and therefore the modesty appropriate to all our human talk of the Holy One. Yet the immediate context of these words is the promise of Israel's release from Egyptian bondage (Exod. 7–13; 15–17), indicating a disclosure of who God is in what God does and will do.

BIBLICAL UNDERSTANDINGS

The understandings of God in the Christian tradition rise out of the cumulative account of the divine deeds in the two Testaments, as this story has been interpreted over the centuries by the church. The narrative appears variously in the Christian community's creeds, liturgies, and theologies. It describes God as the Creator and Sustainer of all that is, the One whose holy love responds to the world's recalcitrance in singular acts of deliverance and disclosure among a particular people, Israel, and whose Word enters the world in the life and ministry, crucifixion and resurrection of Jesus Christ to liberate and reconcile. From within this track of revelatory history, God is perceived as working redemptively throughout the world toward the goal of *shalom*, the life together of God, humanity, and nature. A foretaste of the promised future is offered in the life of faith through the witness and worship of the body of Christ on earth, the church.

In the Christian narrative, God is known as triune. "Father, Son, and Spirit" refer to the three acts of God in the divine drama: creation, reconciliation, and sanctification. In the outworking of the divine plan (*oikonomia*), these "missions" of the "economic Trinity" are not just phases of God's life (the teaching of modalism rejected by the church). Rather, Father, Son, and Spirit are each fully God, eternal "Persons" that constitute the "immanent Trinity." Their harmonious life together—a total "co-inherence"—is such that the three *are* one. In the language of John's letter: "God is love." Hence the special triune name in which Christians are baptized.

Christian theology seeks to identify the attributes ("perfections") of the triune God as these emerge in the biblical narrative. In the story no foe is so strong that the divine purpose can be frustrated, therefore God is almighty. No depth or height can obscure the divine purview, therefore God is all-knowing. No length or breadth is inaccessible to the divine reach; therefore God is all-present. The saga tells of the being and doing of God in and beyond this world—God is immanent and transcendent. In the events that transpire, deity is not bound by time or space—God is eternal and infinite. As the One who authors and is the biblical tale's chief figure, God is personal, albeit far more so than we in our limitations are or understand persons to be.

The specific content poured into these general qualities of omnipotence, omnipresence, omniscience, immanence, transcendence, eternity, infinity, and personality is established by the ways they are exercised in the economy of God. These ways are sometimes called the "ethical" attributes while the abstract perfections are denominated the "metaphysical" qualities. Preeminent among them are the love of God and the holiness of God.

The divine love (*chesed, agape*) is the total self-giving that bonds the Trinity in unity and the spontaneous, unmerited care that creates the world, watches over it, suffers its rebuke and rejection, forgives its sin, and restores it to wholeness. The divine holiness (*kadosh*) is the glory and purity of the God "high and lifted up" (Isa. 6:1), a perfection and separation from taint that expresses itself in our own call to righteousness. The destiny of a world, created by love but found wanting before holiness, is the plot of the Christian story. Its centerpoint is the reconciliation of the attributes of holiness and love as a holy love in which the divine wrath against sin is absorbed by the divine mercy to sinners in the cross of Christ. Thus the righteousness of God is reinterpreted as a suffering love that takes upon itself the consequences of the world's scorn for the divine glory, making possible the final "reconciliation of all things."

CHALLENGES AND NEW CONCEPTUALIZATIONS

God, as described in the biblical narrative and revered by the Christian community, is the subject of doubt and denial by powerful alternative readings of the human condition, past and present. In the West since the eighteenth century Enlightenment, both an intellectual and political atheism have vociferously questioned the existence and beneficence of God. Can reason tolerate such a belief when there is no persuasive proof of transcendent reality? When God appears to be a projection of human needs (Ludwig Feuerbach), wish fulfillment (Sigmund Freud), resentment (Friedrich Nietzsche), or vested interest (Karl Marx)? Are not all kinds of theism dubious before the magnitude of human suffering? Isn't the "justification of God" (theodicy) impossible before the slaughter of innocence? Are not now the raised stakes of the world's peril and promise of such compelling importance that any focus on transcendent reality becomes a distraction?

Modern religious pluralism adds another challenge to that of the secular critics of Christian belief in God. The range of world religions and the claims of nontheistic worldviews have come into high profile in our age. Different conceptions of the divine and apparent lack of interest in and need for God on the part of otherwise moral persons and movements pose sharp questions to Christian belief.

Challenges to faith have prompted efforts in reconception. Secularization and pluralism provide the framework for various modifications and reinterpretations. Thus God is conceived as active in secular history (either a particular "acts of God" theology or a theology of "universal history"); engaged in the world's creative transformation (process theology); oriented to the future (theology of hope); encountering humans in their personal decision and anguish (existential theology); concerned about wholeness and healing (therapeutic theologies); at work in social change (political theology); in solidarity with the oppressed and delivering from bondage (Third World, black, feminist, and other varieties of liberation theology); protector and restorer of the good earth (ecological theologies); present in the secularization process (secular theology) or completely identified with secularity ("the death of God theology"); or active savingly in universal religious experience and in non-Christian world religions (various pluralist theologies).

Others view secularization and pluralism as a threat to Christian belief, believe the critics to be foes of faith, and reject efforts at reconceptualization. These understandings of God accent the uniqueness and overagainstness of Christian identity, stressing either Protestant distinctives (evangelical theologies, orthodox and neoorthodox Protestant theologies, neofundamentalist theologies) or the Roman Catholic or Eastern Orthodox heritage (traditionalist Roman Catholic and Eastern Orthodox theologies). And yet again, various kinds of ecumenical theology strive to maintain both the classical Christian understandings of God and an openness to new implications evoked by the changing secular and pluralist scene.

Representative of the effort to honor both the heritage and the horizon of Christian belief in God is the debate about the best language for deity, one prompted by a feminist critique of usage scored as patriarchal. The spectrum of response runs from a call to abandon all belief in a supreme Being because it represents a pattern of control in which the male is ascendent and the female submissive, through the substitution of Goddess for God language, or the pairing of Mother and Father and "he" and "she" terms for God, to the use of "God" as a proper noun in the place of all pronouns, or the balancing of male and female metaphors from Scripture in description of or prayer to God. Others defend the inherited language as integral to Christian belief and interpret any change as a defeat by contemporary cultural trends. Ecumenical theologies, sensitive to those who point to the norm of Christ in whom "there is neither male nor female" (Gal. 3:28) struggle to render language about and address to God in an inclusive way, but reject ideologies that would abandon either the reality or name of God, including the trinitarian formula in which the church baptizes and expresses its God-story.

TEACHING ABOUT GOD

Teaching about the nature of God in religious education groups requires that educators and leaders take into consideration the age, developmental level, and conceptual abilities of those they teach. Even two year olds have heard God spoken about at home and in the toddlers' group. They attach meaning to the word from the context. God is thanked for food and asked, in prayer, to take care of the child. It is reassuring when told by an adult that God loves, cares about, and hears children. Conversely, children learn a different understanding of God if told that God doesn't like

certain actions or will punish those who do them. The small child's knowledge of God is experiential.

Ideas about God become concrete in religious education classes for preschool children. They learn verses from the Psalms about God's love and continuing care. They learn that God created the world and is near to people. Bible stories tell them how God took care of Abraham, Jacob, and David.

School-age children become aware of the perplexities of life and begin to realize that people have responsibilities for showing God's love. From the stories of the prophets, children learn that God expects people to be faithful to the covenant and to show their love by dealing justly with their neighbors. In Christian communities, the story of Jesus will be taught and children begin to see how God's love can be shown through suffering.

Adolescents, able to reason abstractly, begin to explore the idea of God philosophically and to learn the different ideas about God that people around the world hold. They will want to discuss these ideas and view them in the perspective of faith commitments they may have made earlier. They need freedom to explore and leaders who can appreciate their search.

Adults sometimes need to be stimulated to rethink their understanding of God in order to grow in faith. They will explore the relationship of knowledge about God to faith in God that propels them into a life-style that reflects religious faith. See also Bible in Religious Education, The; Cognitive Development; Creation; Doubt; Faith; Faith Development; Language Analysis; Moral Development; Symbolism; Theodicy; Trinity.

FOR FURTHER REFERENCE

Anderson, B. W. "God, Names of." "God, Old Testament View of." Moule, C. D. F. "God, New Testament." Trible, Phyllis. "God, Nature of in the Old Testament." In *Interpreter's Dictionary of the Bible.* Suppl. vol. New York: Abingdon, 1962, 1976.

Brunner, Emil. *The Christian Doctrine of God.* Translated by Olive Wyon. Philadelphia: Westminster, 1950.

Küng, Hans. *Does God Exist?* Translated by Edward Quinn. Garden City, NY: Doubleday, Inc., 1980.

Russell, Letty M., ed. *The Liberating Word.* Philadelphia: Westminster, 1976.

Ward, Keith. *Holding Fast to God.* London: SPCK, 1982.

G. Fackre

Gospel

The English word "gospel" (Anglo-Saxon "godspell," "God-story") translates the Greek *euange-*

lion, which in the New Testament means the "good news" of God's saving action in Jesus Christ. The noun is rooted in the Old Testament verb "to bring good news," a term that is particularly prominent in Isaiah 40–66 for the announcement of the impending return from the Babylonian exile.

THE HISTORICAL JESUS

Jesus was deeply influenced by Isaiah 40–66, and especially 61:1, as shown by his sayings recorded in Matthew 5:3 and 11:5. According to Luke, Jesus cited Isaiah 61 in the sermon at Nazareth (Luke 4:18–19), though the citation's absence from the Marcan account (5:1–6) makes it uncertain whether this is historical. But this citation is true to Jesus' understanding of his mission, which was to announce the coming of the kingdom of God. Mark has the noun "gospel" in five sayings of Jesus, but the specific phrasing of the sayings may be Mark's.

THE EARLIEST COMMUNITY

As a result of the Easter event the disciples continued Jesus' message but with a new content. The proclaimer became the proclaimed: whereas Jesus had preached the coming of the kingdom, the early community preached the act of God in Christ's sending, death, and resurrection. They probably continued to use the verb "to preach the good news," although clear evidence of this is lacking.

The noun "gospel" (*euangelion*) appears to have come in with the Hellenistic (i.e., Greek-speaking) mission. It had already been used in secular Greek for imperial proclamations, such as the emperor's birthday or a military victory. Now the Christian meaning of the word would be colored by Jesus' use of the verb from Isaiah 61:2 to proclaim the acceptable year of the Lord; it means a proclamation of the saving act of God in Christ.

Evidence for the content of the preaching of the Hellenistic mission is found in Romans 1:3, "the gospel concerning his Son, who was descended from David according to the flesh and designated Son of God in power according to the Spirit of holiness." Another form of the gospel of the Hellenistic missionaries is cited in 1 Corinthians 15:3–7. The formulae may vary but the content remains the same: the life, death, and resurrection of Christ (i.e., the Christ event), always interpreted as the saving act of God.

PAUL

Having cited the traditional gospel of the Hellenistic mission at the beginning of Romans, Paul proceeds to reformulate it in his own terms in Romans 1:16–17, "I am not ashamed of the gospel: ... For in it the righteousness of God is revealed through faith for faith." When Paul speaks of "my gospel" he does not mean that it is a different gospel from that of his predecessors. He means that he was directly commissioned by the risen Lord to proclaim the gospel. Although different in its formulation, it is in substance identical with the gospel preached by the other apostles. The only difference in content was that they spoke of the Christ event itself; Paul spoke of its saving effects.

The gospel is also "preaching" (kerygma) or the "Word." The preaching, though a human activity performed by the apostles and their assistants, is at the same time an act of God. It makes the saving act of God effective in the present (1 Cor. 1:21). It is an act of power (1 Cor. 1:18; Rom. 1:16). Hearing the gospel leads to faith and to the gift of the Spirit (Gal. 3:3). The gospel brings the church, the people of God, into being as a community or partnership in the gospel (Phil. 1:5).

THE GOSPELS

"Gospel" is a favorite word of Mark (seven times). It is used in the title (1:1), in Mark's summary of Jesus' message (1:14), and in five of Jesus' sayings, where it is also probably the evangelist's editorial work. Mark deliberately adopted the language of the Hellenistic mission, which used "gospel" for the proclamation of the Christ event in its totality, because he conceived the telling of the story of Jesus to be itself proclamation of the gospel. Mark did not mean to call his actual work a "gospel"—that usage did not come in until the second century—but he laid the foundation for it. Matthew includes only two of the five Marcan sayings of Jesus where the term occurs, while Luke does not use the word "gospel" at all. Perhaps Luke wished to restrict the word "gospel" to the post-Easter community's proclamation (Acts 15:7; 20:24) and regarded it as inappropriate for Jesus' message of the kingdom before Easter. On the other hand, Luke uses the Greek verb *euangelizesthai*, "preach the good news," quite generally: for angelic annunciations (1:19; 2:10), for the Baptist's preaching (3:18), as well as for Jesus' message (e.g., 4:18), for the Twelve during his earthly ministry (9:6), and for the post-Easter preaching (Acts 5:42). Luke seems to use the verb in the general sense of "to announce"—what is announced being defined in each context by the object of the verb (see the references above).

The Fourth Gospel uses neither the noun nor the verb. Perhaps this is because it presents Jesus not as one who proclaims the kingdom but as one who is himself the revealer and the revelation.

In the later New Testament writings the term "gospel" survives in traditional contexts (1 Tim. 1:11; 2 Tim. 1:8, 10; 2:8; 1 Pet. 4:17) but it has lost the living actuality it had in Paul and Mark. The gospel is now not seen as proclamation but as "doctrine," "tradition," "deposit of faith," to be preserved inviolate from generation to generation (thus often in the Pastorals, e.g., 2 Tim. 2:2). It is the "faith once delivered to the saints" (Jude 3). Faith has become not so much a personal acceptance of the saving act of God in Christ as the intellectual acceptance of the truths of the gospel enshrined in traditional formulae. Such concerns became necessary in the period when the original apostolic witnesses had died and false teachers threatened the church.

There is an exceptional use of the word "gospel" in the book of Revelation. In 14:6–7 an angel proclaims an "eternal gospel." Note that it is *a* and not *the* gospel. Also verse 7 seems to indicate that it is an announcement of the last judgment, which in the seer's vision is just about to take place. It is unclear why it is called an "eternal" gospel. Perhaps the meaning is that it is the announcement of the final fulfillment of God's eternal purpose. *See also* Jesus Christ; Kerygma; Preaching; Reign of God.

FOR FURTHER REFERENCE

Bornkamm, G. *Paul.* New York: Harper & Row, 1971. Pp. 109–10, 248–49.
Dodd, C. H. *The Apostolic Preaching and Its Developments.* London: Hodder & Stoughton, 1949.
Marxsen, W. *Mark the Evangelist.* Nashville, TN: Abingdon, 1969. Pp. 117–50.

R. H. Fuller

Grace

Grace is God-in-action, as God works through personal relationships to forgive and strengthen God's creatures. Grace is often mediated through other people and to children through their parents. We can do nothing to merit God's favor or grace, for grace is always something more than we deserve, thus putting the emphasis on God's loving good will rather than upon God's justice. The only human response is trust in God.

In relation to grace Paul was skeptical of any works of the law and of human merit. "Therefore, since we are justified by faith, we have peace with God through our Lord Jesus Christ. Through him we have obtained access to this grace in which we stand, and we rejoice in our hope of sharing the glory of God" (Rom. 5:1–2). However, Paul kept grace in balance by bringing in moral law, as opposed to the ceremonial and ritualistic laws by which people sought merit. Grace is associated with a divine calling or vocation, wherewith God calls us and sends us and provides the means for doing God's work, for "God is able to make all grace abound to you, so that in all things at all times, having all that you need, you will abound in every good work" (2 Cor. 9:8, NIV).

Grace is basically a source of power. Grace is not a way to escape pain and travail, but a means for transcending them. Grace as power is inescapably associated with the cross of Christ, so that any suffering now present is not comparable to the glory that is God's gift. It is God who lifts us from the depths of our own misery and sin and suffering and raises us to the heights. Grace is the power to complete daily tasks we could not do on our own. God brings power out of weakness and makes our powerlessness effective in a violent world.

The power of God's grace does not eliminate the possibility of further evil and sin, for no possibility of good can ever be divorced from the inclination toward sin. Thus grace always involves forgiveness, and before forgiveness there comes judgment. But God as judge is different from a human judge. In a law court, we would have no defense and therefore be condemned. But with God as judge, we can throw ourselves on the mercy of the court, and contrary to all expectations God will forgive us.

It is possible to fall from grace, because grace is persuasive and influential rather than irresistible. Paul urges his readers "to continue in the grace of God" (Acts 13:43).

In the synoptic Gospels, the view of grace is much simpler. Human beings have real freedom to turn to God or away from God, and thus they have genuine integrity and responsibility. A religion of grace begins with human intention. Grace is seen as a gracious personal relationship that is uplifting and power-giving within an organic framework of Creator-creature and creature-creature societies. Thus grace is persuasive rather than irresistible. It is not a matter of stimulus and response, and there is nothing impersonal about it. When grace is irresistible, it cannot be gracious. God's grace preserves our freedom and therefore is both moral and religious. Thus grace may carry human beings beyond the meanings of their own making and alert them to goodness and beauty beyond their own imagination or willing. What has been called "grace under pressure" points to God's work in us to achieve something far beyond what we had hoped for. When God dwells within us as the Holy Spirit, we may be "justified by faith."

Grace, then, is God's gift, not something human beings can earn. As John Oman writes, "grace is precisely grace because, *though wholly concerned with moral goodness, it does not at all depend on how moral we are*" (*Grace and Personality*, p. 164 [his italics]). Acceptance of grace is so simple that a little child can experience it, but it is so mysterious that the learned are often confused by it. We respond to God as a little child responds to his or her mother, trusting that a gracious and steadfast love will be offered in return.

Religious education needs not only to teach about grace, connecting it with God's love and favor through Scripture stories and verses, but also to provide an atmosphere in which grace flourishes. This is never something impersonal but always involves human and divine relationships. The grace of God should always be in evidence in the relationships between teachers and learners, between learners themselves, and indeed in how the members of the whole religious community interact with each other and with others in everyday life.

As educators, we need to pray for those we teach, "Give them grace, we pray thee, to stand fast in thy faith, to obey thy word, and to abide in thy love; that, being made strong by thy Holy Spirit, they may resist temptation and overcome evil, and may rejoice in the life that now is, and dwell with thee in the life that is to come" (*Book of Common Prayer*). *See also* Faith; Freedom; Justification.

FOR FURTHER REFERENCE

Oman, John. *Grace and Personality.* Fontana, 1917.

R. C. Miller

Grade Levels

See Grouping.

Graduate Study

See Higher Education, Religion in; Professional Study.

Great Britain and Northern Ireland

The United Kingdom has three separate systems of state education covering the three divisions of the country for legislative purposes: England and Wales, Scotland, and Northern Ireland. All three systems make provision for religious education as an integral part of the curriculum for all pupils.

ENGLAND AND WALES

In England and Wales a unique educational system has developed taking account of the original denominational provision of schools through the National Society and the British Foreign School Society. Controversy about the place of religious teaching in state-funded schools was finally resolved in the Education Act of 1870 in the famous Cowper-Temple Clause, which established that the state would allow only nondenominational religious teaching in its schools. Meanwhile, growing partnership between church and state in the provision of schools was eventually secured through a dual system in which schools provided

by the county education authorities coexist with voluntary schools provided by religious denominations. In practice the bulk of these schools are provided by the Church of England, the Roman Catholic church, and to a much lesser extent the Jewish community.

The 1944 Education Act made religious instruction compulsory in all county schools. A daily act of worship was also required for all pupils. The act was passed with a high degree of consensus among the churches and prescribed that every local authority should make its own syllabus for religious education or adopt one made by another authority.

Between 1944 and 1988 British society became more pluralist as a result of immigration and secularization. While most Christian denominations declined in numerical strength, membership of other world religions grew in numbers. The syllabuses of religious education reflected these changes and provided for the teaching of other religions as well as Christianity. Whereas in 1944 it was assumed that religious education in schools would help to nurture children in the Christian faith, by the 1980s the intention was to help pupils to appreciate the variety of religious belief and practice and to become tolerant of differences.

The 1944 act required that every school day should begin with collective worship not distinctive of any particular religious denomination. This requirement was observed until the 1960s but then gradually gave way to school assemblies that lost much of their religious content. Moreover, changes in the size and design of schools often made it impossible for the whole school to meet together.

The Education Reform Bill, debated in Parliament during 1988, provided critics of trends since 1944 with opportunity to restore religious education to its former privileged position. The government at first proposed only minor changes concerning school worship, but after widespread pressure from some Christians the churches were forced to accept new interpretations of both the content of religious education and the style and frequency of school worship. Both have a statutory place in the school curriculum and both have to reflect a mainly Christian emphasis, although concessions can be made to reflect predominant religious traditions other than Christianity in schools in some areas of the country.

To regulate religious education and worship in schools each local education authority in England and Wales must appoint a Standing Advisory Council for Religious Education (SACRE). Each SACRE must reflect the prevailing political, educational, and religious views in the area concerned.

Since 1944 parents have had the right to withdraw their children from religious education and school worship. Those rights have been maintained under the 1988 act.

SCOTLAND AND NORTHERN IRELAND

Although Scotland and Northern Ireland are governed from Westminster as part of the United Kingdom, legislation affecting them often takes a different form from that affecting England and Wales. Their different religious histories have also led to considerable variations with regard to religious education.

In Scotland the traditional influence of Calvinism meant that the teaching of the Bible and the catechism had pride of place in the school curriculum. A 1972 report, "Moral and Religious Education in Scottish Schools," prepared by a committee appointed by the secretary of state for Scotland to review the provision and practice of religious instruction in Scottish schools other than Roman Catholic, led to new developments. In 1974 the Scottish Central Committee on Religious Education (SCCORE) was set up to enable educationists, as opposed to church representatives, to play the determinative role in regulating religious education in both denominational and nondenominational schools. Roman Catholic teachers were appointed to serve on SCCORE, thus paving the way for increased Protestant and Catholic cooperation.

Such cooperation has not been possible in Northern Ireland. The deep political and religious divisions there are reflected in the schools. Almost everyone is identified as Protestant or Roman Catholic. Almost all Protestant children attend state or Protestant voluntary schools, and almost all Catholic children attend Catholic schools. Religious education in such a divided society is regarded as a means of induction into a particular religious, and often denominational, tradition.

Religious education in the Protestant community for the younger pupils is substantially based on biblical knowledge with little reference to their contemporary social context; for older pupils it largely ignores the Roman Catholic tradition of Christianity, even though at that level the syllabus purports to relate the faith to today's world. The Roman Catholic church provides schools for nearly all its children, and religious education is a vehicle for Catholic teaching with little attempt to promote understanding of Christians who are not within that tradition.

PROFESSIONAL EDUCATION

In all parts of the United Kingdom, because of the statutory place that religious education has in the school curriculum, with its development also as a public examination subject at the ages of sixteen and eighteen for those who choose it, specialist teachers with professional training are required. Teachers of religious education are trained either through a religious studies course as part of a general teaching qualification at a college of higher education or on a postgraduate teaching course with a specialization in religious education.

With the renewed emphasis on religious education in the 1988 Education Reform Act and similar developments elsewhere in the United Kingdom, many more specialist teachers will be required to sustain the subject in the curriculum.

EDUCATION IN THE CHURCHES

In the churches there is a strong emphasis on Christian education for children. The Sunday schools of the nineteenth century, originally formed to teach children to read and write in the absence of formal schooling, gradually concentrated on Bible teaching and worship as day schools increased. Links with the churches became stronger, and Sunday schools provided the main setting for education of children by churches.

During the twentieth century national organizations have provided lesson material graded according to the ages of children. The majority of Sunday schools have moved from Sunday afternoons to Sunday mornings and have become closely associated with the worship and life of local congregations. The concept of the church as a family has been developed in various ways by most denominations, and Sunday worship and education increasingly integrates adults and children. Denominations have, separately and together, developed training courses for local teachers, all of whom are voluntary and unpaid. More recent developments in all denominations emphasize all-age learning, and the Anglican report "Children in the Way" explores the concept of the whole church as a pilgrim community.

For the churches' own ordained ministry, theological colleges provide professional training. Many colleges use faculties of theology in the universities for the more academic parts of the training, while some provide their own similar courses. Some colleges remain denominational, but there is increasing ecumenical cooperation through schemes like the Cambridge Federation of Theological Colleges and a more integrated scheme in Manchester and through the creation of Queen's College, Birmingham, recognized by several denominations. Social institutions, industry, and local churches are widely used for practical and pastoral training. *See also* Anglican Education; Reformed Education; Sunday School Movement.

FOR FURTHER REFERENCE

General Synod Board of Education, The National Society. "Children in the Way." London: Church House Publishing, 1988.

J. P. Reardon

Greek Education (Ancient)

Ancient Greek education was always marked by high seriousness. Heraclitus (ca. 540–475 B.C.) declared it "a second sun to its possessors." Subsequent Greek philosophy and politics bear him out. Education in preclassical and classical Greece exhibited both informal and formal aspects. Homer (before 700 B.C.) provides glimpses of informal instruction of youth in oratory and martial skills through the counsel and example of an older soldier. Informal education was generally the only kind permitted to girls (a fact deplored by both Plato and Aristotle), for they were expected to excel as adults only in childbearing and domestic skills. Women played little part in rearing boys after their seventh year.

Formal education was recognized as necessary for boys and youth, however. Schools are mentioned by both Herodotus (ca. 484–425 B.C.) and Thucydides (ca. 460–399 B.C.), and schooling of some kind seems to be presupposed by Heraclitus's statement. The goal of education in Greece was to produce useful citizens. Because the economy was built on slavery, useful citizenship was concerned not with basic maintenance of life, but with pursuit of social values. The rival states of Sparta and Athens shared the same understanding of the purpose of education but held quite different views of useful citizenship.

Sparta aimed for soldier-citizens to defend the state and glorify it through conquest. Aristotle, though judging as an Athenian, was no doubt correct in holding that Spartan education and laws were framed mainly with a view to war. For the first seven years of life, boys and girls lived at home, but their parents' educational role was, at best, incidental. Children were placed under the care of nurses, who trained them toward physical excellence and self-reliance.

At seven, boys began their formal education in state-run schools under the direction of a *paidonomos*, or supervisor of education. The school reflected the culture's interest in little beyond preserving the state and extending its dominance, even though all three customary branches of learning were included—letters, music, and gymnastics. Letters was part of Spartan education, but only enough reading and writing for basic functioning; literature was valued for its stories of great warriors and bold exploits, but these were known mostly through song. Music was highly regarded in the form of choral singing, which provided both soldierly camaraderie and the means to recall past heroes, to inspire their emulation, and to stir up zeal for going into battle. Gymnastics was central in Spartan education, and Spartan athletes won more than their share of Olympic victories; the purpose of gymnastics, however, was not to gain individual or even Spartan renown but to produce more able soldiers.

At twelve, the boys, still supervised by the *paidonomos*, were placed under the charge of older youth, who put them to tasks and exercises that would toughen them in body and spirit. These included hardship, thievery, the suffering of organized flogging, and engagement in savage fighting, sometimes to the death. Spartan education thus produced what was wanted: useful citizen-soldiers, culturally limited, but disciplined, courageous, self-reliant, cunning, and devoted to Sparta.

In Athens the useful citizen was a cultured person—a man in whom individualism and service to the state (developed individual talents and love for Athens) were held in balance.

Education began early in Athenian children's lives with disciplined games and carefully chosen stories (true ones, says Plato). Boys entered and departed programs of formal education at varying ages, depending on their fathers' ability to pay for them.

Usually by age seven a boy was enrolled in at least one class run by a *paidagogos*, or tutor. A class was only as good as its tutor, who charged a fee commensurate with his competence. The state maintained moral oversight, but curriculum was not prescribed. Nevertheless, a standard pattern was generally followed. Each boy worked under three tutors, one for each branch of learning. He studied letters—reading, writing, and arithmetic—and read and memorized great poetry. He studied music, learning to play the lyre and to sing songs of the lyric poets. And he studied gymnastics, training his body to serve his mind.

In the fourth century B.C. *ephebic* (young men's) colleges were organized for training youth eighteen years and older in democratic citizenship, but they deteriorated over time into schools of extended gymnastics. At its best, Athenian education produced the useful citizen who was like an active philosopher, competent in liberal arts and generous in serving both the state and culture in general.

But Athenian education was not always at its best. The competence of tutors was frequently poor, and individualism sometimes was carried to extreme. In response Plato (427–347 B.C.) urged a "philosopher-king" to promote stability, and Aristotle (384–322 B.C.) argued for standard education for all. Civic life disintegrated, however, and the individualistic Athenians could not agree on whether to unite with other city-states to defend themselves against invaders from the north. In 338 B.C. at the battle of Chaeronea the cities of Greece fell to Philip of Macedon. *See also* Pedagogy.

R. R. Sundquist

Group Dynamics

Contrary to a common notion that group dynamics pertains to techniques for controlling groups and manipulating the masses, the term has its source in social science in the search for an understanding of the forces and conditions that make groups productive or cause them to be ineffective or destructive. Consequently, the principal focus of this branch of social science is not so much on techniques for social change as it is on procedures for observation of group behavior and the development of sensitivity to forces in group behavior that influence group cohesion or disintegration. The data and knowledge that emerge from such studies, of course, can be used constructively or otherwise, as in every other walk of life.

UNDERSTANDING GROUPS

Pioneer work in this particular field of social concern had a significant beginning with the observations of Charles H. Cooley at the turn of the twentieth century, although it could be said that the entire discipline of sociology had its foundations in the philosophical system of Auguste Comte and in the nineteenth-century early sociological studies of Max Weber in Germany and Emile Durkheim in France. Cooley's work and that of others constituted the speculative era, when creative conceptualization of group behavior began to make specific inroads on the broad field of sociology.

An era of empirical study was blooming by the second quarter of this century with the work of a number of social scientists principally at the University of Iowa, the University of Michigan, and M.I.T. in the United States and at Tavistock Institute of Human Relations in the United Kingdom. Out of these empirical studies emerged a growing body of research theory that has become a guide for continuing research in the social sciences and a resource in the field of adult education.

All such theorizing has its origin in some definition of a group and, in turn, each body of research sheds light on the adequacy of that definition. One of the early definitions that was consonant with some of the concerns of the pioneers of group dynamics in church educational programs was proposed by Raymond B. Cattell of the University of Illinois; he said a group is a collection of organisms in which the existence of all, in their particular relationships, is necessary to the satisfaction of certain individual needs in each member. The study of what these needs are, how the group meets them or fails to do so, and the role of the individual in the process is the basic exploratory function of group dynamics. While the satisfaction of individual needs is by no means the complete raison d'être of a religious community, certainly it is an essential if not central part of the purpose of any religious education program.

In practice, group dynamics is a way of exploring the interaction of persons within a group. This entails examining direct and indirect ways that individuals exercise leadership or other forms of influence in the group, how they are persuaded to agree to a group decision or block such a decision, and ways of handling conflict. Role playing, brainstorming (in which ideas are first gathered without comment; discussion and evaluation follow), "if you could do this" scenarios to facilitate imaginative future planning, or expecting a group to evolve leadership when starting without a designated leader are processes in which it can be particularly clearly seen how members are functioning in a group. A process observer is one who watches from the sidelines and takes notes and tapes, so that he or she can be called upon at particular points to recapitulate not the content, but the dynamics, i.e., the interactions, that are taking place.

The carryover is into committees, where awareness of group dynamics helps members become more sensitive to ways in which to facilitate the process of working together. Teachers in religious education classes also find these techniques, including the observer, helpful in assessing the kinds of class participation and reasons for participation (or lack thereof) as an evaluative tool for restructuring.

APPLICATIONS TO RELIGIOUS EDUCATION

The branch of this science that most directly affected educational work in religious communities stemmed from the field studies of Kurt Lewin in Iowa, later at M.I.T., which led to the development of the National Training Laboratory for Group Development at Bethel, Maine. Here teachers gathered for conferences at which techniques arising from group dynamics were practiced in order to be used later in their own schools. In the early 1950s the Episcopal church initiated the first use by churches of training laboratories modeled after the Lewin-oriented NTL laboratory. These church models were designed to assist clergy in becoming sensitive to the forces that are cohesive or destructive, positive or negative, in the group life of the church. The emerging new educational program of the Episcopal church during that decade depended heavily on learning and development taking place through group experience within the parish family and in the community. Within four years more than twenty-five hundred clergy, including almost sixty bishops, plus a growing number of lay leaders, participated in these "labs." In 1956 the first of a series of interdenominational group development laboratories was sponsored by the National Council of the Churches of Christ at Green Lake, Wisconsin.

During the 1960s and early 1970s the investment of almost all national church structures in parish education gave way to needs in other areas, especially the needs of the inner city. Departments of education essentially disappeared. While concern for "process" carried over into other areas of the church's life, intensive training conferences as a part of the church's education program became rare. Similarly, the contact between church education and what was happening in the social sciences lost much of its substance, retaining only minimal influence on the program of the churches.

What was happening in the social sciences during these years was also undergoing change. In keeping with the nature of empirical research, the study of group dynamics, and even more, its application, went off in several major directions, the principal ones being personal growth and organizational development. Some church leaders and their agencies are still in contact with these professional sources of research in group life, for it remains a cardinal fact that the church is a "group," a body, whose practicing members are closely bound to one another by their Lord, but whose relationships to one another can be cause for scandal rather than an example of wholeness.

In general, the kind of assistance religious institutions and their educational enterprises can receive from the technical science of group dynamics can sharpen their ability to recognize what people do to one another in both church and society when they are joined in a common enterprise. The meticulous observation of the scientist and the procedures employed to effect change can, together, assist people to respond to their calling as creatures within God's creation. *See also* Conflict Management; Engagement; Human Relations Training; Leadership Development; Management; Staff Relationships.

FOR FURTHER REFERENCE

Human Relations: Studies Toward the Integration of the Social Sciences. New York: 233 Spring St., NY 10013; London: 88/90 Middlesex St., E1 7EZ.

Journal of Applied Behavioral Science. Arlington, VA: NTL Institute, P.O. Box 9155, Rosslyn Station 22209.

D. R. Hunter

Grouping

A group is a social unit with a number of individuals in more or less interdependent relationship to one another. The group may have formed or been appointed for various reasons. The principles of forming a group or grouping have implicit or explicit values or norms that regulate the behavior of the members for the life of the group. Grouping is often done with the hope of achieving compatibility, homogeneity, or complementarity.

Grouping is done according to various aims. Learning groups may be formed by age, level of ability, level of attainment or grade, sex, race, language, socioeconomic status, or special needs. Some groups are formed because of geographic locations, as in the case of busing or consolidation of smaller schools. Some grouping is done in larger groups because there are not enough teachers. Grouping practices sometimes attract criticism and disapproval, often with intense emotional responses. Attitudes people hold toward particular grouping practices appear to be partly determined by social and cultural factors and be rooted also in the deeper levels of the personalities of the individuals concerned. If chronological age is the only consideration in forming learning groups, the mental age level may vary as much as eight years within the same group. Age grouping may be a more reliable factor for socialization. It is the one most used in schools and churches.

BASES FOR GROUPING

In many schools or churches an orderly progression of the majority of persons through a program that is designated for a stipulated period of time is expected. Although most persons are expected to progress at the predetermined rate, provision is sometimes made for the exceptionally able pupils to be more rapidly promoted and for the slower learners to remain behind and to repeat a grade.

An alternative to chronological age as a system is that of arranging for persons to belong to a relatively homogeneous group with respect to their levels of ability or attainment and thus to progress at their preferred rates in different "tracks" or "streams." If this is allowed, some classes will contain children differing in age by two or more years. In practice, however, "streaming" by ability tends to be used where larger numbers of children are already grouped by age; e.g., when there are a sufficient number of six year olds to form three separate classes, they are often grouped by ability.

In small churches there are educational advantages to permitting activities among persons of different ages for the benefit of all concerned. Larger groups can be formed that share space, equipment, and teachers. And it has been found that in mixed age groups, younger children learn more from those slightly older than they do from same-age children; similarly, older children have the opportunity to practice different interactional skills with those slightly younger. The criticisms against this wider age range are made by teachers who find this arrangement unmanageable.

Those persons who prefer learning to happen in homogeneous groups believe that such factors as mental age, physical maturity, social and emotional development, or a child's aptitude or readiness for a specific educational activity must be considered in the grouping. Grouping by chronological age is administratively simple and is usually accepted more widely.

If education is to be concerned with emotional and social development as well as scholastic progress, coeducation would seem to be the best arrangement. Not only do boys and girls enjoy the social benefits of growing up together, but they have the advantage of being taught by both men and women, giving a wider range of views and modes of thought.

The opponents of coeducation point out difficulties in this form. Educational needs of boys and girls are dissimilar in some respects. They may be interested in different subjects. They may during the early years of secondary school tend to develop, both intellectually and emotionally, at markedly different rates. Yet differences in rates of development occur to people as individuals, and with the changing roles of both men and women in society today, there may be less reason for separating the sexes. The interaction will help in later understandings of male and female roles.

When there are racial, language, or socioeconomic differences, fewer reasons exist for persons' segregation into separate groups than the values gained by interaction in the same group. It has been argued that if members of a racial minority have been underprivileged, improvement can be made more satisfactorily in their own group. The stronger argument that prevails today is that segregation tends to perpetuate discrimination and groups need to be racially mixed as well as mixed as to socioeconomic levels in order to motivate acceptance and understanding.

Problems in some communities also arise in regard to language differences. When a different language is spoken at home, children will be learning in a language other than their native tongue. This means moving toward bilingualism or the adoption of one recognized official language. The latter could be viewed as working contrary to attitudes needed for group harmony. In some places schools have opted for the use of two languages.

Grouping on the basis of socioeconomic status happens in a self-selective process when there is a wholly independent system of schools. Some special privately supported schools have tended to continue segregation practices or have sorted people into socioeconomic classes. Any socially divisive plan makes grouping in the churches even more difficult.

Special classes may need to be provided for those who are severely disabled. An issue arises with regard to those children, youth, and adults whose disabilities are of a less severe kind. Some believe that these special persons will become insecure and poorly motivated if they are put into groups that are largely not impaired. The other side of the argument is that when impaired persons mingle only with others of their own kind, their progress may well be impeded. The decisions about how inclusive groups are to be must be made by the teachers in conversation with the members of the total community.

OTHER FACTORS

Grouping has been considered largely from the learner's needs. Grouping procedures may also be affected by the requirements of the community or the congregation. The number of leaders available and the needs and abilities of those leaders may determine the style, size, and inclusiveness of the grouping.

THE PROBLEM OF ABILITY

Some measure of the person's aptitude or the person's faith development is employed in many places for the purposes of educational grouping. It is particularly difficult in religious groups to develop a measurement for such grouping. This practice involves intensely controversial issues. To make a judgment concerning another person's faith stage or spiritual ability is easily attacked as unfair or biased. Churches have to this time not provided good assessment means to group persons according to maturity or faith levels. A range of courses or experiences can be offered allowing persons to select their own level. This kind of grouping may be more possible when several church schools cooperate and work out a plan together.

Grouping within religious education classes by ability requires either complete honesty about the titles and purposes given to groups or specific testing instruments. Any grouping by ability tends toward some dissension between teachers and other educational planners. Those who oppose "streaming" advocate teaching in heterogeneous groups or organizing small ad hoc groups for various activities. Those who favor the practice insist that working with people of comparable ability provides greater motivation. If progress is hampered by the presence of those who work at a slower rate, they may fail to reach their full potential.

SOME MODELS

In planned heterogeneous groups alternative patterns may include:

1. Parallel classes with a mixture in each of ability, age, sex, race

2. Ungraded classes that allow for persons to help each other around a particular interest

3. Multigrade groupings that deliberately plan for older and more experienced persons to gain their knowledge by sharing and teaching the less experienced

4. Intergenerational (interage) grouping to provide a rich experience in questioning and sharing (these groups offer the best experiences in sharing faith because of the different levels of experience and knowledge and the support and modeling provided)

5. Groups internally balanced to match equal numbers of men and women or of various cultural or racial groupings

The most common grouping for religious education classes is as follows:

1. One teacher for each six pupils at preschool level through grade 2
2. One teacher for eight to ten pupils in grades 3, 4, 5, and 6
3. One teacher for fifteen in youth and adults

Another model is based on the use of teams for teaching. It would include three grades in a group with a team of leaders. Teams could allow for as many as four grades in a group. In very small churches grouping may be done with three year olds in a separate group, four and five year olds with grades 1 and 2, and the others in a third group. In some cases all those from grade seven could be with adults.

Grouping is considered best if it provides encouragement to form the individual's own thoughts. Persons are encouraged to share ideas and are constantly helped to see and compare alternative perceptions and plans for action. The grouping is most useful if it invites persons to an experience that is individualized, creative, and humanizing. *See also* Adolescence; Adult Development; Child Development; Cognitive Development; Faith Development; Intergenerational Approach; Psychosocial Development.

H. L. Miller

Guidance Counseling

Guidance means helping a person become a self-directed individual, and *counseling* takes place within a direct, one-to-one relationship. These two terms are used both interchangeably and together.

The goal of guidance counseling in the business, education, personal, legal, social, or family arenas—is to help counselees become more self-directed and aware of the options in their lives. The guidance worker does not make decisions for the counselee but helps to strengthen the problem-solving process in the individual. In most types of counseling, there are elements of education or training. Guidance also is a perspective, a general way of looking at a total situation, whether in business, education, or home life. In many places where people come together, they are carrying out the counseling process with each other. But when more than just informal help is needed, one goes to a trained professional.

Guidance counselors use a variety of methods in their work:

1. giving tests and interpreting results
2. following up with student records
3. designing forms and checklists
4. developing methods of shaping behavior
5. talking with and helping teachers and parents
6. interviewing
7. carrying out actual one-on-one counseling sessions
8. interpreting the counseling program to the school, business, or community as a whole

The main theme of guidance counseling is holistic development. One of the tasks of the guidance counselor in America from the beginning has been to keep before the public the fact that individuals, although they may be seen in various roles—worker, student, parent—are ultimately to be regarded as whole beings. Every effort must be made to help individuals develop their human potential, in order to retain the "stuff" that makes each person a unique part of humanity.

HISTORY

Guidance counseling began with Frank Parsons of Boston, who wrote a book called *Choosing a Vocation* in 1909. Eli Weaver developed a vocational guidance program about the same time in New York. In 1913, the first guidance association was founded, the National Vocational Association. Other associations were formed, but in 1950, all the groups came together under the name the American Personnel and Guidance Association.

The leading figure in the development of the guidance movement in America was John Dewey, who stressed the importance of human potential and experience, or learning to do by doing. His ideas fit in perfectly with the emerging guidance and counseling emphasis.

The two world wars brought the need for guidance to the fore, in the wake of technological changes in the workplace. America was faced with the problem of guiding and training large numbers of workers, especially returning soldiers, to enter the postwar world.

PROGRAMS

Guidance counseling programs exist in a variety of settings. High schools have active guidance counseling programs because students at that age—between twelve and nineteen—are making important choices. In light of the changing economic, political, and social scene in America today, many programs have emerged to address the needs of special groups: high school dropouts, non-college-bound students, culturally disadvantaged students, rural students, college-bound students, college dropouts, women students, and handicapped students.

Colleges are the arena in which the guidance counselor is most influential; counselors help students choose a study program, provide personal counseling, and do academic and vocational placement. The attempt is now made to infuse the curriculum as a whole with the counseling perspective so that teacher and paraprofessional might help the professional guidance counselor.

Graduate and professional schools have extensive guidance counseling programs. Among these are programs in schools of law, medicine, business, and theology. Business schools have been particularly active, especially after the world wars, when soldiers had to be helped to return to society.

Personal counseling programs have also developed. The modern world is stressful; often an individual needs a sounding board or someone with whom to share feelings and pain rather than conventional psychotherapy. Different specialities and emphases have emerged. Counselors may concentrate their work on children, youth, or adults, or may specialize in certain problem areas—sex, teenage pregnancy, abortion, drugs—or the problems faced by certain groups—single people, the aged, the terminally ill.

RELATIONSHIP TO RELIGIOUS EDUCATION

The relationship of guidance counseling to religious education is meaningful and valuable. Counselors, with their emphasis on the primacy of the person and innate human potential, join hands with religious educators, who speak of the kingdom of God and human beings as sons and daughters of the kingdom.

In the community guidance counselors have linked their efforts with those of churches on problems like stress management, chemical addiction, child and wife abuse, husband abuse, teenage pregnancy, abortion, marriage enrichment, and mid-life crisis, and on programs to serve the aged and the terminally ill.

Guidance counseling and religious education have also come together in the matter of career counseling and religious vocations; the principles of guidance counseling can be useful in helping those who wish to enter the ministry. Many churches have set up departments of church vocation in their corporate bodies, and such departments often exist at the local church level as well.

On college campus too the religious educator joins hands with the guidance worker. This working relationship is most often seen in campus ministry programs, in which the leader works closely with student workers on matters of worship and counseling and on programs of a religious nature. Sometimes campus ministers serve on guidance counseling committees.

The guidance counselor approach has developed recently on the campuses of theological seminaries as well, where student personnel workers have even been employed to look after health, employment, academic, and career needs. Some seminaries have developed what is known as a spiritual director—not a guidance counselor but a professional who regards religious vocation from the point of view of mission, ministry, the church, and the gospel. Operating from the holistic perspective, these workers emphasize the primacy of the human person and try to promote a society in which persons can grow in their own unique way *and* with others, to indeed open up to the kingdom of God.

TRENDS

A number of trends in the field are discernible:

1. helping teachers to be more responsible for guidance

2. developing a life guidance focus rather than a vocational or educational guidance focus

3. stressing the developmental aspects of guidance wherein guidance is fashioned for the individual at different stages of life

4. basing choices on knowledge of the self rather than on outside expectations

5. training guidance workers as facilitators rather than persuaders or manipulators of what they *want* the counselee to do

6. training guidance counselors to include in their work with people the social as well as the personal dimension

General trends are also important to the field. Writers such as Alvin Toffler (*Future Shock*, 1970), Marilyn Ferguson (*The Aquarian Conspiracy*, 1981), Marvin Cetron (*Encounter with the Future*, 1983), and John Naisbitt (*Megatrends*, 1988) describe waves, shifts, encounters, and megatrends that provide a framework for the future for business, education, and the church—and for guidance counseling.

Toffler writes of the "third wave," Ferguson, the "paradigm shift," Cetron, encounters with the future, and Naisbitt, megatrends and the reinvention of the corporate body. Each says in his or her own way that people-helpers can no longer do business with the same kind of worldview. Instead, they must design goals, projects, and mission by considering that we are moving into a new way of perceiving reality. Ferguson insists that we are shifting from a world in which the main emphasis is on being comfortable, secure, and static to one of risk, relationship, and growth.

Naisbitt provides a series of megatrends for the guidance counselor to reflect upon. Using megatrends as a framework for looking at present and future, he speaks of our present society moving from an industrial to an informational society; from forced technology to high tech/high touch; from institutional help to self-help; from representative democracy to participatory democracy; from hierarchies to networking; from short-term to long-term planning; from centralization to decentralization; from north to south and west; from national to world economy; and from either/or to multiple option. Study of each of these trends provides valuable lessons to those who develop the theory and practice of guidance, whether personal, vocational, or educational.

These four theorists have different ideas, but they prod both the guidance counselor and the religious educator to raise relevant questions about the culture and to search for authentic answers. *See also* Psychological Testing; Psychotherapy; Vocation.

J. Jackson

Guilt

The word "guilt" is derived from the Anglo-Saxon word "gylt," which means "to pay." Originally, the word meant payment of a fine for an offense. Today it may refer to punishable conduct, the state of having broken a law, crime, or wickedness. It also may refer to feelings of guilt, that sense of responsibility for wrongdoing or the emotional conflict arising out of real or imaginary infractions of rules or mores. Guilt may be discussed from a variety of perspectives: legal, psychological, moral, or theological. Guilt may be individual or collective.

TYPES OF GUILT

Legal guilt refers to that objective state of affairs when a specific act contrary to a written law is committed. It is wholly objective, involving culpability and punishment. Subjective considerations such as motivation are not important, but legal guilt may be mitigated by insanity or ignorance; in such cases we speak of "diminished responsibility."

When we speak of psychological guilt we are referring to feelings of guilt that may be appropriate or inappropriate. It is appropriate that we feel an inner sense of wrongdoing, self-blame, or guilt when evil has been done or good not done. The development of a moral consciousness or conscience depends on appropriate feelings of guilt. Such feelings of guilt are an impetus to atone, seek forgiveness, and turn from evil.

Inappropriate guilt feelings are those feelings that arise out of a scrupulous or misinformed conscience. Anxiety about imagined or exaggerated wrongdoings as well as neurotic feelings of self-loathing are not conducive to authentic atonement, forgiveness, and conversion from evil.

Moral guilt is incurred when what is deemed ethically wrong or evil is chosen over what is right or good. Moral guilt presupposes freedom to choose what one ought; one cannot be held morally responsible for an act performed under force or duress.

Problems arise in assigning moral guilt because there is disagreement about what is right and good. Because cultural conditions differ from society to society, what is morally abhorrent in one may not be so in another. Even if an act is believed to be objectively wrong, subjective considerations may lessen the degree of moral guilt. Motivation and individual circumstances must be considered in assigning moral guilt. What is considered morally wrong in one circumstance may be considered morally good in another. The works of Lawrence Kohlberg and Carol Gilligan explore degrees or morality from this subjective point of view.

Theological guilt is guilt that results from a sense of sin. An act or the omission of an act believed to be an offense against God or God's law is considered to be sin. It is because we consider human acts to have consequences bearing on our relationship with God that we have developed a theology of sin and guilt. What we do or do not do in our interrelationships with other individuals and with all of creation has an impact on our relationship with God. It is the fracturing of this relationship that is the subject of theological or religious guilt.

Thus, because Israel understood that their God was a God of history, intimately involved with their lives, they believed that whenever Israel as a nation or in the person of its leaders committed evil, it turned its back on Yahweh. Sin resulted, guilt was incurred, and reparation demanded.

Christianity has sometimes taught that the guilt resulting from sin was such that it demanded the death of Jesus on the cross. Only by the death of the Son of God could atonement and reconciliation with God be accomplished. It is more generally held today that the life, death, and resurrection of Jesus served God's salvific purpose in history.

While contrition and reparation are necessary for the overcoming of guilt, forgiveness and grace are the free gifts of God and are not the result of our works.

Recent developments in theology have introduced the idea of corporate or collective guilt that results from an awareness of systemic sin. Institutions, organizations, and communities may be sinful insofar as they oppress, cheat, manipulate, or misuse people. All who are involved in such collectives are proportionally responsible for the evil done and share in the guilt.

TEACHING ABOUT GUILT

Children may begin to feel guilt by the age of three. At first they know that something they have done has disturbed the person who loves them. When they find out what has happened, they may want to change their actions. When it is explained what brought this response, they learn how to avoid the actions or words that bring unpleasant results. Thus the two year old learns not to bite mother. This can be construed as moral guilt only when the child is old enough to understand some reason for the difference between right and wrong in specific actions, at age five or six (biting hurts another person). With rational grounds for choice, children's actions become deliberate. The rules of the playground preclude pushing and hitting other children.

Theological guilt connects wrongdoing with sin, which is disobedience to God. God loves people and does not want them to hurt one another. To do so is wrong because it is sinful. It is a refusal to love as God loves people. The Bible has verses that assure people of God's forgiveness and stories of how God forgave disobedient people who were sorry and asked to be forgiven. Jesus taught people to forgive each other.

School-age children can be taught about guilt, sin, and forgiveness in terms of concrete actions, putting biblical stories in the context of their life situations. In the story of the forgiving father (Luke 15:11–32) children can act out the parts of father, younger son, and older son to see how they may sometimes feel forgiving, unforgiving, or in need of forgiveness.

The role of the group in the formation of guilt feelings is experienced to some extent during the early school years, but definitely during adolescence. Sometimes peer pressure may lead to conflict between received family and religious standards and those practiced by the group. Guilt can result whether the young person opts for a group standard that will disappoint a family or for a family standard that will bring isolation from the group. This is one area for discussion in religious education groups, where life experience stories and role playing become useful methods.

Adults, in their study, need to make distinctions among psychological, moral, and theological guilt, but also to see the connections. While inappropriate guilt feelings can occur, the tendency today is to avoid feelings of moral guilt, focusing on mistakes or bad judgment. Religiously motivated people will want to examine these factors in the light of biblical assertions about the moral goodness of God and God's expectation that faithfulness means recognizing one's sin, repenting, seeking forgiveness, and accepting restoration.

Whether we speak of objective or subjective guilt, legal, psychological, moral, or theological guilt, we must consider culpability and corresponding responsibility. Freedom from guilt demands repentance and atonement. *See also* Moral Development; Nurture; Reconciliation; Salvation; Yom Kippur.

R. Coll, I. V. Cully

Habits

Habits are customs or practices one performs with such regularity that one can scarcely consider not doing them. The term may also be used to refer to one's dress and especially to particular forms of religious dress. However, in religious education the term is usually used to refer to religious practices or conduct done with some regularity.

Habits sometimes are viewed negatively to refer to practices in which we engage with little thought in a somewhat rote manner. If one engages in habits that have negative consequences for oneself or others, they are obviously of negative value. However, what of those routinely engaged in with little rational thought or planning? Religious educators are divided as to the value of such habits.

For example, is prayer or attendance at Sunday school performed in a routine way out of habit of significant value to the person who is so engaged? Some would say it has become perfunctory and, though engaged in with great regularity, it has little value for the person. Others would say that such habits are good. They demonstrate commitment to one's religion, and they place one in a position to receive religious insights and perform religious service. Certainly good habits in the practice of one's religion are to be preferred to habits in the neglect of the same.

Some habits may be decided upon by an individual, for example, a daily exercise routine, but most habits do not develop by themselves. People (parents, teachers, employers) train other people in habits of expected behavior by a process of conditioning. Behavior that wins approval from significant other persons tends to be repeated and to become habitual. Behavior that brings reproof or disapproval tends to be avoided. Behavioral theory affirms that positive reinforcement is more effective than negative reinforcement. The fear and confusion engendered by the latter can interfere with learning new behavior patterns.

Parents and teachers may be unaware that they are influencing habits. When constant attention is paid to the disruptive child without trying to find the root cause of the behavior, such actions are actually being encouraged. When creative thought or probing questions are welcomed, this mode of learning is encouraged. B. F. Skinner, noted for research in conditioning, contends that creativity is not "innate" but develops only if encouraged, and creativity can be stifled by disapproval.

Patterns of moral behavior, both personal and social, tend to reflect the expectations of a culture. People belonging to a religious culture that has specific moral requirements may find themselves at odds with the surrounding community and have to find their own ways of instilling their moral habit patterns into their children. For example, the Amish, preferring not to use electricity or automobiles, live in their own communities.

Expectations of how to behave in church (the limits of restlessness, the emphasis on quiet) are habit-forming. So are expectations of how to behave in a social group (repress anger, express feelings). Thus habits in one person may differ from place to place. A child habituated to remain silent while one teacher speaks may habitually interrupt with questions where another teacher permits.

Educators need to realize that the formation of habits is an educative process and it is important to be deliberate in what habits are formed and how they are formed. See also Attitude Formation; Behavior; Conditioning; Culture; Learning Theory; Motivation.

J. J. Sowell

Halevi, Judah

See Judah Halevi.

Handicapped

See Exceptional Persons.

Hanukkah

From the Hebrew word for "dedication," Hanukkah is known in English as the "Feast of Lights" or "Feast of Dedication" and celebrates the Maccabean victory over the Syro-Greeks under Antiochus Epiphanes in the year 165 B.C. This minor Jewish festival commemorates the cleansing and rededication of the ancient Temple in Jerusalem by the rekindling of the *ner tamid*, the "eternal light," symbol of the presence of God in the Jewish sanctuary. The festival commences on the twenty-fifth day of the Hebrew month of Kislev, corresponding to November-December on the Gregorian-secular calendar, and runs for eight days.

The first book of Maccabees tells the story of the oppression of the Jews of Palestine by Antiochus. Though not a Greek himself, Antiochus's love for Hellenism caused him to undertake strenuous efforts to make the territory under his control a model of Greek culture. He forbade the teaching of Torah, attempted to erect a statue of Zeus in the Holy of Holies within the sacred precincts of the Temple, and demanded that the Jews bow down to the god Zeus—a direct violation of their religious tradition.

In the village of Modin, Mattityahu (Gk. Mattathias), a priest of the Hasmonean family, slew the messenger sent by Antiochus with the orders and, together with his several sons led by Judah, organized a guerrilla army in 168 B.C. that continually attacked the armies of Antiochus until they were successful in 165 B.C. The term for this guerrilla army was "Maccabee," which means "hammer" in Hebrew. From all available evidence, this conflict was the first in recorded history primarily for the cause of religious freedom.

According to Jewish tradition, when the Maccabees entered the Temple sanctuary in Jerusalem to repurify it after it had been desecrated, they found only enough pure, beaten oil to rekindle the *ner tamid* for one day. That this minimal quantity of oil burned continuously for eight days is the miracle commemorated by this holiday.

Today, Hanukkah is celebrated primarily in the home with the kindling of an eight-branched menorah or *chanukiyah*, the number of candles lighted corresponding to the night being celebrated. Gifts are exchanged, usually from parents to children, and a popular game with a spinning top (*dreidel* in Yiddish, *s'vivon* in Hebrew) is played.

Its accidental proximity to Christmas on the calendar, coupled with the pluralism of American society, has encouraged the evolution of Hanukkah into a far more significant Jewish holiday in America today than it was in previous generations. The very evident nationalistic echoes of Hanukkah have also contributed to its increasing importance in Israel. See also Jewish Festivals and Holidays.

FOR FURTHER REFERENCE

Goodman, Philip. *The Hanukkah Anthology.* Philadelphia: Jewish Publication Society of America, 1976.

Solis-Cohen, Jr., Emily. *Hanukkah: The Feast of Lights.* Philadelphia: Jewish Publication Society of America, 1937.

S. L. Jacobs

Hartshorne, Hugh

As a teacher and writer in the first half of this century, Hugh Hartshorne (1885–1969) applied contemporary insights from psychology and education to the development of religious education. As principal of the Union School of Religion (1912–1922), he supervised the introduction of progressive educational innovations into the teaching of religion to children. As research associate of the Character Education Inquiry at Teachers College, Columbia University (1922–1929) and as research associate in religion at Yale University (1929–1951), he demonstrated the value of social science research for religious education. He was a prolific writer on the religious education of children and youth, worship in the church school, character education, and the organization and administration of the church school. He contributed frequently to the journal of the Religious Education Association from 1914 through 1954 and served as its president from 1935 to 1939. In 1951 he was appointed professor of psychology and religion at Yale, a position he held until his retirement in 1954. *See also* Character Development; Progressive Education; Research; Social Sciences.

C. R. Foster

Herbart, Johann Friedrich

German educator and philosopher, Johann Friedrich Herbart (1776–1841) studied at Jena, after which he tutored in Switzerland. While in Burgdorf he became acquainted with Johann Pesta-

lozzi, an educational reformer. Early in his career Herbart was appointed to the chair of pedagogy and philosophy at Königsberg formerly occupied by Immanuel Kant. In 1833 he went to Göttingen as professor of philosophy and there developed the theory known as the "Herbartian principle"— that new knowledge should be presented to the child in a fashion that will relate it to what has already been learned and associated with the pupil's whole experience. This method of teaching was introduced into the Sunday schools of the United States by early leaders of the movement. In higher education Herbart emphasized the adjustment of the student to society through the study of literature and history. Much educational innovation today derives from Herbart's theories. *See also* History of Christian Education; Pestalozzi, Johann Heinrich; Sunday School.

L. G. McAllister

Heresy

"Heresy" is from the Greek *hairesis* meaning, literally, "choice" or "that which is chosen." This term originally applied to a choice between different schools of philosophical thought but was used by the early church fathers to mean a deviation from pure doctrine. The word is sometimes used in a secular sense to mean a radical straying from some accepted orthodoxy (e.g., in science), but its primary connotation today is theological.

It is perhaps best understood, according to Roman Catholic canon law, as the willful denial or doubt by a baptized Christian (thus a member of the church) of an article of faith that is defined as such by the teaching authority of the church (dogma; Matt. 18:17).

From this definition it may be observed that only those who are baptized may fall into heresy and the denied or doubted truth must be proposed by the teaching church as having been revealed by God. There is thus a close relationship between heresy and dogma, and much doctrinal development and the proposing of dogma has taken place in response to the need to combat heresy. In the definition doubt is to be understood as an obstinate withholding of acceptance and not a mere mental puzzlement or hesitation. And the denial must be free and deliberate; unconscious error does not constitute heresy.

For Christian churches where Scripture alone is the rule of faith and the validating source for doctrine, where there is strict adherence to the principle of private interpretation of Scripture, and where the teaching authority of the church is not clearly defined, the words "heresy" and "heretic" logically cannot have the force they have in the Roman Catholic communion. Thus, exclusion from church fellowship, while being rather infrequent, is more likely to occur for disciplinary reasons than for rejection of Christian faith. In the Catholic church the ecclesiastical penalty for heresy is *ipso facto* excommunication, provided the heresy has been externally manifest in some way (spoken or otherwise indicated). *See also* Biblical Authority; Doctrine/Dogma; History of Christian Education; Magisterium.

I. Knox

Hermeneutic

Hermeneutic means interpretation. It is the discipline whereby one attempts to translate or make meaningful an otherwise obscure text. Translation itself might seem simple enough, inasmuch as it is often thought of as the mechanical process of replacing the word in the original language with today's English equivalent, but words have shades of meaning that change from one culture to another and within cultures over time. Choosing the "right" translation still involves human judgment and interpretation. And then once one has the best or "most accurate" English translation, there still remains the matter of interpreting the biblical material for life and faith today.

Nineteenth-century hermeneutical studies brought out and took seriously the gap between our modern worldview and the worldview we have constructed for the writers of antiquity. Yet there was also interest in preserving the historical character of the narrative. For that reason, there was a tendency to say, "Yes, the things in the Bible happened, but not in the way in which they are depicted."

In the New Testament, for example, Jesus is depicted as curing people by casting out demons and evil spirits. Today most people do not think of demons and evil spirits; they think instead of physical and/or psychosomatic illnesses. Does that mean we must dismiss these stories as unreal or irrelevant and restrict ourselves to those passages that speak primarily of ethical human conduct?

Not at all. In fact, to do so misses the point of the Gospel narratives. The strength of the narratives lies in the fact that the authors most certainly believed that Jesus was capable of performing the feats they ascribe to him, that he in fact cured maladies (whichever view one holds of the cause of the maladies), and that he was able to cure them because he was the Savior, the Son of God, the Messiah. To say anything less than this is to do injustice to the faith of the Gospel writers.

Each author's message was his expression of his faith in Jesus. Hermeneutic allows us to see that the fact that an author formed his expression in terms familiar to him from his particular worldview need not hinder our appreciation and appropriation of his message for the building of faith.

Hermeneutic therefore permits the text to speak to us today with something of the immediacy with which it spoke in its own time. The question of whether or not the event depicted in a particular narrative actually happened or whether it happened in exactly the manner in which it is depicted must be addressed differently by historians, who use the ancient texts as historical resources.

Religious educators, who must attempt to interpret biblical passages for faith education today, must be faithful to what is understood as the intention and purpose of the writer, have an appreciation of biblical culture and worldview (and where there are parallels to modern life and where there are not), and be reminded that human nature remains the same and the message of the Bible is addressed to people. *See also* Bible Class; Bible in Religious Education, The; Bible Study; Biblical Authority; Biblical Criticism; Biblical Translation; Exegesis.

FOR FURTHER REFERENCE

Palmer, Richard E. *Hermeneutics*. Northwestern Studies in Phenomenology and Existential Philosophy. Evanston, IL: Northwestern University Press, 1969.

Stuhlmacher, Peter. *Historical Criticism and Theological Interpretation of Scripture*. Translated by Roy A. Harrisville. Philadelphia: Fortress, 1977.

J. S. Ruef

Heschel, Abraham Joshua

An outstanding Jewish theologian and philosopher, Abraham Joshua Heschel (1907–1972) was descended from two lines of Hasidic rabbis. While contributing to every field of critical Jewish scholarship, Heschel maintained the Hasidic spirit in his systematic theology of Judaism, especially in *God in Search of Man* (1955) and other major works. His doctoral research, published in English as *The Prophets* (1962), his childhood background, and his survival of the Holocaust inspired his emergence, for Jews and Christians, as a powerful religious presence on the American scene. Professor at the Jewish Theological Seminary, consultant on Jewish affairs to Vatican II, active with Martin Luther King in the civil rights movement, and leader in opposition to the Vietnam war, Heschel championed the causes of Soviet Jews and the state of Israel. His legacy for religious education is great. Educators may draw from his explication of awe and wonder as responses to the mystery of being. His development of the phenomenology of prophetic consciousness and the correlative task of witnessing God's presence in the world through holiness are rich and suggestive resources. *See also* Buber, Martin; Existentialism.

J. Lukinsky

Higher Education, Religion in

Historically, education has been deeply influenced by religious concerns. This has been true especially in Western Christian societies. With the advent of Christianity, education came increasingly under the control of the church. From the sixth century, monasteries, cathedral schools, and universities emerged as Christian forms of education. The early universities were often founded by religious orders. Although concerned primarily with religious and moral training, the university continued the liberal arts tradition advocated by the Greco-Roman scholars of an earlier age.

EARLY RELIGIOUS TIES

Many of the great universities of Europe were founded, in part at least, from religious motivations. The Sorbonne, the famous university in Paris, was first organized in the thirteenth century as a residential hall for students in theology. It served as a major intellectual center in religious thought until about 1888, when the university disposed of religious studies in order to become a secular institution.

Oxford and Cambridge in England are two of the oldest universities in Europe. Scholars are actually uncertain as to which is the older as both schools date to the twelfth century. The tradition at both schools is that they grew from religious orders or monasteries located in the two towns. Students gathered in the housing of the orders to live and to read theology under the leadership of masters, or tutors. The religious foundations of Oxford were dissolved and the school became secular during the Reformation years. About the same time the patronage of Cambridge shifted from the church to the ruling monarch.

Harvard University is the oldest university in America. It was founded in 1636 by the Puritans or Congregationalists who wanted in the New World a school to continue in the tradition of Oxford and Cambridge. The earliest curriculum at Harvard made the study of Bible and theology central and served largely to train persons for the ministry. The other colonial schools, such as Yale and Princeton, were founded also to train people to serve the needs of the church and civil state. As people moved westward, the churches' schools went with them in the form of frontier colleges designed to provide higher education within a Christian environment.

THE MOVEMENT AWAY FROM SECTARIANISM

Thomas Jefferson was a major leader in the development of public universities free from sectarian control. The University of Virginia was founded in 1819 without the traditional department of theology. Jefferson advocated that religion, if taught at all, should be integral to the other departments of study. He proposed that the different sects or denominations be encouraged to establish alongside the university and offer courses of study having to do with their own religious tradition. Although this proposal for dealing with religious pluralism was rejected, the Jefferson plan for a chaplain to care for the religious life of the students was funded.

The model proposed by Jefferson led in the latter nineteenth and early twentieth century to the rise of the public, state-supported universities. Politically the churches continued to seek to influence these nonsectarian schools. Much of the nineteenth century was occupied with the struggle over who was to control higher education, the forces of religion or the forces of the secular state. Public institutions continued to spread, especially in the West, and they enrolled an increasing number of students. At first, the state schools continued to require chapel services and some forms of Bible study. In time the denominations fulfilled their responsibility for meeting the religious needs of students by locating churches or chapels near the campuses. In addition to social and devotional programs, these small congregations formed houses or centers for the teaching of Bible and religion courses. The courses were generally accredited by the university for academic degree credit. One of the earliest of these centers was founded by the Methodists at the University of Illinois in Urbana in 1892. In 1898, the Episcopal church opened a chapel at the University of Texas in Austin, and the same year the Presbyterians employed a minister to serve the religious needs of students at the University of Colorado.

These attempts by denominations to establish sectarian programs adjacent to the centers of higher learning have gradually given way to ecumenical ministries. This cooperative strategy has become the major focus of most major mainline Protestant groups, who have joined together to serve college campuses as United Ministries. The church's fear of university has diminished, and the focus has shifted from protecting the religious faith of students in a "home away from home" to serving a mission that has concern for the whole campus and the total intellectual enterprise of education. This has included a concern for both students and faculty, an emphasis upon justice issues, and a desire to advocate for free and open intellectual inquiry. Also currently emerging are new patterns of partnership in which mainline Protestants are finding compatible ministries with evangelicals and Roman Catholics, as well as with Jewish and other religious traditions.

THE SCIENTIFIC STUDY OF RELIGION

The discussion as to the appropriate role that religion should have in higher education continues to this day. Is it to serve primarily for training in faith or as a mode of scientific inquiry? To a large extent the major emphasis today has shifted to the study of religion as an objective field of inquiry. This is illustrated by the prominence of the American Academy of Religion with its scientific emphasis. Many modern universities have developed programs of religious studies in which the content is derived from all of the disciplines of the humanities.

STUDENT ORGANIZATIONS

Student religious societies have always been indigenous to higher education. The "Holy Club" at Oxford in the early 1700s is only one historical example. Such groups have provided students with a way to express their religious and spiritual insights. These have sometimes emerged as the by-product of classroom teaching and at other times emerged as protests against the restrictions imposed upon students by the university or the society at large. Christian student societies of varying kinds have been a part of American higher education from the early part of the eighteenth century. Almost always these groups were inter-denominational in character. Most notable are those societies sponsored by the YMCA and what came to be known as the Student Volunteer Movement. These early associations contributed to the formation of the World Student Christian Federation in 1895. The federation was an international association of campus religious movements and became one of the major forerunners of the World Council of Churches. See also Colleges and Universities, Church-Related; Colleges, Black; Religious Studies; Student Christian Movement; Theological Education; University.

A. J. Moore

Hinduism

R. C. Zaehner, the late Spalding Professor at Oxford, defined Hinduism as "the 'ism' of the Indian people." This definition suggests a more extensive complex—one that encompasses the totality of mores and customs that constitute an ethos or worldview—than that which the conventional notion of a religion denotes. For Hinduism the parameters of this worldview are considerable, having been drawn from the innumerable distinct cultures, both indigenous and nonindigenous, that have coexisted on the Indian subcontinent from prehistoric times into the present century. Although these groups may have at one time maintained distinct beliefs and practices, a gradual process of synthesis led by the first centuries A.D. to the establishment of pan-Indic tradition. The Indian tendency to syncretism is already apparent in a text from ca. 800 B.C.: "The one called 'Agni' [the god of fire], the priests worship him as the sacrifice, because he ties together this whole universe. . . . Those skilled in sorcery worship him as a spirit, because by him this universe is kept together. . . . Thus, according to whatever form they worship him, so he becomes" (Satapatha Brahmana 10.5.2.20). In much the same manner the thirty-three gods of the Rigveda-samhita, a text composed ca. 1200 B.C., become in the texts of the first centuries A.D. a largely symbolic thirty-three thousand.

The vehicle that facilitated much of this synthesis is Sanskrit, which refers to a culture as well as a language. Sanskrit's roots are not Indic, but rather lie in the central Asian steppes, the homeland of the nomadic tribes that at the close of the third millennium B.C. migrated to Europe, Asia Minor, and India. Symbolic of the Indian melting pot, the culture and language of these migrating tribes, who referred to themselves as arya ("the noble"), provided a base to which the diverse beliefs and practices of the subcontinent adhered. This process is apparent in the history of the gods Siva and Vishnu, one or the other of whom virtually all Hindus view as supreme deity (a third sect devoted to Devi, the goddess, is often tied to the worship of Siva). The mythology of the Rigveda-samhita, the text that most closely reflects Hinduism's non-Indic Aryan substratum, only vaguely depicts these two deities. Yet, over the centuries, these bits of Rigvedic mythology lent themselves to a process of identification and assimilation in which innumerable indigenous Indian deities were conjoined in a universal Indian mythology—one that broadly depicts Siva as an unpredictable destroyer-creator and Vishnu as the benevolent preserver of the cosmic order. Thus, although certain of the structural elements of Hinduism originated outside India, the tradition grew and developed organically within the subcontinent, eventually overwhelming these non-Indic structures. It is worth noting that, in evidence of this relationship to the subcontinent, Hinduism has neither been a missionary religion nor engendered a significant number of communities in diaspora.

Any attempt to view Hinduism as a single entity necessarily risks ignoring those disparate elements that have imbued the tradition with a certain tension and, hence, a certain vitality. For the conflation of traditions that underlies Hinduism continues to enliven its variously diverging and intersecting concerns both this-worldly and otherworldly.

KEY DEVELOPMENTS

Many of the beliefs and practices recorded in the earliest Vedic texts (*veda* meaning "knowledge") look back to the non-Indic Aryan past. The *Rigveda-samhita*, a collection of hymns that, in the main, extol the gods and thereby seek their favor, clearly reflects this heritage. Among the deities Dyaus Pitr, "Father Sky," is equivalent to the Greek Zeus; Varuna, upholder of cosmic order (*rta*), equivalent to the Greek Uranus and the Iranian Ahura Mazda. Indra the warrior god, who slays the demon Vrtra and so releases the ordered cosmos from the primeval chaos, is himself a reflection of the Aryan people as they battled their way into the Indian subcontinent. Indra's battles thus occur not only on the cosmic level but also on the more immediate level of subduing the Dasas, the Aryan name for India's indigenous dark-skinned inhabitants—to the Aryans, the representatives of primeval chaos. (It is worth noting that this indigenous population, who lived in the Indus Valley, possessed from at least the third millennium B.C. a remarkably mature urban culture, with cities characterized by uniform brick construction, regular streets with drainpipes, and houses with indoor bathrooms.)

The Vedic religion underwent a substantial transformation toward the close of the *Rigveda*'s composition (ca. 900 B.C.), perhaps because of the Aryan encounter with the inhabitants of the Indus Valley. This transformation is apparent in particular in the development of the Vedic sacrificial ritual. Initially, the chief ritual purpose of the *Rigveda*'s hymns was to invoke the gods and thereby win from them the goods of life. The gods' provision was won through the mechanism of the sacrifice at its simplest an exchange in which, for example, a cow might be offered up to gain more cows. The transformation in the nature of the sacrifice occurred when the Vedic thinkers

began to extend this notion of exchange, in particular, from one that exchanges food for more food to one that exchanges (human) life for more life.

The creative potential of such an act is the subject of a late Rigvedic hymn (10.90) that describes the creation of the cosmos through the sacrifice of a primordial being, Purusa, the "Man." Purusa's dismembered body gives rise both to the various elements of the cosmos—his head becomes the heavens, his trunk the atmosphere, and his feet the earth—and to the social order—his mouth becomes the priests (*brahman*), his arms the warriors (*ksatriya*), his thighs the merchants (*vaisya*), and his feet the peasants (*sudra*). This is the first reference in Indian literature to caste (*varna*), and the notion that it is established as a part of the cosmic order underpins for the Hindus the absolute nature of carrying out their societal duty.

The immediate consequences of the Purusa mythology are seen in the *Brahmana* and Upanishad texts, the texts that follow chronologically the *Rigveda-samhita*. The chief concern of the *Brahmana* texts (ca. 900 to 700 B.C.) is the sacrificial ritual, its ideology as well as its technique. The ideology centers on the possibility of renewing the existence of the cosmos (and thereby, human existence) by recreating the events that led to its creation; as the authors of the *Brahmana* texts often state: "This ritual act done now is that which the gods did then." The technique is more problematic, for the replication of Purusa's primordial act would, in the opinion of some scholars, seem to require that in performing the sacrifice humans must offer up human sacrifice. To circumvent such an offering a complex technique was developed whereby various substitutes—ranging from grain and animals to a gold effigy—were employed in place of the human victim.

This complex, and not entirely satisfactory, solution (for it does not actually fulfill the requirements of the sacrificial theory) seems to have led to the idea of "ritual interiorization," an idea that is explored in detail in the Upanishad texts (ca. 700 to 500 B.C.). In this type of ritual activity physiological functions stand in the place of the physical objects of the sacrifice. The interiorization of the sacrifice focuses on knowledge (*jnana*) rather than action (karma). Whereas the path of action seeks to realize the identity of human and cosmos through physically replicating the events of the cosmogony, the path of knowledge seeks this realization through an internal process that identifies the microcosmic self (*atman*) and the macrocosmic ground of all existence (*brahman*).

The reenactment of the cosmogony, whether through the path of work or the path of knowledge, suggests a rigor that precludes normal societal existence. Yet Hindu society is founded upon the same event that led to the creation of the cosmos: the failure to fulfill societal duties, and thus to "act rightly" (*dharma*), breaches the cosmic order. The *Bhagavad-Gita* (ca. 200 B.C. to A.D. 200), certainly the single most influential texts in the Hindu tradition, iterates this point: "Better to do one's own duty, though imperfect, than to do another's duty, however well performed. . . . One should not lay aside the works that are inborn in each of us" (18.47–48). In Hindu thought, the consequence of not acting according to one's inborn nature—defined by caste—is continual rebirth in an "unreal" cosmos; that is, a cosmos with which one never realizes one's essential identity. The integral relationship expressed here between this-worldly and other-worldly concerns—for the creation of the cosmos is at the same time our own creation, and its nature defines our nature—is perhaps what best defines Hinduism throughout the vicissitudes of its long development.

RELIGIOUS EDUCATION

Hindu writers often speak of the "forest universities" of ancient India, as described and illustrated in the Upanishads. Teachers (gurus) withdrew from society, gathering students around themselves and teaching the texts and values of Vedic literatures.

Later ages of Hindu tradition, as depicted in the *Manushastra*, show a system of individual tutorship or education for the upper two castes. Families secured the services of a learned Brahman priest, who instructed male children in the duties and learning of the tradition.

In modern times two of India's great universities are devoted to education in the Hindu tradition. Annie Besant in 1898 founded the college that later became Banaras Hindu University as a tribute to Hindu thought and devotion. Rabindranath Tagore founded a school at Santiniketan that later became the international university called Visva-Bharati; it was dedicated to social reform and world unity.

H. Tull

Hispanic Americans

A distinct effort that can be called religious education among Hispanic Americans is a recent phenomenon. Until the mid-1960s, there was no religious education outside religious education in general for this group, which numbers about 14.6 million, 80–90 percent of them Roman Catholics. In Roman Catholic circles the ferment caused by the Second Vatican Council in every area of the church's life, altered the situation radically. The most important of these changes for the religious education of Hispanics were the adoption of ver-nacular languages as the medium for liturgy and the publication of the first Bible in the Spanish of Latin America rather than that of Spain.

INITIAL RELIGIOUS EDUCATION EFFORTS

As Catholic parishes began to change from Latin to English, Hispanics began to feel the need to worship in their own language, too, and many churches responded accordingly. The appearance of these services in Spanish highlighted in a new way the growth of the Spanish-speaking population in the United States and their desire to maintain cultural and religious links with their countries of origin. This Hispanic awakening within the church was strengthened by parallel movements in the society at large, made concrete in the struggle for civil rights and in the increased availability and acceptance of music, clothing, and foods characteristic of ethnic and racial groups within the country.

As demand grew for religious educators prepared to work with the growing Hispanic population, many dioceses in California, Texas, Illinois, New York, New Jersey, and Florida began offering continuing education programs designed to enable priests to perform the basic sacramental services in Spanish. These programs were implemented by sending priests and sisters to the Latin American countries from which the Hispanic population of those states came. In addition, native priests were recruited from Mexico, Colombia, Puerto Rico, and Spain. But that was not enough; besides language, cultural and historical understanding and appreciation were needed. Hispanics come from an area of the world that in the late 1960s and early 1970s was bursting with religious and political ferment. The Latin American Episcopal Conference (CELAM) meeting in Medellin, Colombia, in 1968, together with the first papal visit to the Western Hemisphere, brought together creative theologians and educators and provided a worldwide forum for their ideas. The seeds were sown for liberation theology, affirming that the gospel promises freedom from injustice; for an integral religious education that includes all aspects of the Christian life, with particular attention to social and political dimensions; and for recognition by educators of the role of popular religious practices such as novenas. These ideas changed forever the religious education task in Latin America as well as the rest of the world.

The two historic events were complemented by important breakthroughs for Hispanics in the United States: the opening of a division for Hispanic Affairs in the Department for Social Action of the United States Catholic Conference (USCC) in 1968; the ordination of the first Mexican-American Catholic bishop, Rev. Patricio F. Flores, as auxiliary of San Antonio, Texas, in 1970; the first Encuentro Nacional (National Meeting) of Hispanic Catholics and the creation of the Mexican-American Cultural Center (MACC) in San Antonio in 1972, with the specific goal of training religious educators for service among Hispanics as well as U.S. missionaries to Latin America; and in 1977, the second Encuentro Nacional and the opening of an office for multicultural religious education within the USCC's Department of Education. The first priority of that office was to identify leading religious educators among Hispanics and to develop guidelines for expanding resources to be used with Hispanics.

GUIDELINES AND RESOURCES FOR RELIGIOUS EDUCATION

The impetus for this endeavor was provided by the first attempts at MACC to identify the elements of Hispanic religious practice for use by religious educators (1974–75) and the publication in 1977 of "Sharing the Light of Faith: The National Catechetical Directory for Catholics of the United States." In the directory, the Catholic church in the United States for the first time acknowledged both the presence of Hispanics and other minorities and their distinctive needs and asked for research and the channeling of funds and resources to provide them with adequate religious education. The need is for recognition of learning styles that emphasize strong relations between church and family, collaboration rather than competition, clear direction and modeling from those in authority, and ample use of religious symbols, music, and poetry from their heritage.

Religious education programs for Hispanics require an emphasis on personal communication between students, teachers, and parents and the inclusion of celebrations and activities that connect with distinctive religious traditions, respect those traditions, and find new ways to nurture and develop them.

Earlier religious educators of Hispanics used materials imported from the countries of origin of the largest groups (Cuba excepted)—Mexico, Puerto Rico, Colombia, and the Dominican Republic—or materials translated from English. After 1977, with a gathering of Hispanic religious educators in Corona, California, a national search began for materials produced by Hispanics for Hispanics; in addition, a methodology began to be developed for preparing Hispanic religious educators. Six regional training institutes were held between 1979 and 1980, with the participation of 350 educators. In 1988, St. Mary's Press in Winona, Minnesota, announced a project aimed at identifying Hispanic religious educators already doing successful work with Hispanic youth and writers to begin producing materials that are not simply translations from English. The goal is to publish the first materials by 1992, the five-hundredth anniversary of the arrival of the Catholic faith in the New World.

This shift of outlook and methodology is only slowly producing new materials. But the search continues, because the translations of English-language materials being produced by major publishers lack historical and cultural roots in the Hispanic reality and fail to inspire and channel Hispanic religious sensibilities.

It is not only the Catholic church that is interested in the Hispanic population. All the major Protestant groups, including the evangelical churches, have made great strides in the last ten years in including program materials in Spanish. Episcopalians, Methodists, Baptists, Seventh-day Adventists, Assemblies of God, Jehovah's Witnesses, and Mormons are all making significant efforts to reach out to Hispanics with family-oriented services that respond to religious and social needs. Storefront churches in the urban centers where Hispanics flock in search of work offer not only Bible classes but also instruction in the English language and assistance in securing housing, employment, and medical services. *See also* Language, Inclusive; Liberation Theology; Multicultural Education; Social Justice, Education for.

FOR FURTHER REFERENCE

Erevia, Angela, and Virgil Elizondo, eds. *Possibilities for Catechetics and Liturgy for the Mexican-American Community*. San Antonio: Mexican-American Cultural Center, 1974.

Methodology and Themes for Hispanic Catechesis. Washington, DC: Department of Education, U.S. Catholic Conference, 1979.

M. A. Herrera

History of Christian Education
The Early Church

A study of the developing content, methods, institutions, media, and personnel of Christian education discloses how information about Jesus of Nazareth was transmitted to generations subsequent to his own. This study should be seen in context of a larger question, the question of how those generations came to know Jesus. In other words, the history of Christian education is part of the history of the possibility of recognizing Jesus as risen Lord.

Teachers within the early church transmitted that possibility in stories and in more systematic discussions. Their narratives and early systematic thought about the resurrection gave Christian history its starting point and became part of the New Testament canon; but at the same time, their work relegated Jesus to the past and put distance between the learners and the Lord. The defining and distancing work of the teachers, however, was always balanced within the church by the ministry of caring for those in need. The immediacy of this care, along with the definitive accounts of the teachers, together presented the possibility of recognizing the risen Lord and of celebrating his presence in the liturgical assembly. Therefore, the history of Christian education is fully intelligible only when viewed alongside the history of charity and the history of liturgy.

THE TEACHING MINISTRY

Jesus, called most often "teacher," received his religious education in Judaism, where home life, ritual, and oral instruction together formed the child in faith. Educational reforms instituted by Simon ben Shetach about three generations before Jesus' birth suggest that there may well have been a primary school in Nazareth; Jesus likely learned to read Hebrew there. We have the texts from which he learned about the reign of God: the Pentateuch, the Prophets, and the Writings. Not far from Jesus' town were Hellenistic institutes of higher education, the Stoic philosophers' schools. Their alumni also traveled and taught moral precepts in Galilee.

The Galileans who first followed Jesus regarded him as a teacher against this background. After Jesus' death, these followers recognized his identity and significance. Moreover, they saw that his presence persisted in their midst, validating itself by the continuation of the works of healing power that the living Jesus had used to inaugurate God's reign. They continued the wandering teaching practice of Jesus; but to his message about the kind of God it was whose reign was beginning, they added the statement that through that God's power Jesus was living. These itinerant Christian prophets visited a circuit of resident communities where they celebrated the Eucharist and were fed. Those communities, however, needed more than a charismatic evocation of the presence of the risen Lord in the breaking of bread; they needed continuity between this presence and their religious past, as well as practical guidance in running the affairs of daily life.

That need gave rise to the differentiation of the teaching ministry from prophecy. Unlike the traveling charismatic prophets, teachers settled down in a community and, in Matthew's words, became scribes learned in the reign of God who could bring forth both the old and the new (Matt. 13:52). There are indications that the teachers' work included interpreting Jesus' career in light of the Hebrew Scriptures, collecting the remembered sayings of Jesus and sorting through the collections, reconstructing the message and career of Jesus in teachable narrative form, applying the gospel message to particular issues, and forging a distinctive Christian self-understanding vis-à-vis Judaism.

Outside Palestine, the gentile Pauline churches also distinguished the work of teachers from that of prophets and apostles; they seem to have been without presbyters (elders, chosen leaders of a church; 1 Cor. 12:28). Later, however, the church to which 1 Timothy is addressed has presbyters who also teach (1 Tim. 5:17). The church from which the Johannine writings come did not establish a teaching ministry at all and suffered schism. The importance of the teacher's ministry in the Matthean communities, quite plain in Matthew's Gospel, is also evident in the *Didache* (*Teaching*), a book written in a Matthean church a generation or two later. That ancient teachers' handbook indicates that the community has come to accord greater authority to its resident teachers than to transient prophets. Prophecy is not self-validating anymore except within the eucharistic celebration; rather, true prophets are distinguished from false by comparing their words and their behavior to an accepted teaching, set forth by the teachers' manual. But in this *Didache*, we also witness the passing of authority from the trusted teachers to bishops and deacons, new ministries of which the people seem wary (15:1–2).

If teachers were important to communities that still had members who had known Jesus, they were indispensable to the increasing numbers who had not. Teachers took on four interrelated functions, which resembled those of the rabbis: to instruct children and other new members of the community; to conserve, interpret, and apply the tradition to new circumstances; to inculcate a distinctive religious identity over against that of the dominant culture; and to answer the attacks of learned nonbelievers.

RISE AND DECLINE OF THE CATECHUMENATE

By the second century, these defenders and appliers of the gospel no longer appear as independent teachers; virtually all are bishops, for the episcopal ministry has absorbed the ministry of teaching. The catechumenate, which took shape about this time, was a period of formal instruction and exhortation by the bishop or, occasionally, a delegated presbyter for candidates for baptism. Content included the Scriptures, Christian life-style, and the creed, but instruction in the sacramental liturgy itself was reserved for a postbaptismal "mystagogy." An eloquent, but probably atypical, example of the intensive Lenten and Easter climax of the catechumenate program is the fourth-century *Catechetical Lectures* of Cyril of Jerusalem (ca. 315–386). Augustine's (354–430) *De catechizandis rudibus* discusses teaching practice at the turn of the fifth century.

Children were primarily influenced by moral and doctrinal formation in the Christian home. The address "On Vainglory" by John Chrysostom (ca. 347–407) offers advice on Christian parenting to the upper classes. Only in a few large cities did anyone attempt to organize Christian higher education on the model of the Greek philosophers' schools or circles. The catechetical school of Alexandria seems to have been one of these under the leadership of its first three teachers (according to Eusebius), Pantaenus, Clement (ca. 150–215), and Origen (ca. 185–254).

The only distinctively Christian educational institution was the catechumenate, which borrowed some elements from contemporary Hellenistic and Jewish institutions while rejecting others. To Judaism, Christians owed the greater portion of their Scriptures, the rabbinic method of applying them, and the custom of meeting for communal reading and homiletic interpretation of the sacred texts. They also owed the concept that God's law was meant to be honored in everyday living, not just in religious observances in the Temple, and that formation in an observant life-style required daily example. In addition, Jewish sects such as the Essenes had provided a period of instructing and testing for new members. Aspects of this novitiate period probably helped to shape the catechumenate. But unlike the Essenes, the early Christian church did not isolate catechumens from the world.

The Hellenistic mystery religions had secret and impressive initiation rites. Christians likely made their own baptismal initiation rites elaborate, sensuous, and secret in response to social expectations based on the mystery cults. However, mystery initiations usually required little or no prior instruction. The long, thorough formation process of the catechumenate was the principle sociological factor distinguishing Christianity from the mystery religions, and this difference helps to explain why they did not survive the persecutions as Christianity did.

Christians participated fully in the primary schools and gymnasia that were functioning in every town where Hellenistic educational ideals had penetrated. Because their sacred texts were Greek, Christians saw no reason to set up a separate school system like that of Rabbi Joshua. The secular schools taught reading, writing, and speaking by means of classic texts containing stories about the exploits of gods and heroes. Like most people, Christians regarded these as literary folk tales, though they disquieted some. Tertullian (ca. 160–220) deemed it improper for a Christian to teach in a secular school but reluctantly admitted the necessity of Christians' learning in them. When the emperor Julian, dubbed the Apostate (ca. 331–363), attempted unsuccessfully to revive traditional Roman piety by forbidding anyone to teach who did not believe that the gods were real, this was seen for what it was: thinly veiled discrimination against the numerous Christians employed in the secular schools.

The teaching task of interpreting the tradition was accomplished principally through the homilies of the bishop and his presbyters. There were no theological seminaries. The clergy received rhetorical training from secular teachers and religious training from association with more senior clergy. (It was the deacon Deogratias's request to the bishop Augustine for advice about how to catechize that had prompted Augustine to compose *De catechizandis rudibus*.)

Constantine's legalization of Christianity in the early fourth century began a brief golden age for the catechumenate. (Constantine built the basilica in which Cyril of Jerusalem conducted his catechumenal lectures.) However, the children of new Christians now were being baptized in infancy. The catechumenate fell into disuse by the mid-fifth century in many cities and disappeared by the seventh. Christianity was still an urban religion. The influx of tribal peoples was weakening the imperial cities, and with them their educational institutions. Christian education so far had depended upon secular society to teach people, or at least the clergy, to read, write, think, speak, and listen. With the eclipse of antiquity's educational institutions and the disappearance of its own catechumenate, the church's educational work was severely hampered. New methods and institutions of Christian education were needed. *See also* Augustine; Baptism; Catechetical School; Catechumenate; Clement of Alexandria; Cyril of Jerusalem; Didache; Joshua ben Gamla; Judaism.

M. Sawicki

The Medieval Period

The medieval period is taken here to mean the millennium in European history that begins toward the end of the fifth century and runs through the fifteenth, roughly from the demise of the organized catechumenate in the West to the eve of the Reformation.

The seventh through the ninth century was a time of intense missionary activity and evangelism among the Germanic tribes. Christianity spread throughout northern Europe.

During the medieval period, becoming a Christian was chiefly a process of acculturation. People were baptized into the church in infancy and no formal catechetical structure took the place of the catechumenate (the process in the early centuries through which people were instructed in Christian doctrine as preparation for baptism). But Christianity permeated every aspect of life, creating a culture that manifested itself in sacred time (Sunday, Lent, Advent, holy days, and saints' feast days), sacred places (churches, wayside shrines, and pilgrimage centers), and sacred persons (clerics and members of religious orders recognized by their distinctive garb). Popular piety and the cult of saints were powerful forces in the formation of culture and religious attitudes.

From the collapse of the Roman Empire until the late Middle Ages, formal education was had primarily by monks and clerics who attended monastic and cathedral schools. As long as most people were largely illiterate, the ordinary means of communicating the faith were *images* and the *spoken word*. The pictures in illuminated manuscripts highlighted themes in the written text but were accessible only to the few. In the great Romanesque churches and Gothic cathedrals, biblical scenes were carved in bas-relief and friezes for all to see. In northern Europe pictures from the life of Christ, the Virgin Mary, and the saints were found in stained-glass windows and in Italy in frescoes. In the "Bible of the poor," as this medieval visual art has been called, each scene illustrated a particular point, and where scenes of the Old Testament were presented together with scenes from the life of Christ the parallel was based on typology.

The principal occasions for the use of the spoken word, or oral catechesis, were (1) the minimal instruction of children and the unlettered to explain the meaning of their baptism; (2) the penitential rites that rose to prominence in the High Middle Ages, particularly confession; and (3) preaching.

EDUCATION AND BAPTISM

As a result of the prevalence of infant baptism and the disappearance of the catechumenate, in the early Middle Ages sponsors—godparents—came to act in the name of baptized children and assumed the responsibility with the parents for teaching them the rudiments of the faith. The fact was, however, that neither parents nor godparents were adequately prepared and the task of instruction fell to the clergy, most of whom were themselves poorly educated. Such formal catechesis that there was consisted mainly of teaching the Apostles' Creed, the Lord's Prayer, the Ten Commandments, and some knowledge of Christian behavior.

One of the rare extant sources from the seventh century, the *Adnotationes de cognitione baptismi* by Ildefonse of Toledo (d. 667), is an explanation of the baptismal rite, the creed, and the Lord's Prayer given to the faithful after the reception of the sacrament. In 734 the English Benedictine the Venerable Bede (673–735) sent Egbert, bishop of York, detailed instructions as to how the Apostles' Creed and the Lord's Prayer were to be taught in rural areas. Priests were to teach the prayers in Latin to the few who could handle it; others were to learn to recite them in the vernacular, though care should be taken that they learn to chant the words. Bede encouraged singing as an aide to memorization.

The *Elucidarium*, an eleventh-century work, was intended by its anonymous author (now thought to be one Honorius Augustodunensis) to be a compendium of theology for use in training young clerics. A dialogue divided into three parts, in it a "disciple" questions a "master" who in turn explains church doctrine. In the first part the questions and answers center on the story of salvation: God and creation; angels and demons; the world and human beings; earthly paradise; the sin of our first parents; the necessity of satisfaction for sin; the incarnation of the Son of God; the Passion, death, and resurrection of Jesus Christ; the church as the body of Christ; and bad priests. The second part takes up practical themes of Christian life: providence and predestination; original sin and baptism; marriage and canonical impediments; forgiveness of sins; the human condition and relationship with God; guardian angels and devil-tempters; and anointing the sick, death, and burial. The third book deals with eschatology: the fate of the deceased (heaven, purgatory, hell); the condition of souls awaiting the final judgment; the Antichrist; the resurrection of the body and final judgment; and eternal happiness. The *Elucidarium* was intended to be a systematic but popular presentation of doctrine stated in formulas that could be easily memorized. The dialogue suggested that there was a clear and concise answer to every question.

Catechetical manuals of this kind, primarily for the guidance of the clergy in the instruction of the faithful, continued to be written through the medieval period. Among the best known and most influential are works by Jean de Gerson (1363–1429), theologian and sometime chancellor of the University of Paris. His works for the clergy are in Latin, but Gerson also wrote in the vernacular. His *ABC des simples gens* is an outline of doctrine for "simple folk."

The ABCs for Simple Folk, a mere listing of church teachings and practices without explanation, illustrates the medieval penchant for groups of seven: the seven deadly sins and the contrary virtues; the seven petitions of the Our Father; virtues (faith, hope, charity, prudence, temperance, fortitude, and justice); gifts of the Holy Spirit; beatitudes; spiritual works of mercy; corporal works of mercy; orders (porter, lector, exorcist, acolyte, subdeacon, deacon, and priest); sacraments; and the seven privileges of the glory of paradise (three of the soul: clear vision of God, love of God, and surety of being always there; four of the body: brightness, sublimity, agility, and impassibility). In speaking of penance, he notes that it too has seven parts: repentance is implicitly understood, and then there is fasting, almsgiving, prayer, contrition, confession, and satisfaction.

EDUCATION AND CONFESSION

Another occasion for formal catechesis in the medieval church presented itself in the practice of auricular confession. Although the practice of confessing to one another as urged by the Letter of James (5:16) continued into the High Middle Ages, ecclesiastical authorities took steps to make it clear that only priests can absolve one from sin in the name of the church.

The Fourth Lateran Council in the decree *Utriusque sexus* (1215) obliged all the faithful of either sex who had reached the age of discretion to confess their sins to a priest at least once a year. Although Lateran IV was the first general council to legislate the matter, provincial councils and local ordinaries had tried to enjoin the practice. Canon 10 of the same council ordered bishops to appoint priests not only to preach but to hear confessions, impose penances, and attend to the spiritual needs of the faithful. The reform legislation of Lateran IV had far-reaching theological and pastoral ramifications not only for sacramental practice but for catechesis.

Many of the *Libri Penitentiales*, handbooks for priests, suggested questions that confessors might ask the penitent. Some directed that the penitents be quizzed on their knowledge of the creed and be asked to recite the Lord's Prayer from memory. More importantly, private confession became an occasion for moral catechesis whereby individuals were instructed about their responsibilities as Christians and members of the church.

PREACHING

Throughout the medieval period, however, the usual means of instruction was preaching. The ecclesiastical legislation of synods and councils and the often repeated admonitions of church and civil authorities indicate the importance attributed to preaching and also suggest that it was neglected by clergy charged with the care of souls.

In the time of Charlemagne, an *Admonitio generalis* (March 789), designed to promote faith in the Trinity, in the incarnation, and in the Passion, resurrection, and ascension of Christ, encouraged preaching. Sermons were to focus on the Apostles' Creed and moral themes (sins to avoid, the commandments and moral norms to be observed). Like many synods of the time, the Council of Tours (813) urged that preachers explain the creed and Lord's Prayer in the vernacular so that the faithful could better comprehend the Christian truths. Although few examples of such vernacular homilies survive, the texts of the creed and the Lord's Prayer are among the oldest surviving samples of writing from the period.

Two sets of Rogation Day sermons in Old English by the monk Aelfric (ca. 955–ca. 1020) provide a good picture of the scope and content of catechesis at the close of the tenth century. They expound the creed, the Lord's Prayer, and Christian morality. With regard to the last they show the unmistakable influence of Gregory the Great in the way they present the last things and the vision of final judgment as an incentive to Christian living. Similarly, the catechetical sermons preached by Thomas Aquinas in the Lent of 1273 centered on the Apostles' Creed, the Lord's Prayer, the Hail Mary, the twofold commandment of love, and the Decalogue. Although Thomas's instructions survive only in the form of Latin summaries, he preached them in the local dialect of Naples.

In 1281 the archbishop of Canterbury, John Pecham, promulgated the canon *Ignorantia sacerdotum*, which became the norm for catechetical instruction in England until the time of the Reformation. One section of Pecham's directives, titled *De informatione simplicium* (*The Instruction of Simple Folk*), stressed the need to teach the fundamentals of faith in the vernacular at least four times a year. Although the contents are similar to topics covered by Thomas in the Lenten sermons, they rather surprisingly omit the Lord's Prayer while the teaching on the sacraments is expanded.

Although the medieval church never developed formal structures for Christian education of the laity, its emphasis on the creed, the Lord's Prayer, and the commandments represents a thread of continuity between the ancient catechumenate and the catechisms of the Reformation period. *See also* Alcuin; Art in Religious Education; Baptism; Creed; Gerson, Jean de; Ignatius of Loyola; Rabanus Maurus; Thomas Aquinas.

FOR FURTHER REFERENCE

Gatch, M. McC. "Basic Christian Education from the Decline of Catechesis to the Rise of Catechisms." In J. H. Westerhoff and O. C. Edwards, eds. *A Faithful Church*. Wilton, CT: Morehouse-Barlow, 1981.

McNeill, J. T., and H. M. Gamer. "Medieval Handbooks of Penance." In *Records of Civilization*, vol. 29. New York: Columbia University Press, 1938.

Sloyan, G. S., ed. *Shaping the Christian Message*. New York: Macmillan, 1958.

B. L. Marthaler

The Reformation

The Protestant Reformation, the sixteenth-century religious movement in opposition to the practices of the Roman Catholic church, began in the schoolroom and the pulpit. Most of the early Protestant leaders were significantly influenced by Renaissance humanism and so expressed a central concern for the reform of education, from early catechetical training to graduate studies.

LUTHERAN AND CALVINIST REFORMERS

Protestantism's founder, Martin Luther (1483–1546), was both university professor and parish priest. His Reformation ideas were closely related to an emphasis on the authority of Scripture and the right and responsibility of all people to have access to Scripture for their own study. Such a perspective resulted in Luther's addressing the need for general education.

In 1522, he published the New Testament in German (the Old Testament was completed in 1534). This was followed by a reform of worship that provided for the use of German in the Mass, so that ordinary people could understand and participate in the liturgy. The place of the sermon was greatly enhanced in Lutheran worship, again in part with an eye toward education.

Perhaps no area of reform was more important than that of catechetical instruction. Luther's smaller and larger catechisms (both published in 1529) provided the basic documents for a Protestant religious education and laid more emphasis on theology than earlier catechisms.

Luther's friend and co-worker Philip Melanchthon (1497–1560) provided directions for the reorganization of German schools, from grammar schools for boys and girls to university curricula. Here the close relationship between Reformation and Renaissance can be seen. The Protestant school reforms included a heavy emphasis on learning the language of classical antiquity, not merely to enhance civil life and personal growth, but to enable the student to spend a lifetime of serious encounter with the Bible.

Changes in the grammar schools also allowed the universities under Protestant leadership to move rapidly toward the study of Scripture in Hebrew and Greek. This in turn was brought to bear in sermon preparation, which was seen in part as a way of educating the people. University reform occurred first at the German universities of Wittenberg, where Luther and Melanchthon taught; Marburg, the first university founded as a Protestant university; and Tübingen.

In Zurich, Ulrich Zwingli (1484–1531) was concerned first of all with reform of the basic education of children and ministers. The traditional seven liberal arts of medieval education were augmented by beginning Greek in the grammar school, so that students who went no further would be able to read the Bible in Latin, in their own tongue, and with some limited understanding of New Testament Greek. Ministerial students would then be able to move rapidly into advanced Latin and Greek, followed by Hebrew. Their roles of preacher and community teacher would also center on biblical instruction for the people. It was only after Zwingli's death that a catechism was prepared for doctrinal education in Zurich. This latter effort, by Heinrich Bullinger (1504–1575), Zwingli's successor, was to be overshadowed by the work of other Reformed theologians.

The Reformation in Geneva, under the leadership of John Calvin (1509–1564), brought new emphasis on the educational ministry of the church. Calvin devised a church structure that included four offices within the order of ministry, one of which was the minister as teacher. Significantly influenced by the educational system devised in Strasbourg, Calvin began first with the formal instruction of small children and continued to what would ultimately be university education. The primary goal of this comprehensive system was to create a truly Christian society. Strong communal control of life through church and state was balanced by the emphasis on individual growth and ability to interpret Scripture and consider matters of the faith.

Calvin's plans were resisted by many in Geneva, partly due to cost, partly due to concerns about the power given to the church in such an educational program. Meanwhile, in 1541 Calvin prepared a catechism in which his vision of the faith was summarized with clarity and vigor. A Latin translation led to numerous other catechisms prepared by followers of Calvin. These were used as basic instruments to teach the faith to children and as fundamental theological texts for candidates for the ministry. One of the most influential of these Calvinist catechisms was the *Heidelberg Catechism* of 1563.

ANGLICAN REFORMERS

The story of the Reformation in England is complicated by intrigue, politics, personalities, and social and class movements. The Anglican tradition that emerged from the Reformation somehow stands between Roman Catholicism and the rest of Protestantism. The compromises involved in that middle position are seen in the efforts to provide a reformed religious education in England.

The Reformation came to England in part through university teachers and students who had studied on the Continent. Oxford and Cambridge thus became centers of pro- and anti-Protestant movements. King Henry VIII (1491–1547) dissolved the monasteries and many other Roman Catholic institutions, using some of the wealth gained to finance his government. New forms of funding education had to be found. The result was that public education, such as it was, increasingly came under the control of private- or community-sponsored schools, reducing the role of the church in general education.

More specifically, religious education was addressed under the reign of the boy-king Edward VI (ruled 1547–1553). Under his authority a catechism was published, along with a book of Scripture readings to be used in the schools and by individuals.

After the death of Roman Catholic Queen Mary in 1558, the direction of religious education, as with all matters of religion, was bitterly debated. Queen Elizabeth seemed to want a very limited Reformation, but many of her church leaders were strongly Calvinistic. For most of her reign, a semiofficial catechism by Alexander Nowell was used in the churches and schools, along with a 1559 primer that was much like a medieval book of hours (with Scripture, prayers, and pious meditations). Nowell's catechism was closely based on Calvin's rigorously Protestant catechism. In addition, a brief catechism in the *Book of Common Prayer* could be used along with the creed and the Lord's Prayer when a simpler educational tool was needed.

The conflict between the various parties in the English Reformation was not to be settled until many years later. The strong Protestants, often called Puritans, found themselves establishing their own schools and writing curricular materials for use with their children and converts. Their work primarily followed the writings of Calvinistic Reformers from the Continent and Scotland.

RADICAL REFORMERS

The Radical Reformation is a term applied to the numerous groups that arose during the Reformation period either apart from or in conflict with the Lutheran, Calvinist, and Anglican strains. These included the Congregationalists (sixteenth century), Baptists (seventeenth century), and Society of Friends (eighteenth century). One distinction often made is that the Radical Reformation rarely included the governing authorities of an area. Because they were so diverse and so very different from each other, only a few general comments can be made here.

Radicals did not want their children in the schools run by their opponents. They found it necessary to provide basic education themselves, especially in areas where they were able to create their own communities. Education generally focused on literacy, for they were as biblically centered as any of the Protestants. Biblical interpretation, doctrinal works, even catechisms became a part of the educational program of some of the groups. In almost all cases, higher education was rejected both as being unnecessary and as creating opposition to the truth as they saw it.

THE ROMAN CATHOLIC RESPONSE

Part of the Roman Catholic response to the Protestant Reformation was to carry out reforms of education within Catholicism. Of the many steps taken, none was more important for the laity than the preparation of a new catechism by Peter Canisius (1521–1597) and the gradual approval of translating Scripture into the common languages of the day. Peter Canisius was a Jesuit priest actively involved in Counter-Reformation activities. In 1554 he published his *Large Catechism*, which provided a form of basic Christian education that was also decidedly Catholic and anti-Protestant.

The publication of Roman Catholic versions of the Bible in common languages occurred over a period of time in various locales. English-speaking Catholics were given a New Testament in 1582 and an Old Testament in 1609. Because the translation and publication had to take place outside of England, this Bible has been given the name of the two French cities in which the work was done: Douay-Reims.

The education of clergy also received a new impetus in the Roman Catholic church as a part of the response to the Protestant challenge. The Council of Trent (1545–1563) included among its decisions the reform of clergy education. Further, and of great importance, Pope Pius IV was asked to prepare a new Catholic catechism. This was done under his authority in 1564–1565. This catechism became a fundamental part of clergy training, summarizing as it did the heart of Catholic theology.

In sum, in the Reformation was included a call for change in education. Those parts of the Reformation that had the support of cities and states were able to provide school systems and curricular materials that would be appropriate. Because the Reformed movement, that of Calvin and others, was more urban than the other movements, it was able to develop perhaps the most thorough-going reform of education. Both Roman Catholicism and the Radical Reformation reformed education by reacting to the works of Luther and Calvin and their supporters. In every case, changes in religious education were affected by politics as well as theology, by economics and social class as well as faith stance. *See also* Anabaptist Education; Biblical Translation; Calvin, John; Catechism; Liberal Arts; Luther, Martin; Lutheran Education; Reformed Education; Zwingli, Ulrich.

FOR FURTHER REFERENCE

Grimm, Harold J. *The Reformation Era, 1500–1650.* New York: Macmillan, 1965.
Spitz, Lewis. *The Protestant Reformation, 1517–1559.* New York: Harper & Row, 1985.

R. L. Harrison

The Eighteenth Century to the Present

The post-Reformation period (seventeenth century) brought work and writings that have continued to influence religious education in Europe and the Western Hemisphere. John Amos Comenius (1592–1670), bishop of the Moravian church, was an educator whose ideas of teaching children had a wide impact on European education. Instead of teaching Latin through its grammar, he devised a method of teaching it through the use of a picture book, in which Latin and the vernacular language were printed side by side and the emphasis was on concrete words illustrated with pictures. He was invited by several governments to restructure their educational systems. Jean-Baptiste de la Salle (1651–1719) established the first schools in France for the instruction of large numbers of children in both religion and practical skills and founded an order to continue the work.

In the late eighteenth and nineteenth centuries in Germany, several educators started experimental schools and their ideas were influential although the schools did not continue long. Johann Heinrich Pestalozzi (1746–1827) sought to bring the affection of family relationships into the school. Friedrich Froebel (1782–1852) and Johann Friedrich Herbart (1776–1841) urged the use of experience-oriented methods. These affected English and American education, notably in the development of the kindergarten and a concern to include the teaching of moral values. Basically education, whether largely under private auspices, as in England until the late nineteenth century, under churches, or under the state, included both religious observance and the study of religion as integral parts of the curriculum.

As with European schools, the first elementary and secondary schools in America were concerned primarily with religious rather than secular education. Established and run by groups, usually Protestant, who had initially come to the United States because of, among other things, a desire for religious freedom, their ultimate objective was to make possible the reading of the Bible so that each individual and family could be led to salvation.

The free, tax-supported public school system that came into being in the United States during the early decades of the nineteenth century continued the Protestant orientation and mission of imparting common religious values. Bible reading and stated prayers continued to be the practice in most public schools. Although Horace Mann (1796–1859), the first secretary of the Massachusetts Board of Education and "father" of U.S. public education, hoped to overcome the divisiveness that had characterized sectarian education with a nondenominational approach, he still held to the school's role in providing education in Christian moral values.

A bitter and prolonged controversy arose during the 1840s between Protestant and Catholic groups, particularly in New York and Philadelphia but in other cities as well, over the reading of the King James Version of the Bible in public schools and the use of public funds for religious schools. Catholic groups sought tax funds for parochial schools or permission to use the Douay translation in public schools. The courts, after years of litigation, ruled that the Bible is a sectarian book, that reading it is an act of worship, and that sectarian instruction cannot be permitted in tax-supported public schools (1890). This led to the exploration of other forms of religious education by Protestants and Catholics.

In the period of Protestant dominance prior to the Civil War, much of religion was under the sway of revivalism. Horace Bushnell (1802–1876), a Connecticut pastor, suggested in his influential book *Christian Nurture* (1847) that under the appropriate influences the child might be led by several stages to religious understanding, avoiding the excessive emotionalism of the revival.

NEW TERMS AND DEFINITIONS

A new understanding of religious education came into being in the early twentieth century. After the development of public school education and its secularization, "religious education" came to have three meanings. It could refer to education that was for the purpose of inculcating religious values and morals; education in the specific traditions, beliefs, and ceremonies of a particular sect or denomination; or education *about* religion such as a comparison of various religions or a study of their literature.

As the disciplines of sociology and psychology were developed, their insights were related to the moral and spiritual values found in religion. Sociologists and philosophers of religion such as Emile Durkeim (1858–1917), Max Weber (1864–1920), W. Paul Douglas (1871–1953), and particularly William James (1842–1910) in his book *Varieties of Religious Experience* (1902) demonstrated the relationship between religion and culture. At the same time John Dewey (1859–1952), a prominent educator, George Albert Coe (1862–1951), Lewis J. Sherrill (1892–1957), and others demonstrated that genuine religious experience involves the recognition of truth and values by the individual followed by a response in changed behavior.

In the United States and Canada the modern use of the term "religious education" is linked to the founding of the Religious Education Association in 1903 and the founding of the journal, *Religious Education*, in 1906. The association is an interfaith and interdenominational organization the purpose of which is to promote religious and moral education, to raise educational standards in religious programs, and to keep the ideal of religious education before the public. It was founded in part to improve upon the Christian nurture philosophy of Bushnell.

By the 1940s the major faiths in the United States were dissatisfied with the term "religious education" because of its limitations and lack of clearly drawn criteria. Protestant groups increasingly used the term "Christian education" in reference to church-sponsored educational programs. "Catholic education" was the term used by Roman Catholics to refer to their educational theories and practices. Because of the large parochial school system, Catholics made a distinction between education as school centered and education that is directly religious.

NEW EDUCATIONAL AGENCIES

The formal educational agencies used by most Protestant churches for the religious education of children and youth are the Sunday school, youth fellowship groups, vacation church schools, and camps and conferences.

The Sunday school movement began as a philanthropic effort to offer a modest amount of education to the children of the poor. Robert Raikes (1736–1811), a printer and publisher of Gloucester, England, popularized the idea. Beginning in 1780 he gathered children who worked through the week on Sunday to instruct them in reading and in church catechism. The idea caught on quickly and by 1786 Sunday schools had been established in Hanover County, Virginia. Sunday school societies were soon formed in New York, Boston, and other cities.

In 1824 a number of city associations organized the American Sunday School Union with headquarters in Philadelphia. By that time the original idea of offering secular instruction had vanished and the Sunday school had become an important part of Protestant religious education.

With the founding of the Young People's Society of Christian Endeavor in 1881 still another means had been discovered by Protestant groups for the teaching of religious values. This program immediately won the favor of youth leaders in most denominations and youth fellowship groups continue today in one form or another.

Vacation church schools, meeting in churches during the summer usually to study the Bible, began shortly after World War I and have become a popular means of teaching religious values. Camps and conferences began in the decade of the 1920s, primarily as a means of educating certain promising youth in leadership for the church. Many church leaders believe that vacation church schools and summer camps and conferences offer better opportunities for teaching and learning than Sunday schools since they make larger blocks of time available for educational purposes.

PUBLIC AND PRIVATE SCHOOLS

Released-time instruction represents a plan whereby public school students are excused part of the school day to attend religious classes. These are taught by representatives of the various faiths and have been considered legal so long as they are held at locations other than the public school, there is parental permission, and the public school does not enforce attendance in any way.

After the controversies over public school education in the nineteenth century, the Roman Catholic church developed a large parochial school system to provide a complete and formal education for Catholic children and youth. Behind the system is a philosophy of education derived from Catholic tradition and belief. Catholic educators believe that education is a process whereby deep and abiding changes are wrought in children and youth, that education is something that happens to human beings as a result of individual endeavor, and that education should be under the direction of the home and church. Schools are established in which the young can be taught the principles of faith and morals while being instructed in other subjects. After-school religious education classes are held for those who do not attend parochial schools.

Because of the separation of church and state in the United States and the continuing tensions between religious groups as the nation moves toward a pluralistic society, it was inevitable that certain controversial issues pertaining to religious education would be brought before the courts. In decisions related to religious education, the U.S. Supreme Court has affirmed a parent's right to send a child to a private school (1925), ruled against the use of public school facilities for released-time religious education (1948), and affirmed public school authorities could excuse children from class attendance in order to receive religious instruction (1952).

In more recent decisions the court has ruled that the school day may not begin with a stated form of prayer (1962), denied the right of a state or locality to require recitation of the Lord's Prayer or Bible readings in public schools (1963), ruled that public schools may not be required to post the Ten Commandments (1980), and decided that a daily "moment of silence for volunteer prayer" may not be required in public schools (1984).

Although public funds are used in some states to provide transportation, books, and lunches to private school students, no use of tax money for the general support of private (including religious) school students has yet occurred. There is, however, continued pressure by certain groups for constitutional change that would affect religious education.

The kind of religious educational developments made necessary in the United States by religious pluralism and no single established religion had little impact in Europe, where it has always been customary to include the study of religion in the schools. In eastern Europe, in the Soviet Union after 1917, and other countries after 1945, restrictions on religious education under Communism brought the means of religious education back to the family and participation in the liturgy.

With increasing Protestant missionary activity in Asia and later in Africa beginning in mid-eighteenth century (Catholic missions had been established much earlier), more schools on the elementary, secondary, and collegiate level were established, with special training for catechists (teachers of religion) and clergy. Americans brought the Sunday school, and teaching materials were developed. *See also* Church-State Relations; Private Schools and Religion; Public Schools and Religion; Sunday School Movement; individual entries on religious education in each of the denominations, e.g., Lutheran Education.

FOR FURTHER REFERENCE

Coe, George Albert. *Social Theory of Religious Education*. New York: 1917. Reprint. New York: Arno, 1969.

Cully, Kendig Brubaker. *The Search for a Christian Education Since 1940*. Philadelphia: Westminster, 1965.

Warren, Michael, ed. *Sourcebook for Modern Catechetics*. Winona, MN: St. Mary's Press, 1983.

L. G. McAllister

History, Teaching of

The teaching of history is an important aspect of religious education. Jewish educators have developed courses of study at various age levels, recognizing the importance of tradition in forming in the young a sense of belonging. Roman Catholic and Orthodox churches also have long had a sense of tradition. But most Christians have a gap in their knowledge of what happened between the return of the Jews to Jerusalem from Babylonian exile and the birth of Jesus. And among Protestant Christians, there is often a second gap in their knowledge of history—a gap regarding the history of Christianity from the Roman persecution in the year 64 to the time of the Reformers, the founders of their traditions.

The methods and content used by religious educators in teaching history necessarily vary depending on the age of students. While child development theory says that a sense of historical time does not develop until about the age of ten, this need not preclude teaching young children about tradition, and tradition (which means "handing over") is what the teaching of history is about. Religious history is the story of the religious family. From past people, all who live today have received the faith.

History can first be taught in that context: stories can be told of people of the past whose wisdom and devotion, like those of biblical people, have been witness to God's work. Traditionally children in the Catholic and Orthodox churches learned stories of the saints, but these frequently seem so unrealistic that teachers today view them less as models than as caricatures for young people today. There is need for story material from all religious traditions that conveys both the humanity and the Spirit-filled lives of such people. ("Saint" means one made holy, and in the writings of Paul this is his address to the whole congregation.) These stories offer identification for everyone, beginning with preschool children.

Eight to ten year olds are ready for segments of history that link people and events in a more developed pattern. Children from eleven on need an overall view. When they reach the age for abstract operational thinking, somewhere around age twelve, boys and girls can begin to wrestle with the ideas involved in religious history. Adolescents and adults can grapple with intellectual history: the theological conflicts of the sixteenth century between Catholics and Protestants, the questions raised during the eighteenth-century Age of Reason that continue today, the effects on the Christian churches of the seventh-century rise of Islam, the work of Maimonides as a leading medieval scholar, the need to reflect on the Holocaust in the perspective of two thousand years of history.

No matter what the age of students, story remains the primary method of teaching. But learners will also enjoy dramatization in various forms and illustrative ways of viewing history. Adolescents and adults need study, presentations, discussion, film, videotape, and drama. There is a further need to view the traditions of each of the world's religions in its own context and all in relation to one another. In a world becoming increasingly international and ecumenical, anything less presents an incomplete view of religious history. Contextual teaching is one key to deeper understanding.

Church history is usually a required course in a theological seminary. When courses on the subject are available at colleges and universities, they are frequently included in the religion department rather than in the history department. Recently there has come an awareness that religion has been largely ignored as a component in history and social studies courses on the elementary and secondary level. Publishers are now revising textbooks to present a more balanced view of this area of culture. See also Archaeology, Biblical; Drama; Dramatization; Time Line.

I. V. Cully

Hofinger, Johannes

Johannes Hofinger (1905–1986) was an Austrian-born Jesuit priest noted for his tireless promulgation of kerygmatic renewal with its emphasis on the relationship between liturgy and catechesis. He recognized that the first part of the liturgy is the proclamation and teaching of the word of God through Scripture and sermon. Catechetics needs to be based on Scripture in the context of liturgy.

Hofinger studied theology at Innsbruck under Josef Jungmann, doing his dissertation (1937) on the history of catechisms in Austria. A peripatetic and charismatic teacher, he taught in seminaries in China (1937–1948) and Manila (1949–1958). As secretary general of the International Catechetical Study Weeks (seven meetings between 1956 and 1968), Hofinger inspired worldwide exploration on catechetical renewal.

Beginning with summer lectures in 1954 and 1955, Hofinger taught in the United States while continuing on the global lecture circuit, last working for the archdiocese of New Orleans, Louisiana.

Hofinger's major publications are *Our Good News* (1945, in Latin and Chinese), *The Art of Teaching Christian Doctrine* (1955), *The A-B-Cs of Modern Catechetics* (with William Reedy, 1962), *Our Message Is Christ* (1974), *Evangelization and Catechesis* (1976), and *Pastoral Renewal in the Power of the Spirit* (1981). See also

Catechesis; Eichstätt Conference; Jungmann, Josef A.; Kerygma; Liturgy; Society of Jesus.

M. C. Boys

Holidays

A holiday is a day or series of days to commemorate a special event with religious ceremonies and traditional practices. The word is also used for secular and patriotic occasions. In Judaism regular observance of festivals and holy days recalls God's intervention in history. The Sabbath is a holy day, a gift from the creator God to set a pattern of work and rest. Pesach (Passover) is observed in homes with a ritual meal to help participants, especially children, learn why "this night is different from all other nights." Other Jewish holidays include Shavuot (Pentecost), Rosh Hashanah (New Year), Yom Kippur (Atonement), Sukkoth (Tabernacles), Hanukkah (Dedication), and Purim (Deliverance).

The Christian church organizes holidays in a church year, a calendar of days of remembrance and celebration of the events in the life of the church. The season of Advent and Christmas Day anticipate and celebrate the coming of Jesus. Some Christian groups observe the Baptism of the Lord, Epiphany, and the Transfiguration of the Lord. The season of Lent, a time of penitence and spiritual renewal, culminates with the holidays of Palm Sunday (or Passion Sunday), Maundy Thursday, Good Friday, and the most important holiday, Easter, which celebrates the resurrection of the Lord Jesus Christ. The season of Pentecost completes the yearly cycle.

Some Christian denominations do not emphasize liturgy and rite yet increasingly emphasize the celebration of the mighty acts of God and the use of ritual to mark significant events in the lives of the people. The intent is to avoid secular customs and to restore to holidays their original meaning. In the spirit of ecumenism, different faith groups have observed Thanksgiving together, and in the spirit of pluralism, churches have encouraged a diversity of cultural and ethnic expression in the observance of holidays. See also Church Year; Jewish Festivals and Holidays.

D. Ng

Holism

Holism is essentially the notion or conviction that wholes, or at least some wholes, are more than merely the sum of their parts; i.e., the parts cannot explain the existence or behavior of the whole. One does not often find the term used in this more formal philosophical sense in the writings of Christian educators, but the idea is frequently implicit. Most often holism has been argued for living beings, particularly human beings, and is set over against all who would seek to explain human behavior, or organic wholes, by reference to simpler parts.

In philosophy, the word and idea of holism were popularized in a book by Jan Christian Smuts, Holism and Evolution, published some sixty-five years ago (1926); thus it is a modern term, but it certainly permeates the thought of many earlier writers on education and philosophy, at least as long ago as Plato. The opposite of holism is individualism, and both crop up in modern forms in historical and social science methodology. More often, perhaps, is there a division between a social explanation of behavior and a psychological explanation of behavior, the sociological view seeking to explain each human as a product of environmental forces found in the society, and the psychologist seeking to explain by searching for the source in the persons for both the behavior of the individual and that of the social order. The former seems closer to a mechanistic or reductionistic pattern. Neither extreme is, however, found in ordinary practice and not much in theory. Both sides seem to want to allow for individual variation and for the power of society to influence and shape the person.

In both the writing and practice of Christian education, the evidence of holism is more pronounced in those approaches that lean toward or upon process theology or nonreductionistic psychology, such as that of Abraham Maslow or C. G. Jung, and those that try to provide more space for individual variation in ways of learning, content, and practice for the student.

What is perhaps most important is for the individual practitioner to be aware of the danger of extremes and to sense the implicit nature of these positions in writings about practice or content so that they can be adjusted or made explicit for the student. Holism argues against all attempts to manipulate the individual by adjusting the environment in ways not approved of or known by the person. Such a practice could be found in an overemphasis on "behavior modification" techniques, although the use of reward and punishment, even as small as a smile or a frown, are such techniques and are unavoidable in any classroom. The issue again is that the teacher should use such methods consciously, intentionally, and responsibly. Responsibility here means deep sensitivity to the effect upon each student and that such acts be carried out with love and care. Teaching such as this requires a high order of self-knowledge on the part of the teacher as well as the highest of motives. Teachers always have considerable effect upon students but are not often aware of all the ways in which they do influence their charges, both for good and for ill. In this case, an emphasis on the whole child, or person, would seem wise and necessary, as well as knowledge derived from a study of behavior modification, which is extremely useful, if not essential, in understanding classroom dynamics.

In modern thought, at least as long ago as the writings of William James, the necessity of the teacher having self-knowledge and intentionality has been stressed. The issue for us now is not only how we can attain such self-knowledge, but how to have responsible intentionality about teaching. For self-knowledge, the new work in Christian spirituality would seem to be the most helpful; for methods in teaching, the classic educational works of the past two decades are rich sources. For responsibility, teachers must look to their own faith and spiritual life. The issue is not as simple as individualism versus holism, but a balance between individual responsibility and social conditioning in a context in which both are recognized as factual and valuable. See also Jungian Influences; Learning Theory; Maslow, Abraham; Process Theology.

G. H. Slusser

Holocaust, Teaching the

Teaching the Holocaust is an imperative task for all educators, but especially for religious educators. The systematic, bureaucratic annihilation of six million Jews and five million other designated "life unworthy of life" by the Nazis and their collaborators during World War II was a crime unique in the annals of human history, different not only in the quantity of violence—the sheer numbers killed—but in its manner and purpose as a mass criminal enterprise organized by the state against defenseless civilian populations. As Nobel Peace Prize-winning author and survivor Elie Wiesel has pointed out, "Not all victims were Jews, but all Jews were victims." The concept of the annihilation of an entire people, as distinguished from their subjugation, was unprecedented; never before had genocide been an all-pervasive government policy unaffected by territorial or economic advantage and unchecked by moral or religious constraints.

THE ROLES OF ALL INVOLVED

Despite its magnitude and uniqueness, public understanding of the Holocaust has remained equivocal and often confused by categorical overgeneralizations about human behavior and morality during the Nazi era. Such generalizations as "good" and "evil" ignore the complex range of human responses during the Holocaust and obscure the difficult reality of everyday life under Nazi rule. Teaching the Holocaust, therefore, requires that one present the entire range of human experience,

taking care to represent the persecutors, the victims, the bystanders, the rescuers, and the global response (or nonresponse) to the tragedy as it was unfolding.

When teaching this historical event, one must always emphasize that the systems and institutions we now hold responsible were created and run by *individuals*. Everyone—from Hitler to the petty Nazi bureaucrat, from Churchill and Roosevelt to every American and British citizen who received news of the concentration camps (well before they were liberated), from anti-Semites in every occupied country (like those who for twenty-five cents "sold" Anne Frank and her family to the occupying Nazis) to those humane non-Jews who risked their lives to aid victims of Nazi persecution—was a *moral actor*. Every individual daily faced moral dilemmas and either participated, resisted, or, through their inaction, contributed to the process of destruction.

A crucial but often ignored response during the Holocaust was non-Jewish resistance. Young people are very curious about the Holocaust and want answers as to why such events can occur. But because many of today's students have lost faith in the future, it is essential that Holocaust education should not solely emphasize horror and destruction and therefore reinforce basic pessimism. The Holocaust should not be used as further evidence that human beings are by nature depraved. Therefore, educators have an obligation to present evidence of the humane response during the Nazi era. Humane behavior can be investigated through the study of two areas: the response of non-Jews to the persecution of victims and the caring human relationships that developed within the concentration camps.

RESISTANCE

Nazi ideology could not tolerate any opposition. The Nazi state immediately monopolized the educational system in Germany, including church youth organizations, and arrested anybody who did not enforce their edicts. When racial laws were established in Germany in 1933, Protestant ministers and Catholic clergy were faced with a grave moral dilemma. Should they obey the state, or should they protect Jews (some of whom had converted to Christianity, but were still considered non-Aryans), defying the Nazis and answering to the higher authority of their God?

In teaching the Holocaust, it is important to emphasize that this decision was an individual choice made by individual clergy and church leaders of every religion. Some remained silent, and others—like German pastor Dietrich Bonhoeffer—waged their anti-Nazi protests from the pulpit, encouraging their congregations to resist inhumane government policies and to aid victims. In 1939, for example, Bonhoeffer, leader of the Protestant opposition, stated, "Truth to tell, I pray for the defeat of my country, for this is the only possibility for atoning for all the suffering which my country has inflicted on the world." Bonhoffer and members of his Confessing church (as well as other individuals throughout Germany) helped Jews go into hiding, procuring for them false identity papers and food ration cards. Surprised by the extent of Protestant opposition, Hitler rounded up hundreds of pastors throughout Germany and interned them. The example of religious leaders such as Bonhoeffer and others like him in every occupied country offers religious educators the opportunity to explore through concrete historical events a myriad of profound moral questions and a range of religious responses.

In addition, many non-Jews who resisted Nazism and aided victims defied their communities' religious leaders who either espoused Nazism or collaborated with Nazis in order to "protect their own." People from all walks of life and in every country the Nazis occupied transcended their own safe community of fate and faith to risk status, possessions, and indeed their lives in the process of saving Jewish men, women, and children. The rescuers of Jews and other victims were extreme individualists. Those who were religious had a deep-felt need to answer to their God by acting on behalf of the persecuted, and they did so, even when this meant alienating themselves from their communities and from organized religion under Nazism.

CHARACTERISTICS OF RESISTORS

In-depth social psychological study of rescuers has revealed that their sense of humanity as all-inclusive and the active need to extend aid to the suffering were often extensions of the rescuer's experience with an altruistic role model—either a parent, a relative, or a religious leader—in childhood or adolescence. In addition, rescuers were frequently raised in homes in which tolerance for differentness was a family value; the very individuals who risked their lives to save others learned humane values in the home. Tolerance, therefore, is a learned value, one that can be cultivated in young people through family relations and through religious education. Teachers and parents need to both teach and model tolerance in the home and in the religious community, where it eventuates in outreach to those under threat.

Finally, all rescuers possessed a strong and certain awareness of the fate of the victims; their ability to bear witness to and to "let in" the suffering of others was often crucial to their acting upon the premise, "If I do not intervene, these people will die." As Rabbi Harold M. Schulweis points out, "The lives of the rescuers help repudiate arguments that a single person caught in a web of totalitarian evil could do nothing except cling to the wheels of the system. The lives of

these rescuers demonstrate the falsity of the generalization of human nature as essentially selfish and cruel, and the untruth that complicity with the savage predator was and is the only real alternative." In teaching the Holocaust, Rabbi Schulweis concludes, one must never obscure the "truths that help restore human compassion, and strengthen the basic trust so indispensable for the vitality of our children's futures. A post-Holocaust world needs the healing that confirms the healthy view of human nature" (*A Jewish Theology for Post-Holocaust History*, pp. 44–46). Educators need to be caring, empathetic individuals who encourage student sympathy for the needs and suffering of others that results in personal response and active service to others.

SURVIVORS

Students often have a mistaken "lone wolf," Darwinian vision of "survival of the fittest" in the concentration camps. But as Terrence Des Pres points out, the survivor is "anyone who manages to stay alive in body *and* in spirit, enduring dread and hopelessness without the loss of will to carry on in human ways." Study of the survivors' existence in extremity must take into account that "human relations in the camps took as many forms as they generally take," and that, as one survivor put it, "survival ... could only be a social achievement, not an individual accident." Most survivors, Des Pres notes, "simply found themselves helping each other, as if by instinct, as if in answer to a need. Their experience suggests, in fact, that when conditions become extreme, *a need to help* arises.... Prisoners survived through concrete acts of mutual aid, and over time these many small deeds ... grew into a fabric of debt and care." Thus, Des Pres concludes, "The survivor's experience is evidence that the need *to* help is as basic as the need *for* help, a fact that points to the radically social nature of life in extremity" (*The Survivor*, pp. 154, 156, 160).

In addition, religious life in the ghettos and camps was maintained. Even in the death camps of Auschwitz and Dachau and in the ghettos of Warsaw, Riga, and Kovno, religious Jews were determined to observe, as much as this was humanly possible, the commandments and prohibitions of Jewish law. As in other periods, the Holocaust era produced its own literature of *sh'eilos u-teshuvos*, rabbinic responsa. How did Jewish law view Jews who, directly or indirectly, assisted the Germans in oppressing and destroying other Jews? Under what circumstances was suicide in the ghetto not regarded as a sin? Was the use of birth control permissible in the ghetto once the Nazis decreed any Jewish woman found to be pregnant would be immediately put to death? As Holocaust scholar and philosopher Dr. Norman Lamm observes in the Introduction to a book by Irving J. Rosenbaum, "Dedication to Torah was

TEACHING THE HOLOCAUST

Age Level	Teaching Goals by Age	Methods and Resources
Preschool and early elementary	Focus on instilling basic trust in and respect for others.	Provide a warm, loving and nurturing environment; discipline by reasoning rather than physical punishment; allow children exposure to people with different ethnic and religious backgrounds and discuss differences in a positive manner; model altruistic behavior for children.
	Allow children some opportunity to observe annual Holocaust re-membrances, but do not press the subject on them in any way.	A memorial candle can be lit at home during Holocaust Remembrance Week, for example, but detailed discussion of the Holocaust should wait until the subject arises in some natural way; answer questions regarding the Holocaust only as the child asks them.
Later elementary and junior high	Children can begin to learn of historical periods when people dehumanized, abused, and killed others who were different in some way from themselves.	The Nazi period and the Holocaust can be introduced with age-appropriate reading materials (such as Anne Frank: The Diary of a Young Girl) on the experiences of children and adolescents; use material as well from history books written for young people (such as those by David Altschuler, Bea Stadler, and Milton Meltzer); films depicting the experiences of children (such as A Miracle at Mirauo, Au Revoir les Enfants, Anne Frank in Maine, and other versions of the story of Anne Frank) may also be used; the Anti-Defamation League of B'Nai B'rith publishes a curriculum combining history and literature on the life of Anne Frank.

Age Level	Teaching Goals by Age	Methods and Resources
High school	The full progression of events in the Holocaust can be taught; details of both the inhumane acts and the many humane responses can be researched and discussed.	Reading material that depicts the persecutions more graphically can be used (books such as Elie Wiesel's *Night* and Primo Levi's *Auschwitz*).
	Moral questions and issues raised by the Holocaust can begin to be addressed.	Students may be asked initially to discuss how the Holocaust could have happened in a civilized world; discussions should eventually address questions of responsibility very directly (including the question of individual vs. institutional responsibility).
Adult	Emphasis should be placed on how future genocides can be prevented.	Adults should be asked to think through the choices they (as responsible individuals) make daily today; they should also think through what and how they are teaching children about this and they should be encouraged to strengthen their perceptions of themselves as role models—not merely discussing moral issues with children but acting morally and at times altruistically.

expressed not in the abstract, but in the minutiae of daily life even *in extremis*. Thus a semblance of normality was restored to the inmates of [concentration camps], as the norms of the Halakhah [Jewish law] provided a minimal psychic structure of human dignity and morale" (*The Holocaust and Halakhah*, p. ix). Rabbinic responsa from the Holocaust era are powerful testimony to how survivors maintained an ethical and spiritual sanctity even under the most brutal and inhumane conditions and should be part of both Jewish and non-Jewish religious education.

In summary, religious educators do more than teach the story of the Holocaust, its causes and consequences. They must also teach, at every age level, how to be people among whom this can never happen again—religious people put obedi-ence to God above all other values, based on the biblical understanding of creation and covenant.

FOR FURTHER REFERENCE

Des Pres, Terrence. *The Survivor: An Anatomy of Life in the Death Camps*. New York: Oxford University Press, 1976.

Hallie, Philip. *Lest Innocent Blood Be Shed*. New York: Harper & Row, 1979.

Lifton, Robert Jay. *The Nazi Doctors*. New York: Basic Books, 1986.

Littell, Franklin, and H. Locke, eds. *The German Church Struggle and the Holocaust*. Detroit, MI: Wayne State University Press, 1974.

Rosenbaum, Irving J. *The Holocaust and Halakhah*, New York: KTAV, 1976.

Schulweis, Harold M. "A Jewish Theology for Post-Holocaust History." *Midstream* (August–September, 1987).

E. Fogelman

Holy Spirit

The Holy Spirit, in the Bible, refers to the way in which God is known and active in the world, in human history, and particularly in the history of Israel and the church. Sometimes the reference is to the Spirit of God or in the New Testament to the Spirit of Jesus. Christians understand the Holy Spirit in relation to God as Trinity. God is known in three ways: as creator, redeemer, and sustainer or sanctifier. The work of sustaining (empowering) and making holy (sanctifying) is that of God the Holy Spirit. The idea of the Trinity is more easily understood as a description of how God acts than as a definition of God. The Holy Spirit is not a separate power but an expression of God. This article deals with the question: What is the work of the church in Christian education in light of its belief in the Holy Spirit of God?

This is a central question for Christian educators. In its answer lies not only the clue to present weaknesses in the educational program, but also the starting point for any revision of it. To fail to take account of the Holy Spirit when planning for any part of the church's life and work is to guarantee failure of its efforts.

The goal of Christian education is that all men and women in God's world may respond to the call of God in Jesus Christ and may live in all of life's relationships as children of God. We may express this same trust by saying simply that the goal of Christian education is the life of faith, or life in the Spirit, life in Christ. These ways of speaking may be used interchangeably, as the apostle Paul uses them in his Letters to the churches. When the New Testament speaks of life in Christ, it is speaking of a completely different kind of life from the life of natural human beings. It uses sharply contrasting words to show this: death and life, flesh and spirit, estranged and brought near.

In view of the work of the Holy Spirit in the development of faith, what can the church do through its educational program? In attempting to answer this question it is necessary to look at three aspects of the work of the Holy Spirit: the Holy Spirit and faith, the Holy Spirit and the Bible, the Holy Spirit and the church. Each of these aspects calls for a theological answer and an educational answer: How does the Holy Spirit act? How does this doctrine affect the work of Christian educators?

THE HOLY SPIRIT AND FAITH

How does the Holy Spirit work to bring us to faith in Jesus Christ? It is impossible to explain the work of the Spirit of God upon the souls of humankind. All we can do is describe what happened at Pentecost when the Holy Spirit was given to the followers of Christ so that they were transformed. This transformation was complete; the followers of Christ were turned inside out. They were concerned no longer only for themselves and their business but gave themselves over to God's business. They had a mission and this mission was to carry out the work of Christ in the world. They made no attempt to explain it; they simply declared it. They knew they were in no sense responsible for the change they experienced in themselves. They knew it to be a gift, a gift from Christ himself, in fact a gift of Christ himself. They knew that in a very real sense Christ was living in them.

What, then, can Christian educators do? Christian educators are caught in the mystery of the work of the Holy Spirit. They know that no human being can bring about such a change in another human being. But they also know that the Spirit comes to us when we know Christ and have given our hearts to Christ. So the work of Christian educators is to teach about Christ in the hope and expectation that the Holy Spirit will use this teaching to bring the learners to faith in Christ and will send them forth into the world in the mission of Christ.

THE HOLY SPIRIT AND SCRIPTURE

How does the Holy Spirit use the Bible in the work of changing a person's heart? The Bible is the story of God's work for our salvation. It is the church's recollection of what has taken place in the past to bring it to the point where it can call itself the body of Christ. It is the foundation for the new life in which members are called to seek the will of God in every situation, knowing that God is as active in their lives as in the lives of biblical people.

Although it can be said that the Bible is the church's recollection of its history, the threefold relation of the Holy Spirit to the Bible must be acknowledged: in the revelation of God in the events of the Bible story; in the inspiration of the writers of Scripture; and in the illumination of the readers of the Bible. Thus the Bible may be regarded as the word God has spoken and the word God is speaking to us today. The Spirit of God has been and is present in Scriptures, in its writing, in its presentations through the ages and in our study of it today. As we read, we find God present to us as earlier to Abraham and Moses. The stories come alive, and God is present in them. Through the story the Holy Spirit will speak to our hearts and we will be comforted and strengthened.

With this view of the Bible and the Holy Spirit the church will treat the Bible as the primary material of the curriculum, and it sets the guidelines for the way in which the Bible will be taught. The Holy Spirit brought the Bible into existence through the community and now uses that community to proclaim and interpret the message of the Bible. The Bible will be taught, therefore, with great sensitivity to the prompting of the Spirit.

Students as well as teachers need to be open to the Spirit. All who read must be ready for the Spirit to speak to and through them. The New Testament church told over and over again the story of what God had done, and as they told it the Spirit of God acted upon the hearts of those who listened. So listeners today must hear with open hearts and identify with the story. Then they must explore the meaning of the story and pledge themselves to obedience to the message. The New Testament church ended each telling of the story with a call to repentance and new life, for one cannot hear the story of the Christ without the necessity for decision for or against him.

THE HOLY SPIRIT AND THE CHURCH

The third question to be dealt with is that of the relation of the Holy Spirit to the church. How can the Holy Spirit use the life of the church in the work of nurture?

Some churches, particularly those in the Pentecostal movement, believe that outward manifestations are essential evidences of the presence of the Holy Spirit. Other churches view the presence of the Holy Spirit in quite different ways.

Two familiar figures by which the Bible describes the relation of Christ and the Holy Spirit to the church are "the temple of the Spirit" and "the body of Christ." These metaphors signify that the presence and power of the Holy Spirit of Christ is present in those who have repented and have been baptized in the name of Christ (Acts 2:38). The members of the church, then, act in fellowship with Christ and with one another. They are not perfect human beings. They are called to continual denial of self, continual acknowledgment of sin and judgment, and continual openness to the Holy Spirit. They do not cease to belong to Christ when they fall short of Christ's perfection. The work of the Spirit is to nurture them as children of God, whom they have already acknowledged. The task of Christian education, therefore, is primarily the task of nurturing the disciples of Christ, reminding them continuously of what God has done for them in bringing them into his family, helping them interpret what that means, and reminding them that their task as children of God is mission to the world.

This same task of nurturing the members of the church in their faith in Jesus Christ becomes the way in which children and unchurched adults may be brought to Christ. When these people are drawn into the body of believers and begin to participate in its worship, study, and fellowship, the Holy Spirit has in the church's life a means by which to extend God's grace to them. So it may be said that the primary work of Christian educators is to nurture members of the church in their faith. The education of children proceeds by including them in the church's life of worship, study, and mission, so that they may be led to identify themselves with the fellowship and heritage of the church and thus to identify themselves as disciples of Christ.

Whatever is done by the church in Christian education rests on and is shaped by belief in the Holy Spirit and the willingness to be open to the presence and power of the Holy Spirit. Its essential task is to bring individuals into the fellowship of the church where they may hear God's call to them in Jesus Christ and may learn what it means to live all of life as children of God. This is a magnificent responsibility, and the church that accepts this responsibility wholeheartedly will find itself fulfilled by the power of the Holy Spirit. *See also* Bible in Religious Education, The; God, Understandings of; Koinonia; Revelation; Trinity.

R. Henderlite

Horne, Herman Harrell

Herman Harrell Horne (1874–1946) influenced a generation of religious educators through his university-based teaching in the theory of religious education growing out of the philosophy of idealism with its emphasis on the reality of the idea.

A native of North Carolina, Herman Horne received his B.A. and M.A. degrees from the University of North Carolina and his Ph.D. from Harvard University. After teaching philosophy at Dartmouth College for fifteen years, he joined the faculty of New York University in 1909 and was professor of the history of education and the history of philosophy until retirement in 1942. He was also a lecturer at the summer sessions of a number of colleges, universities, and theological seminaries.

Among his many books was *The Philosophy of Christian Education*, published in 1937, in which he developed the concept of Jesus as teacher and philosopher. His lecture "Jesus as a Philosopher," on 13 February 1924, was believed to be the first radio broadcast from a university classroom. When his radio talks were published in 1927, he wrote: "Without doubt the time will come when, by means of television, you will be able to see as well as hear the distant lecturer." Horne was a charter member of the Religious Education Association in 1903. *See also* Idealism.

B. W. Kathan

Human Relations Training

Group interaction has been studied for a long time by social scientists. The MIT professor, Kurt Lewin, a refugee from Nazi Germany, raised significant questions about human relations based on that experience in his book *Resolving Social Conflicts* (1947). Training to improve human relations has been carried on in many universities. The National Education Association, through its Adult Education Services Division, founded the National Training Laboratory in Group Development in Bethel, Maine, in 1947. The directors of the laboratory trained leaders to create conditions conducive to the most effective personal interaction, especially when change is necessary on the part of one or more members of the group for that interaction to take place. Sensitivity and the training of effective leadership were stressed.

Harrison Elliott (1882–1951) introduced group discussion to religious education in 1920 as a tool for better communication. From this beginning, many church groups began to make extensive use of the insights of human relations training. The church is a group, and this training facilitated the functioning of the group. Church leaders could and did profit from increased sensitivity.

Human relations training events held currently for religious education teachers and other leaders help them learn the techniques of listening to each person, affirming all efforts of learners, being aware of the interaction among group members, and bringing to the attention of a group potential tensions with ways these can be lessened. Insights from such events, carried into classrooms and other meetings, enable teachers and leaders to develop a climate in which learning and productive work are facilitated.

Problems have arisen, however, when leaders have forgotten that, while the human relations training can facilitate group interaction, it does not and cannot convey information. It cannot provide the content and practice of faith, which are what religious education is properly concerned with teaching. It does, however, furnish an effective tool or technique for processing that information.

Recently, concerns similar to those that produced human relations training have been focused on human systems. A human community is a system organized to accomplish some purpose. Input, what is fed into the system or community, the functioning of the systems (throughputs), the outputs or products of the system, the environment within which the system is placed, and the boundary between the system and its environment are all considered. Human relations training assists in effective management of a system. When carried on mechanically, it can ignore persons. When viewed organically, it can facilitate interaction of processes.

The theological implications of human relations training need to be studied carefully. Religious education has a different purpose than group interaction. Salvation is not the same as therapy. The church must become aware of what it means to be truly human. Sensitivity and true humanness are related, but not identical. While the truly human individual will always be sensitive, the sensitive person is not necessarily truly human. For the Christian, Jesus Christ is the paradigm of true humanity. Religious education must lift up, clarify, and enflesh the paradigm so that hearers are not only challenged but enabled to become Christlike. The insight of human relations training can become the servant of the church in helping develop groups, group leaders, and goals so that the genuine humanity of all its members is realized, but it must never be an end in itself. *See also* Engagement; Group Dynamics; Systems Theory.

L. A. Myers

Humanism

Humanism is a term that has been applied to a number of historical movements with somewhat different emphases. The point of agreement among them has usually been an exaltation of human values and the cultivation of the free, responsible individual. Humanism is usually associated with the ethos and culture of the Renaissance and with such modern movements as Christian humanism (combining Christian and classical themes) and scientific humanism (usually antisupernaturalistic and relativistic in character).

Protagoras' dictum, "Man is the measure of all things," may be taken as a basis for humanism. Greek and Roman anthropomorphism with regard to the gods, art, literature, philosophy, and government produced cultures that have been used to define humanism and to provide resources for its nurture in subsequent cultures. Classical humanism, with its high conception of the human and its relatively low idea of the divine, is often contrasted with the Jewish-Christian high estimate of the divine and relatively low idea of the human when unaided by the divine.

CLASSICAL HUMANISM IN HISTORY

Classical humanism was fed into the stream of Western civilization and thought partly through Celtic influence (the Celts preserved fragments of classical literature and the skills of classical learning), partly through medieval monasticism on the Continent (the monasteries acted as repositories for ancient documents and as centers of literacy), and partly through the penetration of Europe by Byzantine culture and by the Arabs (who had preserved and developed Aristotelian philosophy and science). When these converged at the University of Paris at the time of Thomas Aquinas (ca. 1225–1274), the result was Scholasticism, destined to be Catholicism's dominant theology, combining the revealed and the natural with a generally less pessimistic view of human nature and human thought than had characterized previous Christian theology.

The Renaissance signaled a full-scale revival of classical learning, scholars devoting themselves to study of the literature and philosophy of the ancient world. In ancient texts and classical artifacts, the humanists of the Italian Renaissance recognized models of government and intellect, literature and philosophy, and art and culture by which their own times might be greatly enriched. The basic humanistic work of the scholars combined two of the most essential educational functions—that of providing texts and other resources through research and creative development and that of conducting schools (not just for the young) in which the "new learning" might be further developed and transmitted.

This intensive intellectual reawakening flowered in the arts. The assertion of the human as one moves from medieval painters to Giotto, Duccio, and Michelangelo becomes more and more pronounced. The contemporary mind is likely to associate the ideal of humanity with Michelangelo's *David*. This burst of creative activity in the arts fed back into the intellectual life of humanism as artists and philosophers theorized under the generally sympathetic patronage of the wealthy and powerful.

So-called Christian humanism flourished in the Northern Renaissance. Influenced by Italy, it was, however, just as interested in digging into the backgrounds of Christian culture as into the Greek and Roman. Consequently, it promoted biblical studies and the study of Christian history using the new critical and historical tools. By all standards, Erasmus (1466?–1536) was the outstanding northern Christian humanist—a student of the ancient classical and biblical languages, translator, and international commentator on public and cultural questions. To be counted among the humanists of this sort were Martin Luther (1483–1546) and John Calvin (1509–1564). The more purely intellectual humanists of the period, however, parted company with the religious Reformers, lacking their zeal for militant change.

The humanists and the humanist-Reformers were passionately concerned with education and educational ideals. In the early sixteenth century Castiglione's *The Courtier* presented the ideal of the cultivated and socially responsible gentleman, while Machiavelli, with his interest in the political forces that militated against human ideals, presented in *The Prince* the human being whose cunning could cope successfully with those antihuman forces. Erasmus himself was the product of the educational system of the Brethren of the Common Life. Luther insisted on the responsibility of the "mayors and aldermen" for the education of the citizenry. Calvin strove for a fully educated leadership for church and state. The humanist educational ideal has persisted in Western culture, a classical education being considered the highest form of education and the proper norm for the preparation of civic and cultural leaders.

HUMANISM IN RECENT THOUGHT

More recently, the term "humanism" has been applied to two divergent positions, classical humanism and scientific humanism. Classical humanism, exemplified in particular by Irving Babbitt (1865–1933) and Paul Elmer More (1864–1937), is closely akin to Renaissance humanism in searching for classical sources and models for culture and education. The emphasis on the humanities in secondary and higher education is probably the most pervasive and powerful aspect of this movement. With More in particular, and in such theologians as Lynn Harold Hough, classical humanism has taken a distinctively Christian form.

Scientific humanism, on the other hand, sees the scientific mind as humanity's greatest achievement and the scientific method as humanity's most powerful tool. The forerunners are the Enlightenment, August Comte's positivism, and British utilitarianism. Among its most eminent recent exponents have been Bertrand Russell (1872–1970) and John Dewey (1859–1952), both of whom wrote extensively on education. Dewey's educational method, set forth in *How We Think* (1910), involves a scientific problem-solving model. His religious views, as expounded in *A Common Faith* (1934), distinguish between "the religious," by which he means a dynamic psychological process of discriminative valuing, and "the religions," by which he means dogmatic and static formulations of belief and practice. The former he accepts; the latter he rejects. This position, essentially agnostic, is promoted by the American Humanist Association.

Certain conservative Protestant groups have recently mounted a vigorous campaign against a position that they label "secular humanism." By this they usually mean a variety of things that run from scientific theories that challenge positions stemming from biblical literalism, through political positions that they consider to be "socialist," to practices like abortion that they see as violations of the sacredness of human life. The focus of their attack is often the public schools, where they would like to see prayer reinstated and where they insist that their creationist views be given equal emphasis with evolutionary theories. So serious have they become that under their sponsorship a fast-growing movement for "Christian schools" has come into being, partly as a shelter for their children from secular humanism and partly as a challenge to the public school system. The movement is their practical challenge to what they see as the threat of the dominance of scientific humanism and thus as agnosticism with regard to religious faith and Christian values in the public schools. *See also* Empiricism; History of Christian Education; Public Schools and Religion; Scientific Method; Secularism; Theology and Education.

D. C. Wyckoff

Hymnody, Christian

From the earliest days of human singing, voices have been raised in rejoicing. God's mighty acts are recognized in Moses' song (Exod. 15), in Psalm 150, and in the canticles of Mary (Luke 1:46–55), and Simeon (Luke 2:29–32). Martin Luther, commenting on 2 Samuel 23:1–2, deliberately implies that all hymns belong to the church, "because the Church accepted them and uses them as if the members had written them themselves, and they were their hymns. That is why we do not say, thus, St. Ambrose, Gregory, Prudentius, but we say, 'So sings the Christian Church, in union with them,' and when they die, the Church remains, singing their hymns forever."

Christian hymnody can be said to begin with the passage from the Letter to the Ephesians that admonishes Christians to address "one another in psalms and hymns and spiritual songs, singing and making melody to the Lord with all your heart" (5:19). Many hymnals include hymns that often date back to the third century, though the music will be of later origin than the lyrics until the sixteenth century, except for plainsong adaptations that may date to the tenth century. Fewer congregational hymns were written during the Middle Ages, a time that saw the rise of monasticism with its daily sung services prepared for monastic congregations. The Reformation brought a resurgence in congregational hymn singing, beginning with Martin Luther and including the Genevan and Scottish psalm paraphrases. Anglican hymnody soon followed, and congregational singing returned to Catholic congregations. The evangelical movement encouraged hymns with themes of personal piety. Gospel hymnody was a contribution of nineteenth century-American evangelicalism. The black churches have added their own rich treasury of spiritual songs. Hymns from around the world enrich more recent collections.

PURPOSE

Singing hymns is done not so much to win converts or souls as to equip Christians to attend to the transforming love of God in a broken and sick world, according to S. Paul Schilling of Boston University School of Theology. We distinguish *hymn* from *song* because the former unifies a singing fellowship in a corporate expression of faith. In these last years of the twentieth century a good contemporary hymn speaks of God to the singers from where we are now, not from, for example, the situation of an eighteenth-century Deist or a Methodist camp meeting out-of-doors with Charles Wesley leading in a thunderous voice. As we sing, our imagination is ignited and we enjoy expressing our faith by what we know *now* to be the world and its humanness. A good hymn is "poetry as the handmaid of piety," as John Wesley wisely said it.

Unison of the singing congregation may not always be easy to achieve, and it is possible for individuals to be so overcome by a certain expression of faith or a particular insight that they momentarily stop singing. But beyond that, both the language and music of hymns make people want to sing them again, and each time new implications arise that can make a particular Sunday memorable indeed. When we sing older hymns, we often feel that our own faith has traveled far to enter the testing of this age; for example, knowing that the faith of early Germany during the Thirty Years War produced "Now Thank We All Our God" can give it special meaning today. Older hymns help singers understand they are giving voice to something far more important than "Hymn Number 145." We love their familiarity. They remind us of the Psalms. They bring forth the glories of a Bach chorale. We gather a glimmer of what it means to be made in God's image and likeness. We sense only through singing, "O Master, let me walk with thee, in lowly paths . . ." what wondrous walking it is.

Theologically and musically nothing in this world surpasses the singing of a great hymn by a great company of believers. The greatest hymn writers have known that: Ambrose, Luther, Wesley, J. S. Bach, Ralph Vaughan Williams, and Erik Routley. If it is memorable in language or in imagery or theology, let it be sung—especially if the music is equally memorable. As he edited that epochal volume *The English Hymnal* (1906), British composer Ralph Vaughan Williams said: "It ought no longer to be true anywhere that the most exalted moments of a churchgoer's week are associated with music that would not be tolerated in any place of secular entertainment." If music and meaning combine in a great hymn to help each other, then those singable statements of faith and hope will bring power to people and a desire to repeat the experience week after week. Even though people say, "I love this hymn because of its melody," if it had no meaning, that hymn would not be sung. What Christians tend to remember are words of Scripture and the rhyming of hymn texts. Learning and teaching and repeating good hymns, memorizing whole stanzas is worthwhile.

PRESENT CONCERNS

In this last quarter century, modern congregations are demanding recognition of God's feminine structure and love. Poet Brian Wren expresses this yearning in two stanzas counteracting centuries of stereotypes: "Strong mother God, working night and day/planning all the wonders of creation/setting each equation, genius at play . . ." And stanza two: "Warm father God, hugging every child,/ feeling all the strains of human living,/caring and forgiving, till we're reconciled . . ." It is not enough simply to say the Bible writers and the hymn writers of nineteen centuries thought in generic terms of God—most of them did not. Nor did we in our Sunday school days. We have been subject to the wrong mental images for a lifetime. Linguistically hymns need to explore new boundaries. Behavior can be molded and emotions triggered by the choice of hymns in corporate Sunday worship.

Another modern rethinking of ancient prejudice comes with the realization of how language sets thought patterns about light and darkness. Perhaps the ancient association of darkness with evil should submit to question. "Joyful is the dark!" affirms one hymn. "Black is beautiful," sing those who gave rise to American spirituals. More hymns that are not tinged with racist language are needed.

Hymns must somehow deal with human oppression, with refugees who have no land to call their home, with exploding technology and its effect on our global home. The air we breathe will be a future concern of those who sing. And somehow we must rid our churches of the glorification of war and invasion, which nineteenth-century writers liked to dwell upon. Romanticism is out of date.

Walter Ong lists four attributes of sound: it always exists in the present; it provides a special path to the brain through the ears; it unites groups of people; and it situates people here and now. When we hear a hymn we are thrust into actuality, and so we sing. And so we sing ourselves into humanness. We have a musical happening before God. Afterward we feel as if our throats are still ringing with rejoicing.

Said college president and teacher Raymond B. Blakney: "In music, as in the rest of life, the difference between the best of us and the worst of us is very small, compared to the gap between all of us and God. On that basis an honest song in a person's heart is a most acceptable offering to the God of all faith and faithfulness." *See also* Language, Inclusive; Music in the Church; Worship.

L. B. Wirt

I

Idealism

Idealism is the theory that reality is primarily mental rather than material: it consists of mind, soul, spirit, or self. This philosophical definition is very different from the everyday one, by which we most often mean guiding one's life by certain principles or ideals.

There are many brands of idealism, no two quite alike. Plato was an idealist, since he believed that "ideas" exist in the cosmos quite apart from brains and that physical objects are only temporary, changing, and finite embodiments of ideas: there is "the idea cat" and "this here and now cat." René Descartes was an idealist in his basic principle, "I think, therefore I am." George Berkeley was an "absolute" idealist since he believed that only minds (God's and ours) exist: because the physical world is a fabrication of my own thinking, only God and I exist. Friedrich Hegel

was an idealist because he believed that the Absolute Mind permeates human activity and that we can "think God's thoughts." Mary Baker Eddy, the founder of Christian Science, was an idealist because she believed that we all exist within the mind of God, the only reality, and that nothing else, including evil, has ontological existence. Asian religions tend to be idealistic since they hold that life's true purpose is achieved only through an odyssey of the mind (or spirit), minimizing the material world and the physical body.

Christian idealism usually begins with the prologue to the Gospel of John: "In the beginning was the *logos*," translated "In the beginning was Idea and Idea was with God and Idea was God . . . and Idea entered into flesh and dwelt among us." European philosophers tended to assume (with the Greeks) that ultimate truth was intellectual. Theologians tended to assume (with the Hebrews) that ultimate reality was spiritual. Most American theologians tended to think of the *logos* as the principle of personhood: God is complete, universal, infinite Personality and we are incomplete, local, and finite personalities. Our partial personality suggests complete wholeness. In the moment I become aware of this projection, I find myself to be part of a greater whole—a community of human persons and the divine Person. God is experienced at this human frontier, Jesus of Nazareth being the primary example of living on that border between divine and human reality.

Many educators find in idealism ground for thinking about and conducting education. Their rendering of the Latin word *educere* is "to lead out—from within." Socrates said that virtue is knowledge, knowledge is teachable, and the knowledge a person most needs is knowledge of oneself. Plato taught that education is "a continuous discourse with oneself." For the idealist educator, the development of the mind is from within outward and educative experiences are interpersonal in character.

Religious educators find their ground in theological personalism. Human personality is of supreme worth because God is personal. Personality is a process of becoming brought about by nurture, linking the developing changes in the individual person with the creative personality of God. This occurs in interaction among persons while making choices, growing, and failing to grow. The content is personal interaction, as recorded in the Bible and as experienced in family and classroom. The goal is that persons may enter the high destiny for which they and the world were created.

Idealism is the actual, even though unrecognized, practice of most Protestant Sunday school teachers in the United States. It has been criticized as subjectivist, substituting immanence for transcendence, nurture for training, democracy for the kingdom of God. However, it is based in a theological idealism that is widely held by American Protestants. *See also* Empiricism; Essentialism; Pragmatism; Realism.

W. R. Rood

Identification

Identification is both a psychological term and a teaching method. It refers to the process by which a person puts him- or herself in the place of another, vicariously feeling as would the other person.

As a psychological process, identification often comes about because of a close relationship, as between spouses, siblings, or parent and child. But reacting to another's desires or tendencies as if they were one's own (and perhaps being unaware that this is occurring) may hamper one's own emotional life or individual action. Identification can make a person so subjectively involved that objectivity and an effective solution to a problem are prevented. On the other hand, identification in the joy of a person or group enables one to transcend the self.

Sometimes people identify with someone they do not know personally—a historical person, contemporary leader, or sports or entertainment figure. This person is held up as a model because something about the person or his or her situation parallels that of the person who identifies. Identification may even be with a group or movement. Charismatic leaders, whether political or religious, evoke such identification.

Literary works such as novels, short stories, plays, films, or television programs are designed to encourage identification. Artists strive to create characters people can identify with, and some characters are more easily identified with because of the attractiveness of their roles or the similarity of their situation with that of the reader or viewer.

In the religious education setting, identification can be used as a tool to help people learn and grow. Providing students with opportunities to experience identification with people and situations both biblical and contemporary can facilitate understanding and foster learning.

Television programs and videotape will provide teachers with a source for helping learners understand a situation in some depth. Film gives opportunity for teachers to prepare for discussion by structuring questions that examine motives and character.

Participation in an event at which an important person is present may bring closer identification than would either a television documentary or a written record. Teachers can find out when important speakers and leaders will be in the area and arrange for a group to attend such a meeting. Discussion can follow at a later time.

Viewing a play or reading a short story provide other opportunities for identification. Teachers can find help from librarians and in resource centers. After the reading, students can discuss the characters and the solution to the situation.

Play reading is another method through which teachers can structure identification. One-act plays or a section of a play can be a focus for discussion of the characters and the solution to a situation offered by the play.

Role playing is a variant of drama in which a life situation is acted out informally so that learners can put themselves in more than one role and explore the feelings and situations of other people. Teachers have an important part in giving learners choice in choosing roles or making suggestions for playing parts, so that everyone will feel comfortable in the role chosen. An important aspect of using identification in this context comes during the ensuing debriefing, in which teachers guide learners in exploring and discussing the people (characters), situation, and their own conclusions.

The purpose of teaching through identification is to broaden sympathies, enlarge perceptions, and enable people to see others not only objectively but subjectively. *See also* Cinema; Drama; Empathy; Role Model; Role Playing; Visual Methods.

I. V. Cully

Ideology

The term "ideology" has unfortunately acquired a wide range of meanings. Ideology can refer to the science of the study of ideas or to the way ideas are expressed in language. Most literally it means, simply, "knowledge of ideas." Not surprisingly, rationalists in several time periods have contributed to its range of meanings by associating ideology with varied forms of nonempirical knowledge. Some psychological definitions point in the direction of projection and wish fulfillment. "Ideology" has even been offered as a substitute term for "metaphysics." The popular use of the concept is commonly traced to Destutt de Tracy (1796) who employed the word "ideologiste" to characterize any thinker who traced ideas back to the primitive impressions from which they arose. In Napoleon's time, "ideologues" were looked upon by the establishment as unrealistic, disconnected from the world as it is. At least from the time of de Tracy and Napoleon, then, the term "ideology" has carried a pejorative connotation.

As a concept, ideology has been useful to scholars in analyzing and critiquing the dynamics (unions and tensions, for example) that exist within and between institutions such as church and state. At an earlier time in history when there was, so to speak, a common ideology in which philosophical and theological bases harmonized, one could safely derive normative social standards as well as axioms for the sciences a priori. However when the unity of the world (of subject and object) was called into question and eventually shattered, the need became evident and the necessary attitude was present for serious thinkers to seek to identify, analyze, and critique the underlying ideologies.

The Christian religion has been a favorite subject of such analysis and critique because it offers a classical form of ideology. Karl Marx (1818–1883) and his followers, for example, offered an extensive critique of Christianity. They argued, as a result of their critique, that the only way to "break the fetters" of an ideology such as they perceived in Christianity was through revolution. The Christian ideology was, for Marx, a sign of an unreal understanding, an unhealthy consciousness of social and economic reality.

For religious educators, the notion of ideology offers a useful critical and evaluative tool. The truth claims of a particular form of religion can be examined with reference to the resulting lifestyle. The question is whether these "truth" statements bind or free followers to actualize their fullest potential. Teachers need to refrain from absolutizing the claims of any ideology because these are human concepts. Yet all people live by ideologies, and ideologies must be evaluated by their results in personal and community life.

H. W. Burgess

Ignatius of Loyola

Founder of the Jesuits (Society of Jesus), Ignatius of Loyola (1491–1556) is perhaps best known for his *Spiritual Exercises*, a systematic series of meditations used in the order and adapted for use today among laity for spiritual formation and sustenance.

Born in Spain in 1491, Ignatius was baptized in the parish church of St. Sebastian. He served as a page and military enlistee to several civic leaders. In 1521 he was injured in battle and experienced a long and fruitful convalescence. During that time he read spiritual writings that ultimately led him to dedicate himself to a spiritual life. That new phase of his life began with an eleven-month stay at Manresa, during which time he wrote the major part of his *Spiritual Exercises*, a work he continued to make minor additions to over the following years until it was approved by the pope in 1548.

Ignatius studied in Barcelona and Paris and was ordained in Rome in 1537. There he and several followers secured papal approval in 1540 for the new order, the Society of Jesus, a group dedicated to the propagation and defense of the faith. To this day Ignatius's spiritual exercises are the heart of the formation of the order's members and the order has distinguished itself in the fields of missions, schools, and studies in higher learning.

Ignatius envisioned his mission and that of the order as that of promoting God's glory (Lat. *ad majorem Dei gloriam*). More specifically he interpreted that as assisting people to know their destiny and teaching them how to attain it. In accord with that he founded the Roman College in 1551. It became the prototype of the Jesuit institutions of higher learning. *See also* Devotional Literature; History of Christian Education; Society of Jesus; Spirituality.

M. C. Bryce

Imagination

The word "imagination" refers at times to remembering something already seen (reproductive imagination) and at other times to creating an image that is entirely new (productive imagination). There is also a range of meaning that stretches from having critical distance on images so they can be distinguished and critiqued to being so fascinated and involved with them that one becomes confused about what is real and crosses over into the realm of illusion. The use of the term shifts about along these two lines of possible meaning suggested by Paul Ricoeur. What is most important is that the imagination at its center is the creative process taking us deeper into reality. Illusion is a defense to avoid reality.

Before the seventeenth century, the imagination was thought to be located in the brain and to regulate visual phenomena, including both dreams and hallucinations as well as emotions. Then when the French philosopher René Descartes (1596–1650) redefined the soul as "immaterial substance," imagination's role in the disease process and in revelation was denied by physicians and theologians. It seemed impossible for an "immaterial substance" to get sick or to know God.

Theologians became especially suspicious about the imagination when Ludwig Feuerbach (1804–1872) said that religion was the projection of our own nature onto the screen of the heavens. God, therefore, was an illusion. Nietzsche, Wagner, Marx, Freud, and others attacked religion on this basis. Today religious educators may still be reluctant to stimulate the imagination because of its association with this attack or the possibility of confusing illusion with the deeper reality of the creative process.

But hostile attitudes toward the imagination in theology began to change in the 1960s or even earlier. In 1976 two popular books by major theologians marked this change, *Ministry and Imagination*, by Urban T. Holmes, and *Introduction to Theology*, by Theodore Jennings. In 1981 appeared *The Transforming Moment*, by James E. Loder, on the structure of the creative process and its relation to religious education and pastoral care.

Loder enlarged the view of the creative process from involving just the mind to involving one's whole existential being. He identified five steps in the process: (1) conflict initiating a need for a knowing response; (2) an interlude for scanning possible resolutions of the conflict; (3) transforming the terms in which the conflict was first felt into ones that can yield a new and constructive way of looking at it; (4) a release of tension and an opening of the knower to this new way of seeing the situation; and (5) interpretation.

While Loder's scheme provides a good working analysis, we know from others how imagination is fundamental to the nature of being human. Perhaps no one has looked more carefully at mothers and babies than psychoanalyst D. W. Winnicott (1896–1971). He found that the mother and child work together to affirm the infant's imagined reality. The imaginative process of the infant conjures up the mother, who sustains the infant's capacity for imagination.

Psychoanalyst Christopher Bollas called the mother a "transformational object" to underline the infant's experience as a process. The first image of the mother is as a source for transformation, not as an organized image of a person. The interplay between mother and infant effects the process of development by means of imagination and play.

Ultimately the mother does not respond completely and the child discovers that the reality of the mother is other than him- or herself. This begins the other side of development, the testing of limits of newly imagined realities. Religious education needs to help guide, nourish, and celebrate this process.

In analyzing the working of the two halves of the cerebrum in adults, however, two kinds of thinking were isolated by researchers—the verbal and analytical versus the visuospatial and intuitive. The use of images might be said to be "located" in the right hemisphere of the brain, while the left hemisphere uses language to articulate them. The full process of the imagination requires the complementary function of both realms. Teaching "both sides of the brain" is a priority, then, for religious education, because of the need to balance both kinds of knowing for the imagination to function fully in all aspects of the religious life.

Both therapists and educators have been interested in how people can impoverish their experience and imagination by deleting the use of one or more of their representational systems. These systems are primarily the kinesthetic system (feeling and touch), the visual (seeing and picturing), and the auditory (hearing and listening, telling and saying). Not only does awareness of these systems help identify a primary communication match in education, but it also helps people change and engage life more fully. This has implications for a multisensorial approach to religious education that stimulates the motivation and will as well as thinking and feeling, so that people will be more likely to do what they think or feel they ought to do.

Unless religious language is learned while using it in creative ways, there is a danger of placing artificial limitations on the development of both children and adults, because it becomes associated with processes other than this constructive one. In addition, the imagination is needed to envision ways of moving beyond where one is developmentally. If one of religious education's goals is to help foster faith development, then the imagination is of paramount importance. The imagination does not deserve mistrust, but consciously creative and faithful stewardship of our freedom to be creatures created in the image of God, the Creator. *See also* Aesthetics; Affective Development; Creative Activities; Creativity.

FOR FURTHER REFERENCE

Gardner, Howard. *Art, Mind, and Brain.* New York: Basic, 1982.
Jennings, Theodore W., Jr. *Introduction to Theology.* Philadelphia: Fortress, 1976.
Lindbeck, George A. *The Nature of Doctrine.* Philadelphia: Westminster, 1984.
Lowenfeld, Viktor, and W. Lambert Brittain. *Creative and Mental Growth.* 8th ed. New York: Macmillan, 1975.
Miles, Margaret R. *Image as Insight.* Boston: Beacon, 1985.

J. W. Berryman

Indoctrination

The concept of education as indoctrination has a long and respected history. It has to do with instruction in a body of doctrine, that is, in a system of religious or philosophical beliefs, political ideology, or economic theory. Indeed, at one time, indoctrination and education were synonymous. But indoctrination also has an ambiguous and controversial history, especially in modern times, and has recently been called into question as a valid educational method. John Dewey (1859–1952), for example, rejected its validity as authentic education since in his view education has to do with freedom of inquiry, examination, crit-

icism, and evaluation. Such values are prized in a democratic society; indoctrination, in his view, can flourish only in an authoritarian society.

EDUCATIONAL MODELS BASED ON INDOCTRINATION

Before considering this debate further, let us review some educational models based on indoctrination in the older, classical sense of the term. Early Hebrew education as reflected in Deuteronomy 6:4–5 is a good illustration of indoctrination. It was the responsibility of the family to teach the children the Shema, "Hear, O Israel: The Lord our God is one Lord; and you shall love the Lord your God with all your heart, and with all your soul, and with all your might." This was the heart and core of Torah. No effort was to be spared in the inculcation of this view of life in the hearts and minds and spirits of the children. It was not only a system of thought but a way of life.

The members of the family were totally immersed in this way of life. They were reminded of it at every turn—when sitting down, rising up, going out, walking by the way, and coming in. The rituals of the household, the clothing they wore, their feasts and fasts all combined to create a comprehensive environment in which this view of life was both lived and passed on.

The criticism that this way of understanding the world and people's place within it was inculcated without critical reflection would be valid but irrelevant. What alternative worldviews would bring the Hebrew people the *shalom* God intended? What was there to reflect critically about? This was the command of God. Critical reflection such as the kind that later arose out of the prophetic tradition had to do not with the possible superiority of the Canaanite over the Hebrew religion but with how faithfully the Israelites were living out the commands of Yahweh.

A second paradigm of indoctrination is the *Didache*, a late first-century or early second-century catechetical manual for the instruction of new believers in preparation for Christian baptism. The first six chapters in particular serve this function. The document begins with the words, "There are two ways: one of life and one of death." Here is no open-ended discussion of the relative merits of these two ways; nor is critical reflection invited on the validity of the assertion. This is indoctrination, pure and simple.

Catechetical instruction in both Roman Catholic and Protestant traditions through the years took shape in another form of indoctrination, the catechism. It contained questions to the asked of candidates for baptism and answers to be memorized by them. When called upon by the catechist to answer, the catechumens would respond word for word as they had been taught. The intention, of course, was that the meaning of the question and the answer had been communicated and grasped. Still, the possibility that the answer had been memorized and parroted without comprehension was always present. In any case, critical reflection, examination, and evaluation were not intrinsic to this model.

NEW PEDAGOGIES

John Dewey's definition of indoctrination is "the systematic use of every possible means to impress upon the minds of pupils a particular set of political and economic views to the exclusion of every other" (*Education Today*, p. 356). This he rejects. True education, in his view, calls for "the active participation of students in reaching conclusions and forming attitudes. . . . The active participation, the interest, reflection and understanding of those taught are necessary" (p. 356).

More recently, the liberation pedagogies of scholars like Paulo Freire have called into question in an even more radical manner the validity of those educational models that have transmission of a heritage as their goal. Some refer to this as the "banking" model of education in which the deposit of knowledge and experience of a society or a generation is made available to others. It is not only the method (whether doctrinaire or democratic) that is at issue. It is the question of the content itself. Liberation pedagogies mistrust such deposits as basically flawed for they are the product of particular ideologies (political, economic, philosophical, religious).

The new pedagogy insists that the learners themselves create their own knowledge through their own methods by means of critical reflection on their own experience. Furthermore, the most authentic knowledge will be created by those who have the least to conserve (the poor, the powerless, the vulnerable). It is the wealthy, the powerful, the oppressors whose interests are at stake and who have created the deposits in the cultural banks of any given society. They have the most to lose when the learners give up their passive, dependent role in learning (enculturation) and become actively involved in the process of critical reflection, analysis, and evaluation.

This brief survey of the concept of indoctrination helps us to see that it is not simply a question of one method over against another. It involves us in such deeper issues as epistemology (how we can know what we do know), the sociology of knowledge, and the politics of education. These questions will not soon be resolved and until they are, educators would be well advised to live with the creative tension between freedom of inquiry and the indoctrination inherent in passing on a systematic body of principles and values. Both of these give the human race a considerable advantage over the rest of God's creatures. *See also* Action-Reflection; Catechism; Dewey, John; Didache; Doctrine/Dogma; Liber-ation Theology; Methodology; Progressive Education; Theology and Education; Tradition; Transmission.

FOR FURTHER REFERENCE
Dewey, John. *Education Today*. New York: Greenwood, 1940.

R. T. Bender

Inductive Bible Study

Inductive Bible study is a methodical approach to the study of Scripture. After previewing the whole, the student focuses on individual words and phrases of a passage without preconceived conceptions and draws conclusions from observations made. It is the opposite of the deductive method, which begins with a generalization and looks for support in the passage for its deduction.

Inductive methodology as applied to the study of Scripture was developed in the early 1900s by Wilbert W. White, founder of Biblical Seminary in New York (now New York Theological Seminary) in an attempt to teach students to study the Bible for themselves. This procedure consists of a three-step process: observation, interpretation, and application. Emphasis is on the primacy of firsthand observation of the text through careful examination and questioning of that text. Students are taught to look at word usage, relationship of terms (contrasts, comparisons, and repetitions), and literary form. This exacting analysis is followed by interpretation of the meaning of the text, defining words, asking "why" questions, looking for reasons behind the words used, and finding principles for personalization. The final step is the personal application of the truth to the life of the learner so that transformation may take place.

For example, a deductive study of Psalm 121 might begin by introducing students to a general outline of the book, the meaning of the word "psalm," the types of psalms, and the place of this particular psalm in the collection before trying to interpret the writing. In the inductive approach, learners read the psalm in its entirety (observation), concentrate on key words and phrases and look at rhythms and contrasts to try to ascertain the writer's intent (interpretation), and ask what it means for the religious life today (application). *See also* Bible in Religious Education, The; Bible Study; Biblical Criticism; Exegesis; Hermeneutic; Teaching Styles.

J. A. Gorman

Infancy

The term "infancy" is sometimes used to refer to the age of persons who have not as yet attained the use of reason. Children up to the age of seven are sometimes included under this definition. More often and in educational circles, however, infancy generally refers to the developmental stage from birth to fifteen or eighteen months that is characterized by the total dependency of the child on the caregiver.

By any definition, the period of infancy is overwhelmingly important in laying the foundation for religious development. The most powerful and influential factor in the infant's development is the family. And religious education has a responsibility to educate parents in such a way that they become intentional about the religious development of their children.

Since infants learn through direct experience with their environment, Jean Piaget (1896–1980) has labeled the early development of the child as the sensorimotor period. Learning occurs when the child sees, hears, touches, smells, tastes, manipulates, experiences, and interacts with his or her environment.

Even though the preschool child generally has little understanding of religious terminology and the infant in particular uses virtually no logical thinking, it is during this early childhood period that the basis for a maturing faith begins. Creating relationships that are loving, dependable, and nurturing provides the young child with the opportunity of attaining the major goal of infancy as argued by Erik Erikson (1902–), that of developing trust. "Nurturing" is a key word. A child needs the warm, secure feeling that comes from being held close to another in a relaxed way, picked up and reassured when crying, changed when wet, and fed when hungry. Caregivers soon learn to differentiate among the cries that make up an infant's language and respond accordingly. When the child's first experiences of life prove relationships to be essentially trustworthy, the seeds of faith, which is the relationship of trust in God, are planted. As the infant grows, structuring positive opportunities for the young child to interact with the environment, to deal with frustrations, and to cope with fears helps the child develop a sense of autonomy (independence) and self-worth that is a vital key for learning to love others and to love God. Feeling secure and being assured of parental love even when disciplinary measures have been experienced is a major step in building an attitude of self-acceptance and love and respect for others.

The child's first images of God are provided by the parents. The worshiping community, however, can help parents by offering a broader context, the family of God, in which the love and care of the family is reinforced. The attitudes engendered by the worshiping community at this early age may serve as a foundation for the child's later participation in the church. When parents attend church with an infant, they need to know by the words and actions of others in the congregation that they are welcome. When they feel accepted, they relax and so does the baby. If the child cries, they can leave calmly and return when ready. Usually the rite of infant dedication or baptism becomes the focus for formal welcome into the congregation. By this act, both infant and family gain a stronger sense of religious community. The attitude and action patterns that the young child develops in the first years also permeate the whole of life and religious development of the growing individual. These patterns of behavior are formed as the family participates in prayers, thanksgiving, praise, worship, and fellowship services.

Religious symbols have little influence on the young child, except for the indirect message received from the parents as they respond to the implicit meaning of the symbols. These items, including the Bible, may become loved and treasured objects because of the way in which the child's parents respect and use them.

As the child grows, new experiences offer a broader challenge for learning in a secure environment. These opportunities should include forming appropriate attitudes about the physical world. To expand a child's trust in the grace of God, we should encourage the child to explore God's world, appreciate its beauty, sense its awe and wonder, and delight in the mystery of all things. We can call attention to natural things and reaffirm the notice a child takes of flower, leaf, or bird. The meaning of Scripture begins to develop as children take pleasure in hearing simple, happy Bible stories from a picture book. Hearing simple songs and following uncomplicated familiar prayers of thanksgiving and assurance increase a child's pleasure in actions associated with God. When children hear about Jesus as a special baby loved by Mary and Joseph, they are helped to develop favorable feelings toward him. Enjoying loving, secure relationships with members of the worshiping community identifies church as a special place where it is good to be.

To get along happily in the first experiences with a group of peers builds attitudes of belonging and develops patterns that may later become more consciously religious. Basic experiences like these form the emotional groundwork upon which faith may grow. In these early years the child who is deprived of such experiences of love and care will find it difficult to give love to others or to God. *See also* Child Abuse; Child Development; Daycare Center; Nursery Education; Parenting; Preschool Children.

FOR FURTHER REFERENCE

Barber, Lucie W. *The Religious Education of Preschool Children*. Birmingham, AL: Religious Education Press, 1981.

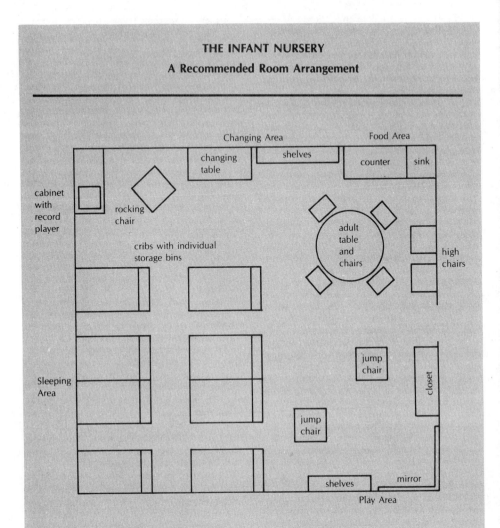

THE INFANT NURSERY

A Recommended Room Arrangement

The space and facilities above have been designed to meet the needs of an infant nursery with an average attendance of 8 infants. Total floor space equals 280 square feet (17½ × 16) to provide the optimum 35 square feet of space per child. All but the Food Area should be carpeted. It is recommended that soft music be played continuously to help infants sleep.

Cully, Iris V. *Christian Child Development.* San Francisco: Harper & Row, 1979.

D. C. Borchert

Informal Education

See Progressive Education; Teaching Styles.

Information Processing

See Computers; Record Keeping.

Inner City

See Urban Church.

Instruction

Instruction is what teachers do as they seek to communicate with learners regarding a subject of importance. However, teachers are more than instructors. In the educational setting they also serve as friends, leaders, mentors, guides, and examples. Even though instruction is a significant aspect of the work of teachers, they should never emphasize the role of instructor so much that the other important roles are neglected.

ASPECTS OF INSTRUCTION

There are at least five aspects to instruction; it is intentional, sequential, purposeful, multidimensional, and personal. Instruction is *intentional* from several different perspectives. Most teachers begin their planning for teaching with a curriculum that has been carefully designed, written, edited, and produced. Some design a curriculum for the situation—an option that can be difficult but satisfying. Churches need to be intentional about the goals they establish for education, the curriculum that is selected, and the recruiting of teachers. Teachers themselves should prepare session plans based upon a specific topic, theme, or passage of Scripture. They will need to determine objectives appropriate for their classes and choose a variety of strategies to help learners achieve those objectives. It is also the teacher's task to gather resources and materials and arrange the furniture in the room.

These are examples of how instruction is a result of intentionality on the part of curriculum producers, staffs, boards, committees of congregations, and especially the teachers themselves. Yet many important things happen as a teacher and class are working together that may not have been intended. There needs to be an openness to the element of surprise and serendipity that occurs naturally and contributes much to the richness of the learning experience.

Instruction is *sequential*. Classes are organized for all age levels, so that over a period of years there is an orderly process to learning and growth. In a given course of study there is development from one session to another. And, in each session, whether it be thirty minutes or two hours, there is a sequence to activities as they are presented by the teacher and experienced by the learners. By presenting subject matter sequentially teachers and learners can be clearer about what they are doing and in seeing the connections between the various concepts, events, persons, or biblical texts being studied.

Even though instruction is organized sequentially, all persons do not gain information, develop skills, or have experiences in the same order or at the same time. Teachers need to recognize that many things occur in a person's life that interrupt and take precedence over a well-defined sequence created by curriculum planners and teachers.

Instruction is *purposeful*. Purposes or goals of instruction are defined differently depending upon who is determining them. Curriculum editors, denominational executives, pastors and educators, congregational leaders, and teachers all influence the purpose of instruction. The biblical interpretations, theological convictions, views of the learner, and educational theories held by these various persons all contribute to determining the purpose of instruction. One purpose of instruction may be to present to the learners the biblical interpretations, doctrines, history, and practices of a particular denomination or congregation so that the learners will come to espouse the beliefs of their church. Another purpose of instruction may be to involve the learners in exploring the biblical, theological, and historical heritage of their faith in order to make decisions about how they understand and respond to that heritage. A third purpose of instruction may be to share with the learners a wide variety of experiences of the practices of their church so that they may become informed, responsible members and participants. Still another purpose of instruction may be to prepare the learners to serve as faithful believers and followers of God as they act out their faith individually and corporately in the larger community.

It is not a matter of a stated purpose being right or wrong for all constituencies, but rather a matter of determining which purpose will best serve the particular church, teacher, and learners. When the purpose of instruction is understood, shared, and implemented by those involved, then that purpose will be well served.

Instruction is *multidimensional*. When instruction deals primarily with information about persons, events, places, concepts, interpretations, and doctrines and that information is organized

325

and analyzed, then teachers and learners are engaged in the cognitive aspects of instruction. On the other hand, instruction emphasizes the affective dimension when learners are involved in activities that encourage them to interact with others, to experience the arts, and to express themselves in ways that enable them to share with others their feelings, values, and beliefs. Another way to identify the many dimensions of instruction is to focus on the variety of strategies available to teachers as they seek to communicate with those in their classes; among them are lecture, storytelling, dramatizing, using audiovisuals, group discussions, creative expression, role playing, and many more.

Given the many dimensions of instruction it is important for teachers to develop skills in a variety of activities, to determine when one activity is more appropriate than another for particular learners, settings, or time frames, and to utilize a variety of activities over the course of study. In so doing, teachers will be able to respond to the diverse skills, interests, and needs of those they teach.

Instruction is *personal*. It is a cliché, but it is also true, "Teachers do not teach lessons, they teach persons." Teachers will be remembered for who they are as individuals far longer than the lessons they teach will be remembered. The relationships that develop between the teachers and the learners and among the learners will enable instruction to take place far more effectively and with greater motivation than if the emphasis is just on the transmission of information. For instruction to have any impact upon learners, it is important for teachers to plan for ways to relate to each individual in the class and to devise strategies that individuals can respond to personally.

THE PROCESS OF INSTRUCTION

From a general perspective, instruction has been described as being intentional, sequential, purposeful, multidimensional, and personal. From a more specific perspective instruction can be described in terms of what happens in the process of a given session plan. Instruction can be planned and implemented in five specific steps. The teacher leads an opening of the subject and the session, decides on ways for presenting the subject of that session, devises several strategies to involve the learners in exploring the subject, provides time and materials to enable the learners to respond creatively and express their own insights, feelings, and beliefs, and selects a means for closing the session. These five parts of a session plan can be rearranged and adapted to fit the time available, the needs of the teachers and learners, and the requirements of the subject itself. *See also* Education, Theories of; Goals; Learning Theory; Les-

son Planning; Methodology; Teaching Styles; Teaching Theory.

D. L. Griggs

Instruction, Theory of

See Teaching Theory.

Inter-Varsity Christian Fellowship in the USA

Inter-Varsity Christian Fellowship in the USA (IVCF), founded in 1939, is an evangelical movement dedicated to working with students on American college campuses. Its purpose is to build collegiate fellowships that engage their campuses with the gospel of Jesus Christ and make disciples who live out biblical values. More than 27,500 students are actively involved with Inter-Varsity, making it one of the largest evangelical college student movement in the United States. IVCF employs more than 800 staff members in all 50 states. More than 400 specially trained Inter-Varsity staff members work on 833 university and college campuses, schools of nursing, and other comparable educational institutions (1986 figures).

Inter-Varsity is a student-led movement. The focus of the ministry is the student-led chapters on college campuses. Chapter leaders plan and carry out each group's activities, which include evangelistic outreach, large group meetings, weekly small-group Bible study, and area-wide and national conferences. Inter-Varsity staff train and teach students and student leaders. They guide, advise, critique, and encourage.

Inter-Varsity Christian Fellowship in the USA traces its roots to the student movement in England, which began in the 1870s. This spiritual awakening gave rise to a movement called Inter-Varsity Fellowship of Great Britain (1923).

In 1939, evangelical students from the University of Michigan invited C. Stacey Woods, then general secretary of the Canadian Inter-Varsity, to help establish an Inter-Varsity chapter there. Similar requests came from other campuses. With the help of C. Stacey Woods, Herbert J. Taylor (president of Club Aluminum Products Corp.), and others, Inter-Varsity–USA was incorporated in 1941. C. Stacey Woods was the first general secretary of the American association.

In 1947 student movements around the world united to form the International Fellowship of Evangelical Students (IFES), of which IVCF–USA is a member. Today, IVCF–USA is a significant part of the IFES global student movement involving more than 85 countries.

The Inter-Varsity movement has continued to

prosper over the years under the able leadership of C. Stacey Woods, Charles Troutman, Charles Hummel, John Alexander, James McLeish, Gordon MacDonald, and Thomas Dunkerton.

Inter-Varsity regularly sponsors a triennial student missionary convention, first held in Toronto in 1952 and later at the University of Illinois at Urbana. This gathering of students (19,000 in 1987) is the largest and most significant student missions convention in America. It has been hailed by missions boards as the major recruiting force for both foreign and domestic missions.

Established in 1936, Student Foreign Missions Fellowship (SFMF) grew out of a gathering of 53 students at Ben Lippen Conference in North Carolina committed to a vision for world evangelism. Formally incorporated in 1938, it merged with IVCF–USA in 1945. SFMF works with students on Christian college campuses, helping them discover their role in world evangelization.

In 1948, Christian Nurses Fellowship, a national movement of evangelical nursing students, merged with IVCF–USA, changing its name to Nurses Christian Fellowship (NCF) in 1952. NCF helps nursing students and nurses identify and meet spiritual needs of patients.

InterVarsity Press (IVP) publishes hundreds of books and study materials specifically aimed at Christian college students. These books cover such vital topics as working through personal relationships, confronting contemporary issues, exploring different worldviews, plans for world missions, and making evangelism a way of life.

Other ministries of Inter-Varsity include: Black Campus Ministry, Latino Fellowship, International Students Ministry, Inter-Varsity Overseas/LINK, Theological Students Fellowship, Faculty Ministry, 2100 Productions, Campus by the Sea (California), Bear Trap Ranch (Colorado), Cedar Campus (Michigan), and the Fort Lauderdale Evangelism Project. See also Evangelism; Mission Education.

A. B. Loux

Interdisciplinary Studies

Religious education, even by name, is an interdisciplinary enterprise. Although religious education theorists differ in terms of how disciplines are interrelated and which ought to be most important, no theorist in religious education can avoid some solution, however expedient or unthinking, to the way in which diverse disciplines are to be interrelated for the tasks of religious education. Assuming the fundamental validity of an established discipline such as theology or psychology, the interdisciplinary issue may be stated as a problem in methodology. How are two or more disciplines to be related so as to allow both to be treated with integrity and both to be mutually enriched, albeit not always directly or equally, by the relationship?

FAILED APPROACHES

Certain approaches to this issue may be dismissed at the outset. The tendency to cross-fertilize disciplines by finding semantic connections must be rejected as trivializing and distorting. For example, "object relations" has opposite connotations in theology and psychology; in the former it depersonalizes, in the latter it designates the focus of one's affections. Terms must be kept in their larger disciplinary contexts if they are to be the focus of an interdisciplinary study. Similarly, one-to-one correlation between stages of human development and theological doctrines must be dismissed. For example, autonomy versus shame in Erik Erikson's writings does not correlate directly with a Christian doctrine of sin or evil. Also to be rejected are tendencies that make another's discipline "nothing but" an aspect of one's own, as when Freudian psychoanalysis makes theology nothing but a symptom of regression and neurotic behavior. Common but less sophisticated forms of reductionalism abound in efforts to deal with pragmatic problems (e.g., for teaching purposes or for curriculum construction) by simply drawing on whatever discipline may be handy, disregarding the question of how separate disciplines, even though effective in their own way, may work at cross-purposes. For example, the learning theory that works best in the short term may be reinforcement schedules, but the learner learns as much from how learning takes place as from what is being taught. This raises a theological implication of learning theory, and we have to question whether, for example, learning Paul Tillich's theology through programmed reinforcement does not present a hopeless contradiction between content and method.

SUCCESSFUL APPROACHES

Following are four methodological approaches that promise to fulfill the conditions for a genuine interdisciplinary exchange and so lay a solid foundation for theory and practice in Christian education. The dialogical relationship between disciplines is a major premise of the following approaches, but it should be clear that dialogue is not enough. Each is attempting to discover the logos in the dialogue that can make it productive and intelligible. Furthermore, theologians are emphasized here because they have done considerably more thinking about theologically related interdisciplinary concerns than those in secular disciplines.

First, the generative methodology behind Paul Tillich's *correlational* approach to theology. It begins with existential questions raised by the inherent ambiguities of human situation. These are answered by the gospel, whose center for human existence is the new being in Jesus Christ. Tillich made considerable use of depth psychology in formulating the questions on an ontic or functional level and thus used them to point to the deeper ontological issues addressed by the gospel. In the history of Christian education Tillich's correlational method has had significant influence on Lewis Sherrill and, in theory design, upon D. Campbell Wyckoff. Currently, practical theology, which embraces Christian education among other aspects of ministry, is being systematically reconstructed on a correlational basis that modifies and extends Tillich's method. *Practical Theology* (1983), edited by Don S. Browning, makes this point clearly.

The second approach, systematically developed by Seward Hiltner, is called *perspectival*. Here the initial focus is upon an experiential phenomenon (e.g., psychopathology), which is first viewed theologically (e.g., under the aspect of sin) and then interpreted psychodynamically (e.g., the pathological potential is blame and guilt); finally the theological situation can be restated with greater sensitivity to the concrete human situation. Thus, one may say, "What is religiously important about sin is not that someone, we or our forefathers, did bad things. . . . It is that the answers of human life, even when they turn out badly, are not above repair if seen in the context of a God who unambiguously wills the fulfillment of humankind so long as he does not have to remove human freedom in the process" (Hiltner, *Theological Dynamics*, p. 107). This perspectival approach that moves from theology to psychology and then back to theology keeps the interdisciplinary circle intact with respect to a given phenomenon, but ontological and existential concerns tend to drift toward pragmatic and empirical criteria. Historically, the more liberal, pragmatic approaches to Christian education growing out of empirical theology tend to be fundamentally consistent with the perspectival approach. Although George Albert Coe's work is not as methodologically self-conscious as Hiltner's, it is probably the best parallel to the perspectival approach in the history of Christian education.

The third approach concerns Roman Catholic theology, where the traditionally positive relationship between nature and grace has made theological correlations with the natural and human sciences less problematic. A key figure here is Bernard Lonergan, whose transcendental Thomism focuses on four phases of knowing that are necessary and sufficient in any field or discipline but need to be restated, depending on the field in question. These phases are experience, understanding, reflection, and judgment. Lonergan uses this necessary (transcendental argument) pattern of cognition as the basis for interdisciplinary study on the grounds that only such an approach allows insight and intelligence to work together for a true knowledge of Being. Lonergan has applied his approach to the structure and sequence of theological curriculum in *Method in Theology* (1972), and the sequence may also have application to educational process, structuring the phases of teacher-student interaction by moving from experience to judgment in relation to any given educational concern.

The fourth approach is structuralism, by which it is assumed that there are universal structures of mind that will inevitably govern thought in all disciplines, theology as well as the sciences. The key figures here, such as Claude Lévi-Strauss, Jacques Lacan, Jean Piaget, Lawrence Kohlberg, and Carol Gilligan, are not theologians. The most widely debated application of structuralism to theologically related study is James Fowler's effort, in *Stages of Faith* (1981), to construct stages of faith development. Since this is a highly debatable position on both theological and developmental grounds, it should be seen as groundbreaking but not as a definitive example of the structuralist methodology in Christian education.

Although many questions follow from these suggestions, perhaps it is best to view interdisciplinary methodology as an effort to make connections between disciplines explicit, cognitively reversible, and open to public scrutiny. Thereby, the disciplines involved in religious education may become mutually critical and corrective for the sake of their mutually enlightening contributions to theory and practice. *See also* Faith Development; Motivation; Psychology of Religion; Social Sciences; Sociology of Religion; Structuralism; Teaching Theory; Theology and Education.

FOR FURTHER REFERENCE

Browning, Don S., ed. *Practical Theology*. San Francisco: Harper & Row, 1983.

Hiltner, Seward. *Theological Dynamics*. Nashville, TN: Abingdon, 1972.

Lonergan, Bernard. *Method in Theology*. New York: Herder & Herder, 1972.

J. E. Loder

Intergenerational Approach

The prefix "inter" means "between," "among," "together," or "mutually reciprocal." A generation is a body of individuals born at about the same time. Intergenerational learning occurs when persons from two or more generations (children, youth, adults) are involved in planned face-to-face sharing and communication that strengthens their faith.

While there is usually a topic or theme for each intergenerational learning experience, an underlying purpose is always the building of community, where all grow in appreciation and

Jesus was a Jew. Only as a Jew can he be understood. So say some. Jesus was a Jew, but he can only be understood as one who transcended the limitations of his Jewishness. So say others. Jesus was a Jew, but what we know of him has been so modified in the gentile, Greek direction that his Jewish background is only barely visible. So say still others.

These opinions come from those who have studied the evidence that can be found in the New Testament and related documents of the period. Such opinions, of course, necessitate a careful sifting of the evidence as well as a degree of selectivity in choosing evidence to support a particular point of view. For instance, it is likely that a Roman Catholic, wishing to support the papal claim to authority, would emphasize the passage Matthew 16:13–19, in which Jesus appears to pun on the name of Peter (rock) and in which he presents to this same Peter the keys of the kingdom of heaven. It is unlikely that a Protestant would emphasize this particular passage, focusing instead on Matthew 18:18–20, in which Jesus appears to be granting this authority of "binding and loosing" to the whole church. Others, eager to avoid this question, attempt to deny that Jesus is making a pun on Peter's name and aver that Jesus is only referring to the "rock" of Peter's faith.

It is, in the last analysis, the connection one presupposes that Jesus had or has to the institutional church that determines, to a large extent, the picture of Jesus at which one ultimately arrives. If one begins with a presupposition that the church is made up of those with direct access to Jesus through the medium of the Bible, then one will discount, for the most part, the idea that the church played a considerable part in the shaping of the New Testament literature. On the other hand, if one tends to place a high degree of importance upon the church as an entity in itself, perhaps even considering it a divine institution, then one will be more willing to see the church as having had a hand in the formulation of the New Testament Scriptures as they now stand. However, as far as this writer is concerned, there can be no doubt that the emerging Christian community, probably in various forms, had a great deal to do with the way in which the New Testament was eventually formulated.

JESUS AS TEACHER

However, there seems to be one area in which most people are in agreement and that is the picture of Jesus as a teacher. There is a wide consensus that in his parables we come very close to the so-called historical Jesus. There is also a considerable amount of agreement that Jesus' point of reference in the parables, whether stated or not, was the kingdom of God. Jesus, in a number of instances, refers quite explicitly to God's kingdom or reign as the point of comparison. Using stories

and situations that would have been understandable if not altogether familiar to his hearers—a farmer planting seed, a woman sweeping the house, a foreman hiring a crew to pick grapes, two men praying in the Temple—Jesus drew word pictures that focused his hearers' attention on a comparison of their situation with that of God (however perceived). Sometimes explicitly religious, sometimes not, Jesus' parables drew the attention of his hearers away from narrow, private concerns to a consideration of how things in general seemed to work.

There were many voices clamoring to be heard during Jesus' time; Jesus' was one among many. Some said that, more and more, religion was the way out of the Jewish dilemma of subjection to the power of Rome. Some advocated cooperation with the Roman authorities, while others urged a program of terrorism. Still others fled to the wilderness where they founded religious communities in which they practiced purity of life and awaited Armageddon. Jesus preached adherence to God's will ("A man had two sons . . .") and faith in God (Which of you by being anxious . . .").

Jesus never claimed to have the answer to Israel's dilemma or to anyone's personal dilemma. He did not claim any particular status either in this world or in the next. But he did point to what he believed was God's creation as a place where one could find answers to one's questions if one "had the ears to hear."

Jesus was not afraid to criticize the religious authorities of his day. His criticism evidently hit home, because they wasted little time in planning to have him eliminated. Jesus died a victim of the religious status quo in league with a local government that was more interested in civil order than in its own imperial justice.

If we have doubts about who Jesus was, the early community of his followers did not. They expressed it in different ways, but of one thing they were sure—that God had acted in the case of Jesus in a way in which he had not acted heretofore. Some said that God had exalted him to heaven. Others said that he was raised from the dead. Others spoke of his resurrection followed by his ascension. However they expressed it, the early followers of Jesus were convinced that God had somehow intervened to vindicate and proclaim Jesus the victor over his foes.

What one thinks of Jesus depends to a certain extent upon how much of the material in the New Testament one thinks has been affected by this extraordinary faith of Jesus' followers concerning what happened to him after his crucifixion. One certainly needs to ponder the question of whether any of the material about Jesus would have survived if death had been thought to have been the end for him.

"Come to Jesus," says the preacher. One cannot dispute the evidence that many hear and respond to that invitation. But to whom are they responding? Whoever he was and is, this one called Jesus Christ remains unforgettable. *See also* Christianity; Gospel; Parable; Reign of God; Trinity.

FOR FURTHER REFERENCE

Anderson, C. C. *Critical Quests of Jesus*. Grand Rapids, MI: Eerdmans, 1969.

Bornkamm, G. *Jesus of Nazareth*. Translated by I. and F. Mclusky with James Robinson. New York: Harper & Row, 1960.
Sandmel, S. *We Jews and Jesus*. New York: Oxford University Press, 1965.
Schweitzer, E. *Jesus*. Translated by D. E. Green. Atlanta, GA: Knox, 1971.

J. S. Ruef

Jewish Education

The history of Jewish education may be said to begin with two well-known passages in the Torah, the Five Books of Moses. The first of these passages follows the charge, "Hear, O Israel," the declaration of faith (as it has come to be called), and refers to our obligation to teach the basic principles of the religion in every time and venue: "And you shall teach them diligently to your children." The second refers to the obligation of parents to instruct children about the liberation from Egypt: "You shall teach your child [about the Passover] on that day, saying . . ." Thus, teaching and learning are seen in the Jewish tradition as basic obligations, which begin with the family.

Jewish schooling, however, must be said to begin at a later date—perhaps around the year A.D. 70, with the destruction of the Second Temple and the concurrent decline of the priesthood as a ruling class. The rabbis and scholars who became the new leaders of the Jewish community left Jerusalem and founded the academy at Yavneh, an institution that was, as far as we know, the first Jewish school. The scholars of Yavneh strove to substitute prayer and the study of Torah for the sacrificial cult of the Temple. Indeed, they saw the establishment of the academy at Yavneh as some measure of consolation for the loss of the Temple.

Under the ensuing Roman rule Jews sometimes studied at their peril, but learning was too important to be given up. A popular legend about Rabbi Akiba illustrates this point. Akiba was asked by his disciples if he were not afraid for his life, because the Romans had forbidden the study of Torah. He answered in terms of a parable: A fox sees that the fish in a stream are struggling to escape the nets of their tormentors. He therefore invites the fish to come up and spend time with him on the dry land—safely out of the reach of the wicked forces. The fish refuse the invitation, saying that no matter how dangerous it is in the water, they would rather remain swimming in the territory that is native to them than attempt to survive in some presumably safer atmosphere that would be totally foreign.

The oral tradition, developed by the rabbis and collected in the Talmud, abounds with legends and sayings emphasizing the centrality of the study of Torah to the Jewish people. Over time, the term Torah itself has been construed far more broadly than its narrow denotation as the Five Books of Moses. For Jews living today, the term "Torah" connotes not only the Bible but the Talmud, later commentaries, and, indeed, the entire body of Jewish learning.

UNDERLYING TENSIONS: ADAPTATION VERSUS RETENTION

Though the study of Torah is essential to Jewish life, it is not an unconflicted endeavor. As the parable of Rabbi Akiba suggests, the study of Torah by Jews in the diaspora was, and is, at times undertaken at the expense of relations with their host culture. In the USSR until recently, for example, the teaching of Hebrew and the Torah was prohibited by law. But even Jews living in more open societies have experienced a tension between the obligation to study Torah and their desire to blend in with their neighbors. This brings us to what might be viewed as an organizing principle for a history of Jewish education. Study in Jewish tradition has been characterized by one of two thrusts: adaptation to the standards of the non-Jewish world, on the one hand, and the retention of traditional norms and values, on the other. Wherever Jews have lived, they have been torn between thinking of adaptation as a compromise and seeing it as an opportunity to enrich learning. In each generation Jewish scholars have wrestled with the need to retain some pure connection to the values of the previous generation while acknowledging in one way or another that accommodation and change are the hallmark of Jewish life. Thus, one is not surprised to find neo-Aristotelian principles at work in the philosophy of Maimonides; Greek notions of the immutability of values in the Talmud and midrash; and, in the modern era, influences from nearly every shade of the philosophical spectrum, from idealism to existentialism.

Judaism has borrowed from other cultures and contributed to them at the same time, searching for principles that transcend time and place and for ways to teach those principles. The tension may best be reflected in the basic Jewish fact of commentary, as exegesis: the hermeneutic tradition. An original text is preserved within the tradition, and generation after generation of Jewish scholars or exegetes expand upon the norms, laws, and spiritual messages embedded within the text. The teaching of Torah throughout Jewish history is an outgrowth of the attitude reflected in that tradition of commentary and exegesis. Each Jewish school strives to maintain the Jewish tradition, while at the same time making a viable Jewish life possible in the various diaspora communities.

TRADITIONAL JEWISH EDUCATION

Traditionally, Jewish education began in the home when a child was about three and was continued throughout childhood and adult life. The study of Torah was a commandment incumbent upon all Jews and was seen as the foundation for the other commandments. Formal schooling usually began at the age of six and was conducted in schools associated with synagogues. Funds to support these schools and pay for communal teachers were generated through internal taxation. In the premodern period, only males attended school, and females were given a more limited education at home.

The curriculum of the Jewish school began with the study of Torah and continued with the study of Talmud and midrash. The older and more outstanding students were eventually enrolled in *yeshivot* (academies of learning) and were supported by the community as they continued their studies into adulthood; these scholars were highly honored in the community. In this manner the continuously growing body of Jewish interpretation was transmitted from generation to generation.

Not only was the subject matter of Jewish education delineated in Jewish texts but treatises were also written about the qualities of good teaching and the characteristics of good students. In *Hukkei Ha-Torah* (rules of the study of Torah), written by Rabbi Eleazar of Worms in 1309, a complete set of regulations dealing with schooling was provided. Though details of method may have varied from community to community, the commitment to the study of the basic texts was always present. Jews were often isolated from, and even persecuted by, their host societies, but the principle of Jewish learning for all males continued unabated from the time of the founding of the academy at Yavneh until the modern era.

Beginning in the eighteenth century, as the restrictions on Jewish participation in their host societies were gradually lifted, the conflicts between adaptation and retention in Jewish life intensified. As more avenues opened up for Jewish entry into the commercial, cultural, and intellectual life of the society at large, increased pressure was brought to bear on Jewish schools to add secular subjects to their curricula.

Thus, Jewish schools of this era struggled constantly with the issue of secular versus Judaic studies. Should the purpose of education be to help young Jews adapt to the new realities of their society? Or should the school continue in its emphasis on Judaic texts, thereby maintaining the continuity of the tradition?

In some cases a particular Jewish community opted for one kind of education over another, but in many, novel solutions to the dilemma of adaptation or retention surfaced. In the late nineteenth century, for example, Hebraic *gymnasia* were formed. The schools emphasized both secular disciplines and Judaic studies, though often Judaic studies focused less on Talmud and more on spoken Hebrew and modern Hebrew literature.

JEWISH EDUCATION IN NORTH AMERICA

Past

The tension between the opposing goals of secular adjustment and traditional preservation is best exemplified in Jewish education in America. Before the first wave of significant Jewish immigration to America in the mid-nineteenth century, Jews were educated mostly by means of private tutors and apprenticeships. Tutors were expected to impart both the secular skills of computation and English reading and the Jewish skills of prayer and Hebrew reading. Children learned the necessary occupational skills through apprenticeships. The few formal schools that were established maintained the same balance between Jewish subjects and secular ones. In the few instances in which teachers were hired for the children of the poor who could not afford private tutors, the teacher was engaged to teach children enough Hebrew to enable them to participate in worship services.

With the German immigration of the mid-nineteenth century, and the arrival in America of approximately two hundred thousand Jews, significant Jewish communities were established in the East and Midwest. At the outset these German Jewish communities established private day schools for their children, in which they sought to impart a set of skills necessary for living in America, a set of skills necessary for participation in their own Jewish communities, and a firm grounding in German culture.

As the common school crusade spread across America, however, it became increasingly difficult for Jews to maintain their private schools. Public schools became the avenue to participation in American life. As these schools became less blatantly Protestant in their orientation, and as they began to recognize the different cultural needs of immigrant groups, the public schools began to absorb increasing numbers of Jewish children. For the time, it seemed that the balance between adaptation to America and retention of Jewish culture and religion had shifted in favor of adaptation.

Concurrent with the decline of the German Jewish day school was the advent of the Jewish Sunday school, patterned after Protestant Sunday schools. Begun in Philadelphia in 1838, Jewish Sunday schools soon spread throughout America. Most of the day schools converted to Sunday schools rather than close their doors permanently. The curricula of the Sunday schools consisted primarily of the memorization of a Jewish form of catechism, in the guise of a series of maxims dealing with Jewish beliefs and proper actions. In addition, the course of study included Bible readings and holiday celebrations. This Judaic education was limited to a few hours on Sunday mornings and thus provided little balance to the massive enculturation provided by the public schools.

The balance remained essentially unchallenged throughout the period of heaviest immigration, the era from 1881–1924, when nearly three million Eastern European Jews came to America. Though attempts were made at transplanting the full-time Jewish schools of Eastern Europe to America, these attempts were few and short-lived. Even the most religious Jews found the possibility of public education, and its promise of a share in the American dream, too alluring to forgo.

It was during this period that the basic pattern of Jewish education in America became firmly established; it has remained essentially unchanged until today. Under the direction of Dr. Samson Benderly and a group of his disciples, an approach to Jewish life in America was forged wherein Jews would send their children to public schools but seek out every opportunity outside public school hours to have their children retain their Jewishness. Benderly and his followers established communal schools called Talmud Torahs (literally "the study of Torah"). The typical Talmud Torah offered its students eight to twelve hours of instruction per week and met on weekdays after school and on Sundays.

As a centralized communal institution, the Talmud Torah was able to maintain relatively high standards and to offer full-time jobs to a small cadre of professional teachers. However, beginning in the 1940s, Jews, along with many other Americans, migrated from concentrated urban enclaves to more dispersed suburban ones. No longer easily accessible to its students, the communal Talmud Torah began to diminish in size and importance; it was gradually replaced by supplementary schools sponsored by individual synagogues. Today, though a small number of communal schools have survived in some parts of the country, the vast majority of Jewish schools operate under congregational auspices.

The shift from communal to synagogue sponsorship of supplementary education had several significant long-term consequences for Jewish education, in terms of curriculum, hours of instruction, and staffing patterns. Nearly all synagogues in the United States are affiliated with one of the four major movements: Orthodox, Conservative, Reform, and Reconstructionist. Whereas the typical communal school offered the same curriculum to all its students, a school under the auspices of a synagogue would tend to reflect the ideology of a particular movement to the exclusion of the others. Even synagogues within the same movement often differ significantly as to their relative emphasis on such subjects as Hebrew, text study, ritual observance, and social ethics. Great variety and accelerated change in the curricula of supplementary schools has been one result of the proliferation of congregational supplementary schools.

A second result of the change from communal to congregational schools has been a sharp decline in the hours of instruction. In 1946, 63 percent of students enrolled in supplementary schools attended five days a week, receiving an average of eight to ten hours of instruction. In 1958 only 6 percent attended five days, and by 1970 there were no five-day supplementary schools in existence. A 1982 census of Jewish schools sponsored by Jewish Education Services of North America (JESNA) and the Hebrew University, found 24 percent of schools operating only one day a week and the remaining 74 percent operating two or three days.

A third consequence of decentralization was the near-total demise of what had been, in the 1930s, a nascent profession of Jewish teaching. Large communal schools, which often operated double or triple shifts, were able to offer their teachers full-time positions, with salaries that were low but still competitive with those of public school teachers. In contrast, the 1982 Census of Jewish Schools found only 7 percent of supplementary school teachers teaching eleven hours or more per week, 9 percent teaching seven to ten hours, 31 percent teaching between four and six hours, and 52 percent teaching fewer than four hours a week.

Present

There exist today approximately 2,066 Jewish supplementary schools in North America. Collectively, these schools enroll 268,000 students and employ approximately 20,000 teachers. Roughly 4.5 percent of these schools are affiliated with the Orthodox movement, 35.8 percent with the Conservative movement, and 48.6 percent with the Reform movement. Eight percent of supplementary schools operate under communal auspices; the remaining 3 percent of schools are listed in the census as "other." The median enrollment in supplementary schools is 100–250 students, but the range in enrollment is large: 17 percent of schools have fewer than 50 students; 21 percent have fewer than 100; 34 percent enroll 100–250 students; 19 percent enroll 250–500; and 9 percent have more than 500 students.

As indicated above, supplementary schools operate independently of one another; their curricula reflect, in part, the ideology of their parent congregations. Nonetheless, some commonalities may be found. Schools that meet one day a week tend to focus on the development in their students of a Jewish identity, through the teaching of holidays, prayer, and stories from the Torah. Schools meeting on additional days tend to add Hebrew to the curriculum. Few supplementary schools are able to give their students a facility with the study of Jewish texts; they aim instead for a broad understanding of Jewish values, beliefs, and practices. Much of the curriculum from grades five through seven is devoted to preparation for the bar or bas mitzvah, the rite of passage that marks a thirteen-year-old's entry into adult Jewish life. This preparation requires the development of functional worship skills, including the ability to read Hebrew, the language of Jewish worship, and at least a rudimentary knowledge of a portion from the Five Books of Moses. In fact, the bar or bas mitzvah ceremony may be said to be the focal point of much of the supplementary school experience; only 18 percent of students continue their formal Jewish education past the age of thirteen.

A loose network of local and national institutions and organizations renders a variety of support services to supplementary schools. Most large cities in North America have a central agency for Jewish education, which offers schools consultation, teaching training, curriculum and media development, and, in some cases, direct financial aid. Each movement has a department of education that develops curricular materials and training modalities of its own. There exists a small number of commercial publishing houses specializing in textbooks and media for Jewish schools.

Though the early trend toward adaptation among American Jews, as represented by full participation in secular education institutions, has remained largely unchanged, a significant countertrend has developed. In the 1940s, the Orthodox community began to establish Jewish day schools for those parents who wished to give their children a more intensive exposure to the Jewish tradition and to Jewish texts than was possible in a supplementary school. Conservative Jews in the 1950s and Reform Jews in the 1970s began to establish day schools of their own. Today day schools account for 28 percent of the Jewish children enrolled in Jewish schools. Though there is wide variation in the type of education provided in the day schools sponsored by different segments of the Jewish community, these schools have in common a responsibility for the total education of the child, in secular as well as Judaic studies.

The shift in the long-standing balance between adaptation and retention, at least for that segment of the population whose children attend day schools, is not surprising: an increasing proportion of American Jewry are no longer immigrants or the children of immigrants. For third- and fourth-generation American Jewish children, adaptation to American life and culture is no longer at issue; they are concerned instead with retaining a connection with and commitment to their Jewishness.

A survey of current educational institutions in the Jewish community of North America would be incomplete without mention of the alternative modes of Jewish education that have developed over the past thirty or forty years. Following Samson Benderly's principle of taking full advantage of the time blocks in which children are not attending public school, Jewish educators have created an impressive network of Jewish preschools, summer camps, youth groups, and trips to Israel of varying duration. Jewish summer camps provide opportunities for Jewish children to experience Jewish life in an environment conducive to the traditional daily and weekly rhythms. Six-week to year-long experiences in Israel help young Jews develop an understanding of and a commitment to both the Jewish state and their own sense of Jewishness. The Jewish preschool offers an unprecedented opportunity for schools to reach parents as well as children. A growing number of family-education and adult-education programs have this goal as well.

Future Trends

Changes in American Jewish life tend to parallel trends in the general American society, and those changes create the context for future developments in Jewish education. As American Jews become predominantly fourth- and fifth-generation Americans, their characteristics will be shaped less by ethnic particularity and more by their integration into the culture of the larger society. Thus, a number of trends in Jewish education can be foreseen.

One such trend is the increasing geographic mobility of American Jews. Career and economic considerations have already led to migration from the established Jewish centers of the Northeast to new concentrations of Jews in the Southwest and West. In these younger communities the patterns of Jewish education may be reshaped by a combination of factors. First, a relatively small Jewish presence will make Jews less comfortable with their ethnicity. Thus, the aims of the supplementary school will move further away from the teaching of content and closer to affective experiences aimed at the strengthening of Jewish identity. This will lead to an even greater emphasis on the informal aspects of Jewish education, both within and outside the school; it may even lead to a reconfiguration of the supplementary school itself.

The question of who will teach in the supplementary school of the future will become increasingly problematic. Women who received some teacher training in college have formed the traditional pool of supplementary school teachers. But as the status of teachers in North America has declined, and as new career opportunities for women have opened up, this traditional pool has dwindled. Because Jews living in outlying areas tend to be less educated Judaically, the shift of Jewish population to these areas will make the current shortage of qualified teachers for supplementary schools even more severe. Inevitably, new staffing patterns will have to be developed.

The proliferation of schools in growing new communities and the shortage of trained teaching personnel is creating an increasing demand for school directors who are well educated in both Judaica and pedagogy. These individuals will increasingly supervise teaching staffs consisting not of professional teachers but of highly motivated members of the community. Thus, although teachers in the supplementary setting will increasingly be laypeople, the professionalization of the Jewish school principal will continue and will take the form of a larger and more prominent professional cadre of American-trained full-time directors of Jewish schools.

The changing Jewish family is a second factor that will lead to new adaptive responses in Jewish education. American Jews, like Americans in general, are marrying later, divorcing more frequently, bearing fewer children, and creating dual-career families. The afternoon school is becoming less and less viable for working suburban parents. The Sunday school, for its part, is becoming less viable for children from divorced families who rotate between parents on weekends. On the other hand, the increase of dual-career and single-parent families has created a need for a far more extensive network of day care, after-school care, and full-time preschool programs than currently exists. Increasingly there is pressure for Jewish schools to fill those needs. Such a development would lead to a significant expansion of Jewish early childhood education, necessitating the development of a professional cadre of Jewish early childhood educators and increased attention to pedagogical issues and learning materials for these age groups.

America is the most open, democratic, and pluralistic society in which Jews have ever found themselves. In such a milieu, the pressures toward complete assimilation are quite strong. The majority of American Jews, who have lived in America for three to four generations, have developed over the years a rather diffuse and content-less sense of Jewish identification. They are united by a general concern for the Jewish people and the state of Israel, a fear of anti-Semitism, some common philanthropic causes, and the maintenance of a few basic life-cycle rituals. Many of these Jews do not belong to a synagogue and do not send their children to Jewish schools or Jewish summer camps. Even those who do provide some sort of Jewish education for their children are not particularly concerned about the diluted curriculum of the supplementary school or about the decline in the hours of instruction. For them, sending a child to a Jewish school is more a symbolic than a substantive act.

At the same time, there is a sizable minority of American Jews who are very involved in Jewish life. These are Jews who send their children to day schools, or to a supplementary school, about whose quality they are deeply concerned. In future years members of this group may find themselves increasingly at odds with one another over a number of ideological issues. With as many as 50 percent of Jews marrying non-Jews, and with Jewish identity traditionally being matrilineal, the issue of the status of the child of a Jewish father and a non-Jewish mother has been hotly debated. The Reform and Reconstructionist movements would consider such a child Jewish; the Conservative and Orthodox would not. A second issue dividing the community is the status of women, with all movements except the Orthodox ordaining women as rabbis. It may be that these ideological differences will lead to a number of Jewish educational systems that are vastly different in ideology and content.

Thus, current and future generations of Jewish educators face a dual challenge. To the unaffiliated or marginally affiliated Jew they must hold out a compelling picture of the Jewish tradition that will inspire in these Jews a commitment to its continuity. For affiliated Jews of all persuasions they must create opportunities and experiences in which the study and preservation of Torah will override ideological divisions.

Although the American Jewish community has thus far succeeded in maintaining the delicate balance between adaptation and retention, its ability to do so in future years is by no means assured. Indeed, some observers foresee an increased state of fragmentation, in which a majority of Jews will become virtually indistinguishable from the rest of American society, while the minority that remains committed to upholding the tradition will be subdivided into contentious factions. The possibility of maintaining a cohesive and vigorous American Jewish community will rest, in some measure, on the vision and leadership of its educators. *See also* Holocaust, Teaching the; Jewish Festivals and Holidays; Jewish Theological Concepts; Middle East; Private Religious Schools; Private Schools and Religion; Rabbi as Educator; Torah as Teaching; Torah, Study and Teaching of.

I. Aron, W. Cutter, S. S. Lee, M. Zeldin

Jewish Festivals and Holidays

Judaism is the religion that began when a specific, identifiable group, the ancient Hebrews, made a covenant with God at Mount Sinai to be his people; it is still practiced today by Jews the world over. Other than the high holidays, which are observed as very personal holidays during which each individual Jew confronts God face to face searching his or her deeds, Jewish holidays are integrally connected with events in Jewish history and given theological meaning as each new generation confronts and celebrates them.

OVERVIEW

Judaism has several yearly holidays and one weekly holiday. The weekly holiday is the Sabbath, in Hebrew *Shabbat*, which occurs on the seventh day of each week from sundown Friday until sundown Saturday. It is a day for rest and re-creation of spirit, a day of worship and, in essence, the nondisturbance of the natural order. It commemorates both creation and the Exodus from Egypt.

The yearly holidays all occur according to the Jewish calendar, in which the years are based on the solar seasons and the months are based on the phases of the moon; each new moon marks the start of a new month. There are five major holidays, four traditional and two recently instituted minor holidays, and a number of fast days. Some holidays are called major because their origins are found in the pages of the Torah, the first five books of the Bible.

The major holidays include three pilgrim festivals, Pesach (Passover), Shavuot (Pentecost), and Sukkoth (Feast of Booths), and two high holidays, Rosh Hashanah (New Year) and Yom Kippur (Day of Atonement). The minor holidays are Purim (Lots), based on the biblical book of Esther; Hanukkah (Feast of Dedication), based on the books of Maccabees in the Apocrypha; Tu B'Shevat (meaning the fifteenth of January or February), the New Year of the Trees; Lag B'Omer, the thirty-third day of the counting of the *omer* or grain sheaves between Pesach and Shavuot; Yom Hashoa (Day of the Holocaust), a memorial day for the victims of the Nazi Holocaust; and Yom Ha-atzmaut (Day of Independence), Israel's Independence Day. Of the fast days, which commemorate sad events in ancient Jewish history, the most significant other than Yom Kippur is Tisha B'Av, the ninth day of the month of Av (late July or August); it commemorates the destruction of the Temple in Jerusalem, both in 586 B.C. and in A.D. 70.

SPECIFIC EVENTS

The pilgrim festivals reflect two different but parallel Jewish traditions. One is the ancient agricultural cycle. Pesach, or Passover, was the time of the first grain harvest of the spring. However, it is better known as the holiday marking the Exodus of the Israelites from Egyptian bondage. The Passover saga then moves to the giving of the law at Mount Sinai, the forty years of wandering in the wilderness, and finally the entry into the promised land. On the first evening of Passover Jewish families have a festive, ritual meal at home called the Seder; there are numerous symbolic foods and a liturgy in celebration of freedom. This message of freedom can be seen as freedom not only from physical slavery but from any other kind of bondage that limits human potential and stifles the growth of the human spirit. In addition to the liturgical message of freedom, there are also references to the ultimate freedom of the messianic age when all tyranny will cease and all humanity will know universal peace and well-being. A further theme of the Seder proclaims that all of the events of the Exodus are directly attributable to God. Moses is never mentioned in the Haggadah, the prayer book of the Seder. And from a theological standpoint, each Jew throughout history is believed to have participated in the Exodus as it is relived by each generation at Seder in its time.

Fifty days, that is, a week of weeks plus one day, after the start of Pesach is Shavuot, another holiday with both an agricultural and a theological-historical message. The Torah refers to Shavuot only as the Holiday of the First Fruits, marking the first harvest of the spring planting. Later Jewish tradition connects Shavuot to the giving of the Ten Commandments at Mount Sinai, for the book of Exodus states that the children of Israel came to that mountain in the third month after the Exodus.

In the fall, fifteen days after Rosh Hashanah is Sukkoth (Feast of Booths), the fall harvest festival marking the conclusion of the agricultural

341

year and symbolically connected with the wilderness period, when the Israelites lived in temporary shelters during their forty years of wandering. This holiday, with its message of thanksgiving, connotes the temporariness and fragility of human existence as well as dependence upon God for the blessings of life. Throughout the eight days of the holiday, psalms of praise known as Hallel are recited in the synagogue. The conclusion of the holiday is marked by Simchat Torah, when the final verses of Deuteronomy are read and immediately thereafter the reading cycle is resumed with the story of creation in Genesis. It is a time of great rejoicing and festivity, denoting the importance of Torah in the life of each Jew.

The high holidays, which occur ten days apart in the fall month of Tishri, are holidays of introspection, contrition, prayer, and spiritual soul-searching. The themes of repentance and atonement are central to both Rosh Hashanah (the New Year) and Yom Kippur (the Day of Atonement). Rosh Hashanah, which occurs on the first day of Tishri, is observed in the traditional synagogue for two days and in the Reform synagogue for one day. Yom Kippur, ten days later, is a twenty-four-hour fast day and is the more somber holiday. Both observances are synagogue-centered today; both include the blowing of the *shofar*, or ram's horn, as part of the observance; both call Jews to consider their lives, what they have done with their days and how they can alter their behavior to be more in line with God's ways; both are holidays of worship with special prayers and special music reflecting these themes.

Of the six minor festivals, Purim and Hanukkah are perhaps better known than the rest. Purim is based on the biblical account of the escape of the Jews of Persia from the evil intentions of Haman, the prime minister, who wished to destroy them because of his hatred of Mordecai, the uncle of Esther the queen. Esther discovers the plot and reveals it to Ahasuerus, her husband, who decrees that Haman be hanged on the gallows he had prepared for Mordecai. The account reminds us of the ever-present need to be alert to counter tyranny and oppression. Purim is a holiday of merrymaking and contains a lesson that has been repeated many times in Jewish history; thus the holiday has held great meaning over the centuries.

Hanukkah, a midwinter festival celebrated for eight days, recalls the struggle of a small band of soldiers led by the Maccabee family to overcome the might of the Syrian king Antiochus Epiphanes in the year 165 B.C. Antiochus tried to impose his form of worship, but the Maccabees and fellow Jews defied him and fought to affirm their freedom to worship God. This is the first recorded holiday celebrating a struggle for religious freedom. The holiday recalls the miracle of a small jar of oil that should have been only enough to light for one day the "eternal light" in the sanctuary but that actually lasted eight days. For this reason, Hanukkah is known also as the Festival of Lights. Today lights from the menorah, or candelabra, symbolize this remembrance.

The other two minor holidays mentioned earlier (Tu B'Shevat, the New Year of the Trees, and Lag B'Omer, the thirty-third day of the counting of the grain sheaves) come from the rabbinic period, after the destruction of the Temple in A.D. 70. Their origins are not entirely certain. Today the planting of trees is symbolic in many climates, and money may be sent to Israel for that purpose. The "counting" is also symbolically done in the synagogue.

The Jewish people have come to celebrate two more modern minor observances since the end of World War II. Yom Hashoa commemorates the deaths of six million Jews during the Nazi Holocaust. It began in the 1950s as a day of memorial. Yom Ha-atzmaut commemorates the establishment of the modern state of Israel in 1948. They are the first new Jewish observances in almost two millennia.

W. J. Leffler

Jewish Theological Concepts

Jewish theological concepts are rooted in the Hebrew Bible and developed by Jewish tradition. Tradition refers to the exegetical-midrashic interpretations and applications of the postbiblical rabbinic sages and their heirs down to our own day, the philosophical thinking of medieval theologians, the mystical speculations of cabalists, and the systematic theologies of modern theologians.

Biblical and rabbinic theologies are not systematic. Theological concepts such as God, Torah, and covenant are implicitly developed in the narrative, poetic, and legal genres that characterize both bodies of traditional material.

DIVERSITY IN SCRIPTURE AND INTERPRETATION

Moreover, within general boundaries it is difficult to identify a single point of view on most issues. The view of God in the Five Books of Moses (the Torah) changes internally and varies further in the Prophets and Writings. All share commonalities and differences. Thus, the view of God's justice in Job is not that of Genesis or Deuteronomy. Parts of the Bible itself interpret other sections, as in the prophets' emphasis upon the ethical import of the animal sacrifices, a view found in the other sources but one that draws new energy in the prophets' response to their own times.

A critical view of this literature is concerned not only with the worldviews of the various sources but also with those of the editors and redactors who combined them. The stance of these writers against their environments is reflected both in what they include (the creation as "good," for example) and in what they omit (the mythological stories of God's origin and life apart from his creation).

The sages canonized the Scripture and promoted their normative interpretation of it in the midrashic and talmudic literature. They saw their task as that of reconciling contradictions, clarifying ambiguities, and striving for an overall consistency. The premise of this literature is of a pervasive, consistent, linear, and normative viewpoint, from the Scriptures to their own time.

Yet the genius of the authors of this rich literature, preserved for us in the Babylonian and Jerusalem Talmuds and in the various collections of midrashim, lay in their preservation of diverse opinions, especially in the more poetic, imaginative interpretations of the *Midrash Aggadah*. To speak of God was ultimately to speak of the "ineffable," but the clues were to be found in the Scriptures and in their interpretations, with their poetic, playful, and metaphoric images (thus, the hundreds of midrashic parables in which God is likened to a king who builds a palace, sends a servant on a mission, gets angry at his child and sends him away . . .).

This diversity was kept alive in the legal (halakic) sections of this literature too, though later authorities developed principles for deciding the law for purposes of unity of practice (the law is followed "according to the school of Hillel when it differs from the school of Shammai," and many other examples). Rejected opinions were not seen as wrong but respected as valid points of view that could be religiously significant even without leading to practice.

THE DEVELOPMENT OF VALUE CONCEPTS AND SYSTEMATIC PHILOSOPHIES

In this respect Max Kadushin (1895–1980) has pointed out that the rabbis crystallized theological "value concepts," terms that function organically but not explicitly in the biblical materials, such as *Malkhut Shamayim* (Sovereignty of God), *Kiddush Hashem* (Sanctification of God's Name), Mitzvah (Commandment), *Berakhah* (Blessing), and many more. Once fully crystallized as rabbinic terms, they function organically as before, but additionally in a more generative style, lead to new legends, legal applications, and interpretations of the biblical text. For Kadushin, as opposed to those who see mysticism as a loss of self-awareness and absorption into the divine, "normal mysticism" is the Jewish view of the experience of God in everyday life, as a dimension of the ongoing study of Torah (here in the broad sense of Jewish teaching as a whole) and of the observance of Jewish law and custom. The "value concepts" animate the study and practice of ordinary people who are neither saints nor mystics.

Medieval theologians influenced by Greek philosophy were constrained to reconcile their systematic philosophical ideas with their commitment to the narrative and poetic traditions of biblical and rabbinic literature. Anthropomorphisms were a central issue. Maimonides' *Guide to the Perplexed* (A.D. 1200) deals with the metaphoric and anthropomorphic language of the Bible and midrash and with issues such as the conflict between God's omniscience and human freedom. Judah Halevi (A.D. 1074–1141) rebelled against the systematization of the philosophical theologians and tried to reinstate the narrative as the authentic source of meaning; he was himself a poet.

Until the modern Western Enlightenment most Jews were not philosophers. They lived within the tradition, a people redeemed by God from Egyptian slavery, commanded, in the Torah revelation they accepted at Mount Sinai, to be "a kingdom of priests and a holy nation" in the land of Israel promised to their fathers, Abraham, Isaac, and Jacob. Their task was to join this narrative with its explicit and implicit theology and, especially after the destruction of the Jerusalem Temple in A.D. 70, to await God's redemption from their dispersion among the nations. Religious education for them was education in Torah, that way of living and thinking in response to God's commandments, as interpreted by the tradition. Theology was embedded in stories, the lives of heroes, and especially in the regimen of practice determined by the tradition for all aspects of daily life. Observance of the Sabbath and the holy days were regular opportunities for enactment of the theological beliefs of Judaism reflected in the paradigm events of biblical history, for example, the Exodus (Pesah/Passover), the Exodus and the creation (Sabbath), the wandering in the desert (Sukkoth/Tabernacles), and the giving of the Torah (Shavuot/Pentecost). The weekly Torah reading in the synagogue was enacted dramatically as a living experience of *the* original revelation. Theology was not, therefore, propositional or catechistic but enacted in daily life. The theological dimension was also reflected in the interpersonal domain, where love and respect were due one's neighbor, who was created in God's image.

THEOLOGY TODAY

Modern theologians have a problem. Historians attending to the worldviews of different periods have not found it necessary to reconcile differences or to sustain normative positions, thereby cutting the tie between historical understanding and normative meaning. In their view the Song of Songs is not, in its origin, an allegory of the relationship of God and the people of Israel as it is in the midrash. Their question, *qua* historians, is to discover why the sages of the midrash chose to interpret a group of love poems in an allegorical way. This may be important and interesting, but it is not necessarily meaningful (though it *could* be, and this is one of the challenges to religious education in the modern period) to those modern Jews who seek personal and communal religious significance.

Responses of twentieth-century Jewish theologians have varied. Abraham Joshua Heschel (1907–1972), a wide-ranging scholar and theologian, sought synthesis in his systematic theology. From his historical work on the prophets he saw them as uniquely empathic of the divine perspective, their message a true if not literal revelation of God's word. The sages' continuing deliberation on this message also has revelatory dimensions. For Heschel, Judaism requires a life of response to the word, expressed in living according to the commandments as viewed by the tradition, leading to a life in God's presence, a life of holiness. For Heschel, memorializing his countrymen who perished in the Holocaust, the most spiritual embodiment of this way of life was the pre–World War II Jewish community of Eastern Europe.

Mordecai M. Kaplan (1881–1983) combined the naturalism of John Dewey with a "functional" view of tradition. The God concept functioned historically to enhance life, to provide for significance. Therefore, those factors that contribute to the quest for meaning, that "transform chaos into cosmos," partake of the divine. Jewish tradition is the record of the Jewish people's struggle for meaning, the terminology of which now needs transformations to which people can respond with integrity.

An educational response to the historian's challenge to Jewish theology would create ways to enable the classic texts of Jewish tradition with their unique perspectives to challenge us as they did when they were responses to the issues of their own times. The recapture of the existential issues to which they responded and the entry into the classic answers would need to draw on the resources of psychology and the arts as a first step toward a new, emergent synthesis.

In the state of Israel today and in the diaspora countries, many Jews do not define their Jewishness in religious terms. Yet they too need to confront Jewish theological concepts if they are to relate seriously to the question of what being a Jew means today. That question can be approached only through a paradoxical confrontation with a tradition that is inescapably religious. The religious educator is challenged to transform Jewish theological concepts so that they speak to Jews of different backgrounds and convictions whether they define themselves as religious or not. *See also* Jewish Education; Systems Theory; Torah, Study and Teaching of.

FOR FURTHER REFERENCE

Fackenheim, Emil L. *God's Presence in History.* New York: Harper & Row, 1970.

Heschel, Abraham J. *God in Search of Man.* New York: Farrar, Straus & Giroux, 1976.
Kadushin, Max. *Organic Thinking.* New York: Bloch, 1976.
———. *The Rabbinic Mind.* 2d ed. New York: Bloch, 1965.
Kaplan, Mordecai M. *The Meaning of God in Modern Jewish Religion.* Wyncote, PA: Reconstructionist Press, 1975.
Rosenak, Michael. *Commandments and Concerns: Jewish Religious Education in Secular Society.* Philadelphia: Jewish Publication Society, 1987.
Schechter, Solomon. *Aspects of Rabbinic Theology.* New York: Schocken, 1961.

J. Lukinsky

Joint Educational Development

Joint Educational Development (JED) is an ecumenical partnership of denominations cooperatively doing church education throughout the United States and Canada. JED grew out of exploratory conversations begun in the fall of 1967 by representatives of the Episcopal church, the United Church of Christ, and the former United Presbyterian Church, U.S.A. [now part of the Presbyterian Church (U.S.A.)].

Joint educational developments began to take shape beginning with four exploratory position papers on the subjects of the nature of the church, theories of education, views of society, and understandings of church education. By the end of 1969, three other denominations had joined further joint ventures, namely, the Christian Church (Disciples of Christ), the Reformed Church in America, and the former Presbyterian Church, U.S. [now part of the Presbyterian Church (U.S.A.)]. The ecumenical partnership was formally organized in May of 1970.

In addition to the six founding denominations, JED's membership has included the following partner or cooperating denominations: American Baptist Churches in the U.S.A., Church of the Brethren, Cumberland Presbyterian Church, the Evangelical Covenant Church, Friends General Conference, Friends United Meeting, Moravian Church in America, the Presbyterian Church in Canada, United Church of Canada, and the United Methodist Church.

JED is a partnership and process for ecumenical teamwork, modeling covenant relationships among denominations to accomplish shared goals that are important in the church's educational mission and ministries. Educational staff persons from the partner denominations have suggested new projects in their areas of ministry, to be approved by the JED executive committee, which includes representatives from the partner denominations. These have included program resources for particular groups (Appalachian, black, Hispanic, and Pacific Asian-American church education), for specific age levels (youth and singles), for leadership development (leader designs and support systems, regional teacher/leader education events, North American Event for Church Educators, *JED Share*, which is a quarterly magazine for church educational leaders, and Ministers Involved in Christian Education), and special subjects (using mass media in Christian education, God language and liturgical language, faith and moral development, curriculum analysis). When projects have been selected, teams of staff persons from the denominations, along with regional and local church educators, carry out the projects. The educational agencies of the JED denominations give funds and staff time to the projects that they want to support, and sometimes one or two denominations carry on a task on behalf of the others in the partnership.

JED's best-known and most extensive project involving a variety of options for teaching/learning has been the curriculum publishing project Christian Education: Shared Approaches. This project was initiated in the early seventies. Formal publication of materials began a few years later, and these materials were widely used by many of the participating denominations for several years.

Recently, however, this curriculum project has been scaled down and others are no longer being explored. Without professional staff, JED operates solely through its denominational networks, and some denominations are more active than others. Some denominations have been involved in internal reorganization. Others have expressed dissatisfaction with one aspect of curriculum materials produced by JED. Despite the variety of curriculum materials, the attempt to be multidenominational left no provision for teaching about a specific tradition—its history, polity, belief system, liturgy, and outreach—except as this might be part of a general course of study. As a result, some denominations withdrew support for particular curricula in order to develop their own. Today there are two JED curricular options: *Bible Discovery*, in which six denominations cooperate, and *Discipleship Alive*, in which three participate. Two denominations are involved in both curricula. In spite of recent changes, JED still provides an important roundtable for a number of denominations to share their common interests and projects. *See also* Curriculum; Systems Theory.

J. J. Spangler

Journal Writing

Keeping a journal is essentially the disciplined and regular practice of reflective writing about one's spiritual journey. Journal writing has for centuries been an important part of Christian history. Augustine's *Confessions* is an early example of this reflective practice, as in more recent years have been Dag Hammarskjold's *Markings* and Thomas Merton's *Journals*. In recent decades there has been a resurgence of emphasis on the practice as an important means for assisting one's spiritual development. Ira Progoff, a psychologist of Jungian leaning, has popularized a complex method of journal writing through his nationwide journal workshops.

Although there is no one proper method for keeping a journal, such writing is distinguished from keeping a diary, because it is not an account of the events of one's life, but a reflection upon their meaning for soul, the heart and center of life, or one's relation to God. A journal may well include such items as life events, ideas, and insights, significant quotations of prose or poetry that have informed one's life, and emotional and intellectual processes, including dreams, that characterize this life period. Attention must be given to unconscious as well as conscious processes that are occurring. The continual quest is to know God's will for one's life.

Keeping a journal could and probably should be taught in the church school and might be begun even in the primary years, but the deeper reflection and spiritual insight that are the goals of the journal would seem to require the intellectual development that begins around age twelve to fourteen; indeed, this might be an ideal time for such training because of the inherent self-consciousness and life questioning that occur at this point of development.

Because of the highly individual and personal nature of journal writing, the most useful training, other than actually writing the journal (perhaps under the guidance of a person wise and experienced in journal writing), would seem to be the reading of some of the classic journals. There are many important authors, in addition to those noted above, e.g., George Fox, Teresa of Avila, John Woolman, Søren Kierkegaard, and John Wesley. The old practice of reading the biographies of the saints might also be very useful for teens and adults. For specific journal writing methods, see Progoff's *At a Journal Workshop*. *See also* Devotional Literature; Spirituality; Writing.

FOR FURTHER REFERENCE

Progoff, Ira. *At a Journal Workshop*. New York: Dialog House Library, 1975.

G. H. Slusser

Judah Halevi

Judah Halevi (A.D. 1074–1141), a Jewish physician and merchant, is remembered primarily as philosopher and poet. Eight hundred of his secular and religious poems survive in the liturgy and in collections. His *Songs of Zion* is particularly well known.

His philosophical work *Kitab Al Khazari*, a polemic against Aristotelian philosophy, Christianity, and Islam, was a popular medieval philosophical study. Apologetic, it emphasizes immediate religious experience over deductive reasoning and claims prophetic religion superior to philosophical religion.

Halevi thought education should combine Jewish and general studies and that language, grammar, and philosophy should be emphasized. He placed little stress on traditional rabbinic learning. *See also* Jewish Education; Jewish Theological Concepts.

W. Jacob

Judaism

Judaism is the historically evolved religious faith, heritage, and tradition of the Jewish people. Its sacred literature is the Torah or "Teachings," comprising the Five Books of Moses, the Prophets, and the Writings—thirty-six books in all.

HISTORY

According to the Torah, Judaism begins with the patriarch Abraham (Abram), who left his home in Ur after glimpsing a singular vision of the Divine Reality, and descends through Isaac (son of his and his wife Sarah's old age), through Isaac's son Israel (who was at one time named Jacob and wrestled with beings both human and divine and prevailed), through Israel's son Joseph (who was sold into slavery in Egypt and rose to a position second only to Pharaoh), and through others to Moses. Moses, with his brother Aaron and sister Miriam, brought together various Israelite tribes who had been slaves in Egypt for a time, and led them as a unified people to a land "flowing with milk and honey" and promised them by God. The people entered this land after wandering in the wilderness between Egypt and Palestine for a generation. Historically, we may date Abraham's journey at approximately 2250 B.C., the beginning of the Egyptian enslavement at approximately 1760 B.C., and settlement in the promised land at approximately 1300 B.C.

The unity of the Israelites ended in approximately 930 B.C. when the nation of Israel divided in two following the death of Solomon, the third king of Israel (after Saul and David). The Assyrians destroyed the northern kingdom of Israel in 721 B.C., but the southern kingdom of Judah remained in Israelite hands until its destruction by the Babylonians in 586 B.C. The people rebuilt their land beginning in approximately 450 B.C. and continued to regard it as their primary place of habitation until its destruction by the Roman oppressors in the year A.D. 70. They did not see their own flag of sovereignty again until 1948 with the creation of the Third Jewish Commonwealth.

The people dispersed, and the story of Jewish history after A.D. 70 continues at various places as time passes: in Babylonia, where the Talmud was produced; in Spain, seat of a "golden age" of Jewish literary creativity; in Poland and Russia during the dark days of the Middle Ages; in Germany, France, and England, where the Enlightenment, World War I, and World War II all had major impact upon Jews; in the United States, today seat of the largest Jewish community in the world; and in a reborn state of Israel.

Worldwide, the Jews alive today number between 14 million and 16 million: approximately 6 million in the United States, 3.5 million in Russia, 4 million in Israel, and 2.5 million throughout the rest of the world.

RECENT INFLUENCES

The contemporary Jewish experience may best be understood as influenced, by and large, by four relatively recent historical phenomena:

1. The rise of Hasidism, a seventeenth-century orthodox pietistic movement that saw its goals as the worship of God through joy (i.e., an eastern European religious movement)

2. The birth of Reform Judaism, an eighteenth-century nonorthodox interpretation of Judaism as historically dynamic and ever-changing to meet new realities (i.e., a western European religious movement)

3. The rise of the Haskalah, a Russian Jewish movement of enlightenment that saw the creation of a nonreligious Jewish and Hebrew cultural expression (i.e., an eastern European secular movement)

4. The birth of modern political Zionism, a nineteenth-century movement of liberation to restore the ancient dream of a Jewish homeland to the Jewish people (i.e., a western European secular movement)

To these four must be added the enormous impact of the Holocaust of World War II, which saw the deaths of six million Jewish men, women, and children, and whose full implications have not even begun to be fully realized. The reborn state of Israel, too, occupies a dominant place in the thoughts and actions of Jews alive today.

PRIMARY RELIGIOUS GROUPINGS

In the United States, the majority of Jews may be identified with the primary religious groupings:

1. Reform (see above)

2. Orthodox or fundamentalist, both Hasidic and non-Hasidic

3. Conservative, which also had its origins in Europe in response to Reform Judaism, serving as a "buffer" between Reform and Orthodox

4. Reconstructionist, an offshoot of Conservative Judaism and a liberalizing of its own tendencies to follow closely an Orthodox line

STATUS IN VARIOUS COUNTRIES

The American Jewish community may be characterized as an "at home" Jewish community, fully participating in the political life of the country and various movements concerned with social betterment (e.g., the civil rights movement). In the process, it has created a plethora of organizations to address every facet of American Jewish life: religious, political, social, fraternal, civil, philanthropic, educational. It is a philanthropic community, directing its largesse to Jews and non-Jews, both in the United States and abroad. It is also an extremely well-educated and well-read Jewish community; Jewish authors and books on Jewish themes are read and admired both inside and outside the Jewish community. In light of the tragedy of the Second World War, it is a Jewish community vitally concerned with and committed to the survival of the state of Israel and the plight of Jews in eastern Europe. It is a community continually confronted by the question of minority status in a religiously free environment, where its own born population does not seem to keep pace with its losses, and where exogamous marriage (i.e., marriage outside the community) is an increasing fact of life.

Israel's four-decades-old struggle for survival increasingly occupies center stage in American and worldwide Jewish life. Of its Arab neighbors, with a combined population of more than seventy million, only Egypt has formally made peace. Much of Israel's thinking and expenditures are concerned with defense: for example, boys and girls upon graduation from high school are required to serve in the armed forces for three or two years and will remain active in the reserves throughout much of their adult lives. Having fought wars in 1948, 1956, 1967, 1973, and 1981, Israel continues to strive to maintain a reasonable state of normalcy for its citizens and to become a "spiritual center" for Jews throughout the world.

The Jews of Russia, from the Stalinist purges of the 1920s through the 1980s, experienced a form of "cultural genocide," which found the demands of the state incompatible with the necessities of maintaining a viable and varied Jewish life. Jewish religious traditions conflicted directly with the political philosophy of communism. Synagogues were turned into museums and factories; publications in both Hebrew and Yiddish (a cognate language) could only be produced underground; teachers of Judaism learned their craft surreptitiously; and Jews wishing to leave were subject to severe economic and social discrimination.

Throughout the rest of the world, wherever Jews dwell, their stories are both positive and negative: The Jewish community of Australia flourishes; the Jews of Syria suffer increasing discrimination. The Jews of South America still maintain creative communities; the Jews of Ethiopia find themselves having to escape the land of their birth in order to survive.

What continues to unite Jews the world over is, first, their history, which brought them into being as recipients of the divine gift of revelation; second, their commitment to the One God; third, their common history, celebratory life cycle, and festival/holiday/calendar cycle; and fourth, their common faith and fate. See also Holocaust; Jewish Education; Jewish Festivals and Holidays; Jewish Theological Concepts; Rabbi as Educator; Torah as Teaching; Torah, Study and Teaching of; Zionism.

S. L. Jacobs

Jungian Influences

The hypotheses and methodology of analytical psychology, pioneered by C. G. Jung (1875–1961), have provided a bridge between the rational-intellectual approach to life and the more nonrational and spiritual approach. His work began the trend toward holistic and transpersonal developments in the field of psychology. Modern practices of therapy and the human potential movement owe much to the foundational work of Jung.

In the book The Death and Rebirth of Psychology (1973), Ira Progoff points out that both pre-Freudian psychiatry and Freud considered the psychological problems of individuals from a limited medical point of view. Broader implications of a historical and social nature were not considered. Therefore, the facts that were examined and the resulting hypotheses were also necessarily limited.

Rejecting the reductionistic and biologically based point of view of Freud, yet retaining an analytical methodology with hypotheses based in experience, Jung opened the way for modern psychology to affirm the experience of people as spiritual beings. As he sees a sense of meaning in life as necessary to psychological health, it is clear that this approach is philosophical and religious as well. As such, Jung's work has implications not only for the field of psychology, but also for history, philosophy, art, literature, and religion.

These implications are explored in depth by

Ira Progoff in his book *Jung's Psychology and Its Social Meaning* (1985), in which he states that social thinkers as diverse as Lewis Mumford, Paul Tillich, and Arnold Toynbee have an affinity with Jung's ideas, although they deal with their own unique considerations. Jung considers the major life task and developmental process of human beings to be that of increasing consciousness by gaining knowledge of the contents and processes of the unconscious, both personal and collective. This drive toward unity and wholeness, which can be facilitated in the analytical process, is called individuation.

ASPECTS OF INDIVIDUATION

The process of healing or the resolution of psychic conflicts can be achieved by an exploration and attentiveness to the natural drive toward wholeness innate to the human psyche. Conflicts and neuroses born in the past might be ameliorated by directing energies toward the future and focusing on finding meaning in one's life. This personal meaning would necessarily be in harmony with the purposefulness of one's own psyche.

Jung's analytical psychology is grounded in individual psychic experience, encompassing humanity as an evolutionary whole and allowing for cultural diversity. This approach is both individual and social.

Jung found that the language of the unconscious, both of the personal unconscious of each individual and of the collective unconscious, which represents the cultural and evolutionary heritage of humanity, expresses itself in the form of image and symbol. A person's quest for wholeness is manifested in dreams as symbols that often compensate for the reality of that person's conscious life. The analytical process helps the person unlock the particular meaning expressed symbolically in the dream. Jung found certain constant images arising that were recognizable in the myths of many cultures. These basic patterns of energy common to all human psyches he termed archetypes. They are psychic parallels to biological instincts and are played out in infinite variation from individual to individual. The basic form is recognizable and is part of the collective unconscious of humanity.

It is through a culture's mythology and religious practice that these archetypes have been expressed and encountered throughout history. For a purely materialistic and scientific culture, access to this depth of human life has been denied. Jung's work provided scientific validation and new language to speak of realities that heretofore were in the sphere of the spiritual and therefore rejected by science. His work showed the common psychic realities shared by all people in all times and so gave a social dimension that had been lacking in psychology prior to that time. Analysis had opened the door to inner life. It proved a path to valid individual religious experience and the God within. What had been lost to modern materialistic people could be recovered through psychology.

Jung's model has allowed the rebirth of God for many contemporary people. His hypotheses tested in personal inner quests have provided a language for people to again consider the spiritual nature of their own being. For some, it has enlivened the symbols of traditional faith and restored religion to its prior place as container and expresser of the real and valid spiritual-psychic process.

Jung's interest in the myths of other and ancient cultures has spawned study of the mythologies by other academic fields such as literature, comparative religion, and philosophy. The study of the nature of symbols and their use is widespread and crosses disciplines.

Reading Jung or commentaries on his work by students and disciples may draw the reader into a personal inner search. This can happen by affinity as well as crisis, which is what brings some into analysis. The path of individuation is not only for the sick, it is the goal of all human psychic development, according to Jung. This path is part and parcel of the task of traditional spirituality and it is not unusual that there is much contemporary writing in the fields of prayer and spirituality that uses Jungian hypotheses as a theoretical base and uses this psychological language to convey traditional spiritual realities.

APPLICATIONS FOR SPIRITUAL FORMATION

Since spiritual formation is the major goal of religious education, Jung's model can serve as a good theoretical base for understanding the human being and behavior. It is because his work does not disregard but in fact emphasizes the spiritual that it is useful and popular. Jung provides a new language and new categories for speaking about spiritual realities. Because of this, his hypotheses, language, and approach can serve as bridges to a depth of spirituality for persons for whom traditional religious language and symbols have lost their vital meaning. Modern people having encountered Jung's work and having reconnected with their own depths can reenter and reclaim their own religious traditions and find again in them healing, growth, and God.

The methodology of working with dreams and meditative states helps broaden definitions and experiences of prayer. Books and workshops on dreams and journal keeping as part of spirituality abound and often are grounded in the Jungian model. This allows people to get in touch with their own personal religious symbols and experience.

As a theoretical base, Jung's work could help define goals and methods of adult religious education that are appropriate and fruitful for mid-life spiritual tasks. His work in personality type is already widely used in leadership training as a basis for better understanding and acceptance of individual differences. This has implications for teaching, learning, and leadership styles as well as for methods of prayer.

Jung has shown that the psychic transformation that is called forth in human beings leads to a religious and ethical stance. Because of Jung, religion has not been replaced by psychology, and religious experience has been validated and enlivened. *See also* Dreams; Freudian Influences; Motivation; Psychology of Religion; Symbolism.

FOR FURTHER REFERENCE

Jacobi, Jolande. *The Psychology of C. G. Jung.* New Haven, CT: Yale University Press, 1962.
Jung, C. G. *Modern Man in Search of a Soul.* New York: Harcourt Brace, 1933.
Singer, June. *Boundaries of the Soul.* New York: Doubleday, Anchor Press, 1972.

M. F. Purcell

Jungmann, Josef A.

Josef Andreas Jungmann (1889–1975) was a pioneer in twentieth-century kerygmatic renewal. Born in the South Tirol, Austria, Jungmann worked as a diocesan priest from 1913 to 1917, when he entered the Society of Jesus. As teacher of catechetics and liturgy at the University of Innsbruck for over twenty-seven years (1925–1952), Jungmann left an indelible mark on generations of students. His *The Good News and Our Proclamation of the Faith* (1936; English trans. entitled *The Good News Yesterday and Today,* 1962)

was testimony to his deep involvement in the renewal of the catechetical apostolate. This book was a watershed in catechetical studies, for it marked a shift from method to content by stressing the kerygmatic (proclamation) dimension that could move hearts and change lives. It was Jungmann's contention that the kerygmatic included above all a clear vision of the good news of God's saving love centered in Jesus. Jungmann's work, including *Handing on the Faith* (1953; English trans. 1959), had a profound impact on catechetics and Vatican II. *See also* Catechesis; Eichstätt Conference; Hofinger, Johannes; Kerygma.

H. C. Simmons, R. H. Cram

Justice

See Social Justice, Education for.

Justification

The term "justification" in biblical and theological tradition has to do with God's saving action in rectifying humanity and creation. The idea is related to the notion of justice, the making right of a wrong situation. In theological understanding, justification also includes reference to God's compassionate and free forgiveness, God's sharing the suffering of fallen or unfinished humanity and creation, and God's decisive work of reconciliation in and through Christ.

The term carries with it both legal and soteriological connotations. Out of its legal roots in Semitic and Greco-Roman backgrounds, justification connotes a verdict of acquittal or vindication by a judge or court. It means to be declared right or innocent or to be absolved, pardoned.

With respect to God's saving action, justification signifies God's work of "making right" the fallen creation. The apostle Paul emphasizes that justification is not a human work, something we can earn or deserve, but that it is solely God's gift in Christ that can be received only through faith, which is itself part of the gift (Rom. 3:23–24, 28; Gal. 2:16; 3:11; 5:4). Yet Paul also emphasizes that those who receive this gift in faith must be active in doing good and will be judged on this basis (Rom. 2:6–10; 1 Cor. 3:12–15; Gal. 6:7–9). Although scholars debate whether justification by faith is the central theme of Paul's message or a polemical expression of it in opposition to views of his opponents, Martin Luther centuries later insisted that it was "the chief article" of Christian faith and made it central in his effort to reform the church. Luther seems to have understood justification as God's free forgiveness and declaration of the sinner as righteous in and through Christ.

In the post-Reformation era Protestant theology often stressed the incompatibility of this view of justification with the view that had developed in Roman Catholic tradition and that was reaffirmed at the Council of Trent, which held that justification includes not only the divine pardon but also actually *making* the recipient righteous or just. Furthermore, in Catholic theology justification embraces the entire salvific action of God in the life of a person from conversion or baptism to final union with God beyond death. In Protestant perspective justification refers to God's decisive action in Christ and the implantation of this in (or "imputation" to) the believer in faith. Hence, in the Catholic view no one can be sure of being justified short of the eschatological perfecting of the believer, whereas in classical Protestant thought the believer trusts in the gospel of God's justification given in Christ.

However, in recent ecumenical studies involving Roman Catholic and Protestant as well as Eastern Orthodox scholars and in ecumenical study groups on many levels, there appears to be increasing convergence in understanding justification as God's action not only to but also within the recipient. This has led some to conclude that there is no longer any substantive theological basis for division of the church over this matter. Although other Catholic and Protestant scholars view such a conclusion as premature, they would generally agree that there have opened possibilities for a new and more harmonious understanding of justification within the church.

As this occurs, new aspects of the meaning of justification may emerge. One instance of this is the perception in liberation theology that justification of the believer is indissolubly linked with the struggle for social justice. Another is the awareness in process and evolutionary theologies of the connection between God's saving action in the individual and in the rest of creation.

Justification is not a word in common use. Young learners may feel that "making just" in the biblical sense (as in the story of the forgiving father of the prodigal son) is unfair. They need to be helped to reflect on how good it feels to be forgiven and restored to favor by parents. Adults will need to struggle with the relationship of love to justice in the dealings of God with a nation (as in the Prophets) or with individuals (as in the Epistles). Teachers use both the biblical word and reflection on experience. See also Faith Development; Grace; Liberation Theology; Salvation; Sanctification; Social Justice, Education for.

FOR FURTHER REFERENCE

Anderson, H. George, et al., eds. *Justification by Faith: Lutherans and Catholics in Dialogue.* Minneapolis, MN: Augsburg, 1985.
Boff, Leonardo. *Liberating Grace.* Maryknoll, NY: Orbis, 1979.
Küng, Hans. *Justification.* Philadelphia and Atlanta, GA: Westminster, Knox, 1988.

W. R. Barr

Juvenile Delinquency

A juvenile delinquent as defined by each state is a person between the ages of sixteen and eighteen who commits a crime. A crime as defined by the U.S. Department of Justice is a behavior for which society provides formally sanctioned punishment.

HISTORY OF LEGAL JURISDICTIONS AND JUDGMENTS

For centuries juveniles accused of crimes were tried in the same courts and imprisoned in the same institutions as adults. Beginning in medieval England, Western cultures began establishing ages under which a child could not be tried or punished for a crime. At that time the minimum age was seven, based on the belief that until that age the child was not aware of the consequences of personal acts. At seven the child was considered enlightened and responsible for behavior. By the middle of the nineteenth century, the age of accountability was changed to fourteen and children over that age who committed criminal acts were considered adults and subject to adult procedures.

In 1899, the city of Chicago (acting for the state of Illinois), the city of Denver, and the state of Rhode Island introduced juvenile court, which established new rules and standards for dealing with youthful offenders. Juvenile court bases its premise on the concepts that juveniles are salvageable human beings who need treatment rather than punishment. Further, this court felt a need to protect children from the stigma of criminal proceedings and to act on their behalf in other situations such as neglect and adoption and for status offenses such as truancy, running away, and incorrigibility, which did not apply to adults.

A significant change occurred in juvenile court in 1967 when the U.S. Supreme Court ruled that a child charged with a crime had the following rights of due process under the Constitution: (1) to be notified of the charges and the dates of the court hearings; (2) to have counsel; (3) to cross-examine and confront witnesses; and (4) to avoid self-incrimination by remaining silent. Thus the new focus of juvenile court became the principle of *parens patriae*, where the court acts as a parent or guardian interested in protecting, helping, and looking out for the best interests of the child—where formerly attorneys had fought to determine the guilt or innocence of alleged offenders.

CURRENT LEGAL PROCEDURES

Presently in the United States, criminal offenses are classified according to their specification in the written law of state statutes. The definition of a given crime varies among federal, state, and local jurisdictions. Most jurisdictions recognize two classes of offenses, felonies and misdemeanors, but they are not distinguished in the same way in all states. However, most states define felonies as crimes punishable by one year or more in prison.

Offenders who are taken into custody and referred to the juvenile division of the court are charged with either a felony or misdemeanor or both, but the proceedings in this division are different. They are less formal, the vocabulary is different (e.g., adults commit crimes, have trials, and are sentenced; juveniles are involved in delinquent acts, have hearings, and receive dispositions or placements), and the usual rules of evidence are not rigidly followed. Younger offenders and those charged with misdemeanors are normally released to the custody of their parents, to return to court later to admit or deny having done the delinquent act. Adjudication in most cases is usually withheld and the juvenile is returned home without further intervention. Occasionally, a first-time older offender will be placed on a short period of probation with a state or local child protection agency as a precautionary measure. This serves as a safeguard against the possibility that the child's delinquent behavior was related to a troubling home or school circumstance that, if undetected, could cause future problems.

Those committing second-time misdemeanor offenses and first-time nonviolent felony delinquent acts frequently are treated as first-time misdemeanor offenders, except that the juveniles are frequently detained in a juvenile detention center until their adjudicatory hearing. A disposition of adjudication of delinquency in such cases frequently involves probation, family counseling, restitution where applicable, and placement in a halfway house.

Juveniles committing many nonviolent felonies and serious delinquent acts are kept in a pretrial detention situation, adjudicated for having committed a delinquent act, and placed in juvenile training institutions, halfway houses, or wilderness camps. These programs provide continued educational and vocational training and frequently include psychological intervention. Most residential placements are followed by lengthy periods of probation or community control once the child is returned to home and the community.

Older juvenile offenders (sixteen–eighteen years) and those charged with serious crimes against persons such as murder and sexual battery and assault are frequently referred from the juvenile division to adult criminal court by judicial waiver. In such a case juvenile court waives its jurisdiction through a process known as "binding over," "certifying," or "direct filing," and the offender is physically transferred from the juvenile holding facility to the adult jail. Federal decree requires separate and individualized housing in jails for juveniles, but standards requiring daily schooling and other juvenile detention requirements such as "no smoking" cease. Adult criminal justice vocabulary is activated as well as adult standards of time for when petitions must be filed or speedy trial waived.

Juveniles tried as adults have a high conviction rate relative to adults, but studies show that for almost half of those found guilty the outcome is a fine or sentence to probation. However, those juveniles who are sentenced to incarceration receive longer sentences than they would have received under juvenile disposition.

STATISTICS

Statistical data from the U.S. Department of Justice for 1979–1984 reveal the following trends in juvenile crime. There was a drop in the total number of arrests of youths under age eighteen during the 1970s, concurrent with a 14 percent increase in arrests of persons over age eighteen. However, part of the decline in number of total arrests under eighteen can be attributed to the fact that fewer young people between the ages ten and seventeen existed at that time. From 1972 to 1981 juvenile arrests increased again but not as much as for those eighteen and older. The arrest rate for adults during that period increased 66 percent for violent crimes and 112 percent for serious property crimes, while juveniles increased "only" 31 percent for the former and 22 percent for the latter. Arrest records for 1981 show that juveniles are more likely than older persons to be taken into custody for crimes against property (36 percent to 14 percent), and for violent crimes 4 percent of juveniles are arrested compared to 5 percent of adults.

Studies of violent juvenile offenders suggest a striking resemblance to adult felons. They are predominantly male and disproportionately black and Hispanic compared to their proportion in the total population; they come from economically disadvantaged single-parent homes where instability and conflict is prevalent and they are more likely than other juveniles to have interpersonal difficulties and behavior problems in school.

The typical juvenile delinquent is a boy. Of all the boys who come before juvenile court, 75 percent are adjudicated delinquent (found guilty) of a criminal offense; 9 percent are there because of noncriminal status offenses (running away, truancy, incorrigibility). Of all the girls who appear before juvenile court, 39 percent are found guilty of a criminal offense and 28 percent are there because of noncriminal status offenses. From 1974 to 1979, the total number of girls in custody declined 28 percent while the number of boys in custody increased 1 percent. More recently, however, the number of both boys and girls in custody has been steadily increasing.

A final and significant difference between

adult and juvenile criminals is the importance of gang membership and the tendency for the young to engage in group criminal activities. National surveys by law enforcement officials found that while a disproportionate number of gangs are found in large cities, gangs are also common in cities with less than half a million persons. Gang members are more likely than other juveniles to participate in violent crimes, particularly robbery, rape, assault, and carrying weapons. Between the years 1973 and 1980 there was a decrease in youthful group crime, but unfortunately, more recent statistics indicate that group crime is now on the rise. *See also* Adolescence; Psychosocial Development; Social Work; Youth Ministry.

G. W. Brandstadter-Palmer

Kaplan, Mordecai M.

Mordecai M. Kaplan (1881–1983), an Orthodox Jew by upbringing, was founder of the Jewish reconstructionist movement, a movement that sees Judaism as an evolving civilization and not just a religion. In this view, Judaism is a synthesis of religion, race, and culture. Practical applications included refashioning the synagogue into a center for the totality of Jewish communal life that stressed humanistic and religious aspects. Kaplan asserted that American Jews must relate to both American and Jewish civilizations and must stop thinking of themselves as a uniquely chosen people.

Kaplan influenced many of the current generation of rabbis, having served as a professor at the (Conservative) Jewish Theological Seminary from 1909 to 1963. Among the many causes he championed was that of equal rights for women in Jewish ritual and practice. As early as 1922 he created the bas mitzvah ceremony for thirteen-year-old girls, marking their arrival at the age of Jewish duty and responsibility. *See also* Bar/Bas Mitzvah; Judaism.

J. M. Epstein

Kerygma

A Greek term meaning proclamation or preaching, *kērugma* (n.; verb, *kērusso*, "to preach"), denotes the core content of the Christian proclamation of faith (see Matt. 12:41; Rom. 16:25; 1 Cor. 1:21; 2:4; 15:14; 2 Tim. 4:17; Titus 1:3).

In religious education, the term is generally used in reference to a movement in twentieth-century Roman Catholicism. Inspired principally by Austrian liturgist Josef A. Jungmann (1889–1975) in his 1936 work *Die Frohbotschaft und unsere Glaubensverkündigung* (English trans. and abridgment, *The Good News Yesterday and Today*, 1962), the kerygmatic movement sought to restore Christ to the center of theology. Jungmann, struck by the vitality of the early church in contrast to what he judged to be the lifelessness of scholastic theological systems, proclaimed the necessity of returning to the biblical sources as a means of ecclesial renewal. He and his followers, most notably Johannes Hofinger (1905–1986), emphasized a clear and effective presentation of the gospel, rather than the delivery of the "truths of the faith" in static, propositional form. Kerygmatic theology was life-oriented, its thrust pastoral rather than research-oriented. Thus, its teachers were to be heralds of the gospel.

Foundational to the kerygmatic approach was emphasis upon the unity of God's all-embracing plan of salvation. This had a quite practical consequence in Catholic life for Jungmann, as he believed that the multiplicity of devotions to the saints had often tended to obscure God's saving acts and the centrality of Christ. Liturgical renewal must be kerygmatic; i.e., it ought to clear away all that obscures the clarity and power of God's love in Christ and to emphasize the evangelical character of Christian life.

Even more significantly, the stress in the kerygmatic movement on the unity of God's plan resulted in appropriation of salvation history (German *Heilsgeschichte*) as the central theme in liturgical, catechetical, and biblical renewal. Salvation history offered Catholics, generally unschooled in the Bible, an overarching concept by which they could understand Scripture. This took on particular importance in the impetus given to Bible study by Vatican II (1962–1965), and numerous catechetical materials produced in the wake of the council featured the kerygmatic approach as the key element in religious curricula.

Furthermore, the salvation history thematic played center stage for Protestant biblical scholars in Europe in the "biblical theology movement" (ca. 1945–1960), especially in the work of Gerhard von Rad, Oscar Cullman, and C. H. Dodd. Kerygma also served as the unifying thread of the United Presbyterian Church's Christian Faith and Life curriculum, initiated when James D. Smart was editor-in-chief. The basic theory was developed in his book *The Teaching Ministry of the Church* (1954). The kerygmatic approach was also basic to Iris V. Cully's *The Dynamics of Christian Education* (1958) and D. Campbell Wyckoff's *The Gospel and Christian Education* (1959). Thus the kerygmatic movement in Catholic circles intersected with Protestant emphases and became one of the first themes of ecumenical biblical study.

The kerygmatic approach, however, came under criticism for its excessively verbal character and for its lack of attention to educational theory. The almost total emphasis on the presentation of the personal message of Christ made it a teacher-centered pedagogy—the teacher as herald—and many critics, though appreciative of its personalist and existential tone, noted the movement's limits as a methodology. Others maintained that people needed to be better prepared—to be "preevangelized"—so as to hear the kerygma; the teacher needed a clearer sense of the person's life situation before proclaiming the gospel.

Moreover, biblical scholars increasingly took issue with the thematic of salvation history with which the kerygmatic movement was so closely linked. While few denied that the Bible does indeed recount the history of salvation, many now claim that the motif is grounded in an inadequate theology of revelation and presents an insufficiently nuanced position both on the relationship between the Hebrew Scriptures and the New Testament and on Christocentrism. To the extent that kerygma is linked with salvation history, it no longer dominates biblical study in catechetics.

Nevertheless, kerygma continues to play a prominent role in the vocabulary of catechetics. It is often used in relationship to two other Greek terms, *catechesis* and *didache* or *didascalia* (teaching). The three are seen as the movements of an educational cycle: the sequence of initial proclamation of the good news of salvation, followed by oral instruction for neophytes, and then by more extensive teaching. Kerygma is also linked with *koinonia* (communion or fellowship) and *diakonia* (service); these three summarize a holistic approach to education in faith: message, community, and service.

Though the kerygmatic movement no longer plays the role it once did, kerygma continues to

be a significant term in Christian education insofar as it highlights the joyful character of salvation. *See also* Biblical Theology; Catechesis; Eichstätt Conference; Gospel; Hofinger, Johannes; Jungmann, Josef A.; Salvation.

FOR FURTHER REFERENCE

Boys, Mary C. *Biblical Interpretation in Religious Education: A Study of the Kerygmatic Era.* Birmingham, AL: Religious Education Press, 1980.

Cully, Iris V. *The Dynamics of Christian Education.* Philadelphia: Westminster, 1958.

Dodd, C. H. *The Apostolic Teaching and Its Developments.* Chicago: Loyola University Press, 1936.

Jungmann, Josef A. *Handing on the Faith.* New York: Herder and Herder, 1959.

Nebreda, Alfonso M. *Kerygma in Crisis?* Chicago: Loyola University Press, 1965.

M. C. Boys

Kierkegaard, Søren

Søren Kierkegaard (1813–1855) was a Danish philosopher and theologian. He has been called the spiritual father of the existentialist school of philosophy because, in an era that was dominated by Hegel's teaching that progress lay through reason, Kierkegaard found reason wanting and emphasized the role of will. It was his conviction that we are presented with certain options in life that call for a "leap of faith."

His publications were not in the typical philosophical mode but rather were written under various pseudonyms and included parables, myths, poems, and dialogues. His intention seemed to be to lure readers into facing themselves and making a choice. For him, truth was subjective; that is, truth is only meaningful when it is true *for me*, when it shapes who I am and what I do because it *is* who I am. This became the basis for the philosophy of existentialism, which influenced Protestant religious education in the 1940s and 1950s because of its distinction between the subjective and objective views of reality as applied to teaching and learning. *See also* Existentialism; Faith.

J. C. Smith

Kindergarten

The kindergarten department is made up of four- and five-year-old children, those youngsters one and two years away from first grade. The exception is when the four- and five-year-old population in the church is large enough to warrant a separate department for each age level.

RELIGIOUS UNDERSTANDINGS

Kindergarten department children are teachable and responsive to God. They are intuitive thinkers who cannot handle excessive symbolism except as it is used in real-life illustrations. Their view of God is anthropomorphic, yet they understand God's love and care, friendship, greatness, protection, and desire for them to respond to him. They readily interchange "God" and "Jesus," usually referring to God as Jesus, no doubt because they are familiar with real-life narratives of Jesus' activities.

Children in this department require that a teacher use concrete language that relates to their experience. This presents a special problem for the Bible teacher, who deals with abstract concepts such as trust, faith, and worship. However, the teacher can illustrate each term with real-life examples—or can involve the child in a learning center that will provide a firsthand experience to which to link the abstract word or concept.

LEARNING ABILITIES

The attention span of the kindergarten child is still somewhat short, no more than ten minutes at a time, usually closer to five. Although the child's ability to listen increases when he or she begins

to attend school, one can expect to change activities several times within a class session.

Some kindergarten children are still socially insecure; others are quite comfortable in new situations. Teachers must be aware of the need to make children comfortable and secure. An attractive, inviting room, interesting activities, and a teacher who is already present waiting to welcome children as they arrive provide the security needed.

Children of this age are beginning to learn values. However, their sense of right and wrong is derived primarily from what they are permitted to do or not to do. Loving, firm, consistent discipline both at home and at church or synagogue is critical for them to develop a healthy sense of justice and morality.

The kindergarten department accomplishes its objectives best when it is organized comfortably and allows the children maximum involvement in the learning process. The teacher/pupil ratio should be low, no more than one to five or six. A department ought not to exceed twenty to twenty-five, even with an appropriate teacher/pupil ratio. This arrangement allows children to receive personal attention.

METHODS FOR LEARNING

The kindergarten room is best organized with learning centers located around the room. One teacher supervises each center, using conversation with the children to teach the biblical truth that provides the focus for the session. Children are allowed to move freely from one activity to another as long as there is room for them in a center. In a classroom with only one teacher, the centers may be set up before class. Then the teacher and all of the children can move from center to center together. This arrangement is used to keep the children's attention and to allow for firsthand experiences.

A home-living center with appropriate equipment is recommended. A book and puzzle center will be used often. Other areas may be for nature objects, art, blocks, and music. Not all centers will be used each week, but three or four will be selected to teach the Bible theme for the day. A story area will be used during each class session. So will small tables, seating no more than five or six, used for take-home activities and some learning centers. A worship area where the group gathers for singing is also needed. Recommended space is thirty to thirty-five square feet per child.

LEADERSHIP

An effective department will be led by a department supervisor who coordinates the work of the staff. The department leader recruits needed teachers (or communicates that need to the person who is designated to do recruiting), meets with teachers regularly to plan weekly teaching sessions

THE KINDERGARTEN DEPARTMENT
A Recommended Room Arrangement

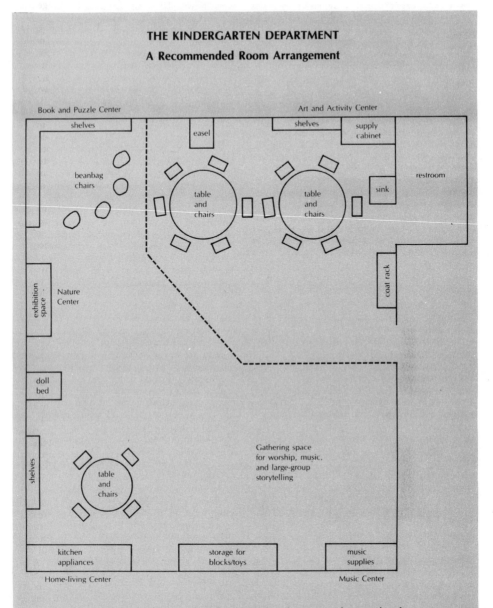

The space and facilities above have been designed to meet the needs of a kindergarten department with an average attendance of 15 children. Total floor space equals 525 square feet (21 × 25) to provide the optimum 35 square feet of space per child. Carpeting is the preferred floor covering in all but the Art and Activity Center where vinyl or some easy-to-clean surface is recommended. Windows provide semidirect lighting.

and special departmental activities, encourages teachers, and makes sure that adequate equipment and supplies are available for teaching sessions.

The key to a strong department is the staff. Teachers must be warm, caring individuals who love children and interacting with them, for kindergarten children "catch" religious faith as much as they are taught it.

CURRICULUM

Curriculum for four and five year olds generally deals with simple Bible stories that acquaint the child conceptually with God and Jesus Christ and a child's response to him. Effective curriculum teaches these concepts using learning centers as described above, effective storytelling, music, and craft activities that involve the child in the learning process and bring the concept into a concrete experience to which the child can easily relate. *See also* Child Abuse; Child Development; Nursery Education; Preschool Children.

E. A. Daniel

Kingdom of God

See Reign of God.

Knowledge, Theories of

What one believes about knowledge—its nature, sources, and how it is organized and acquired—will profoundly affect the way one goes about developing a program of religious education.

To know is to be actively involved in searching out factual data and meaning. To have knowledge is to possess the product of that active search. Knowing is a process of intellectual activity; having knowledge is the acquisition of a treasury of accumulated perceptions and concepts.

At the outset, it is useful to distinguish between perception and conceptual content. A perception is an immediate sensing of phenomena, while conceptualization is the organizing of one's perceptions into permanent classifications of acquired knowledge. For example, a child entering a church might perceive that people pray there, that songs are sung, that there are various signs, symbols, and actions not seen anywhere else (or at least not quite in that same way). But until a child can name and classify all these perceptions, describing them accurately to others, one cannot say that a concept of churchly liturgy has been formed.

Philosophers have long debated whether certain types of knowledge could be classified as either "objective" (resting in the qualities and properties of the objects of our knowing) or "subjective" (resting primarily in the person of the one who knows). That most knowledge is both objective and subjective and that it is not possible always to distinguish between these components is the more widely held view. When, for instance, we speak of "knowledge of the love of God," we affirm the objective reality that has been attested by witnesses in the generations of our religious history/heritage. But we also recognize that this is something we affirm because we personally have felt it (subjectively).

SOURCES OF KNOWLEDGE

The sources of knowledge are outlined in clear prose in *Philosophy of Education* by Philip H. Phenix (1958). The *human senses* are a source of knowledge. All that we see, hear, handle, taste, and smell comes into our consciousness and is organized by our nervous and endocrine systems into a body of patterns and structures. (When Helen Keller, deprived of both sight and hearing, was first able to connect the splash of water from a pump with the word "water" spelled into her hand by her teacher, her whole world became different.)

Reason as a source of knowledge is closely linked to the senses but includes more. We have memories and also a variety of mental states (joy, depression, anxiety, hope, and the like) that combine to make it possible for us to puzzle through our life experiences and form hypotheses, to test out a variety of ways to live and act and relate to others, and to solve problems. The study of theology and the development of tools for interpreting the Bible are the products of reason; they challenge us to search the many sources of recorded information about how others have reasoned in other generations.

Another source of knowledge can be labeled as *intuition*—a kind of direct, immediate knowing that seems to short-circuit the usual processes of thinking and learning. When we speak of the precepts of God that are "written on the hearts" of God's people, this is a kind of intuitive knowledge. The educator Jerome Bruner wrote of knowledge structures formed by learners as the result of "intuitive leaps" whereby a collection of perceptions are somehow formed into a rational whole without the necessity of explaining tediously the interrelationships of thought that are involved.

Considerable weight has been given in our century to *existence* as a source of knowledge. This theory holds that we know simply by being. This existential view, taken to its extremes, tends to reject institutional norms and the wealth of accumulated culture in favor of urging each human being to strike out and learn by immersion in the world's suffering and struggles, triumphs and victories. Existentialism in religious education would tend to reject organized schools and programs in favor of "being the church in the world" through social action and a congregational life that focuses continually on being for others.

In contrast, *tradition* as a source of knowledge is the repository of derived wisdom about manners and morals, customs and rituals. Religious bodies have their "ways of celebrating" that involve practices handed down through the generations. Most of our knowledge is not original with any one of us; we have it secondhand as part of a passed-on tradition. Even statistical tables and calendars and the like are a part of that type of heritage.

All the foregoing have primarily to do with knowledge that is natural—a part of the nature of human beings and the world in which we live. Processes can be identified and named whereby we possess such natural knowledge. But for members of the Judeo-Christian tradition, there is another kind of knowledge based on faith in God as its only Source. This is the knowledge of *revelation*.

Revealed knowledge (such as Abraham's knowledge of the one God who led him and his family to move out in faith, not knowing their destination; Moses' receiving of the Tablets on Mt. Sinai, from which were derived all the codes of law treasured by the Hebrews; or the witness of the apostles to the fact that Jesus Christ is Son of God and Savior of humankind) transcends all other kinds of knowledge. Faith, said St. Anselm, is always in search of "understanding." He meant that our knowledge of God is in itself a revealed, given object of our life devotion. We proceed from that "given" to the task of trying to discover, in our own lives and in every generation, just what it is that God is actively doing.

FORMS OF KNOWLEDGE

The twentieth-century theologian Karl Barth described faith itself as a "form of knowledge." To know something, truly, means to plunge deeply into understanding what we first accept on faith. We trust what comes to us, and we build our structures of knowing on that foundation of primary trust.

A popular way of speaking about knowledge is to distinguish between knowledge in its "pure" form (intellectual propositions, theoretical models, and the like) and knowledge that is "applied," or actively utilized in dealing with real, everyday problems. We might speak of a theologian's complex labor as a function of pure knowledge, while the work of a church school teacher in a parish church (no less important, by any measure) might be characterized as applied knowledge.

Contemporary research in the field of knowledge is peripherally concerned with the relationship between scientific and religious knowledge. Frequently one hears it said that science is verifiable, "real" knowledge about all that exists, whereas religion tends to be regarded as vague, personal, and not subject to the same rigorous application of intellect. The work of the Academy of Science and Religion and other groups is designed to bring these two long-separated disciplines into more intense conversation with each other. That such a conversation is needed is clear; we have only to witness the controversy over evolution and creationism in public education in order to illustrate the breach that exists.

It should be evident to those who teach in the church that this role requires a healthy respect for all forms of knowledge and for every source of human knowing. We speak of knowing what is true, what is good, what is right "in the eyes of God." Such knowing can only be possessed as a consequence of prayerful weighing of all the stimuli that come our way and sorting out and classifying the perceptions until concepts are formed that become "ruling principles" of our lives. Scripture, tradition, reason, and experience combine to help us in our formation as people of God. Such knowing and being are not achieved alone; they are possible, in their fullest sense, when we take our places in a community committed to learning "what is the will of the Lord." *See also* Empiricism; Epistemology; Existentialism; Faith; Learning Theory; Phenomenology; Revelation; Tradition.

L. E. Bowman

Koinonia

Koinonia is a Greek word derived from *koinos*, an adjective meaning "common or shared," and from the verb *koinoneo*, which means to "share, communicate, contribute, or have fellowship with." It is related to *koinonoi*, a noun meaning "partners or partakers." *Koinonia* is a term used by Greek and Roman philosophers and by the apostle Paul and others in the New Testament to describe the nature of community.

Plato, in *The Republic*, demonstrates the need for a common feeling or harmony among citizens in order to provide a foundation for political order. In *Nicomachean Ethics* Aristotle discusses friendship and love, especially of parents for children and children for parents. He wrote: "For children are a blessing to both parents, and this community of interest (*koinonia*) binds them together" (7.14).

Marcus Aurelius, a Roman emperor and Stoic philosopher, wrote in *The Meditations:* "Society (*koinonia*) therefore is the proper good of a rational creature. For that we are made for society (*koinonia*), it hath long since been demonstrated" (5.15). Pythagorean thinkers expanded the use of the term to include people, the gods, and even animals because they all shared in life.

Whereas these philosophers used *koinonia* to describe a human creation or social construct, the

New Testament writers understood it as a gift of God through the Holy Spirit and a characteristic of the early church. *Koinonia* appears nineteen times, primarily in the Letters of Paul, but also in Acts, Hebrews, and 1 John, and is translated in different ways depending on the context: fellowship, partnership, sharing, communion, participation, contribution. One can distinguish at least five different uses, but they are all interrelated.

Fellowship, or a description of the common life of the early church, is found in Acts 2:42: "And they devoted themselves to the apostles' teaching and fellowship, to the breaking of bread and the prayers." In 1 John 1:3, 6–7, *koinonia* is used four times, twice as fellowship "with us" or "one another" and twice as fellowship with God.

The term also refers to the mystical or spiritual *relationship* with God, Christ, and the Holy Spirit. 1 John 1:3b reads: "And our fellowship is with the Father and with the Son Jesus Christ." This is echoed in 1 Corinthians 1:9. In 2 Corinthians 13:14, the word is used in the often repeated Pauline benediction that concludes "and the fellowship of the Holy Spirit be with you all." In Philippians 2:1 the RSV translates *koinonia* as "participation in the Spirit." In another place (2 Cor. 6:14) Paul asks, "Or what fellowship has light with darkness?"

Participation, or sharing in the sufferings of Christ, is another use. In 1 Corinthians 10:16 *koinonia* is translated as "participation" or "communion" in reference to the cup of blessing and the bread of the Lord's Supper. In Philippians 3:10 the same word is translated as "sharing" the sufferings of Christ.

Partnership, or sharing of the gospel and faith, appears in the Letter to the Philippians. Paul expresses his thanks for their partnership (*koinonia*) in the gospel (Phil. 1:5), and in his Letter to Philemon he prays that the sharing (*koinonia*) of faith "may promote the knowledge of all the good that is ours in Christ" (Philem. 6). Another use of the word is found in Galatians, where Paul recalls that James, Cephas, and John gave to Barnabas and himself the "right hand of fellowship" (Gal. 2:9).

And finally, *koinonia* means *contribution*, or sharing of gifts and goods. In four places (Rom. 15:26; 2 Cor. 8:4; 2 Cor. 9:13; Heb. 13:16), the word is used in reference to the sharing or contributing for the relief of the poor.

Theologians have commented on the richness of the term as a description of the ideal church. There are dangers with the word "fellowship," but we must remember that *koinonia* is a gift and not just a natural outcome of a social process. It is given by Christ and maintained by the Holy Spirit.

These biblical meanings—"fellowship" as mutuality in the presence of God through worship, "participation" as identification with Christ, and "sharing" what we have with others—enrich a commonly used word that usually relates to good times together or enjoying a group. Religious education teachers, understanding these meanings, can deepen the awareness of the relationships within the religious community. *See also* Congregational Life; History of Christian Education; Holy Spirit; Liturgy; Worship.

B. W. Kathan

La Salle, Jean-Baptiste de ————

Pioneer educator and founder of the Christian Brothers, Jean-Baptiste de la Salle (1651–1719) was born in Rheims, France, and ordained in 1678. About 1680 he organized a group of laymen principally to give an education in the fundamentals of Christian faith and morals to the sons of the poor and of the working class. He introduced the teaching of a suitable trade along with religion and in 1685 established the first of a new kind of training college to better prepare teachers. In 1684, to ensure a wider mission for the work, La Salle formed the Institute of Brothers of the Christian Schools (the Christian Brothers).

He wrote a rule for his order and insisted that those who joined take a vow, along with the usual vows of poverty, chastity, and obedience, to persevere and to accept no income for teaching. La Salle was canonized in 1900 and declared patron of all Christian teachers in 1956. *See also* Christian Brothers; History of Christian Education.

L. G. McAllister

Laboratory School

A laboratory school is a teacher training session that includes actual practice with a sample class and feedback on technique. Many churches have adopted the laboratory school as a strategy for training teachers and leaders serving the whole spectrum of classes and programs in the church. Some denominations, most notably the United Methodist, have developed a nationwide program of laboratory schools, which are planned and conducted according to clearly stated standards. They are led by instructors who have demonstrated competence in teaching a particular age group as well as the ability to assist other teachers to develop those skills in teaching. These leaders are carefully evaluated and guided in their work and only those who fulfill all the prescribed requirements are recognized and certified as laboratory school leaders.

There are many different strategies and settings for training teachers and leaders in the church. Workshops, seminars, institutes, classes, conferences, and retreats are examples. The laboratory school differs from all other strategies of teacher and leader training in several ways.

Laboratory schools are usually held for an extended period of time, often in the summer, when participants are able to commit themselves to a week of focused, intensive practice and reflection on the activities of teaching in the church. Another format that has worked well is to conduct a school one day at a time over a period of six to ten weeks. The extended period of time is necessary in order to provide all of the participants ample opportunities for discussing, observing, practicing, and evaluating the many skills involved in the teaching/learning process.

Laboratory schools emphasize teaching skills in the context of actual teaching situations. Children, youth, or adults are recruited to serve as students for a typical church school class. They are taught initially by experienced teachers who demonstrate effective teaching strategies. The teachers-in-training observe the class session and afterward participate in a period of debriefing and evaluation to learn from the experience as many insights and helpful suggestions as possible. To be most effective it is important that the classroom setting and those recruited as students represent as closely as possible the actual at-home situation the teachers will face.

A key element of a laboratory school program is observation of competent, experienced teachers by those who are seeking to develop their skills. The observers (the teachers-in-training) use prepared observation forms or instruments to guide them to look for specific actions of the teachers and the learners. So much happens in any given time frame that teachers are helped most when they can focus their attention on something specific: giving directions, asking questions, guiding discussions, relating to learners with particular needs, transition from one activity to another, and other important aspects of the teaching process.

One of the main benefits from attending a laboratory school is gained from the actual ex-

perience of practicing the skills of teaching. The participants are prepared for their turn of teaching by observing others teach, by participating with the trainers in planning a session, by assisting in teaching one or more sessions, and by assuming major responsibility for some important part of a session, if not the whole session.

After doing the teaching, teachers and leaders spend time debriefing and evaluating the process in order to gain new insights about teaching as well as about themselves. The teachers-in-training are helped to learn both from their strengths and from their weaknesses. The school leaders, in addition to being outstanding teachers, must also be sensitive, capable persons who are able to support and encourage others who may be anxious about what they are doing. There are schools where the leaders serve in both roles; in others, one set of leaders does the actual classroom teaching and another set leads the evaluation and debriefing process with the adult participants. Some laboratory schools have found video recording of a teaching session to be very helpful. It is possible to use the video in the debriefing time as an instant recall of what happened. Not all teachers, however, are comfortable being the subjects of a video and feel embarrassed when they see themselves in the replay.

Those who have had a year or more experience as teachers benefit most from a laboratory school. Persons who have not had any experience as teachers in any setting will likely be too anxious and self-conscious about themselves and their teaching to be able to gain from what such a school has to offer. Even experienced teachers become a little unsettled when they are the focus of another's observation and evaluation.

Teachers who participate in a laboratory school often describe their experience as one of the most stimulating and helpful learning opportunities they have ever had in serving in the church. *See also* Evaluation; Leadership Development; Supervision; Teacher; Theology and Education.

D. L. Griggs

Language Analysis

Language analysis is a philosophy that studies the relationship between words and meaning. It has affected philosophical discourse by concentrating on the structure of words in contrast with classical metaphysics, which explores the meaning of existence.

Language analysis is associated with Ludwig Wittgenstein (1889–1951), who in his early writings insisted that only verification through the senses gave meaning to a sentence. Sentences not so verified have only emotive (i.e., emotional) meaning; as a matter of rationality they are literally "nonsense." Later, Wittgenstein proposed that there are many "language games," by which he meant that there are different levels or categories of language in which sentences have meaning in terms of their use. Language becomes a part of an activity or a form of life. People back up their language by their life as a whole and thus participate in many language games. Thus key words used in religious discourse have meaning in that context.

Horace Bushnell (1802–1876) anticipated similar problems in 1849. He proposed that religious language is secondary to language about things. In every language there are words for literal use and for figurative, metaphorical, and analogical use. Religious words are derived from those used to point to the physical state, but they do not correspond with any exactness; such words impute form to what has no form. Because of the peculiarity of religious language, it is necessary to make use of many words or figures of speech to ensure that clarity will increase and falsifications will cancel each other out. Bushnell, however, saw that relationships were essential to the nurturing process and emphasized the place of family and church as organic systems supporting religious growth. Religious words are important when the person using them stands behind them and guarantees them by conviction and integrity of action.

The linguistic philosopher Ian T. Ramsey (1915–1972) stressed that religious language uses odd, peculiar, and unusual phrases that may "come alive" in moments of discernment or disclosure. Such discernment may result in commitment as one responds in terms of freedom, which may or may not be based on a sense of duty or loyalty. The objective reference in theology is mystery, and therefore there is always a logical gap between the model used and the disclosure that occurs. Theology thrives on a diversity of models, and because a single one is inadequate, every model needs "qualifiers," which point the model in such a way that a disclosure becomes possible. The purpose of religious education, in Ramsey's view, is to teach insight and evoke disclosures by using words that come alive, so that this response leads to commitment centered in Jesus Christ as discovered in the Bible, in doctrine, and in worship, which is empirical "fit" and key to the process.

Religious education theory has been only slightly influenced by language analysis. There has been an emphasis on analyzing the terms used and an effort at clarification of concepts. It has been helpful to clear away the obscurity made by trying to fit religious language into the confines of language analysis. Ramsey's insights have given religious educators a clue into both the limitations and the descriptive possibilities of religious language.

Much religious language is self-involving and performative. When one says "I thank," "I sub-

mit," "I pray," or "I appoint," one is performing a speech act. It is neither true nor false but is liable to infelicities. The statement may misfire because one is not able to carry it through or act it out, or one is mistaken. Words may do things, express feelings or reveal opinions or values. David Evans has coined the word "onlook" to express how we "look on" some aspect of the world. There are self-involvement and a degree of autobiography, and one takes a stand. Good teaching, especially when it operates within an atmosphere in which logically odd situations are evoked, may lead to a response that is self-involving and thus to a deeper commitment in words and deeds. *See also* Commitment; Communication Theory; God, Understandings of; Semiotics; Symbolism.

FOR FURTHER REFERENCE

Miller, Randolph Crump. *The Language Gap and God.* New York: Pilgrim, 1970.

R. C. Miller

Language, Inclusive

Human language is just that—human. It has been and is still being constructed by men and women to enable them to communicate about the reality of which they are a part. Language facilitates the development and sharing of culture. Language is created by human beings to enable the exchange of ideas, meanings, and feelings. The words and phrases that compose language are arbitrary; by themselves they do not name reality. That naming comes about by the agreement of the community that uses the language.

As a human construct, language reflects the values important in a society. It is, as it were, a verbal artifact by which we may learn about the society from which it springs. Language helps to transmit and maintain social positions and power relationships as well as economic and political structures.

Language, like other human institutions, often takes on a life of its own and begins to define the very people who created it. Thus language has a double function: it expresses what human beings think and feel about their culture and it helps to shape both the persons who use it and the culture in which they live.

Words and images are sometimes used to present one group of the human family as the standard against which all are to be measured. For instance, women, members of racial and ethnic minorities, people with disabilities, and elderly people have been stereotyped as somewhat inferior because they are different from the dominant group constituting the norm. Such groups can be excluded by mentioning them, by using stereotypical labels to highlight their difference, or by not mentioning them, by using terms, phrases, or descriptions specific to the dominant group to represent the whole.

Feminists were among the first to call attention to this latter form of exclusion in the use of masculine nouns and pronouns to refer to both men and women, e.g., "man" was used to mean all people everywhere, humankind. Studies show that such sexist language has served to make women invisible and to reinforce male dominance in our culture.

Inclusive language, on the other hand, consciously uses words and phrases that include women as well as men. Expressions such as "God made man" are reworded so that it is clear that women are included in the meaning: "God made human beings (or men and women)."

IN RELIGION

The realization of the impact of inclusive language has led publishing houses and professional and business organizations to adopt an inclusive language policy. The issue of inclusive language has been a struggle in religious communities, but churches and synagogues have begun to recognize the need for change in this regard. Many denominations have issued guidelines for worship. In 1983, the National Council of the Churches of Christ published the first of three volumes of *An Inclusive Language Lectionary*.

Already in 1895 Elizabeth Cady Stanton published *The Woman's Bible*, in which she excised biblical passages she felt demeaned women and placed men in dominant positions. But her radical approach did not take into account the primacy of the canonical Scriptures in the religious community. In translations today, specifically the latest edition of the Revised Standard Version, attempts have been made to eliminate male-biased language in passages dealing with human beings (sometimes using the plural, sometimes changing from third to second person), but traditional language about God has been retained.

Today inclusive language seeks not only to further gender equality, but also to promote cultural and social equality. Language that suggests that Western European culture is the norm by which other racial and ethnic groups are to be judged reinforces prejudices and stereotypes. Expressions and images that present all members of a particular racial or ethnic group as having the same characteristics, temperament, and talents validates and perpetuates the exclusion of those groups from participation in the larger society.

As people became aware of sexist and racially and ethnically exclusive language, awareness has also grown of other patterns of language that exclude persons. When we define people by one facet of their being we deny the richness of their personhood. Thus, to speak of the poor, the handicapped, the epileptic, the blind, etc., is to define persons by only one aspect of their lives. Such stereotyping makes it difficult to see other characteristics of persons, to appreciate their whole personhood. Such expressions as "persons who are poor," "a woman who is deaf," or "a man who is blind" may be more appropriate.

Inclusive language also refers to language we sometimes use when referring to God. The images and metaphors we use when referring to God are incomplete and limited human attempts to better understand the reality we call Ineffable. Scripture supplies a rich treasure of metaphors that may be applied to God: Rock, Fortress, King, Mother, Lord, Love, Spirit, Father.... Exclusive use of one kind of terminology limits our ability to image Divinity; using only one metaphor for God suggests that that metaphor captures God's essence and is therefore a kind of heresy.

IN RELIGIOUS EDUCATION

Religious educators already have a head start in the use of inclusive language, for many publishers of curricular materials are conscious of the need to be inclusive and this is reflected in published texts. Teachers need to explore their own feelings and habits in the use of language to see to what extent they are willing to be inclusive, not only with reference to persons, but with reference to God. People have individual tolerances for change in religious terminology and need to respect each other's views. At the same time, children and adolescents today live in a culture increasingly affected by the pressures of women and minorities for full inclusion and will expect to find this attitude in their religious community. The phrasing of hymns and prayers in liturgy and study are other ways by which people learn attitudes. Religious educators need to be aware of changes and interpretations that affect inclusiveness and the effect of language on learners. *See also* Communication Theory; Culture; God, Understandings of; Hymnody, Christian; Liturgical Movement; Metaphor; Singles; Social Justice, Education for; Symbolism.

R. Coll

Latin America

Latin America, which includes Mexico and the countries of Central and South America, has a combined population of approximately 400 million, of whom over 360 million (90%) are Roman Catholics. Each country to one degree or another faces the problems of extreme poverty and political turmoil, and it is these challenges that have helped shape the churches active in Latin America today.

THE CATHOLIC CHURCH

The Catholic church in Latin America makes its presence felt among the people in the perspective of its historical context. A new focus appears in the Puebla document "On Evangelization in Latin America's Present and Future," final document of the Third General Conference of the Latin American Bishops, held in Mexico in 1979:

> Catechesis . . . must be a priority activity in Latin America if we wish to achieve a deep-rooted renovation of the Christian life, that is to say, if we wish to arrive at a new civilization that signifies communion and sharing between persons in the Church and in society. (p. 977)

"Catechesis" rather than "religious education" is the term used to describe ongoing education in the faith. In the Latin American church, catechesis takes place primarily in seminaries, academic and nonacademic institutes, catechist formation programs, youth ministries, public elementary schools, and Catholic schools.

As more and more laypeople are becoming aware of their role in the church, committed Christians are searching for new ways to pursue education in their faith and in its deeper life response. There is a strong call for renewal in Latin American seminaries. Seminarians feel they lack preparation for pastoral ministry and lack the pedagogical skills needed to communicate the message. Too much emphasis is placed on systematic theology, they feel.

Catholic institutes are today being encouraged to offer undergraduate degrees in a specific religious field. In Venezuela, for instance, such an institute is linked to the diocesan seminary Santa Rosa de Lima, and its program, whose goal is to train pastoral ministers, has been registered in the National Department for Higher Education. At present, there are hundreds of clergy, religious, and laypeople enrolled in the religious pedagogy undergraduate degree.

The Council of Latin American Bishops founded the Theological-Pastoral Institute located in the Archdiocese of Medellin, Colombia. It offers a nine-month training program for active pastoral ministers from all over Latin America. The program's purpose is to provide intellectual stimulation in an environment that fosters community and a great spirit of solidarity with the Latin American church. The program includes social science and theological and pastoral courses; a certificate is given to each participant at the close of the program.

Other programs are offered through correspondence courses from Spain consisting of a series of folders addressing topics such as Christology, catechesis, ecclesiology, and anthropology. A professor accredited by the Spanish institute meets with participants to clarify material and evaluate learning.

CATECHIST FORMATION

Parents are the first teachers of their children. In the Latin American church, parents not only catechize informally but are beginning to assume greater responsibility for their children's ongoing education in the faith. The Chilean church is considered to be one of the pioneers in developing a "parents as catechists" program; it has become a model for programs in other Latin American countries.

In a typical program parent-catechists (five to seven families) meet weekly with a facilitator to study, reflect, share testimonies, and pray about the Christian message they will be presenting to their children that week. A study guide for parents might have lesson plans to help them prepare their children for the sacraments of Eucharist and penance. In addition, parish catechists coordinate social and religious activities among the family members and the parish community in order to foster a spirit of unity. After their children receive the sacraments, the parents become parish catechists or facilitators for a parent-catechist session held in their homes.

Catechist formation is one of the most critical needs in the Catholic church in Latin America. In order to foster the participation of the laity, the diocesan catechetical office in the Archdiocese of Caracas, Venezuela, has developed a master teacher program, whose goal is to teach others to teach prospective catechists. The program includes the following elements: (a) basic orientation and preparation in catechesis, Christology, Scripture, ecclesiology, liturgy, sacraments, sociology, psychology, pedagogy, and methodology; (b) weekly meetings to reflect on and evaluate their catechetical experiences; (c) participation in the planning of catechetical events; (d) special study in one subject; (e) teaching of one's area of concentration in the basic catechetical courses at the parish and deanery levels; (f) opportunities for retreats, prayer, and reflection according to the liturgical season; (g) opportunity to take an in-depth course each semester in one of the areas already mentioned.

YOUTH MINISTRY

More than half the population of Latin America is under twenty-five years old; therefore one of the main priorities for the Catholic church in Latin America is youth ministry. As the Puebla document states:

> The Church has confidence in young people. They are a source of hope for it. In the young people of Latin America it sees a real potential for the present and future of its evangelization. Because they inject real dynamism into the social body, and especially the ecclesial body, the Church assumes a preferential option for the young people. (p. 1186)

However, youth ministry has also been one of the most neglected areas in the church. Frequently, youth groups come together looking for mutual support from their peers and playing music for the youth Sunday liturgy. Sometimes, they offer services in their own parish community. Yet youth groups are expressing a deep thirst for a closer relationship to Jesus, and what it means to be his disciple. There is an urgent need to promote youth ministry and to train prospective youth ministers.

PUBLIC SCHOOLS

In some Latin American countries, religious education is permitted in elementary public schools. Usually it is the responsibility of the Christian community to prepare and send catechists to the public schools. The national catechetical office in some countries publishes a series of religious texts for each grade to correlate with the regular school curriculum.

Public schools have been great avenues for inviting children as well as parents to participate in the sacramental preparation program in the parish to which they belong.

CATHOLIC SCHOOLS

In Catholic schools in Latin America religion is given as much importance as any other subject in the curriculum. Religious educators do not limit themselves to the programmed courses in religion; their goal is to encourage growth in the faith.

Education in general, as well as Christian education, is being challenged not to operate out of a worldview that fosters individualism, paternalism, or maternalism but to awaken an authentic Christian concern about building a more just and humane world.

TRENDS IN CATECHESIS

An effort is being made to bridge the gap between faith and life. Catechesis is therefore focusing on everyday experiences in the light of God's Word in order to elicit a faith response in day-to-day life.

To carry on Jesus' mission in this historical moment, the church recognizes that catechists must pay attention to what is going on in the society and in the world. It is essential for them to recognize the suffering Christ in the faces of abandoned children, homeless people, confused young adults, laborers who are treated unjustly, and indigenous people marginalized by the society. Catechists must be aware of malnutrition and of health problems as well as of violations of human rights on both the national and the international levels. They must see that inhuman poverty is a product of economic, social, and political structures. Catechists are called to become aware of the values of the existing culture and to nourish the seeds of hope already present among the people.

Catechesis is called to strengthen communion and collaboration among the people of God: laity, clergy, and religious women and men. It is the responsibility of the whole ecclesial community. The community of believers gathering for worship and service to others is an important means to foster a mature faith. To build up the Christian community is one of the main tasks of catechesis, and it is the mission of families, schools, parishes, the lay apostolate, and the basic ecclesial communities.

The basic ecclesial community (base community) is the experience of being church at the grass roots level. It is a model of church that is intended to respond to the challenges of Latin America at this moment in history. Some of the essential elements of these communities are: creating a more interpersonal relationship with one another; acknowledging and empowering the different gifts and charisms in the community; taking on the attitudes of Jesus; reflecting on personal and communal experiences in light of God's word; celebrating faith life; being missioned as a community to evangelize and be evangelized by those who are marginalized by society—the poorest among the poor.

Over the last twenty years, the basic ecclesial communities have multiplied and flourished especially in some Latin American countries. They are one of the joys and hopes of the church.

The ultimate goal of the ministries of evangelization and catechesis is to *uncover the reign of God* so we recognize our solidarity as brothers and sisters and share the goods of creation.

PROTESTANT EDUCATION IN LATIN AMERICA

There are approximately twenty-one million Protestants in Latin America today. Protestants came to Latin America as immigrants around the 1830s, bringing from various European countries their cultures, their languages, and their home churches, including the Lutheran, Reformed, Anglican, and Methodist churches. Later in the nineteenth century, the mainline American Protestant denominations—Methodist, Presbyterian, Disciples, and Baptists—entered. They adopted the language and culture of the country and established indigenous churches. Their purpose was evangelistic.

By the turn of the century, there was a small but growing middle class in Latin America who were liberal and progressive in their values and valued that approach for their children's education. At the Panama Conference in 1916, influenced by the thinking of a Disciples missionary, the Reverend Samuel Guy Inman, evangelicals began to establish private elementary and secondary schools of high academic quality.

Early in the twentieth century, Pentecostal groups appeared, serving and appealing to the large proletariat: the urban poor. Some churches were founded by missionaries; others were indigenous. Although primarily concerned for evangelism, many of these churches also established literacy programs and popular education with a goal of "uplifting" this group they served. Although they keep no official records, the Pentecostal is clearly the fastest growing religious sector in Latin America.

The evangelical (that is, Protestant) churches sponsor more than three hundred seminaries and Bible institutes. Seminary associations are grouped in Brazil, The River Plata (Argentina, Paraguay, Uruguay), and the Caribbean. A series of strategy conferences beginning in 1916 created the Commission on Cooperation in Latin America. There is also a Council of Latin American Churches (which was preceded by national councils in most countries) and an Evangelical Council of Christian Education for all Latin America. The latter sponsors curricular materials in Spanish and Portuguese. As early as 1917 a training school was established in Buenos Aires to prepare women for educational ministry in parishes.

Sunday schools are the basic agency for religious education of Protestants.

The publication of literature has been an important element in evangelical education, and evangelical publishing houses have flourished in Latin America for many years. *See also* Hispanic Americans; Liberation Theology.

FOR FURTHER REFERENCE

Brown, Robert McAfee. *Theology in a New Key.* Philadelphia: Westminster, 1978.
LaFeber, Walter. *Inevitable Revolution.* New York: Norton, 1983.

R. S. Toledo

Latter-day Saints, Church of Jesus Christ of

See Mormon Education.

Lay Ministry

Lay ministry is the work of Christ delegated to his followers, the church. This ministry is directed to both the membership of the church and to those outside and is carried out corporately and individually. Clergy and laity participate in it together as a joint effort. Thus lay ministry refers to the work of Christ performed by laypeople, whether it is done in the life of the church, in the home, or in the societal setting where they live and work. Recent changes in the understanding of lay ministry have had a significant impact on the design

and goals of Christian education programs on all levels.

The common usage of the word "lay" denotes one who is untrained in a given vocation or one who is not a professional. In the church the laity refers to those people of the church who are not the professional clergy. Unfortunately this use of the term is different from its original meaning.

HISTORY

The term "lay" is derived from the Greek word *laos* meaning "people." Often it is used to designate the people of God, as in *laos theou*. When used as such, the term refers to all the people of God whether they be professional leaders or not. By the end of the first century, Christian literature showed a distorted use of the word. Instead of designating all the people of God, it came to refer only to the nonprofessional, hence the current usage. By the first century the professional leaders in the church were called the *kleros* (from which the present term "clergy" is derived), and this also represents a distortion of the root meaning. In biblical usage *kleros* designates all of God's people; all clergy and laity are called his inheritance or portion. Thus the two terms commonly used today to designate the professionals and nonprofessionals in the church both carry a meaning that is a distortion of the original.

Church historians describe the early Christian church as a movement in which the professional leaders and nonprofessionals were both active in the church's mission and ministry. Both shared in doing the work of the kingdom of God. Leaders had a different function than the nonprofessionals, but they shared a common calling and task. There was a difference of function but not a difference of status or essence.

Life of the church from the second century onward showed an increasing trend toward clericalism, in which the status of the laity was demeaned and their role was relegated to that of passive spectators. The clergy moved to prominence as doers of ministry. They developed into an elite group with special titles and privileges. The laity became the objects of ministry with no recognition or standing as ministers in their own right.

The erosion of the identity of laypeople as participants in ministry greatly diminished the practice of lay ministry in the centuries leading up to the Reformation. Laypersons no longer saw themselves as the people of God with gifts for ministry and a calling to serve him. They were left unequipped and uneducated. They could not understand Latin, the language in which Scripture was transmitted throughout the Middle Ages. Therefore, regarding Scripture they were illiterate.

The sixteenth-century Reformers brought renewal to the concept of lay ministry. Church leaders courageously reaffirmed the biblical teaching regarding the laity. Martin Luther led the Reformers in teaching that all believers were ministers of Christ. In 1520, he wrote a treatise entitled *Address to the Christian Nobility of the German Nation* in which he stated, "there is . . . really no difference between laymen, priests, princes, bishops, or . . . between religious and secular, than that of office or occupation, and not that of Christian status. All have spiritual status, and all are truly priests, bishops, and popes." Thus the popular statement of the Reformation, "the priesthood of all believers," was born.

Lay ministry, after many centuries of dormancy, began to make a comeback in the churches. The Bible was translated into the language of the people so that they could read and study it in their homes. Catechisms were written and used to educate the people. The "priesthood of all believers" meant that each person could approach God directly through Jesus Christ without a human intermediary. All believers were priests regardless of theological training or church-sponsored ordination and each had a service to perform in the whole economy of Christ's kingdom. The Reformers taught that this ministry, or calling, had a double focus—to the church and to the world. This ennobled the so-called secular tasks of the laity performed in the world.

Many noted post-Reformation movements have taken the lay ministry concept seriously. Nikolaus von Zinzendorf (1700–1760) in Germany, John Wesley (1703–1791) in England, and John R. Mott (1865–1955) in America are among the well-known leaders of the past. As a whole, however, the church in the centuries following the Reformation has not implemented lay ministry adequately.

Renewed interest in lay ministry in the last half of the twentieth century in many churches has brought significant impetus to the movement. Biblical and theological writings have stirred the church to continue the work of restoring lay ministry to the life of the church. Lay academies have been established. Local churches have found practical ways of implementing the priesthood of their membership.

Vatican II's "Decree on the Apostolate of Lay People" has encouraged many kinds of lay actions such as assisting at the liturgy, catechetics, and service in the Roman Catholic Church as well.

BIBLICAL TEACHINGS

The biblical teachings that inform the lay ministry movement are: The work of Christian ministry and service is committed to all believers, laity as well as clergy (1 Pet. 2:9; Matt. 5:13, 14; Acts 1:8). God's grace is the basic motivation for ministry (2 Cor. 5:14, 15; Eph. 2:8–10; 1 Cor. 15:10). All believers have received ministry gifts (abilities) enabling them to minister (1 Cor. 12:4–31; Rom. 12:3–8; 1 Pet. 4:10, 11). Pastors and teachers of the church are responsible for equipping believers so as to develop their ministry gifts (Eph. 4:11, 12; Mark 3:4; 2 Tim. 2:2). Believers are to be cared for and held accountable in their ministries through the support of fellowship groups (1 Thess. 2:7, 8; Heb. 10:24, 25). And Christ's servant-heartedness is the manner in which his followers are to minister (John 13:14, 15; Luke 22:24–26; 1 Pet. 5:1–5).

PRESENT ISSUES

Several practical issues converge to enliven the lay ministry venture in the contemporary church. First, there is much more ministry that needs to be done than a paid church staff can accomplish. Sheer demands of ministry require that the ministry tasks be shared with the laity. Second, laypeople are in the right place. The greatest opportunities and needs for ministry are in the settings of the home, workplace, and structures of society where the laity function in the normal course of their daily life. The church's potential for witness resides in the laity. Third, lay ministry works. The history of the church is replete with evidence that the laity can carry out effective ministry. The early Christian church is looked upon as normative for the life of the church today. Another point is that church growth is positively correlated to lay ministry. Research indicates that sustained church growth tends to occur where there is an involved and equipped laity. And finally, an equipped and involved laity manifest phenomenal personal growth. Those who become a channel of God's grace are graced in the process. Nurture takes place best in the context of ministry.

All of this sends a strong signal to leaders of Christian education to see their primary task as designing an education ministry in the local church that will equip the laity for their ministries in the church, home, and society. The design of the equipping process is to be informed by the needs and challenges faced by the laity in their daily encounter with the pressures of society and the pragmatic demands of their workaday world. The church thus becomes the equipping center out of which lay ministry emanates. *See also* Cursillo; History of Christian Education; Ministry; Peer Ministry; Sunday School Movement; Vocation; Volunteer Principle.

K. Van Wyk

Leadership Development

Congregational leadership development is a process of finding, enlisting, training, and supporting leaders for the ministry of the church. Individual leadership development is a lifelong process of setting and achieving short-range and long-term goals for oneself.

Leadership is a process that happens in a group rather than a property of some individual. Dimensions of leadership include:

1. Embodying in some way a vision that others are willing to follow

2. Sensing what others are willing to risk

3. Holding a self-image that may be experienced by others as confidence

4. Being willing to take responsibility in a specific situation

5. Having skills that enable participation

Different people in a group may fulfill these functions at various times. Since leadership is a function rather than an attribute of a person, anyone can be a leader. The Bible tells us that even a little child can lead us (Isa. 11:6). But many people seem more ready to be followers than leaders. The question then is how people can come to exercise the functions of leadership with ease.

CONGREGATIONAL LEADERSHIP DEVELOPMENT

Leadership development is an ongoing process in the congregation. Assumptions influence the process whether they are stated or not. Among those assumptions are what the congregation as a whole and those in it understand about the purpose of the church, what is appropriate to achieve that purpose, who is allowed to provide leadership, and how leadership functions in the congregation. Answers to questions like these provide the basis for a planned program of leadership development.

The first task is to find and enlist leaders. Romans 12 and other passages describe the variety of gifts present among those in the body of Christ. Various ministries are also needed in order that God's realm might become reality for all people everywhere on earth. A checksheet can help people indicate their gifts and preferences in relation to the dimensions of the congregation's life and work.

People need to know the time, energy, and skill required for a job before they can decide responsibly about the appropriateness of that task for them. People are more likely to say yes to a certain job if it appears to meet personal, interpersonal, and church needs.

Providing a variety of ways of working may ease the enlistment task. Two- or three-person teaching teams work in some situations. Recruiting for specific short-term tasks like leading a group may be easier if leaders are found for whom the area is of particular interest. To handle the reluctance to "being tied down every Sunday" teachers can be rotated and reliable substitutes found.

People are also more likely to respond positively to doing a job when they know that training and support are available. Training can include any or all of the dimensions described below under individual leadership development. People need personal support from the pastor and others as well as institutional support such as adequate resources, time off, and ways of communicating their ideas to others.

Apprenticeship and other in-service training allows people to move at a comfortable pace. Regular meetings and workshops can provide training, support, and motivation for teachers. Church officers are more likely to perform effectively if they are trained for their specific role and if they experience themselves as being personally supported in their expenditure of time and energy.

INDIVIDUAL LEADERSHIP TRAINING

Some research done in a college program for teacher education found that people went through several stages as they moved from identifying themselves as not being teachers to knowing themselves to be teachers. The stages are marked by the questions discussed below.

Who am I? Identity of oneself as a person of worth is apparently a required first step on the journey toward effective leadership. Reflection from trusted others is one way in which positive change in self-image happens. People need to have experiences in which they can examine again who and whose they are.

Many people talk of the significance of being in a small group of people for a long enough time that they come to trust each other. Such small-group programs appear to be more effective if they have up to eight people who meet together for at least twenty hours. That period of time can be in several sessions, but the same people need to participate the whole time. Essential in such groups is the agreement that whatever is said is confidential. Otherwise, trust is not built.

Struggle with self-identity is often identified as the crucial issue of adolescence, and so it is. But it is also a recurring uncertainty throughout life. The focus of the identity question shifts with different ages and situations: "Who am I as a parent?" "Who am I as a responsible member of the church board?" "Who am I as a leader of the study group?"

What is to be taught? What is the vision to be shared? For people of faith, the same answer might be possible to both of these questions. The vision of a world in which God's shalom is experienced by all people everywhere can be the foundation out of which any particular content can be taught. To be a leader, one must have convictions, a faith to share as a base out of which to work. Specific situations then require differing content that the teacher or leader must learn in order to be able to share with others.

The church school and other groups of the church have facts, ideas, concepts, and values that are the medium with which the participants work as they seek to accomplish their goal or manifest their vision. Leaders and teachers must know or be able to find what the group needs in order to keep itself moving toward its goals.

Who are the learners? Who are the participants in the group to be led? Leaders are more effective when they know about the people with whom they will be working. Much information is available to help the leader know about the physical, emotional, social, psychological, and spiritual phases through which many people move as they mature.

One difficulty is learning how to identify and work with the amazing diversity of being human without placing people into inappropriate categories. Some physical and social development is readily observable—though it is always open to misunderstanding by an observer. Wrong assumptions are even more easily made about psychological, emotional, or spiritual understandings out of which a person may be living. Every life is or can be grace-filled. Sensitivity to such possibilities within each person can be both taught and learned.

How can a certain content be taught to particular learners? What processes will help a group move toward its goals? Processes for teaching/leading are usually more effective if those involved participate in making decisions about how their life is to be lived. Even very small children can make choices about what they want to do.

One of the ways in which people differ is in how they like to learn. Leaders and teachers can learn to identify how those in their groups like to learn and to work in groups. They can also figure out what is most effective with the particular people they are teaching or leading.

Some learners need an overview before they are comfortable working on details. Others start with pieces and create their own structures.

The different physical senses are windows to learning for different people. Some pick up information through their eyes and learn more readily through pictures and images. Some find hearing and listening more accessible channels. Some must talk through the content. Some need to work with their hands to create ways of holding the content being provided. Some learn more effectively if they can dance or move in some way. And, to make it even more complicated, some people learn best through various combinations of these sensory approaches.

Where can I get help so I continue to grow as a teacher, a leader? Those who want to develop their leadership skills can find help both within themselves and from others. Self-help books, tapes, and videos abound. Almost everything has been packaged in some way: "Improve Your Self-image," "Tell Stories Better," "Learn to Work with People More Effectively," and so on. Doing learning alone carries with it the difficulty of maintaining the discipline required for growth and change to happen. Working with others—even one other—provides accountability and motivation to continue toward intended goals.

Learning with other people is possible through the congregation and other denominational structures, at colleges or universities, in community educational programs, at museums, and with institutes of various kinds. Costs for such training and learning experiences vary from absolutely nothing except the time involved to several hundred dollars for an experience.

Growing teachers and leaders can continue throughout their whole lives to increase their facility with various methods. Programs of leader development can assist people during the journey toward more effective leadership. *See also* Lay Ministry; Management; Professional Study; Staff Relationships; Systems Theory; Teacher; Volunteer Principle.

S. J. Heckman

Learning Center

As currently used in religious education the term "learning center" refers to a cluster of processes and materials intended to help individuals or groups learn, explore, or reinforce a specific skill, area of content, or experience. Often a learning center is a particular location: a room, a portion of a room, a space marked off in some way from other similar spaces. Learning centers may also be portable: a suitcase or box with the essential equipment and printed or media directions and resources, a film or videotape that contains the process and content for a desired learning objective.

The learning center approach to education is based on two fundamental convictions. The first is that learners are different and have different styles of learning that are most useful and satisfying to them. The second is that most of what any institution would teach can be approached in a variety of ways and from a number of perspectives. A third conviction emerges when the first two are taken seriously and that is that people like to have some freedom in choosing the ways in which they will learn. Self-choice is thought to heighten motivation and to produce learning that is more gratifying to the learner.

For nearly two decades, religious education has taken the learning center experiences of secular education and translated them into the settings of the Sunday morning church school, intergenerational education, and other special educational endeavors. Regional and local workshops have offered training in the theory and management of learning center–based religious education. Curriculum resources have utilized the approach and one curriculum, Creative Curriculum (P.O. Box 612, Portland, ME 04104), has been constructed almost exclusively around the use of learning centers.

VARIETIES

A pedagogical step in the direction of the learning center approach might be illustrated by a teacher saying to a group of young children following the hearing of a Bible story: "Some of you might like to draw a picture of the story, some others of you might like to act out the story, and some of you can make up a list of questions to ask your parents about how they feel about this story." In this instance the learners are given an opportunity to choose what they will do from a list of possibilities, but the primary reference and control points are the teacher and the story. A series of learning centers would build, in more significant ways, on the basic convictions about learning that were identified earlier. Each center would have a well-articulated objective or series of objectives. These might be posted, included on the film, or spoken on a tape. The learner would know specifically what he or she might gain by way of knowledge, skill, experience, or insight in this learning center. The objectives might be directly related to the particular class session or might be a part of a unit of study that could continue for weeks or months. Within a particular center there might be one way of exploring and discovering, such as researching a historical event and recording findings, or there might be choices in discovery, such as reading, listening, interviewing, composing, analyzing, etc. The work of each learning center might be an end in itself or, in combination with other work, define, describe, or depict a whole comprised of many parts. An example of the latter would be the pulling together of the factors that led to the Reformation, the interpretation of those factors, and the implications for the future of the Christian church. Such a gathering of individual and group work on various dimensions of a large issue might be the culmination of a unit of study in which each person had done one or two tasks in depth and was the recipient of the results of others' work in other areas.

The previous paragraph suggests that learning centers may be created around the topic to be studied and may include varieties of ways to take hold of the topic. They may also take shape in terms of degree of difficulty in comprehension, skill requirements, independent work habits, knowledge, patience, persistence, or other factors in which there are great variables among learners. Frequently in intergenerational contexts or where multiple grades meet together such gradations are acknowledged by designating certain learning centers for those who like to read, act, or draw, for those who like to work alone, for those who like

to work with someone else, or for those who expect to be here for three sessions and can spend the time needed to solve this problem. In some instances certain centers are designated as Step One centers and others as Step Two, etc.

TEACHER AND STUDENT CONSIDERATIONS

The activities of the teacher or teaching team change when learning centers are utilized. While learners may do more work "on their own" than in a traditional classroom approach, teachers are in no way less involved or busy. A thorough grasp of what is to be taught and what one hopes the learners will experience is essential before the task of developing learning centers can be undertaken. Concurrent with this, the teacher must be convinced that learners are able to work on their own and that, in fact, such work might be as valuable or more so than what a teacher might tell them. Once the learning centers are conceptualized, putting together the directions and resources so that learners of a particular age, skill level, and interest can use them is time-consuming and careful work.

Some teachers as well as some students find it difficult to function effectively and happily in what may seem, initially, to be an unstructured environment. Some will find themselves adapting to what may seem a better way to teach and learn but others may never come to appreciate this new way. Young children who are unusually active or other children who are easily distracted may find the apparent freedom too much to deal with and teachers may find it better to keep them in a more controlled environment in which limits are reinforced more visibly and more often. Children and young people who grow accustomed to the learning center approach are often appreciative of the opportunity to work more at their own pace and with processes and materials that are theirs to control for a period of time. While students are thus engaged, teachers and their aides move among the learning centers ready to answer questions, assist where stumbling blocks in comprehension or use of materials have been noticed or mentioned, encourage efforts, and help groups to work more cooperatively on their specific tasks. Because teachers are not dealing with large groups, more individual attention is possible and teachers are also able to make note of learners as individuals. Frequently the sharing of faith questions and the witnessing to God's activity in one's life are made more possible in the smaller contexts of learning centers that are physically set apart from the rest of a larger classroom. It is possible that the use of learning centers will also facilitate more immediate and direct feedback to the learners so that satisfaction at accomplishment is experienced or remedial activity is quickly identified and can be pursued while interest and motivation may still be high. *See also* Cognitive

A SAMPLE LESSON PLAN
For Adults

Title: Who Do You Say That I Am?

Scripture: Mark 8:27-38

Central Truth: The most crucial question anyone can answer is that of Jesus, "Who do you say that I am?"

Lesson Aims: After having examined Mark 8:27-38, the adults will be able to:
1. Identify the various responses cited by the disciples in answer to the question, "Who do men say that I am?"
2. Explain the significance of the answer an individual chooses for a life-style.
3. Identify an area of their lives that will be affected as they follow Jesus.

Lesson Plan:

Introduction (10 minutes)

Write the word "Jesus" on the chalkboard and ask class members to suggest thoughts that come to mind. Write responses on the chalkboard.

Transition statement: The response we give to this name determines our direction in life.

Bible Study (30 minutes)

1. Read Mark 8:27-30

   On a map, indicate that Caesarea Philippi is located outside of Galilee, in the area of Philip. Link that to the lesson from Mark 6:14-29.

   List the eight key tenets of messianic expectations in the days of Jesus.

   Develop a discussion by using the following questions:
   - What were the responses given by the disciples to Jesus' question?
   - Why were these particular responses significant?
   - How much did Peter understand when he said that Jesus was the Christ?

2. Read Mark 8:31-33

   Continue the discussion by asking:
   - How would this teaching have affected the disciples? How does it strike you?

3. Read Mark 8:34-38

   Continue the discussion by asking:
   - How would this teaching have affected the disciples? How does it affect us in the age in which we live?
   - Why would this teaching directly follow the statement that Jesus is the Christ?

Application (10 minutes)

Discuss the following matters:
   - C. S. Lewis gave a set of contemporary responses to Jesus. He said that we judge him to be a legend, a liar, a lunatic, or Lord. Do you agree? Why?
   - If you decide that Jesus is the Christ, what will that mean for your life-style?
   - What does it mean, practically, to lose our lives? How does that demonstrate our commitment to Christ?

Commitment (5 minutes)

Ask again, "Who do you say that Christ is?" Then say, "Having answered that question, what change will that require in your life-style this week?" Encourage people to ask God to provide insight into the ways they need to change to follow him. Close with a prayer of commitment.

past), and/or too secular in approach because of the openness of the inquiry. The arguments vary in specifics, but the issues often center around the value of history, authority, the goals of education, and the role education plays in society.

Historically, liberal arts can be traced to the Greeks—Isocrates, Plato, and especially Aristotle. Aristotle's *Organon* urges the development of a body of knowledge by inductive reasoning. Knowing this body of knowledge develops intellectual virtue and liberates persons to be actors and producers of events rather than unfeeling reactors. The Pythagoreans had given form to mathematics (including arithmetic, geometry, astronomy, and music), which produced content for education. Rhetoric (the preparation of wise organization of ideas) and dialectic, to which Aristotle added rudimentary forms of grammar, provided the methods of ordering the content. These became the seven liberal arts that have become central in educational thought to this day.

If the purpose of Greek education (*paideia*) was for the good of the public, Cicero in the republic of Rome urged the development of orators who by learning and character could represent *humanitas* (humanity) and carry on public life in a just way. For Cicero the study of liberal arts was foundational toward developing *humanitas*.

Imperial Rome, in need of support for the state, moved away from the open inquiry the liberal arts had provided toward an approach that turned liberal arts into an encyclopedic exercise of making compilations of past knowledge. Taking the need for organization of knowledge to an extreme, the Romans developed the *compendium*, which ordered knowledge. However, the process became rigid, inquiry was stifled, and the compendium was rotely learned without relevance and application. By the sixth century, Roman education had lost the vitality of the original conception of liberal arts.

Classical learning and the liberal arts were part of the significant background in the Greco-Roman world of the early Christians. While church fathers like Augustine in the fifth century saw value in liberal studies as preparatory for a Christian life, the eschatological and ascetic perspectives overwhelmed Greek ideals of education. The monasteries that arose as an outcome of the ascetic dimension of the Christian faith ironically were major centers of preservation of classical learning.

It was not until the recovery of the classical traditions in the movements that became the sixteenth-century Renaissance that liberal arts were widely viewed to be important again. Reaction to the conservatism and control by the church was intensified as classic views were recovered. Humanism, which focused on development of the well-rounded person, insisted on the return to the study of the liberal arts.

Martin Luther (1483–1546) made much use of humanistic studies in his scriptural work in particular and encouraged wider education in the liberal arts. Erasmus (1466?–1536) attempted to fuse classical views and Christianity.

Liberal arts were organizing curriculum once more. Nineteenth-century science posed a new test of the value of the liberal arts in seeking practical rather than abstract learning. The debate was a strong one. Cardinal John Henry Newman in *The Idea of a University* (1852) was a strong advocate of the liberal arts as the way to cultivate the mind. Robert Hutchins in the twentieth century made similar arguments in opposition to John Dewey and others who urged more pragmatic studies. *See also* Curriculum; Greek Education (Ancient); History of Christian Education; Humanism; Roman Education (Ancient).

R. A. Olson

Liberalism

Liberalism is a positive attitude toward change expressed in both philosophies and policies. Liberal philosophies emphasize freedom of individuals to act or express themselves in a manner of their own choosing. Liberal theologies emphasize humanitarian values and a loving and continuously creating God. Liberal political philosophies emphasize representative forms of government, and liberal social programs emphasize nonrevolutionary progress and reform.

Liberalism in modern times began with the French philosopher René Descartes (1596–1650), whose statement was, "I think, therefore I am." This sense of individual identity and freedom was at the root of both the French and American revolutions with their emphasis on individual liberty. In the nineteenth century, Charles Darwin established the working principle of evolution and some theologians adapted it as "God's way of creation." They applied the principle of progression to peoples and societies: human beings were growing morally better and their societies were becoming progressively more benevolent. Albrect Ritschl (1822–1889) presented the task of religion to be "God and man working together to bring better things to pass." William Ellery Channing (1780–1842) urged the humanitarian principle as a "ray of divinity in man." Although influenced by these foundations in the nineteenth century, in American Protestantism liberal theology is a twentieth-century phenomenon, beginning with the social gospel.

The social gospel was distinctively American and simultaneously a theology and a program for social progress. After the Civil War, Washington Gladden (1836–1918) glimpsed a religion that "laid hold of life with both hands" and proposed to "realize the kingdom of God in this world."

Walter Rauschenbusch (1861–1918) met "a terrifying insight into the condition of the working classes" in New York City and was convinced that society must be remodeled through Christianity as a philosophy with the church as an agent and the kingdom of God as a model. It has been said that the social gospel died in the Wall Street crash of 1929 and the Great Depression of the 1930s, but even the European neoorthodoxy that replaced it was strongly modified by the American liberal demand for practical and social relevance. It reemerged in the strategies of the civil rights movement, which insisted that segregation and poverty were not the intention of God, and in the philosophy of the death of God movement, which announced the demise of a deity isolated from the events of this world.

Liberal theology stresses divine fatherhood and human brotherhood rather than transcendental justice and majesty, portraying God as immanent in the world and permeating every part of human life. It rests on an understanding of Jesus as a man who labored in a carpenter shop and whose words about the dignity of human life and work could be taken as literal truth applicable to human affairs. It seeks to relate the message of salvation to society, to economic life and social institutions as well as to individuals. It tends to emphasize the obverse of the traditional doctrine of original sin, pointing to the inheritance of virtue and imagination by humanity as well as sinfulness. Both evil and good are the product of social conditions as much as inherent in human nature. It is humanity's sacred responsibility to lessen the causes for sin and to increase the causes for virtue. The kingdom of God is not a heavenly realm of another and far distant future life, but rather the reign of love and justice on this earth, as completely as possible as soon as possible. All human relationships and institutions should and can be brought under the control of love, sympathy, and service.

Liberal religious education is a practical expression of liberal theology. The classroom in the local church is where the kingdom of God begins, because there children who are physically and intellectually changing may be most effectively exposed to the possibilities of changing the world for the better. Exploring positive human relationships under the guidance of loving teachers is the basic strategy. Jesus and the ethical prophets are examples to be known and admired as role models. Learning is indicated by an increasing independence of response from the limitations of past and present circumstances. Religious education should give pupils, young and old, respect for and confidence in their capacities as children of God. They learn to think together about human conditions. The church should provide a set of observable and workable models that will enable a clear analysis of the shortcomings and possibilities of the social and political world. Education should

equip students with a sense of the unfinished business of the kingdom of God and prepare them to be effective in pursuing it.

In recent years, liberalism has come under attack. It is said to be unrealistic and permissive. Liberal movements for social change are said to be indistinguishable from far Left radicalism and simplistically interested in "doing good." Liberal theology is criticized as merely humanistic and secularized. Progressive education is said to have failed to teach "the three Rs." Liberal religious education is said to be "sub-Christian," producing adolescents and adults incapable of making moral choices. Though these criticisms may be justified, the distinctive emphases of the American liberal experience on historical change, personal growth, divine-human partnership, and social responsibility are permanent influences in twentieth-century life and thinking. *See also* Freedom; Liberation Theology; Neoorthodoxy; Progressive Education; Social Gospel; Theology and Education.

W. R. Rood

Liberation Theology

Liberation theology is reflection about God that emphasizes the freeing of people from their oppressions. These theologies (it is better to recognize a number of them) emerged in the last two decades as Christians struggled against oppressive forces holding them captive and saw God's action in Jesus Christ as being involved in their liberation. That reflection about God came from the actual involvement of Christians as they tried to do God's will in this world.

DEVELOPMENT

The impetus arose from several Christian traditions, but the term itself refers directly to the work of Latin American Christians, lay, clergy, and professional theologians, who found their life situation increasingly opposite to the biblical pictures of God's love and righteousness at work in the world. As they analyzed their dilemma, they described the saving action of God in terms of liberation—liberation from personal sin, from oppression under the structure of society, and from the powerlessness of their condition.

The most obvious oppression in the Latin American situation was political and economic. The majority of people were hungry. In most countries the gap was wide between rich and poor. Relatively few people or families owned most of the land and wealth, while the large majority of people were poor, many of them desperately poor. The government and the military supported the status quo. Harsh oppression and torture were not unusual. As a result the people, led by their priests, began to ask why God allowed such a condition to exist.

Since Vatican II, the Catholic church had been increasingly sensitive to the plight of the poor, as faithful Catholic people who were suffering in Latin America and elsewhere increased in numbers. The Latin American Bishops' Conference at Medellin in 1968 proclaimed that God was on the side of the poor. The fatalistic use of the concept of "God wills it" began to be challenged.

Small groups called Christian base communities began to form in many countries. They studied the Bible and talked about their situations. Many priests and religious sisters took part in those groups, and they began to share the emerging interpretation that the situation was not the way God willed it, but that God willed their liberation from the injustices under which they suffered. That growing sense of restlessness and protest came out of the experience of oppressed people.

Leaders who had studied Marx in their higher education training led people to understand their situation in that way. They found Marx's social analysis helpful in interpreting their situation, in part because Marx described how the capitalistic system bore heavily upon the poor and powerless and used religion as a way of keeping people passive under the injustices of the system. Most powerful church and political leaders saw great danger, however, in the Marxist analysis. They accused liberation theologians of following Marx instead of Christ. So the debate has raged over many years.

Liberation theologians, as they came to be called, used the social sciences as their tools for analysis. They found insights of sociology helpful in understanding why people are kept under subjection and how the social structures perpetuate that subjection. They agreed with Marx that conflict is present in society because power is used to establish and to maintain an unfair status quo. They believed people came to know through action and emphasized praxis, a term that included both action and reflection, not just what Westerners mean when they say "practice." Their different starting point—with the poor—meant they began their theologizing with the experience of powerlessness.

The foundational work was Gustavo Gutierrez's A Theology of Liberation, published in Spanish in 1971 and in English in 1973. In that book and later writings by him and other theologians the basic theological positions have been developed. Liberation includes historical liberation from oppression and a chance at a more fulfilled human life on this earth. It also includes liberation from sin and names both personal and social sin as being involved in the injustices from which God is working to liberate people.

Following the lead of Latin American liberation theology, other theologies began to arise from oppressed people in society. Black theology posed a clear challenge to the identification of God with the status quo and affirmed a God of the blacks who was working to liberate them from sins of racism. Women who shared their stories began to articulate their opposition to the dominant theology, which they saw as supporting the patriarchal structures of power in the church as well as in society. Christians who were gay and lesbian reflected in the same way on how their oppression was against the will of a liberating God. In Germany, "political theology" sounded some of the same themes.

Soon many Africans and Asians were analyzing their dependence upon Western theologies and beginning to publish their own theologies from their situations of oppression. Minjung theology from Korea recently has appeared, representing reflection about God's action in the liberation efforts of the poor and powerless in Korea. A Third World theology organization has sponsored meetings in different continents, so a network of liberation theologians is taking shape.

RESPONSE

At first the dominant theologians of the North Atlantic world did not respond seriously to liberation theology. Only gradually did they begin to face the implications of it for the church at large. That their power to define and legitimate theology was related to the power of the dominant socioeconomic and political structures of the global economy was a challenge difficult to deny. Political liberation for former colonies had not resulted in economic freedom from the global system, nor had it led to a better life for most people in the new countries. That was one reason Christians and their local leaders who lived in those situations had begun to ask questions about the church's position and its role in the struggle. Liberation theology had helped to articulate that challenge.

Conflict with the Catholic church also came. Although at the Puebla Conference in 1979 the Latin American bishops reaffirmed one of the central positions taken at Medellin more than a decade earlier—that God has a bias for the poor—the Vatican began to give warnings against liberation theology primarily because of its use of Marxist social analysis. Some of the leading Latin American and other "liberation theologians" were told to minimize their public theologizing.

Similar strains appeared in Protestant churches, as many conservatives and people on the "religious Right" showed their deep fear of communism in criticizing liberation theology as they interpreted it. On the other side were the black and other ethnic theologians, feminist theologians, the "religious Left," and other oppressed groups in the churches. Under such pressures many people felt that the church was losing its leadership role in U. S. society. Others felt it had long since lost that power, and that the theological arguments over liberation and salvation merely demonstrated it.

IMPLICATIONS

Implications of the theology of liberation abound for the church and for Christian life and challenge much of "business-as-usual" Christianity. Although the call to liberation includes liberation from historical oppression and from the consequences of social as well as personal sin, liberation theologians do not see their work as outside the theological traditions of the church. They find the Exodus story a fundamental biblical base and see their orientation as recapturing a divine bias for the poor that is deeply rooted in Scripture. They assert that biblical faith both includes and transcends the demand for social liberation, but they emphasize the social dimensions of faith.

Action-reflection is the method. This approach is reflection on praxis, thinking in the midst of action, rather than starting with doctrine and trying to "apply" it to life. Education utilizing action-reflection invites learners to begin with their own experience—to name their own reality—and then critically reflect on that reality. Adding the scriptural dimension, the story and vision of the faith tradition, provides learners with the framework for decision, action, and commitment on behalf of justice. *See also* Action-Reflection; Conscientization; Consciousness-Raising; Praxis; Salvation; Social Action; Social Justice, Education for; Teaching Theory.

FOR FURTHER REFERENCE

Boff, L. and C. *Liberation Theology from Confrontation to Dialogue.* San Francisco: Harper & Row, 1986.

Brown, R. McA. *Theology in a New Key: Responding to Liberation Themes.* Philadelphia: Westminster, 1978.

Gutierrez, G. *A Theology of Liberation.* Maryknoll, NY: Orbis, 1973.

Lara-Braud, J. *What Is Liberation Theology?* Atlanta, GA: General Assembly Mission Board, Presbyterian Church in the U.S.A., 1980.

W. B. Kennedy

Library

See Resources and Resource Centers.

Life Map

A life map is the pattern of a person's spiritual journey. The term is the key concept in the book *Life Maps: Conversations on the Journey of Faith* by James Fowler and Sam Keen (1978).

Fowler's life map is structural developmental. A person's faith, or way of being in the world, develops in stages according to a predictable structure and shapes one's character, relationships, and life orientation. This life map of the faith journey has seven stages—primal, intuitive-projective, mythic-literal, synthetic-conventional, individuative-reflective, conjunctive, and universalizing.

Keen understands faith as the transformation that occurs when one surrenders control and begins to trust. The stages of his life map are child (construction of character), rebel (doubt), adult (self-confidence), outlaw (exploring, transcending), and lover and fool (openness, enlightenment).

While the term "life map" is not generally used by other theorists, developmental patterns or models have been proposed by such writers as Erik Erikson, Lawrence Kohlberg, Daniel Levinson, Roger Gould, and Robert Kegan. *See also* Faith Development.

D. E. Wingeier

Life-style

Life-style is the distinctive and therefore recognizable way in which an individual or society conducts its life. It is an intentionally consistent way of life or pattern of behavior that expresses one's attitudes, values, and goals, and reflects one's fundamental orientation to life.

The term was coined by psychoanalyst Alfred Adler to describe the constancy of an individual's personality that remains basically the same once it is firmly established in early childhood. One's life-style is formed through interaction with the environment and becomes a unique, personal result of the need for both adaptation to and differentiation from one's surroundings.

The growing child selects from among firsthand experiences, family interactions, observations of significant adults, and formative events those aspects that best fit into his or her own developing self-concept and need for effective functioning. Through this gradual, step-by-step process, a consistent, coherent pattern of behavior develops.

One's life-style, therefore, is an expression of one's personality structure, goals, coping system, and characteristic pattern of perceiving oneself and life's problems. It is an underlying, unifying pattern or direction that embraces both knowledge and feeling and influences all behavior. Each individual's life-style is unique and creative and provides stability to one's life.

Life-style is reflected in the kinds of goods and services acquired, the ways they are used, and how one's time is spent. It may be oriented toward gaining and consuming material things, developing and enjoying physical fitness and exercise, the pursuit of the arts, learning, or culture, the values of group sharing and community service, personal achievement and success, a concern for family and loved ones, or other values and goals.

Life-styles are influenced by cultural norms and expectations. Individual personality, character, and direction of life are shaped by the ethos, customs, and values of one's society. The view of time in a culture affects the pace of life. Patterns of communication influence the nature of relationships. Whether communities are organized hierarchically or democratically affects attitudes toward power, authority, and leadership. The status and roles assigned to men and women, young and old, insiders and outsiders shape the goals and expectations of individuals. The value placed upon persons and their uniqueness determines the balance between conformity and self-expression, compliance and assertion.

Life-style, whether individual or cultural, is composed of several elements—self-image, beliefs, attitudes, morals, relationships, behavior, and habits or customs.

One's self-concept shapes the way one lives. To see oneself as fun-loving and outgoing leads to a different life-style than a view of self as humble and dedicated. Persons growing up in a society that emphasizes obedience and uniformity will tend to accentuate their similarities, while individuals socialized to value uniqueness and novelty will be more likely to stress individual differences.

Life-style is also shaped by worldview. Whether one believes in an expanding universe, freedom of speech, a loving God, family loyalty, the dependability of technology, or the pursuit of happiness will have great impact on one's style of life. A social order that teaches belief in the ultimate authority of the state will foster a very different life-style than one that stresses belief in individual dignity.

Attitudes are mental positions and/or feelings toward a particular fact or state. Life-style is strongly influenced by the posture taken toward such matters as health, education, family, money, sex, and work. Positive or negative feelings toward these things may be a matter of individual choice or cultural conditioning or both, but they do shape life-style.

Views of right and wrong also help determine life-style. One's ethical ideas and moral standards affect both the ends one seeks and the means used to achieve them. Such moral qualities as integrity, justice, generosity, and compassion will dictate one type of life-style, while values like self-aggrandizement, control, comfort, and security tend to form a quite different pattern of living.

Relationships are another component of life-style. Some persons and cultures encourage intimacy in relationships, others are more distant and reserved. Relationships may be caring, conflicted, exploitative, nurturing, respectful, structured, or harmonious. They may be largely determined by social roles and expectations or open to individual initiative and exploration. One's life-style is strongly influenced by family relationships in childhood and is expressed through a network of relationships throughout life.

The ultimate indicators of life-style are behavior and habits. Self-image, beliefs, attitudes, morals, and relationships—all are expressed through the way we act. Our conduct and habits are the outward manifestation of life-style, the formulation in concrete actions and customs that makes it possible for different life-styles to be identified and described. They are the outward signs of our inner identity and character.

The way an individual or society conducts its life—that is its life-style. The way a religious person conducts his or her life in response to a faith commitment is a life-style, and one by which outsiders come to view that religion. The way a religious community conducts its life-style expresses its faith, whether this is viewed through attitudes and actions directed toward individual growth, concern within the community, involvement in the wider community, or a combination of these. Religious educators have always viewed the development of attitudes and actions as essential to real religious education, knowing that the form of a religion needs to be expressed in actions. Curriculum, Bible study, and activities are selected with this in mind. *See also* Behavior; Belief; Culture; Ethics; Personality, Theories of; Values.

D. E. Wingeier

Ligon, Ernest M.

Ernest Mayfield Ligon (1897–1984) is notable for a theory of character education developed both through a religious education curriculum and continuous research. The son of West Texas pioneers, he was a graduate of Texas Christian University (A.B., M.A.) and Yale University (B.D., Ph.D.). A Christian Church (Disciples of Christ) minister, he taught psychology at Yale, Connecticut College, and Union College (1929–1962). He was also founder and director of the Union College Character Research Project, a semiindependent affiliate sponsored by Eli Lilly and the Lilly Foundation, for some forty years (1935–1982).

Ligon was heir to Hartshorne and May's *Studies in the Nature of Character* (1928–1930), carrying that concern into new frontiers for psychology and education. For thirty years Ligon's books were influential, including *The Psychology of Christian Personality* (1935), *Their Future is Now* (1939), and *Dimensions of Character* (1956). In his later years he was increasingly interested in questions of developmental theory and posited hypotheses that can still challenge researchers or theorists. *See also* Character Development; Hartshorne, Hugh.

J. H. Peatling

Liturgical Movement

Liturgical movement is the name given to the Christian church's effort, in recent times, to recover an understanding of its worship and to renew liturgical ritual and language so as to enhance meaning and encourage fuller participation.

The movement's origin is most often attributed to Dom Prosper Guéranger and the Benedictine monks of Solesmes Abbey in France toward the middle of the nineteenth century in their work for the restoration of the liturgy generally and of Gregorian chant in particular. In the Roman Catholic church the movement was given impetus by the instructions of Pius X on church music and frequent Communion at the beginning of the twentieth century. The encyclical *Mediator Dei* (1947) of Pius XII is regarded by some as the most fundamental document in the movement's history in that it lays out the basic principles for the recovery of a truly participatory liturgy. Finally, the *Constitution on the Sacred Liturgy* of Vatican II has profoundly affected liturgical celebration.

Although beginning within the Roman Catholic communion, the liturgical movement has spread to most Christian churches. To a certain extent the work of the tractarian movement in nineteenth-century England paralleled that of Guéranger and the Benedictines, albeit with less success. Revisions of the *Book of Common Prayer* early in the twentieth century, the work of scholars such as Gabriel Hebert, and the liturgy of the Church of South India and of the Taizé community in France have all contributed to liturgical renewal and to its deeply ecumenical thrust. The Reformed churches too have participated in liturgical renewal through revisions of texts and hymnals, more frequent celebrations of the Eucharist, and a milder view of the Puritan strictures against formalistic worship.

The fundamental purpose of the liturgical movement is to give the liturgy back to the people of God as a source of spiritual nourishment and greater meaning in life, as a means of promoting an experience and understanding of church as Christ's work in the world, and as a ritual expression of committed Christian service.

In accomplishing this purpose the movement is concerned with the following:

1. The modification of esoteric rites, texts, and song so that they more clearly express what they signify and so that they are made more accessible to ordinary people with a view to greater liturgical participation (a difficult but all-important aspect of this is the honing of a language that worshipers understand but that also is adequate to symbolize God who is mystery, but mystery present)
2. The undertaking of a pastoral work of instruction, by word and example, as to the meaning and significance of liturgical ritual and the importance of active participation
3. The search for indigenous cultural forms (art, drama, symbols, music) that are adequate to and can be adapted for divine worship
4. Careful preparation and performance of the liturgical rite
5. The training, instruction, and commissioning of competent and dedicated liturgical leaders

See also Language, Inclusive; Liturgy; Vatican II; Worship.

I. Knox

Liturgy

"Liturgy" comes from the Greek *leitourgia* meaning, literally, "work done on behalf of or pertaining to the people," a public service. The Septuagint translators gave the word a religious connotation by making it refer to divine worship, perhaps in keeping with the notion of a Jewish theocratic state whose ruler is Yahweh and whose people belong to Yahweh.

In the modern context it is best understood as the public worship offered to God by the church. Thus, private prayer is not liturgical prayer except for those moments of silence and private devotion that are integrated parts of a whole, properly constituted liturgical service. Further, the church must exist as a group of the faithful legitimately assembled and usually led by a designated minister in the worship of God. Thus, there is no liturgy without community; liturgy is community prayer.

Rules for what constitutes true liturgy and for the conduct of liturgical worship are laid down by church authorities more or less strictly in different denominations. One's view of what constitutes authentic liturgy will depend to a certain extent on how far one sees the need for its control by church authority.

LITURGICAL ELEMENTS

The basic elements of the liturgy are those of word and sacrament, by which we give expression to our need to symbolize God's supreme worth and dominion and to express our fealty through the virtue of religion. The word of the liturgy must be the word of God in Scripture, or firmly based therein, while the act or sacrament should express the ongoing life of the Christian community. Word and sacrament are used to give expression to the four basic thrusts of prayer, adoration, contrition, thanksgiving, and supplication.

The major liturgical work of the Christian community is the celebration of the Eucharist, the reenactment of the Lord's Last Supper with his disciples. At the Eucharist the church is most perfectly "one" (see John 17:21), gathered together in the Lord and blended as the grains of wheat in the eucharistic bread.

An essential aspect of liturgical service is ritual. Ritual expression is fundamental to the life of the community, and particularly to a faith community. The community must share its faith story by repetitive symbolic acts. Thus, music, drama, poetry, and dance as expressing the faith life of God's people have an important place in the liturgy, along with storytelling and the retelling of the Christian story. Also, liturgical rituals should be related to the cultural life of the people if they are to remain effective in helping to transmit the Christian faith story from generation to generation.

Liturgical ritual should lead beyond itself to the mystery of who God is. Thus, it should be familiar and unself-conscious. A balance must be found between the need to change symbols and rituals to meet new cultural expressions and the need for ritual to be familiar and unobtrusive.

"Celebration" and "worship" are words that are frequently used to describe what is taking place in liturgy. These words engage different human emotions and evoke various sets of responses corresponding to different experiences—veneration, awe, wonder, and deference, on the one hand (worship), and joyful conviviality and enthusiasm (celebration), on the other. Both these aspects of the human response to the presence of God must find their place in a well-enacted liturgy. God who is the transcendent "other" is also the God of immanence in Jesus Christ at the heart of all human life.

LITURGY AND RELIGIOUS EDUCATION

Since we make our personhood and enhance our self-understanding by our life rituals, it follows that for people of faith liturgical rituals, the rituals of worship, are an essential part of the Christian formative process and thus become eminently educational. This does not mean that liturgy is to be used merely as a pedagogical tool. Rather it means that liturgy teaches and it is through liturgy that the Christ story is experienced and expressed in the life of the church. We learn through experience and reinforce that learning by expression, or doing, thus providing further experience.

Thus, for example, liturgy brings us into contact with the mystery of God who is present. This experience finds expression in a life-style marked by an appreciation of and a reverence for the sacred in all of life. Again, by immersing us in the Christ story through the word in Scripture and through the sacramentality of ritual the liturgy provides an experience of the "nowness" of Christ's gift of himself. In reality, we meet Christ our Savior. Such experience finds expression in a life marked by meaning and a sense of the grateful acceptance of his gift of life. It also finds expression in the imitation of Christ's life of service, his work for the establishment of the kingdom of God. Further, by living, worshiping, and celebrating together the community experiences itself as *koinonia*, that is, fellowship, oneness in the Lord—in short, it experiences itself as church.

To experience we must participate, not simply wait to be entertained. Meaningful participation requires preparation. By suitable preparation the liturgy is made more relevant and instructive and thus the teaching role of the liturgy is enhanced.

Part of the preparation must include instruction that centers in the meaning of the liturgical symbols and the ritual undertaken. The understanding and appreciation of the role of story is also extremely important. Young children can be encouraged, at home and in religious education classes, to ask about these actions and symbols. They can be taken into the church to look more closely at the objects and vestments used and to note how the arrangement of space is related to liturgical use. Children and young people usually receive specific teaching at the time of first Communion or confirmation/church membership. New or returning adults are incorporated more fully into the faith community by having such information as part of their instruction.

As our liturgy remembers and reenacts the life of Christ and retells the Christian story so is the expression of our liturgical experience as Christian life-style similarly a reenactment by the church of the life of Christ. We live our liturgy and thus bring to life the old pedagogical maxim of learning by doing. *See also* Church Year; Eucharist; Koinonia; Lectionary; Liturgical Movement; Sacraments; Symbolism; Worship.

FOR FURTHER REFERENCE

Davies, J. G., ed. *A New Dictionary of Liturgy and Worship*. London: SCM, 1986.
Irwin, Kevin W. *Liturgy, Prayer and Spirituality*. New York: Paulist, 1984.
Micks, Marianne H. *The Future Present*. New York: Seabury, 1970.
Price, Charles P., and Louis Weil. *Liturgy for Living*. New York: Seabury, 1979.
Westerhoff, John, III. *Learning Through Liturgy*. New York: Seabury, 1983.

I. Knox

Locke, John

The first of the great empiricists, John Locke (1632–1704) spent most of his life in public service in England. He criticized the prevailing philosophical realism that defined reality in mathematical and mental models dependent upon "innate ideas" and deductive reasoning. In contrast, while recognizing the limitations of human experience and understanding, he argued that knowledge is acquired through sense experience and thorough reflection. Beneath his philosophical reflection was the concern to combat authoritarianism. In political and religious writings, Locke pleaded for tolerance as a means of overcoming sectarian disunity within English society and the imposition of "reality" by the politically powerful. He thereby provided the philosophical resources needed for scientific expansion and the extension of democratic institutions. In education he advocated using the actual experience of children and encouraging reflection on sense experience. In religion Locke used the empirical method to demonstrate the reasonableness of Christianity. *See also* Education, Theories of; Empiricism; Experience; Knowledge, Theories of.

J. L. Seymour

Long-range Planning

Long-range planning for religious education envisages the future. A committee given the responsibility for such planning has numerous options for approaching the task and numerous influences to consider.

THINKING THE FUTURE

To *plan* the future one first needs to *think* the future. And our thoughts of the future are heavily influenced by our current situation and viewpoints. As David Loye pointed out in a recent issue of *The Futurist*, our future forecasts differ dramatically depending on whether we are liberal or conservative, activist or inactivist, leader or follower, power-seeking or power-possessing.

Arnold Mitchell, in his book *The Nine American Lifestyles*, projects four general scenarios for the future. The Renaissance Future anticipates no great shortage of energy resources and fewer radical shifts in economics and leadership by the thinker-doers than the intellectuals. The Bouncy Prosperity Future projects that business will pick up, energy situations will get no worse, and prophecies of a doomsday will go unfulfilled. The Hard Times Future is just that; it projects one recession after another, rising crime, and an economy out of control. The Transformation Future expects shifts away from highly centralized government toward voluntary simplicity where people choose to live a more frugal life using the earth's resources responsibly.

A long-range planning committee attempting to think the future would want to use all available information and all such forecasts.

RETREAT TO PROJECT

Long-range planning can be a creative process, and creativity is enhanced when some or all of the process can be done in a retreat setting away from the demands of everyday life. Depending on the planning to be done, a Saturday or Sunday in such a setting may provide a planning committee adequate time and the environment necessary to draft some basic plans. A full weekend may make it possible to accomplish some more extensive planning.

The planning committee should be chosen well in advance and should be representative of parents, teachers, administrators, congregational members, clergy, and others who will ultimately be affected by the outcome of planning. Subcommittees should then be appointed to research specific matters that will bear upon the long-range planning. The work of these subcommittees may take weeks or perhaps even months, but the information and data gathered by them will be useful tools in long-range planning. The subcommittees should do all of the following things:

1. Establish the theological foundations important to the congregation and consonant with its faith tradition

2. Describe educational understandings on which curriculum decisions and methods for teaching will be based

3. Determine goals for the educational enterprise

4. Get statistics on the present size and ages of the congregational members and determine probable future statistics based on projections for the local community

5. Decide upon an optimum size of the congregation and possible means for reaching this goal

6. Review present religious education classes and curriculum and prepare suggestions for changes that may be required

7. Consider the possibilities for satellite religious education programs

8. Plan for necessary leadership recruitment and development for the coming year, and for three to five years ahead

9. Inventory the current physical space and condition of facilities and prepare conditional recommendations for renovations, replacements, and additions

10. Evaluate current ministry to the congregation, community, and world, determining what proportion of budget and personnel is involved in each sector

11. Examine patterns of financial giving over the past five years, and suggest what financial planning needs to be done to encourage development

During the planning retreat itself visual rehearsal can be a useful tool. As a result of thinking in pictures, minute planning can often be done. People should be encouraged first to use their imaginations to solve problems and create scenarios for future action. Their images are then shared with the group. The feasibility of these images and ideas is not the point initially; these are meant to be visions through which the group can be challenged to think in pictures of new ministries. Evaluation comes later.

A desirability-feasibility grid is the next step. Possibilities envisioned in the previous exercise can be placed on a grid plotting both desirability and feasibility. The horizontal axis of the grid ranks desirability and the verticle axis ranks feasibility. A scale of one to five is used on each axis, with one as low value and five as high value. The suggestions accorded the highest combined values are the ones that the group will want to give the greatest consideration for implementation.

Open discussion and mutual acceptance are essential if the process of long-range planning is to go smoothly.

Long-range planning is accomplished when goals, dates, tasks, funds, and personnel are attached to each future event.

Once plans are complete, the planning committee will want to present findings and recommendations to the religious education committee, the governing board, and either the whole congregation or specific groups such as an adult forum or a parents' class. This gives the committee the opportunity of being heard, publicizes their work, and invites everyone to help implement plans for the future. *See also* Evaluation; Finance; Goals; Lesson Planning; Management; Planning; Statistics.

FOR FURTHER REFERENCE

Brown, Marion E. and Marjorie Prentice. *Christian Education In The Year 2000.* Valley Forge, PA: Jackson, 1984.

Hortin, John A. and Gerald D. Bailey. "Visualization: Theory and Applications For Teachers," *Reading Improvement* (1981).

Loye, David. "The Forecasting Brain," *The Futurist* (February, 1984).

Mitchell, Arnold. *The Nine American Lifestyles.* New York: Warner, 1984.

M. E. Brown

Lord's Supper

See Eucharist.

Love

Love as used in Scripture means a relation to another that appreciates and seeks the good of the other. The term "love" is used to translate a variety of Hebrew and Greek terms in the Hebrew and Christian Scriptures. Among the most important of these are *ahab* (outpouring love; Deut. 7:8), *hesed* (loving-kindness, loyalty; Ps. 36:7), *hen* (favor, grace; Prov. 8:35), *raham* (mercy, compassion; Deut. 30:3), *philia* (friendship; John 5:20)—and the key word for love in the New Testament, *agape* (self-giving love; e.g., John 3:16).

God's compassionate love for the world is emphasized throughout the biblical narrative, to be sure in integral relation with God's holiness and righteousness; and in 1 John 4:16 it is boldly asserted that "God is love." Yet God's love is not a weak and sentimental love but rather a "tough love" that feels the hurt of the world and works to heal it. Human love is seen as both a gift of and a response to God's love. In the Christian life such love is also to manifest God's loving work of reconciliation in Christ. "If God so loved us, we also ought to love one another" (1 John 4:11).

Such love has many facets; it includes respect for and appreciation of others, concern for their well-being, self-giving service, rejoicing and suffering with others, allowing them the freedom to be themselves, sharing with them in the struggle for a better life, and a wise care of creation. *See also* Ecology; God, Understandings of; Grace; Reconciliation.

FOR FURTHER REFERENCE

Haughton, Rosemary. *The Passionate God.* New York: Paulist, 1981.

Nygren, Anders. *Agape and Eros.* Chicago: University of Chicago Press, 1982.

Outka, Gene. *Agape.* New Haven, CT: Yale University Press, 1972.

Song, Choan-Seng. *The Compassionate God.* Maryknoll, NY: Orbis, 1982.

W. R. Barr

Loyola, Ignatius of

See Ignatius of Loyola.

Luther, Martin

Martin Luther (1483–1546), through his challenge to the theology and practice of the sixteenth-century Roman Catholic church, was largely responsible for the Protestant Reformation. He insisted that justification by grace through faith was the center of Christian faith. Luther saw salvation as a sheer gift of God. Human beings have no contribution to make to their own salvation. Christ bestows that gift of freedom from sin. Freed from sin, humans then can serve their neighbors without needlessly worrying about God's reward. The power of the theological ideas unleashed far-reaching changes in church and society.

A biblical scholar, theologian, and active preacher, Luther was an educator in the university and parish. He urged academic reform, particularly the inclusion of insights from humanism. He found that the study of primary sources through classical languages was essential to study of the Bible. His German translation of the Bible determined the shape of the German language. He published over six hundred works plus hymnody and liturgies.

In parish visits in 1528, Luther noted the lack of education among the laity and clergy. As a result he produced the *Small Catechism* with illustrations, simple language, and practical applications for the laity. It was designed for use in the home. The instructional method included memorization of the Apostles' Creed, Lord's Prayer, Decalogue, and prayers plus learning and discussion of Luther's "positive" explanations that focused on practical Christian living. He developed the *Large Catechism* for clergy who were poorly prepared to teach. Clergy were also urged to preach catechetical sermons. Luther's catechisms were the paradigm for catechisms by Calvin and later Catholic efforts in style, form, and to lesser degree theological content.

Luther's interest in education was not merely sectarian or parochial. As early as 1520 in *An Open Letter to the Christian Nobility of the German Nation* and in *On Christian Liberty*, Luther pleaded for university reform for the sake of the future of the nation and the development of universal education. He suggested that ample funds would be available to provide for education for all people if indulgences were stopped. His theological concern was knitted to his concern for the whole community.

In *To the Councilmen of All Cities of Germany That They Should Establish and Maintain Christian Schools* (1524) and *On Keeping Children in School* (1530) Luther encouraged the state to develop schools for all children even though parents are primarily responsible for their children's education. His curriculum included Latin, Greek, history, mathematics, singing, physical training, and practical duties of life.

His vision of education assumed that each person was called by God to offer service to others. Thus he insisted on skilled teachers who in turn could assist pupils to become good clergy, civil servants, and citizens. *See also* Catechism; Faith; Grace; History of Christian Education; Lutheran Education.

R. A. Olson

Lutheran Education

The Lutheran church is named for its founder, Martin Luther (1483–1546). At present, there are 8 million Lutherans in the United States.

MARTIN LUTHER'S INFLUENCE

Lutheran religious education properly begins with Luther himself, who, though renowned as a Reformer, was an educator as well as a theologian, scholar, musician, translator, and prolific writer. While his concern in reforming the church was theological, he realized that its success depended on education.

Luther wrote three major essays relating to education: *To the Councilmen of All Cities in Germany That They Establish and Maintain Christian Schools, On Keeping Children in School*, and *On Christian Freedom*. He argued that (1) education in the vernacular be compulsory for both boys and girls; (2) education be supported by the city or state since their officials were responsible for the general welfare of the community; (3) education was necessary for secular and church vocations, especially in leadership development; (4) scholarships be provided for needy students; (5) the curriculum include all disciplines: classical languages, dialectics, rhetoric, music, poetry, literature, history, mathematics, gymnastics, and, of course, theology and the Scriptures, which he considered the central core of education; and (6) libraries were essential for education.

Christians should be able to read the Scriptures in their own language, investigate the meaning, and make decisions regarding their faith. Luther had experienced the freedom to investigate and the right to debate under Renaissance teachers at the University of Erfurt. He translated the Scriptures into the vernacular so that all Christians could have that privilege.

Since Luther did not separate religion from education, all the statements above apply to his concept of religious education. In addition, based on his theology, Luther believed that God's word found in the Scriptures is God's message to humankind, the central Word is Jesus Christ, and the gospel, the good news of God's love and forgiveness through Christ Jesus, is the church's central message. Salvation is by faith alone, a gift of God's grace—works cannot make one righteous before God. The word has two dimensions: law, God's word of judgment, and gospel, God's word of love, forgiveness, and hope—grace. The Scriptures are definitive, the source and standard for faith and life, and the Holy Spirit calls persons to faith by the gospel.

Regarding methodology Luther suggested principles that teachers still use today:

- Provide simple instruction for small children.
- Provide materials appropriate to their development and ability.
- Recognize students' needs and that they really like to learn.
- Make learning enjoyable.
- Use concrete examples to illustrate abstract ideas.
- Teach language by speaking, not only by grammar.
- Provide multilingual instruction.
- Teach science and nature by observation.

In the twentieth century Lutherans extended Luther's ideas by developing carefully researched age-level characteristics and objectives, as well as coordinated curricula for the various educational agencies being used in the churches. The findings of researchers in educational philosophy, psychology, human development, and methodology have been included in these curricula and applied to the teaching of religion. Lutherans in many Third World countries have developed religious curricula appropriate to their culture.

In general, Lutherans throughout the world still hold to the idea that religion is central to education because it provides a purpose for life. Lutheran religious education is based on the Bible and continues to emphasize Luther's themes of Scripture, faith, and grace alone.

Wherever Lutherans went they took their Bible (in the vernacular), their hymnal, and Luther's *Small Catechism*, a summary of biblical doctrines he had prepared so that pastors, teachers, parents, and children might learn the main teachings of Christianity. That catechism is still a basic textbook for Lutherans in many countries throughout the world. Lutheran religious education meant studying the Bible, singing hymns, and memorizing the catechism.

SCHOOLS

Wherever Lutherans immigrated to, they also started schools in which religion was one of the basic subjects. In many countries the pattern of state-supported schools that had developed during the Reformation was followed. In other countries the schools were supported by congregations. Lutheran missionaries followed the same pattern of starting schools, which were welcomed in many countries where few schools were available to the general population.

Several theological movements have affected Lutheran religious education. The evangelical orthodoxy of the sixteenth century was followed by a scholasticism in the seventeenth century that became very stiff, formal, and intellectual. A. H. Francke and other Pietists at the University of Halle tried to counteract the intellectual "religion of the head" of the Scholastics with a personal approach and an appeal to emotions and evangelical concern, "religion of the heart." Later this group supplied many teachers and pastors to the Germans who migrated to America and Australia in the eighteenth and nineteenth centuries because of the theological rationalism that had taken over in the state churches. In America and Australia they were free to set up their own schools to preserve their theology.

In colonial times and in the early nineteenth century, Lutheran immigrants in America started schools that served the general public as well as their own children. Later when the states assumed responsibility for education, many Lutheran and other Protestant churches gave their schools and teachers to the state. The teachers continued to teach religion, thus accounting for the Protestant flavor of American public school education that lasted until the middle of the twentieth century.

The Lutheran church–Missouri Synod kept its schools because the founders had come to America for religious freedom and established schools to protect that freedom. Today its school system is the largest Protestant system in America. Several other Lutheran church bodies also have schools. Together these Lutheran schools serve nearly 500,000 children through more than 2,000 preschools, 1,500 elementary schools, and nearly 100 secondary schools.

The Lutheran church–Missouri Synod has founded nine colleges for the training of teachers for its schools. Curriculum guides, catechisms, Bible histories, hymnals, and music books were produced for the teaching of religion. This school movement developed *Lutheran Education*, the oldest professional educational journal in continuous publication in the United States, a descendant of *Evangelisch Lutherisches Schulblatt* (1865).

CHURCH PROGRAMS

Churches who had given their schools to the state participated in the Sunday school movement and later in other part-time agencies such as vacation Bible school and after-school weekday instruction. The Lutheran churches developed their own curricula in order to accommodate their concern for the sacraments.

The part-time agencies generally used volunteer teachers, many of whom were not professionally trained. Teachers' manuals, training courses, magazines, and in-service programs for local and national conferences and conventions were developed in an attempt to help the nonprofessional volunteers.

The limited time available in these agencies also led the Lutheran churches to develop weekday programs for children and comprehensive biblical study courses for adults. The Bethel Bible Series, "Word and Witness," and "Search" are examples of such adult programs.

Next to Luther's *Small Catechism*, the most universal program of religious education among Lutherans is the practice of confirmation and the instruction that precedes the ceremony. Over the past four centuries Lutherans have refused to call confirmation a sacrament, even though they often treat it as one. Until very recently it was a requirement to qualify persons for participation in the Lord's Supper, which became the final goal for religious education. Confirmation was graduation. Once young people had access to the sacrament, many felt no need for further education.

After World War II many Lutherans in Europe and America were concerned about the practice and did extensive research that resulted in some new directions. Confirmation is now defined as a lifelong educational and pastoral ministry of the church. It was removed as a prerequisite for participation in Holy Communion. Instead, congregations were encouraged to offer the Lord's Supper to children prior to the rite of confirmation and to lengthen the time of instruction, beginning earlier and continuing longer. New learning materials helped to implement the changes.

GENERAL CONTRIBUTIONS

Lutherans have a long history of educational concern at all levels: elementary, secondary, college, seminary, university, and most recently preschool. They have four and a half centuries of educational experience and tradition throughout the world following the direction set at the time of the Reformation, namely, a theology based on Luther's three themes: Scripture, grace, and faith alone, with Jesus Christ as the central Word.

Lutheran religious education has the potential to make some serious and important contributions to the modern scene. First, its emphasis on the need for a clear distinction between law and gospel, shows that the law serves theologically to convict the sinner and serves in a civic way to control and regulate society. It is not intended to serve as a way of life; Christians are to live under the gospel, exercising love and forgiveness. Lutheran educators understand Christians to be both sinners and saints, sinners because they are still in the flesh and daily sin much, saints because they daily receive the assurance of God's grace and forgiveness and thus stand justified. Lutheran education stresses that the gospel is the power that can affect growth in faith and make it effective in the lives of children and adults.

The gospel of love and forgiveness is the key for developing relationships through which learning and growth in faith take place in the community of believers, the Christian church. *See also* Catechism; Confirmation; Grace; History of Christian Education; Luther, Martin; Private Religious Schools; Public Schools and Religion.

D. Schulz

Magisterium

"Magisterium," taken from the Latin word *magister*, "teacher," refers to the teaching authority of the church. It is a term more significant in Roman Catholicism than in other Christian communions. The Catholic church teaches that in matters of faith or morals the authority and responsibility to teach the faithful resides with the bishops. The authority of the magisterium stems from the belief that the pope and the bishops are successors of Peter and the apostles. The biblical roots of this authority are drawn from Jesus' conferring authority on Simon Peter as leader of the Twelve. The passage most often used in support of this claim is Matthew 16:18–19: "I for my part declare to you, you are 'Rock' and on this rock I will build my church. . . . I will entrust to you the keys of the kingdom of heaven. Whatever you declare bound on earth shall be bound in heaven; whatever you declare loosed on earth shall be loosed in heaven" (NAB). The claim that the bishops also share in this teaching authority rests on such passages as Matthew 18:18 and 28:18–20. The third chapter (especially #24 and 25) of the *Dogmatic Constitution on the Church (Lumen Gentium)* spells out the teachings of Vatican II (1962–1965) on the magisterium.

Extraordinary magisterium and ordinary magisterium refer to the official forms in which the teaching of the hierarchy occurs. Extraordinary magisterium is exercised when the pope and bishops together as in an ecumenical council or the pope acting alone as head of the universal church teaches solemnly in a formal, public, and definitive way and declares that teaching binding in faith. Vatican I (1869–1870) declared such pronouncements infallible.

Ordinary magisterium is exercised when the bishops or the pope interpret and express the Christian message in the course of performance of their pastoral responsibilities. Such things as encyclicals, pastoral letters, universal catechisms, and dogmatic and pastoral constitutions fall into this category.

In the strictest sense, the magisterium refers to those who possess teaching authority in virtue of their office, that is, the pope and bishops.

In a broader sense and following the lead of Thomas Aquinas, the teaching authority lies in the magisterium of the cathedral chair (office of the bishops) and in the magisterium of the professorial chair (expertise of theologians). Thus the hierarchy and theologians working together are both responsible for teaching the faithful.

An even broader interpretation of the word "magisterium" has developed, especially since the Second Vatican Council. According to this interpretation, the whole people of God share in the teaching authority of the church. The *Dogmatic Constitution on the Church* states: "[The laity] are in their own way made sharers in the priestly, prophetic, and kingly functions of Christ. They are to carry out their own part in the mission of the whole Christian people with respect to the church and the world" (n. 31).

A tripartite pattern emerges then with those whose authority is derived from office (as with the pope or bishops) and those whose teaching authority is derived from expertise (as with theologians) sharing the responsibility for teaching authority with all members of the church. Thus the *sensus fidelium*, or "consensus of the faithful," contributes to the authority of the whole church to teach in the name of the whole church. This is not to suggest that the role played by bishops, theologians, and the whole church is the same. Each makes its own contribution to the magisterium.

Protestant denominations do not ordinarily speak in terms of magisterium and the obligation to give assent to the pronouncements of the bishops. Martin Luther rejected the infallible authority of councils and popes with the statement: "Unless I am convinced by the testimony of Scripture or by evidence of reason (for I do not believe the pope or the councils alone since it is proved that they have erred frequently and contradicted themselves), I am convicted by the Scripture I have quoted and held prisoner by conscience in the words of God." Calvin argued that there are good and bad councils depending on the reason and motivation for which they are called and the character of the bishops involved. Scripture has supremacy over councils; therefore councils do not merit blind obedience but rather a testing in the light of Scripture and of the above-mentioned criteria (motivation and character of participants).

The differences between the teaching of Luther and Calvin and that of the Catholic church appear fewer now than they did in the sixteenth century. Belief in the magisterium does not demand blind obedience but rather a general attitude of religious assent. Each person is endowed with free will and is responsible before God for judgments of conscience. Catholics agree that conscience is supreme before God, but they also believe that they have an obligation to seriously listen to and consider the pronouncements of the hierarchy in spite of past errors. *See also* Biblical Authority; Doctrine/Dogma; Heresy; History of Christian Education, Reformation; Lay Ministry; National Conference of Catholic Bishops; Tradition; Vatican II.

R. Coll

Maimonides

Moses Maimonides (1135–1204) is recognized as one of the most brilliant, original, and influential scholars of Jewish law and philosophy. He is often called in Jewish circles RaMBaM, an acronym for Rabbi Moses ben (son of) Maimon. Born in Cordova, Spain, he spent most of his adult life in Fostat (Old Cairo), Egypt, as a royal court physician and as the unofficial religious and political head of the Egyptian Jewish community. His important writings include a commentary on the Mishnah, responses to Jewish legal questions, and medical treatises.

Maimonides' outstanding work in Jewish law is the *Mishneh Torah* (lit., repetition of the Torah), a massive, comprehensive legal code. The Talmud, the primary source of postbiblical Jewish law, is not a systematic compendium of legal rules or decisions; therefore, Maimonides extracted the final decided laws from the other material in which they were buried. He also codified post-talmudic legal decisions, including his own. He arranged these according to a topical classification system that he created to facilitate ascertainment or study of the law for those without the time or competence to learn the Talmud and its commentaries. Maimonides also included the rationale for many laws, as well as considerable spiritual, ethical, and philosophical comments. This work was written in concise but elegant Hebrew so as to be accessible to all Jews. While provoking criticism from some rabbis, the *Mishneh Torah*'s fame and influence spread quickly, making it an authoritative source of Jewish law and itself the subject of voluminous commentaries.

The Guide for the Perplexed, Maimonides' preeminent philosophical treatise, seeks to refute the troubling, but superficial, belief that traditional Judaism and Aristotelian philosophy are incompatible. Maimonides sought to demonstrate this by explaining how correct biblical interpretation reveals "the secrets of the law." *The Guide* discusses, accordingly, such problematic topics as God's names, attributes, knowledge, will, and providence, as well as creation and prophecy. Not purely abstract, these secrets are the theoretical foundation of practical Jewish law (codified in the *Mishneh Torah*). Maimonides wrote *The Guide* in a complex, nonstraightforward style using Judeo-Arabic so that only those expert in both the rabbinic and philosophical traditions would understand the true meaning of these profound, but easily misunderstood, secrets. Modern scholars disagree on exactly how Maimonides synthesized Judaism and philosophy, and whether or not he ympathized more with one of the two traditions. *The Guide* was first translated into Hebrew in Maimonides' lifetime. It was so influential that virtually every subsequent work of medieval Jewish philosophy is in some way a response to it. Its espousal of Aristotelianism led to such vitriolic criticism from theological traditionalists that they excommunicated its readers. Many medieval Christian scholastics also knew *The Guide* through a Latin translation.

Maimonides had specific ideas on education: the content of curriculum, class procedures and methods, the character of a teacher, and even a teacher's classroom deportment. But this would be too rigid a schema for modern Jewish education. His importance for education today lies in the content of his philosophical and theological writings.

N. D. Goldberg

Mainline Church

The term mainline generally refers to several Protestant denominational groups of long standing on the religious scene. An alternative sometimes used is "mainstream."

While the exact groups referred to may vary depending on the user of the term, the establishment Reformation churches are most often intended. These include the Lutheran, Presbyterian/Reformed, Christian, Episcopalian, Methodist, Congregational/United Church of Christ, and Baptist churches.

The designation is not primarily based on numbers, for other Protestant religious groups may be larger. There are other significant Protestant groupings, each with a distinctive emphasis: evangelical, some of which would be included as congregations within each of the mainline groups; Pentecostal, whose distinctive characteristic is the charismatic witness; and many Anabaptist, who have traditionally cultivated apartness, with particular emphases on nonviolence and simplicity of life.

I. V. Cully

Management

Management is the process of evaluating, planning, organizing, staffing, leading, and directing the efforts of colleagues, and of employing all other resources in achieving stated goals. Management has no existence in and of itself but is dependent on an institution or organization, and more importantly, people. It is people who manage and carry responsibilities, perform tasks, and execute functions. Managers lead by arranging for people to execute whatever tasks may be necessary—most often delegating tasks to others rather than carrying them out themselves.

Unfortunately, the church and its ministries have tended to adopt business practices with only incidental reference to their suitability biblically. Shorthand definitions of management stress working with and through individuals and groups to accomplish organizational goals. A more Christian perspective may be that of meeting the needs of individuals as they work at accomplishing their tasks.

Foremost to the notion of a Christian view of management and leadership is the biblical concern for persons. Manipulation of one's colleagues is utterly unacceptable; the *imago dei* renders all people to be valued highly. Scripture is replete with models for conduct in human relationships. See, for example, Matthew 20:20–28; 23:1–12; Romans 12:3–21; Philippians 2:3–18; Acts 6:1–7; 15:1–21; and Exodus 18:9–26. Nehemiah is a case study in group management; Proverbs speaks to the issues of planning, staff selection, decision making, problem solving, and the process of change. Christians do well to reflect in particular on the management ministry of the Master of Managers.

The basic components of every organization are people, ideas, and things. Ideas create the need for conceptual thinking; things, for administration; and people, for leadership. Most management authorities state that the four central sequential functions are planning, organizing, directing, and controlling. In this model, activities such as evaluating and staffing are subsumed under planning and organizing, respectively. Because of their pertinence to religious ministries they will receive special attention.

PLANNING

The forgotten function of management is evaluation, particularly in churches and synagogues and their agencies and organizations. Poor managers fail to confront people and face facts realistically; they either dispense with or underplay evaluation. When evaluation is treated cavalierly the entire planning function is distorted; when it is conducted with compassion and objectivity, achievement and growth become possible. Evaluative instruments that hold excellent potential for accurate assessment have been developed and field tested by denominational bodies, American Baptists and Southern Baptists in particular.

Evaluation and planning are predicated on carefully structured purpose and mission statements. They themselves may not be readily measurable, but they must provide clear direction for where the institution wants to go. Religious organizations have an unfortunate tendency to define their purposes but never get around to stating clearly what they intend to do.

The more precisely stated the purposes, the greater the possibility for setting measurable objectives. While there should be room for the faith dimension of goals and objectives, the more definable and measurable they are in terms of time and performance the greater the likelihood of accomplishment. Goals, then, should be realistic, identifiable, and achievable. Long-range planning goals should be set in five-, three-, and one-year increments and reviewed at least annually.

Once accurate goals have been developed, effective strategies, programs, and budgets will flow readily. Strategies determine how and when to achieve goals. Programs establish priorities and dictate sequence and timing of the implementational steps. Budgets should allocate not only financial but all other resources—personnel, facilities, equipment, and so on.

After evaluating, forecasting, setting objectives, developing strategies, programming, and budgeting resources, one sets procedures and develops policies. Procedures describe the steps to be taken in order to accomplish a task. Policies are guides for making decisions. Policies are established by the appropriate leadership team after reviewing input from representatives reporting to them. Good policies encourage the delegation of decision making and do not try to predetermine all decisions. Policies concentrate on basic general approaches; procedures emphasize details.

ORGANIZING

The second sequential function in the management process is that of organizing, which includes four activities:

1. Establishing organizational structure
2. Delineating relationships
3. Creating position descriptions
4. Establishing position qualifications

Religious institutions tend to answer organizational problems with spiritual solutions and handle spiritual problems with organizational answers. With this caution in mind we turn to specifics.

With objectives established and plans in place to achieve them, an organization must be designed and constructed. When objectives are well honed they give shape to organizational structures. The next step, delineating relationships, introduces the inherent complexity of working with human beings. Good people relationships affect the facilitation, coordination, and definition and clarification of lines of responsibility and authority. Ideally, people should interact and connect effectively, but they cannot be organized like an assembly line. Administrators must be alert to ego and other psychological needs. Wise managers will also be sensitive to personality and skill differences in creating position descriptions and establishing qualifications; some flexibility should be built in.

An organization is its people. The religious institution is particularly vulnerable at the point of staffing. It must choose people of religious commitment and maturity who are fully competent and capable of discharging their tasks.

After staff members are selected, they must be given a thorough and sensitive orientation to familiarize them with the service/ministry situation. Performance evaluation is a necessary part of the accountability process, but to demand adherence to standards without adequate information and preparation is unfair.

Training programs aim at maintaining and improving current job performance; development programs seek to improve skills for future jobs. The need to train new or recently promoted volunteers or employees is self-evident. Such staff people usually need to learn new skills, and since their motivation is high, they welcome training. Training experienced people can be problematic.

Four procedures might be considered for assessing training needs:

1. Performance appraisal
2. Analysis of job requirements
3. Organizational analysis
4. Survey of human resources

Managers should then choose the appropriate on-the-job training vehicle:

1. Job rotation, in which one works on a series of tasks
2. Internship, in which job training is combined with related classroom instruction
3. Apprenticeship, in which one is trained under the tutelage of a highly skilled co-worker

DIRECTING

The third sequential function is that of bringing about purposeful action toward desired goals. When evaluating, planning, organizing, and staffing are under way we are ready for the implementational steps of the process of directing. They are delegating, motivating, coordinating, managing differences, and managing change.

Delegation is the assignment of formal authority, responsibility, and accountability for specific activities from one person to another. The extent to which managers delegate authority is influenced by such factors as the specific situation, the relationships involved, personalities, and the capabilities of the participants in a given situation. Delegation transfers and decentralizes legitimate organizational power.

The classic biblical incident is the delegation of the juridical power of Moses to others through the suggestion of his father-in-law Jethro in Exodus 18. But delegation is one thing; motivation is another.

Motivation is that which energizes, channels, and sustains an individual in performing goal-directed actions. While motives are difficult to discern we are not short on motivational theories. In essence, though, managers know that people are generally motivated to do something that will satisfy their own needs. People are responsive to praise and encouragement; they need to feel successful and fulfilled in their tasks; and they tend to be motivated intrinsically if they have the freedom and autonomy to perform their jobs in their own way.

When managers speak face to face with people and affirm them with genuinely respectful words and actions, people are more readily persuaded and inspired to take action, whether mutually agreed upon or not. Goals that motivate are goals that workers see as their own, especially goals they helped formulate.

Coordination is the integration of the activities of the separate parts of an organization into the combinations most effective in achieving organizational goals. Without coordination, individuals and departments lose sight of their place in and contribution to the institution. The relationship of coordination to motivation is obvious.

Communication is the key. The organizational structure and design determines how well information is transmitted and processed. Factors complicating the task usually fall into four areas:

1. Differences in perspective regarding particular goals
2. Differences in time dimensions
3. Differences in interpersonal working styles
4. Differences in methods and standards for evaluating progress

Despite similar religious commitment by staff members, failure in coordination may lead to major problems. As people present their viewpoints and make certain they are heard, managers must attempt to manage differences, that is, to resolve conflict in healthy ways. Conflict causes even colleagues to fabricate and magnify the faults and weaknesses in others. Energy is expended on nonproductive activities. Divisions are created. The real issue(s) must be identified and treated.

A step-by-step method of handling confrontation might be the following:

- Make sure you are dealing with facts, not guesses or hearsay.
- Make the initial confrontation in private.
- If private confrontation fails, take someone with you and try again.
- If the person resists resolution of the conflict, consider dissolving the relationship.

Matthew 18 addresses the last three steps.

Managing change is equally important. People frequently are unwilling to alter long-established attitudes, and change is often temporary. People resist change.

Kurt Lewin has developed a three-step sequential model of the change process. Unfreezing makes the need for change so obvious that the individual or organization can readily see and accept it. Through the process of identification and internalization a competent change agent fosters new values, attitudes, and behavior. Refreezing locks new behavior patterns into place by means of supporting or reinforcing mechanisms, so that they become the new norm. The change process is fraught with possibilities and problems. Religious leaders should become students of this process and of the ways their own leadership style may influence it.

CONTROLLING

The very term *controlling* is almost repugnant to those guided by biblical principles. Rightly understood, however, its negative overtones of domination and manipulation can be greatly diminished. Controlling means setting standards, measuring performance, and taking corrective action.

A reporting system will determine what critical data are needed and when and how tasks will be done and by whom. By measuring results, leaders gain the knowledge they need to take corrective action and to appropriately reward good work. This affirmation and encouragement of colleagues completes the controlling process.

RELIGIOUS EDUCATION

The enterprise of management in an educational agency is that of providing a bridge between policy and practice. Theological and biblical constructs must inform the church and its organizations as they develop philosophies of management. As the people of God the church is a redemptive fellowship, a *koinonia* that is indwelt by the Holy Spirit. The entire church should be viewed as the core and foundation of Christian education. If Christian education is to give people a liberating perspective on life, a balanced and comprehensive program is necessary, a program whose leaders have analyzed their goals and have structured a ministry toward their achievement. Good management facilitates the "works of service" that build the church (Eph. 4:12, 13). *See also* Director of Religious Education; Finance; Goals; Long-range Planning.

FOR FURTHER REFERENCE

Callahan, Kennon L. *Twelve Keys to an Effective Church*. San Francisco: Harper & Row, 1983.
Doll, Ronald C. *Supervision for Staff Development: Ideas and Application*. Boston: Allyn & Bacon, 1983.
Drucker, Peter F. *Management: Tasks, Responsibilities, Practices*. New York: Harper & Row, 1973.
Lewin, Kurt. In Paul Hersey and Kenneth H. Blanchard, *Management of Organizational Behavior: Utilizing Human Resources*, 4th ed. Englewood Cliffs, NJ: Prentice-Hall, 1982.
Rush, Myron. *Management: A Biblical Approach*. Wheaton: Victor Books, 1983.
Stoner, James A., and Charles Wankel. *Management*. 3d ed. Englewood Cliffs, NJ: Prentice-Hall, 1986.

W. S. Benson

Mann, Horace

Horace Mann (1796–1859) was a key figure in developing the public school system in the United States and moving the schools toward nonsectarian values. Born in Massachusetts, he studied and taught at Brown University and practiced law in Dedham and Boston. Between 1827 and 1837, he served in the Massachusetts legislature and state Senate.

Mann's educational career began in 1837 when he became secretary of the newly created state board of education. In his efforts to reorganize the schools, he held hopes that free, common education could improve the human race. He became a controversial figure as he worked to ensure public education for all children and to establish in the schools nonsectarian religious and moral values. He was concerned about public responsibility, so he published annual reports and advocated public taxation to support the schools. He also instituted reforms in textbooks and discipline to support what he called Christian, nondenominational values. The common schools of Massachusetts became a model emulated around the United States.

Mann returned to politics in 1848, serving in Congress until 1853. He ended his career as president of Antioch College in Ohio, where he cultivated his educational values in a black, coeducational context. *See also* History of Christian Education; Public Schools and Religion.

M. E. Moore

Map

A flat, generally two-dimensional visual aid that outlines, in graphic form, the boundaries, topographical features, and location of a particular geographical area is a map. A map is drawn to a selected scale demonstrating the relative positions of important features within the whole area being studied. Maps generally include such features as major cities, rivers, lakes, highways, mountains, and valleys. Maps may also chart other infor-

mation such as population, climate, cultural traditions, movements, and so on.

Because maps are useful in helping students visualize large land areas and the relative locations of neighboring nations, they serve as excellent supplementary aids for lectures. Further, because maps may be reproduced in several sizes, they are useful as research tools in books and other printed material. Many Bibles, for example, include maps of the ancient Near East in biblical times. Maps, along with charts, diagrams, and illustrations, provide much helpful supplemental information for several teaching methods. *See also* History, Teaching of; Visual Methods.

W. A. Smith

Marriage Enrichment

Marriage enrichment is an educational design for couples intended to improve the quality of their marital relationships. It is education, not therapy or counseling for troubled marriages. Constructed (in the words of various programs) "to make good marriages better," it concentrates upon communication skills and helps couples to more clearly identify their marital goals.

THE BASES

The procedures emerged during the 1960s when marriages seemed to be deteriorating under increasing stress, despite efforts of marital counselors, pastors, priests, and other professionals. The programs offered help to "subclinical" marriages (those with low-level, debilitating problems, those that are functioning well below the optimum, but that do not need the clinical help of a counselor). Such "subclinical" marriages seemed to be on the increase because of a large shift in societal expectations of marriage, including eroding roles of male and female, greater sexual satisfaction, more employment outside the home for the wife, and increasing awareness of the goals of women's liberation. Such changing expectations lead to greater confusion among couples and a heightening of stress. These problems are compounded in the cultures of North America by taboos against talking with other people about problems or difficulties in one's marriage.

According to *Toward Better Marriages: The Handbook of the Association of Couples for Marriage Enrichment*, the marriage retreat experience produces three results: "It enables the couple to make an honest assessment of where they now are in their marriage; to identify together the directions in which they want to seek future growth; and to learn new skills that will aid them in the growth process" (p. 12).

Churches and synagogues have provided the primary impetus and locus for the developing systems of marriage enrichment. One reason for this is that these groups have been achingly aware of the deteriorating quality of much of married life and are determined to do something about it. Also, marriage enrichment seems to be based upon understandings of human relationships that are theological in essence. Marriage is not simply physical or philosophical. It is a bond between two individuals with social consequences. Family is a profoundly central human organization, and marriage is the key to much of its success or failure.

Two people united in marriage are not simply "married singles," each with his or her own continuing set of values; in some mystical sense they become "one flesh," male and female, both made in the image of God. The object of the marriage is not primarily that of happiness and individual fulfillment, but that of building a relationship of supreme value.

Marriage enrichment is founded upon those dialogue patterns that Martin Buber described as "I and Thou." The purpose of marriage is communion—the need to share not simply thoughts and concepts, but feelings. Feelings are innate and are not to be judged; they just *are*. They are not controlled by an act of will. It is the action that follows the feeling that is shaped by will. In the "communion" of marriage, the skill of interpersonal communication is founded upon acceptance of these realities.

TYPES OF PROGRAMS

Three distinctly different types of marriage enrichment programs emerged during the 1960s.

One used a large-group format, with lectures and demonstrations followed by private discussion by each couple. This type was developed by Father Gabriel Calvo in Barcelona, Spain, as part of the Christian family movement in 1962. Known as "Marriage Encounter," it was brought to the United States by Father Calvo during the Christian family movement meetings at Notre Dame in 1967. Marriage Encounter was soon adapted by Protestant denominations, and in 1974 Jewish Marriage Encounter was developed by Rabbi Bernard Kligfield. The Marriage Encounter system is by far the largest of the various styles.

A second style uses small, intimate groups exclusively, in which couples discuss and share together with leaders a part of the group. This model was developed in 1962 by David and Vera Mace for the Society of Friends and became known as the "Quaker Model."

The third type combines both elements, presentations by leaders and involvement of couples with each other. This style, known as "Marriage Communication Labs" and launched nationwide in 1965, emerged in the model developed by Leon and Antoinette Smith for the Methodist church.

Consider briefly the salient features of each type. The Catholic expression of Marriage Encounter uses a married couple and a priest as the leader team. Their presentations and demonstrations systematically move from self-examination to the spiritual dimensions of the marital relationship. The "encounter" takes place between the wife and husband only, in private. Heavy use is made of writing, with each partner responding on paper to many questions posed by the leaders and then sharing their responses with their mate.

The Quaker Model has a minimum of organized structure. Groups are small in size (five to eight couples) and no prepared program is presented. The agenda is developed by the expressed needs of the couples for specific areas of marital growth. The leader (or lead couple) must be skilled in small-group leadership dynamics. Extensive use of couple dialogue (in front of the other couples) builds trust and accountability.

The Marriage Communication Model uses lead couples exclusively and is flexible in size (one lead couple with five or six other couples, or up to twelve couples with two lead couples.) As in Marriage Encounter, the lead couples provide minilectures and demonstrations. As in the Quaker model, much of the interaction of spouses is in the presence of other couples. If it is a larger group with two lead couples, much of the time the group is divided, each half with a lead couple.

All three models are basically designed around a retreat or weekend of about forty-eight hours. All permit other forms, however, such as one night per week for several weeks; but these do not seem to be preferred. Each insists upon private sleeping rooms for each couple, and each provides time for the couples to be alone in work and play.

THE ORGANIZATION

The burgeoning growth of these marital programs led to the founding in 1973 of the Association of Couples for Marriage Enrichment (ACME), "to work for better marriages, beginning with our own." This organization sets leader standards, sponsors training programs for leaders from provisional to advanced, and provides leader certification for a number of denominational programs. It also has strongly emphasized the need for continuity through support groups for couples beyond the original retreat. Increasingly each of the systems has done this, building "Encounter Renewals," "Image Groups," and "Havurot," following the lead of ACME with its chapters in cities across the country. Further coordination and cross-fertilization occurred in 1975 with the creation of the Council of Affiliated Marriage Enrichment Organizations.

As might be expected, a certain amount of convergence among the three designs continues to evolve. Despite some obvious competition, each is strengthening the others with the wisdom of its own experience.

Although little evaluation of marriage enrichment programs was done in the early years, by the mid-1970s some groups were using evaluation forms, questionnaires, and subjective written feedback and a few were moving into more objective research. A decade later research into the effectiveness of programs indicated that marriage enrichment can be an effective agency for improving relationships, that relationship skills can be taught, and that the new openness to communication learned in the experience can be maintained over time. *See also* Adult Education; Communication Theory; Counseling; Human Relations Training.

FOR FURTHER REFERENCE

Gallagher, Fr. Chuck. *The Marriage Encounter.* New York: Bantam, 1978.

Hopkins, LaDonna and Paul, and David and Vera Mace. *Toward Better Marriages: The Handbook of the Association of Couples for Marriage Enrichment.* Winston-Salem, NC: Association of Couples for Marriage Enrichment, 1978.

Mace, David and Vera. *We Can Have Better Marriages—If We Really Want Them.* Nashville, TN: Abingdon, 1974.

Otto, Herbert A., ed. *Marriage and Family Enrichment: New Perspectives and Programs.* Nashville, TN: Abingdon, 1976.

T. McConnell

Marx, Karl

Born in Trier and educated at the universities of Bonn and Berlin, Karl Marx (1818–1883), in collaboration with Friedrich Engels and, revisionist scholars now say, with the significant contributions of his spouse, Jenny von Westphalen, is the father of Marxism, a revolutionary movement of social and economic theory.

Influenced in his early years by Hegel's (1770–1831) dialectical understanding of history and by the materialism of Feuerbach (1804–1872), Marx, at Berlin, embraced the atheism of the Left Hegelians and their call to constant criticism of and revolution against every status quo.

In Paris (1843–1845) Marx wrote a series of essays, *The Economic and Philosophic Manuscripts,* often referred to as the "early Marx" because of their humanistic tone and concern for the alienation of the individual person. But they contain the beginnings of Marx's economic interpretation of history, which receives mature expression in the "later Marx" as a "scientific" analysis of the economic laws (class struggle, class consciousness, etc.) that govern all historical evolution.

The best known works of the "later Marx" include *The German Ideology* (1846) and *The Communist Manifesto* (1848), both written in Brussels; *The Critique of Political Economy* (1859); and *Capital* (vol. 1 published in 1867 and vols. 2 and 3 edited by Engels and published in 1885 and 1894), which Marx wrote in London where he lived with Jenny from 1849 until his death in 1883.

The central principle of Marxism is dialectical materialism. Marx accepted that all reality is reducible to matter, that all ideas are reflections of the material conditions of life, and that history evolves dialectically by a process of class conflict. History, the product of human labor, began, Marx claimed, with classless societies and evolved to class forms of slave-master, serf-lord, and worker-capitalist in bourgeois society. Now, Marx promises, capitalism will inevitably destroy itself by its own inherent contradictions to usher in, through the revolution of the proletariat, a new classless and communist society of corporate ownership. Therein one will contribute according to one's ability and receive according to one's needs.

While Marx's atheism and materialism inevitably clash with basic tenets of Jewish and Christian faith, aspects of his system of analysis have been used by some theologians and religious educators. Liberation theologians concerned with economic oppression sometimes use Marx's critique of capitalism as a tool of social analysis. Marx contended that human labor has a surplus value (i.e., we produce more than we need to live), but that in a capitalist economy the surplus value is unjustly retained by the employer while the worker becomes an "object" paid only enough to keep on producing. This exploitation can be redressed only by common ownership of the means and goods of production.

Religious educators committed to social justice and consciousness-raising education have also learned from Marx the extent to which all human ideas, laws, politics, and social and religious structures are a superstructure that reflects the economic infrastructure of society, i.e., the economic forces of production and economic relations expressed in systems of ownership, exchange, distribution, etc. This realization helps to promote a healthy skepticism of all ideology and encourages social analysis of historical structures to promote critical consciousness by asking, of every arrangement or idea, whose interest is being served and whose interest is being forgotten. *See also* Dialectic(s); Liberation Theology; Social Justice, Education for; Structuralism; Teaching Theory.

T. H. Groome

Maslow, Abraham

Abraham Harold Maslow (1908–1970) was an influential humanistic psychologist who developed a "third force" psychology distinct from deterministic behaviorism and Freudian psychoanalysis. His best-known books are *Toward a Psychology of Being* (1962); *Religion, Values, and Peak Experiences* (1976); and *Motivation and Personality* (1970).

His theory of human nature emphasizes the themes of meaning, responsibility, value, and self-actualization. His research showed fully actualized persons to be characterized by clear vision, acceptance, purpose, autonomy, compassion, moral conviction, and creativity. They also enjoy "peak experiences," which are personal moments of intense joy, awe, clarity, and ecstasy, without fear or inhibition.

In Maslow's theory of motivation, behavior is caused by a hierarchy of needs—for survival, safety, belonging, esteem, self-actualization, and aesthetic experience.

These theories were developed during and after World War II, in an effort to show that hu-

man beings are capable of much more than hatred and prejudice—the openness, unselfishness, care, and love of the self-actualized person. *See also* Personality, Theories of.

D. E. Wingeier

Maturation

Maturation may be defined as the process of coming to a relatively advanced level of physical, emotional, intellectual, and spiritual development as defined by the norms established for that level. The ground plan for the process of maturation is found in the genetic code of each individual. The way the process actually unfolds is in interaction with environmental factors such as the adequacy of nutrition, physical and emotional care, the quality of intellectual stimulation and interaction, and the depth of the spiritual life of those who take responsibility for nurture.

Maturation focuses on both the differentiation and the integration that take place at each of the stages of human growth. As the child grows, unique characteristics bud, bloom, and become a part of the whole organism, making possible more and more refined skills and abilities. At each stage, the varying aspects of growth (physical, emotional, intellectual, and spiritual) need to be interrelated so that the individual is not advanced in one area and retarded in another. In actuality, it is rare for any person to be maturing in all areas at the same pace. Growth itself is characterized by spurts, plateaus, and sometimes apparent periods of decline prior to growth again. The rhythm of maturation, discovered epigenetically in terms of optimum times for certain kinds of growth, makes possible educational and socializing experiences that help persons become both more differentiated and integrated (appropriately mature for their age and experience).

In all stages of maturation there is an implied norm of what mature life is—some end stage at which growth has reached the maximum level, when the person is considered highly developed or advanced, a fully functional adult.

THEORIES OF HUMAN DEVELOPMENT

Each theory of human development has its stages of maturation and its implied norms for the mature human being. The following theories of development have been influential in religious education. The implied views of maturation and maturity inherent in each have been combined with varying biblical, theological, and educational assumptions in defining appropriate strategies for the religious education of persons at each of the stages of life.

One of the earlier developmental stage theories was that of Sigmund Freud. He focused on the stages of psychosexual development. These stages were related to age and were based upon biological growth but with profound psychological impact. Since Freud saw sexuality to be the central arena for self-definition and relationships, his implied norm for maturity in life was what he termed genital sexuality, in which the individual has developed positive feeling about his or her own sexuality and is able to express such affirmation with someone of the opposite sex in a context of love and productive work. The goal of maturity for Freud was for the person to be able "to love and to work" in the context of a healthy heterosexual relationship. The process of maturation points to important dynamics to work through in a positive way at each of the stages from the oral (birth to two years), anal (two to three years), phallic (three to five years), latency (six to eleven years), to the full genital stage (from puberty on to adulthood).

Carl Jung's four-stage theory of psychological growth has an implied norm of maturity that emphasizes the development of clear spiritual values. The four rather broad stages (childhood, youth, maturity, old age) have norms for successful maturation that are shaped in the light of the human pilgrimage toward spiritual values that are adequate for the second half of life and death. For example, stage three is actually called "maturity" (from thirty-five to forty on to sixty through sixty-nine). Here the individual faces a mid-life crisis during which he or she recognizes how distorted and lopsided life may have been with its emphasis on physical security and begins a spiritual pilgrimage in earnest. Mid-life is also a time of experimentation and acting out patterns that are counterproductive but actually quests for ultimate meaning. Stage four is old age (from sixty through sixty-nine on to death). In this stage, which Jung called the evening of life, mature persons seek deeper awareness of the collective unconscious, out of which they came at birth and to which they return at death.

Probably no theory of human development has been more influential in religious education than that of Erik Erikson. His eight-stage theory, presented in his book *Childhood and Society* (1950), and his interpretation of the virtues needed at each stage, found in *Insight and Responsibility* (1964), project not only the primary human issues for each stage but also norms for maturation at each stage. For instance, stage one is basic trust versus basic mistrust (birth to two years). The child who is nurtured and affirmed by his or her mother and others develops a sense of stability, a feeling of being loved and wanted, a sense of the numinous, and a sense that the environment is trustworthy. The child who does not experience such love, care, and trust can become physically and psychologically disabled. There is evidence of high infant mortality, autism, and re-

tardation when these primary needs are not met. The norm for evaluating the successfulness of the first two years of life is whether or not the child has a sense of hope and drive about moving on. The list of virtues at each of the stages becomes a set of norms for evaluating the degree to which each person matures appropriately. Success with early tasks makes it easier to negotiate later tasks. Each task is present in some way all through life.

The other stages (Autonomy vs. Shame and Doubt, Initiative vs. Guilt, Industry vs. Inferiority, Identity vs. Role Diffusion, Intimacy vs. Isolation, Generativity vs. Stagnation, and Ego Identity vs. Despair) are well known. The norms of successful maturation are not as well known. In addition to hope in the first two years of life, the other norms for evaluating maturity in subsequent stages are self-control and willpower, direction and purpose, a sense of competence, fidelity, love and affiliation, care and generativity, and wisdom.

The overall vision of the maturity in Erikson's work has been the development of a clear identity that encourages creative self-giving or generativity at each of the stages of life. These norms for growth have been very compatible with various curricular goals for many faith groups and have appeared repeatedly in leadership training designs and resources. Erikson's stages tend to be seen as providing norms and goals primarily for emotional development ("psychosocial" in his language).

Another theory that has influenced religious educators as well as other developmental theories is that of Jean Piaget. His theory of cognitive development with its four stages, the sensorimotor (birth to twenty-four months), the preoperational (two to seven years), the concrete operational (seven years to twelve years), and the formal operational (twelve to adult) is based on the following understandings concerning the maturation process. A central concept is the nature of a mental operation. A mental operation is a process of logical thought in which the person is able to say, "Because this is true and that is true, therefore, something else is true, logically." For instance, children in the preoperational stage have not developed the structures in the mind that allow them to relate items to one another logically. They tend to think with their perceptions without reference to cause and effect. Fact and fantasy get mixed up.

The process of maturation involves several principles. A child grows in mental ability as the child comes up against an experience that puts him or her into a state of disequilibrium. In that state of need the child discovers that his or her previous way of thinking (based on the schemas that have developed in the mind) is not adequate to solve the problem and put the individual back into a state of equilibrium. Disequilibrium opens the child to new ideas. So, the principles of assimilation and accommodation become operative. In the state of need the child's mind assimilates new information that can be tried out to see if it works. As this is done, the mind accommodates itself to the new approach by developing a new schema, which, in turn, becomes the construct through which the child perceives the incoming life of the world. This new schema, then, provides a workable solution to the disequilibrium. Therefore, the child goes back into a state of equilibrium and can function until the next problem arises to cause disequilibrium again. These steps are fundamental to the maturation process at each stage of mental development. The whole process is dynamic, cumulative, and interactive between assimilation and accommodation. Piaget calls this ongoing mental activity the adaptation process. This same pattern of maturation, with certain important variations, is found in other theories of development that have grown out of Piaget's work, especially Ronald Goldman's theory of the stages of religious thinking (*Religious Thinking from Childhood to Adolescence*, 1964), Lawrence Kohlberg's theory of moral development (*The Philosophy of Moral Development: Moral Stages and the Idea of Justice*, 1981), and James W. Fowler's faith development theory (*Stages of Faith: The Psychology of Human Development and the Quest for Meaning*, 1981).

It is important to note that there is increasing evidence that there are differences between the maturation of females and males both in terms of the dynamic factors at work and the vision of a fully mature male or female. The work of Carol Gilligan is promising (*In a Different Voice*, 1982). Another theory sensitive to these differences is Gabriel Moran's theory of religious education development (*Religious Education Development*, 1983). *See also* Adolescence; Adult Development; Aging; Child Development; Cognitive Development; Faith Development; Moral Development; Psychosocial Development; Young Adults.

R. L. Browning

Measurement

Measurement is a process of examining and judging concerning the worth, quality, significance, amount, degree, or merit of something. Measuring becomes a basis or standard for comparison. In measurement value judgments become an inescapable concept. Even when measuring is producing pure, cold, scientific data it has little meaning unless it can be applied to valuing components. The religious educator cannot escape valuing by simply burrowing into data. The information being gathered must have meaning if it is worthwhile.

Traditionally, measuring devices have been used in evaluating predetermined goals and objectives. The traditional question wrapped around an educational goal or outcome is, "Can it be measured?" A program, lesson, or session would be judged successful according to the extent that objectives could be measured and attained. Since educational objectives are essentially changes in people, measurement becomes the process for determining the degree to which these changes in behavior actually take place. This measurement of predetermined behaviors offers an educational approach that is systematic, formal, precise, and internally logical. For these reasons it has prevailed in all fields of educational endeavor including religious education.

But there are problems. Such an approach of measuring objectives is often authoritarian, discourages flexibility, and takes little account of the learner's experiences. Depending on how it is employed, it may contradict many of the central principles of learning—a collaborative environment, flexibility of format and direction, and the encouragement of experiential and self-directed learning.

If value questions (what is important and has meaning) are at the center of measuring devices, the unplanned results of the learning process are taken seriously. In valuing judgments a strong affective dimension becomes a part of the evaluating process. While some information and skill-based data can be measured, other outcomes will result in feelings of increased confidence, better interpersonal relationships, a new sense of purpose, and a changed self-concept.

VARIETIES OF MEASURING DEVICES

The explosion of instrumentation for educators in recent years has explored both objective and subjective criteria in measurement. J. W. Pfeiffer and J. E. Jones in *The 1982 Annual Handbook for Group Facilitators* define instruments as surveys, questionnaires, or inventories that have no predetermined correct answers. Instruments generate data for personal growth, teaching and learning, measurement, and research.

Measurement takes on a broader educational function when personal growth issues emerge. Instruments can be used to promote self-awareness and an analysis of personal growth issues in the area of attitudes, values, and personality characteristics. Many instruments also provide clear guidance on what the user can do with the results through a program for self-development.

When specific changes in the learner are the focus, instruments are helpful in teaching and training methodologies, primarily as feedback devices and self-directed plans for making changes.

When instruments are used for measurement they are used to assess, analyze, and diagnose personal, interpersonal, and group dynamics. Finally, instruments used for research generate, validate, or test theories. When used for theoretical rather than practical purposes, they become tools for more formal academic pursuits.

The four purposes for instruments are not mutually exclusive. Many instruments can be adapted into multiple uses. For example, the Thematic Apperception Test (Atkinson, 1958), once strictly a research instrument, is now used as a personal growth tool and can be used in a modified form to teach people about human needs such as achievement, affiliation, power, and the avoidance of failure.

There are numerous informal paper-and-pencil instruments that can be developed by teachers and leaders in religious education. Informal opinion surveys may be used regularly in classes or groups to secure views on a subject under discussion. The number of people to be surveyed, the means of tabulating results, and the way questions are stated are important facts in measuring and reflecting any significant consensus. Questions may be designed to produce yes-or-no or multiple-choice answers. Other questions can be designed that call for a brief response. Open-ended responses are more difficult to tabulate, but can be most helpful in obtaining the thoughts and feelings of persons. Some opinion surveys are designed as intensity scales. The responses on a five-point scale may range from "strongly agree" to "strongly disagree."

Another way to measure the more subjective values and meanings of the learner is through an attitude scale. Since attitudes are learned, they may be evaluated and unlearned. One way of doing this is through the use of a checklist of attitudes—a scale. Such a checklist may be made up of a series of statements about a subject with a multiple-choice answer scaled to show varying reactions.

An exciting educational process in measurement is the development of instrumentation "on the spot" with participants actually writing the items. An added advantage to this practice is that often the teacher or leader cannot locate (or did not anticipate the need for) an instrument that is appropriate to the situation. Few of these scales would stand up to statistical scrutiny. But spontaneously derived instruments are helpful in exploring concepts, generating here-and-now data for discussion, and developing new models for exploring interaction and learning.

An example comes from a group-building session. Group members are instructed to recall an individual in their past who has influenced them significantly and positively and then to write down two or three adjectives that describe how they experienced that person. Then the process is repeated for a person who influenced them both significantly and negatively. These two lists are called out, alphabetized, and posted. This instrument can then be developed into a three-to-five-point scale and used to guide discussion.

SELECTING A MEASURING DEVICE

The number of published and unpublished instruments for learning has become so great that selecting the right one for a particular use may be confusing. In more technical kinds of measuring devices the issues of reliability and validity become critical. Reliability simply means that the instrument will yield the same results for the same people on separate occasions, given the same conditions. Validity means that the instrument measures what it claims to. Another issue is the instrument's transparency, that is, how obvious it is that a leadership-style instrument is intended to measure leadership. If the instrument is transparent it will be easier for people who take the test to understand and trust the results.

But there are other questions that must be asked in selecting measuring instruments for learning:

1. Is the scoring dependent on the judgments of the scorer, or is there a standard key?

2. Is the instrument written at an appropriate reading level? Does it use a technical vocabulary?

3. Can the items be adapted to fit a particular situation?

4. Can it be reproduced or edited without special permission?

5. How much time is needed to prepare, administer, score, and interpret the instrument? Can the instrument be self-scored?

6. Are interpretive materials available and easily understood?

Although measurement devices may vary greatly, they all provide assessment and data gathering tools as well as a teaching- and learning-centered focus. They become a necessary part of the religious educator's repertoire of methodologies and can be effective in the most simple or more sophisticated learning settings. *See also* Evaluation; Goals; Methodology; Psychological Testing; Questionnaire; Research; Scientific Method; Statistics; Taxonomy; Teaching Theory.

FOR FURTHER REFERENCE

Atkinson, J. W., ed. *Motives in Fantasy, Action, and Society*. Princeton, NJ: Van Nostrand, 1958.

Oppenheim, A. N. *Questionnaire Design and Attitude Measurement*. New York: Basic Books, 1966.

Pfeiffer, J. W., and J. E. Jones, eds. *The Annual Handbook for Group Facilitators*. San Diego, CA: University Associates, 1972–1987.

Pfeiffer, J. W., R. Heslin, and J. E. Jones. *Instrumentation in Human Relations Training*. San Diego, CA: University Associates, 1976.

J.D. Hendrix

Media

Usually media are thought of as the mass media, particularly newspapers, radio, and television. But the mass media are only a portion of the media vehicles with which educators work.

A medium is a tool that literally stands between two or more people in a communication process. Its use influences the shape and thinking of the group and individual. As H. Marshall McLuhan has said, "The medium is the massage." Therefore, Christian educators need to ask what impact using a certain medium will have on the shape and thinking of society and on the shape and theology of the church.

Christian educators encounter and use media in three primary ways:

1. The mass media (such as newspapers), which are aimed at and create large audiences of people

2. Group media, which may include the tools of mass media but are directed at a smaller, select audience and may be used in more dialogical and community-building ways (for example, congregational video programs use televisions for display)

3. Personal media, which are primarily for internal reflection and self-communication (such as journal keeping)

MASS MEDIA

Concern about the content of mass media programming has been high for Christians. Exploitation of sex and violence and the use of racial and sexual stereotypes have been topics for education and action. Some attention has been given to the issue of the monopoly of mass media limiting diverse political and social viewpoints. As one reporter put it: "The media do not tell us what to think, but they do tell us what to think about." This is a concern for Christian education.

More subtle is the model the mass media have become for communication and education, even from the time of introduction of the print medium. The classic description "sender-message-receiver" presumes a one-way thrust (dialogue is essentially a double monolog). It supports dominance of information, tending to equate message with a quantity of information. Finally it suggests that the receiver is essentially a consumer and the sender is the source of knowledge.

Christian educators nevertheless have appreciated the benefits of mass media's reporting worldwide events and thereby minimizing isolationism. Awareness of human interdependence has been deepened with the advent of television and of satellite communications. But while mass media, from church curriculums to "MASH," provide many fine program resources, they have often resulted in passive education programs in the local setting.

GROUP MEDIA

Group media activities offer an alternative use of many of the same tools used by the mass media. They also employ many programs from mass media in alternative ways. *Probe*, the sharing newsletter developed ecumenically in the Pittsburgh area, is an instance of group media educational use of the print medium. Educators shared their resources and insights in a network fashion.

Cable TV has been used as a group medium in ecumenical worship dialogues. In Dubuque, Iowa, church services were taped and cablecast on Monday evenings primarily for dialogue discussion groups. Members of each tradition took turns responding to questions others had about their worship and faith. One large Roman Catholic church later adopted the Food Pantry offering element they had first seen in the cablecast service of a small United Methodist congregation.

Initial use of video in most local settings has usually been passive: the group views a presentation and then discusses it. Some are beginning to see that even pretaped programs can be used more actively and are encouraging participants to stop the videotape whenever they wish to ask a question or make a comment. In this way an essentially monological program can stimulate group discussion and the group begins to employ the program as an outside resource rather than as an expert guide for unquestioned information.

Low-cost and low-light videocameras are beginning to offer congregations or clusters opportunities to use video tools as group media. One confirmation class studied worship by taking a video recorder into the community and taping what they saw people worshiping, that is, valuing highly. They noted money, clothes, cars, and other material things. The camera aided their perception and the program they created undergirded their memory. Others are beginning to learn again from the elderly by videotaping intergenerational interviews and sharing them with classes and congregations.

The computer, initially put to work as a record keeper, is being used for education in many congregations. Many fear individualized instruction will further isolate members from each other and that doctrinal positions might be hardened if computers teach tractable students. Others have shown that computer-assisted education can leave educators time for group-building and reflection-stimulating activities while giving students help with the building blocks of dates, places, names, and events of history. They have used computers with small groups rather than individuals and have discovered that carefully constructed programs can stimulate small-group discussion and even occasion conceptual rethinking. It is also true, however, that programs could reinforce unthinking absorption of narrow viewpoints, as printed curriculums have.

But computers linked by telephones have enabled diverse views to be shared in group discussion of faith issues in small communities and nationwide. Computer networks now allow group-mediated sharing of the sort *Probe* represented in print. Local communities and even congregations have established their own networks.

PERSONAL MEDIA

Personal media uses are not new: the personal Bible, the devotional booklet, and a personal journal have long-standing histories. Now individuals and families have available video recorders and computers. Some may deepen their own isolation by turning still further inward, occupying their time with video and computers rather than being engaged with other people. Different users may find that their eyes are opened to a wider world as they are stimulated to ask others questions and to explore wider fields.

There are critical theological, educational, and ethical issues to be considered in every use of a medium. This is as true of the medium of print as it is of the newer mediums such as photography, television, video, radio, audio recording, and the computer.

Christian educators will need to participate reflectively and actively in appropriate use of the various media tools and to assist the people of the church in their own thoughtful use of these creative gifts. Each medium can be used to manipulate or to enable, to isolate individuals or to build community, to control thinking or to stimulate reflection, to immobilize people or to encourage them to act. Christian educators can provide tools to critique misuse and to enhance appropriate use of the media. A continuing source of perspective on media is the World Association for Christian Communication (122 King's Road, London SW3 4TR). *See also* Audial Methods; Books, Children's; Books, Religious; Cinema; Communication Theory; Computers; Journal Writing; Periodicals, Religious; Radio; Television; Visual Methods.

FOR FURTHER REFERENCE

Rossman, Parker. *Computers: Bridge to the Future.* Valley Forge, PA: Judson, 1985.

B. Everist

Meditation, Forms of

In most forms meditation entails discipline of mind and body for spiritual development through silence and an inward focusing of thought. Although primarily an Eastern religious custom, it has attracted interest among Christians at different periods of history and been adapted to Christian usage, particularly in the contemplative tradition. In the twelfth century Hugo of St. Victor in Marseilles, France, outlined the three phases of prayer as *cogitatio* (thought), *meditatio* (inward reflection on the *imago Dei*), and *contemplatio* (mystical experience). At various periods subsequent to this Westerners have looked with serious interest at meditative techniques used in Eastern religions, especially Hinduism and Buddhism. During the 1960s, Thomas Merton (1915–1968) led the way in study of Zen meditation as a possible cure for violence, racism, and other social ills of Western culture. Western appropriation of Eastern forms ranges all the way from simple exercises for the purpose of relaxation and collection of faculties to serious efforts to become swamis and rampoches.

YOGA

Some forms of yoga entail meditative exercises. Hatha yoga, perhaps the most common form employed in the West, concentrates exclusively on physical postures and breathing exercises. Fakirs can do remarkable feats in body control, such as allowing themselves to be buried for long periods. There is no directly religious purpose in these exercises; they are preparatory for other forms of yoga.

Bhakti yoga, a more developed system, pursues religious objectives such as merger with the "all-life" and the final synthesis as one probes into one's inner self. This form of yoga uses exercises similar to Buddhist ones.

ZEN BUDDHIST MEDITATION

An outgrowth of Hindu yoga, Zen envisions an eight-step ladder reaching toward the ultimate goal of nirvana ("extinction [of desire] and rebirth"). Step one involves a search for moral purity beginning with the five great commandments—not to kill, steal, commit adultery, lie, or drink intoxicating beverages. Compassion for one's fellow human beings is also viewed as an essential attitude for meditators.

Step two concerns common practices of piety and asceticism such as recitation or (preferably) loud chanting of litanies or scriptures. Meditators are also advised to repeat one of the short prayers that encompass the whole meaning and purpose of life. In India the sacred "Om" or "A-U-M" is often used.

Step three has to do with proper body posture. The most popular position is the lotus, in which the meditator sits crossed-legged with the soles of the feet resting on the thighs. Since this is quite uncomfortable, many sit on benches with hands resting on the thighs.

Step four entails regulation of breathing. Meditators begin with deep, quiet breaths, which gradually diminish until breathing reaches a minimum.

Step five initiates strictly inward and spiritual work as meditators begin to regulate thought processes. Meditators review their past life, particularly in its weakness. Not only the physical body but even the soul is seen dissolving as this unhappy *samsara*, the continual cycle of birth, misery, death, and rebirth that all must go through, runs its course. As this happens, however, they realize that liberation can be achieved if they submit joyfully and faithfully to the ethical duties of life. By lifelong meditation of this type, they may perceive the essence of their true nature or "original countenance." For Buddhists, therefore, meditation is the most important "work" human beings undertake. They forbid worship, prayer, praise, or similar activities in the hall of meditation precisely for this reason.

Step six is called *dharma*, a stage in meditation where meditators no longer depend on the outer senses but rather begin to experience new powers in the soul. Images and objects from the outer world, such as a sprouting seed or a crystal, may be compared with those from the spiritual sphere. Some schools also use mantras, words, or *objets d'art* at this stage.

Step seven is *Dhyana* or, in Japanese, *Zen*, the stage of contemplation or intuitive gazing. Here meditators are able to view life without being distracted by selfish desires. Things appear as they are in the inner world of the soul.

Step eight brings meditators to the consummation, called *samadhi*, where subject and object are completely merged and the self-consciousness of the subject disappears entirely. Selflessness takes the place of self-consciousness, effecting a cosmic "breakthrough." *Samadhi* is, of course, a transient state and thus leaves the still higher goal of *nirvana*, a permanent state of selflessness, the *summum bonum*. Contrary to earlier Western interpretations, *nirvana* does not mean complete extinction of being but only of the personal, self-centered life to which human beings cling; it is life completely purged of everything egocentric.

TRANSCENDENTAL MEDITATION (TM)

Transcendental meditation, popularized in the West by Maharishi Mahesh Yogi, stresses selection of a proper thought under guidance of a trained master of meditation. The thought, according to the maharishi, must be "harmonious and useful to the thinker and his or her surroundings." Since thoughts rise like ever larger bubbles from the subconscious to the conscious, meditators can ride the waves they create back into the subconscious and thus arrive at the state of pure consciousness or self-awareness. The result is an expansion of the capacity of the mind that will affect a meditator's whole mental and physical existence. Psychologists have shown measurable beneficial physiological effects of meditation such as decrease of the heartbeat, increase of the electrical resistance of the skin, and changes in body metabolism. The maharishi insisted that meditators learn from trained guides who could check their experiences.

CHRISTIAN MEDITATION

Christian meditation shows obvious affinities and even direct borrowing from Eastern types of meditation. The most direct heir of this influence is the contemplative tradition that began with the Gnostics, the Alexandrian Platonists, and the desert fathers and continued through the Middle Ages to the present day. In one respect, however, thanks especially to Origen (182–254), Christian meditation has differed significantly from Eastern, that is, in emphasizing Scriptures, or at least scriptural motifs, in meditation.

Origen inaugurated the practice of meditating on the Song of Songs as the discourse of Christ with the church of the individual soul. This method reached its peak in the sermons of Bernard of Clairvaux (1090–1153) and in the poetry and prose of John of the Cross (1542–1591). In meditation on this love poem one listens to the lover speaking to his beloved as if it were Christ saying loving things to the person meditating. In imagination the meditator, as it were, "makes love" to Christ as Christ "makes love" to the meditator. Imagination, of course, is key to what happens here, unlocking the emotions and enabling even the simplest person to open to the love of God.

Francis of Assisi (1182–1226) developed a simple form of meditation on the life of Christ that achieved its classic expression in the *Imitation of Christ* (ca. 1425) attributed to Thomas à Kempis and in Ignatius of Loyola's *Spiritual Exercises*. The object is to have the mind of Christ formed in one so that one would act like the Master himself. In the *Spiritual Exercises* (1540) Ignatius delineated specific exercises centering on the Gospels (especially Luke) to be followed during a four-week formation retreat. During the first week, one focuses on human sinfulness; during the second on the life of Christ; during the third on the Passion of Christ; and during the fourth on the resurrection and the kingdom of Christ. Through use of vivid imagination retreatants put themselves in the scene depicted in the Gospels, picturing the actual physical location. When the text does not describe a scene because the subject matter is not physical, they are to imagine themselves in surroundings that would produce the necessary emotional response. For example, if a text discusses deliverance from sins, one might imagine oneself surrounded by wild animals and from that situation entreat God's help.

Ignatius stressed both control of imagination by "consideration" and guidance of a director. Imagination can be very erratic and thus requires control.

From ancient times exploration into the subconscious has taken the form of analysis of dreams. Employing insights of psychotherapist Carl Jung, many Christians rely on experiences in dreams to interpret and to understand what is taking place deep within and to help them cope with the world around them, viewing dreams as a means of revelation. Since dreams mirror the inner condition, according to the Jungian view, when properly interpreted, they may serve as guideposts along the path of life and speak to human beings about their relationship with the Transcendent. Interpretation, of course, depends on intuitive understanding of the symbols that characterize dreams, somewhat as one might interpret a great painting or drama. Because it is highly subjective, however, most persons require the help of experts in dream interpretation.

In their concern for spiritual renewal the Puritans returned during the sixteenth and seventeenth centuries to medieval methods for the cultivation of piety, including meditation. In *The Saints' Everlasting Rest*, composed in 1648, Richard Baxter proposed a method quite similar to Ignatius of Loyola's. Meditators must free themselves first from "worldly" preoccupations. By "consideration," rational control of the process, they can safely release imagination to "open the door between the head and the heart" and make possible devotion. Baxter urged use of biblical images, soliloquies, and "sensible objects" to incite love, desire, hope, courage, and joy. Puritans, too, relied on the Song of Songs as well as New Testament images.

Members of the Society of Friends, or Quakers, have surpassed other Protestants in consistent concern for meditation. Their silent worship is a time of listening or expectant waiting. Friends employ a variety of methods, including oriental, during their worship. Often, however, they simply speak of "centering down," which means yielding to the "Light Within" in quiet resignation like a swimmer trusting the body to the buoyancy of the water.

LEARNING MEDITATION

These many forms of meditation are taught in the religious communities in which they are practiced. A guru or teacher accomplished in meditation leads the disciple(s) or community. Novices entering a religious order often undergo intensive training in the meditation techniques of their order, although today such training is being widely sought by laypeople as well.

Quaker meditation is taught to children in the family and as they participate in Sunday worship, remaining for increasingly longer periods.

This custom is finding wider usage among other traditions where meditation as a form of prayer is being encouraged. Today many of the growing number of prayer groups in Christian parishes are making use of meditative techniques. Some help participants prepare for personal and intercessory prayer; others, like the Ignatian method of picturing oneself in a biblical situation and responding to it, are aids to Bible study as well as devotion. *See also* Devotional Literature; Prayer; Retreat; Spiritual Direction; Spirituality.

E. G. Hinson

Memorization

Memorization is the process of learning material by heart in a way that it is understood, related to life, and retained for future reference. Scriptural material is basic, but in many traditions affirmations of faith and liturgical materials such as canticles, psalms, and hymns are memorized. In time past, but infrequently today, the questions and answers in the catechism were memorized.

Memorized Bible verses have long been valued for their guidance in daily decisions, for encouragement, and for providing resistance to temptation. Christ's defeat over Satan during his temptation in the wilderness was assisted by his facility with memorized Scripture. Memorization of biblical passages is commanded by God (Deut. 6:6), helps avoid sin (Ps. 119:11), and can lead to spiritual prosperity (Ps. 1:2, 3).

The ability to memorize does not depend on intelligence or an inherently good memory. Rather, it depends on development of the capacity for memorization. Memory is more than a repository for facts. It is a collection of experiences and information that are housed in the mind if the learner realizes they are needed for the future and if they are seen as important. This suggests that we can assist learners in memorization by impressing on them, in ways that are meaningful and important to them, the significance of material to be memorized.

Two types of memory can be identified: short-term and long-term. While short-term memory retains material only briefly, it serves to channel information into long-term memory. Material is more permanently retained if it is repeated or rehearsed. It also is remembered long-term when associated in some way with other parts of long-term memory. This suggests that the instructor should relate what is being memorized to other experiences stored in a learner's memory. Long-term memory, not short-term, appears to decline with age. However, as age advances, problems are experienced in retrieval from long-term memory, suggesting that assistance should be given to develop memory cues that help recall.

All leaders have experienced the problem of students who don't remember. Greatest memory losses occur within forty-eight hours. Apparently what is not quickly and frequently brought to mind tends to fade, making repetition and review essential. Memorized material that does not fade often becomes distorted by interference from previous learning, particularly if what is being memorized has similarities to things learned earlier. This can be avoided by careful distinction between previously memorized material and new.

When Scripture is being memorized, decisions will have to be made concerning which version to use. Here, the practice of the church and the age of learners will provide guidance. Leaders will have to decide whether memorization should be word for word or basic thoughts and ideas. Usually word for word is the accepted practice, but it should be recognized that understanding and application to life are ultimately more to be desired than word-perfect memory. It is best to have a memorization plan, assigning scriptures that are related to lessons or units being studied. Assigning a passage of verses to be memorized for a unit of lessons is generally preferred rather than assigning individual verses for each lesson. Care must be given to selecting scriptures appropriate for the chronological and spiritual development of the learners.

Rote memorization is in most cases counterproductive. It requires a great deal of effort, generally involves poor comprehension and meaningless (to the learner) recitation of words, and results in poor retention. Greater long-term memory comes from gaining learners' interest by using unique or novel stimuli related to what is being memorized, by identifying the main concept, and by repetition. Learners need to understand meanings of words and phrases in relation to everyday experiences. Involvement and assistance of parents at home aids in the process.

Use of a variety of media will also help. For children, materials can be printed on poster board and cut into pieces for students to reassemble. Word puzzles can be made by selecting a key word, cutting large letters from poster board to spell the word, and cutting each large letter in pieces, again for learners to assemble. Bible string-a-verse games have words of a verse printed on poster board in scrambled order. Each word has a brass brad that children connect with yarn to provide the correct order. A rebus format can be used, substituting pictures for words. These and other memory devices are explained in curriculum materials or in age-level methodology books for religious education. See also Bible in Religious Education, The; Bible Study; Learning Theory; Methodology.

D. H. Dirks

Men's Organizations

Historically men's organizations and the educational mission of the church, the people of God, have been closely related. The call came to Moses for a kind of organization of the men of the nation to stand with him in the leadership of the people. "And the Lord said to Moses, 'Gather for me seventy men of the elders of Israel . . . and let them take their stand there with you' " (Num. 11:16). In the twentieth century men's organizations related to the educational mission of the church range from loosely organized men's Bible classes in some local churches to highly organized bureaucracies found in others. Since this article treats men's organizations in general terms, it is suggested that those who seek more detailed knowledge turn to denominational sources.

Perhaps the most important concern religious education brings to men's organizations is the same concern it would bring to all organized groups within the church. A basic presupposition of religious education is that the community itself teaches by its life together. As important as any formal instruction is the learning that takes place in the very manner of life of the community. Education in the Christian community must never be thought of as accomplished by a set of rules about "how to teach." The educational mission of the church is the same as the mission of the church itself: to provide the opportunity for hearing and responding to God's offer of salvation and new life in Jesus Christ as he is made known in the Scriptures. The community that responds to the justice, grace, and forgiving love of God teaches by its life in community as well as by its words.

There have been men's organizations, particularly in the churches' Sunday schools, that have encouraged loyalty to their own organization above loyalty to the whole communion. They have had a complete worship service, their own music, their own offering unrelated to the needs adopted in the church budget, often their own service projects and their own "preacher," ordained or not. This type of organization of men within the church has often seemed to encourage more and more passive listening on the part of men rather than participation as advocated in religious education.

The Laymen's Missionary Movement in the early years of the twentieth century did much to arouse interest in organizing men of the church for committing themselves to the larger mission of the church. Celebrating the one-hundredth anniversary in 1906 of the famous "Haystack Prayer Meeting" did much to arouse the concern of these organizations of men for foreign missions. It was at this time that men's organizations began to appear in several denominations and to encourage men's work organized across denominational lines. The watchword was the popular slogan of the day—"evangelization of the world in this generation."

The general secretary of the Laymen's Missionary Movement (interdenominational) reported in 1911 that in the five preceding years there was seen the most extensive and inspiring missionary interest in modern times. But World Wars I and II seriously affected the continuance of men's organizations in the churches. Although that interest was revived for a while after the wars and some very important developments resulted, organized men's work seemed to have difficulties not found in organizations for women or young people. The men's group was at one time the place for informal discussions about issues which the men alone would later decide at a meeting of the governing board. But the men's group could no longer function in this regard as women came into the parish power structures. In this, men's church groups mirrored similar groups in the community today.

Some denominations continue to promote men's groups through a national office. The United Methodist Church has such an office and aims to have a men's group in each local church with emphases on evangelism, mission (service), and spiritual growth. Prayer and Bible study groups are developing, and retreats are being held. The Presbyterian Church (U.S.A.) has a national office for men's groups that sponsors an annual nationwide conference. There are similar conferences on synodical and presbytery levels. Area retreats have attracted interest and local church groups of men frequently gather for a breakfast meeting with Bible study. The Southern Baptist Convention has a similar national office, and it too is encouraging spiritual life emphases. The Christian Reformed Church publishes Bible study material for men's groups.

Among evangelical churches, prayer breakfasts have become an avenue for gatherings of men. Similarly a United Church of Christ pastor tells of having a good response by inviting men who wish to join him for breakfast "downtown" on Friday mornings. Informally they discuss the theological implications of some recent event. The informal breakfast group seems to be one of the most viable options currently for a gathering of men. See also Conference; Retreat; Bible Study; Women's Organizations.

C. E. S. Kraemer

Mentor

Mentor was a character in Homer's *Odyssey*, a friend left in charge of Odysseus's household during his absence and responsible for the education and guidance of Telemachus, Odysseus's son. Mentor served as a faithful friend, adviser, helper, and educator. The goddess Athena took the form of Mentor when she intervened on behalf of Odysseus and Telemachus. The word "mentor" has come to mean a faithful friend and adviser, a master or sponsor.

The term today is used in business and education to describe the role of teacher, role model, and sponsor. A mentor is an important factor in career development. Expertise alone will often not suffice, and an older experienced person is needed to facilitate learning and advancement. Younger people, especially women in many professions, need the personal involvement and nurturing of a seasoned and successful professional. Although the word "mentor" implies a one-to-one relationship, the function has been institutionalized in the form of development teams in some corporate organizations.

As a teacher and role model, the mentor challenges and motivates the protégé, recognizing potential. The mentor endeavors to draw out those latent gifts and encourages their fledgling use. The mentor teaches necessary skills and jargon and sets standards of performance, introducing the other into the new social environment and sharing the benefit of prior experience that will make progress in the system possible.

As a helper and guide, the mentor becomes a facilitator, through position and experience opening doors for the younger one and giving guidance and support while new skills are exercised. The protégé benefits from power that is reflected if not shared outright. The mentor sees the protégé as who that person can become and structures experiences to bring this to pass. Seeing in the mentor an example of values, virtues, and achievement, the protégé is drawn toward what is now seen as possible. The mentoring relationship requires care, expertise, and commitment.

As a faithful friend, a mentor provides an emotional bond and support for the protégé. This personal quality of the relationship is important. The younger person often has feelings of respect, gratitude, and admiration for the more experienced guide, although at times there may be conflict in the development of the relationship.

If control or constraint rather than guidance is exercised by the mentor, the protégé may resist or withdraw. And if the protégé outdistances the mentor or reaches the point when support is no longer needed, the mentor may feel envious or unappreciated and abandoned. Both mentor and protégé must keep in mind the goal of the mentoring process—to have the protégé advance to the point that mentor and protégé can meet as equals.

The mentoring relationship is common in biblical literature and is well illustrated by the prophets. One might consider the schools of prophets rather like the corporate development teams. The one-to-one relationship is more common and can be recognized between Elijah and Elisha, Eli and Samuel, and Samuel and Saul.

Moses' relationship to Joshua, his hand-picked successor, expresses the mentoring relationship as well.

The New Testament provides other illustrations of such relationships, for example, Paul and Timothy. Barnabas was a mentor to Paul, interceding with the community at Jerusalem on Paul's behalf and facilitating Paul's development as an apostle. Paul himself saw his role as evangelist and teacher in this same way, and he expected the new Christian communities he founded and nurtured to use him as a role model. As the church developed, many others served as models of behavior and values, teaching by their own personal care and example and inspiring many to depth of Christian life and commitment.

The best example is Jesus himself in relationship to the disciples. As Athena took the form of Mentor aiding the human protagonists, so God, becoming one with humanity in Jesus, aids, guides, and protects as well as challenges and motivates humanity. The myth prefigures the function of Christ to the church.

The person of the Holy Spirit is in relation to the people of God in such a mentoring capacity, as teacher and guide expanding and completing the work of Jesus and remaining with us as Jesus departs to the Father. In everyday teaching and nurturing relationships it is possible that God is present and working in the caring and personal involvement.

An aspect of the role of a mentor that is not immediately evident in its modern counterparts but is very valid in the context of the church is the function of Mentor as steward for Odysseus. Mentor was made responsible for what belonged to Odysseus during his absence and was entrusted with the care and development of both persons and things. This sense of stewardship arising from commitment to a friend has the potential for personalizing our current understanding of stewardship. To understand a steward as one who not only guards, but guides and develops what has been entrusted to that steward raises the relationship above the level of merely caretaking. The mentoring relationship is an image of the guide and steward, through whom and in whose actions God remains at work creating and developing. See also Leadership Development; Role Model; Stewardship.

M. F. Purcell

Merici, Angela

Angela Merici (ca. 1470/1475–1540) was an Italian educator and founder of the Company of Saint Ursula. A mystical experience as a young adult convinced Merici that it was God's desire that she initiate a society of consecrated women. In the meantime, she devoted herself to charitable work, joining the Third Order Franciscans. After going to Brescia in 1516, she made many friends among members of the "Company of Divine Love," apparently collaborating in their work at the hospital of the "incurables" and in a broad range of charitable activity.

In 1516 Merici formed a group of twelve girls to assist her with activities of religious instruction; twenty-eight formalized their association by signing their names in the "Book of the Company of Saint Ursula" on 25 November 1535. Members of this company pledged to live simply and chastely; they lived at home and devoted their lives to education and charity, departing from the restrictions of women's cloistered communities. Especially notable was Merici's attentiveness to the formation and education of the members of the company. Believing that the renewal of family life and society would begin with the Christian education of future wives and mothers, she taught them how to teach the women whose lives they touched: family, friends, and the neighborhood children.

M. C. Boys

Metaphor

A metaphor is a figure of speech that asserts similarity between essentially unlike things. Religious metaphors draw images from everyday realities to express God's indirect and partial presence in the world. For example, "A mighty fortress is our God" and "God is my rock and my salvation" transfer words or phrases from the objects they usually designate (fortress and rock) to another reality (God) in order to convey the notion of God more vividly. Religious language is inherently metaphorical because the reality of God's transcendence cannot be literally expressed in human terms. Religious metaphors are therefore meant to be more than the poetic embellishment of a meaning that could be stated more directly. They are figures of speech used to formulate a human awareness of God. To this end, they move between a literalism that reduces God to human terms and a fanciful poetry that conveys nothing conceptual about God.

Because religious educators' primary purpose is to teach about God and God's revelation in Scripture, an understanding of metaphor is essential. This enables teachers to explore biblical metaphors with a class in order to better understand their meaning. See also Bible Study; God, Understandings of; Symbolism.

J. H. Stone

Methodist Education

The Methodist movement stems from the evangelical renewal begun by John Wesley (1703–1791) in England that soon spread to the American colonies. The present U.S. membership of the denomination is about nine million.

THE INFLUENCE OF JOHN WESLEY

The central role education has had within the Methodist tradition can be attributed to the importance that John Wesley gave to education. He inspired a popular education movement that led to extensive reform in the English system of education. Many considered Wesley to be the most important leader in education in eighteenth-century England. He was concerned with the widespread ignorance and illiteracy of his day and provided practical leadership in promoting new forms of education for both children and adults who had been denied schooling.

Central to Wesley's evangelistic movement was the belief that education and religion needed each other. Wesley taught those who came to hear him that they had within them the capacity to change, to read and to improve their minds, and to grow in the knowledge of God's love. The Methodist understanding of education was grounded in John Wesley's oft-quoted words: "Let us unite the two so long divided—knowledge and vital piety."

Wesley's concern for education led to four important developments. The first was the founding of schools for elementary and secondary instruction. The most important and permanent of these was the Kingswood School opened in 1784 near Bristol. Wesley envisioned Kingswood as a model for Christian education. The plan for the school included a highly organized community, a rigid set of rules to guide the religious life, and a curriculum of classical studies, language study, science, and Christian literature. In his *A Plain Account of Kingswood School* (1781) he wrote that the purpose of Christian education is to form the minds of the pupils in both wisdom and holiness "by instilling the principles of true religion, speculative and practical, and training them in the ancient way, that they might be rational, scriptural Christians."

Second, Wesley was a significant leader in the development of the Sunday school. It is reported that the Methodists organized more Sunday schools in England than any other group. The first Sunday school group of children in England was gathered together by Hannah Ball in High Wycombe eleven years before the Robert Raikes's school of 1780, which began the Sunday school movement. Inspired by Wesley's emphasis upon education, Hannah Ball conducted a school to train children in the Scriptures as well as in reading and writing. At a time when only one in fifty persons in England was literate, the growing Sunday schools became the forerunner of the English day school system.

A third contribution that Wesley made to education was a system of bands and classes for adults who had come under the influence of his preaching. He saw conversion as only the beginning of salvation and believed that faith was a lifelong process of growth. These small groups under the leadership of a layperson met weekly for prayer and Bible study. Unique to these groups was a system of accountability in which persons could remain members only as they continued to study and to grow in their Christian faithfulness. The phenomenal growth of the Methodist movement in England and America is often credited to the effectiveness of these class meetings in forming the minds of the Methodist people.

A fourth contribution to education by John Wesley was in the area of publishing and distributing popular literature. Wesley is credited with being the first in England to provide cheap and readable literature for the populace. Wesley not only wrote hundreds of tracts for distribution but arranged for the publication of cheap editions of some of the best books of his day. He disliked large books and did not hesitate to abridge any book he believed worth reading. His goal was to "furnish poor people with cheaper, shorter, and plainer books." He believed that "the work of grace would die out in one generation if the Methodists were not a reading people."

EARLY AMERICAN METHODISM

John Wesley's concern for education and its practical application to life was readily transferred to the new church in America. At the first Christmas Conference of American Methodists, it was voted on 1 January 1785 to establish a college patterned after Wesley's Kingswood School. Although short-lived, Cokesbury College was started in 1787 at Abingdon, Maryland. It was the hope of the first American bishop, Francis Asbury, that each conference would establish a boarding academy for the education of Methodist youth.

By the Civil War, the Methodist Episcopal church had founded more than two hundred schools in thirty-three of the thirty-four states. These included colleges, secondary schools, and seminaries. As the Methodist preachers followed the people westward, so did their educational institutions. Many of these schools were frontier institutions designed to train youth who were too poor to travel back East to the more established schools. Methodism located colleges near the people most in need of educational opportunity and innovated with work-study programs that would allow sons and daughters of poor farmers to get an education.

In spite of John Wesley's insistence on the training of preachers, ministerial education in

American Methodism was slow to develop. Favored was practical training that could be had while engaged in the work of ministry. The frontier conferences were hesitant to require a college education for ministry. The general sentiment was expressed in the *Discipline* of 1784, in which preachers were advised not to let education interfere with saving souls. In time, largely due to the influence of John Dempster, the first Methodist theological school was founded in 1839. First located in Newbury, Vermont, the school was moved to Boston in 1867 and became the Boston Theological Seminary.

The first Methodist Sunday school in America was founded by Bishop Francis Asbury in 1786 in Hanover County, Virginia. As in England, here the motivation was to provide both Christian education and literacy training. The General Conference in 1790 called for the establishment of Sunday schools for both white and black children: "Let us labour, as the heart and soul of one man, to establish Sunday Schools in, or near the place of public worship." Asbury urged that the preachers work to bring Christian education to all, including those in the most isolated hamlets.

At the 1827 meeting of the General Conference, the first general agency in Christian education was voted into existence with the establishment of a Methodist Sunday School Union. Dr. Nathan Bangs was elected the first correspondence secretary with responsibility to promote Sunday schools churchwide and to create and promote instructional materials in the Holy Scriptures for use by teachers.

These early developments in the Methodist Sunday school movement led at the same time to increased attention to Sunday school literature and to book publishing. *The Christian Advocate and Journal* had a column called "Sunday School Department" and the church called for books and tracts that would serve reading needs, especially of people living on the frontier. By 1844, the Methodist Episcopal church had in publication 352 Sunday school tracts and a number of general Sunday school periodicals, including *Children's Magazine*, *Youth's Instructor*, and *Sunday School Advocate*.

DIVISION AND UNION

Slavery and the Civil War were among the factors that led to church division in 1844. In 1846, when the first General Conference of the Methodist Episcopal Church, South, met, it was voted to continue the promotion of Sunday schools, and T. O. Summers was elected editor of a proposed new Sunday school paper. The Reconstruction years were difficult, and it took five years for *The Sunday School Visitor* to get out a first issue. A permanent Department of Sunday School Literature and an Office of the Sunday School Secretary were not established until 1870.

Possibly the most important leader in the development of the Sunday school movement in the Methodist Episcopal church was John H. Vincent. In 1868, Vincent was elected secretary of the Methodist Sunday School Union and editor of Sunday school literature. He popularized the Sunday school and developed a churchwide program that led to growth both in Sunday school attendance and in church membership, developed a system of teacher training, and expanded the publication of Sunday school literature.

In the Southern church, under the leadership of John W. Shackford, elected general secretary of the General Sunday School Board in 1922, great strides were made in leadership training and in encouraging churches to meet high standards in a program of education.

Another split within the ranks of Methodism led to the formation of the Methodist Protestant Church, organized in 1830 largely over the issues of bishops and the assignment of pastors to churches. Because of divisions caused by the Civil War and inadequate financial support, it was 1884 before this group developed a general agency for the promotion of the Sunday school and the publication of literature.

By the end of the 1920s, all three Methodist branches had become leaders in the Sunday church school movements. Together they created in 1939 a single board of education, the Methodist Union, to oversee educational functions, thereby giving education a central place in the Methodist church. It was organized into three divisions: educational institutions, local church, and editorial. Included under the local church was a new youth agency that was to bring together the Christian Endeavor and Epworth League into what was called the Methodist Youth Fellowship.

In 1968, the Evangelical United Brethren Church, itself a product of a long series of church mergers and maintaining a tradition dating from the early 1800s of Sunday school associations, Bible study groups, lay movements, and young people's work, and the Methodist church united to form the United Methodist Church. The United Methodist Church in 1972 established a program board for the local church called the Board of Discipleship. Education and church school publications were made sections in a board that included a dozen other "discipleship ministries" including lay life and work, stewardship, evangelism, worship, spiritual life, youth work, and family life. Education, rather than having a central place, became one of the elements in a total ministry of the local church. Also in 1972, a new General Board of Higher Education and Ministry was established to plan and guide the work of schools and colleges, theological education, special ministries such as chaplaincy, and lay church careers.

Among other American churches that have roots in the Wesleyan tradition are the African Methodist Episcopal Church, African Methodist

Episcopal Zion Church, Christian Methodist Episcopal Church, Free Methodist Church, and the Wesleyan Church. Each has unique doctrinal and ecclesiastical emphases, but they share a continuous concern for education—education at the local church level, higher education, and ministerial education. *See also* Bible Class; Black Experience and Religious Education; Class Meeting; History of Christian Education; Sunday School; Sunday School Movement.

FOR FURTHER REFERENCE

Encyclopedia of World Methodism. 2 vols. Nashville, TN: United Methodist Publishing House, 1974.

Schisley, John Q. *Christian Education in Local Methodist Churches.* Nashville, TN: Abingdon, 1969.

A. J. Moore

Methodology

Methodology is the science of method; it is wisdom about *how* something is done. Method is a systematic procedure for reaching a goal or doing inquiry into an area of study. It includes techniques and particular practices used to carry out a method.

In education, methodology includes wisdom about how teaching and learning take place and, also, wisdom about how research is done in the teaching/learning process.

TEACHING METHODOLOGIES

Until the 1930s most religious teaching was centered on transmitting knowledge of religious texts with the help of instruction by a teacher. The influence of such leaders as George Albert Coe (1862–1951), John Dewey (1859–1952), and William Clayton Bower (1878–1982) led to a greater stress on learning through experiences. In the years since 1930, an explosion has taken place in the psychosocial study of learning and motivation; the research indicates that learning is facilitated and motivation enhanced by certain teaching techniques and leadership styles. This research has fostered the use of many new techniques as well as shifts in the structures of the educational process.

Added to this has been considerable theological reflection on the authority of the Bible and historical tradition relative to the authority of the life experience of individuals and communities. This methodological question—whether the starting point of religious education should be the historical texts of the religious tradition or the life experience of the present community—was the focus of the debate between neoorthodox and progressive religious educators in the 1940s and 1950s. Since the 1970s, liberation theologians have encouraged religious communities to engage in theological reflection on social structures and actions. The accompanying methodological question is how persons can identify and analyze these social realities in the educational process.

Educational methods have been developed that are compatible with these and other educational and theological positions. Some of the basic methodologies commonly used in religious education include socialization, critical reflection, aesthetic, instructional, developmental, phenomenological, and humanistic methodologies.

Socialization methodologies are those focused on the transmission of culture and the incorporation of people into the culture. This was an early concern of John Dewey and of his contemporary Emanuel Gamoran, who saw the role of Jewish education as the transmission of Jewish civilization. The methods of socialization are basically embodied in the ordinary life of the religious community, especially in relationships and in rituals such as worship, the celebration of high holy days, and rites of passage. Socialization theorists usually emphasize the structures and relational patterns of the community, as well as the transmission of historical traditions through the life of the community.

Critical reflection methodologies begin with identification and analysis of the social situation, usually with the aim of critiquing and reforming it. Critical reflection has become an important means for analyzing social structures and how they affect the lives of people. It often includes dialogue comparing the existing social situation with the religious ideal, or vision. Critical reflection can be a method of approach to historical religious texts (through literary or sociocultural criticism), to the life of the present religious community, or to social realities past or present.

Aesthetic methodologies are those that utilize the visual arts, drama, dance, and literature in communication. Many religious educators have urged the use of these methods for the sake of stirring imagination and vision and for the sake of addressing the emotive and imagistic capacities of persons. The underlying assumption is that some knowledge is beyond linear, rational expression.

Instructional methodologies are almost taken for granted since they are so dominant in religious communities. These are the methods by which the knowledge, values, and actions of the religious community are transmitted by a teacher to learners, using the most effective methods of presentation known. Religious educators who have emphasized instruction have usually given careful attention to the findings of educational and psychological research on how people learn and on the effects of different modes of instruction.

Developmental methodologies include exploration of the environment, social activity and discourse, group decision making, and communication that is aimed at the developmental level of the learners. These methods are designed to promote growth. The focus is on the inner capacities of the learners and the nurture of these capacities in a wise and caring environment, rather than on teaching the community's knowledge and values. Two educational techniques that are often important in developmental methodologies are group discussion and free play in a safe and rich environment.

Phenomenological methodologies are those that encourage persons to name and interpret the meanings in their lives. The heart of the method is to observe and listen to oneself and others and to share one's perceptions in dialogue with others; hence, it is intersubjective. Persons often share their experiences or stories and, with others, interpret the deep meaning in those experiences for themselves. The purpose is to deepen one's sense of self and one's relationship with God and others.

Humanistic methodologies, influenced by humanistic psychology, focus on self-growth. Since they are based on trust of the learners, they are student-centered. Students create their own goals and environments for learning, and the teacher's role is to be accepting and to facilitate the student's goals. These methods attempt to address the many dimensions of human wholeness, usually giving special attention to the emotional dimension.

These methodologies overlap, and they are amenable to various combinations. Furthermore, some techniques (such as lecture or discussion) can be used with more than one methodology. The selection of a methodology is based on the aims of the educational process, on the nature of the social context, and the particular learners and teachers. Whether choosing one methodology over another rests with teachers or others setting educational policy, a knowledge of the subject is helpful in understanding the perspective from which methods supplied in the teaching material were formulated.

RESEARCH METHODOLOGIES

The purpose of research in education is to understand better the dynamics of teaching and learning and the meanings persons find in the teaching/learning process. Research includes study of the various factors influencing the educational process and also study of the perceptions and values of the teachers and learners. Research methodology, therefore, needs to be inclusive of those experimental methods designed to study cause and effect and those humanistic methods designed to study internal meanings. Some methods have been particularly common and useful in educational research.

Naturalistic observation has been used in education for teacher training and for exploratory research. In naturalistic observation, an observer makes systematic observations in a natural social setting on the basis of predecided categories or questions. The observer is typically an outsider to the setting and makes the observations as unobtrusively and with as much standardization as possible. Some basic limitations in this kind of research are the inevitable influence of the observer on the situation, the observer's lack of access to internal meaning information of the persons studied, and the minimal control of situation variables. Some strengths of naturalistic observation are the potential for observing individuals' behavior in a social setting and the lack of artificiality typical of experimental research.

Another research method is the *interview*. This has been used in the study of faith development and of interpersonal dynamics in teaching and learning. The interview gives information not usually available by direct observation, and it offers a way to collect a vast amount of data with minimal costs and practical problems. It also avoids some of the ethical problems of invading persons' privacy or misleading them as to the nature of the research. Much recent study of interview research, however, has shown how limited the perspectives of self-reports can be and also how easily the conclusions can be shaped by the sample of subjects and the context in which the interviews take place (such as a real decision-making context or a hypothetical context).

Longitudinal study, or *psychohistory*, is the study of one individual over a period of time in different situations; it has been particularly helpful in learning how persons develop and how they are influenced by their religious and interpersonal experiences. Psychohistory provides access to some of the internal aspects of a person's behavior. The primary difficulty in any longitudinal research is the difficulty of generalizing from one person to another. Added to this are the practical problems of time, money, and communication with the subjects over an extended period of time.

In the *laboratory experimental method* are a wide variety of approaches in which the researchers typically create social situations in a laboratory with volunteer subjects and observe the behavior of the subjects under various stimulus conditions. One or more independent variables are manipulated, and the other dependent variables are held constant. The subjects are chosen as much as possible by standardized sampling procedures. This kind of research is valuable in studying memory, motivation, and the effectiveness of different instructional techniques and schedules of reward. The advantages of such laboratory research are that extraneous variables are more tightly controlled and one can pinpoint more closely which stimuli are "causing" which behavior. The findings are situation-specific, however, and do not take account of the influence of varying social elements in the natural setting. Thus, the findings in the laboratory may not be highly generalizable to the natural social settings were people live. Another related danger in laboratory experimentation is its tendency to be oriented toward human engineering of social behavior. Though this can be useful information, it is inadequate to provide depth understanding of human social behavior.

The *questionnaire* is common in the research of denominations and religious publishing houses because it provides a large amount of data quickly and inexpensively. The questionnaire is often used to identify patterns of religious participation, personal religious preferences, and dominant beliefs and values. The gathered data is then used to guide decisions about denominational programs and curriculum content and design. Unfortunately, questionnaires can yield data on simple opinions, but can give little or no indication of the meaning of those opinions for the people; also, questionnaires cannot tell the researcher anything about the cause and effect relationships among the different factors studied.

One less used, but very promising method for educational research is the *ethnographic*, or *participant-observer, method* characteristic of social anthropology. The basic approach is for the researchers to become involved in a community, make detailed observations, and write the story of the people. This method is increasingly used in congregational studies, and it yields the kind of contextual detail that helps explain the functions of the rituals and behavior observed. The limitations are the possible distortions introduced by the researchers' biases and their interactions with the community studied; also one faces the difficulty of generalizing from one community to another.

This brief review of research methods suggests the complementary value of different approaches to educational research. In choosing a method, the most important criterion is that the values and assumptions of the method be consistent with the goals of the research. Also important is researchers' restricting their conclusions to what is appropriate within the strengths and limits of the method(s) chosen and being self-critical about their own prejudgments and research methodology. *See also* Affective Development; Cognitive Development; Discussion; Education, Theories of; Enculturation; Faith Development; Humanism; Learning Theory; Measurement; Moral Development; Phenomenology; Process Observer; Psychology, Educational; Psychology of Religion; Questionnaire; Research; Sociology of Religion; Teaching Theory; Theology and Education.

FOR FURTHER REFERENCE

Eisner, Elliot, ed. *Learning and Teaching the Ways of Knowing.* Chicago: National Society for the Study of Education, University of Chicago Press, 1985.

Groome, Thomas H. *Christian Religious Education.* San Francisco: Harper & Row, 1980.
Harris, Maria. *Teaching and Religious Imagination.* San Francisco: Harper & Row, 1986.
Joyce, Bruce, and Marsha Weil. *Models of Teaching,* 3d ed. Englewood Cliffs, NJ: Prentice Hall, 1986.
Seymour, Jack L., and Donald E. Miller. *Contemporary Approaches to Christian Education.* Nashville, TN: Abingdon, 1982.

M. E. Moore

Mexico

See Latin America.

Middle Childhood

Middle childhood is a life period in between early childhood and adolescence. It is not thereby an intermediate or transitional stage, for it is characterized by dynamics peculiar to its character. Its boundaries are elusive and unstable because of shifting social phenomena and developmental changes.

SOCIAL, PHYSICAL, AFFECTIVE, AND COGNITIVE DEVELOPMENT

Socially, this life period is associated with schooling, thus beginning and ending according to the schooling pattern. The period begins with entrance to kindergarten or first grade. In the K-6 pattern children leave middle childhood at the end of the sixth grade. In the K-5 pattern children move into middle school at sixth grade. Where middle-school social settings resemble elementary more than high school, the transition is not as radical as it once was from sixth grade to junior high.

Church organizational patterns as a rule acknowledge middle childhood as beginning with the first grade, then generally attempt to adjust to the public school patterns to mark the end of the period. Additionally, larger churches provide for multiple groupings within the period.

By reference to physical development, the beginning of middle childhood is difficult to establish, but puberty marks its end. Children are taller now than their counterparts at the beginning of the century. However, the age is still one of steady growth and maturation until near its end when children enter an accelerated growth period that leads eventually to sexual maturity. Girls begin the growth spurt earlier than boys. Boys and girls are equally strong through most of middle childhood, but in late childhood girls are stronger.

They also have an edge on intellectual accomplishments.

Middle childhood is a latency period with regard to sexuality, but the period is not free of crises around sexuality. Sexual fantasies and fears from early childhood persist. For example, internal changes, such as menarche in female children, which may occur as early as ten years, generate recognizable behaviors. Sex, along with age, race, and social status, is a determinant in the spontaneous grouping of children. The evidence is mounting that some dimensions of sex grouping are the result of social conditioning rather than the fruits of normal development. While some homogeneous groupings are necessary for identity formation, the emerging wisdom is that some structuring against these natural groupings and the positive modeling of counterattitudes will encourage inclusion over exclusion, mutuality over isolation, and realistic sexuality over stereotypical behavior.

Affective development during middle childhood is characterized by strong identification with the adult world. Children want to do what they see adults doing. A wide range of exposure to social and vocational roles will provide children with models by which to explore the world. In such activity children are working through issues of competence and belonging. One goal of education is to help children feel worthy in the successful completion of activity. When children consistently fail in their performances, the expectations should be altered to provide the opportunity for children to complete tasks successfully at their level of skill. Another goal is for children to sense that the adults around them accept them as valuable to the whole.

Children in contemporary society are under special stresses. In deprived circumstances, middle children are just beginning to sense the limitations their environment places on them, a beginning that too soon will draw them into the full implications of growing up poor. Privileged children seem only faintly aware that their lives are overstructured. Some without the skill to analyze their hurried pace experience frustration and anxiety. These already stressful conditions are complicated by the fact that the children's parents are caught up in the same dynamics.

Middle childhood is a period of progress in cognitive growth. Middle children gradually discard some and expand other modes of thinking that characterized their preschool years and develop strong cognitive skills. They leave behind the illogical mental processes that were determined by what the eye perceived rather than by any consistent rules of thinking; e.g., that larger means older. This intuitive approach to processing reality gives way to a more logical mode, but the goal of education here should be to blend the intuitive into the concrete rather than to nullify it. The middle childhood thinker works with experience and data and forms a view of that part of the world that is accessible to concrete thinking. This development makes it possible for children to learn mathematics, grammar, and facts of history and contemporary life and to participate in experiential approaches to problem solving.

RELIGIOUS DEVELOPMENT AND RELIGIOUS EDUCATION

The religious feelings of middle children are pliable and trusting. In their need to assume the roles they see adults acting out and in their penchant for peer association, they test their personalities. These relations are genuine and on analysis have the character of mutual exchange. While they love their parents and feel close to their peers, middle children cannot endure relationships that do not meet their expectations.

Children can identify with the actions and feelings of the characters in the good Samaritan parable but still not be capable of ferreting out their motives or sense the broad emotional use to which Jesus put this parable. Affect and cognition are inseparable, of course. Children who are predisposed to a learning event enter into it more fully. Warm feelings about the church's sanctuary, the worship leaders, and the worshipers facilitate children's worship experiences. The objective content of a learning event leaves imprints on children's religious feelings. When children are exposed to content that matches their readiness, they will most likely also develop good feelings about the experience. This includes material and experiences that are appropriately accelerated to draw children toward a higher proficiency or maturity.

Religious development in early middle childhood follows the intuitive character of the life period. Cognitively this means that these young children exhibit egocentric and disconnected thinking. Because they cannot analyze their own thought or take the viewpoint of another, they will not be expected to engage in theological reflection beyond what they can experience directly. They can understand that the good Samaritan helped the hurting man in the road and can make fledgling promises to do the same for others, but they cannot be expected to live into this parable in any reflective sense. Because they reason from one fact to another and do not attend to the intervening process or put the facts together to form a larger picture, these younger middle children need curriculum experiences that do not require induction or process analysis. The simple facts of the life of Abraham, Moses, and Jesus are sufficient to the developmental readiness of the younger middle child.

The intuitive character of religious development in this early period soon gives way to the predominant concrete mode of thinking. In this middle and later part of childhood children begin constructing religious reality that is more logical and stable. Whereas earlier they made no connection between the Jesus at Bethlehem and the Jesus in Jerusalem, they can now do so along with associating the intervening events. Their emerging sense of time makes it possible for them also to begin to grasp the historical breadth of the life of Jesus. However, middle children cannot step outside these concrete events in order to form general meanings. Thus the concept of Jesus as Savior, for example, forms slowly and in the concrete, thus laying the ground for a later appreciation of and commitment to the meaning of that saviorhood. Children can now reflect on the concrete meaning of the parable of the good Samaritan but are not yet capable of engaging the subtleties of this parable.

Faith development in middle childhood, in the sense of meaning making, is concurrent with story and sociality. Children construct the world, as they understand it, through narratives that are less fantasy-filled and thus more realistic. Children live within their stories because they are yet incapable of understanding them as parables or symbols of reality. The meaning is in the story itself, not in its universal extension.

Middle children construct meaning according to the social bounds within which they live, including family, peers, teachers, ministers, and other significant persons or groups within their world. Within these bounds, children make moral judgments, draw circles of inclusion, and relate to authorities.

Middle children belong in the worship services of the church. This inclusion does not require that worship be translated into a childhood idiom, although periodically it should provide experiences suited directly to their developmental needs. Children will appropriate faith through prayers, hymns, lessons, sermons, and celebrations.

Basic religious education is accomplished during the years of middle childhood. The foundational knowledge from which to reason and reflect on their faith during adolescence will be gleaned during these earlier years. The concern for relationships among peers and with adults that characterized preschool religious education continues. Now, however, the interest in concrete learning and the growth in reading and writing skills, in addition to oral expression, presents opportunities for biblical learning, learning of worship materials, stories about historic figures and events, knowledge about religion around the world, and sensitivity to the concerns of war and hunger that children face in many parts of the world.

Religious education classes need knowledgeable teachers. The children in them want to learn, ask questions, and explore. Younger children are usually content with whatever transpires in class, but older children may indicate their restlessness at superficial teaching by absence or subtle forms of disruption, thereby calling attention to themselves and upsetting the teacher.

Used to visual stimuli and varied equipment in daily school, they may find the sameness of some religious education classes boring. It is important to have charts and posters on walls, books, cassettes, films and videotapes, and occasional field trips or visitors for further enrichment. Learning activities involving graphic materials are popular with the younger group, but older ones prefer more inventive methods such as devising a television or video cassette program from a Bible story, writing their own impressions of an event, or dramatizing a situation through role playing, plays, or puppet shows.

While public school levels are usually followed for class placement, smaller congregations may put two or even three grades together. Very small classes make these boys and girls uncomfortable; they prefer company, ten to fifteen members in a class. Some schools have co-teachers or helping teachers for flexible class time when the group can be subdivided. This is also important when one child in a class is frequently disruptive and needs personal attention from a teacher. *See also* Affective Development; Child Abuse; Child Development; Childhood Education; Cognitive Development; Faith Development; Moral Development; Psychosocial Development.

G. T. Sparkman

Middle East

Religious education in the Middle East is conducted at the crossroads of conflicting national, ethnic, cultural, and religious identities. The politics, social life, culture, and education of the people have been shaped by the three great religions rooted in the region: Christianity, Judaism, and Islam. Each community has developed a certain social cohesion and clings to its own particular religious identity. Ninety percent of the population is Muslim.

THE ISLAMIC COMMUNITY

There is immense diversity in the Islamic world, although all Muslims are committed to the same basic tenets of Islam. The central affirmation, "There is no God but God," is whispered in the ear of the newborn child. From that beginning, the Qur'an (the Holy Book) and the written sayings and examples of the Prophet Mohammad (the *Hadith*) influence the entire life of the child. The Qur'an is the source of all knowledge and the inspiration and guide of all education. The *Hadith*, together with the Qur'an, is the source of the Shariah, the large body of law that constitutes

God's commands that Muslims must obey as a sign of their submission to God.

The Qur'an is recited as a religious activity. For Muslims, it is God's speech, God's final revelation, God's infallible word. Qur'anic Arabic, its eloquence, its beauty, its lyric style cannot be fully translated. Children must learn to read the Qur'an in Arabic. The mosque becomes a place not only for prayer but for recitation and learning.

Women and girls do not usually attend Friday prayers, but girls receive instruction from their mothers in manners and Islamic observances and conduct their prayers in their own homes.

With the introduction of Western-style school systems and modern subjects, the usual channels of oral and formal Islamic studies have been partly destroyed. Muslim leaders prepare lessons in Islam for instruction in both government and private schools. It is not uncommon, however, to find a circle of boys in the larger mosques seated on carpets surrounding their teacher for instruction.

Religious law and science (the Qur'an, theology, the *Hadith*, Islamic history and literature) are taught at universities and Islamic institutions. Al Azhar in Cairo, founded over eleven hundred years ago, is a major university and the seat of modern Islamic thought and learning. In 1961 the government reorganized the university to include modern subjects as well as traditional religious studies.

The Islamic response to Western education and influence is sometimes disillusionment and a deep distrust of the West. Many believe Western ways have seduced their youth and destroyed Islamic values; they demand an Islamic alternative. Muslims have a powerful desire to establish a single community, Islamic in character. A secular approach to education is foreign to Islamic thinking.

Religion is more than personal faith in God. Islamic education must encompass a legal system, codes of behavior, family life, business practices, social and international relations.

Some new traditional Muslim scholars advocate a return to strict observance of Islamic law and religious practices. A larger number of Muslim educators advocate Islamization of education (return to the Shariah) with the integration of modern science toward the creation of a single Islamic educational system. The current resurgence of Islamic thought and the vitality of Muslim society is likely to produce change.

THE CHRISTIAN COMMUNITY

There are an estimated twelve million Arab Christians in the Middle East representing various traditions and observing ancient ceremonies. The largest churches are the Eastern Orthodox and the Oriental Orthodox (Armenian, Coptic, and Syrian churches). Their differences stem from ancient controversies over the nature of the person of Jesus Christ. Each maintains its own seminaries, schools, and church life.

Corporate worship has a large part to play in education through the celebration of the liturgical year in its sequence of feasts and fasts. Holy days are lively intergenerational learning events in a social context of praise and celebration. At baptism, infants are given the name of a saint whose icon is kept in the child's room, inviting prayer, reverence, and familiarity.

Schools from kindergarten through secondary grades are built on church property. The parish priest as catechist both protects and transmits to the students the rich heritage of the church. A boarding school at the site of Orthodox seminaries instructs and nurtures boys at an early age in preparation for later study for the priesthood. The theology and creativity in seminary education is in rediscovery and reapplication of the heritage of the church to contemporary issues. Reading in Orthodox history and the church fathers is a chief source of inspiration.

The Eastern Orthodox church has experienced renewal in recent years through the Orthodox Youth Movement. A lay movement founded by a group of students in 1942, its educational activities include catechism schools, Bible studies, and production of religious material in Arabic.

Catholic churches in the Middle East (Greek, Syrian, Armenian, Coptic, Latin) are largely the result of missionary endeavors. The Maronite Catholics with monophysite roots (i.e., a primary emphasis on the divinity of Christ in his incarnation), in conflict with the Byzantine church in the fifth century and under pressure from Muslim armies in the seventh century, fled from Syria to the mountains of Lebanon for safety. Never fully at ease with the culture and religion of the area, they developed a close relation with Europe during the Crusades. In 1736, abandoning their monophysite view, they united with Rome, developing strong relations with the French, who provided for them Jesuit teachers. Learning French and enjoying French culture, their traditions continue at the University of Saint Joseph in Beirut.

The Protestant (Evangelical) churches grew out of missionary activity among Arabs and Armenians in the nineteenth century and resulted in the establishment of churches and schools in the Reformed and Episcopal traditions. Christian education takes place in Evangelical schools, in Sunday schools, and through youth groups, retreats, and parish activities. Special attention has been given to schools for girls. Protestant schools enroll students from all religious backgrounds. Often a majority of the students are Muslims. Only the Christian children attend Bible classes, however, since many countries of the Middle East require children be given instruction in their own religion. Beirut University college serves both men and women with instruction in English. It is the site of the Institute for Women's Studies in the Arab world.

Two seminaries, the Near East School of Theology in Beirut and the Evangelical Theological Seminary in Cairo, Egypt, prepare men for parish ministry and both women and men for teaching Christian education in churches and schools. Graduates serve Evangelical churches in Iraq, Jordan, Kuwait, Lebanon, Syria, Egypt, and South Sudan.

Christian missions have developed through the generations points of contact across language barriers, cultural differences, and geographical settings where differences are confronted and dialogue can take place. The Middle East Council of Churches (Eastern and Oriental Orthodox and Protestant churches) maintains an ecumenical learning center at the Orthodox monastery in Aiyia Napa, Cyprus. Crossing parochial boundaries, searching together out of mutual suffering produces education for peace and reconciliation. The Council serves to educate Western Christians on issues of justice and peace for all the people of the Middle East.

Currently moves are being made toward membership in the Council by the Catholic family of churches. Such a step would signal a new era of cooperation in the Middle East.

THE JEWISH COMMUNITY

There is no significant Jewish religious education in the Middle East except in the State of Israel. With the establishment of the State of Israel in 1948, Jewish communities in other areas of the Middle East and such cultural and religious institutions as then existed in those areas began to disintegrate as Jews increasingly emigrated to Israel. At the same time, Middle Eastern governments restricted programs of religious education for the small remaining groups of Jews in each country.

The Proclamation of Independence of the State of Israel guarantees freedom of religion and education to all citizens of the country. The schools in the elementary and secondary education system of the State of Israel are administered by the Ministry of Education and Culture and are divided into four sectors each, with the indicated enrollment in grades one-twelve during the 1987–88 school year: State Education (593,144), State Religious Education (158,156), Independent Religious Education (43,780), all comprising the Jewish school system; and Arab Education (202,661). The schools in the Arab sector, attended by Muslims, Christians, and Druze, provide a secular education for the students. Religious education is left to the mosque and the church. Schools in the three sectors of the Jewish system provide a secular education and some religious education as well.

While the state education schools, in which the majority of Jewish children study, are usually characterized as "non-religious," because the Jewish religious tradition is an integral part of the cultural and national heritage of all Jewish Israelis, students are required to learn a significant amount of religious information. In these state schools, the teaching of the Bible, the Talmud (post-biblical Jewish law), the Jewish religious calender, and other Jewish religious traditions all are an integral part of the curriculum prescribed by the Ministry of Education and Culture, and the compulsory matriculation examinations in the academic high schools include one on the Bible.

Students in the state religious schools study an array of general and Judaic subject matters, similar to what is studied in the State schools; however, teachers are required to observe the precepts of Orthodox Judaism in their personal lives, a higher percentage of hours are devoted to religious subjects, and Judaism is taught as a guide to personal behavior. The independent religious schools place greater emphasis on religious observance and maintain control of teachers' qualifications, teaching materials, and curriculum. There are also a number of unofficial, unrecognized schools under ultra-Orthodox auspices which are essentially independent of state control and receive no state funding.

Reform and Conservative Judaism arrived in Israel only in the 1950s and have yet to establish officially recognized formal programs of religious education for Israeli children; however, they have established successful informal programs of religious education in the form of youth movements and summer camps. The conservative movement has taken the initiative to establish a network of schools in the state education sector for parents who wish their children to study an enriched Judaic curriculum without being subjected to the stringencies of the religious schools.

The only type of rabbinic training that is recognized by the State of Israel is ordination from an orthodox *yeshivah*. There are many such *yeshivot* in Israel; ordination is usually awarded after a student has shown proficiency in a prescribed course of study in Talmudic literature. The international Reform and Conservative movements have each established a rabbinic training institution for qualified Israelis in Jerusalem; the courses of study in these institutions resemble those in the American seminaries of these movements. Graduates serve in rabbinic and educational posts that do not require government recognition. Overseas rabbinic students from all branches of Judaism come to Israel to augment the rabbinic studies in their home countries.

In innumerable ways, opportunities to learn the Jewish religious tradition permeate all aspects of Israeli life. The holy days of the Jewish religious calender are observed by governmental and other public institutions. The state radio and television begin and end each day with readings from the Bible and present programs in observance of the Jewish sabbath and holy days. When high school graduates are drafted for military service, they have the option of serving in a unit which combines military training with a rigorous program of Talmudic studies. All Israeli universities offer courses in Jewish studies.

The State of Israel is a center of religious education for world Jewry as well as for Israeli Jews. Tens of thousands of Jewish high school and university students from throughout the world come to Israel each year in order to participate in short-range and long-range programs of religious education under the auspices of international organizations and Israeli educational institutions. *See also* Christianity; Islam; Judaism.

FOR FURTHER REFERENCE

Adar, Zvi. *Jewish Education in Israel and in the United States*. Jerusalem: Melton Center of the Hebrew University, 1977.

Haddad, Yvonne Yazbeck. *Islamic Values in the United States*. New York: Oxford Univ. Press, 1987.

Haines, Byron L., and Frank L. Cooley. *Christians and Muslims Together*. Philadelphia: Geneva Press, 1987.

Kleinberger, Aharon F. *Society, Schools and Progress in Israel*. Oxford: Pergamon Press, 1969.

State of Israel Central Bureau of Statistics. *Statistical Abstract of Israel, 1988*. Jerusalem: Central Bureau of Statistics, 1988.

Ware, Timothy. *The Orthodox Church*. New York: Penguin Books, 1983.

B. I. Cohen, C. S. Weir

Military Services

A military base is more than a workplace; most service people live on base, or at least depend on base facilities for recreational, educational, and spiritual needs. It is a world of young women and young men; most people in military service are young adults, physically fit, highly trained, highly mobile. They are volunteers in this duty, working long hours, away from their hometown and many traditional support systems. Depending on where they are stationed they may be offered a seemingly unlimited variety of entertainment in free time, or in stark contrast, very limited options for recreation. The contrast with a civilian church community is startling. Most churches do not have large numbers of young adults; their members are predominantly children, preteens, and people over forty.

CONTENT OF RELIGIOUS EDUCATION

Religious education in the military services takes life as a text. People in uniform, many with families, find that service life and experiences help develop their spiritual and religious life. The opportunities for multiethnic and multicultural experiences far exceed those in most civilian settings. Their duty assignments in this country and abroad expose them to people from other backgrounds and cultures. This exposure stimulates spiritual growth. However, it is up to the individual how to respond to these opportunities. Simply being with other groups or living in a certain place does not guarantee learning. Some people withdraw to a narrowly controlled environment; others go to the other extreme and plunge headlong into a new culture or new activities.

To provide some continuity of learning for Protestants in this transient community, the Armed Forces Cooperative Curriculum provides a structured curriculum for religious education. It is published by the Protestant Church-owned Publishers Association (PCPA), a trade organization of publishers from the Protestant denominations that endorse clergy for service in the Army, Navy, and Air Force. (The Navy provides chaplains to the Marines and the Coast Guard.) This curriculum is two-tracked—Bible to life and life to Bible—and covers pre-elementary through adult age groups on a graded basis. Special attention is given to materials for adults and young adults to assist them in relatively isolated settings like ships, foreign assignments, and remote duty posts.

TEACHERS AND TEACHING METHODS

As it is with most religious education, the essential skills and spiritual dedication of teachers is of the ultimate importance. Special attention is given to teachers, not only in the PCPA resources, but by individual chaplains and the resource agencies of the chaplains (the chaplaincy boards of the Army, Navy, and Air Force), which contract with civilian church and private agencies for teacher training.

Methods of teaching are various and include seminars, workshops, and highly popular retreats. Retreats are of particular importance for the morale and enrichment of individuals and families far from hometown and part of a community mostly without resident grandparents or people of grandparent age.

Over the course of a several-year assignment service personnel often outdistance the training they received in their family or local church. Religious education is thus particularly dependent on self-directed study and the acquired or taught ability of individuals and families to interpret their experiences and to develop skills such as prayer, Bible study, worship, and the ability to address issues related to families and other religions.

The chapel program that becomes their "church" in the United States and overseas often resembles a fine-quality parish church with worship services, Sunday school study groups, and special events. Most remote situations offer at a minimum a circuit-riding chaplain who teams with lay leaders for worship and small group study. Also, through their various chaplaincy boards, the military services have made available extensive film libraries and audiovisual support. Equipment and films on a large variety of topics are available for use by informal and organized groups, either indoors or outdoors, depending on the troop setting. All chaplains, and in many cases, directors of religious education, have available what is called a religious program specialist in the Navy and a chaplain manager in the Air Force, a position peculiar to the services. These are enlisted women and men who are available as resource persons and enablers paid by the services to assist individuals and families to develop and experience their religious faith.

Chapels and fellowship halls are available at government expense. Often in combat settings the need is met creatively through troop-designed and -equipped chapels and fellowship areas. Indeed, religious leaders in the military are particularly innovative in transforming field and garrison into splendid settings for religious education. Less creative, but highly practical, are the use of the Department of Defense school system facilities, which often provide shared space for graded Sunday school experiences.

Military families, however, like missionary families overseas, have the opportunity to learn by living in a different culture—through, for example, day trips, festivals, lay-planned interreligious experiences, shared worship. Here people learn from their own faith experience and that of others. Most military people have had an opportunity to hear and see people of different faiths, as well as to work side by side with them.

Particularly important in the military services is the role of lay leadership in the many small and scattered communities where people gather in work and fellowship. Often it is the presence of one single lay leader on a post or in a military unit that becomes the catalyst for drawing leaders and people together in a religious learning community. For the many service people who live off base and gravitate to civilian churches it is particularly important to relate to small churches with less transient members and with middle-aged and "grandparent-age" people with whom they can identify. See also Chaplaincies.

W. E. Foreman

Ministry

Ministry is a central category in the Christian church's self-understanding. The word "ministry" has its Christian origin in the New Testament, where the Greek term is *diakonia*. Sometimes *diakonia* refers to one of the church's activities, namely, the serving of those who are in need (see Rom. 12:7). At other times, *diakonia* is a comprehensive term for all of the church's activities, as when Ephesians 4:12 refers to God's gifts "for the equipment of the saints, for the work of ministry, for the building up of the body of Christ."

This double use of the term is not an accident. The New Testament can be read as an argument about the nature of power. Its message is a challenge to the widespread assumption that power means only might, domination, and coercion. The New Testament offers the paradox that greater power is found in receptiveness, obedience to God, and service to one's neighbor—that is, in ministry. The willingness to be called or chosen by God for a demonstration of power out of weakness is found throughout the Hebrew Bible. The early Christians saw this paradox embodied in the person of Jesus.

Christian religious educators are interested in ministry because this idea describes at least some of their work. One aspect of the church's life is the education of its members, and the Christian religious educator can be one of the ministers in a pastoral team. The name for such a ministerial role is usually "minister of Christian education," an indication that ministry has an appropriately specific focus when used with the word "education." Religious education as a whole cannot be subsumed under ministry. For example, Jewish religious education does not come under the term, nor does religious education in the English state school.

Even some of church-related work in religious education is considered by some people to be outside church ministry. There is a difference here between Protestants and Roman Catholics. In general, Protestants use the word in a more encompassing way, so that an individual may refer to his or her ministry, even when the work is outside any direct church involvement. In contrast, a teacher in a Roman Catholic high school may resist the naming of his or her work as ministry, wishing to keep the academic study of religion free from church control.

It should be noted that some Roman Catholics are moving in the opposite direction, that is, trying to get the teaching of religion in parishes and schools explicitly recognized as church ministry. Thus, the disagreement over what to include under ministry is between churches and also within churches. All of the parties refer to the same passages in the New Testament, but the problem is not the correct translation of Greek terms. The very idea of ministry is embedded in the changing conceptions of church over the centuries.

The three passages that provide a list of church ministries are Romans 12:4–8; 1 Corinthians 12:4–10; and Ephesians 4:11–14. These lists are probably intended to be illustrative rather than exhaustive; they reflect to some degree the social environment of particular churches. The individually named ministries include apostle, prophet, evangelist, pastor, teacher, and healer. Some of these ministries are internal to the church's life and others are directed beyond the church. Within the educational part of ministry, some education is for articulating the beliefs of the congregation and other education is for dialoguing with the nonchurch world.

The chief limitation on the idea of ministry has been the historical tendency to equate the term with a social class. Already by the third century, *ministerium* was the name for the clergy: bishops, priests, and deacons. The Protestant Reformation was in part an attempt to recover ministry as an activity in which all Christians can participate. The attempt was only partially successful. In modern times, ministry has generally been taken to mean the church professional. The Second Vatican Council used the word "ministry" as practically equivalent to ordained priesthood. However, the council did open the door to a new use of "ministry" by Roman Catholics and fruitful conversation between Roman Catholics and Protestants.

In summary, Catholic and Protestant churches have been moving toward some agreement on using "ministry" to describe activities central to Christian existence. Ministry can therefore be described as activity on behalf of a Christian community for the advent of God's kingdom; it is a gift received in baptism that may be further specified by ordination. Christian religious educators play two important parts in the rethinking of this idea. They exemplify an aspect of church life distinct from the pastoral or priestly role. And their activity is needed for the continuing clarification of the meaning of teaching both within and beyond the church. *See also* Diakonia; Director of Religious Education; Lay Ministry; Peer Ministry; Vocation; Youth Ministry.

G. Moran

Mission, Education for

Mission education is a particular focus of Christian education with concentration on mission outreach. In recent years it has come to be called education for mission with an emphasis on what Christians can do in mission personally as well as in support of organized mission activity in their own national settings and overseas. The degree of emphasis on mission education varies in mainline Protestant churches, in the Roman Catholic church, and in more conservative evangelical churches. More traditional churches tend to center around the interpretation and support of the activities of overseas missionaries, although in all churches there is more attention to the work of indigenous churches and leaders than to that of missionaries.

HISTORY

The era from 1500 to 1750 was an era of great expansion of the Christian church. In the Roman Catholic church, orders such as the Jesuits, the Franciscans, and Dominicans were the great missioners. In the eighteenth century establishment of Protestant and Anglican mission societies in Great Britain and on the continent of Europe was accompanied by a great deal of energy and enthusiasm for the work of those who went to declare the gospel in non-Christian lands.

The growth of modern mission education parallels the growth of organized missionary activity. Very often growth in missionary activity followed the establishment of colonies and the flag and gospel often went together. In Latin America where Spanish and Portuguese explorers went, Roman Catholic missionaries followed. In Asia and Africa where Britain was the main colonizer, the Church of England and the Protestant churches of England and Scotland developed.

In the late eighteenth century in the missionary societies in England, Switzerland, the Netherlands, and Germany, Christians wrote about, sang about, and gave money for the support of "foreign" mission work. In North America domestic mission activity flourished as well. The emphasis on personal salvation in theology gave the supporters of mission a burning zeal to take the message of Jesus Christ to the millions who had not heard. Missionaries from North America and Europe went to Asia, Africa, and Latin America.

Women, excluded from participation in male-dominated mission societies, began their own societies in the latter part of the nineteenth century. In North America the initiative for mission education passed to them. Bands of children devoted to bringing the gospel to the pagan sprang up in Protestant churches. Mission materials were created for them and for Sunday schools and women's societies. Among Protestant churches in the United States today, the activity of mission education still emanates largely from women's groups. Roman Catholic missionary orders have had their own publications and lay support groups. The Orthodox churches, while they spread from Europe to North America, Alaska, Japan, and South America, did not have the same kind of separate organized missionary activity.

In 1887 at a student conference held at Mount Herman, Massachusetts, under the leadership of evangelist Dwight L. Moody, the Student Volunteer Movement was founded. This group had the slogan "To evangelize the world in this generation" and recruited thousands of young persons to take the gospel to those who had not heard it. As it swept college and university campuses, one of the young persons touched was Methodist layman John R. Mott. Mott became the initiator of several ecumenical organizations including the World Student Christian Federation, the World Young Men's Christian Association, and the World Council of Churches.

The zeal for mission of these educated young people of the Student Volunteer Movement was accompanied by a parallel Missionary Education Movement in which Protestant churches joined together to produce study resources, training events, and missionary education. When the National Council of the Churches of Christ (NCCC) was formed in 1950, the Missionary Education Movement was one of the ecumenical agencies joining to make the new body. Located in the council's Division of Christian Education, the program department for Education for Mission is the place where mainline Protestant churches come together under the name of Friendship Press to prepare mission materials.

DEFINITIONS AND IMPORTANCE

In *Being in Mission*, a 1987 Friendship Press book, Lutheran mission educator Arthur O. F. Bauer distinguishes between the task of the local church's *ministry* and nurture of its own membership and its *mission* to the community beyond. In recent years Christian education curriculum has tended to have less visible mission education as the definitions of mission and ministry have become blurred. Part of this is the success of the mission educators who have taught "mission is at your doorstep" and "everyone is a missionary." A result has been less attention to the organized mission work of the church in some curricula. Many churches are reworking and reformulating their theologies of mission. Work for peace, development, and justice and "deed" evangelism are considered mission. At the same time churches, particularly mainline churches, have been called to renew emphasis on proclamation of the Word to those who have not heard.

Education for mission builds on basic Christian education, which teaches the faith, supplies biblical information and interpretation, and involves learners in the Christian community. This is augmented by education for mission directed outward to evangelistic and service efforts beyond the Christian community.

In a February 1983 statement on mission education the program committee of Education for Mission of the NCCC affirmed the importance and necessity of education for mission, saying it enables people to discover the meaning of mission, to learn about the church's involvement throughout the world, to prepare themselves for ministry in mission, and to engage individually and corporately in expressions of mission. The ecumenical consensus statement defined education for mission as equipping people so that they may widen their vision and invest their strength in meeting opportunities for mission now before them. Under the heading "organizing principle," the NCCC document says education for mission is necessary because of the "tension, incongruity, and contradiction" individual Christians and local congregations experience between the gospel proclaimed and the realities of life. Deeming inappropriate such ways of dealing with that tension as "to conform, to condemn, to retreat," the statement asserts that the only acceptable relationship between the gospel and the world is "to live in the midst of the world as ambassador for Christ; to love the world as God loves it; to serve in the world in such a way as to witness to God's love." And the statement stresses that education for mission is not to educate *about* mission but to educate toward the goal of active participation.

At a World Council of Churches (WCC) European seminar on education for mission held in 1977 in Aarhus, Denmark, under the sponsorship of the council's Commission on World Mission and Evangelism, church mission executives and local congregational leaders explored the meaning of the Christian community in mission. The point was made that education for mission is no longer a "transport" problem (How do I bring the gospel to the other person?); it has to do with mission to persons' own places and societies.

TEACHING METHODS IN THE CONGREGATION

Mission education in the congregation needs to be done in special ways when the regular Sunday curricular materials do not include it. A unit of study could be inserted, for example, during Lent. The subject could be explored for weekday sessions or vacation church school.

Preschool children enjoy stories of children who live in other countries, thereby getting to know something of their culture. The use of songs, games, and foods from another country makes this vivid. School-age children can learn more about children and families in other countries, and older children will have some background from social studies to help them with geography. Some will even have travel experiences, and members of the congregation may have slides or videotapes to share. Stories of missionaries who in the past shared their faith through schools, hospitals, agricultural stations and churches enrich the study. Visitors home from mission stations can bring firsthand information. Adolescents can study the spread of Christianity from New Testament times to the present, learn about other religions, and have interfaith dialogue with other young people. Many young people's groups have summer work and study projects in places where the work of mission is being carried on in their own country or overseas.

Adults can study about the mission of the church in relation to their congregation's and denomination's support of the enterprise around the world. They can be encouraged to ask themselves the place of the Christian church in the world scene, the locations where it is growing, and its interactions with other religions. Such adult study can be carried on in a series of Sunday classes or weekday evenings. Increasingly these are interge-

EDUCATION FOR MISSION

Age Level	Understandings	Teaching Methods
Preschool	Children gradually realize there are people other than themselves, and they begin to learn how to relate to others; through experience, they also begin to learn about the religious community and the love of God.	Adults must meet the basic needs of children, providing them with love, care, and security; model acceptance of and concern for others; allow even very young children to experience the religious community; tell them stories of God's love and care and begin to teach them Scripture verses of assurance and thanksgiving.
Grades 1–3	Children gradually realize differences between themselves and others, including differences in religious belief and practice; they can begin to learn concretely about other people and places; they can increasingly participate in and understand their own religious community; they begin to understand the importance of giving to the church and to others.	Tell stories about children in various cultural settings, and teach songs and games from those cultures; discuss differences and similarities between children; teach Scripture verses of God's care for all people; tell stories about both home and overseas missions; encourage children's increasing participation in the religious community; provide opportunity for their direct participation in mission efforts (praying for others, giving to the offering, helping with food and clothing drives).
Grades 4–6	Children can better understand history and geography; they can begin to understand the concept and importance of mission.	Foreign missionaries and visitors can be invited to speak at home, school, and church; foreign languages and further details of foreign cultures can be taught; Scripture passages about mission and missionaries (i.e., Luke 2:1-4; Acts 12:25; 20:35) can be taught; encourage further participation in the religious community and mission projects.
Grades 7–8	Children continue to learn about other people and places; they can begin to comprehend the concept of stewardship.	Encourage further study of other people and places; organize field trips to and participation in local service projects; further discuss Scripture verses about mission and stewardship.

Age Level	Understandings	Teaching Methods
High School and Adult	Different cultures, life-styles, and beliefs can be better understood; global interrelationships can be better understood as well; the mission of the church in the world can be discussed as well as the relationship between an individual's work and the church's mission; concepts of stewardship and mission may continue to broaden.	Youth and adults may travel overseas to gain increased understanding; they may participate directly in short- or long-term mission projects at home or abroad; they may attend mission conferences; Scripture references on mission and stewardship should be studied regularly, and individual and corporate actions reevaluated in this regard.

nerational studies that may even include a meal together, games, songs, and other methods of learning. The background for all such study is Matthew 28:19–20, the command to make disciples of all nations.

A useful source for materials is Friendship Press, publishing arm of the NCCC, which brings out materials on two themes each year; for 1989–1990, for example, it will be the Philippines and Islam.

FORMAL STUDY, INSTITUTES AND CONFERENCES

In addition to the popular education of persons in local congregations, there is a scholarly field of mission education. This academic discipline—missiology—includes the history, theology, and practice of mission. Missiology as a discipline has declined in many mainline Protestant seminaries (no longer are there many professors of mission) but academic research continues. *The International Review of Missions*, a quarterly that reports the studies of the Commission on World Mission and Evangelism of the WCC, and *Missiology*, the international quarterly of the American Society of Missiology, are among the key resources. *The Evangelical Mission Quarterly* is published by the Evangelical Foreign Mission Association and the Interdenominational Foreign Mission Association in Wheaton, Illinois. A respected quarterly publication is the *International Bulletin on Missionary Research*, published by the Overseas Ministries Study Center, New Haven, Connecticut. *MARC* is a monthly newsletter from Mission Advance Research Corporation, Monrovia, California.

Mission institutes and conferences are still held in the summer in the United States. The largest of these among mainline Protestant churches are the schools of mission held by United Methodist Women, which attract some twenty-five thousand persons every summer. The Southern Baptist mission agencies have a strong missionary support program. Various Roman Catholic orders like Maryknoll have monthly publications, films, and publishing ventures. Orbis Books of Maryknoll has published much Third World liberation theology.

As the number of missionaries in mainline Protestant churches has declined, the number going under conservative evangelical auspices has greatly increased. Student mission conferences sponsored by the Inter-Varsity Christian Fellowship draw as many as eighteen thousand young people every three years at Urbana, Illinois. Independent mission societies and churches related to the National Association of Evangelicals are among the 160 mission sending agencies that have displays at the conferences.

Mission education has been defined as being education *about* mission, including information about involvement in structural mission organizations; education *for* mission, including preparation and involvement of people in service locally, in the nation, and across the world as lay and professional workers; and education *in* mission, action-reflection of persons involved in mission, either as volunteers or professionals. Mission education also informs persons *about* the planned program of mission carried out by their church's formal mission agencies or ecumenical groups.

The great mission thinkers of the twentieth

century whose thinking has influenced mission education are such Third World theologians as D. T. Niles of Ceylon, Kosuke Koyama of Japan, Ruben Alves and Don Helder Camara of Brazil, Emilio Castro and Philip Potter, general secretaries of the WCC, and Mercy Amba Odoyaye of Nigeria. *See also* Bible Societies; Evangelism; Inter-Varsity Christian Fellowship in the U.S.A.; Liberation Theology; Ministry; National Council of the Churches of Christ in the U.S.A.; Student Christian Movement; Teaching Mission; Vocation; World Council of Churches.

FOR FURTHER REFERENCE

Barrett, David. *World Christian Encyclopedia*. Nairobi and New York: Oxford University Press, 1982.

Bauer, Arthur O. F. *Being in Mission*. New York: Friendship Press, 1987.

Beaver, R. Pierce. *American Protestant Women in World Mission*, rev. ed. Grand Rapids, MI: Eerdmans, 1980. A revision of *All Loves Excelling*.

Neill, Stephen. *A History of Christian Missions*. Baltimore, MD: Penguin Books, 1986.

B. A. Thompson

Modeling

Modeling is the construction of interpretive schemes through which one engages reality. Models are imaginative tools for ordering experience. They provide both the condition for and content of our experience. By adopting a model through which concrete and conceptual environments can be grasped, our experiences gain clarity and meaning. Abstract or concrete activities are possible through modeling activity. Persons are enabled to deal more directly and deeply with intention and potential, because they can represent and articulate in advance many possible combinations and propositions. Through modeling, individuals can join with others to hypothesize, deduce consequences, and test for truth, with the awareness that new data can affect existing realities, disproving some and proving others. Recently the term "modeling" has come to be used in religious education to avoid the purely cognitive or linguistic significance that appears to be attached to "theory," to connote some effort toward explanation or understanding so as to resist confinement to the notion of predictability or control sometimes associated with the scientific endeavor, and to suggest some kind of holistic interpretive scheme of reality.

G. Durka

Montessori, Maria

Maria Montessori (1870–1952) made creative contributions to religious education through attention to the learning environment and the use of sensorial materials. Although she was the first woman to earn a medical degree in Italy (1896), she devoted herself to education, child advocacy, peace, and religious education from about 1906 on.

Montessori stressed the same things in religious education as she did generally for early childhood learning: the maximum amount of freedom to make *constructive* choices in a social setting appropriate for the child's developmental level, and an enormous range of activities and materials for learning in a spiral curriculum extending from early childhood through high school.

Jean Piaget, born the year Montessori graduated from medical school, attended the 1934 Montessori Congress in Rome. His work focused on the developmental structures of thinking while Montessori focused on the optimum environment and materials for learning at each stage. Sofia Cavalletti's Catechetical Center in Rome is the primary center for the expansion and interpretation of this work in the world today. *See also* Child Development; Education, Theories of; Piaget, Jean; Preschool Children.

J. W. Berryman

Moral Development

The term "moral development" has come to refer almost exclusively to a set of findings from social science research and the theories based on them about the way the thinking that motivates or underlies moral behavior develops from childhood to adulthood. Jean Piaget (1896–1980) experimented in street conversations with children in Switzerland, publishing his summaries of children's responses to moral questions in his classic *The Moral Judgment of the Child* in 1932. Replications of his work were conducted among English-speaking children and in an American Indian tribe in the next two decades, but it was the work of Lawrence Kohlberg while he was finishing doctoral study at the University of Chicago in 1958 that brought widespread attention to the moral reasoning of children. He studied seventy-five boys in his dissertation research. Replications have now been completed in numerous cross-cultural settings, and more continue. In addition, Kohlberg continued to follow his original sample and also to recalculate his original measurements and revise his earlier pronouncements.

Moral development has become the centerpiece for "structural development" and for developmental psychology, sometimes referred to as a "third force" in psychology, compared to behaviorism and psychoanalytic psychologies.

THE WORK OF JEAN PIAGET

Jean Piaget found that children develop ways of moral reasoning that move from "objective responsibility" to "subjective responsibility." For example, a child of six will almost always judge the wrongness of an act by the physical and material consequences of the act: ten broken dishes, though accidental, prove more immoral than one dish broken in the course of disobeying a parental rule or expectation. The transition to subjective responsibility, Piaget found, occurs around the age of ten, plus or minus about two years. From this key finding, Piaget experimented to find how children explained the rules governing moral issues. Here he found that they move from "motor rules" to "the practice of rules," which, he found, precedes "the consciousness of rules." He identified early rule concepts as egocentric and blurred, with more attention to going through the motions of rule obedience than to intentional attention to them. There followed a "heteronomous" period when rules were regarded as originating from external authority and when obedience was held in place by that external expectation. Finally the "autonomous" rule found the later child and early adolescent realizing that the making of rules was through cooperation. This cooperation, the basis of orderly community, set the children up for making rules, modifying rules, and doing so by consensus for the common good.

Piaget theorized that the growth or change in moral reasoning proceeded along a path he described as the adaptation process. He envisioned the human agent as simply "assimilating" the fa-

miliar experiences of life and filling up the structural understandings through simple cognition. But he saw critical events—the "disequilibrating" moments—as triggering the "accommodating" phase of adaptation. During accommodation there is temporary disequilibrium, confusion, even depression, as old structures collapse and newer, more efficient and expanding structures are developed to meet the more complicated challenges of the recent experience. This "construction" aspect of Piaget's theory has earned it the title "structuralism."

Piaget concluded that humans interact with their environment and are not simply shaped by it. This active role of humans has earned for structuralism a reputation for a "high view of persons" compared to more deterministic views of people expressed by behaviorism (experience shapes the person) and by psychoanalytic theory (your options are limited by other people who have determined your potential and your future).

Perhaps most significant of all for religious educators, Piaget found that all children construct their moral reasoning around issues of "justice." This universal core of morality turned out to be "layered" in developmental stages that moved through two dimensions of justice: retributive and distributive. Here unfold developmental sequences moving from (1) punitive and expiatory justice options, to (2) reciprocal and equality choices, and finally to (3) commutive and equitable visions of justice in action.

THE WORK OF LAWRENCE KOHLBERG

Lawrence Kohlberg based his University of Chicago experiment on Piaget's findings, but many people who are familiar with Kohlberg have neglected to examine the Piaget base, which may have more significance for religious education than the Kohlberg replications and elaborations taken by themselves. One can see the "three levels" of Kohlberg and their roots in the three layers of justice reported by Piaget. The first level in Kohlberg's scheme, preconventional moral reasoning, consists of judgments based on physical consequences (stage one) and on "what feels good" in interpersonal transactions, often characterized by "I'll scratch your back if you'll scratch mine," a sort of "good-old-boys'" morality (stage two). The second level, conventional moral reasoning, consists of judgments based on respect for external models, rules, and authorities. Early signals are those of wanting the approval of respected models, either peers or parental generation types (stage three), while the more ripened signs are those of keeping social rules and expectations out of respect for the orderly functioning of the group or the society (stage four). The third level, postconventional moral reasoning, consists of full participation in articulating and codifying moral rules and expectations that are rooted in unchanging universal principles and that take an objective stance to protect the worth, dignity, and potential of all persons and all entities affected by the moral choice. At the corporate level, this shows up as high participation in generating community consensus based on such principles (stage five), while at the private level it appears as a deep commitment to what is true, beautiful, just, and good, even though the commitment must be held as a solitary covenant with truth, sometimes in conflict with the corporate vows one has made with a community (stage six).

THE RESPONSE OF RELIGIOUS EDUCATORS

Religious education has been attentive to the Piaget/Kohlberg research base and theory. Responses range from the uncritical assumption that moral reasoning and the goals of religious education are equivalent to each other, on one end, all the way to rigorous rejection of "moral development" as irrelevant to the goals of religious education, on the other. More often religious educators have concluded that all issues of human growth and development have potential enrichment for a theory and practice of religious education in any faith tradition and that the findings about justice and unfolding patterns of moral reasoning must be taken very seriously in a more comprehensive ministry of religious education.

Among those religious educators who find some validity in moral development theory, applications can be found in working with people of all age levels. Beginning with young children, who are egocentric in their ways, teachers and parents can encourage mutual concern. They will understand why children who still view justice as keeping the rules will see some Bible stories as unfair, for example, the parable of the workers in the vineyard, in which those who came last get the same pay as those who worked all day. Alertness to where children are in moral understanding will prevent teachers either from unrealistic expectations or distress that particular concepts are not understood. Admittedly adults frequently seem "immature." They too are still in an unfolding pattern of thinking with regard to moral issues, and the mutual reasoning and action of the faith community can assist them in the process.

Those who reject moral development findings do so on various grounds. One objection is that moral growth cannot be categorized in carefully described stages. Human sin, repentance, and grace are factors, and human perfection is neither a goal nor a possibility. In this view, empirical validation is useless. Another theological view sees "stage theory" as relativism, humanism, and liberal atheism.

Faith development is a related but quite different empirical model. James Fowler, its primary researcher, seems to ground his theory more in Erik Erikson's psychodynamic model than in the justice core model of Piaget and Kohlberg. The six stages of faith development theory bear some resemblance to Kohlberg's stages and to Piaget's three levels, but they do not correspond at important points. *See also* Character Development; Child Development; Cognitive Development; Faith Development; Maturation.

FOR FURTHER REFERENCE

Joy, Donald M., ed. *Moral Development Foundations: Judeo-Christian Alternatives to Piaget/Kohlberg.* Nashville, TN: Abingdon, 1983.

Kohlberg, Lawrence. *The Philosophy of Moral Development: Moral Stages and the Idea of Justice.* San Francisco: Harper & Row, 1981.

Piaget, Jean. *The Moral Judgment of the Child.* New York: Macmillan, 1931.

Stonehouse, Catherine M. *Patterns in Moral Development: A Guidebook for Parents and Teachers on Facilitating the Christian Moral Development of Children, Youth, and Adults.* Waco, TX: Word Educational Products, 1980.

D. M. Joy

Moravian Education

Education has remained a vital part of the ministry of the Moravian church since its founding in the fifteenth century. John Hus, a rector of the University of Prague, became outspoken about the need for reform in the Roman Catholic church of his day, especially about the need for the gospel in the language of the people. He preached in Czech at the Bethlehem Chapel in Prague and advocated lay partaking of the cup as well as the bread of Communion. He was burned at the stake by the Council of Constance on 6 July 1415, but his followers organized the *Unitas Fratrum* (Moravian church) by 1457. They translated and published the Czech Kralitz Bible (1579–1593).

It was John Amos Comenius (1592–1670), a bishop of the Moravian Unity, who became known as "the father of modern education" with his concepts of worldwide education of all peoples. Exiled from his Moravian homeland, Comenius was welcomed in Poland, England, Sweden, and Holland where he wrote and published educational works such as *Gateway of Languages, Orbis Pictus (The World in Pictures*—the first illustrated textbook), and his *Great Didactic*, which called on educators to view knowledge from a global perspective.

The Counter-Reformation saw the Moravian church nearly wiped out in its homeland, although Comenius prayed that a "hidden seed" might come to life. This was realized as Moravian refugees found a benefactor in Count Nikolaus von Zinzendorf (1700–1760) and established the Herrnhut community in Saxony. The count inspired his Moravian colleagues to spread the gospel in mission efforts around the world, first going to the West Indies in 1732.

A part of each Moravian mission enterprise was education, and the mission workers became the teachers of the peoples they went to serve in Greenland, Africa, South and North America, Asia, and around the globe. Valentine Haidt, a seventeenth-century artist and preacher, painted biblical scenes to assist American Indians in understanding the gospel message. The Moravian schools became the backbone of educational systems in such countries as Surinam and Labrador and on many islands of the Caribbean.

In the settlement congregations of Germany, England, and North America, the schools founded in the eighteenth century have continued to provide high-quality education. In America schools continue at Moravian College and Theological Seminary, Moravian Academy, Bethlehem, Pennsylvania; Salem College and Academy, Winston-Salem, North Carolina; and Linden Hall School for Girls, Lititz, Pennsylvania. In every congregation there is an active educational program along traditional Sunday church school lines. In the tradition of John Hus's desire to educate the laity, Comenius's commitment to world education, and Zinzendorf's dream of an ecumenical church in mission, the Moravian church today continues to support ecumenical efforts in Christian education with a cooperative curriculum.

At present, the Moravian church has 54,000 members in the United States and 1,250,100 members worldwide. *See also* Comenius, John Amos.

B. E. Michel

Mormon Education

The origins of the Church of Jesus Christ of Latter-day Saints are rooted in young Joseph Smith's quest for learning. In response to the assurance that "if any of you lacks wisdom, let him ask God" (James 1:5), the boy prayed to know which church was right and which one he should join. The answer to his prayer set him on the path to what he saw as his mission—restoring the gospel of Jesus Christ to the earth. The answer also established the foundations for education in the Mormon church and established the priority of spiritual over secular sources in the search for truth.

THE IMPORTANCE OF EDUCATION

Subsequent revelations to Joseph Smith, the founding prophet of the Mormon church, which

today numbers 3,680,000 in the United States, outlined its educational philosophy—learning is essential to spiritual progress. One revelation states that "the glory of God is intelligence, or in other words, light and truth" (*Doctrine and Covenants* 93:36). This revelation confirms the church belief in omniscience as a primary attribute of deity. Another revelation states that "whatever principle of intelligence we attain unto in this life, it will rise with us in the resurrection. And if a person gains more knowledge and intelligence in this life . . . than another, he will have so much the advantage in the world to come" (*Doctrine and Covenants* 130:18–19). This revelation extends the importance of intelligence from God to personal progress in the life to come.

Education, therefore, lies at the core of Latter-day Saint theology as a religious requirement and as a vital action required to bring one into God's presence. Joseph Smith taught that God requires people to learn about him so that they "may understand and know how to worship, and know what [they] worship, that [they] may come unto the Father in [Christ's] name, and in due time receive of his fulness" (*Doctrine and Covenants* 93:19).

The Mormon search for truth is undertaken by both mind and spirit, and encompasses both spiritual and secular disciplines. Joseph Smith taught, "And as all have not faith, seek ye diligently and teach one another words of wisdom; yea, seek ye out of the best books words of wisdom; seek learning, even by study and also by faith" (*Doctrine and Covenants* 88:118). Latter-day Saints are to be instructed not only "in theory, in principle, in doctrine, in the law of the gospel, in all things that pertain unto the kingdom of God," but they are also to learn "of things both in heaven and in the earth, and under the earth; things which have been, things which are, things which must shortly come to pass; things which are at home, things which are abroad; the wars and the perplexities of the nations, and the judgments which are on the land; and a knowledge also of countries and of kingdoms" (*Doctrine and Covenants* 88:78–79).

Joseph Smith taught the purpose for this combination of earthly and heavenly learning: God wants us each to learn for our personal benefit in both this life and the life to come. Through Joseph Smith, the Lord told the Saints that he wanted them to "be prepared in all things" to fulfill the mission with which he had commissioned them (see *Doctrine and Covenants* 88:80). Education helps a Mormon prepare to be a better servant of God.

But intellectualism for its own sake is rejected emphatically in the Mormon church's teaching. The apostle Paul warned Timothy to reject those "doting about questions and strifes and of words" (1 Tim. 6:4, KJV). The Book of Mormon, which Joseph Smith translated in a revelation, warns of "the vainness, and the frailties, and the foolishness of men! When they are learned they think they are wise, and they hearken not unto the counsel of God, for they set it aside, supposing they know of themselves, wherefore, their wisdom is foolishness and it profiteth them not" (2 Nephi 9:28). Mormon scriptures provide the proper priorities for learning: "To be learned is good if they hearken unto the counsels of God" (2 Nephi 9:29). God requires us to "study it out in [our] mind," and then ask him "if it be right" (see *Doctrine and Covenants* 9:8). Though reasoning has a role in the learning process, it always must yield to revelation for a person to gain an assurance of truth.

HISTORY

The earliest educational programs of the church were centered in the family with Scripture study sessions in the home. This practice was expanded worldwide throughout the church into the family home evening, a weekly gospel instruction and activity program held by families. In 1833, Joseph Smith organized a School of the Prophets in Kirtland, Ohio. It provided instruction for adult males in gospel doctrines, political science, literature, geography, and Hebrew. About sixty students attended. This school was replicated later in 1833 in Independence, Missouri, and in other American frontier settings as church members moved westward during the 1840s. In November 1837, the church began classes of the Kirtland High School in the attic story of the Kirtland Temple. About 135 students studied the classics, English, and such things as deportment and doctrine. On 16 December 1840, the Illinois state legislature granted a charter for the University of the City of Nauvoo, the first municipal university in America. The Mormon church established and operated this university during 1841 and 1842.

During this same period, the church established the women's Relief Society on 17 March 1842. One of its founding purposes was to foster love for religion, education, culture, and refinement. The first courses of study included home ethics, gardening, literature, art, architecture, and genealogy. This organization has grown to be a worldwide society of Latter-day Saint women who attend weekly courses on family and parenting skills, theology, and related areas.

When the Mormon pioneers moved west to Utah in 1847, Brigham Young, second president and prophet of the church, instructed them to take textbooks and other instructional items with them. They established the first elementary school in a tent just three months after their arrival in Utah. During the next ten years, Brigham Young directed the colonization of nearly one hundred new towns in the intermountain West. Each town had a teacher and school soon after it was established. When the territorial legislature met in

1850, its second act was to create the University of Deseret, later to become the University of Utah, which opened in November 1850 and enrolled forty students the first year.

The pioneers did not neglect spiritual education. In 1848, a Scottish emigrant, Richard Ballantyne, began holding Sunday school in his home. It soon spread throughout the church. Today, Sunday school provides Sabbath instruction in gospel principles and practices for all members twelve and older.

As the Mormon church grew and the educational needs of children and youth expanded, it organized a Young Woman's Mutual Improvement Association in 1869, with a counterpart organization for the young men in 1875. The church established a Primary organization in 1878 for younger children. The Young Women, Young Men, and Primary organization also have expanded throughout the church. They continue to provide weekly instruction in gospel doctrine as well as opportunities for service and character development.

As the Church of Latter-day Saints continued to grow in the western United States, it organized secondary schools and, eventually, schools of higher education, including twenty-two academies (eleven in Utah; four in Idaho; three in Arizona; and one each in Wyoming, Colorado, Canada, and Mexico). The church established the academies between 1875 and 1911 to provide schooling beyond the elementary level. The academies were later turned over to local governments as high schools or junior colleges when operating costs outweighed their benefits and when public schools became adequate to serve church members.

To continue providing spiritual education concurrently with the secular education provided by public schools, the church organized the seminary program in 1912 and the institute of religion program in 1926. The seminary provides religious instruction at the secondary level and the institute at the higher-education level. This weekday instruction complements and, where necessary, counters secular education. The seminary and institute programs have been expanded to meet varying student circumstances throughout the world, including all fifty of the United States and seventy-two other countries or territories.

PRESENT ORGANIZATIONS AND PROGRAMS

At the high-school level, more than 215,000 students are enrolled in seminary. Most of these students attend classes held in church-owned buildings located adjacent to the public schools. They are released from public school to attend seminary classes. Where released-time classes are not available, students attend early morning classes or complete home-study seminary courses. At the higher-education level, the Mormon church operates institutes of religion at more than 1,400 colleges and universities, providing religious instruction to more than 135,000 students. In addition to the seminary and institute programs, the church provides continuing education opportunities that reach adults in many parts of the world.

The church also has developed a higher education system, including Brigham Young University in Provo, Utah, the largest church-operated university in America; Brigham Young University-Hawaii Campus at Laie, Hawaii; Ricks College in Rexburg, Idaho; and the LDS Business College in Salt Lake City.

Today, the Mormon church offers a wide array of educational programs that meet both secular and spiritual needs. In addition to the universities and colleges, the church operates eight elementary schools, thirteen middle schools, and nine secondary schools. These schools, located in Latin America and the South Pacific, provide educational opportunities to many who would otherwise be deprived of education.

Within the church, families receive spiritual instruction at least monthly from priesthood home teachers; women receive similar instruction, along with instruction in provident living, from Relief Society visiting teachers. All male members who hold the priesthood meet in quorums each Sunday for gospel instruction. Families and individuals search the Scriptures for eternal truth at their own initiative.

Elder Boyd K. Packer, a member of the Quorum of the Twelve Apostles of the church, summarized the importance of education for church members when he wrote, "In the Church of Jesus Christ of Latter-day Saints, daily religious instruction is not just a frill or an embellishment. It is not just an appendage to a sound program of education. It is the very core of it" (*Instructor* [Sept. 1959]: 289). *See also* Colleges and Universities, Church-related; Private Religious Schools; Private Schools and Religion.

H. W. Pinnock

Moses ben Maimon

See Maimonides.

Motivation

Motivation, a psychological term, has been widely used in religious education since the 1930s. The root meaning of the word "motivation" is derived from the more common English noun "motive," denoting (from the Latin verb *movere*) movement or action. A motive is said to be a force or drive within a person impelling him or her to act in a particular way. For example, the motive hunger causes a person to seek food to satisfy (or diminish) the hunger. Likewise, the affiliation motive causes persons to seek the company of others. Some synonyms used for motive or motivation are: drive, need, impulse, desire, wish, urge, instinct, purpose, and value.

But do motives really exist? Long lists of supposed motives have been compiled by psychologists, beginning with "biogenic drives" like sex, thirst, and hunger and extending to "psychogenic needs" for dominance, aggression, nurturance, and even play. Skeptics claim that such motives are the figment of psychologists' imagination, since no one has ever seen or touched a motive. Motivation psychologists reply that since people behave in different ways at different times, there must be "something" inside of us that causes this different activity. The theory of motivation, they say, explains better than any other theory the probable cause of so wide a variety of human behavior. While the existence of motives must be inferred from observed behavior, psychologists claim that the strength and quality of motivation can be scientifically measured.

Scientific measurement of motivation is easiest at the biogenic end of the motive spectrum. For example, the strength and type of an animal's food-seeking response can be calibrated. If a rat eats twice as much cheese as it did the day before but only half as much grain, it can be said that the rat's motivation to eat cheese has doubled but its motivation for eating grain was reduced by 50 percent.

Psychogenic motivation is less easily described and measured. We are physically aware of most of our biogenic motives because we experience them directly in the feelings of hunger, thirst, the desire for sex, etc. But of our psychogenic motivations to acquire possessions, order our lives, and nurture, dominate, or affiliate with others we have little or no conscious awareness. Some people may be able to describe an "urge" to nurture or a "longing" to affiliate, although these feelings are vague and hard to measure. Such psychogenic motives are usually identified and measured not by experienced feelings, but by the behavior they elicit. For example, if a person is observed taking care of cats, plants, children, and even organizations, motivation psychologists might have reason to assume that these actions are the result of a strong nurturance motivation. This would be a guess (or inference) and it might be wrong. Such behaviors could be the result of habit, monetary reward, or other motives unknown to the psychologist.

It seems likely that most behavior is motivated by something "inside" us, but that something may be far more complex than first supposed. Even so simple a behavior as petting a cat may be caused by as many as ten or fifteen different motives. The increasing complexity of motivation theory makes it less amenable to scientific verification.

Despite difficulties in describing the nature of our motivations, in scientifically measuring them, or even proving they exist, concern with motivation has not diminished. The reason seems simple. Even guesses about motivation are a way of answering the "Why?" raised by our observations of behavior. Someone does something that affects us and we want to know why. Before modern psychology, the answer was either that the person "willed" that action, that it was an accident, or that it was caused by a good or bad spiritual force acting through them. Sigmund Freud and many of the "analytic" theorists who followed him have argued that all behavior is motivated (and therefore nothing is done by accident), that some behavior is unconscious (and therefore not willed), and that spiritual forces have no bearing upon motivation. Although Carl Jung and a number of modern psychologists have challenged some of these claims, the psychology of motivation remains today essentially a secular and deterministic enterprise claiming a scientific basis.

MOTIVATION AND RELIGION

An interest in the sources of human behavior has not been lacking in religion. Traditionally, religious motivation has been thought to be of two kinds. Most like psychological motivation theory is the religious assumption that virtuous behavior results from a "pure heart" (Ps. 24:4) or similar image denoting a total orientation of body, mind, and spirit toward benevolence. The saints of all religious traditions are understood, at least in part, as possessing a unique center characterized by this simplicity, purity, holiness, and goodness—sometimes called the human spirit.

The other traditional source of religious motivation has been a transcendent power acting through persons. In Judaism and Christianity this transcendent power is most often seen to be God's Spirit acting on and with the person's own spirit. The prophets claimed that they acted at God's behest, at times against their will. Paul's personality and motivation were reshaped in a moment of divine intervention; thereafter he explained the source of his new life as "no longer I who live, but Christ who lives in me" (Gal. 2:20). And the mystics of all ages and faith traditions have described their experience and actions as emanating directly from the power of God's Spirit.

Most religious thinkers today see these two sources of religious motivation acting together, God's Spirit inspiring (or in-spiriting) our human spirit to make it simple, pure, holy, and good. From this center then flow the fruits of the Spirit such as love, joy, peace, patience, gentleness, and self-control (Gal. 5:22–23). Less traditional religious thinkers have suggested that the confluence of God's Spirit and the human spirit produce a motivational state characterized more by its radical sense of security and openness to life than by a pure heart from which flow the traditional virtues. However described, the motivational state produced by the interaction of God's Spirit and ours is usually known as faith.

Evil raises a particular problem for religious motivation. Scripture and our own experience warn of an evil within us and perhaps beyond us. In most religious traditions, evil is seen as a disordering or perversion of the good ordained by God. Even the cosmic source of evil, Satan or Lucifer, is said to have been a fallen angel. If the human source of religious motivation is the pure heart, the seat of evil motivation cannot be the heart itself but that which lies within the heart. This means that God's power for good ultimately has the upper hand, although evil motivation continues to be expressed in the world. A partial explanation of this curious relationship between good and evil (at times called grace and sin) is found in Paul's claim that the increase of sinful behavior actually attracts God's grace to oppose it (Rom. 5:20).

MOTIVATION AND RELIGIOUS EDUCATION

Religious education has struggled since the 1930s to devise a theory of motivation that reflects the wisdom of its own religious traditions as well as what is most valuable in the secular field of motivational psychology. Most modern denominational religious education curricula in the United States have been influenced by theories of learning and motivation derived from post-Freudian developmental psychology. Each age level has been carefully studied to discover what motivates those at that level to seek approved religious goals. The most common motivators (or "conditions") of religious behavior discovered range from unconditional parental love to a personally meaningful understanding of Scripture and a positive relationship to a church or synagogue.

Important as these findings are, their usefulness has been limited by two factors. The first is that most new curricula developed to take account of these findings have had limited success in embodying them. It is one thing to know what a six year old warms to interpersonally and can intellectually grasp and another to recreate that in the classroom, the sanctuary, or even the home. The second difficulty lies in the great importance developmental psychology places on creating the appropriate environment for learning and growth. Lost sight of too often is the inner life of the learner understood from a religious, and not simply a psychological, point of view. In recent years there has been a shift in religious education thinking and teaching to address these problems.

Theories of motivation have played an increasingly important role in religious education.

These theories have helped the church better understand why religious persons and others behave in certain ways. They have given greater clarity to what moves us to pray, to read Scripture, and to live out other aspects of religious life. But because motivation theory has developed out of twentieth-century psychology and not religious thought, this theory is better suited to understanding psychological motivation than what moves a person religiously. Attempts to find religious equivalents for psychological terms have not satisfied scholars of either religion or psychology. As we approach the twenty-first century, there is obvious need for a theory of motivation grounded more basically in Scripture and religious tradition. *See also* Attitude Formation; Behavior; Faith; Faith Development; Grace; Interdisciplinary Studies; Jungian Influences; Learning Theory.

FOR FURTHER REFERENCE

Allport, Gordon W. *Becoming*. New Haven, CT: Yale University Press, 1955.
Fowler, James W. *Stages of Faith*. San Francisco: Harper & Row, 1981.
Gilligan, Carol. *In a Different Voice*. Cambridge, MA: Harvard University Press, 1982.
James, William. *The Varieties of Religious Experience*. New York: New American Library, 1958.
Maslow, Abraham. *Motivation and Personality*. New York: Harper & Row, 1954.

D. C. Duncombe

Multicultural Education

The lamentable, often stated comment still holds that "Sunday morning is the most segregated hour of the week." This is because religious institutions are part of a whole society. Multicultural religious education is the infusion of the traditions of ethnically diverse people into religious curricula and educational settings. This is a recently developing area of concern for religious educators.

A HISTORY OF DIVERSITY

Biblically, this diversity is chronicled in the story of the Tower of Bable, when there came a confusion of language and the resulting multiplicity of tongues (Gen. 11). The obverse is noted in the Pentecost experience, when the apostles were made to speak in many tongues so that people from many different lands could all understand them (Acts 2). The Bible is the story of many peoples, from Semitic to Greeks and Romans.

In the United States, long-standing immigration patterns and the resulting treatment of minority groups brings this concern to the forefront. The Native American population was subjugated beginning with the arrival of European colonists in the seventeenth century. Tribes were destroyed or relocated on reservations with few resources for survival.

African slavery was introduced in 1609 and the importation of slaves continued until 1819. Even after emancipation in 1863, segregation laws separated freed slaves and their descendants from the white society and perpetuated discrimination.

During the nineteenth century, Chinese laborers were brought to North America under slavelike conditions to build railroads. As late as 1941, during World War II, Americans of Japanese ancestry were forced to dispose of their property and moved to internment camps.

During a major immigration period, 1824–1924, thirty-six million new arrivals mainly from Europe, but also from Africa and Asia, changed the ethnic balance. Often finding themselves victims of fear, ignorance, suspicion, and exploitation, immigrants were encouraged to become part of a "melting pot" as "Americans," blending into the existing dominant, white Anglo-Saxon English-speaking culture. In spite of this effort, ethnic identities remained strong.

Before World War II Jewish families fled Germany, the occupied countries, and later Eastern Europe. Since the war there have been two large immigrating groups: Hispanics and those from the Pacific Rim.

In an effort to lessen discrimination and open more opportunities, action was taken toward racial desegregation. Racially separated military units were disbanded after World War II. The Supreme Court in 1954 ordered the desegregation of the public schools. The civil rights movement in the 1950s and 1960s accented the thwarted aspirations of blacks for a just society. The civil rights legislation of the 1960s offered hope to minorities for economic, educational, and political opportunities. The black power movement fostered black pride and awareness and pointed out the need for continuing watchfulness in the area of discrimination.

With this kind of multiethnic background and the turning away from the "melting pot" concept to the encouragement of ethnic pride within American society, much needs to be done educationally and religious communities have a part arising from their theology of creation and redemption as the gift of God to all peoples.

TEACHING PLURALISM

Keeping ethnic pluralism alive is enhanced by the use of language. A person's deepest meanings about culture and beliefs are frequently not translatable into other languages from the one first learned. Seeking to be sensitive to language backgrounds in learning groups and give assistance in looking for effective ways of expressing diverse faith understandings is helpful work for religious educators. Today materials are being prepared in

MULTICULTURAL EDUCATION

Age Level	Understandings	Teaching Activities
Preschool	Children gradually realize there are people other than themselves, and they begin to learn how to relate to others; they are too young to understand concepts of difference and similarity.	Adults should model acceptance of and concern for others; demonstrate and teach cooperation and constructive methods of conflict resolution.
Grades 1–3	Children gradually realize differences between themselves and others.	Tell stories of children from different cultures; encourage children to talk about differences and similarities; discuss Scripture verses that tell of God's care for all people; neighboring families with different cultural backgrounds may visit and learn from each other; children from urban areas may visit a rural family for 1–2 weeks during the summer (and vice versa).
Grades 4–6	Children gain a sharpened awareness of differences; tension over differences may increase in neighborhoods, in school, and in church.	Tell stories related directly to the children's experience of cultural differences; encourage children to share their experiences; role play and discussion may be used to help children search for mutual understanding; discuss Scripture verses about God's creation of all people (i.e., Mal. 2:10; Acts 17:26); foreign visitors can be invited to the home, school, or church; foreign languages and details of foreign cultures can be taught.
Grades 7–8	Children further explore and understand concepts of friendship and cooperation; tensions over majority/minority status may increase.	Role play and discussion continue to be of help in accepting others and understanding differences and similarities; study of other cultures and people should be encouraged.

Although the Hebrew Scriptures describe the use of various instruments in Jewish worship, Christians have had a checkered past with the acceptance of instruments in worship. The first organs used in worship appear in the eighth century. The primary use of the organ in the Roman Mass and office worship of the church from the eighth century on was to supply organ versets of polyphonic music when choral forces were limited to monophonic chant. This alternation, based on the chant melodies, took place during the ordinary and proper of the Mass and during the psalm, canticles, and office hymns of the daily office. It was well into the seventeenth century (and a hundred years after Luther's creation of congregational song) that the organ came into its present role as a leader of congregational song. This helped to create the need for another style of composition for the organ, called the organ chorale. These organ chorales were based on the German congregational songs, as has continued with English and American hymn tunes. The organ chorale functioned in worship as organ introductions to congregational singing as well as in the style of alternation mentioned before and eventually as organ solos in the liturgy.

Other orchestral instruments began to be employed in worship, especially in the period following the Reformation. The German cantata and English anthem both used instruments in addition to the organ. Instruments in worship were forbidden by Calvin and Zwingli in their branches of the Reformation. In England, many organs were closed or destroyed during the Commonwealth period. The Restoration period saw organs restored to worship, and the English voluntary emerged as a vital musical offering in Anglican worship. In America, Puritanism and Calvinism rejected instruments and organs well into the nineteenth century. Other Protestant groups began to use other instruments such as cellos, flutes, oboes, and brass to support their singing. The reed organ, harmonium, and pipe organ gradually became accepted in the second half of the nineteenth century by American Protestants.

HYMNS

The congregational participatory strain of church music that received its impetus from Luther and Calvin has continued in Protestant churches without interruption since the Reformation. The German hymn or chorale flourished in Germany alongside the great motets and cantatas of nonparticipatory church music. The Calvinistic tradition of psalm singing adopted by the Anglicans, Calvinists, and Puritans in England and America has continued without interruption into the twentieth century, as evidenced by the Presbyterian *Psalter* of 1912.

The great contributions to English hymnody of Isaac Watts (1674–1748) and Charles Wesley (1707–1788) were gradually ecumenically accepted into denominational hymnals in America and England during the nineteenth century. Social movements and liturgical reforms in England and America in the twentieth century have added to the wealth of congregational song. Hymn texts have been composed by Washington Gladden, Frank Mason North, William P. Merrill, and in our time, Fred Kaan, Brian Wren, and F. Pratt Green, to name but a few.

Church music (both the music and the poetry in the case of hymnody) is an artist's expression of faith. Therefore, it must be taken seriously in the life and ministry of the church. Hymns are theology, and our standards both with adults and children must be high. Music that helps to inspire and comfort also helps to make texts memorable. Either good music with poor text or a poor text with good music is unacceptable. The "marriage" of music and text as well as thoughtful placement of music in a worship service or educational curriculum are essential. Music speaks to the soul, but it also speaks to the mind.

MUSICAL EDUCATION

The highest regard for the quality of music and text must govern church programs, especially with the education of youth. The graded choir programs in American churches over the past half century has helped to raise the quality of musical adoration, reflection, inspiration, and theological insight for the young people engaged in them. Music educators employing the Orff-Schulwerk method, a way of teaching young children basic rhythms and tone blocks through the use of percussion instruments, have invigorated children's musical choral programs. It must become a priority of the broader spectrum of religious educators to engage youth and adults alike in the inspiration and didacticism of the best congregational song of the church. On another level, our rich Christian heritage of choral and instrumental music should enter the religious education of all Christians for their spiritual inspiration and edification. A curriculum of religious education that includes church music of the highest quality will certainly minister to the growth and development of the contemporary Christian community.

Church music is ministry. While striving for excellence, it is important to maintain a balance of nurture and care in music ministry. The church of our time must continue to seek to find artists of the highest quality to call into service as composers of music and poetry. The best church music is always vital and alive. It is music of faith in which the performers have committed their special gifts to ministry and service, to the glory of God, and the edification of God's people. *See also* Choir; Choir, Children's; Choir School; Hymnody, Christian; Liturgy; Worship.

FOR FURTHER REFERENCE

Laurence, Joy E., and John A. Ferguson. *The Musicians' Guide to Church Music.* New York: Pilgrim, 1981.
Routley, Erik. *Christian Hymns Observed.* Princeton: Prestige, 1982.
———— . *Church Music and Christian Faith.* Carol Stream, IL: Agape, 1978.
Schalk, Carl, ed. *Key Words in Church Music.* St. Louis, MO: Concordia, 1978.
Sydnor, James R. *Hymns and Their Uses.* Carol Stream, IL: Hope, 1982.

D. A. Weadon

Myth

Myths are the language of religion par excellence. They are stories that reveal the mysterious nature of the most basic human questions: Why are we here? Where are we going? What is the meaning of life? They are stories that portray the values that give significance to people's lives.

Myths may be religious for many reasons. Some are stories about divine actions and sacred realities. Others fulfill spiritual needs, helping humans cope with the limiting situations of suffering, evil, and death. Some encapsulate rituals that help humans pass through important transitions in life, especially birth, puberty, adulthood, and old age. Myths may be religious because they convey concrete notions about how to approach that Absolute Reality (e.g., God, Allah, Brahman) that is both transcendent (beyond space and time) and immanent (active at the core of the human self).

Contrary to common perception, myths are not primitive or mistaken ways of relating to the world. They are neither unscientific accounts of imaginary persons or things nor antiquated efforts to explain the world with a naive philosophy that may have been true at one time but can no longer be taken seriously. Myths are classical stories that provide reflections on the constants of human experience. They narrate a message that is permanent and universal; they never belong solely to the past ("once upon a time") but always to the present.

Myths are similar to, yet essentially different from, other literary forms such as sagas, legends, or fairy tales. Myths are cosmic in scope, unlike sagas, which are more closely bound to a specific locale and connected with definite historical events. As the revelation of mysteries, myths differ from legends, which serve primarily to edify by holding up human models who inspire admiration and are worthy of imitation. Because of their sacred character, myths are distinct from fairy tales, which are products of fantasy that furnish entertainment, nostalgia, and amusement by evoking a make-believe world.

SCIENTIFIC STUDY

Tremendous advances have been made in the development of a science of mythology in the past century. Religious scholars have charted the relationship of myths to rituals, traced the diffusion of myths from one culture to another, and developed elaborate typologies. They have taken advantage of the research, insights, and special focus of academic areas as diverse as psychology, cultural anthropology, structural analysis, and phenomenology. Among those writers on the religious nature and functions of myth who have contributed much to the reevaluation of myth are Mircea Eliade, Joseph Campbell, and C. G. Jung.

For Eliade, myths are stories that are sacred, exemplary, and significant. They narrate those primordial events when sacred beings brought order out of chaos, thus constituting and inaugurating reality. Myths reveal the true nature of the here-and-now world by relating it to metaempirical reality. They articulate those sacred deeds that are models of meaningful human actions and that become real each time they are faithfully repeated in rituals.

For Campbell, myths are vivid stories that elicit awe, gratitude, and even rapture in relation to the mystery of the universe and human existence. They provide models of the universe that support and are supported by a sense of the sacred. Myths serve a social function by integrating individuals organically within the group. They guide individuals stage by stage through the inevitable crises of life, from the childhood condition of dependency, through the traumas of adolescence and the trials of adulthood, to the deathbed.

For Jung, myths use the language of symbols to manifest the hidden transcendent world to human consciousness. Similar to dreams, myths give expression to certain unconscious processes and content—archetypes—which are innate in each person. These archetypes bring the psyche some awareness of and insight into the constantly repeated experiences of humanity, thus aiding each individual's growth into wholeness.

TYPES

Some myths are cosmogonic, others are heroic, and still others utopian or eschatological. Some myths are oriented to the past, others to the present, still others to the future. Some are agricultural, others are more appropriate to a hunting culture. Most such divisions are really quite artificial, and the distinctions should not be too neatly drawn. Still, since classifying myths helps us see their similarities in different cultures, we may conveniently divide them into myths of gods, heroes, and saviors.

Myths of *gods* (for example, the Babylonian Tiamat struggling with Marduk, the Chinese Pan Ku and Nukua impregnating the world with the forces of yin and yang, the Polynesian Maui slowing down the sun) provide some sense of cosmic order and meaning. They help people come to terms with the mystery of their environment and with the powers that lie outside human control. In this category are myths of the past, particularly of the creation of the world and of the first humans. Also included are myths that give expression to the Absolute Reality, which is often both personal and impersonal, masculine and feminine, austere and intimate. Here too are myths of human separation from the Absolute Reality, perhaps due to fate, a mistake, or a desire to be independent. Included, finally, are trickster myths, which usually highlight the dilemmas that accompany growth into conscious awareness of freedom or account for the arbitrariness of life in spite of the human pursuit for cosmic order.

Myths of *heroes* (for example, the medieval Parsifal seeking the Holy Grail, the Greek Psyche enduring trials to regain her husband, Eros, the Hindu Rama rescuing Sita from the demon Ravana) give glamor and panache to the struggles of ordinary humans, enabling them to participate in a life cycle greater than their own. They ease human stresses and fears by providing models of exemplary activity. Here myths include stories of virgin births and confrontations with monsters. They portray the quest of the hero, often mounting a charger, galloping off to conquer an enemy at great sacrifice, and bringing a boon back as a reward to the community. They include other, gentler quests where there is no rivalry or competition, for example, quests for success in love or knowledge.

Myths of *saviors* (for example, the Zoroastrian Ahura Mazda struggling with the devil Ahriman, the Babylonian Gilgamesh seeking immortality, the Egyptian Isis restoring Osiris to life) are stories that help humans overcome—that is, make sense of—the perennial mysteries of evil and death. In this category of myths are theodicies (stories of why there is evil in the world) and soteriologies (descriptions of a strategy to follow to overcome evil). Here too are stories of the origin of death or of a descent to the abode of the dead.

Also common are the savior's death (often in tragic circumstances), eventual restoration (through resurrection or reincarnation), and consequent dominion over death. These myths include stories that look to the end of the world when judgment will be rendered on good and evil alike and a new world will be created, whether as heaven, utopia, nirvana, or return to a lost paradise.

CONVEYING TRUTH

The stories in myth are not usually factual, nor do they usually have a historical basis. Their truth is of a different order, dealing with values and meaning. Myths are not antithetical to the more abstract philosophical teachings found in a culture's religious doctrines: they exist alongside each other, employing different modes of expression.

When myths are located in and derive their authority from the sacred books, or scriptures, of the world's religious traditions (for example, the Muslim Qur'an, the Buddhist Lotus Sutra, the Hindu Bhagavad-Gita), their truth is said to be inspired. Because Jews and Christians have considered their Scriptures to be historical as well as historic, they have often claimed that their myths contain a higher level of truth than those in other traditions. Still, since all myths are veiled explanations of the truth, it makes no sense to say that one myth is better or truer than another.

Some Christian and Jewish traditions do not recognize the category of myth within Scripture. Where it is recognized, teaching must make clear the understanding used here of myth as a language and form for conveying truth. Stories are received

by children at face value, for they accept the mysterious and do not always ask for rational explanations. Older children, more keyed in to rational explanations, need to learn about the distinctions made here so that they can recognize truth in varied forms. Adolescents and adults, having a better grasp of literary forms and various modes of conveying truth, can more easily appreciate the reason why the mystery of God's dealings with human beings is couched in many ways.

By studying the heritage of myths, persons attain a different perspective on their familiar world. By appropriating the truths in the myths of other religious cultures, they acquire new insights into the truths of their own mythic tradition. The gods, heroes, and saviors in myths all provide glimpses of the Absolute Reality. The challenge and legacy of myths is to recognize and consent to this Reality. *See also* Bible Study; Narrative Theology; Storytelling; Symbolism.

FOR FURTHER REFERENCE

Biallas, Leonard J. *Myths: Gods, Heroes, and Saviors.* Mystic, CT: Twenty-Third Publications, 1986.

Campbell, Joseph. *Myths to Live By.* New York: Bantam Books, Viking Press, 1972.

Dunne, John S. *Time and Myth.* Notre Dame, IN: University of Notre Dame Press, 1973.

Eliade, Mircea. *Myth and Reality.* New York: Harper & Row, 1973.

Jung, C. G., ed. *Man and His Symbols.* Garden City, NY: Doubleday, 1964.

L. J. Biallas

Narrative Theology

Narrative theology focuses on the power of stories to shape the quality of human life. It defines "story" or "narrative" as the ordering of human experience within the framework of time and space. It assumes that the human mind is structured or conditioned to think in narrative form, so that stories influence our comprehension of existence, our sense of place in the world and history, and our moral awareness. It affirms Stephen Crites's observation that "the formal quality of experience through time is inherently narrative" ("Narrative Quality of Experience," p. 291).

EMPHASIS ON STORY

For narrative theologians, the biblical stories are richly textured and subtle expressions of meaning that are not reducible to the religious propositions often derived from them. The Bible is not, therefore, best understood as a compilation of religious beliefs illustrated by stories. Christian doctrines, creeds, and principles, important as they all may be, remain abstractions from the narratives that give rise to them. Narrative theology does not challenge these abstractions as such, but it does question their value when severed from their roots in the biblical stories. It believes that God approaches readers most directly in these stories, to which the readers best respond by remembering, understanding, and feeling the impact of the stories as a whole. "Biblical story," then, does not here mean "just a story." It is not the anecdotal recital of some incident, legend, or "Aesop's fable," the meaning of which resides in the moral it contains rather than in the story content itself. Instead, "biblical story" refers to that purported divine wisdom and truth that unfolds as historical narrative within the Bible, such as the accounts of the Exodus events.

The historical narrative is distinguished from the legendary or mythic narrative in that its truth unfolds through real actions within historical time. For example, Christians consider St. George's slaying of the dragon as legend while they regard Christ's victory over death as historical narrative. Some biblical stories are considered fictional by scholars today, but even as such they derive authoritative meaning from the larger narrative that contains them; an example might be the parable of the good Samaritan, the meaning of which unfolds within the context of the Gospel of Luke as a whole. Given this distinction between historical fact and fiction in the narrative form, even fictional narratives often touch human experience more intimately than the morals or principles we abstract from them. For instance, Herman Melville weaves textures of experience into his *Moby Dick* narrative that can only be felt in the full reading of it. Similarly, whether the Jacob and Esau story in the book of Genesis is fact or fiction, we diminish its power when we miss the nuance of the narrative in the hurried search for its moral.

Narrative theology is not so much a separate theological movement as it is the effort to recover this neglected dimension of theology and to regenerate its power to inform and influence us. It suspects that the biblical narrative itself often receives superficial attention from biblical critics and theologians because they look for a meaning behind or outside the story and therefore give insufficient attention to the story itself. For instance, the historical critics search for the original "life situation" that gave rise to the narrative and in doing so sometimes miss the narrative's meaning. Similarly, structural critics look for the "deeper meaning" behind both the "life situation" and the narrative, often dismissing the content of the story as either irrelevant or subsidiary to the deeper truths, which are presumably concealed from us behind the surface meanings of all narratives. Further, theologians can so concentrate on the theological import of the "acts of God" they find in the biblical stories that they miss the intended subtleties of God's action described in them. In short, the preoccupations of critics and theologians can divert them from the narrative's meaning, just as an obsession with photography can divert tourists

from the meaning of the monuments they visit. And yet, even though the narrative may approach the "original experience" more closely than does the doctrinal or moral principle, it also remains an abstraction from that experience. The immediacy of human experience always evades the subsequent articulation of it.

Major twentieth-century literary critics such as Erich Auerbach and Northrup Frye have enriched narrative theology by demonstrating the influence of biblical literature on its secular counterpart. Frye traced the origins of comedy, tragedy, satire, and romance to biblical literature, while Auerbach informed us that the modern notion of the realistic character who is transformed by the vicissitudes of life and the erosion of time is a biblical creation—David and Saul are examples. If the biblical narratives do carry such richness, say the narrative theologians, then we should search for the levels of meaning within them rather than use them as flat-surfaced springboards to theological propositions.

CONCERNS

Problems of religious meaning arise for the narrative theologian, however. Is it possible to know that a particular religious narrative refers to the "real truth" about ultimate reality—about God? We may internalize the story so that it carries affective (emotional) power to shape our own lives—so that it becomes our "own story"—but can we know that the story truthfully represents God's presence in the world? The response of most narrative theologians is this: if the story's plain meaning includes the historical presence of God, such as the Exodus events in which God delivers Israel from its bondage to the Egyptians, then to judge it false or incredible from our contemporary perspective is to violate the story's integrity by reading into it a different meaning than the author intended. But can we reasonably expect modern people to accept the original meanings of the biblical stories? And even if Christians "know" the biblical stories are "true" for them, are they also willing to grant Muslims and Zen Buddhists the truths of their stories? Do the stories from all religions, although different in their content, point to the same reality? And if so, are the stories themselves relative? Van Harvey's "soft perspectivism" is perhaps the narrative theologian's best answer to most of these questions. "Soft perspectivism" entails an ultimate commitment to one's own story, yet the imaginative openness to appreciate another's perspective—a kind of "self-transcendence" that allows for both conviction and tolerance. From this "soft perspective," narrative theology can study appreciatively the narratives from other cultures and religions.

Narrative theology is especially relevant for religious educators. If we learn about God and discover elements of life's meaning through stories, then religious education should give serious attention to them, asking the following questions: How do we grasp the meaning of a religious story when we read or hear it? And how do we incorporate that meaning into the felt experience of our own personal stories? *See also* Bible in Religious Education, The; Bible Study; Biblical Criticism; Storytelling.

FOR FURTHER REFERENCE

Alter, Robert. *The Art of Biblical Narrative.* New York: Basic, 1981.
Auerbach, Erich. *Mimesis: The Representation of Reality in Western Literature.* Translated by R. Trask. Princeton, NJ: Princeton University Press, 1953.
Crites, Stephen. "The Narrative Quality of Experience." *Journal of the American Academy of Religion* 39, no. 3 (Sept. 1971).
Goldberg, Michael. *Theology and Narrative: A Critical Introduction.* Nashville, TN: Abingdon, 1982.

J. H. Stone

National Association of Directors of Christian Education

See National Christian Education Association; Professional Societies.

National Association of Evangelicals

The National Association of Evangelicals (NAE) is a Protestant interdenominational movement founded in 1942 to promote interchurch fellowship and cooperation on an evangelical theological basis. Its membership includes 42 denominations plus individual churches in 33 other fellowships. All of the historic Protestant denominations are represented in NAE, and many of the smaller groups as well. It is estimated that there are some 3.5 million people from about 38,000 local churches in the organization.

The National Association of Evangelicals adopted a doctrinal statement in 1943 that remains unchanged to this writing. It is committed to conservative theology which sees the Bible to be "inspired, the only infallible, authoritative Word of God," and affirms the deity of Christ, the lostness of humanity apart from the efficacy of Christ's death and bodily resurrection, and spiritual unity of believers.

Among its affiliates is the National Religious Broadcasters, which represents approximately 85 percent of all religious broadcasters in the world. Initially, its World Relief Corporation responded to the Vietnam conflict by establishing a Christian Lay Leadership Training Center. By 1982 it had served 51 nations and had assisted 32,000 refugees in resettlement in the United States.

In 1946 the Commission on Educational Institutions sponsored the volume *Christian Education in a Democracy,* edited by the late Frank E. Gaebelein. This commission became the National Association of Christian Schools. It eventually merged into the National Christian Education Association.

The NAE organized meetings leading to the formation in 1945 of the National Sunday School Association (NSSA). The NSSA continued through the early 1960s and served with distinction as a catalytic agent to start city and area associations. Most of these associations remain vibrant while NSSA has been reorganized as the National Christian Education Association in a weaker form. The National Association of Professors of Christian Education (formerly the Research Commission) was an affiliate of NAE/NSSA but disaffiliated in the period of the demise of NSSA. Christian Camping International (CCI) has its roots with the NAE/NSSA as well. CCI was founded in 1961 and later severed its ties with NAE. CCI remains a very effective arm for evangelical camping ministries around the world.

While NAE's influence has waned in the area of Christian education, it continues to be a viable alternative to the National Council of the Churches of Christ for denominations and individual churches that are conservative in theological concerns. The national headquarters office is in Wheaton, Illinois, and its magazine is entitled *United Evangelical Action.* It sponsors commissions in the areas of world relief, international relations, spiritual life, social action, chaplaincy, educational institutions, radio, and television. A public affairs office in Washington, D.C., provides liaison with the government.

After World War II the NAE assisted missionaries in obtaining visas. Eventually NAE formed the Evangelical Foreign Missions Association, which today represents 81 denominational and nondenominational agencies that send out more than 10,000 missionaries to over 130 countries. NAE is one of 50 national bodies that are related to the World Evangelical Fellowship. *See also* Evangelicalism; National Christian Education Association; Professional Societies.

W. S. Benson

National Association of Professors of Christian Education

See National Association of Evangelicals; Professional Societies.

National Catholic Education Association

See Professional Societies.

National Christian Education Association

The National Christian Education Association was established in 1945 under the title of the National Sunday School Association with the purpose of revitalizing the Sunday school and returning to an evangelical message and biblical interpretation. By the 1940s certain leaders of the more conservative denominations were convinced that an apparent decline in the membership and effectiveness of the Sunday school was due to the liberal theological influence then prominent in the religious education movement. They were especially critical of the International Council of Religious Education (now the Division of Christian Education of the National Council of the Churches of Christ) and its Uniform Lessons Series.

The desire to develop a new uniform Bible lesson series along distinctively evangelical lines led to a number of meetings in 1944 and early 1945 sponsored by the Commission of Church Schools of the National Association of Evangelicals (NAE). Those present were convinced that a new uniform Bible lesson series should be produced and that the task should be assigned to a new national association organized on evangelical principles. The National Sunday School Association (NSSA) came into being in Chicago, Illinois, on 1 May 1945.

The new lesson committee immediately adopted the statement of belief of the National Association of Evangelicals as a minimum basis of theological agreement. The object of the lessons was a Bible-centered content and their purpose was evangelism—the winning of every pupil to the Lord Jesus Christ and to his service. Topical lessons were to be limited and the schedule of lessons related to major observances of the church year. A new series of uniform lesson outlines was put into preparation and first published in 1948. Several publishers were authorized to use the lesson outlines cooperatively developed and the lessons reached approximately four million pupils.

In addition to the new series of uniform lesson outlines, other means for revitalizing the Sunday school included the promotion of Sunday school conventions, the production of books and pamphlets as aids to evangelical Sunday schools and their teachers, and the provision for research in Christian education. National conventions of the NSSA were held annually beginning in 1946, and the association sponsored a National Association of Directors of Christian Education and promoted a Youth Week, a National Family Week, and a National Sunday School Week.

The association was administered by a general council composed of representative denominations; regional, state, and city Sunday school associations; and Sunday school publishing houses. Among member groups were the larger Assemblies of God, the Free Will Baptists, the Wesleyan Methodists, and conservative congregations from a number of other denominations. The general council sponsored specialized commissions for such groups as professors of Christian education, denominational executives, and publishers. The association was financed by gifts from individuals and by contributions from local congregations and Sunday schools, denominations, and publishing houses.

The association ran into difficulties when its head, Dr. Clate Risley, left in the mid-1960s. By then the national conventions were drawing fewer people (although the area conventions continued to be well attended), and there were financial problems. The National Association of Evangelicals decided to disband the National Sunday School Association and let the matter rest for a while. The National Association of Professors of Christian Education, the National Association of Directors of Christian Education, and the National Association of Denominational Executives of Christian Education all continued—first as part of the NAE, but growing more autonomous with time—and each eventually became independent. Other functions of the NSSA continued under various commissions of the NAE.

In 1978, the NAE sponsored area workshops and a national congress on Christian education. In 1980, it established the National Christian Education Association as a commission of the NAE. This commission includes one representative from each affiliated denomination as well as members-at-large from non-member denominations who wish to participate. The chair is appointed by the Board of Directors of the NAE. The commission publishes a quarterly newspaper and is concerned with the work of Directors of Christian Education, Sunday Schools, youth work, religious clubs, and religious day schools. *See also* Evangelicalism; National Association of Evangelicals; Professional Societies; Sunday School Movement.

L. G. McAllister

National Conference of Catholic Bishops

The National Conference of Catholic Bishops (NCCB) is simply the name given to the Roman Catholic bishops of the United States when they come or act together in attending to church affairs in this country. The United States Catholic Conference (USCC), again, is simply the name given to the Roman Catholic bishops of the United States when they come or act together to attend to public policy issues that have an impact on the Catholic church in this country or on which the Catholic church in this country should have an impact.

STRUCTURE

The NCCB is a canonical body established in accord with church law as found in the revised code of canon law. The USCC, on the other hand, is a civil, nonprofit organization, which has been incorporated in the District of Columbia. Neither the NCCB nor the USCC are legislative bodies, except in rare cases delineated by the revised code of canon law. Despite their consultative nature, however, the presumption is that plenary decisions of the bishops (a two-thirds majority) will be carried out by the individual members in a collegial spirit.

Both the NCCB and the USCC share the same elected president, vice-president, secretary, and treasurer, who serve for a three-year term. The NCCB and the USCC also have the same general secretary, who, as the chief executive officer of the national staff headquartered in Washington, D.C., serves for an appointed term of five years.

Since all the bishops, the full membership of both conferences, ordinarily meet only once a year, forty-nine of them come together three times a year to carry on the interim business of the conferences. These forty-nine members are the elected chairmen of the NCCB and USCC standing committees, the two elected bishops on each of the three USCC committees, and thirteen bishops from the thirteen episcopal regions in the United States. When this forty-nine-member group deals with NCCB agenda items, they are called the administrative committee. When they deal with USCC agenda items, they are known as the administrative board. The administrative committee/board approves the agenda for the annual meeting of the bishops, reviews any decisions made between their three meetings by the executive committee, and oversees the work of the general secretariat and national staff.

While the administrative committee/board attends to matters between the annual meetings of the bishops, emergencies do arise between the three meetings of the administrative committee/board. To provide for these emergencies there is an executive committee for both the NCCB and the USCC composed of the four elected officers of the conference and one of the bishop members of the administrative committee/board elected by that group.

It becomes evident from the composition of the administrative committee/board membership, that the NCCB and the USCC structure is composed of committees. The NCCB committees are composed of bishop members only. Nonbishop participants in the NCCB committee meetings are nonvoting consultants. The USCC committees, however, allow for as many as twenty-one voting members. The USCC by-laws designate that, within the twenty-one members, there be a bishop chairman, ten bishops (two of whom are elected by the full body of bishops with the other eight being invited by the chair), and ten nonbishop members selected from the ranks of the clergy, religious, and laity.

CONCERNS AND RESPONSIBILITIES

The NCCB committees number twenty-three and are concerned about a myriad of issues touching church life as can be seen from the following enumeration: American Board of Catholic Missions; Bishops' Welfare Emergency Relief; Boundaries of Dioceses and Provinces; Canonical Affairs; Church in Latin America; Conciliation and Arbitration; Doctrine; Ecumenical and Interreligious Affairs; Human Values; Laity; Liaison with Priests, Religious, Laity; Liturgy; Men Religious; Missions; North American College (Louvain); North American College (Rome); Pastoral Research and Practices; Permanent Diaconate; Priestly Formation; Priestly Life and Ministry; Selection of Bishops; Vocations; and Women Religious. Some of these committees have full-time staff and others do not.

The USCC has three committees that are also staffed full-time by three corresponding departments: Communication, Education, and Social Development and World Peace. The Committee and Department of Communication is responsible for attending to the church's apostolate in and through the media, both printed and electronic. The Committee and Department of Education is charged to provide leadership in collaboration with other national and professional Catholic organizations in educational and catechetical areas. The Committee and Department of Social Development and World Peace is responsible for representing the concern of the bishops for domestic and international peace and justice.

The range of the NCCB and USCC committees indicates the concern of the bishops for the church and the modern world. The changing needs of the contemporary scene demand that both conferences with their committees constantly adjust and evolve to fulfill their responsibilities. Those basic responsibilities, however, remain constant. They are, first, to assist the bishops in their teaching office and ministry. Second, they are responsible for providing the bishops with action plans to address contemporary needs. Finally, the conferences are to establish and implement policy concerned with matters that touch on Catholic life in the modern world.

HISTORY

The two conference structures explained above were created after the Second Vatican Council. In that council's *Decree on the Bishops' Pastoral Office in the Church*, #37, the council fathers stated: "Since episcopal conferences—many such have already been established in different countries—have produced outstanding examples of a more fruitful apostolate, this sacred Synod judges that it would be helpful if in all parts of the world the bishops of each country or region would meet regularly." That statement was a recognition and an encouragement for what had been done in the United States, for the current NCCB and USCC structure had actually been conceived at the beginning of World War I. At that time, the Catholic hierarchy in the United States had been convened by James Cardinal Gibbons of Baltimore to form the National Catholic War Council. This council became the channel whereby Catholics put their funds and personnel into the spiritual and recreational service of servicemen engaged in the European conflict.

At the end of the war, in 1919, Pope Benedict XV wrote to the hierarchy in the United States to encourage them to work with him for peace and justice. The U.S. Catholic bishops rallied to this call and decided to continue meeting on an annual basis. On 24 September 1919, they resolved to form and name their organization the National Catholic Welfare Council. They also elected a seven-member administrative committee to carry on the council's business between their annual plenary meetings. This action was soon followed by the establishment of a national headquarters with a general secretary and staff in Washington, D.C.

Subsequently, the bishops changed the title of their organization from "council" to "conference" so as to reflect more adequately the consultative rather than legislative nature of their common action. Over the course of the years, the bishops then saw a need to distinguish between their internal and external church concerns. And so, while they already saw themselves as the National Catholic Welfare Conference, they saw themselves working through their staff in areas like education, immigration, and social action as the National Catholic Welfare Conference, Inc. And so the stage was set not only for this collegial enterprise to be affirmed and encouraged by the Second Vatican Council, but to give birth to the NCCB and USCC structures that serve the church in the United States today. *See also* Vatican II.

T. G. Gallagher

National Conference of Diocesan Directors of Religious Education

See Professional Societies.

National Council of Religion and Public Education

See Public Schools and Religion.

National Council of the Churches of Christ in the U.S.A.

The National Council of the Churches of Christ in the U.S.A. (NCCC) is an organization of cooperating denominations that meet together, communicate their views to each other and to the world, and work together on programs and projects. Membership in the council is an expression of unity and common mission.

HISTORY

By the beginning of the twentieth century, ecumenical movements brought together Christian agencies engaged in common tasks such as home and foreign missions, interseminary programs, stewardship education, and especially religious education, as seen in the International Sunday School Association and the International Council of Religious Education. In 1908 the Federal Council of Churches was created, which led to the formation of the NCCC at a meeting in Cleveland, Ohio, in 1950, bringing together twelve interdenominational agencies and twenty-nine denominations. In 1981 the NCCC, now consisting of thirty-one "communions" of Orthodox, Protestant, and Anglican church bodies, with a combined church membership of forty million persons, expressed its identity in a revised preamble to its constitution in this way: "The National Council of the Churches of Christ in the U.S.A. is a community of Christian communions which, in response to the gospel as revealed in Scriptures, confess Jesus Christ, the incarnate Word of God, as Savior and Lord. The communions covenant with one another to manifest ever more fully the unity of the Church. Relying upon the Holy Spirit, the Council brings these communions into common mission, serving in all creation to the glory of God."

Adjusting organizational and programmatic emphases to meet the needs of the current situation, the NCCC underwent restructuring in the 1980s to shift from being a council to a "community of Christian communions." For most members this meant "being" as well as "doing," manifesting among the communions a unity that was itself a worthy task and achievement. Efforts at achieving this goal continue today.

ORGANIZATION

The current organization of the NCCC can be described in two related levels. At one level there is a governing board of about 260 persons and an executive committee of about 50 persons representing the member communions. At semiannual meetings the governing board establishes policy, discusses common concerns, develops and distributes policy statements and resolutions, reviews the work of the program units, and worships together. At the other level, program units are organized into clusters, planning and implementing programs and projects as agreed upon by the members of the program committees, which consist of representatives from the member communions.

The forty or so program units are organized into five clusters. The cluster on Unity and Relationships fosters ecumenical ties. In that cluster the Commission on Faith and Order sponsors theological dialogue on Christian unity; the Commission on Local and Regional Ecumenism relates with 250 city and state councils of churches; and the Commission on Justice and Liberation monitors the NCCC's work in the light of ethnic and racial minority concerns.

The cluster on Education and Ministry, which connects a broad range of education programs for all age groups, has programs for church support of public and higher education, education for mission, and recruiting and training of professional church leaders. This division sponsors Bible translation work such as the Revised Standard Version and creates the Uniform Lessons Series which are the basis for religious education curricula used by forty million Christians. In this cluster the Commission on Stewardship provides training and materials on the theology and practice of the stewardship of all of God's resources. The Communication Commission deals with issues in mass communication and helps create mass media programs that raise issues for public consideration.

The cluster on International Ministries works with organizations in countries outside the United States in fields such as human rights, agricultural development, economic justice, and leadership development. The cluster on Church World Service raises money for disaster relief and enables churches working together to encourage development in other countries, particularly those in which poverty and hunger are severe problems.

The cluster on Church and Society works on projects to bring about a just society. This cluster seeks to change the systems and institutions that perpetuate injustices such as sexism, racism, and poverty. Civil and human rights, evangelism, and economic and ecological justice are dealt with in this cluster.

Funding for a large and complex organization such as the NCCC is itself varied and complex. Major sources of funds include contributions from participating communions designated for programs and projects to which they are committed and for which they have shared in planning and development. The sales of resource materials produced by NCCC units usually cover the cost of production but in some cases, such as royalties from sales of the Revised Standard Version Bible or the outlines of the Uniform Lesson Series of Bible studies, have been substantial and have supported related programs. One of the program

units, Church World Service, receives contributions from individuals and churches, government payments for certain programs involving refugee resettlement, and other sources amounting to $25 to $30 million annually, about 70 percent of the total NCCC budget.

AGENDA AND ISSUES

While any area of Christian life and witness could be considered by the governing board and program units, the NCCC generally concentrates on those areas in which a united effort is needed and for which there is a commitment of resources and leadership by the member communions. Often programs are created only after a long process of consultation, decision making, and planning, as well as fund-raising. For the current decade an "ecumenical agenda" has been established to guide the NCCC in its work:

1. Christian unity—growing in commitment to the visible unity of the church

2. Peace with justice—growing in commitment to the whole human family

3. Ecumenical learning—growing knowledge of one another in Christ

4. Stewardship of nature—growing in commitment to God's creation

5. Ecumenical spirituality—growing in knowledge of God in Christ and the Holy Spirit

6. Cultural renewal—growing in capacity to reveal the glory of God in the fullness of human life

Throughout its history the NCCC has engaged in activities at the forefront of Christian witness and social action. Often the member communions participate in social justice programs through the NCCC instead of working through their own agencies. The NCCC has been involved in the struggles for civil rights, world peace, and the reduction of military arms, and for dialogue between churches or nations who are at odds with each other. In recent years the NCCC has drawn both praise and criticism for creating an inclusive language lectionary and advocacy on behalf of people in North America who are suffering from injustices, such as farmers, racial minorities, immigrants, and the urban poor.

The NCCC faces a number of issues at this time. It is struggling with the issue of being versus doing, seeking to decide how limited human and material resources are to be allocated either to programs expressing an ecumenical ideal of unity or to social service and justice programs. The issue of limited resources is very real for the NCCC, which depends greatly on the contributions of church agencies who themselves face shortages of resources. At issue also is the constituency of the NCCC, which has a great variety of members, including large Protestant denominations, historic black denominations, Orthodox communions, but few evangelical denominations and no Roman Catholic members. The debate over accountability continues, as member communions seek to assert oversight over the program units through the governing board but find it difficult to do so because of the complexity of NCCC organization and funding patterns. Another issue is how to assert leadership among the churches and to express a public moral and theological voice in the political, social, and economic areas of life. *See also* Councils of Churches; Ecumenical Education; Mission, Education for; Peace, Education for; Social Justice, Education for; Uniform Lessons Series.

D. Ng

National Sunday School Association

See National Christian Education Association.

Native Americans

The native peoples of North America have not traditionally separated sacred and secular. Consequently religious education is not categorically distinct from other forms of education. When the entire universe is seen as the continuing expression of a creating God and humans are viewed as brothers and sisters of all other creatures, then education of the young is a seamless fabric.

To European settlers immersed in a dualistic worldview of sacred and secular this view was puzzling, if not actually demonic. They saw the new continent as a wilderness occupied by wild animals and dangerous humans to be tamed and domesticated. The inhabitants, by contrast, perceived it as a garden in which they were to live in harmony. The spiritual realities of life for them flowed from the earth.

The development of cultural anthropology in the late nineteenth century gave birth to an awareness that there are many human cultures existing parallel to and somewhat independently of one another. Before this discovery, social organizations were thought to be part of a single human culture with various societies strung along a continuum from "primitive" to "civilized."

Initial efforts to extinguish the cultural, economic, and religious base of Native American life were seen as benevolent, as ways of enlightening the natives, bringing them to modern Christian civilization. But Native Americans had their own distinct cultures with values in many cases more advanced—more "civilized"—than those of their conquerors, so they have resisted strongly for four hundred years these efforts at assimilation.

The struggle intensified during the western expansion of "manifest destiny" and culminated in the Indian Wars of the nineteenth century. When the U.S. Army failed to create farmers from the hunting tribes of the Great Plains, government officials turned to the churches. In 1869, under President Grant, responsibility for educating and assimilating the tribes was given to Christian denominations. Within three years seventy-three Indian agencies had been apportioned to them. Denominational efforts assumed a standard pattern: take the children away from their homes; place them in boarding schools; cut their contacts with parents; deny them the right to speak their native language; and drill them in European Christian cultural values and traditions.

Under "freedom of religion" guarantees, the government scrupulously protected the right of every denomination to receive these permits. But no freedom of religion was granted the Native Americans, because it was held that their beliefs were primitive superstitions, not religion.

The mood of the European Americans gradually shifted, however, and in 1934 John Collier, superintendent of Indian affairs under President Franklin Roosevelt, was able to secure passage of the Indian Reorganization Act. One provision of this act permitted Native Americans to practice their native religion unmolested.

This change slowly brought native practices "above ground." Oral tradition, songs, dances, and sacred rituals have increasingly come back into visibility.

These practices are often intermixed with Christianity. In New Mexico, for example, the Pueblo Indians have lived with Roman Catholic influence for nearly four hundred years; they count themselves Christians even as they continue many ancient traditions.

From the 1960s to the present, a slowly developing respect for Native American views has begun to permeate American consciousness. But this movement is hampered among many Christians by the lingering fear that Native Americans will lead us back into worship of animistic nature spirits or even into satanic worship. Nevertheless as knowledge slowly replaces prejudiced views born of ignorance, religious groups have frequently become the community leaders in recognizing the great accord that exists between basic Native American beliefs and those of the Judeo-Christian tradition.

Religious education informed by the wisdom of Native American tradition would likely include the following features:

- Respect for every person (for one never knows who might bring salvation to the community in the future)
- Respect for the wisdom of children and of old people, because they are close to the hand of God
- Respect for the land, our mother

- Respect for the right of all animals and plants to exist as fellow creatures
- Awareness of our communal dependence upon one another in a fabric of human relationships
- Harmony between the needs of the individual and of the group
- Gratitude for the gift of continuing life granted to us by the death of plants, fruits, seeds, and animals
- Gratitude to God for bringing together all these elements so that we might live this day

See also Multicultural Education.

FOR FURTHER REFERENCE

Bowden, Henry Warden. *American Indians and Christian Mission: Studies in Cultural Conflict.* Chicago: University of Chicago Press, 1981.

Deloria, Vine, Jr. *God Is Red.* New York: Dell, 1983.

Josephy, Alvin M., Jr. *Now That the Buffalo Is Gone.* New York: Knopf, 1982.

T. McConnell

Natural Law

See Ethics.

Naturalism

Naturalism is that interpretation of reality that has taken sensory experience of the physical world and its scientific formulation as the comprehensive access to truth. The word "natural," from which naturalism derives, has a veritable sea of meanings, but the latter word is much more specific.

In Christian theology in the Middle Ages a basic differentiation developed between nature, on one hand, and grace or the supernatural, on the other. This terminology has continued in Roman Catholic theology to the present. While it is helpful to keep in mind that in religious matters naturalism has typically been contrasted with any view that admitted the existence and operation of the supernatural in human life and the world, this contrast can also seriously mislead because in the medieval tradition "nature" included matters about God, immortality, and human destiny, which naturalism has rejected along with supernatural matters like the triune nature of God, the incarnation, etc.

The discussion that follows focuses on the "ism" of naturalism and the allied word "naturalistic." Naturalism can be found in some thinkers of ancient Greece, but the general meaning of the term as we know it today arose in the eighteenth century with the empiricism that was fostered by the arrival and successes of modern science.

For instance, in French philosophy of two centuries ago a most prevalent manner of interpreting the world of nature was as a vast machine. So also the human was thought of as a machine and everything about the human was described in terms of physical matter and its movements. The human soul and mind were not in contact with anything eternal, spiritual, or divine, and right and wrong were matters of transitory pleasures and satisfactions. Seeing the human being as a machine was insisting on the identity of the human with the world of nature at large. This is the key to understanding modern naturalism. The being called human and its history, culture, knowledge, and morality are interpreted by means of that which ostensibly made sense of the nonhuman world of nature. The religious consequences of the position have usually been atheistic.

Such naturalistic thinking was given powerful support by the biological theories of Charles Darwin shortly after the middle of the nineteenth century. Now it was no longer the human as a machine but as an animal evolving from so-called lower or more primitive forms of life on earth. Evolution provided an embracing category that could be utilized to see human beings as an instance of nature and no more. Evolution itself did not require such a conclusion and consequently many people accepted the evolutionary framework as correct but insisted that the human spirit could not be comprehended within this biological development.

In Europe and America just prior to 1900 the lines of intellectual controversy were most often drawn between naturalism as the view of reality based upon the knowledge of nature and idealism as the view of reality that took the human self and mind as the touchstone for the character of the real. Most prevalently, Christian thinkers were advocates of the latter position, although some forms of idealism were thought to be incompatible with Christian affirmations. Naturalism, rather than being oriented to human self-consciousness of freedom and the apprehension of spiritual realities (including the communication of a transcendent God), attempted to base itself upon the five points of human contact with the environment, the senses, and the experimental knowledge gained through the exercise of these senses in science.

Twentieth-century thought has brought new departures in naturalism. Sigmund Freud broke new ground in exploring the subconscious realm of the human self, but some of his philosophical interpretations of its implications appear as extensions of the tenets of naturalism, especially with respect to religion. Yet naturalism has taken new forms that are concerned not as simply to reduce the spiritual life of humanity to categories of the nonhuman world. Much American philosophy in the first half of this century in George Santayana, John Dewey, Frederick Woodbridge, and others represents such an expanded and reformulated naturalism. Religion is given a positive and beneficial role in human life when properly exercised, in contrast to the nineteenth-century and Freudian versions that presented religion merely as superstition or a sickness of civilization. The continuity with older naturalism is evidenced in that this naturalism still has no place for God as one transcendent to the world of nature. Matter is the ultimate reality.

The use of the word "naturalism" has sharply receded from the prominence that prevailed in 1900. Christian thought has been able partially to appropriate insights of naturalism. Some thinkers have forged categories that attempt to overcome the split between the human self and the natural world by interpreting nature in a manner much more in continuity with human experiences of freedom, morality, and religious communion with God than was possible in the older forms of naturalism discussed above. *See also* Atheism; Empiricism; Experience; Idealism.

FOR FURTHER REFERENCE

Krikorian, Y., ed. *Naturalism and the Human Spirit*. New York: Columbia University Press, 1944.

Otto, Rudolf. *Naturalism and Religion*. New York: Putnam, 1907.

Weiman, Henry N. *American Philosophies of Religion*. Chicago: Willet & Clark, 1936.

J. C. Verheyden

Neo-Thomism.

See Thomism.

Neoorthodoxy

"Neoorthodoxy" means "new orthodoxy" and designates a school of theological thought that dominated Protestant theology from 1919 to the mid-1950s. It left its mark on the worldwide church through the ecumenical movement, where it was a strong force, and it also had a considerable impact on the life of the churches in this period, especially on such church activities as preaching and Christian education.

BEGINNINGS

Neoorthodoxy arose as a protest against liberal theology and its attempt to unite religion and culture, throne and altar, God and humanity in a natural and unbroken harmony. Yet it did not discard the historical-critical approach to the Bible (the study of biblical documents from historical and literary viewpoints) or reject the application of the Christian faith to social and political issues. The leader of this school was the Swiss theologian Karl Barth (1886–1968), who was regarded by many as the most creative theologian of the century. He made his break with theological liberalism as a result of his great concern with the need and task of Christian preaching. After becoming a village pastor in Safenwil, Barth began to question both his preaching and the liberal theology on which it was based. The problems of human life drove him to the Bible and gradually he became convinced that the true preacher must have the Bible in one hand and the newspaper in the other. Therefore, Barth immersed himself in the "strange, new world of the Bible" and also in the life of his people. He earned the nickname "the red pastor" for helping to organize a trade union in Safenwil.

The catastrophic event of World War I helped to crystallize matters for Barth and many others. When ninety-three German intellectuals, including a few of Barth's revered teachers, came out in support of the war policy of the German kaiser, Barth was appalled. He concluded that if this was what the great cultural synthesis of liberal Protestantism meant in practical terms, then a theological renewal was necessary.

Paul's Letter to the Romans proved to be the doorway to this theological renewal. Barth began an intensive study of the Letter and when his commentary was published in 1919, it landed, as Karl Adam aptly put it, like "a bombshell on the playground of the theologians." In the commentary, Barth reaffirmed the Reformation principles of grace alone, faith alone, Scripture alone. Under the influence of the nineteenth-century thinker Søren Kierkegaard, he stated some things one-sidedly, as he later admitted, by insisting on the "infinite qualitative distinction" between time and eternity.

Barth's theology was also called the "theology of crisis" since it dealt with the crisis of European society and also the crisis of the individual before God. Another label that was used was "dialectical theology." It referred to Barth's method of statement and counterstatement. For Barth, theological truth is like a bird in flight; no still photograph can capture it, only a moving picture. Neoorthodoxy was also called "Neo-Reformation theology" to emphasize the strong influence of Luther and Calvin. While this influence was great, Barth was also severely critical of Reformation thought, concerned as he was to provide "a corrective theology" for his day.

DIVERSE THINKERS

Neoorthodoxy was not a united and uniform theological movement, including as it did such diverse thinkers as Emil Brunner, Friedrich Gogarten, Rudolf Bultmann, and Paul Tillich. These theologians felt the influence of Barth but they diverged from him later and developed their own theologies. The German church struggle brought some of these differences to the surface. While some theologians hailed the rise of the Third Reich, Barth opposed the Nazi regime. It was during this time that he made his break with Gogarten on the relation of anthropology and theology, always concerned to stress the transcendence of God in relation to humanity, and with Brunner on the question of natural theology, insisting that biblical revelation alone was the medium of God's self-disclosure. When the German Confessing Church met at Barmen in May 1934, Barth wrote most of the text of the *Barmen Declaration*. Against the claim that God had revealed himself in German "blood and soil" and in the rise of Hitler to power, the declaration stated: "Jesus Christ, as he is attested in Holy Scripture, is the one Word of God which we have to hear and which we have to trust and obey in life and death."

In North America, neoorthodoxy took a less radical form and was commonly associated with the Niebuhr brothers, H. Richard and Reinhold. The latter's Gifford lectures, *The Nature and Destiny of Man* (2 vols., 1941–1943) became a landmark of American theology. Reinhold Niebuhr and Barth did not see eye to eye particularly on the Christian's attitude to communism, Barth's position being more tolerant of this ideology. Under the editorship of James D. Smart, the Presbyterian *Christian Faith and Life* curriculum was influenced by the neoorthodox approach as was also the Presbyterian *Confession of 1967*, both of which had a strongly biblical approach. Neoorthodoxy, particularly in its Barthian form, concentrated on taking God rather than the human person as the starting point of theological inquiry. One does not speak of God, Barth said, by speaking of the human person in a loud voice. Neoorthodoxy sought to formulate a theology centered on God and Jesus Christ and it did much to restore theology as a central activity of the church, serving its teaching and preaching.

IN RELIGIOUS EDUCATION

Neoorthodoxy has had a lasting influence on religious education curriculum among the denominations that have tended to work cooperatively (as in Joint Educational Development). It has continued to form the theological/biblical foundation for the Presbyterian curriculum. It brought to other denominations a stronger emphasis on the biblical story and interpretation, rather than putting a primary emphasis on life experience. The difference between this approach and evangelical curricula (also biblically based) lies in its accep-

tance of historical and literary scholarship as tools for interpretation and in not trying to make immediate applications of the biblical material to personal situations. The design is for learners to identify with biblical people and hear God's word spoken to them and their times through these stories. *See also* Biblical Authority; Ecumenical Education; Liberalism; Theology and Education.

FOR FURTHER REFERENCE

Barth, Karl. *Evangelical Theology.* Translated by Grover Foley. New York: Holt, Rinehart and Winston, 1963.

Busch, Eberhard. *Karl Barth: His Life from Letters and Autobiographical Texts.* Translated by John Bowden. Philadelphia: Fortress Press, 1976.

Smart, James D., trans. *Revolutionary Theology in the Making: Barth-Thurneysen Correspondent.* Richmond, VA: Knox, 1964.

W. Klempa

New Zealand

Of New Zealand's population of 3.3 million, the largest religious groups are Anglican (29%), Presbyterian (18%), and Roman Catholic (15%).

British settlers arriving in New Zealand in the nineteenth century brought with them the trappings of Victorian church life, including, for Protestants, the Sunday school, which continues to be the most obvious and enduring agent of church education. Anglican (from 1814), Methodist (from 1822), and Roman Catholic (from 1838) missionaries to the Maoris, the *tangata whenua*, or "people of the land," trained native catechists, who could be regarded as the earliest indigenous agents of deliberate Christian education. Roman Catholic missionaries set up parochial schools that have remained the major agency of Catholic religious education for children. A 1975 act of Parliament enabled private and church schools to be integrated into the state system while safeguarding their special religious character. A smaller number of Protestant and Anglican schools have joined the far larger group of Catholic schools in being so integrated, leaving independent only a small group of well-endowed church schools.

GENERAL EDUCATION

Early New Zealand schools were church sponsored, but by the 1870s a secular state education system was in place. Since the 1877 Education Act New Zealand education, to avoid sectarian disagreements among believers, has been officially "secular." (In fact, it was not until after the Second World War that theology and religious studies were taught in New Zealand universities, which are part of a state system.)

The New Zealand Bible in Schools League was formed in 1912 "to secure for the Bible its proper place in education." This movement failed in its immediate aims, but by 1962 the "Nelson System" whereby schools would be closed for half an hour a week to permit religious instruction by volunteer teachers was incorporated into the Education Act. Use of an agreed syllabus prepared under the guidance of the Churches Education Commission remains mandatory. The Commission represents Anglican, Presbyterian, Methodist, Baptist, and Congregationalist churches along with the Salvation Army, Society of Friends, Associated Churches of Christ, Apostolic church, and Open Brethren Assemblies.

PROTESTANT RELIGIOUS EDUCATION

By the early twentieth century the Methodist and Presbyterian churches had organized Sunday school or youth departments with full-time advisers attached to them. Anglican dioceses and the Baptist Union followed. Interdenominational Sunday School Unions (Auckland, 1865, Wellington, 1880) had an important influence.

Arguably the most significant and uniquely New Zealand Protestant educational venture was the Bible Class movement for youth and young adults (Presbyterian, 1902, Methodist, 1905, Baptist, 1905). Features of the movement were evangelistic youth camps at Easter (which still continue), full-time organizers, and a sturdy independence. The movement's decline in the post–World War II period deprived these churches of a significant source of leadership and vigor. Christian education departments were unable to generate the same enthusiasm or loyalty.

By the early 1960s each of the denominational youth departments had become departments of Christian education seeking to promote educational opportunities for all ages.

Over the last three or four decades, the Sunday school and youth groups have declined in numbers and effectiveness within mainline Anglican and Protestant churches.

The work of the denominational Christian education departments demonstrates the unfocused understanding of education and its role in the church that has bedeviled Protestant Christian education in New Zealand. At various times they have been understood as agents of evangelism, supporters of missionary work abroad, encouragers of Sunday school, sponsors of group life laboratories, stimulators of social action, and agents of parish development and of various church renewal movements. In 1976 the Presbyterian church renamed their agency the Department of Parish Development and Mission. Some Anglican dioceses have replaced Christian education advisers with ministry development officers responsible for the encouragement and development of nonstipendiary clergy.

Generally educational understandings have followed trends found elsewhere in the Western church. Since the 1960s a number of leading Christian educators have done postgraduate study in the United States. It was not until the 1960s and 1970s that specialist Christian educators were appointed to theological college faculties. Until that time child development taught within pastoral theology tended to be the only specific preparation for educational ministry given to ministry trainees.

New Zealand churches have valued educational links with Australia. Baptist and Anglican churches have shared curriculum development with their Australian counterparts, but the most significant cooperation between Australia and New Zealand has been through the Joint Board of Christian Education, involving Anglican, Methodist, and Presbyterian churches in New Zealand. This board has been the major producer of written curriculum materials for use in New Zealand churches, and specifically New Zealand content is included. North American material from theologically conservative sources is used in some Protestant congregations and denominations.

ROMAN CATHOLIC RELIGIOUS EDUCATION

With Roman Catholic parishes the Confraternity of Christian Doctrine, a program of weekday Christian instruction for children, came into common use in the 1960s. To support this work CCD resource centers were set up, and since the 1970s these centers have become involved in adult education and assisting parishes to implement the insights of Vatican II. In 1985 the sole Roman Catholic teachers' college was closed, with state colleges of education providing a catechetical studies course for those preparing to teach in state-integrated Catholic schools. A decline in numbers of people offering themselves for teaching orders has meant an increasing reliance on lay teachers.

TRENDS

Within the Roman Catholic church the Young Christian Workers movement in the 1960s and more recently the Evangelism, Justice, and Development Commission have helped give a social justice focus to church education. Within Protestant churches the National Council of Churches had supported the denominations in this area. The formation of the Council of Churches in New Zealand, Aotearoa (1987), bringing together the Roman Catholic church and members of the National Council of Churches (and therein replacing this council), will enable increased cooperation in education on justice and social issues.

In the 1980s a number of additional significant trends and issues can be identified. The churches, most notably the Anglican, Roman Catholic, Methodist, and Presbyterian, are deeply involved in a search for a more bicultural New Zealand, based on a more faithful response to the 1840 Treaty of Waitangi signed by Maori chiefs and representatives of the English crown and safeguarding Maori prerogatives and land. Theologically this has meant a new awareness of distinctive Maori spirituality and forms of church life. The *marae*, a large hall that serves as the focus of Maori life in community, is being recognized as an ecclesial model of potentially great significance for European understanding of the church as an educational environment. The Marae is used for worship, study, socialization, and business. On some occasions, meetings last through the night and people eat and sleep in the marae. The current Western socialization or acculturation of models of religious education is evident in contrast, and the narrower "Sunday school" understanding of education is increasingly regarded as deficient. Maoris' respect for the "ancestors" is alerting educators to the role of the saints in Christian education. Educational programs on racism and cultural awareness are now common in the churches, and there is considerable debate about the most appropriate and effective educational methods.

Significant communities of Pacific Island migrants (particularly from Samoa, Tonga, Fiji, and the Cook Islands) with strong church allegiance (Methodist, Presbyterian, Roman Catholic, Congregationalist) have brought with them nineteenth-century missionary patterns of church life and education. How best to provide educational resources appropriate for migrant communities anxious to preserve their way of life and expression of faith in a new environment is an ongoing issue. The large majority of Protestant and Anglican churches are small, unable to maintain inherited models of Sunday school and youth education programs. Considerable attention is being given to ways whereby the small church can become a truly educative environment. In some places all-ages worship and education is developing. The Sunday school and traditional youth programs remain strongest in conservative churches with large regional congregations. A renewed emphasis on adult lay education is seen in the formation of lay education centers and programs in Protestant churches, in increasing lay enrollment in extramural studies based at theological colleges, in the use of the North American "Education for Ministry" program, and in the work of Roman Catholic diocesan centers for education and spiritual formation.

The ecumenical movement has been enhanced by considerable cooperation and cross-fertilization between churches in the area of Christian education. *See also* Australia; Pacific Islands.

B. K. Rowe

Nursery Education

The nursery of the church or synagogue is the designated setting for the youngest members of the community of faith—infants, toddlers, twos, threes, and fours. When a faith community speaks of nursery education, it is generally referring to a program of religious education for the two-, three-, and four-year old children.

PARTNERSHIP WITH PARENTS

When the covenant community accepts the responsibility of the religious education of its children, it is acting as an extension of the home and family; and the family in its role of nurturing children in religious faith is serving as an extension of the covenant community. The family and the religious community are partners in providing the environment and the means by which children may grow up in the faith of the parents.

THE UNIQUE RESPONSIBILITY OF TEACHERS OF THE YOUNG

Young children, whose language and thought processes are far different from those of adults, are influenced more by their interactions with significant persons in their lives than by verbal teaching. Since the first years of a child's life are crucial in the child's development, it is vital that the teachers of young children be chosen with care. These teachers should not only love children and seek to understand them and their needs but be persons growing in their love of and relationship to God. They need to have a deep commitment to the faith community as well as to the responsibility of teaching.

NATURE OF YOUNG CHILDREN AND HOW THEY LEARN

Any effective program of religious education for the young child must take into consideration the characteristics of children and the ways they learn. It is generally agreed that the young child's thinking is based on feeling rather than knowing, that these children have no concept of time and space, and that they learn by what they experience rather than by what people say.

Physically, the children are very active, and they tire easily. They need vigorous, large muscle activity, frequent changes of activity, and times of quiet work.

Socially, the older of the children in this group are becoming increasingly interested in interaction with peers but often do not know how to relate, share, and take turns. They need many opportunities for practice of such skills in a supportive environment. Sometimes they require a teacher's help in working out problems and at other times they need encouragement to talk things out with another child.

Emotionally, children at this age are self-centered, seeking much attention and praise, and therefore need affirming relationships with adults who understand their need for assurance. The children are becoming increasingly independent and need opportunities to do things for themselves.

Mentally, threes and fours are interested in using language, carrying on conversations, creating songs and poems and stories, and in making their own choices of activities, resources, and friends. Freedom to enjoy unstructured play with limited guidance by friendly teachers helps children feel relaxed and find stimulating work to do.

The toddler, in the early stages of walking, talking, and relating to people beyond the immediate family, needs a protected environment with a watchful, helping teacher and toys for experimentation. These children will more likely play alone or with the teacher than with peers.

The two year old is developing autonomy. While parallel play is often observed, twos watch and sometimes participate with other children. Their need to develop independence is often indicated by aggressiveness, and the phrase "terrible twos" reflects adult consternation at their almost continuous use of "no" to indicate the wish to make decisions. Twos need the opportunity for making choices within boundaries, a key to socialization at this age. They are interested in and capable of participation with many of the play materials and activities of their older peers, the threes and fours, but will not usually display the same degree of skill. Some preschool programs are structured to include a range of age levels with the idea that twos are stimulated in their socialization by the presence of older children and the latter learn how to adapt to younger children (as in a family).

Religiously, children have an increasing capacity for wonder and are naturally trusting, hopeful, loving. They learn to appreciate and respect God's creation, begin to talk about the God who loves them, and often reach out to others, reflecting the caring attitude they have observed in adults.

Though children share many personality characteristics in common, it is also true that each child has special characteristics, interests, capacities, and prior experiences that make the child a unique person. As religious educators begin to know children as individuals, they can better offer opportunities to help children grow into the persons God intends them to be.

THE NATURE OF THE PROGRAM

The typical nursery education program includes a large block of time for children to choose freely among playtime activities. For those with participatory skills this is followed by a five-to-ten-minute group time and finally a time for rhythmic movement, a group game, or a simple project such as planting seeds.

Curriculum resources developed for the nursery age child usually provide a central idea around which the play activities and group activities may be planned. Stories, poems, fingerplays, games, and music are suggested as well as ideas for helping the children derive the most benefit from the play areas.

The Bible, a primary resource for religious education, is essentially an adult book. Much of it is beyond the comprehension of young children, and its stories and teachings must be used in a way that respects the integrity of the Bible and reflects an understanding of the needs of the child. Verses from the Bible that express thanksgiving and assure children of God's love and care are appropriate, as are stories about God's help and faithfulness. Stories that are the foundations for holidays (Hanukkah, Christmas, Purim, Easter) add religious meaning to these days.

The largest portion of the educational period is devoted to play, since play provides the most effective avenue of learning for young children. Youngsters are most comfortable in an informal play environment that provides for freedom of movement, time to explore and try out new things, and opportunities to engage in activities of their own choosing. Twos and younger threes normally enjoy playing "alongside" another child while older threes and fours can work cooperatively with two or more other children. Interest centers for play often include a building area, a home-living area, a book center, an art center, and a nature center. A new interest center, such as a music center or game center, may replace an old one from time to time, but too frequent changes are not desirable. The children need the security of the "expected" in their classroom environment as well as in the teaching staff. This general nursery classroom arrangement can be seen in diagrams accompanying this article.

ENVIRONMENT TEACHES

The physical environment itself carries a message to young learners about the importance of the religious educational enterprise. Children respond positively to a homelike environment, clean and orderly space, sunny windows, inviting colors, resources placed within easy reach, comfortable nooks, linoleum-floored areas to allow for spills, carpeted areas that keep the play from being too loud and provide a cozy place for pillows and books. Toilet furnishings, tables, and chairs should be child-sized, and work and play materials should be large enough to accommodate large muscle activity.

The psychological environment is even more important. Consistency of staff is absolutely essential to give the children a sense of belonging. There should be two teachers in the classroom no

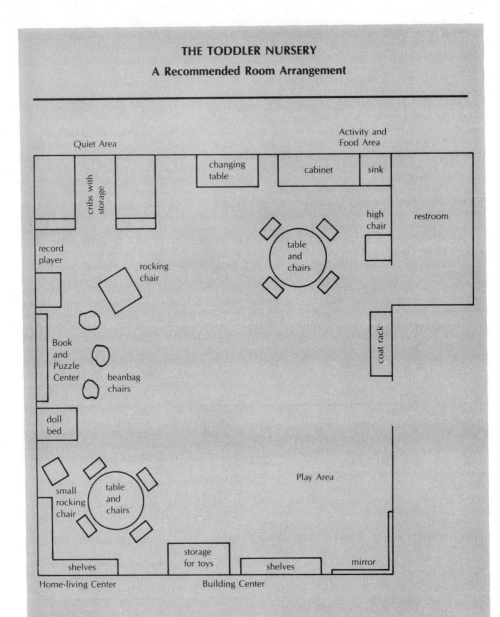

THE TODDLER NURSERY

A Recommended Room Arrangement

The space and facilities above have been designed to meet the needs of a toddler class with an average attendance of 10 children. Total floor space equals 350 square feet (17½ × 20) to provide the optimum 35 square feet of space per child. All but the Activity and Food Area should be carpeted. Windows should provide semidirect lighting.

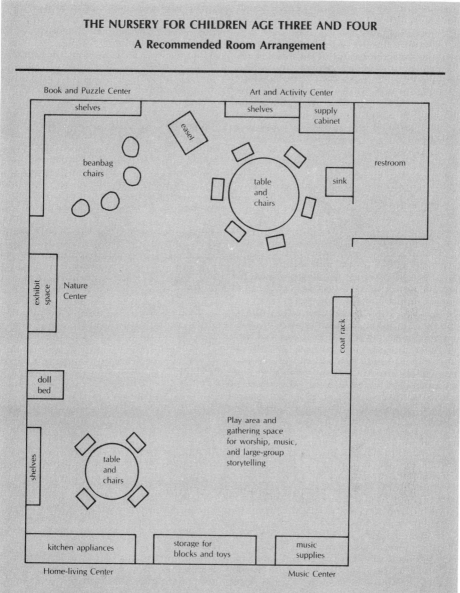

THE NURSERY FOR CHILDREN AGE THREE AND FOUR
A Recommended Room Arrangement

The space and facilities above have been designed to meet the needs of a nursery department with a maximum attendance of 12 children. Total floor space equals 420 square feet (17½ × 24) to provide the optimum 35 square feet of space per child. Carpeting is the preferred floor covering in all but the Art and Activity Center (where vinyl or some easy-to-clean surface is preferred). Windows should provide semidirect lighting.

matter how small the group to allow for special one-to-one needs, and a ratio of one teacher for every five children. A maximum of fifteen children in a class is suggested.

Young children need teachers who are warm, accepting, and appreciative of the gifts children offer to adults—affection, joy, spontaneity, honesty, openness. Teachers should provide an atmosphere in the classroom that communicates acceptance and caring, no matter how unacceptable a child's behavior may be. Members of the teaching staff need to realize the importance of comforting and giving attention to children who cannot control their behavior. A child who has needs for behavioral change requires teachers who believe in the child and support the child's efforts. Occasions when boundaries have been overstepped give a teacher and child an opportunity to talk together about the reasons a particular behavior cannot be allowed and about other options available to the child for getting needs met.

THE COVENANT COMMUNITY EDUCATES

Since young children are a part of the community of faith, there need to be times when children experience the life of the whole church or synagogue family as part of their education and as part of their sense of belonging. Such experiences might include attendance at weekday meals and programs, with some programs being intergenerational ones; attendance for a portion of corporate worship on special occasions; visitation to their classrooms by the rabbi, minister, minister of music, or custodian; development of special relationships with individuals of all ages in the faith community and taking on the task of meeting a special need of the congregation.

CHALLENGES

Parents need the strong support of the family of faith to meet the demands of their vitally important responsibility of child rearing. Adults with young children often feel overwhelmed with their responsibility, yet do not want to bother others with their problems. Members of the covenant community should take initiative in providing love and support to these families. Perhaps the church or synagogue can offer classes to assist parents, provide a baby-sitting pool, or organize small community groups whose members support one another in times of need, pray for one another, and make themselves available to one another.

Further, adults in the faith community should recognize the need children have for models. The faith of children is shaped to a large extent by the faith of their parents and other significant persons in their lives, including their teachers and adult friends. Of particular importance to the young are the actions of the adults in their lives. Words and actions must be congruent to be taken seriously. Adults who have committed themselves to an ever-growing faith of their own have already provided a solid foundation for the religious development of the children in their care. See also Child Abuse; Child Development; Children's Church; Day-care Center; Infancy; Kindergarten; Parenting; Preschool Children; Worship, Children's.

E. A. Ramsey

Nurture

Nurture in religious education literature means the process of acquiring—or the effort to inculcate—faith in God, a religious understanding of the world, and a set of moral principles and practices from adult caregivers and the church.

The idea of nurture is best described in the Old Testament Shema. In Deuteronomy 6:4–9 the Hebrews were told, "And these words which I command you this day shall be upon your heart; and you shall teach them diligently to your children, and shall talk of them when you sit in your house, and when you walk by the way, and when you lie down, and when you rise." In the New Testament nurture lies behind the story of Jesus in the Temple at the age of twelve (Luke 2:41–52); the passage ends with these words: "and Jesus increased in wisdom and in stature, and in favor with God and man" (Luke 2:52). Nurture assumes that if the right environment is provided, children will become religiously oriented persons because they grew up in the faith (Prov. 22:6; Eph. 6:4).

Use of the term "nurture" was activated in the modern era by Horace Bushnell (1802–1876) with his book *Christian Nurture* (1861). Bushnell lived in New England at a time when the theology of the Great Awakening led by Jonathan Edwards (1740s) had hardened into dogmas stressing the sovereignty of God, the total depravity of humans, and people's inability to be saved unless they were converted by the Holy Spirit—usually in a revival. Since these dogmas also applied to children, there was little parents could do for their children except to explain the beliefs and urge children to expect salvation through a conversion experience. Bushnell reacted to these rigid beliefs by insisting that parents and the influence of the home and church could and should produce an environment such "that the child is to grow up a Christian, and never know himself as being otherwise" (Bushnell, *Christian Nurture*, p. 4).

The theology to which Bushnell responded was about human nature and the controversy continues into our time. In contemporary terms there are three major views of human nature, each of which has a direct bearing on religious nurture.

The first is the classic view that humans are prone to sin. This view is attributed to the apostle Paul (Rom. 5–9). Paul was deeply influenced by

At the beginning of the third century, the Alexandrian school seems to have had primarily a lay-oriented curriculum. However, Origen took his duties as chief catechist so seriously that he sold his library, gave up scholarly pursuits, adopted an ascetic life-style, and devoted himself to exhaustive Bible study. According to Eusebius, Origen's fame as a teacher eventually drew "thousands," even of the intelligentsia, under his influence.

Origen's writings have left him with an enduring reputation as the first true textual critic, the most influential commentator of the early church, the first theologian to offer a systematic exposition of the Christian faith, and a great apologist for the faith. He is popularly remembered for his allegorical method of interpreting Scripture, but his own literalistic interpretation of Matthew 19:12 caused him to castrate himself. Origen's writings and asceticism seem to have spawned and nurtured the monastic movement that flourished in succeeding centuries. *See also* Catechetical School; History of Christian Education.

H. W. Burgess

Orthodox Christian Education Commission

See Orthodox Education.

Orthodox Education

The Eastern Orthodox churches continue in a line from the earliest Christian congregations, and their liturgical practices trace back to the earliest Christian traditions. Initially concentrated in the Middle East, these churches then spread to Eastern Europe and later to the western world. They now have 123 million members worldwide. The churches recognize basic doctrines from the first seven ecumenical councils as does the Roman Catholic church, but they deny the jurisdiction of the pope. Independent within each nation today, Orthodox churches are linked by their bishops, the patriarch of Constantinople being the "first among equals."

EMPHASIS ON EXPERIENCE

"O taste and see that the Lord is good!" (Ps. 34:8). This simple statement from Psalms summarizes the Orthodox approach to religious education: one's experience (taste) of the life of the church precedes the process of understanding (seeing) the content and meaning of that life.

From the time of birth, the sacramental life of the family and parish community is the context for education and spiritual nurture. The child is integrated into the community as an infant—being "named" on the eighth day, and baptized in water and chrismated (confirmed) with the "seal of the gift of the Holy Spirit" several weeks later. At the same time, the infant is "churched" and receives Holy Communion as a full member of the community. Sensory experiences in worship and family life contribute to educational and spiritual nurture throughout childhood and adulthood. Surrounded by images of Christ, Mary the mother of God, and the saints, a person grows in participation and awareness of the church through the ages. Incense, icons, water and oil used in blessings, physical activity (kneeling, standing, prostrations, processions, making the sign of the cross on oneself), bread, wine, and other liturgical acts and symbols involve the whole person (body, soul, and spirit) in the act of worship and personal prayer. The rhythm of the liturgical cycles of feasts and fasts engage a person throughout the church year and over the years not only in liturgical celebration but also in reflection and action concerning the Christian's responsibility in the world. From this central, communal action of the worshiping community comes the vision and motivation to witness to the risen Lord and give oneself in service to others in his name.

The integration of worship, teaching, and practice (praxis) within the context of personal and community life is the key to education in the Orthodox church. The aim of all religious teaching, as expressed by Alexander Schmemann, is to integrate the person from childhood "into the life of the Church—the life of grace, communion with God, love, unity and spiritual progress towards eternal salvation, for such are the essential aims of the Church" (*Liturgy and Life*, p. 23).

The Christian community from its very beginning set the pattern for this method of sacramental integration and socialization: "And they devoted themselves to the apostles' teaching and fellowship, to the breaking of bread and the prayers. . . . And all who believed were together and had all things in common; and they sold their possessions and goods and distributed them to all, as any had need" (Acts 2:42–45). By medieval times, however, the fullness of this life (and of the educational nurture that proceeded from it) had broken down. Worship was often reduced to meaningless rites; teaching, to the repetition of standard formulas; and Christian praxis, to minimal codes of conduct. Scholasticism and Pietism, in opposition to each other, completed the disintegration of a holistic approach to the Christian vision of life. Though predominant in the West, these trends also affected the churches of the East.

Only with the rediscovery of the centrality of liturgical worship through the biblical and patristic studies of the late nineteenth and twentieth centuries was the fullness of church life and thought recovered, and with it the renewal of Christian education.

RENEWAL AND RECENT DEVELOPMENT

Several movements led to the renewed awareness of holistic or "total parish education" that guides the thinking of Orthodox educators today. The first is the theological reawakening that came with the rediscovery and translation into modern languages of the writings of the church fathers. Stimulated by the work of several Russian theologians in the second half of the nineteenth century, this recovery of "Orthodox" theology flowered in the period of Russian emigration following the revolution of 1917 and was centered in the St. Sergius Theological Institute in Paris, which produced many of the noted Orthodox leaders, bishops, and theologians of today.

The second major influence was the development of Orthodox youth movements in Western Europe and the Middle East: the Russian Student Christian Movement (RSCM) in France, Zoe (Gk.; "life") and movements developing from it in Greece, and the Orthodox Youth Movement (MJO) in Lebanon and Syria. Although each movement had a slightly different emphasis, the results were similar: a eucharistic renewal, educational programs for all age levels, and a commitment to mission and social responsibility (which also included the restoration of the monastic life). Contemporary leaders whose early formation came from these movements include Patriarch Ignatius IV of Antioch, Metropolitan Georges (Khodre) of Mount Lebanon, Bishop Anastasios (Yannoulatos) of Greece, Abbot Vasileios of Mount Athos, Nikos Nissiotis (d. 1986), Alexander Schmemann (d. 1983), John Meyendorff, and Nicholas Lossky. Today, a new generation of theologians, educators, and youth leaders trained by them carry out the education and mission of the church on nearly every continent. This work is supported by the efforts of several institutions (in addition to the continuing work of the movements previously mentioned): Syndesmos (Gk., "bonds"), the International Fellowship of Orthodox Youth; St. Vladimir's Orthodox Theological Seminary and its SVS Press (the largest publisher of Orthodox books in English) in Crestwood, New York; the Orthodox Christian Education Commission (OCEC) in the United States; and Apostoliki Diakonia, the ministry and mission outreach of the Church of Greece.

The development of modern religious education curricula, methods, and materials is being accomplished slowly in North America and in other areas of the world where formal educational programs are established. The rethinking of Or-thodox Christian education in contemporary society has been going on for less than fifty years and has been slowed by a number of factors. Emigration from Old World "Orthodox" areas to the West has been accompanied by traditional emigré problems: assimilation into new cultures, the struggle with foreign languages, problems of identity, the secularization of culture itself, pluralism, etc. In the Old World countries, the church has been confronted with other challenges: atheistic or totalitarian governments, the abolition of religion in the schools, civil unrest, and the cultural change that comes with increasing secularization. In some Western countries, the Protestant model of Sunday schools was adopted uncritically, and what is basically an anomaly in Orthodox thinking and practice—the conducting of educational programs during the same hour as the celebration of the Eucharist—can still be found in some Orthodox churches today. Consequently, the development of current Orthodox educational thinking has necessitated a process of reflection on "tradition," inductively drawing from the theological sources and practice of the church through the ages the principles and concepts that would enable a reconstruction (or transformation) from tradition of an educational model for today.

Among the pioneers who began this process for the Orthodox was Sophie Koulomzin, whose initial work in Paris was further developed upon her emigration to the United States. The founder of the Orthodox Christian Education Commission (OCEC), she gathered a group of Orthodox educators and theologians to reflect upon tradition in the contemporary cultural context, which led to a renewal of Orthodox educational practice combining modern psychological insights and educational methodology with essential theological concepts and insights that approach the spiritual nurture of persons holistically. Among others involved in this process were the archpriest Alexander Schmemann, her colleague; Constance Tarasar and John L. Boojamra, her successors in the OCEC; the archpriests Stephen Sedor, Thomas Hopko, and George Nicosizin; Xenophon Diamond and Cornelia Hategan, in the United States; and individuals in the Orthodox churches abroad: Jean Tchekan in France; Metropolitan Georges (Khodre), Maud Nahas, Salma Fayad, Frieda Haddad, and others in Lebanon; Alexandros Papaderos of the Orthodox Academy in Crete; and several young priests and educators in Finland. Three international conferences have stimulated a cooperative effort to continue the dialogue and exchange of research worldwide. These conferences have also involved members of the Oriental Orthodox churches, notably Metropolitan Paulos Gregorios of the Orthodox church in India, Bishop Anastasios and Maurice Assad of the Coptic church in Egypt, and members of the Armenian church in the Middle East.

As we look to the future of Orthodox Christian education, the goal of total parish education requires an evaluation of the church and its mission in society. The Orthodox in America are just coming to terms with their situation in the American context and the attendant responsibilities involving witness, mission, and service. The integration of worship, teaching, and practice for the spiritual development of persons of all ages will be the key to a truly Orthodox understanding and practice of education in the decades to come. *See also* Liturgy.

FOR FURTHER REFERENCE

Koulomzin, Sophie. *Our Church and Our Children.* Crestwood, NY: St. Vladimir's Seminary Press, 1975.

Schmemann, Alexander. *For the Life of the World.* Crestwood, NY: St. Vladimir's Seminary Press, 1973.

――― . *Liturgy and Life: Christian Development Through Liturgical Experience.* Syosset, NY: DRE-Orthodox Church in America, 1974.

Tarasar, Constance J., ed. *Perspectives in Orthodox Education.* Syosset, NY: DRE-Orthodox Church in America, 1983.

C. J. Tarasar

Outdoor Ministries

Most people think of children camping by a lake for a week when they think about religious outdoor experiences. That image is appropriate, but religious outdoor ministries now encompass much, much more.

Now people of all ages enjoy getting away from their normal daily routine for a time of meditation, prayer, recreation, and learning. Activities may include not only the traditional ones of hiking, swimming, and Bible study, but also computer training, ecological study, leadership training, worship, music, special service projects, and a variety of others.

GOALS

One basic philosophy of outdoor ministry is that it is not only important what people do, but important in what setting the activities take place. To "go apart" from the world to deepen one's relationship with God is an ancient and time-proven tradition. The deepening understanding of God is the first and primary goal of religious camping.

A second primary goal of outdoor ministries is helping participants learn to live interdependently. Many people find this community building changes their perspective on what it means to live cooperatively with others.

A third goal of outdoor ministries is enabling participants to appreciate creation and to embrace a holistic view of creation. In a setting apart from city and suburbs, participants feel more at one with God's created world.

ORGANIZATIONS

The Council of Religiously Affiliated Camps (CRAC) is part of the national 5,000-member American Camping Association. Other groups dedicated to outdoor ministries are Christian Camping International, which certifies Christian camps at three levels of work and publishes a *Journal of Christian Camping,* and the National Council of Churches Committee on Outdoor Ministries, which helps coordinate educational efforts and publishes both materials for directors and counselors and administrative and leadership training materials.

A number of Roman Catholic leaders and programs have mobilized and organized Catholics Involved in Outdoor Ministries (COM), a "kindred" or affiliate of ACA, which recognizes and adheres to the high standards, philosophy, and ethics of the American Camping Association. COM and CRAC hold their annual meetings in tandem with ACA and also interact with each other.

The Jewish Welfare Board located in New York City publishes a national directory of Jewish camps and their programs. Though quite comprehensive, the directory does not include the whole range of religious camping programs sponsored by Jewish groups and movements. Within Judaism there are camps related to the various movements: Reform, Conservative, Orthodox. In philosophy, camps range from those with a cultural emphasis or a religious orientation to those with community-oriented programs or programs of academic study.

HISTORY

The camping movement in the United States began over a century ago. Robert Allen, president of the Presbyterian Church (U.S.A.) Camp and Conference Associates outlined this development:

- 1860s: The church camp movement began. Families gathered in "camp meetings" for several days to hear evangelists.

- 1900s: Sunday school classes went to camps as outdoor classrooms for Bible teaching and recreation.

- 1910s: Scouting and Camp Fire programs were imported from England, setting a style of youth camps that continues to be popular today.

- 1920s: College campuses were put to use for camps and conferences.

- 1940s: Camps were being built by the churches for their own camping programs.

- 1950s: Camps began to develop decentralized

OUTDOOR MINISTRIES

Age Level	Goals	Appropriate Activities
Preschool	To learn about God by learning about God's creation, observing and experiencing the outdoors, discovering plants and animals; to provide opportunities for physical exercise and group interaction	With close supervision, children can play outdoors and visit farms, parks, and zoos; older preschool children can attend outdoor day camps.
Grades 1–8	To learn more about God's creation and to begin to develop attitudes and habits of care for it; to adjust to being away from home; to learn interdependence and cooperation with others; to learn outdoor skills; to provide time and opportunity for serious biblical study and special worship	With decreasing supervision, children can play outdoors; classes should provide opportunity for more formal observation and study of nature; field trips can be taken to parks, zoos, museums, and planetariums; children can be given increasing responsibility for tending a garden or caring for animals; early elementary children can attend summer day camps and older elementary children can attend one-to-eight week residential camps.
High School	To increasingly accept and learn how to undertake the role of steward of God's creation; to increasingly understand interrelationships and develop further skill in cooperation; to provide time and opportunity for serious biblical study, worship, and reflection; to further develop outdoor skills	Formal study of the outdoors should continue, with a focus on environmental problems and possible solutions; formal study of biblical passages regarding creation and stewardship (i.e., Gen. 1; Ps. 8; Ps. 24:1, 2; Matt. 6:25-33) should also be undertaken; opportunities should be provided for youth to work together on environmental projects; general residential camps, special camps (i.e., music camps), and special outdoor trips (i.e., skiing or biking) can be enjoyed.
Adults	To provide the opportunity to examine and better our stewardship of all things in both our communal and our individual lives; to provide both solitary and communal time and opportunity apart from the daily routine for recreation, study, and worship	Stewardship and personal life-style considerations can be directly discussed; congregations as a whole should regularly assess their stewardship of all resources; outdoor events and ministries should be tailored from various options to fit specific needs.

Questions from the audience may be written out and given to the panelists ahead of time, providing them a chance to decide who will field each question. Or the moderator can read the questions to them after they have expressed their own viewpoints. This would depend on the maturity of the speakers. Students can use their curriculum material to help clarify problems or to answer questions.

The panelists sit facing the audience. The moderator introduces the panelists and their topic. The moderator also watches the time to allow all the panelists an equal opportunity to speak.

The moderator calls time and then involves the audience by asking for comments or questions from them. At the close of the time, the moderator summarizes the major points given and thanks everyone for participating.

A panel may also be used for peer-group problem solving. In some communities, the municipal judge turns some of the teenage misdemeanor cases over to a panel of teenagers. They hear the cases and decide on the sentences, usually some needed community service work. It is sometimes proving to be more effective than the adult-made decisions.

Children sometimes like to play "stump the panel" as a way of reviewing some of the factual material in the church school curriculum. After reading the material, pupils write out questions and turn them in. After the panel is chosen, the moderator reads a question and one panel member tries to answer it. If this panelist does not know the answer, he or she takes a seat and the question is given to the next panelist. At the end of a given time, if any panelist still remains, the panel wins. If all have returned to their seats, the panel is "stumped."

In adult groups the panel could be organized similarly to television quiz shows. The material covered should have relationship to topics that have been studied by the group. This would be an evaluation tool for the teacher who could then provide opportunities to reinforce problem areas.

Another effective way to use a panel is to present new informative material to the group, discuss it among the panel, and then open it to the total group for comments and/or questions. If this were done as a symposium before a large audience, the entire assembly could be divided into small discussion groups for more involvement with the ideas presented.

Well-known community leaders could be invited to be on a panel to present points of view on a topic of interest to the group, or the panel can be used to clarify congregational issues. One church was considering hiring a woman minister. They invited area women in ministry to form a panel to discuss their specific experiences. Their moderator, a man from a church who had not had a woman as minister, kept a lively discussion flowing.

The panel discussion is only one among many methods in the teaching/learning process. It teaches the participant to do critical thinking and to gain experience in public speaking. *See also* Discussion; Symposium.

D. K. Wolcott

Parable

Parables are probably the most characteristic form of Jesus' teaching. They make up about one-third of the synoptic Gospels. This makes parables one of the most important kinds of teaching/learning that Christian religious educators are called to deal with. Despite this, there has been a reluctance to present Jesus' parables to children, because their symbolic nature makes them easily misunderstood.

It is difficult to neatly define a parable. The narrow view sees it as a comparison between what is known (a mustard seed) and what is unknown (the kingdom of heaven). The Greek word *parabole*, used to translate the Hebrew term *mashal* in the Septuagint tends toward this narrow meaning, while *mashal* indicates a broader literary type that includes proverbs, satire, taunts, words of derision, riddles, stories, allegories, comparisons, figurative sayings, and extended metaphors.

Parable use during the centuries since Jesus has not clarified this definition. They have continued to generate meanings and theories about how those meanings are made. One cannot begin to think about the best way to teach about parables, to teach the art of using them, or to do research about teaching methods until one decides what hermeneutic (i.e., way of interpretation) is appropriate.

For example, German scholar A. Jülicher rejected the allegorical method of interpretation about the turn of the century. He said parables have a single point and are not an allegorical code that needs to be translated at every point and level into another kind of language to be understood appropriately. This "point" was a moral proposition that could be applied to the present. Another German scholar, Joachim Jeremias, agreed with Jülicher but thought that the single point was more theological than ethical. In 1935 C. H. Dodd said that parables are metaphors from nature or common life that leave the mind in sufficient doubt that they "tease the mind into active thought." Much of contemporary parable scholarship has studied and broadened how this "teasing into active thought" takes place.

Suppose the "point" of a parable is an experience rather than a thought? The Chicago-based parable scholar Dominic Crossan suggested in his early work that it is the parable maker's experience of God that awaits us "in parable."

If Jesus had wanted to teach ethical or doctrinal points he could have spoken directly and used parables to ornament or to illustrate his ideas. This kind of education is direct and easily measured, but it does not exhaust the way parables work. The history of parable interpretation shows that they have generated new meanings and even new views about how they make meaning for nearly two thousand years!

Jean Piaget, a Swiss psychologist and philosopher, found that children are not able to make conscious analogies until late childhood or early adolescence. In the early 1960s, an English scholar, Ronald Goldman, applied Piaget's work to religious education and seemed to confirm that children should not be given parables until adolescence. He assumed that parables have a single point that needs to be understood by an analogy from the known to the unknown and from the past to the present.

If parables are a unique kind of language that enables us to encounter the mystery of God, then this changes the approach of the teacher. Instead of closing the mind and memory around a thought, the teacher shows how to love parables and how to be playful and open to them. When children enter parables in this way, the concern about misunderstanding can be relaxed. Similarly, adolescents and adults are free to go beyond cognitive understanding and be confronted by the life-changing challenge of parables.

Regardless of what approach one takes to parables, it is clear that we cannot apply what works in secular education to religious education without due consideration. The language of God—sacred stories, parables, and liturgical acts—requires a psychology and pedagogy all its own. *See also* Cognitive Development; Metaphor; Myth; Storytelling; Symbolism.

FOR FURTHER REFERENCE

Crossan, John Dominic. *In Parables: The Challenge of the Historical Jesus.* San Francisco: Harper & Row, 1985.

Kissinger, Warren. *The Parables of Jesus: A History of Interpretation and Bibliography.* Metuchen, NJ: Scarecrow, 1979.

Perrin, Norman. *Jesus and the Language of the Kingdom.* Philadelphia: Fortress, 1976.

Stein, Robert. *The Method and Message of Jesus' Teachings.* Philadelphia: Westminster, 1978.

J. W. Berryman

Parapsychology

Parapsychology is the study of psi or the psychic powers of the mind. Psi researchers increasingly dislike the term "parapsychology," because it implies that psychic powers are beyond the realm of normal human experience. The term "psi research" is preferred because it includes the idea that all persons have some psychic powers and that these abilities can be increased with practice.

Psi research focuses on mental telepathy (the ability to sense the thoughts, feelings, and perceptions of another person at a distance), clairvoyance (the ability to perceive events, objects, or people in ways not available through the use of the five senses), remote viewing (the ability to see a mental picture of a place many miles away and to describe it in considerable detail), and precognition (the ability to perceive future events). Other phenomena associated with parapsychology are hypnosis, psychokinetics, seances, psi healing, out-of-body experiences, and so forth.

If the findings from such research were to be confirmed scientifically a Copernican revolution would take place in our understanding of the nature of the mind, with profound implications for education in general and religious education in particular. The phenomena studied by psi research have been experiences more traditionally attributed to divine intervention, special spiritual gifts, or special training. *See also* Knowledge, Theories of.

R. L. Browning

Parenting

Parenting is the process by which parents or other significant caregivers rear children in their heritage and for life in their society. It seems to be widely agreed that the word crept into common speech in the late 1970s and is probably here to stay. It is used interchangeably with words like "bringing up," "raising," or "rearing" in relation to creating a family, the leadership of a family, and programs in family education.

The importance of parenting is usually taken for granted. The constant oversight of infants and small children is necessary for their survival and later for their safety. They learn trust from the security given them as infants by concerned people. They learn autonomy by the careful guidance that permits choices within limits. They learn initiative by being given freedom with responsibility. They learn the basic skills necessary to life in their society because parents and teachers help them to learn. They develop self-identity when their independence as persons is encouraged during adolescence. Parenting is the process by which these developments take place.

Parents do this through the kind of family life they structure. Their affection for their young ones, which bonds the children in love yet frees them to grow as individuals, encourages wholeness. Parents accomplish the task through interaction with other persons and agencies within their culture: educational, religious, and social. Relationships within their own wider family and friendship networks enlarge children's growing ability to relate positively to other persons.

Breakthroughs in the behavioral sciences in understanding the dynamics of the family have resulted in an increased amount of material in practical form. Conferences, sponsored mainly by academic agencies, have been developed and expanded into a greater number of events, more popular and less clinical, that welcome not only professionals but others concerned with parenting.

The negative aspect of the situation arises from the fact that the turmoil of the 1980s has had an impact on all areas of human society, including the family. To be sure, the family has always been changing, but many factors—such as the high divorce rate, shifts in traditional patterns of authority, sexual freedom, and the drug crisis— have been cause for general anxiety about the status of the family. Among parents themselves there is a fervent search for direction on coping. Hence a huge variety of groups are producing materials to promote their point of view as to how, in a time of chaotic change, the needs of parents can be met more completely.

ISSUES FOR RELIGIOUS EDUCATION

In the religious community today, parenting is considered to be one of two major pillars (together with marriage enrichment) of family ministries. Because family ministry is understood today as a style of total congregational life, i.e., a pervasive emphasis or way of ordering the household of faith (rather than merely an occasional potluck supper), attention to parenting is part of programming for the family life cycle (marriage, young children, teenagers, empty nest, retirement) in the diverse kinds of contemporary families (nuclear, single parent, blended, and so forth).

Thus, parenting is mainly thought of in terms of parent education, parent support groups, and family counseling, reflecting the impact of the family systems theory from the behavioral sciences. It is understood that the members of a family and their life-style as well as their total environment act on each other and all affect the development of each one. Hence, education, support, and counseling may be needed together or at separate times.

In addition to the traditional ministry for crisis, today there is also a new emphasis on family "wellness" parenting, i.e., parenting that is preventive and supportive on an ongoing basis. This is a way of integrating family life and putting the emphasis on wholeness, both of the family entity and each individual within the family constellation.

One area of parenting under the heading of family ministries within any religious education program is the developmental understanding of human growth. A study group might use either a book or a cassette program over a number of weeks to learn about and discuss the stages of human development, both cognitive and emotional. Integral to such a program is the religious development of the child and its relation to other kinds of development.

Family relationships is another area for religious education. Since "family" is a justice issue and also an integral part of adult education in its parenting aspects, a theology of family is critical to the values and style of parenting that occurs. When taken seriously, the biblical hermeneutic of a denomination or a congregation largely determines the relationship in a family where parenting is thoughtful and intentional. Leadership of parenting groups that hear the biblical message of mutuality, equality, and liberation will urge increased responsibility and partnership for every person in the household. The Bible is filled with material for study both of families depicted and admonitions for ordering family life, although a theology that seeks to build directly on biblical family models must carefully consider before assigning roles and responsibilities the influence of patriarchal structures, adversarial relationships, and even corporal punishment in society in ancient times.

Family activities is another area for study and parents can help each other by sharing experiences that might be of mutual interest. There are a variety of indoor, at-home activities: playing games, preparing meals, carrying out special projects, reading out loud, or listening to music or viewing television together. Outdoor activities like gardening, swimming, or games are also vehicles for family sharing. Pleasure and enrichment are to be found in exploring a wider area with walks in parks, visits to museums, or discovering landmarks. A study group on family activities might have people present their areas of interest or research materials frequently issued by communities about places of interest.

A good example of parenting at its best is the positive experience of families for which the regularly scheduled family meeting is a sturdy tradition. This forum for the sharing of plans, problems, and concerns belonging to any family member is successful only when parents engage in and teach a process of openness, honesty, fairness, and concern. Those taking part in parenting groups that view the live, unrehearsed video of the McGinnis family meeting in *Parenting for Peace and Justice* do not find it difficult to discern what is happening: listening, respect, participation, encouragement. It is evident that the parents share a mature marriage relationship, creative parenting skills, and an unmistakable faith journey.

Another area of parenting lies in religious nurture. Traditional forms are teaching children to pray, giving thanks before a meal, forms of family worship at home, taking children to worship as a family, and seeing that children attend religious education classes regularly. Parents look for examples and resources. They can be offered guidance upon the arrival of the new baby, for this is a time when parents are most eager to have information. A parent support group can be helpful. Materials on prayer and family worship may be available through denominational sources or the local congregation. A study group will find this one area in which experiences can be helpfully shared or a resource person can offer new insights.

Peace and justice issues of the wider community are areas of concern to families, if only because examples are seen daily on television. Families in need all over the world are torn apart by war, oppression, and poverty. Churches and synagogues are involved in local programs like food banks, homeless shelters, and educational programs as well as overseas programs for the victims of war, famine, disease, and illiteracy. In the doing of these programs as well as reflections upon them, religious education is accomplished.

RESOURCES

The most widely admired religious program is the multimedia implementation of the book *Parenting for Peace and Justice* by James and Kathleen McGinnis. Through video, filmstrip and worksheets, this resource deals in detail with themes rooted in the Scriptures: nonviolence, prayer, stewardship/simplicity, prejudice and racism, sex-role stereotyping, and family involvement in social action. *Active Parenting* by Michael Popkin is a video-based, seven-session program that seeks to enable parents to foster quality relationships in the family. It is considered by many in the church to be the best secular parenting skills course in the tradition of Adlerian psychology—out of which in the past came pioneering programs such as Thomas Gordon's *Parent Effectiveness Training* (PET) and Dinkmeyer and McKay's *Systematic Training for Effective Parenting* (STEP). *Active Parenting*'s philosophy, values, and techniques are compatible with Christian theology. And one denomination is producing a supplemental publication, *Active Parenting in the Faith Community: A Biblical Theological Guide to Active Parenting* (Presbyterian Church, U.S.A.).

Two very durable Protestant adult curriculum resources, cooperatively produced, are *The First Years of Parenting*, by Frances Johns, and its theological companion *Belonging/Growing in the Christian Community*, by Walter Brueggemann (Presbyterian Church, U.S.A.). Both are widely used for pre/post–parental baptismal instruction and preschool parent groups. *Christian Parenting: Resources for Group Use* is a detailed teachers' manual for a twenty-four-session course that includes sections on "The Bible and Self-Esteem," "Parents as Communicators," "Spiritual Development," "Discipline," and "Parents as Sex Ed-

ucators." *Parenting Your Disabled Child* by Bernard Ikeler is a semiautobiographical manual that deals not only with the basics of a special parenting task but also the spiritual dimension and the theology of suffering. Periodicals like *Marriage and Family Living* (St. Meinrad Archabbey, St. Meinrad, Indiana) and *Family Relations* (National Council on Family Relations, St. Paul, Minnesota) frequently contain articles on parenting. *See also* Child Development; Family Life Education; Parent-Teacher Relations; Peace, Education for; Psychosocial Development; Social Justice, Education for; Worship, Family.

FOR FURTHER REFERENCE

Brueggemann, Walter. *Belonging/Growing in the Christian Community*. Atlanta, GA: Presbyterian Church, U.S.A., 1979.

Carlson, Lee, ed. *Christian Parenting: Resources for Group Use*. Valley Forge, PA: Judson, 1985.

Ikeler, Bernard. *Parenting Your Disabled Child*. Philadelphia: Westminster, 1986.

Ikeler, Carol Rose, ed. *A Guide to Parenting Programs: An Assessment of Seven Major Parenting Programs Currently in Use in Local Churches*. Atlanta, GA: Presbyterian Publishing House, 1984.

Johns, Frances. *The First Years of Parenting*. Atlanta, GA: Presbyterian Church, U.S.A., 1979.

Larson, Jim. *Church Guide to Family Ministries*. Minneapolis, MN: Augsburg, 1986.

Leonard, Joe. *Planning Family Ministries*. Valley Forge, PA: Judson, 1983.

McGinnis, James and Kathleen. *Parenting for Peace and Justice*. Maryknoll, NY: Orbis, 1981.

Popkin, Michael. *Active Parenting*. Atlanta, GA: Michael Popkin, 4669 Roswell Rd., 30342, 1982.

Sawyers, Lindell. *Faith and Families*. Philadelphia: Westminster, 1985.

C. R. Ikeler

Parent-Teacher Relations

Throughout history, parents and teachers have shaped the structure and destiny of the human race. Parents are involved because of their child-bearing and rearing functions. Teachers are those outside the family who teach the children.

In much of today's world teachers are formally trained in colleges and universities. They are licensed by state agencies of education and hired by local boards to teach.

However, parents are still the primary teachers of children, preparing them from birth until the age of independence for a successful transition to adulthood. They guide children in the art of loving themselves and others and in the skill of balancing dependency with independency tempered by interdependency. Foundational to all these are the language skills, religious belief system, personal and group identity, positive self-concept, sensitivity to others' needs, and social skills and competencies the young must possess to reach their fullest potential.

Parents and teachers employ similar strategies to accomplish the goal of equipping children to be productive, adjusted adults. Both use techniques of discipline: rewards and denial of privileges. Both give support to children so that they can learn trust, not mistrust. Both transmit values to the young. Often teachers' and parents' values are mutually supportive; at other times they may differ. However, the most effective parent-teacher relations are formed when parents and teachers see each other as partners. Whenever they become opponents because of differences about curriculum content or classroom methods, they frustrate each other's efforts. The learners' future is then at risk.

MUTUAL RESPECT

A main factor in good parent-teacher relations is mutual respect for each one's basic function. Parents realize that they quite often lack the training needed to give children a formal education. Conversely teachers lack the intimate knowledge of child and family background that parents know from their life together.

The classroom by its very nature becomes a small example of the varied personalities, social philosophies, religious beliefs or nonbelief systems, and moral values of the society. The family milieu provides a more integrated set of experiences that each child brings to school. This task of bringing commonalities from differences requires skill and diplomacy on the part of teachers. They need to provide for free interchange on the part of children while avoiding directly imposing their own positions. If, in the discussion of social, religious, and moral issues, teachers honestly feel some position needs to be considered that is not accepted by some parents, they need to do so in a way that respects parental views. Conversely, parents need to respect the teacher's function of providing learners with an information base upon which to form opinions. Each needs to be sensitive to the other so that children retain confidence both in their parents' ways and in their teachers' views.

Teachers need to be sympathetically knowledgeable about the basic beliefs and attitudes held by parents, and the latter need to be aware of the perspective from which teaching takes place in the school. These views are usually less divergent in private schools or religious education programs chosen by parents than in the public school situation.

MUTUAL SUPPORT

Learning is facilitated when the parents actively support the teacher's educational efforts. For example, if the teacher assigns homework, parents structure family life and the learner's free time away from home to ensure that it is done. Time with friends or television viewing is delayed until the homework is completed. Teachers and school, through their information network, can find ways of getting important information to families (children sometimes forget). They need also to realize that stresses in family life such as parental working hours, crowded houses, or parental priorities might militate against the completion of assigned homework.

Families enrich the lives of children in accordance with their economic means and their interests. It might be through encouragement of local baseball teams or out-of-town ski trips, through hunting and fishing or visits to museums. The school can supplement these with field trips or visiting resource persons that will further widen perspectives for children.

Parents support teachers by consistently participating in parent-teacher conferences as scheduled. Parents learn from the teacher how he or she views their child. The learner's strengths and weaknesses, potentials, and adjustments to other persons can be discussed. A mark on a report card or a short note sent home is a poor substitute for such meetings. Teachers view this as a time to get acquainted with parents, sense through conversation their understanding both of the child and the school, and explore ways they can mutually assist in a child's growth.

Another benefit of these conferences is that teachers and parents meet face to face. Parents talk with a person and "teacher" becomes more than a name. They can begin to view the teacher through the eyes of their child. Teachers, in seeing parents, begin to understand how some ways a child acts in class might be an effort to respond as his or her parents would expect.

One of the more difficult areas for parents and teachers to develop mutual support is in the discipline of children at school. When a learner misbehaves and has to be disciplined, parents often resent a teacher who does this to "my good child." They may go to the school and confront the teacher in anger or accuse the teacher of bias. Or parents may have adopted a permissive discipline at home. When put into the structured classroom in which others' rights and freedoms have to be observed, children of such parents may become disruptive. When the teacher responds with disciplinary action, the child does not expect it and resents it as unfair. Some children learn that disruptive behavior brings them more attention and use nonconformity to fulfill their needs. When a teacher alerts parents to this situation, the parents may resent it and blame the teacher for picking on the child. When to share information and when to deal with situations in a particular setting—home or school—is a decision that requires good judgment for both parent and teacher.

If parents understand that teachers see their children in the broad perspective of a classroom where each child is different, they can develop a more supportive attitude. Parents tend to observe their children within the narrower bands of family relationships at home and during playtime with friends. Each is a different context.

Parents also see the child with a bias that comes from attachment. The teacher's way of dealing with their child may come as a surprise and be taken as an affront to their parenting ability. To the degree that parents realize their children may behave differently in other out-of-home situations where parents cannot see them, they will welcome the teacher's efforts. Rather than feeling that a teacher is being critical of their parenting efforts, they will welcome this new dimension of insight. Teachers who remember this bias will attempt to help both parents and children view necessary restrictions in a positive light. They will also constantly reassure parents that they are doing their task well. It may help to remember that many teachers are also parents and are fully aware of how parents view children as well as how children may differ in responses in classroom and family.

When parents and teachers accept their different roles but mutually respect each other's goals, their relations are at the highest level. Learners are deeply enriched by their cooperation. *See also* Discipline; Parenting; Teacher.

F. F. Wise

Passover/Pesach

Passover (*Pesach* in Hebrew) is the archetypal redemptive experience of the Jewish people and, ultimately, of all humankind. It is celebrated for seven days (according to biblical tradition) or for eight days (in the postbiblical/rabbinic tradition) beginning on the eve of the fourteenth of the Hebrew month of Nisan (occurring generally in March or April), historically the first month of the ecclesial Jewish calendar. It is the oldest religious celebration of any Jewish group in the world.

HISTORY

The biblical book of Exodus provides the setting and rationale for the celebration, detailing the enslavement of the Hebrews by the Egyptians after they settled in Goshen during the reign of Ramses II and the rise to political power of the former Hebrew servant Joseph. The turnabout in Hebrew-Egyptian relations is epitomized in 1:8: "There arose a new king over Egypt, who knew

not Joseph." It is only with the appearance of Moses, born of Jewish parents and raised in the Egyptian court, that the fortunes of the Hebrew slaves begin to turn for the better. It is Moses, together with his brother Aaron, who liberates the children of Israel despite the obduracy of the pharaoh and leads them into the freedom of the desert, where they wandered for "forty years" (a biblical generation). Moses, because of his own failings, does not lead them into the promised land of Canaan. Thus Passover celebrates the redemption of the Jewish people from their slavery in the Egyptian "house of bondage," their freedom, and their arrival in ancient Canaan.

The term itself, Pesach, stems from the Hebrew verb *lifsoach* ("to pass over"). The "Angel of Death" "passed over" the houses of the children of Israel on its way to the homes of the Egyptians to slay their firstborn sons. This was the penalty for Pharaoh's refusal to allow the Israelites their freedom even after experiencing the power of Yahweh through nine previous plagues (i.e., blood, frogs, lice, wild beasts, blight, boils, hail, locusts, and darkness).

THE SEDER

The heart of the celebration of the Passover for Jews ever since early rabbinic/Talmudic times has been the home celebration appropriately named Seder (Hebrew for "order"). The meal and liturgy of the Seder follow a prescribed outline. The "prayerbook" for the home is known as the Haggadah or "Story" and serves the primary purpose of retelling the story of the Exodus narrative together with the various accretions of generations—both rabbinic commentaries and additional historical experiences. The Haggadah is itself an evolving repository of Jewish historical consciousness, reflecting in each generation the events germane to it.

The order of the home Passover service follows a prescribed outline, regardless of the creativity of the Haggadah used. Even where there were deletions (e.g., the omission of the ten plagues in early Reform Jewish texts) or additions (e.g., the Matzoh of Hope for the still-unliberated Jews of Soviet Russia), the order remains the same:

1. *Hadlakat Hanerot*, the lighting of the festival candles

2. *Kiddush*, recital of the sanctification of the festival wine

3. *Karpas*, partaking of parsley dipped in salt water

4. *Yachatz*, breaking the middle matzoh and hiding one part to be eaten at the end of the festival meal as the Afikoman (possibly a Greek derivative for "dessert")

5. *Maggid*, telling the story of Israel's deliverance from Egyptian bondage

6. *Motzi Matzoh*, reciting the blessing before the meal, including the particular blessing over the matzoh, or unleavened bread, itself

7. *Korach Maror*, combining the matzoh, *maror* (bitter herbs), and *charoset* (nut-apples-wine mixture) and eating them together

8. *Shulchan Orach*, serving the festival meal

9. *Tzafon*, concluding the festival meal by finding and eating the Afikoman

10. *Baraych*, reciting the benedictions after the festival meal

11. *Hallel*, reciting the remainder of the psalms praising God for his deliverance of the children of Israel from slavery to freedom

12. *Nirtzach*, concluding the experience with a prayer for the acceptance of the entire celebration

Traditionally, the entire event is concluded with the refrain, "*L'shanah ha-ba-ah b'Irushalayim*," "Next year, may the Jewish people come to celebrate the Passover in freedom in Jerusalem." The evening continues with the singing of a number of songs associated with the Passover, foremost among which are "*Echad mi yodea*," "Who knows one?" and "*Chad gadya*," "One Kid," both of which are madrigals of numbers.

Equally associated with the celebration of the Passover are the symbolic foods, eaten in the reclining position assumed in ancient times by free people. The most well known is the matzoh, or unleavened bread, eaten during the entire period as a reminder of the hurried preparations of the Israelites for their departure from Egypt. By extension, those who observe most strictly eat no products whatsoever relating to the five grains—wheat, rye, barley, oats, or millet. One of the ways of preparing for the Passover, a kind of "spring cleaning," is the ceremony of *Bedikat chametz*—going throughout the house looking for any evidence of leaven and then either storing or disposing of it.

Maror, or bitter herbs (usually horseradish), is a symbolic reminder of the bitterness of the Egyptian enslavement. *Charoset*, a mixture of apples, wine, nuts, and cinnamon, is said to resemble the mortar that cemented the bricks made by the Israelites. *Z'roah*, or the roasted shankbone, is a reminder of the Paschal sacrifice offered up in the ancient Temple in Jerusalem in celebration of the Passover. *Karpas*, or the green, leafy vegetable, usually lettuce or parsley, is dipped in salt water twice to remind Jews of the tears shed at the bitterness of their lot as well as of their meager diet (it is also said to symbolize the renewal of life in the spring). A *beitzah*, or roasted egg, is usually included among these foods on the Seder plate as a reminder of both the wholeness of life and its association with mourning for the destruction of the Temple.

Also included in the preparations for the Passover meal is the setting aside of the *Kos Eliyahu* or "Cup of Elijah." According to Jewish religious tradition, the prophet Elijah serves as a harbinger of the long-awaited messiah whose coming will take place during the Passover season. Thus, a cup of wine is set out for his messenger to aid and refresh him on his journey, visiting Jewish homes to announce his arrival.

Those who participate in the Passover Seder also enjoy four cups of wine, joyfully "toasting" God for the words used to describe the deliverance of the children of Israel in the Exodus text: "take you out," "save you," "free you," and "take you" (Exod. 6:6–7).

Because the celebration of the Passover is vitally concerned with the education of Jewish children, the core of the experience remains two moments: when the youngest child present recites the *Mah nishtanah*, or "Four Questions," about the unique nature of the evening meal (Why matzoh? Why *maror*? Why dip vegetables twice? Why recline when eating?) and when all the children are assembled to go on a "treasure hunt" to find the Afikoman, without which the Passover meal and liturgy could not conclude.

The Jewish celebration of the Passover event is at the very heart of the Jewish religious tradition and is symbolic of the values sacred to Jews over the generations. *See also* Jewish Education; Jewish Festivals and Holidays; Judaism.

FOR FURTHER REFERENCE

Goodman, Philip. *The Passover Anthology*. Philadelphia: Jewish Publication Society of America, 1971.

Poisson, Joseph A. "Passover: A Teacher's Outline." In *Compass: Directions in Jewish Education*. New York: Union of American Hebrew Congregations, February 1975.

S. L. Jacobs

Peace, Education for

The point of education for peace must be not simply appreciation of peace as a desirable ideal, but indication of directions to take for getting there. In biblical understanding, peace does not refer to an internal state of mind, but a relationship of wholeness, fulfillment, justice, and freedom in community with God, neighbors, nature, and oneself. In our time of unimaginably expensive and destructive weapons and unconscious, debilitating spiritual compartmentalization, peace must be relational and whole, as the biblical story suggests. The direction to take for getting there must be both an inward journey and an outward journey. Peace is not merely a state of mind. Religious education for peace must have a variety of objectives.

PEACE EDUCATION

Age Level	Understandings	Teaching methods
Preschool	Children gradually learn there are people other than themselves, and they begin to learn how to relate to others; they are too young to understand concepts of difference or similarity; conflict with others is likely to center on sharing things.	Adults should model acceptance of and concern for others; demonstrate and teach cooperation and constructive methods of conflict resolution (sharing, taking turns, and saying "I'm sorry").
Grades 1–8	Children gradually realize differences and similarities between themselves and others, and tensions are likely to result; conflicts are likely to occur over words and actions as well as possessions; relational attitudes and skills continue to develop; concepts of friendship and cooperation, fairness, and justice are gradually explored and understood.	Through story, discussion, and role play, children can better understand their differences and similarities; through correction and practice, they can be taught to avoid hurting others or causing disputes with their words and actions; teach Scripture verses about peace and reconciliation (i.e., Gen. 33; Matt. 5:9, 38-48); tell and read stories of recent peacemakers (i.e., Martin Luther King); discuss news stories of various conflicts and efforts at resolution.
High School	Interrelationships are better understood, and the causes and complexities of war and peace can therefore begin to be examined.	Ongoing discussion and study of past and present conflicts can further understanding of the causes of conflict, the progression of conflict once begun, and methods of resolution rather than escalation; students can begin to determine ways they might act individually and with others to further peace; the biblical vision of peace (see Isa. 2:1-4) should be discussed.
Adult	Understandings of peace and justice, relationship, and community continue to deepen; the effect of individual and corporate actions on peace and justice are increasingly understood.	Scripture references regarding peace and justice should continue to be studied; workshops can be given on conflict management at home and at work; actions already taken for peace and justice should be affirmed and further action encouraged; knowledge of present conflict and injustice should continually be updated and ongoing action taken.

OBJECTIVES

The objective of some education for peace is to teach why war is wrong or why some wars are wrong. Pacifism teaches that all war is wrong, because of its terrible consequences, or because of general philosophical or religious principles, or because of specific scriptural teachings. The main rival to pacifism is just war theory, which gives reasoned principles for deciding which wars are unjust and which are just.

Another objective is to redeem our image of our enemies. Francis A. Beer, in *Peace Against War* (1981), presents results of extensive political science research showing that the spread of hostile and dehumanizing images of the enemy usually precedes war. Khadafy of Libya was first labeled as a nonhuman, a "mad dog," before the United States bombed Libya. The Scriptures of most religions point to conversion of our image of the enemy as an essential part of becoming an obedient disciple.

Injustice, oppression, and the violation of peoples' human rights cause war. Political science and the Scriptures agree on that. Education for peacemaking includes much about world hunger, human rights, racism, and love and justice for people in need. According to the teachings of all the major religions, discipleship without compassion and deeds of mercy is false religion. It is also the cause of many wars. An objective is to engage students in the struggle for compassionate justice.

Another objective is to learn to practice skills of conflict resolution. Jesus' teachings about talking with your brother and your accuser, going the second mile, turning the other cheek, giving to the person who begs, and loving and praying for your enemy all emphasize specific steps of positive conflict resolution. Jesus does teach peacemaking as *not* judging and *not* setting yourself against those who are evil; but he emphasizes much more the constructive, transforming initiatives that can resolve conflict and dissolve enmity. To teach conflict resolution skills is to teach peacemaking. To teach people, including children, not only about conflict resolution, but actually to practice conflict resolution in the family, in school, at work, and among friends is to build the experiential base for expecting political leaders also to be better peacemakers. And good teaching helps people make that connection.

"Being religious," in the pejorative sense used by Dietrich Bonhoeffer, focuses only on achieving private peace of mind while handing the world over to the devil. Religious education derived from such "religiousness" does not help people cope with a world threatened by nuclear war and by the widespread poverty that accompanies wasting one trillion dollars each year on military expenditures. It teaches unhealthy denial.

True religious education that is faithful helps people comprehend their world and be empowered, rather than powerless, to change it, in concert with others. This includes an interpretation of the power structures so they can be understood. The biblical understandings of the principalities and powers and of the powerlessness of idolatry are far more important than is usually recognized.

Many are now beginning to understand the human condition as a bondage or addiction to powers that lead us to make war against our interest and against our created good purpose. It is more like alcoholism than like a free choice. This suggests a more profound religious understanding of the condition of sin, or idolatry, or alienation, or powerlessness. Regeneration or recovery comes not from blame, shame, and condemnation or from trusting our own power to save ourselves, but from admitting our powerlessness, beginning to trust in a higher power, and following specific steps of personal growth and conflict resolution. The process of recovery then must resemble the Alcoholics Anonymous process. One must be a member of a recovery group and follow specific steps of inner spiritual recovery and outer change in behavior. Religious education on peacemaking then becomes a group process of sharing and mutual support.

In sum, the objectives of religious education for peacemaking are far more extensive than many imagine. The process can be immensely inspiring and can involve the full breadth of religious faith. Many persons are finding their faith much deepened and enriched—even experiencing something like a Great Awakening—as they allow a fuller experience of peacemaking to be born in them. And they are sharing it with their fellow pilgrims.

Two biblical passages are keynotes for peace studies. One is Isaiah 2:1–4, paralleled by Micah 4:1–5, envisioning a time when God will rule the earth and people will live obediently and in peace with one another. Another is Luke 6:27–36, where Jesus enjoins his followers to return good for evil and to love their enemies, being merciful as God is merciful. The first passage may be discussed by young people's and adult groups in the context of world tensions. The second is the context for dealing with conflict situations among people at all age levels. Children act in momentary anger and "turning the other cheek" needs thoughtful consideration where questions of fairness and justice arise.

AGE-LEVEL APPROACHES

Preschool children begin to learn skills of conflict resolution as teachers help to adjudicate and defuse anger over materials that are not shared. Discussion on the spot and agreement for changed actions begin the learning process.

School-age children find conflicts not only in actions but in words that escalate tensions. They can begin to analyze feelings and look more precisely at meanings. Biblical passages can be thoughtfully used as a way of approaching problems. As children grow in an understanding of relationship to God, they become more aware that God loves everyone without regard to specific actions. Children today watch television, see views of children and families hurt, and know that something awful called war is going on somewhere in the world. They need their questions and confusions cleared up in a forthright but non-frightening way. Through stories and role playing, work can begin on the causes of war and the benefits and necessity of peace.

Adolescents are even closer to these situations as they watch young people engaged in armed conflict. They are capable of thinking beyond immediate situations to the roots of war, the political, social, and economic factors involved. The biblical understandings about God's purposes for creation can be brought into discussion.

Adults, with their own involvements in wars, their awareness of the costs of war, and their understanding of political realities can study war and efforts toward peace in depth. Individuals and parishes may belong to organizations striving for peace. Units of study on conflict resolution as it affects their personal, family, and professional life are also useful.

These are approaches to the four goals of understanding peace through relationship to God, establishment of justice, redeeming the image of the enemy, and conflict resolution.

Although not enough curriculum materials for different age groups have been produced, some useful materials and recommendations are available from the offices of the Presbyterian church, the United Church of Christ, the United Methodists (Cokesbury Press), the U. S. Catholic Conference, the Church of the Brethren, and the Mennonite Central Committee, among others. Especially useful for youth and children are *Try This: Family Adventures Toward Shalom* and *Shalom Age Level Guidelines*, both from the United Methodists; *Why People Fight*, and *Peace Futuring* from the United Church of Christ; Dr. Seuss's *The Butter Battle Book* (New York: Random House, 1984); Stanford Summers, *Wacky and His Fuddlejig* (New York: Red Ink Productions, 1980); and Bernard Benson, *The Peace Book* (New York: Bantam Books, 1982). *See also* Social Action; Social Justice, Education for.

FOR FURTHER REFERENCE

Beer, Francis A. *Peace Against War*. New York: Freeman, 1981.

Mott, Stephen C. *Biblical Ethics and Social Change*. Oxford University Press, 1982.

National Conference of Catholic Bishops. *The Challenge of Peace*. Washington, D.C., 1983.

Sider, Ronald. *Rich Christians in an Age of Hunger*. 2d. ed. Downers Grove, IL: Intervarsity, 1984.

Stassen, Glen. *Journey into Peacemaking*. Brotherhood Commission, Southern Baptist Convention, 1987.

Yoder, John H. *Nevertheless*. Scottsdale, PA: Herald, 1982.

G. H. Stassen

Pedagogy

In modern usage, pedagogy refers to the instruction given pupils by teachers who follow accepted principles. Often it is referred to as the "art of teaching." It also means systematized instruction in the methods of teaching. The term "pedagogy" has a long history, growing out of the educational practices of ancient Greece between 600 and 400 B.C.

One of these emerging developments was the use of slaves to supervise the training and behavior of the boys of upper-class Athenian families. Each family hired one male slave to oversee all of its sons. He took charge of the boys from the time they awoke in the morning until they went to bed. Throughout the day, he accompanied them everywhere they went, carried their tablets and musical instruments, and made sure they did not eat too much. He was chaperone, teacher, and nurse to his charges, and was totally responsible for their moral training.

The slave was called the *paidagōgos*, from which the word "pedagogy" comes. It literally means "to lead the child." Paul, no doubt, had this practice in mind when he said to the Galatian church, "So the law was put in charge [as our schoolmaster] to lead us to Christ. . . . Now that faith has come, we are no longer under the supervision of the law" (Gal. 3:24–25, NIV).

For many generations pedagogical instruction was mainly concerned with the transmission of knowledge. Children were expected to learn facts and concepts and then to repeat that information back to their teachers correctly. Failure to do this satisfactorily incurred a whipping.

Modern pedagogy has moved in the direction of fulfilling the original concept—"to lead the children." Rather than stressing the learning, storing, and recalling of facts and concepts as its goal, education is reducing the amount of facts learned to essential tools—reading, spelling, arithmetic—and then training children to know how to find and retrieve knowledge and to do critical, evaluative, problem-solving thinking. In this way the learners' potentials are "led out" or developed.

This shift has been accelerated by technical advances such as computers and word processors, coupled with awareness of the fact that the amount of new knowledge increases so rapidly, learners cannot remember it all. They must know where to find what they need and how to retrieve it, so they can use it as the basis for sound decisions.

In summary, pedagogy today has returned to its original pattern. Learners are the focus of its efforts. They are not to be merely receptacles of information, molded in a shape determined by society, but are to become informed, trained, and self-disciplined to fulfill their inherited potential. *See also* Education, Theories of; Greek Education; Problem Solving; Teaching Styles.

F. F. Wise

Peer Ministry

Peer ministry is a process of mutual support between or among people of similar age, concerns, or needs. In one sense peer ministry is not a recent development. People have always ministered to each other in informal ways, equal to equal. Peer ministry covers a spectrum from peer groups through peer counseling. Four levels can be identified: first, informal interaction as part of normal community relationships; second, formal groups structured around age, interest, or gender; third, groups specifically designed for peer interaction; and fourth, counseling programs.

Neighbors wrestling with community problems across the fence or on the stoop and members discussing with one another the challenges of raising children are examples of informal interaction. In magazines and discussion groups church bodies and congregations have sought to assist their members in helping each other directly.

In congregational women's groups, men's clubs, and youth organizations more formal kinds of peer ministries are offered. In more recent years the elderly have formed their own organizations in congregations, another form of peer ministry. These are usually formed more for programmatic purposes, such as mission outreach or recreation, but they have often provided peer ministry. In some instances this peer ministry has been formally nurtured, such as in Women to Women, developed by the American Lutheran Church Women in 1985.

Another specially developed program was the Peer Program for Youth, which was called "a group interaction plan to develop self-esteem, self-understanding, and communication skills." It was intended for use within existing groups or for use by specially formed groups. It was built on the achievement motivation program and Dr. Thomas Gordon's parent effectiveness training model. PEER, which stood for "Positive Educational Experiences in Relationships," was one of three training programs used in Youth-Reaching-Youth, a project funded by the National Institute of Mental Health. PEER's accent was primarily on personal growth within a peer community.

Alcoholics Anonymous groups offer an intensive kind of peer caring and have provided models that have been adapted within and outside the churches. These groups define "peer" finely, limiting participants to those who have experienced the same struggle. They stress accountability of the participants to each other.

Campus ministries have developed peer Bible study training and support groups to enable students to lead studies in their dorms where professional leaders were not allowed. It has also been found that such peer study groups were more freely received by students.

In counseling, the term "peer ministry" is contrasted to service rendered by a professional (particularly a counselor) toward a patient, considered to be a relationship of academic unequals. Yet peer counseling as developed in the community is more than simply one person helping another. There is an intentionality, training, and accountability structured into peer counseling programs.

In high schools and colleges students have been trained with counseling skills, including the ability to recognize when referral is necessary. This is not simply for convenience or economic savings. Students will often talk more readily, easily, and openly to other students. They will also assume their peers share their challenges and experiences and therefore respond to them more readily.

James C. Fenhagen includes some discussion of peer ministry approaches in his book *Mutual Ministry, New Vitality for the Local Church* (1986). Two structured programs that provide training and support for peer ministry by church laity are Caring Community, led by Harry Hinrichs of Milwaukee, Wisconsin, and Steven Ministry, based in St. Louis, Missouri. The work of the Youth Research Center is thoroughly outlined by Ardyth Hebeisen in *Peer Program for Youth* (1973). Many high-school and college counseling centers and some church social service agencies offer training in peer counseling and are often willing to assist churches wishing to participate or to develop their own programs. *See also* Counseling; Lay Ministry; Ministry; Youth Ministry.

B. Everist

Penance

See Reconciliation.

Pentecost

Pentecost, also known as Whitsunday, is an annual feast of the Christian year that falls on the fiftieth day after Easter. In Christianity Pentecost is celebrated as the anniversary of the descent of the Holy Spirit on the disciples.

The Christian celebration of Pentecost can trace its origins to the Jewish Festival of Weeks (Shavuot), which originally marked the beginning of the wheat harvest in ancient Israel. It is celebrated on the day that falls seven weeks (fifty days) after Passover (indeed, the Greek word *pentecost* means "fiftieth day"). The Feast of Weeks was one of the great "pilgrimage feasts" of Israel, a day on which devout Jews traveled to the holy city of Jerusalem to offer sacrifice at the Temple. It was established as a day of rest in all the land of Israel and has always been one of the most joyous Jewish festivals.

By about the time of Jesus, however, the Feast of Weeks had begun to take on new meaning for the Jewish people. In addition to its agricultural significance as a thanksgiving celebration for the wheat harvest, it also began to be looked upon as a thanksgiving celebration for the giving of the law on Mount Sinai, for the joy of Jewish identity as the chosen people of Yahweh.

Shortly after the death of Jesus, Pentecost came to have still another meaning for his followers. The Christian celebration of Pentecost is rooted in the account in Acts 2 of the events that occurred on the first Pentecost following the resurrection. On that day, according to the writer of Acts, the disciples were gathered together in Jerusalem. Suddenly, there was the sound of rushing wind, and the Holy Spirit appeared to the disciples looking like tongues of fire.

For the church, then, the Day of Pentecost marks the day when those whom Jesus had left behind were filled with the power of the Spirit, just as he had promised them before his death (John 14:25–26). It is in this sense the birthday of the church, the anniversary of the day on which Christ's disciples first knew themselves to be not simply a band of religious individuals but a community at one with its Lord, enlivened and empowered by the same Spirit that was in Jesus Christ. In this way the church incorporates the Jewish notion that it is one's identity as a people that is celebrated at Pentecost. However, it is not the law that makes Christians one but the Holy Spirit bringing them together in one body.

In the early church, the Day of Pentecost commemorated not only the indwelling of the Holy Spirit in the church but also the ascension of Jesus into heaven. As late as the middle of the fourth century, Christian writers describe the ascension of Jesus and the descent of the Holy Spirit as more or less simultaneous events. The "forty days" during which, according to the book of Acts, Jesus remained with the disciples after the resurrection was taken in the figurative sense of "a long time." It seems that no attempt to correlate the date of the ascension with the account in the book of Acts was made until the end of the fourth century, when Pentecost and Ascension began to be observed as separate feasts, with Ascension fixed at forty days after Easter.

Originally, the entire period of fifty days from Easter to the Day of Pentecost was referred to as "the Pentecost" and was seen to reflect the joy of the resurrection. Fasting was prohibited, and prayer was offered in a standing posture instead of kneeling as a sign of our participation in the triumph of Jesus Christ.

Since the fourth century, the liturgical character of the Day of Pentecost has been guided by lessons and prayers that focus on the work of the Holy Spirit. Traditionally included in addition to readings from the account in Acts of the first Pentecost after the death of Jesus and his promises regarding the sending of the Holy Spirit (John 14:15–18) are lessons from the Old Testament prophets that refer to the ways in which the power of the Spirit is to shape the future of God's chosen people.

Pentecost also came to have important baptismal associations. Those individuals who were unable to be baptized at Easter were commonly baptized on the Day of Pentecost, and the paschal candle, which had been lighted at the Easter Vigil and kept burning on the Sundays thereafter, was removed to a place near the baptismal font. As confirmation came to have a ritual identity separate from baptism within the Western Christian church, it was natural to liken the work of the Holy Spirit in the disciples at Pentecost to the work of the Holy Spirit in an individual at confirmation, and the Day of Pentecost became a traditional occasion for confirmations. The practice of dressing the candidates for confirmation in white garments is the source of the English term "Whitsunday" (White Sunday) as a synonym for Pentecost.

Pentecost also has been a traditional time for other observances especially associated with the work of the Holy Spirit within the Christian community. Ordinations, revivals, homecomings, and the commissioning of individuals for certain forms of Christian service are appropriately celebrated on the Day of Pentecost.

In addition to ceremonies such as these, the distinctive liturgical character of Pentecost is reinforced by a number of special signs and symbols. At least two biblical accounts refer to the descent of the Holy Spirit as being like fire, inspiring the use of the color red. Also, the references in Mark 1:10 and Matthew 3:16 to the Holy Spirit's descending on Jesus "like a dove" have made the dove another symbol of the day. *See also* Church Year.

S. J. White

Pentecostal Education

Pentecostals, taking their name from the earliest experience of the outpouring of the Holy Spirit in a God who is nonmaterial and abstract. So the parent becomes the first theologian to the child.

This stage is followed by the crisis of autonomy versus shame and doubt. Here the child is attempting to master his or her own body and learn control of self and social world. It is the period of "holding on" and of "letting go," a period marked by independence and demand in behavior but also when shame and doubt of self might emerge. Acceptance and restraint are the key parental virtues for the caregivers of the toddler. This is followed by the crisis of initiative versus guilt. In Western, industrial societies many neuroses are rooted in the failure of the child to resolve this conflict. New muscular and mental abilities invite initiative taking, but failure is at hand. Also great energy is available for activities, but it must be curbed and disciplined or guilt overcomes the child. Industry versus inferiority is the stage of grade-school children, in which they master the use of symbol systems and tools in order to deal with the exterior world. But they may not be proficient in these tasks; thus feelings of inferiority may persist.

The adolescent faces the bipolar task of ego identity versus role diffusion: sex roles versus bisexual ambiguity; leadership versus authority confusion; self-certainty versus self-consciousness; role experimentation versus fixation or confusion; and ideological commitment versus a confusion of values or value rejection. This is an explosive time in the life of the youth. The role of peers and mentors becomes quite important in helping one through these tasks. In the field of religious education, youth leaders and teachers have the opportunity of mentoring and providing role models as well as "the practice of valuing," which comes in serious yet open conversation. The young adult period, with its crisis between intimacy and isolation, follows. Here the individual must choose relationships in sexuality and in camaraderie. The capacity to commit oneself requires the identity task to have been resolved adequately. In this period, the opposition forces can lead to isolation, promiscuity, or other rejecting behaviors.

Adults experience the stage of generativity versus stagnation. That is, they devote their energies to procreation, productivity, and creativity or they know the remorse of stagnation and failure. In older age, the adult deals with ego integrity versus despair. If the person accepts the result of adult generativity and holds to an ego identity that is still functional, then there is integrity; otherwise there is despair and thus fear of death. In recent years, Daniel Levinson, Gould, and others have added greater sophistication in describing these adult stages, with an emphasis on the major transitions in adult experience.

Some theorists have paid closer attention to biology, including Gardner Murphy, Gordon Allport, Carl Rogers, and most clearly William Sheldon. Humanistic psychology led by Abraham Maslow and Fritz Perls has emphasized the self-actualization of the adult. O. Hobart Mowrer has related traditional learning theory to the development of the personality. George A. Kelly introduced a structural theory in which the individual constructs a personality out of structural relationships. Jane Loevinger has provided a description of cognitive stages that give rise to certain personality profiles.

TOOLS

This plethora of personality theories provides to general or religious educators a rich set of tools for understanding the learner and guiding the learning experience according to the learner's abilities and needs. Although there are numerous instruments for describing personality profiles, the most widely used are the Minnesota Multiphasic Personality Inventory and the Myers-Briggs Personality Indicators. *See also* Adolescence; Adult Development; Behavior; Child Development; Erikson, Erik; Freudian Influences; Jungian Influences; Maslow, Abraham; Motivation; Psychological Testing; Psychosocial Development.

FOR FURTHER REFERENCE

Burger, Jerry M. *Personality Theory and Research*. Belmont, CA: Wadsworth, 1986.
Erikson, Erik. *Childhood and Society*. New York: Norton, 1963.
Jones, Ernest. *The Life and Work of Sigmund Freud*. 3 vols. New York: Basic, 1957.
Maddi, Salvatore R. *Personality Theories: A Comparative Analysis*. Pacific Grove, CA: Brooks/Cole. 1980.
Progoff, Ira. *The Death and Rebirth of Psychology*. New York: McGraw-Hill, 1973.

C. H. Snelling

Pestalozzi, Johann Heinrich ⎯⎯⎯⎯

Although educated for careers in law and ministry, Johann Heinrich Pestalozzi (1746–1827) spent his life challenging traditional views and approaches to education. This Swiss educational reformer first attempted to apply principles from Jean Jacques Rousseau's *Emile* to the education of his own child. When he found them to be impractical, he decided to study children himself. Between 1774 and 1779 he developed an educational program for neglected children he had taken into his home. He later drew on this experience when he wrote *Leonard and Gertrude*. From 1805 to 1825 his association with the institute for training teachers in Yverdon, canton of Vaux, attracted educators who introduced his ideas throughout Europe and the United States.

Pestalozzi believed society could be regenerated through the educational efforts of parents and teachers. To this end he contended that all children should receive an education from birth respecting their growth and development and related to their experience. His distinctive contribution to education was to insist that children learned through experiences that approximated methods of teaching in the family, that they were encouraged by loving (rather than aversive) discipline, and that they needed a Christian environment. *See also* Froebel, Friedrich; Herbart, Johann Heinrich; History of Christian Education, Eighteenth Century to Present.

C. R. Foster

Phenomenology

"Phenomenology" means different things to different people. It has been called a study of the logic of meaning, a theory of abstraction, and an inquiry into the character of human consciousness. The simplest definition is to say that it is above all a descriptive science concerned with the appearance of things as perceptual wholes. It sets out to classify and describe various phenomena, which it sees not as isolated objects but as clues to ultimate essences. In order to record the authentic appearance of any object, it deliberately avoids bringing into play any ideas of it that precede the actual observation. This means that it will not be distracted by such factors as metaphysical presuppositions, mental states of the observer, or causes, origins, and consequences—it lets the object show itself. There is no room in phenomenology for the concealments and distortions that sometimes keep us from seeing what the world is actually like.

The science was restated, if not originated, by Edmund Husserl (1859–1938) at the turn of the century. His book *Logical Investigations* (1900) was very influential, changing the methods used in a number of studies. He described his aim as the effort to make sense of existence without leaning on authority or memory, but simply by looking at the world as it appears in order to discover by intuition its universal essences. It was to be a nonempirical method, meaning that essences were to be encountered intuitively. He was convinced that there was only one way by which essences could be found and that was by observing objects as they appear. He used the Greek word *epoche* to describe the method of what the mystics called purification, purging, or bracketing irrelevant considerations that could only distort the observation. And he used the word "eidetic" to describe the freshness with which the universal essence could appear by intuition. He thought Plato's ideas could be discovered not by studies in the Academy, but by confrontations with the object as though on the first day.

Husserl was primarily interested in logic and in the technical problems of philosophic method, but the method he described had great appeal and was found to be widely useful. Sociology cannot be carried on in any other way, nor can the humanities. It has had a striking influence on religious and theological studies as well as on philosophy. Carroll A. Wise and Seward Hiltner have shown how it can have a liberating effect on the whole field of pastoral counseling. Martin Marty uses it as his chief method in his many studies of the American religious scene. Theologians have found it useful as well. Max Scheler (1874–1928) used it for his important studies of religious values. Rudolf Otto (1869–1937) wrote *The Idea of the Holy* (1923), the classic phenomenological account of the varieties of religious consciousness, the feeling-states of numinous experiences. John Macquarrie, influenced by both Heidegger and Husserl, has made it one of his primary tools in several books. Mircea Eliade (1907–1986) made careful scrutinies of myths and ritual events, finding them clues to archetypal events of the distant past. Phenomenology and existentialism are mutually helpful allies. *See also* Epistemology; Existentialism.

P. Elmen

Piaget, Jean

Jean Piaget (1896–1980) was a Swiss genetic epistemologist (as he termed himself) who formed a theory of cognitive development based on the idea that the origin of intelligence lies in sensorimotor activity. According to this theory, a child's cognitive and intellectual development proceeds in a specified order based on genetically determined stages. These stages are the sensorimotor (birth to age two), the preoperational (ages two to seven, in which the child thinks intuitively and prerationally), the concrete operational (ages seven to eleven, in which the child can respond logically to concrete objects and relations), and the formal operational (ages eleven to fifteen, in which the child is now capable of abstract reasoning). Certain developmental tasks accompany each stage; their accomplishment enables progress from one stage to the next.

In the 1960s and 1970s some religious educators sought to apply Piaget's developmental tasks of intelligence to religious education. But story (especially biblical story), art, dance, dreams, play, myth, song, morals, and liturgy are learned primarily through participation and are not amenable to tasks of logical reason, as Piaget made clear in his book *Play, Dreams, and Imitation in Childhood* (1962). In early childhood, he writes, preverbal structures (through imitation, imagination, images, participation, and repeated interaction with environment) take shape. These preverbal, nonconceptual structures shape linguistic patterns leading to reason and speech. Recognition that the origin of intelligence roots in sensorimotor activity tends to overcome dualism in religion and goes far toward creating a dynamic whole of theory and practice and action-reflection. *See also* Adolescence; Affective Development; Child Development; Cognitive Development; Maturation; Moral Development; Preschool Children.

N. Morton

Pioneer Clubs

Pioneer Clubs, based in Wheaton, Illinois, is a church-sponsored weekly program for children in kindergarten through the twelfth grade. Its purpose is to help children and youth integrate their knowledge and experience of Christ into every phase of life. An age-graded curriculum allows participants to study and apply Scripture in their lives.

The goals are to enable children and youth to enter a personal relationship with Christ, to foster healthy relationships with others, and to grow as whole individuals. Sound educational principles are incorporated into a program of Bible exploration, creative projects, learning activities, and recreation. Integral to this learning is a merit system in which participants earn awards for specific achievements. Materials are age-graded into six divisions and separated into curricula for boys and girls.

Pioneer Clubs are found in 90 denominations incorporating 2,500 churches. Approximately 100,000 members are registered in the United States and 15 foreign countries. A camping program includes 28 camps located in the United States and Canada. *See also* Awana; Youth Ministry.

J. A. Gorman

Planning

Over a quarter century ago Louis Allen in *The Management Profession* defined planning as "the work a manager performs to predetermine a course of action." In that classic volume he identified seven components of the planning process:

1. Forecasting (estimating the future)

2. Establishing objectives (determining end results)

3. Programming (establishing the sequence and priority of steps to be followed in reaching objectives)

4. Scheduling (establishing a time sequence for programming)

5. Budgeting (allocating resources essential to achieve objectives)

6. Procedure (applying standardized methods of performing specific work)

7. Policies (developing and interpreting decisions)

In the modern and much more sophisticated systems approach of today, Allen's analysis, far from being archaic, still forms the basic foundation of how we understand planning. A major scholarly text by Carl Anderson entitled simply *Management* and published in 1984 defines strategic planning as "deciding how to allocate resources (people, capital, etc.) to bring the organization into alignment with its environment, especially its industry, so that long-term goals and objectives can be reached."

LONG-RANGE AND SHORT-RANGE PLANNING

One way in which the concept of planning has changed measurably, however, is in the identification of the difference between long-range planning and short-range (project) planning. Generally speaking, project planning in churches and religious organizations will focus on one year, while long-range planning can commonly reach three to five and in major organizations such as colleges and universities must normally be done at least ten years in advance.

The major value of planning is the avoidance of crisis management, the ability to actually ensure the vitality of the organization by giving it direction and vision as well as some strategy whereby the vision can be realized. Planning is a process not an event. Necessary steps are laid out (whether for long- or short-range planning), sequences are designed, evaluation systems are built in all along the way, and the organization begins to focus on *then* rather than *now* and to change things from the way they *are* to the way they *ought to be.*

In a very real sense, the short-range plan is simply one step down the road of the long-range plan. A ten-year long-range plan will identify those objectives the organization expects to achieve within the first year, second year, third to fifth year, etc. As the plan stretches out it moves from the most specific to the least specific. But perhaps it is better to see that process in reverse: the broad general vision as the long-range plan giving birth in turn to objectives, more specific goals, and very definitive implementation steps.

Certainly it is easier to move from a successful experience in project planning (a leadership development retreat for elders, deacons, Sunday school teachers, and other lay leaders to be held next August) to the much more difficult prognostication of where the church or organization must be ten or fifteen years from now. On the other hand, a well laid out master plan for the future makes possible year-by-year project planning.

What kinds of things fall into the category of short-range (project) planning? Obviously the staff retreat mentioned above would be a good example; also such things as a curriculum reevaluation, a membership drive, initial research on a building program, the institution of a new educational ministry such as a boys' or girls' club, the development of a singles or single parent ministry, or the hiring of a new staff member.

CONSIDERATIONS AND PROCESS

The ingredients commonly associated with any kind of planning—philosophy (mission), objectives, programs, organization, staffing, and financing—force several questions early in the planning process. The question of *mission* is always there, though not necessarily rethought or restructured on an annual basis. What is the purpose of this organization? Why does it exist? What does it intend to achieve? There is also the question of internal posture. What capabilities does the institution have to develop its opportunities? Does it have the resources to achieve the goals it has set for itself?

External environment, though more a factor in long-range than short-range planning, certainly affects all kinds of planning. How are the demographics of the community changing? What is different about the makeup of the congregation or constituency when compared with five years ago? What economic, denominational, political, or religious trends are significant in relation to planning?

Planning is inseparably related to goal setting. Someone has suggested that the future is like a funnel and the next three months can be thought of as the neck of the funnel. Within this narrow confine we can see and predict rather clearly. But as the funnel of the future opens, even six, nine, and twelve months ahead become somewhat obscure. Lack of planning causes us to stumble down the funnel encountering whatever might be there and coping with it when it appears. Such leadership is often called "crisis management" or "problem orientation." The reverse is objective orientation, in which we make every effort to see what lies further down the funnel and how we can change our current postures to deal more effectively with what we see.

In a religious organization goals are statements of faith. They suggest what people might be able to do at a certain point in the future if God makes it possible. Scripture passages like Matthew 6:25–34 and James 4:13–16 are not injunctions against planning but rather commands to submit our human plans to the overall plan and power of God.

If goals really are statements of faith, then the absence of goals (the failure to plan) may represent an absence of faith. Churches and religious organizations fall short on planning for several reasons. One seems to be that they simply do not know how to go about the process. Another is a misinterpretation of Bible passages such as those mentioned above. Fear of failure also plagues religious as well as secular organizations. After all, if no goals are set, the group is under no obligation to achieve any goals.

Increasing specificity in the planning process is one of its most strategic components. The overall mission statement gives birth to a series of objectives, which are specific events measurable in future time. These in turn break down into even more specific goals, which give way to realization procedures in the form of very definitive implementation steps. One good way to measure the latter is to apply the simple yes or no evaluation question: "Did the official board gather six resumes by January 1 in its search for a new minister of education?" "Have we announced the dates and site for the family camping weekend in June?" "Has the Sunday school superintendent issued a list of substitute teachers for every class?" "Are the minutes of the elders/deacons meetings being distributed within one week after the meeting?"

Obviously built into the above gridwork are decisions and programming, schedule and budget. It is important that people to be involved in the leadership retreat be consulted along the way regarding needs and interests. Planning is a process conducted with people and aimed at a specific product. *See also* Finance; Goals; Lesson Planning; Long-range Planning; Management; Record Keeping; Systems Theory.

K. O. Gangel

Play

Play is an activity, often contrasted to work, that is characterized by pleasure, lack of goals beyond itself, spontaneity, and voluntary and active player participation.

Various theories have considered play a discharge of excess energy, the practice of activity for later adulthood, the reliving of human history (e.g., using a baseball bat could replay early hunting with a club), a way to bring balance between feelings of overstimulation and boredom, and, in psychoanalytic thought, a way to master frightening events and emotions.

Play is the way infants and young children learn. Free play, that is play activities in which each child has choice, takes up the predominant amount of time in church and synagogue day programs for preschoolers. When religious education classes, limited in time, focus instead on other activities, they ignore the learning that takes place in play. The Bible teaches that persons are to live with mutual concern toward each other as children of God. Play helps children to do so. In learning how to share toys, take turns, settle quarrels, and enjoy group activity, they are learning how to live constructively.

For the purposes of free play, there need to be a variety of toys consonant with the space available. Housekeeping toys give children an opportunity to play family situations and teachers the chance to observe the kinds of family situations being enacted. Blocks give opportunity for constructing and destructing at the will of the young builder. Cooperation is often a necessary skill here. Toys on wheels encourage interaction with other children, both in the choice of vehicle and the direction of the course.

Other preschool activities such as fingerplays, action songs, games, rhythmic instruments, and activities involving graphic and molding materials (paints, playdough) are also forms of play. These sometimes fit more comfortably into what is viewed as a Bible class because the songs and constructive activities can contain biblical content.

Play develops in social stages described as: solitary or onlooker (two year olds playing alone or merely watching), parallel (three year olds engaging in similar pursuits without real sharing), associative (threes and fours exchanging ideas but doing their own projects), cooperative (fours and fives planning and carrying out an activity by assigning roles, e.g., "You be the mother and I'll be the child"). These forms of play are also interactive. A five year old may prefer to play alone for a while; a two year old may try to join a group.

The structures of play change as children grow. Functional or practice play involves muscles or handling of play materials with no further intended goal, such as kneading clay just for fun rather than for making a dish (ages three–five). Constructive play, the most common play in kindergarten, involves plans for completing a project such as a castle or airplane (kindergarten and older children). Symbolic or dramatic play uses imagination and fantasy, such as in "Let's pretend" (five–eight). Games-with-rules use instructions agreed upon ahead of time for the goal and permitted play action, such as in hide-and-seek (begins at age six or seven). The play of older children and adults usually involves games.

Play as games is used in religious education when there is a longer session with need for a relaxing break. It is an essential part of the schedule for vacation church schools.

Play as recreation is one of the activities of youth groups as well as of family and intergenerational events, but usually when the term "play" is used it is more narrowly described as a learning activity of children.

Information about the value of play comes from direct observation of children's actions and from structured experiments to discover what children learn from particular kinds of play. Although research does not provide clear-cut answers, it does confirm some observations.

In play children practice many skills, such as learning to initiate and complete projects; to identify, compare, choose, or reject objects for special use; to experiment; and to put thoughts into words. Children also use their senses and enjoy the feel of sand running through fingers, the muscular movement of climbing, and the sounds of bells or cymbals. After enjoying these experiences in religious education, children may be gathered together to thank God for giving them the ability to think, see, touch, hear, smell, taste, and move.

For older children games also encourage important qualities for living such as cooperation, fairness, persistence, and accepting success and failure. Games from other nations, if explained, can also provide a wider view of God's people.

PLAY

Age Level	Appropriate Toys and Games and Their Benefits
2–3 years	Push and pull toys help build large muscle coordination. Toys that fit together in specific ways help children distinguish between shapes and sizes. Dolls and stuffed animals provide children with something to carry, cuddle, and play "make believe." Rhythm instruments help teach rhythm. Crayons and paper stimulate the imagination.
4–5 years	Outdoor equipment and toys with wheels can further physical development, promote interaction between children, and provide the opportunity to learn to take turns or share. Blocks provide the opportunity for children to use their imagination and build something on their own or with others. Playing "house" or "family" teaches children about roles and relationships. Graphic materials provide the opportunity for children to retell stories and experiences or use their imagination. Puzzles help children to further distinguish between shapes and sizes.
Elementary	Bicycles and gym equipment further coordination and provide exercise. A variety of arts and crafts stations and sessions encourages experimentation and creativity and allows children to gradually discover their own likes and talents. Field games and games-with-rules further physical and mental skills, teach the value of rules and organization, and encourage participation, cooperation, and friendly competition. Symbolic or dramatic play may help children better understand or resolve various situations; it also increases group cooperation and social participation.
Adolescent	Individual and team games and sports develop individual skills and sportsmanship and continue to teach the value of organization and the importance of having and keeping rules; team games and sports additionally develop an appreciation of and skill in teamwork. Symbolic or dramatic play continues to be of value in understanding or resolving situations.
Adult	Individual and group games and sports further develop individual skill and can provide exercise and emotional release; group sporting and social events additionally promote positive group interaction and strengthen social bonds.

The role of the teacher is important in play. The teacher defines the objectives (to learn how to cooperate with other children, to learn how to care for materials, to make choices) and provides the setting and materials (kinds of toys and other equipment), structuring the times for play in the total schedule. The teacher guides individual children, both encouraging new experiences and redirecting them if their chosen play is too difficult. The teacher also adjudicates conflicts and reconciles children to each other. Teachers thereby teach how God accepts, forgives, and reconciles.

Because play develops many skills for living, it can make valuable contributions to religious education at any age. *See also* Kindergarten; Nursery Education; Preschool Children; Recreation.

FOR FURTHER REFERENCE

Garvey, Catherine. *Play.* Cambridge, MA: Harvard University Press, 1977.

Weininger, Otto. *Play and Education.* Springfield, IL: Thomas, 1979.

J. B. McCandless

Pluralism

See Multicultural Education.

Poetry

Poetry is a linguistic expression of experience that communicates a rhythm of ideas, sounds, and shapes. Something of what the poet perceives in everyday experience is rhythmically felt by something perceived in the experience of the audience. Poetic writing is generally distinguished from prosaic writing, the latter being linear and discursive in its rational arrangement of words. Poetry is, however, deliberately intuitive and creative in its choice and positioning of words. Words are selected both for their sounds and their meanings and are then placed into a pattern that will elicit a rhythm. Often figures of speech, such as a simile or a metaphor, are used to break up the logical and objective character of prosaic thinking.

Poetry is often understood as a language of images. Actually the subject matter of poetry is presented by creating illusionary events. These illusions are felt and perceived in forms that become symbolic in the mind of the audience, giving the audience the possibility of creating images. The structure of these images highly depends on the expectations aroused in the mind of an audience. Thus, the poet speaks to an audience's understanding of experience in structuring the poem. Although there are various understandings of experience within the same audience, structure can be pliable enough to be felt universally. That is

why the meaning appropriated from the images can differ from person to person and from moment to moment. Even more, images can take on very different meanings when the audience is made up of various cultural backgrounds. The images projected by the early nineteenth-century English poet Shelley and received by his audience carry different meanings than those images shaped by a twentieth-century female Asian-American poet and received by her audience.

The tension produced by multiple meanings, shaped similarly, speaks positively to the transcendence of poetry from experience to experience. Despite the tension between various meanings there is a unity within the poem communicated by its rhythm. Because rhythm is the basic mediator of the form received, it is at this level that the greatest number of people can enjoy a poem. That is why it is helpful to read the poem aloud or listen to the poem being read. The unity of that rhythm produces an indescribable feeling that can be understood as joy. Even when a feeling of sadness is produced, the lack of joy is felt.

Lyric poetry expresses the poet's emotions and thoughts. Sonnets, elegies, odes, and hymns are examples of lyric poetry. Because lyric poetry deals with creating surprises and satisfying the expected immediately, it has the quality of timelessness. Narrative poetry, on the other hand, is concerned with telling a story and deals with the unfolding of events and the development of characters.

A good deal of poetry employs verse, which divides a line into metrical feet and defines its metrical rhythm by the length and intensity of accents within those feet. Words are then given a sequence according to the metrical design. There are several types of verse—iambic, trochaic, dactylic, anapestic, spondaic, and blank. Blank verse is an unrhymed iambic verse of five metrical feet, used especially in English dramatic and narrative poetry. Free verse has no regular meter and breaks away from a strict sequence of sounds. Free verse began as a protest against metrical form that bore no identification with the rhythms experienced in life. However, the revolutionary quality of free verse also prepared the way for both new forms and the revival of older forms.

Poetry of the English language has been a mixture of rhythms of Anglo-Saxon, Celtic, Norman French, Middle English, and Scots, together with the rhythm of Latin and, at various points, of French, Italian, and Spanish (T. S. Eliot). Recently, English poetry has received new rhythmic strains as speakers of English from marginalized cultural groups begin to express their rhythms poetically.

The creation of ideas, sounds, and shapes, whether versed or unversed, carries an expectation of repetition. If a rhythm is uneven, then the poem creates a feeling of fluctuating emotion. Even free verse expects a rhythm although its expectation is left unfulfilled. Common to all nondiscursive linguistic expressions is, then, a sense of recurring elements in its composition, known to poetry as poetic rhythm.

The use of poetry in religious education begins with the Bible. The psalms express many moods: despair, anger, joy, confidence. Passages from the prophets are in poetry. Luke's Gospel contains several hymns (poems) in the first few chapters. Rhythm accentuates the mood of a poem and also makes memorization easy. With biblical poetry, learners are participating in the life of the community that listened to the prophets and the early church that wrote these songs. Hymnals are collections of poetry set to music; the verse is usually suitable for use with most age levels.

Some poets like John Donne (1572–1631) and Francis Thompson (1859–1907) wrap their thought in obscure images. Their poetry can be used with selected adult groups willing to probe the deeper aspects of religious experience. Contemporary poetry may seem to some hearers to be harsh, expressing the darker side of life, yet the religious implications of these feelings also need to be explored.

Teachers using poetry need to distinguish between sentiment and sentimentality. The former is an expression of real feelings in many moods. The latter expresses unrealistic feelings, usually described as overoptimistic. There is nothing in them with which to identify in reality. Sometimes easily rhymed verse fits this pattern. To write expressive verse is a skill as well as an art. *See also* Aesthetics; Bible in Religious Education, the; Metaphor; Symbolism.

C. W. Spanier

Poster

A poster is a flat, often stiff, piece of material displayed publicly to communicate a message in word, picture, or symbol (e.g., graphs, charts, or time lines). Posters may be made by anyone from professional printer to classroom student.

Posters have an infinite variety of uses in religious education. Posters may announce meetings—time, location, activity, purpose, cost, intended audience. Posters may illustrate a theme, such as discipleship, announce an event, such as a work camp, or carry short, catchy messages like, "Life is precious. Handle with prayer."

Posters may highlight past, present, and future events—past events such as retreats or service projects; present activities such as welcoming new members or celebrating a member's service to the church; present local and world needs or service activities for decent housing, food, or physical and spiritual healing; and future goals like increased evangelism or social action.

Posters should have a central focus of interest, use a few strong colors, have wide margins, and be uncluttered, neat. They should be placed in a public spot and be removed when outdated. *See also* Visual Methods.

J. B. McCandless

Practicum

A practicum is a program or plan of study that supplements theoretical training with hands-on experience. The practicum flows from the student need to experience or become proficient in performing certain tasks related to a particular discipline of study or theory. The emphasis is on action, practice, and implementation.

A practicum might be used in several settings. A senior-high youth group is engaged in a unit on "Faith in Daily Life." They have studied the biblical and doctrinal meaning of "calling" and discussed implications of this for their daily life. Their practicum includes an instrument by which each student will determine his or her skills and gifts that may be clues to the type of occupation or other service eventually pursued. Interviews of people in those occupations, role plays, and simulation games will give youth opportunities to experience some of the situations they might encounter in these work settings.

A seminary might offer a teaching practicum for students on the use of media in developing theological concepts in parish settings. A two-day practicum is prepared that will incorporate several biblical and theological concepts that have been studied by the students. Using the case study method to identify several different parish settings, the participants experience how various media programs have accented these biblical or theological themes, learn how to use the equipment, visit a museum to study the artistic expressions of these themes, and prepare media resources for different age groups. During the practicum participants reinforce and strengthen their theoretical study as they develop the concepts through a variety of forms.

A congregational intergenerational practicum on worship might include activities in which all ages could learn, experience, and practice worship. In this practicum participants could write prayers, hymns, and liturgies for home, retreats, personal devotions, and congregational worship. Activities could include practice of leadership roles, liturgical dance, drama, poetry reading, making banners, painting, and drawing. Time for reflection and corporate worship would be an integral part of the practicum.

J. Bozeman

Pragmatism

First used by the American philosopher Charles S. Peirce (1839–1914), the word "pragmatism" refers to that philosophical movement during the first quarter of the twentieth century that was heir of Darwin's theory of evolution and vigorous actor in the transition of American society from a primarily agricultural social orientation to an industrialized and scientific one. Generally speaking, pragmatism became known primarily for its understanding of the relationship between ideas and action (ideas that did not effect or transform action were of no practical value); more specifically, it addressed the relationship between truth and action (truth was viewed as a changeable but satisfactory hypothesis resulting from careful scientific analysis and active experimentation) and the relationship between knowledge and experience (knowledge could not be dehumanized; rather, humans were the ground of all knowledge). Thus, it is clearly seen that while pragmatism refers to a particular method of analysis and active experimentation, it also carried within it metaphysical (concerning the nature of reality) and epistemological (concerning the nature of truth and knowledge) assumptions that bear directly upon an understanding of human being.

In its popular manifestations, pragmatism has become associated with usefulness, practicality, and experience-based education. It would not be unfair to suggest that for most practitioners in religious education during the twentieth century the question, "Does it work?" has played a central role. Results are "the proof of the pudding," and in this sense pragmatism entered religious education because it confirmed the American common-sense notion that what really counts (i.e., the truth) in the end are affirming, positive, and acceptable results. This popularized view of pragmatism affirms the centrality of Darwinism for education, for the determination of truth becomes a matter of devising a process whereby the fittest truth survives and the weaker truths perish.

How did pragmatism enter the arena of religious education? A simple but perhaps the most adequate answer would be "by osmosis." Philosopher and educator John Dewey (1859–1952) was instrumental in popularizing the basic ideas of pragmatism within an educational framework. Reared in Burlington, Vermont, Dewey viewed the rapid urbanization and industrialization of America and realized that traditional ways children learned by doing in the chores of everyday farm life were passing away. Dewey argued that the new society of cities and machines required a new approach to education (*School and Society*, 1899). It would not be too reductionistic to suggest that Dewey's new approach to education was an attempt to project and perpetuate the values and social relationship patterns of the old New England family farm into an urban industrial setting.

George Albert Coe, the dean of twentieth-century religious education theory, was fundamentally informed by Dewey when he wrote his highly influential *A Social Theory of Religious Education* (1917), especially when it came to an understanding of experience. Add to this the fact that pragmatism had made its way, thanks to the progressive movement, into the public school system by such means as the "project method," field trips, infusion of the curriculum with real-life questions, etc., and it is no surprise that religious education—sometimes critically, most times uncritically—and pragmatism became associated in practice, if not in name.

The metaphysical and epistemological bases of pragmatism present serious problems for the thoughtful religious educator. "Does it work?" and "Is it faithful?" are often seen as opposing questions by teachers and learners in religious educational program settings. Yet, the widespread influence of popular pragmatism is not unexpected within the American setting. It was received, however imperfectly, because it conformed to socially accepted plausibility structures already in place—politically, economically, symbolically, and militarily.

Some current American religious curriculum publishers, no doubt spurred on by capitalistic economic considerations, are often more concerned with "user comfort" (what works and therefore what sells) than with rigorous educational and theological integrity. Certain forms of church growth and evangelistic efforts also fall into this trap. Pragmatism in its rawest and most popular forms in religious education has become a synonym for mindless, "feel good" functionalism—something philosophical pragmatism, with all of its limitations, would never tolerate.

While some religious educators such as Jacques Maritain (*Education at the Crossroads*, 1943) and James Loder (*The Transforming Moment*, 1981) have argued against various epistemological and metaphysical assumptions inherent in pragmatism, it is unlikely that the question, "Does it work?" will be budged from its central place in grass-roots religious education any time soon because of the pervasive and powerful place "it works" has in the core values taken for granted by American society at large. Pragmatism will remain a primary focus of professional and volunteer reflection as the American industrial age passes and pragmatic presuppositions fail to provide adequate avenues for knowing truth. *See also* Dewey, John; Empiricism; Experience; Knowledge, Theories of; Progressive Education.

R. H. Cram, H. C. Simmons

Praxis

While the word long predates him in pre-Socratic philosophy, Aristotle was the first to make wide usage of the term "praxis" in his writings. Aristotle said that a free person has three distinctive options for relating intelligently to life and, conversely, there are three human activities from which "knowing" can arise, namely, the lives of *theoria, praxis,* and *poiesis.*

Theoria is the speculative life in which knowing is by means of contemplation, reason, and reflection detached from historical engagement. *Poiesis* is the productive life of "making" in which the knowing involved is the "know-how" of the artisan or poet. The middle way, *praxis*, is the public life of the citizen in which knowing arises from one's reflective engagement in a social context. *Praxis* is social action that is reflectively done and reflection upon what one is doing as a social being in order to promote further reflection-action in an ongoing cycle. While the term "praxis" has had significant shifts in meaning since Aristotle, it has always retained the basic structure of his understanding—action-reflection united to lead to further praxis.

After Aristotle, and especially with the influence of the Neoplatonists, praxis as a valid way of knowing suffered an eclipse in Western metaphysics. It was revived in the post-Enlightenment era by Friedrich Hegel and Karl Marx but with rather narrow meanings. For Hegel, praxis does not arise from the agency of human action-reflection but is the historical expression of the Universal Spirit (*Geist*) in the world. For Marx, praxis *is* human action-reflection, but he tended to reduce action to productive labor and reflection to production feedback.

Contemporary scholars have broadened both the reflective and active components of praxis. The active dimension is now taken to include any intentional human activity in the world, but especially those actions that attempt to make and keep life human—the struggles for freedom. The reflective dimension is also deepened to mean the kind of critical reflection that unmasks and critiques hidden assumptions, controlling interests, and ideologies of oppression. The contemporary understanding also attempts to transcend Aristotle's dichotomy of theory from praxis by holding them in a dialectical and mutually correcting unity with each other.

The confidence is that praxis as critical reflection–social action can be emancipatory and humanizing for its participants and for our social structures. This is why a praxis epistemology is now favored in the methodologies of critical social science, liberation theologies, and consciousness-raising pedagogies.

In liberation theologies, a praxis methodology means taking as one's starting point a particular historical struggle for emancipation, e.g., the struggle against sexism (as in feminist theology), against racism (as in black or other minority of ethnic theologies), or against economic oppression (as in Latin American liberation theology), and

"doing theology" out of the critical consciousness that emerges from those struggles for freedom in the light of Christian faith.

In education, a praxis approach to pedagogy was revived in this century (Aristotle always referred to education as a form of praxis) by the great Brazilian educator Paulo Freire. Freire has developed a praxis pedagogy ostensibly for teaching literacy, but with other far-reaching educational possibilities. In his praxis-based and problem-posing process, people are brought to name and reflect critically on their own historical struggles in the world in order to come to a critical consciousness that acts to change their conditions toward freedom.

While a "reflection on experience" approach is not new to religious education, either Jewish or Christian, more recently a "shared praxis" approach has been developed for education in religious faith as a step beyond what is commonly called the "experiential" approach. In "shared praxis," the active historical agency of the participants is more obviously honored as they are brought to name and express their own present action in faith. Second, the reflective moment is deepened as the participants use critical reason, analytical memory, and creative imagination to appropriate their own praxis in the world and come to "know" their own stories and visions. The story and vision of the faith community is then made accessible in the pedagogical context and the participants are invited to place their own conscious praxis in dialogue and dialectic with "the faith handed down" with the practical interest of coming to decision for a *lived* faith response in the world. *See also* Action-Reflection; Dialectic(s); Liberation Theology; Social Action; Teaching Theory.

FOR FURTHER REFERENCE

Freire, Paulo. *Pedagogy of the Oppressed.* New York: Seabury, 1970. A praxis approach to consciousness-raising education.

Groome, Thomas H. *Christian Religious Education: Sharing Our Story and Vision.* San Francisco: Harper & Row, 1980. The "shared praxis" approach to religious education.

Lobkowitcz, Nicholas. *Theory and Practice.* Notre Dame, IN: University of Notre Dame Press, 1967. A historical overview of the term praxis.

Segundo, Juan. *The Liberation of Theology.* Maryknoll, NY: Orbis, 1976. An excellent explanation of a praxis method in theology.

T. H. Groome

Prayer

Prayer is communion, communication, or conversation with God as the ultimate personal reality in the universe. Both individual (private) and corporate (public) prayer involve different forms or dimensions: praise or adoration, thanksgiving, confession, petition or intercession (a type of petition), and surrender or dedication.

RECITING THE PSALMS

Through the centuries Christians have developed numerous approaches to prayer. From Judaism they inherited the psalms of the Old Testament. Early Christian congregations recited these in worship with Christian hymns and "spiritual songs" (1 Cor. 14:15; Eph. 5:19). The desert fathers, early Christian hermits, used the psalms as their chief mode of prayer, some attempting to recite all 150 psalms every day. Benedict of Nursia (ca. 480–547), as a part of his reform of monasticism, made chanting of psalms the heart of the "divine office," in which the monks gathered eight times a day for prayer. The Benedictine rule required recitation of all 150 psalms once a week. Throughout the Middle Ages, monks leading the way, psalmody continued as a central corporate exercise in prayer. Although Protestants closed monasteries and dismissed the monastic regimen, most of them continued some type of psalm usage. The psalms have obvious value for corporate prayer, many originating as community praises, thanksgivings, or laments, but the "I" psalms, written in the first person singular, teach much about the transparency needed to commune with God.

PRAYER	
Age Level	Teaching Goals and Methods
Preschool	Children learn to pray through example and experience; adults should pray with them at home and in church regularly; mealtimes, bedtimes, celebrations, and specific occasions provide the opportunity for such shared prayers; simple prayers giving thanks, asking for forgiveness, and petitioning for specific things are most easily understood; older preschool children can begin to learn about and memorize the Lord's Prayer (Matt. 6:9-13; Luke 11:2-4).
Grades 1–8	Children become increasingly familiar with the various forms of prayer, the history of prayer, and its role in both individual and corporate communion with God; biblical examples of prayer and biblical stories about prayer should be read and discussed; the Lord's Prayer can be taught and memorized more specifically as an example of prayer and a compendium of doctrine; other classical prayers can be taught as well; adults should continue to pray with children and children should be encouraged to pray on their own, with others, and for others.
High School	Students continue to increase in their understanding of the meaning and role of prayer; a discussion of seemingly unanswered prayer may help students better understand prayer and suffering; a discussion of the interaction between God's purpose and human will may help students better understand prayer and justice.
Adult	Adults should be encouraged to continue to pray regularly on their own and with others; suffering, injustice, and seemingly unanswered prayer can continue to be discussed; discussions can also focus on the theology of prayer, the psychology of prayer, and the relationship between prayer and worship; prayer groups and prayer chains may be established.

RECITING THE LORD'S PRAYER

Early in their history, Christians also began to recite the "Our Father," or Lord's Prayer, both privately and corporately. The early manual called the *Didache*, or *Teaching of the Twelve Apostles*, commanded recitation at the third, sixth, and ninth hours (nine o'clock in the morning, noon, and three in the afternoon). By the early third century converts received instruction in the Lord's Prayer as a "compendium of doctrine" as well as the most perfect way to converse with God. Cyprian of Carthage (ca. A.D. 250), evidently fearful of heresy, discouraged laypersons from spontaneous prayers; the Lord knows his own words best, he insisted. Most Protestants and Anglicans continued recitation of the prayer as an established part of the liturgy, but some radical Reformers opposed it along with all set forms. John Bunyan, a Puritan and Baptist, for instance, denied that Christ intended it "as a stinted Form of Prayer." Thence developed a tradition emphasizing reliance on the immediate inspiration of the Spirit.

REPETITION

In a quest to fulfill 1 Thessalonians 5:17 ("pray without ceasing") or Luke 18:1 ("men ought always to pray and not to faint"; KJV), the early monks developed the "Jesus prayer" or "prayer of the heart." They repeated over and over the words, "Lord Jesus Christ, have mercy on me," in rote manner. The object was to keep their minds focused always on Jesus, whom some envisioned in anthropomorphic form, as their guide and protector. The Jesus prayer has had especially extensive usage among Eastern Christians. An obscure Russian treatise entitled *The Way of a Pilgrim*, probably composed in the nineteenth century, laid out a precise method for etching the prayer on the subconscious. One should pray three thousand times a day the first week, six thousand times the second, and twelve thousand times the third; after that, the prayer would synchronize with one's heartbeat. Whether one was awake or sleeping, the heart would be entreating, "Lord Jesus Christ, have mercy on me." In the West a Carmelite lay brother named Nicholas Hermann, or Brother Lawrence, worked out a less mechanical method for "prayer of the heart" while washing dishes in a monastic kitchen. In whatever he did, he tried to maintain an attitude of attention to the presence of God or direct "a sweet and loving gaze" toward God. A simple person, he fell head over heels in love with God and let that transfuse everything he did, even to turning his "little omelette in the pan for God."

CONTEMPLATION

In the monastic tradition, which was in itself essentially a calling to perfection through prayer, contemplative or listening prayer gradually dom-

inated. Underlying the monastic approach was the conviction, based on Matthew 5:8, that the pure in heart alone would see God. Solitude, self-denial, and prayer were the means through which God could transform sinners. To pray means, above all, to listen, to open oneself to the love of God, which can cleanse and purify. Listening requires silence and solitude; Jesus withdrew to the mountain or the desert to be alone with God. The monastic ideal dominated the medieval church. Somewhat more secular usage appeared among the Platonists during the Renaissance, who emphasized contemplation as the way human beings could achieve their full potential. The Protestant Reformers, of course, took a very negative view of the whole approach as a type of works salvation, insisting on a return to simpler forms of prayer of a conversational type. The Quakers alone, in the seventeenth century, revived and continued the contemplative tradition in their silent meetings. Since the Second Vatican Council (1962–1965), however, other Protestants have been rediscovering this approach to prayer through such gifted teachers as Thomas Merton, a Trappist monk (1915–1968).

During the Middle Ages, contemplatives gradually devised a scheme indicating levels or stages of prayer. Although subjected to numerous adaptations by many writers, the scheme laid out by Teresa of Avila (1515–1582) entailed four levels, which she illustrated with analogies drawn from a Spanish garden. On the lowest level prayer is a laborious mental exercise—like water being hoisted by bucket from a cistern. Discipline is required, for a person wanting to pray must put forth effort and keep going despite disappointment. Teresa confessed that it took her twenty years to learn how to pray. On the second level "the prayer of quiet" grows less difficult—like water assisted by a water wheel. God touches the soul with a "spark" as a pledge of better things to come. On the third level prayer becomes nearly effortless as human faculties "sleep" and respond to the divine grace that pours over them—this is like water running from a river or a stream. Here union with God occurs, but human faculties still have sufficient awareness to know what is happening. Teresa depicted this as "nothing less than an all but complete death to everything in the world and a fruition of God" (*Life*, chap. 16). On the fourth level prayer becomes totally free—like rain pouring down on parched soil. This, too, involves union, but the soul no longer can comprehend what is happening.

READING SCRIPTURE

From the beginning of Christian history reading of Scriptures has constituted a form of prayer, as it did in Judaism. Early congregations read and reflected on the Old Testament and eventually the New, as it was formed. The desert fathers, many of whom were illiterate, memorized large portions and recited them. The monks gradually developed a style of reading known as *lectio divina*. This entailed reading and pausing at length to let "the word" soak in. The collapse of education as a consequence of the barbarian invasions in Europe in the fifth century naturally caused this custom to diminish even in the monasteries. Much of the struggle of the church in the late Middle Ages, therefore, had to do with a recovery of this approach to prayer. Protestants fancied themselves "people of one book," the Bible. The Puritans especially emphasized constant praying through the Bible as the way to salvation.

Recent decades have opened a new chapter in the history of prayer. In his classic work, *Prayer*, published first in 1932, Frederick Heiler took a dim view of all non-Protestant forms and approaches to prayer. Today Christians of all persuasions are learning not only from one another but from people of other faiths as well.

TEACHING PRAYER

The teaching of prayer, even within monastic communities, usually comes about through involvement. Children learn how to pray as parents pray with them before meals, at bedtime, or in particular situations. Similarly prayer is taught in a religious education class when the class engages in prayer during the session. Religious education classes also teach about prayer by explaining the meaning of the forms used. In some traditions, particularly the Jewish, Orthodox, Roman Catholic, and Anglican traditions, children learn classical prayers, including those from the liturgy. Teaching meditation as an approach to prayer takes place at home, at school, and in the community of Quaker worship. Young people and adults explore various forms through units of study that combine both background and practice.

Congregational worship is a concerted act of prayer, and the depth of an individual's life in prayer is strengthened by regular participation in weekly worship. Similarly, the worship of a religious community is strengthened by the depth of devotion of those who participate. *See also* Meditation, Forms of; Retreat; Spirituality; Worship.

E. G. Hinson

Preaching

Preaching is the church's proclamation of faith to call forth and to inspire faith. Rightly understood, preaching takes seriously three elements—the hearers, the preacher, and the revelation of God in the Bible. Who are the hearers? Are they baptized or unbaptized? Are they comprehending the message for the first time? How do they understand and express their needs, their pain, their faith? Taking into account the nature of the audience is a prerequisite for the communication of a message. The character of the preacher, the second element, also plays a significant role in preaching. Today the preacher's openness and solidarity with the congregation are more valued than in past generations. And finally there is the message. A sermon is not a preacher's opinions, however clever or relevant, about a certain topic. A Christian sermon seeks to expound an understanding of God's revelation to humanity, primarily as manifested in the Bible. However, despite the crucial importance of the hearers, the speaker, and Scripture, preaching is essentially an activity of God's Holy Spirit, offering the gospel of God as known in Jesus Christ for the salvation and sanctification of humanity.

HISTORY

The roots of Christian preaching are in the first-century synagogue practice of reading from the Scriptures and explaining their meaning. The early church apparently continued this tradition, using not only the Hebrew Scriptures but also the Letters of Paul (1 Thess. 5:27; see also Col. 4:16) and later the Gospels and other writings that became canonized as the New Testament. Justin Martyr wrote (ca. A.D. 150) that admonition based on the writings of the prophets and apostles was a practice in the Sunday service of his day.

Throughout the eras of church history, preaching has waxed and waned. There were great preachers of the early Christian centuries like Origen, John Chrysostom, and Augustine of Hippo. During the Middle Ages theologians such as Bernard of Clairvaux, Anselm, Abelard, and Thomas Aquinas were known for their effective preaching. However, there were long periods when no sermons were heard in cathedral or parish church. The Protestant Reformation restored preaching to a place of importance. Key Reformation leaders like Martin Luther, John Calvin, and Ulrich Zwingli all insisted on the necessity of preaching in public worship. Since the Reformation the sermon has been a, and often the, characteristic feature of the Sunday worship service in many Protestant denominations in the United States. At times Sunday worship has been called a "preaching service," indicating that the sermon has been the essential and usually the climactic element in the service.

As a result of the liturgical renewal movement of the twentieth century, many Protestant denominations have begun to reassess the relationship between the sermon and the sacrament of the Lord's Supper. Do the two belong together in the normative Sunday worship service as attested to, for example, in Acts 20:7–12, where after the apostle Paul's speaking the community "broke bread," or in Justin Martyr's description of Sunday worship? If so, is preaching primary, with the Communion added as a sealing of the benefits offered by the word? Or is the Eucharist primary, with the sermon as preparation for intelligible reception of the elements? Or are the two inseparable, complementary, each offering the life-giving Word in a different guise? The Christian church worldwide is divided as to the answer to these questions. It is noteworthy that another consequence of the liturgical renewal movement and of Vatican II has been the rediscovery in the Roman Catholic church of the significance of preaching. In both branches of the Christian church the linkage between preaching and the Eucharist is being reaffirmed.

PURPOSE

Another lively topic of discussion among Protestant homileticians in recent years has centered on the purpose of preaching. Is preaching a means of grace, offering Jesus Christ and the benefits of faith? Until recent years the sermon fell under the overarching category of rhetoric, the primary goal of which is persuasion, the audience's assent to the truth of the speaker's statements. The Protestant sermon, like Protestant theology, principally engaged the mind, with illustrations designed to clarify the issue, elicit the concurrence of the emotions, and/or drive home a point.

Such an understanding of preaching has theological implications: God's revelation is understood to be the divine communication of knowledge, and faith, thus, involves the acceptance of these suprarational, authoritative truths.

Many scholars and practitioners are questioning this singular understanding of the sermon. Drawing from the insights of narrative theology, studies in the parable and metaphor, and communication theory, they claim that preaching is more "sacramental," effecting change in the hearers as divine grace uses the ordinary elements of human words to save and sanctify. Just as sacraments consist of two parts, the outward sign and the inward grace, so the sermon consists of the ordinary, everyday words of human speech and the activity of the Holy Spirit. As in the sacraments there exists a sacramental union or a spiritual relation between the common elements and the thing signified, so in preaching the words not only point to God but also become instruments for God's addressing God's people. These homileticians speak of preaching as "encounter" or "word-event."

Part of the theological basis for this understanding of preaching is that revelation consists not of timeless, static truths, but of God's self-disclosure through a personal encounter. God as Subject confronts the individual as subject through the medium of normal, natural words. The essence of faith is not content but relationship, fellowship with the One who claims the individual's allegiance as Lord. The response of faith is not primarily assent and conformity to truth, but prayer and obedience to God as a Person. A sermon, therefore, is a means of grace as "Christ crucified" is offered and received in faith. Holding the two in tension is probably the most effective means for communicating the variety of faith's responses to the word of God.

FORM

This disagreement about the purpose of preaching has led to divergent understandings of the form a sermon should take. The standard structure has been "three points and a poem," a deductive approach designed to lead the truth out of the biblical passage and apply it to the hearers. In recent years homileticians have explored the use of an inductive approach, designing the sermon to lead the hearers into engagement with the biblical passage or the sermonic material. Those who espouse this approach have benefited from research into the literary shape of the Bible. They suggest that sermons take the shape of the Scriptures on which they are based. For example, a narrative passage lends itself to a narrative type sermon, one that follows the story line of the biblical passage. Or a sermon based on a parable might aim to create the same surprise or shock that the original story would have had on its first audience.

Preaching under the heading of rhetoric, more deductive preaching, seeks to *organize ideas* for the most persuasive communication of the message. The paradigm is the lawyer delivering a final appeal to the jury. Preaching that espouses the "new homiletic," more inductive preaching, seeks to *shape an experience* so that the sermon interacts with the hearers much as do other art forms that involve time such as music or drama. The paradigm is the story teller weaving a captivating tale with the hearers leaning forward, caught up in a world of possibility and imagination. Some call this latter approach "narrative preaching," meaning that the sermon borrows many of the techniques of narration, e.g., plot and movement.

Although the preacher may be called teaching elder, preaching should not be confused with teaching because of its essentially proclamatory nature. However, hearers are taught by preaching, and they learn about God's revelation even while caught up in its exhorting power. This is the role of preaching in nurturing faith. Many hear biblical interpretation only through this weekly exposition of the text or of biblical passages used to illumine a theme. The theological understanding of the preacher influences that of the hearers, and their understanding of a particular faith tradition is formed in part by preaching.

Although there is no unanimity among homileticians regarding the purpose of or pattern for preaching or regarding its relationship to the Eucharist, there is no doubt that preaching is a central function of the Christian church for converting unbelievers and for nurturing the faith of believers. *See also* Communication Theory; Eucharist; Grace; Kerygma; Liturgical Movement; Narrative Theology; Sacraments; Sermons, Children's; Worship; Worship, Children's.

L. A. Rose

Preadolescence

See Middle Childhood.

Prejudice

Prejudice is the belief that those different from oneself in some way are inferior. Prejudice is an idea, but it is expressed in words and actions that harm others. Religious educators sometimes transmit prejudices along with religious beliefs, especially if they attempt to teach beliefs without reference to the underlying faith experiences that the beliefs describe and evoke. Since prejudice is based on fear, what dispels prejudice is experience: gaining a firsthand knowledge of the other so that one can view reality from the other's perspective and thereby come to care for the other's concerns and needs.

Jewish and Christian traditions teach that God created all living things. Therefore, religious education in these traditions should seek to instill the idea that all people are brothers and sisters who must care for one another, the animals and plants, and the environment. Yet this teaching is forgotten when the religious community places utmost value upon maintaining its own structures, cohesion, and boundaries. When this happens, socialization into the community will stress the differences between those within the religious group and those outside, rather than their common origin from the Creator God. "We" will be "the good people," and everyone else "bad."

Religious prejudice shows itself in numerous ways. For example, the belief that only in one's own church can salvation be found may lead to the idea that other branches of Christianity are devoid of God's grace. Religious bigotry is abhorrence of different religious tradition, but it can also occur between groups that share a common heritage. Bigotry increases in virulence to the extent that someone else's beliefs seem to threaten one's own, as, for example, when a child of Christian parents worships God in the person of the Hindu deity Krishna.

Besides specifically religious prejudices, other biases exist in society. Nationalism is the belief that one's own country ought to be more powerful and richer than any other, no matter what the cost to poorer nations. (Nationalism should be distinguished from patriotism, love of country that inspires one to do everything possible for the welfare of its people but does not imply injuring others.) Racism and ethnic prejudice are hatred of those whose heritage is different from one's own, and it finds many expressions: violence against those of another color or tongue, laws that separate races and give privileges to one race over others, negative attitudes and expectations that affect hiring and promotion decisions in the workplace, insulting portrayals of disadvantaged races in the mass media—the list could be greatly expanded.

Sexism is approval of disequitable relations between the sexes, and it resembles racism in many of its economic, social, and psychological manifestations. Fear, and consequently hatred, of women (or of men) forms its basis.

Ageism is believing that someone must be "too old" or "too young" to do, be or know something, without bothering to discover an individual's particular capacities.

Because nationalism, racism, sexism, and ageism are present in our society, they deeply affect religious communities and their educational efforts. History provides examples of religious teaching that defended and praised ideas that we now recognize as prejudice.

Honest assessment of past and present prejudice within religious education seems a prerequisite for addressing prejudice in society at large. Fortunately, resources are at hand for this work; for example, the studies of Latin American, feminist, and black theologians of liberation. The opposite of prejudice is not liberalism or relativism, but fidelity to the teaching of the universal parenthood of God.

Teaching about prejudice begins with an acknowledgment of the forms of prejudice being practiced. Elementary-age children can share their own examples; individuals frequently feel left out, even within a homogeneous group, because of their need for acceptance. Teaching becomes especially important in changing communities where new residents from another culture evoke protective actions within the community. Prejudice in such situations is conveyed to children through parents.

Churches and synagogues, as keepers of the biblical tradition, will teach acceptance of all people through their affirmations of God as creator and redeemer, through the example of biblical peoples who were received when strangers, and through biblical teachings on responsibility toward strangers. The biblical perspective can be brought to bear on the practices of a community.

Working with adolescents brings a different dimension; parents are fearful of intercultural dating, and the community may keep groups segregated socially even though frequently they attend the same high school. Adults have pragmatic concerns about jobs and housing values that need to be discussed openly. Religious education in this area is seldom an academic exercise. There is plenty of material in the existential situation to be viewed in the light of the biblical understanding of God. It is important, however, to remember that people need the security of being accepted where they are in their thinking before they will be able to consider other viewpoints and ways of acting toward those against whom they harbor prejudice. See also Feminist Movement; Language, Inclusive; Liberation Theology; Multicultural Education; Social Action; Social Justice, Education for.

M. Sawicki

Presbyterian Education

See Reformed Education.

Preschool Children

Preschool children are those between the toddler stage and the age of mandatory school entrance. Usually kindergarten children are considered to be in preschool since, although kindergarten may be required for entrance into first grade, five year olds do not have to be enrolled in a kindergarten. The statutes of the various states specify either six or seven as the age for compulsory school attendance. In practice therefore preschool children are three, four, or five year olds.

HISTORY OF KINDERGARTEN

In Western society, until fairly recently, early childhood was not considered a special period in human development. Until the fifteenth century children were expected to behave like adults and were dressed in grown-up fashion as soon as they had left the infant stage. In the dame schools of Colonial America, located in the kitchens of New England housewives, three and four year olds were taught along with their older siblings. The younger children too were expected to learn the alphabet, to recite Bible verses, and to write sums on their slates. The practice continued in the common schools of New England and by 1850 15 percent of the children enrolled were younger than five.

Although as early as 1813 Robert Owen proposed infant schools to provide a separate education for young children, these schools, which were radically different from the common schools, did not find ready acceptance. It was not until later in the nineteenth century when Friedrich Froebel established the first kindergartens that the education of preschool children was generally realized as something unique. Froebel understood that young children differed from their older siblings and his schools used concrete materials to help children discover "inner truth" through self-activity in pleasant surroundings. These "child gardens" were instituted to help children weed out bad tendencies while cultivating those considered desirable. In the United States Elizabeth Peabody was instrumental in establishing kindergartens and teaching Froebel's ideas to others.

These first kindergartens had served mainly middle- and upper-class families, but the idea of educating preschool children was soon borrowed by those in the United States who were concerned with the Americanization of immigrant children. Froebel's kindergarten thus became the model of the "day nurseries," those institutions set up to care for and socialize the poor. These nurseries, similar to our present day-care centers, were operated by settlement houses and religious groups; the former met social and physical needs while the latter added religious precepts. The purposes of the nurseries differed according to their sponsorship: the churches and synagogues emphasized education while the settlement houses emphasized the social welfare of their families. In 1873 the first public school kindergarten was started in St. Louis and the social welfare aspect of the kindergarten, with its concern for the "whole child," was modified by the academic constraints of the school. The tension resulting from this marriage of elementary school and kindergarten has lasted until the present day.

RESEARCH AND OBSERVATION

Along with the inauguration of the kindergarten, two other developments important for preschool education took place in the early years of the twentieth century. One was the child study movement, whose stalwarts included G. Stanley Hall and Arnold Gesell. This movement was instrumental in founding nursery schools, mostly associated with universities around the country. Unlike the day nurseries of earlier days these schools were half-day programs. The purposes of the schools were to provide practice for home economics teachers to observe normal children at play, and to provide laboratories where curricula and teaching methods could be researched. The science of child development had begun with preschool children as the focus of much study.

The other influential development for preschool children during these years was progressive education, begun at the University of Chicago by John Dewey (1859–1952), who stressed that the curriculum for young children should be an outgrowth of their own ideas and interests rather than the ideas of the teachers. For Dewey education was a process, not preparation for living but life itself. Such a philosophy was readily accepted by those concerned with the needs of young children.

In Europe at about the same time, Maria

500

Montessori (1870–1952), the first woman physician in Italy, had begun to establish schools to help children become "normalized." She had worked with children who were considered to be mentally handicapped and found that with a different style of teaching they were able to achieve at a higher level than many so-called normal children. This led her to develop a system and materials that took advantage of "sensitive periods," those times when she believed children were particularly able to learn certain material. The early religious education of children was an important concern to Montessori and with it she used the same approach she took toward education in general—letting children experience as they learn.

During the second quarter of the twentieth century in Europe the ideas of Jean Piaget (1896–1980), a Swiss epistomologist, gained a large following. By the middle of the century, Piaget's work was rediscovered in the United States by early childhood educators. Piaget believed that children passed through unvarying stages of development and that their styles of learning differed according to each particular stage. Thus preschool children had progressed from the sensorimotor stage, with its emphasis on developing reflexes and eye-hand coordination and the recognition that objects still exist when out of sight. In the preschool years, or preoperational stage, children are particularly involved in developing symbolic thought, especially in the tremendous growth of language and through the use of symbols in play. Piaget believed that children around the age of four gradually entered the stage of intuitive thought with a primitive logic system whereby events are explained in terms of other events and children can concentrate on no more than one aspect of a problem at a time.

Piaget developed his ideas through careful observation of children and through listening to their explanations of their actions. Although he did not directly discuss education, his emphasis on the child's own mental actions had a profound effect on the education of preschool children. It tended to confirm what preschool teachers had been saying all along: children are not empty vessels to be filled with factual material; they are active explorers of their environment and can only assimilate much knowledge through action. Since this is the case, schools where preschool children sit and listen to the teacher or simply recite material are not effective. In order to develop their understanding of the world, preschool children must be allowed to actively explore.

They learn by doing: through experiences of handling materials, hearing music, looking at books, and making a variety of drawings and constructions. Given freedom to explore, their exuberance leads to creative activities. They discover new ways to build with blocks, imagine routes for trucks, trains, and planes, or re-present family life. They can make up their own songs and tell their own stories. Through interaction with other children and adults they become aware of the limits of individual freedom and learn habits of cooperation, mutual help, and delayed gratification. Preschool education is best accomplished when a variety of materials are made available to children and teachers become facilitators, encouraging more than telling, guiding rather than directing, sensitive to individual needs within the larger context of the group.

RECENT EDUCATIONAL TRENDS AND CONCERNS

By 1985 40 percent of all three and four year olds were enrolled in some form of preschool, while the figure reached 96 percent for five and six year olds. This was partly due to the publicity surrounding the results of programs specifically designed to counteract the effects of poverty, such as Head Start and the Perry Preschool Project. No research has shown preschool to be beneficial for middle-class children, but a majority of middle-class parents enroll their children in some form of preschool. Many preschool children are cared for in day-care centers while their parents are employed and since most licensed day-care centers have an educational component, these children are considered to be in preschool along with their counterparts in nursery school and kindergarten.

Today's trend in preschool education is toward providing full-day kindergartens instead of the previously typical half-day programs. At the same time there has been a tendency to push some of the more academic curricula of the elementary school into the kindergarten. This has been strongly resisted by early childhood educators and others who are familiar with the research, since there is much concern that the pressure on young children produces undesirable side effects and is actually counterproductive academically.

Another recent trend is for public schools to provide preschool for three and four year olds. In some states this is available mainly to children deemed to be "at risk" because of certain factors in their home environments. Preschool education for these children can be a cost-saving measure in the long run, since it results in fewer children assigned to special education classes, less retention in grade, lower high-school dropout rates, higher employment in high-school years, and fewer arrests for juvenile delinquency. For this reason other states have made a verbal commitment to begin public preschool education as soon as the necessary funding can be found. Experts favor this preschool education provided appropriate curricula and methods are used.

Some recent books on preschool children (e.g., Valerie Suransky's *The Erosion of Childhood*, 1982, and David Elkind's *The Hurried Child*, 1988) suggest that the preschool years have become a time of many demands on youngsters, who are often hurried through their childhood without the chance to be children. Partly this is due to the influence of television, which exposes children to material once considered beyond their years, but it also stems from the pressures that parents and teachers exert as they try to have children learn more at an earlier age. This too is a concern of early childhood educators.

Recent research in psychology tends to support the view that heredity has a stronger effect on personality than we had believed. Some preschool children may be shy and others outgoing by nature. While environmental influences can shape these tendencies, it is probably difficult if not impossible to reverse the trend and change a shy child into one who is outgoing. We no longer think of intelligence as a fixed concept unable to be modified by careful nurturing. Neither do we believe that intelligence is infinitely malleable. It may well be that personality is a similar construct, with both heredity and environment playing their part in its development. The age-old question of which is the most potent factor in the development of preschool children will probably never be resolved. Since there is nothing preschool teachers can do about heredity, it behooves them to concentrate on making the environment as satisfying as possible.

Constructing an environment conducive to preschool learning might begin with a large, cheerful, well-lighted, temperature-controlled room. Materials can be arranged in interest centers: a music center with tapes and/or recordings, players, and earphones, illustrated songbooks, and instruments both for accompanying singing and the children's use; a reading corner with cassettes and books; and an activities center with materials for creative work (crayons, paints, felt-tipped pens, clay or other molding material, colored paper and scissors, magazines for cutting out pictures, and three-dimensional materials for constructions). Children also enjoy a housekeeping or dress-up center, blocks, and wheeled toys. Pictures, posters, and other learning materials will enliven the walls. An outdoor play space and equipment encourage motor activity. A nondisciplinary, indoor "quiet corner" will give children a place for that time apart occasionally needed amid much activity. *See also* Affective Development; Child Abuse; Child Development; Cognitive Development; Day-care Center; Kindergarten; Montessori, Maria; Nursery Education; Piaget, Jean; Psychosocial Development.

FOR FURTHER REFERENCE

Leeper, Sarah Hammond, Ralph C. Witherspoon, and Barbara Day. *Good Schools for Young Children: A Guide for Working with 3, 4, and 5 Year Old Children.* New York: Macmillan, 1984.

Mussen, Paul H., ed. *Handbook of Child Psychology.* 4th ed. New York: Wiley, 1983.

A. H. Brautigam

Prisoners

Religious education for prisoners includes all programs of worship, study, counseling, and fellowship in U.S. prisons and aftercare facilities that further prisoners' religious understanding and commitment.

CHAPLAINS AND PRISON ADMINISTRATIONS

There are roughly 2,000 prison chaplains in 659 state prisons and 47 chaplains in 86 federal prisons, appointed by state and federal authorities and usually paid by prisons. The majority of these chaplains represent the three major faiths, Christianity (Protestant and Roman Catholic), Judaism, and Islam.

Chaplains serve either part- or full-time, some in more than one institution. In many prisons, religious "centers" of several rooms allow inmates of a faith to meet in an informal atmosphere for study, fellowship, and counsel as well as worship.

Some prison administrations cooperate with religious programs in the belief that they promote rehabilitation, such as Attica Correctional Facility (New York), Huntington Correctional Facility (Pennsylvania), Oahu Community Correctional Center (Waikiki, Hawaii), and San Quentin Correctional Facility (California). Some administrations are less cooperative and limit various gatherings and celebrations traditional to religious faiths in the belief that anything beyond constitutional obligations unnecessarily reduces security.

Policy in federal prisons provides for equal opportunity to worship freely (with necessary accoutrements), appropriate accommodations for meetings, worship, and study, and reasonable observance of special holidays, including at least one full day a year with an appropriate meal. Many state prisons are emulating the federal pattern.

PRISON MINISTRY'S, PURPOSES AND PROBLEMS

Aside from the usual motivations for teaching religion, there is an added aim in the case of prisoners—to help change their lives so they will not return to prison, to reduce the 80–90 percent rate of return (recidivism).

Religion is not just theoretical beliefs and principles. It includes the skill of living out those beliefs in everyday life and it can play a most significant role in effecting behavioral changes in prisoners' lives—changes in the deeply rooted attitudes, morals, and reactions that caused their incarceration and that, if not changed, will ensure their future return to prison. Experience has shown that lasting and permanent changes in such areas have been effected within the context of religious teaching and ministry, both in prisons and in aftercare.

Christians teach prisoners that God's loving forgiveness can be received upon repentance and turning from sin to obedience and that a new life in Christ can be lived with changed attitudes and reactions. Also, they are shown that adverse circumstances, even their prison experience of punishment, can produce constructive growth.

The teaching of Jewish inmates emphasizes the need for change based on increased obedience and respect for God and family, and Islamic teaching stresses the requirement of absolute obedience to Allah.

One of the greatest problems in prison religious ministry is that the practice of any faith within prison walls is "sheltered" by having time to pursue it in close fellowship with others and by a freedom from most of the personal burdens, responsibilities, and temptations in the world outside. On release, the latter will assume crisis proportions, time for study will evaporate, and even finding an "accepting" congregation for spiritual nourishment and fellowship can be very difficult for ex-offenders.

Unless prisoners have been taught in prison how to cope with such circumstances, or have entered a teaching program of aftercare, or at least have set up a detailed support system of relatives, friends, churches, or other groups, it is difficult to "make it" outside. Most fail within a few weeks or months and join the number headed back to prison. Hence, there is great need both in prisons and aftercare facilities for teaching offenders to use their faith to bring about the changes in their everyday thinking and acting that will prevent their return to prison.

CHRISTIAN EDUCATION

Both chaplains and volunteers conduct religion and Bible study courses, some of which are prepared by denominational churches or national prison ministries. The Baptist churches and Baptist Home Board of Missions, Mennonite Church (Gospel Echo publications), Good News Prison Ministry, Salvation Army, Prison Fellowship, and Teen Challenge all have courses specifically prepared for prisoners. Also, monitored correspondence courses, some in Spanish, are available from many of these, as well as from schools and colleges such as Moody Bible Institute, Columbia Bible College, and Trinity Seminary. Roman Catholic REC Program (Residents Encounter Christ) is outstanding for its teaching and three-day, in-prison retreats.

Prison Fellowship (Washington, D.C.), founded by Chuck Colson following his Water-gate prison experience, initiated in 1976 the "Washington Discipleship Seminars" for eight to ten federal prisoners taken out of prisons countrywide on furlough for fourteen days. Six seminars are held each year. Later, the three-day "In-prison Seminars" were introduced, with 407 held in 1986, and ten to twenty trained volunteers assisting teaching teams in each seminar.

Formal theological courses are also available. New York Seminary conducts a one-year, forty-two-credit course in Ossining Correctional Facility (New York) yielding a master's in professional studies degree in prison ministry. Based on this, a master of divinity degree can be completed in approximately one year after release. Baptist seminaries, and others, also make seminary extension courses available through prison chaplains, and inmates may enroll in religion courses offered in most prison college courses.

In addition to formal training there is experiential education, which includes programs aimed at teaching prisoners to live out religious principles in everyday life and to change old habits, attitudes, and reactions. For example, some chaplains create whole church communities with inmates assuming real responsibility for all the usual roles, including pastoral functions and governing bodies.

Intensive work is being done with prisoners' families, since approximately 85 percent of marriages fail upon incarceration. Family Reunion Programs in New York and other states, allowing three-day trailer visits with families, become, after counseling, opportunities to begin to live out religious beliefs and principles being learned together. In prison, Roman Catholic Marriage Encounter and Cursillo programs, Protestant Tres Dias programs, and Episcopal Kairos programs have great impact on prisoners, spouses, and families. The Salvation Army, as well, has a teaching program for women prisoners and their children in a religiously oriented camping weekend.

Prison Fellowship's community service projects take inmates on two-week furlough releases to do public work projects. These are practice periods for living out the seminar and other teachings and were held in over fifty communities in 1986. Their care groups assist prisoners in life problems both in prisons and in aftercare.

There are a growing number of groups functioning both in the prisons and in aftercare facilities that aid inmates in replacing, through God's power, old attitudes and emotions, such as taking responsibility for their actions instead of being "victims," and in learning to respond constructively to adverse situations. These groups can drastically reduce recidivism and include, among others, Cephas-Attica (Rochester, New York); Christian Prison Ministry, "The Bridge" (Orlando, Florida, and Framingham, Massachusetts); Mennonite's "Hopeway" (Lancaster, Pennsylvania); Helps Ministry, "Alpha House" (Mount

Vernon, New York); and Yoke Fellows (Williamsport, Pennsylvania).

In 1986 there were approximately 60,000 Christian volunteers for prison ministry, of which about 25,000 were associated with Prison Fellowship. There were approximately 1,500 prison ministries, of which 40 were organizations of national impact and over 700 were known as "Mom and Pop" small groups.

Prisons must often screen groups to avoid unaccredited sects or cults, to ensure well-rounded religious teaching of spiritual depth, and to avoid mere "head knowledge" that does not survive release. The same tension between traditional and fundamental teaching exists in prisons as on the outside.

Other well-known ministries include: Chaplain Ray's International Prison Ministry (Dallas, Texas), providing Bibles, books, visits, teaching; Billy Graham Evangelistic Association (Wheaton, Illinois), supporting 300 chaplains, Bibles, books, and over 100 individual responses to prisoners' questions per day; Youth for Christ, Youth Guidance Program (Wheaton, Illinois), juvenile corrections; Full Gospel Business Men's Fellowship International, Prison Ministry Program (Santa Ana, California), Bible studies, 34 prison chapters; Institute for Prison Ministry, Donald Smarto, Director (Wheaton, Illinois), serving prison ministries; Good News Prison Ministry, teaching; M-2 (San Quentin, California), one-to-one "friendship" teaching relationship in prison and aftercare; Covenant Players (Reseda, California), presenting the gospel nationwide in simple, forceful drama.

JEWISH EDUCATION

Rabbi prison chaplains, now numbering 200, have been active for over 100 years; they are few in number due to the low number of Jewish prisoners: 5,000 out of total prison population of 500,000. Teaching involves Hebrew, Torah, law, liturgy, and holiday observances, together with counseling and worship.

Aleph Institute (Miami, Florida), founded in 1983 by a Hasidic group, teaches "The Living Torah," a study of Jewish law and heritage, in a setting of caring service to the needs of inmates of all faiths and also conducts two-week furlough release seminars for federal prisoners in Yeshiva College (Morristown, New Jersey) each year.

Experimental work was done at Comstock Correctional Facility (New York) with a program and service of Jewish mysticism, a study of ethics and cabala.

Correspondence courses are also available and there is lay prison ministry involvement, including work with families, through the Prisoner Outreach Program of B'nai B'rith, International Coalition for Jewish Prisoner Services, and other agencies.

MUSLIM EDUCATION

The first two Muslim chaplains were appointed in 1975, and by 1986 twenty chaplains were serving. Their teaching includes concentrated Islamic studies stressing disciplinary principles, the "Ju'muah" (Friday worship service, frequently with an inmate Imam), the "Da'wah" (introductory instruction for others), observance of Ramadan (annual thirty-day fast) and two other feast days. Reports indicate that the recidivism rate for "on-record" Muslims is below the national average of 85 percent.

OTHER FAITHS

Minority faiths without chaplains are served by volunteers of such faiths and upon request prisons provide individuals with representatives of their faith for counseling or teaching. At least one federal prison even provided an American Indian sweatlodge, a small stone hut for an Indian sweating ceremony.

RESOURCES

The American Protestant Correctional Chaplains Association (5235 Greenpoint Dr., Stone Mountain, GA 30088) coordinates member chaplains of all denominations and faiths. Other organizations to contact include the American Catholic Correctional Chaplains Association (4455 Woodson Rd., St. Louis, MO 63134), the American Jewish Correctional Chaplains Association (c/o New York Board of Rabbis, 10 East 73rd St., New York, NY), the American Muslim Correctional Chaplains Association (New York State Department of Corrections, Ministerial Services, Bldg. No. 2, State Office Building Campus, Albany, NY 12226), and the Federal Bureau of Prisons (320 First St., N.W., Washington, DC 20534). *See also* Chaplain; Ministry.

FOR FURTHER REFERENCE

Smarto, Donald. *Justice and Mercy*. Wheaton, IL: Tyndale, 1987. Covers religious ministry to prisoners, historical and current, with comprehensive lists.

G. H. Henley

Private Religious Schools

Private religious schools—also called parish schools, parochial schools, day schools, or independent schools—are sponsored and funded by local congregations or associations of congregations for the general and religious education of primarily elementary age children of the congregation or surrounding area. Weekday classes cover basic studies such as English, mathematics, history, and sciences. Religious education is integrated into each subject area or special time is set aside for religious instruction on a regular basis.

In the United States, typically the private religious school develops to counteract prevailing social or religious norms, to make religious education available in a specific theological point of view, to be an outreach ministry for the congregation and community, or to provide alternative education that connects religion and all areas of life. Schools vary in size, curriculum offerings, educational standards, teacher performance, tuition costs, and admission policies. The intensity of the commitment toward alternative schooling by the leaders and congregational members, funding, and the educational ramifications of theological and ideological points of view shape the style and character of schools. Each school governing board determines response to educational issues related to general education and administration of a school plus the role of religion in the school.

The parochial school emerged as a distinctive educational agency in the 1840s as the "common" school (or public schools as we know them) began to be the prevalent school model. Most Protestants gave up their struggling schools to support the larger, publicly funded weekday schools. These schools, given the predominantly Protestant nature of the society, included Bible and moral teaching. Sunday schools became an additional means of religious education for the churches. Thus the "parallel" or "dual" system of public schools and denominational Sunday schools emerged as the most favored of the Protestant strategies in education.

CATHOLIC SCHOOLS

Catholics rejected the dual approach and insisted on developing weekday parochial schools to counteract the powerful influences of Protestant-dominated common schools. They found the use of the King James Version in public schools particularly irksome.

Catholics struggled to provide schools that taught Catholic views to the millions of immigrants in the nineteenth century. Anti-Catholic sentiment by the Protestant majority fueled the desire to have a Catholic school in every parish and requirements that Catholic children attend Catholic schools. Increasing secularization of the public school and modernizing within the Catholic church brought vigorous reaction from the pope and further impetus toward parochial education, including the development of Catholic high schools in the late nineteenth century. An impressive system of schools developed that fostered a high degree of loyalty, quality programs, and increasingly high professional standards for teachers.

In the 1960s Catholic schools were criticized because of the overwhelming attention the schools required of parishes, the difficulties in supporting urban schools for non-Catholics in poor neighborhoods, increasing costs, labor disputes, decreasing enrollment, and research results on the mixed impact of Catholic schooling on behavior and belief. The critics contended that earlier needs of preserving Catholic loyalties, countering anti-Catholic sentiment, and providing ethnic and language identities were no longer required.

Proponents insist on the indispensability of schools; however, they agree that schools should be more clearly recognizable as faith communities that make unique contributions to society. Staffing schools with competent teachers and committed Catholics while maintaining adequate salaries for the larger numbers of lay teachers and serving poor residents in urban parishes are no easy tasks. Catholic schools remain the largest alternative to public schools in the United States, with nearly three million participants.

LUTHERAN SCHOOLS

German immigrants who formed the Lutheran Church–Missouri Synod (1847) and the Wisconsin Evangelical Lutheran Church (1850) came with the mission of preserving Lutheran doctrine against the attacks of rationalism. Parish elementary schools became key agencies for maintaining confessional orthodoxy, opposing "unionism," and "upbuilding Christ's kingdom." Reacting to negative experiences of state control of education in Germany, they saw in America the opportunity to develop schools that would resemble German models but be free to teach Lutheran points of view.

Textbooks were carefully chosen; languages were required for the university-bound. Teachers were trained in and certified for theological orthodoxy by the denominational colleges. German was the language of the classroom.

The introduction of the English language was a turning point. The English debate concerned such issues as church-state relationships, the value of Sunday schools, theological correctness, the value of public schools, compulsory school laws, and anti-German attitudes in society.

In the twentieth century, Lutheran schools, like the Catholic schools, made strong efforts to fight off government control of schools, developed stronger teacher education, and took advantage of population growth to begin more schools. The focus remained providing congregational children with a Christian education.

More recently, controversial research suggested that Lutheran parochial school children are not markedly different in religious practices and beliefs from other Lutheran children who go to public schools. Funding is a continuing concern, yet Lutheran schools continue to be viewed as vital for congregational mission and congregations are eager to support them. By the 1980s, however, over 40 percent of elementary students in Lutheran schools were non-Lutheran, which poses a new challenge. In urban areas, the schools become an important alternative as a more manageable educational environment. Over 195,000 elementary pupils are served by Lutheran schools.

REFORMED SCHOOLS

The Dutch Secessionist Calvinists who came to America in the 1830s established Christian schools because of negative judgments about state control of education in the Netherlands. Schools were begun in 1856 in Grand Rapids, Michigan, and were forerunners of the Christian Reformed Church and its schools.

Other Calvinists influenced by Abraham Kuyper developed schools that were related to churches but were controlled by groups of parents and laypersons and were called "societies." These societies maintain considerable autonomy even though there is national support in the Christian Reformed tradition for curriculum development and teacher education.

The theological perspectives of Christian Reformed–related schools argue that all areas of life are under the sovereignty of God, schools should be independent to avoid both church and state control, truth can be found in general and special revelation, and the school has a mandate to help students learn to transform society. Integrating these ideals into curriculum has been a major undertaking. Nearly 75,000 pupils are involved in Reformed schools.

ADVENTIST SCHOOLS

The Seventh-Day Adventist church, founded in the 1840s on the basis of a belief in the immediate return of Christ, began to establish schools in the late 1800s. Because of the theological position there was disregard for education early in the movement; however, later that same unusual theological position made it necessary to develop schools. The denomination has nearly 60,000 elementary pupils.

JEWISH SCHOOLS

Jewish day schools, while rarely congregational schools, but rather sponsored by independent groups, are a growing phenomenon in the United States. The struggle for identity in the face of anti-Semitism has increased interest in such schools.

EVANGELICAL SCHOOLS

The most recent large-scale effort to establish religious schools is the Christian day school movement by evangelical Protestants. Occasioned by reevaluation of public education, many elementary schools have been begun by independent congregations. Some estimates suggest from 250,000 to 1 million students attend. Issues of authority, social standards, government control, and the role

of evangelicalism in shaping American life are part of the powerful motivation.

Born of frustration with current societal trends, the Christian schools can be marked by controversy. Admission policies have been questioned for racial bias, standards have been low in some schools, high in test results in others; the interaction with the state over minimum standards has been sometimes acrimonious. These schools, like those parish schools in the past, represent strongly held views and fierce loyalties, provide options to standard practice, and test new ideas about education. *See also* Colleges and Universities, Church-Related; Jewish Education; Private Schools and Religion; Public Schools and Religion; individual entries for each denomination, e.g., Lutheran Education.

FOR FURTHER REFERENCE

Carper, James C., and Thomas C. Hunt, eds. *Religious Schooling in America.* Birmingham, AL: Religious Education Press, 1984.

Kennedy, William Bean. *The Shaping of Protestant Education.* New York: Association Press, 1966.

R. A. Olson

Private Schools and Religion

Religion plays an important role in the educational programs of denominationally linked private schools. A church school demonstrates its religious commitment in five aspects of its work: in its governance, religious identity, and school climate; in its curriculum—the teaching of theology, ethics, history, and the like; in its liturgy—its worship services in a chapel, classroom, or elsewhere; in its approach to service, outreach, and mission; and in pastoral counseling, the use of religious faith as the basis for helping students understand and deal with problems and challenges.

SCHOOL GOVERNANCE

Most religious private schools in the United States are governed by a denomination or religious group. The Roman Catholic church maintains the largest group of such schools. The large majority of these are elementary, closely associated with a parish. Most Catholic secondary schools are either diocesan or private, the latter often administered by a religious order.

Many Protestant church schools, too, are associated with and administered by an individual parish or church. The Lutheran Church–Missouri Synod governs 1,750 schools, mostly elementary. These schools are overseen and financed by a congregation, which assumes total responsibility for educating its children. Episcopal elementary schools are often closely allied to a parish, but they tend to be more independent financially. Quaker schools may profess an informal affiliation with the Friends Council on Education, but most are totally independent. Thus religious schools may be organized and totally controlled by a denomination or religious group, or they may affiliate in name only.

A school's association with a denomination, parish, diocese, or order influences its religious identity, which in turn helps determine its "climate." A church school may, in itself, constitute a religious community organized around its curriculum, its mission and religious purpose, and the faith it professes.

Some religious denominations govern schools as they would missions. For some groups, particularly conservative Christian groups, schools function as instruments of evangelization. With education a primary goal of most families, the private school may attract children first and adults later. Whereas conversion to the faith may not be a central goal of the school or an announced goal at all, religious schools can play an effective role in the evangelical work of the denomination. Church people supporting schools thus view their broader religious purpose as the education of the entire family, with the school serving as the instrument of education for the young.

CURRICULUM

In Roman Catholic parochial schools, the curriculum includes preparation in the sacraments; it provides a powerful influence in shaping the school's religious identity. Instruction in the catechism and other religious doctrines is provided by the parish priest, who fulfills the teaching mission of both school and parish. Religious instruction remains important in Catholic secondary schools, with required church history, theology, and Bible classes complementing the standard liberal arts as part of college preparation.

Protestant schools differ widely in the degree and type of religious instruction offered. Some conservative groups prepare and present curricular materials with a Christian perspective; reading, social studies, even science texts bear the clear imprint of the Christian faith. In these schools, usually elementary schools, group prayer, theology, and the reading of Scripture routinely supplement other instruction. Less conservative denominations, Lutherans and Episcopalians, for example, offer a foundational curriculum that is similar to that used in the public schools; however, they supplement the teaching of standard subject areas with Bible stories and the history of the church— lessons intended to develop a theological awareness. The Lutheran Church–Missouri Synod prepares "curriculum guides" to assist in the teaching of religion and in presenting the church's faith. These guides are intended as aids to worship, not as substitutes for curricular materials in the basic disciplines. Thus supervision over religious curriculum tends to reinforce a denomination's official ties with its schools.

WORSHIP

Roman Catholic, Lutheran, Episcopal, Seventh-Day Adventist, and more conservative Christian schools all integrate worship into the normal school day. Although their liturgies differ extensively, these denominations all view corporate worship as the school's responsibility. Moreover, for all these denominations worship provides an essential teaching medium, with the Bible and its stories and theology at the heart of the school's educational purposes. Corporate prayer allows the community to give thanks for special events and to acknowledge God's influence in the lives of children.

Liturgy in school worship programs also creates a sense of community, and thus it influences the atmosphere and character of the school. In some religious schools, those of the Seventh-Day Adventist church, for example, worship and other aspects of the curriculum merge, so that the educational purposes of the schools can be largely defined by their character as worshiping communities. In other schools, such as those with Episcopal ties, worship takes place at a set time in the day and can be seen as distinct from the rest of the educational program.

Schools vary widely in the religious affiliation of the students they enroll. Jewish, Seventh-Day Adventist, and Lutheran schools, like many Roman Catholic parochial schools, primarily enroll students brought up in the faith they profess. Thus the purposes of worship require little explanation to families enrolling children or to the children themselves. The school's program reflects or replicates that of the local church or synagogue, just as its goal is to reinforce adult worship. Schools of these denominations are worshiping satellites; they use songs, psalms, and prayers found in the liturgies of the adult worshiping communities supporting the school. Some Protestant denominations, on the other hand, enroll students with a diversity of religious backgrounds. Most students in Quaker or Episcopal schools are unfamiliar with the liturgical traditions of those denominations; many are not Christians. Worship in such schools is designed not to maintain or reinforce a specific faith tradition so much as it is to introduce students to a broader Christian perspective.

Thus worship in religious schools as well as the specific elements of liturgy complement the educational purposes of the sponsoring faith.

SERVICE AND OUTREACH

Private schools may be considered satellites or missions of religious denominations. They also may engage in missionary or outreach work of their own. Worship programs provide the primary means for evangelization and conversion. The curriculum may also be designed to promote the faith. Some religious schools view homogeneity of belief as essential to their mission, so children from other backgrounds are assimilated quickly. Other church schools accept or even promote a variety of religious expressions, so assimilation is not a goal.

In recent years, service to the local community and beyond has become an important end of many private schools. In some, graduation requirements include participation in an outreach program. A commitment to Christian social service lies behind the development of such programs, although the ideological motivation may be more apparent than actual meaningful service.

COUNSELING

A school's religious context determines the nature and extent of counseling to students and their families. Elementary school parents often find in their children's schools a source of information on child rearing that is oriented around the faith perspective of that denomination. The more theologically conservative schools tend to view education in its broadest context, introduction into the faith, with proper parenting an essential aspect of that developmental process. Here the ideal approach is for school, church, and family to work in harmony, so that children receive a consistent explanation, usually theological in perspective, for whatever issues they may face. This goal exists for denominations that view their schools as the means for socialization into a particular faith context.

Teachers and chaplains in religious secondary schools may use faith as the context for pastoral counseling. Informed by a theological perspective, they help young people understand and deal with the challenges and issues of adolescence. Here again, the school's overall orientation as a religious institution will inevitably influence the student's outlook on life. *See also* Colleges and Universities, Church-Related; Jewish Education; Private Religious Schools; Public Schools and Religion; individual entries for each denomination, e.g., Lutheran Education.

P. W. Sipple

Problem Solving

Problem solving is the process by which a person seeks an answer to a question or problem by examining a number of alternatives and choosing one or more leading to what is considered a desirable goal or solution. After the problem has been correctly defined, input may be found by speaking with other people, reading about options, or trying various possibilities (trial and error) until something leads to a solution.

GENERAL USE

Problem solving is something people do every day, in ordinary situations (how to arrange the day's work) and special circumstances (how to find a new job). The infant's problem is reaching a toy and she tries various methods within her limited range of locomotion to get it. If these fail, she cries for assistance. Small children early learn how to solve problems of interrelationships (how to persuade a parent to buy candy; how to persuade a playmate to give up a turn on the bicycle). Problem solving never ends. Only the methods change with mental development, observation of other people, and experience.

The process is defined educationally as an approach to learning. Sometimes it is called "discovery learning," because the learners themselves are involved in discovering answers. A problem may be set to the class and each student instructed to find an answer by working alone. This encourages individual initiative and reveals to the teacher the student's ability to organize information toward a goal. Or the problem may by worked out by small groups of two or three students, who divide the responsibilities and take joint credit for the solution. This encourages cooperative effort and teaches them how to listen to others, build on their contributions, and find satisfaction in the completion of a joint effort.

USE IN RELIGIOUS EDUCATION

Problem solving is a useful method in religious education because it engages the attention of the learners. They have to become involved; therefore both curiosity and interest are aroused. The problem-solving approach can be used in Bible study by putting learners in the situation of biblical persons. What would they do when the spies returned from viewing the land of Canaan? A teacher can tell or read the story from Numbers 13:1–39, then stop with the report. After students have considered the options and made a decision, the teacher continues the story with the two opinions in the camp and the eventual decision. In the account of Paul deciding to return to Jerusalem (Acts 20), the reasons why he should or should not have done so can be looked at. Problem solving can also be used to involve learners in key points of religious history through decisions leaders had to make. The role of the teacher in this approach is to make available resources, receive and write down for all to see the questions posed by the problem, and guide learners to probe more deeply, welcoming any ideas rather than discouraging students by objections and receiving with approval their various solutions—still asking the reasons for their choices.

Problem solving is frequently used as both a way of ascertaining where learners are and a way of exploring possible solutions to ethical situations in the light of religious understandings. The possibilities are unlimited. Elementary children face problems in relating to a new child who may be "different" in some way from the rest of the class. Or they are torn between the use of force and other ways of maintaining themselves in the face of verbal or physical abuse from another child. The question of receiving information from other students becomes acute in high school and college—the problem becomes, "How is cheating defined?" Adults deal with moral and ethical problems that can cause painful consequences for themselves and others.

So problem solving in this domain becomes involved in the approach to ethics: whether it is to be situational (in each situation one must ask what is best for everyone with the least damage to anyone); contextual (what the best solution is in the framework of one's religious understandings and social and cultural life); or rule (what principles from religious and civil law govern one's life). The approach affects both the options considered and the solution made.

The role of the teacher or mentor is a sensitive one. This is a person to whom one can verbalize the problem and who will react to the options in a way that affirms the person but does not offer solutions. The reason for this is that persons must, in the end, be responsible for solving their own problems. This is one factor in maturity. But persons are strengthened when dependable people can listen, respond, and stand by whatever results come from the decision made. Clergy, religious education teachers, and congregational friends all may be called upon to assume a role in helping others with decision making.

The basic field of exploration before us is a God to be known and with whom to relate, the human person developing, intuiting, grasping, and moving toward that God, and the responsibility we have toward one another for growth in this project. In this exploration questions are constantly posed, our lives call for clarification, and modes of response in action are called forth. From the human mind's first sense of God to our present formulations of insight born of revelation, prayer, and interpretation, we see a constant, persistent effort at problem solving through our questions, choices, and testing in an effort to bring precision to our perception.

We are persons of action, enlightened action. And so, following upon our insights, we find ourselves constantly facing the question of choice in ways of living. We are comfortable only when our living is guided by our clearest thought. As circumstances around us change, so the mind is called to find more adequate solutions for action. The guidance of professional moralists and caring friends notwithstanding, we are constantly called upon to make uniquely personal choices. As insight develops, so does this power of discerned action. Students learn this process through ex-

ample and guidance, and so they need practice and constant encouragement.

Catechetics as a science has, since the 1930s, exemplified the role and responsibility of search and decision and has served as the stimulus for theological renewal. The project was to first rediscover the joy of the Good Tidings and then to find ways of guiding learners developmentally through this journey of discovery. This called for and still calls for ongoing questioning in theology and research into learners' progressive readiness for religion. The many aspects of this double project make constant call on the processes of problem solving. *See also* Creativity; Discovery Learning; Ethics; Learning Theory; Progressive Education; Scientific Method; Sociodrama; Teaching Styles.

I. V. Cully, T. A. Francoeur

Process Observer

A process observer watches a group of people interact while they make decisions. The purpose of process observation is to identify and to improve the methods used in making decisions. Attention focuses on group and individual behavior to gather data. Process observers identify groupings and relationships, assess individual performance, note decision-making processes, record leadership styles, identify present and absent group functions, and assess group development.

Observers record what is said and how people act. Task functions are noted—seeking and giving information, summarizing, synthesizing, testing for consensus, etc. Group maintenance needs are recorded—standard setting, mediating, relieving tension, etc. Individual behavior is described—aggression, withdrawal, gestures, competition, etc. The data gathered are openly discussed so that all participants may contribute to improving the group's process. Process observation enables individuals and groups to modify behavior so that the process used will be more effective and satisfying to all group members. *See also* Group Dynamics; Management; Problem Solving.

FOR FURTHER REFERENCE

Johnson, David W., and Frank P. Johnson. *Joining Together*. Englewood Cliffs, NJ: Prentice-Hall, 1975.

L. Broadus

Process Theology

Process theologians develop an understanding of Christian faith through the central insight that all existence is relational and interdependent. This insight is fundamental to many modes of doing physics and psychology in our time, but it received its most rigorous philosophical development through Alfred North Whitehead's *Process and Reality*, published in 1929. Drawing on the categories of Whitehead and on the work of his younger philosophical contemporary Charles Hartshorne, a number of theologians have developed the theological implications of relational existence. Doing so is consistent with the understanding that the Christian tradition, informed by its Scriptures, is built up by the continuous interpretation of faith in the thought forms of a contemporary time and place. Relational existence, expressed in the categories of process philosophy, has developed as a major worldview in our own time and hence becomes a contemporary vehicle for giving a critical understanding of Christian faith.

THE PHILOSOPHICAL MODEL OF RELATIONAL EXISTENCE

Whitehead's model of relational existence portrays a dynamic flow of energy given and received from multiple sources. The model is that of an "actual entity," by which Whitehead means an event, a process of the coming together of energy from past actualities. In this convergence of energy, a new actuality comes into being. The many patterns of energy are unified in a unique way by the new entity, but once that unification takes place, the entity contributes its own energy to the forming of its successors. Thus there is a rhythmic reciprocity of existence, a giving and receiving and giving again, that marks the internal constitution of all things. The many become one, and the new one is thus added to the many, qualifying it anew and calling yet again for a new one.

The model is meant to define the substrata of ordinary existence such that it can apply to the most minute particle of reality. However, it is best illustrated from the world of personal experience. Each person appears to be a discrete reality living an autonomous mode of existence. Yet such autonomy is clearly illusory, since we are dependent upon the environment and others for such basics as food and shelter. Process thought pushes this dependence even further to note that the more personal a subject is, the more clearly it is formed self-consciously through relation to others. Further, these relations are internal to personhood—not external or tangential.

For example, consider the commonplace that love opens our own well-being to some mode of dependence on the well-being of the one loved. Parents lie awake at night waiting for the sound of the front door opening to signify that their seventeen-year-old son is safely home from the party: their own well-being is dependent upon the well-being of that youngster, and this dependence strikes to the core of who they are. It is internal to their personhood, constitutive of it, and not accidental. But in the very reality of that love, they encourage growth toward interdependent adulthood for their son. His well-being requires the ability to develop friends, a life's work, and eventually a home away from that of his parents. Given their love for him, the parents' well-being also requires this. But they wait for the safety-signaling sound of the door at night. Existence is interdependent, and the relationships of existence are internal to who we are in receiving and giving, giving and receiving.

THEOLOGICAL IMPLICATIONS

What are the implications for theology? Foremost, they affect the development of the doctrine of God. If existence is necessarily relational and if relationships make up the heart of each reality, then an existing God is also essentially relational. The covenantal aspects of the biblical tradition become particularly prominent in process theology, for God exists interdependently with the world. "God so loved the world" is interpreted to mean that God's own well-being is affected by the condition of the world. In the process dynamic, God is affected by the world by receiving the actuality of the world into the divine nature. For most process theologians, such as Schubert Ogden, Delwin Brown, and to an extent Lewis S. Ford and John B. Cobb, Jr., this reception into God is the transition of the world into God's own memory. God preserves the world within everlastingness as vivid, objective memory. For others, such as Marjorie Suchocki and Joseph Bracken, God receives the world in its subjectivity, constituting judgment and everlasting life for the world.

But God also affects the world. As Charles Hartshorne notes, God is the most relational of all. Finite actualities are affected by a closed past and then affect an open future, but this influence on the future fades with time. God, as the everlasting entity, is continuously open to every actuality as it completes itself in the world and affects every reality as it comes into being. God, knowing the entire circumstances of each becoming entity's past, gives that entity an optimum possibility for unifying that past and thus creating its own satisfaction and its own mode of influence. Thus God's effect on the world is creative providence.

Process theologians view evil as dependent upon the limitations of finitude, on the one hand, and on the free response of each actuality to its situation and to God, on the other. Finite circumstances, including the mortality of all things finite, limit what kind of possibilities can be received and actualized in the world. At times, even the best possibility is nonetheless painful. The best is inescapably relative to circumstances, even while it offers concrete ways of moving toward transformation of circumstances. Thus the best is inescapably contextual and therefore social.

Christology, in such a relational world, is God's revelation of the divine nature in history, or, as Schubert Ogden presents it, the "re-presentation" of God in history. In David Griffin's further development, this revelation of God in time makes a concrete difference in the internal constitution of those who receive it by faith, creating a greater openness to the providential possibilities given them by God for their own redemptive existence.

Redemption from evil is partial in the finite world, but complete in God. The partiality in history is simply because the conditions that make for evil are the conditions of existence. However, redemptive living is openness to that "best" that God continuously makes available, so that one weaves it into oneself. Since the best is contextual, actualization of that best brings an openness to what is also best for others and the recognition that their best, like one's own, is conditioned by context. There will be pluriform manifestations of what is good. Thus redemptive living is an openness to interdependence and a sensitivity to those things that make for well-being in various ways throughout the world. Hence process theologians are deeply involved in issues of political, economic, personal, and ecological interdependence.

The church is that community that, through history, is open to God through the empowering revelation of God in Jesus Christ. Theologians such as Bernard Lee and William Beardslee have developed doctrines of the church as an agent of hope and transformation in the world.

Prayer in a process world is the intentional openness to God's guidance, but it is also an openness that in itself creates a change in the world. In process thought, God works with the world as it is in order to bring it to that which it can be. Since prayer is an act in the world, it changes what the world is and to that extent changes what kinds of redemptive possibilities the world can receive. Thus prayer, particularly intercessory prayer, is given particular development by process theologians such as John B. Cobb, Jr., Martha Graybeal Rowlett, and Marjorie Suchocki.

While the schools and emphases of process theology vary widely, the common theme is that God and the world are interdependent and that God is active in history for creation's good. *See also* Covenant; Creation; Dialogue; God, Understandings of; Prayer.

M. H. Suchocki

Professional Societies

Professional societies are formed for the purpose of fostering interchange among people engaged in a common work and may, by the requirements they set for admission, encourage particular standards for the profession. The Religious Education Association of the United States and Canada (REA), founded in 1903, is the only interfaith organization serving professional religious educators. Begun under the influence of William Rainey Harper, it soon became the champion of liberal religious education dominated by the thought of George Albert Coe. Always open to all faiths, the REA began in 1952 under the leadership of Herman Wornom to include many Catholics, Orthodox, and Jews in its membership. Its journal, *Religious Education*, founded in 1906, provides articles and book reviews of high caliber. The REA promotes research, supports advanced study, and holds conferences and conventions throughout the United States and Canada. It is supported financially by its members, and there are regional chapters in some cities.

Another organization, the Association of Professors and Researchers in Religious Education, meets annually for exchange of papers and discussion. Its precursors were two separate groups (researchers and professors) that assembled annually at the midwinter meetings of the Division of Christian Education of the National Council of the Churches of Christ (est. 1950). One group was engaged in research for denominational or interdenominational agencies; the other taught religious education in colleges and seminaries. The two groups combined to establish an independent group in 1969. It has met frequently in conjunction with the REA, with which it now shares the journal *Religious Education*. Started as a Protestant group, it now has Catholic and Jewish members.

Evangelical Protestant professional associations have their roots in the shared history of the Sunday school movement. The National Association of Evangelicals was formed in Columbus, Ohio, in 1942 in reaction against the perceived liberalism of the National Council of the Churches of Christ, the International Council of Religious Education, and the Religious Education Association; and in 1945 the National Sunday School Association (NSSA; now named the National Christian Education Association [NCEA]) was formed. It has spread into a blanket of state- and citywide organizations. The National Association of Professors of Christian Education and the National Association of Directors of Christian Education are two professional groups that move under NCEA motivation. Each holds annual professional conferences. Both are significantly supported by evangelical denominations and publishing houses.

The National Catholic Education Association (also the NCEA) is a volunteer professional association of personnel and supporters of educational efforts within the Roman Catholic church in the United States. Meeting as a federation, it is composed of eight departments: colleges and universities, seminaries, CACE or chief administrators of Catholic education, special education, elementary, secondary, boards, and forums. The underlying purpose is to improve the distinctive character and quality of the educational mission of the Catholic church. The association is engaged in the preparation of administrators, the spiritual and professional formation of teachers, Catholic curriculum development, evaluation processes, data gathering and dissemination, planning for the future in a new era, governance of educational institutions and programs, adult religious education, effective education of Hispanics, financial development, education of the economically deprived, global understanding and international education, public relations, and peace and justice education.

The National Conference of Diocesan Directors of Religious Education consists of Catholic directors and associate and assistant directors from around the country. The NCDD assists them in carrying out their work in their own dioceses, fosters communication and community among them on the provincial and national levels, and provides them with the opportunity of addressing the larger catechetical needs and problems with a united voice. Since 1982 it has become an independent organization with its own Washington office. Within the forum of the NCEA are also the National Conference of Directors of Christian Education (NCDCE) and the National Association of Parish Coordinators/Directors (NPCD).

There are many Jewish organizations. The Jewish Educators Assembly (JEA) consists of principals of Conservative Jewish day schools. NAPE (National Association of Professional Educators) is made up of professors of Reform Jewish education. The Conference on Alternatives in Jewish Education (CAJE) is a grass-roots organization in the Reform tradition. ECA is the Educational Council of American Orthodox Educators. JESNA is the Jewish Educational Service of North America and is an umbrella organization for policy making.

Some Protestant denominations have organizations for professional and paraprofessional religious educators. Usually sponsored by the denomination, the groups elect their own officers and plan their own annual gatherings. The purpose is to strengthen morale among church educators as well as to maintain and strengthen professional preparation for this vocation. *See also* National Association of Evangelicals; National Christian Education Association; Religious Education Association.

R. C. Miller

Professional Study

Religious education is a relatively new field of professional study. The field had its beginnings with the founding of the Religious Education Association in 1903. The first person hired as a director of religious education was quite possibly James W. Thompson, who was called in 1906 to serve Christ Methodist Church in Pittsburgh, Pennsylvania. By 1910 there were enough persons in the profession to hold the first national meeting of directors of religious education. The forces that brought the new field into being included, first of all, the failure of revivalism to stem the tide of perceived moral decline in the nation, so the churches turned to education, especially the Sunday school, as the instrument of change. Second, there was a new thrust in religious education that emphasized a scientific method of learning built on the theories of John Dewey. Learning was to build on experience and involve problem solving through development of a hypothesis related to the problem, testing of the hypothesis, and conclusions based on the test. And, finally, there was a new educational psychology that did not view children simply as "little adults" but took their developmental needs seriously.

The first permanent general secretary of the Religious Education Association, Henry F. Cope (general secretary, 1907–1923), also set some of the first standards for professional study in the field. He stated that, in addition to the usual courses in religious history and literature, there should be courses in psychology, the history of education, pedagogy, educational method and organization, the psychology of religion, and Sunday school methods and organization. Practitioners in the field of religious education set their own standards for professional study in 1914 in the constitution of the Association of Church Directors of Religious Education. An active member of that association was required to have four years of college and either three years of seminary education with courses in religious education or two years of study in an approved school of religious pedagogy. The expectation that directors of religious education should have three years of seminary or two years of graduate study in religious education was a much higher goal than many of the early educators ever reached. Congregations were willing to hire persons with far fewer qualifications than the professional organization called for.

The entire profession of religious education was shaken by the depression of the 1930s. In the face of that disarray the directors of religious education in the Methodist Episcopal Church, South, proposed certain standards for professional preparation in 1934: a bachelor's degree; at least one year of graduate work in religious education; and at least two years of actual, successful experience in religious education in an approved situation. The example of the Methodist Episcopal Church, South, in its adoption of the standards was followed by other denominations in their expectations for religious educators.

In the next thirty years there was a trend toward raising the level of professional preparation by the churches. By 1965 a director of religious education was expected to have an undergraduate bachelor's degree and either a graduate degree in religious education or a Bachelor of Divinity degree from a seminary.

GRADUATE DEGREES IN RELIGIOUS EDUCATION

At present it is usually expected that directors of religious education will have a four-year college education and a two-year master's degree or a three-year seminary degree. The master's degree will usually be either a Master of Arts in Religious Education or a Master of Religious Education and is expected to take two years of full-time graduate, professional study beyond an accredited B.A. or its equivalent. The Association of Theological Schools has a set of standards for both degrees. The 1986 standards state the goals for the M.A. and M.R.E. programs as developing the ability to:

1. See educational mission within the larger context of the religious community's total mission

2. Function professionally in the light of sound educational theory

3. Evaluate one's performance from the discipline of education's perspectives

4. Communicate one's faith so as to enlist commitment from others

5. Work effectively and harmoniously with other professionals and laypersons in developing and pursuing educational objectives

6. Function effectively in a variety of interrelated roles, such as teachers of teachers, program designer and administrator, age-group specialist, and regional educational worker

The standards state that the content of the programs should include three things: the opportunity for acquiring the varied understandings required by the religious educator, for supervised practice in educational ministry, and for the personal and spiritual growth. For the first there should be a balance of offerings and requirements between the religious heritage (Scripture, history, theology) and educational theory (religious, psychological, philosophical, and sociological dimensions) and attention should be given to the role of knowledge in these areas in forming the religious community and the profession of the educator. To fulfill the second requirement, programs should include apprentice experience or internship in educational ministry settings supervised by both full-time and adjunct faculty, and this field experience and the supervisors should function as integral to the total educational program—there should be colloquia in which full-time faculty (from varied fields), adjunct faculty, and students seek integration of the academic and experiential

knowledge. And for the third component, programs should have an adequate counseling program, provide opportunity for spiritual formation, and attend to the personal and spiritual qualities necessary for effective educational leadership. The program for personal and spiritual development should also be integrated in the total life of the school, including courses of instruction and field learning experiences.

DIVINITY DEGREES

The other route for professional preparation is that of the Master of Divinity degree (formerly the Bachelor of Divinity degree). More and more students preparing to serve as religious educators are electing this route. It has two benefits. The first is that the religious educator is at the same level of academic preparation as the other persons on the church staff. The second benefit is that ordination is a possibility, should the religious educator seek the office. However, the student preparing to be a religious educator via the route of the Master of Divinity degree should major in religious education. Most seminaries have only one required course in religious education. Sometimes the required course can be selected from a number of offerings. In other instances, there is only one choice. In many seminaries the course will be offered in conjunction with field education in a local congregation. Most seminaries offer an array of elective courses in religious education from which the student can choose.

Whichever route the student takes in preparing for the role of religious educator, it is important to consult with denominational authorities, when appropriate, about their expectations for preparation and certification. *See also* Bible College; Director of Religious Education; Professional Societies; Religious Education Association; Theological Education.

FOR FURTHER REFERENCE

Association of Theological Schools. *Procedures, Standards, and Criteria for Membership.* Bulletin 37. Part 3. Vandalia, OH: Association of Theological Schools, 1986.

Furnish, Dorothy Jean. *DRE/DCE—The History of a Profession.* Nashville, TN: Christian Educator's Fellowship, United Methodist Church, 1976.

Harris, Maria. *The D. R. E. Book: Questions and Strategies for Parish Personnel.* New York: Paulist, 1976.

R. L. Conrad

Programmed Learning

Programmed learning, a concept of the late 1950s and early 1960s, is a method of self-instruction based largely on the theories of B. F. Skinner. Key ideas to be taught are arranged in a "program" in such a way that the learner is required to repeat each one in sequence until all are firmly fixed in the memory. The process of repetition and the built-in reinforcement techniques in the programs were intended to help learners acquire a solid base of information they would not easily forget.

Advantages to programmed learning were said to be that it allowed teachers to focus on class discussions and other activities rather than taking so much time making sure students learned the basic data (factual information) needed in a subject area. Skills for studying could be communicated in such programs, and students would be helped to concentrate on clear outlines of subject matter content.

A famous program used in public schools for a number of years was "English 2600," consisting of 2600 "frames" of instruction in the rudiments of English grammar. The program was tested repeatedly and proved to be an effective means of inculcating vital information so that learners could make effective use of it.

But could such a methodology be employed in religious education? Inasmuch as religion, like all subject areas, has certain outlines of key information, would it be possible to prepare programs that could be used by church school teachers?

Between 1961 and 1965, the United Presbyterian Board of Christian Education, then in Philadelphia, undertook a major research project to test the effectiveness of programmed learning. For an experiment in adult education they were joined by the curriculum editors of the Episcopal Church, New York. With assistance from staff of the Battelle Institute, Columbus, Ohio, and consultants at Temple University, the project produced programs for use with children, youth, and adults in a variety of subject matter areas. A published report on this project indicated that the method held "promise," especially for junior-age children (grades 4–6).

The effort was abandoned after the research was completed. No denominational publishers took up programmed learning as an option for regular instruction in the churches, and today it is rarely mentioned among religious educators.

The reasons most commonly cited for abandoning the concept of programmed learning are four. First, it is very costly in time and money to write, test, and publish effective programs. Churches with limited funds have not wanted to invest heavily in this endeavor. Second, church educators have a theologically based resistance to the use of programming. Its reliance on the Skinnerian idea of "shaping behavior" through "conditioning" of the learner seems to deny the spirit of freedom and creativity that religion seeks to espouse and foster. Third, it has not been clear how such a method could be integrated into the limited time spans of typical parish education programs. And finally, the use of the programs seems "wooden" and individualized rather than lively, group-oriented, and designed to encourage social interaction. (Senior highs and adults in the research project mentioned above reported they could remember a lot of facts, but they were uncertain about the value of the acquired information. They felt frustrated about not having time to discuss the materials with other learners.)

Most of the published programs have been "linear," in contrast to a more interesting format of "branching," that is, each frame builds directly into the succeeding frame. In a "branching" program, learners are encouraged to "skip" familiar information and explore further options. The argument for "branching" has been that it encourages dialogue and allows the learner more opportunity for self-expression.

Although the term itself may no longer be a popular one, certainly the limited experiments thus far in the use of computers for instructional purposes have employed similar principles. What makes computers more enjoyable, especially for younger learners, is the interaction between the machine and its screen with a learner or a group. Gaming devices can be intermingled with questions and answers and blanks to be filled in. For reasons similar to those cited above, many religious educators have been lukewarm toward the consistent use of computers for use in church education. *See also* Computers; Conditioning; Learning Theory.

L. E. Bowman

Progressive Education

The term "progressive education" is associated with the philosophy of John Dewey (1859–1952), whose work focused on the process by which learners are engaged in directing their own growth and development in relation to subject matter competency. He sought to counter authoritarian methods in which learners' activities were undertaken at the command of teachers who functioned as repositories of knowledge, often to the neglect of their responsibility for assisting learners to be self-regulating in a democratic community. (Dewey's work followed that of such European pioneers as Jean-Jacques Rousseau and J. H. Pestalozzi and American experimenters like Horace Mann and Francis W. Parker.)

Progressive education, in simplest terms, focuses on the whole learner, emphasizing problem solving, decision making, and self-expression in all its forms—in contrast to an educational approach that focuses primarily on the accumulation of factual knowledge. The progressive principles, although sometimes criticized by religious conservatives, have been so uniformly accepted and put into practice that they are currently viewed as desirable norms.

Subject matter is now generally integrated so that a unit of study moves around a theme. There is more action on the part of the learner: searching for information, drawing or writing an impression about a story, participating in open discussion, or working in a small group as well as individually. Freer interaction between teacher and learners has repositioned the teacher from a desk at center front to various activity centers around the classroom, facilitating instruction as well as small group and individual attention and fostering an atmosphere of cooperative learning. *See also* Confluent Education; Creative Activities; Learning Center; Learning Theory; Pragmatism; Problem Solving; Teaching Styles; Theology and Education.

L. E. Bowman

Project

A specific task done by an individual or group employing physical and mental skills for the purpose of supplementing or applying classroom studies is termed a project. Projects are related to developmental abilities and are therefore age specific.

The purpose of a project is to provide an opportunity for students to "get into" the subject. It is an arena in which the imagination can be stretched as the subject is looked at from many angles during the doing or creating of the project. For example, a religious educator teaching older elementary students about life in biblical times might choose to have the students build a Palestinian village. To build a Palestinian village, one would need to know how people made a living, what they ate, what tools they used, what the geography of the area was like, and how their families were organized. A project helps people assimilate what they have learned, and involvement in the "doing" helps people learn.

The following elements are part of planning a project:

The *purpose* of a project is why it is being done, the goal of the activity. It could be to initiate a new study unit or to summarize the learning at the end of the unit. The "why" is very important because it determines the rest of the planning.

What is to be done is the overall view of the project. In the previous example, the decision was made to create a Palestinian village representing as many aspects of living as possible.

The *structure* is the order in which the various elements of the project are done in the separate sessions available. In our example, the first part might be creating the environment—learning about the geography and finding some way to create it. Another part would be housing. What did the homes look like and what kind of construction did they have? Another part could be the customs about relationships, eating habits, raising children, and so forth. Having a general time structure enables the planning of one segment at a time.

The *resources* are the people and supplies needed to accomplish this project. Extra help may be needed for the building of a rather elaborate village. Parents or other helpers may need to be recruited. The supplies should be listed for each segment of the structure, each step in making the village. Trying any new methods before using them with children is recommended.

Some way should be planned for *sharing the outcome*, for others to enjoy the project, perhaps an open house for parents and friends or visits by other classes. Children should be given an opportunity to talk about what they have created to reinforce what they have learned.

Evaluating the process allows an educator to see what he or she has learned about how or how not to do a project. The children's evaluations about their likes and dislikes in doing the project are helpful. Evaluation will provide valuable information on which to build further plans for learning activities for classes. *See also* Constructive Activities; Crafts; Creative Activities; Demonstration; Dramatization; Field Trip; Map; Pageantry; Time Line.

S. H. Matthaei

Providence

The biblical doctrine of providence claims less than some of its theological restatements of later times. Providence in the Bible affirms the care of God for the creation, in its totality, but according to the divine purposes for the creation. Human beings are intimately involved with God in God's providential care of the universe.

This partnership is well illustrated in reference to God's guidance of the historical process. One of the unmistakable instances of divine providence is the portrayal in Exodus of God's coming to deliver the Israelite slaves from bondage in Egypt. That deliverance is effected through the hardening of the Pharaoh's heart. But the way the Bible describes that hardening is threefold. Pharaoh hardens his own heart—acts stubbornly against the best interests of his own people and his own best interests to hang onto the slaves, even in the face of the destruction all around him (Exod. 9:34). God also hardens Pharaoh's heart, we learn (Exod. 4:21). God makes it hard for Pharaoh to let the slaves go, both because Pharaoh needs to be taught a lesson and because the nations need to see God's power to deliver from oppression. Other Bible texts record that Pharaoh's heart simply gets hard. He does not harden his own heart; it just gets hard—unaccountably but unmistakably (Exod. 7:13). Providence is like that: sometimes God works through human beings directly in the realization of the divine purpose for the world. Sometimes God directly acts upon the historical process, according to biblical faith. And on other occasions, divine providence operates more mysteriously, not explicitly as God's act, but also not explicitly as a conscious human act.

Providence is God's mysterious care for the universe, then, using the universe's own realities, using human activity, using irruptions of divine power and presence and caring, and also acting through mysterious doings and dealings that are not alien to God but are not simply the product of divine causation.

When one does not allow for this third kind of divine engagement with the world and its created beings, the doctrine of providence can become too mechanical or too flat and lifeless. The mystery needs to be retained and affirmed when teaching a doctrine of providence.

Children are taught about providence indirectly through every assurance of God's love and care, which they learn about through happy experiences in the world around them and with the people they know. Older children learn the biblical story of God's care for Israel and for the early church (Paul had a clear sense of providence).

Young people and adults will need to be reminded of the biblical story so that they know the roots of this understanding about God. They may question the idea of providence in the face of situations that seem to be outside God's care. "Why does God permit this to happen?" they ask. The mystery of suffering gets caught up into the doctrine of providence and can be answered only in the biblical assurance that God's purpose is, in some way, being worked out through all events. The teacher's task is to guide people as they find satisfying answers to such difficult questions. *See also* God, Understandings of; Theodicy.

W. Harrelson

Psychological Testing

Psychological testing is the use of various methods of evaluation to determine the degree to which an individual possesses personality traits, employs psychological mechanisms, or manifests psychological conditions as defined by psychologists and psychological theory. The five most common methods of psychological testing are self-reports, projective tests, performance tests, experience reports, and independent observation.

METHODS

Self-reports or self-rating measures are the most common of all psychological tests. Most of these measures come in the form of paper-and-pencil inventories, questionnaires, and scales asking for information concerning the test taker's personality characteristics, behavior, feelings, attitudes, opinions, or beliefs. The accuracy of these tests depends primarily upon the skill and honesty of the test taker in reporting facts about his or her life. Normal intelligence, recall, and discrimination are required, which makes their use with small children or mentally impaired persons difficult.

Projective tests present the test taker with a series of ambiguous pictures or other objects to be identified. Although there is no "correct" response, the kind of response given is interpreted by the test giver as having a particular psychological meaning. The most well-known projective test is the Rorschach ink blot test. Psychologists claim to be able to identify psychological phenomena such as controlled anger, intolerance of ambiguity, sexual disturbance, or schizophrenic thinking from the associations made to parts of each ink blot. The accuracy of projective measures depends on the interest and cooperation of the test taker and the skillfulness of the test interpreter. Children like projectives and do well with them.

In *performance tests*, the test taker is given a task that may involve difficult motor, cognitive, or perceptual skills. For example, children may be handed a school transcript showing the courses they took in years past minus their grades. They are then asked to recall the grades they received. Those children remembering grades higher than they actually achieved are assumed to be less secure than those remembering their grades accurately or remembering just as many bad grades as good grades.

Experience reports expose one to unusual and often unrealistic sensory experiences. For example, as a result of the autokinetic effect, a stationary point of light in a darkened room appears to move for most people. One's psychological makeup influences the way the light moves. For insecure and defensive persons the light moves in a constricted and similar pattern each time it is turned on; for more secure people it often appears to move wildly and unpredictably. The test taker need only report what he or she sees and the psychologist makes the interpretations.

With *independent observation*, one is simply observed by the test giver and psychological meaning is ascribed to what is observed. Children are observed at play through a one-way mirror or an adult is observed by her or his therapist and certain conclusions drawn by the observer regarding inferred psychological traits. The accuracy of independent observation depends solely on the methods and skills of the observer.

A good testing program often includes one or more measures from each of these five testing methods in order to take advantage of the strengths of each and to minimize the weaknesses of individual tests.

Useful psychological tests are those that have validity, reliability, and generalizability. A valid test is one that measures what it claims to measure (like anxiety) and not something else (such as fear). A reliable test will identify the same psychological trait(s) in a person or group each time it is administered. The results of a generalizable test apply not only to the person or group tested, but more broadly to similar persons and groups.

What purpose do psychological tests serve? Four general uses are recognized:

1. Psychological tests are employed by counselors to identify personality traits of patients in psychotherapy so that treatment can be more effective.

2. Psychological tests can indicate the prevalence and intensity of psychological phenomena among groups of persons (example: tests show that women between fourteen and eighteen years tend to be more depressed than men at this age).

3. Psychological tests provide those considering committed relationships (employment, marriage, religious life, etc.) a way of determining which areas of personality functioning are most and least compatible with such a commitment.

4. Psychological tests are used to determine the degree to which a particular event or experience affects the psychological functioning of a person or a group; for example, the effectiveness of a teaching method or curriculum can be determined by administering the proper psychological tests before and then after its use.

IN RELIGIOUS EDUCATION

Psychological testing became popular among religious educators in the 1930s. Its primary use was to develop psychologically sound Sunday school curricula. The classic psychological research of this period in religious education was done by Hugh Hartshorne and Mark May (*Studies in Deceit*, 1930). Through skillfully designed experiments, these psychologists tested children in various curricula to see which one best taught the value of honesty (the result: students in no curriculum were found to be more honest, even than those who had enrolled for Sunday school but did not attend classes). Almost every new curriculum series designed by the major Christian denominations since the 1940s has incorporated sophisticated psychological testing procedures to determine the readiness and capacity of various age

and socioeconomic groups to understand and respond constructively to religious content.

It is not inappropriate to ask, as do some religious educators, what tests and measures designed to reveal psychological dynamics and traits have to do with religious life or learning. Or more simply, what religiously significant information do psychological tests or terms convey? Religious educators have been split on the issue and can be found in at least three groups.

Separationists include some religious evangelicals and fundamentalists (as well as orthodox psychologists) who maintain a strict separation between religion and psychology, claiming that religious and psychological concepts or states are not interchangeable. Psychological testing is seen as of no value and often misleading.

A second group may be termed *accommodationists*. Many liberal Christians and Jews (as well as spiritually attuned psychologists) see striking similarities between religious and psychological terms like sin and alienation, grace and self-esteem, faith and trust. This group often tends to "psychologize" religion and use psychological testing uncritically.

A growing number of serious religious and psychological practitioners and scholars are discovering ways that religion and psychology influence one another. Loath to imply simple identities between religious and psychological terms or states, these *integrationists* look for religious "threads" or theological "themes" in psychological traits as well as for the psychological dynamics in religious experience. This group endorses a selective and careful use of psychological testing.

In summary, it can be said that psychological testing as a respected professional discipline has found a place in religious work of many kinds. However, great care must be taken to ensure that the integrity of neither religion nor psychology is compromised by inducing a premature or superficial synthesis of the two. Sensitively done with an eye to the theological meanings behind psychological tests, measures, and concepts, psychological testing can prove an invaluable resource to religious educators and counselors. *See also* Evaluation; Interdisciplinary Studies; Measurement; Psychology of Religion; Psychotherapy.

FOR FURTHER REFERENCE

Cronbach, Lee J. *Essentials of Psychological Testing*. New York: Harper & Row, 1960.

Duncombe, David C. *The Shape of the Christian Life*. Nashville, TN: Abingdon, 1969.

McGuigan, F. J. *Experimental Psychology*. Englewood Cliffs, NJ: Prentice-Hall, 1968.

Strommen, Merton P. *Profiles of Church Youth*. St. Louis, MO: Concordia, 1963.

D. C. Duncombe

Psychology, Educational

Psychology is the study of human nature and behavior with special focus on the self-consciousness of the human mind and the inner working of the mental processes. Inasmuch as "self-consciousness" was rather late in arriving as a subject for human scientific research (a great deal more was known about plant and animal development in earlier centuries), psychological studies of human nature and behavior tend to have their beginnings in the early twentieth century.

Religious education is informed by many psychological disciplines—most immediately that of educational psychology (and some theological seminaries include a course derived from this discipline called the psychology of religious education). Educational psychology is the study of how people learn. The purpose is to develop learning theory and to assist educators in understanding learners and developing methods for teaching.

Educational psychology has embraced concerns about establishing "a scientific approach to educational issues." Thus linked with empirical sciences, educational psychology has tended to reorganize itself periodically with emerging new research.

The early influence of Sigmund Freud on educational psychology established a pessimistic view about learning, largely based on early childhood experience and the continuing shadow of dark and sometimes obscene complexes that may motivate but more often interfere with learning. Freudian insights have helped religious educators to understand that what learners say or how they act is not always what they really mean and that one must probe beneath the surface to gain a deeper understanding of the person.

Studies in behaviorism by B. F. Skinner emerged in the mid-twentieth century as a positive base and educational psychology was almost entirely behavioristic during the period from 1950 to 1975. Behaviorism essentially holds that learning is shaped by the reward and reinforcement conditions in the environment. The learning aspects of behaviorism were validated primarily with animals and continue to be regarded as highly effective with very young children and children with certain kinds of disabilities.

Religious educators have found value in the positive aspects of reinforcement conditioning. Teachers have been alerted to the fact that acceptance of learners and their viewpoints encourages further learning. They also realize that there is value in habit formation and that, for example, attending worship regularly is not simply an exercise in conformity, but a constantly reinforced attitude.

Both psychoanalytic and behavioristic contributions will be seen in educational psychology today, but since the early 1970s developmental psychology has encroached on the educational field, and today's texts tend to show many developmental and "structural" contributions. These have come largely from a modification of Freud's work by Erik Erikson and from the work of Jean Piaget and Lawrence Kohlberg in the development of moral reasoning. Structural psychology of this developmental sort holds that each person uniquely interacts with the environment and "constructs" knowledge and skills through adapting to present and new experiences.

From Erikson's psychosocial stages, religious educators have become aware of strengthening factors that need to be encouraged at each age level, beginning with nurturing in infants. From Piaget they have affirmed the value of play as an instrument of learning in preschool children, the need for concrete learning in early childhood, and the gradual development of abstract learning in later childhood. *See also* Adult Development; Behaviorism; Child Development; Education, Theories of; Freudian Influences; Learning Theory; Moral Development; Psychosocial Development; Structuralism; Teaching Theory.

FOR FURTHER REFERENCE

Anderson, Richard C., and Gerald W. Faust. *Educational Psychology: The Science of Instruction and Learning.* New York: Dodd and Mead, 1974.

Cronbach, Lee J. *Educational Psychology.* 2d ed. New York: Harcourt, Brace & World, 1963.

Schneider, Allen M., and Barry Tarshis. *An Introduction to Physiological Psychology.* 2d ed. New York: Random House, 1980.

Schuster, Clara S., and Shirley S. Ashburn. *The Process of Human Development: A Holistic Approach.* Boston: Little, Brown, 1980.

D. M. Joy

Psychology of Religion

The psychology of religion is the scientific discipline that uses psychological categories of thought and research methodologies for the purpose of increasing the understanding of those human beliefs, experiences, and behaviors associated with the divine or with other systems of ultimate meaning in given cultures. The term "social psychology of religion" refers to the dimension of psychology of religion that focuses on the shared beliefs and behaviors of religious groups and on the interaction between psychological and social dynamics in religion. The term "sociology of religion" refers to the companion discipline that uses the methods of sociology to study religious institutions, communal experiences of religion, and the social influences on religious communities.

HISTORY

Religious thinkers throughout the centuries have reflected critically and in depth on their own inner experiences and those of their religious groups. The precursors of modern psychologists of religion include the prophet Jeremiah, Augustine, John Bunyan, Julian of Norwich, Catherine of Siena, Søren Kierkegaard, Hildegard of Bingen, and Friedrich Schleiermacher. The dawning of psychology as an experimental science and its separation from its roots in philosophy in the closing decades of the nineteenth century gave birth to psychology of religion in its modern form. The motivating purpose and hope was to understand the religious life of human beings from the scientific perspective of psychology rather than from theology.

The major pioneers in the formative period of psychology of religion include G. Stanley Hall (research on conversion, 1881; launched *The Journal of Religious Psychology* and *Education*, 1902); Edwin D. Starbuck (*The Psychology of Religion*, 1899); George Albert Coe (*The Spiritual Life*, 1900; *The Psychology of Religion*, 1916); William James (*The Varieties of Religious Experience*, 1902); James B. Pratt (*The Psychology of Religious Belief*, 1907; *The Religious Consciousness*, 1920); and James H. Leuba (*A Psychological Study of Religion*, 1912). It was William James's *Varieties of Religious Experience* (depending heavily on Starbuck's earlier research) that brought psychology of religion into major prominence in the burgeoning discipline of psychology.

From their radically different perspectives within depth psychology, Sigmund Freud and Carl Jung contributed to the early flowering of exploration of and reflection on religious beliefs and behavior as legitimate objects of psychological investigation, thus laying the foundation for the stream of psychology of religion that developed within psychoanalysis. Freud made important contributions to the understanding of the pathogenic, growth-inhibiting religion that constricts the spiritual and psychological health of so many people in our society. Freud recognized that our religious beliefs and feelings are deeply influenced by early life experiences with personality-shaping adults. He saw that we tend to project our infantile need for a perfect parent figure onto the universe in the ways we image deity. He saw that magical, infantile feelings continue to dominate the religious lives of many people long after they accept reality in other areas. He also identified the process by which the conscience is formed and its initial contents determined, as children internalize the values of their culture through the reward-punishment controls of their parents.

The inadequacies of Freud's understanding of religion include his lack of awareness that salugenic (growth-nurturing) religion exists. He was led by his instinct-oriented, biological reductionism to a mechanistic model of human beings that left no room for the profound human capacities for transcendence and freedom.

In contrast to Freud, Jung believed that spiritual growth leading to a basic sense of identity and meaning is an indispensable aspect of the process of psychological maturing (which he called individuation), particularly in the second half of life. He saw the mythical, symbolic, mystical, nonrational aspects of religion as healing and growth producing, the way by which the riches of the unconscious can be claimed and the threat of mass-mindedness in our culture diminished.

There was a decline of interest in scientific research on religious issues between the two world wars. The increasing emphasis on animal psychology (in the functional school) and the dominance of behaviorism both contributed to the sharp curtailing of the scientific study of religion by psychologists. In the 1920s and 1930s, some interest continued within certain psychoanalytic schools, stimulated by the writings of Freud and Jung. George Albert Coe, a leading religious educator, produced a book in the psychology of religion area (*The Motives of Men*, 1928). It was mainly in a few seminary departments of religious education that courses with a psychological orientation were taught during the 1930s.

In the late 1940s and early 1950s, there was a dramatic wave of revived interest in psychology in general and in its use within religion and religious congregations, in both education and counseling. Erich Fromm brought together a psychoanalytic and a cultural orientation, applying this dual focus to religion as well as ethics in several influential books such as *Escape from Freedom* (1941), *Man for Himself: An Inquiry into the Psychology of Ethics* (1947), *Psychoanalysis and Religion* (1950), and *Zen Buddhism and Psychoanalysis* (1964). Like Jung, Fromm saw religion (broadly defined) as a fundamental need of all human beings. His crucial distinction was between authority-centered, growth-blocking religions and religions that increase inner freedom, self-esteem, and power.

The post–World War II surge of interest in applying psychology to practical problems of living produced what might be called "religious psychology," the use of psychological insights and methods by religious writers to help people with their problems. Influential books included Joshua Liebman's *Peace of Mind* (1946) and Leslie Weatherhead's *Psychology, Religion and Healing* (1952). The growing interest in the uses of psychology in understanding religion and doing ministry resulted in such books as Paul E. Johnson's *Psychology of Religion* (1945) and Gordon Allport's *The Individual and His Religion* (1950). The founding of a new journal, *Pastoral Psychology*, in 1949 was both an indication of and a stimulus to the integration of psychological insights and methods with the work of clergy and other religious professionals.

The groundswell of interest in applying psychology to religion helped to ignite new fires under a revival of scientific, empirically focused psychology and sociology of religion. The founding of the *Journal for the Scientific Study of Religion* in 1962 both resulted from and became a stimulus to increased scientific research by psychologists and sociologists on religious behavior and issues.

CONTEMPORARY ISSUES AND IMPACT

The rich variety of issues on which contemporary psychologists of religion are focusing include: operational definitions of religion; the psychological roots and functions of religion; religious and moral development; personality dynamics and religion; religious experience, mysticism, altered states of consciousness, the parapsychological, conversion; religious ritual; religion and mental and holistic health; gender differences and religious-moral development; social class religious differences; religion and psychotherapy; pastoral psychology; and interreligious and cross-cultural religious differences.

Increasing the constructive impact of the discipline of psychology of religion on the religious lives of individuals and congregations depends on at least these factors:

- Strengthening of the knowledge base in the field by increasing research done by scientists from a variety of interrelated psychological, sociological, and anthropological disciplines

- Increased dialogue and collaborative thought among psychologists of religion and scholars in the religious and theological disciplines

- Increased application of relevant insights from psychology of religion research to the practice of all dimensions of religious work and ministry

- Increased attention to religious experience that is beyond the reach of positivistic sociopsychological methods, such as mystical experiences or spiritual experiences that take on unique interpretations within their cultural contexts

- Increased research from a social systems perspective, and cross-cultural research by anthropologists focusing on comparative sociopsychological factors in diverse religious systems

- Increased attention to the insights and research findings of psychologists studying women's experience and feminist psychologists of religion who bring the perspectives of women's spiritual experience and of living in a sexist society to their research and understanding

Psychology of religion is an invaluable resource for those who function as religious teachers and leaders. Here are some of the important uses of the methods and findings:

1. As an alternative framework for evaluating the understandings and interpretations of theological reflection, in terms of their sources in human dynamics and their impact on wholeness

2. As a resource for facilitating religious and moral development

3. As a way of establishing criteria from the psychosocial sciences for identifying sickness-causing versus health-enhancing systems of belief and religious practices

4. As a way of discovering the generic factors in the diverse religions of humankind as a means of avoiding divisive religious exclusiveness and condescension toward other faith and value systems and building bridges of mutual understanding, respect, and cooperation

5. As a way of understanding and modifying the destructive ways of searching for meaning (e.g., worshiping money, power, position, social class, or "success")

A radical holism is emerging simultaneously in a variety of fields in our times—in medicine, psychotherapy, biology, physics, ecology, and spirituality. Within this pregnant and hopeful social context, discovering the nature of health-enhancing religion and its crucial role in motivating self-care and increasing human wholeness becomes even more urgent. Scholars in the discipline of psychology of religion and practitioners using their insights and findings can make crucial contributions to enhancing wholeness centered in healthy spirituality in our society with its epidemic of religiously spawned brokenness. *See also* Conversion; Faith Development; Freudian Influences; Interdisciplinary Studies; Jungian Influences; Moral Development; Religious Studies; Social Sciences; Sociology of Religion; Spirituality.

FOR FURTHER REFERENCE

Maslow, Abraham. *Religions, Values, and Peak Experiences.* New York: Viking, 1964.

Oates, Wayne E. *The Psychology of Religion.* Waco, TX: Word, 1973.

Pruyser, Paul. *A Dynamic Psychology of Religion.* New York: Harper & Row, 1968.

Spilka, Bernard, Ralph W. Hoo, Jr., and Richard L. Gorsuch. *The Psychology of Religion: An Empirical Approach.* Englewood Cliffs, NJ: Prentice-Hall, 1985.

Tisdale, John R., ed. *Growing Edges in the Psychology of Religion.* Chicago: Nelson-Hall, 1980.

H. Clinebell

ordained or lay. The American Association of Pastoral Counselors is the professional guild that sets standards for such specialized ministries. *See also* Behaviorism; Counseling; Emotionally Disturbed Children; Freudian Influences; Gestalt; Jungian Influences; Psychosynthesis; Transactional Analysis.

FOR FURTHER REFERENCE

Clinebell, Howard. *Contemporary Growth Therapies.* Nashville, TN: Abingdon, 1981.
Harper, Robert. *Psychoanalysis and Psychotherapy, Thirty-six Systems.* Englewood Cliffs, NJ: Prentice-Hall, 1974.
Kovel, Joel. *A Complete Guide to Therapy.* New York: Pantheon, 1976.

H. Clinebell

Public Relations

Public relations is the term used to indicate the ways by which an organization relates to the community. Through public relations religious organizations explain who they are, what they stand for, and what they do. The purpose is to be understood, accepted, and have cooperation in some areas of their work. Key questions of public relations are: What do people believe about the congregation and its members? How did they acquire that viewpoint?

The goal of public relations is to create and maintain a context favorable to the growth of the congregation and those in it. Growth means increasing the number of members but it also refers to growth toward individual and corporate shalom.

Public relations involves information and communication. Communication flows among those who are members and friends of the congregation as well as those who are outside of it. There are many avenues for such communication.

Spoken words convey information—in conversations of members, in pastors' sermons, on radio or television, and in visits with both members and prospects. *Written words* appear in bulletins, the yellow pages of the phone book, newspaper ads, reports or correspondence, and stories about the congregation's activities in newspapers, denominational publications, and popular magazines. *Images* on the sign at the church or synagogue entrance, on letterhead, in informational brochures—even the appearance of the congregation's property—also communicate.

The kind of *events* the congregation sponsors or takes part in tell much about it: holding a Lenten series, participating in a hunger walk, providing shelter for the homeless, being a polling place, running a day-care center, maintaining an ongoing education and witness program or a study-action series on peace, or even sending members to clean up flood damage. The life-styles and daily actions of *people* known to be members are telling as well. The pastor and others may call on the sick and homebound, and members may participate in community activities such as Campfire, Boy Scouts, the city council, or the school board.

PLANNING CONSIDERATIONS

Planned programs of public relations are more effective if they address what is important to different people. Some are concerned about the goals toward which the congregation is moving. Some want to know how decisions are made in the congregation. Some want to know what vision or dream underlies the congregation's activities. Some care mostly about the relationships between people.

It is also important in planning for public relations to take account of the process through which people move in their journey from knowing nothing about the congregation to being actively involved. Most people move through four phases. First, people find out about the congregation in some way, either from members or from any of the variety of sources mentioned above. Then they attend an event, often at the invitation of a member, or check with the pastor for help. What happens to and with them persuades them either to continue or not. The next phase involves a decision. If they feel comfortable and if their involvement in the congregation meets some of their needs, they might decide to become members. And finally, whether people stay actively involved in a congregation depends upon how deeply they become related with others. Those within the congregation are nurtured and sustained by participating in events in which they encounter a range of faith experiences and by receiving information about such events. They can find out about them and other matters of congregational interest through newsletters, announcements in newspapers and on television and radio, talking with other members, and by being called upon in their homes on a regular basis by the pastor and others.

The style and quality of communication often determines whether a person moves to the next stage of the process. Both planned and unplanned public relations play a role in each of these stages of involvement. How much information people have and the form in which it comes provides either positive or negative influence upon the participant, the member, or the prospective participant.

FORMAL AND INFORMAL EFFORTS

Public relations or communication is carried through both words of witness and deeds of service. It is useful to have a sense of identity that can be communicated in a few words such as "we are a friendly church." But printing that phrase in the bulletin, newsletter, or newspaper ad is useless if members speak only to those they know, if children are ignored, if the building is not accessible to those in wheelchairs, if only those of the same race or economic class are welcome. The words said or written must be consistent with the lifestyles of those of the congregation.

Public relations is a significant factor both in gaining new members and sustaining those already involved. Planning that people both within and outside the congregation have a positive image and belief about the congregation deserves more attention than is given in most congregations.

A conscious effort at outreach through public relations will mean continuing work by a small group with some abilities in planning and using the various methods noted here. The whole congregation will need to be aware of a desire to become better known in the community, increase membership, and be recognized as having concerns outside itself. Start with the simplest methods: those with which the congregation will feel most comfortable. Ask help from professionals in the media who can make visual, written, and oral communication inviting. Realize that when new people come, only a warm reception by the whole congregation will persuade them to return.

Formal public relations efforts have been used in religious education most frequently for announcing and inviting children to attend vacation Bible schools. In the fall, new children in the community can be invited to attend religious education classes through newspaper ads and stories, through an "open house" welcoming event, or by personal invitation by member families. Teacher training events need publicizing. Class attendance is encouraged and the need for helpers in the religious education program made known through the bulletin, visits from teachers, and invitations to watch a class at work.

The opening of classes in the fall, parents' meetings, and a closing program are all publicized more widely through promotional efforts. The "taken for granted" attitude toward religious education can be mitigated and new awareness of its importance aroused through such activities. *See also* Communication Theory; Congregational Life; Management.

S. J. Heckman

Public Schools and Religion

Public education in the United States is an evolving phenomenon that has had a continually changing relationship with religion. The early colonies continued the European pattern of schools sponsored by the established church. Thus the first schools were by intention religious, not secular. The favorite textbook was the *New England Primer*, which provided instruction in catechism as well as spelling. The alphabet was taught in rhymed couplets: "A. In Adam's fall/We sinned all. B. Heaven to find/The Bible mind."

Various colonies, like Massachusetts in 1642, enacted laws "to assure that children learned to read and understand the principles of religion." "Religion, morality, and knowledge being necessary to good government and the happiness of mankind," the Northwest Ordinance of 1787 set aside federal lands in the territory for schools.

Although Thomas Jefferson conceived the idea of free, tax-supported public schools, Horace Mann is considered the "father" of the common school. In 1837 he was appointed secretary of the Massachusetts board of education. He sought to maintain Christianity in the public schools, but minus sectarianism.

Nonsectarianism was understood as "pan-Protestantism," and it exerted a pervasive influence over public schools. For instance, between 1836 and 1920 *McGuffy's Readers*, full of eclectic aphorisms and moralisms, were the best-selling textbooks. Prayers were said; the Bible was read; and clergy frequently directed the schools. The Protestant character of the public schools has been recognized as a central reason for the growth of parochial schools sponsored by the Catholic church and other religious groups who did not find their beliefs and values reflected in the government-sponsored schools.

Waves of immigrants in the 1880s and 1890s increased the debate about whose religion was to be taught in the public schools. As religious consensus decreased, emphasis on the principle of separation of church and state increased.

Societal changes accompanying World War I reversed the trend. Starting with Pennsylvania's law in 1913 requiring Bible reading, at least half the nation's school districts eventually instituted some form of devotional exercises involving Bible reading and/or prayer.

In an effort to maintain separation of church and state while providing religious education, released-time programs were developed in which students were excused from school for religious instruction. Released time was begun in Gary, Indiana, in 1913. By 1948 all but two states had some released-time programs. Some continue despite tighter legal restrictions.

Since mid-century attention has been focused on constitutional issues concerning rights of individuals. As well-publicized court cases have challenged assumptions about religious practices in schools, local and state education agencies have increasingly tried to avoid controversy; policies have swung over to virtually total avoidance of religion—textbooks have rewritten history deleting all references to religion and neither God nor religious beliefs are mentioned in classrooms for fear of offense.

CONSTITUTIONAL ISSUES

Constitutional issues have been hotly contested in matters of religion and public education. The Bill of Rights begins: "Congress shall make no law respecting an establishment of religion, or prohibiting the free exercise thereof."

The Supreme Court has sought to clarify the proper relation between religion and education in a long list of cases involving the public schools. *Abington* v. *Schempp* (1963) is the most often quoted. That decision banned Bible reading and recitation of the Lord's Prayer from public schools not only because it favored one religion over others, but because prayer is a religious act and cannot be sponsored by the state without violating the First Amendment. The Supreme Court decisions specify over and over that the church and home are the appropriate places for religious practice, which is no business of government.

The *Schempp* ruling does address the danger of establishing "a religion of secularism," by showing hostility to religion and "preferring those who believe in no religion over those who do believe." But in the Court's opinion on *Schempp*, Justice Clark stated, " . . . it might be well said that one's education is not complete without a study of comparative religion or the history of religion and its relationship to the advancement of civilization. It certainly may be said that the Bible is worthy of study for its literary and historic qualities. Nothing we have said here indicates that such study of the Bible or of religion, when presented objectively as part of a secular program of education, may not be effected consistent with the First Amendment."

Teaching of religion as a subject in school has had great success in some districts but has not been widespread. The National Council of Religion and Public Education, an interfaith group, was founded following *Schempp* to develop curriculum, oversee training of teachers, and to establish a proper climate for the teaching of religion in the public schools. The study of religion is usually undertaken in social studies, while the Bible is studied as literature in English courses.

The matter of what is finally permissible in either curriculum or school activity in any specific community is to be determined by the local school board. Continual shifts in policy and interpretation by the courts make it impossible to give general answers or point to standard procedures.

RELIGIOUS ORGANIZATIONS

Religious organizations entered a new phase in their relationship with public education in the 1980s. Immense problems in public schools were documented in dozens of reports published by prestigious commissions during the first half of the decade. The most pervasive problems were identified as low achievement as demonstrated in test scores, lack of discipline, substance abuse, and segregation by class or race. Reformers, including religious activists, gravitated toward either of two poles. Some advocated replacing public education with private education to be accomplished by redirecting tax dollars through tax credits for tuition or vouchers for education. Others advocated reforming the public system.

Evangelical churches that had opened from ten to thirty thousand Christian academies in the 1970s and 1980s joined the Roman Catholics and others with established parochial school systems in calling for support of private education. Bible was integrated into the teaching of every subject, and creationism replaced evolution as the key scientific teaching. Utmost value was placed on instilling discipline and respect for authority. Controversy swirled around many of the schools, especially in such matters as teacher certification and other forms of state control.

During the same period mainline Protestant denominations evidenced increasing commitment to advocacy for public education. A dozen denominations and the National Council of the Churches of Christ passed policy statements extolling the principle of free public education, advocating access for all to quality education within a multicultural context. These organizations, in coalition with other religious groups and secular agencies, became particularly active in the desegregation of schools. They worked to maintain the separation of church and state and fought tuition tax credits and funding to assist parochial schools. Because a predominance of teachers, administrators, and school board members were also members of the mainline churches and synagogues in each community, their values tended to be reflected in the educational leadership.

The public schools are a primary arena where the nation works out its values and beliefs. What the next generation is to learn becomes a test of what the adult population considers important. The governance and funding of public education are political matters, and shifting political balances are a primary factor in whose value system, including religious values, guides the formation of the next generation. *See also* Church-State Relations; Higher Education, Religion in; History of Christian Education; Mann, Horace; Private Schools and Religion.

M. L. Shafer

Publishing, Religious

See Books, Religious; Periodicals, Religious.

Puppets

Puppetry is a creative art form, an expression of meaning, and a learning tool quite useful in religious education. Puppetry helps persons of all ages get inside religious literature, imagining what happened and understanding how participants felt. This art form can also be used to solve problems and help people express themselves. Puppets are also entertaining; a group can use puppets to communicate a message as they entertain other groups.

The best rule for preparing a story for puppets is to keep it short and simple. Begin by hearing the story. Talk about what happened in the story and then divide the story into scenes or parts. Make a list of the characters in the story. Talk about how they acted and how they felt. Talk about the different ways the character could have responded to the situation. Assign characters to members of the group. Have them practice working with the puppets to express various emotions like anger, joy, and love. Decide if there will be a written script or a narrator with the puppets speaking spontaneously. No script is needed for open-ended skits because the puppets solve problems by working out the endings.

Making puppets can be fun, but it can also be time-consuming. With some imagination puppets can be made out of almost anything—popsicle sticks, paper bags, socks, and hands. The type of puppet determines how many sessions construction will take. For dramatizing anything from Bible stories to dilemma stories, simple, faceless puppets can be used. It is surprising how the character of these puppets can change just by their actions.

The simplest puppet stage can be made from two expandable curtain rods placed in the door frame. The bottom rod should be about shoulder high for the group. Hang a piece of material on this rod that reaches the floor. The upper rod holds a piece of material that hangs just below the bottom rod. Puppeteers can stand behind this curtain and work their puppets in front of the top curtain and not be seen.

Remember that puppetry is not just another craft. The purpose of the art form is to express a special meaning, to tell the story of faith, to deepen understanding, to provide a vehicle for the expression of emotions. Puppetry can be a form of ministry.

Simple puppets (stick, bag) can be made and used by children in early elementary grades. They can operate the puppets while the teacher tells the story, or they can be responsible for the conversation of their puppets. Older elementary children can make puppets, devise stories, and give a performance for a group. Puppetry has for centuries been a sophisticated and elaborate art form, so its use by a special adolescent or adult group for serious biblical storytelling should be considered. See also Dramatization.

S. H. Matthaei

Purim

Purim (in Hebrew, literally "lots," Esther 3:7) is the holiday celebrating the rescue of the Jews of ancient Persia from the evil Haman, as related in the biblical book of Esther.

The holiday is celebrated on the fourteenth day of the Hebrew month of Adar (usually in March). The key commandment is the reading of the book of Esther from a parchment scroll. Other observances include charity to the poor, exchanging gifts of food, special prayers, and a spirited feast. Children dress in costumes, often as characters mentioned in the book of Esther.

The fact that God's name is not mentioned in the book of Esther makes this holiday Judaism's most "secular" and presents the challenge of religious life in a world where God seems absent, and highlights the precarious status of Jews outside the land of Israel. See also Jewish Festivals and Holidays.

FOR FURTHER REFERENCE

Goodman, Philip. The Purim Anthology. Philadelphia: Jewish Publication Society, 1949.

D. A. Resnick

Q

Quaker Education

The Society of Friends (sometimes called Quakers) grew from a group in England gathered around George Fox (1624–1691), who preached awareness of the "inner light," God present in and directing the life of every person. For the Friends, religious practice is a preeminently communal experience in which individual revelation is tested against the authority of the group rather than the authority of a priest or accepted dogma. The perpetuation of such a tradition depends not on the mastery of sacred texts and sacraments but in embodying a way of life grounded in silence, divine revelation, and faithfulness to the internal guidance that can come when one sits in stillness with others. Finding ways of transmitting this culture and spiritual practice to the young is the task of Quaker education.

Fox was responsible for the establishment of the first Quaker schools in 1668: Waltham for boys and Shacklewell for girls. Within a hundred years, twenty-one small Quaker boarding schools were operating in England; the same phenomenon was duplicated in the United States. Most of these schools specialized in elementary education, instructing children in "whatever things were civil and useful in creation." In time, Quakers moved into secondary, higher, and adult education; each level of learning was informed by a set of attitudes characteristic of Quaker practice. These include the nurturing of community, simplicity, equality, respect for the individual, and the maintenance of social harmony. Underlying all was a sense of the abiding presence of the divine, referred to by Friends as the Inner Light, in the lives of individuals and the entire group. This cluster of attitudinal habits is what distinguishes Friends' schools from most other educational settings.

Mature Quakers need to be able to function within each of the two expressions that evolved from Fox's insight that there is that of God in every person, the liturgical and the social. The first, meeting for worship, involves sitting with others in prayerful silence, collecting oneself, and remaining open to reflections that demand to be shared. In the second, meeting for business, Friends engage in a corporate search for that point of consensus upon which future action can be built. Both gatherings demand a sensitivity to the needs and wisdom of others, a sensitivity that can develop best when a child is raised in a caring and conscientious community. It was the job of Friends' education to cultivate such sensitivity.

COMMUNITY AND SIMPLICITY

To achieve this end, Quaker schools recreated the communal setting of the extended Quaker family. They operated as tightly knit educational communities made up of teachers, students, bakers, and janitors. Solidarity was built through shared labor, worship, and decision making. People learned to know one another in a variety of contexts and experience in concrete ways their common identity. By being exposed on a regular basis to meeting for worship and meeting for business, young Friends were given practical training in the religious and social forms they would use as adults. By being isolated from secular influences, they were drawn into an empirical understanding of the peculiar nature of the Society of Friends and encouraged to remain loyal to the religious path of their parents.

Part of what separated early Friends from the surrounding society was their reaction against the unessential, be it church rituals or personal habits. Friends sought to celebrate simplicity in all areas of their lives. Their choice of plain clothes reflected this concern, as did their choice of curriculum. They saw the arts, music, and literature as distractions, forms of knowledge that were frivolous and ostentatious. To take the place of these traditional academic disciplines they substituted the sciences, mathematics, surveying, and practical skills. Only in the nineteenth century did Quakers reintroduce the humanities. Today the curriculum of most of their schools resembles that of any mainstream educational institution, though in some schools the Friends' testimony regarding simplicity can still be seen in the teaching of practical skills in conjunction with school-based work programs, the construction of adequate but unadorned physical plants, and the encouragement of life-styles that focus more on the quality of personal relations and commitment than on consumption.

EQUALITY AND MUTUAL RESPECT

In addition to community and simplicity, belief in equality is another essential Quaker attitude. If that of God is present in all people regardless of sex, race, or social position, then all must be treated as equals. The Quaker avoidance of the formal "you" was an early demonstration of this concern. Rich and poor alike were to be treated the same. Education, likewise, was to be given to all Quaker children, regardless of station. To make this possible, Friends' meetings have traditionally set up funds to provide for the schooling of children of less affluent members. This belief in essential equality led Quakers to provide education for both boys and girls at a time when formal learning was nearly exclusively a male domain. Friends were also among the first to address the educational needs of blacks and Native Americans. Quakers in Barbados set up schools for the nonwhite population in the 1670s and ran afoul of the law because of it. A hundred years later, American Quakers took responsibility for educating the blacks they had freed.

Related to equality is the emphasis placed in Quaker schools on the cultivation of mutual respect between teachers and students. Because every person, adult and child, embodies that of God, students came to be treated more as people than pupils. The formal patterns of authority and dominance typical of most school settings were replaced in Friends' institutions by personal involvement. In terms of educational practice, Quakers were quick to abandon corporal punishment and the harsher forms of student control that had become standard practice in most British public schools. They sought instead to maintain social harmony through reconciliation rather than punishment, to draw out what was best in their children rather than repress the worst. In doing so, they taught their young concrete rather than merely abstract lessons in peacemaking.

In the twentieth century, Quaker schools have continued to proliferate and evolve. Currently, Friends are affiliated with over 160 schools around the world. In the United States, Westtown, George School, Bryn Mawr, Swarthmore, Haverford, Earlham, and Pendle Hill are among the more commonly known. As the Society itself has changed, however, and as its members have become less "peculiar," Friends' schools have stopped preparing children for a unique way of life. Now most Quaker schools are recognized as excellent educational institutions, but the more visionary aspects of their earlier history have generally been set aside. Still, traditional Quaker concerns relating to equality, justice, and peace turn up in community service programs, student exposure to the social activism of Quaker organizations like the American Friends Service Committee and the Friends Council on Legislation, and student involvement in decision making related to the operation of the school itself. Even meeting for worship continues to be given a place in the weekly schedule, though its meaning is often poorly understood by students and faculty trained more in reason than revelation.

Quaker schools no longer lead their students into membership in a unique religious society; they lead them instead into an active and thoughtful engagement with the world based on a recognition of the underlying commonality that links all people regardless of class, race, faith, or nationality. Rather than withdrawing from secular society to create the society that should be, Quakers have turned their attention to reforming the larger world in whatever ways they can. Whether the Society of Friends or its schools can resist secularization given this changed perspective remains an open question. See also Private Schools and Religion.

G. A. Smith

Questionnaire

A questionnaire is a device used to collect factual data or opinions in order to gain useful information. Such an instrument usually consists of a set of questions and may be printed for written response or asked orally face to face or over the telephone. In preparing a questionnaire, it is necessary to identify the purpose of the research. A clear sense of purpose enables the identification of what information actually needs to be collected. Balanced and fair questions are effective means to gaining an accurate response. Questions should be stated in their most neutral form and avoid emotionally laden or threatening words. Several forms of each question should be written and the best chosen; then they need to be tested on several different people beforehand to see whether all understand the questions with the same sense of meaning. Before finalizing the questionnaire, all questions should be checked to make sure that they will provide the information needed to satisfy the original purposes. See also Evaluation; Measurement.

J. D. Ban

Questions

A question is a sentence, usually in interrogatory form, designed to elicit a response to the issues raised. With the exception of the rhetorical question, a question anticipates the giving of an answer, which requires the one being questioned to address the issues in the question itself.

The use of questions and the solicitation of answers to them is one of the most common teaching methods. Studies of classroom discourse have indicated that questions account for approximately one-third of all such conversation. Questions are successful in teaching because they tend to take advantage of people's natural curiosity and to draw students from a strict dependency upon facts contained in books and lectures to applying them to their own experience.

Questions may be raised by anyone in a teaching/learning situation. The student may raise questions to get clarification of points made in a lecture or in a reading assignment. Students may also address questions to each other in a discussion in an attempt to understand more clearly what is being said by others.

The most common examples of questions in a teaching/learning situation are those directed to the students or learners by the teacher. Questions have many purposes. They can initiate further discussion, find out the level of factual knowledge possessed by the class or the student, draw a particular person into the discussion, identify weaknesses in knowledge for further classroom work, review work previously covered, and build up the confidence of persons the teacher is certain will answer correctly.

The use of questions is not limited to obtaining factual information. Questions are more frequently asked in order to challenge students to build upon previous information and make new connections based upon their own reasoning and problem solving. Rather than depending upon the recitation of memorized facts, the use of questions challenges the student to think about the implications of the relationship between facts and personal experience.

Many types of questions are commonly used in education. One set of questions may be verified by personal investigation. Among these types of questions are: *analytic* questions, which may be verified by consulting books, definitions of terms, the application of scientific principles, etc.; *empirical* questions, which appeal to one's investigation of sense experience and personal experimentation; *valuative* questions, which elicit responses based upon the values one places upon certain events, ideas, or concepts; and *metaphysical* questions and questions dealing with one's faith (although the question of verification here is unclear in many instances).

There are also questions that call for the student to make direct use of previous knowledge and to develop new ideas on the basis of that information and their own understanding of the world. One type of such questions is *cognitive-memory* questions, which require the student to utilize cognitive operations to answer the questions posed. There are also *convergent* questions, which call for comparisons, conclusions, or summaries of previous information, and *divergent* questions, which encourage the student to elaborate upon previous statements or responses. *Evaluative* questions elicit personal opinion and decisions on the basis of the information given in previous discussions.

Other questions seek to lead the students to probe more deeply into their own thinking on a given subject, to focus their thinking and clarify their previous answers, and to challenge long-held beliefs and opinions. Questions serve to stimulate the individual's own thinking and are therefore helpful in promoting education in its fullest sense.

Questions have been a significant part of religious education for much of its history. The catechetical approach in particular has relied upon a series of standardized questions and answers memorized by students to give them the basic elements of the historic faith and help them become full members of the church.

Teachers need to frame questions according to the context or situation. If information is expected, students need to have or have had access to it; otherwise a feeling of failure may be engendered. Valuative or metaphysical questions should be asked only if there is enough rapport among participants to encourage answers. And questioning is not only a teacher's function; students who question are seeking information or clarification or may be open to further discussion. *See also* Discussion; Disputation; Evaluation; Indoctrination; Methodology; Socratic Method; Teaching Styles.

W. A. Smith

Quiz

The quiz is a brief form of examination, testing the retention of facts and information in a particular subject area. Given on a regular basis, the quiz measures the factual retention of students and offers a continuous record of evaluation in the subject matter being presented. A number of positive characteristics are evident in this method of testing. The quiz, when frequently administered, may act as an energizing agent in the student's daily preparation.

When followed by a discussion of the results and remedial work, the quiz may be an effective tool in selecting correct study skills. Teachers may find the quiz helpful in seeking an objective determination of the growth and level of achievement of each student. The results of the quiz may point to specific concepts that need to be emphasized without reiterating others. It may assist in establishing certain tangible goals and objectives toward which progress can be measured by the students, teachers, and parents.

The quiz also has some obvious disadvantages. It measures the mastery of facts and retention of information without evaluating growth on a significantly broad basis. Rote learning seems to be the objective rather than perceptional understanding. The frequency with which quizzes must be administered in order to validate the evaluation procedure is time-consuming. Even the brevity of the test itself brings into question the validity of its results. Individual differences within students are not taken into consideration and the teacher is placed in an autocratic role. *See also* Evaluation; Measurement.

D. C. Borchert

Rabanus Maurus

Rabanus Maurus (780–856) of Mainz, Germany, contributed to the cultural development of modern Europe as monk, priest, abbot of Fulda, and finally archbishop of Mainz. Rabanus was most noted as a teacher, drawing students from far distances to study with him at Fulda. He himself was a student of Alcuin at Tours, who named him "Maurus" after St. Benedict's favorite student.

Rabanus's scholarship and teaching were influenced by his own administrative responsibilities and desire to spread learning. His writing included biblical commentaries, a martyrology, collections of hymns and prayers, and commentary on ecclesiastical organization and worship. He translated some of his work from Latin into vernacular German and wrote a Latin-German glossary of the Bible. Among his better known works are the hymn "Come Holy Spirit" and his books *On the Universe* (an encyclopedia), *A Book of Martyrs*, and *On the Formation of Clerics. See also* Alcuin; History of Christian Education.

M. E. Moore

Rabbi as Educator

The Hebrew word *rabbi* means "teacher," and since the beginning of rabbinic Judaism two thousand years ago the rabbi has been the principal vehicle for Jewish education. The rabbinic role of educator remains primary today despite added modern duties.

In the synagogue scriptural readings, from both the Pentateuch and the prophets, central to the service on Shabbat, Monday, and Thursday, provide the rabbi with a vehicle for exegesis and education. The vast midrashic literature (commentaries on the Torah) attests to the popularity of this form of education. The prayerbook (Siddur) incorporates classical texts from the Bible, Mishnah, and Talmud in regular communal worship, providing another educational vehicle for the rabbi. Special liturgies for holidays and commemorative occasions provide still another. Because study is considered an obligation for all male Jews, much of the activity in the synagogue revolves around education. (Women's education was largely neglected until the nineteenth century, with some notable exceptions.) Historically, rabbis have been the principal teachers for communal

male education on the advanced level and frequently the supervisors of education. It was not until the nineteenth century that the additional duties were added that are typical of the rabbi of today.

EARLY RABBINIC PERIOD (200–900)

During the period from 200 through 900, universal education was an ideal and study of the Scriptures was supposed to begin at age five, Mishnah at ten, and Talmud at fifteen. There is, however, no detailed description of the lower educational system during this period, nor do we know the extent of literacy. The Talmudic literature mentions elementary schools and academies in a wide variety of places, but we are unable to trace their history consistently in any one site.

We do know about education at the highest level in this period, the rabbinic academies at Sura, Pumbeditah, Nahardea, and elsewhere. Those who were later to become judges and communal leaders throughout the Jewish world were trained there. The curriculum represented a mixture of scriptural exegesis and learning from various chains of tradition loosely organized into subject areas by the teachers (rabbis). Mnemonic devices were frequently employed to assist memory. Discussion and debate were part of the process. Students arrived with a good preliminary education achieved at the lower level, but little is known about it. Some of this preparation of students for the rabbinic academies was done by rabbis, but most seems to have been done by teachers who were not rabbis.

Beginning around 600, broader adult education took place at the biennial three-week *kallahs*, during which rabbis led participants in study of an entire tractate of the Talmud. At times more than two thousand attended, but it is not known how they were chosen or what level of scholarship they had previously attained.

MIDDLE AGES IN MUSLIM AND CHRISTIAN LANDS (900–1700)

The centralized educational system and the role of the rabbi in this effort continued in the Muslim world. As the Abassid and Ommiad dynasties faded and local sovereignty expanded, the power of the centralized rabbinate and the great ancient Talmudic academies gave way to more local authority. The position of the rabbi continued. In most instances the rabbinate was not a full-time occupation; the rabbi made his living from a trade or profession. This continued to be true through the following centuries for all except those in the advanced schools or in the highest judicial positions.

During these centuries more attention was given to scriptural exegesis in an effort to ward off the threat of various schismatic movements that sought to eliminate the rabbinic traditions. As part of the emphasis on biblical exegesis, much of the midrashic literature reached its final form in this period. These commentaries provided the text for primary education. The material that combines scriptural citations and weaves a fairly complex net indicates that Scripture was often taught through this indirect method. Saadiah ben Joseph (892–942) and Maimonides (1135–1204) presented the Jewish legal tradition in a newly systemized fashion to meet educational needs. At the same time the philosophical writings of Ibn Gabirol (ca. 1020–ca. 1057), and Judah Halevi (1075–1141) and the sophisticated poetry, both religious and secular, of other scholars, as well as their linguistic studies, indicate that eduction was influenced by Arabic patterns. The teachers at all levels had to concern themselves with introducing students to philosophy, Hebrew and Arabic linguistics, and complex poetry. The relatively affluent and highly developed communities of the Mediterranean basin must have had a sophisticated educational system for boys of all ages.

The concerns of the more isolated, smaller communities in northern Europe were different. Up to the time of the French Revolution and the beginning of modern Jewish life the rabbi taught at the higher levels, and other teachers took care of elementary education, often under the supervision of a rabbi in their own or a nearby community. Such a system required that traditional biblical and rabbinic literature be made available to teachers of varying abilities. The eleventh-century French scholar Rashi (Solomon ben Isaac, 1040–1105) made a systematic exegesis of the entire Hebrew Bible and the Talmud, effectively opening them to mass study. The guidance of Rashi and his disciples made it possible for scattered communities not served by rabbis to attain a higher level of learning. The texts themselves were emphasized, in contrast to the midrashic method, and a logical progression was encouraged. The commentaries of Rashi continue in use to the present time.

THE MODERN RABBI (1800 TO THE PRESENT)

The role of the rabbi has changed radically in modern times. Judicial functions initially handled by rabbis have been largely taken over by the secular state, pastoral duties of various kinds have been added, and the rabbi's position as communal leader has been enhanced. Rabbis are prepared for these new roles in professional schools that include departments of education. Being a rabbi has become a full-time profession for most. The education of both men and women has become part of the rabbi's task, beginning with the Reformed movement in 1800 and gradually spreading to all Jewish groups.

The size of the modern congregation makes the use of volunteer and professional teachers necessary for the education of both children and adults. Rabbis may continue to teach, but they are primarily responsible for the curriculum and its implementation and, frequently, the administration of schools. Curricula have been developed by the various movements: Reformed, Conservative, Reconstructionist, and Orthodox. They have been greatly influenced by the philosophies of Mordecai Kaplan (1881–1983) on Jewish unity, peoplehood, and folkways; the contemporary Eugene Borowitz on covenant theology, history, and social action; Soloveichik (Joseph Baer of Volozhin, 1820–92) on the traditional curriculum; and various Zionist thinkers on Hebrew language, and the land of Israel. Contemporary educational methodology has been employed and modified through the decades. Much of this education takes the form of after school or Sunday classes, and the methods mirror those used in the public school systems.

Orthodox, Conservative, and Reformed day schools with full curricula of Jewish and secular education have been developed throughout the United States and the Western world. Rabbis are involved in curriculum development and often serve as principals of such schools, where they may also teach. Several hundred rabbis teach at the college level, some at secular universities.

A new dimension has been added to the modern rabbinate with the ordination of women, which began in the 1960s within the Reformed, Reconstructionist, and Conservative movements. Women have entered every aspect of rabbinic life; their role has not been limited to that of educator. *See also* Jewish Education; Jewish Theological Concepts; Judaism; Torah as Teaching; Torah, Study and Teaching of.

W. Jacob

Radio

Radio is one of the most influential media forms in existence and can be an excellent tool in religious education. There are more radios, three hundred million sets, than citizens of the United States. Not only is it a widely used medium during the daytime hours, but it serves as the primary source of music for all ages at any time.

The most dominant radio format, contemporary music, often referred to as middle-of-the-road music, reaches mainly twenty-five to fifty-four year olds. Album-oriented rock stations reach the eighteen to thirty-four year olds, while the top forty stations reach primarily teenagers. These factors are important considerations when drawing upon radio for religious education purposes, whether it is used as a form of instant curriculum or as an opportunity to develop a group's own program.

Radio provides numerous resource options waiting to be creatively tapped into for religious education. It can be used at home for gathering data to bring to a group for discussion. For instance, a group of youth or adults studying a unit on being created in God's image could keep a log for one or two days of what they listened to on radio and then reflect on what their radio preferences said about themselves. Or for several weeks a youth group could listen on their favorite radio stations for the pop songs that best illustrate the Bible lesson of the past week. Such an assignment would help young people clarify their personal values in comparison to those reflected in contemporary music. *Cultural Information Service* is a periodical that provides regular reviews of popular music and occasionally discusses value questions in connection with a hit album.

Radio also offers an abundance of news, features, talk shows, and information programming that can provide illustrations for a study group. National Public Radio (NPR) has several features daily that deal with societal and moral issues of everyday life.

Because radio is local in nature, it provides more opportunities for organizations such as the church and synagogue to produce programs of religious interest. The first place to look for assistance in developing a program is the local ministerial group or council of churches, which may already have a good working relationship with the radio stations. The person to meet at the local radio station is the public affairs director, who is responsible for how the station uses its time for public service programming and determines what public service announcements it will run for nonprofit organizations.

But before contacting anyone, take time to consider the reason for developing a radio program, the target group of people to be reached, and the goals to be accomplished. *Get the Word Heard* radio kit is one of the best aids in dealing with these questions. The manual and cassettes are a guide through eight radio program formats. Step-by-step instructions are illustrated by examples of actual programs.

Your religious education goals may suggest either a talk show or feature format. Several years ago one community organized a weekly program for church school teachers based upon the interdenominational Uniform International Sunday Lesson. On each radio program a minister from the community provided both biblical interpretation and practical illustrations for teachers.

Another potential program series might be a talk show with guest panelists. Each week a program host can interview authorities such as child psychologists, educators, or other religious leaders. Such programs work best when they focus upon a particular theme. The liturgical seasons work very well, but sometimes current events or an ecumenical curriculum emphasis dictates the topic.

Several communities over the years have reached the youth audience most effectively by producing a program with a music and commentary format. In many localities young people were actually involved in the production by interviewing other youth and interspersing these pieces between current hit songs.

Although today many people are used to television with its visual component (even discussions with little action are available on videotape), the possibilities of radio as an effective religious education resource should not be underestimated; they are limited only by one's imagination and creativity. Radio regularly provides curriculum resources and is available for local religious programming on an ecumenical basis at little or no cost. *See also* Audial Methods; Media.

FOR FURTHER REFERENCE

Brussat, Frederic A., ed. *Cultural Information Service: Resources for Lifelong Learners.* P.O. Box 786, Madison Square Station, New York, NY 10159.

Olson, Lani L. J., and Fred Erickson. *Get the Word Heard.* Indianapolis, IN: Office of Communication, Christian Church (Disciples of Christ), 1983.

N. E. Topliffe

Raikes, Robert

Robert Raikes (1736–1811) is credited with starting the Sunday school movement. A publisher and philanthropist, he was born in Gloucester, England, and educated locally in the Cathedral College School. On the death of his father in 1857, Raikes became editor and publisher of the *Gloucester Journal,* a weekly newspaper owned by the family. Raikes early became a supporter of prison reform and, seeking to get at the root causes of crime, decided to try to provide a modest education for the children of the working classes. Although most children worked six days a week, their Sundays were spent in aimless play. Developing an idea earlier tried elsewhere, he began to have them taught reading and the catechism in the afternoon to keep them out of mischief, thus developing Sunday schools. A half dozen such schools were organized in Gloucester between 1780 and 1783. In spite of some opposition, the movement spread widely and rapidly. *See also* History of Christian Education; Sunday School; Sunday School Movement.

L. G. McAllister

Reading in the Classroom

While reading—both silently and aloud—by children is an inevitable and invaluable part of most classroom instruction, certain practices must be observed so that children feel comfortable in the religious education classroom.

READING LEVELS

Use texts at the correct reading level for the class. Most curriculum publishing houses follow guidelines for reading levels but these may not fit a particular class. Each class has its own special characteristics.

With the help of one willing child, there is a practical way to determine in advance whether reading material fits reading abilities in a particular classroom. Choose a passage of about 100 words and ask the child—preferably an average reader from your class—to read the passage aloud to you. Record the number of missed words, and if the child misses five or more words out of 100, the material is too difficult. If the child reads the 100 words fairly easily, then ask the child to tell you what the lines are about. Unless the child can verbalize what's going on in the passage, it is too difficult.

In addition to this practical solution to the question of readability, there are several professional formulas for determining the readability of printed materials. These formulas depend on analyzing two or more factors, such as sentence length and familiar words. These formulas must be studied carefully to avoid misinterpretation and some are complicated to figure. Moreover, none measures density of ideas. However, they are used by educators, publishers, and others in evaluating reading difficulty of printed materials. Some of the authors of readability formulas are George Spache, Edgar Dale and Jeanne S. Chall, Edward Fry, Albert J. Harris, and Milton D. Jacobson. Their works are commonly found in college libraries and education offices.

Several factors in child development affect ability to read and understand material, and these are discussed in a table accompanying this entry. One of the primary factors is the child's attention span. This is particularly important to remember in typical once-a-week religious education classes which are seldom as structured as five-day classes. The same trial and error strategy recommended above to determine reading level also applies when determining attention span for different ages. Most three- and four-year-olds have an attention span of five to ten minutes for any activity. Through second grade attention span continues to be very limited. Third graders begin to show increased ability to sustain attention on one activity and fourth graders show even more. Fifth and sixth graders enjoy acquiring information and this will help hold their attention when reading and discussing something interesting to them. Since each child matures at his or her own rate and since each classroom has its own characteristics, teachers learn by experience how long a reading activity can continue without a break.

OTHER CONCERNS

When asking children to read aloud in class, don't call on single children unless they have volunteered. The practice of going around in a circle having each person read in turn often puts pressure on the child who is behind the others in reading skills or who is shy. An alternative is to have the class read aloud as a group.

Helps for silent reading and subsequent discussion include:

- Print key words on a chalkboard or large piece of paper for all to see.
- Pronounce the words and tell the children that these are important words they will find in the printed material.
- Ask for volunteers to say what the words mean.
- Supply meanings for any words the class doesn't know.
- Put key questions on the chalkboard before the children begin to read as a guide to finding the main ideas.

READING ABILITY

Age Level	Developmental Considerations
Preschool	Children learn primarily through experience with their physical senses; they think concretely, cannot understand abstract thought or symbolism, and do not recognize cause and effect; they enjoy repetition and rhyme, but have limited memory; they have an attention span of 5–10 minutes.
Grade 1	Children continue to learn through experience; they continue to think concretely and cannot understand abstract thought or symbolism, but they begin to recognize cause and effect; they also begin to recognize sequence; they perceive things with a single focus, one thing at a time.
Grade 2	Children continue to learn best from concrete experience; they can recognize cause and effect; their memory is improving and they can recall simple sequences, though they may forget minor points in a sequence; they require a lot of repetition and review; they can respond to stories providing role models for desirable moral growth, but may focus on one minor detail of a story rather than the main concept; they enjoy fantasy and imagination.
Grade 3–4	Reading abilities may differ widely among children; they can begin to perceive more than one idea at a time; they begin slowly to use symbols (in a concrete and literal way), to make metaphors, and to infer meaning from symbols, images, and rituals they experience; they love to know and explain facts and collect and classify information, but they do not yet think abstractly and do not generalize, synthesize, deduce, or think critically about data or truth; they understand cause and effect and they think increasingly well in sequence, but they are not yet capable of understanding history in the broad sense; they can recall, create, and compare stories; they become conscious of literary forms; their attention span lengthens to 15–20 minutes.
Grade 5–6	Children begin to gain a sense of geography and history; they begin to generalize and draw conclusions, and they are on the threshhold of abstract thinking; they continue to make slow progress in their ability to infer meaning from symbols and symbolic language; they can begin to discover meaning beyond the literal meaning in stories.
Grade 7 and older	Above listed reading skills may continue to increase, but many people continue to read at the level of a 13-year-old student.

- During the discussion of what was read, ask for volunteers to respond or have the children break into groups to find answers together.

Readers having difficulty can be helped in inconspicuous ways and their strengths in other areas recognized. All-important is the teacher's contribution to a child's sense of self-worth, one of the keys to a continuing life of faith. A child's later understanding of what it means to belong to a religious community is being shaped from the earliest years in the religious education classroom. *See also* Books, Children's; Child Development; Cognitive Development.

M. Hanson

Realism

Realism is essentially a philosophical term. In metaphysics (the study of the nature of reality), realism is the position that reality exists apart from our perception or desire. This position is in contrast to idealism, for example, which maintains that what we regard as reality is largely a projection of our own thinking processes.

In epistemology (the study of how we know reality), the position of realism is sometimes divided into naive and critical. Naive realism teaches that there is a reality apart from our perception and desire, but that we have access to that reality through our perceptual faculties. The naiveté is considered to be present in the conviction that these faculties deliver reality to us *as it is.*

Critical realists take into consideration that the reality we know we only know after we have processed it, that is, only after our senses and interpretive schemes have worked on it. These epistemologists recognize that evidence indicates our senses are quite limited in the range of reality to which they have access. Moreover, our interpretive schemes reflect our socialization and expectations more than the actual imprint of reality on our minds. In other words, there is a subjective dimension to everything that we think we know; what we know, in everything we claim to know, is an aspect of ourselves.

Naive realism is sometimes called unreflective realism, since in the light of all we have learned about perception to date, it is hard to deny the fact that we do not have access to reality *as it is.* Resistance to critical realism, especially in religious circles, seems to stem from the fact that one must give up the notion of certitude if one is a critical realist. While this is so, in the sense that one cannot claim to have *the* truth because one does not have access to an unfiltered reality against which to measure the accuracy of one's interpretation, it need not lead to relativism. The Hebrew notion of truth is helpful here. The true is what is dependable. An interpretation of reality acquires truth or credibility as its dependability is verified in various circumstances and over time.

Conversationally, realism is usually contrasted with optimism and pessimism. The realist claims to see things as they actually are as opposed to the optimist, who is said to have too rosy a view of reality, or the pessimist, who has too gloomy a view. In the arts, realism is the aesthetic tradition that purports to represent people and situations as they are, that is, not romanticized or distorted by any other unrealistic prism. Both of these common uses of the word "realism" are based on the more technical use of the term in philosophy.

Most people tend to be functional realists, at least on a day-to-day basis—they tend to think they see things as they really are. An understanding of critical realism prompts religious educators to remind themselves and make their students aware that one's own interpretation of reality is not absolute and that all human perceptions are to some extent subjective, that the self is part of what is seen. *See also* Epistemology; Idealism; Knowledge, Theories of; Romanticism.

J. C. Smith

Reasoning

To reason is to use the mind for sifting facts, making inferences, and drawing conclusions; known propositions are used and reworked to form new ones. Reasoning is the way in which this process is carried on.

From the biblical "Come now, let us reason together" through the history of religious institutions, reasoning has served a central function for religious communities. A concern for religious educators is awareness of the propositions known or assumed from which new propositions are developed. The first step is determining what propositions are both known and assumed in the life of a religious community. The second is facilitating the reaching of new operational propositions.

In teaching/learning situations time must be spent in determining individuals' relationships to the propositions by which reasoning is accomplished. The heritage of the teaching community needs to be examined for its impact upon how reasoning is accomplished. Does the institution seek to build upon what has been? Or is the past abandoned to allow the organization to follow a new way? What is the response of the adults to change? Is there a correlation between what is stated by the adults and how they actually practice their faith? Is the reasoning process open to the pursuit of truth, wherever it may lead? Are appropriate evaluation methodologies used to check out the validity of propositions known by the community of faith as well as those propositions operating out of the assumptions held by the community?

The second step, the facilitating of the reasoning process to teach new propositions, requires openness of mind and spirit, since the natural reaction of people and institutions to change is to resist it. A critical question in this struggle is: "So what?" Having shared the known and assumed propositions, what do they mean to the life of the religious community as well as the wider community within which the institution exists? The thrust of this reasoning process should lead to new areas of service and ministry.

While the field of psychology, building upon the work of Sigmund Freud, Erich Fromm, and C. G. Jung, deals with the rational and nonrational and their influence upon the reasoning process, many religious communities still hold that the teacher provides the appropriate reasoning for the students. In this style of education, few, if any, new propositions are discovered; rather, old and little tested propositions are reinforced. This method must be contrasted with that of inductive reasoning, in which learners observe phenomena and draw possible conclusions. This approach is more often found in general education than in religious education, but religious education teachers need to open their minds to the possibility of change and learning if students are expected to do so.

Reasoning demands a variety of strategies as well as the ability to know when and how to use them. There is often a lack of awareness of the abilities people use in solving life problems. Religious education needs to help students discover the reasoning skills they use daily but rarely think about, including the learning skills being used, in the case of children and adolescents, in school programs. For example, the computer has great potential for exploring systems of thought and reinforcing newly acquired propositions with implications for the religious community.

The tasks of working with preschool and adult learners pose a somewhat different problem. While much has been discovered about how preschoolers learn and their utilization of the affective domain to experience a reasoning process, it is difficult to overcome stereotypes of learning deeply embedded in the minds of people working with preschool children. A source of help is the trained preschool teacher in the community. Adults, with their tendency to address serious learning only when it affects their employment, present other difficulties. Time spent learning about the daily lives of adult learners will provide the designated teacher with information about reasoning skills already resident within the class members. Reasoning skills used in daily living can be utilized within the religious setting. For those adults who are less comfortable with conceptual learning, experience-oriented teaching and concrete examples often facilitate access to the reasoning process.

The reasoning process often encounters opposition from those who prefer to base decisions on feelings. Others point out the limits of reason, especially in today's highly technological Western society. Nuclear danger may also cause people to feel that reasoning is useless in the face of overwhelming power. Such rationalization has allowed the religious community to avoid intentionally addressing many of the injustices of the world. In fact, the injustices have often been supported by religious rationalization.

Groups holding a liberal theology may find it more comfortable to discuss such issues on an intellectual plane that does not involve emotional response or action. This is rationalization rather than reasoning. Conservative groups may stress a structured theological belief or an equally structured code for moral living. These also may evade the task of giving reason to belief and reasonableness to morality.

Reasoning is essential today when the prevailing structures of inductive thinking cause people to want to explore religious meanings, but the corrective influence upon the reasoning process, from the earliest time of the human race to the present, is the presence of the mystery of faith. *See also* Adult Education; Cognitive Development; Knowledge, Theories of; Learning Theory; Teaching Styles.

M. F. Hatch

Reconciliation

The reconciliation of God and the world and people with each other are central themes of most religious traditions. In one way or another, religions confess an experience of separation from the deity that is mirrored in the fractures and alienations of everyday life. With the rise of psychological insight, the alienation and reconciliation of what has been called our "divided self" (R. D. Laing) have emerged as grounding motifs in both religion and psychotherapy.

Reconciliation from estrangement can take forms that move from relative acceptance of our feelings of separation from God, each other, and self to positive efforts of bridging the gaps through various religious interpretations and rituals, practices that foster communication and community building, and any number of psychotherapies. Either through acceptance or positive effort, overcoming this sense of estrangement is a major part of the human agenda.

RECONCILIATION IN BIBLICAL RELIGION

Biblical religion teaches in its creation accounts that God's intentions and providence for the world offer an invitation to peaceful and loving presence with God and each other. The account of the human fall (original and originating sin) from this graced presence suggests an alienation and estrangement that ground human history as we know it. In the biblical account, the first significant act of the now estranged human condition is the fratricide of Cain against Abel. The image that Scripture suggests as the epitome of human alienation and sin is the murderous assault of one person against another, both of whom are members—as are we all—of God's family. As human conditions and manifestations in particular acts, alienation, estrangement, and negation require, in biblical religion, both a reconciler and a reconciliation. Estrangement is therefore associated with sin and a reconciling redeemer. God will not abandon those who have become estranged.

Christianity confesses that such reconciliation has been accomplished in the life, death, and resurrection of Jesus Christ. The Spirit of the reconciling God in Christ remains in Christian faith as the foundation of the church. The community of the church thus has, as part of its nature and function, the ministry of forgiveness and reconciliation.

As a necessary first step in all acts of reconciliation, both religious and psychotherapeutic, those estranged must become aware of their own state. Christianity in all of its forms promotes the practice of confessing sin and estrangement as part of its ministry of reconciliation.

Protestant Christianity has traditionally understood this confession to be one of general sinfulness that can be overcome through acceptance of faith in Christ. Such an act of faith-confession is itself a grace of God. Being "lost and found" have been constant themes of Protestant piety. Being "born again" is another common expression of this kind of confession and reconciliation. Baptism is the central liturgical act that celebrates this movement from estrangement to reunion.

The Catholic traditions (Roman, Orthodox, and, in part, Anglican) generally have more of a sense of ongoing renewal than of single rebirth. In them and in many Protestant traditions baptism, administered in infancy, is a general entrance into the graced community of the church. After baptism, new acts of sin and estrangement can be particularly confessed in special liturgies of repentance. Thus, what is traditionally called confession, the sacrament of penance, and now, more commonly, the sacrament of reconciliation is part of the special liturgical life of the Catholic traditions. Whereas there has been some historical debate about the underlying theologies of faith, sin, and appropriate liturgies of reconciliation between the Catholic and Protestant traditions, the central elements of confession, forgiveness, reconciliation, and renewal in Christ are common to Christianity in general.

The Roman Catholic practice of confessing particular sins before a priest (also part of Anglican and Orthodox traditions) has undergone significant theological and liturgical renewal since the Second Vatican Council (1962–1965). The priest functions now more generally as a representative of the community of the church that welcomes those who seek reconciliation after their self-confessed sin and estrangement. While still requiring a particular confession after serious sin (in most circumstances), the Roman Catholic church has developed new services and liturgies that also stress the corporate and communal nature of sin and reconciliation. Celebrations of the Eucharist and Lord's Supper in most traditions contain a corporate confessional ritual that intends a reconciliation before the communion of the table.

TEACHING RECONCILIATION

For Protestant religious educators, reconciliation is taught in a general sense; the parable of the prodigal son reconciled to the family and the prophet's promise of God's reconciliation with Israel signified by the return from Babylonian exile are prototypes. Life experience examples are mutual forgiveness and acceptance of friends or family members after a quarrel, marital reconciliations, or tensions within a congregation that find resolution. This is not simply person-to-person reconciliation, however—the ability to forgive and become reconciled is a gift of God's grace. Humans are enabled to forgive because God does.

In traditions where reconciliation is a liturgical act, children are prepared for participation through a unit of study. Adults preparing for baptism (as in the Catholic Rite of Christian Initiation for Adults), are similarly instructed. After participation in the rite, people are able to reflect in a new way, with teachers, about its significance. *See also* Faith; God, Understandings of; Grace; Psychotherapy; Sacraments; Vatican II.

J. Monti

Record Keeping

Well-kept records are an invaluable tool when planning for and evaluating activities intended to meet the needs of any individual or group of people. Records can provide the facts needed to assess individual growth and nurturing needs, to assess the quality and extent of a group's changes and interactions, and to make financial and administrative decisions.

TYPES OF RECORDS

"Records are kept to keep the seed from falling by the wayside," wrote John Wesley. Wesley, whose interest in small group functioning was evident in his class meetings, developed an elaborate system of accountability for the bands and class meetings that were organized. He made certain that every leader carefully checked the status of each member at each meeting. He required not only an attendance record (attendance was rewarded with tickets), but an account of the status of each person's faith. In churches and synagogues today records are more likely to be kept only of significant events in the minutes of groups. The value of such minutes—and of any other records kept—is closely related to their purpose.

Several records may be kept for assisting the growth of persons and knowing what programs are needed next. Basic records are often kept by households, often including all the members in a household whether or not they attend organizational functions. The record on each person might include dates of birth, baptism, confirmation, and/or church membership. The giving record of families might also be kept. Offices or leadership roles need to be recorded as well as community activities, conference appointments, or honors for service. There may also be space on such a record for the calls made by pastors or supervisors. These family records may require cross-referencing for families where children are related to a parent from a previous marriage. The neighborhood where people live, the employment record, and other churches to which they have belonged might be helpful. The purpose of this complete record is to give an accurate picture of the environment of each person as well as achievements to date.

A related record that is rarely kept is the faith history of each member. This record could be a combination diary, journal, and album of spiritual landmarks, perhaps in the form of a notebook in which special events or particular times of reflection are recorded. At one church notebooks, kept at the church, were started at the beginning of junior high for each student. In addition to the person's own contributions, anyone could add pertinent items to the book. These were returned to the persons at the end of high school graduation for their own continued use. The development of a recorded faith history is of great assistance in planning activities for the faith development of persons.

Another kind of record is the class or group membership list. These lists supply data concerning enrollment, attendance, and participation in groups. These records could be referenced to the family records. The attendance records will only be useful if they are studied for trends or patterns that inform planners. The revealing of absentees requires quick follow-up, so records must be readily accessible. For purposes related to gaining new members, a list of visitors and persons who attended special events such as vacation church school, camps, and church dinners should be kept and referred regularly to those who make calls and enlist people for their groups.

For administrative uses, records of insurance for workers and equipment, taxes paid, and compensations for particular workers should be kept. Budgets should be kept for comparison planning. Resources such as equipment, tools, and gifts to the church such as windows, crosses, offering plates, or Communion equipment all need to be inventoried in a permanent record book.

HELPS FOR RECORD KEEPING

Some general suggestions for record keeping are:

1. Keep the system simple.
2. Limit what is kept. Keeping copies of everything is more a sign of anxiety than of care. One needs to ask the question, "Will anyone care about this information in one year or in five?"
3. Be specific in listings.
4. Keep nonconfidential records accessible.
5. Put someone in charge of each kind of records, perhaps the church secretary, an officer of the group, or a person who has a special aptitude for records.
6. Carefully date and keep confidential concise and specific evaluation records such as personnel files and leadership information.
7. Keep a duplicate copy in another location of any records that have legal implications.

USE OF THE COMPUTER

Today many records can be more efficiently compiled and stored on a computer. Computers may be used for indexing, filing, and for producing reports by reordering, sorting, selecting, counting, and adding information.

All three kinds of records (information helpful in determining individual growth and nurturing needs, group information, and administrative data) can be kept on the computer. In addition, a computer can be used to record: worship details such as hymns, Scripture lessons, and other resources used; inventories of choir music, audiovisual equipment, and resources; financial reports over a period of years to determine trends; spread sheets to show bookkeeping procedures; calendars of ministerial and church activities; minutes to be produced for meetings; and a talent bank cross-referenced to positions to be filled or tasks to be done.

Developing adequate computer programs to meet the record-keeping needs of a congregation will save hours of time and storage space. Creating new programs and updating existing ones should be done on a regular basis. Ideally, information to be stored should be entered only once and the computer made to do the work of sorting, selecting, listing, and rearranging.

Record keeping done either with careful files and notebooks or on the computer are the essentials for keeping relationships vital and evaluating group performances. Records that are well kept will keep the "seed from falling by the wayside." *See also* Attendance; Computers; Finance; Management; Planning.

H. L. Miller

Recreation

Recreation is engagement in those activities that give balance to life, provide for meaningful relationships with others, promote opportunities for creative experiences, and enhance self-understanding. Its root meaning is re-creation, creating again, restoring, and it is through this meaning that recreation takes its place as a learning strategy in religious education.

The religious community is a natural setting for recreation. Throughout Scripture people are challenged to a life full of joy, caring, and sharing. As the community of faith goes about its routine of study, worship, fellowship, and service, it is reminded that life is to be lived as a whole; that is, all activities reflect the way faith commitment is understood. Therefore, a program of recreation is not merely incidental to the life of the congregation, an "added extra"; instead it is an integral part of the total life of the community and its planning and implementation within the area of religious education are of utmost importance.

Before considering a program of recreation, we must first examine the concept of practicing recreation within ongoing activities of the congregation. There are times when the concept of "moments for recreation" may help fulfill Scripture that charges people to "make a joyful noise unto the Lord" or "praise God with cymbals and dance." Examples of moments of recreation include having a community sing before a banquet program, using a group mixer while people stand around waiting for a program to start, or beginning study sessions with a game that helps individuals relax, thereby opening themselves to relating within the whole group. Generally, a program of study is designed to help people relate day to day, as they encounter self and others. A serious look at how and why people play can help add that dimension to the ongoing fellowship of the institution. A study of recreation may help heighten the realization that a commitment to a religious conviction includes the whole of a person's relationships and activities.

One does not go to the Scriptures to find proof for participation in recreation. Rather, one goes to Scripture and discovers that there are guidelines for living a full and abundant life. The guidelines that Paul gives in Philippians (4:8) may serve as mirrors in which to reflect one's choice of recreational activity. Are they honorable, true,

just, pure, lovely, and gracious? Is there any excellence? Anything worthy of praise?

Decisions regarding specific recreational activities will also be influenced by the availability and practicality of activities, the number and ages of potential participants, and the leadership available.

Participation in recreation may take many forms—as part of a large group, a small group, or individually. However, one must remember that what might be renewing for one person may not be renewing for another. One person may find renewal in backpacking into the wilderness, another by participation in a drama-in-the-park group. Both enjoy the outdoors but the choice of activity is different.

Recreation is a necessary part of the educational curriculum for children. Young children need physical activity and learn through it. Through games older children learn what it means to play fairly, have regard for other people, and win and lose gracefully.

Activities for youth and adult groups (large and small) or for the congregation as a whole include dinners, family outings, games, tournaments, and other sports events, musical and dramatic events, craft groups, camping trips, field days—opportunities for recreational fellowship are limited only by interest of the participants, imagination of the planners, and resources. One parish gathers a group annually for a whitewater rafting trip. Another group goes to a conference center for a weekend of individual relaxation, meeting together only at meals. Bowling and skating parties are popular with young people. Needlework guilds and other painting, writing, or ceramic groups provide enjoyment for participants but may also raise money for outreach projects with their work. It must be remembered that what might be renewing for one person may not be for another—providing a variety of forms of recreation ensures that its purpose will be achieved for all members of the community.

When the religious community takes seriously its responsibility to provide experiences of enriching participation in play, the results will be new avenues of praise and worship opening to them, new inner peace and satisfaction that enhance individual lives, and the development of cohesive relationships that will strengthen the faith community. Playing together opens doors for further relational growth and development between age groups, sexes, and cultural and racial groups. *See also* Outdoor Ministries; Play.

G. Q. Bannerman

Redemption

See Salvation.

Reformed Education

Education in the Reformed tradition includes the teaching ministry of Congregational, Presbyterian, and Reformed churches. If Baptist churches are known for their emphasis on evangelism, it could be said that the unique thing about churches in the Reformed tradition is the importance they attach to education. The Reformed family of churches value education, insisting on college and seminary training for their clergy and education to equip laity for leadership in the instruction of children and youth. It is not by accident that the minister's office at the church is often called the "pastor's study."

HISTORY

Education lies close to the heart of the Reformed tradition. The reason for this can be traced back to the Reformation and to the Reformers' conviction that Scripture should order and guide the life of the church. But for reform to succeed, both clergy and laity needed to be able to read and understand Scripture for themselves. Education became the means for producing a biblically literate people. The success of the Reformers' educational efforts may be seen even today in the high literacy rate in countries where the Reformation movement was strongest.

The Reformed churches stem mainly from the work of John Calvin (1509–64), who fled from France to Geneva under persecution and established a Reformed church there. He affirmed the Bible to be central to faith and practice and based the church on this affirmation. Followers of Calvin—particularly those who tried to establish the French Reformed Church (the Huguenots)—were alternately persecuted and tolerated. Many fled to Germany, the Netherlands, England, and later the American colonies. Early Dutch settlers in the United States established what is known today as the Reformed Church in America. The Christian Reformed Church in the United States also has Dutch ties.

John Knox (1514–72), fleeing persecution in Scotland, came under the influence of Calvin in Geneva and later returned to Scotland to establish the Presbyterian church. There have been several branches of the Presbyterian church in the United States. In 1983 the Presbyterian Church (U.S.A.) was formed by the reunion of the Presbyterian Church, U.S. (Southern), and the United Presbyterian Church, U.S.A. (Northern), thereby healing a Civil War division.

Teaching was central to the ministries of both Calvin and Knox. John Calvin began the day with lectures for the laity. The *Institutes* served as a text for teaching theologians, pastors, and adults, and a catechism served as the teaching resource for the young. Calvin also wrote numerous tracts that had an instructional purpose. His commit-

ment to education included the establishment of the College of Geneva in 1559.

As the Reformation spread from Geneva across Europe, it took with it a commitment to education. Like Calvin in Geneva, John Knox in Scotland expected adults to instruct the young in the home setting. Pastors were to use the catechism to prepare the young for admission to the Lord's Table. Knox's goal was to establish a school in every Scottish parish and to have a schoolmaster next to each minister. Knox also advocated group Bible study. These beginnings helped establish the pattern that is still discernible in the Christian education programs and curricula of churches within the Reformed tradition.

DISTINCTIVE FEATURES

When the designers of a new Reformed and Presbyterian educational curriculum (1988) thought about the distinctive features of education in the Reformed tradition, they named five adjectives: biblical, historical, ecumenical, social, and communal. They saw a Reformed-Presbyterian education as being grounded in the Bible, informed by the history of the church, committed to the unity of the church, engaged with the issues of contemporary society, and nurtured within the faith community. The educational resources growing out of their design will reflect these five elements.

Three other elements could be added to their list: the role of the minister as teacher, the catechetical method as an instructional approach, and the confessions of the church as the content of teaching. Liturgically speaking, the minister is the "pastor and teacher." The liturgy of the Presbyterian Church (U.S.A.) asks the candidate for ordination or installation, "Will you be a faithful minister, proclaiming the good news in word and sacrament, teaching faith, and caring for people?" (*The Worshipbook* [Philadelphia: Westminster Press, 1972], p. 91). And the liturgy of the Reformed Church in America ends its Declaration with the words that the minister is "the lawfully installed pastor and teacher of this church" (*Liturgy and Psalms*, ed. Gerrit T. Vander Lugt [New York: Board of Education, 1968], p. 100).

The Reformers made use of the catechetical method for instructing the young. Calvin wrote a catechism for children that was to be used by parents for instruction in the home setting and by the elders in their visitation of families as an evaluation of the progress being made by the children. The Synod of Dort (1618) emphasized a threefold approach to catechizing. Parents were to catechize in the home, teachers in the school, and ministers and elders in the church. While the emergence of developmental psychology and new pedagogical insights and practices have tended to push this method aside, within more conservative denominations like the Christian Reformed church, this instructional approach is still used by some congregations in conjunction with the Heidelberg Catechism in preparing youth for communicant membership.

Catechism, however, is more than an approach to education in the church or a method of instruction; it can refer to the content of Christian education as well. When some people speak of "catechism," they mean "Christian doctrine," and they have in mind the confessional character of education in the Reformed tradition. To speak of catechism as a characteristic of Christian education within the Reformed family of churches is to speak of the Scots Confession (1560, Scotland), the Heidelberg Catechism (1563, Germany), the Belgic Confession (1566, the Netherlands), and the Westminster Shorter Catechism (1646, England). These confessional documents represent the consensus of the church around the interpretation of Scripture and are either tacitly or expressly embedded in the curriculum of Christian education.

In the late 1800s, the Sunday school began to replace such doctrinal instruction with a more biblically oriented curriculum. While the Sunday school continues to be the major agency for Christian education in Congregational, Presbyterian, and Reformed traditions, there has been a shift in curriculum from a broadly ecumenical scriptural focus to a more denominationally defined view of biblical content. In the late forties, the United Presbyterian Church, U. S. A., developed its own curriculum, Christian Faith and Life. Several other denominations, including the Presbyterian Church, U.S., and the Reformed Church in America, joined together to produce the Covenant Life Curriculum. Unlike earlier Sunday school curricula, these curricula reflected a more Reformed point of view.

Higher education has been important in the Reformed tradition, and colleges were established with the western migration across the United States. The oldest Presbyterian college is Tusculum, Greenville, Tennessee (1794); there are sixty-nine colleges today. There are also six secondary schools. The oldest of the ten theological seminaries is Princeton, established in 1812. Presbyterian College of Christian Education was established by the General Assembly for the specific purpose of preparing people for educational ministry.

The Reformed Church of America has three colleges: Pella and Northwestern in Iowa and Hope in Michigan. The two seminaries are New Brunswick (in New Jersey), established in 1810, and Western in Michigan. These represent two strands of that tradition: the earliest settlers who came from Holland to the New York area in the seventeenth century and a later nineteenth-century settlement in the Midwest.

The Christian Reformed church, dissenters from the established church in Holland (and later from the Dutch Reformed church in the U.S.) established Calvin College and Calvin Seminary in Grand Rapids, Michigan. They have a strong tradition of parent-sponsored (in contrast to parochial) schools for the education of children. The Sunday school curriculum, titled "Bible Ways," was revised and rewritten (1988–89) with Scripture references using the New International Version.

Education in the Reformed tradition centers in the ministry of the Word. In shaping their educational ministries, Congregational, Presbyterian, and Reformed churches look to their roots in the Reformation era and to the challenges contemporary society presents. *See also* Catechism; Private Religious Schools; Sunday School; Sunday School Movement; United Church of Christ Education.

FOR FURTHER REFERENCE

Brouwer, Arie R. *Reformed Church Roots: Thirty-five Formative Events.* New York: Reformed Church Press, 1977.

Dendy, Marshall C. *Changing Patterns in Christian Education.* Richmond: John Knox Press, 1964.

Purdy, John C., ed. *Always Being Reformed: The Future of Church Education.* Philadelphia: Geneva Press, 1985.

G. Brown

Reign of God

The Hebrew *malkuth Yahweh* or the Greek *basileia tou theou* seems to be best translated by "reign" of God rather than "kingdom," since it refers to an active ruling rather than to a particular "realm" or "domain." Scholars today agree that the symbol of the reign of God represents the central theme in the life of Jesus and his conscious purpose.

That God now reigns and is to reign in fullness are convictions rooted deeply in Hebrew consciousness. *Malkuth Yahweh* refers to the actual sovereignty of God in the world now as its Creator and Sustainer and to the complete and universal goal of that divine rule at the end of history. Later Judaism refined those two distinct but related meanings of the symbol into two forms: the eschatological reign of God to be inaugurated by final judgment on the nations and an end to the world in its present form, and an earthly reign of God to be established by the triumph of the messiah. Whether it is happening now or promised later, in the Old Testament God's reign is always of both heaven and earth and is God's willing of peace, justice, mercy, and wholeness (*shalom*) of life for all. Because God is active in history on behalf of those values, they are a sure promise but also, in the covenant, a responsibility to be lived by God's people.

NEW TESTAMENT UNDERSTANDINGS

Less frequently used in the other books of the New Testament, in the synoptic Gospels the reign of God (or in Matthew, reign of "Heaven," a circumlocution for God in later Judaism) is presented as the raison d'etre of Jesus' life. From Jesus' opening proclamation in Mark 1:14–15, the reign of God was his constant theme and operative self-understanding. He understood the symbol in continuity with his Jewish roots— God's will being done now and all creation being brought to wholeness and completion. And yet Jesus understood himself and the event of his life as bringing a whole new level of meaning to this ancient symbol.

He considered the reign of God to have already arrived and pointed to himself as the definitive agent in whom God is acting to bring it about. Second, Jesus' word and work tended to make more explicit the radical aspects of the symbol. He called all to the reign, but seemed to favor the socially marginalized, the disadvantaged, and those who suffer for justice's sake (Luke 6:20). Admission demands becoming like a little child (Mark 10:15), living with justice (Matt. 5:20), doing the will of God instead of merely talking about it (Matt. 7:21), and abandoning one's wealth (Luke 18:24). It demands repentance (Gk. *metanoia*), a moral revolution, and a total change of life. Further, scholars generally agree that Jesus radicalized the love commandment of God's reign by making more explicit that one cannot love God without loving one's neighbor and that "neighbor" knows no limits; in fact it includes even one's enemies.

There is also a tension in Jesus' preaching of the reign, one evident in his Jewish roots, but heightened by him and bequeathed to Christians thereafter. The tension has at least three related expressions: between "already realized" or "not yet fulfilled"; as coming solely by the gift of God's grace or requiring human agency; and between an eschatological event promised outside of history or as a demand that places personal and social responsibility upon us now. While biblical scholars of the past tended to favor an either/or solution to the tension, contemporary scholars favor a both/and response, saying that there is ample evidence to support each side of the tension in the New Testament. Jesus preached the reign as already present in him (e.g., Matt. 3:2; 4:17) but also not yet completed (Matt. 6:10). Both present and future themes are evident in many of the parables, his favorite way of preaching the reign. He preached the reign as the gift of God's grace (e.g., Luke 12:32) but also as demanding a lived response from his followers now (e.g., Matt. 6:33). He spoke of the reign as a sure promise to be completed at the "end time" but also as demanding that God's will be done on earth, as it is done in heaven.

UNDERSTANDINGS THROUGHOUT CHRISTIAN HISTORY

That tension concerning the reign of God continued to be represented, however, throughout almost every period of Christian history. The first Christians expected the final manifestation of the reign in the near future (see Mark 9:1). When that imminent expectation waned, it seems that the focus of the church's preaching shifted to Jesus himself. This central theme became more implicit in the preaching of Jesus as Lord and when reign was mentioned it referred either to the church or to the rule of Jesus over the individual believer. Rudolf Schnackenburg writes, "God's reign recedes into the background of the apostolic preaching until it is scarcely noticeable" (*God's Rule and Kingdom*, p. 259).

The symbol, while never completely lost, re-emerged for attention with the Reformers; but here again the tension is evident. Luther, in rejecting the notion that the church is synonymous with the reign of God, posed it as the realm of grace created for us by Jesus but not to be identified with any human arrangement, effort, or organization. Calvin, on the other hand, said that the reign could be embodied in part in a theocratic society—thus raising again the issue of whether the reign is entirely in God's hands or we are to work toward it in society. Immanuel Kant, Friedrich Schleiermacher, and Friedrich Ritchl favored the latter interpretation, saying that as a symbol it stands for the ideal Christian society on earth, thus helping to secularize the symbol in terms of human progress and development. That "secularized" understanding continued on in liberal theology and in the social gospel movement.

Beginning about 1900 and aided by the tragedy of World War I, German Lutheran theologians (Johannes Weiss, Albert Schweitzer) pushed back against the liberal social interpretation and emphasized the eschatological and future dimensions of the reign, to be brought about only by the mighty and apocalyptic act of God; a position amplified further by neoorthodox and dialectical theology (Karl Barth, et al.).

UNDERSTANDINGS TODAY

There now seems to be emerging, however, a consensus position that takes a more both/and approach, as Scripture scholars advise, and can be summarized as follows: that the preaching of Jesus as Lord and Savior requires the preaching of what Jesus preached—the reign of God; that the reign has already come definitively in Jesus, God's irrevocable promise of it; that it will come, by God's grace, completely and with newness at the end time; but that its working out is an intrahistorical enterprise as well in which human agency contributes to its final perfection. Thus, the reign of God is now more readily understood

Community. Their aim is to promote the vision of the council—that the church is the people of God.

RELIGIOUS ORDERS AND RELIGIOUS EDUCATION

Religious education has always been a concern of religious orders. Elizabeth Ann Seton, founder of the Sisters of Charity, opened the first Catholic school in Baltimore in 1808. By 1900 U.S. nuns operated 3,811 parochial schools, 663 girls' academies, and by 1915 fifteen colleges for women. Orders of brothers took up the education of boys. The parochial school system was built primarily to provide religious education to immigrants, commonly of the same ethnic background as the sisters or brothers and often with limited education. In the 1950s the Sister Formation Conference led the movement to secure for women religious a preparation equal to that expected of teachers in the public system. The orders then began providing gifted members with the highest level of preparation, including doctoral degrees in theology.

Religious education in Catholic schools always had a twofold thrust—education of children in the Catholic faith through catechizing and a controlled environment and ministry to the poor of whatever faith. But by the 1950s the majority of parents of Catholic schoolchildren were no longer poor, and sisters began to object to "subsidizing the rich" with contributed services. Many religious took up new ministries, witnessing to Christian compassion without regard to the faith connections of those in need. Furthermore, women in religious orders in particular were no longer content to serve under male pastors who often had less education than they did. In the decade of the 1960s over one-fourth of U.S. sisters left their orders. Others remained in parishes in the office of director of religious education. Some sisters now teach in theology departments of universities, in all-male seminaries, and in programs for male deacons. The leadership of these better-educated religious women enriched theology, liturgy, biblical studies, and the development of resources for religious education.

Thus the orders were radically changed by a decisive shift in the models of church that required contrasting forms of religious education. In the hierarchical model, authority over knowledge rested with priests and bishops without regard to their educational level. But Vatican II stressed the adult character of Christian life, which needed to be fostered by ministry training. Under a perception of the church as a community of believers, all groups were encouraged to learn from one another, with the aim of coming to act in a Christ-committed way. Religious education often took the form of ministry training, enabling parents to teach their children and teams of laypersons to assume leadership roles in the parishes.

The decline in membership in religious orders since Vatican II has caused alarm among church authorities. History, however, attests to a remarkable ability of orders to adapt to changing times. *See also* Christian Brothers; Roman Catholic Education; Seton, Elizabeth; Society of Jesus; Teresa of Avila; Vatican II; Vocation.

FOR FURTHER REFERENCE

Abridged Guide to the Archives of Religious Communities of Canada. Ottawa, Canada: Canadian Religious Conference, 1974.

Barrett, Deborah, ed. *Guide to Religious Communities of Women.* Chicago: National Sisters Vocation Conference, 1983.

Canu, Jean. *Religious Orders of Men.* New York: Hawthorn, 1960.

Chittister, Joan. "Communities of Women Religious: Paradigms of Oppression and Liberation." *Religion and Intellectual Life* 4 (Fall, 1986):84–104.

R. Bradley

Religious Studies

Approximately one thousand colleges and universities throughout the United States and Canada offer academic programs in religious studies leading to the Bachelor of Arts degree. About fifty of these institutions also provide graduate programs leading to Master of Arts and Doctor of Philosophy degrees in the various specializations encompassed by religious studies: philosophy of religion, history and literature of religions, sociology of religion, psychology of religion, and numerous other subfields and specializations such as Buddhist studies, Judaic studies, Islamic studies, Native American Indian studies, Myth studies, Medieval studies, Ritual studies, and so forth. Moreover, these programs in religious studies are to be distinguished from theological studies programs at the some two hundred and fifty seminaries and divinity schools in the United States and Canada leading to such professional degrees as the Master of Divinity, Master of Theological Studies, Doctor of Ministry, and Doctor of Sacred Theology.

DEFINITION

The term "religious studies" is not without a certain ambiguity, however, even though it now appears to be the designation of choice for the academic study of religions in the college or university setting. This ambiguity lies in the fact that the noun "study" modified by "religious" can imply that personal belief or piety is necessary for and/or prerequisite to this kind of academic inquiry. But precisely the opposite meaning is intended, since religious studies is meant to identify an objective, scientific, nonbiased study of religion as distinct from a "theological" and/or "confessional" study for the purpose of increasing the faith, understanding, and institutional commitment of individual degree candidates in a particular religion. And while it is probably unlikely that entirely anti- or nonreligious individuals will seek to become specialists in religious studies, it nevertheless needs to be stressed that personal religiousness is not a formal necessity for and it may, in fact, be viewed as an impediment to objective, critical scholarship. From a practical standpoint it can be asserted, therefore, that those seeking advanced degrees in religious studies (as this designator is today understood) usually do so for the purpose of teaching and research, whereas those who seek theological degrees usually do so for the purpose of pursuing a specifically religious or clerical vocation such as the ministry.

There are, of course, many examples of individuals with both kinds of degrees and, indeed, individuals with both religious and secular vocations engaged in religious studies. The essential point, however, is to understand that religious studies has been struggling to separate itself, both formally and materially, from theological studies for more than a century. And although this history is exceedingly complex, the nature and meaning of "religious studies" can best be clarified, perhaps, by briefly sketching this development.

SCIENTIFIC, COMPARATIVE STUDIES

Religious studies, especially in America, has passed through two distinct stages. For the sake of convenience, the first stage may be identified as beginning in 1870 when the noted historian and philologist Max Müller (1823–1900) addressed the British Royal Institute calling for a new, scientific study of religion. It was Müller's notion that the world's religions are much too important to be neglected by critical scholarship or simply to be left to their partisans in theological schools. He also believed that since the post-Enlightenment world was rapidly outgrowing all forms of religious superstition, the time was ripe for religion to be investigated scientifically, analytically, and comparatively in the university. Müller and his supporters were also of the view that, given autonomy, the scientific, comparative study of religion could develop the discipline proper to its own needs and that it could, thereby, rightfully exist in the academy alongside other established disciplines.

During the seventy-five years following (or roughly to the mid-twentieth century), it became manifestly clear that Müller's dream would not be realized—at least not in its original form. First, the scientific and/or comparative study of religion was unable to develop the value-free discipline or methodology originally envisioned. Indeed, the intellectual horizon of Müller and his contemporaries was largely bound to an evolutionary notion of religious history, with Christianity, both *de facto* and in many cases *de jure*, being viewed as the superior standard of development to which all other religions (especially so-called primitive religions) were subordinate. Such a progressive or crypto-evolutionary approach to analysis and interpretation, both in the history of religions and elsewhere, was progressively discredited during the first half of the twentieth century as being subtle forms of neocolonial imperialism and cultural domination by post-Enlightenment European Christians.

Second, the romantic positivism of the evolutionary comparativists was both theoretically and personally objectionable to many scholars in the United States engaged in religious and theological studies, for in the United States, the academic study of religion was, from the outset, almost exclusively the province of those teaching in religiously founded, denominational colleges and universities, in divinity schools, or both. In these settings (and here especially conservative or confessionally identifiable liberal arts colleges), the academic study of religion was by design and intention the study of the founding religion, namely, Christianity. In Protestant colleges this study consisted in the main of required courses in the Bible, and in Catholic colleges of required courses in dogmatic theology—in each instance the purpose being twofold: the preparation of young people for religious vocations and the further grounding of all graduates in the beliefs of the host religion, that they might more effectively function in the service of the church as articulate, influential laypeople. In sum, not only did many American religionists object to what was frequently viewed as the "relativizing" effects of the comparative, historical study of religions and the corrosive influence of the so-called higher-critical methods on traditional religious authority, but they also believed that a strictly academic approach to religion was in many ways contrary to their basic purpose, namely, strengthening the faith of their students.

INTERDISCIPLINARY STUDIES

By the middle of the twentieth century, however, prevailing attitudes regarding the academic study of religion and the proper organization of curriculum began to change rather dramatically. First, increasing numbers of scholars began to realize that it was important, if not essential, for more than one religion to be studied in a department of religion if such departments were to have legitimacy in colleges of arts and sciences, for apart from this modification and expansion, there was nothing to distinguish departments of religion from departments of theology. Second, specialists in religious studies were faced with the dilemma of losing the academic study of religion to other departments in those instances where Christianity was not the primary object. And while this was especially true at advanced, graduate levels of instruction and research by way of the establishment of independent centers for South Asian studies, Near Eastern languages and literatures, African studies, and the like, it also raised questions regarding the proper training of undergraduates for these specializations and whether this training would be given over, by default, to other departments and disciplines. Third, the post–World War II period introduced a new spirit of ecumenical liberalism, especially in mainline Protestant and Catholic institutions, and with it the general recognition that Americans (given their new role as world leaders) should know something about the rest of the world—including religions other than biblical Judaism and Christianity. This attitude, combined with other postwar social and cultural changes, including urbanization and the rapid expansion of higher education in both the public and private sectors, led increasing numbers of American religionists to recognize that Max Müller's axiom "He who knows one, knows none" is as true of religion as it is of language.

The net result is that religious studies, since the 1950s, has emerged as an important interdisciplinary, polymethodological, and cross-cultural area of academic inquiry. All religions have material manifestations and expressions including ritual acts, mythical narrations, dogmatic explanations, moral interpretations, social constructions, and profound personal experiences. These various and diverse material dimensions cannot be properly elucidated by a single discipline or method but require the combined expertise of social scientists, literary critics and historians, philosophers, psychologists, and also theologians.

This new recognition is well evidenced in the development and organization of the principal learned society in religious studies, the American Academy of Religion, which was initially founded in 1909 as the National Association of Biblical Instructors. Its name was changed by the action of its members in 1964 to better reflect the new professional self-consciousness, and its diverse program of publication and research is characteristic of the manner in which religious studies curricula are ordered today. By these developments, religious studies has greatly contributed to the growing awareness that true science does not have to do with the development of a monolithic discipline, but with the collective efforts of a community of scholars illuminating one or more facets of the truth. *See also* Higher Education, Religion in; Psychology of Religion; Social Sciences; Sociology of Religion; University.

FOR FURTHER REFERENCE

Directory of Departments and Programs of Religious Studies in North America. Edited by Harold Remus. Waterloo, Ont.: Council on the Study of Religion, 1981, 1985.

A. M. Olson

Research

Research in religious education is designed to examine the ways that a religious community teaches, demonstrates, and communicates its own faith and life and the extent to which persons of all ages in that community learn about, appropriate, and participate in that faith and life.

Diverse forms of religion have generated even more diverse expressions of religious education, because each body of religion has developed a number of ways and resources to achieve its own unique educational objectives. Consequently, research in religious education is both very diverse and multifaceted.

Projects are designed to examine factors that range from those that are very private and personal to those that are corporate and institutional. Religious education research relates to the effect of religious education on persons and their response to it. Such research focuses on meanings and experiences, interpersonal and divine relationships, being and becoming, attitudes and beliefs, and practices and behaviors.

Research designed to examine the religious education endeavor of a religious body includes such factors as teaching and administrative skill development, settings and groupings, curriculum resource evaluation and utilization, physical facilities, and others.

Religious educators believe there are ultimate values and experiences that are of divine origin and that transcend normal educational achievements. Therefore, a distinctive characteristic of effective religious education is that persons of all ages are expected not only to learn about and appropriate the meanings and content of the faith, but also to experience it as a dynamic force affecting them in all their relationships.

Since the indicators for measuring and assessing the effect of any educational enterprise are determined by the objectives of that enterprise, it follows that the development of a clear and comprehensive statement of the above double-faceted objective of religious education is exceedingly important. A persistent task of religious education researchers is that of identifying goals and objectives that will be commonly accepted in the religious community and that at the same time lend themselves to the formulation of researchable hypotheses.

Most religious education research examines the data from one of three perspectives. A few studies may include some components from all three perspectives, but those are the exception rather than the rule. The usual practice is to examine the areas of investigation from essentially only one perspective.

PERSONAL PERSPECTIVE

The first perspective focuses on the personal and individual aspects of religious education. Some very noteworthy efforts have been made to identify specific personal dimensions or criteria of religious faith and commitment. In most instances three to nine discrete dimensions or criteria have been identified. What follows is a composite clustering of the dimensions or criteria most frequently cited.

One group of studies relates to the possession of basic knowledge and understandings about the Bible, history, biography, and basic moral principles. Another cluster of personal faith dimensions focuses on doctrinal beliefs about God, humankind, sin and salvation, the meaning of life and death, and the levels of commitment persons have made to them. A third cluster revolves around the spiritual disciplines and practices that the learner affirms and that are evident in related behavior. Values and attitudes about cultural, social, political, and religious issues constitute what religious educators consider to be a very significant fourth cluster of personal religious education concerns. A fifth area of investigation from the personal perspective is closely related to many of the focal points mentioned above but is a distinct area known as faith development.

Researchers who investigate personal and individual dimensions of religious education are frequently confronted with the difficult task of identifying and measuring some characteristics or qualities of the faith life that are private and subjective. Some critics believe that since God is the ultimate source of all religious experience and faith-motivated behavior, such experiences and behaviors are so very personal and private that they cannot be fully understood or measured with real objectivity. Furthermore, some who believe that God is actively present in the learning process feel that it is an act of supererogation for researchers to circumscribe the range of learnings, behaviors, and experiences that are found among the faithful.

RELATIONAL PERSPECTIVE

A second perspective from which religious education is examined is that of relationships. The basic tenet of the Judeo-Christian tradition is one of love—love for God, for others, and love for self. Consequently, even though the meanings and experiences of the faith life lie deep within each individual person, they cannot be fully understood or adequately examined apart from the whole field of relationships.

Although many studies related to different aspects of interpersonal relationships have been conducted, only a small number of them focus specifically on interpersonal relationships in religious education settings. Many of the findings from other studies of interpersonal relationships can be applied to religious education groups; nevertheless, religious educators believe that the essential nature of religious education groups and settings is such that a unique set of dynamics are operative in those groups and settings and they warrant special attention from the research community.

The dimensions that have been singled out cluster around three kinds of relational factors. The first cluster is made up of those factors related to group climate or atmosphere. It is difficult to measure this characteristic in specific terms, yet it can be sensed and does have an overriding effect on every religious education effort. Some indicators are friendliness, ease of conversation, openness to persons and ideas, and warmth and acceptance of all persons.

A second cluster of relational characteristics are those related to the perceived needs and expectations of those in the group. These determine to a large extent the group self-image; the types and styles of leadership and teaching that are effective; the relative importance that is attached to serious study, action projects, social events, and worship; and the relationship of the group to others.

A third cluster of relational characteristics revolves around the norms and life-style of the group. Included in this cluster are such things as verbal and nonverbal communication patterns, physical arrangements, facilities, how decisions are made, ways designated leaders and teachers are selected, and group traditions and customs.

ORGANIZATIONAL AND INSTITUTIONAL PERSPECTIVE

A third perspective of much research in religious education is related to organizational and institutional factors. The large amount of research in this area is undoubtedly due to readily accessible reports and records (most of which contain numerical data), the tendency to measure effectiveness and "success" by numbers, the impact of such research on policies and programming, and the ease with which organizationally based research can be reported and interpreted.

Organizational or institutional research in religious education can be grouped in five major clusters. The first and most common base for examining religious education from the organizational perspective is that of membership and attendance. Such data are readily available and lend themselves to rigorous statistical analyses that can be used to chart trends, distributions, projections, and the positive and negative effects of changes, membership, and attendance.

The second cluster of organizationally centered research is related to the organizing principles that underlie the various types of religious education efforts. Organizing principles determine the ways persons are distributed in different classes and groups, the kinds of curricula offered, and the types of groups, classes, and settings provided.

A third cluster of organizational factors often investigated are those that focus on leadership. Areas that have received considerable attention include assessment of leadership needs, and the recruitment, training, and supervision of leaders.

Operational and administrative factors constitute another cluster of concerns viewed from the organizational perspective. Included in this cluster are cost, schedules, pupil-teacher ratios, employment of professional religious educators, and physical resources and equipment.

A fifth group of organizational factors might be called environmental factors. These include such areas of study as demographic factors—economic, political, and social developments; shifts in public education sector; and the general mood and prevailing attitude of persons who may affect religious education endeavors.

USE IN RELIGIOUS EDUCATION

Probably more research has been conducted in the area of religious education than in any other area of church and synagogue life. The findings provide reliable information that is used by planners and practitioners who are responsible for administering and conducting religious education efforts locally as well as regionally and nationally. Research data inform editors and curriculum planners. Evaluation of programs, resources, and training events provides continuing guidance for those who design, develop, and reshape religious education programs and resources. Through research, knowledge about faith development is enhanced. Those who teach in academic institutions and those who write rely heavily on research for reliable and accurate information. Indeed, research provides the foundational bases for most of the cutting edges in religious education. *See also* Evaluation; Goals; Measurement; Methodology; Psychology of Religion; Social Sciences; Sociology of Religion; Statistics; Teaching Theory.

W. J. Hartman

Resource Person

Every religion teacher has need for resources to help support and extend the effective communication of the message of faith to others. These resources are both material supplies and the services of other people. Behind a material resource there is often a resource person who is prepared to assist the teacher in a special way. Hence, there

are as many different resource persons as there are needs for a variety of resources.

Not all situations require a resource person, but it is important to know who is available in a congregation. The use of resource persons has a double benefit—they gain the opportunity to contribute their talents to the religious education program part-time, and the program itself is enriched by their contributions.

The primary resources for every teacher are the student text and the teacher's manual that elaborates on the use of it, and there are almost certainly resource persons available to help teachers successfully utilize these primary resources. There is first the director of religious education, Sunday school superintendent, religious education committee, or other teachers responsible for selecting the course of study. The publishing companies that produce these resources also generally have personnel who are specialists in explaining and demonstrating possible creative uses of the material.

Most teacher's manuals list a wide range of supplemental resources to encourage enrichment by individual teachers. The religious education center's librarian can help teachers locate and use the materials. The librarian can also guide the teacher in using reference and other materials the library has available.

Another resource is the person who keeps class records and mimeographed references handy and posts events and other relevant information on bulletin boards. A secretary often performs these duties.

Other resource persons are the helpers who obtain and care for classroom equipment and arrange the room. They may order and distribute general classroom supplies that are kept in a central place. Others operate audiovisual equipment and keep it in good condition.

A variety of teaching techniques challenge a teacher to develop skills that stimulate pupil participation. In the process of planning lessons teachers must choose among visual and audiovisual aids, arts and crafts, music, song, drama, and other modern-day communication media, overwhelming to a teacher without the assistance of those who are proficient in these areas.

Besides the resource persons already mentioned there are, first of all, master teachers who are willing to demonstrate techniques proven effective over years of experience. They may be day school teachers willing to meet with and advise religious education teachers. Family members and friends of both teacher and pupils may help supply materials, share ideas, or assist in carrying out projects in which they have a special interest or ability. The students themselves can also be resource persons. Teachers can draw on their talents, experiences, and knowledge. They can be encouraged to collect and bring into class at scheduled times pictures, photos, records, or tape recordings. They can be given opportunities to report on specified radio, television, or video programs, or to share stories about travel, sports, and other life experiences—all with a view to analyzing them from the perspective of the religion curriculum.

Guest speakers are frequently used. They may be representatives of charitable or religious organizations or members of other civic groups. Judicatory offices or central agencies often furnish the names of persons whose services may be called upon at a minimal fee. Regional centers offer consulting services and help in the pooling of resources. Clergy can be particularly helpful because of their theological and ecclesial knowledge.

Finally, but not least important, as resource persons are church members. A listing that includes occupational data might reveal a number of persons who would be willing—even delighted—to share and volunteer their expertise on a topic with which they are familiar. Such persons will be known informally within the congregation.

We are living in an age when the power of mass media as channels of communication has the potential of shaping character and building community or of destroying it. There are a number of suppliers for media resources, but teachers also need someone who can evaluate quality with reference to the intended use and help them understand how to use these resources effectively. *See also* Resources and Resource Centers.

M. Timmerman

Resources and Resource Centers

The needs of a contemporary church school for resources far exceeds the old-time Sunday school library that consisted of a collection of storybooks for children. Today's church educator requires not only books on many subjects for all ages, but also nonprint media and consultants who can assist in planning for their use. There are at least three places to which church educators should be able to turn to help meet these needs: the local church library, the local church resource center, and regional resource centers, both denominational and ecumenical.

THE CHURCH LIBRARY

Major responsibility for administering the church library generally lies with a library committee that is accountable to the religious education committee or some other administrative structure of the church. Library committee members should recognize the importance of the library in the educational program of the church, and they should be knowledgeable about the educational program as a whole, including the curriculum resources being used in all church school classes.

A major task of the library committee is to establish the policies under which the library operates. Church librarians are usually volunteers who must be recruited and taught the necessary library skills. Criteria must be developed for the selection and purchase of books. Procedures must be established and enforced.

The collection of a modern church library includes a wide variety of printed materials. Of primary interest are those books needed to supplement the curriculum resources approved by the religious education committee. These books may be checked out by the teacher for use in the room for the duration of a unit or made available for general circulation.

One important aspect of a leadership development plan for a local church is the library collection of books especially for teachers. These should include books on teaching methodology and age-group characteristics.

Crucial for both teachers and students are the reference books such as concordances, atlases, commentaries, Bible dictionaries, and word books and current religious periodicals. Some church libraries also include a section of religious and other relevant contemporary fiction.

Although books are expensive, there are several possible ways to secure funds for library acquisitions. The best approach is to include the library in the church or church school budget. Gifts of money for book selection and purchase by the library committee may be made by individuals or groups within the church. Purchases of books themselves should be made from a list of approved books provided by the library committee.

From time to time churches receive "gift libraries" from individuals, families, or estates. While these often contain valuable and useful volumes, care must be taken to ascertain in advance the donors' wishes concerning the books that the library cannot use. If the library is to be patronized it must be seen to be both attractive and useful. The library collection must be kept up to date by regular and judicious elimination of books no longer appropriate. A policy that keeps to a minimum the giving of specific books as memorials makes the discarding of ancient volumes less difficult.

Some method of cataloging and circulating the collection is necessary, regardless of the size of the library. The less complicated the cataloging system, the better, since a complicated system will produce a backlog of uncataloged materials and will be difficult for library patrons to use. A card catalog is necessary for knowing what volumes the library holds, as well as for ease in locating the books themselves. However, since many people choose books by browsing, books should be shelved by both age level and subject. While some church libraries always have a person available for checking out books, others use the "honor system," letting users sign out their own books, al-

THE CHURCH RESOURCE CENTER

audiovisual equipment
for classroom use

consumable
teaching supplies

rolling table

Storage Area for Teachers' Supplies

shelves

shelves

audiovisual resources

teachers' resources

audiovisual equipment

computers

children's books

librarian's
desk

card
catalog

children's
table
and
chairs

table
and
chairs
for
adults

general books

beanbag
chairs

return
book
bin

Library

The church resource center above doubles as both the church library and teachers' resource center. The floor area of the library portion is 400 square feet (20 × 20), and there are 100 square feet of additional storage space in back.

though users should never reshelve their returned books.

Frequent library use is encouraged when the church library is located close to an entrance with easy access and is open at times other than Sunday morning.

AN EXPANDED CHURCH LIBRARY

Modern libraries are no longer limited to print media but have expanded to include videotapes, filmstrips, slides, films, audiocassettes, records, computer disks, as well as flat pictures. The church library may also contain the equipment necessary for use of nonprint media, including projectors, record players, and computers. A decision needs to be made about whether access to these materials will be limited to teachers, or be offered to children and other adults. In addition to its other responsibilities, the library committee must also provide for maintenance of the required equipment and training of persons authorized to use it.

THE CHURCH RESOURCE CENTER

A library contains a collection of resources that may be borrowed and returned. A resource center includes, in addition, supplies that are to be consumed: paper, paste, scissors, paints, and masking tape, for example. It is a common practice to combine the "expanded library" and the room for supplies and call this the church resource center. This center is staffed with consultants who know what resources are available and who are skilled in assisting teachers' planning. The resource center should be located so as to be easily accessible to church schoolteachers both during the week and during the church school sessions.

REGIONAL RESOURCE CENTERS

A growing trend has been the establishment of regional resource centers, similar to the local church resource center but much more extensive. These centers combine many features found in the local church resource center and add others: an extensive library, audiovisual resources and equipment, workrooms where art-and-craft activities may be learned and practiced, lectures and workshops by prominent religious educators, curricula—all under the supervision of a staff of professional religious educators.

One such regional resource center, sponsored by four denominations, contains three thousand books, plus records, tapes, filmstrips, and curricula on a variety of subjects, including Bible, beliefs, worship, hunger, peace, justice, and the aging. Another nationally known resource center serves 240 churches from eighteen denominations and has 500–1,000 users each month. While most regional resource centers put major emphasis on religious education, many seek to be resources in other areas as well: such as liturgy, church music,

and leadership development for the total life of the church. The growth of regional resource centers is a phenomenon of the 1980s that has potential for dramatically changing the way in which local church schools do curriculum planning and provide skill training for teachers. *See also* Resource Person.

FOR FURTHER REFERENCE

Hammack, Mary L. *How to Organize Your Church Library and Resource Center.* Valley Forge, PA: Judson Press, 1985.
Smith, Ruth S. *Running a Library: Managing the Congregation's Library with Care, Confidence, and Common Sense.* New York: Seabury Press, 1982.

D. J. Furnish

Resurrection

Resurrection is the rising to life from death. The concept derives from Jewish apocalyptic writings (third century B.C.–second century A.D.) in which the faithful elect were believed destined to be raised from death at the end of the ages (cf. Dan. 12:2).

JESUS OF NAZARETH

That Jesus died, was buried, and was raised to life is a fundamental affirmation of Christian tradition in continuity with Jewish apocalyptic hopes. This affirmation, according to the earliest testimonies found in the New Testament, always centered, however, not on modern-day questions—on what actually happened on the fateful day in question in the tomb (the historical facts), or on how such an event could have occurred (the phenomenological problem), but on the actual testimonies of those who were convinced that the Jesus whom they had known and who had died and been buried in a tomb was alive. Such testimonies were based on eyewitness accounts of postresurrection appearances.

The earliest references to the resurrection of Jesus of Nazareth from the dead do not derive from one who had known him personally. In a pastoral letter to the Corinthian church written about A.D. 55, the apostle Paul provides the earliest extant written reference to the death and resurrection of Jesus (1 Cor. 15:3–7). There is consensus among New Testament scholars that this reference is primarily the quoting of a Christian liturgical and/or creedal formula that is older than the letter it is preserved in. (This of course also means that it is even older—by twenty to forty years—than the resurrection narratives in the canonical Gospels.) What this formula as the earliest extant statement about the resurrection of Jesus indicates is that early emphasis was placed upon the appearances of Jesus to his followers. There is no mention of the empty tomb or any other historical data that would normally be deemed important in establishing the historicity of an event. What was most important at the earliest stage of reflection upon the death and resurrection was the corroboration of testimonies from followers of Jesus that they had seen alive the Jesus whom they had known to have died.

Paul is also important because he is one of those followers who makes the claim that Jesus appeared to him, and so with him we have direct testimony about and reflection upon the experience. At the end of the quoted formula in 1 Corinthians 15 Paul includes himself as one of those followers to whom Jesus made an appearance (v. 8). In this passage, along with Galatians 1:15–16, 1 Corinthians 9:1–2, and Philippians 3:7–11, Paul provides us with the only extant direct eyewitness account of a postresurrection appearance of Jesus. Again, these references make it clear that at the earliest stage in the traditions about the resurrection of Jesus what seemed to be of importance in terms of evidence were the appearances or the appearance accounts.

The canonical Gospels (except the genuine text of Mark) preserve the tradition of attaching importance to Jesus' appearances to his followers in the form of extended narratives (Matt. 28:16–20; Luke 24:13–53; John 20:19–30; 21:1–23 = redactor). But what also assumes importance at this stage in the development of the tradition is the reference to Jesus' body missing from the tomb (cf. Matt. 28:1–10; Mark 16:1–8; Luke 24:1–12; John 20:1–9). Mary Magdalene and the other women are the important witnesses for the empty tomb reference. Alone this testimony did not establish the resurrection of Jesus; it only aroused suspicions (cf. Matt. 28:13). It was likely that such testimony became important alongside the stories of the appearances not in order to relate "what really happened," but to make the connection between the earthly Jesus of Nazareth whose death and burial had been witnessed (Mark 15:47) and the resurrected Jesus. Thus, what was being claimed about the appearances of Jesus was that they were more than spiritual intuition or psychological insight; they were appearances of the Jesus who had died but was not in the tomb.

That a narration of the facts, of "what really happened," was not of concern to the earliest Christians is indicated by the confused and conflicting details of the testimonies in the New Testament. Chronological distance from the time of the event is not an adequate explanation; it is clear that both Paul's reflections upon Jesus' appearances to him and the Gospel writers' narratives of appearances and the empty tomb are controlled by theological motives. The belief that Jesus of Nazareth was alive was not the clear belief statement that explained everything about Jesus; it was rather the inspiration for imagining and realizing new things—a new community, self-understanding, destiny, and missionary activity.

TEACHING THE RESURRECTION

Teaching about the resurrection includes biblical, theological, and ecclesial factors. The church has been called an Easter community. Every Sunday is a little Easter and always a day of the celebration of the resurrection because it comes on the first day of the week.

In traditions where Easter is celebrated as a season, the New Testament accounts are read on successive Sundays and Easter hymns sung during that seven-week period. The affirmation of the resurrection is repeated in the creed and in the eucharistic response: "Christ has died, Christ is risen, Christ will come again." Liturgy teaches all participants through the weekly repetition of words and actions.

In religious education classes preschool children hear the Easter story in their lesson on that day. Preschoolers do not usually ask for explanations, so in the telling teachers need to focus on conveying the sense of wonder and joy that the first witnesses experienced. Easter hymns echo the feelings.

School-age children will need to hear the story of the crucifixion and of the resurrection in related sessions so they can grasp the fact that both were necessary: suffering came before joy. The obedience of the cross was fulfilled in the affirmation of the resurrection. Interpretations will vary, but the two events need to be seen together. All the biblical stories of resurrection experiences need to be told including Paul's, so that children can begin to understand how the Christian community grew from the belief in Christ's resurrection.

Adolescents and adults, familiar with the resurrection accounts, may have questions about historicity (place, time, manner) for which the Bible does not give answers. These groups can compare and study the New Testament accounts. They can trace what the resurrection has meant for the church since its beginning through studies in the book of Acts, where it is the keystone of the preaching of the apostles, and passages in the Letters of Paul such as 1 Corinthians 15:14. Further study will indicate the effect belief in the resurrection has had on conversions, the lives of believers, and the life of the whole church. *See also* Easter; Jesus Christ.

V. L. Wimbush

Retardation

See Exceptional Persons.

Retreat

A retreat is a time of withdrawal from normal everyday activity for the sake of inner refreshment, clarity, and discernment with regard to one's religious commitment. The Christian life, as classically understood, presupposes a rhythm of withdrawal from and engagement in the affairs of the world. Fullness of life requires the maintenance of such a rhythm if the believer is to avoid two deadly traps of the spiritual life. The first trap is the attraction of a life of activity that is either mindless or simply in the service of the ego. The second is the lure of a spiritual laziness or passivity masquerading as "faithfulness." Really knowing what one is up to takes a great deal of wisdom, testing, and rest.

A retreat, therefore, has a double purpose: rest and struggle. Two important scriptural models point to this double purpose. The first is found in Genesis, where God rested on the seventh day after the six days of creation (Gen. 2:3). Another name for this refreshing rest is Sabbath time. The observance of the Sabbath, though much misunderstood, is a weekly retreat for the sake of personal and communal renewal. The second purpose of a retreat is to provide an opportunity for inner struggle for the sake of clarity of commitment and vocation. Jesus was driven by the Holy Spirit into the wilderness to be tempted (Matt. 4:1–11). A retreat can, therefore, be a time of crisis as well as rest.

It is a pity that the word "retreat" is used loosely today to mean any kind of time out from our usual routine in order to be refreshed. Parish workshops and weekend conferences are often mistakenly referred to as retreats. While such things are good of themselves, the word "retreat" describes a quite different activity. A retreat in the traditional sense of the word is a time away in silence. It is "time in the desert" alone or with others. The point of a retreat can be summed up in one of the sayings of the desert fathers: "Go, sit in your cell and your cell will teach you everything." Silence is hard for many people today and a retreat is often punctuated by addresses or meditations from a leader. Nevertheless, silence is the most important ingredient of this time away. The retreat leader is usually available for counsel or confession and can often be helpful to someone going through a time of crisis.

Retreats can be as short as one day (often called a "Quiet Day") or as long as many weeks. The most common length is three days and normally this is the minimum time required for a person to derive any benefit. We need a day to get into the spirit of a retreat and come to a place of inner silence. Retreats based on the *Spiritual Exercises* of Ignatius of Loyola lasting eight or thirty days have become very popular and are offered in various centers all over the world.

It would be a mistake to define a retreat too rigidly, provided that its double purpose of rest and struggle is observed and silence is at its heart. Retreats take on many forms today and are shaped by many traditions. The setting can vary from a quiet place in the country to a house in the city. Many monastic houses offer hospitality for people seeking a retreat, and retreat centers are often found in Christian or Zen monasteries and other religious centers.

The Protestant denominations are coming to value a silent retreat, which hitherto has been almost exclusively found in the Roman Catholic, Anglican, Orthodox, Buddhist, and other non-Christian traditions. Retreats are becoming more and more important in the lives of men and women in an age of high stress and deep insecurity.

There are two dangers in people's attraction to retreats. The first is the trivializing of a retreat to serve a narrowly psychological end. A proper retreat is to be grounded in a particular tradition or discipline. The second danger lies in a retreat becoming an escape route from responsibility. It is seen as an opportunity to "tune out" of a difficult and sometimes hostile world. That, however, would be to misuse the purpose of a retreat, which is for deeper engagement with life's opportunities and responsibilities by means of "sitting quietly in one's cell." War and conflict begin in the human heart and the human heart is where the peace of the world also begins. The opportunity for genuine and long-lasting spiritual renewal through the agency of the retreat movement cannot be overemphasized. *See also* Ignatius of Loyola; Meditation, Forms of; Prayer; Spiritual Direction; Spirituality.

A. W. Jones

Revelation

In most of the religions of the world, revelation refers to the deity's self-disclosure or communication with humankind or, from the other perspective, to humankind's elevation and empowerment through its reception of the knowledge of things beyond its realm and capacity to control and understand with reason alone. The religious communions of the world differ not in their basic claims about what is involved and at stake in this phenomenon, but in their translations of the context of the disclosure or communication and in claims regarding the media through which divine communication is effected.

The Judeo-Christian tradition is distinguished by its translations of various Hebrew and Greek terms in the Bible originally connoting the act of "uncovering," "revealing," or "disclosing."

Where the matter pertains to fundamental and ultimate truths, God is always seen as the actor, the one taking the initiative. God's initiatives are also always seen as expressions of love for humankind, even when the content of the communication is judgment.

DISCLOSURE AND DISCERNMENT

The self-disclosure and truths of the God of the Judeo-Christian tradition are thought to be communicated through different media. The Bible records God's communication through prophets, seers, special anointed individuals, angelic intermediaries, the creation, historical events, and, for Christians, Jesus of Nazareth. And as the record of God's various initiatives in communicating with humankind (the chosen people and the church), the Bible understood as Holy Scripture is itself a medium through which God communicates.

The variety of types of agencies and modes through which God's self-disclosure is effected is both suggestive and problematic. It suggests that different media and agencies were required for communication with different peoples, with different generations at different times and in different places, perhaps on account of the different translations of the disclosures. It also suggests a hierarchy of disclosures and points to the problem of the recognition and evaluation of disclosures that are claimed to be divine. Without recognition of the problem inherent in the variety of agencies and media of divine disclosures there can be no clarity about what God communicates.

The Jewish and Christian response to the problem over a considerable period of time was, first, to develop and preserve the writings that recorded the types of God's self-disclosures and their agencies. Second, over an even longer period of time were developed interpretive principles by which some writings, as types of disclosures, could be experienced as true and articulate reflectors (canonical Scriptures) of the ways in which God communicates. This complex selection process implied an understanding of disclosure that goes beyond recognition and acceptance of various media and agencies, insofar as the latter can be separated from the content of disclosure. What was already at work in the preservation and selection process of God's self-disclosures was a notion about what God discloses. The Jewish canon indicates an understanding of the unique, loving, sovereign God who demands radical allegiance and obedience from humankind. God's demands and character are reflected through multiple agencies, which are collectively experienced as history. All other disclosures are judged against this notion. The Christian canon shows an understanding of the same God, but now God's demands and character are most clearly reflected in the historical person of Jesus of Nazareth. All other disclosures are judged against this person.

The process of coming to recognize the parameters within which God has been communicating within the two traditions led to the codification of the communication itself. In Christian theology especially, but also in some circles within Judaism, it became important to isolate and make claims to authority to recognize true and false interpretations of the distinct features and content of God's disclosures. So not only was a canon required, but in both the Jewish and Christian religions beginning in different periods of their histories creedal formulations and theological arguments and theologians were seen as necessary in order to make explicit the content of God's disclosures. The problematic effect this shift toward a narrowing of the understanding of the possibilities for God's disclosure has had is now part of cultural history: it has ranged from the artificial dichotomy between reason and faith (as the content of revelation) to the actual attempt to limit the range of possibilities—in terms of media, agencies, and content—for God's disclosures. The challenge must be to avoid the frustration of God's communication by circumscribing it in terms of media, agencies, or content in absolute codes.

TEACHING METHODS

This challenge comes to religious education teachers. When they understand the Bible to be the primary medium for God's self-disclosure, the content of the Bible will be basic to their teaching. The purpose is to show through biblical stories and teachings how God and God's purposes are being revealed.

Simple stories and biblical verses can be used for teaching young children. The continued biblical story and other passages can be used with older children for retelling and discussion. From the seventh grade through adolescence the idea of revelation as God's self-disclosure can be explored in the context of the understanding of who God is and how God acts. The teachings of the prophets, the meanings of the gospel, and the story of the community of Israel and of the early church (the book of Acts) become seen as media of revelation. Adults are able to encompass the sweep of history in the Bible, separating the various forms the revelation takes and exploring their significance for today's world.

This broadening of the scope of the teaching about revelation points to the idea that God's revelation in the Bible is seen as action: in the covenant community of Israel, in Jesus, and in the community of the church. This raises for adult students the question of whether God's self-disclosure in history ended with biblical events or if revelation may still be seen today, both in individual lives and in nations. It invites exploration of the idea of the prophet as one who discloses God's word and the uses of prophecy today in some religious groups.

Jesus as the self-disclosure of God is taught in children's stories of Jesus in which the love and mercy of God are portrayed. It is taught for older children, adolescents, and adults with reference to the Passion and resurrection as a unique way by which God, through Jesus, participated in and overcame sin, suffering, and evil in the world.

The revelation of God in all creation is learned by young children in stories and experiences through which they are alerted to their enjoyment of the natural world and connect this with thanksgiving to God, the giver of all life. Older children begin to puzzle about "natural" events that cause widespread destruction. Some are recognized today as the result of human activity, but others, such as tornadoes, are perplexing evidence that not all of nature reveals the goodness of God and that God's care is shown through the strength given to surmount natural events.

Adolescents and adults will want to explore the idea of "natural revelation"; that is, God is self-revealed to all people in some way through the world in which they live and not only in the specific forms of religious tradition. The interaction of these two modes of God's self-disclosure is subject for serious deliberation. *See also* Bible in Religious Education, The; Biblical Authority; Doctrine/Dogma; God, Understandings of; Knowledge, Theories of; Theodicy.

FOR FURTHER REFERENCE

Jeske, Richard L. *Revelation for Today: Images of Hope.* Philadelphia: Fortress, 1983.

Pannenberg, Wolfhart, ed. *Revelation as History.* Translated by David Granskou. New York: Macmillan, 1968.

Schillebeeckx, Edward, ed. *Revelation and Experience.* New York: Seabury, 1979.

Thiemann, Ronald F. *Revelation and Theology: The Gospel as Narrated Promise.* Notre Dame, IN: University of Notre Dame Press, 1985.

V. L. Wimbush

Rogers, Carl

Carl Ransom Rogers (1902–1987), clinical psychologist, is noted for his client-centered approach to therapy, which has implications for education as well as for treatment. Born in Oak Park, Illinois, he attended the University of Wisconsin and earned graduate degrees at Columbia University. Professor of clinical psychology at Ohio State University (1940–1945), he later served as professor of psychology and executive secretary of the counseling center at the University of Chicago (1945–1947). He was professor of psychology and psychiatry at the University of Wisconsin

(1957–1963) and resident fellow, Western Behavioral Sciences Institute, La Jolla, California (1964–1969). Until his retirement, he was with the Center for Studies of the Person at La Jolla.

In therapy Rogers's emphasis is on permitting the client the initiative; the therapist does not analyze or direct but maintains an attitude of unconditional positive regard and responds only to affirm or question. *Client-Centered Therapy* (1951) and *Becoming a Person* (1961) give the basics of his therapeutic model. His approach to education in which the teacher is guide to student exploration, is outlined in *Freedom to Learn* (1969) and *Freedom to Learn in the 1980s* (1983). It is a pragmatic approach in which the student's own insights are affirmed and encouragement given to continual exploration. *See also* Affective Development; Counseling; Learning Theory.

L. G. McAllister

Role Model

An individual who serves as a pattern of behavior for another individual or a group in relation to one or more of the social roles carried by that person or group is called a role model. There are two aspects to this phenomenon, the "model" about which a great deal of theory has been built and the "role," which also has a considerable body of literature, often referred to as role theory. The role is an important aspect of administration and leadership development. Although some work has been done in religious education with respect to role theory and administration, most uses of the term have centered around the various roles persons assume in the educational situation, on the one hand, and certain individuals in history who may serve as models for living, on the other.

The word "role" is adapted from the vocabulary of the theater, and it is used by sociologists to denote the part or pattern of behavior one is expected to play in social interaction. The term is used with two meanings. One meaning relates to the way persons respond to social situations; the other consists of a set of expectations and ways of behaving associated with a specific position in a social system. The first is called an individual or an interpersonal role; the second is called a social role. It is this latter meaning that is usually intended when one speaks of a "role model"; that is, the role model provides a set of expectations and ways of behaving.

The term "model" also connotes a pattern for behavior when referring to a role model. However, there are many usages of the term in both the natural and behavioral sciences, as well as in philosophy and religion. Ian Barbour points out that there are a number of different kinds of models in science and there are also a number of types of models in religion (*Myths, Models, and Paradigms*, 1974), but his own work is related primarily to models in relation to language. Marc Belth (*Education as a Discipline*, 1965) distinguishes types of models as found in the educative process, and he uses this discussion of models as a framework for examining the discipline of education. In religious education, the use of role model is more sociological in nature, denoting a pattern of behavior expected in a social situation. The pattern may cover the total behavior and various roles of an individual, or it may be limited to one role.

Although the role model is assumed to be a person to be followed, it should be noted that individuals choose particular models, even negative ones. Moreover, following a role model does not mean achieving what the role model accomplished. The desire, even intention, to do so can cause guilt and disillusionment. The person who seeks to follow a model will need to choose elements in that life that are helpful and be willing to forgo complete identification. Modeling and identification are not the same, although there may be common elements. The role model, wisely considered, can be an encouragement, strengthening a life purpose.

There are many live role models in religious education, not to mention historical ones. Ministers, priests, rabbis, nuns or monks, teachers, parents, leading laypersons, choir directors, missionaries, directors of religious education, and other staff members—all may provide role models around whom members of a congregation, adults as well as children, pattern their behavior. Important role models are drawn from history—the apostle Paul, Francis of Assisi, Martin Luther, Moses, Maimonides, Mohammed, the Buddha, Swami Prabhupada.

In the Christian religion, Jesus Christ has been the prime role model, both as a total pattern for living and as teacher or preacher. The range of interpretations of Jesus' life in social interaction is wide—hymn writers sing of "Gentle Jesus, Meek and Mild" and "Jesus Thou Divine Compassion" while liberation theologians interpret his radical call to social justice.

Jesus is considered the Master Teacher. Much has been written on his use of parables, allegories, metaphors, and similes; his informal approach to teaching in whatever setting persons were gathered; his concentration on the small group, his twelve disciples; and his teaching by actions.

Jesus is the role model for the preacher, but his roles as healer, exorciser, and servant are less popular, though they have emerged from time to time as important patterns for Christian leaders. In the contemporary situation Jesus' role as champion of social justice has become pivotal in the new theologies that have arisen among minority groups and Third World countries. Liberation theology, black theology, feminist theology—all emphasize those sections in the Gospels in which Jesus shows concern for the poor and needy, sets prisoners free, heals the sick, and "sets at liberty those who are oppressed." In each case, the theologians have related the role of Jesus to the peculiar experience of the group.

Perhaps in no other faith has a religious leader been associated with the term "role model" as has Jesus Christ in Christianity, but it should be pointed out that the compassionate Buddha has been the ultimate portrayal of the Enlightenment from the beginning of Buddhism, and other leaders like Mohammed have been the examples held up to followers throughout the years. As educators in other religions develop the theoretical foundations of religious education, it is likely that the term "role model" will be used as widely to describe founders and other great leaders as is now current in Christianity. *See also* Identification; Mentor.

N. H. Thompson

Role Playing

Role playing is the acting out of the behavior of one or more characters in a specific situation. The situation is often one in which conflict is experienced. The purpose of the role play is to help the participants understand the situation and/or the people involved in it through the experiencing of feelings; the emphasis is on the individual and what is learned from one's reactions in a particular situation. Role plays are spontaneous, improvisational, and brief. They consist of dialogue and movement. They often lack plots and props, unlike some other forms of dramatization.

Role playing can be used as a technique for helping persons express their own feelings. It is therefore helpful in religious education when there are conflicts within a class or other kind of group. It is also of use when studying topics dealing with emotional and moral issues, such as cheating, sexuality, death, loneliness, etc. In these kinds of situations, a person or several persons can be asked to spontaneously and briefly act out the characters involved in the conflict or dilemma. A deeper experience can sometimes happen if the actors are then asked to switch roles. In the ensuing discussion, the actors can share the feelings they experienced as they acted. Possible solutions can be studied.

The role play is also a method to help people understand feelings, situations, and roles different from those with which they are familiar. A teenager can begin to understand a parent by playing the parent role in a conflict situation. A North American can gain insight into an Asian culture by acting the role of an Asian. A contemporary student can start identifying with a historical matriarch or patriarch, such as Ruth or Moses, by acting the part of one in a chosen situation. In this type of role play, it is important to provide the actors with accurate information about the characters and the situation they are attempting to portray.

Role playing can also be a tool for teaching information in an interesting manner. Teachers can provide information about persons or situations and students can discuss how the roles should be played, or students can research the parts themselves. Thus they can learn facts as well as experience the attitudes, values, and beliefs of the people they are playing. This kind of experiential learning will be remembered far longer than learning merely presented through hearing or reading.

Role playing is also a way to teach new, more appropriate behavior, behavior expected in the community of faith. Students can be asked to act out a situation as they normally experience it, for example, that of a parent with a misbehaving child. The teacher can then enter the role play with the more appropriate behavior. The students reenact the situation once more, with the new behavior. A discussion should follow, in which the reactions of the participants are expressed, and the new behavior explained. This kind of modeling can be more effective than telling students how to behave.

It is important that role play be well prepared as an integral part of the lesson plan. The characters must be briefly but fully described for each actor. Often one actor will not be told what the other character is planning to do. The situation, including time, place, and problem or issue, is usually described to all the participants, including the observers. The results can be informative and humorous.

A role play should not be allowed to go on too long. It should be stopped by the teacher before it becomes a futile argument or wanders off the subject. It is important to have an immediate debriefing. The actors can be invited to share the feelings they had as they played their parts. The observers can then share their impressions. If the role play deals with current conflict, the group can use these feelings as data to help them in their search for resolution. If the role play deals with a historical situation, students can hypothesize about how the situation was actually resolved. They can contribute their opinions of what they feel they would have done in that situation. Many opinions and resolutions may surface. Students will have learned that their opinions are important and that they are not alone in their anxieties. They will have experienced themselves as members of a faith community. *See also* Dramatization; Identification; Simulation; Sociodrama.

FOR FURTHER REFERENCE

Johnson, Bev. *Drama in the Church*. Minneapolis, MN: Augsburg, 1983.

Schaupp, Jack. *Creating and Playing Games*. Nashville, TN: Abingdon, 1978.

C. E. Blair

Roman Catholic Education (USA)

Roman Catholic education is diverse. Coming to the United States from European backgrounds, it has adapted itself both to the culture and the needs of its people. Three comments will establish a context. First, education in the United States is primarily a state and local responsibility, not a federal one. This fact explains some of the diversity that is part of the U.S. Catholic response to the secular and religious education of its members. Second, two fundamental questions underlie this diversity: How should the Catholic religious vision relate to the culture in which it finds itself, and what are the implications of the answer for the Church's educational mission, a mission that involves creating educational contexts within which a synthesis occurs between culture and religious vision? Third, elementary and secondary schools are a significant part of the U.S. Catholic educational story; nevertheless, there are and have been other agencies that educate Catholics. Though most of this discussion focuses on schools, reference is made to a wider network. U.S. Catholics today number about 78,991,000; the worldwide Roman Catholic population numbers about 926,194,600.

BACKGROUND

The story begins in the late sixteenth century with European Catholic settlements in the borderlands of what later became the United States. Spanish and French mission colonies had little concern for formal schooling. Education was directed to "civilizing and Christianizing" native inhabitants. Later, in the English Atlantic seaboard colonies, though Protestant denominational schools existed, in contrast, the Catholic effort to found schools was sporadic.

Prior to mass European immigration, roughly from 1790 to 1830, the Catholic church was small compared to other denominations. It had few clergy and relied on books for religious guidance and inspiration. Major responsibility for religious and secular education rested with the family. John Carroll, chosen the first U.S. Catholic bishop in 1784, spoke strongly about the family's educational role in one of his first pastoral letters. The 1829 U.S. bishop's pastoral letter echoed this theme. Complementing it was the notion of the woman as moral guardian of the family and chief domestic educator.

The institutional church engaged in some educational activities, at the core of which were preaching, parish missions or revivals, and the Sunday school or catechism class, the catechism itself, as a basic formulation of the faith, being the content. After 1810 Catholic newspapers appeared. In addition, religious and doctrinal books, catechisms, and pamphlets circulated.

Three types of schools existed. The first, for boys and girls of the parish, were diverse structurally and more integrated into the local community than in later times. The line between public and private schools was not well defined. For example, some Catholic schools received financial support from the local government, true in New York City until 1825. The core of elementary education was "reading, writing, arithmetik, and Catechism," with moral and religious training the central purpose of the school.

Another type of school was the women's academy, appearing in the early nineteenth century. Key to establishing these was the availability of women religious, who later became the primary means of staffing schools. Third were men's colleges, the most important schools during this period in the opinion of the bishops. They were vehicles for recruiting and training men for the priesthood. Academies and colleges were mixed institutions with various grade levels, young and old, Protestant and Catholic, boarding and day students.

Catholic higher education had its origins during this period. In 1785, John Carroll proposed that an academy be opened to provide boys with a basic seminary education. This led to the founding of Georgetown College (later University) in 1789, primarily for theological students. Carroll's idea was that the primary form of Catholic higher education was to be theological. Other Catholic students and teachers could attend existing non-Catholic colleges. In 1790 he reached an agreement with the Sulpician Fathers to open a seminary for students from Georgetown. He then began to stress Georgetown's character as a preparatory school rather than a seminary, a distinction that gradually developed into the idea that the secondary schools could prepare students for a higher education that was not exclusively theological.

DEVELOPMENT

The century of immigration began in the 1820s and extends to about 1920. This immigration transformed the U.S. church, increasing its population from roughly 318,000 in 1830 to almost 18 million in 1920 and creating a new context for the church's educational work.

In addition to preaching, parish revivals, Sunday schools, and parish schools, other educational agencies arose: the parish library and reading circles, the devotional society, men's and women's benevolent organizations, summer schools. All formed a loose collection of institutions whose purpose was to foster intellectual and religious growth.

During the nineteenth century, though, the parish school became the church's principal educational institution. Changes occurred in the general world of education that influenced Catholic education. The most significant was the growth of common public schools serving children in a geographic area. Rooted in a Protestant context with little tolerance for Catholicism, these schools were part of one of the reform movements occurring during the pre-Civil War period. By 1860, local and state supported public education for elementary schoolchildren was generally accepted. This movement combined with other strong anti-Catholic sentiments to create an impetus for the rapid growth of Catholic schools.

As mentioned earlier, Catholic schools did exist prior to this time but not on a massive scale. In the 1830s and 1840s Catholic leaders were ambivalent, one group promoting Catholic schools, others seeking a compromise with local public schools.

As local and state supported public education grew in the 1850s and 1860s, so did the establishment of parish schools. In 1852, the First Plenary Council of Baltimore urged the foundation of parish schools. The second in 1866 issued a similar statement. The third, meeting in 1884, had a vigorous debate on the issue that split the bishops into bitterly opposing factions. A majority approved legislation that focused on the importance of establishing schools in *every* parish and the obligation of pastors, people, and parents to support these schools.

By the end of the nineteenth century, having a parish school was the norm for a majority of the bishops, but not for every immigrant group. For example, the Germans, French Canadians, and Poles were strong advocates, with the Italians and Mexicans much less so. In fact, only 35 percent of U.S. parishes supported a school by 1920.

The same trends toward centralization, professionalization, and specialization affecting public schools in the late nineteenth and twentieth centuries also influenced Catholic schools. These led to a more systematic organization of schools at the diocesan and national levels, though they would retain more autonomy and never be as "system-oriented" as public schools. An example of this movement to organize nationally is the 1904 merger of several existing organizations to form the Catholic Educational Association.

In the first two decades of the twentieth century, the public high school became a more distinct institution, though high schools had emerged early in the mid-nineteenth century. Catholics were slower to organize these, with the first central high school established in 1890 in Philadelphia. The private academy as the context for secondary education inhibited the growth of Catholic high schools. Not until a clear differentiation between collegiate and secondary education occurred in the early 1900s did high schools begin to exist more generally.

Another educational agency was the Confraternity of Christian Doctrine (CCD), responsible for providing religious education to students not enrolled in Catholic schools. Old in origin, the modern version dates from 1905 when Pope Pius X directed that CCD programs be established in every parish. It was an after-school program taught by parish school teachers; the original content was the catechism. This catechetical movement supported vacation schools, discussion clubs, and other activities, as well.

During this period, Catholic higher education was also undergoing changes. A Catholic layman, Orestes Brownson, was the most influential exponent of the idea that Catholic colleges should abandon seminary connections, and become centers of higher learning. Yet by the end of the nineteenth century, few of the two hundred men's colleges (including Catholic University, established in 1884) were without seminary affiliation. The first women's college, the College of Notre Dame, was founded in Baltimore in 1896. Today there are 235 Catholic colleges and universities.

Training for the priesthood today is provided in graduate institutions that may or may not be located on the campus of a college or university. Some are staffed by orders; others are diocesan institutions. Some include graduate theological programs (Ph.D.) in addition to basic preparation for parish clergy (M.Div.), and most are members of the Association of Theological Schools.

PRESENT SITUATION

The immigrant church developed a devotional style that was at its peak for thirty years after World War I, fostered by a variety of institutions and activities, including the popular devotion to Mary supported by a ritual form called the novena

and the Marian sodality movement directed to high school students. Youth organizations multiplied; parish missions continued to be popular; and retreats became a major new form of religious education. All were supported by religious magazines, books, radio programs, and national publicity campaigns.

The 1930s and 1940s also saw the growth of the U.S. liturgical movement. Rather than emphasizing the private dimension of religion, it fostered community and the public quality of religion. This emphasis on the public influenced the organization renamed the National Catholic Welfare Conference in 1922. It became an important educational agency promoting social action and the reform of society. This orientation led to the foundation of many activist lay groups, including Catholic Action, the Christian Family Movement, and the Catholic Workers Movement.

Through it all, the school remained the center of the Catholic educational network. But a crisis occurred in 1922 when Oregon passed a law requiring almost all eight- to sixteen-year-old children to attend public schools. In 1925, the U.S. Supreme Court in *Pierce v. Society of the Sisters* ruled that no state could mandate attendance at public schools. *Pierce* was a major victory for Catholic school advocates.

During the next forty years, enrollment in Catholic schools grew, as did the number of schools. By 1959, about 59 percent of Catholic parishes had elementary schools serving about half of Catholic elementary schoolchildren. Moves were made toward accreditation, testing, and certification of teachers. Though a substantial majority of elementary schools continued to be parish schools, high schools were of three types: religious order, diocesan, and single or interparish. Enrollment peaked in 1965 when approximately 4.5 million elementary students and 1.1 million secondary students were enrolled in approximately 10,880 elementary schools and 2,415 secondary schools.

During the 1960s the event that had the most profound influence on Catholic education was the Catholic church's Second Vatican Council from 1962 to 1965. It issued a *Declaration on Christian Education* that spoke strongly in support of Catholic education and the schools. Another strong statement, *To Teach as Jesus Did,* was issued in 1973 by the U.S. National Conference of Catholic Bishops. In 1977, the U.S. Catholic bishops issued a national catechetical directory entitled *Sharing the Light of Faith.*

Since the council, much discussion has occurred on the function and role of U.S. Catholic education, especially the schools. Research has shown the schools to be successful both academically and religiously. Religiously, they have been shown to influence positively the adult beliefs and behaviors of graduates. By contrast, there are virtually no general, statistically significant correlations between attendance at non-school-based religious education programs like CCD and later religious beliefs and behaviors. This information has led to another controversy about the place of schooling in the Church's educational mission.

Many involved in CCD and its more recent versions have been critical of the lack of Church resources committed to its activities, compared with resources available to schools. These programs have been enlarged to include religious formation from early childhood to old age. Non-academic formation groups may meet in retreat-like settings over lengthy periods of time.

Several profound changes have taken place in the schools. A major change has been in staffing. In about twenty years, schools have gone from a staff of about 20 percent laypeople to about 80 percent laypeople, because of a decline in the numbers of religious since the mid-1960s. Another change has been the dramatic increase in non-Catholic and minority enrollment within a more general picture of enrollment decline. In 1985 there were approximately 9,250 schools enrolling 2.82 million students (down from nearly twice that enrollment in 1965); for 1988–89, enrollment figures were 1,911,911 in parish schools, 639,208 in secondary schools (NCEA). Though school financing has always been a major concern, this issue has been complicated by the loss of contributed financial services made by priests and religious, and by delayed capital expenditures.

Catholic colleges and universities also underwent changes during recent decades. The early 1900s saw reforms intended to separate the high school from the college into two distinct educational institutions; it would no longer be assumed that students would go from the high school to the adjacent college. College curriculum became standardized with fewer required theology courses, more variety in religion courses, and more emphasis on departments outside the classical curriculum such as the sciences. The 1950s and 1960s saw further curricular modifications and growth, especially on the doctoral level. The 1960s also brought changes in the composition of staff as lay scholars were added to what had been predominantly clergy faculty, changes in the student body, as colleges became co-educational and more non-Catholic students were enrolled, and as new financial problems arose. The late 1960s saw what is perhaps the most profound change yet, when legal control, vested in the religious order that founded the institution or in the diocesan bishop, often advised by laypeople, began to pass to a predominantly lay board of trustees. This change in structure, brought about by a broadening in the understanding of authority and how it is to be shared, raised new questions about the purpose and identity of Catholic higher education, especially as it pertains to issues like academic freedom and the teaching of biology. *See also* Catechism; Colleges and Universities, Church Related; Confraternity of Christian Doctrine; National Conference of Catholic Bishops; Private Religious Schools; Private Schools and Religion.

FOR FURTHER REFERENCE

Buetow, Harold A. *A History of United States Catholic Schooling.* Washington, DC: National Catholic Educational Association, 1986.
———. *The Catholic School.* New York: Crossroad, 1988.
Dolan, Jay P. *The American Catholic Experience.* New York: Doubleday, 1985.
Hassenger, Robert, ed. *The Shape of Catholic Higher Education.* Chicago: University of Chicago Press, 1967.
Hennesey, James. *American Catholics.* New York: Oxford, 1981.

B. V. Manno

Roman Education (Ancient)

Roman education at its best sought to prepare citizens for active and wise participation in all three offices of government: legislation, administration, and adjudication. Rome's genius was to develop and codify law, and it is suitably reflected in the content of education. The *Laws of the Twelve Tables* (449 B.C.) were memorized by Roman boys as the *Iliad* and the *Odyssey* had been laid to heart by Greek boys.

The history of Roman education, like the history of Rome itself, is divided into the era of the republic and the era of the empire or, to be more accurate, the era of imperialism. During the republic, education was marked by two primary characteristics. First, as conservative as the countryside in which it flourished, it passed on a traditional way of life. Second, it centered in the family; there it took place, there lived the virtues to be taught, and there ruled the *paterfamilias*. Emancipation passed from landowners to sons. No son was emancipated so long as his father lived. (A daughter never became eligible for emancipation.) Yet the boy was so revered that his parents spent generously—time, effort, and, as available, money—on his nurture and education.

Roman education during the republic was not rigidly standardized; each family had its idiosyncrasies. So great was the power of custom, however, that recognizable patterns prevailed. For the child's first seven years his education was at the hands of his nurse, almost always his own mother. She shared with him the family mores and wisdom, as much by her presence as by deliberate teaching.

When the boy was about seven, his father assumed the active role. He represented authority, tradition, and religion, and his power and influence were immense. Often he was the only teacher his son would have, and if book learning was to be included, he was the one to teach it. He exacted his son's help in observing the family's numerous religious ceremonies, and he took the boy with him as he went about personal and civic duties. He also set the boy to memorizing the *Laws of the Twelve Tables*, which both reflected and carried forward their way of life.

At about sixteen years, usually not before fourteen or after seventeen, the boy was recognized as having grown up. He was robed in an adult's toga and ceremoniously enrolled as a citizen, and he began a new phase of education, coming under the charge of an elder (usually a friend of his father), one distinguished, experienced, and wise. For at least a year, the young man lived beside this man, absorbing his way of doing things and becoming both familiar with his role in public service and acquainted with other distinguished persons.

Imperialism came to Rome in the middle of the third century B.C., though the empire was not officially affirmed until 27 B.C. After 241, when Rome defeated Carthage in the first Punic War, it was recognized as a power in the Mediterranean world. Society was in upheaval; the senate debated problems and sought new ideas and ways of persuasion. At hand, having come to Rome about 270 B.C., were the language, eloquence, and literature of Greece. Interest in Greek philosophy and education followed, and by the middle of the next century schools had been organized on the Greek model.

At age seven, the boy began school, entering the first of three stages of education. The master of this first stage was the *litterator*, the teacher of reading, writing, and arithmetic. For most students this stage constituted the whole of their formal education, and usually it offered just enough knowledge to get by.

The next stage was directed by the *grammaticus*, who taught literature and language. During the early years of the schools, the literature was Greek, for the initially Roman literature lacked sufficient quality. In time, however, Roman literature came also to be included in the curriculum. The final stage, which relatively few boys attained, was under the *rhetor*, whose subject was the art of eloquent and persuasive speaking.

Quintilian (ca. A.D. 35–95), an exceptional *rhetor*, described an ideal school in which well-educated teachers held children in high esteem and would work at relating education to life and at developing the character as well as the oratorical skills of their students. Even he looked on every subject in terms of its usefulness to oratory: knowledge of right speaking (grammar, etymology, and diction) to provide its obvious skills; the interpretation of poets to supply ideas and ways of presenting them; music (knowledge of melody and rhythm) to enhance gracefulness in speech;

geometry (mathematics) to exercise the mind and to quicken perception; and gymnastics to improve gestures and bodily movement in speaking.

Education under the Roman Empire was not controlled by the state, and schools varied greatly from one another. Usually, however, they were far from ideal. Often the inherited curriculum was treated simply as something to be memorized. The students' days were long and dull, meeting places noisy and badly equipped, and schoolmasters badly paid and no better than their remuneration. They were notorious for cruelty with the ferule and even the lash.

Like Rome itself, Roman education declined from its distinguished beginnings during the republic. In spite of exceptional students and teachers like Quintilian, the people whose gift to the world was written law ultimately fell short both in empire and in education.

R. R. Sundquist

Romanticism

Romanticism is a mode of writing or vision of the world controlled by imagination, emotion, and a subjective point of view, often aiming to suggest the ineffable. The romantic movement is characterized by an emphasis on a return to nature and reliance on human self-sufficiency. Romantics have developed private belief systems expressed in symbolic forms but generally fail to construct a theology commensurate with their psychological insights. Since the eighteenth century many poets and mystics have adopted the romantic mode, rejecting rationalism, putting faith in feeling, and attributing a semimystical value to nature. The early poetry of William Wordsworth (1770–1850) embodies nature mysticism. The poet William Blake (1757–1827), who was influenced by the mystic Jacob Boehme (1515–1624), denounced the constrictions of an objective creed and the claims of reason. Blake contemplates "Heaven in a Wild Flower" (*Auguries of Innocence*) and affirms that "Imagination . . . is the Divine Body of the Lord Jesus" (*Jerusalem*).

Inevitably religious education was influenced by the romantic movement. In Catholic education this took the form of pious stories of the saints, a certain type of "holy picture," and sentimental hymns and other religious music.

In Sunday schools it could be observed in the pictures of imagined Palestinian scenes and Jesus (of whom we have no pictures) used in teaching. Children's songs, both words and music, have tended toward the sentimental (which is not necessarily a hallmark of the romantic movement but may be an expression of it). Romantic music on religious themes has long been part of youth conferences and gospel music continues the tradition.

New church hymnals continue the use of some familiar nineteenth-century hymns while adding new ones in a contemporary idiom.

The new emphasis on the aesthetic and the emotional in religious education will see new interpretations of romanticism. See also Aesthetics; Affective Education; Realism.

R. Bradley

Rosh Hashanah

Rosh Hashanah (in Hebrew, literally, "the head or beginning of the year") is the Jewish New Year, emphasizing divine judgment of human actions and the need for repentance, prayer, and acts of charity to ensure human survival for the year to come.

Since ancient times, the holiday has been celebrated on the first two days of the Hebrew month of Tishri (generally during September) as fulfillment of the biblical command, "In the seventh month, on the first day of the month, you shall observe complete rest, a sacred occasion commemorated with loud blasts" (Lev. 23:24b, JPS). The second day was added when difficulties arose in determining exactly when the new moon appeared, and now Rosh Hashanah is the only holiday generally observed for two days (though some Reform Jews celebrate only a single day). The holiday is also known as the "Day of Remembrance," the "Day of Judgment," and the "Day of Loud Blasts (of the ram's horn)."

The commandment of the day is the blowing of the *shofar* (usually a ram's horn) in a traditional pattern of whole and broken blasts, an act that has been given numerous interpretations. Three of the key interpretations coincide with the special additional prayers that are recited: Kingship (the trumpets of coronation), Remembrance (the merit of the binding of Isaac, which concluded with a ram caught in a thicket by its horns, Gen. 22:13), and Ram's Horn (which will sound the redemption, returning the Jewish people to their land). Medieval commentators emphasized that the blasts rouse us from the slumber of routine and insensitivity, awakening us to our responsibilities toward others and toward God.

Though much of the day is spent in prayer in the synagogue, a number of customs are observed outside the synagogue. Holiday meals are celebrated at home, with foods symbolic of what is hoped for the new year: it will be sweet (apples and honey), abundant (like the seeds of a pomegranate), and successful (the head of a fish, rather than its tail). On the afternoon of the first day, people congregate near a body of running water to recite penitential prayers, including the verse, "You will hurl all our sins/Into the depths of the sea" (Mic. 7:19b, JPS). Greeting cards are also exchanged, though that is a recent custom. Overall, the mood of the day is serious, not somber, tinged with joy in the certainty that God sustains all those who repent.

Rosh Hashanah is one of the high points of a seven-week penitential (Days of Awe) and festive season. During the month preceding Rosh Hashanah, the *shofar* is blown at the conclusion of each morning's synagogue service (excluding the Shabbat, or Sabbath). During the week before Rosh Hashanah, predawn penitential prayers are recited before the regular morning service. Rosh Hashanah begins the Ten Days of Repentance, which culminate in Yom Kippur, the Day of Atonement and final judgment. Psalm 27 is recited morning and evening from the beginning of the season until the end of the Sukkoth festival seven weeks later.

Rosh Hashanah, together with Yom Kippur, are unique among the holy days on the Jewish calendar in that they do not commemorate a specific historical event or agricultural season. Rather, they require that individuals scrutinize their relationship to God in the context of the Jewish people as a whole, since nearly all prayers are recited in the first person plural (e.g., "*Our* Father, *Our* King, inscribe *us* in the book of good life"). What historical connections exist are largely symbolic; e.g., Rosh Hashanah commemorates the creation of the world and, specifically, the judgment of Adam for his transgression. So are his descendants judged on this same day and, as later commentators have added, on every day of the year. Hence, key parts of the liturgy composed originally for Rosh Hashanah have been carried over to the regular daily liturgy.

The essence of the day is the "reenthronement" of God as king, with all the consequences that must have in the life of each person and that of the community as a whole. That coronation began with the *shofar* blasts at Mount Sinai (Exod. 19:16) and will conclude with those to accompany the end of days (Isa. 27:13). Moreover, the liturgy recognizes the unique kingship of God in accepting the inevitability of human shortcomings. This is symbolized in the broken, wailing sounds of the *shofar*. Yet the theme of the day is not so much a wallowing in the sins of the past year (though that point is driven home), as it is resolve for a new course of life in the year to come. That resolve is tested in the week between Rosh Hashanah and Yom Kippur, which is a prototype of the new year. Final judgment is rendered on Yom Kippur, which concludes with a final blast of the *shofar*. See also Jewish Festivals and Holidays.

FOR FURTHER REFERENCE

Goodman, Philip, ed. *The Rosh Hashanah Anthology*. Philadelphia: Jewish Publication Society, 1970.

D. A. Resnick

Rural Church

Picture a country setting with trees and grass and large fields; at the edge of the field facing the road is a one-room white building with a small steeple and bell tower—that is the rural church. Normally this church will have twenty to two hundred members who live nearby. Often, the members of the church are descendants of those who formed the first congregation; three or four generations of one family may all attend the same church. Rural churches make up a large proportion of the congregations in most denominations.

The farm population of the United States in 1986 was listed at five million, or 2.2 percent of the country's population. Almost three million people are employed on farms: 1.8 million family members and another million who are hired help. Today the rural church is under stress as it tries to help its people deal with a time of social and economic crisis among farm families and farm communities.

CHARACTERISTICS

Fundamental to the life of the rural church is worship, preaching, and fellowship of the congregation. Members of the church usually are rooted in the land and particularly value kinship ties and personal independence. Maintaining tradition and a sense of community are important priorities of the rural church.

Activities of rural churches vary. The church may be open only on Sunday mornings for Sunday school and/or for worship and remain locked during the week. Church activities promote community life: typically homecoming, when families and pastors who are part of the history of the church gather for worship and dinner on the grounds; covered-dish meals, where family specialties are shared; and revivals, in which a visiting preacher and song leader seek to motivate and inspire the congregation. Sometimes the church serves also as a meeting place for general community gatherings or town meetings.

Adult and family activities may include Wednesday night prayer meeting and Bible study. There is usually a youth group, perhaps an evening youth fellowship. Children normally attend the worship services with their families and attend Sunday school. Vacation Bible school is usually held for children. Because of the importance rural communities place on the family, children, youth, and adults generally are not as separated at gatherings as they may be in urban or suburban settings. Members of the rural church know each other and develop a caring environment among members; an informal network of persons in the church makes sure that members are cared for. Birth, marriage, illness, and death are community affairs, and often a member of a rural church will be baptized, confirmed, married, and buried in the rural church of his or her parents.

Worship in the rural church is usually less formal than worship in urban and suburban areas. Members feel free to speak from the congregation remembering members of the church or the community at large in their prayers. There are distinctive differences among rural churches, however; most carry out their own local traditions and rituals as well as those of the denomination.

Leadership of the rural church is usually held by influential persons in the rural community. The church may have a full-time pastor or may be served by an intern from a nearby seminary or a person with a lay pastor's license. Sometimes a retired pastor takes an appointment in a rural church. Often, several churches form a charge or parish and share one pastor who visits each church each Sunday. If these churches are at great distance from one another, the pastor may alternate Sundays, with a layperson presiding on the Sunday when the pastor is with another congregation in the parish. Since the rural church is usually in a small community, a resident pastor is expected to be involved in community life as well as in church functions. The pastor's spouse also plays a crucial role in promoting church events and helping the pastor to care for the congregation.

A rural church may have an office for the pastor and sometimes a few rooms for classes. Frequently, a cemetery spreads out on land adjacent to the church with burial spaces for church members divided into family plots. In addition to the church building and cemetery the rural church may also have an arbor—an open shelter outside that serves as a place for family get-togethers, covered-dish suppers, and evening revivals. If the congregation has one full-time pastor there is usually a parsonage on the church property; in this case, the pastor will conduct most church business from home.

TENSIONS

The rural church, usually old and small, is a familiar part of the American landscape. As the country becomes urbanized and farm life is threatened, rural churches lose members and often must close or join with other churches to form one congregation. Some rural churches are subsidized by their general church body. Some exist only as legal entities for the congregation to own its cemetery; these congregations may have a service only once or twice a year.

In the latter part of the twentieth century the loss of farm land and the bankruptcy of many farmers has focused concern on rural life and the rural church. The problems are not new. The depletion of farm land through urbanization goes back thousands of years and may be found almost anywhere on earth. Global awareness of the problem is new, however, and is only beginning. The World Council of Churches and governments around the world are only now becoming sensitive to the issue. It is an economic problem, for food production is at the base of all economic security. It is also a tragic human problem, as famine stalks multitudes of people.

In the United States, unfavorable weather that has cut production has come after years of falling prices for the land itself as well as for farm products. Farmers who had expanded their land holdings have faced bankruptcy and the loss of both land and home—all that they had hoped to have for themselves and their children. For people proud of their independence, going to others for help has been a painful necessity.

The church becomes pivotal in communities where people are in trouble. It includes among its members both farm families and those who run the banks, stores, and other businesses and agencies. It is made up of people who have known and trusted each other; it has a pastor who knows everyone. The church can help people in pain express their fears and anger in ways that will prevent breakdowns and promote strength. Churches provide help through support groups as well as individual and family counseling.

But the problems will not go away, and rural churches, acting together, are becoming advocates in a time when farming is in transition and the future of the family farm seems to be in question. They ask for study of the proper place of agribusiness and the small farm.

Recent discussion of the total ecology of earth influences the discussion. The biblical assertion that God created the world and found it good and gave it into the care of human beings "to till and keep" is foundational. Recent experiments in farming techniques have disclosed that ecologically sound agricultural practices can bring comparable yields with fewer harmful side effects. Churches can affirm these insights through preaching, teaching, and the use of their own land, as they encourage families in the congregation to try new ways.

The rural church today, in the midst of new tensions, is ministering to people in acute need. At the same time, it is challenged with the opportunity to encourage people to face the future in new ways, strengthened by their biblical faith in God the creator and provider.

FOR FURTHER REFERENCE

Dalglish, William A. *Models for Catechetical Ministry in the Rural Parish.* Washington, DC: U.S. Catholic Conference, 1982.
Dudley, Carl S. *Making the Small Church Effective.* Nashville, TN: Abingdon, 1978.
Ray, David R. *Small Churches Are the Right Size.* New York: Pilgrim Press, 1982.
Schmidt, Karla, ed. *Renew the Spirit of My People: A Handbook for Ministry in Times of Rural Crisis.* Des Moines, IA: Prairiefire Rural Action, 1987.

M. S. Goodson

Sacraments

The sacraments (also sometimes called "ordinances") are sets of explicit liturgical words and actions that function within the Christian church as special mediators of the relationship between God and human beings. Although each individual sacrament has a distinctive character, mode of administration, and meaning within the Christian life, all sacramental activity has as its source and foundation the saving life and work of Jesus Christ.

HISTORICAL UNDERSTANDINGS

Although there are many New Testament accounts of events that would later come to be called sacraments, especially of baptism and the Eucharist (for example, Acts 8:36–38; 1 Cor. 11:17–34), there is neither a definition of precisely which actions of the church are to be considered sacraments nor any systematic theological treatment of their meaning in Scripture. *Sacramentum* (meaning an oath of allegiance), from which the word "sacrament" is derived, is the later Latin translation of the Greek word *mystērion* in many New Testament passages. Whenever the word *mystērion* is found, it describes a hidden part of God's plan of salvation that is being communicated to human beings in some tangible way. In many places in the New Testament (for example, 1 Tim. 3:16; Eph. 5:32) it is the life, death, and resurrection of Jesus that is described as the primary *mystērion*, the physical presence of God's willingness to forgive and redeem all of humanity. From this understanding is derived the most persistent definition of a sacrament, namely, "an outward and visible sign of an inward and spiritual grace."

Quite early in Christian history the church began to reflect upon what it was experiencing in its corporate worship and to try to understand what distinguished a sacrament from other forms of Christian practice. Because the New Testament is not explicit about what constitutes sacramental activity or how such activity operates, the term "sacrament" remained a rather fluid one for some time. In the late fourth century, Augustine referred to more than thirty ecclesial practices as sacraments, because each one was experienced by faithful people as giving visible form to the redeeming love of God in Christ. The imposition of ashes on Ash Wednesday, the installation of a local pastor, and the taking of monastic vows, as well as the Lord's Supper and baptism, were among those actions called sacraments by Augustine.

No systematic attempt to enumerate or codify the sacraments was made until the early Middle Ages. In the mid-twelfth century, theologian Peter Lombard wrote an influential textbook in which exactly seven actions of the church were declared to be sacraments by virtue of their institution by Jesus or by the apostles. These actions were baptism, the Eucharist, penance, ordination, anointing of the sick, confirmation, and marriage. Within a short time, this had become the definitive list, expounded upon by theologians and affirmed and reaffirmed by successive ecumenical councils of the church.

During the centuries that followed, the sacraments provided a comprehensive system of Christian pastoral care that carried the faithful from birth to death. But the sacraments themselves became increasingly privatized, and theologians focused their attention on the minimum requirements necessary to ensure that divine grace was properly mediated by each sacrament, creating a system both rigid and complex. By the beginning of the sixteenth century, abuses of the sacraments were widespread, and they had become the occasion for a certain amount of misunderstanding and superstition.

To many, these abuses of the sacraments were clear evidence of the need for the reform of the church as a whole. In his zeal for reestablishing the church on its biblical foundations, Martin Luther (1483–1546) effectively dismantled the medieval sacramental system by proclaiming that only baptism and the Eucharist could be considered sacraments, since no explicit words of Jesus Christ could be found in Scripture as institution for the other five. Above all, Luther and the other Reformers of the sixteenth century were emphatic that the sacraments are the work of God, not the work of human beings. In the sacraments, the promises of God are made visible and operative in the lives of faithful people.

But two centuries after Luther's death, the Enlightenment altered the traditional understanding of the sacraments. Unwilling to accept the idea that God might use physical realities (bread and wine or water, for example) to convey divine grace and love, Enlightenment Christians transformed the sacraments from acts of God's self-communication to acts of human beings by which they remember what God has done for them in the life and death of Jesus.

CONTEMPORARY UNDERSTANDINGS

Christian bodies continue to debate the meaning of the sacraments in their corporate lives. Most Protestant denominations have accepted Luther's claim that only baptism and the Eucharist can be regarded as sacraments, while Roman Catholics have generally continued to insist that the grace of God is definitively operative in no more or no less than seven actions of the church. Two Protestant denominations, the Society of Friends (Quakers) and the Salvation Army, both of whom consider outward sacramental signs superfluous, have eliminated any overt sacramental practice from their gatherings for worship. The Brethren Church and the Church of the Brethren consider footwashing and anointing of the sick to have been instituted by Jesus as well and practice both with regularity. Although some Protestant denominations, such as Lutherans and Episcopalians, have retained the more traditional understanding of the sacraments as special moments in the work of God in the lives of human beings, many mainline Protestants have been heavily influenced by the thinking of the Enlightenment and view the sacraments as useful ways by which human beings remember the sacrificial life and death of Jesus.

In recent times, however, serious efforts have been made to rethink the nature of sacramental activity within the church. Modern attempts to balance the concern for retaining the priority of God's action in every time and place and in the life of every human person expressed in the traditional view of the sacraments with the concern for active human participation in the work of salvation expressed in the Enlightenment view have led to new models of sacramental theology.

Much of this work is based upon the idea that the sacraments cannot be seen in isolation but must be understood in the light of Scripture study, Christology, and the theology of the church (ecclesiology) and in light of the human person, time, and history. Contemporary biblical study has yielded important insights about the ways in which God's self-communication is mediated to humanity. Throughout the Old and New Testaments, we find the principle underlying the theology of the sacraments at work: God using ordinary things to convey redeeming love to humankind. People, places, events, and objects—indeed the whole of the created order—are viewed as the material by which God's self-giving is accomplished (this is generally referred to as "sacramentality").

Recent work in the area of Christology has also come to have important implications for contemporary thinking about the sacraments. Increasingly, Jesus himself is viewed as the primordial sacrament, the most complete and definitive presence of God's love in time and space. The individual sacraments are to be understood as derivative of and dependent upon the sacramental life and work of Jesus, as actions by which the church, the body of Christ, expresses itself. Because of this broader understanding of the term "sacrament," the question of the exact number of individual sacraments has become less and less of an issue in recent years for Protestants and Roman Catholics alike.

Insights from the social sciences have also made a significant impact on modern sacramental theology and practice. The work of sociologists, anthropologists, and psychologists has made it plain that human beings naturally use symbolic action to relate to one another, to convey to one another those things beyond words—love, fidelity, and compassion, for example. From this understanding has come renewed concern for the clarity with which the sacramental action speaks within the church, the honesty of the materials used, and the forthrightness of the gestures employed, all of which contribute to the effectiveness with which the sacraments communicate meaning.

After a long period of relative neglect by many Christian bodies, the sacraments are beginning to return to a more central place in corporate worship. New rites based upon the most recent generation of theological reflection and historical research have been produced by nearly all of the major Protestant denominations, and there is a concomitant increase in sacramental piety. Indeed, a return to common sources, biblical, historical, and theological, has allowed Protestants and Roman Catholics to move closer to one another in their practice and theology of the sacraments, contributing to the ecumenical climate of the late twentieth century.

The various denominations usually provide instruction about particular sacraments for individuals or groups about to participate in them (e.g., believer's baptism, confirmation, marriage) or about to participate in them for the first time (e.g., the Eucharist). Given are doctrinal positions, procedures, and the meaning of the rite for persons as individuals, as members of a particular faith tradition, and as members of the church as a whole, the body of Christ. Yet true learning about sacraments comes when people experience them, when participation in the liturgy brings a personal dimension to teaching. After the experi-

ence, reflection on the event in religious education groups can deepen understanding. The liturgy can be reviewed from the standpoint of involvement and additional scriptural resources brought to bear. *See also* Baptism; Confirmation; Eucharist; Liturgy; Symbolism.

S. J. White

Salle, Jean-Baptiste de la

See La Salle, Jean-Baptiste de.

Salvation

Religion is the human attempt to overcome the separation from God, and salvation is the religious event through which this happens. For many people salvation means having one's sins forgiven or getting to heaven. It is actually a broader process, a movement of life and liberation central to all world religions. Salvation is essentially a healing process with a common structure: a problem to be overcome, a solution to this problem, and a strategy to achieve this solution.

The problem lies in the fundamental fact of human existence—that something has gone wrong with creation. Somehow the original closeness with God has been lost, whether due to human ignorance of the true nature of the world or a proud desire to be self-sufficient. This essential flaw—this original evil or sin—is manifested in a multitude of experiences, for example, alienation and failure, social injustice and war.

The goal of religion is the transformation of the human plight and the restoration of the lost harmony. It may be the personal experience of peace, liberation, joy, or ecstasy, or it may be the communal sharing in a golden age, utopia, new heaven and earth, or final resurrection of all the dead.

The strategy or process of salvation to achieve this goal has several aspects. The process is initiated by God and human involvement consists in openness to this divine activity and in obeying certain standards of behavior. One follows the way of a savior, who provides a final vision of salvation, and participates in the moral discipline and ritual life of the community.

In the Jewish Scriptures, the problem is seen as enslavement or oppression by the enemies of Yahweh. The solution is a home in the promised land and a messianic era of peace and justice, prosperity and posterity. The strategy is total obedience to the covenant with Yahweh.

Redemption means to free, and this is a basic element in the doctrine of salvation (the technical name is "soteriology"). The Christian tradition has its own expressions of the process of salvation, emphasizing the unique role of Jesus. He is Savior by his incarnation, for being both God and human he can heal the separation between God and humans. Jesus is Savior in his public ministry by his acts of compassion. Finally, he is Savior in his sacrificial death and resurrection, which effect deliverance from evil and reveal God's merciful act of love and reunion.

There are several interpretations of what this means, and no one has ever been accepted as "final," although particular Christian groups may prefer one to another. The "ransom" theory takes its name from the Gospel saying that the Son of man came "to give his life as a ransom for many" (Matt. 20:28; Mark 10:45). The problem is that human beings are enslaved to sin and therefore to Satan, and only divine intervention can free them to live in joyful obedience to God. Only God, who judges sin, can effect this (i.e., ransom them). Jesus is the ransom. The second-century theologian Irenaeus is linked to this view.

A second interpretation is the "satisfaction" theory. Jesus is the vicarious sacrifice (as the lamb slain for the Passover, or those sacrifices regularly made at the Temple) as a propitiation to effect atonement for sin. He gave his life freely and obediently as a way by which God and humanity could be reconciled. This interpretation is linked to the eleventh-century theologian Anselm of Canterbury.

A third interpretation is the "moral influence" theory, linked to the twelfth-century monk and scholar Abelard. For him, the life, death, and resurrection of Jesus move hearers to repentance, through which they find forgiveness and restoration from God (salvation) and the power to live the new life in Christ.

A contemporary expression, in liberation theology, locates the problem in the structures of human society that crush or dehumanize people; the solution is the liberation of the oppressed, a sign of the reign of God; and the strategy is the practical struggle to overcome injustice. Jesus suffers in the suffering of God's people and his resurrection promises the power to overcome evil.

Christian salvation also stresses its universal and eschatological nature, a time when Satan will be definitively defeated and all people will share in the coming reign of God. The final glorification is anticipated when any person imitates the exemplary activity of Jesus. At such graced moments the strategy and the solution coincide. See also Bible in Religious Education, The; Eternal Life; Jesus Christ; Justification; Liberation Theology; Reconciliation; Resurrection; Sanctification.

FOR FURTHER REFERENCE

Hellwig, Monika. *Jesus: The Compassion of God*. Wilmington, DE: Glazier, 1983.

Knitter, Paul. *No Other Name?* Maryknoll, NY: Orbis, 1985.
Küng, Hans. *On Being a Christian*. Garden City, NY: Doubleday, 1976.
Thompson, William. *The Jesus Debate*. Ramsey, NJ: Paulist, 1985.

L. J. Biallas

Sanctification

Sanctification is the process of making a person, place, or object "holy" (Lat. *sanctus*), set apart for God's purpose. With respect to people it also describes the process of becoming more and more godlike. Because only God is intrinsically holy, people, places, and objects are holy only to the extent that they are brought within the sphere of God's activity. Hence, God (as Father, Son, or Spirit) is the primary agent of sanctification; although God may also work through people who themselves have been set apart first.

When applied to Christians, sanctification has a double meaning. It denotes the transition of human nature from the realm of the profane to that of the sacred; a transition only fully achieved by Christ who is "our sanctification" (1 Cor. 1:30). It also denotes the responsibility placed on the recipients of the conferred status of sanctification to live out the implications of this gift—including the moral implications (see Rom. 6:19–22; 1 Thess. 4:3–4; Heb. 12:14). God's sanctified people are called upon to be holy even as God is holy (Lev. 19:2; 20:26; 1 Pet. 1:15–16; cf. 1 Thess. 4:3). In this sense, sanctification is an eschatological concept: Christians are already what they shall be, but, both personally and corporately, they need to appropriate their transformed nature.

The twofold dimension of sanctification as status and goal links it with other theological terms such as salvation and justification. In Protestant theology, sanctification is often described as the continuation of the process of salvation inaugurated by God in the lives of individuals when they have been justified by grace through faith. Catholic and Orthodox theologians have not distinguished as sharply between justification and sanctification, preferring the latter to describe both the fundamental gift of salvation and its continuing transformation of human nature.

Eastern Orthodoxy's doctrine of *theosis*, the deification of humanity, expresses the transforming character of sanctification most clearly: Christians are able to live out their true nature because they are "partakers of the divine nature" (2 Pet. 1:4). The extent to which this is attainable has been debated vigorously. Apart from the teachings of some rigoristic sectarians, John Wesley's "perfectionism" and the resultant Holiness movement have probably come closest to claiming the possibility of living a completely holy life. Other Protestants have normally argued that, because of the reality of sin, even those "who are in the process of being sanctified" (1 Cor. 1:2; Heb. 2:11; 10:14) continue to have a tendency to want to be separated from God rather than be drawn to God or for God. Despite a highly developed doctrine of grace, including that of "sanctifying grace," Catholic theology has also recognized the persistence of human sinfulness. Consequently, Christian tradition, as a whole, has been somewhat skeptical about the possibility of attaining total sanctity in this life, even though it has argued that, as a gift, sanctification describes the status of every Christian.

The understanding of sanctification comes to young children indirectly. They know people who have a special quality of life that exhibits love, kindness, forgiveness, and gentleness and learn that this is what it means to follow Jesus. They are told stories about Bible people whose lives showed that they were acting as they thought God would want them to act.

School-age children can understand in a concrete way how the people's actions indicate their awareness that God is working through them. They begin to understand that God is also with each of them and that God's Holy Spirit is acting through them. Traditional stories of the saints may seem unrealistic today, but there is a need to recover for teaching fresh interpretations of the lives of people through the centuries whose lives were expressions of sanctification by God, along with stories of people today who live and work in the power of the Holy Spirit. The Orthodox church is rich in the tradition of the staretz, or holy man. The full stories of the lives of biblical people also illustrate the process of sanctification.

The prophets regarded Israel as a holy people, set apart by God. Similarly, Paul addressed the people in his churches as "saints." All believers are, in this sense, "saints." Adolescents and adults will want to consider what it means both that individuals are made holy by God and that the whole religious community is holy, i.e., set apart for God's purposes. Studies of Acts and the Pauline Letters are ways of considering sanctification.

The liturgies of baptism and confirmation both point to and provide a framework for study of the process of sanctification. "Let us go forth into the world, rejoicing in the power of the Spirit," is a liturgical dismissal. Adults will want to discuss what it means to live in the world in the power of the Spirit and to what extent a person can fulfill this gift through his or her life. *See also* Baptism; Confirmation; Faith Development; Justification; Salvation.

W. Tabbernee

Scientific Method

The scientific method is a way of thinking about problems and solving them that has been developed by many theorists and experimenters over hundreds of years. Although scientists do not agree completely on the sequence and names of the steps, they generally identify five operations: (1) stating the problem or question, (2) forming the hypothesis, (3) observing and experimenting, (4) interpreting data, and (5) drawing conclusions. After the problem is solved, the scientific method can be used to explain both the problem and its solution. Thus the scientific method may be used as a way of investigating and refining the use of the scientific method.

INFLUENCE ON EDUCATION

In the first half of the twentieth century, John Dewey (1859–1952) claimed the scientific method for education, conducting a laboratory school and eventually developing a philosophy of education through interpreting his conclusions. His questions were: what do children learn and how do they learn it?

Dewey understood that the way people, especially Americans, do everything in daily life is instinctively scientific. It is the way they think. In the first place, thinking does not happen in a vacuum. Thinking is not contemplation, as some of the Greeks had thought. It does not arise from merely amassing sensations and sorting them into categories, as Francis Bacon (1561–1626) had suggested. There must be something to cause thinking, some change in circumstances that renders merely habitual reactions inappropriate. In short, thinking begins when people are challenged, when a problem arises and continues until something works to solve or shift the problem. Then the process begins all over again. Thinking, according to Dewey, is a universal and continual process of experimentation exercised in the theoretical issues of life as well as in its practical affairs.

From his experience Dewey concluded that learning follows the same pattern as effective thinking. Learning is lifelong, beginning at birth and enabling the person at each moment of life to discover what knowledge is needed in order to proceed to the next set of problems. The purpose of the school is to increase the learner's effectiveness in problem solving. The task of the teacher is to assist the child in discovering and applying the steps of the scientific method in daily life. This is done best, Dewey observed, together with other children who are solving similar problems, that is, in a social context. The strategy of education is to help order these problem-solving experiences so that the child is always being presented with problems that, as they are successfully solved, lead the learner to increased skill and confidence. The world will thus be continually supplied with people equipped to keep the society changing and growing. The school is social laboratory rather than information channel or tradition conduit.

APPLICATION TO RELIGION AND RELIGIOUS EDUCATION

When the scientific method is applied to the field of religion, the emphasis is shifted away from traditional theoretical issues like whether God exists or what God is like. Though Dewey defined God as the connection between the unsatisfactory present and the desirable future that tends to change the unsatisfactory into the desirable, he preferred to talk about the connection rather than about God. Alfred North Whitehead (1861–1947), his contemporary, in laying the foundations for what is now known as process theology, emphasized the advance of actuality toward novelty rather than static ontological reality. Later philosophers with a grounding in science, such as Ian Ramsey, Teilhard de Chardin, and Ian Barbour, have found connections between the data of science and the affirmations of religion. Another strategy has been to restate nonverifiable theological assertions so that they can be studied empirically. The process of exploring empirical data may be regarded as spiritual discipline and the results valued as revelatory.

The scientific method has also been applied to the observable data of religious behavior: what happens to a person in religious experience? Early in the twentieth century, William James (1842–1910) observed and analyzed his own change from despair to hope. Edwin Starbuck (1866–1947) studied the results of hundreds of questionnaires from people who claimed a conversion experience and concluded that it was an adolescent phenomenon. George Albert Coe (1862–1951) added personal interviews to Starbuck's method and developed a philosophy of scientific education in religious values. Later researchers have refined these techniques with the application of the methods of statistics, factor analysis, and the like to study the influence of things like home, peer pressure, advertising, and television on value formation and choice making.

One outcome of all this research was to restate the question, "What is faith?" as "How does faith develop?" Early researchers asked, What are the kinds or traits of character desired by churches? How can they be identified? And what favors or hinders their development? One such program was elaborate and extensive, the Union College Character Research Project, begun in 1935 in Schenectady, New York, by Ernest M. Ligon and continuing until 1982. A more philosophical approach was taken by Lewis J. Sherrill (1892–1957), who observed and classified the changes that take place during the course of a life-

time, in a religious person's relationships with God, the church, other persons, and the physical world. Jean Piaget's study of the cognitive development of Swiss children produced a summary of sequential stages that others have correlated with moral development (Lawrence Kohlberg), religious thinking (Ronald Goldman), and faith (James Fowler). These studies have been influential in the development of curriculum materials for children and youth. The content of these studies also is used to develop units for adult religious education groups.

Educators, whose primary concerns are classroom sessions and individual learners, ask, What can be taught? How shall it be taught? What do learners learn? Both commercial and denominational agencies design materials and strategies and conduct programs of testing and evaluation.

Application of the scientific method to the study of ancient documents and artifacts and to the comparison of world religions, though not directly related to educational research, enriches the resources available to educators. Frontier research into micro- and macro-space dynamics provides data for religious philosophy. Research into personal wholeness, political power, and social issues, for example, concerns religious educators.

Though sharpened by the results of areas already investigated and by the refinement of technique achieved, the issues for scientific method in the field of religious education have remained unchanged: What are the most important questions to be asked and what are the most promising ways of seeking answers to them? *See also* Dewey, John; Education, Theories of; Learning Theory; Problem Solving; Progressive Education; Psychology of Religion; Research; Social Sciences; Sociology of Religion; Statistics.

W. R. Rood

Second Vatican Council

See Vatican II.

Secularism

Beginning with the Enlightenment—an eighteenth-century European philosophical movement that sought to examine and to criticize all assertions on the basis of human reason—the Western industrialized world has become more secular. Secularity refers to a wide array of tendencies, thought patterns, and practices whereby persons in the modern world seem to live by temporal rather than spiritual values. What can be known through reason or through day-to-day human experience or observation of the natural world is, to the thoroughgoing secularist, all there is to know.

Many modern people appear to live their lives as if God did not exist and there were no values other than those of their own creation.

Some observers of contemporary Western society question its alleged secularity. Sociologists like Peter Berger (*The Sacred Canopy*, 1967) question the conventional modern assumption that the world is in the process of becoming progressively more secular, that religion is being discarded by modern people in technological societies. Some believe that what is being interpreted as growing secularity may be a shifting of the forms and practices of religion. They argue that religion is still a lively and dominant experience of life, except that it is now being practiced in unorthodox ways. They warn us against interpreting an apparent decline in mainline Protestant church attendance or the apparent secularity among the academic or artistic elite of a society as indicators of growing secularity in the society as a whole. With resurgent fundamentalism (both Christian and Moslem) and the veritable membership explosion within the more conservative Christian bodies both here and in the rest of the world (particularly the Third World), many question whether increased secularity is indeed a fact of modern life or simply an isolated phenomenon among certain cultural-economic groups within Western society.

For a time, some liberal Christians argued that secularity, far from being a foe of Christianity, is a new friend to be embraced. They noted that the Christian faith, in its emphasis upon the worth of the individual, the goodness of creation, and the value of human intellect, was a contributor in the movement toward increased secularity (Harvey Cox, *The Secular City*, 1966). These commentators urged the church to prepare its members to deal with a world where older viewpoints emphasizing the transcendent and the supernatural were declining. Other Christians saw secularity as a corrosive, destructive force to be resisted.

Depending upon one's assessment of secularity, educational responses within the church will be influenced by the nature of the modern world. The church, a body within but not of the world, has a stake in understanding this world, making judgments about it, and teaching its people to live within, for, and despite the world. *See also* Fundamentalism; Humanism; Public Schools and Religion.

W. H. Willimon

Semiotics

"Semiotics" comes from the Greek words *sēma* and *sēmeion* meaning "a sign [from the gods], signal." The field of semiotics includes studies in a wide range of sign systems that make possible communication between people. This article will limit itself to aspects of words as signs in the Scriptures.

One fundamental understanding of God in the Old Testament is that God is transcendent; therefore no representation of God in stone, on canvas, or in the human mind can be adequate. The Hebrews believed that they had been forbidden to give God a name or represent God by any kind of image. But the latter did not exclude that revelation of God that is found in human language.

Words are signs. The letters "b-r-e-a-d" put together in that order signify a certain reality. They stand for an article of food prepared by moistening, kneading, and baking meal or flour, generally with addition of yeast or leaven. But the choice of these particular letters, b-r-e-a-d, to symbolize that reality is an arbitrary one, so that the meaning of a given selection and ordering of letters has to be learned. Moreover, the word has been variously spelled "bred," "bredd," "bryad," and so on and has also passed through various meanings from "piece of bread" and "broken bread" into that of "bread as a substance."

Some words have one basic everyday meaning. "Flour" is a fine powder made from grain. (Though that does not tell us whether it is plain or self-rising flour, corn or wheat flour.) It is important in many areas of life, e.g., law and medicine, that given words do have a single, commonly accepted meaning.

But many words have more than one meaning. Thus poets, novelists, and mystics use words that move us beyond the accepted to the surprisingly new. The writers of Scripture use human language to convey a sense of the One whom words cannot contain.

"Bread" may mean a kind of food that is for many the staff of life, money (slang), one's livelihood, the wafer used in Holy Communion, or what Jesus is said to be to people, "the bread of life."

What the word "bread" means in a given statement depends on how it is associated with other words in a sentence or paragraph, and depends, too, on the reader's being imaginatively engaged with the text. The teaching of Jesus is couched in poetic imagery and the meaning of sayings and stories attributed to him is found in the relationship between the reader and the author of the text, and that calls for the involvement of both.

Semiotics has practical implications for religious educators. It suggests the need for an awareness of the many possible meanings of words, both in their everyday use and in the uses that hearers may have in mind. Frequently a teacher will use a word implying one meaning, only to discover that hearers were responding to other meanings and had other identifications with the word. The use of symbols (including words as symbols) can be rich because they gather many meanings, but those who use symbols in teaching need to be alert to the possible implications of each word. *See also* Communication Theory; Language Analysis; Symbolism.

FOR FURTHER REFERENCE

Scott, Bernard Brandon. *The Word of God in Words: Reading and Preaching.* Philadelphia: Fortress, 1985.

R. W. Graham

Sermon

See Preaching.

Sermons, Children's

The children's sermon is an act of worship that is a brief, carefully focused presentation of the Christian gospel to children. It is usually placed within a larger order of worship, either the central worship of a congregation or a time of worship just for children.

ISSUES FOR CONSIDERATION

Three issues need careful consideration before a children's sermon is included in the main worship service of a congregation. First, how is the presence of children in worship understood? Are children included willingly and with careful thought about how they will experience worship? Biblical foundations that support the presence of children can be found in Mark 9:33–37 and 10:13–16. Jesus cared for children and included them among his followers as valuable persons. A theological foundation that supports the presence of children is the sacrament of baptism. If children belong to the church through baptism, they should be included in worship. In churches where believers' baptism is practiced, children need to feel that they are included and welcome in worship. Children's early religious experiences can be lastingly influenced through the impressions they receive in worship. Care should be taken that these early experiences are positive and help children grow in faith.

Second, how is the involvement of children in worship understood? Children need help to understand what is happening. Young children's parents can help them to participate in worship by active guidance in acts of worship such as prayers, hymns, and offerings. As they grow older, children can be given specific roles of responsibility in worship, such as acolytes, ushers, and choir members.

Third, when a congregation wishes to directly address children through a specific act of worship,

a children's sermon may be considered as an option. The children's sermon is an act of worship intended specifically to reach children within the range of their abilities to know and understand life and the world in which they live. The inclusion of a children's sermon in the order of worship requires careful thought and is best approached after both the presence and involvement of children in worship have been considered.

There is an important distinction to bear in mind between the children's sermon as an entire act of worship, on the one hand, and as the delivery of a message to children, on the other. As an entire act of worship, the event includes children's involvement from beginning to end—from the moment they are perhaps invited to leave their pew and move forward to the chancel until they arrive back in the pew. As the delivery of a message to children, the focus is upon the content and methods that are used to communicate with children in the form of a presentation by a worship leader.

DELIVERY AND FORM

Four criteria can be used to evaluate the delivery of a children's sermon in terms of content and message. First, it should carry the meaning of the gospel. Scripture is the place to begin since it represents the standards by which faithful communication of the gospel has been measured for centuries. Biblical faith is the richest resource of images, stories, and teachings. Resources that rely solely upon personal and social values often tend to trivialize the content of the children's sermon. The issue of how to use the Bible with children is of special importance and needs careful attention (see Gobbel and Gobbel, *The Bible—A Child's Playground*).

Second, the children's sermon should address children in terms they understand. Language, concepts, and forms of communication should be within children's ability to comprehend. A theory of faith development such as James Fowler's (*Stages of Faith*, 1981) is helpful. Young children ages four to six particularly benefit from a message directed to them in a concise episode. Jean Piaget's stages of cognitive development are a reminder that children up to the age of eleven best understand words and ideas that are concretely stated. Older children are increasingly able to comprehend the main sermon, especially if it includes narrative.

Third, the children's sermon should stir the imagination and feelings of everyone who hears it. Adults are often as involved as the children. Imagination and feelings are at the core of the creative process that leads to change and growth. If imagination and feelings remain untouched, the gospel will have a poor chance of being involved in a person's responses to life or in the way the world is viewed.

Fourth, the children's sermon should aim at having an influence upon the ways in which people, and children in particular, view the world and respond to life. "Entertainment"—doing something cute for children—is not a worthy goal of a children's sermon. Children's understandings can be enriched with stories, images, and teachings that are rooted in biblical faith. The incorporation of these contents into actual responses to life will depend upon children's relationships with adults who love them and who truly care that children grow in a faith that is Christian. The content of the children's sermon can provide a common place in worship for children and adults to begin a process that runs deep and takes time to nurture.

The delivery of children's sermons takes various forms. In the twentieth century, object lessons and moral lessons dominate the literature of published children's sermons. Object lessons rely upon children being able to understand an analogy between an object and a meaning. The meaning is usually abstract. Moral lessons as they appear in the literature tend to be didactic in nature, and they cover a wide range of moral categories from "smile at people you meet" to "be kind to one another."

Stories appear in the literature, but not as often as object lessons and moral lessons. Recent attention to developmental theory and to narrative theology tends to indicate that the story is the most significant form for children's sermons. Stories draw the imagination to experiences told through plot and characters. This provides a bridge for listeners to think of their own lives in terms that the story presents.

Other forms of children's sermons include dialogue conversation with children, dramatic presentation by actors or puppets, and simulated experience in which children role-play the content of the sermon. Because learning for children is primarily through experience, actual participation in the sermon can increase its teaching value.

Visual aids can enhance the presentation of children's sermons. Visuals are helpful in claiming and holding the attention of young children. However, visuals should stimulate children's imagination to fill the gaps with their own images as much as possible. Storytelling in its purest form does not rely upon visual aids.

Forms for children's sermons can be as varied as the imagination allows. Care should be taken that the form adopted will effectively carry the content of the message.

There are good reasons for inclusion of a children's sermon as an act of worship within the worship service. The children's sermon deals with the way children think, allows forms of communication that appeal to children, influences impressions through feelings, movement, and closeness to a worship leader, tells children they are included and that someone thinks of them as wor-

ship is prepared, and allows young children to be involved in the word-event in worship.

There are important precautions to note about the children's sermon. The children's sermon can be inappropriate for children if its content is adult-oriented and if its forms are trite, moralistic, demeaning, or manipulative. It can focus attention on children rather than on God. It can place children in a vulnerable position where their self-esteem can be hurt by insensitive actions of adults. It can be theologically and spiritually shallow.

How well children's sermons serve the purposes of worship depends upon how seriously and creatively they are used to serve all the people who worship. If they truly nurture children, they will nurture everyone. The presence of children serves the whole people of God. *See also* Affective Development; Bible Study; Child Development; Children's Church; Cognitive Development; Drama; Faith Development; Liturgy; Moral Development; Narrative Theology; Object Lesson; Preaching; Puppets; Role Playing; Storytelling; Visual Methods; Worship; Worship, Children's.

FOR FURTHER REFERENCE

Foster, Charles R. *Proclaiming the Word with Children*. Worship Alive! Nashville, TN: Discipleship Resources. Worship Alive! is a series of undated leaflets on worship and the arts.
Gobbel, A. Roger, and Gertrude G. Gobbel. *The Bible—A Child's Playground*. Philadelphia: Fortress, 1986.
Smith, W. Alan. *Children Belong in Worship: A Guide to the Children's Sermon*. St. Louis, MO: CBP Press, 1984.

J. A. Carr

Seton, Elizabeth

Elizabeth Bayley Seton (1774–1821) founded a sisterhood, was the first American-born Roman Catholic saint, and is credited with beginning parochial education in the United States. Born in pre-Revolutionary New York, her family was loyalist and Anglican. Her father, Richard Bayley, was a physician; her mother, Elizabeth Ann Bayley, died when she was three.

Elizabeth married William Magee Seton, and they had five children before his early death in Italy. She came to know Roman Catholicism through a family with whom she lived there. When she returned home, she converted.

Faced with supporting her children after being cut off from her family because of her conversion, she opened a school in New York City. It was designed to teach basic skills in reading and writing, pass on culture, and foster piety. Many of the pupils were orphans. She later moved to

Baltimore, then Emmitsburg, Maryland. There she opened the first Catholic free school and founded St. Joseph's College (for women).

Elizabeth later took her vows and founded the American Sisters of Charity, which grew to twenty communities before her death. Besides her school, care of orphans, and leadership of the sisterhood, Elizabeth Seton was known for being a friend and an inspiration to others as a model of holy living. She was beatified in 1963 and canonized in 1974. *See also* Religious Orders; Roman Catholic Education.

M. E. Moore

Seventh-day Adventist Education

The Seventh-day Adventist Church, organized in 1863, has historical roots in the Advent awakening of 1841–44. Though sharing soteriological beliefs (beliefs about salvation) with many mainline conservative Protestants, it is distinguished by its belief in the imminent premillennial Second Advent (return of Christ), observance of the seventh-day (Saturday) Sabbath, and belief in the ultimate utter extinction of the incorrigibly evil. At the end of 1988 the church had 5,749,735 members (675,702 in the United States) and was working in 184 countries in 671 languages.

A concern for religious education dawned only gradually for pioneers whose zeal was centered in eschatology (doctrine about final events). It has developed in three dimensions: denominationally-sponsored schools (kindergarten–university), Sabbath schools (comparable to Sunday schools) and youth societies centered in the local congregation, and home and family life education.

KINDERGARTEN–UNIVERSITY SCHOOL SYSTEM

At the end of 1988 Adventists operated 79 universities and colleges, 689 secondary and worker training schools, and 4,450 primary schools. Graduate work was based in 10 institutions and offered elsewhere by extensions with 3,366 enrolled. At all levels 773,633 students were enrolled with 43,474 teachers. The educational system was most fully developed in North America (13 colleges and universities), the Far East, Latin America, Africa, and the South Pacific. Andrews University (Berrien Springs, Michigan) includes the most prominent Adventist theological seminary. Andrews also offers degrees in religious education; through 1989, seventy-three had received the M.A., and fifty-six the doctoral degrees. The religious education department is based in the School of Education and offers specializations in the church, school, and family settings.

SABBATH SCHOOLS AND YOUTH SOCIETIES

At the end of 1988 Adventists reported 56,568 Sabbath schools with 6,619,940 members (children 0–18 are 49 percent, adults 19 and older, 51 percent). There were 44,846 Adventist youth and Adventist junior youth societies with 1,859,033 members and 11,693 Pathfinder Clubs (coeducational clubs similar to Boy Scouts and Girl Scouts) with 511,643 members. During 1984 (latest data available) the church held 1,925 camps with 149,560 youth and junior campers.

HOME AND FAMILY LIFE EDUCATION

Programs in home and family life education are on three levels: leadership training, broad-spectrum programs, and specialized seminars. Professionals are trained in graduate programs in family life at Andrews University and Loma Linda University in California and in extension programs in other countries. Certificates of family life educator are awarded, and annual family life conferences are held. Broad-spectrum programs include weekend seminars presented for the entire congregation for family wellness. Home and Family Day twice yearly is in the recommended church calendar, and materials are prepared for Home and Family Week for all denominational elementary schools. Specialized seminars are given in marriage, parenting, singles ministry, divorce recovery, drug dependency, family worship, and other areas.

HISTORY

Adventists are indebted to Luther, Methodism, the Sunday school movement, and other influences in the development of their concepts of religious education. James White (1821–81), leader, publicist, administrator, and initiator of almost every enterprise in the fledgling Adventist Church, was first to advocate religious education. Deeply concerned for the children of believers who many times were not adequately nurtured by parental example and instruction, he prepared the first religious education publications for youth, writing with notes propped on his lunch basket while his horses fed and rested. Thus *The Youth's Instructor* was born in 1852. He prepared the first nineteen Sabbath school lessons. Although White's own formal education lasted only twenty-nine weeks, he nevertheless spearheaded the drive for the first Adventist elementary school and marshalled forces for the first Adventist college, established in 1874 at Battle Creek, Michigan.

Ellen G. White (1827–1915), wife of James, as early as 1852 wrote of the need for religious education in the family. In 1872 she published her testimony "Proper Education" setting forth educational ideals. By 1910, through struggle and experience, the Adventist school system was in place. Many of White's 119 books, 160 pamphlets, and over three thousand periodical articles deal with education. An overview of her evolving thought (from 1872 to 1915) is found in *Fundamentals of Christian Education*; her most advanced, polished concepts are found in *Education* (1903) and *Ministry of Healing* (1905). White's educational thought could be summarized as follows: Every school has its organizing principles. For some these are the Greek and Roman classics, human speculation, and competition. However, this is not "proper education." The cross is the center of Christian education. Education has as its purpose the restoration of the student to the image of God and should be organized around the service principle with love as the primary motivator. The goal of education is right morality based on freedom of choice and the right exercise of willpower. Education is the harmonious development of the physical, mental, spiritual, and social powers. It prepares students for usefulness in this life and for fuller joy and wider service in the world to come. Teaching and practicing health principles are integral to education. Schools, as well as the home, should preferably be in rural environments so as to enhance work-study, meaningful cross-generational relationships, and the ability to see God in his handiwork. The Bible is to be the chief, but not the only, textbook. Parents and teachers must model the values they wish to transmit. Parents are primarily responsible for religious education, over half the character is formed, White believed, before schooling begins. The individual is also responsible, and the role of the teaching institution is supportive. Reflection, investigation, and individuality should be fostered, and excellence should be the watchword in education.

YOUTH AND FAMILY MINISTRIES

The first SDA youth society was organized in Hazelton, Michigan in 1879, somewhat along the lines of the Christian Endeavor. The Seventh-day Adventist General Conference of 1901 made youth societies a recognized part of the church. Currently Adventist youth rally under the banner of AYA (Adventist Youth Association) or AJYA (Adventist Junior Youth Association). In 1913 Ellen White asked Arthur W. Spalding to do something for the families of the church, and in 1919 he founded the Home Commission of the General Conference to coordinate the nurture and outreach programs of the congregations. By 1975 this had grown into the Home and Family Service and leaders were named in conferences and churches. This commission was merged into the Church Ministries Department in 1985.

RELIGIOUS EDUCATION CURRICULA

Goodloe Harper Bell (1832–99), teacher of the first denominationally sponsored school, molded the Adventist Sabbath school more than any other person in the early days, and prepared throughout the 1870s and early 1880s the first graded series of Sabbath school lessons. By 1892 each age level had its own published curriculum. Adventists continue to publish their own Sabbath school curricula at all levels. With some adaptations the same lessons are taught around the world at a given age level. Elementary and secondary schools have their own religious education series in English. An international edition serves other languages. Denominational science textbooks present the creationist alternative. Delmer and Betty Holbrook beginning in 1975 spearheaded efforts to develop family life curricula. More than a score of curricular programs have been developed on a broad spectrum of marriage and family topics for use in local churches.

THEOLOGICAL AND PHILOSOPHICAL BASIS

Adventist religious education could be described as theologically conservative but pedagogically progressive. Theologically it sees the learner as born in sin but capable of infinite development. Through Christ every individual has some perception of right, a desire for goodness. However, individuals struggle against an antagonistic power that they cannot resist alone. According to Ellen White, "To withstand this force, to attain that ideal which in his inmost soul he accepts as alone worthy, he can find help in but one power. That power is Christ." An appropriate philosophical label for the Adventist religious educational stance is "redemptive holism." The individual is an indivisible entity, a whole. Sin places individuals in the midst of a cosmic conflict between good and evil. Our human nature tends to alienate us from God and other people and to fracture our own personalities. Christ enters our lives to restore physical, mental, emotional, and spiritual wholeness in *at-one-ment*. The *kerygma* (proclamation) proclaims the good news to the individual; the *didache* (teaching) nurtures him or her into the way of life of that gospel. Religious education in all its facets and agencies has the purpose of bringing the individual to a saving and deepening relationship with Jesus Christ. *See also* Eschatology; Private Religious Schools; Private Schools and Religion; Salvation.

FOR FURTHER REFERENCE

Knight, George R., ed. *Early Adventist Educators.* Berrien Springs, MI: Andrews University Press, 1983. Chaps. 1–4.

Spalding, Arthur W. *Origin and History of Seventh-day Adventists.* Washington, DC: Review and Herald Publishing Association, 1962. Vol. 2, chaps. 3, 5, 6, 19; vol. 3, chaps. 7, 12.

White, Ellen G. *Education.* Mountain View, CA: Pacific Press, 1942. P. 29.

———. *Fundamentals of Christian Education.* Nashville, TN: Southern Publishing Association, 1923. Pp. 15–46.

———. *Ministry of Healing.* Mountain View, CA: Pacific Press, 1905.

J. B. Youngberg

Sexuality

A person's sexuality involves the sum total of that individual's sexual characteristics, traits, feelings, attitudes, and behavior. From both spiritual and psychological perspectives, sexuality is viewed as an important aspect of a person's created being. It heavily impacts one's body image, self-concept, self-esteem, social relationships, and even worship of God.

BIBLICAL UNDERSTANDINGS

The Bible presents principles to guide and increase understanding of sexuality. It first presents our sexual nature as an integral aspect of the way that God created human beings. Genesis 1:27 ends with the phrase "male and female he created them," indicating the deliberateness of the sexual design. It is also apparent from this same verse that sexuality is, in some way yet to be fully understood, reflective of God's image. "So God created man in his own image, in the image of God he created him; male and female he created them." God approves of sexuality in the inclusive evaluation of the whole creation that "it was very good" (Gen. 1:31). Prior to the entrance of sin into the world, Adam and Eve were at ease with and accepting of their own and each other's sexuality. "And the man and his wife were both naked, and were not ashamed" (Gen. 2:25). The equality and value of both men and women is noted in Galatians 3:28.

Scripture also indicates that God's original creation of sexuality included sexual intercourse. The phrase "they become one flesh" (Gen. 2:24) refers specifically to genital sexual intercourse. Since this occurs prior to Adam's and Eve's first sins, sex cannot be considered an impure addition to God's original plan. Much of the Song of Solomon emphasizes the importance and value of finding pleasure in sex.

An important biblical principle regarding sexuality is that sexual intercourse is to occur only between husband and wife. Various biblical passages condemn adultery (Exod. 20:14; Matt. 5:27–32), fornication (Eph. 5:3), homosexuality (Lev. 18:22; 20:13; Rom 1:26–27; 1 Cor. 6:9–10), and bestiality (Exod. 22:19; Lev. 18:23; 20:15–16). There are no biblical references to the sexual practice of masturbation.

Within marriage, sexual union is symbolic of the man and woman becoming as one (Gen. 2:24; Matt. 19:5). The importance of a husband loving his wife and a wife loving her husband is noted in Ephesians 5:25, 28, and Proverbs 5:15–19 emphasizes the value of a married couple finding pleasure in sex. The Bible supports mutuality and equality in the marital sexual relationship (1 Cor. 7:3–5; Eph. 5:21).

The sexual relationship between husband and wife is also used in both the Old and New Testaments as a symbol of God's relationship with his people (Isa. 62:5; Eph. 5).

PSYCHOLOGICAL UNDERSTANDINGS

Psychologists vary widely in their understanding and treatment of sexuality in their theories of personality. For Viennese neurologist Sigmund Freud, sexuality was central to human personality development and psychological functioning. In his theoretical framework, psychic energy, which connects with sensual and somatic satisfaction, is sexual energy. The developing human passes through stages during which sexual energy is associated with different erogenous zones: oral, anal, and genital. He associated sexual energy with *eros* or life instinct, which is in opposition to *thanatos* or destructive instincts.

Most psychological theorists since Freud see sexuality as less central to personality development. C. G. Jung believed that sex played a widely varying degree of importance in human behavior. Sometimes everything depends on the individual's sexuality and at other times its importance is minimal. Alfred Adler believed that sexuality had psychological significance especially as it related to the person's feelings of inferiority or personal strength. Carl Rogers gives sexuality psychological significance primarily as it impacts and plays a part in the individual's identity and level of self-esteem.

STAGES OF DEVELOPMENT

Sexuality during the infancy, toddler, and early childhood years should be viewed as being generally related to children's feeling pleasurable physical sensations, feeling secure, experiencing warm and loving contact with parent figures and exploring, discovering, and feeling comfortable with their own bodies. During the elementary school years sexuality is associated with identifying with parent role models, developing peer friendships, further development of childhood masculine or feminine behavior and habit patterns, and gaining confidence in personal abilities and skills. The onset of puberty brings renewed focus and intensity to the young person's sexuality. The physiological ability to function sexually, the ability to impregnate or to become pregnant, strong feelings of sexual arousal, the development of secondary sexual physical characteristics, and increasing interest in developing relationships with the opposite sex are important aspects of sexuality during the adolescent years.

Adulthood brings the opportunity for the integration of sexual loving into a long-term relationship. The development of a long-term sexual relationship, procreation, and nurturing the next generation are important aspects of adult sexuality. Mid-life and old age also bring certain challenges to the individual's sexuality. Coping with mid-life issues often causes a person to confront the consequences (positive and negative) of earlier sexual choices. Successful adjustment in old age requires further adaptation to lessening sex drive and, at a more general level, acceptance of life as it has been and as it is with its limits.

An important aspect of the development of mature sexuality is learning how to establish increasingly intimate relationships with the opposite sex. As romantic, loving relationships become more intimate and the degree of commitment increases, it is normal and healthy for the degree of sexual intimacy to increase also. Sexual intercourse is ideally a comfortable next step after the marriage ceremony.

Autoeroticism, self-stimulation, and masturbation are normal and healthy aspects of sexuality. Active and frequent masturbation is common in childhood and adolescence but should diminish during adulthood as the individual learns better self-control and establishes a meaningful sexual relationship in marriage.

Sexually deviant behavior can be classified in four different categories. Sexual deviance may involve inappropriate intensity and frequency (e.g., satyriasis), mode of expression (e.g., sadism), object of affection (e.g., pedophilia), or context (e.g., prostitution).

Sexual dysfunctions can occur between married sexual partners. Problems with arousal, pain, and orgasm are experienced by both men and women. These difficulties can be caused by physiological, anatomic, relational, or psychological sources. Effective specific treatments for many of these dysfunctions are offered by urologists, gynecologists, and psychotherapists who specialize in the treatment of sexual dysfunctions.

CURRENT TRENDS

Religious education regarding sexuality must respond to current trends in the social context in which the church ministers. A brief discussion of four of the most salient of these trends follows.

In large part stimulated by the women's liberation movement, a much-increased focus has been placed on female sexuality. Particular emphasis has been placed on women's needs, pleasures, and rights to sexual fulfillment. As a result of this important change, men have been challenged to become more aware, sensitive, and responsive to their sexual partners. This trend enhances the opportunities for both genders to increase the pleasure and fulfillment in their sexual loving.

The social and religious sanctions regarding sexual intercourse only in marriage are becoming more relaxed. Factors influencing this change include easily accessible and effective birth control methods, legalized abortion, a growing single adult population, and an increasing divorce rate.

Inflation and other economic issues are making the original purchase of housing more difficult. Single adults often join together with two or more other singles to purchase a residence with their pooled resources. Gender frequently is not an issue in these primarily financial alliances.

Many other couples are purposefully living together in order to be more assured that they are sexually and otherwise compatible before entering into a marriage commitment. Some of these couples decide to continue residing together without marrying for various reasons, considering marriage an unnecessary or negative issue.

As society moves toward accepting and expecting sex between adolescents and adult singles, the religious community also is becoming more tolerant. Though in most religious circles adultery is still considered sinful, sex among unmarried singles adults and older adolescents is expected in many denominational groups. Sanctions regarding remarriage after divorce are also becoming more permissive.

Churches in America are also becoming more tolerant toward homosexuals. The rise and growth of the gay rights movement has won increasing political and social benefits for the homosexual community. Homosexuals can adopt children and win custody of their children. Both the American Psychiatric Association and the American Psychological Association have determined that a homosexual or bisexual orientation does not constitute or indicate sexual deviance or any other mental disorder.

Though there continues to be much conflict within the church community about whether homosexual acts are sinful, there is growth toward more tolerance and acceptance of homosexual people. Ordaining homosexual ministers is a major issue in several denominations. Acceptance of the homosexual is the central purpose of a few groups like the Metropolitan Community Churches.

Increasing concern about sexually transmitted diseases is also influencing sexuality. Though gonorrhea and syphilis are still important medical problems, little social concern is generated by their presence. Much public attention has been given to the spread of infection with the herpes virus. This usually nonfatal disease causes many people to determine whether or not they would warn a possible sexual partner of the danger of infection.

AIDS (Acquired Immune Deficiency Syndrome) is a life-threatening disease that is contracted primarily through sexual contact, contaminated blood transfusions, and the use of contaminated needles to inject illicit drugs. Though first transmitted primarily through homosexual contact, the heterosexual community is increasingly at risk through exposure from bisexuals and prostitutes. "Safe sex" and "You are going to bed with every one your partner has gone to bed with before you" have become ingredients of the current sexual mind-set.

RELIGIOUS EDUCATION

Focus on sexuality as a part of religious education should be directed in several important areas. Generally, it is important not to desexualize biblical characters during Bible studies. Churches must wisely determine how sex education should be handled in their religious training. Training both of children and of adults might be considered as well as training parents how to educate their children in healthy sexuality. Issues relating to abortion and contraception must be handled carefully to ensure accurate fit with theology. *See also* AIDS; Language, Inclusive; Personality, Theories of; Psychosocial Development; Sexuality Education.

G. K. Olson

Sexuality Education

Sexuality education is more than teaching young people about the physical aspects of reproduction. It is a process, beginning at birth and continuing throughout life, of acquiring information and forming values, attitudes, and beliefs about personal identity, relationships, and intimacy.

Parents are the primary teachers of these attitudes and values for their children, who continually absorb and internalize them, although they learn from others too, including friends and teachers. Almost as powerful as parents in teaching values and attitudes are the media: television, movies, music, advertisements, and even toys.

Often the messages given through the media are contradictory to those given within the family. Both sets of messages are subject to evaluation by the church or synagogue on the basis of religious teachings. The Scriptures provide basic general guidelines for sexuality education. These basic principles are given more specific meaning as they are combined with reliable information from current medical, psychological, and sociological research.

Many denominations provide curricula for use within the home or by the church or synagogue. These may always be adapted to fit the local situation and combined with materials from other sources.

Teachers of sexuality education in the religious setting need to be familiar with the teachings of their particular group. It is also important that teachers be comfortable with their own sexuality and with both scientific and colloquial terms needed to talk about sexuality. Their comfort level needs to be such that they can discuss openly, without embarrassment, any questions or concerns their students may bring up. There are no "bad" or "stupid" questions; however, there may be wrong answers that youth will continue to believe if their concerns are not discussed. Students are often more comfortable talking about some concerns with persons other than their parents.

Any sexuality course for children or youth has greater effectiveness if parents are also involved in parallel and joint sessions. This not only gives the parents the same information their young people are receiving, but most importantly, it opens up communication within the family, even long after the sessions are over.

Sexuality education with older children and youth may be done as a series on a weekly basis, but for the cumulative effect, an intensive weekend provides the better format for learning. In a five-session weekend youth and parents might be separate for the first four sessions. Possible themes might include:

- The meaning of being male and female in today's society

- The physiology and anatomy of the reproductive system

- Understanding the meaning of love, intimacy, and relationships

- Clarifying values and understanding the decision-making process based on those values, including religious values

- Facilitating communication within the family (for the final session with youth and parents together)

SEXUALITY EDUCATION

Age Level	Developmental Considerations	Teaching Goals and Methods
Preschool	Children experience both pain and pleasure through their physical senses; they will explore their own bodies and begin to form a self-image based on their explorations and experiences; as they grow, they will differentiate themselves from babies and ask questions about babies (particularly if they have younger siblings); they also learn to differentiate between boys and girls; they begin to learn about sex roles and relationships based on adult role models.	Children should be provided with care, love, and security; under close supervision, they should be allowed to explore their surroundings; as they grow, they should be assured that their family loves them and that God created and loves them; their questions about physical differences between boys and girls and about babies should be answered simply and directly; positive roles and relationships should be modeled.
Grades 1–4	Children's self-image continues to form; competition between boys and girls is high; they continue to learn about sex roles and relationships through adult and media models; they gradually begin to learn about the role of males and females in conception and about prenatal stages of growth.	Children should continue to be provided with love and care, and all should be treated equally; Scripture verses on creation and God's care should be related and memorized; the wonder of creation can be taught through stories, museum exhibits, and nature walks; children's questions regarding sexuality should be addressed directly; varieties of families and family roles should be discussed; positive role models are key.

(continued)

All of these sessions should also provide opportunities for youth and parents to enhance their own self-esteem. When persons feel good about themselves they are less apt to be coaxed into behaving in ways contrary to their values, and they are less likely to "use" others for their own gratification. Responsibility and mutuality are two values that can be reinforced through a course in sexuality. Providing knowledge is not giving permission to act out that knowledge. On the other hand, knowledge *is* power—power to stand up against peer pressure to behave contrary to one's own value system. Knowledge gives power through an understanding of the issues involved, before any situation arises in which a person's values might be compromised. Thus it is never too early to begin sexuality education.

For older youth, additional topics can be in-

Age Level	Developmental Considerations	Teaching Goals and Methods
Grades 5–8	Children's secondary sexual characteristics develop and they gain the ability to function sexually; with the development of reason, they can better discuss and understand such things as love, intimacy, mutuality, relationship, and responsibility; they are in the process of clarifying their values and establishing a decision-making process based on those values.	Children should be taught more explicitly about the anatomy, physiology of the reproductive system; Scripture passages regarding sexuality and relationships should be studied; family and community mores and values should be openly discussed (perhaps during an intensive weekend workshop on sexuality attended by both parents and children); attention should be paid to maintaining open communication between the generations.
High School	Understandings of the meaning of love and sexuality deepen, and values continue to be clarified.	Family and community mores and values should continue to be affirmed; discussion might address such traditional topics as appropriate sexual expression or such controversial topics as birth control, abortion, and sexually-transmitted disease; individual experiences can be related and role play used.
Adult	Single adults gradually discern the role of sexuality apart from a long-term relationship; married adults move from initial sexual intimacy to long-term relationship, procreation, and nurturing; older adults adapt to physical changes and increasing physical limitations.	Adults with similar concerns should be encouraged to meet together for biblical study and discussion regarding their sexuality; parents should additionally be given instruction regarding their role in the sexuality education of their children.

cluded. Important are not only traditional topics such as appropriate expressions of sexual intimacy and the importance of monogamous relationships, but also more controversial issues such as birth control, abortion, and sexually transmitted diseases including AIDS.

Taking developmental stages into consideration, it is probably best in a single course to combine youth of no more than two or three years spread in age. There are wide differences between seventh graders and ninth or tenth graders, for instance, in interests and experiences. Graded courses in sexuality education are available from some denominations for older elementary, younger youth, older youth, and adults.

Parents of young children are a group with special needs and concerns. They appreciate help in knowing how and when to bring up the subject of sex with preschoolers and what words are appropriate to use. They can also be helped to watch for the "teachable moment" for moving naturally into a conversation about sex by building on a child's interest, for example, on hearing sanitary napkins referred to as bandages.

In such a parent class each parent might anonymously write out questions that seem troublesome. The teacher should also be prepared with appropriate questions frequently asked by children, for example, "How can a girl have a baby without being married?" As each question is read, the group may discuss possible responses, or two parents could role-play the questions as being asked by a child and answered by a parent, followed by general discussion. *See also* AIDS; Parenting; Sexuality.

L. C. Seifert

Sherrill, Lewis

Lewis Joseph Sherrill (1892–1957) contributed to the understanding of the psychological and theological roots of religious education. A Presbyterian minister, he was professor of religious education at Louisville Presbyterian Theological Seminary (Kentucky) and Union Theological Seminary (New York).

In *Guilt and Redemption* (1945) he combined psychological and theological insights to interpret educationally the basic Christian doctrine of salvation. In *The Struggle of the Soul* (1951) he interpreted the crisis at the beginning of each psychosocial stage as a time when a person is particularly open to the guidance of God. His final book, *The Gift of Power* (1955), was a comprehensive theory of Christian education. Adapting Paul Tillich's method of correlation, Sherrill found eight biblical themes (affirmations about God's self) that corresponded to human predicaments. For example, the theme of "creation" is related to the predicament of human beings rejecting God's rule and using the resources of the world in a selfish way. *The Rise of Christian Education* (1944) is a volume of history that begins with the Jewish educational experience and traces Christian education from the early Christian period up to the Reformation. No sequel was written. *See also* Education, Theories of; Psychosocial Development; Theology and Education.

C. E. Nelson

Shinto

Shinto is the name usually applied to the ethnic religious tradition of Japan. The word is ironic, for it is Chinese, *shen* and *tao* meaning in the Chinese language "the way of the gods or good spirits." The Japanese for this name is *kami no michi*. Whatever the label, the roots of this tradition go back to Japan's prehistoric past, or as Shinto puts it, to the Age of the Kami. The *kami* are gods or spirits inhabiting objects or events of nature and society that elicit responses of awe or reverence.

HISTORY

By the first century A.D. the sun-goddess, Amaterasu, the deity of the dominant Yamato clan, had assumed dominance over this populous pantheon. To this day the Japanese flag still bears Amaterasu's image.

Civic myth tells the story that in 660 B.C. Amaterasu sent her grandson, Ninigi, down to earth to rule the Japanese islands. The sword, jewels, and mirror of Amaterasu and of the imperial family are still central objects of devotion in the great shrine at Isé.

Buddhism came to Japan from the Asian mainland in the sixth century A.D. and soon combined with Shinto to form Ryobu Shinto, literally "two-way Shinto," Buddhist saviors being combined with Shinto kamis. During the ages of Buddhist dominance, Shinto receded to the background as an ethos or climate of natural and civic piety. Shinto shrines with their distinctive *torii* gateways continued to dot the Japanese landscape, and the kamis persisted as objects of devotion and allegiance. Shinto sacred writings, the *Kojiki* and *Nihongi*, date from the eighth century and show strong influence from Tang dynasty China.

To Shinto piety and Buddhist symbolic forms were added still a third element, namely, Confucian ethics and philosophy, interpreted, be it added, in distinctively Japanese ways. One such interpretation of Confucian and Neo-Confucian thought produced in Japan the code of *bushido*, literally, "the fighting knights' way."

During the Tokugawa period (1603–1867) these developments stimulated a notable revival of Shinto devotion and thought known as the School of National Learning. Rejecting the alien, Chinese ways of other scholars, the leaders of this school pored over ancient Japanese texts, seeking roots in their own land and culture. Once Kado (1669–1736) had founded this school, others, notably Motoori (1730–1801), carried it forward. Motoori spent thirty years on a commentary on the *Kojiki* and wrote critical interpretations of the *Tale of Genji*, an early eleventh-century proto-novel.

In 1853 Commodore Perry opened the closed kingdom of Japan to foreign influence, and in 1868 the Tokugawa shogunate gave way to the restoration of the emperor Meiji. During the Meiji Restoration, under the devoted leadership of young samurai, Japan modernized. Shinto was seen as a living, powerful, and true value system. At first attempts were made to make Shinto the established religion, with accompanying hostility to both Buddhism and Christianity as foreign faiths.

THREE DIVISIONS

When this attempt failed, Shinto was divided into three aspects, shrine Shinto, sect Shinto, and domestic Shinto. The second and third were designated as religious, and the first was interpreted simply as civic allegiance. However, shrine Shinto soon became state Shinto with governmental support of more than a hundred thousand shrines and priests. With governmental support came governmental control. This system continued until 1946, when the shrines were disestablished and the emperor renounced his divinity. Since World War II, shrine Shinto has had the same relation to government as churches have to the government of the United States.

Meanwhile, sect Shinto has continued to play a significant role in Japanese religious life. During the Meiji period there were thirteen officially recognized sects, and doubtless others that were unrecognized. These were popular religious movements that arose spontaneously under charismatic leaders. Several were so-called mountain sects, celebrating one or another of Japan's mountains. One Meiji sect that continues in vigorous life to the present is Tenrikyo. It was founded by a peasant farmer's wife, Miki Nakayama (1798–1887), who arose as a charismatic leader. She is said to have miraculously healed her husband, providing a model for continuing faith healing. Receiving revelations from deities whom she called Divine Parents, she gathered followers and spread her message. Tenrikyo survived governmental persecution in World War II and today reports more than two million followers as well as an active missionary movement both in Japan and overseas.

Once the clamp of governmental control was removed after World War II, new sectarian groups, sometimes called "new religions," flowered in great profusion. Most of these movements combine elements of Buddhism or Christianity with a Shinto base and charismatic leadership. One of the largest of these groups is Soka Gakkai, also sometimes known as Nichiren Shoku. Another is PL Kyodan, the PL standing for "Perfect Liberty," which is featured in its creed.

Domestic Shinto continues its quiet existence as the "godshelf," or *kamidana*, in many Japanese homes. Often is the *kamidana* is added a *butsudana*, or Buddhist shelf. Either is a kind of family altar for daily devotion, prayer, and ceremonial offerings.

What the future holds for Shinto is a matter for much speculation. One Japanese scholar has written that the kamis are traditional residents of Japan's rural landscape who will not survive the massive urbanization of the present age. Others argue that Shinto meets a felt need of Japan's people and will endure as long as this need lasts.

Shinto, consisting as it does of ethnic myths and rituals of the Japanese people, has generated its own ways of communicating these forms to each generation. For example, the populace throngs to Shinto shrines to celebrate the New Year. People continue to go on pilgrimage to the Imperial Shrine at Isé and to other holy places. Schoolchildren honor the flag with its symbol of the sun-goddess, Amaterasu, and the names of Japanese soldiers who have died in war are inscribed in a book of the Yasakuni Shrine, which is somewhat analogous to America's Arlington National Cemetery.

During the Tokugawa age the so-called School of National Learning pursued research and scholarship in the Shinto tradition. Since World War II Kokugakuin University in Tokyo has pursued similar educational goals.

J. A. Hutchison

Simulation

A simulation is the imaginative reenactment of a past event or of a possible future event so as to allow the free interplay of defining characteristics. A simulation does reenact an event, but it is designed to do more than repeat what has already occurred or what is expected. The defining factors or characteristics of an event are given free play so that their interaction can be experienced and the outcome can be better understood.

Educators use simulation because they can give participants a deeper understanding of how things happen and why. To simulate the conflict within a group may help persons understand better why it is happening. Before visiting a public official, a teacher may simulate the conversation to help students prepare for the encounter. Law students simulate a court session in order to learn about court procedures and history students simulate a historical event in order to better appreciate why it happened as it did.

Religious educators use simulation in many of the ways mentioned above. They simulate an event such as an encounter between youth and parents to prepare for such a conversation. They reenact past events to better understand why they happened. They may simulate an overseas event to better understand world problems. Biblical events can better be understood by simulating them. Religious educators are also using computers to simulate biblical, historical, contemporary, and possibly future events.

In religious education the use of interpersonal simulations is like theater, except that the interaction is spontaneous rather than by a prepared script. It is like role play, except that a simulation involves a larger event with various interacting roles. The situation is established, the various participants are given instruction for their own roles, and then they play out the situation freely and spontaneously until they reach some predetermined conclusion.

A group may simulate almost any biblical story. To simulate the story of the prodigal son a particular setting must be agreed upon. For example, the group may have the conversation between the father, younger brother, and older brother as the latter returns from the field to find the welcoming party in progress. One person should try to understand the attitude of the father, another the younger brother, and a third the older brother. When they are prepared, the older brother arrives and the conversation takes place spontaneously. The conversation may stop after an agreed time, say, ten minutes. After the simulation the participants discuss what happened in the simulation and why. This debriefing is very important from an educational point of view.

The parts of a simulation are four: the agreement about the scene, the background study for various roles, the spontaneous interaction between characters until a predetermined conclusion, and the debriefing about what has happened and what has been learned. More persons can be involved by letting a whole group prepare for each role and having them choose one of their members to play the role. They may even take turns playing the role as the simulation continues.

An interpersonal simulation has a structure that defines and relates the interacting roles, although the action and conversation is spontaneous within the established characteristics. For a biblical simulation the story itself should set the structure. If the structure is historically accurate, then participants can gain historical understanding. For example, the trial of Jesus before the Sanhedrin can be simulated by having Herodians, Sadducees, and Pharisees represented.

The structure need not always be historical. It may include a fictional situation to allow the characters in the story to interact. For example, Isaac may call a family counsel with Rebecca, Jacob, and Esau after discovering he has been tricked into giving the blessing to Jacob. The spontaneous interaction can give insight into the story even though such a family council is not described in the biblical account.

Structures that work well in biblical simulations are trial scenes, councils, debates, town meetings, paired discussion, and conventions, to mention a few. In the book of Job each of the friends attempts to counsel Job. A simulation may begin with a statement by Job. Then persons representing each of Job's friends try to counsel according to the relevant text. Finally someone paraphrases God's response to Job.

Dramatic simulations are used by religious educators because they can stimulate great insight into a situation, whether contemporary, historical, or biblical. Simulations as here described are for junior high or older youth, although simpler simulations can be used with children. Clarity of purpose, good direction, adequate preparation, spontaneous interplay, and careful discussion are vital elements. *See also* Dramatization; Role Playing; Sociodrama.

FOR FURTHER REFERENCE

Miller, Donald E., Graydon F. Snyder, and Robert W. Neff. *Using Biblical Simulation*. Valley Forge, PA: Judson, 1973.

D. E. Miller

Singles

The word "single" presents a challenge. What does it mean to call someone "single"? Webster's dictionary first defines single as "one not married," a definition that expresses a negative condition and carries the inferred assumption that marriage is society's norm for personal worth. But should it be, or have we overvalued being "coupled" or married? We too easily define ourselves by roles: wife, husband, single. We need to examine critically the underlying assumptions surrounding our use of the term "single," because we share responsibility for the resulting effect on us all.

Singleness is a birth-to-death issue. We are born single and many of us die alone. We all pass through many stages of singleness in our lives. Even in permanent primary relationships there is aloneness that can lead to loneliness, lack of self-esteem, and the lack of security that many singles experience. Indeed, in a culture that soon may be more single than coupled, singles and marrieds may have a lot more to share in common than differences that warrant separation into two categories.

Statistics vary according to the source, but about 40 percent of the U.S. population is single according to a 1980 report by the U.S. Census Bureau. This means that there are roughly 59 million unmarried adults over the age of 18. Fifty-nine percent are always single. Eighteen percent are divorced. Five percent are separated, and 22 percent are widowed. Twenty-five million are men, and 34 million are women. A study by the U.S. Department of Commerce in 1981 looked at single people age 15 and older and found: 39.6 percent are 65 years of age and older; 24.6 percent are 45–64; 8.7 percent are 35–44; 18.4 percent are 25–34; and 8.7 percent are 15–24. The

A SINGLES MINISTRY

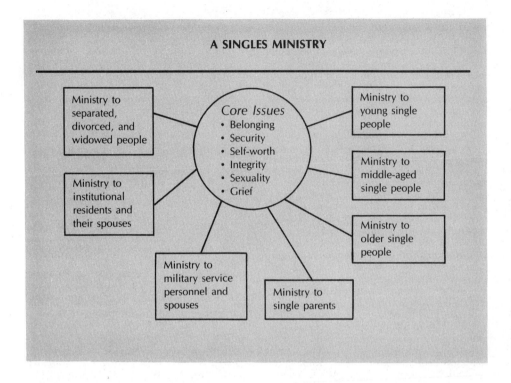

Ministry to separated, divorced, and widowed people

Ministry to institutional residents and their spouses

Core Issues
• Belonging
• Security
• Self-worth
• Integrity
• Sexuality
• Grief

Ministry to young single people

Ministry to middle-aged single people

Ministry to older single people

Ministry to military service personnel and spouses

Ministry to single parents

largest group of singles by age are those over 65, most of whom are women. Many of these people are living on less than adequate income in less than adequate housing. Singleness is everybody's issue.

In the church, repeated efforts have been made to work with singles. Some have focused exclusively on those eighteen to twenty-six years old, i.e., those called "young adults." This group has often included singles as well as young married couples without children. Seniors are the other age group of singles on which much ministry has been focused. Many congregations or coalitions of congregations have provided physical, emotional, and political resources for the concerns facing this growing population. In recent years, as the divorce rate has risen, the church has also focused attention on the needs of the divorced and divorcing. However, many groups dealing most effectively with support for these people are outside the church, e.g., Parents Without Partners, Beginning Experience, and We Care. Widows and widowers comprise another group of singles whose immediate needs at the time of the spouse's death are met very well by the church community, but possible ongoing needs are often not considered; in most cases the message is that people who have lost a spouse by death should have dealt with that loss in a year or less. Another group either ignored or assumed to be well integrated

are those who are married but participate in church life as "singles." The spouse may be of another faith or absent for a significant part of the marriage. Single parents can be in any one of the groups above. Within the church community, single parents are primarily women.

CORE ISSUES FOR MINISTRY

The fact of being single itself is not the issue around which effective singles ministry should happen. More important are the core human concerns that affect all those in effect living in the single state—belonging, security, self-worth, etc. These concerns can rightly be isolated and made the central issues in singles ministry, but most of them need a larger frame of reference, because they relate to the attitudes, practices, and programs of the church and its leadership as they either enable or block singles from having their needs met as an integral part of the congregation. Certain groups of singles also have specific needs that the church can assist with by encouraging a particular ministry activity for that group of singles. A diagram accompanying this entry shows how a singles ministry might look overall.

The core issues of singles ministry include:

1. Belonging: Belonging means achieving a sense of community and intimacy within the congregation. This involves changing the attitudes

within the congregation so that singles are recognized and affirmed as belonging to the group.

2. Security: People in a single life-style look for stability and security in a home, job, and friends just like anybody else. They look for support and affirmation of their stability and maturity as responsible members.

3. Self-worth: Single persons are whole persons and seek to be valued for who they are with gifts and personhood as singles. They are not of less value because they are not married or "paired" in a traditional way.

4. Integrity: Singles seek a life purpose and vocation with meaning and to contribute to society in a full way. The church needs to support this venture of single persons.

5. Sexuality: Singles seek to be healthy in all aspects of their single life-style and struggle to live a sexual life that is wholesome (healthy) in the midst of ethical ambiguities and relatively little help and guidance from the church.

6. Grief: Grief is another significant but sometimes elusive issue. Often singles over the age of thirty indicate by the stories they tell in the privacy of one-to-one counseling that they have awkward, complex feelings when the reality confronts them that their singleness may simply not be a stage as much as a life-style. A single in a congregation who asks for a singles group may be trying to articulate the loss felt at not being part of a couple. This is a grief cycle and needs to be processed. Logically, not everybody can be a part of a couple. Twenty-five million singles are male and thirty-four million are female. To tell someone that he or she has just not found the right person is deceiving.

These core issues are involved in daily and weekly ministry of the congregation's ongoing life and program. It is also a ministry of changing attitudes, language, and practices within the congregation. But singles of all types may also need to be brought together to share their experiences in the congregation and develop strategies to improve their acceptance and integration into the congregation. Opportunities for core issue studies include retreats, Sunday morning class, weeknight classes, one-day seminars, and intergenerational opportunities.

PARTICULAR NEEDS

When the issue of singles programs, activities, and organizations is raised, the focus shifts from general concerns of all singles to particular needs that exist among groups identified in the outer groupings (single parents, separated, divorced, etc.). These programs are developed according to the specific needs that may exist—support groups, growth groups, skill or information, life-style adjustment, biblical studies, etc.—for the particular persons who may be divorced, always single, or single for a specific period of time.

It needs to be said that there are many singles for whom no special or particular ministry is needed and there are congregations who have made adjustments toward the inclusion of singles.

THE NEED FOR INTEGRATION

The major component of ministry with single people is movement toward integration. Unlike some other situations in a congregational setting, the singles issue could be solved if and when the church and its members become better educated about the issues and become part of the dialogue that helps all people to be a community. The integration model involves paying particular attention to new members who are single, listening to them, and helping them find the resources they need to feel welcome. Unlike marrieds, they do not have another person to rely on during the sometimes awkward "getting to know you" stage of being a new member. Integration involves intentional singles leadership, making sure that singles are represented on the church council, committees, and planning groups in the same ratio as they are present in the total membership of the congregation. Integration means linking people by their issues. A single person may not have a support system to talk over child problems, job insecurities, aging parent issues, a recent divorce, the breaking up of a relationship, grief, and other concerns. People in ministry can often introduce people with similar concerns to each other with a simple word or phone call.

Inclusive use of language is an important aspect of an integrated ministry among singles. People who are single not by divorce or death are always "single," not "never married" or "not yet married." In a culture that defines family over and over again as being a permanent primary relationship with children, the "Family Pot Luck" and "Family Devotions" probably mean that as well. If a congregation "family" means the whole family of God, that must be stated clearly again and again. We can never assume inclusiveness. In teaching illustrations and sermons it is helpful to move beyond illustrations of our own families and intentionally include images and stories about individuals who are identifiably single. Not all of us can understand the love of God in terms of love of a spouse. Equally difficult is the use of divorce as the only example of the way in which we experience alienation or sin. Awareness is the key to all of the above and does not require a complex structure or a new organization. Changing language most often needs to be modeled first by the professional staff.

The church is called to be a community of persons bound together in Christ Jesus, experiencing trust and love in fellowship. The church is to be more than a clustering of families or collection of individual persons. It is to be a family in itself that gives life to other families and individuals. This means valuing singleness in the environment of our gatherings. *See also* Adult Development; Language, Inclusive; Lifestyle; Systems Theory; Young Adults.

FOR FURTHER REFERENCE

Brown, Raymond K. *Reach Out to Singles*. Philadelphia: Westminster, 1979.

Johnson, Douglas W. *The Challenge of Single Adult Ministry*. Valley Forge, PA: Judson, 1982.

Timmerman, Joan. *The Mardi Gras Syndrome*. New York: Crossroad, 1984.

C. C. Peter

Skill Training

Skill training is one of several approaches to education that seek to provide the student with the means of acquiring mastery of an appropriate set of habits in a limited situation. A more adequate definition requires a discussion of "skill" prior to elaboration of training in skill.

"Skill" refers to an acquired proficiency or competency in relation to a specific, limited goal. There are at least five steps involved in the development of skill, whether one discusses skill in athletics, an academic subject, or a technical field. A first step is the identification of a goal or objective the student wishes to pursue. Each area of study represents a discrete, limited field and carries with it a specific set of tasks that must be mastered for skill within that field to be acquired.

A second step in the acquisition of skill is the identification and analysis of the many tasks required for progressive competency in the field. This may be accomplished by observation, instruction, research, or other means. This identification and analysis helps the student become aware of the complexity of the skill itself and the approximate hierarchy or order in which the tasks should be mastered.

A third step is practice in the various tasks involved in the selected skill. Each skill involves the sequencing of tasks in a consistent and reliable manner. Practice in the performance of the various tasks involved familiarizes the student with the execution of each task, the sequence in which the tasks are performed, and the sensorimotor functions involved. Through practice, the student becomes progressively more proficient at the tasks in the field.

A fourth step involved is feedback. Here the student has the chance to compare his or her abilities or performance in a given task with the stated goals and objectives set at the beginning of the learning process. This comparison allows the student to alter the goal or objective, reevaluate the component tasks involved in proficiency in the field, adjust the practice routine, or recondition her- or himself to better achieve the goal or objective. Feedback allows one to assess one's progress toward the goal or objective and adjust one's training toward that goal or objective appropriately.

A fifth step is the ability to extrapolate from one specific ability to other similar or closely related abilities (e.g., the application of mathematical skills in physics) or to interpolate from a general ability to more specific and component abilities (e.g., the application of one's general skill at golf to the task of putting). Skill is more than the acquisition of knowledge or information. It includes the ability to move beyond the limited field of study and the application of the principles or tasks involved in learning to a wider field of related knowledge.

There are a number of specific, identifiable skills related to learning as well. Skills are often identified with habits but may be distinguished from the latter in several ways. A habit generally involves only a conditioned response to certain stimuli and may or may not involve the development of a specific motor skill. A skill involves the patterning of both specific sensorimotor coordination and an intentional cognitive action directed toward mastery of the field. A skill involves the intelligence in a way quite distinct from the development of a habit.

The number of skills involved in education is limited only by the imagination, one's physical abilities, and one's societal constraints. The following list, while not exhaustive, suggests a number of skills that may be identified with particular attention to religious education:

1. Information-gathering or heuristic skills: proficiency in the ability to make observations about one's environment, to find biblical and historical references, to listen carefully to information shared orally, to ask questions, and to search out further implications of information received

2. Problem-solving skills: the ability to develop, test, and evaluate hypotheses in response to problems posed within one's experience in the world

3. Interpretive or hermeneutical skills: the ability to receive information about the world through such sources as the Bible, one's own or others' experience, and find meaning in that information for the way one lives one's life and makes sense of the world

4. Critical skills: the ability to weigh evidence, assess the relative merits of various arguments, make distinctions between opposing

positions, and form one's beliefs following a careful sifting of the available data

5. Symbolic skills: the ability to appreciate and be receptive to the power of symbols to communicate through word, art, music, liturgy, dance, etc.

6. Affective and social skills: the ability to relate to others as persons of worth, to experience the total range of elements involved in being human (i.e., emotional, spiritual, cognitive, symbolic, etc.), to develop a respect for all God's gifts of life, and to be tolerant of the differences between various social, ethnic, religious, and political groups

7. Skills of precision: the ability to sharpen one's beliefs and thoughts through openness to other opinions and further evidence, the drive to push beyond the immediate answers that are apparent in "raw" experience

8. Communicative skills: the ability to express one's beliefs, opinions, and feelings in a clear, concise manner, the ability to share oneself with others openly and honestly

9. Evaluative and moral skills: the ability to make decisions about the way to live one's life and relate to others in a way that respects their rights and the commonly accepted patterns of behavior in life, to engage in discussions about moral responsibility on a regular basis

10. Transformative skills: the ability to allow one's interpretive skills to influence one's understanding of the world, to combine one's construction of reality through beliefs and theory making with one's actions, to commit one's skills to work toward the cause of human liberation and transformation

Skill training can be either an external involvement in the development of skill in a particular field or the process of developing skill or a skill itself. Each of the five steps in the development of skill allows an opportunity for the involvement of a teacher or trainer. Teachers may help learners identify the goal or objective to be pursued through lecture, example, discussion, or any number of other methods. They may help learners identify and analyze the component tasks of a skill and help organize these tasks into an effective learning or training model. Teachers may assist learners in their practice routine, making suggestions for more effective use of the hierarchy of tasks and their energy. Feedback may be one of the more useful functions of the teacher or trainer as learners assess their progress toward the goal or objective. And the teacher or trainer may help learners make the connections between the specific skills and the wider related skills and component skills that allow them to transcend the limited scope of skill training.

In the final analysis, however, the acquisition of skill occurs when the external, observable standards identified with a particular skill become internalized in the understanding of the person and incorporated into the interdependent functioning of motor skills, intellectual processes, and interpretive functions of the one who learns these skills. The function of the teacher or trainer in skill training is primarily that of establishing a positive learning environment, providing an occasion for the steps of skill development to occur, supporting the person at every stage of the process, providing the tools and materials required for the effective learning of the skill, and offering constant feedback to assist the learner's evaluation of her or his progress. See also Competency-based Education; Feedback; Learning Theory; Transfer of Learning.

W. A. Smith

Smart, James D.

James D. Smart (1906–1982), Canadian theologian, scholar, prophet, and educator, was the architect and first editor-in-chief (1944–1950) of The Christian Faith and Life Curriculum: A Program for Church and Home, developed by the United Presbyterian Church, U.S.A.

This enterprise was launched at a time when rigid conservatism in the church scorned education, and education was severed from revelation. Smart challenged the Presbyterian church to assume its responsibility in God's purpose: to produce attractive materials that were theologically and educationally sound, backed by a regional network for leadership training and comprehensive participation in church and home.

He was the author of many scholarly and popular books for ministers and laity. But his pivotal breakthrough volume, The Teaching Ministry of the Church (1954), influenced thousands, including church educators, seminary students, and theologians, for whom church education had previously been a dead end. See also Curriculum; Reformed Education.

C. R. Ikeler

Social Action

Social action is the fruit of religious belief. For many religions, social action is a duty in response to a divine command; for others, it is a virtue, the result of aspiring toward a holy life. Social action takes many forms, from the personal giving of alms to the corporate reform of unjust governments. Religious social action, as it reflects the desire to create conditions of truth, goodness, and justice in human society, provides a basis for ecumenical cooperation among denominations and religions despite theological differences. It can also be the basis for division within a particular tradition if it involves siding with one political party or social class. Action thus forms one pole in the dynamic character of religious life, the other pole being belief.

RELIGIOUS BACKGROUND

Both holy scriptures and the ethical teachings of religious traditions teach service to other human beings and proper attitudes toward others. The Ten Commandments given by Moses in the Hebrew Bible form the basis for Jewish and Christian ethical conduct and include the individual's attitude and behavior toward God and toward other human beings. In the New Testament, Jesus simplified these commandments into two great commandments, "You shall love the Lord your God with all your heart" and "You shall love your neighbor as yourself" (Mark 12:28–31). It is this second commandment that serves as the basis for Christian social action. Jesus attempted to define "neighbor" in the broadest possible way, to mean all people, including, like the Samaritan in his day, those of other class, national, or ethnic backgrounds—even "the enemy."

Throughout most of recorded history, religious social action has consisted of care for the hungry, the sick, the poor, the uneducated, and the homeless. Religious bodies have for centuries established schools, hospitals, and charitable institutions. Even in the modern welfare state, most religious social action involves contributions of food, clothing, education, and medical supplies to people who suffer from famine, disease, and war.

All of the world's major religions have taught that rulers have a particular moral obligation to the ruled. For example, the right relationships taught in Confucianism dictate specific responsibilities that a ruler, as a kind of parent, has for the welfare of the ruled. In the Christian tradition, theologians like Augustine, Thomas Aquinas, Calvin, and Luther have elaborated the responsibilities of kings, princes, and other rulers. In Islam, writers like Abu al-Qasim al-Husayn al-Maghribi (d. 1026) and Abu al-Hasan al-Mawardi (d. 1058) have done the same. In modern times, with the rise of industrialization and democracy, religious people have engaged in social action aimed at changing government policy. From a historical viewpoint, this is a recent phenomenon.

MODERN MOVEMENT

In nineteenth-century America, Christian social action took the form of campaigns to abolish slavery, to prohibit the drinking of alcohol, to establish norms for industrial justice, and to give women the right to vote. These social reform measures drew upon Christians from the ranks of all Protestant denominations and formed the basis for a movement known as the Social Gospel. There was an optimistic attempt, prior to World War I, to establish a Christian civilization in America through this social action. The Federal Council of Churches of Christ (FCC) formed around common commitment to social action and a predilection to eschew questions of theology that kept the churches divided into denominations. The Social Creed of the Churches affirmed by the FCC (1912) included principles of industrial arbitration, a minimum wage, and the end of poverty. Walter Rauschenbusch (1861–1918) provided a capstone for this movement with *A Theology for the Social Gospel* (1917), a reexamination of Christian theology guided by the principle of progress through social action.

For Roman Catholics, the papal encyclical *Rerum Novarum*, 1891, affirmed the Vatican's concern for social justice. While condemning socialism, it also condemned exploitive forms of capitalism, insisting on the responsibility of the state for the welfare of all its citizens.

But the dreams of the nineteenth-century social activists were shattered with the outbreak of World War I. The most advanced "Christian" nations were suddenly engaged in the most massive human murders in history. New "neo-orthodox" theologians added a corrective to the humanistic social gospel by calling attention to the necessity of faith in a transcendent God and a profound awareness of human sin. Reinhold Niebuhr, professor of applied theology at Union Seminary in New York, provided the theological underpinning for twentieth-century social action with *Moral Man and Immoral Society* (1932). The basic premise of this book is that even if individuals act morally, collective human behavior, as it is manifest in Western industrial democracies, contains a profound depth of evil and sin. Niebuhr advocated a new Christian realism that combined the social analysis of Karl Marx (critique of industrialism) and Max Weber (critique of bureaucracy) with his own concept of sin, particularly his criticism of individual and collective egoism and the will to power. Niebuhr provided a theological basis for Christian social action to enter the political world of power politics, the world of political lobbying by the churches on issues of social justice.

Nonviolent resistance, developed by Mohandas K. Gandhi in South Africa and then applied in India, was an effective tool for social change in the British Empire. Gandhi's actions were rooted in spiritual discipline and love, which he saw as common to all great religions. Martin Luther King, Jr., a student of Reinhold Niebuhr, was converted to the philosophy of nonviolence after studying Gandhi. In the civil rights movement King maintained that the goal was not defeat of the white man but the natural coming together of the souls of white and black alike. King believed that nonviolence was the ethic of Jesus; it required "noncooperation with evil" and "cooperation with the constructive forces of good." He stood in opposition to revolutionary violence.

Twentieth-century Christian social action has largely followed traditional patterns; in the National Council of the Churches of Christ in the U.S.A., for example, the majority of funding has gone to Church World Service (CWS), which distributes food, clothing, and medical supplies. However, a new layer of social action that stresses government reform has been superimposed on the traditional. In the 1920s and 1930s there were large campaigns by the clergy against militarism. In the 1940s religious leaders urged governments to participate in the establishment of a just world order. The United Nations was the fruit of the combined action of political leaders and the cooperative efforts of Protestants, Catholics, and Jews. In the 1950s racism and the nuclear arms race were the focus of much religious social action. The tumultuous 1960s brought campaigns for civil rights legislation and against the war in Vietnam. The 1970s followed with advocacy for the rights of all minorities and for the human rights of victims of other governments.

Mater et Magistra, issued by Pope John XXIII in 1961, reaffirmed the call for social justice earlier heard in *Rerum Novarum*. The Second Vatican Council, in the Constitution on the Church in the Modern World, addressed the issue in *Gaudiumet Spes* (1965), noting the present imbalances, recognizing the aspirations of people, and affirming the solidarity of the church with the whole of the human family. A third important statement was *Economic Justice for All*, a pastoral letter on Catholic social teaching and the U.S. economy issued by the U.S. Council of Bishops in 1986.

PRESENT SITUATION

Liberation theologies, which developed out of the experience of oppression of minorities, had roots in the social action aimed against status quo powers. The most important expositions were Gustavo Gutierrez's *A Theology of Liberation* (1971) and James H. Cone's *A Black Theology of Liberation* (1970). These works argue that revolutionary social change is the moral responsibility of Christians. Liberation themes are used in recent social activism for women's rights, racial justice, migrant farm workers' rights, gay and lesbian rights, Third World liberation, native American rights, and ecological stability. With the new claims by different social groups came conflicts between groups competing for political power, jobs, and social benefits.

Social action connected to political change has also had the effect of creating factions within denominations and across the religious spectrum.

The problem was illustrated by competition for and politicization of funding within the National Council of the Churches of Christ in the U.S.A. in the 1970s. In the 1980s the abortion issue typified the debate between two groups of Christians, both arguing on the basis of human rights, conservatives for the rights of the unborn and liberals for the rights of the mother. Social activists have also been divided over whether a free market economy or socialism is a better basis for a just society. They are divided on the issue of whether the military budget should be increased or reduced. The growing movement to stop the nuclear arms race in the 1980s is a social action coalition largely composed of the middle and upper classes. A number of minority leaders, who feel priorities should be on social justice issues, feel the peace movement draws too much attention away from liberation issues. Thus, although social action in the nineteenth and early twentieth centuries provided the basis for ecumenical cooperation, the twentieth century has brought together several competing ecumenical alliances divided along political lines.

Social action is therefore not an easy area in religious education. On the parish level, for example, careful education is required in order to bring understanding of the positions taken by church bodies. People may find it difficult to struggle with the social, economic, and political issues that are factors in social injustice; they may be more willing to act as citizens affirming their faith than to accept positions taken by the institutional church. Discussion, research, and observation are all important. Groups willing to discuss issues may not be willing to act; parishes active in supplying food banks and homeless shelters may not see the need for legislation. People need, first of all, to be affirmed in what they are already doing; only out of this acceptance will they be willing to look at alternatives.

Seminaries and religious schools, which were primarily formed for the creation of denominational ministers, have become more ecumenical and more involved with social action issues in the twentieth century. Many seminaries now award divinity degrees to students who, for their field training, elect to work in a social action ministry instead of a church. In addition to the type of knowledge they impart, individual seminaries are now also characterized by the type of social activists they produce. *See also* Liberation Theology; Social Gospel; Social Justice, Education for.

FOR FURTHER REFERENCE

Beach, Waldo, and H. Richard Niebuhr. *Christian Ethics: Sources of the Living Tradition*. New York: Ronald Press, 1973.

Ferm, William Deane, ed. *Contemporary American Theologies: A Book of Readings*. New York: Seabury, 1982.

Handy, R. T., ed. *The Social Gospel in America, 1870–1920.* New York: Oxford, 1966.

Hollenbach, David. *Claims in Conflict: Retrieving and Renewing the Catholic Human Rights Tradition.* New York: Paulist Press, 1979.

Khadduri, Majid. *The Islamic Conception of Justice.* Baltimore: Johns Hopkins, 1984.

Miller, Robert Moats. *American Protestantism and Social Issues, 1919–1939.* Chapel Hill, NC: Univ. of North Carolina Press, 1958.

Niebuhr, Reinhold. *Faith and Politics.* Edited by Ronald H. Stone. New York: George Braziller, 1968.

G. L. Anderson

Social Gospel

The social gospel was a movement in American Protestantism that flourished late in the nineteenth and early in the twentieth century. The goal was to apply the Golden Rule and biblical understandings of justice to the social and economic order. Numbers of seminary professors like Walter Rauschenbusch (1861–1918) of Rochester Seminary and pastors like Washington Gladden (1836–1918) of First Congregational Church in Columbus, Ohio, were the visionaries and leaders who prompted colleagues and laypeople to revise their understandings of the social order.

The social gospel leaders found counterparts in movements like Anglo-American Christian socialism and various liberal Continental agencies for social reform. They partook of the same climate but seemed generally unaware of or were distanced from Roman Catholic impetuses like those that issued from Pope Leo XIII and his social encyclicals. Similarly they took little notice of and remained independent of evangelistic and conservative Protestant forces like the Salvation Army and early Pentecostalism, forces that in their view charitably brought acts of mercy to victims of industrial change but did not address the structural problems of the age.

CHARACTERISTICS

These social gospel pioneers began with a comprehension of what modernity did to traditional human arrangements and economic understandings. In town and country life individuals could transact on independent terms. In the late nineteenth-century industrial city, large corporations, led by men of great wealth who had no reason to deal with individual workers, held power. These required restraints of a sort that no private citizen, however moral, could bring. At the same time, employees of corporations and factories needed to have the power to form labor unions and bargain collectively. These rights and powers were often denied them, sometimes in the name of Protestant-based individualist and laissez-faire doctrines. These workers needed empowerment and theological legitimation that the social gospel set out to help provide.

A characteristic term for Walter Rauschenbusch and other leaders appeared in one of his book titles. It spoke of "Christianizing" the social order. That word provided a clue to the ethos of the movement. It was progressive and in its own way optimistic, though its leaders grounded their views in realistic understandings of human nature and social structures. They were influenced by evolutionary approaches but were put off by social Darwinism, which turned out to be antisocial, "survival of the fittest" individualism.

Some social gospel leaders were influenced by economic thinkers like Henry George (1839–1897), who advocated that all land be taxed and all other taxes be abolished in order to encourage development and break up the monopoly power of landholders. Yet it cannot be said that leaders of the movement were united around any economic or political program; they were often accused of vagueness in respect to policy. At times they would unite with "trustbusters" in the White House and Congress to further counter the power of large corporations and monopolistic trusts. Some borrowed notions of workers' cooperatives from British Christian socialism. None united with the few Marxist or other radical socialist organizers or agitators in proposing resort to violence in class warfare. They were instead meliorists who would work inside the existing political order, which Rauschenbusch and others considered partly "Christianized" along with the family, public education, and other institutions or agencies. There were a few socialists among them, notably George Herron (1862–1925). Herron, a professor at Iowa College (later Grinnell), disgraced himself, however, through personal scandals and was not long to be reckoned with among the leaders.

Theologically the social gospel pioneers saw themselves as retrievers of early Christian and other ancient themes. Josiah Strong (1847–1916), an editor, minister, and pioneer bureaucrat, particularly insisted that it was theological conservatives who had been the modernizers through their departures from biblical views. In the eyes of Strong and others, what became the social gospel was an attempt to retrieve all orders of life for the Christian sphere. Believers could not serve only personal, private, individual, familial, and leisure aspects of life. They must reenter the political, social, and economic orbits. To the end of pursuing such a "holistic" vision, Rauschenbusch and others drew on classic sources. There was much recourse to the Hebrew prophets because they challenged earthly powers and sided with the poor and oppressed. Jesus and images of the simplicity and common life of early Christians were prime. Rauschenbusch as a church historian also resorted to medieval sects, Anabaptist Reformation thought, and other selected exemplars.

Despite their long memories and claims, however, the social gospel leaders were perceived and sometimes dismissed as liberals and modernists. They did draw on liberal European thought, particularly in respect to the proclamation of the fatherhood of God, the "brotherhood of man," and the coming kingdom of God (a favorite symbol). They did favor liberal views of Jesus, being more preoccupied with "the historical Jesus" than with what looked to them like irrelevant views of Christ based on Greek philosophy. To promote social change, most of them also criticized doctrines like original sin as limiting.

IMPACT

The social gospel made its way through major seminaries, periodicals, and prime pulpits. It is hard to measure its power or limits, since it was contemporaneous with various progressive movements that had their own momentum. Yet there were institutionalizations of its impulses, as in the social creed of the Methodist Episcopal church and in the ethos and program of the interdenominational Federal Council of Churches, formed in 1908.

There were blind spots in the social gospel. In retrospect, many leaders in the train of Josiah Strong sounded racist and were in fact Anglo-Saxon imperialists. There was almost no reference to the plight of emancipated but discriminated-against blacks, whether in the rural South or, increasingly, in the urban North. The spokespersons were all men and, hence, spokesmen who cherished Victorian views of woman and the home. Few of these leaders became public advocates of women's suffrage and some were explicit about keeping women out of public roles.

In conventional accountings, the social gospel came to its crest during Rauschenbusch's prime years before World War I. By the time he wrote *A Theology for the Social Gospel* in 1917 the good times were past. World War I offered setbacks to progressives and the 1920s in America presented an uncongenial social climate. When Christian social realist movements of the sort that the brothers Reinhold and H. Richard Niebuhr advocated in the 1930s came to prominence, the social gospel was in eclipse, often dismissed as simplistic. Yet some of its motifs and tendencies lived on. Thus Martin Luther King, Jr., for instance, explicitly drew on Rauschenbusch and the movement to help give energy and direction to the civil rights movement in the 1960s, and there are periodic recoveries of interest in the piety, program, and achievement of the Rochester professor and some of his colleagues. *See also* Social Action; Social Justice, Education for; Liberalism.

FOR FURTHER REFERENCE

Fishburn, Janet Forsythe. *The Fatherhood of God and the Victorian Family: The Social Gospel in America.* Philadelphia: Fortress, 1981.

Gladden, Washington. *Recollections.* Boston: Houghton Mifflin, 1909.

Handy, Robert T. *The Social Gospel in America.* New York: Oxford University Press, 1966.

Hopkins, C. Howard. *The Rise of the Social Gospel in American Protestantism, 1865–1915.* New Haven, CT: Yale University Press, 1940.

Rauschenbusch, Walter. *Christianity and the Social Crisis.* 1907. Reprint. New York: Harper & Row, 1964.

M. E. Marty

Social Justice, Education for

Social justice is the effort to deal justly with people through the social, economic, and political systems in which they live. A fundamental teaching of the Jewish and Christian traditions is that all human beings are made by God and are formed in God's image. Thus, by virtue of creation, all human beings have dignity—not a dignity dependent on social class, race, color, sex, or national origin, but a dignity that is their birthright conferred by God.

Because they are created and formed in God's image, human beings share a common nature that transcends all differences. This is the basis for the relationship they have to God and one another. The Jewish and Christian traditions teach that religious institutions have no meaning or purpose in and of themselves. They exist to remind us of our sacred origin and bond.

Our understanding of human persons and relationships has expanded in this century primarily because of advances made in the social sciences. Human beings, it is argued, are fundamentally social, born into a particular social, economic, and political context. That context affects understandings and relationships. Moreover, human relationships extend well beyond the private or personal realm. Human beings relate to and affect the lives of one another through the intricate web of economic, social, and political structures and systems.

The social sciences have also provided a fuller understanding of the nature of structures and systems, which are more than the individuals they comprise. They have a history that predates individuals. They have goals, objectives, values, and agenda of their own, and have within themselves power to destroy or enhance life. They are the mediators of human dignity. Consequently, the structures and systems themselves as well as the individuals within them must be brought under moral scrutiny.

EDUCATION FOR SOCIAL JUSTICE

Age Level	Understandings	Teaching methods
Preschool	Children begin to form a positive or negative self-image based on their experiences and their treatment by others; they gradually learn there are people other than themselves, and they begin to learn how to relate to others; they are too young to understand concepts of difference or similarity.	Adults must meet the basic needs of children, providing them with love, care, and security; model acceptance of and concern for others; demonstrate and teach cooperation and constructive methods of conflict resolution.
Grades 1–8	Children gradually realize differences and similarities between themselves and others and tension may result; relational attitudes and skills continue to develop; they gradually explore and understand concepts of friendship and cooperation; they also gradually understand the concept of and the need for justice (initially between themselves and others, then on a more global basis).	Younger children can be taught Scripture verses about God's creation of all people and care for them; differences and similarities between children should be discussed; role play may help children above grade 3 to better understand each other; children can be taught Scripture verses about God's justness and God's call to us to be just (i.e., Ps. 72:1-4; Amos 5:24; Mic. 6:8); they can hear and read about biblical people who were just (i.e., Exod. 18:13-26; Ruth 1:22-2:7); encourage younger children to practice justice by sharing toys and materials, abiding by the rules of games, and seeking a fair solution to quarrels; older children should discuss news reports about such issues as hunger, homelessness, and refugees; anxieties the children might have about such things happening to them should be discussed as well; children should be given the opportunity to participate directly in social actions such as food and clothing drives.

Age Level	Understandings	Teaching methods
High School and Adult	They are increasingly able to understand interrelationships and value cooperation and justice; they are increasingly able to examine causes of injustice and seek justice through both individual and corporate action.	Scripture verses about justice should be further studied and discussed; social justice actions already taken should be affirmed and further actions encouraged; the relationship between personal lifestyle and social justice should be examined, as should corporate responsibility; discussions might also address concepts of the reign of God, the role of the church in the world, and the teachings of liberation theology; nonviolent action and other methods of seeking social change can be taught.

Despite this growing awareness of the public and political nature of human existence and the effect social structures have on human dignity, religious institutions have preferred to focus on the interpersonal and private dimensions of human existence; they have particularly been reluctant to come to terms with the public and political nature of their own structure and to assume responsibility for it. The Holocaust, white racism, sexism, global poverty and hunger, the threat of nuclear annihilation, all carried out through the normal operation of social structures and systems, have usually been met by religious institutions not with bold initiatives but with timidity.

RELIGIOUS EDUCATORS

It should come as no surprise then that social justice has not been central to religious education. A review of the themes of major conventions of professional religious educators and the attention given to issues of social justice in professional journals suggests that social justice is not a matter of central concern.

Yet there have been in the past and continue to be prophetic voices calling religious institutions and religious education to accept responsibility for all dimensions of human existence, including the public and political. From the past the voice of George Albert Coe (1862–1951) particularly stands out. A leader in the religious education movement in the United States, he was the author of several volumes, including *A Social Theory of Religious Education*. He believed that human beings are characterized by the ability to critically

reflect on and transform themselves and society. He saw religion as a process of valuation. Religious education provides the structure for coming to terms with the ultimate ends and values of life. It enables people to critically evaluate themselves and society in light of ultimate ends and values, and it also enables people to intervene in society and transform it. Coe's insights into the nature of the human person, the role of religion and religious education in society, and the structural and systemic forces that threaten human dignity are being heard today by religious educators writing on justice.

A voice from the Third World, Paulo Freire, is having the greatest impact on social justice theory in religious education today. Freire, a Brazilian educator, is best known from his work *Pedagogy of the Oppressed*, which emerged out of his experience working on the problem of adult literacy in Brazil. Freire believes that education is never a neutral process; it can be a tool for enslavement or for emancipation. The goal of all education, Freire maintains, is to humanize. But in order to humanize, the obstacles to humanization must be analyzed, confronted, and transformed. Traditional education, he believes, does not have within itself the power to transform because it is essentially "banking education." Its purpose is to pour information into the student, who then gives it back to the teacher. It is not education geared to enable the student to critically intervene in and transform reality.

In the emancipating educational process Freire calls "conscientization," the hierarchical relationship between teacher and student is radically altered. The teacher becomes not a depositor of information but a problematizer. That which is perceived to be unproblematic—the normal, natural, acceptable, and inevitable—is posed as a problem requiring critical intervention by teacher and student alike. For Freire, it is in the actual critical intervention in reality and reflection upon it that we begin to understand the economic, political, and social obstacles to human liberation and acquire the ability to transform them.

EDUCATION FOR JUSTICE

Despite the task so clearly laid out by Coe and Freire, much work remains to be done in educating for justice in religious education today. The relationship of the private to the public and political dimensions of human existence, for example, needs to be taken seriously. Human beings are never merely private beings; they are at one and the same time private, public, and political. The point is to seize and direct the public and political dimensions of existence and educate through them.

Religious education must also come to terms with the nature of structural and systemic injustice. It must face head on what is involved in social change. Can education for justice be done without developing the skills of social analysis? Justice education, however, must move beyond consciousness raising and analysis. Attention must be given to the kind of action required to change structures that threaten human dignity. Charity, traditionally promoted and sanctioned by religious institutions, although ameliorative, does little to address the imbalance of social power and may actually perpetuate it. Effective education for justice must also reckon with the fact that power is seldom dislodged through moral persuasion alone; conflict and confrontation are inevitable.

Religious education for justice begins when the young child protests "That's not fair!" As parent or teacher deals with the immediate situation, the parameters of what is considered fair or unfair are established.

Children learn first through immediate interrelationships. The circle becomes extended when religious education teachers refer to news reports that many children see on television. They see hunger, war, and other forms of violence of which children are victims. Their own anxieties (Could this happen to me?) must be explored constructively by the teacher's asking why this can happen and what we can do about it. Helping to buy food for the food bank or participating in a hunger march can be a visible symbol of connection to other people.

Adolescents and adults are mature enough to explore the way in which structures impede or enhance justice. They can face the indifference through which those who are comfortable insulate themselves from injustice. Basic biblical material

from the prophets is essential at this point, because they did not mince words in describing both injustice and indifference as disobedience to God. Gospel teachings from Mary's Song (Luke 1) through Jesus' proclamation of the reign of God are further biblical bases. Recent statements by religious bodies are also bases for further study.

The next step is for people seriously to confront the possibilities for intervention in behalf of social justice by their religious communities, locally and nationally. Are they content with ameliorative efforts? Are they willing to act individually as agents of change or willing that the congregation or national body should assume such a role? Actual participation in projects for hungry, homeless, or war-displaced people both expresses concern and encourages ever deeper wrestling with issues. This is action-reflection as a method of learning. *See also* Action-reflection; Coe, George Albert; Peace, Education for; Moral Development; Social Action; Social Gospel.

S. C. Toton

Social Science

"Social science" is a generic term for the collection of those disciplines that are focused on the detailed, systematic, and empirical study of human beings and their interrelations with individuals, groups, and institutions.

The social sciences embrace all or major portions of anthropology, economics, education, geography, history, law, nonmedical psychiatry, psychology, and sociology. Sometimes the term "behavioral science" is used synonymously with "social science." At other times, behavioral science is used to signify a group of disciplines including psychology and sociology, which form a generic subdivision of social science.

PURPOSE, METHODOLOGY, AND CHARACTERISTICS

The purpose or goal of social science is to empirically examine human activity in order to ascertain the behavioral nature and functions of the person. The human activity that social science studies directly or indirectly takes place within social circumstances or in one way or another relates interactionally to social activity. The behavioral nature and functions of the person that social science endeavors to discover do not comprise ultimate nature or ultimate functions, but rather those dimensions of human nature and functions that can be unearthed by scientific observation and analysis.

Social science proceeds from, works through, and is validated by empirical methodology because social science strives to discover what is actual and real in human activity, as contrasted to ideology or to philosophy and theology. Ideology examines human behavior in order to elaborate what its proponents would like to see become actual and real. Philosophy and theology study human behavior (among other things) primarily to discover what ought to be true in personal activity.

There are at least seven major characteristics of social science research and activity, namely empiricalness, quantitativeness, replicability, publicness, objectivity, conditionality, and value freedom.

Social science is *empirical* in that it is characterized by close adherence to observable phenomena, so that whatever conclusions are reached from the investigation follow naturally from these empirical procedures rather than from sources that are speculative, self-authoritative, uncontrolled, external, or a priori.

Social science is *quantitative* in that it assigns numerical values to observations in order to attain greater precision in measuring both the data and the differences between and among various classes or related data.

Social science is *replicable* in that its procedures are reproducible under the conditions operative in the original investigation. This characteristic enables social science to be independent of the personal vision, experiences, biases, or lifestyle of the researcher.

Social science is *public* in that its procedures and results are completely communicable and communicated. This characteristic facilitates freedom of inquiry and rigorous examination of results by any interested person.

Social science is *objective* in that its procedures and findings can be empirically tested. By use of carefully constructed methodological controls, social science can free itself from the inevitable tilt of the personal subjective judgment of the researcher and so can attain a more or less objective approximation of the personal and/or social phenomenon under investigation. Objectivity in social science is not the same as objectivity in philosophical science. Social science objectivity is admittedly as close an approximation of the actual or real as imperfect human endeavor can attain. Objectivity in philosophical science is total detachment and complete isolation from human subjective influence. Indeed, research data from both the social sciences and the physical sciences indicate that philosophical objectivity is not attainable by human beings.

Social science is *conditional* in that the explanations it offers hold true only for a certain range of phenomena and are generalizable only when specified conditions are realized. Theories and other types of social scientific explanations are provisional and are revised as new and expansive data arise.

Social science is *value free* in that it is concerned with an impartial investigation and explanation of phenomena, without regard for any system of thought or for any group of people that would assign value judgments to either the phenomena or to the conclusions of the research. Social science, therefore, is not normative. It does not make statements about what ought to be. Value freedom in social science means that the methodology of social science research is of such a nature as to render more or less inoperable any human or group values of the investigator during the course of the research procedure. (Value freedom in philosophical science is absolute in that it denotes the total absence of values in research methodology.) Social science does indeed investigate the norms and values of persons and groups, but in a way that seeks to discover what exists rather than what ought to exist.

ROLE IN RELIGIOUS EDUCATION

The role of the social sciences in religious education is probably the most foundational and hence the most practical issue facing the field. Virtually every religious education practice is determined by the response which one gives to this absolutely cardinal issue.

Historically, two principal positions have been taken in religious education, namely, the theological approach and the social science approach. The theological approach to religious education is centered on the premise that the social sciences play either no role or an ancillary role in the work of teaching religion. According to this perspective, religious education is a branch of practical theology. As a macrotheory of religious education, theology is stipulated as possessing the power of explaining, predicting, and verifying the entire range of religious education phenomena. In this view, theology and theology alone is capable of devising and testing effective teaching techniques, of explaining the conditions under which religious learning can or cannot take place, of directly devising successful religious curricula, and predicting who will or will not be an effective religion teacher. The theological approach regards religious education as a way of doing theology, as theological method.

Leading religious educationists in the second half of the twentieth century who adhere to the theological approach to religious education include Randolph Crump Miller, D. Campbell Wyckoff, Johannes Hofinger, Berard Marthaler, and John Westerhoff.

The social science approach to religious education holds that social science forms the basic ecology, essential structure, and foundational processes of all forms of religious education. According to this position, religious education is a branch of social science in general and of education in particular. In this view, "education" as a noun ontically and hence properly situates its qualifying adjective "religious." As a macrotheory of religious education, social science is stipulated by this approach as possessing the power of adequately explaining and predicting and verifying the whole range of religious education phenomena.

Of the three fundamental forms of religious education (religious instruction, religious counseling, and the administration of religious instruction activities), only the area of religious instruction has not completely deserted the theological and embraced the social science approach.

The formal beginning of the social science approach to religion teaching occurred in 1971 with the publication of a book entitled *The Shape of Religious Instruction* by James Michael Lee. A few of the social scientific criticisms of the theological approach to religious education include the following. First, theology does not possess the methodological tools capable of adequately explaining how teaching/learning takes place, of predicting which teaching procedures will fail or succeed, and of verifying the degree to which teaching/learning takes place. Second, theology of practice is different from the practice itself (in this case the practice of religious instruction); otherwise theology would automatically be all sorts of practice, something which is as impossible as it is imperialistic. Third, theology provides only a theological description of any particular reality such as religious instruction; it does not provide a description of the nature and workings of a particular reality itself. Fourth, theology inherently is not value free; hence it cannot be an adequate theory for religious instruction because the content it may provide to religion teaching has only limited generalizability to teachers/learners from differing religious denominations and theological persuasions.

Leading proponents of the social science approach to religion teaching include James Michael Lee, Thomas Walters, Timothy Arthur Lines, Harold Burgess, and David Bickimer. *See also* Interdisciplinary Studies; Learning Theory; Psychology of Religion; Research; Scientific Method; Sociology of Religion; Theology and Education.

J. M. Lee

Social Work

Social work, one of the major professions concerned with the well-being of humanity, is defined by its purpose, objectives, values, focus, population groups served, fields of practice, and problem areas. Social workers seek to improve the quality of life of all persons by providing rehabilitative and preventive services and supports to individuals and groups. They also work to bring about needed changes in society. Most social workers provide services directly to their clients. However, many social workers perform other roles, including administration and management, consultation,

policy analysis, research, professional education, and social action. Social work is a mosaic of methods and skills based upon many kinds of knowledge and guided by multiple theories. It is carried out with populations of every age and type.

The desire to help one another in times of need and stress is deeply ingrained in the human race. Throughout the ages and in all parts of the world, these humanitarian impulses have marked the beginnings of social service. Mutual aid and individual charity can be considered early social service. The giving of alms was accepted as a religious duty or a self-imposed obligation of the privileged toward the underprivileged. Recognition of deficiencies in almsgiving came early to the countries of the Western world. As early as the sixteenth century, Juan Luis Vives in Belgium and a little later St. Vincent de Paul in France sought to relieve destitution through orderly methods of investigation of the needs and problems of the poor. The Elizabethan poor law of 1601 in England established the principle of public responsibility for those in need, a principle that was adopted by the American colonists who carried the English poor law to the new land.

Changing economic and social conditions in nineteenth-century England and America brought new problems of massive poverty and, also, new approaches toward solutions. These attempts flowed from compassion and paternalism, strongly tinged with a desire to protect society from the risks and consequences of pauperism. In 1819 in Glasgow the Reverend Thomas Chalmers concluded that public poor relief was fostering dependency and initiated a private program of direct service combined with careful assessment of needs and resources. This convinced many that private methods of charity were superior to public. The charity organization movement in Britain and America took over this idea and helped establish a new conception of social service as organized activity designed to lead individuals and families to self-help and independence through thrift, industry, and strength of character. By 1900 in the United States there were over 150 "societies" incorporating these notions into "charity" employing a common method, self-discipline, training, and the use of "friendly visitors." This laid the foundation for the later development of a body of knowledge and method for the profession of social work.

The first program for training social workers was established in 1899 as the New York School of Philanthropy, now the Columbia University School of Social Work. Soon afterward paid staff had largely replaced the volunteers. Today practice is carried out by social workers from three levels of professional education: baccalaureate, masters, and doctorate. In 1986 to supply these workers there were 434 accredited social work professional and 51 doctoral degree programs in the United States in which 38,450 undergraduate,

21,569 graduate, and 1,825 doctoral students were enrolled. More than 98,000 social workers belong to their professional organization, the National Association of Social Workers.

Religious agencies have long been involved in many forms of social work. Professional training for social work has been combined with professional training for ministry. Day-care centers and preschool programs in churches and synagogues, sometimes specifically designed for children with special needs, are also forms of religious education. Social workers work with religious educators, as with children who have special family or learning needs. Summer programs may combine social services and religious education.

BELIEFS

Social workers believe that individuals have inherent value and dignity, that they should have equal opportunity to provide for their common needs and the chance to achieve to their fullest potential. Social workers believe that their clients should be as fully involved as possible in solving problems. Consistent with social work's purpose, social workers hold that relations between people should promote the dignity, individuality, and self-determination of everyone. People should be treated humanely and with justice.

OBJECTIVES

The focus of social work is neither simply the client nor the environment but person(s)-in-situation, a dynamic reciprocal relationship in which it is assumed that persons affect and are affected by their environment in a continuing process. Social work accomplishes its purpose by helping people to cope better with life's tasks and to get needed resources, by making organizations responsive to people, by influencing transactions between organizations and institutions, and by influencing social and environmental policy.

LOCATIONS

There is almost no place, from Native American reservations and urban ghettos to banks and blue-chip corporations, where social workers do not practice. They practice with every age, ethnic group, economic class, and sexual orientation. In clinics, community mental health agencies, mental hospitals, jails and public welfare agencies, social workers practice mainly with the poor, the disturbed, the homeless, and the deviant, with those characterized by their poverty, by their alienation from the community, and their powerlessness. Social workers in day care, in facilities for the aged, in hospitals, and in family service agencies work with a cross section of the population. In private practice social workers are apt to work mainly with upper-middle-class people. Most social workers are employed in host rather than social work settings unless they serve in a family or chil-

dren's agency, a neighborhood center, or a community mental health clinic. Host settings, controlled by other professions, provide a variety of jobs but tend to fragment the social work profession and may constrain social work roles. Social workers have less job security and less influence in host settings than elsewhere.

FIELDS OF PRACTICE

Currently social work covers several overlapping fields of practice: family and children's services, health and mental health, aging, education, juvenile and criminal justice, and occupational or industrial social work. Effective work within any of these fields requires that the social worker be knowledgeable about the range of problems encountered, the resources and populations specific to that field, relevant legislation, funding sources, the work of other disciplines, and the typical services provided.

POPULATIONS SERVED AND PROBLEM AREAS

Social work practice has become specialized according to populations served. Thus the social worker becomes expert in knowledge and skill about groups of people variously defined according to age, class, ethnicity, or gender. This may be useful when services are organized around such situations as poverty, racism, or oppression. Social work practice is also organized around problem areas such as child abuse, substance abuse, spouse abuse, runaways, unwed mothers, crime, delinquency, and mental illness. Specialization according to problem focuses practitioners' knowledge and skill but sometimes fails to address the organization, research, interdisciplinary, and policy considerations involved.

METHODS

The first step of the social work helping process is careful study and assessment of the problem or situation. When goals have been identified, services are planned and implemented according to clients' aims and needs and available resources. Final steps include evaluation of outcomes, feedback, and application of results to future practice. This is an attempt to apply a more or less systematic, scientific, problem-solving process to the accomplishment of social work purposes in a manner that maximizes client involvement and facilitates accountability to ensure that the promised service is in fact delivered. The practice of social workers is of roughly two kinds: direct and indirect. Most social workers are involved in practice with individuals, singly or in groups, which is increasingly supported by empirically based knowledge and theory. The major underpinnings for direct practice are personality, cognitive, behavioral, social learning, communications and organizational theory.

Theories from social science and social work itself help to explain the persistence of poverty, injustice, and other social problems and suggest how social workers and others may attempt change. While the concerns and activities of most social workers focus on service delivery, there is increasing emphasis upon prevention along with greater sophistication about and willingness to engage the political process in seeking to redirect our social priorities. *See also* Child Abuse; Counseling; Exceptional Persons; Juvenile Delinquency; Ministry; Social Justice, Education for; Social Science.

R. K. Brautigam

Society of Friends' Education

See Quaker Education.

Society of Jesus

The Society of Jesus (Jesuits), a Roman Catholic religious order acknowledged as a leader in Catholic education since its founding, was formally approved by Pope Paul III in 1540. In 1522 in Spain, its founder, Ignatius of Loyola (1491–1556), had begun catechizing children and adults, sharing with them the fruits of his own experience of God and of the discernment of spirits, especially through the *Spiritual Exercises*, a biblically based series of prayerful reflections on salvation history, sin, and the life, death, and resurrection of Jesus. Dedicating himself to the ascetic life and concerned for the cultivation of the whole person for God, Ignatius gathered a group of men who took religious vows in 1534, were ordained in 1537, and formed the core of the new order.

These earliest Jesuits shared the dedication to religious education and wrote into the Jesuit Constitutions in 1539 the obligation to study catechetical methods and to teach catechism. Peter Canisius (1521–1597) was the first Jesuit to respond directly to Luther's catechism, imitating his popular question-and-answer format. In 1555 Canisius produced his large catechism for preachers and teachers, with references to the Bible, tradition, and canon law. In 1558 he wrote a catechism for youths. This set the tone of Catholic religious education in Germany for the next 200 years. By 1597, 134 editions had been published. His longer book was used as a model for the *Roman Catechism*, mandated by the Council of Trent and completed in 1566. His arrangement of material significantly differed from Luther's: faith and the creed; hope and the Lord's Prayer; charity and the commandments; sacraments; sin; and good works.

Perhaps the most influential Catholic catechism was done by Jesuit Robert Bellarmine (1542–1621) in Italy. He wrote a text for pupils in 1597, followed by a teacher's manual in 1598. By the middle of the nineteenth century this catechism had been translated into more languages (over sixty) than any other book except the Bible and the *Imitation of Christ*. Many of these translations had ecumenical and missionary purposes. At the First Vatican Council (1869–1870) it was recommended as a model for a universal catechism.

Over six hundred catechisms and catechetical books have been produced by Jesuits, but of course Jesuit involvement in religious education took and takes many other forms: prayerful celebration of the sacraments, preaching, teaching in Catholic schools, religious books and articles, radio and television programs, drama, music, art, architecture, and especially directing people as they follow the *Spiritual Exercises*.

A series of international congresses organized by Johannes Hofinger (1905–1986), Jesuit, from 1956 to 1968 reformed Catholic religious education by building in elements from the biblical and liturgical movements and anthropology. The deductive structure of classical catechesis yielded to an inductive, experiential basis, focusing more on adults than children and later incorporating the practical orientation of liberation theology. At these congresses Jesuits promoted ecumenical understanding and cooperation in translating the Bible, producing audiovisual aids, and using mass media both to prepare the way for the gospel by promoting general human development and to clarify and reinforce religious insights, attitudes, and values.

The Jesuit order has also been active in establishing schools. Secondary (frequently residential) schools have been noted for the classical education given students preparing for college. Universities like Loyola (Chicago) and Fordham (New York City) excel in teacher-scholars and programs. Theological schools are usually participants in theological consortia as at Chicago and Berkeley. *See also* Catechesis; Catechism; History of Christian Education; Hofinger, Johannes; Ignatius of Loyola; Religious Orders.

F. J. Buckley

Sociodrama

Sociodrama is a method for creative group problem solving through drama that can be used by teachers with students of all ages from kindergarten through adult. Sociodrama was developed in the 1940s by J. L. Moreno as an extension of his psychodrama but was revised and further developed by E. P. Torrance. It is distinct from role playing in that the emphasis is on group (rather than individual) situations and it seeks resolution, even if provisional, to issues with social implications.

As developed by Torrance, sociodrama focuses on a conflict suggested by the group that, although relevant to the group, is generally not a current pressing concern to a group member. In contrast, psychodrama usually focuses on a current problem of a particular individual and is thus far more intense than sociodrama. Although sociodrama can be used by a leader after several hours of training, psychodrama should be used only by a well-trained leader.

The purpose of sociodrama is to help a group examine a social problem and then propose and test out varied solutions through drama. Sociodrama can occur in a classroom or any other setting, with or without props.

Sociodrama uses steps familiar from problem solving:

1. Defining the problem. The leader asks questions to help the group set forth facts and general information relevant to the conflict situation.

2. Stating the problem or conflict in clear language.

3. Casting the characters. Characters must be volunteers.

4. Warming up actors and observers. Actors leave the room to plan their own approach to the problem while the leader encourages the audience both to suggest alternative solutions to the problem and also to choose an actor to identify with. Actors then return and describe their identities.

5. Acting out the problem. Dramatization may last seconds or several minutes. The leader must not suggest a solution to actors but, if the action bogs down, may ask, "What happens next?"

6. Cutting the action. The action should be cut when the actors reach a solution, drop out of their roles, or are totally blocked.

7. Discussing and analyzing the situation. The audience discusses and evaluates the solution and may suggest other solutions.

8. Making plans to test new ideas through further dramatization or in real life.

To stimulate deeper thinking, other techniques may be added. An actor may give a soliloquy, turning to the audience and expressing feelings not spoken in the dramatization. An actor may have a double, the actor's "other self," who talks to the actor as the actor is quietly reflecting after the conflict has ended. Roles can be reversed—a mother plays the role of a child or a child plays a mother.

In religious education sociodrama can help children and youth search for solutions to problems such as dealing with peer pressure to engage in forbidden or damaging behavior (such as that of using drugs) or handling conflicts with parents (over such things as curfew or use of a car). Sociodrama can also help adult committee members to analyze various sides of a controversial issue. Sociodrama can thus provide a creative tool for group problem solving in the church. *See also* Dramatization; Group Dynamics; Problem Solving; Role Playing; Simulation.

FOR FURTHER REFERENCE

Torrance, E. P. and R. E. Myers. *Creative Learning and Teaching.* New York: Dodd, Mead, 1970.

J. B. McCandless

Sociology of Religion

The sociology of religion examines the relationship between religion and all dimensions of society: government, the economy, family life, education, health services, recreation, sports, the military, law, art, and all the elements of culture, including language itself and communication systems. It is done comparatively across space and as far back through time as known artifacts allow us to go. Anthropological digs provide the oldest materials for comparison and reveal that the many separate dimensions of society as we know them today—the divisions of labor into separate functions as listed above—were not so distinct in tribal societies. Furthermore, qualities we would now define as religious, such as invocation of the gods, pervaded the practice of all other functions.

VARIETIES OF FOCUS

Much of the analysis in the sociology of religion is devoted to the differentiation of specifically religious functions from other aspects of society. This task is not only one of analysis but of historical development. The pursuit of the holy, the transcendent, the sacred, ultimate reality, the divine, or God and the linkage of that pursuit with everyday life, ferreting out what is commonly understood as the religious factor, is not merely an analytic task. The very pursuit itself is caught up in the current faith, beliefs, experience, and historical period of the observer. Sociologists study the content, variations, transitions, and interpretations of religions as they are institutionalized in societies and are available for analysis in extant artifacts and recorded data. Because religion has for its object the mysterious, the unknown, and totally other, it is manifest to researchers only through symbol, myth, and ritual as these are invented and displayed in ceremony; expressed in prayer; acted out in worship; portrayed in church architecture, statuary, painting, and design; and interpreted in Scriptures.

The sociologist observes groups that gather for religious services; studies their creeds, codes, and ceremonies; compares churches, denominations, cults, and unique religious expressions of individuals in roles of priest, prophet, shaman, and mystic; and examines the reality of major world religions as they link with and inform civilizations. Thus, Hinduism in Indian culture, Islam in Muslim nations, Shinto in Japan, native religions in the Americas, and Christianity in Western Europe and in its extension along the trading, colonizing, and migration routes are objects of sociological analysis.

The sociology of religion examines the linkage of the gods of ancient Greece and Rome with family life, governance, warring, and recreation practices, noting specifically the way work got done, and discovers, for example, that hand work was done by the slave labor of captured peoples who did not share in the common worship. The sociology of religion studies the rise of Christianity in Europe as ancient tribes gave up their local gods and came to worship the Christian Trinity. It notes the link of the Protestant reform with the rise of modern nations and the establishment of national churches—the Anglican in England; Lutheran in Germany, Norway, Sweden, and Denmark; and Calvinist in Switzerland. Sociology pursues the movement of denominations of these groups into France, Scotland, and Holland and then to the United States. It perceives the clear links of government types with Catholicism in Italy, Spain, and Portugal; the distinctly Greek Catholic style moving eastward; and the emergence of Russian Orthodoxy, noting the influence of belief and ritual on art, education, and the practice of healing. As it does so, sociology sees the specific influence of European religions on the native cultures of colonized peoples in Africa, Asia, and Latin America. In these locations ancient tribal religions mesh with the new religions and not only form distinctive ritual and worshiping styles but come to legitimate divisions of labor (apartheid in South Africa, the Chicano land struggle in Mexico, the institution of the Protestant ethic in the United States), in each case establishing through language, belief, and religious practice class structures confirmed in word and worship. Sociological analysis reveals the link of the organization of labor in the United States with Catholic and Jewish groups in a management system predominantly Protestant. It then notes the shift in control as immigrant church groups become secure and religious solidarity moves from inner city to suburb. Critical social analysis eventually becomes an analytic tool of sociologists.

Today, sociologists note also the vigor of new life in Islamic fundamentalism in Iran; the persistence of struggle among Christians, Muslims, and Jews in the Middle East; the division of Catholic and Buddhist in the Vietnam struggle; and the conflict of Buddhist and Hindu in Sri Lanka and of Catholic and Protestant in Northern Ireland, noting in each case links of wealth and power against poverty and powerlessness.

It is the task of the sociology of religion to account for observed connections and to determine causes for group solidarity around religious assembly and support of other institutions of the society. Furthermore, the sociology of religion also studies the rise of new religious movements, such as the Unification Church, the Hare Krishnas, the Children of God, Scientology, and the charismatic movements within older established religions. The growth of conservative churches and the initiation and development of liberation theology in Third World countries, especially in Latin America, where the special option for the poor and the decisive affirmation of a social justice and world peace agenda are affirmed by the Catholic church, the World Council of Churches, and a national organization of several Protestant denominations call sociologists to examine group and class linkages. Sociology invites religious reflection on the phenomenon even as it researches correlations and causes.

Sociological research is designed to gather evidence about these several trends, to relate them to larger movements of social change, on the one hand, and to the preservation of social structures, on the other. The labels of politics—conservative, liberal, and radical—are used more neutrally by sociologists to examine the patterns of norms and values associated with the formation, development, preservation, and/or decline of religious groups acting to provide social control or to foster release from cultural commitment. When experiences of anomie, alienation, and rebellion, on the one hand, and pressures to conform reinforced through ritual or the exercise of power, on the other, link the existing class, ethnic, or sexist exploitation to traditional religious practice, sociologists note these correlations and propose hypotheses to test for causal relations derived from theories of society.

The sociology of religion in Europe focuses more on national differences and the secularization process, that is, the desacralization of society. In the United States, however, the focus has been the study of the influence of religion on the emergence of the conscience of the nation, thereby both expanding Rousseau's concept of civil religion and accounting for the growth of pluralism, individualism, and secularization. Denominational differences within Protestant churches and between Protestantism, Catholicism, and Judaism have been a main focus of research in the United States, thus giving the discipline a distinctly American orientation. Both foci tended to render the study of religion peripheral to the study of society in the mid-twentieth century, until recent developments highlighted the mutual influence of social interaction and the religious factor.

HISTORY

The founding scholars of sociology recognized the significance of religion in the development of societies with their distinct cultures, the force of religion in social control, and its dynamic in social change. Emile Durkheim (1858–1917) examined the link between institutionalized conceptions of God and abstract conceptions of society itself, the need of periodic celebration to energize a community to keep on living in the face of disenchantment that can generate anomie and ultimately induce trends to suicide. Karl Marx (1818–1883) observed how the eschatological vision was used to control the labor of the hand workers within a given society. Max Weber (1864–1920) saw the prophet as an agent for social change leading the worshiping community to question the entrenched ritual presided over by the priest. Bronislaw Malinowski (1884–1942) made clear distinctions among magic, science, and religion, often obscured in religious practice. Sigmund Freud (1856–1939) focused on the psychic cooptation of God to superego. Using the insights of these founders of modern sociology in their unmasking of unintended functions that religion has come to have, Talcott Parsons (1902–1979) linked and distinguished the search for ultimate meaning and expression from other levels of institutionalization. Clifford Geertz (b. 1926), noting that each religion has its own surprising message, provided an insight to distinguish the work of the theologian and true believer from the research task of the sociologist, that is, to examine the reality that has come to be and to leave the pursuit of the holy to the faith community. What subsequent analysis indicates is that the links between religion and society are real and need to be examined and understood by theologians, by those who profess specific religious beliefs, and by those who work with the religiously committed.

IN RELIGIOUS EDUCATION

Adults in religious education classes need units of study in sociology of religion to help them understand the formative place of religion in society. A sociological approach to the Bible—the religious situation in which biblical religion developed, the world in which Jesus lived, and the environment of the early church—will enrich study. Adolescents are interested in studying various religious traditions and the sociological dimension can enable them to understand the distinctiveness of each religion. Teachers of children will find that some knowledge of biblical sociology helps them to introduce background material to enliven biblical stories. Some familiarity with Canaanite religion, including the worship of Baal, for example, will put in perspective the insistence of the biblical writers that the people of Israel worship the Lord who is one God. *See also* Archaeology, Biblical; Cultic Religious Movements; Culture; Interdisciplinary Studies; Liberation Theology; Psychology of Religion; Religious Studies; Research; Scientific Method; Social Science.

FOR FURTHER REFERENCE

Durkheim, Emile. *Elementary Forms of Religious Life.* 1915. Reprint. New York: Free Press, 1965.

Glock, Charles, ed. *Religion in Sociological Perspective: Essays in the Empirical Study of Religion.* Belmont, CA: Wadsworth, 1973.

Hammond, Phillip E., ed. *The Sacred and the Secular.* Berkeley and Los Angeles: University of California Press, 1985.

Malinowski, Bronislaw. *Magic, Science and Religion.* Garden City, NY: Doubleday, Anchor Books, 1955.

Weber, Max. *The Protestant Ethic and the Spirit of Capitalism.* 1904. Reprint. New York: Scribner, 1958.

M. A. Neal

Socratic Method

The Socratic method is a thinking strategy originally devised by Socrates in the fifth century B.C. to pursue truth by means of questioning. There are certain assumptions underlying this strategy: personal opinion is not an adequate basis for knowledge; what is to be learned is not a static body of knowledge to be transmitted to the learner; and the role of the teacher is to engage the learner in a maieutic process of coming to "know" that which is implicitly accessible to the seeker. The movement is from assurance to doubt to humility and tentative clarity. The teacher uses systematic questioning to probe ever more precise levels of expression of knowledge available to humans as rational creatures. Both teacher and learner stand before truth and are changed by that truth. The use of questioning to "test" students' assignments, to compare answers with predetermined concepts, or to engage participants in vigorous group discussion are all contradictions in principle to the Socratic method. In fact, the method itself is based primarily on vigorous probing of the thought of one person at a time, although a group may benefit from listening. The Socratic method is for serious students and perceptive teachers who are willing to risk seeking deeper meanings. An article in a creedal statement as basic as "The Lord our God is one Lord" (Deut. 6:4) can be probed word by word and then in its entirety. Both biblical passages and theological affirmations will reveal layers of meaning. In the final analysis, the student learns what it means to be a responsible thinker. *See also* Knowledge, Theories of; Questions.

S. P. Little

South America

See Latin America.

Spiritual Direction

Spiritual direction is a popular umbrella term used mainly in the Roman Catholic, Anglican, and Orthodox traditions to cover a variety of ways in which people give and receive spiritual guidance. Protestantism, with its historical emphasis on the doctrine of justification, does not have as developed a tradition of spiritual direction as does its Catholic counterpart. The companion doctrine of sanctification is now being given more attention and the whole realm of spirituality is being seen in a more sympathetic light by Protestants as the churches move closer together. The Protestant tradition has much to offer in the realm of the inner life and spiritual direction is becoming part of Reformed spirituality.

The word "direction," however, can be off-putting and misleading—off-putting because it suggests giving the "director" a great deal of authority over the seeker and misleading because, in the end, the director is not a human being, but the Holy Spirit. The Christian tradition, for example, does not concern itself with gurus. Rather, a director is, to use a sixteenth-century term, "God's user."

The birth of the tradition of spiritual direction is to be found in the fourth century in the Egyptian desert, where the disciple went to the master with the fundamental request: "Give me a word, Father, that I may live!" Here we have a clue as to the purpose of spiritual direction—the imparting of a word of life through the agency of another. The spiritual director is a diagnostician, that is, someone who can "discern spirits" and point to the Word of Life who is Christ. The director is able to "read souls" and intuitively see what is going on. Our capacity for self-deception seems infinite and we need companions and guides to help us discern true spirits from false. Spiritual direction is, therefore, to be understood as taking place within the context of a community of faith. It is an "act of worship" in that it openly acknowledges the presence of God as the third in the midst of an encounter between two people. Depending on the maturity of the one seeking direction, the relationship can be one between master and pupil, one between friends, or anything in between. Spiritual direction is usually, although not always, conducted on this one-to-one basis.

There are dangers to be faced. Spiritual direction is an art and a great deal of harm can be done by well-meaning but inexperienced practitioners. The tradition insists that the director be a "theologian" (not in the academic sense, but one who is steeped in prayer and in the love of God) and a person who is well versed in the Scriptures. The Bible is important because spiritual direction is based on the belief that the life of every person and every community has a dramatic shape directly related to the Bible. Each has a story to tell and every individual story is tested by and finds its meaning in the gospel story. In spiritual direction there is a fourfold model that involves the telling of the story, the sharing of one's vision for the future, the placing of the life and the vision in the context of the gospel story, and finally discerning the next step along the way. In this fourfold model one can see that psychological skills are as essential as the gift of spiritual discernment. People tend to want instant answers and easy solutions to their inner yearnings and conflicts and this makes them vulnerable to unskilled and even unscrupulous self-appointed guides. For this reason contemporary spiritual direction is also committed to psychological knowledge.

Pastoral counseling is an important ally of spiritual direction although they are not identical. Pastoral counseling tends to emphasize self-expression and self-fulfillment. It concerns itself with the functioning of the ego so that it can cope and flourish in the world. Spiritual direction, on the other hand, while acknowledging the importance of the above, puts its energy toward self-surrender and self-abandonment in its concern for the discipline and glory of the life promised by the death and resurrection of Christ. It is sometimes useful to think of pastoral counseling as a necessary preparation for spiritual direction. Both are under pressure today to endorse people's goals of self-improvement and personal happiness as a right. Both traditions are being called upon to deal with people's sense of disappointment and outrage at not getting what they want. In short, both disciplines have to deal with people's naive and infantile expectations in the context of faith, hope, and love. *See also* Counseling; Retreat; Spirituality.

A. W. Jones

Spirituality

Spirituality may be described but is not readily defined, for the boundaries are broad. It is a sense of relatedness to that which is beyond the self yet approachable. For some, the spiritual is around or within the self. This may be personal or nonpersonal, named God, power, or presence.

In a basic sense, religion meets needs for orderliness in human life, offering guidelines for personal and group living, mutual strengthening, and a relationship to the transcendent. Many people seek a quality beyond the mundane that is referred to as "spiritual." They are impelled by various needs. Some yearn for peace and tranquility in the confusion of social and personal life. Others hope for security from anxiety and fear. Some, troubled by the potential for harm in their own hostilities and anger, seek a way of controlling these impulses and using them for more productive living. They desire renewed strength as well as a reflective approach to daily life.

The spiritual dimension has been recognized in all religions, from the major world religions to those described today as animistic. Animism holds that the vital principle of life is immaterial spirit, which gives dynamic to all creation and can be apprehended in every area of life. Eastern religions like Buddhism and Hinduism have highly developed forms of physical discipline and meditation to promote access to the spiritual. The religions with Middle Eastern roots include groups with special emphases on the cultivation of spirituality. In Christianity the tradition that began with the desert fathers developed over the centuries into the various monastic orders. Within Islam, the Sufis, best known for the rhythmic, whirling dance they participate in as part of a yearly festival, originated in the seventh century in Konya, Turkey. The mystical side of Judaism is represented by the Hasidic movement, which began in Catalonia and Provence in the thirteenth century but found its modern form in eighteenth-century Poland under the leadership of Ba'al Shem Tov.

TRADITION

The spiritual life is more easily developed among people who are conscious of a tradition. The monastic way both in Eastern Orthodoxy and Roman Catholicism has given those religious cultures a design for the cultivation of the spiritual life. The "staretz," or holy man, an itinerant spiritual guide who was not usually a member of a monastery, has been a revered figure in Russian Orthodoxy. Those who did not take monastic vows were conscious of the life and were drawn into its periphery as they attended liturgies and served or were served by the members of the monastic community. The Buddhist monastic tradition influences its culture as townspeople receive the monks on their daily rounds seeking food and travel to monasteries for special festivals.

The English Reformers tried to preserve some of the monastic tradition by retaining the two offices of Morning and Evening Prayer for use in the parish churches. Other spiritual traditions have been nurtured among Protestant groups at various times; some include the Moravians, the Mennonites, and the Society of Friends. Living in community or proximity, adherents strengthened one another in their particular spiritual disciplines and were a witness to the surrounding community by their lives. In the beginning of the Methodist movement, the class meeting assisted in the cultivation of the spiritual life of members. The Hutterites today are a tightly knit group whose cohesiveness is due in part to their shared disciplines.

Spirituality is furthered through knowledge of the examples of people who have been practitioners. They may be known through historical remembrance, via biography and autobiography, and through writings in which they have shared their spiritual quest. Early writers included the fourth-century Cappadocians Basil of Caesarea and Gregory of Nyssa, who documented their quest for spiritual perfection. From the medieval Western tradition come the illuminating writings of Bernard of Clairvaux, Francis of Assisi, Meister Eckhart, and Julian of Norwich. These sought, through a process of self-emptying, to receive divine illumination that would transfigure their lives. The ecstasies of the contemplative life are most vividly described in the writings of two sixteenth-century Spanish mystics, Teresa of Avila and John of the Cross. Their compatriot, Ignatius of Loyola, founder of the Society of Jesus, has left a legacy in his *Spiritual Exercises,* describing a method for meditation.

George Fox, founder of the Society of Friends, and John Wesley, founder of the Methodist movement, bring seventeenth- and eighteenth-century Protestant insights to spiritual development. The examples and the writings continue into the twentieth century with Rufus Jones, Simone Weil, Thomas Merton, Dag Hammarskjold, and Martin Luther King, Jr. The spiritual tradition has always been a blend of the active and the contemplative.

The second half of the twentieth century has often seen the various historical forms of spirituality influence each other in unprecedented ways. Eastern forms have been adapted to Western culture, beginning with Zen Buddhism and including theosophy, a westernized form of Hinduism. Yoga, a meditative technique from Hinduism, has become recently popular as a spiritual aid among Westerners. Since Vatican II, the Catholic church has established links with both Buddhists and Hindus, participating in joint study conferences where similarities and differences in the cultivation of the spiritual life have been explored. Out of such exploration have come books on such topics as "Christian yoga" and "Zen Catholicism."

POLARITIES OF UNDERSTANDING

Two aspects of the understanding of God are present in the spiritual quest: the transcendent and the immanent. The Bible affirms God to be the creator of the universe, the redeemer of all creation, and the sustainer of all life. God is separate from creation, and this fact makes possible a personal relationship between Creator and creatures. God is Spirit, and those created by God may receive the Holy Spirit, be indwelt by the Holy Spirit, yet maintain individuality. God may dwell in all creation (theologian Teilhard de Chardin names this "panentheism") but is not merged into the creation (pantheism). The separateness of God is essential to the biblical understanding of spirituality.

At the same time, God is related to the creation. The Bible affirms that God loves all creatures and that humans can respond to God in love. This represents the "immanence" of God, the nearness of the creator, redeemer, to those who are dependent upon God for the gift of life. These two aspects of God are held in balance in a developed spirituality. The believer has a sense of awe and wonder in the presence of the Holy One—profoundly expressed in Isaiah 6:3 and in Revelation 4:8: "Holy, holy, holy, is the Lord of hosts," the *Sanctus* of the liturgy. At the other pole, the believer can affirm that "the Lord is my shepherd, I shall not want" (Ps. 23:1).

These polarities are paralleled by the understanding of the objective and subjective elements in spirituality. The immanent sense of the presence of God brings to the spiritually sensitive person a feeling of intimacy that gives reassurance in every need. The subjective element stresses the personal quality of God. But to confine the relationship to God at this pole would be to bring God totally into the human dimension and miss the important insight that God must be beyond human understanding. The transcendent holiness of God is an essential dimension in biblical understanding and makes more wonderful the love of God for creation. This is the objective pole of spirituality. The mystic combines these elements in a unique way, being at the same time totally filled with the presence of God and overwhelmed by the holiness of God.

To some, the transcendence or "otherness" of God suggests One who is far off. This can lead to the objectifying or intellectualizing of the understanding of God that avoids any relationship to God. Yet it can also make relationship possible because only two who have separate existences, an I and a Thou, can become related. Conversely, the immanence of God, with the possibility of intimacy, can be thought of as confining God. One could retreat into a form of spirituality that permits one to avoid ordinary life. The mystics have been among the most energetic and active people in history. Spending long hours in retreat, they have come forth to lead all kinds of renewal efforts. It is no accident that Teresa of Avila reformed the Carmelite order and that Ignatius of Loyola founded the Society of Jesus.

FOUNDATIONS FOR THE SPIRITUAL LIFE

The spiritual life requires nurturing from childhood through adulthood, although in different forms for different ages. Developmental psychology gives clues to the foundations on which spiritual development is built. Infants who learn through caring adults how to trust can more easily put their trust in God. Children who develop autonomy and initiative can more easily make faith commitments. Adolescents who have a sense of their own identity may thereafter be able to understand the relationship between the closeness of God and the otherness of God.

FORMATION

In adulthood, the spiritual life is developed through deliberate formation, a term Protestant Christians have tended to avoid, lest the freedom of the Holy Spirit be denied in an effort to develop the spiritual. But through the centuries, spiritual growth has occurred as people have simultaneously learned about it and practiced it, for cultivation is a deliberate process. In eighteenth-century France, two noted spiritual directors, Francois de Sales and Francois Fenelon, assisted devout women of the French court with the task of formation. They answered a question similar to that asked by Westerners today: how can one cultivate quiet in the midst of a busy social schedule? They insisted that a regularly planned time for meditation, prayer, and spiritual reading be written into the daily schedule and the cares of everyday life be considered in the light of that reflection.

AVENUES FOR GROWTH

One of the most widely available avenues for spiritual development is the community of faith, primarily the *worshiping congregation*. The use of Scripture, the forms of prayer, the content of hymns, and the celebration of sacraments are all powerful expressions of and aids to the spiritual life. To try to practice spirituality alone is to cut oneself off from such human contact and to deny the potential in a group gathered for worship. As the monastic orders have long known, the power for growth lies in the interaction of community, worship, and personal devotion. Every branch of the Christian church has recognized the power inherent in the Lord's Supper for mutual strengthening. Varied forms of prayer are first learned within the service of worship: the collect, the litany, the pastoral prayer. The Quaker tradition of silence, basic to their congregational worship, is a pattern internalized in childhood.

Scriptures are a primary source for the cultivation of the spiritual life, both during worship and privately. In meditation on Scripture, believers participate in the biblical story. Here are the examples of those who heard and responded to the voice of God:

Abraham, called from his ancestral home; Moses, accosted in the desert; Isaiah, standing in awe in the Temple; Amos, given a word he dared not ignore. Mary received the angel's message and responded with willing praise; Jesus accepted his calling first in the desert and again in Gethsemane. Paul struggled along the Damascus road.

The Psalms have expressed the spiritual longings of people for millennia. The psalmist struggles with God: protesting the evil that has been done; petitioning for redress; affirming trust and hope; expressing thanksgiving for deliverance. No other writings plumb the depths of human experience so extensively. The raw emotions make some readers uneasy. Such honesty in the presence of God seems astonishing. Here is a secure faith that is the very essence of the spiritual.

The riches of a *hymnal* need not be confined to liturgical use. The hymnal is a source of materials to voice in prayer or to lead to meditation. From biblical times to the present, hymnody has been a witness to the faith on the part of hymn writers and an affirmation of faith on the part of those who read or sing hymns. *Collections of prayers* have commended themselves for the deepening of the spiritual life, among these the *Book of Common Prayer* for four centuries. Although most Protestants have been hesitant about "set" forms of prayer, many have found that the phrasing and the insights of others who have walked in the spiritual way can enrich their own lives. Those in liturgical traditions have the treasury of daily and weekly collects as food for meditation. *Poetry*, too, can become a source for spiritual renewal: in the obscurity of the metaphysical poets such as George Herbert, the struggle for faith in Francis Thompson, and the sometimes hidden spirituality of contemporary poetry. This has been a neglected resource.

Particular *groups* encourage participants in the spiritual life. Prayer groups have become common in churches, meeting regularly for intercessory prayer and mutual strengthening. Such groups become training grounds when the members engage together in the practice of specific forms of meditation.

One form of group *meditation* is based on the reading aloud of a verse or passage from Scripture. Each person then reads it silently. This is followed by silence to reflect on and receive insights from the passage. The amount of time allotted to silence lengthens as the group becomes more practiced in meditation. Such a session begins and ends with prayer.

Another form of meditation deriving from the Ignatian method is to hear a biblical story read and to put oneself in the situation not as one of those described in the narrative, but as one who might also have been among those present. Reflection for some hinges on how one would have responded in that situation. Others will leave themselves open to guidance on an immediate problem or a task. Only practice leads to depth. What is begun in a group can be continued individually.

Formation may also be aided by a *spiritual director*, spiritual guide, or "soul friend"—to use both traditional and new terminology. Such a person is deeply aware of the spiritual dimension of life through study and practice but has the added gift of being able to guide others in spiritual growth. Some people meet regularly with a spiritual director; others seek such help at specific points in the journey. There has been a newly developed interest in the spiritual director recently, particularly among Protestants not familiar with the tradition.

The *retreat* is another avenue for spiritual growth. The word comes out of military terminology, where retreat after a battle was for the purpose of regrouping in order to venture back into the fray with new strength. In order to accomplish the purpose of spiritual renewal, a retreat needs to be held in a place apart from everyday life where there is space and quiet. The retreat leader is a guide who speaks briefly and is available for counsel. Most of the time is free for the retreatants to use for rest, reading, prayer, meditation, and reflection. The regular times for worship bring mutual strengthening as the group sings, prays, hears Scripture, and participates in the Eucharist together. Long a familiar avenue of renewal for Catholics, Eastern Orthodox, and Anglicans, it is now becoming better known among Protestants, who are developing their own forms of retreat. Retreats should not, however, be confused with conferences, which have different goals and therefore employ different methods.

The *liturgical year* is an enrichment for spiritual growth. The Jewish calendar begins in late fall where "Simchat Torah" or the second reading of the Law climaxes the New Year–Yom Kippur–Feast of Booths cycle of festivals. Through the year, the lectionary provides for serial reading of Scripture, punctuated by the lesser celebrations such as Hanukkah and Purim and the great festival of Passover-Pentecost. The Christian calendar also begins in late fall with the Advent season. The believer relives the Gospel story from the nativity of the Lord, through the Epiphany season of the "showing forth" of Jesus at his baptism, his teaching and his mighty works, into the Lenten preparation as he and the disciples turn their faces toward Jerusalem. This is climaxed by the Great Three Days of the Passion and the triumph of Easter, the forty-day celebration that, with an added ten days after Ascension, culminates in Pentecost. By reliving the story each Sunday in the congregation, and daily in the devotional life, the believer becomes participant with those who first lived it and all who have followed down through the centuries.

Spiritual growth develops through an openness to the leading of the Holy Spirit. Life becomes both a quest and a pilgrimage. There can be hope without certainty. One lives in the present and accepts the future. The ambiguities of life are part of its mystery. Both Abraham and Moses went out not knowing where the journey would end, but trusting in the word of God. Jesus becomes the example for Christians who, identifying with his life and death, find meaning to suffering in the cross and victory in the resurrection.

The spiritual life is not confined to a few who spend their lives practicing it intentionally in committed groups, whether monasteries or communities. It is a possibility for all believers who accept the resources offered them within the worshiping community, small groups, individual guides, and the written resources of Scripture, hymnal, prayers, and the writings of those who have intensely cultivated this way of life. Each generation adds to the storehouse of experience and witness. *See also* Church Year; Devotional Literature; Hymnody, Christian; Jewish Festivals and Holidays; Meditation, Forms of; Prayer; Retreat; Spiritual Direction; Worship.

FOR FURTHER REFERENCE

Cully, Iris V. *Education for Spiritual Growth*. San Francisco: Harper & Row, 1984.
Hinson, E. Glenn, ed. *Doubleday Devotional Classics*. Garden City, NY: Doubleday, 1978.
Holmes, Urban T. *A History of Christian Spirituality: An Analytical Introduction*. New York: Seabury, 1981.
Payne, Richard J., ed. *Classics of Western Spirituality*. New York: Paulist, 1978–.

I. V. Cully

Staff Relationships

The most valuable resource of any organization is its people. No amount of equipment, hardware, software, or facilities can replace a caring and competent leadership staff in church work. The leadership staff includes all persons accountable for the congregation's program: pastors, lay professional staff (musicians, education, youth, and volunteer support directors), and office and facility support staff. Staff members may be full- or part-time. The staff is, of course, supplemented by regular interaction with committed volunteers, many of whom are leaders in their own professions. All of these persons need an organized and concerted effort to help one another feel good about their personal and professional effectiveness. A leadership support system enables staff members to interact in such a way that they effectively meet their individual and collective needs. These needs may be simple or complex, including such items as:

- Professional recognition and approval
- Feelings of well-being—better health and less stress
- More time for planning
- Better relationships with colleagues
- Help with program planning and implementation
- Fewer interruptions
- More resource helps to work with
- Improved staff meetings
- More space in which to work
- A place to park

The list could include countless items all as unique and varied in value as the members of any given church staff. Identifying the most common needs is the first step toward establishing successful staff relationships. Step two relates to the establishment of a team effort.

According to Roman Catholic writer Matthew Fox (*A Spirituality Named Compassion*, 1979), the Christian life may be seen either under the symbol of the ladder or the circle. The ladder is hierarchical, suggesting individualism and competition. The circle leaves room for others; it suggests cooperation as people see each other face to face.

Effectiveness and satisfaction are dependent upon teamwork. The four ingredients that enable a staff to function as a family show us how to participate in or support an effective staff team.

A COMMON SENSE OF MISSION

An effective staff has a clear sense of mission and an understanding of the work it hopes to accomplish. The mission should be written, regularly reviewed, and updated. The mission stance provides the criteria for program development, resource selection, and guidance regarding the use of leadership resources and the perception of trends. The stance provides a solid frame of reference for the constituents, because they can anticipate the actions and leadership of their staff. The stance also builds a positive and constructive staff, because it knows what it as a staff stands for. The mission stance provides a sense of direction and facilitates planning. Staff members realize that priorities for programs will vary and priority opportunities for staff members will shift from time to time according to the mission.

Often a leadership staff comes together with little mutual understanding of why it is there. Members rehearse a pattern or tradition that was established for them by prior staff teams. In some cases autocratic leaders have provided the direction and purpose for the staff's existence without taking into consideration the unique gifts and current concerns of the staff. A staff needs to have ownership of its mission and ministry. Ownership is established when members of the staff commonly determine the direction and purpose of their being together.

Criteria that should guide the mission of a staff include:

- The congregation's or constituents' priorities and expectations
- Denominational accountability
- The gifts, the experience, and the interest of individual staff members
- Particular needs and resources of the community

A mission statement establishes specific goals that give meaning to who members are as a staff among God's people. Leadership with a vision for mission is based on an understanding of God and a sharp awareness of the world in which we live.

ORGANIZATION FOR ACTION

A congregation's staff members may be feeling stress and exhaustion. They may be continually running into each other at the same meetings with the same tasks with the same people. It may not always be clear who is responsible, and individuals may often be embarrassed because certain activities and reports are not attended to. Some staff members may be overloaded with responsibilities while others may be frustrated with extra time and energy. Staff meetings may tend to focus more on frustrations than the tasks at hand. In such cases the staff probably is not effective because it is not organized for action. For sure, we should not organize for the sake of organization or hold staff meetings for the sake of having meetings, but organization for the purpose of enabling staff to be accountable for ministry is necessary.

All staff persons should have a *job description*. The job description should state clearly the agreed upon expectations of a position and it should clarify for all concerned the work a person is to do. The description should state how the accomplishment of these tasks will be evaluated and what compensation and benefits will be provided for the staff member.

Regular meetings should be held (biweekly to monthly) primarily to help the staff grow in harmony and mutuality. The agenda should include opportunities for sharing work and personal related concerns, an update on budget and program progress, special concerns of the governing body, and an opportunity to celebrate the lives and progress of the staff members.

There should be careful *communication and interpretation* of the work of staff members to the constituents. Sometimes the work of a staff member is misunderstood because it has not been interpreted appropriately, and some important work does not give persons an opportunity to be visible. Communication to the public should affirm all staff persons for their work.

A COVENANT OF MUTUAL RESPECT

To nurture staff relationships that upbuild the "body of Christ," certain principles must be adhered to. Staff members should agree to the following principles:

1. Never publicly talk negatively about a colleague; all such discussion should be private and confidential.

2. Never demand special privileges that are not available to all colleagues.

3. Support the leadership of others; it may not be possible to like every colleague, but staff members must respect another member's position or function, or that position or function is undermined.

4. Work with integrity; be professionally honest and do not ask other colleagues to cover up for negligence.

CELEBRATION OF LIFE TOGETHER

A staff is called together at a particular place at a particular time. Celebration is an act of reverence or appreciation for the present time. Celebration enhances the moment—it is a recognition that what is shall not be again. Celebration gives praise to God for these people, one's colleagues, in this time, in this place. Effective staff relationships should include the following aspects of celebration.

Humor is a gift of God—the spirit of joy and enthusiasm. One of the beautiful things about the faith community is that members both weep with those who weep and rejoice with those who rejoice. Both need to be done with vigor. The capacity to see the humor in certain situations, to enjoy the funny side of life can brighten the day for everyone.

The capacity to leave and let go should be developed. We all have people and things that we care about very strongly. But the day comes when they are no longer part of our lives. A loved one departs, a good job is lost, a valued situation changes for one reason or another. When that time comes, a period of grieving may be in order but it should soon be set aside. The past is over and done with—it's time to celebrate.

A common prayer life provides a good opportunity for a staff to share openness to God and to one another about hopes, dreams, failures, and hurts. Thankfulness and expressions of gratefulness to God give focus to belief in the Giver. Prayer spreads the spirit of love. Prayer is the means by which the will and love of God are brought to bear on a staff and on the world through Jesus Christ. *See also* Conflict Management; Congregational Life; Leadership Development; Management.

C. C. Peter

Starbuck, Edwin D.

Edwin Diller Starbuck (1866–1947) was a pioneer in the field of psychology of religion and in developing programs of character education. A native of Bridgeport, Indiana, he attended Indiana University and received an A.M. and Ph.D. from Harvard University with postgraduate work at the University of Zurich, Switzerland. He taught at Stanford University (1897–1904), Earlham College (1904–1906), Louisiana State University (1906–1923), and the University of Iowa (1923–1930) before becoming professor of philosophy and later of psychology at the University of Southern California.

He wrote a book on character education in 1898, and *Moral Education in the Public Schools* in 1904. From 1912 to 1914 he worked with the Unitarian churches on a curriculum for character education. He started the Institute of Character Research at the State University of Iowa while teaching there. With a strong interest and research in the psychology of the conversion experience and in religious development, he wrote the first book in that field, *Psychology of Religion* (1900). *See also* Character Development; Conversion; Psychology of Religion.

L. G. McAllister

Statistics

Statistics is a branch of mathematics that gathers and analyzes data with a view to revealing relationships among these data, determining causes of these relationships, and clearly noting apparent relational occurrences due solely to chance.

The simpler calculations deal with distributions within a given population or sample, describing these according to the bell-shaped curve of normal distribution (i.e., in any sample, numbers tend to be distributed in a bell-shaped curve—most bunched in the middle, fewer at each end). Measures of tendency may be calculated, the most common being the average, or mean. Measures of dispersion, the most common of which is the standard deviation (the area either way from the mean into which two-thirds of the sample will fall), may likewise be calculated and these describe the magnitude of dispersion or distance of individual measure from the mean. Other indices may measure the degree of correlation between groups of measures.

Reliability of measures depends on distinguishing between true causes or influences and chance occurrences, and mathematical procedures exist that attempt to study these situations for an indication of reliability. Statisticians are constantly devising new procedures to enable more accurate study of true causes and factors in a growing variety of seemingly unmanageable data.

REPORTING RELIGIOUS RESPONSE

The phenomenon of human religious response presents little difficulty for the science of statistics when it is a matter of reporting numbers of adherents to various faiths and their distribution as to geographic location, age, sex, or race. Here the meaning of religious response is not questioned, nor is its degree of presence discussed. For religious educational purposes, surveys produce statistics on attendance and enrollment as well as parallel figures as to age levels in the community and its schools. From the study of such data, conclusions are drawn to discover whether enrollment could be larger or attendance better. It may suggest the need for outreach, better programs, or parental cooperation.

Numbers and their distribution patterns are helpful in certain investigations, but different kinds of information are often sought and notions, characteristics, or traits are not easily quantifiable. Here the study of religion, religious response, and religious education presents difficulty to those who seek to use scientific method. Keen observation and clear intuitions are required in generating and testing all hypotheses.

ASSESSING FAITH AND MORAL DEVELOPMENT

Maria Montessori (1870–1952) remains an accepted authority in her observations and discussion of the child's earliest experiences of awe, followed by wonder. Her descriptions of the child's developmental response to the innate sense of God are widely accepted and respected. Following a more statistical approach, Ronald Goldman, in England in 1959, studied readiness for religion in children of different ages, presenting highly sensitive guidelines for assisting religious response without doing violence to the child's natural, developmental rhythms. The study includes observations concerning the Bible and its stories, prayer, and the church. Later, David Elkind, in Boston, studied religious development through Piagetian categories using verbal questions as the basis for observation. Other researchers have used such well-established projective tests as human figure drawing, "House-Tree-Person," and finger painting, as well as responses to pictures and stories, and interviews. Such analytical studies of the child enable religious educators to prepare curricula consonant with needs and readiness. They help in the writing of developmental profiles for teachers and in choosing methods in religious education, thus making these findings important for the classroom teacher.

Moral education and faith development have always been integral parts of religious education, but today feelings or intuitions about readiness and levels of responsibility have not sufficed. With the growing interest in child development, distinct populations at specific levels have been studied and hypotheses generated and tested by means of reliable instruments fashioned expressly for the purpose. As a result, moral development has emerged as a distinct discipline. The work of Lawrence Kohlberg in Chicago resulted in categories that are used for curriculum development both in schools and in religious education programs. In a parallel way, James W. Fowler's work in faith development has entailed not only a close study of the nature of faith but a careful observation and description of its expression at different ages and levels of psychological development. Such investigation employs a methodology that starts with interviews through which measurements, validation, and conclusions are made.

PSYCHOLOGICAL TESTING

In the late 1950s and early 1960s, psychologists in Europe and North America began to study the personality patterns of seminarians and novices in religious communities. Practical and reliable indications were sought in such matters as personality profiles of seemingly well-adjusted applicants and psychological patterns of persevering and nonpersevering candidates at different stages, including the years after ordination or profession. Specific trait measurement was also attempted, such as of value patterns, sexual orientation, generosity, and introversion/extroversion. Existing tests were used in many cases, including the Rorschach Ink Blot Test, and new measures using statistical methods were devised. Today psychological testing is a routine prerequisite for entrance into theological seminary among most religious groups as a way of ascertaining potential fitness for ministry and discovering needs that can be met during seminary preparation.

Problems in the field include choosing appropriate statistics for the information with which a researcher is working. Interpreting statistics is the core of the matter, and this may depend on inferences. Moreover, much of the statistics in religious education or development comes from clinical or "soft" data. It does not provide statistics covering large numbers, but instead depends on a sampling of persons who are interviewed in depth.

NEW RELIGIOUS RESEARCH USING STATISTICS

New research through statistics continues. The Search Institute in Minneapolis has been at work, with foundation money, on an analysis of questionnaires to predict the success of church youth programs. In Finland, a study of religious experience is being made through open-ended responses to projected photos. Because religion is a school subject, researchers have a large sample through which to study children's religious understanding (of God, prayer, and death) in relation to the understanding of other subjects. They are interested in both the emotional and cognitive dimensions of belief. They are correlating aptitudes in science and mathematics with kinds of religious belief and worldviews, in order to ascertain how a scientific approach affects religious faith.

Other areas of investigation, perhaps even more difficult to probe, are those of growth in spirituality and pastoral counseling and spiritual direction. Researchers have been looking for reasons and situations promoting growth, collecting data, experimenting, and drawing conclusions for further testing. As in the study of psychotherapy, the factors contributing to growth are difficult to name, difficult to measure, and difficult to control. However, inasmuch as grace builds on nature and scientific methodology now allows for study of the controllable bases for spiritual growth, research may help practitioners supply for grace a favorable ground in which to grow.

Most religious educators, counselors, and spiritual directors are not trained in research methodology and statistics. However, they need to develop an appreciation for such work and an ability to use the results. This will encourage statistical study among religious education enterprises on the local, regional, and national levels. *See also* Evaluation; Measurement; Methodology; Psychology of Religion; Research; Social Sciences; Sociology of Religion.

T. A. Francoeur

Stewardship

A steward is one who cares for the properties or business of another, an owner. While stewards do not have "ownership" they do have responsibility for the appropriate care or management of that property or business on behalf of the owner: stewardship.

Technological advances have brought us a new understanding of the concept of ownership. When the first color photographs of earth from space were published, we saw no color-coded nations, no borders, no walls—only beauty. "And God saw everything that God had made and behold, it was very good" (Gen. 1:31). And as communication satellites have brought us instant news reports of world hunger, natural disaster, and the ravages of war, graphically portraying the results of human hatred, envy, and greed, we have come to see our world as a kind of global village. With this growing awareness that all life on earth exists in a delicate balance and that what we do affects that balance, our secular world has rediscovered the ancient religious concept of stewardship, which derives from humankind's position at the top of God's created order, in the place of "dominion." Our dominion requires us to be stewards of God's creation.

As a religious concept, stewardship is directly related to religious doctrine regarding creation, providence, sin, and redemption. Most religions have a doctrine of creation which asserts that God did indeed create this universe. "In the beginning God created the heavens and the earth" (Gen. 1:1). Inherent in this act of creation is the sense that God has a purpose for creation.

The Judeo-Christian tradition teaches, moreover, that God gave humankind a position of "dominion" over the rest of creation (Gen. 1:26), and that position requires us to be stewards of creation. Humankind has failed God, but God has promised to redeem his creation; the Lord God Omnipotent reigns, and humankind's position in relation to God is a position of dependence. That life is a gift—given and given anew by God—undergirds our desire to be good stewards.

Religious educators deal with God's love for us and our love for others. In an age marked by narcissism and a decline in personal morality, the religious community has a unique opportunity and responsibility to teach and model stewardship in all its aspects.

We begin with Planet Earth. Study of issues from acid rain to nuclear power belong within our purview. What is our proper role in the use of available resources? Proper use of our environment—land, water, air, animals, minerals, fuels, and appropriate technology—is a topic for study, reflection, and action for stewards.

If all that we are and all that we have—our time, talents, and possessions—are gifts from a loving Creator God, we must give our attention to all of humankind. We can no longer ignore an earthquake in Colombia, acid rain in Canada, or nuclear testing in the Pacific Islands. As an interdependent world community we must respond to the needs of all people, with peace as our common goal. Crosscultural communication is no longer a luxury, it is a necessity if we are to survive. In addition to the story of creation, religious education offers study and discussion of human groups and the tenets and practices of the major world religions.

Liberation theologies have been influential. These affirm that all people must be freed from political, economic, and social restraints (oppression) in order to fulfill their God-given potential. Dealing realistically with our current life condition requires us, informed by our religious faith, to act out our beliefs in practice (praxis). Stewards must address their personal and community responsibility for time, talents, and possessions.

Time is one thing that each individual shares equitably: twenty-four hours each day, 365 days each year. How shall they be used? For what purpose?—simply to survive, or for the advancement of human civilization? Stewards regard time as a precious gift from God.

Talents—"the fruit of the spirit is love, joy, peace, patience, kindness, goodness, faithfulness, gentleness, self-control" (Gal. 5:22, 23)—are to be used in behalf of others.

With regard to possessions psychologists and sociologists report what religion has known all along: people are concerned for themselves. Of our resources 98 percent go toward ourselves, with only 2 percent for others freely offered. Religious educators have the responsibility to openly deal with the hard issues: how one uses resources (for self or others); what one believes about money (tool or goal). Stewards know for whom they live. They care for others' needs and share their possessions.

Teaching about the use of time, talents, and possessions begins early in the family and in the religious community. Religious education can point out that allocation of time reflects priorities and can encourage individuals to see both talents and possessions in terms of how they may be constructively used to carry out humanity's stewardship responsibility in the world. Religious educators themselves need to learn to discern and actively appreciate their students' special gifts and to encourage their use in family, work, and society.

The agenda for stewardship nurture and education affords both challenge and opportunity for religious educators. If we are committed to the fulfillment of God's vision for God's world, as we understand that vision from our religious heritage and literature, then we have no choice but to assist God's people to become faithful stewards. *See also* Creation; Liberation Theology; Peace, Education for; Social Justice, Education for.

FOR FURTHER REFERENCE

Hall, Douglas. *The Steward*, Library of Christian Stewardship. New York: NCCC, 1982.
———. *Images of Life*. New York: Friendship Press, 1982.

D. A. Wright

Storytelling

Story has a vital function in religious education because the message of the Bible is told as story. Story is a high art and a folk art, an expression of the sublime or simple instruction. Storytelling helps people to penetrate into themselves and shape how they perceive the world and their own lives.

HISTORY

Storytelling is an ancient art. There is ample evidence that from 50,000 B.C. the Neanderthal held beliefs about individual personality, the cosmos, and death, for in graves that have been excavated bodies have been aligned to the east or curled as in sleep, precious objects enclosed, and in one instance flowers strewn on the body. The Neanderthal had the vocal organs and mental capacity to speak, so it is hard to believe they did not tell myths or stories about life and death, day and night, waking and sleeping that were reflected in their burial customs.

The advent of writing in Sumer, about 3000 B.C., almost immediately documents myths and epics of creation, gods, goddesses, and dragons that had long been sung by priestly castes, perhaps preserved for millennia in oral tradition. Sung poetry was not only the professional storyteller's easiest method of relying on memory, but it was a safeguard of the stories themselves, so our earliest narratives are of unknown age.

Epics related noble events and thoughts, but Sumerian cuneiform tablets also reveal fragments of fables. Fables were essentially cautionary tales and were informally told by parents, guardians, and lesser functionaries. Fables protected hearers from direct admonition by disguising story characters as animals or even trees (see Judg. 9:8–15), but a moral was always implied if not explicitly appended. Epic material and myths were the stories of professionals, such as priests and bards, and were appropriate to liturgy and other communal occasions, while fables were homespun and told by the folk without pretense in the course of daily life.

Court records or chronicles are another kind of story. In the Bible these are found in 1 and 2

STORYTELLING

Age Level	Guidelines for Content and Presentation
Preschool	Biblical stories of God's love and care and present-day stories of people, particularly children and their families, are appropriate; stories should encourage identification and imagination and should avoid moralism and symbolism; they should not be so simplified as to lose all memorable details; stories should be told or read vividly in no more than 2 to 3 minutes, often using flannelgraph or other illustrations.
Grades 1–3	Stories of specific events and challenges in the lives of biblical and present-day people are appropriate; stories should be told or read vividly in no more than 5 minutes, often using illustrations or dramatization.
Grades 4–8	Longer stories set in specific places and historical periods can be used, as can continued stories that took place over a period of time (i.e., the biblical story of Moses and the people of Israel, or stories of families and nations traced through several generations); symbolism and abstract material can begin to be used and understood; stories can be read or told by students as well as teachers, and discussion and dramatization might follow.
High School and Adult	Anecdotes and illustrative material are enjoyed; stories can be read or told for their own sake or as the basis for further thought and discussion; reasoning and abstract thinking can be used to grasp both past and present meanings of stories; additional resource materials can be used to further understanding.

Samuel, the story of the United Kingdom; 1 and 2 Kings, the history of Israel to captivity; and 1 and 2 Chronicles, the story of Judah to captivity.

The Bible begins with creation and other stories of early experience such as the Flood and continues with the patriarchal saga of the family of Abraham and Sarah. Exodus recounts the story of Israel in Egypt and the wilderness journey until the promised land is reached.

Stories of heroes are found in Judges, as the settlement of the land is recounted. The story of Deborah is told both in poetry (Judg. 5) and in prose (chap. 4). There are also the stories of Gideon (chap. 6) and Samson (chaps. 13–16).

The New Testament presents the Gospel form of narrative. There are four retellings of the life, teachings, death, and resurrection of Jesus. The purpose is to strengthen the faith of believers and to appeal to potential believers. The book of Acts is the story of the spread of the Christian community from Jerusalem into the Greco-Roman empire.

Parables, which came thousands of years after fables, also use the elements of everyday life, but while fables are concerned with the practicalities of getting by in this world, parables convey sublime ideas, usually by way of analogy, such as the nature of God and his kingdom, that perhaps could be expressed in no other way. Unlike fables, parables do not give their meaning at the end; interpretation often rests with the teller or hearers. Although there was a tradition of parabolic teaching before Jesus (2 Sam. 12:1–4, the oldest biblical parable, recounts the story the prophet Nathan used to show David the error of his ways with Bathsheba), Jesus brought the parable to perfection and made the form his chief method of teaching. Jesus' parables deal with such things as a lost coin, a pearl of great price, and a prodigal son in order to explain about the nature of God and his kingdom and remain the primary story material in Christian education, whether from a pulpit, in a course of instruction, or in family life.

STORYTELLING IN MODERN TIMES

Stories extend beyond the Bible to encompass significant people and events in the life of the religious community through the past nineteen centuries. Stories can also represent the experiences of hearers and contemporary situations. Anecdotes are a form of story much used in sermons. Storytelling appeals to all ages and is a useful form of approach for intergenerational events.

Jewish storytelling tradition has been more creative than the Christian one and Jews continue to create new stories and forms of stories to illuminate the Torah. Many of these stories were preserved in the haggadah of the midrash and Talmud, and the inventiveness continued as late as the eleventh or twelfth century. During the eighteenth century a radically different type of teaching tale arose among the devotional sect of the Hasidim, usually in the form of an anecdote about a famous rabbi. Hasidic and similar tales continue to be useful in teaching the faith of the Jews and have even engaged the interest of theologians such as Martin Buber.

The Protestant Sunday school movement, which began in England and spread to the United States in the early nineteenth century, produced, in 1872, the International Uniform Lessons Series. While the series made use of weekly printed Bible stories, story*telling* as a medium of communication was not promoted. Edward Porter St. John's *Stories and Storytelling in Moral and Religious Education* in 1910, however, recognized the importance of telling and broadened the range of material of the Sunday school storyteller to include folk and fairy tales.

The emphasis during these years was on the teaching values of stories, whether biblical or nonbiblical. There was also an appreciation of the appeal inherent in stories that made teaching and learning more attractive. The culminating book of this period was Jeanette Perkins Brown's *The Storyteller in Religious Education* (1951).

An important turning point came in 1961 at the midwinter meeting of the Division of Christian Education, National Council of the Churches of Christ, when the Swiss theologian Markus Barth presented his views on storytelling (published as "The Cowboy in the Sunday School," *Religious Education*, January/February and March/April 1962). Barth recognized the uniqueness of storytelling and the singularity of its meaning. The monumental shift Barth proposed was from using stories as a way to make a point or press a lesson home to appreciating what a story is of itself. Barth's stress was on telling stories and leaving them to work their own powers without trying to explicate.

Subsequent writers on storytelling include John Harrell and Bruno Bettleheim. Harrell's *To Tell of Gideon* (1975) makes use of cassettes to include examples of storytelling skill. In *The Uses of Enchantment* (1976) Bruno Bettleheim gave the first clues as to how fairy tales can operate healingly in the lives of children. How all stories in our rich heritage function in the lives of youth and adults is covered in Harrell's *The Man on a Dolphin* (1983).

THE ROLE OF STORYTELLER

At the same time that storytelling was being investigated, the nature of the storyteller also became clearer. For the ancient Greeks, the storyteller was inspired by the mother of the muses, Memory. The storyteller was the living repository of the community's lore, which included the secrets of life. When an *aoidos* sang an epic, the activity was not merely a reprise, but a living event being shared between teller and audience in the present moment. To the Greeks, when stories were written down and memory no longer called upon, the life went out of them. It is no wonder, then, that storytellers were special persons in society. This function does not and cannot come about if storytellers see themselves as actors or clowns (these involve impersonation and are different arts), but only when storytellers remain themselves and speak directly to the audience. Storytelling then becomes an interpersonal activity, a direct personal encounter between the teller and each of the hearers, and when the material that is shared has depth and substance, the relationship takes on a sacred character and "religious education" takes place.

The training of storytellers, then, becomes important. Books by Marie Shedlock (*The Art of the Storyteller*, 1915) and Ruth Sawyer (*The Way of the Storyteller*, 1942) are valuable for beginners. In 1975 the National Association for the Preservation and Perpetuation of Storytelling came into being and has grown into a significant force in storytelling today. From the beginning, religious educators have been important members and many have been nurtured through the association's conferences, workshops, and its *National Journal of Storytelling*. In recent years there have also been independent conferences on storytelling and the religious message.

Today among religious educators there is an intellectual appreciation of storytelling, especially of telling their own stories or listening to others' stories. But they need to gain the security that only comes from personal experience to trust in the unique nature of storytelling and the insights of our story heritage. Then they will make even more use of storytelling for religious education. This was its original function. *See also* Bible Study; Books, Children's; Narrative Theology; Sermons, Children's.

J. Harrell

Structuralism

Structuralism as a form of literary criticism examines the structures that presumably reside beneath the surface meanings of a literary text. We can think of structuralism through the analogy of the loom, which places controls on the weaver's tapestry. The author's written text, just as the weaver's finished work, is a creative expression within the bounds of structural constraints (Daniel Patte). Moreover, these structures lie hidden beneath the literary form of the text itself, present in primal myths as "binary oppositions," which are the opposing forces of life and death, good and evil, and the divine and the human, according to Claude Lévi-Strauss.

Because structuralism traces meaning beneath the surface expressions of a biblical text, it presumes that this meaning is largely inaccessible to the traditional forms of biblical criticism, which focus on a literary text's form and content, the life situation giving rise to a text, and the author's intention. Instead, readers discover the text's "meaning effect" in their own understanding of it once they grasp the deeper, ahistorical meaning. In a structural approach to New Testament literature, this deeper meaning is found in Christ, the hero who mediates and resolves the "binary oppositions." Christ as the preexisting "Word become flesh" in John's Gospel, as God's "beloved Son" in Mark, and as the product of a virgin birth in Luke (Dan Via's grouping) are all surface, historical expressions of the Christ who reconciles these deeper "binary oppositions." Once we are privy to these somewhat arcane truths, we recognize the common underlying patterns on which the separate Gospel narratives are constructed, say the structuralists. Radical structuralists usually disregard the historical significance and surface meaning of the Gospel narratives in their focus on these patterns, while the more moderate, "eclectic" ones view structuralism as an addition to, rather than a replacement of, the traditional forms of criticism.

Some structuralists contend that structural elements are present in all areas of human thinking, not just in an author's narrative ordering of a text. They cite as examples the class struggle proposed by Marxism and the unconscious mind portrayed by psychoanalysis as structures that shape history beneath the sequence of surface historical events.

Structuralist discourse can be incomprehensible for the outsider because of its technical language. Consider this array of terms: "synchronic," "diachronic," "paradigmatic," "syntagmatic," and "actantial." Still, an acquaintance with structuralism is important for religious educators even though they may seldom use its technical terms and procedures, for if the forces that shape the meaning of religious texts reside even partly beneath the surface of their literary expression, then educators who teach these texts should be aware of them. See also Bible Study; Biblical Criticism.

J. H. Stone

Student Christian Movement

Subsuming a number of campus organizations, particularly the intercollegiate YMCA/YWCA, the Student Volunteer Movement, the World Student Christian Federation, and several regional Student Christian Movement groups, the Student Christian Movement is an evangelistic effort by students on college campuses that had its beginning in the late nineteenth century.

During the nineteenth century, young people's societies in the United States met in the local church for worship, fellowship, and service. But in higher education, students who had often been influenced by religious awakenings seemed naturally to join together for reasons of evangelism and missions. These voluntaristic lay groups eventually moved to encircle the globe.

While founded in England (1844), the YMCA quickly spread to the United States. Later, from his Princeton College base, Luther D. Wishard, first secretary for student work, began to recruit on other college campuses and the intercollegiate work known as the Student Christian Movement was underway. Eventually, the student departments of both the YMCA and the YWCA shouldered much of this program. Christian discipleship, the authority of Scripture, and leading youth to faith in the triune God were key principles.

The Student Volunteer Movement became the mission arm of the overall Student Christian Movement. Through the purpose of Wishard and the inspiration of evangelist Dwight L. Moody, more than 250 students convened at Mount Hermon (Massachusetts) for Bible study and produced a missionary awakening with the watchword: "The evangelization of the world in this generation." Students traveled to campuses to promote and recruit, and in 1889 the Student Volunteer Movement organized formally.

As the movement spread to Europe and the non-Western world, a single man rose to prominence. When the revivals of Moody swept American and British youth along, John R. Mott was taken up in the tide. He began in university Y work at Cornell, became the executive secretary of the Student Volunteer Movement, and did more than any other individual to found the World Student Christian Federation in 1895. The world was his field and federation was his idea. He traveled the world and brought the various student movements of America, Britain, Germany, and Scandinavia into one organization. Mott aimed at winning the students of the world for Christ; they in turn perpetuated that evangelism.

The philosophy of the Student Christian Movement changed over the decades. While begun by Christian individuals through a voluntaristic effort, the movement became more church-centered as each major denomination attempted to follow its students to college. Nevertheless, university pastors and students began to cooperate, and the earlier interdenominational spirit again flourished. Tensions between Y work and church agencies sometimes developed. Yet, as decline set in, the very names indicated the cooperative nature of campus work in the United States: the United Student Christian Movement, the National Student Christian Federation, the University Christian Movement, with some programs supervised by the National Council of the Churches of Christ in the U.S.A. To the students, then, the modern ecumenical movement owes a substantial debt. Today, the Student Christian Movement is organized regionally, with the North American group headquartered in New York City. *See also* Evangelism; Mission, Education for; Young Men's Christian Association; Young Women's Christian Association; Youth Ministry.

W. J. Schmidt

Suburban Church

Suburban churches, as we have known them in recent years in North America, are a new phenomenon. In Europe and in colonial America, the important churches were to be found in the center of a town or city, along with the best houses or palaces.

BACKGROUND

Colonial American churches were built without endowment in land, drew little or no support from public taxes or tithes, and lacked the royal patronage normal in Europe from the time of Constantine and Theodosius. But they did not have public responsibility for operating schools and caring for the poor as did the churches in Europe, so their physical plants were simpler. At first they consisted solely of a building for worship and possibly a sacristy or vestry room. Parsonages were added later.

After the Civil War, congregations began to build halls for social gatherings and for Sunday school. Although at first these halls were simple, as time passed they came to include stages, kitchens, and a multipurpose room with space for lay-led worship and Sunday school classes.

PRESENT SITUATION

Changes in educational theory in both public and church schools following World War II required churches and synagogues to build special educational buildings or wings with separate classrooms, offices, and libraries as well as space for social events. This is the type of church plant that became characteristic of the rapidly growing suburbs of the 1950s and 1960s.

The suburb was a place of privilege, a dream of upward mobility, a clean place where children could be safely raised among home-owning neighbors and friends of similar status and class. It had no factories and no working-class or service-class people, and it was often racially segregated *de facto*. It took education to arrive there, and education was also one of its greatest concerns and products. The suburbs revolved around children and their schooling. In contrast to the Europe of the Middle Ages, where, in Charles Beard's description, the typical institution was the parish church, in America the typical institution was the local public school. Suburban schools were handsomely supported by property taxes, the assumption being that large expenditures would ensure high-quality education. Suburban churches took their cue from the schools, investing heavily in new curricula as well as in expanded buildings and administrative and committee structure. Buildings and programs were financed by capital fund drives and by mortgages similar to the ones suburban parishioners had on their own houses.

Unlike small town churches, which typically include people from all social classes, suburban churches have built their religious communities on a limited section of the population. Typically, they have been segregated by class as well as by race. Their religious education programs have done a good job of transmitting peer culture, which tends to identify religion solely with the beliefs of "people like us" rather than with the whole common people of God.

PROBLEMS AND POSSIBILITIES

The early Sunday school movement often included adult classes that continued for decades. Attending such classes even after completing formal secular education was common for the faithful and the leaders of the local church. This pattern was not repeated in the suburbs. Although secular education for most children in the suburbs extended well beyond high school, religious education did not.

Youth activities did not typically center on the study of the Bible or theology but on discussion about life adjustment, tending to be concerned with the problems of making choices within the peer group. Youth activities were designed to build loyalty and community rather than to impart information about a faith tradition. Yet even these intensive activities often involved only about 20 percent of those who had been received into full church membership at junior high school age.

As a result, suburbs produced people who were highly educated in scientific method and historical criticism through the college level but had only a grammar-school level of learning in the core studies of Bible and religious tradition. They were well initiated into grammar-school and youth-activity worship experiences but uninitiated into the patterns of traditional adult worship and activities. Moreover, the growing influence of television, with its brief scenes promoting short attention spans, made young people cultural foreigners to highly verbal worship centering on sermons of classical length.

The result is a congregation of adults who, faithful in attendance at worship and active in congregational affairs, grasp biblical references in hymn, sermon, or even Scripture reading in only the most general way. Even in churches with a participatory liturgy, one cannot be certain that people fully understand the words they speak.

An encouraging sign, however, is that although serious Bible study among the high school group seems to be waning, there is increased interest among adults, indicated by the popularity of national programs, for which churches enroll and buy specific study materials.

This problem is less apparent among evangelical churches, where it is expected that biblical content and interpretation are basic to curriculum at all age levels. Nor is it as evident in synagogues, where preparation both for bar and bas mitzvah and confirmation follows a prescribed course that acquaints young people with both Scripture and liturgy.

Sunday schools and other religious educational activities have traditionally found teachers primarily among women who stayed at home to raise children. Today many of these women find the pressures of outside jobs and homemaking make it necessary to cut down on other commitments. This decrease in the number of available leaders has affected weekday and vacation school activities, some of which have been moved to evenings or concentrated on weekends. It has also—encouragingly—begun to bring men into the teaching process, to encourage team teaching, and to stimulate thinking about further possibilities, such as short-term assignments or larger class groupings.

Religious education programs in suburbs as elsewhere are also under siege from the rising divorce rate. Children who share living arrangements with two parents (or sets of parents) living at a distance from each other will be found spending some time in each of two congregations. This pattern is disconcerting to teachers, who hope for the stimulus to both themselves and the class of regular attendance. The children involved may welcome the variety of experiences, but they could also become confused by different approaches, if the two programs vary considerably.

With the insistently busy schedules that both parents and children keep in suburban families has come an increasing emphasis on devoting weekends to the maintenance of their own family's affectional ties. Frequently, given the level of affluence, activities will include out-of-town weekends at a second home or a variety of recreational activities that have replaced the former longer summer vacations. Plans may be as simple as a nearby one-day excursion, entertaining friends or relatives, or enjoying an afternoon at the family pool. Whatever the plan, however, it frequently omits religious activities. There is a noticeable decrease in attendance on holiday weekends or during school vacation periods, as well.

CONCLUSION

In the past generation or two, suburban churches have exerted a disproportionate influence on denominational concerns and policies. Their educated, articulate members have furnished so much of the leadership at the judicatory level that among mainline denominations the suburban church has become normative.

Yet not everyone in the country has access to higher education, a high-paying job, and a house in the suburbs. While the suburban church or synagogue has an authentic mission in the suburbs, it is only a partial sample or segment of the people of God. It cannot serve as a model for the rest of society.

Changes are coming to the suburbs as housing growth slows down and stops and as the economy changes from production to service industries with their lower rates of pay. At the same time, a movement back to the cities is beginning, and suburban culture is being imported into slum areas undergoing gentrification.

The suburban church in America has been one distinctive outreach in the church's history of mission, catechesis, and evangelism. Like the base communities of Brazil and Latin America, it has much to say to the whole church, but it cannot be copied directly outside its native habitat.

FOR FURTHER REFERENCE

Brueggemann, Walter. *Hopeful Imagination: Prophetic Voices in Exile.* Philadelphia: Fortress Press, 1986.

Newbigin, Lesslie. *Foolishness to the Greeks: The Gospel and Western Culture.* Grand Rapids, MI: Eerdmans, 1986.

Sample, Tex. *Blue-Collar Ministry: Facing Economic and Social Realities of Working People.* Valley Forge, PA: Judson Press, 1984.

Schreiter, Robert J. *Constructing Local Theologies.* Maryknoll, NY: Orbis Books, 1985.

S. W. Martin

Suicide

Suicide is the intentional killing of oneself. Suicide is often attempted as a means of resolving problems arising from the human condition: an exceedingly harsh life; the exhaustion of all other alternatives to life's problems; social glorification of those who have committed suicide; repeated breaching of thresholds for coping with the human condition; isolation from love and support; and membership in the high risk groups of the elderly or young males who seem otherwise unable to cope with life's reality.

Students of suicide place causes either within the self or as a result of outside factors. The classical view of external etiology is sociologist Emile Durkheim's *Suicide* (1897). Failure to establish successful social relationships eventuates in self-destructive behavior. This failure may be due to social factors beyond the control of the individual or inner dynamics of a person's psyche or spirit. More recent investigations have added the biological dimension to the possible causes of suicide: chemical or biological factors so disturb a person's equilibrium that suicide seems to be the only viable alternative (e.g., chemically introduced depression becomes so severe that suicide is attempted).

Only unsuccessful suicide attempts permit observations of the consequences of self-destructive behavior. The impact of an attempted suicide demands the attention of all participants in religious education both for the individual and for all relations, family, and friends. The attempt is a signal that the balance between creative and destructive forces in the life of the individual are precarious. A new life situation devolves from the experience of attempted self-destruction. Timely professional intervention in the family dynamics may prevent a successful suicide, but it is not guaranteed. The process of coming to grips with this new complex of interrelationships is not unlike the grief process made familiar by Elizabeth Kübler-Ross—denial, anger, bargaining, depression, and acceptance—in some undetermined order.

Of unique importance for religious education is the question of God's responsibility in death, including suicide. Some religious traditions view the time of death as God's action and condemn suicides for interfering in the divine process. The issue of God's power in relationship to the power each person has over his or her life is at the center of many Western religious explanations of suicide. Those who emphasize God's omnipotence and original creation hold suicide as morally unacceptable. Moral culpability diminishes as mitigating causes explain the action; social, psychological, and physical causes may excuse behavior. These reflections have not been applied to those who allow themselves to be killed in the line of duty to state, church, or family. Such self-sacrifice has sometimes raised suicide as an act of heroism. The martyrs of early Christianity or the Jews of Masada who killed themselves in order to avoid the ravage of Roman armies demonstrate that self-destruction for a higher cause is sometimes acceptable in religious terms. But accidental self-destruction and intentional self-destruction without such a purpose have not enjoyed the same high regard. People are disturbed by the victory of destructive forces when moral calculations do not perceive a balance in favor of creativity.

Suicide prevention demands a realistic appraisal of the psychological, spiritual, and physical conditions of certain age groups as well as individuals who appear to be suicide-prone. Programs abound for the purpose of preventing suicide. Individual counseling and public teaching in the form of lectures and workshops either directly in classroom contact or through telecommunications media provide many opportunities to educate the public. Some authorities argue that silence about this possible solution to life's problems is a better tool than attempting to raise the consciousness of those who might in fact engage in suicide.

The stage of life at which an individual contemplates or attempts suicide is an important factor. Teenage suicide in general seems unacceptable when compared to suicide of a person in the later stages of life, though even here there are many who find this solution to the problems of aging to be equally unacceptable. Religious education needs to include consideration of all the factors that might influence a person's attitude toward the preservation of his or her life. Consultation and open support provide the first line of reaction; a deep spirituality based upon a realistic assessment of the present world and individual conditions provides the society with a means to combat what in most cases is a tragic event.

Religious communities too often hope that the mutual support of members will prevent suicide and are shocked when it does not. Members need reassurance for what they have tried and an opportunity to grieve and confess what they feel they might have done. Adolescents (since this is a high-risk age) need to discuss the issue frankly both in the light of the situation as they know it, including the tensions of their lives, and the assurances religious faith gives of the sustaining power of God for life. Older people's groups (the other high-risk age) will also need to make this a subject for reflection. For all adults, the related question of euthanasia cannot be avoided, and this brings in questions about suffering and the love of God. These are not easy questions for religious educators, but they should not be avoided. Pastoral counseling of people who come in despair has educational components as the counselor tries to affirm the person's self-worth and give assurance of God's sustaining care. *See also* Aging; Counseling; Death; Theodicy.

R. E. Keady

Sukkoth

Sukkoth (Heb., "booths"; singular *sukkah*) is the Jewish fall harvest festival also commemorating the temporary dwellings the Israelites lived in during their desert trek to Canaan. Sukkoth is one of three pilgrimage festivals (together with Pesach and Shavuot), when Jews in ancient times traveled to the Temple in Jerusalem (Deut. 16:16).

The holiday is seven days long (eight days outside of Israel), beginning on the fifteenth day of the Hebrew month of Tishri (September/October). The first day (second, outside Israel) is a full holiday, with the remaining days celebrated as half-festivals (Lev. 23:39–43). Sukkoth is also known as "the time of our rejoicing" or simply as "*the* holiday," because of its joyous nature. Immediately after Sukkoth is Shmini Atzeret, "the eighth day of Assembly," the festival that concludes the fall holiday season. It is also Simchat Torah ("rejoicing in the Torah"), marking the end of the annual cycle of reading the Torah.

Sukkoth is rich in commandments. The obligation to live in a *sukkah* requires each family to construct a temporary hut with a flat roof covered with greenery, leaving the sky still visible. The minimum requirement is to eat in the *sukkah*, though the more observant sleep and spend leisure time there as well. Decorating the *sukkah* with harvest produce and homemade decorations is another family activity. The other commandment is "the four species": citron, palm, willow, and myrtle (Lev. 23:40). The latter three are bound together and known as a *lulav*. All four species are held during the daily Hallel (thanksgiving) prayers (Pss. 113–118) and the other special festival prayers (Hoshanot, "hosanna").

The festival has a complex combination of meanings. Foremost is the commandment to be utterly happy (Deut. 16:15), thanking God for his harvest and Torah. (Some see Sukkoth as the source of the Pilgrims' Thanksgiving holiday.) The *sukkah* symbolizes our closeness to nature but also the fragility of human existence and our dependence on God. Thus, Ecclesiastes is recited on the holiday, adding a note of skepticism. The four species, too, indicate the beauty of nature, and have been given symbolic—even mystical—interpretations. One interpretation is based on the fact that each of the four differs in having a distinctive fragrance and/or taste. The four are likened to four types of Jews, possessing both knowledge of Torah *and* good deeds, neither, or one but not the other. Yet all four species must be clasped together in order to fulfill the commandment, just as the Jewish people must be united despite their differences. Finally, it is the Jewish festival with the most universal element, looking forward to the time when all peoples will come together to Jerusalem to give thanks to the Lord (Zech. 14:16).

D. A. Resnick

Sunday School

The Sunday school is most often perceived as a major teaching arm of the Protestant churches. It has been viewed at various times as a school for the poor, the evangelistic outreach of the church, the exclusively educational unit of the church, and a church growth organization. In most denominations the primary function of the Sunday school is stated as being for the communication of the faith.

STRUCTURE, LEADERSHIP, AND RESOURCES

Since its inception in the late 1700s, the organizational structure the Sunday school assumed has basically followed age-group divisions ranging from preschool through children, youth, and adults. A normal grading pattern within the Sunday school includes preschool (ages 1–3), kindergarten (ages 4–5), primary (grades 1–3), juniors (grades 4–6), junior high (grades 7–9), senior high (grades 10–12) and adults (age 17 and older). In the children's department another frequent pattern is the two-year grading pattern (grades 1–2, 3–4, 5–6). Larger Sunday schools are often closely graded, with each age group constituting a separate department. Adults sometimes are divided by sex, age, and/or marital status, although elective courses may be offered that tend to mix the various groups.

Leadership positions in the Sunday school vary with the size of the church. Certain officials seem to appear regularly. The head of the Sunday school is generally called the superintendent. This individual is responsible for carrying out the policies established by the appropriate church committee, such as the Christian education committee. A superintendent's responsibilities may include assignments in the areas of literature, supplies, budget, membership, personnel, planning worship experiences, and leadership development. These areas may also be assigned to assistants. Each age group division (preschool, children, youth, and adults) also may have a divisional superintendent or coordinator. Often every department within a division is headed by a department superintendent or director. Other personnel may include class leaders, teachers, outreach leaders, social chairpersons, unit leaders, and secretaries. Their duties involve convening the class sessions or business meetings, teaching, visiting prospects, arranging social events, contacting absentees, keeping records, or collecting and caring for audiovisual materials and equipment.

Denominations often prefer that their churches use denominational curriculum materials when these exist, but independent publishers also produce curriculum materials that are broadly used. Several basic organizational patterns of curriculum materials dominate the field. Smaller churches that choose to incorporate more than one age in each class often use the broadly graded materials, while larger churches may choose to use the closely graded materials that have separate classes for each age or school grade. Most materials are written on a three-year cycle, repeating the same material every three years, while kindergarten materials are usually published on a two-year cycle.

For many years the basic outlines of many denominational materials were prepared cooperatively by the Division of Christian Education of the National Council of the Churches of Christ under the leadership of two large committees. One committee designed the outlines for the graded series and the other designed outlines for the uniform series. Representatives from participating denominations staffed these committees. The Uniform Lessons Series is still one of the most widely used series spanning many denominations. It provides materials that develop the same Scripture passage or theme for all age groups.

Independent publishing houses produce complete sets of materials for churches. Most of the larger denominational groups publish their own materials or form cooperative groups to publish materials suited to the needs of the participating denominations. A few local churches choose to produce their own materials privately with the professional guidance of a director or minister of Christian education. All of these curriculum materials are designed to be used by volunteer teachers within local churches.

Although churches have been hiring Christian education professionals since the 1920s, the overall educational program of the church remains in the hands of laypeople. Consequently, the vitality of the Sunday school is dependent largely upon these volunteer teachers. Criteria for selecting teachers usually include their character and skill in teaching. Training is an essential ingredient for increased effectiveness of the Sunday school. Concern and love, however, are, generally speaking, the most important factors for the success or failure of the Sunday school.

With limited space or resources to accommodate growing church memberships, Sunday schools have initiated flexible scheduling. The normative hour for Sunday school would be before the worship service. Today many churches have multiple worship services and multiple Sunday school hours. Large suburban churches have two or three complete Sunday school sessions, each fully staffed and having its own particular students. The students generally are in the children's division, with some youth and adult classes being offered. The multiple sessions are usually conducted during the same hours as the worship services.

Some churches offer extended sessions that take a two-hour period of time for Sunday school. These are usually offered for younger children but may involve children up to the fourth or fifth grades. One of the hours of the extended session usually overlaps with the worship service. Part or all of the first hour's staff may continue during the second hour and curriculum materials are provided to ensure a consistent learning experience during the second hour. Sometimes this includes a worship service. Some local churches have tried Saturday morning or weekday classes in order to expand the Sunday morning opportunities. Some adult classes begin with a collective worship service, but others gain additional teaching time by dispensing with this and giving the complete hour to classroom study. These classes are often smaller in size and use discussion methods as a regular teaching technique rather than the strictly lecture method, which is traditionally associated with adult Sunday school teaching.

CHARACTERISTICS AND CONTRIBUTIONS

Some characteristics of the Sunday school have continued to persist throughout the more than two hundred years of its existence. These include the Bible as the basis for instruction, concern for the moral character of its members, an emphasis on the motivational system of awards, leadership by the laypeople, and an emphasis on children's work. Youth and adult ministries have long been a part of the Sunday school, but recent trends seem to show a growing concern for the needs of single and senior adults. Statistics show evidence that those Sunday schools that focus on outreach and evangelism sustain continued growth.

The Sunday school has made various contributions to the life of congregations. At one time it was seen as the agency that could bring moral improvement to society by uplifting the lives of the poor. At another time the Sunday school was viewed as the agency to develop disciples, emphasizing the numerical growth of the church. It gives instruction, deepens faith, helps to form character, sensitizes people to ethical questions, and provides awareness of the role of the church throughout the world. Imported from England, the Sunday school is one of the longest lasting vital religious movements in American Protestant history. It is an institution in which all members may participate responsibly. In fact, it is one of the largest organizations in the nation staffed entirely by volunteers. *See also* Bible Study; Bus Ministry; Curriculum; Departments, Sunday School; Discussion; Sunday School Movement; Superintendent, Sunday School; Time Arrangements; Uniform Lessons Series; Volunteer Principle.

FOR FURTHER REFERENCE

Cully, Iris V. *New Life for Your Sunday School.* New York: Hawthorn, 1976.
Lynn, Robert W., and Elliott Wright. *The Big Little School.* Birmingham, AL: Religious Education Press, 1980.
Piland, Harry M. *Basic Sunday School Work.* Nashville, TN: Convention Press, 1980.

D. C. Borchert

Sunday School Departments
See Departments, Sunday School.

Sunday School Movement

An organized effort, usually formed across denominational lines, to improve the effectiveness and extend the influence of the local Sunday school eventuated in the Sunday school movement.

BEGINNINGS

In Britain, the name of Robert Raikes (1736–1811) has been firmly linked to the Sunday school movement, although there have been other claimants to the title of "founder." In 1780 this Gloucester newspaper publisher, already committed to efforts at prison reform and the education of offenders, established for poor children a school in "Sooty Alley" of that city. The purpose of the school was to teach working children the rudiments of learning on Sunday, their free day.

Raikes was a devout Anglican layman, but before long the idea of Sunday schools spread to Baptist, Congregational, and Methodist churches throughout England. Anglicans in the Sunday school movement remained more prominent in England than Episcopalians appeared later in America, although many prelates in the Church of England opposed the movement, often with strong charges and outright suppression.

As became the case in America as well, British Sunday schools were often organized along territorial lines and denominational differences were usually ignored. The slogan, "Doctrine divides, service unites" became almost a password. It was a movement largely in the hands of the laity of the churches and formed for many years one of its chief involvements with the work and mission of the church.

In the early 1800s, local and county Sunday school associations were formed to carry on the work of Raikes and other early leaders. In 1803 the London Sunday School Union was created, and in time a national body came into existence. In 1880, the centennial year of the Sunday school, it was estimated that there were at least twelve million persons enrolled in the Sunday schools of the nation.

EARLY U.S. DEVELOPMENTS

The movement found its fullest expression, however, in the United States. It is difficult to assign firm dates and localities for the origins of the movement in America, but by 1790 a group of prominent Philadelphians had founded the First Day or Sunday School Society there. The purpose (as in England) was to provide the rudiments of elementary education to indigent children, thereby keeping them off the streets on Sunday.

The American Sunday School Union was founded in Philadelphia in 1824 and was characterized by strong missionary and evangelistic zeal. This group was busy organizing and caring for Sunday schools on the frontier, penetrating into the territory west of the Appalachian Mountains. Resolved to establish Sunday schools in every frontier settlement in the Mississippi Valley, it pursued its goal with a staff of three and a large group of volunteers. With readers, song books, Bibles, and other materials in their saddlebags, they made the Sunday school an established part of each pioneer village at an early stage of its settlement.

By 1830, these and other efforts had grown so much that the leaders of the American Sunday School Union called a national Sunday school convention to meet in the Chatham Street Chapel in New York City. It was attended by workers from fourteen of the twenty-four states of the Union and became the first of a series of annual conventions that extended to 1960, after which time other agencies matured to carry on the work. At the core of the early meetings were the reports from frontier missionaries giving encouraging witness to the establishment of Sunday schools across the expanding nation.

The mid-1800s and the period after the Civil War were times of expansion for the Sunday school. Local, county, and state Sunday school associations were formed in virtually every state in the Union. Less liturgical churches, such as the Methodist, Baptist, Congregational, and Presbyterian, were most prominent in these associations, the Lutheran and Episcopal less so, and the Roman Catholic almost not at all.

INTERNATIONAL AND LATER DEVELOPMENTS

The first World Sunday School Convention was held in London in 1889. Others followed at stated intervals until 1958 when Sunday School workers joined together in Tokyo for the fourteenth of such gatherings.

The World Sunday School Association was formed in 1907 to organize and promote these large gatherings. It was initially a split structure with two general secretaries and two offices, one in London and the other in New York. In 1950, the association changed its name to the World Council of Christian Education, and a more unified structure was established in 1950, though for many years the unification was more an ideal than a reality. Nelson Chappel, a Canadian, was the first general secretary of the unified organization. He was succeeded in 1965 by Ralph N. Mould, an American Presbyterian minister.

In 1971, after a protracted period of negotiation, the World Council of Christian Education merged into the World Council of Churches' newly organized program unit on education.

In North America, meanwhile, cooperative ties underwent many changes. The influence of the American Sunday School Union declined as denominational influence increased. The International Sunday School Association, a nondenominational organization with Canadian participants as well as those from the United States, began in the 1890s and helped to organize subsequent World Sunday School Conventions prior to the formation of the World Sunday School Association in 1907. In 1922, the International Council of Religious Education was formed from the International Sunday School Association and a recently formed cooperative group of American denominations seeking to counterbalance the American Sunday School Union. In 1945, conservative and fundamentalist churches, desiring closer adherence to traditional biblical curricula and a more vigorous sense of evangelistic outreach, founded the National Sunday School Association (now the National Christian Education Association).

UNIFORM LESSONS SERIES

One specific contribution of the American Sunday School Union was in curriculum development. Recognizing the needs of an expanding Sunday school movement for usable teaching materials, B. F. Jacobs, a Chicago businessman and ardent Sunday school worker, teamed up with a friend, Edward Eggleston, a writer, to urge the development of such a program at the annual Sunday school conventions. They were joined by a Methodist minister (later bishop) John H. Vincent who had already started Sunday school teachers' training institutes in Illinois and pioneered a uniform lesson outline. First proposed in 1869, the project was accepted in 1872 and the Uniform Lessons Series was launched. Its success was indicated when it was used in Canada, Australia, and Asian countries where missionaries were working. In the 1960s a survey showed that more than a hundred denominations were using it and on every continent. This continued despite criticism since early in the twentieth century of the weakness of a uniform graded series and the development among denominations of graded materials more in line with child study guidelines concerning the learning needs of children at various age levels. (The series provides materials for learners from preschool through adults).

THE MOVEMENT TODAY

It has not always been clear as the Sunday school movement developed whether it was an agency concerned with general social uplift (personal hygiene, literacy, personal morality), with the evangelization of the unsaved, or with the education of believers. Many Sunday schools persisted for years in doing a little bit of all three, though the slow trend has been in the direction of the third task. From the turn of the century, teacher training was seen as an important task and Sunday school conventions addressed themselves to that persistent responsibility.

Today in Britain, because the study of religion is included in the school curriculum, the Sunday school is viewed as less important for religious education than it is in the United States, where it is the basic form. Also today, with the concentration on religious education as a denominational task in both Britain and the United States, there is a lessened sense among church people of being engaged in a common enterprise that crosses these lines. On neither the local, area, state, nor the national level are there conferences equivalent to those of the past, although cooperation continues in some sectors through a religious education committee (ecumenical) in a local council of churches. *See also* History of Christian Education; National Christian Education Association; Raikes, Robert; Sunday School; Uniform Lessons Series.

FOR FURTHER REFERENCE

Ferguson, John, ed. *Christianity, Society, and Education.* London: SPCK, 1981.

Knoff, Gerald E. *The World Sunday School Movement.* New York: Seabury, 1979.

Lynn, Robert W., and Elliott Wright. *The Big Little School.* 2d. ed. Birmingham, AL: Religious Education Press, 1980.

Seymour, Jack L. *From Sunday School to Church School: Continuities in Protestant Church Education in the U.S. 1860–1929.* Washington, DC: University Press of America, 1982.

G. E. Knoff

Sunday School Superintendent

See Superintendent, Sunday School.

Superintendent, Sunday School

Within the Sunday school movement in the United States, the position of superintendent has developed as one of leadership for growth and mission. The superintendent is a significant partner in the ministry team of a congregation, involved in administration, teacher training, mission outreach, and volunteer coordination. In the congregation of any religious body, one is likely to find a similar lay position.

In the mid-nineteenth century, lay leadership in the Sunday school movement envisioned a future of boundless possibilities. Well into the twentieth century, the laity collaborated across church body lines to promote uniform lessons and to break down sectarianism.

With the rise of professional religious educators in the early twentieth century, the laity maintained the quiet, steady influence throughout the introduction of graded lessons and new teaching methods. The lay, volunteer Sunday school superintendents remained the closest to the grass roots, sometimes resisting attempts to professionalize church school education, but always remaining a link between the people, the professionals, the home, and the community. Their commitments and efforts to improve their work are reflected in books printed in the 1920s such as *How to Run a Little Sunday School* and *Church School Administration*.

Through the years, administration has been key. Superintendents fifty years ago may have led the opening exercises, including songs, prayers, the collection, and memory work. Today superintendents are concerned about theories of group work and decision making. But their work continues to include teacher recruitment and training, attendance and promotion, development of courses of study, and overall curriculum, as well as making sure supplies are ordered and rooms ready.

A superintendent may head a staff of three or a team of one hundred teachers. The job is a supervisory task, particularly on Sunday morning, but it is also a linking role between the church council, the board or committee of education, and teaching staff. It requires skills in management, diplomacy, and communication, as well as in education. Personal attributes of love, patience, and leadership are important.

Whereas the superintendent may sometimes feel frustrated as the one who receives the emergency call when a teacher is sick or materials have not arrived or criticism when rooms are not arranged or programs fail, the long-term, wise leader learns to delegate, to build cadres of substitutes, and to be constantly discerning people's gifts and empowering them for their own teaching and leading tasks. Through ongoing efforts, including much affirmation and support, this leader builds an atmosphere that challenges everyone in the community of faith to be a teacher and a learner. Such an approach multiplies ministry. The laity develop their teaching abilities through new-teacher training events, ongoing staff meetings, and introduction of new and creative resources, methods, and multimedia. The superintendent may facilitate teaching arrangements whereby mentors and models serve to induct new people into the excitement of educational ministry.

The superintendent is a linking person between professionals and laity, and also between church and home, and church and society. The superintendent is intentionally concerned that the babies born to church members and the children of new members are added to church education rolls as soon as possible and that parents become partners with teachers as nurturers in the faith. The superintendent helps envision an overall ministry of education for adults, youth, and people with special needs. Such educational ministry is inward-directed in that this leader tries to assure that everyone in the congregation has at least one educational opportunity a week.

Such educational ministry is outward-reaching as well. Since the 1960s and 1970s Sunday schools have come full circle back to Robert Raikes's and Hannah Balls' efforts to provide schools for the poor. A superintendent today will not just be concerned about providing a well-run Sunday school for the congregation, but help in setting goals for mission. This might include a neighborhood literacy program, efforts to increase awareness of global issues, or a visitation and care project in which people learn through their care for others. The superintendent is often a liaison in the community in discerning the need for such projects. The superintendent may also meet with representatives from other congregations to sponsor a joint Vacation Bible school or teacher training event.

The superintendent affirms, builds, links, and organizes, and through such ministry often develops greater skills. He or she finds strength in attending churchwide and regional workshops, through such resources as books, journals, and courses, and in peer consultation. The nurture of the superintendent is an important responsibility of the pastor, who in turn often finds in this person a strong partner in ministry. The Sunday school superintendent through committed and skilled leadership facilitates the ongoing growth of the overall educational ministry program of the congregation.

When a professional religious educator comes to a staff, the role of superintendent becomes more specialized. Knowing the congregation, the superintendent already has general support for working with parents and teachers and welcoming new families. Continuing tasks are to see that supplies are easily accessible to teachers, to keep weekly attendance and enrollment records, and to be a general liaison with the congregation.

The professional educator does long-range planning in cooperation with committees, plans an overall teacher development strategy, reviews curriculum options, develops resources, orders supplies, keeps permanent records, and, with the superintendent, reports to the appropriate governing board. The interaction between professional and volunteer requires skill and mutual understanding in order to work out responsibilities and relationships to mutual satisfaction. The key is in deciding who has the best access for fulfilling a particular responsibility. *See also* Director of Religious Education; Leadership Development; Sunday School; Sunday School Movement; Volunteer Principle.

N. C. Everist

Supervision

Supervision is a professional service providing evaluation and direction for teachers-in-service in view of the goals of a well-organized program of instruction. The chief purpose of supervision is to enable teachers to develop self-evaluation skills that will be a means of helping them tap their own creative uniqueness and measure their own growth process.

THE NEED AND RESPONSIBILITY

In view of the value that should be placed on the teaching of religion in organized religious centers, supervision should be considered an essential corollary to any teacher formation program. In centers primarily staffed by volunteers, who often serve on a temporary basis, it is all the more important to provide supervision for the guidance and support that leads to higher motivation and continuing perseverance.

It is one of the responsibilities of the director of religious education to provide for the supervision of the performance of religion teachers according to established norms and procedures. In smaller centers the director usually assumes this role. In larger centers it may be delegated to others who are prepared to specialize in this field. In broader administrative districts involving a number of centers, supervision is often conducted periodically by designated representatives. In all of these circumstances supervision is a professional service by one who not only has the essential educational credentials (e.g., in theology, psychology of learning, and communication skills), but also has had practical teaching experiences in classroom situations.

Supervision begins with inexperienced teachers who have presumably received basic preparation for using a prescribed course of studies. Its value is to help them better understand how to apply practically the principles learned in the orientation courses, how to develop skills in their own unique way, and how to find and use resources not always specified in manuals. However, supervision should also be valued as a continuing process, along with program planning and goal setting, as a helpful means of promoting communication and accountability needed at all levels. Experienced teachers can profit from it when they recognize their need to grow continually in the art of teaching and are open to learn new ways of meeting new challenges from year to year. With continued supervision they acquire the facility to feel comfortable in using helpers or co-teachers and inviting parents or other visitors to observe classroom demonstrations.

The director of religious education who assumes the role of supervision has the distinct advantage of having personally become acquainted with prospective teachers through the recruitment process. This involves individual interviews, orientation sessions, and perhaps an opportunity for the prospective teacher to observe or assist experienced teachers. As a result of this initial relationship, the director is in a better position to determine whether or not the person recruited may have the potential qualifications for placement on any particular grade level. If so, the follow-up supervision is then built upon a stabilized foundation in keeping with the established goals of the center.

Because of many other administrative duties, especially in larger centers, the director may find it necessary to appoint one or more trained supervisors to carry out the task of ongoing supervision. In this case the supervisors must first become acquainted with the program and be prepared to communicate not only with the director but with other staff members, with parents, and with policy-making committees.

THE PROCESS

The first task of a supervisor is to establish a relationship with each teacher that is nonthreatening and affirming. Many teachers have a built-in fear of supervision and are plagued by nervousness or self-consciousness based on the mistaken notion that they are being tested by the random observations or judgments of strangers. This can be averted at a get-acquainted session with all of the teachers before the program is initiated. The supervisor then creates an atmosphere of confidence, explains the purpose of supervision, and helps them to realize the positive assistance it can provide.

The next step is to arrange for personal interviews during which the supervisor is prepared to listen to the teacher's aims, hopes, recognized abilities and difficulties, and sense of mission. Regularly planned follow-up meetings form the core of the supervision process. They provide the opportunity for the supervisor to listen to the teacher's assessment, to offer practical suggestions in lesson planning, to refer the teacher to other available resources, to recommend a possible change in the classroom environment, to suggest the need for a helper, and other similar directives.

Visits to the classroom for observation should never be unexpected. They are helpful only when they are in response to the invitation and readiness of the teacher to demonstrate a particular technique being given special attention at any given time, for example, a demonstration of a small-group discussion, the use of a particular visual aid, or a student involvement in some creative activity. It is only rarely that a supervisor would be requested to observe an entire class period. More than likely the purpose of this would be to observe student behavior or interaction. Every observation should be followed by a meeting with the teacher, either immediately after the class to affirm a successful effort or within a reasonable time for further evaluation of felt needs.

A general evaluation at the end of the school year is often a valuable means of promoting the development of a religion program. An essential part of this evaluation is to give teachers an opportunity to respond to a thoughtful questionnaire intended to help them measure their progress in the perspective of overall goals. This may be handled on a group basis when each teacher can benefit from the contributions of others or individually with the supervisor when there is a need for further clarification or direction.

In regional areas where a central office directs the education and supervision of teachers in a number of religion centers, supervisors may be assigned to visit these centers periodically. In this case the process of supervision is necessarily modified. Usually time is arranged for meetings with the teachers at a particular center before and after the scheduled classes. Before the classes the teachers are given opportunity to express their assessment of the total program, their participation in it, and their hopes or fears with the supervisor as an understanding and empathetic listener. The teachers may be asked to leave their doors open during the class sessions so the visitor could observe from the halls the general atmosphere prevalent in the classrooms. The supervisor might sit in the classrooms of those who request this for a brief period. Afterward, further discussion takes place when group dynamic techniques can be used to draw out favorable comments, questions, felt needs, and significant problems. Again, the chief task of the supervisor is to listen, to encourage all that is positive, and to offer practical suggestions. Whenever possible time is allowed for any teacher desiring to have a personal interview.

There are many centers of religious education where there is little or no opportunity to obtain or afford the services of professional supervision. However, there is always the possibility of seeking the aid of dedicated teachers who have successfully mastered the art of teaching over a period of years. With the understanding of the value of personal relationships that form the basis of supervision, they may be an asset to any program and find it a pleasant way in their years of retirement to help other teachers and to continue being a witness to the faith they share. *See also* Director of Religious Education; Evaluation; Group Dynamics; Laboratory School; Leadership Development; Management; Process Observer; Teacher; Volunteer Principle.

FOR FURTHER REFERENCE

Manternach, Janaan, and Carl J. Pfeifer. *The Creative Catechist*. Mystic, CT: Twenty-Third Publications, 1983.

Sullivan, Gertrude Ann, and the San Diego Education Team. *Teacher as Gift*. Dubuque, IA: Brown, 1979.

M. Timmerman

Symbolism

Symbolism refers to the relationship obtaining between a transcendent reality and the particular concrete instances in which that reality becomes itself through expression in a medium. From Greek stems meaning "to throw together," the term "symbol" connotes a gathering or a connection: both the gathering of diverse elements into the symbol's meaningful pattern and the intrinsic connection between the symbol so gathered and the symbolized reality it mediates. Thus in Luke 2:19 the verb *symballein* describes Mary's pondering of the events of Jesus' birth; her heart "symbols" as it makes connections among events and as the emergent pattern presents the transcendent reality of Jesus' identity.

This general meaning is the basis for the more specific Christian senses of the term. However, in the Septuagint the verb *symballein* has a different connotation. In Isaiah 46:6, it describes the clinking together of pieces of silver being weighed before they are cast as an idol. Although the term "symbol" comes into modern languages through the cultural influence of Christianity, Jews also now use it in speaking of God's self-expression in creation. Torah, or law, is the principal symbol God has given to Jews. Observing Torah gathers them together and makes them a holy people among whom God dwells. But God's presence through symbol is not understood as incarnational within Judaism, Islam, or religious traditions other than Christianity.

In early Christian liturgical use the creed, also called the symbol, allowed the church to become itself as a community of faith through the articulation of its beliefs. The common creed, with its pattern of statements, pulled the community's diverse members together in faith and actualized the transcendent reality of the church. Elements of Christian sacramental celebration, such as the eucharistic bread and wine and the baptismal water, are symbols that are understood to allow the saving act of God in Jesus to be expressed and available in the concrete circumstances of the lives of individuals and communities. Jesus himself is regarded as symbol of the Father's creative love, which is to say that he is the concrete incarnate expression through whom the transcendent reality of God constitutes itself as parent by embracing the medium of humanity.

As Christ, then, Jesus becomes for Christians the gatherer of humanity and their connection to divinity. The pattern of divine-human relationship established in Christ is rendered explicit in the four narratives called Gospels and in the other books of the New Testament. Like any literature, these texts refer to realities apart from themselves; but beyond mere referring, these texts are symbols that, in expressing the Christic relationality of God and humanity, also present the invitation to join oneself to the reality of that relation. Therefore Christ, as person and as pattern, is accessible to the generations subsequent to Jesus thanks to a network of symbols that express and extend his personal availability to them: the church, the church's sacramental celebrations, and the Bible.

Other Christian symbols (such as the cross or the communion cup) derive from these.

Symbolism in the Jewish and Christian traditions, then, does more than artistic or literary signification does. The symbol not only points to God from afar but also brings God within reach. Symbol "makes present" in two senses. First, the symbol—Torah, temple, *halakah*, community, Scripture, Christ, sacrament, church—provides a point in the material world where the personal being of God becomes present, active, and available for the sake of relationship with other persons. Second, the symbol projects upon our present reality an ideal vision of future relationship, so that whatever is out of line with the vision can be changed as we build the future into a transformed present.

DEVELOPING SYMBOLIC UNDERSTANDING

Although symbol does more than communicate, the capacity to engage with symbols seems to have something to do with the capacity for language and develops along with it. Some hold that symbolic competence actually precedes linguistic competence and founds the latter. Thus Jews circumcise infants, and in the earliest centuries of the church, new Christians experienced the rites of initiation before receiving a verbal explanation of them.

Other educators hail the advent of language as the first step toward developing symbolic competence. Before becoming able to talk, about two years of age, children give no indication that they can imagine a thing standing for anything other than itself. To speak is to be able to refer, that is, to be able to hold with a word or concept those things that one previously could hold only with hands, eyes, or other senses. The verbal/mental grasp is constructed by internalizing the manual/ visual grasp. The exercise play of the infant, who delights in the simple movement of muscles, is displaced by the symbolic play of the preschool child, who delights in making all kinds of things stand for other things. The "standing for" is accomplished through linguistic competence, that is, through the conceptual or verbal/mental grasp. This grasp is the key to mastering the physical and later the social world, as every child must learn to do; but it can also impede understanding of realities that do not fall under human control.

The preschooler's thought is intuitive, or preoperational. It goes forward without keeping track of itself and without being able to retrace its steps. Children are easily frightened or can frighten themselves by thinking of something like "a dog as big as a house" because they cannot run the thought backward to discern whether it began in perception or in imagination. They do not yet distinguish the real from the imaginary. (Indeed, something of this confusion must endure into adulthood for people to be able to imagine the nonexistent for the purpose of making it real.)

About the age of seven years, intelligence has matured to the point where thought becomes reversible and operational, as in the arithmetic operations of addition and subtraction. School-age children can "take away" what they have "added to"—not just physically but mentally as well. Like their younger siblings, they have a mental grasp of the concrete objects and relations they have perceived, a grasp that persists even after the perception has ended. Now, however, they develop a repertoire of logical and perceptual means to test the adequacy of propositions that purport to describe the world of concrete experience. Symbol is grasped *literally*, as a concept referring to or a statement describing the physical world.

Adolescence brings the capacity to think about thoughts, to relate relations. Where the grade-school child turned away from the imaginary in order to explore and understand the real, the adolescent may turn away from concrete, real experiences in order to explore the realm of possibility through imagination. Youth seek to understand the part in relation to the whole and themselves in relation to the groups of which they are a part. They are interested in abstracting relational truths from the concrete stories in the Scriptures. Symbol is grasped *conventionally*, as the principle of unity that holds the parts in relationship or the general rule of which concrete events are but instances.

Thus far, the maturing of the cognitive grasp of symbol has meant gaining better control over symbol. But with early or middle adulthood may come the need to think about thought itself, as well as thinking about things and thoughts. The critical thinker is less concerned with the real or the ideal than with the knower's subjective contribution to the reality of the real. One notices, with a sense of suspicion and dismay, the uncanny fact that the whole seems to be more than the sum of its parts. The "extra" ingredient is what the knower has added to the known in the act of understanding it. Reality now seems encumbered by the alien bias of one's own and others' perceptions. The grasp implicit in the concept seems to have mangled reality; one wishes to know it "raw," untouched, without interpretation. Symbol is grasped *critically*, so that one seeks to peel back the skin of the symbol from the reality that supposedly lies beneath it.

But symbol eludes this attempt so to dissect and control it. The critical attempt to get behind the symbol always fails. Out of the failure, another modality of cognition may emerge. The subjective grasp now is experienced as partnered with, wedded to, indeed itself grasped by a transcendent other. The Christic relation cannot be held at arm's length by the knower. It imprints itself upon the knower's own hold upon all reality and possibility. Subjectivity's influence upon the message, far from being an interference, now seems a gift. As medium becomes message, so teacher becomes Shema or gospel insofar as one's knowing is grasped by what one knows. Symbol grasps the one who would grasp it, transforming subjectivity itself and becoming the pattern of any knowing.

DEVELOPING SYMBOLIC UNDERSTANDING THROUGH RELIGIOUS EDUCATION

Competence to engage with symbol develops gradually and is carefully nurtured at each stage. This nurture is twofold: practice in grasping the symbol and exploring it within the present competency level and a challenge to cooperate as the learner is lured onward to more complex modes of engagement. One fosters a literal grasp of symbols in children and a conventional grasp in adolescents. Adults are invited to go beyond conventional understanding to critical examination of the symbols and from criticism on to the capacity to know self, others, and things in the symbol's light.

In seeking to describe symbolism and how it works, one is acutely conscious of standing at some point in one's own developmental journey and articulating a theory that will be inadequate for the experience of those whose understanding is more mature than one's own. But Jewish and Christian teachers have called upon the transformative power of symbolism throughout their history even when they had no good theory of how it worked. For Christianity, the fourth-century catecheses of Cyril of Jerusalem provide one excellent example. The creed supplies the outline for his course of lectures. The talks are delivered in the liturgical setting of the basilica of the Anastasis, where Cyril points out the sites of the events of Jesus' Passion and resurrection. Scripture is mined for themes and details that, allegorically interpreted, give detail to Cyril's portrait of Christ. The lectures lead up to a liturgical experience of initiation, and the mystagogical or postbaptismal talks play upon the symbols of the ritual to reinforce the meaning of new Christian life.

Liturgy, then, is the primary bearer of the meaning of symbols. Believers grow up conscious of the presence of these visual, spoken, and enacted signs. For the young they appear as word pictures, speaking their concrete meaning. Beginning with adolescence, community and personal meanings become attached in an unfolding process.

Teaching about symbols takes place in homes and in religious education classes. They are connected with Scripture and liturgy, but teachers verbalize meaning and give learners opportunity to express their responses in verbal, written, or graphic form. The symbol becomes connected with broader meanings for adults, for their lives are touched by the implications of the sign. Such meanings become expanded beyond the immediate context to include all of society and world. The power of symbols lies in the fact that they continually gather new meanings. *See also* Child Development; Cognitive Development; Faith Development; God, Understandings of; Liturgy; Sacraments.

M. Sawicki

Symposium

A symposium is an educational technique for the presentation of a topic to a moderately large audience. It consists of several brief statements of approximately ten or fifteen minutes by persons knowledgeable in their fields and under the leadership of a moderator. The objective of the symposium is the presentation of authoritative and analyzed information for discussion and decision.

There are several things to be done in preparing for a symposium: develop a topic and rationale; divide the topic for presentation and discussion; select qualified speakers and an astute moderator; and develop program notes and a printed piece.

A symposium event usually proceeds as follows: a formal statement of the topic and a brief overview of the major issues involved by the moderator; introduction of the presenters with attention to their areas of expertise; presentations by the symposium panelists and perhaps summary statements by the presenters; and a discussion period for clarification and other input. *See also* Panel Discussion.

G. S. Shockley

Systems Theory

Modern systems theory (also referred to as systems analysis, social systems methods, and systemic approaches or orientation) asserts that no singular aspect of life can either exist or be understood as an isolated entity, but that each is connected and integrated with others in a larger, whole system of complex realities. Systems theory suggests an updated, paraphrased version of John Donne's famous lines: "Nothing is an island, entire of itself; everything is a piece of the continent, a part of the main." According to systems theory religious education is a "living" enterprise, as complex and dynamic as any living organism.

EXPLANATION AND EXAMPLES

Several key, related concepts help to explain systems theory. The term "holism" emphasizes that each system is a complex reality that can be understood only in its wholeness or completeness of many interdependent subsystems. The term "synergy" emphasizes that the "working together" or combined actions of all these subsystems produces a total outcome that is far greater than the sum total of the separate efforts of the different parts.

Everything in both the natural and social or organizational worlds exemplifies key aspects of systems theory. The natural environment consists of many ecosystems, such as a forest, lake, or ocean. Each ecosystem involves various subsystems (of different kinds and measures of air, water, land, plants, and animals) that are so systemically (meaning, from the Greek term, "placed together") interconnected and interdependent that any change in one part is bound to have multiple effects on all of the other parts. For example, an oil spill on a lake does not just create a temporary eyesore; rather, it causes countless effects, in time and space, on all of the people, animals, and other environmental elements that interact with the polluted lake.

Perhaps the natural world's most readily understood example of systems theory is the human being. Each person is an amazing system made up of many subsystems: of body, mind, and spirit; of different parts and pieces, both internal and external; of vast, interconnected networks of blood, bones, nerves, tissue, chemicals, and electrical impulses. Even a slight illness or injury of any sort causes dysfunction of all kinds throughout the body. Conversely, successful treatment restores not just the ailing part, but also brings new health and wholeness to the total system of body, mind, and spirit.

Groups of people and organizations of all sorts form the unique, innumerable systems of the social world. They are living organisms whose shared, organizational health and well-being depend on the harmonious interactions of multiple internal and external factors. They do so in an ongoing process of "forming" and "being formed by" the quality and degree of the hopes, plans, images, and values of one group of people and of the other common systems (such as family, neighborhood, workplace, community, nation, etc.) in which they are involved. When any one of these elements is missing, ill-balanced, or dysfunctional, then the whole social system's health and well-being are threatened.

Every congregation is just such a living organism. It is a complex and dynamic social system in which religious education is one major subsystem that interacts with evangelism, youth ministry, stewardship, worship, and numerous other subsystems. Religious educators cannot act as if their ministries (particularly the church or Sunday school) are autonomous, self-supporting systems. Nor can other church leaders and programs function as if religious education was merely a peripheral component in the church's total mission.

When this happens, the congregation becomes an unhealthy and dysfunctional social system. On the other hand, health, vitality, and growth are natural outcomes whenever the many subsystems recognize the special gifts and needs of each other and intentionally cooperate to nurture and sustain one another.

APPLICATION TO RELIGIOUS EDUCATION

Religious education, however, may properly be understood as a system by itself, in the sense that it is a ministry of the church or synagogue that consists of many specialized subsystems. Both in theory and practice, these religious education subsystems or components have been identified and described in various ways. For example, Christian Education: Shared Approaches, the major educational systems project of Joint Educational Development, clearly and intentionally defined five interactive, interdependent components:

1. Biblical, theological, and educational affirmations
2. Teaching and learning opportunities
3. Leader development and support
4. Material or curriculum resources
5. Planning and evaluation

Further, the Christian Education: Shared Approaches project emphasized the importance of maintaining a balanced sense of interdependence, integrity, coordination, and harmony among all of these religious education subsystems. From a systems theory approach, creative and effective religious education does not simply happen by selecting the "right" curriculum, or choosing the "best" teachers, or any other seemingly simple and singular activity. Rather, creative and effective religious education happens only when consistent and careful attention is given to all aspects of these key educational components as they interact with all the other vital subsystems in the life of the church.

To illustrate this approach, the governing body of a congregation, desiring to improve the educational program, would need to work through the religious education committee, in five areas simultaneously. All groups (congregation, leaders, teachers, clergy) need to think through and write out the biblical, theological, and educational components on which their program rests. They chart the educational opportunities now available and decide what, for effective education, needs to be added, deleted, or changed. They set in motion a program both for training teachers and other leaders and for giving them support—not only in words, but also by supplying needed equipment, space, etc. They select curricular materials that would enlist the enthusiasm of teachers, use the new skills they were learning, and be consonant with the biblical, theological, and educational affirmations. Finally, this work would be outlined in a plan to be implemented over six to twelve months. Essential to the effectiveness of this plan is a careful instrument for evaluation that would ascertain what had gone well, what did not work and should be deleted, and what needed to be added.

Despite confusion and doubt in some quarters about systems theory, there are sound biblical and theological affirmations of its vital application to church life. The apostle Paul clearly portrayed (notably in 1 Cor. 12:12–31) the church as the holistic "body of Christ," which consists of many different but essential parts. And Paul proclaimed (Rom. 8:28) that everything "works together" for good (namely, evidences a systemic synergy and holism) among those who cooperate with and love God. *See also* Curriculum; Evaluation; Interdisciplinary Studies; Leadership Development; Learning Theory; Management; Methodology; Planning; Social Sciences; Theology and Education.

J. J. Spangler

Taoism

Taoism is the label often applied to a tradition of Chinese mystical thought and devotion, and of related arts and practices, that has exercised pervasive influence in China, Korea, and Japan. The word *tao*, in Chinese, means "way," and it applies to literal streets and paths but is also extended metaphorically to ways of life or in characteristic Taoist metaphor to "the great way of the universe."

HISTORY

The origins of this tradition lie in the *Tao teh ching* ("the classic of the way and its virtue"), traditionally attributed to Lao tzu (ca. 550 B.C.), and in Chuang tzu (399–295 B.C.), author of a book of mystical thought and wit that bears his name. The *Tao teh ching* is a poem of some eighty-one stanzas (sixty-five in a different edition) and exists in over forty translations into English. The basic image and concept is the Tao, usually translated as Way, though one translator has rendered it as System. In contrast and opposition to the reigning Confucian rationality, the Tao is declared to be inexpressible. However, as the *Tao teh ching* declares, we can know it negatively as the unknowable, the invisible, and the inaudible. From the *Tao* comes one, from one come two, and from two come the myriad things of the world of everyday existence. In two of the favorite metaphors of the *Tao teh ching*, the Tao is said to be like water, and like vacuity or emptiness.

The fulfillment of human life, according to the *Tao teh ching*, does not consist in Confucian social activism but in the naturalness, simplicity, and acquiescence of the Tao. From this is derived an ethic of *wei wu wei*, "doing by not doing," whose content is a peaceful, quiet life in small rural communities.

Chuang tzu's book carries these views of Lao tzu to paradoxical and extreme conclusions. It scornfully rejects governmental service for the simple, natural life. It attacks the extensive and expensive funeral rituals of the time. Chuang tzu exclaimed, "Once I dreamed I was a butterfly. Then, I awoke and there I was. I do not know whether it was Chou dreaming he was a butterfly or the butterfly dreaming that it was Chou."

The insights of Lao tzu and Chuang tzu were woven into the philosophical synthesis of the Han dynasty, adding both a mystical and a metaphysical dimension to the Confucian core of thought. Also during this period there arose a popular Taoist movement, thus effecting a division between philosophical and popular religious aspects of the Taoist tradition. One leader, Chang Ling, was given by his followers the title Heavenly Teacher. He collected as pay for his teaching five bushels of rice, so his society became known as the Way of Five Bushels of Rice.

After the fall of the Han dynasty in early third century A.D., there followed in China three centuries of great disorder and disintegration. Two responses to this dark age were the rise of Chinese Buddhism and a revival of Taoism, called by the Chinese "the dark learning" and by Western scholars, Neo-Taoism. Taoist texts were studied and meditated over. Confucian rationalism was rejected in favor of Taoist intuition. Earnest and ethical Confucian humanism was rejected in favor of the pursuit of pleasure. The Yang Chu chapter of a book by Lieh tzu advised momentary pleasure as the one true good, saying that if by pulling out one hair a person could save the world, a true sage would not do it. The Seven Sages of the Bamboo Grove, as they were called, gathered for wine and for witty conversation as the sole ends or goals of life. Truly in this age of disorder, the alternative to a Buddhist monastery was a Taoist garden of pleasure. Seldom if ever in human history have mysticism, wit, and pleasure met and mingled as they did in Neo-Taoism.

Confucian ethics and philosophy resumed their central place in China in the Song dynasty (960–1268). Although the philosophers of Neo-Confucianism were anti-Taoist, they showed Taoist influence in their presupposition of an intuitively apprehended totality of things that formed the context for their philosophical thought and ethical action. Taoism also exercised an observable influence in that most Chinese forms of Buddhism called Chan in China and Zen in Japan.

While these developments were taking place in high intellectual society, popular Taoism continued on its way among the populace. A descendant of Chang Ling of the Five Bushels of Rice Way was installed in Dragon and Tiger Mountain in central China, where he and his line gained the title of Taoist "popes." They had little real authority and were chiefly the blessers of Taoist charms and potions.

MAGIC AND EDUCATION

For many centuries popular Taoism has been little more than an accumulated system of magic charms, fetishes, and potions, all designed to ward off ill fortune and to secure good fortune and long life. In recent Chinese history, for example, the Boxers were firm in their faith that Taoist charms would render harmless the bullets of "foreign devils." Evidence from Marxist China indicates that popular Taoism is either dead or dying.

The relation between mysticism and magic is not unique in the world's religious history, among many other illustrations being the alchemists of the early modern West. Mystics speak perforce in metaphors, and if they are aware of the metaphorical character of their words, literalist followers forget it and take their words literally. So indeed the precious metal of mysticism is transmuted to the baser metal of magic, in China and elsewhere.

In contrast to the mandarin sages of the Confucian tradition, the Taoist wiseman appears antiintellectual and antieducational. Indeed, at times the appearance has been in fact true. However, the project of communicating the distinctive values of the Taoist tradition has asserted itself as an educational task. Scorning the heavily ethical out-

look of Confucianism, the Taoists sought to communicate their values in pictures (notably landscape painting), in poems, and even in enacted parables. In the course of time many of these intuitive values found embodiment in Chan or Zen Buddhism.

The revival of Zen Buddhist philosophy and practice in twentieth-century Japan and elsewhere has underscored the continuing vitality of Taoist concepts and images.

J. A. Hutchison

Taxonomy

"Taxonomy" is a term borrowed by education from biology, where it denotes the scientific classification of plants and animals by species. In education, the term is used in connection with the classification of educational objectives for testing purposes, although taxonomies of educational objectives have also proven useful in curriculum design and construction. The attempt is to sort out all possible educational goals and to organize them into a coherent scheme that is both operational and logical. Operationally it develops a systematic analysis of the operations to be performed on and with knowledge, attitudes, and skills. Logically it shows the detail of these operations as they move from the simple to the complex.

TAXONOMIES BY DOMAIN

Benjamin S. Bloom and his associates set out in the early 1950s to develop a taxonomy of objectives for three "domains": the cognitive, the affective, and the psychomotor. The practical use they saw for the taxonomy was to assist teachers to locate their objectives by domains and by degrees of simplicity or complexity and to provide specific examples of how to test the degree to which learners had achieved the objectives that had been set.

Work on the cognitive domain eventuated in the publication of *Taxonomy of Educational Objectives, The Classification of Educational Goals. Handbook 1, Cognitive Domain* (1956). The major categories for classification were:

- Knowledge (from knowledge of specifics and terminology, through knowledge of processes and methods, to knowledge of theories and structures)

- Comprehension (from ability to explain, through ability to interpret, to ability to determine implications and consequences)

- Application (the ability to use general ideas, methods, and principles in specific situations)

- Analysis (ability to analyze elements, relationships, and principles)

- Synthesis (from ability to convey ideas, feelings, and experiences to others, through production of plans, to derivation of sets of abstract relations)

- Evaluation (ability to make judgments on the basis of both internal evidence and external criteria)

With examples provided of ways to test for each level in these categories of knowledge and ability, the use of the taxonomy by teachers in test construction and evaluation was clear. In addition, however, the taxonomy, being comprehensive, contributed to curriculum construction by suggesting objectives that teachers might have overlooked and by indicating logical sequences of objectives.

Work on affective learnings proceeded very slowly, due to misgivings as to the propriety of specifying objectives related to values and beliefs. Nevertheless, the work was done, and David R. Krathwohl and his associates published *Taxonomy of Educational Objectives, The Classification of Educational Goals. Handbook 2, Affective Domain* (1964). Here the major classificatory categories were:

- Receiving (from awareness, through willingness to receive, to controlled or selected attention)

- Responding (from acquiescence in responding, through willingness to respond, to satisfaction in response)

- Valuing (from acceptance or belief in a value, through preference for it, to commitment to it; commitment relates to faith and involves a firm emotional acceptance of a belief upon admittedly nonrational grounds; there is loyalty, furtherance, and deepening and the seeking of converts to the belief; motivation is intense)

- Organization (the development of a system of values, determination of their interrelationships, and the establishment of dominant and pervasive values)

- Characterization by a value or a value complex (consistency of behavior in terms of internalized values)

Completing the series of taxonomies is Anita J. Harrow's *A Taxonomy of the Psychomotor Domain, A Guide for Developing Behavioral Objectives* (1972).

IN RELIGIOUS EDUCATION

Religious knowledge of a cognitive sort is learned through the same psychological processes as other cognitive knowledge, indicating that the analysis of the cognitive domain is applicable both to the curricular organization of religious knowledge and to testing for the degree to which it has been attained by the learner. In *Tools for Curriculum Development for the Church's Educational Ministry* (1967) the following sequence is suggested as part of a taxonomy of the learner's engagement in the learning tasks (cognitive domain):

- Translating, identifying, and interpreting to discover meaning and value

- Systematizing meanings and information into sets of meanings and values

- Testing and experimenting personally with discovered meanings and values

The relevance of the analysis of the affective domain is direct. Both the most general statements of objectives for Christian education and the most specific statements are built within a context of awareness, response, discriminating commitment, and consistent behavior (character). In *Tools for Curriculum Development* taxonomies for the affective domain are outlined with reference to the learner's basic needs, the learner's engagement in the learning tasks, and the possible results of learning.

LeRoy Ford, of the Southwestern Baptist School of Religious Education, Fort Worth, Texas, has led the field in the direct use of Bloom's taxonomy of the cognitive domain. Many years of development and experiment have gone into Southwestern's production of a handbook by which faculty and students may see how each unit of each course contributes to the mastery of the field, the sequences by which knowledge of the field is to be achieved, and how and when that achievement is to be tested. The result is a completely rationalized curriculum of professional religious education. Ford's *Design for Teaching and Learning: A Self-Study Guide to Lesson Planning* (1978) enables the parish teacher to use the taxonomical system. He has also been influential in promoting the use of the taxonomy internationally in theological education by extension. His present work deals with the detailed practical application of the taxonomy of the affective domain to religious education. *See also* Affective Development; Cognitive Development; Evaluation; Goals; Measurement.

FOR FURTHER REFERENCE

Bloom, Benjamin S., et al. *Taxonomy of Educational Objectives, The Classification of Educational Goals. Handbook 1, Cognitive Domain.* New York: Longmans, Green, 1956.

Cooperative Curriculum Development. *Tools of Curriculum Development for the Church's Educational Ministry.* Anderson, IN: Warner, 1967.

Ford, LeRoy. *Design for Teaching and Learning: A Self-Study Guide to Lesson Planning.* Nashville, TN: Broadman, 1978.

Harrow, Anita J. *A Taxonomy of the Psychomotor Domain, A Guide for Developing Be-*

havioral Objectives. New York: McKay, 1972.

Krathwohl, David, et al. *Taxonomy of Educational Objectives, The Classification of Educational Goals. Handbook 2, Affective Domain*. New York: McKay, 1964.

D. C. Wyckoff

Teacher

A teacher is an instructor whose duty is to impart knowledge about a particular subject following a systematic, methodical procedure. A teacher of religion has a call to be more than an instructor of the truths of faith. It is a call that involves the goal of motivating and inspiring learners to be prepared to make an active response to those truths in their practical application to life. The term "catechist" is applied to teachers who proclaim the word of God in such a way as to enable the faith already possessed to become "living, conscious, and active through the light of instruction," as stated in the National Catechetical Directory, *Sharing The Light of Faith.*

Formal teachers of religion are those persons affiliated with a church community and appointed to teach in church-related schools or in local community religion centers whether conducted in church facilities, in private homes, or elsewhere. They may hold classes for children as well as for adults or may provide tutoring when needed. They may be called upon to participate in team teaching programs or in other related learning experience groups, such as liturgical ceremonies, study clubs, forums, and similar controlled situations.

Other persons who indirectly give public witness to their faith as they serve in various ministries may be considered informal teachers of religion, insofar as religion is sometimes "caught rather than taught." Parents who realize their vocation to hand down the tenets of faith from one generation to another by their word and example also fit in this category. They teach more formally when they consciously plan ways of sharing their faith convictions with their children, for example, by arranging specific times for family discussions on matters of faith and morals as they relate to current events in everyday living.

Whether or not one is reimbursed for a teaching assignment, whether or not one is experienced in the art of teaching, certain personal qualifications and competencies are expected to be manifested and developed. A teacher should have sufficient familiarity with the subject matter to be able to adapt it to the principles of growth and development as they ordinarily apply to the learning ability of students at a given level.

Student texts and teachers' manuals that for-

mulate content and arrange lesson plans based on the above principles are prescribed in most organized centers for religious instruction. A teacher should be able to use these tools with flexibility, realizing that no printed material can be applied indiscriminately to every individual situation.

To meet these basic requirements, a prospective teacher should be willing to be interviewed and tested and be open to the need to participate in whatever courses or programs of study may be recommended or deemed necessary as adequate preparation by those in charge. Most inexperienced, volunteer teachers need some training in both content and methods of teaching and the opportunity to do practice teaching under supervision.

Teachers are expected to work closely with other teachers and helpers and to collaborate with the staff in the development of goal-directed programs. Periodic joint sessions may be required when the contribution of teachers is needed for an adequate evaluation of policies, schedules, resources, reports, etc. Opening channels of communication with parents is a further means of achieving goals.

While a person may be willing and able to meet the above requirements, not everyone can approach a teaching situation with the same degree of competency. To create a controlled environment that fosters learning through group interaction and through a variety of creative expressions and problem-solving techniques is an art that can only be attained by experience, by developing skills over time. It is also a precondition for maintaining class discipline, which is a chief concern of every teacher. For this reason it is important for the teacher to cultivate a pleasant disposition that is characterized by enthusiasm as well as by calmness and firmness and to manifest a basic respect for the uniqueness of individual pupils.

In view of future trends resulting from such phenomena as population mobility and rapidly developing communication technology, a teacher of religion may need to cultivate the all-important role of a prophet—one called to interpret the revelation of God as manifested through the signs of the times and in contemporary situations.

It is to be understood that no one teacher can be expected to excel in all of these qualifications, but that all are challenged to be open to the Spirit, to people, and to new ideas, and to be ready and willing to grow in the art of learning even as they expect their students to do so. A learning experience is one that effects a change in a person. This not only applies to students, but to the teacher as well. It has been aptly said that a good teacher is simply a more experienced learner and an expert is one committed to continuing self-improvement. *See also* Curriculum; Evaluation; Instruction; Laboratory School; Learning Theory; Methodol-

A TEACHER'S SELF-EVALUATION GUIDE

Assess yourself in each of the following areas:	Always	Nearly Always	I Need to Work on This
1. Goals and Their Implementation			
I understand the stated goals of the religious education program as a whole.	___	___	___
The content of my teaching is in accord with these goals.	___	___	___
The methods of my teaching are in accord with these goals.	___	___	___
2. Organization			
I plan sessions in advance, familiarizing myself with each lesson's content and method and adapting it as needed for my students.	___	___	___
I request, collect, and test all needed supplies and resources well in advance.	___	___	___
I proceed in class in an orderly fashion.	___	___	___
3. Attendance and Punctuality			
I myself have close to 100 percent attendance and when I need to be absent I make arrangements for a reliable substitute.	___	___	___
I am punctual, arriving in class in advance of the first students.	___	___	___
4. Teacher-Student Relations			
I am in touch with the contemporary situation and life circumstances of my students.	___	___	___
I try to understand my students' needs and actions.	___	___	___
In class, I cultivate a pleasant disposition, maintaining enthusiasm, calmness, and firmness.	___	___	___
I am able to manage the class as a whole.	___	___	___
5. Creativity and Growth			
I actively seek and consider suggestions from others regarding my teaching.	___	___	___
I am increasing in the creative use of teaching materials.	___	___	___
I read one or more books annually to enrich my teaching.	___	___	___
I attend one or more teacher's workshops annually.	___	___	___
6. Cooperation and Collaboration			
I attend regular teachers' meetings.	___	___	___
I collaborate when needed to develop goals, choose curriculum, evaluate programs, etc.	___	___	___
I work closely and cooperatively with other staff members.	___	___	___
I maintain open communications with the parents of my students.	___	___	___

To assess your performance on the whole, count the number of times you placed a check under the category "Always" or "Nearly Always." If 16-20, you are doing very well. If 12-15, you need to work to improve your performance in areas where you scored poorly. If below 12, you should perhaps seek help from others to improve your performance.

ogy; Parent-Teacher Relations; Professional Study; Teaching Theory; Team Teaching; Theology and Education.

FOR FURTHER REFERENCE

Manternach, Janaan, and Carl J. Pfeifer. *The Creative Catechist*. Mystic, CT: Twenty-Third Publications, 1983.

Sharing the Light of Faith, National Catechetical Directory. Washington, DC: United States Catholic Conference, 1979.

Sullivan, Gertrude Ann, and the San Diego Education Team. *Teacher as Gift*. Dubuque, IA: Brown, 1979.

M. Timmerman

Teaching Mission

Teaching mission is a term used to refer to a variety of types of concentrated efforts of a congregation or group of churches in a community or geographical region to relate education and outreach. In the 1940s and 1950s, the National Council of Churches of Christ developed a program called the Christian Teaching Mission, paralleled by similar approaches in denominations. An outside leader made presentations to participating congregations, either denominational or interdenominational, held study sessions, and trained persons to study the community and develop appropriate ways to meet opportunities for enlistment, fellowship cultivation, and service. The overall goal was that a congregation would be led to improving its total program. The many modifications of that plan all include an intensive focus on teaching by an outside leader, and a plan comparable to a preaching mission or an evangelistic mission. Two characteristics usually mark the teaching mission as distinctive: it helps relate education and evangelism and it is intended to develop leadership among laity for communication of the gospel. In more recent developments, the term has come to refer in general to a week of enrichment, workshops, intensive study focused on a theme, or even a school of religion. *See also* Evangelism; Lay Ministry; Mission, Education for; Workshop.

S.P. Little

Teaching Styles

Styles of teaching, at every age level, can ultimately follow only one of two pathways: either the teacher and learners begin with an established proposition, thesis, or "point," *or* they begin with a period of investigation that will finally lead them to a conclusion (thesis, proposition, or "point").

Consider, for instance, the task of teaching children about sizes and shapes. Concepts of roundness, squareness, and triangularity are involved. So are the concepts of small, smaller, smallest, and large, larger, largest. A teacher may elect to "tell" the learners by showing examples of these concepts and explaining repeatedly. Learners would, in turn, be invited to identify additional examples—to demonstrate that they had indeed understood what was presented by the teacher. (This approach, quite legitimate as a style of teaching, moves from the presentation of truths to a process of involving the learners in reiterating the material for themselves.)

On the other hand, another teacher might choose to provide the learners with opportunities to handle a variety of objects of differing sizes and shapes, then to sort them out in some way that might be meaningful. Through a process of questioning and reexamination of data, the learners are assisted by the teacher in articulating their "discovery" of the concepts of roundness, squareness, triangularity, and gradations in size. (This approach, also valid, moves from the students' observations to an eventual "closing in" on a defined area of truth.)

The time-honored names for these alternative styles of teaching are "deductive" (moving from a point to an application in the students' lives) and "inductive" (moving from investigative procedures to an articulated conclusion). Both styles have their place, and the more effective teachers are gifted at employing both approaches.

Indeed, teachers soon discover that they are moving back and forth, repeatedly, from moments of "closed" presentations to moments of "open" investigation. The rhythmic movement between logical induction and deduction is at the very heart of the teaching/learning enterprise.

TEACHING STRATEGIES

Within the two basic approaches, teachers may opt for a wide variety of strategies. The notion that deductive teaching inevitably involves only the method of lecturing is erroneous; teachers may elect to present key concepts in a variety of ways. Similarly, it is a mistake to think of inductive teaching as invariably unstructured and freewheeling; a considerable amount of carefully planned activity may be involved. It is essential for teachers to distinguish primarily between the patterns of logic that are involved.

In the teaching of religious subject matter, teachers may choose between curricula that are best characterized as "Bible-to-life" materials (more deductive, on the whole) or curricula that are "life-to-Bible" in their primary orientation (more inductive). Or, in the case of theological material or other "churchly" subject matter, teachers are always faced with the choice of approach—either from "where the students are" at the moment or from the "givens" of content.

In the choice of curricular resources that contain suggested teaching procedures, it is a mistake to rely too heavily on promotional descriptions provided by the publishers. One must read through a considerable number of the proposed units of study to discern the teaching styles that seem to get preferential treatment. Often, within the same curricular stream, readers discover the writers' and editors' wisdom in including both inductive and deductive approaches to teaching.

Only minimal attention has been given to the fact that learners show, early in life, their preferences for one or the other of the styles: some young persons, like the adults they become, prefer teachers to introduce the key concepts along with pertinent examples; they can then take the next step of making application to their own life scene. Other youth and adults are much more comfortable in a setting that allows for experimentation, projects, and much openness of style on a teacher's part before they are assisted in drawing together their discoveries.

Years ago, in *Two Modes of Thought*, J. B. Conant reflected on the need for more research into this interesting phenomenon of human preferences for either inductive or deductive teaching styles. The matching of teachers' preferences to the preferred styles of their students would be a possibility in some settings, but this has seldom been considered.

MODELS OF TEACHING

Bruce Joyce and Marsha Weil in *Models of Teaching* classified teaching/learning under these headings:

- Social interaction—emphasizing relationship of persons to one another, with attendant values inherent in such give-and-take

- Information processing—in which learners are helped by teachers to hear, respond, and reflect upon provided data

- Person-orientation—spotlighting individuals' development of self-concepts, self-images, lifestyles, and the like

- Behavior modification—involving the communication of how-to procedures, attainment of skills, and the changing of learners' ways of undertaking tasks

At first blush, one might conclude that the models of social interaction and person orientation would be more "open" (inductive) and that information processing and behavior modification would lend themselves more readily to "closed" (deductive) approaches. But this conclusion would be premature. Within all four general models it is possible for teachers to operate with a wide variety of teaching strategies, some of them inductive and some deductive. Sometimes teachers themselves are not certain where they fall in the continuum; their styles are best evaluated by independent, objective observers.

In religious education, the greatest need is for teachers to be exposed to a variety of logical approaches to the teaching task; their greatest temptation is to teach without adequate planning and consequently to operate without sufficient attention to logic. This makes for student confusion and dissatisfaction and often leads to disciplinary problems.

OPEN CLASSROOM

Beginning in the early 1970s, religious bodies began to experiment in earnest with the "open classroom" as an approach to teaching. Classrooms were filled with a variety of learning centers (or stations), in which learners would follow the provided directions at the pace of their choosing in whatever order they might prefer. The centers (stations) in themselves varied widely in their approach. Some required observations and reflection; others involved a variety of "right-brain" activities (art, music, creative imagination).

These open-classroom experiments have met with varying degrees of success. Teachers who implement them successfully must be careful planners, devising ways to achieve a balance between individualized learning and the need for group sharing. The idea that an open classroom is "easier" to do is erroneous; much planning must be done in advance if it is to be successful. But where adequate preparation has taken place, many teachers have found that the methodology frees them to relate more successfully with each student on a one-to-one basis.

Few publishers have supplied curricular resources that are expressly prepared for the open classroom, although most materials can be adapted by local teacher groups for use in such settings.

To summarize teaching styles, consider a class session devoted to the prophet Amos and his theme of "justice." One possibility would be to summarize the prophet's message, share readings from the Scripture that bear his name, and give examples of both injustice and justice today, perhaps including apartheid or the plight of the homeless in American society. Students would then be invited to undertake projects or discuss key questions (or both) that would enable them to demonstrate their understanding of Amos's message. This would be a deductive style of teaching.

Another possibility would be to devise a variety of activities that would expose the learners to present-day issues of justice. Students might go on a field trip to a soup kitchen, listen to a videotape about events in South Africa, or consider some other current issue. They might examine clippings from news magazines or local journals. Through guided discussion, they close in on the

639

theme of justice, and the teacher brings in Amos's story at the relevant moment. This would be an inductive style of teaching.

If an open-classroom setting were employed, the learning centers would include well-designed, manageable blocks of learning that contained some or all of the suggested activities in both examples above; some would focus on contemporary life, others on biblical texts. The learners would be trusted to make the connection. *See also* Discovery Learning; Inductive Bible Study; Learning Center; Methodology; Teaching Theory.

FOR FURTHER REFERENCE

Joyce, Bruce, and Marsha Weil. *Models of Teaching.* Englewood Cliffs, NJ: Prentice-Hall, 1972.
Little, Sara. *To Set One's Heart.* Atlanta, GA: Knox, 1983.

L. E. Bowman

Teaching Theory

Teaching theories attempt by means of explanation, criticism, and imagination to direct and promote educational practice and methods as well as educational norms and procedures of evaluation. They test the practice of education according to accepted criteria and standards. They ask whether education achieves the goals it sets out to reach and probe the fundamental rationale and assumptions of a particular curriculum or program.

Although teaching theories are most often used to explain educational practice, it is helpful to make use of the explanatory nature of practice to understand the theories themselves. One can begin to understand teaching either by theorizing or by practicing, but practice often supplies the concrete examples needed to give insight into theory.

CLASSICAL THEORY

Ancient Greek philosophers grappled with the issue of theory and practice in an attempt to determine what kind of knowledge was most worthwhile. The classical understanding of theory and practice is found in the writings of Aristotle.

He described three types of human life and activity: *theoria, praxis,* and *poiesis. Theoria* (contemplation) was the speculative life in which one searched for truth solely by an intuitive process. To theorize was to achieve an wisdom by understanding the most basic principles of life. The achievement of theoretical knowledge was the most complete form of happiness. Aristotle called the practical life *praxis* and described it as a reflective engagement in some area of society. *Praxis* included two parts: action and reflection. *Poiesis* was Aristotle's term for the productive life.

Through it a person developed a craft, a skill, or an art.

Despite Aristotle's careful distinctions about these terms, his legacy to Scholastic philosophy included a number of dualisms, notably the opposition between theory and practice and the superiority of theory over practice. Scholastic philosophy in the Middle Ages continued and reinforced this tradition. Theory, which was the activity of the speculative or contemplative life, gave "true" knowledge. The practical life afforded only the experiences out of which opinions could be formed.

This classical position of Greek and Scholastic philosophy led to the notion that in knowing and acting it is always best to go from theory to practice. It devalued common experience and practice as sources of true knowledge and exaggerated the value of theory and speculation. In education it has led to the belief that certain subjects are in themselves more valuable than others.

The result of this viewpoint in religious education has been a one-sided relationship between theology/Scripture and education. Theology and Scripture are viewed as providing the teachings (theories) that practical-minded religious educators must find ways to transmit to others. This viewpoint emphasizes religious education as a content-oriented subject.

Religions do have a content, and this is the tradition that needs to be handed on to each generation. When the emphasis is on learning and understanding this content (Scripture, theology, history, liturgy), lecture and other forms of presentation are used, with discussion to help learners clarify the material. Then the material may be applied to the life situation. This is also referred to as "deductive" learning: going from the general to the particular.

DIALECTICAL THEORY

Another way of understanding the relationship between theory and practice is to view them not in a relationship of opposition or superiority but in a dialectical one. Friedrich Hegel (1770–1831) made one of the first moves in this direction when he rejected the separation of theory from practice and emphasized the unity of the two. He attempted to maintain the productive tension between practical life experience and the theories derived from the experiences of previous generations. Hegel utilized the three movements of dialectic—thesis, antithesis, and synthesis—to show how theory and practice criticized each other and resulted in new truths.

Hegel's analysis of practice was criticized by Karl Marx (1818–1883) for being overly idealistic and contemplative. For Marx, theory represented the consciousness that arises from practical involvement. Once a theory has evolved, it must inform further practice, and in that way is dialectical unity posited between the two.

This dialectical approach to theory and practice has received its strongest educational development in the writings of Paulo Freire. Freire advocates a dialogical approach to education in his theory of conscientization. The purpose of education for Freire and others who share his liberational approach is to bring people to critical consciousness of the social realities in which they are immersed. Critical consciousness entails the denunciation of oppressive reality and the prophetic announcement of a utopian reality that is free of oppression. To conscientize others is to assist them in "decoding" reality and in stripping it of the deceptive myths that both distort a vision of reality and prevent social action for change. This conscientization is made possible through praxis, i.e., reflection on and action in the world with the intent of transforming it.

The dialectical approach to theory and practice is a challenging one for religious educators since teaching theories have the important function of directing action. There is a close connection between the explanatory and directive functions. Whoever theorizes in education should not have the elaboration of theory in mind as the end product, but rather the development of guidelines for educational practice.

PRAGMATISM

Pragmatism arose through the thinking of the nineteenth-century American philosopher and psychologist William James (1842–1910). He affirmed that experience must precede theory and that the latter is a reflection on experience. Theories demonstrate their validity by their successful transferral into practical life. John Dewey (1859–1952) adapted this idea to educational theory, and his formulation is known as "instrumentalism": the means are instrumental to the end and must be constantly evaluated in terms of their effects. Dewey's counterpart in religious education, George Albert Coe (1862–1951), considered this to be a continuing process of re-creation and reconstruction. Values were in this sense relative, but he believed that constant reevaluation brought a better understanding of and higher standard of values. Their approach was that of "inductive" learning: going from the particular to the general.

This is the basis for progressive education that evolved in the United States during the first half of the twentieth century. Classrooms became environments for learning about a community, society, or enterprise, and every subject—reading, writing, geography, history, arithmetic—was related to and learned from that context. Although it is rarely found today in this complete form, its legacy includes more pupil-oriented teaching methods and the integration of subjects such as geography with history and literature with art.

In religious education there has been a similar broadening of learner experiences as demonstrated in curricular materials since the early part of the century. Learners move around in the classroom at their work, teachers are facilitators, resource materials are available, and a variety of methods are employed.

THE EFFECT OF PRACTICE ON THEORY

Educational practice also provides direction for theorists and researchers. Practice directs theorists to facts, phenomena, and events that must be explained and reveals incongruities that are not accounted for in existing theories. Practice provides the material for the exercise of the three components of teaching theory's critical function: analysis, evaluation, and synthesis. Analysis describes the concepts, definitions, models, arguments, and slogans that are used in educational practice. It subjects these to careful scrutiny. Evaluation is concerned with determining the validity of practices, whether or not practice achieves its stated goals. Synthesis attempts to put together the findings of practice into a fully integrated theory. Practice also has potential for offering constructive criticism to teaching theory. Practice may show that theories are inadequate for explaining or imaging reality. By putting a teaching theory into practice, one often sees ways in which the theory should be modified. It is the failure of a theory to meet the test of practice that often leads to its abandonment.

CONCLUSION

A mutual utilization and critique of both teaching theory and practice is needed in the field of religious education. Curricula and programs need to be put to the test of theories, with probing into aims, objectives, and assumptions, and theories need testing by both formal and informal experimentation.

Practitioners need to take direction from theorists and theorists must look in the direction of practioners. At times, teaching theories can take the lead in innovation and creatively imagine or construct new realities or possible practices. So also at times can concrete practical situations stretch the imagination of theorists; imagination is often found in the person of action who develops concrete solutions to particular problems, creates a unique educational experiment, or fashions a new type of relationship with learners.

In our theorizing about teaching and in our actions, we need to maintain the dialectical tension between theory and practice. In education, teaching theory without practice can become irrelevant and practice without theory can become mindless. *See also* Action-Reflection; Aristotle; Coe, George Albert; Conscientization; Dewey, John; Dialectic(s); Education, Theories of; Goals; Inductive Bible Study; James, William; Learning Theory; Liberation Theology; Methodology;

Pragmatism; Praxis; Progressive Education; Teaching Styles; Theology and Education.

T. M. Eugene

Team Teaching

Team teaching happens when two or more adult leaders or teachers participate in the planning and actual presentation of a learning activity. Team teaching can be used effectively with any age group.

Team teaching is more than having a regular teacher with a designated substitute or two persons alternating lessons or units. Team teaching is the joint involvement of two or more adults in each phase of the learning project from planning to evaluation. All team members help set goals and plan each session's activities. All are present for each class session with either a directing or helping assignment in each phase of the lesson. Finally, all contribute to the evaluation of each event and unit.

Serious attention should be given to recruiting teams, especially those that will teach together for extended periods, as in the Sunday school. Personalities, goals of the activity, as well as size of the learning group guide the selection process. Sometimes one member is recruited first and asked to suggest other members of the team. Other times, the team is specifically selected to create a balance of ideas, or ages, or to be sure that both men and women are on the team. A caution is raised about using a husband and wife couple as a team. Often only one member plans and the other "sits" through the lesson. When the family goes on vacation or has another reason for absence, the class loses all of its team. Generally a three-member team is best when a married couple is involved.

Team teaching begins with shared planning. Every member of the team must participate in setting the goals for the whole unit and for each session. A clear understanding of the purpose of each class period helps the team work together.

Leadership for the planning sessions is often rotated among team members. One member may serve as the convenor of the planning sessions for a unit or a quarter. Since team teaching involves everyone, the feeling of lead and subordinate roles on the team is avoided.

Teams find it helpful to set general goals for a unit and specific goals for each lesson. Goals (or objectives) tell what students will learn or will be able to do, based on participation in the studies. Planning for individual sessions tends to be two to four weeks in advance with details clarified shortly before the session. The team needs to set clear goals for each session. Goals guide the choice of learning methods or activities as well as resources needed for the session.

When the lesson is presented every leader has an assignment: there is no lead teacher and no "sleeper." If the class is discussing a topic, the co-leader listens for other points that need to be raised or watches the group to see who would like to share an idea. One leader may present information while the other may outline the ideas on a chalkboard or hold a chart. Building on each other's ideas, helping students understand instructions, and encouraging attention are easily focused when the team knows the goal for each part and how it fits with the whole.

Team teaching improves as the members share experiences and friendships over a period of time. Trust must be developed relating to the acceptance of ideas and ways of teaching. Creativity can be encouraged as risk taking is done in a supportive atmosphere.

Students benefit from team teaching. The psychological result of working together challenges the team members to be creative. Ideas that might be too difficult for one leader are now developed as two or more share in the development or presentation. Each teacher does not have to be an expert in every activity or have all the resources. A wide variety of experiences are possible for the class. Teachers can use individual strengths and share alternative roles.

Another benefit to students is that greater support for each class member is available. It is the automatic duty of the "nonpresenting" teacher actively to look for student cues. Restlessness, failure to understand directions, or the need for any kind of special attention become the teaching concern of the other team members.

Team teaching offers opportunities for students to hear contrasting ideas on a topic. Personality differences are normal among teachers. Some persons are quiet, others may be very outgoing; some may be very organized, others flexible. This provides alternative role models for students to observe.

Team teaching takes time for planning. It requires leaders to spend time face to face coordinating ideas and plans. As students observe a successful teaching team, they also see a model of the faith community in action as people learn and worship together and manifest mutual care. *See also* Leadership Development; Lesson Planning; Teacher.

D. G. Emler

Television

Television is a communications tool that bridges time and space and enables religious educators to bring outside resources of persons, places, and events to their work with the excitement of moving images and sound. It provides a wide variety of exciting opportunities to educators and has become an essential resource.

TELEVISION IN SOCIETY

When we consider the role television plays in the informal education of virtually all children, youth, and adults in our society, we can understand the context in which television is used by religious educators. Television has become the most pervasive communication medium of society and much of the enculturating process takes place through television. Because television is such a dominant communication tool, significant personal learning comes through this medium and individuals begin to expect that important information for living will be communicated through television. The implications of this are important for educators. If religious education is important for life, then it must be communicated, at least in part, through the medium of television. Educators also need to be aware of the television programs their students watch and take advantage of opportunities to discuss these programs, examine their messages, and, where possible, build on these messages in positive ways.

Television, like other teaching tools, has limitations for use in religious education. Television is not to be construed as an effortless, entertainment device. It requires preparation on the part of the teacher in selecting programs, and skill in leading groups through the transition from viewing to thoughtful discussion and/or action. Television should not replace the use of print media or other forms of storytelling and discussion in the classroom, but it should be used regularly as an interactive method of teaching. Television in religious education should not be a replacement for persons, but a communications tool used by educators to more effectively inform, motivate, persuade, comfort, and express care.

At present, there are few religious television programs broadcast or videotaped for preschool children, but a careful search will uncover material for children of early elementary age. Most of this material centers on classical biblical stories such as those of David or Daniel. There is more material and more possible use of material with older children and adults.

VIDEOTAPED TELEVISION

Videotaped television is all television distributed on videocassettes and played in one location on a videotape player. At the present time, videotaped television is the most usable form of television for religious educators because of availability and low cost. Videotape players and recorders are widely available and inexpensive for purchase or can be borrowed for use in education. A wide variety of videotape programs are available to rent or purchase, some programs can be recorded off the air for educational use, and programs can be produced locally.

Videotaped television can have great variety, combining still and moving images with sounds to provide a learning experience. It can present dramatic action in movies, plays, and cartoons. One has only to experience the power of a great movie on video to be reminded of the potential of videotaped drama.

Videotapes can present music with images of the musicians as they create the music or music with images of any other type. The importance of music videos, especially to young people, and the quantity of time spent watching the same ones over and over attest to the power of music and images.

Videotaped presentations can cross barriers of time and space, bringing us events from the past and current data from faraway places. There are times in the educational process when there is no substitute for seeing and hearing an event from the past or from across the world. When people watch Martin Luther King's "I Have a Dream" speech, they are reminded of the power of this medium.

Videotaped television is flexible and can be played at any time convenient to the educator, can be stopped for discussion and then continued, or backed up and restarted. Not having to plan around a broadcast time is an obvious advantage, but selecting segments from longer programs and stopping, starting, and backing up are often overlooked as teaching devices.

For example, one scene from a feature-length movie can be selected, a short introduction given to set the context for the scene, and the scene shown. Usually, there are persons who have already seen the movie and the discussion that follows will reflect the total film but focus on the desired point.

Videotaped television can make an emotional impact. This characteristic is so obvious that it may seem unnecessary to point out, but television does have unusual potential in this area. Emotional impact is important to the learning process, and too often we do not plan for emotional experiences.

The number of sources for the purchase and rental of videotapes is growing. Religious publishing houses and bookstores have videotapes and many denominations have film and video libraries at the national, regional, or local level. Libraries often have a resource person available to help with the selection of materials.

Resources available at local secular book and video stores can also be explored. Movies are the most available and least expensive source and can be used in a variety of ways. Occasionally complete films can be viewed and discussed, but short segments from movies are usually more effective. Secular stores also have a growing number of videotapes on a wide range of educational subjects produced for individual and group use.

The following steps are helpful in using videotaped television.

Design the session. Select the videotape and preview it to be sure that it meets your needs and to get the information necessary for planning the session. The videotape is only one part of the total plan and its usefulness will depend on the total design of the session. In some cases the videotape will play a small part and on other occasions it will be a major contribution, but it is essential that the introduction to the videotape and the follow-up be carefully planned.

Check the equipment. Set up the equipment and check it out in the teaching room early enough to work out any problems. Let the tape run long enough to be sure that the fuse or circuit breaker is adequate and plan seating so that everyone can see and there is no glare on the screen. If the group is too large for one television set, make arrangements to have a second or third set.

Use the videotape. Show the videotape according to your design and do not give in to a request to show more of the tape than you have planned to show. Although some may resist stopping for discussion, they usually enjoy it and learn from the sharing as much as from the videotape.

Follow-up and evaluation. Discuss or follow-up the videotape according to your design. Evaluation of the use of the videotaped television will help you in your planning for future sessions.

It is also possible, with proper permission, to record a broadcast program or segment from a program for use at a later time. Some programs that are copyrighted give permission in the credits for you to record them and keep the program for a video library. Many copyrighted programs can only be videotaped for educational use in the immediate future and then erased; if you desire these programs for a videotape library, they should be purchased from the producer.

Television guides that describe broadcast television programs are helpful in selecting which programs to videotape for use as educational resources. Religious education literature also alerts educators to coming broadcasts that may be useful and tells if a leader's guide is available. Special attention should be given to programs that students watch regularly because they have unusual potential as resources.

After a broadcast television program is recorded, previewed, and a segment of the program is chosen for use, the process is the same as for other videotaped television. One can expect to record many programs that are not useful, but when a program or segment really works as a resource, it will make the total effort worthwhile.

Videotaped television production by teachers, students, and others in the local church cannot be considered here in depth but its tremendous potential must be emphasized. Television does not have to be professionally done to be valuable as an educational resource and local production has the added advantage of providing a production process that is a valuable learning experience in itself. After a videotaped television program has been prepared, its use can be planned in the same way as other videotaped television.

BROADCAST TELEVISION

Broadcast television includes television distributed over the airwaves on VHF or UHF stations, television distributed through cable systems, and television distributed by satellite and received on a satellite dish. It too is useful, although there are fewer direct applications for educators because of difficulties in scheduling and planning around set broadcast times.

In spite of scheduling difficulties, regularly scheduled religious education programs are available over satellite on a nationwide basis in some denominations and more work is being done in this area all the time. Educators are encouraged to use the programs live or videotape them for later use. The quality of these programs has been mixed, but it is improving and they are fast becoming a major contribution to religious education.

Although most broadcast television relies on videotaped programs, some broadcasts, usually news or sporting events, are live, so that the viewer watches as the event actually takes place. Live broadcasts are exciting because of their immediacy, and, as technology provides more economical ways to do live broadcasting, educators should take advantage of its possibilities.

There have been some exciting religious education experiments with live television broadcasts via satellite with two-way audio so that the students can see, hear, and discuss with a teacher not present in the same place. These experiments have enabled a teacher or team of teachers in a television studio to work with students in a dozen or more widely separated locations. At the present time, the cost is less than it would be to bring all the students to one location or take the teacher to all the locations, and the cost will gradually be coming down. In one such experiment a teacher worked with groups in Arizona, California, Hawaii, Montana, and Washington and the evaluation of the process by students was very positive.

In the future more individual churches and denominations will broadcast television, providing more opportunities for religious educators. Although broadcast television may never replace the use of videotaped television, the use of both will continue to grow as a major resource for religious educators. *See also* Media; Visual Methods.

S.F. Jackson

Temperance Education
See Addiction.

Ten Commandments

Of all the legal type literature in the history of Western thought none is more revered than the Ten Commandments found in Exodus 20 and Deuteronomy 5. The texts of the two decalogues are very similar. A traditional explanation for the differences is that the Exodus account was spoken by God, while the Deuteronomic account was Moses' repeated version. A modern interpretation holds that they reflect different time periods in history (the one in Exodus is perhaps earlier).

There is a difference between Jewish and various Christian traditions over the numbering of the commandments. According to Roman Catholic tradition, Exodus 20:1–6 is one commandment and verse 17 is divided into two commandments; Protestantism holds verse 3 to be the first commandment, with verse 2 as part of the introduction and verses 4–6 separate commandments; Judaism makes verse 2 the first commandment and verses 3–6 into the second commandment. These differences cause confusion when one refers to any commandment by number rather than by content.

For Judaism the first commandment, "I am the Lord your God" is a credo, acknowledging a historic event as the basis for its religion. Christianity holds a different view of its history and does not include this commandment among the ten.

The second Jewish and first Protestant commandment deals with the relationship of God to other gods. It does not deny other gods but delineates proper worship. There are to be no idols; God will punish his followers who worship idols. It appears to be a polemic against the pagan idolatry of ancient times and a way to separate Israel from the surrounding peoples.

The next commandment refers to the misuse of God's name, not only in an oath; when it is viewed with the previous commandment it teaches that God's image and name are sacred and neither should be abused.

The commandment dealing with the Sabbath is the only one to mention cultic practice. This commandment is one of the bases for the high esteem the Sabbath is held in Jewish and Christian tradition.

The remaining commandments all deal with human relationships. Respect for God complements respect for human beings. Traditionally parents are the link between God and each individual. God is often referred to as "Father." Thus the commandment to love one's parents is a natural bridge between the two sections of the Decalogue. All the succeeding commandments tell what not to do. They are statements of limitation, not exhortations. While they appear to be guides to behavior, more accurately they are points from which to expand and expound upon life. Their open-endedness provides opportunities for an ever-widening understanding of proper behavior.

In some traditions, the basic statements of the Ten Commandments are taught to children at the age of seven or eight because they are basic to the understanding of biblical faith and life or because they are part of the liturgy. As nearly as possible they need to be connected with children's experience. Hence, adultery is explained in terms of faithful family life, and children learn that icons or sacred pictures are illustrative or symbolic and not portraits. "Keeping the Sabbath" varies with culture and religious tradition. Not "coveting" may be in conflict with cultural values. Older children can discuss in more depth the full wording of the Decalogue, studying the two biblical contexts: Exodus 20 and Deuteronomy 5.

Adolescents and adults can, through discussion, probe the meaning of the commandments both to those to whom they were addressed and for life today. What, for example, does it mean to "have no other gods" or to "make a graven image"? How does one interpret the command not to kill (or not to murder)?

In some traditions the Ten Commandments are part of the liturgy and people grow up viewing them in the context of worship. To them, the Ten Commandments have a meaning beyond attempts to give reasoned interpretations or fit them into life patterns. God's purposes are expressed through the words themselves. *See also* Behavior; Bible Study; Covenant; Moral Development.

W. J. Leffler

Teresa of Avila

Teresa of Avila (1515–1582) was a saint, mystic, and leading figure in the Catholic Reformation in her restructuring of the Carmelite order. Born Teresa de Cepeda y Ahumada in Avila, Spain, she entered the Carmelite order in 1536. After a "second conversion" after an illness (ca. 1555) she began a period of intense mystic spirituality that included visions. Yet Teresa is a classic example of one who combined a life of prayerful contemplation with intense activity—she reformed the Carmelite order in Avila and went on to do so in other locations. A tireless and able manager, she led the nuns back to the full observance of their original rule. The reforms included a return to a more strict way of life: silence, solitude, strict enclosure, and more prayer and fasting. Under her influence the reform spread to the men of the order, outstanding among their leaders being John of the Cross.

The most important of her writings are *The Interior Castle*, with its seven stages or "mansions of mystical prayer," the work that above all makes her a master of the spiritual life, and the *Way of Perfection*, for the most part a commentary on the "Our Father," which she wrote to instruct her nuns in prayer and which has served so many generations of Christians. *See also* Devotional Literature; Religious Orders.

T. M. Eugene

Theodicy

The reconciliation between the notion of God's justice and the existence of evil in the world is the substance of theodicy. According to the Genesis account of creation, everything that exists in the world is a creation of God and therefore "good." By definition, then, evil too would fall under the category of "good creation" and in some way be part of the divine schema.

The Hebrew Bible's discussion of the tension between good and evil reaches its apex in the book of Job, an account of the sufferings of the righteous or good man. The "friends" of Job—including his wife—present to readers the various philosophical and theological responses to the problem of evil, all to no avail. The ultimate resolution is that people are ignorant of the ways of God (Job 38–41).

Postbiblically, the rabbis of Talmudic tradition built upon their own scriptural understanding, but focused more on the evils human beings do to each other rather than on the speculative existence of evil in the world. Their resolution was that each human being has the innate ability to perform acts of both evil and good, though like the biblical text they too rejected the notion of humanity as inherently sinful from birth and therefore evil.

In our own day, the Holocaust of World War II has again raised the entire question to painful awareness requiring, for many, a rethinking of both the biblical and rabbinic positions. Jewish thinkers such as Eliezer Berkovitz, Martin Buber, Emil Fackenheim, and Richard Rubenstein, among others, have all attempted to address the concept of theodicy in light of these events.

Christian understandings begin with the interpretation of the crucifixion and resurrection of Jesus Christ as God's vindication of evil. Paul writes that "in everything God works for good with those who love him" (Rom. 8:28). Fourth-century theologian Aurelius Augustine formulated what became the basic Western theological tradition, that evil is a corruption of original nature in the exercise of God-given free will. The justice of God will be most fully revealed in the day of judgment. In Eastern Christianity free will offers the choice of living apart from God or growing in fuller communion with God. *See also* Death; God, Understandings of.

S. L. Jacobs

Theological Anthropology

Theological anthropology represents a field of study that has come to include many of the themes examined in traditional tracts on revelation, creation, human freedom, sin, grace, soteriology, and moral theology. On the one hand, it recognizes the futility of studying these major doctrines apart from one another and apart from their relationship to God, Creator-Sanctifier. On the other hand, theological anthropology represents a reaction against an approach so dominated by the doctrine of God as to overlook the theological significance of human phenomena.

Theological anthropology accepts the premise that humans are at once both subject and object of the inquiry into the purpose and meaning of the created universe. It draws from a wide and complex variety of sources that includes sacred texts (e.g, the Hebrew Scriptures and the New Testament) as well as natural sciences, social sciences, secular literature, and the arts. Theological anthropology is the formal study of human phenomena from a religious point of view as they raise liminal questions and stand in a dialectical relationship to history, culture, and the entire cosmos. In religious education at all age levels, whenever human beings are the subject—in their relationships to self and others, in their social and psychological contexts, and in their relationship to God seen through the understanding of God in Scripture and tradition—it may be termed theological anthropology. *See also* Behavior; Ethics; Social Sciences; Values.

M. C. Bryce

Theological Education

Theological education prepares men and women for ordained ministry, for vocations such as religious education, and for other work done under religious auspices.

EARLY HISTORY

Theological education in the Western religious tradition may be said to have begun with the Levites (Exod. 32:29; 2 Chron. 35:3) and in the postexilic period with the scribes as interpreters of the Torah, but nothing is known of their training. The rabbinate developed during the first century A.D., and after the fall of Jerusalem (A.D. 70) the center for scholarship moved to Jamnia on the border of Judea, where the rabbinic academy was a center both for the education of rabbis (teachers) and for scholarship. During the Middle Ages, yeshivas developed to give both basic education and specific rabbinical training.

Christian theological education began with the catechetical schools of Alexandria (late second century) and Antioch, first for the training of catechists and later as centers for scholarship and education. These centers declined after the eastern Mediterranean area became part of Islamic culture, but by then scholarly enterprises had begun in Europe. The monasteries, beginning with that of Benedict of Nursia (480–547) in Italy, were training grounds for parish clergy as well as their own members. Schools connected with the large cathedrals of Europe flourished starting in the eighth century. The curriculum included both classical and theological studies.

These were succeeded by the universities, beginning with the Sorbonne in Paris in 1257, which offered the liberal arts and sciences in addition to biblical and theological studies. The separation of clergy from laity for education was a post-Reformation phenomenon, resulting in university theology departments designed for clerical studies, either Protestant or Catholic depending on the religion of the country. Today many European universities have both Protestant and Catholic faculties.

Jewish rabbinical training in the eighteenth century was affected by secular trends, and under the influence of the philosopher Moses Mendelssohn (1729–1786) theological schools were established that combined general learning with biblical studies.

IN THE UNITED STATES

In the American colonies, Harvard College was established in 1636 to help prepare a literate ministry, and theology was part of the preparation of most A.B. degree candidates even in the eighteenth century. Harvard established a chair in divinity in 1721, as did Yale College in 1756. Between 1820 and 1840 about 50 American Protestant seminaries were established. More than 120 were founded between 1850 and 1890, many of which have since merged with others or been discontinued.

With the increasing number of Roman Catholic immigrants into the United States in the mid-nineteenth century, there was a need to train Roman Catholic clergy locally. Some seminaries were founded by monastic orders, others by the church itself. In 1986 they numbered forty-seven.

Today most Catholic and Protestant and some Jewish seminaries are members or associate members of the Association of Theological Schools in the United States and Canada. Its yearbook lists 201 graduate seminaries (schools of theology) with a total enrollment for 1986–1987 of 64,328 students, 4,370 on the postgraduate level (Ph.D. or D.Min.).

In the 1960s a significant ecumenical movement began that led to alignment of schools of the various Christian denominations into clusters of consortia that enabled them to benefit from one another's resources and thus enrich their own programs. In 1986 fifteen such arrangements were functioning in the United States and Canada. The development of common library and media resources, joint use of faculty, and freedom for students to take courses in any constituent seminary have been a benefit to participants and have furthered ecumenism.

CURRICULA

The modern rabbinical seminary retains the study of the Hebrew Scriptures at the center of the curriculum. Students also learn Jewish theology and philosophy, both medieval and modern, Jewish history, and Hebrew language and literature. Seminaries today, apart from those of the most orthodox groups, also require courses in education, homiletics, and pastoral psychiatry.

Roman Catholic institutions are divided into major and minor seminaries. Each diocese is expected to have a seminary, whether it is under the supervision of the diocese, a monastic order, or the Holy See, and the larger dioceses are expected to have both a minor and major seminary. The minor seminary is a preparatory college offering a preseminary curriculum that includes philosophy, Latin, Scripture, theology, and general college studies; it is designed for those who desire this specialized education before entering seminary. Major seminaries offer a three-year graduate course that includes philosophy, humanities and sciences, dogmatic and moral theology, canon law, Scripture, and auxiliary ecclesiastical studies and leads to the Master of Divinity degree, which is customarily prerequisite to ordination to the priesthood. In 1964 the seminary course of studies and the regime of spiritual exercises were fundamentally modified by the directions given by the *Constitution of the Sacred Liturgy* (15–17) promulgated by Vatican II.

The Protestant curriculum has traditionally included courses in three major areas: biblical studies, theology (including ethics), and church history. Some schools require Greek and/or Hebrew upon entry or provide for work in these languages during the course of study. A number of additional courses have been added to most curricula in the practical or pastoral field, such as religious education, parish administration, pastoral counseling, world religions, the arts and religion, media and communication, and religion and society.

The patterns of Protestant seminary education vary, but almost all follow a three-year course leading to a Master of Divinity degree. Some have developed an intern year under supervision in a parish after the second or third year. The Council for Clinical Training offers a thirteen-week program in a hospital or other institution for students who serve as assistants to a supervising chaplain. Most students also experience some form of contextual learning in assignments to parishes or institutions on weekends.

As in other fields of learning, there has been an awareness of the need to keep up with change and develop lifelong learning. Most denominations assist clergy by providing study time and money for this. The seminaries provide programs on campus and near major population centers for clergy. The Doctor of Ministry degree program offered by many seminaries is this kind of program, designed to encourage postordination growth. It is a professional degree, in contrast to the Ph.D., which is an academic degree. The program includes the completion of a chosen project that enables the person to explore some aspect of ministry at greater depth. Several years may be needed to complete the work.

CURRENT ISSUES

A number of issues face theological education today. There are now too many seminaries with too few students and too little money. Integration is needed, but merging schools is always a painful decision for those involved. In addition, half the present senior faculty will retire by the mid-1990s and there does not seem to be a sufficient number of highly qualified younger scholars to replace them.

Intercultural factors have become important. Not only are there more women bringing their own perspectives; there are increasing numbers of students from Asian, African, Hispanic-American, and black American contexts. They need an educational experience that will give them the best of "mainstream" thought yet prepare them to adapt this to meet the needs of those to whom they minister.

The question of what is quality theological education is perennial and involves continuing discussion concerning curriculum content, methods of grading, and meeting the expectations both of the academic and the religious community. Theological schools are always balancing the need for academic excellence and pastoral skills. Concomitantly this means decisions as to how far to stress the classic disciplines of Scripture, theology and history, along with the practical disciplines noted earlier to develop competence in counseling, education, administration, preaching, and worship.

There is serious concern about the spiritual and character development of students preparing for ministry. Roman Catholic schools have found that traditional methods are less suitable today. Protestant seminaries are aware of the need for spiritual disciplines. New patterns are emerging.

A recent note has been added with the inquiry as to whether theological education should be planned entirely from the perspective of clergy, including faculty, judicatory heads, and most administrative and governing board members, or whether congregations should be involved in decisions as to the nature of preparation for ministry. *See also* Colleges and Universities, Church-Related; History of Christian Education; Ministry; Ordination; Professional Study; Religious Orders; University; Vocation.

FOR FURTHER REFERENCE

Farley, Edward. *The Fragility of Knowledge: Theological Education in the Church and the University*. Philadelphia: Fortress, 1988.

Hough, Joseph, and Barbara Wheeler. *Beyond Clericalism: The Congregation as a Focus for Theological Education*. Decatur, GA: Scholars Press, 1988.

Wood, Charles M. *Vision and Discernment: An Orientation in Theological Study*. Decatur, GA: Scholars Press, 1985.

J. P. Stump

Theologizing

"Theologizing" is a term sometimes used to refer to theological reflection and judgment. The process of theological reflection is an attempt to offer some conceptual framework for the basic confessions of faith. As a reflection consequent to the experience of faith, "theologizing" is an intellectual activity that intends to give basic religious convictions sense, meaning, and an orderly exposition of reality and truth.

Even amid its various forms and methods, "theologizing" is grounded in a critical correlation between the core elements of religious faith and contemporary issues and questions. Therefore, "theologizing" requires an open and critical dialogue between one's past religious heritage and the cultures of contemporary life. The dialogue always intends a renewed understanding of God and world that will have positive effects in the future. *See also* Belief; Theology and Education; Tradition.

J. Monti

Theology and Education

A discussion of the relationship between theology and education is an investigation of the relationship between the study of God or knowledge of God and the study of formation and transformation of persons in the light of that knowledge and interactions with other facets of human becoming.

Actually, the literal meaning and original usage of the term "theology" to refer to knowledge of God has gradually broadened to mean "rational interpretation of religious faith, practice, and experience" (Webster). However, there is a sense in which the doctrine of God is still the basis for any understanding of the meaning of human existence and of those formulations resulting from "faith seeking understanding." To the degree that theology is concerned with "understanding," it is inevitably related to the educational enterprise, where the focus is on intentional efforts to help people understand and be shaped by that understanding. Such an approach goes beyond the view of education as educing, or bringing out potential within the person, as suggested by the Latin roots of the term, but does recognize the capacities of the human being as offering both constraints and potential for response to God's self-revelation. In fact, one of the critical factors in the self-understanding of those in the field of religious education has been the nature of that relationship between theology and education. After commenting on some of the alternatives as they have existed and presently function, we shall consider, in order, recent historical developments, the contemporary situation, and then the prospects for the future.

ALTERNATIVES

Theology as Source

Probably the most prominent and continuous understanding of the relationship of theology and education is the view that theology provides the content to be taught and education works on settings, processes, and the like, critically reflecting on utilization of policies and procedures from secular disciplines. Even in early Hebrew history, before any distinction was made between theology and education, the stories and interpretations that developed in response to the question, "What is the meaning of this?" gradually became a content to be repeated and reinterpreted and thereby reappropriated. By the time the new Christian religion came in contact with the Greco-Roman world, it became important to specify the doctrines that distinguish Christianity and to develop a system for initiating newcomers into the beliefs and practices of the community. Theology, viewed as doctrine, as creeds and confessions, as systematic formulations of belief, became distinct from education, with its patterns of transmission, training, and developing the "fruits of the Spirit" in Christian living. In a sense, the one presupposes the other. Theology is the source of the goals of education as well as the determiner of content. It promotes the common language and is the source of the common memory of the community. There are variations in that basic relationship: some groups view education as an instrument for indoctrination and others view education as an activity of inquiry,

649

finding present meaning in the interpretation of heritage. In the latter approach, learners listen to the biblical story and are helped to respond in terms of its own meaning and its meaning for them. Story is one important method among others.

Theology as Resource

In this view, education, with its accumulated insights from relevant social sciences, has implicit goals and learning theories that are determinative for both structure and content. Where theology helps meet goals or provides perspective and interpretation for the meaning of present experiences, it is a worthy resource. In fact, it is even a necessary resource, to the degree that one seeks to build continuity with the past in moving responsibly into the future. Adherents of this approach are more likely to prefer the term "religious education" to "Christian education," and professionals identify with "education" as the overarching discipline. This is not the prevailing approach in the late twentieth century, but because theology is optional and because there is no one unifying approach to curriculum development, to give only one example, there is a resulting pervasive confusion in the field. This approach begins with questions the learners are asking. They go to the Bible and theology to seek answers.

Theology as Norm

Subject areas to be included in the teaching ministries are selected and interpreted in relationship to theological formulations. Programs and practices are reflected on theologically to ascertain their appropriateness for religious education. Given the origin of education as an indispensable aspect of theology and its evolution into a separate discipline, it is not difficult to see how this particular approach developed, in which theology should screen and shape content. The hierarchical relationship, in which there is a deductive move from theology to education, in all its aspects, is perhaps verbalized more often than it is enacted, but it still exists as a viable option. In this approach, basic theological understandings such as creeds, confessional statements, and other forms are normative teaching materials. Methods for teaching will be consonant with the theology: for example, if theology is understood as revealed truth, it will be taught per se. Interpretation and application will arise from this fact.

"Doing theology" as Educating

When one engages in critical reflection on the meaning of experience and on decisions to be made in relationship to God's presence and purpose, one may be said to be "theologizing," using a term devised in the twentieth century to reflect an activity of theological reflection. Such an activity is to be distinguished from the methodology of the discipline of theology. In other words, theological reflection becomes educative. Certain theories of education utilize such processes, not in isolation from tradition, but in engagement with it. Here, teacher and learner probe the meaning of life situations in the light of generally accepted theological understandings. This kind of reflection on theology, which begins with experience, can bring new perspectives on a situation. Theology becomes "alive" because it speaks to the present.

Theology and Education as Interactive

Three assumptions characterize this alternative. Theology and education are separate but related disciplines, each with its special contribution and functions. Each draws on a cluster of related disciplines from which it utilizes appropriate contributions. And the educative processes not only educate, but also make a substantive contribution to the ongoing development of the theological formulations of the church. In such an interactive, dialogical process, plans for educational ministry develop. To some extent, theology is normative, but only to the degree that it bears an intrinsic authority resident within the commitments of the community of believers. Here the overarching rubric is ministry, rather than education, and the intention is to equip all believers for the ministry to which they are called. This approach accepts the integrity of each discipline. Whichever is chosen initially, the other approach is drawn upon for its contribution.

RECENT HISTORICAL DEVELOPMENTS

For the major part of the twentieth century, at least up through the mid-1980s, the question of the role of theology and religious education has been one of the continuing issues. During the first quarter, in the U.S. scene, the emergence of progressive education and of "modern" religious education coincided with the widespread liberal theology that eventuated in a new congeniality between theology and education. Although a recurring critique of the period was that religious education had "no theology," the fact is that the presuppositions and goals of liberal theology were so similar to those of education that disciplinary boundaries were blurred. Critiques of education that came from conservative traditions were primarily theological in substance.

Responses in religious education theory and practice to the confrontation by neoorthodox theology and biblical theology centered on the "rediscovery of the Bible" were far-reaching. Randolph Crump Miller captured the dominant mood of the time in his 1950 statement that the "clue" to Christian education is theology. The vitality of the period and the productivity of eminent Christian education theorists like Randolph Crump Miller, Lewis Sherrill, James Smart, and others converged to give the impression of consensus and stability. But the "turbulent sixties," as historian Sidney Ahlstrom calls them, were marked by distrust of both theology and education. Social activism characterized the period, and to the degree that Christian education had an emphasis, it was on Christian education as engagement in mission. Theology was unimportant, almost irrelevant.

Chastened educators thus entered the decade of the 1970s. Iris Cully wrote an article in 1971 in *Religion in Life* entitled, "What Killed Religious Education?" Denominational and interdenominational offices of religious education were dismantled or so restructured that limited staff time and financial undergirding severely limited activities. But religious education was not dead, after all. What was being experienced in educational circles was similar to what was being experienced in theological circles— disruption, confusion, lack of moral clarity, sporadic efforts on the part of scholars to assess the situation and propose directions for the future. Furthermore, strength lay in evangelical circles, where the two alternatives, theology as source and theology as norm, functioned with increasing strength to give direction to a multifaceted, active educational program. Bernard Ramm, in *The Evangelical Heritage* (1973), recognized the millions of evangelicals both in mainline denominations and in independent or sectarian groups and found growing concern for historical study of theology and for social concerns. What is to be observed is that the content of theological emphases coincided with cultural trends and values to give a conservative theological outlook and educational theory the congeniality that liberal theology and religious education had shared earlier in the century. It was in evangelical circles that vitality was to be found in the 1970s. On the other hand, such neat distinctions between liberal and conservative are inadequate. More accurately, there are numerous complex combinations and variations with respect to the interrelationship of theology and education along a continuum. On the one end of the continuum fundamentalist theology offers security within an authoritative theology combined with media use as a form of education. On the other end, secular humanism (or some other focus) offers its hope of educational reform.

Even in the midst of these shifts of more than a decade, it is to be noted that both religious education and theology were moving in new directions, or at least toward constructive reformulations. Education was again becoming "respectable" and moving into the use of new concepts that reflected an exploratory spirit. For John Westerhoff, education was intentional socialization or catechesis. For James Michael Lee, education was a subset of the social sciences that could be planned and implemented without dependence on a particular theological system. For Thomas Groome, Christian religious education was "shared praxis." There were others. Theology was similarly exploratory and fragmented. There was James Cone, with his black theology, Gustavo Gutiérrez with his liberation theology, Rosemary Radford Ruether with her feminist theology. The list could go on to include the theology of play, the theology of leadership, the theology of hope. Although the past tense is used here, descriptively, it should be noted that in the present all these developments continue. What becomes evident is that, as has been true for much of history, theology arises out of reflection within particular situations. In church curriculum developments, it is easy to see parallels between Paulo Freire's *Pedagogy of the Oppressed* (1970) and liberation theology. The point, however, is that they are parallel and not sequential developments.

What can be said, then, about the relationship between theology and education? First of all, it is quite clear that by the 1970s and early 1980s, theology was no longer the "clue" to Christian education. At least two efforts have been made to bring order out of the seeming confusion about how to understand religious education. In 1975, Harold Burgess published his analysis of the existing theories and patterns of religious education (*An Invitation to Religious Education*). He identifies four approaches: traditional theological, social-cultural, contemporary theology, and the social sciences. Even though Burgess does not identify theology as a critical factor in any one category, it is clear that in both the traditional and the contemporary groups, the content of theology is of major importance. In fact, all the alternative relationships between theology and education mentioned earlier in this article may be found in the contemporary theology group. By 1982, Jack Seymour and Donald Miller (editors), in their analysis of an expanding field, found five different approaches to Christian education (*Contemporary Approaches to Christian Education*). They are religious instruction, faith community, developmental, liberation, and interpretation. Although there are implicit theological assumptions in every approach, those assumptions are often not specified, and the source for the focus or image of what education is all about includes a variety of disciplines. Theology has become one influence among many.

At the same time, theology was undergoing a similar process. The title of David Tracy's *Blessed Rage for Order* (1975) captures an underlying motivation for the effort to discern patterns in the theological scene. Tracy presents five basic models he sees in contemporary theology: orthodox, liberal, neoorthodox, radical, and revisionist. His attention is directed primarily to the fifth, revisionist, which he calls a revised correlation model. A difference he sees in his and Tillich's version of correlation is that he sees both questions and answers in both Christian texts and common human experience and language, whereas Tillich focused more on the correlation of human and existential questions with gospel answers. Tracy sparks educational questions and insights, inevitably.

What becomes evident in the analyses cited and elsewhere is that concern for theology is imperative for the educator, influencing how one selects content and chooses an appropriate and consistent process for education. Therefore concern should be brought to the level of consciousness and clarified in dialogue both with other educational theorists and with theologians. Particularly in those periods where it is difficult to find compatible systems of theology and educational theories, the educator and learners in the church should together develop the skill of theological inquiry. In such a process, we have a way of maintaining continuity of tradition, of appropriating that tradition, and of moving into the emerging new world of the future.

What began as a recognition of diversity has moved to full-scale theological and educational pluralism, rejected by some, tolerated by a large group, embraced as the inescapable direction for the future by others.

THE PRESENT: POSTMODERN, POSTLIBERAL

With increasing frequency, scholars from various disciplines are referring to the last decades of the twentieth century as postmodern or postliberal. What is being said is that fundamental shifts in values, beliefs, and perceptions accompany fundamental shifts in societal processes, economic and political, and in modes of communication made possible by the "Information Age" with its media revolution. The shifts spring partly from the religious situation worldwide. David Barrett, in his monumental *World Christian Encyclopedia* (1982), points out that Christianity's base in North America and Western Europe is rapidly shifting to the south and east. At the same time that Western churches lose members at the rate of approximately 7,600 per day, African churches gain approximately 16,400 per day. From 83 percent of the world's Christians located in the West in 1900, Barrett predicts that by 2000, the shift will leave only 40 percent in the West. Not only is there a shift in the geographical centers of Christianity. Of equal importance is the steady decline of the number of Christians in relationship to the whole population. From 34.4 percent in 1900, according to Barrett, by the year 2000 there will be 32.3 percent of the total world population that will be called Christian.

Referring to the United States, it might be said that population shifts are accompanied by the loss of language, symbols, and moral values springing from the Christian tradition. Such a content has functioned in public, even though not always recognized formally, and helped shape the way persons perceived and interpreted experience. We learn from the field of sociology of knowledge (see Peter Berger and Thomas Luckmann, *The Social Construction of Reality*, 1966) that reality "is socially constructed." That is, any given society shapes the perception of its members, creating paradigms or interpretive frameworks that become filters for processing events and experiences. What comes out of that processing is knowledge, that which is assumed to be real. Consider prospects for the future as structural paradigms disintegrate and competing new ones emerge. The problem created is comprehensively societal, as well as specifically theological and educational.

Looking at the long history of Christians' efforts to witness faithfully to their God, a task that involves both theology and education, several guidelines for this postmodern period emerge. First of all, enough great church theologians have viewed themselves as "teachers of the church" to suggest that theology always has the possibility of a teaching orientation. These are days when that orientation is needed. Augustine was aware even of how he organized ideas to facilitate learning and of ways he could help doctrine to be clear to ordinary people. Calvin was no less conscious of his role of teacher for and to the church. Other examples could be cited, not only in the past, but in the present.

Second, theologians and educators must work collegially to enable persons to be aware of their conceptual inheritance and be able to use it in their "social construction of reality." Stephen Toulmin, in *Human Understanding* (1972), says that the power of thought characteristic of humans depends on working with and through that conceptual inheritance, not simply to transmit it, but to recreate and build on it. The difficulty of building on the past in a rapidly changing present calls for every conceivable aid in achieving clarity about the doctrines constituting that inheritance. Unless people have a *name* for an object, an experience, they cannot be related to it, comprehend it, or act in response to it. The importance of naming cannot be overemphasized. And when a "name" from the Christian tradition supplies understanding and connection with some new event or object—and notice that often the concept or name precedes the experience—a person learns, acquires meaning, can assume responsibility. Paulo Freire sees a kind of power attached to one who is able to "name." Is it possible that, in the effort to understand what is happening, people may work together to reinterpret and interrelate concepts, thus becoming better able to deal with new developments? The collaboration of theologians and educators is essential in this task.

And finally, the various possible alternative relationships delineated earlier in this article should be investigated as to their appropriateness for various situations. Already the fifth option, education and theology as interactive, seems to present itself as a valid and basic pattern of relationship. Learning the skills of theological reflection and exploring the pedagogy of obedience, of "doing the truth," provide both the testing for articulated doctrine and a deep knowing that relates theology and education in a profound way. There are even times when theology functions as norm, calling to attention implicit assumptions in the thoughtless adoption of techniques in a faddish effort among educators to maintain interest and produce results. In any case, efforts to choose purposely from among alternatives can only contribute to the health of the church.

A FUTURE POSSIBILITY: RECONCEPTUALIZATION

In this postmodern age, education and theology are already at work in reconceptualizing their fields, but only in beginning stages. Is everything that happens education, or is only instruction education, or is socialization to be equated with education? Certainly traditional schooling is only one setting among many. Increasingly, the congregation is seen as basic. But snippets of ideas detached from comprehensive theories or systems are inadequate. What is called for is a view of a whole ecology of religious education, held together by metaphors or images or concepts that make thought possible and that hold motivational power. Whatever that image is, it may well emerge out of the dialogue between theologians and educators.

Two encouraging developments in the realm of theology already offer promise. One has to do with the rethinking of theological education, referring to preparation for ordained ministry. Edward Farley seeks to find ways to overcome the fragmentation of theological education and to regain that underlying unity found in the view of theology as *habitus*, or "wisdom," a disposition and orientation of the soul itself (*Theologia*, 1983, and other writings). Moreover, even the use of the term "theological education" for clergy is absurd, he says. *All* Christians need theological education, with the wisdom that unifies life. Reconceptualization that includes both lay and clergy is Farley's present task, and for laity he sees attention to "ordered learning" as central to education. A part of this same development, attending to graduate professional theological education is a new attention to "practical theology." Friedrich Schleiermacher's *Brief Outline of the Study of Theology* in 1811 presented theology as having three parts, philosophical, historical, and practical—with practical theology as the "crown." That set of categories and interrelationships is being analyzed and evaluated anew, with the resulting emergence of practical theology viewed as a new genre. In the attempt to find ways of relating theory and practice, of expressing ultimate goals in proximate terms that take into account social, cultural, and psychological factors, a step is being taken in developing modes of theological reflection that structure analysis of experience. What is happening in theological education is of importance to congregational education, both because education in that setting will reflect changes in preparation of pastoral leaders and because the insights are directly applicable to the theological education of laity.

A second development is the effort of theologians to find new ways of conceptualizing the theological task. David Tracy's "revisionist" has already been mentioned. George Lindbeck's *The Nature of Doctrine* (1984) offers one of the most stimulating proposals yet to appear. He sees that traditionally theologians have approached doctrine as the cognitive aspect of religion, understood primarily in propositions or as the "experiential-expressive" interpretation of religion in symbols and existential orientation. Some scholars have sought to combine the two. What Lindbeck does is to propose another alternative, the cultural-linguistic approach. Theology is to be undertaken not in cognitive isolation, but in the context of history, anthropology, sociology, philosophy, and other disciplines. Formulations of meaning are to be viewed not as truth claims nor as expressive symbols, but as "communally authoritative rules of discourse, attitude, and action." Such an approach endeavors to take into account both pluralism and ecumenical concerns. Those who explore his approach will see possibilities for dealing with theology in a way that does link tradition with change and that does at least begin dealing with some of the problems faced in a rapidly changing culture. Moreover, education can share Lindbeck's concern for linking theory and practice.

What can be said in the final analysis is that the pluralism and new environment of the postliberal age call for and point to new possibilities and a close collaboration between theology and education. *See also* Education, Theories of; History of Christian Education; Interdisciplinary Studies; Methodology; Professional Study; Teaching Theory; Theological Education.

FOR FURTHER REFERENCE

Browning, Don S., ed. *Practical Theology*. San Francisco: Harper & Row, 1983.
Lindbeck, George A. *The Nature of Doctrine*. Philadelphia: Westminster, 1984.
Thompson, Norma H., ed. *Religious Education and Theology*. Birmingham, AL: Religious Education Press, 1982.

S. P. Little

Thomas Aquinas ▬▬▬▬▬

Thomas Aquinas (ca. 1225–1274), Dominican philosopher and theologian, was one of the great teachers of the Middle Ages, both by his example and by his writing. He is primarily known for the *Summa theologica* (*Summary of Theology*), which is a complete systematic exposition of theology and a summary of Christian philosophy. Many medieval theologians wrote *Summae* but his unique contribution was to reconstruct Catholic theology on a foundation of Aristotelian metaphysics. Almost every topic treated is discussed in Aristotelian terms: matter and form, potency and act, essence and existence, efficient and final causality. Thomas's other theological syntheses are a commentary on Peter Lombard's *Book of Sentences*, and the *Summa contra Gentiles*, written for those unfamiliar with Catholic doctrine. There are a number of volumes of *Quaestiones disputatae* (*Disputed Questions*) dealing with a variety of topics. Other works include commentaries on Scripture, on Aristotle and other authors, polemical writings, and devotional works. The works of Thomas Aquinas are impressive not only for their quantity but for their systematic, closely reasoned exposition.

Thomas Aquinas was above all else a teacher. He studied under Albert the Great, taught in Cologne, Paris, and various Dominican houses in

In using the prayers and moral code as the text, Thomas takes the order of catechesis from the message itself. He practices his own principles of pedagogy by expanding and explicating what has been familiar to the people since they were children. The Lenten sermons begin with a profound biblical and patristic understanding of faith, appeal to human experience, and employ a frequent use of examples and analogies to replace scientific definitions and explanations. *See also* Aristotle; Disputation; History of Christian Education; Thomism.

FOR FURTHER REFERENCE

Ayo, Nicholas, ed. and trans. *The Sermon Conferences of St. Thomas Aquinas on the Apostle's Creed.* Notre Dame, IN: University of Notre Dame Press, 1988.

Weisheipl, James A. *Friar Thomas d'Aquino: His Life, Thought, and Work.* Garden City, NY: Doubleday, 1974.

C. Dooley

Italy, and established a house of studies in Naples. He died on his way to the Council of Lyon in 1274.

Thomas's principles of psychology and pedagogy influenced subsequent Christian education. His treatise *De magistro* (*Concerning the Teacher*, ca. 1257) contained basic principles of education. According to Thomas, learning is self-activity on the part of the student who, through natural reason, comes to a knowledge of the unknown. Teaching is the process of drawing out the natural reason of the learner and leading the student from the known to the unknown. The *Summa theologica* expands and develops the educational principles of *De magistro*. His teachings on the nature and operations of the soul, the acquisition of knowledge, human acts, the training of the will, the development of habits, and the emotions were the basis of the explanation of Christian doctrine for many centuries. The code of canon law (1917) mandated the study of Thomas for the theological and philosophical formation of Catholic clergy. The current code (1983) recommends that seminary students study dogmatic theology "with St. Thomas as their teacher in a special way" (Can. 252).

Although Thomas did not formulate a series of catechetical principles, he is often accorded a place in the history of catechetics because of the sermons preached during the Lenten season in Naples in 1273. These fifty-nine sermons, recorded by a scribe, are simple and clear explanations of the creed, the commandments, the Our Father, and the Hail Mary. Thomas said that there are three kinds of knowledge necessary for salvation: what to believe, what to hope for, and what to do. The first is taught in the creed, the second in the Lord's Prayer, and the third in the Pentateuch.

Thomism

Thomism is a school of theological and philosophical thought based on the works of Thomas Aquinas, an Italian Dominican priest and teacher (1225–1274). In 1879, Pope Leo XIII, in the encyclical *Aeterni Patris*, proclaimed Thomism the recommended theology and philosophy of the Roman Catholic church. The effects of the Second Vatican Council (1962–1965) ended the singular domination of classical Thomism in the schools of the church, yet its influence remains strong as an enduring heritage for Catholic theology. Thomism has also been influential in Anglicanism. The Anglican divine Richard Hooker (1554–1600) was influenced by Thomism, as was Kenneth Kirk in his work in moral theology in the early twentieth century.

FRAMEWORK AND CONTENT

Aquinas shared the medieval worldview of a rather closed and orderly universe. He found the works of classical Greek philosophy, especially Aristotle, persuasive in the building of his philosophical and theological synthesis. The world was in orderly motion with each visible effect traceable to a knowable cause and all action oriented toward proper and discernible ends. Both the intellect and the will could be properly formed in truth and right by understanding the potentialities inherent in nature and acting according to their proper motion and direction. Thomistic thought was grounded in a highly developed metaphysics that claimed insight into the essential structures of reality through the operations of the human intellect.

Despite his debt to Greek thought, Aquinas was first and foremost a theologian. All of his works intended to offer rational foundation and explanation for the central confessions of the faith, first for nonbelievers (e.g., *Summa contra Gentiles*) and then for Christian students (e.g., *Summa theologica*). Thomism is the most important example of the systematic and orderly Christian philosophy and theology known as Scholasticism, i.e., philosophy and theology of and for "the schools."

The first premise in Aquinas's theological system suggests an analogy between the discernible world around us and the nature of God and God's will "above" us. Such a principle of analogical relation—not correspondence—between God and world was firmly rooted for Aquinas in the Christian doctrine of creation. God, who created the world, is not totally lost to the world through sin. Though alienating (both clouding the intellect and binding the will), sin does not obliterate the ongoing sacramental disclosures of God's presence in the physical universe. The world itself—its nature and essence—remains disclosive of God's presence and will and is thus a sacramental dwelling. The ability of the intellect to know God and of the will to act virtuously according to the divine will and providence is a continuing gift and grace of the Creator. Therefore, in Thomistic thought physical and human nature and divine grace, though alienated, are not totally separated. Human reason is a primary gift of God—the mark and image of God upon the human soul and the ground of the spiritual life. Because of this grace, divine revelation and its mysteries can be given an adequate, though incomplete, rational theological foundation. As a guide for a life of virtue (habits of moral interpretation and judgment), a rational "natural law" exists that forms a connection between divinely revealed law (Scripture) and civic law for the common good.

Aquinas's Christology is set within this sacramental framework. Jesus, as the Christ, is the perfect reconciliation of fallen human nature and originating grace. What had been torn apart by sin was now brought together in Christ, whose redemptive work was effective in the world from the beginning of human time. Brought to its fullness in Jesus Christ, human life in the world is now a work of entrance into this renewed and sanctifying reconciliation of nature and grace, reason and revelation, humanity and divinity. In this way, Aquinas, and Thomism in general, attempts to interrelate the Christian doctrines of creation, redemption, and sanctification.

MODERN INFLUENCES AND UNDERSTANDINGS

While Thomism's influence has been great in Catholicism, especially among Dominican and Jesuit teachers, other approaches were present, notably the Franciscan, whose debt was more to the rather "mystical" Platonic traditions than to the more "empirical" Aristotelian. In later years, some of Aquinas's followers often lapsed into unsophisticated interpretations and reduced his work to poorly formed manuals of doctrine, morality, and piety.

In the nineteenth and twentieth centuries, the rise of new philosophies and modern critical theologies of history, Scripture, and doctrine influenced a reconstruction of the work of Aquinas known as neo-Thomism. While accepting the major premises of Thomism, these teachers and theologians began to take seriously the shifts in understanding of the world and our place in it that had occurred since the Middle Ages. The rather vertical framework of God "above" and humanity "below" gave way to a more horizontal image for understanding the role of the graced and fallen human subject in the divine economy (household) of salvation. This "turn to the subject" had important effects, reemphasizing the human experience of the liberating grace of God's presence amid the sinful enslavements of human history. Thus, theological anthropology—the nature and role of humanity in the divine economy—became a major subject of the neo-Thomistic revival. The neo-Thomists taught that a necessary first subject of theology, correlative to the word of God, was the human hearer of that word. The works of the Jesuit Karl Rahner (e.g., *Spirit in the World*, 1968; *Hearers of the Word*, 1969) have been the most influential twentieth-century contribution in the neo-Thomistic revival. Other important proponents of neo-Thomism are the Roman Catholics Joseph Maréchal, Étienne Gilson, Jacques Maritain, and Bernard Lonergan.

The religious education of adults, when it involves serious theological study, will include some work from the neo-Thomist tradition, difficult as it is. Studied in theological schools, this thought has become synonymous with study that stretches the mind and impels learners to view the Christian faith in relation to the intellectual endeavors of the day. Some introduction to the contemporary writers noted here would be included. *See also* Grace; Roman Catholic Education; Thomas Aquinas; Vatican II.

J. Monti

Time Arrangements

The time arrangements for religious education are both challenging and limiting in their definiteness. Educational influences are inherent wherever persons meet, the faith is proclaimed and celebrated, and encounters with daily living force rethinking of old patterns and responses. However, religious education cannot be left to happenstance; it must be intentional and every effort made to make it truly life-changing, productive of reflection, experience widening, enlarging to the understanding, and motivating for action.

Three concerns focus the attention on time arrangements for religious education: the desire to make the time allotment more effective, the desire to extend the time available for education in religion, and the desire to provide additional experiences in faith for greater growth in the faith. Once an individual or a group discovers the inner joy and satisfaction that comes with new understandings of the rich heritage and relevance of faith for daily living, enthusiasms for new adventures in such growing will give momentum for further study and action. Time must also be allotted and seen to be educational time for follow-up, i.e., formal and informal evaluation, both during and at the conclusion of units of learning.

To make the time allotment (usually one hour a week on Saturday or Sunday morning) more effective, the recruiting of creative leaders must accompany the analysis of current progress, the needs of the congregation, and the setting forth of goals for specific groups within a congregation and for the congregation as a whole. In implementing units of study, activities, and programs directed toward achieving these goals there must be an atmosphere that acknowledges the importance of education in the faith and promotes openness to change, the willingness to adapt to new situations as they arise. Challenges to creative sharing of time, talents, gifts, and commitment will call forth leaders who are seeking unity and strength for living in these demanding and chaotic days.

A number of schemes for extending the time available for religious education have come into use. Released time is still an option in some areas. In this plan, a public school agrees, with parental permission, to release children in particular grades for one class period a week to participate in a program of religious education, usually ecumenical in nature, off the school grounds. In some states, teacher training programs for the teaching of religion as a second field have made possible objective teaching about religion in the school class (frequently as a unit within literature or social studies). An organization, the National Council of Religion and Public Education, works in making this option open and effective. And in recent years, the number of evangelical Protestant schools has grown, joining other long-established traditions (Roman Catholic, Lutheran, Episcopal, Christian Reformed, and Jewish) of having all of a child's education under direct religious influence.

Conducting a program on a weekday after school or in the early evening or on a Saturday morning is still an option, used primarily by Confraternity of Christian Doctrine (CCD) programs, children's choirs, and confirmation classes, although these must compete with secular activities held during the same times. Summer vacation schools, summer camps and conferences, and work camps provide further extensions of time for more intensive study, discussion, and fellowship. Work camps often give youth opportunities for service and interaction with youth from other cultures.

Providing additional, nonclassroom experiences in the heritage and mission of the faith requires the leader of the congregation to be committed to the teaching ministry. Those in the decision-making body of the group need to recognize the importance of providing growing experiences for the gathered group, so that an atmosphere flourishes in which learning, practicing, serving are seen as a responsibility under God for all members.

The great festivals of the faith—Christmas, Easter, Passover—can be enriched as children and parents participate in liturgies and act out for the present the meaning of the festivals. Here the setting of goals and planning are imperative so that the group can process the meanings in the event, take roles, challenge each other to deeper commitment. Significant events in individual and group living will be seen as opportunities for recommitment, challenges to further growth. Baptisms, bar/bas mitzvahs, times of confirmation, anniversaries, and special meals are all times when the congregation as a whole can grow in personal understanding and renewed vows.

Intergenerational events invite older members to share memories and knowledge. Developing volunteer patterns to help with the congregational and community needs calls for seminars, teaching, and learning that is reciprocal and relational. The setting of goals, planning, and being faithful in tasks must be seen as educational time. Small neighborhood fellowship groups provide opportunities for growth in prayer, information, and understanding, call for support relationships, and lead to creative service and further growth. The families in the congregation are a fundamental unit of growth. In this day families need undergirding and help. Activities for single parents, singles, the elderly need special planning.

Time arrangements for all forms of religious education can be as flexible as educators and leaders are willing to plan and implement. *See also* After-school Center; Conference; Planning; Private Religious Schools; Sunday School; Vacation Church School; Workshop.

FOR FURTHER REFERENCE

Brown, Marion E., and Marjorie G. Prentice. *Christian Education in the Year 2000*. Valley Forge, PA: Judson, 1984.

Wyckoff, D. Campbell. *Renewing the Sunday*

School and the CCD. Birmingham, AL: Religious Education Press, 1986.

L. C. Olds

Time Line

A time line is a linear graphic form that pictures the flow of historical events. In Bible study, depicting both biblical events and general history helps students understand how biblical history fits into the flow of the total history of the world. The present is usually designated on the graph as well.

Time lines may simply include words and numbers to designate the gradations in history that are relevant to the study. However, pictures are often used to depict some or all of the events of importance and are especially useful for teaching children.

Time lines are valuable to use for all age groups beginning with third and fourth grades and extending through adults. These should be used for lesson series dealing with biblical history to assure understanding of chronological development. *See also* Bible Study; History, Teaching of; Visual Methods.

E. A. Daniel

Torah as Teaching

"Torah" comes from the Hebrew root *yarah* meaning "to teach." Thus, Torah—the Jewish scriptural tradition—becomes a teaching and learning vehicle, imparting to its adherents over the course of the generations the fundamentals of the Jewish religious faith, heritage, and tradition.

In its briefest formulation, Torah is understood to be the Five Books of Moses (i.e., Bereshit/Genesis, Shemot/Exodus, Vayikra/Leviticus, Bamidbar/Numbers, and Devarim/Deuteronomy). Understood, however, as the Jewish Holy Scriptures, it likewise encompasses the books of the Prophets (Neviim) and Writings (Ketuvim), thus, thirty-six works in all. The mnemonic Tanach is often used for the three parts of the Torah: *Ta,* Torah; *Na,* Neviim; and *Ch,* Ketuvim. Understood in its widest sense, Torah includes *all* Jewish writings subsequent to the canonized text whose purpose is the expansion and explication of Jewish religioethical values.

TRANSMISSION AND CANONIZATION

According to Jewish scriptural tradition as recorded, and still today believed by many within (and without) the Orthodox Jewish communities, Moses, in private communion with God for forty days and forty nights atop Mount Sinai, in fasting and in prayer, functioned as "secretary" to God and returned to the children of Israel with the complete text of the divine revelation—the Humash, or Five Books of Moses—symbolized by the Ten Commandments. Upon seeing the sinning of the children of Israel in worshiping the golden calf under his brother Aaron, he shattered and thus destroyed the original tablets and returned to Mount Sinai in order to replace them, both sets to be kept in the Ark of the Covenant, lost to us today despite the persistance of many in attempting to unearth it.

An alternative understanding, the result of both modern critical biblical scholarship and a rejection of traditional thinking, is that Torah resulted from the evolving nature of the Jewish people over the course of approximately a thousand years (2,000 B.C.–1,000 B.C.) in response to what is perceived to be the divine call and "inspiration" of God. Thus, it is held by the majority of the nontraditional communities, primarily Reform, Conservative, and Reconstructionist, to be a *human* document rather than a divine pronouncement. The two views are ultimately irreconcilable.

There is mention of the Torah of Moses in 2 Chronicles 25:4 and 35:12. King Josiah (622 B.C.) was brought a copy of the Torah during the repair of the temple (2 Chronicles 34:14), and this was read later at the renewing of the covenant. The canon was probably established during the exilic period (beginning 586 B.C.).

The acceptance of the Neviim (Prophets) as canonical took place after the exile but before the Greek period (late fourth century B.C.). This chronology is probable because they are not accepted as such by the Samaritans, those Jews who had intermarried with the people of the land in Samaria during the exile. Daniel, Ezra–Nehemiah, and Chronicles are not in this group.

The Ketuvim (Writings) were accepted still later. Esther, for example, was not found among the Dead Sea Scrolls. A council of the Sanhedrin met at Jamnia (Jabneal), in A.D. 90, and tradition says that the present limits of the canon were established then.

STUDY AND INTERPRETATION

The people of Israel were excluded from the community of humankind subsequent to the destruction of the Second Temple by the Romans in the year A.D. 70, and Torah became the primary vehicle of both general Jewish education and Jewish religious education, later supplemented by the Mishnah (the first compilation of the Jewish legal tradition, finished in Palestine in A.D. 220) and the Talmud (compilation of the academy discussions of the mishnaic tradition in both Palestine and Babylonia, finished initially in approximately A.D. 500, though continuously enlarged upon up to the present time).

From the standpoint of Jewish pedagogy, the

serious study of the Torah enables the Jew to become knowledgeable in the primary resource of the Jewish people and alert to his or her responsibilities as a Jew. It is instrumental in enabling the committed Jew to achieve the goal of making a positive Jewish commitment. It does this through:

1. Promoting an understanding of historical Jewish expectations
2. Rooting the individual Jew in a historic community
3. Fostering a positive relationship between the individual Jew and God
4. Providing historic Jewish answers to some of life's most challenging questions and dilemmas

So significant did the study of the Torah become in the life of the Jewish people and Jewish community that a system of fathoming out its meaning known as midrash (from the Hebrew *drsh*; to "search out" or "draw out") was developed early on in postbiblical rabbinic Judaism and continues to this day. Its frame of reference is Torah as the literal Word of God that has meaning down to each individual word, grammatical construction, and particular phraseology. Those rabbinical authorities who commanded the respect of their communities were thus regarded by the populace and chose to perceive themselves as interpreters of biblical tradition rather than innovators who built upon biblical tradition to meet the exigencies of the day.

The method of doing midrash is best summed up in the Hebrew acronym *pardes*, "orchard." Indeed, the Jewish Bible is likened to an orchard from which truths may be harvested. The word itself is said to remind Jews of the four ways in which a given biblical verse may be interpreted:

● *Pa*, *p'shat*, the *simplest* level of meaning of a given text
● *R*, *remez*, the understanding that a given text is an *allusion*, hinting at some truth not readily apparent
● *De*, *drash*, the meaning that will become apparent to the student only when he or she truly understands the meaning of the words
● *S*, *sod*, the *mystical* meaning of text only apparent to those well versed in the mystical traditions of the Jewish people

Together with the legal traditions of Judaism, embodied in both Mishnah and Talmud, the literature of the midrash was said to comprise the "oral Torah" of Jewish religious tradition, also given by God to Moses at Mount Sinai. Regardless of whether or not one accepts this explanation of its origins, the oral Torah was, indeed, at first an *oral* tradition passed on from rabbinic teachers to rabbinic students who, in turn, became teachers

and passed these traditions on to their students. Only when the very real threat of Jewish survival became of paramount importance, beginning with the Roman period of oppression, were these traditions written down.

Liturgically, selections from Torah (here the Five Books of Moses only) are read during the daylight hours at these worship services: Mondays and Thursdays (the old market days in Jerusalem), Sabbaths and festivals, and the appearance of the new moon, which marked the beginning of the new Hebrew month. An additional passage of Jewish scriptures—usually from the Prophets and thematically related to the first selection—was called the Haftarah, which is now understood to mean "conclusion" and may very well have marked the actual conclusion of the worship service. Today, within both Orthodox and Conservative traditions, the entire selection of verses of both Torah and Haftarah are read, while in Reform Jewish tradition, at the discretion of the reader, usually the rabbi, the essential verses of each are read. Within all branches of the Jewish religious tradition, the Torah continues to serve as the fundamental source of preaching and teaching within contemporary Jewish congregations.

The current debates within the Christian communities between literalist and nonliteralist interpretations of Scriptures do not occupy the same place in the Jewish communities, though, as was mentioned above, there are two significantly different understandings of the nature of divine revelation and the role of Torah as the medium through which that revelation took place. Historically and contemporarily, the Jewish people have *not* demanded adherence to a single set of beliefs and understandings as regards the texts of Scripture. To be sure, however, up until the rise of modern, critical scholarship in the mid-1700s, the overwhelming majority of Jews accepted the transmission of the Torah as it presented itself, rather than the alternative view briefly described above. Difference in interpretation of given scriptural passages has a long and honorable tradition among the Jewish people and continues even today with the publication of an ever-increasing number of volumes dealing with Torah.

FOR FURTHER REFERENCE

The closest to an "official" publishing house for the American Jewish community is the Jewish Publication Society in Philadelphia, Pennsylvania, which first published The Holy Scriptures According to the Masoretic Tradition in 1917 in the highborn English style of the King James Version and subsequently published The Torah (1962), The Prophets (1978), and The Writings (1982), all three of which rendered the Hebrew text into contemporary English.

Additional publications of Torah with commentaries are *The Pentateuch with Haftorahs*, by

Joseph Hertz (London: Soncino Press, 1964), an Orthodox publication; *The Pentateuch*, by A. Cohen (London: Soncino, 1966), also Orthodox in its orientation; *The Torah: A Modern Commentary*, by W. Gunther Plaut and Bernard Bamberger (New York: Union of American Hebrew Congregations, 1981), a liberal commentary; and the ongoing series of publications of individual volumes under the title Artscroll Tanach Series by Mesorah Publications in New York, all within the Orthodox tradition. *See also* Jewish Education; Jewish Theological Concepts; Judaism; Torah, Study and Teaching of.

S. L. Jacobs

Torah, Study and Teaching of

Torah is one of the most important symbols and concepts in the Jewish tradition. This article will describe the study of the Torah, the teaching of Torah, and the Torah's meaning for religious education today.

Like central concepts of other religious traditions, Torah has several meanings. At its most basic level "Torah" refers to the first five books of the Hebrew Bible, which are also referred to as the Five Books of Moses (Genesis, Exodus, Leviticus, Numbers, and Deuteronomy).

"Torah" also refers to "the teaching" or "teachings." It comes from the Hebrew root *Yud Resh Hay* (denoted at times by the acronym *yarah*), meaning "teaching, doctrine, or instruction." In this context, Torah refers to all of the teachings of both the written Torah (Torah, Prophets, and Writings) and the oral Torah (the Mishnah and Gemara, the two parts of the Talmud). For liberal Jews the use of Torah in this context also includes the midrash (other exegetical commentaries that were more concerned with creative interpretation in order to understand the law) and the more modern writings.

"Torah" is also used to refer to a specific set of laws such as Torat Cohaneem (the Torah of the Priests, usually the book of Leviticus) and Torat Mishpacha (Laws of the Family). This use of Torah can also refer to a system of thought of a particular commentator, e.g., the Torah of Maimonides or the Torah of Rashi.

The canonization of the texts of Torah took place in Babylonia during the exile (586 B.C.). We have records that at least part of the text was recited previously by Samuel. Ezra also read from a text of the Torah to those Jews who returned to Judah and Jerusalem. There seems to be evidence from discussion in the halakah (legal discussions in the Talmud and midrash) that there was a single official text during the Second Temple period (515 B.C.–A.D. 70).

Biblical scholars suggest that the canonization

took several of the epic narratives and the stories of the older northern and southern kingdoms and interwove them into one story text. Later additions of laws were made. An area of canonical criticism has developed that parallels the study of how the text developed. The important issues for religious education with regard to the canonization still center on the authority and sacredness of the text itself.

STUDY OF TORAH

Jews engage in the study of Torah as one of their most important activities. A child is blessed by wishing him a life of *torah* (meaning study), *chuppah* (marriage), and *mitzvah* (good deeds). The Torah is read aloud weekly: in traditional synagogues on Monday, Thursday, and Saturday; in less traditional synagogues on Sabbath (usually Friday evening or Saturday mornings) only. The Torah is divided into portions so that it can be read in its entirety every year. Some synagogues follow a triennial reading pattern in which one-third of the portion is read and studied each year so that over a three-year cycle the whole Torah is read. The portions are called Parshat HaShavuah or "portion of the week." There are also special Torah readings for festivals and for the new month or new moon.

Torah study has continued throughout the ages. As a result there are many important interpreters and interpretations of Torah. An interpreter may take any of several approaches to the text. There is a difference between reading the text as a literal document and attempting to find the plain meaning (*p'shat*) and reading the text as an allegorical or philosophical work. In rabbinic terms the controversy is about whether the Torah was written *b'lishon ha'adam* or *lo bilshon ha'adam* ("in the words of man or not").

Some of the most important early Torah commentators and interpreters were Philo (ca. 20 B.C.–A.D. 50), who taught that Torah was the ideal law of the philosophers; Josephus (ca. A.D. 38–100), whose interpretation of the Torah represented a moral and universalistic reading; Saadia (882–942), who understood the Torah as a nationalist text, both ethical and religious, whose understanding was possible through reason. Also in the rationalist tradition of Saadia were such greats as Bahya ben Joseph ibn Pakuda (eleventh-century Spain) and Joseph ibn Zaddik (d. 1149). One of the most famous commentators of the rationalist school is Abraham ben Meïr ibn Ezra (1089–1164). He emphasized clarifying the grammar in order to understand the text. Judah Halevi (ca. 1075–1141) opposed the rationalist school and proposed that the divine laws could not be comprehended by reason alone.

Three other commentators who are well-known took markedly different positions with regard to interpretation. Rashi (Rabbi Solomon ben

Isaac, 1040–1105, France) was interested in the plain (*p'shat*) meaning of the text and used grammar and analysis along with the older rabbinic materials (*d'rash*). David Kimhi (otherwise known by the acronym RaDaK, 1160?–?1235) used grammar and lexicography in his commentaries but also wrote with clarity and passion in relating the Torah to issues of his time. And last, Nachmanides (Moses ben Nachman, otherwise known by the acronym RaMBaN, 1194–1270, Spain) conveys philosophical ideas but also wove cabalistic (mystical) elements into his reading. He suggests that everything might be found in the Torah, including science and astrology, if we only knew how to discover it.

Notwithstanding their different approaches, all these commentators still believed that the Torah was the word of God directly passed to Moses and then to the elders and onward down the line. Although there was controversy about how the revelation was done—word by word, by phrases, or in whole books, in dreams or orally—the divine nature of the revelation itself was never questioned. Only in modern times has literary or higher criticism (which deals not only with date but also with authorship and editing) developed. Modern interpretations and readings are often combinations of the historicocritical methods, the documentary hypothesis (explored by the more "scientific" historical scholars), and the old *p'shat* and *d'rash* methods. W. Gunther Plaut, Harry M. Orlinsky, J. H. Hertz, and E. A. Speiser and Nehama Leibowitz are fine examples of this modern style of commentary and Torah study.

TEACHING TORAH

Jewish religious educators have developed a numbers method for the teaching of Torah. Many still use the Parashat HaShavuah pattern, in which the portion of the week is discussed during the week it is read in the synagogue. In this form either the narrative as a whole or a line by line, word by word (exegetical) approach may be used. Others have reorganized the stories and teachings in the Torah by theme such as covenant, peace, family, caring for the widow and orphan, the Mishkan (Tabernacle), military tactics, festivals, holy days, sacrifices, and agricultural rules. Other teachers attempt to organize the stories and laws in chronological order; still others break down the text into its original sections according to the documentary hypothesis and teach sections that were attributed to one editor or another.

Whichever approach is adopted, various techniques of teaching have been employed. Debates, discussions, and reading the text alongside its commentaries are common practice. Examination of the language, poetry, literary images, and metaphors is a frequent technique. Drama and role playing are methods employed to make the text and characters come alive for students. Creating artistic projects (sculpture, drawings, paintings, models) helps enhance other teaching techniques, as do the more recent audiovisual interpretations of the text itself. In using each of these techniques the teacher is helping the student to participate in the ongoing process of interpreting the text and connecting the new generation to those who have studied Torah in the past.

Since Torah is such a central part of Jewish life it is taught in many settings. Whether in Jewish day schools and yeshivot (institutions of higher Jewish learning), adult education classes, supplementary religious schools, Sunday schools, or in summer camps, Torah is a major topic. Many Jewish organizations begin their meetings with a *d'var Torah* (literally, "a word of Torah" but usually referring to a short lesson about Jewish values or a portion of Jewish law), and some families have developed time (usually on the Sabbath) when Torah is discussed. According to the verses in Deuteronomy 6:6–7, "And these words which I command thee this day shalt be upon thy heart, and thou shalt teach them diligently unto thy children," (JPS) to learn and to teach Torah is one of the highest forms of religious education in which a Jew can participate.

IMPORTANCE FOR TODAY

Torah is still the center of most Jewish religious education. However the text is read, whether as the word of God or the story of a people, the Torah remains a source of inspiration and connections to the past, present, and future of the Jewish people. That the Torah has become a living foundation for both sister faiths (Christianity and Islam) and still remains a vital work of literature demonstrates the wisdom of its canonization. It is a record of a people's encounter with God and of the ongoing covenant that God has forged with human beings. For the Jew, "It is a tree of life to those who hold it fast. Its ways are ways of pleasantness and all its paths are peace" (Prov. 3:18, 17, author's paraphrase). *See also* Jewish Education; Jewish Theological Concepts; Judaism; Torah as Teaching.

FOR FURTHER REFERENCE

Hertz, J. H., ed. *The Pentateuch and Haftorahs.* London: Soncino Press, 1966.

Leibowitz, Nehama. *Studies in . . . Bereshit.* (One for each book of the Torah.) Jerusalem: World Zionist Organization, 1980.

Orlinsky, Harry M. *Understanding the Bible Through History and Archaeology.* New York: KTAV, 1972.

Sanders, James A. *Torah and Canon.* Philadelphia: Fortress Press, 1972.

The Torah: A Modern Commentary. (With commentaries by Plaut, Bamberger, and Hallo.) New York: Union of American Hebrew Congregations, 1980.

S. H. Blumberg

Tradition

Tradition and experience form the components that define the meaning and describe the function of religious education. The discussion of tradition, therefore, requires a prior consideration of religious education.

"Religious education" is the most comprehensive term for all the many conscious and customary, but always intentional, activities by which the members of a community of religious people promote the belief, belonging, behavior, loyalty, and mode of consciousness they believe constitute faithfulness to the sacred mystery and precious meaning of that people.

TRADITION AND EXPERIENCE

In the many activities of religious education, activities ranging from consciously reflective theological inquiry to customary everyday patterns of relationship, the meaning of the activity is defined by and in the polarity: tradition and experience. Rich religious life as well as expert theological work both require knowledge of and loyalty to an inherited way of life and a worldview the cumulative message of which is understood to be the revelation of what it means to be truly human in God. So, too, religiousness in the normative sense entails a special alertness to the voice of God in contemporary experience, both interior and social experience. Where religious life gravitates to one or the other pole, breaking the creative tension between tradition and experience, it becomes archaic or faddist.

In the common era, dramatic examples of the tension between tradition and contemporary experience begin with the controversy between Paul and the Jerusalem church concerning gentile converts (Acts 15:1–35). In Saint Anselm's thirteenth-century formulation of the function of theology, the polarity is also present. In the formula "faith seeking understanding," faith stands for the "given" of tradition and understanding for the contemporary experience. In Anselm's time part of that contemporary experience was the use of Aristotelian categories of rational inquiry as helpful tools for rendering revelation more vivid. In the sixteenth century, Martin Luther evoked the power of Scripture—traditional message—against the contemporary experience of the church.

ITS DYNAMIC CHARACTER

In our time there are a variety of illuminating expressions of the polarity. It is crucial at this point, however, to understand that the polarity, tradition (understood as that which is handed on) and experience, is itself tradition! The deposit of inherited beliefs, behaviors, and loyalties receives its normative expression through a process of interpretation influenced by the experience of the church in each historical epoch: it is, as well, perennially reinterpreted in the light of what contemporary believers experience as the working of the Holy Spirit through the "signs of the times" in their historical moment.

Nowhere is the dynamic character of tradition more in evidence than in the revelation of layers of tradition in the formation of Scripture made available by modern scriptural scholarship. This same source also underlines the dialectical function of religious education as the midwife of new and richer belief, of belonging and behavior, of religious loyalty and consciousness that result when inherited tradition and contemporary experience are forced to modify each other.

Richard P. McBrien speaks of three layers of tradition uncovered by the three methods of critical analysis of Scripture. Historical criticism, revealing the first layer, discloses the basic historical foundation and context within which Scripture was written. Form criticism is "concerned primarily with the formation of the Gospel tradition which occurred through catechesis and liturgical expressions roughly between A.D. 35 and 60." Form criticism analyzes "typical features of biblical texts (hymns, acclamations, confessions, sermons, instructional materials, editorial remarks, descriptive narratives, sayings of Jesus, dialogues, Old Testament allusions and quotations)" (*Catholicism*, vol. 1, p. 395). The many insights resulting from form-critical scholarship are proof of the long period of oral tradition preceding the writing of both Hebrew and Christian Scripture. Finally, redaction criticism tries to discover ideas governing the final editing of the Gospels as we have them today. In each of these specialties the interplay of contemporary experience and inherited belief, which find expression in Scripture itself, is fully revealed and the dynamic and dialectical character of tradition affirmed. It is for this reason Klaus Koch can write convincingly, "The biblical word has proven to be not truth in a fossilized, unchanging sense, but truth which is constantly adapting itself to the circumstances of the time" (*The Growth of the Biblical Tradition*, p. 100).

RELIGIOUS EDUCATION AS FORGE FOR AUTHENTIC TRADITION

The point bears repeating: living and authentic tradition is forged in the polarity of inherited tradition and contemporary experience. Every activity that enables this encounter, from the most sophisticated theological inquiry to simple patterns of healthy family life, is religious education.

The contemporary theological and religious educational expressions of the truth that tradition is a composite of the inherited and the contemporary are many, varied, and rich. The best-known theological expression of this truth in our time is probably that of Paul Tillich. Tillich's method of correlation requires that theological work be done in the light of the "message" and the "situation" (*Systematic Theology*, vol. 1). An expression of the notion by a religious educator in our time and culture is probably that implied in George Albert Coe's well-known rhetorical question, "Shall the primary purpose of Christian education be to hand on a tradition or to create a new world?" (*What Is Christian Education?*, 1929). The writings of Gabriel Moran contain a remarkably subtle and nuanced treatment of tradition and experience when he deals with the notions of "religion" and "education."

Sometimes religion is understood as resistance to arid traditionalism. Its function in relationship to education is to keep human beings open to insight and to revelation available through our presence to experience. In this formulation, education is society's—including the religious institutions'—instrument of orthodoxy; it functions to answer the questions raised by life with inherited traditional answers. Elsewhere in Moran's writings, it is education of a certain quality that is the instrument of creativity in human life and religion that functions to provide orthodox answers to life's questions. Thomas H. Groome has expressed this insight in a theory of religious education in which a normative story and vision are in dialectical interaction with personal and contemporary story and vision (*Christian Religious Education*, 1982).

Among the most expressive and compelling formulations of this issue are those by theologian David Tracy and religious educator Mary C. Boys. In *Blessed Rage for Order* (1975), Tracy explicates a "revisionist" theological model calling for a critical correlation between contemporary human experience and the Christian fact. His is an especially subtle advocacy for a theological method and means of religious living that honor both inherited tradition and contemporary experience. At every point in the conversation, the Christian fact is modified by contemporary experience and this experience purified in dialectical encounter with the Christian fact. In *The Analogical Imagination* (1985), Tracy illuminates this same issue by exploring the nature of the classic person, text, or event. The classic, he tells us, is the person, text, or event that contains inexhaustible excess of meaning. It is available to each generation for deeper revelation of what it means to be human. This is yet another expression of the interplay of tradition and experience, for classic persons, as in Jesus of Nazareth, text, as in Hebrew and Christian Scripture, and event, as in the Passion, death, and resurrection of Jesus the Christ, are the very foundation and essence of what is inherited. The meanings of these classics are endlessly reinterpreted and deepened in each generation.

For Mary C. Boys religious education makes tradition "accessible," and in the very process it renders tradition's transformative power accessible as well. She writes, "If religious education is

to avoid the pitfalls of fossilization and an uncritical pursuit of relevance, then it must both serve and change, continue ancient symbols and explore new possibilities, hand on tradition and transform the world. Traditions, like roots, are lifelines to vital sources from which new entities develop. Tradition exists to make transformation possible" ("Access to Traditions and Transformation," p. 14). Boys makes explicit the means religious education has at its command to render traditional wisdom ever new and a vehicle of transformed lives and consciousness. "Accessibility is best seen in its exemplars: erecting bridges, making metaphors, building highways, providing introductions and commentaries, translating foreign terms, mapmaking and ice-breaking (literally and figuratively) are all instances. Destruction is also an exemplar; it offers a way of removing obstacles. Demolition experts, for instance, use radical means in a controlled fashion as the initial step in providing access" ("Access to Traditions and Transformation," p. 15).

The consideration of tradition, in the context of the desire to understand theological inquiry or the broader human activity of religious education, is an opportunity to reaffirm our openness to change. Under its influence, religious persons will neither retreat from loyalty to the sources of their historical identity nor from a really profound act of faith in the ongoing presence and work of God's Spirit in human history, for it is the reality of God's continuing engagement in human history that is at stake in insisting on the relationship between tradition and experience. *See also* Action-Reflection; Culture; Doctrine/Dogma; Indoctrination; Methodology; Theology and Education; Transmission.

FOR FURTHER REFERENCE

Boys, Mary C. "Access to Traditions and Transformation." In *Tradition and Transformation in Religious Education*. Edited by Padraic O'Hare. Birmingham, AL: Religious Education Press, 1979.

———. *Educating in Faith: Maps & Visions*. San Francisco: Harper & Row, 1989.

Groome, Thomas H. *Christian Religious Education*. San Francisco: Harper & Row, 1985.

Koch, Klaus. *The Growth of the Biblical Tradition*. New York: Scribner, 1968.

McBrien, Richard P. *Catholicism*. 2 vols. San Francisco: Harper & Row, 1980.

Moran, Gabriel. *Interplay: A Theory of Religion and Education*. Winona, MN: St. Mary's Press, 1981.

Tillich, Paul. *Systematic Theology*. 3 vols. Chicago: Univ. of Chicago Press, 1967.

Tracy, David. *Blessed Rage for Order*. New York: Seabury, 1975.

———— . *The Analogical Imagination*. New York: Crossroad, 1985.

P. O'Hare

Training

See Teaching Theory.

Transactional Analysis

Transactional analysis offers a way of understanding, analyzing, and improving interpersonal relationships. The basic theory and practice were developed by Eric Berne (1910–1970; *Games People Play, Transactional Analysis in Psychotherapy, What Do You Say After You Say Hello?*) and successfully popularized in the 1970s by Thomas Harris (*I'm O.K.—You're O.K.*). Other authors, educators, and therapists have used it in relation to child rearing, family counseling, marriage enrichment, and personal counseling. It was initially developed as a therapeutic tool to be used in a group setting. Within the church, books by Muriel James (*Born to Win* [with Dorothy Jongeward], and [with Louis Savary] *The Power at the Bottom of the Well*), Thomas C. Oden (*Game Free*), Valerie Sherwood (*Born to Love*), and others have helped make the insights of transactional analysis available to the church in its pastoral and educational life.

THREE EGO STATES

According to transactional analysis theory, within each person are three ego states, the "Parent," the "Adult," and the "Child." Each represents a source of human feelings and behaviors and each is needed for healthy human life. Personal malfunctioning and destructive relationships are the result of one of these states being underdeveloped or overly dominant.

The "Parent" carries the parenting style that one experienced as a child and represents the behaviors, attitudes, and viewpoints of one's parents or childhood authority figures. Through the "Parent" one's parents continue to influence one's behavior. The "Parent" carries a strong awareness of right and wrong but may lapse into moralism, domination, and the language and behavior of "should." The "Adult" represents the capacity to gather information, to evaluate, and decide. It acts on facts rather than feelings and is realistic and rational. The "Child" carries the memories and the attitudes of childhood. It tends to be impulsive and fun loving but may be irresponsible and suffer from feelings of inadequacy. The "Child" develops first, then the "Parent," and finally the "Adult."

Each state has a vital role to play in life but each can become distorted and so contribute to personal difficulties and impaired relationships. The "Parent" may become swollen so that the person tends to dominate others and to be overly strict and controlled. If underdeveloped, a person may lack a sense of moral responsibility. If a person lives out of the "Adult" alone, life may be sober and safe but lack imagination and joy. The "Child" may so dominate that a person becomes flippant and irresponsible or conversely may feel insignificant and without value in an adult world. Each ego state is important and psychic health results from a harmonious balance among the three.

INTERPERSONAL RELATIONSHIPS

Interpersonal relationships are affected by the ego state that people are operating out of at the time. Healthy relationships are marked by openness and a lack of hidden meanings. Typically healthy transactions are "Adult" to "Adult," "Parent" to "Child," "Child" to "Parent," and "Child" to "Child." Crossed transactions lead to inappropriate and potentially destructive relationships. If an adult person speaks to another adult from the "Parent" state, the other may respond inappropriately from the "Child" state or may ignore the attitude of the other and respond as an adult. A person may relate appropriately to another, but because of low self-esteem that person may respond from the "Child" state. Transactional analysis is aware of the possibility of deliberate or unwitting breakdowns in relationships. Relationships may also be impaired because the words of a person may on the surface appear appropriate but carry a hidden meaning intended to hurt or embarrass. Thus a comment that superficially arises from the "Adult" state may in fact carry a parental message treating another as a child.

All people have a need to be affirmed and if this need is not met, damaged and damaging relationships will occur. To know one is valued and affirmed is to know one is "okay." Mature relationships exist between people who are both "okay." A person may seek after "okayness" by putting others down (an "I'm okay–you're not okay" relationship) or have such a low self-esteem that all relationships are experienced as "I'm not okay—you're okay." So great is the human need to feel "okay," that persons will go to great extremes to gain "positive strokes." The task of the therapist is to assist persons to feel "okay," so they may be able to enter into positive, life-enhancing relationships.

Relationships are adversely affected by "games people play," habitual ways of acting that reinforce their sense of inferiority or superiority. A mature relationship is one marked by an absence of "game playing." Therapists assist people to identify the "games they play," take steps to avoid them, and learn to relate in a more honest and open manner.

A person may become locked into a pattern of behaviors (or "life script") that may owe more to childhood experience than to adult decision. Therapists help people identify and modify their "life script."

The relative simplicity of transactional analysis has commended it to many church educators, pastors, therapists, and preachers, and there have been attempts to develop a theology of relationships based on it. Some have identified a sense of "okayness" with the Christian experience of being loved and forgiven by God. Others have warned against such a simple identification. Educators influenced by the dialogical model of education associated with Reuel Howe or engaged in group life laboratories have found in transactional analysis helpful clues to the improvement of relationships and the development of authentic love. In the latter 1980s the trend among Christian educators was away from dependence on therapeutic models such as transactional analysis. *See also* Counseling; Psychosocial Development; Psychotherapy.

B. K. Rowe

Transfer of Learning

The influence of prior learning on subsequent learning or behavior or the influence of existing habits on the acquisition, retention, or performance of other habits is known as transfer of learning. Transfer can be positive, as when a person who has learned to kneel and bow her head when praying at home finds it easy to pray in a similar way at church. Transfer can be negative, as when such previous learning interferes with the expectation to stand with lifted head when praying in an Orthodox context.

It used to be thought that transfer is general and automatic. The classical doctrine of "formal discipline," for instance, justifies the study of subjects such as Latin and geometry by arguing that the mental faculties of memory and reasoning will be strengthened, thereby facilitating an easier grasp of other subjects. This was disproved in the early twentieth century by Edward Lee Thorndike, whose experiments showed that in order for transfer to take place there must be "identical elements" in the two tasks. A capacity for memorizing poetry does not necessarily mean an equal facility in memorizing Bible verses. This stance advocates intensive practice in specific learning tasks.

Other research has shown that understanding the general principles of a task makes for improved performance; that one can "learn to learn" by practicing within a category of experiences or problems; and that the more completely one learns an initial task, the greater the transfer effect on other, more complex tasks in the same category.

It would seem, then, that more positive transfer could be obtained by encouraging learners to try different ways of carrying out one particular activity in religious education rather than changing activities too often or too soon. Similarly, it would be worth one's while to make sure that basic skills are first mastered before moving on to more sophisticated or complicated ones.

In the area of teacher/leader training, one might emphasize the development of transferable skills in planning a lesson, leading a Bible study, or using a curricular resource by following the same principles. In our rapidly changing world, learning and teaching for transfer are probably as important as training for and in specific tasks.

How is transfer affected by stages in moral and faith development? By personality type? How does it function in the spiritual life? These and other areas await further research by the religious educator. *See also* Habits; Learning Theory; Skill Training.

G. A. Ng

Transmission

Transmission is the process by which the religious community passes on a living, vital faith from the older to the younger generation. The most prominent command to transmit the faith is found in a portion of Moses' address to Israel recorded in Deuteronomy 6:4–9. This is the first part of the classic confession of Judaism called the Shema (the imperative form of the Hebrew verb "to hear") which begins, "Hear, O Israel: The Lord our God is one Lord; and you shall love the Lord your God with all your heart,... soul, and... might," and continues, "These words... shall be on your heart; and you shall teach them diligently to your children." The passage specifies the times, "when you sit,... walk,... lie down,... and rise," and the placement of copies of the written words (wear them "on your hand," "between your eyes," and place them at the doorway). Family nurture was to be complemented by corporate worship and communal life. Thus, the prescription for responsible faith transmission includes diligence, repetition, materials, and acts involving many senses both at home and with the support of the community.

According to the book of Judges, successful transgenerational faith transmission was rare. The generation that was saved by God's judges (and occasionally their children) remembered and kept the faith, but the next forgot and turned to the Baals. Hence the saying, "We are always just one generation away from paganism." Had the New Testament covered a longer time span, the issue of faith transmission would have been articulated just as extensively but with some different nuances because the early Christians lived in a predominantly pagan culture in a time punctuated by persecution.

The church has taken at least four broad positions on the best way to transmit the faith within culture. The first is the attempt to develop a Christian culture. The emperor, king, and clergy, for instance, saw this as part of their responsibility in medieval Europe. This vision of a Christian civilization was strong in most of the United States until early in this century because the schools, most of the community and its organizations, and "the church" in the broad sense agreed on a grand purpose of life and values. The finale of this era was symbolized by the fact that President William Howard Taft chose to address the World Sunday School Convention that met in the United States in 1910. Many argue that when American culture became pluralistic in values, as it did from the 1920s on, faith transmission began to fail. In other words, the Sunday school, which received so much credit for faith transmission by Taft and others, required the support of a broad Christian culture. When the culture changed, the Sunday school was no longer effective.

A second alternative is to develop a Christian culture isolated within a pluralistic culture. This view argues that creating a relatively closed subculture is the best choice when the dominant culture is pluralistic or pagan. Thus, day schools, camps, youth organizations, and colleges that are uniformly Christian must be provided to supplement and support the influence of home and church. Given limited resources, the priority would be to give the children, and then youth, a "complete" Christian experience.

Another stand recommends developing a Christian counterculture interacting with the larger pluralistic culture. The common conviction in this position is that the resources of the faith community are adequate for faith transmission if they are fully utilized. Some have the resource of day schools while others "support" the public schools. The aggressive version of this interactive view seeks to influence a pluralistic culture to make it more moral and even Christian, if possible. This is seen in two versions, conservative (e.g., the antiabortion movement and the movement to return the Bible and prayer to the schools) and liberal (e.g., liberation education, released time religious education, and social action). Some argue—from a Christian education perspective—that the American church's darkest day was when it retreated from the responsibility of trying to influence or dominate cultural values. The clearest choices and, therefore, the best faith transmission occur within the clash of these cultures because of the dichotomous nature of the choices, Christ or the world.

The version of this position that is less directly involved in secular culture emphasizes being "in" but not "of" the world by enabling persons to understand the choices they make in a seductive culture. Several different educational implications of this version stand out: some emphasize spiritual development; others values clarification; and others concentrate on evangelism/discipling. This last group typically has the fastest growing, largest Sunday schools.

Finally, there is the development of an underground Christian subculture in a hostile culture. A common global-historical observation is that perceived threat, persecution, and even poverty are often associated with growing churches that effectively transmit faith almost regardless of the methods employed. The biblical warnings about the dangers of ease, wealth, and dead tradition are well founded. *See also* Culture; Secularism; Sunday School Movement; Theology and Education; Tradition.

J. R. Presseau

Trinity

Christian faith is at the same time monotheistic and trinitarian. Theological explanation of such monotheistic trinitarianism has been both varied and complex. What the earliest Christians confessed about Jesus, the Christ, the Son of God whose spirit remained with them, led to the ongoing challenge of trinitarian theological explanation. The liturgical phrase, used in creed and prayer, is "God the Father, Jesus Christ, the Son, and the Holy Spirit, one God."

The New Testament speaks of God in terms of God's presence in the world. God is the source and origin of all that was, is, and will be. Traditionally, the male image of parent was used and God has most often been spoken of as "Father" in the Christian tradition. As traditional and revered as the name "Father" for God may be, much of contemporary theology sees both the possibility and the necessity of including the name "Mother" as equally disclosive of the revelation of God as loving and caring parent. Since the mystery of God's presence with us requires the use of images of speech and thought, Christians can and ought to give serious consideration to the use of more inclusive names for God that broaden and deepen the experience of the divine-human relationship.

The core of the New Testament revelation is that God, whose presence is manifest in all creation, is now centrally manifest and proclaimed in Jesus, the Christ. New Testament Christology thus confesses God's presence in Christ as the central point of Christian faith. All of New Testament faith is a post–passion and resurrection confession: the man Jesus is now confessed by the earliest believers to have become the Christ, the chosen one, the Son of God. Christ is the Lord of the heavens and the earth and remains with them in the Spirit. Thus, the Christian theology of the Spirit that completes the images of trinitarian faith is based on the confession that the Spirit of God in Christ is a continuing presence in the community as the foundation of the church.

TRINITARIAN THEOLOGY

The earliest New Testament theologies are therefore trinitarian in nature: God's manifestation to and in the world is revealed as a threefold presence. Further developments of this monotheistic trinitarianism came later in the classical doctrinal formulations.

The classical doctrine of the Trinity takes formal shape in the creed of the Council of Nicaea (A.D. 325) and later in the Council of Chalcedon (A.D. 451). These councils used the then contemporary Greek philosophies of persons, essences, and natures, which became the basis for trinitarian theology for most of the generations of Christian history that followed. Even with some remaining theological debate between the Western and Eastern churches about whether the Spirit proceeds from both the Father and the Son (Western church) or only from the Father (Eastern church), the standard trinitarian theology of the conciliar period rather successfully accomplished an explanation of three distinct but interrelated persons sharing a common divine nature or essence. The singularity of the divine nature upheld monotheism, while the division of persons attempted to maintain fidelity to the New Testament confessions of the Christ and the continuing presence of the Spirit of God in Christ that formed the church.

With the coming of modern philosophy, and thus theology, the classical Greek foundations of trinitarian doctrine were called into question. Contemporary trinitarian theology makes use of a variety of philosophical categories and cultural images to maintain the same monotheistic and trinitarian confession. For example, the three persons of the one God could be explained through a reformulation of the *persona* in classical Greek drama, i.e., they can be seen as "character masks" of God's continuing presence with us in the divine-human drama, a drama initiated by the Creator-God, centered in Christ, and maintained by the Spirit. While God's presence with us finally remains a mystery of love, care, and forgiveness for the Christian church, theology cannot shirk its responsibility of vital and contemporary explanation.

TEACHING ABOUT THE TRINITY

For teaching, it must be remembered that the doctrine of the Trinity is not a definition but a description, and there are many ways to assist learners of all ages in understanding the three modes of God's presence in the world.

Preschool children take delight in experiencing the sights, sounds, and tastes of the world firsthand; they enjoy growing plants and caring for small animals. Parents and teachers can connect these positive experiences of joy and wonder to God as the Creator and Sustainer of all life. Stories of Jesus' love, care, and forgiveness show God in Jesus. Discussion of how God is with us today and how God works for good through people show the action of the Holy Spirit. Teachers need not use the term "Trinity" to teach God's various ways of acting in the world to young children.

The linking of the three modes of the action of God is made with older children either through their curriculum or their preparation for church membership. For those preparing for believer's baptism, the baptismal formula "in the name of the Father, the Son, and the Holy Spirit" needs explanation. For those whose confirmation rites include confessing the creed, it is important to clarify the meaning of its affirmations. The diversity in unity can be approached through the metaphor of masks (personae) or of interrelationships (one can be at the same time child, sister, and friend); role playing may be helpful here. Writing or drawing expressions of the activity of God could be used. Discussions in which the leader helps learners explore the mystery of God are important.

Adolescents and adults may be puzzled if they see the Trinity as a matter of arithmetic, so to speak, especially in view of the modern need for clear explanations. While the analogies used above may be helpful, teachers need to be aware that more basic questions may be the meaning of the divinity of Christ (to use the technical term) or how to comprehend God's activity in today's world as the doctrine of the Holy Spirit affirms. Biblical reading and discussion about how Jesus revealed God in his life, death, and resurrection and how the apostolic church demonstrated the work of God through the Holy Spirit offer bases for understanding. Where liturgies use one of the creeds regularly and forms of prayer (such as the collect) that usually address God in three persons, worshipers absorb the form descriptively, and the meaning will be enriched by thinking about these dimensions. See also Baptism; Confirmation; God, Understandings of; Holy Spirit; Jesus Christ.

J. Monti

U

Undergraduate Study

See Higher Education, Religion in; Professional Study.

Uniform Lessons Series

The Uniform Lessons Series, a series of outlines of recommended Sunday school lessons designed to cover the whole Bible in six-year cycles, was established at the National Sunday School Convention assembled at Indianapolis, Indiana, in 1872. The resolution that was passed stated: "Resolved, that this Convention appoint a committee to consist of five clergymen and five laymen, to select a course of Bible Lessons for a series of years not exceeding seven, which shall, as far as they may decide possible, embrace a general study of the whole Bible, alternating between the Old and New Testaments semi-annually or quarterly, as they shall deem best, and to publish a list of such lessons as fully as possible, and at least for the two years next ensuing, as early as the 1st of August 1872; and that this Convention recommend their adoption by the Sunday-schools of the whole country; and that this committee have full power to fill any vacancies that may occur in their number by reason of the inability of any member to serve."

The first International Lesson Committee was appointed at that convention, and thus began the historic work that continues to be carried on by the Committee on the Uniform Series today, a committee that meets annually for a one-week work session followed by interim assignments.

In 1940 the International Council of Religious Education, which evolved in 1922, approved a plan for a comprehensive curriculum to be known as "The International Bible Lessons for Christian Teaching." The Committee on the Uniform Series was one of those committees charged with a specific part of a total curriculum enterprise. The Committee on the Uniform Series was instructed to develop outlines that would be the basis for "a system of lessons" biblical in content, maintaining the principle of uniformity by including a core of common material and emphases to be developed in all age groups, but providing for a graded approach through supplemental materials and adaptations within the several age groups. The first outlines prepared by the new committee were for 1945. The Uniform Lessons begun in 1872 were modified to include specific materials for each of four age groups: young people–adult, intermediate-senior, junior, and primary.

After a period of careful preparation, the 1948 Committee on the Uniform Series produced a *Handbook of Principles and Procedures*. This first draft of the handbook helped to determine the direction of the committee's work and stated its method of operation. The handbook continues to be used although often revised. One such revision occurred in 1981 when, at the recommendation of a special committee, the term "age group emphases" was changed to "life concerns" that would be appropriate to each age level (adults, youth, children). Life concerns are those concerns that are relevant to those of a particular age level in their personal and social setting. Attention to these concerns should help persons grow in faith and respond to life situations out of that faith.

The Committee on the Uniform Series in implementing the 1986/1992 cycle of the Uniform Lessons reflected the conviction that the Bible is "the major source of understanding and meaning of the Christian faith, and . . . the most effective means of confronting persons with the great concerns of the gospel." It also affirms the fact that learning is an ongoing process. Biblical words may remain constant but every new day brings with it new ways of perceiving and responding to God's revelation.

Each cycle attempts to provide a plan for reading and studying the entire Bible over a span of six years. Nearly every book of the canon is dealt with in some fashion, even though it is not possible to include something from each book in one of the passages printed at the beginning of each lesson. Since not all passages are of equal applicability to the learning process, print passages have consistently been selected because they "seem most fruitful for study."

The proposal for the 1992/1998 Uniform Lesson Cycle states in the foreword: "We are now well into the second century of the Uniform Lessons, which began in Indianapolis in 1872. This series continues to be the most widely used form of Bible study. Its popularity is due partly to the careful way in which the cycle and the individual courses are outlined. The fact that these outlines are used in various ways by many denominations and many writers provides great variety. At the same time, there is a basic uniformity that embraces many points of view. All who participate share an interest in comprehensive, continuous Bible study for all ages."

The current Committee on the Uniform Series is composed of twenty-four denominations whose representatives meet annually to review the cycle outlines, finalize outlines for three years ahead, do detailed drafts of outlines to be used four years hence, and finalize outlines for Home Daily Bible Readings to be used four years hence. In addition to the denominations using Uniform Lesson outlines, several independent publishers also develop curriculum based on the outlines. It is estimated that forty-four million persons on any given Sunday use Sunday school lessons based on the Uniform Lesson outlines. The Committee on the Uniform Series is administered by Education for Christian Life and Mission, the National Council of the Churches of Christ in the U.S.A. *See also* Bible Study; Curriculum; National Council of the Churches of Christ in the U.S.A.; Sunday School; Sunday School Movement.

A. O. Van Eck

Unit of Study

A unit of study uses a central theme developed over a number of sessions that combine to make a whole. It makes use of numerous resources, including student experience.

Unit planning is a type of organization that sets the overall purpose or long view for a program. A unit plan identifies the broad picture and becomes the umbrella under which all study, research, activities, and discussions stand. It gives a sense of direction or cohesion to the program and then allows freedom and flexibility as the leaders and participants are sensitive to individual needs and experiences. Unit planning enables the leader to approach the topic from various perspectives and methods and encourages participants to make correlations to daily life.

Units may vary in length. Unit planning allows time for development and maturing of thoughts and experiences as reinforcement from different perspectives can be built from session to session. Each session within a unit will have specific objectives and methodology that combine to make the whole—the unit of study. *See also* Curriculum; Lesson Planning.

FOR FURTHER REFERENCE

Paulson, Donna. *Unit Planning: A Guide for Effective Training.* Philadelphia: Lutheran Church Press, 1970.

J. Bozeman

Unitarian Universalist Education

The Unitarian Universalist Association was created in 1961 by the merger of the American Unitarian Association and the Universalist Church of America. Present U.S. membership is 173,000.

Both the Unitarian and Universalist denominations had roots in New England Congregationalism. Reacting against the Calvinism of the eighteenth-century revival movement, some ministers stressed the use of reason and the response of moral living. Unitarians ultimately trace their roots to the third-century Arian movement, which affirmed the created rather than the divine nature of Christ and to several groups during the Reformation period. Eighteenth-century English Unitarianism grew out of Calvinism, as in the United States. Universalism similarly was a reaction against Calvinism stressing universal salvation. The first Universalist churches were founded in the late eighteenth century, and Universalism flowered in the following century.

GOALS AND CONTENT

Both denominations founded Sunday schools during the late eighteenth and early nineteenth centuries, catechism being the educational method of choice. Eventually both denominations made efforts to create curricula, which began by focusing on the Bible and the history of Christianity. At a time when the educational emphasis was on the imparting of information, with no opportunity for questioning the meaning of the content, William Ellery Channing, speaking to the Unitarian Sunday School Society in 1837 said, "The great end in religious instruction, whether in the Sunday school or family is not to stamp our minds irresistibly on the young, but to look inquiringly and steadily with their own ... in a word, the great object of all schools is to awaken the intellectual and moral life in the child." And A. A. Gould writing in 1899 about the accomplishments of the Universalist Western Conference Sunday School Association said, "First, it had helped our schools beyond the idea that all religion was confined to a chosen people and their scripture. Second, it had taught the idea that all life is religious, and that our own social institutions have fully as great religious lessons for our children as had the tabernacle of Moses. Third, it had shown that all nature is religious ... and fourth, it was showing that all true art is religious."

In the first half of the twentieth century the pedagogical ferment caused by the work of John Dewey, the great amount of research on child development, and the growing influence of psychology contributed to the development of child-centered curricula and experience-centered teaching.

In 1953 the Council of Liberal Churches was voted into being by a joint assembly of Unitarians and Universalists, charged with administering the public relations, publications, and education materials of the two denominations. One Division of Education was formed under the direction of

Ernest Kuebler, with Sophia Fahs as curriculum editor. Both had worked together in the Department of Education of the American Unitarian Association and together with a creative group of religious educators produced many books for children, and guides for parents and teachers, that helped teachers and children together find religious meaning in their lives. In responding to the question, What shall children study? Fahs wrote (Today's Children and Yesterday's Heritage, p. 176):

> All that quickens sympathetic imagining, that awakens sensitivity to other's feelings; all that enriches and enlarges understanding of the world; all that strengthens courage, that adds to the love of living; all that leads to developing skills needed for democratic participation—all these put together are the curriculum through which children learn.

When Dorothy Spoerl succeeded Sophia Fahs as curriculum editor she emphasized the need for children to learn the history and traditions of their religious community, and for them to be helped to form their religious, social, and ethical values.

During the 1970s, the curriculum format was changed, and multimedia kits of curriculum resources were developed by teams of educators, writers, and theologians under the guidance of Hugo Hollerorth. The kits addressed the subject areas of ethics, religious heritage, social relationships, personal religious development, and the Unitarian Universalist heritage and were designed to provide volunteer teachers with resources (books, activities, audiovisual aids, and lesson plans) that would enable them to teach a class. One of the kits, "About Your Sexuality," a course on human sexuality for adolescents, was also widely used by schools and health agencies.

Criticism that the kits did not adequately address religious ideas and, specifically, did not address Unitarian Universalist religious ideas, led in 1980 to the formation of the Religious Education Futures Committee. As part of its charge, this committee was asked to assess the needs of the Association in religious education in light of the many societal changes that have occurred in recent decades. The findings and recommendations of the committee reflect the pluralistic nature of the Association, the wish for life-span religious education, and the "design of curricula in spiral rather than in linear terms. This means reintroducing the values, concepts and functional principles of the faith that we affirm at each developmental level of understanding."

INSTITUTIONS

The Unitarian viewpoint became predominant at Harvard University during much of the nineteenth century, and Harvard Divinity School reflected its theology until the 1940s. St. Lawrence University

(New York) and Tufts (Massachusetts) were established by Universalists. The two Unitarian Universalist theological schools today are Starr King (California) and Meadville/Lombard (Illinois).

Unitarian Universalism stresses the individual search for truth and commitment to living and acting from the core of that truth. The community of faith, in turn, supports the search of each individual, of whatever age, as he or she struggles with the meaning of relationship to self, to religious community, to the larger world, and to the transcendent. See also Fahs, Sophia Lyon.

FOR FURTHER REFERENCE

Anastos, M. Elizabeth. Unitarian Universalist Religious Education: A Brief History. Working paper for Religious Education Futures Committee.

Fahs, Sophia Lyon. Today's Children and Yesterday's Heritage. Boston: Beacon Press, 1952.

Gilligan, Carol. In a Different Voice. Cambridge, MA: Harvard University Press, 1982.

Noddings, Nel. Caring: A Feminine Approach to Ethics and Moral Education. Berkeley and Los Angeles: University of California Press, 1984.

T. Evans

United Church of Christ Education

The formation of the United Church of Christ (UCC) in 1957 by the union of the Congregational Christian Churches and the Evangelical and Reformed Church brought together rich traditions of Christian education having their earliest roots in colonial America.

The Congregational Churches, stemming from the English separatist movement, first arrived in America with the settlers at Plymouth, Massachusetts, in 1620. Congregations were independent although cooperative, and a National Council was not established until 1871. In 1931, it merged with the Christian Churches, which had grown out of several independent groups that had withdrawn from Methodist, Baptist, and Presbyterian denominations in the late 1700s and early 1800s. Church government was congregational; the Bible was the primary rule of faith; and freedom of belief was allowed within that framework.

The Evangelical and Reformed Church was a merger in 1934 of two denominations of European background. The Reformed Church in the United States was begun by eighteenth-century Pennsylvania settlers originally from western Germany and Switzerland. The Evangelical Synod of North America traces its roots to an 1840 meeting of German immigrant ministers who had been influenced by earlier Prussian efforts to unite Lutheran and Reformed churches in the Evangelical

Union of Prussia. Both the Reformed Church in the United States and the Evangelical Synod of North America affirmed confessions from the Lutheran and Evangelical traditions based on the Apostles' Creed.

The Congregational heirs of the English Puritan Reformation and the German Evangelical and Reformed offspring of the continental Reformation held in common a belief in the transformation of society. From this shared faith flowed a commitment to education as a means of transformation and the conviction that faith and learning are inseparably joined.

HIGHER EDUCATION

A 1643 account of the founding of Harvard College in 1636 sets the educational priority of the Massachusetts Bay Colony in clear relief: "After God had carried us safe to New England and wee had builded our houses, provided necessaries for our livelihood, rear'd convenient places for God's worship, and settled the civill government: One of the next things we longed for and looked after was to advance learning and perpetuate it to posterity; dreading to leave an illiterate ministry to the churches, when our present ministers shall lie in dust." For this purpose, John Harvard, minister of the Congregational church in Charlestown, Massachusetts, willed his library and half his estate. In 1701, Yale followed the founding of Harvard, until today there are more than eighty postsecondary institutions of higher education rooted in the tradition of the United Church of Christ in the United States and Puerto Rico. Through the Council for Higher Education of the UCC Board for Homeland Ministries, forty-seven of these accredited institutions are officially related to the United Church of Christ: thirty colleges and universities, fifteen theological seminaries, and two college preparatory schools.

The UCC theological seminaries reflect the early Congregationalists' recognition that education, particularly the education of a learned clergy, was necessary for the building of a Christian nation. Andover Newton, founded in 1807 by orthodox Congregationalists as a result of Harvard's drift toward unitarianism, was the first separate, permanently located theological school in the United States. The concern for an educated clergy was shared by the German Evangelical and Reformed tradition. Lancaster Theological Seminary, founded in 1825 at Carlisle, Pennsylvania, by the German Reformed Church, grew out of the church's struggle to become an American denomination and the need for a clergy educated in America. Eden Theological Seminary, founded in 1850 near St. Louis, represented the Evangelical Synod's recognition that the church's future in America depended upon provision of theological education equalling that of the established Ger-

man universities. Of the fifteen UCC theological seminaries, seven have been designated by the General Synod as "closely related": Andover Newton, Bangor, Chicago Theological Seminary, Lancaster, Eden, Pacific School of Religion, and United Theological Seminary of the Twin Cities.

Also among UCC-related schools are those founded by the American Missionary Association (AMA) during the latter half of the nineteenth century. Although nonsectarian, the AMA received most of its support from the Congregational churches. As an abolitionist organization of both black and white members, with most of the whites being Congregationalists, it represented an extension of Reformed faith in the transformation of society through education. AMA colleges and universities now related to the UCC are LeMoyne-Owen (1862), Fisk (1866), Talladega (1867), Dillard (1869), Tougaloo (1869), and Huston-Tillotson (1876).

The Thirteenth General Synod of the UCC meeting in 1981 affirmed "A Statement on Meaning, Purpose, and Standards of the Relationships Among Colleges, Academies and the United Church of Christ." The statement contained "long held" theological bases for the mission of the UCC in higher education, including a reaffirmation of belief in the transformation of society: "The fullest possible development of the intellectual, moral and spiritual resources of the human family must remain a major dimension of the work of the church as it attempts to minister to the needs of all people and to proclaim the Good News of hope and of humane community based on love and justice." The statement, "intended as a new covenant between the Church and the member colleges and academies of the Council for Higher Education," affirms that those institutions maintaining an official relationship with the UCC are "able to realize more fully their essential educational mission . . . ; the affirmation of ethical values for the renewal of society." Officially related institutions are those that have entered into covenant with the UCC and who join in actualizing the covenant through reciprocal acts of mutual support between the denomination and the institution.

EDUCATION IN CONGREGATIONS

The early Congregational commitment to education also gave impetus to Christian education in local congregations. In the Plymouth and Massachusetts Bay churches, teaching was an integral part of worship and preaching. Children were often specifically addressed in the midst of lengthy sermons. At points of sermonic instruction for children, the preacher "rapped" upon the pulpit calling children to attention in their family pews. This alliance of religion and education was supported not only by churches and families but also by the colonial schools that were part of the New England religious establishment.

When the "half-way covenant" was adopted by representatives of the Congregational churches meeting at Boston in 1662, granting permission to baptize children of parents not "in full communion," the need for the churches themselves to provide religious instruction became even more apparent, since the parents were not necessarily churchgoers. By the late eighteenth century, when the Sunday school movement took hold in the United States, the concept found fertile soil in churches of the English Puritan and German Reformed traditions. As in most Protestant denominations, the Sunday school evolved into a regular feature of the local church Christian education programs of those traditions that form the UCC.

Another profound influence upon Christian education in the Congregational tradition was Horace Bushnell, best known for his book *Christian Nurture* published in 1847. This Congregationalist pastor and theologian rejected the notion of total depravity from birth and maintained that a child should be nurtured in Christian faith as a lifelong process. His emphasis upon "nurture" rather than a datable conversion represented a far-reaching shift in both theology and educational philosophy.

In 1947, ten years before the formation of the UCC, the Congregational Christian churches and the Evangelical and Reformed Church began cooperation in their Christian education programs. The "United Church Curriculum" grew out of the Congregational Christian "Pilgrim Series" and the Evangelical and Reformed "Church and Home Series." In subsequent years, the UCC has used the curriculum of JED (Joint Educational Development), developed by an ecumenical partnership including the UCC. In 1988, the "Discipleship Alive" curriculum was introduced, published jointly by seven denominations, including the UCC.

Resources and support systems for Christian Education are provided congregations through the United Church Board for Homeland Ministries (UCBHM), Division of Education and Publication. According to the mission statement of the UCBHM, "the task of this division is to develop an educational concept, a program and adequate resources based upon: (1) an understanding of how the church is empowered to educate persons for Christian life, faith and discipleship amidst the various settings of life, including the church school, other dimensions of congregational life, and higher education; and (2) life span approaches in education that are informed but not limited to knowledge about the human family life cycle or by cultural and environmental factors affecting human learning." *See also* Reformed Education.

FOR FURTHER REFERENCE

Gunnemann, Louis H. *The Shaping of the United Church of Christ*. New York: United Church Press, 1977.

Shinn, Roger L. *The Educational Mission of Our Church*. New York: United Church Press, 1962.

Zikmund, Barbara Brown. *Hidden Histories in the United Church of Christ*. New York: United Church Press, 1984.

H. D. Henderson

United States Catholic Conference

See National Conference of Catholic Bishops.

University

A university is an institution of higher learning made up of undergraduate and graduate colleges of arts and sciences, together with professional schools such as law, theology, medicine, engineering, and the like. In the United States, the first universities began as colleges and, with the exception of the University of Pennsylvania (chartered in 1740 as a nonsectarian college), they all had religious or denominational foundings and continue to maintain prestigious programs in religious studies. Harvard College was founded by the Puritans in 1636, Yale by Congregationalists in 1701, Princeton by Presbyterians in 1746, and Columbia (originally King's College) by Anglicans in 1754. Harvard and Yale have divinity schools, and Princeton and Columbia have affiliated, though structurally separate, theological schools in Princeton Theological Seminary and Union Theological Seminary, respectively. All of these universities, together with Brown (founded by Baptists in 1764), offer advanced degrees (M.A. and Ph.D.) in religious studies through graduate schools of arts and sciences.

The oldest universities in the Americas, however, have Spanish Catholic origins. The University of Mexico (Mexico City) and the University of San Marco (Peru) were both founded by the Spanish crown in 1551. And the University of Laval in Quebec, the oldest in Canada, was established twenty-seven years after Harvard in 1663 by the French Catholic Bishop Laval from whom it derives its name.

PRIVATE AND PUBLIC INSTITUTIONS

During the late eighteenth century and throughout the nineteenth, two new types of universities came into being in the United States: private universities founded by wealthy benefactors and public, state-supported "land grant" universities. Among the former type are Cornell, Johns Hopkins, Tulane, Stanford, and the University of Chicago, the latter of which also maintains a distinguished divinity school. The University of Chicago may also be credited with having played the major role in the development of the comparative study of religions through the influence of the late Joachim Wach and Mircea Eliade and what is now commonly referred to as the "Chicago school" of the history and phenomenology of religions.

Public "land grant" universities during their formative periods, by contrast, tended to avoid religious studies out of fear of violating the "separation clause" in the First Amendment to the Constitution. There have always been those who maintain that an academic treatment of religion in any form whatever is objectionable on the notion that purely objective, nonbiased approaches to religion are either formally impossible or unlikely in practice. Hence the regents and administrators of public universities have frequently avoided the establishment of programs in religious studies in order to avoid criticism by believers and nonbelievers alike. But it also made little sense, for the fledgling public universities to compete against the strength of the private sector (which was very frequently in the humanities) and a great deal more sense to concentrate upon cultivating technical fields in the natural sciences and the new and rapidly developing opportunities in the social sciences. Also the influence of scientific positivism, in its various forms, was particularly strong in the public university during the first part of the twentieth century. This general mood, combined with what is outlined above, strongly militated against the establishment of programs in religious studies in the private sector and reinforced the notion among many regents and administrators that religious studies should be avoided altogether in order to maintain an official posture of neutrality in matters religious.

RELIGIOUS STUDIES PROGRAMS

As Reinhold Niebuhr observed, however, the constitutional "wall of separation" regarding religion and the state in America is not to be taken as a warrant for the de facto establishment of "secular humanism" as the only ideology that can find official representation in public education. This observation fell upon increasingly responsive ears during the 1950s and 1960s for the following reasons. First, the tremendous expansion of public higher education after World War II brought with it the need to compete with private institutions in all areas including the humanities, and instruction in the humanities cannot be pursued apart from sustained attention to religious values and the history of religions. Second, and perhaps more importantly, the postwar period was accompanied by a growing spirit of liberality in mainline Amer-

ican religious institutions (Catholic, Protestant, and Jewish) and an adumbration of apprehensions regarding the academic study of religions. Thus what began, in the public university, as the fear of being identified as fostering "religion" during the first half of the twentieth century was reversed in many instances during the latter half out of the fear of being identified as fostering "secularism."

This new ecumenical impetus to know more about "other faiths" (if for no other reason that it behooved Americans, given their new position of world leadership, to know something about other cultures) may be viewed as culminating in the early 1960s, for it was during this period that many public universities established programs in religious studies. One of the pioneering institutions in this regard was the University of California at Berkeley through its affiliation with the cluster of theological schools in the Bay Area known as the Graduate Theological Union in the granting of advanced arts and sciences degrees in religious studies, as well as developing other self-contained programs in religious studies on other campuses including the highly distinguished program at the University of California at Santa Barbara.

Denominationally founded universities, however, also continued to proliferate throughout the nineteenth century. Among the most notable are universities of Roman Catholic origin, such as Catholic University, Fordham University, and the University of Notre Dame, Georgetown, Villanova, and Boston College, and universities of Methodist origin, such as Boston University, Syracuse University, Emory University, Northwestern University, Vanderbilt University, Southern Methodist University, and the University of Southern California. All of these institutions maintain distinctive programs in religious studies, whether in arts and sciences or divinity schools or both. Among these, Boston University contributed a unique chapter in American philosophical and religious history by way of the late nineteenth- and early twentieth-century scholars Borden Parker Bowne and Edgar Sheffeld Brightman and what has come to be known as the school of "Boston personalism." Two individuals in religious studies at Boston University have received the Nobel Peace Prize: Dr. Martin Luther King, Jr., a graduate of its Division of Religious and Theological Studies, and Dr. Elie Wiesel, a Professor of Judaic Studies in its department of religion. *See also* Colleges and Universities, Church-Related; Higher Education, Religion in; Religious Studies; Theological Education.

A. M. Olson

Urban Church

To sense the diversity of religions and the variety of churches in the urban areas of the United States one has only to inspect the yellow pages of the telephone directory or the church advertisements of the Saturday newspapers in any city.

THE URBAN ENVIRONMENT

For statistical purposes the city has been defined as a large population nucleus having a high economic and social integration. The largest U.S. cities are New York, 15.6 million; Los Angeles, 10.5 million; and Chicago, 6.9 million. The people living in urban areas in the United States number 172 million, or 76.6 percent of the total population (1980 census). In area, cities occupy only 16 percent of the land.

It is sometimes asserted that there are primarily two economic groups in a city: the rich and the poor. A high proportion of the urban population is made up of the newest and poorest immigrants—people from other parts of this country as well as from foreign countries. In addition, there are young adults who choose city life, excited by the city's diversity and its cultural and business opportunities. Cities continue to maintain areas of high-priced residences. In addition, the "gentrification" process has preserved and renewed old, once decaying buildings.

Violent crime is highest in cities of more than one million population, and property crime is higher in cities between 250,000 and a million. In addition to crime, cities are beset with many continuing problems: housing, transportation, health care, the physical environment, and education. Today the traditional "melting pot" theory of integration is in tension with resurgent pride in ethnic heritage; the resolution is not clear.

THE SITUATION OF CHURCHES

There are many kinds of urban churches (sometimes three and four within one city block): a mainline denominational church with three ministers and a ministry in a residential part of the city; another church with multiple staff, open and alive on Sunday morning only, whose members are heads of corporations; a large interdenominational church whose membership is interracial and multicultural and whose program includes new forms of witness and presence that are ecumenical and outreaching; or a black mainline denominational church with one full-time pastor attempting to minister in the inner city within the restrictions of form and doctrine of the white denomination, and an aging, tired, and increasingly poor congregation.

To this list can be added hundreds of independent, evangelical, Pentecostal, or Holiness storefront churches whose drums and guitars can be heard by those who pass their doors on Sunday mornings. These are filled mainly by blacks and Hispanics and seem to minister to the experiences and needs of people who are new to the city.

In addition, migrants from the Caribbean and Latin America have brought Neo-African religious beliefs and practice. Immigrants from Asia have brought their own faiths: Buddhism, Hinduism, and Islam. Jewish immigrants come both from eastern Europe and the Middle East. A number of people from Third World countries bring to the city the forms of Christian faith they inherited from missionaries.

Many mainline churches have moved out of the city to follow their congregations to the suburbs, selling their property to independent, former storefront churches that seem to thrive where others have not.

Thus, the gathering of the urban church for worship reflects in a massive way the disunity of the church—racially, culturally, socially, economically.

The nonwhite minority churches today are the dominant Christian force in the heart of the metropolis. These, with a few traditional Roman Catholic and downtown mainline Protestant churches and synagogues hold the key to the influence of organized religion upon the public and private institutions that never left the city, and the city's political, economic, and cultural structures.

MEETING THE CHALLENGES

Cities continue to be places of transition and dislocation. Population change, change in racial composition, socioeconomic change are all endemic to the context. The realities of racism, sexism, militarism, and neocolonialism still exist in American society and in cities across the country. Some minority people have achieved significant positions in business, professions and political office, but most still suffer great disabilities in terms of housing, education, medical care and income.

However, in the very midst of destruction, decay, and alienation, we find striking evidence of community, birth, and life, and sometimes this appears in churches.

There has been a boom in storefront churches, so-called because worship takes place in abandoned stores or, when they overflow, in refurbished theaters. Many storefront churches are in forsaken, depressed neighborhoods. And in this inhospitable environment, they flourish, somehow restoring dignity to dislocated people and obtaining commitment.

The storefront is the church of Hispanics and Blacks who seek comfort, joy, hope, and community in fundamental, communal faiths that are celebrated with laughter, tears, prayers, and sometimes hell-fire preaching. Often emotional in atmosphere, the storefront churches place a low priority on doctrine and frequently emphasize the gift of speaking in tongues. Some have as few as eight or ten members, others have hundreds. They are attended almost exclusively by poor people, and the pastors are often women and men who have jobs during the week to support their families—and sometimes to help support the church. There may be as many storefront pastors as there are ministers and rabbis in traditional churches and synagogues.

In times of need, these storefront churches become voter registration centers, day-care centers, health centers for pregnant teenagers and their babies. They organize protest marches to city hall and become advocates for children in the courts and schools. Their activities represent a new understanding on the part of the urban storefront church—from the church as *koinonia* only, to service for one's own, to influencing economic and political structures.

Some of the denominational urban black churches (representatives of six all-black denominations) are finding a new mission as well as they help minority men and women in the urban ghetto live with dignity and hope under the Lordship of Jesus Christ.

Churches of all types establish day schools, with licensed teachers; build residences with apartments for senior citizens at minimal cost; maintain nursing facilities with multilevel care for senior citizens; dispense scholarship funds for young people entering college; and establish savings and loans funds for their members.

These activities show how urban churches are now "seeking the welfare" of the city in which God is creating new community; worship, study, and action are coming together in new ways. Cities today, and their churches, are new creations. They require creative clergy and lay leadership who can make use of the experiences and gifts of people who are often neglected by traditional churches and society.

Particularly in West Coast cities, Asians, both long-established residents and newcomers, are seeking to meet the needs of their constituencies through religious institutions. Buddhism becomes revitalized as an association combining many groups is formed and a new temple is built in southern California. Christian churches organize cultural centers, assist members in learning English, and help their families meet the demands of a new culture within a caring community.

RELIGIOUS EDUCATION

Religious education continues in some city churches with traditional Sunday schools in the large, stable churches. Increasingly, denominations are publishing materials in Spanish and Korean. Most denominations include multicultural materials and illustrations in their curricula, and black denominations are structuring materials that will incorporate black history (so much of which comes from Christian motivation) and black experience.

Because many inner-city children lack the educational stimulation that middle-class parents can provide, churches have tried to assume this socializing role through tutoring, courses in English as a second language, or creative activities groups. Day-care centers, Head Start programs, and kindergartens are further evidence of this concern. Where poverty means lack of food, breakfasts, snacks, or other meals in connection with educational activities make the difference between a tired child and an alert one. Varied activities including athletic programs reach out to adolescents. A scholarship program encourages future planning. Churches also run programs on sexuality and family life and drug prevention programs.

Given the wide variety of concerns in the urban environment a dilemma of the theological seminary is how to educate men and women for urban ministry. To equip this leadership, the seminary must enter the life of the communities and share their struggles for survival and liberation. In addition to traditional roles, those who lead the urban church must be empowered as agents of social, political, and economic benefits for its people. A few interdenominational nontraditional seminaries that have sought out in faculty and student body the diversity of the urban scene are beginning to produce clergy and laity adequate for the urban church. Some of their graduates, making an effort to accommodate the needs of minority churches, are becoming the primary representatives of organized religion in central cities. In West Coast seminaries, Korean-speaking faculty are being engaged to oversee the programs of students who are being taught in two languages and prepared for ministry to Asian congregations in America. In these and other ways, theological schools are seeking to meet the needs of religious and cultural groups that have previously been submerged and to learn from them. Thus is education for ministry becoming more accountable to the congregations and neighborhoods of the city that once went unheard—storefront churches, racial and religious minorities, the diverse congregations of urban religion. *See also* Asian Americans; Black Experience and Religious Education; Black Theology; Hispanic Americans; Language, Inclusive; Multicultural Education.

E. V. Gibbes

V

Vacation Church School

Vacation church school, also known in some denominations and geographic areas as daily vacation Bible school, refers to a one- or two-week summer program of religious education for children and youth.

HISTORY

Believing that the traditional one-hour or less Sunday morning education program was inadequate, church leaders, looking for additional opportunities, saw the summer vacation from public school education as an excellent possibility. In the 1940s and 1950s only the very wealthy seemed able or interested in extended vacations, and communities and secular organizations serving middle-class America had not yet begun to see summer as optimal program time. Congregations, clusters of churches within the same denomination, ecumenical gatherings of churches in a neighborhood developed multifaceted programs that drew children and young people, not only from the participating churches but from the surrounding community as well.

Programs usually included some form of lesson not unlike the Sunday morning church school lessons, music, arts and crafts, recreation, refreshments, and worship. Closely graded in larger churches and communities and more loosely graded in smaller ones, the programs were generally highly structured and required a significant number of teachers, assistants, administrators, and specialists in art, music, drama, storytelling, etc. Pastors were often included, particularly to lead worship. The programs usually had a concluding event in which all the participants presented their experiences and what they learned in a closing program to which parents and interested church members were invited.

Special curriculum materials for such vacation schools were produced by many denominations, by independent publishers, and by cooperative ecumenical efforts. Care was taken, wherever possible, to avoid the content areas that particular groups might have just completed in Sunday morning programs or might be taken up in the coming year. As indicated by the alternate name, some groups went to great effort to ensure that the Bible was the central focus of every session and program.

During the 1940s and 1950s and into the 1960s many vacation schools had classes for children as young as three years and as old as senior

highs. The dropout of youth, already affecting the Sunday church school, began to shrink the summer program also, but many adolescents stayed on to serve as assistants or even teachers. Job opportunities, public education summer schools, more available transportation to recreational facilities, coupled with youths' reluctance to be a part of something that children do, continued to erode attendance. By the 1970s, when more people had summer homes, longer vacations, cars, and more money to travel, scheduling and staffing vacation church schools became more difficult. Summer camp programs with a wide variety of purposes and enticements competed with church members' desires for religious education for their children. The creative activities of the early church summer programs, new and exciting to many children of traditional or inadequate public schools, were no longer as attractive to children who were experiencing such activities in school or had become spectators from years of television exposure.

PRESENT PROGRAMMING

In spite of the forces working against it, the vacation church school continues to exist in traditional and innovative forms and may be experiencing something of a rebirth. Local churches or groups of churches write their own curriculums so that the programs can, in fact, be an extension of the year-long religious education offerings. Ethnic and urban churches have developed programs that explore the cultural heritage of a people or a community. Suburban churches may focus on mission, music, or drama as a way for children and others to explore the meaning of discipleship or to become more deeply involved in Bible study. Some congregations have left the one- or two-week models for one afternoon and/or evening per week for six or eight weeks or for four consecutive evenings of intergenerational vacation schools. Vacation periods other than summer are being utilized for supplemental or primary education programs. These variations have, in many instances, been easier to staff and more easily integrated into the diverse life patterns of those who might participate.

Like the earliest vacation church schools and like all educational programs, the effectiveness of present programs is largely dependent upon careful planning, integration with other existing programs, clear articulation of objectives, sound enlistment procedures, and substantive leader education. Programs may have education as a primary or secondary focus, with fellowship sometimes taking precedence. Whether churches develop their own curriculum or choose from specific available vacation school programs, the objectives should be compatible with the church's self-understanding and with the overall educational ministry rationale. Asking about what a church is called to be and to do may lead a planning group to explore how that particular church has been gifted for ministry. Because vacation programs are usually limited, it often becomes possible for a church to recognize gifts among its members that might not be able to be called on for longer time commitments. Likewise, people with little experience in teaching may find a shorter time commitment an excellent opportunity to discover many gifts for the educational ministry. Preparatory teacher training and serving as an assistant may raise up new educational leadership for the ongoing education program of a church. Clusters of churches or denominational offices may provide training for vacation church school leaders as well as make available for study a wide variety of resource materials.

The extended period of time available in a vacation church school program as well as the "vacation" mentality allows, in many churches, for educational activities that might be frowned upon in the more traditional Sunday morning context. Even in more formal communities it becomes more appropriate for children and adults to dress casually and thereby to engage more freely in some activities. Because most schools meet on weekdays or evenings the possibilities for field trips, excursions, outdoor activities and recreation, and cooperative efforts are increased. If dramatic or musical productions are envisioned, the requisite rehearsal and preparation time is available within the program structure and additional demands on participants' and leaders' time are not required. In some formats eating together becomes an important means of building a learning community and the congregation as well. Physical labor on behalf of shut-in or less privileged members of the church or larger community may be incorporated in an action-reflection model of learning as well as providing a means for younger and older members of a church to engage in the mission of the church together.

Looking at the life and rhythm of a particular congregation may provide planners with insight into alternative education patterns for the whole church or for groups within it. There are congregations today where a majority of people take winter vacations and are at home in the summer. College students may be at home for much of January and away during the whole summer. Spring recesses may send children of more affluent families off to resorts but be a time available to other children and teens when projects, trips, experiments with theater and music may become new opportunities to learn and grow in faith. Knowing well what is intended and openness to new contexts and formats for achieving it may suggest vacation church schools as a significant component of educational ministry. *See also* Childhood Education; Time Arrangements.

F. A. Gardner

Values

The term "value," one of the most basic concepts in the English language, refers in its most general sense to what is good, desirable, and worthwhile. In an objective sense, it refers to things, activities, persons, or experiences of individuals or groups that are deemed good. In a more subjective sense, it refers to personal or group preferences from among a number of possibilities. The concept of values differs from knowledge in that it has a normative element (things and actions are judged according to some norm) in addition to a cognitive element. "Values" is a broader term than "morals" since it includes not only moral values (moral goodness and moral badness) but aesthetic, cultural, educational, political, and economic aspects as well. No sharp distinction, however, should be made between moral values and these other values, since moral judgments are often included within aesthetic, educational, political, and economic concerns.

UNDERSTANDINGS OF VALUE AND VALUES

Values are the concern of many academic disciplines. The longest and most sustained treatment of values has come from philosophers, beginning with Greek philosophy and extending to such modern philosophies as positivism, existentialism, phenomenology, and Marxism. Early philosophies emphasized the objectivity of values as something established in the very nature of things. In addition, values were seen by some to be of transcendent origin, rooted in the very nature of God or in God's will. More recent philosophies have paid more attention to the subjective element in values, i.e., the role of persons and cultures in the creation of values. Data from the social sciences have forced philosophers to deal with the relativity of values within and across cultures.

An important philosophic distinction is made between *instrumental* values (means values) and *intrinsic* values (ends values). The former are means to worthwhile ends, while the latter designate what appear to be the ultimate values of the majority of persons. Suggested as ends values are survival, health, happiness, friendship, wisdom, freedom, self-respect, and a sense of meaning in life. For many individuals religious values such as love of God and love of others are considered the highest human values. Although people differ on the hierarchy and interrelationships of these values, it appears that such values are sought within and across cultures.

Philosophers have proposed different theories or grounds for determining whether things are good, desirable, and worthwhile. These theories tend to take one ultimate value and attempt to connect all other values with it. Hedonism contends the view that pleasure or happiness is the good, the goal of all persons, something all should strive for, and the ultimate criterion by which values are determined. Utilitarianism sees that of value which promotes the good of the greatest number of people or the greatest possible balance of good over evil. Libertarianism judges the value of things ultimately by their capacity to promote the greatest amount of human freedom. A social contractualism based on fairness judges all human arrangements and experiences in their capacity to foster a basic fairness in society.

The term "value" is not used in the Bible in a general or philosophical sense; the infrequent references are with a concrete and specific meaning: "It [wisdom] cannot be valued with the gold of Ophir" (Job 28:16). In modern times, with the secular use of the term in education, the Ten Commandments and the Sermon on the Mount may be considered basic teachings on values, but to the biblical writers and believers these were concrete expressions of how people live faithfully to God under Torah and covenant. Hence "values," meaning qualities or actions held to be valuable by a particular society, are viewed in a religious community in balance with the requirements of Torah or gospel.

The modern debate over values is centered in the issue of the relativity versus universality of values. Logical positivists have denied all meaning to propositions about value. Many psychologists espouse determinism by which what people value is determined by biological or environmental causes. While some social scientists adhere to a theory of a core or consensus of values that keeps a society together, others, especially Marxists, take it for granted that values are determined by class and economic factors. From many anthropologists has come the conclusion that all standards and values are relative to the culture from which they are derived. These and other viewpoints cast doubt both on the objectivity of value and on the power of individuals to make or choose their own values.

EDUCATION IN VALUES

Education in values takes into account these recent developments both in philosophy and the social sciences. This is also true where this education takes place in religious contexts. Some theologians and religious educators take approaches to values that reflect the wide diversity of thought in this area. While there is a recognition of the values of religious traditions and authority, there has been an increased sensitivity in many parts to the complex process by which values are transmitted and formed. While some religious educators adhere to an education in values rooted in an absolutist understanding of religious literature, human nature, tradition, or authority, many others have recognized and deal with the tension that exists between these and more relativist understandings of persons, values, and cultures.

Education in values takes various forms. All of these forms accept that persons are socialized into values by both personal, cultural, and institutional factors. Values clarification seeks to bring persons to an awareness of the values they hold. Value analysis supplements this with a study of the ground for one's value judgments. Developmental values education seeks to create cognitive dissonance in order to move persons beyond their present level of reasoning. Social action education makes active commitment to deal with injustices the principal means of enabling students to form proper values.

These forms can be used for values education at each age level. Preschool children, faced with sharing toys, can be encouraged to tell their teacher what is important to them about holding or sharing (clarification). Next they discuss what the alternatives to sharing are and what alternative they are likely to follow (analysis). Finally, from differing value viewpoints they move toward consensus as to what is best in their situation.

Similarly older children may discuss, for example, being friends and how it feels to be left out of a group, talking about the factors that guide them in choices to befriend or ignore others (clarification). Examples from the situation in their school or neighborhood can be brought up and Bible stories read to help them bring in the dimension that God loves and cares for all people (analysis). Then, facing differing viewpoints both personally and in their social context, they can suggest guidelines for their own treatment of other people.

Adolescents face ethical questions about whether to stay in school or to leave, do minimal course work or strive for high achievement. The same steps in clarification and analysis help members of a group examine how each of them feels about personal and/or school goals and the bases for how they act; they look at this in the light of their religious commitments and make decisions toward positive action.

Adults face many ethical decisions on personal and social levels. The issue as to whether to intervene in alleviating poverty situations through personal and community action or legislation needs to be analyzed in the same way: by examining how and why people take the stands they do; analyzing the grounds for such viewpoints; studying the biblical teachings on poverty, wealth, and justice; and making decisions for action. *See also* Action-Reflection; Cognitive Dissonance; Ethics; Moral Development; Social Justice, Education for.

J. L. Elias

Values Clarification

See Values.

Vatican II

The Second Vatican Council (1962–1965) was a worldwide council of the bishops of the Roman Catholic church that validated certain theological and pastoral changes in the church and instituted additional ones. It began under the pontificate of John XXIII, who espoused the policy of *aggiornamento* (bringing the church up-to-date), and was completed under Paul VI, who was instrumental in directing the council to the church's role in the modern world. The formal results of the council are found chiefly in the sixteen documents officially promulgated by the bishops of the church. Although these documents are basic for understanding the council, one must also recognize the spirit of updating and the concrete reforms that were fostered by postconciliar activities at all levels of the church.

The council fostered reforms and understandings in a number of areas. The liturgical reforms promoted by the council included the introduction of the vernacular language, an authorization to reform liturgical rites of the Eucharist and other sacraments, an emphasis on a liturgically based piety, the principle of accommodating the liturgy to local cultural situations, the importance of the Liturgy of the Word, and a clarification of the structure of the liturgical year. The council set in motion a process by which liturgical life is constantly being reformed both in its rites and in the spirit in which worship takes place.

The council emphasized a number of theological understandings: revelation as essentially constituted by the Scriptures, the church as the people of God as well as a hierarchical institution, the church's cooperative task in working for justice and peace in society, and the role of the laity in the church and the world. The council was interested both in a reform of the inner life of the church and in a reconsideration of the role of the church in dealing with pressing problems in the world. At the basis of this new understanding was a more biblical approach to comprehending the church and a recapitulation of the social theology of recent popes, especially that of John XXIII as enunciated in the encyclicals *Pacem in Terris* and *Mater et Magistra*.

The chief structural or organizational dimension introduced by the council was the principle or doctrine of collegiality, i.e., the participative role of the whole college of bishops in governing the church in union with the bishop of Rome. The council set in motion a periodical synod of bishops in Rome with representatives from churches throughout the world. The principle of collegiality is also manifested in the importance given to meetings of bishops in different regions of the world, e.g., U.S. National Conference of Catholic Bishops, the Conference of Latin American Bishops, etc. Collegiality is also present at diocesan and parish levels where representative councils and committees are now a common feature of church life.

From its beginning the council sought to promote ecumenical understanding and dialogue with Christian and non-Christian churches. The presence of observers from other Christian churches as well as non-Christian religious bodies highlighted this intention of the council. A strong statement on the right of religious freedom in society undergirds the ecumenical dialogue fostered by the council. While postconciliar efforts have waned somewhat, the church through these documents stands on record as seeking the widest possible ecumenical effort and cooperation.

The remaining documents of the council include statements on communications in modern society, relationships with Christian churches of the East, the formation of priests, the promotion of religious life among men and women of religious orders and communities, an understanding of missionary activity in the church, and the nature and purposes of education in the church. In these areas the council did not forge new understandings but rather summarized existing insights and teachings. Postconciliar efforts have been made in all of these areas.

Although the council was not remarkable in what it said directly on catechesis or religious education, the whole thrust of the council demanded and actually produced significant changes in catechesis. A catechetical movement that was inspired by the new theology of the council began in Europe. A sound catechesis was to be based on a contemporary understanding of the Scriptures. The aim of all catechesis was to aid persons to participate more fully in the liturgical life of the church. The doctrinal component of catechesis was to come not from catechism formulas of the past but from the more contemporary theology of the council. The full impact of catechesis was to be judged by the witness of Christians to the faith within them as they attempt to bring salvation both to themselves and to the world. The educational impact of the council is seen in the General Catechetical Directory (guidelines for catechists) issued in Rome, the documents of the worldwide synod on catechesis, and the appearance of catechetical directories in various national churches. *See also* Catechesis; Liturgy; National Conference of Catholic Bishops; Roman Catholic Education.

FOR FURTHER REFERENCE

Documents of Vatican II, with notes and comments by Catholic, Protestant, and Orthodox authorities. Edited by Walter M. Abbott. Piscataway, NJ: New Century, 1974.

J. L. Elias

Vieth, Paul

Paul Herman Vieth (1895–1978) was a professional religious educator who was always concerned about the educational work in the congregation. Vieth's *Objectives of Religious Education* (1930) provided educational guidelines for twenty-five years for the International Council of Religious Education and its successor, the Division of Christian Education of the National Council of Churches, as well as for curriculum developers of the major denominations. After working in research, Vieth taught at Yale Divinity School from 1931 to 1963. He was an early leader in visual education. He served as an adviser in Japan in 1947–1948 and as a teacher there in 1954–1955. He maintained a mediating role as a leader in the field of religious education and has been called "the symbol of a field in transition" by Sara Little. He edited *The International Journal of Religious Education* and three times was acting editor of *Religious Education* (1959–1960, 1966–1967, 1970). He served as teacher, department principal, superintendent, director of Christian education, and member of committees on Christian education in local churches throughout his career. His many books were both theoretical and practical and useful for practitioners. *See also* Curriculum; Goals.

R. C. Miller

Visual Methods

"One picture is worth a thousand words" has long been accepted as a truism. Nonetheless, many Protestant Christians have continued to be bound by a tradition in which the ear is dominant over the eye. This has been changing, though ever so slowly, the glacial speed due partly to the ancient suspicion of the seductive power of the visual image. The second commandment of the Decalogue has been overemphasized in those Christian churches influenced by Calvinism. The phrase

"People of the Book" is as apt for this branch of the church as for the Jewish people. Thus the renewed emphasis upon visual methods for many religious educators is a catch-up movement, since Roman Catholics, Anglicans, Lutherans, and Greek Orthodox never abandoned the long, rich visual tradition.

By visual methods is meant that part of communication dependent upon the eye. It is an important part of audiovisual (or the more current term "media") methodology, in actual practice scarcely to be separated from it. Such separation, desirable only for the purpose of analysis and discussion, is possible in that the visual deals with shape and form, size and spatial relationship, and color. It is unique in that such properties as color can only be communicated through the eye.

Visual methodology begins with words, since intellectual concepts are needed for the mind to sort out and interpret the information taken in by the eye, but words that are concrete and descriptive, rather than abstract and general.

HISTORY

Most of the biblical writings are visual. The psalmist's poetry speaks of God in pictorial rather than the abstract, philosophical terms. (For an example of this, contrast the language of Psalm 139, Genesis 1–2, or Isaiah 55 with that of the Westminster Confession of Faith, the *Shorter Catechism*, or a treatise by Thomas Aquinas.)

The teaching method of the prophets, the rabbis, and of Jesus was also visually oriented, dependent upon parables, objects, and dramatic actions. Good preaching and teaching continue to appeal to the imagination (note the root word here—"image") as well as the intellect for their impact. The emergence of "story" in theology and teaching is a recovery of an ancient, visually oriented tradition.

The early church embraced the visual as it began to use symbols to express its doctrines. The fish, the cross, the lamb, the shell, the dove, and the triangle were simple signs conveying complex meaning. These grew in richness along with the work of the representational artist, so that by the Middle Ages the church building had evolved into a glorious treasure trove of images for inspiring the illiterate congregation and teaching the great truths of the faith. Carved in wood and stone, cast in bronze and brass, emblazoned on banners and in stained glass, woven into tapestries, and painted on canvas and walls and ceilings were the great doctrines and stories of the faith for all to behold and contemplate.

Other visual methods were important, too. Movement and dance, mime and drama contributed vitally to the liturgy, celebrations, and instruction of the church. The procession into the chancel, and even through the streets, the raising

VISUAL MATERIALS AND METHODS

Age Level	Appropriate Materials and Methods
Preschool	Pictures, mobiles, flowers, and interesting objects will help make a room appealing to children and encourage creativity; a class enrollment chart with pictures of the children themselves might be posted; flat pictures and flannelgraph illustrations should be used often when stories are told; projected visual aids can be used occasionally; language itself should be very visual (concrete and descriptive).
	Children should be given toys and encouraged to play games that further visual skills discerning color, shape, size, and spatial relationship; they should also be given the opportunity to create visual objects (pictures and sculptures) themselves.
Grades 1–3	Use of a chalkboard and simple charts and diagrams can aid children in learning and recalling lessons; projected visual aids (slides, filmstrips, films, and videotapes) can be used more often to help focus attention and further interest; stories can be dramatized; works of art with biblical themes can be displayed and responses sought.
	Children can create posters, banners, murals, and sculptures and participate in group dance, drama, and mime.
Grades 4–8	Lessons and specific lesson material can be outlined for children; maps and time lines can now be used; charts and diagrams increase in importance; symbols and symbolism can now be understood and appreciated.
	Children can be taught to develop their own outlines, maps, time lines, charts, and diagrams; their participation in dramatizations and role plays can greatly increase understanding and cooperation.
High School and Adult	Renewed attention should be given to use of visual language, symbolism, parable, and story; attention should also be given to the continued importance of physical surroundings and movement in engaging and teaching learners; the use of outlines, maps, time lines, charts, and diagrams continues to be important in conveying specific information; projected visual aids continue to be enjoyed; dramatization and role play continue to be useful.

up of the host at the moment of consecration, the making of the sign of the cross, kneeling for prayer, and standing (when chairs and pews finally were introduced) for the reading of the Gospel lesson, the acting out of Old Testament and Gospel stories—each of these conveyed great meaning beyond mere words.

THEIR USE TODAY

This dependence upon the visual is just as important today for church educators. Both children and adults live in an image-charged world. They consume thousands of hours of television and films, and they buy large numbers of magazines and comic books, all filled with eye-appealing images and colors. The gospel must be presented in as attractive a way as the filmmaker presents us with an exciting mystery or adventure story or the professional photographer offers us an exquisite flower or a breathtaking landscape. Although it is true that "In the beginning was the *Word*," the passage goes on to declare that "the Word became flesh and dwelt among us ..." (John 1:1, 14). In other words, the Word took on visual, concrete form.

Thus education benefits from the use of a variety of visual methods in the classroom. For many years educational psychologists have been telling us that the learner retains more information when both the "eyegate" and the "eargate" are engaged in the learning process.

The visual method can begin with the classroom itself. Even the drabbest of rooms can be enlivened with pictures and maps placed on the walls or on easels, banners and mobiles hung from the ceiling, flowers or sculpture on a table, a decorated bulletin board, and attractive books placed about. The class enrollment chart can say that this is a caring, lively fellowship by the placing of pictures of the students by their names. A religious education school could even have a parent or teenager serving on the staff as photographer to record the school activities and see that the pictures are frequently displayed on the church bulletin boards.

Teachers can frequently resort to maps, charts, diagrams, posters, and pictures as they teach. Most children love maps and are eager to look up and point out the places mentioned in the lesson. Such visuals are often included in the curriculum packets. Instead of being discarded at the end of the school year, these could be collected and stored in an organized file in the church library, education office, or other accessible location. At the beginning of each quarter or semester teachers can be shown the file and encouraged to use its contents for their rooms. The church educator, superintendent, and teachers can see that this is not a neglected resource—they can continue to cut out and mount pictures from magazines or pick up reproductions of biblical paintings at museums and stores to add to the file collection and encourage others to also contribute.

The blackboard and newsprint pad are valuable tools that can be used to catch the eye. Diagrams can help clarify hard to understand doctrines such as the Trinity, and time lines can help put the various biblical events and characters in chronological order. And the flannelgraph, even in this sophisticated era of VCRs, is a helpful visual tool for telling stories to young children. A well-chosen picture cannot only help the student to visualize a story, it can also evoke a response. A sensitive teacher can draw out quiet or shy students by helping them to respond to a painting or news photo. (We must never forget that education is not just pouring information into passive students, but is a process in which learners are enabled to express their ideas and feelings, to discover wells of creativity within themselves through which the Creator Spirit can move and engage them.)

Projected visuals are also an important part of education. For some reason young children are more delighted by a filmstrip or set of slides than by the same visuals presented to them through a series of flat, nonprojected pictures. Thousands of filmstrips are available on every subject, and a camera with a close-up lens can enable the educator to make slides of virtually any picture in a book or magazine or to capture the colorful events in the life of the church. Films and videotapes are a little more expensive, but they are well worth their cost because of the impact they can have on a class. A lecture might convey something of the meaning of Christ's death on the cross, but a showing of a classic film like *Parable* can move the viewer to tears. The former method can reach the head, the latter the heart—which, as professional educators have been telling us, is the difference between cognitive and affective learning.

Visual methods that directly involve the students add even more to the effectiveness of the learning process. Even young children can learn how to dramatize or mime a Bible story, how to take pictures of their church activities to share with others, how to create murals, collages, banners, videotapes, and clay sculptures. Worship becomes more than listening through group dance or movement, mime and drama, or the use of write-on slides. Educators, however, must keep in mind that the goal in using such visual methods is not to produce great art or artists, but to encourage creative abilities. Excellence in creating, for example, a banner, collage, or group dance should be striven for, but the process itself is more important than the end product—or rather, what happens to the learner is more important. Do the students learn to relate to each other in loving, accepting ways? Is their own self-esteem and confidence in their abilities built up? Can they accept their limitations and appreciate the different gifts of their peers? The answer to these questions tells more about the "success" of the method than the quality of the completed work.

Such visual methods are not novelties tacked onto the "legitimate" ear-centered methods, but are the outgrowth of the church's reclaiming of its biblical heritage, a heritage too rich to be channeled only through the ear. We must recover the excitement of that word we see so often in the Scriptures, "Behold ..." Or, as the psalmist puts it, "O taste and *see* that the Lord is good!" (Ps. 34:8). *See also* Art in Religious Education; Audial Methods; Bulletin Board; Crafts; Creative Activities; Dance; Drama; Flannelgraph; Map; Poster; Television; Time Line.

E. N. McNulty

Vocation

The word "vocation" in today's usage often means a person's occupation, profession, or trade, in brief, how a living is made. A "vocational counselor" normally tries to match a person's qualifications, skills, experience, and personality with the opportunities that society offers at that moment. The word so used is practical, without the magic it has had in former times.

To be sure the word has had nonreligious connotations in the past. Immanuel Kant made much of *Plikt*, the duty one has been called to simply by being alive. For him it is a "feeling of necessitation," because the call to duty is categorical, a person's capacity for recognizing and obeying an unchanging moral law. Sigmund Freud spoke of compulsions arising from the superego or from impulses deep within one. Rainer Maria Rilke spoke of the call as a summoning *Lockruf* from all creation: "Das alles war Auftrag," he said ("All this was mission"). Matthew Arnold spoke of "something not yet yourself which makes for righteousness." The ambiguity of the summons was caused by its problematic source—one's inner psyche, the outside world, or some divine compulsion.

THE CALL TO ALL CHRISTIANS

The Christian sense of "vocation" relies heavily on the etymology of *vocare* (Lat., "to call"), and sees it as the call to everyone to become members in the church. This is the sense of Ephesians 4:1: "I therefore, a prisoner of the Lord, beg you to lead a life worthy of the calling to which you have been called." The call from the heavens such as Paul had heard on the way to Damascus had a spectacular, adamant quality, and the appropriate response was also decisive. A certain limitation of work chosen ought to be observed after the call of baptism. This call, like the one Jesus was given when he was baptized, is from beyond history, just as Socrates' daimon, which called to him at various junctures of his life, came from beyond history. But Socrates' demon simply forbade certain actions, while the Christian call is a summons to a new life.

The new life called for by this ghostly summoning is extended to all men and women. It is simply a summons to membership. Its sacramental initiation is baptism, but conversion might serve the same end. The general appeal is what John Donne spoke of, "to everyone some errand, some task for his glory." The Reformation reaffirmed this call to everyone, not simply those destined for holy orders. Farmers, fisherfolk, housewives, people of all occupations were invited to transfigure their occupation, thinking of it as the place in the cultural sphere assigned to them from which to proclaim the kingdom of God. They were to be the *laos*, the people of God, not separating the secular from the sacred, not thinking of the Sabbath as more sacred than the rest of the week. The call came from above and so was transhistorical, but it was also embedded in history and was not a flight from human existence. The call

was devoid of content, specifying only the form, summoning believers to Christian living in whatever situation they found themselves, something Jacques Maritain later would call "secular sanctity." It was a person's conviction that a certain occupation represented God's will and had his blessing.

So understood, the calling was simply to make the world chosen by one's own free will an appropriate way for proclaiming gospel truth. It involved the paradox that by surrendering oneself, the self would be finally fulfilled. Answering yes to this summons implied the priority of the moral law. No longer need the self feel lonely, having answered yes to a call based on divine concern. The response implies also responsibility, since life lived after such a summons implies an elevation not known before. The response involved stability in the responder, making an appointment to meet oneself at some later time or place. The agreement is to perform acts consonant with the disclosure and to be prepared for a later judgment.

As Martin Luther insisted, the person responsive to the calling has a stand, a position equally as holy as any ordained person. A holy shopkeeper is higher than a worldly priest. If a man meant to be a banker becomes a priest, his station is lower. If a priest is meant to be a banker, his station is lower. The consecrated life of a person considering his or her identity as a divine vocation is itself deeply symbolic, its message sacramental. Such a profound call to identity should be considered lasting, and this is what is meant by 1 Corinthians 7:24: "So, brethren, in whatever state each was called, there let him remain with God."

THE CALL TO PROFESSIONAL RELIGIOUS WORK

The Bible speaks of vocation as membership, but it also uses the word in the special sense of a summons to professional religious work. In this sense it is more specific in both form and content than the call to Christian living. The question of the source of the call, whether from outside or within, has been much discussed in both the general and specific calling, though the truth is that what seems an outer source may take an inner form.

W. H. Auden quotes Kierkegaard's distinction between a genius (one who is summoned by one's own natural abilities) and an apostle (one who is called by God to deliver a message, regardless of personal ability). Apostles need have no special talent, like the fishermen Jesus called, but need only be committed to proclaiming the Holy Name. Nor do they measure success by earthly standards and may in fact find as their own reward what the earth calls failure, suffering, and even death. Their achievement is to be faithful in uttering the name of God.

TEACHING ABOUT VOCATION

Because the call to be a Christian begins with baptism or conversion, teaching about vocation is teaching about the meaning of baptism or conversion. When infants are baptized, this first teaching is entrusted to parents and sponsors to give to children. Some congregations customarily invite all Sunday school children to be present for a service of baptism, so that they can witness an act they may not remember and be able to learn its meaning later in class and at home as reflection on the liturgy. Sunday school materials, beginning with kindergarten, may speak about baptism. Older boys and girls, particularly in traditions that prepare them for confirmation, will review the baptismal service and its meaning in order to understand similarities and differences from the promises to be made in confirmation.

In traditions stressing a conversion experience, there may be careful preparation by parents and Sunday school teachers who feel responsible for encouraging children in this commitment. In these decisions, people are learning what it means to be called to be Christian.

Stories of biblical people who responded to the call of God are useful material: Abraham, Moses, Samuel, Amos, Jesus, Paul. Stories may be dramatized or portrayed visually. Having boys and girls write out these stories and their meaning personalizes the identification.

The life of Jesus has always been for Christians the primary source of identification for vocation: Christians are called to follow him and seek God's purposes for life. All Christian education uses the New Testament as primary material for teaching vocation.

Vocation in terms of life work becomes a subject for reflection with adolescents who are beginning to sense their gifts. Units of study both for classes and fellowship groups can be designed to include opportunities for teachers and leaders to share their own sense of vocation and encourage young people to explore their responsibilities. Adults, who today frequently experience changes in work, are beginning to rethink the idea of vocation, although specificity is replaced with the idea that the call is to fulfill God's purposes in whatever work one is doing. Marriage and parenthood can be considered part of vocation, so many churches provide educational efforts in parenting and marriage enrichment.

Specific vocations to religious work are strongly emphasized in some traditions. Clergy are the models for children and young people and Sunday school teachers speak about the work of ministry. Missionaries, returning on furlough to speak in churches, encourage attention to this calling by their lives and work. Sunday school materials can include units on mission work.

Religious education as a church vocation is modeled by directors and ministers of Christian education, as well as teachers and administrators in religious schools. Campus ministers in college religious programs are influential in counseling young people who feel vocationally drawn toward forms of ministry.

In today's world, skepticism has allowed the unqualified notion of occupation to be the definition of vocation and has blurred the distinction between commitment of daily life and commitment in holy order. The full meaning of *vocatio* is difficult to explain and may better be kept secret, the soul listening in silence. *See also* Lay Ministry; Marriage Enrichment; Ministry; Mission, Education for; Ordination; Parenting; Religious Orders; Theological Education.

FOR FURTHER REFERENCE

Auden, W. H. "Genius and Apostle." In *The Dyer's Hand*. New York: Knopf, 1968.

Wingren, Gustaf. *Luther on Vocation*. Translated by Carl C. Rasmusson. Philadelphia: Fortress, 1957.

Thielicke, Helmut. *Theological Ethics*. Vol. 1. Edited by Wilson Lazareth. Philadelphia: Fortress, 1966.

I. V. Cully, P. Elmen

Volunteer Principle

The principle of voluntary service, which may be defined as unpaid service to other persons, is grounded in the character of the Christian church and many other religious traditions and is often considered appropriate social behavior in a democratic society. The primary example in the Christian tradition is the statement by Jesus, "even as the Son of man came not to be served but to serve . . . " (Matt. 20:28). Jesus himself identified the principle of loving one's neighbor as central to the Ten Commandments of the Hebrew tradition. Many of the world's religions have expressed the truth that those who would find themselves must first lose themselves in a cause greater than self-interest.

Dietrich Bonhoeffer in *Life Together* (1954) defined voluntary service as active helpfulness and said that it began with simple assistance in trifling, external matters which there are a multitude of wherever people live together. He seems to be suggesting that mutual assistance is close to the core of what it means to be a human being. In contemporary society even the government takes an active role in fostering volunteerism to strengthen agencies that provide social services because of the weakening family system.

During the eighteenth century in England and America many social institutions like schools, hospitals, orphanages, and homes for the aged were established and maintained by concerned persons, often apart from the formal organizational structures of the church. Persons were organized into "voluntary societies" based on financial contributions and public service. Such societies cut across denominational boundaries and enabled committed persons to respond to the critical social needs of health, education, and welfare.

The churches in America, of whatever denomination, are also voluntary societies because they receive no direct government subsidies or profits as businesses do. Some denominations are governed more by lay members than by professional clergy. All, however, are highly dependent upon the service of volunteers, whether to maintain their internal needs for leadership in worship, education, and ministry to their own members or the external mission to the wider community. Three issues related to volunteerism will be considered: motivation, recruitment, and management.

MOTIVATION

Both the religious and the psychological traditions affirm that self-identity and maturation are related to finding a person or cause worthy of one's ultimate commitment. Most persons have a need to be needed by someone. Motivation may be grounded in the need for achievement, power, or affiliation; however, the importance of each of these factors varies with the individual. A volunteer is seeking to meet some of his or her personal needs as well as responding to the needs of others. Marlene Wilson in *How to Mobilize Church Volunteers* reports reasons why most people volunteer. They want to:

1. Be needed
2. Help others and make a difference
3. Learn new skills or use skills they already have
4. Belong to a caring community and feel accepted as members
5. Experience self-esteem and affirmation
6. Grow in their faith and share their God-given gifts
7. Keep from being lonely
8. Support causes in which they believe

Such persons are self-giving but hope to receive something positive from the experience. Youth may be seeking self-confidence. Women may be testing skills with the intention of reentering the job market. Many people do not find great satisfaction in their work and look for opportunities to volunteer in order to find deeper satisfaction in life.

The importance of recognition and appreciation has frequently been identified as a factor in increasing the motivation of workers. Where there is appropriate recognition of volunteers for job performance, whether in public events or in personal words of encouragement, motivation will likely be high. Where such recognition is minimal or lacking altogether, volunteers will express dissatisfaction. Churches frequently fail to give appropriate recognition or rewards for volunteer service. It is assumed that the service was rendered to God and, therefore, satisfaction is found in the service as an end in itself. In fact, volunteers are persons seeking meaning, purpose, and self-affirmation, as are paid employees. It costs a volunteer to contribute service to a church or community agency. The church might well consider reimbursing volunteers for their out-of-pocket costs for child care and other expenses.

RECRUITMENT

It is commonly assumed that there is an increasing shortage of volunteer workers for churches and related organizations primarily as a result of the increasing percentage of women who are employed outside of the home. However, the source of volunteers is not limited to a single sex, social class, or economic group. The popularity of volunteering among the elderly continues to grow, with high-school and college youth the second most representative group. These groups perceive volunteering as a means of achieving vocational identity during a life period when employment is not readily accessible. The church likely needs to broaden its image of potential leaders.

Douglas V. Johnson in *The Care and Feeding of Volunteers* estimates that between 30 and 65 percent of the members in a typical congregation would be willing to serve as co-workers and leaders if they knew they were needed. The willingness to volunteer is related to the attitude of the pastor and church leaders toward the importance of the task and the clarity with which the task is defined. Clear job descriptions, matching a person's interests and capabilities with the task and offering a person experience different from their occupation are important factors in the recruitment of volunteers.

Recruitment is made easier if the volunteer is recruited for a specific time commitment, since a person's life situation frequently changes. Persons may prefer specific periods of service with opportunity for periodic time off and alternates to cover their assignments. Assigning persons to work groups or task forces may minimize the absence of any particular person. A safe assumption to make is that the time commitment of a volunteer is temporary.

MANAGEMENT

Management of volunteers in a nonprofit organization is very different from supervising employees. Ministers and other staff members cannot simply issue directives. Supervision has to be by persuasion and shared commitment to institutional goals. A mutual covenant of agreement describing job expectations in writing with periodic review of job performance is possible if the volunteer is convinced that the organization is concerned about the development of the person. Volunteers need to be comfortable with their job assignments and with the staff persons with whom they are associated. Freedom should be granted to change job assignments by mutual agreement. Although the church seldom uses written contractual arrangements for volunteers, social agencies frequently do so and find the practice helpful in clarifying expectations. Harriet H. Naylor in *Leadership for Volunteering* encourages the evaluation of the job performance of volunteers and their assignments. Periodic review should be done with, by, and of volunteers. Such evaluations focus not only on the volunteer but also the impact of the volunteer's work on the agency as a whole and the paid staff.

Volunteering is an opportunity for achieving personal meaning and growth, companionship, and comradery through serving others whether in a local community or a distant part of the world. Those who give also receive. *See also* Evaluation; Lay Ministry; Leadership Development; Management; Organization in Religious Education; Staff Relationships; Supervision.

FOR FURTHER REFERENCE

Ilsley, Paul J., and John A. Niemi. *Recruiting and Training Volunteers*. New York: McGraw-Hill, 1981.
Johnson, Douglas W. *The Care and Feeding of Volunteers*. Nashville, TN: Abingdon, 1978.
Naylor, Harriet H. *Leadership for Volunteering*. Dryden, NY: Dryden Associates, 1976.
Wilson, Marlene. *How to Mobilize Church Volunteers*. Minneapolis, MN: Augsburg, 1983.

E. A. Jenkins

Weigle, Luther Allan

Luther Weigle (1880–1976), religious educator and executive, chaired the committee that produced the Revised Standard Version of the Bible (published between 1946 and 1952). He taught at Carleton College (1905–1916) and at Yale Divinity School (1916–1949), where he was dean (1929–1949). He was responsible for the Yale Studies in the History and Theory of Religious Education, a series of twenty-three remarkable volumes. He served as chairman of the executive committee of the Association of Theological Schools (1928–1948), of the executive committee of the World Sunday School Association (which became the World Council of Christian Education; 1928–1958), of the planning committee of the National Council of Churches (1941–1950), and of the Revised Standard Version committee (1930–1970). For his work on the Bible, he was decorated a Knight of St. Gregory the Great by Pope Paul VI after the translation was adopted by the Catholic church. Later the RSV was approved by the Greek Orthodox patriarchate, making it truly an ecumenical translation. Like that of Paul Vieth, Weigle's position was a mediating one, with its roots in Horace Bushnell's *Christian Nur-* *ture* and its basic faith centered in the vision of God in Christ. *See also* Biblical Translation.

R. C. Miller

Wesley, John

John Wesley (1703–1791) is the recognized founder of Methodism.

The son of an Anglican clergyman, Wesley was educated at Oxford University and ordained upon completing his studies. He thereafter became an instructor of Greek at Oxford and assisted his father in pastoral duties for a time.

While at Oxford, Wesley, with his younger brother Charles, led a small religious society whose purpose was to combat religious apathy and strengthen Christian life for its participants. The group became known as the Holy Club, and members were derisively called "Methodists" because of their uncompromising religious observances. Wesley gained some notice for his leadership of this group.

In 1735 Wesley and three other members of the Holy Club went as missionaries to the newly founded English colony in Georgia. The time in Georgia was marked for Wesley by trouble over his use of elaborate liturgical practices amidst frontier surroundings and an unhappy courtship. A sustained encounter with a Moravian missionary community from the pietist center of Herrnhut in Germany convinced Wesley that the Moravians were in touch with a dimension of the Christian life he did not have—an experience of assured justification by God's grace.

Returning to England early in 1738, Wesley was instructed further in this by the Moravian, Peter Böhler. Although convinced of its accord with the New Testament, Wesley said that he had not then had such an experience of assurance. At the end of May 1738, while attending a religious society meeting in London and listening to a reading from Martin Luther concerning justification by faith, Wesley came to an experience of personal assurance of the grace of God.

Throughout 1738, Wesley was regularly preaching in churches around London and Oxford, but he was increasingly told by those congregations that he would not be invited to speak again; his message of sin and justification by faith was uncongenial to the English parish church of his day. His increasing exclusion from preaching in parish churches led him to follow the example of a former Holy Club colleague, George Whitefield, preaching in fields, town squares, mining developments, and parks. His audiences were the lower classes of English society, and they gladly heard his message of sin forgiven and the grace of God experienced.

Wesley thereafter became a central figure in eighteenth-century religious revival, but unlike many other revival leaders, he organized those who responded to his preaching into small religious groups—first at Bristol, then throughout England and Wales, and across to Ireland. Com-

bining his knowledge of religious societies with his study of Moravian organization, Wesley developed an elaborate structure of small groups—classes and bands—within a religious society. He saw such small groups as a necessary support network for Christian living, complementary to the public worship and sacraments of the church. Wesley thought that a Christian believer without such support would be overwhelmed by the spiritual apathy of the time.

One function of the small classes was educational instruction in the Christian faith. Hannah Ball, a member of one of the societies, organized a group of children for Sunday instruction eleven years before Robert Raikes' Sunday school began the movement which spread throughout England. *See also* Class Meeting; Methodist Education; Sunday School; Sunday School Movement.

J. C. Verheyden

Whitehead, Alfred North

"The essence of education is that it be religious," wrote philosopher Alfred North Whitehead (1861–1947; *The Aims of Education*, 1929). The son of an Anglican clergyman, he began his career as a mathematician and taught in England until 1924, when he came to Harvard as professor of philosophy; he taught at Harvard until his retirement in 1947.

His philosophy of organism, which provides a worldview based on interrelationships and a process of becoming and perishing, is the background for an educational philosophy dealing with living, growing, active organisms who find meaning in the present. Such education is useful and leads to specialization, which is socially valuable. The rhythmic periods of romance, precision, and generalization lead to freedom and discipline. The outcome should be a living religion, aesthetic enjoyment, and creative adventure. Religion is a vision and the response to that vision is worship. God acts through persuasive love, and the power of God is the worship God inspires.

Important among his publications are *Process and Reality* (1929) from his Gifford Lectures, *Essays in Science and Philosophy* (1940), and *Religion in the Making* (1926). *See also* Process Theology.

R. C. Miller

Whitsunday

See Pentecost.

Wisdom

Wisdom literature is a body of writings based on the tradition of the wise man or sage in the ancient Middle East. Sages were valued members of society, sought after because they possessed wisdom—deep understanding, keen discernment, sound judgment, and knowledge of fundamental truths about life. They often filled such roles as royal adviser, judge, teacher, or scribe. The wise looked deeply into things and could to some degree perceive the pattern or ordering eluding most people by which the course of human and natural events could be understood. They could often interpret dreams and other mysteries. Following their counsels helped one cope with the human condition or pursue a life of ethical conduct and also set one on the path to acquiring wisdom for oneself; the opposite, folly, brought destruction.

IN THE OLD TESTAMENT

Wisdom literature, found in the Bible in such books as Proverbs, Ecclesiastes, and Job, is an international literature. Its piety and sentient pronouncements occur in the literature of Sumeria and Egypt as well as that of later Greece and Rome. In a very real sense it is quite secular: human reason is relied on rather than revelation (although that reason is informed by piety, not divorced from it) and it depends for its credibility upon the human propensity to observe and generalize. For that very reason, there was some question initially as to whether the wisdom books were to be included in the canon of the Hebrew Bible.

The writings themselves were probably intended for the upper classes, for the edification of those in positions of leadership in government—those connected with the royal court or what we

today would call the bureaucracy—and, to a lesser extent, in business. The emphasis is on how the individual in a position of responsibility should behave rather than on what happens to a group, the nation of Israel, for example.

In Israel, there would have been little need for the sort of admonitions to "practical wisdom" found in the Old Testament wisdom books prior to the establishment of the United Kingdom under David and Solomon. The fact that Solomon is credited both with extraordinary wisdom as well as the authorship of a number of books in the Bible gives ample evidence to the movement, which probably hit its peak during his reign. Although the final editing of the wisdom books had to wait until the postexilic period, the literature itself undoubtedly experienced its initial impetus with the emergence of an organized government once the tribes were united under one central ruling house. Stated rather simplistically, one might say that in order to legitimate the rule of the Davidic house and under the influence of the demands of a centralized government, one group of writers set about to write the history of the people of Israel (which eventuated in Old Testament books like Samuel and Kings), while another began the task of enumerating those virtues that were proper to those in charge of public affairs.

Within Old Testament wisdom literature itself, one notes a certain disparity of outlook on the subject of retribution. Some writings follow the tradition established in the early strata of Israelite history and continued on in the Deuteronomic writings: when Israel obeyed the commandments of God, it prospered; when it failed to follow the dictates of the Almighty, it inevitably fell upon bad times. Such is the attitude of Proverbs and the apocryphal Ecclesiasticus. This attitude is disputed, however, in the books of Job and Ecclesiastes and one encounters a depth of realism that runs counter to the acceptance of conventional wisdom.

One finds in the wisdom writings what must have been some current mythology about wisdom. Wisdom is seen as personalized and divinized, a kind of *ancilla domini* or handmaid of the Lord. She finds "her place" in Israel and rests there. Eventually in later writings, Wisdom is seen as identified with the prescriptions of the Torah. What started out as an international commodity, the stock in trade of those who had the responsibility of ruling, is now coopted into the religious particularity of Judaism.

This shift to identifying Wisdom with the prescriptions of Torah parallels a shift from an emphasis on the nation to an emphasis on the individual in Judaism after the experience of the Exile and return under Persian domination. Since this had always been the emphasis of wisdom literature, it is not surprising that this literature found its way into the canon of Hebrew Scriptures. That the wisdom books are found in the third part of the Hebrew canon, the Writings, after the Pentateuch and the Prophets, may indicate that wisdom takes over where prophecy leaves off, although the tradition had been around for quite some time in its international form.

IN THE NEW TESTAMENT

Christianity has been heir to much of the Judaic tradition. The development of Wisdom as a person or divine hypostasis reaches its climax in the writing of the Fourth Gospel with its notions of Jesus as the Logos. With God from the beginning, Jesus the Word (wisdom) is God's agent in creation, through whom one has access to the Father.

It is clear from the early writings of Paul, however, that the emphasis on the keeping of the statutes and ordinances of the Pentateuch was not to be the form of early Christian piety. In time, Christianity would create its own set of prescriptions to see church and society through the dark time of the Middle Ages. The Pauline Letters were, after all, succeeded by the post- or pseudo-Pauline writings of the "Pastor," which are not at all out of keeping with a certain kind of conventional "wisdom." However, it is significant that in this early formative period, Christianity saw fit to maintain intact the whole of the Hebrew Scriptures, including the wisdom literature. But the New Testament, no less than the Old, finds its focus not in wisdom per se, but in the action of God (in the Old Testament, the Exodus; in the New, the death and resurrection of Jesus). As Paul says, "the foolishness of God is wiser than men" (1 Cor. 1:25). The question asked by wisdom literature at its greatest, in the book of Job, is given its most profound answer in the death and resurrection of Jesus. *See also* Bible Study; God, Understandings of; Theodicy.

FOR FURTHER REFERENCE

Brueggemann, Walter. *In Man We Trust.* Atlanta, GA: Knox, 1972.

Morgan, D. F. *Wisdom in the Old Testament Traditions.* Atlanta, GA: Knox, 1981.

Scott, R. B. Y. *Proverbs and Ecclesiastes.* Anchor Bible, vol. 18. Garden City, NY: Doubleday, 1965.

J. S. Ruef

Witness

A witness is a person who saw or heard something and can give a firsthand account of the experience, especially in the formal setting of a courtroom. In the verb form it also means testifying to one's religious beliefs. The word will forever be identified with Christians because the risen Lord commanded his disciples to be his "witnesses" to the whole world (Acts 1:8). It is the personal and corporate responsibility of the believer and the community of the faithful (the church) to proclaim God's good news to the world. It is the task of all the people of God (all baptized believers), not just clergy or professional church leaders, to engage in witness and ministry to the world in faithfulness to Jesus Christ.

Some people have understood witness to be "saving souls" for a future life, and others perceive it as primarily participating in marches or boycotts for social protest. These two extremes are challenged by biblical and social perspectives that affirm the necessity of both personal conversion and radical change in social structures. God's vision of freedom, justice, right relationships, and equality of all persons challenges all Christians to be self-critical and discontent with the status quo.

PERSONAL RESPONSIBILITY FOR WITNESS

As followers of Jesus Christ, we are responsible for who we are, what we say, and what we do. The first disciples were called to follow him, to be like him, and to do the works that he did. They were promised his Spirit following his death and resurrection and were transformed from a fearful into a joyful witnessing community. They endured imprisonment rather than keep silent about the wonders and signs that God did through Jesus (Acts 2:22). Early Christians were encouraged to speak the truth, to do right, to seek peace, and to turn from evil. They were to be prepared to give an account for the hope they had and to share it with gentleness and reverence (1 Pet. 3:10–15).

The Christian's witness is not a memorized formula or bumper-sticker theology, "Christ is the answer." It is sensitive listening to the other's situation; it is sharing one's own deep need for God's grace and forgiveness offered in Jesus Christ. It may require actions like feeding the hungry, treating the sick, housing the homeless, or giving a job to the unemployed (Luke 4:18, 19). It may begin more as a matter of "showing" than "telling," seeking to live Christ's kind of loving, compassionate, forgiving life.

Learn to share your own life story. The New Testament is filled with stories about what Jesus did for people. The apostle Paul used every connection to get a hearing for the gospel: his Roman citizenship, his knowledge of languages, his training as a rabbi; tales about shipwreck, stonings, imprisonment; his calls to appear before magistrates and kings. Who can match his story?

We can share the difference that Jesus Christ has made in our own lives. Begin by writing your own Christian pilgrimage. Share it with your spouse and children. How many Christian parents never uncover their religious roots with their children? Recall how Timothy's faith was shaped by his mother, Eunice, and his grandmother, Lois (2 Tim. 1:5). Faith sharing may then move to the extended family, the friendship group, or the neighbor. We learn to listen to other person's cries of despair and cynicism, share others' joys and sorrows, and hear their complaints and their excitement at achievement. Our most effective witness is made by the way we ourselves cope with the pain and anguish of our own lives through God's loving mercy.

Teachers also share in the task of encouraging witness. They tell the story of biblical people and later Christians who shared their faith with others, even when it meant persecution. Role-playing may help learners feel able to share their faith and invite others to attend church. Discussion, particularly with adolescents and adults, may help uncover the reasons why talking about faith is so difficult and suggest ways to do so.

CORPORATE RESPONSIBILITY FOR WITNESS

As members of Christ's body, the church, we have responsibility for one another and the corporate witness that the church makes to all the families of the earth. As the whole people of God we share a common ministry (Eph. 4:12). Our individualistic understanding of the faith must be transformed until all Christians learn to exercise gifts for ministry. Our faith is nurtured in the congregation, but that is not the primary context of our ministry. Christians minister in the world as they serve humanity through their vocations, and as the church acts in behalf of the oppressed, the poor, and the marginalized. Included is the responsibility to witness for peace and justice in the world, reflecting the words of the prophets and of Jesus.

Corporate witness is evident in the outreach programs of churches individually and ecumenically. Parishes are also involved, through the work of denominational offices. This witness is learning by doing. Teachers need to interpret these actions. As parish committees develop projects, reflection on the work—in planning, implementing, and evaluating—is a matter of teaching and learning. Adolescents and adults are involved in such efforts, but special projects can be designed for the religious education of children.

No political, social, or economic system deserves the ultimate loyalty of the Christian. While the Christian church engages in actions that challenge poverty, ignorance, racism, and sexism, it bears witness to God's intention to ultimately rule in righteousness and peace. *See also* Action-Reflection; Evangelism; Experience; Gospel; Liberation Theology; Social Justice, Education for.

E. A. Jenkins

Women's Organizations

Women's organizations are groups that specifically include women in membership and leadership. Their administrative relationship to congregation and judicatory may vary.

HISTORY

"Female societies" were first formed in the United States early in the nineteenth century. A Presbyterian church in Newark, New Jersey, records one in 1803, and Congregational women in New England were also among the earliest to form such groups. These organizations provided a unique avenue for the expression of women's concerns and abilities. At a time when women had no official place in the church power structure, it was in women's organizations that their gifts could be exercised and recognized.

With the beginning of missionary work abroad, women's groups were formed to support this work. Letters were exchanged, money raised. Church women thus gained a glimpse of a wider world, in itself an education. In time cooperation among groups developed, and associations formed, culminating in the formation of national denominational women's missionary associations. They held, invested, and sent overseas large sums for the support of the missions enterprise, and they received firsthand accounts from visiting missionaries. Money-raising projects developed leadership and cooperation on the regional and national levels.

A second area to concern women was that of domestic needs, leading to the formation of ladies' home missionary societies to support educational services for the newly freed blacks in the south and amelioration of conditions for factory workers living in the North. Advancing industrialization led to a focus on the needs of immigrants. Church women expressed their concern by giving food and clothing for those living in poverty, assisting in health care, promoting literacy, and focusing on the particular needs of working women and children. Some of the immigrant groups arriving in mid-nineteenth century and later were Catholic, stimulating concern among women's groups in Roman Catholic parishes.

Westward migration brought other needs that particularly engaged the interest of Protestant women's groups. Evangelistic outreach by the established eastern denominations sought to bring the church to these outposts of civilization. Sunday schools were established, books sent, missionaries and theological students supported. The horizons of women were enlarged as letters were exchanged, missionaries reported on their work, and links were forged among groups across the nation.

Church women's groups were not involved—as organizations—in the women's movement or its specific purpose of securing the vote for women. Active church women were among the leaders, but groups in congregations and on the judicatory and national levels avoided controversial issues. Their efforts were expended toward the improvement of present situations rather than the analysis of root causes and solutions.

Hadassah, an international movement of Jewish women, arose in the late nineteenth century in connection with the Zionist movement and has always had as an objective the care for immigrants to Israel. The two Hadassah hospitals in Jerusalem are the most visible sign of this support for the land and its people. Specific concerns are for the welfare of children and the establishment of schools. Although chapters may meet in temples or synagogues, they represent areas, not congregations. The administration is independent of the national synagogue organizations that represent the several branches of Judaism.

Concern for local needs has always been part of the work of women's groups, indicated by names such as Ladies' Aid or Dorcas Society. Sewing has been important both during meetings and at home, to meet the needs of the poor for clothing and the need for objects to sell at money-raising events. Money earned by women's organizations has sometimes become part of the regular parish budget but sometimes has been designated for special projects—thus maintaining the autonomy of the group and reinforcing the expectation that the governing congregational body (on which for a long time there were no women) would be responsible for maintenance of the building and the general needs of the congregation.

Through money administered by the national body, women's groups by the late nineteenth century had established periodicals and were supporting schools and hospitals. They maintained independent national denominational boards and treasuries. But later drives for efficiency and the consolidation of overlapping agencies led to overtures from national boards of domestic and overseas missions inviting the women's groups to amalgamate. The request was logical in view of their common objective—to make the best use of money sacrificially given. But the women found that without control over money they had lost their power base and with it a representative place on the national boards. Few Protestant church women's groups today maintain their original independence.

Dissatisfaction among women surfaced during the post–World War I women's movement. The Presbyterian Church (U.S.A.) responded with a commission that issued a report in 1927 entitled "Causes of Unrest Among Women of the Church." Among those identified were the church's unwillingness to allow women to be ruling elders (who make up the Session, the governing body of the parish, and are the elected delegates to the national assembly) and its refusal to allow women to be ordained to the ministry. Admission as elders was granted first; ordination took longer. This process has since been repeated in some other denominations.

Women have long been associated with ecumenical work. The World Day of Prayer on the first Friday of Lent has been held community wide

since 1920 (more informally, since the 1890s). Councils of church women were an outgrowth of their common interest in the mission of the church.

ORGANIZATION

In synagogues they are called sisterhoods; in Roman Catholic parishes individual groups may be subsumed under the name Council of Catholic Women; in Protestant churches they may be called guilds or societies. Among Protestant women the trend has been to merge separate groups in an effort to unite in common work women of differing ages and to bring a consciousness of varied tasks to the attention of all women. The larger group may meet monthly or less often, with smaller groups, commonly called circles, available to meet particular needs for association according to age or interest. Sisterhoods too usually have an overall group and smaller constituent groups.

Parish groups in Catholic churches tend to be specific in name and purpose but cooperative through the Council of Catholic Women. Catholic parishes are usually much larger than Protestant or Jewish congregations. There are also groups independent of the parish (such as Catholic Daughters), which draw members from several parishes and raise funds nationwide for the support of priests. Catholic Daughters also supports a retirement home for members. Ladies of Charity, a Catholic group, works within the diocese. An independent Protestant women's group, King's Daughters, with chapters in local parishes, has national fund-raising projects, most visible in its hospitals.

Churches within liturgical traditions include among their women's organizations an altar guild, a group whose function is to prepare the altar for all services. Membership is considered an honor, and the work is viewed as a devotional task.

Women's groups in the Protestant and Catholic churches are further organized on the judicatory level. The Council of Catholic Women is basically an affiliative grouping, an overall organization headed by an executive who is part of the diocesan framework. Among Protestant groups, larger judicatories may have a person designated to help local groups with programs.

Protestant groups are also organized on the level of the national denomination, which usually has an office for women's concerns. Study materials are developed and distributed; national conferences planned with the head as facilitator, and basic work done by an elected committee.

Sisterhoods among Reform groups also have an overall organization, the National Federation of Temple Sisterhoods.

RECENT CHANGES

The changing role of women in society has had an effect on church and synagogue, bringing con-

troversy to governing bodies that do not want to change as well as from men and women who affirm traditional roles. Women are serving in greater numbers on lay governing boards. More denominations are ordaining women to the ministry, and more congregations, Jewish and Protestant, are calling ordained women to head congregations. Women's groups have not always been supportive of efforts by their own members to enter the power structure of the church, nor have they always voted to call women as their pastors.

The increase in the number of women who work outside the home has an effect on women's groups. Work takes time that used to be free for attending meetings. Shifting to an evening meeting or having an additional group for working women have not been solutions. These women do not need an extra meeting; they want more time for their families.

Women who are achieving significant roles in society no longer need the stimulus of being in the governing structure through a voluntary women's group, nor do they need to find satisfaction through raising and spending money. They do not need educational programs to expand their horizons.

Is sisterhood important, as those in the women's movement say? Support groups of varying kinds are arising in congregations to meet specific needs. Mothers' groups, for example, take a new form: mutual aid groups for child care and the establishment of services for children. Temple sisterhoods have taken stands on social issues, including affirmation of the Equal Rights Amendment and support for the United Nations. Protestant and Catholic groups have not usually taken stands on social issues, although their educational programs may include studies and speakers on such issues, and individual members may be active. *See also* Church Women United; Feminist Movement.

I. V. Cully

Workbook

A workbook is a learner's individual activity book that is generally a supplementary component of a curriculum. The workbook provides space for the learner to practice what is taught in the curriculum. Because the learner can write directly in the book, the workbook is considered to be a consumable item and is, therefore, usually paperback and not very thick. To make the learner feel comfortable about writing in the book, the size often corresponds to that of standard paper (8½ by 11 inches) customarily used for writing activities. Furthermore, the standard size provides flexibility. For example, sometimes there are holes on the bound side of the workbook so that the whole workbook can be placed into a ring notebook. Or individual pages of the workbook can be torn out along a perforated edge and either used separately or also placed into a ring notebook.

Although most workbooks focus on writing exercises, some include oral exercises. As an accompaniment to teaching cassette or tape recordings, a workbook can offer pronunciation and comprehension practice by asking the learners to repeat and write what they hear. Similarly, written or oral responses to statements made on the cassette or tape can be a meaningful workbook activity.

As the general purpose of the workbook is to practice problem solving, the format is usually geared toward a progressive learning process. What is taught in the first lesson can be practiced in the workbook by completing various learning activities. Information from the first lesson, practiced and correctly completed, becomes the basis for learning the information of the next lesson. For practical reasons workbooks are not available in all areas of study. Workbooks function very well in the language arts because much can be learned by repetition. Although it might seem that the student of mathematics would also benefit from a workbook, the nature of solving mathematical problems takes up much space, making math workbooks cumbersome and expensive. Sometimes a workbook might look like a laboratory manual, especially if the learning activities involve technical or scientific problems.

Popular learning activities for a workbook are oriented toward content recall or toward logical transfer or substitution of information. Typical workbook activities include questions to be answered, identifications, substitution drills, multiple choices, fill-ins, and phrase, clause, or sentence completions. Since learning is to be attractive and fun, a workbook often includes games such as crossword puzzles or dot-to-dots. Creating captions or developing descriptions for a picture or a series of pictures are activities that involve the learner very responsibly in working in a book.

Use of the workbook begins at the first- or second-grade level because some knowledge of reading generally is needed in order to follow directions. In various fields, it is even used with adults. With children in religious education, however, interest in workbooks may diminish by sixth grade. The size of the group is not a factor in the use of this method.

C. W. Spanier

Workshop

The religious education workshop is an intensive short-term experience of "learning by doing."

Some workshops present themselves because a particular task needs to get done, a family festival needs to be planned for, a visitation ministry must be prepared for, or teachers need to be trained in the use of a newly adopted curriculum. Others arise because potential participants express interest in an intensive learning experience in a certain area: teachers investigating the possibility of team teaching may feel the need to have a workshop on the method.

BACKGROUND

As an educational model the workshop has its theoretical roots in the experiential education movement in the early twentieth century. More recently, the behavioral and humanistic sciences have contributed especially the disciplines of counseling and group dynamics.

The workshop makes the assumption that learning is a natural, self-motivated, and self-directed process for solving problems. Reflective thinking applied to the process (i.e., imagination, past experience, memory, and reason) projects discipline into the tendency to learn by trial and error. The indeterminate situation is analyzed for the factual circumstances, and ideas are proposed, tested for their probable consequences, and prioritized; from these a "solution" decision is made and acted upon.

William Heard Kilpatrick, a colleague of John Dewey's, proposed an inherent procedural structure for experiential, problem-solving learning: purposing, planning, executing, and evaluating. Workshop procedure follows closely this project method, as Kilpatrick called it.

Kilpatrick also embraced the concept of "concomitant learning," i.e., subjective learning that influences the self-concept and behavioral attitudes. Concomitant learning during a serious decision-making experience affirms the self as free, rational, responsible, cooperative, and creatively competent, essential qualities of a democratic people, but qualities desirable too in a religious people.

Modern religious education has adopted Dewey's experiential model of education with the additional theological claim that in and through such instructional-nurturing experiences God becomes known. Reflective thought on Scripture, experience, and other resources guides the process. The presumption is that such creative experience, ongoing as spiritual pilgrimage, gives rise to faith as concomitant learning and shapes vision and life-style.

PLANNING

To plan a workshop, a committee meets to make initial decisions: define purpose, plan for time and place, and secure resource leadership. They will give attention to the setting by providing pleasant and comfortable accommodations, teaching equipment, and supplies, e.g., chalkboard, newsprint, easels, projectors, and recorders, including for research purposes books, periodicals, monographs, and liturgical aids.

While a workshop can be held at home, a site removed from the familiar and its distractions, such as a camp or retreat center, may be preferred. A full day, preferably a weekend, allows for unhurried work, leisure, and fellowship. A workshop may be planned as a series of sessions over a period of weeks, especially when the praxis model of learning—reflection and action, action and reflection—calls for progress reporting, further evaluation, and replanning.

LEADERSHIP

Leadership requires experience and procedural skill, especially the ability to communicate well. Personal qualities of perceptual and relationship sensitivity are equally important. Group dynamics have demonstrated the effectiveness of the leader as facilitator/enabler. Such leadership is the art of perceiving the creative potential of the group and employing techniques that motivate and involve participants at their level of readiness and ability to take hold of their own learning.

Following a time for socializing and orientation, the leader tests the initial purposing and planning with the group, gives time for any "corrections and additions," and initiates project procedure. The usual techniques of lecture, question and answer, and discussion are used as needed. The leadership team may include a process observer and recorder who offer feedback on progress. Members themselves can become increasingly observing and articulate about how the process is leading toward goals and how the relationship among participants is contributing to the work.

THE GROUP

The group needs to be small enough in number to engage in face-to-face communication. A large workshop will subdivide at appropriate points into groups of two and three to ensure full participation. Plenary sessions bring these "labs" back together to report, to show and tell, and to prepare for the next procedural step.

A workshop's primary purpose, as the name implies, is to get work done: to produce that much-needed new curriculum or to develop that strategy for aid to the hungry and homeless. On the other hand, fellowship "while we work," as concomitant learning, is no less important, certainly from a religious perspective. Talk that may begin haltingly and superficially can become dialogue. Dialogue is an "entering into" experience, a sharing with one another out of individual private worlds.

The ideal of dialogic encounter and emerging fellowship must be realistically balanced by an understanding that tension and conflict can occur when the openness of the process allows and encourages differences. The use of process observation and feedback together with role playing and simulation games help a group "in crisis" become increasingly self-aware, objective, and accepting. Resulting insight, consensus, and mutual affirmation can bring a group to a new level of relatedness and productivity. In this creative manner a group may indeed become an authentic fellowship.

A CONCLUDING WORD

A workshop viewed from a religious perspective is more than work accomplishment, important as that might be. A workshop is rather conceived as creative engagement and as such a human response to the divine creativity. Method thus calls for an accompanying interpretation and celebration of its significance. Planning for beginnings and endings of a devotional nature thus becomes essential to round out the experience appropriately.

When articulated confessionally, mutually shared with the emerging, caring, covenant community, and given corporate liturgical expression, the workshop reaches its climax as a model for creative productivity and concomitant religious learning. The workshop as a model for religion's institutional ministry of education has this potential.

When evaluation is completed at the end of the workshop, responses from participants will guide planners in understanding what has been most helpful, what was not useful, and what might be tried in future planned workshops. *See also* Conflict Management; Dialogue; Group Dynamics; Learning Theory; Problem Solving.

P. B. Irwin

World Council of Christian Education

See Sunday School Movement.

World Council of Churches

The World Council of Churches (WCC), linking 330 national and regional churches totaling 360 million Christians from more than 100 countries, was founded in 1948. Although the organization is sometimes criticized for its challenge to the status quo in church and society, it is intended to be a symbol of hope, a lightning rod for controversy, a forum in which the life and work of every church are subject to scrutiny and mutual correction, an instrument for effective cooperation in service to human need, and a constant source of fresh ideas and new vision. Although there had

been other international Christian organizations at work during the fifty years before 1948 (the World Movement for Faith and Order, the World Movement for Life and Work, the International Missionary Council, and the World Council of Christian Education—all of which have now been incorporated within the structure of the WCC), in the World Council of Churches for the first time whole churches (as distinct from individuals, congregations, or councils of churches) had covenanted to work together to overcome ancient divisions and to be more effective in mission and ministry to the world.

PURPOSE

The purpose of the WCC is set forth in its constitution in the "basis for membership" and in other articles summarizing its functions. The basis describes the WCC as "a fellowship of churches which confess the Lord Jesus Christ as God and Savior according to the Scriptures, and therefore seek to fulfill together their common calling to the glory of the one God, Father, Son and Holy Spirit." As a fellowship and a council the WCC does not supersede the authority or independence of any member church, but as the common voice of many churches its statements and actions carry a moral authority that must be taken seriously. The purposes of the WCC are:

1. To call the churches to the goal of visible unity in one faith and in one eucharistic fellowship expressed in worship and in common life in Christ, and to advance toward that unity in order that the world may believe

2. To facilitate common witness of the churches in each place and in all places

3. To support the churches in their worldwide missionary and evangelistic task

4. To express the common concern of the churches in the service of human need, the breaking down of barriers between people, and the promotion of one human family in justice and peace

STRUCTURE

To give concrete expression to these broad goals and to maintain a balance between them, the WCC has developed both an elaborate system of policy formation and a complex bureaucracy of experts at its headquarters in Geneva assigned to program units and subunits that cover almost the entire range of church activities and concerns. Although the staff of approximately three hundred persons must direct the day-to-day work of the council, care is taken that ultimate responsibility for WCC policy and program rests with the member churches through their officially appointed delegates. Care is also taken that governing bodies, staff, and most committees are representative of the diversity of the whole people of God throughout the world, by region, race, gender, age, confessional affiliation, and status as lay or ordained persons. The representative principle assures that minority voices will be heard and that the concerns of small or impoverished churches will be taken as seriously as the concerns of the rich and powerful. This makes for tension within the council that is often painful yet uniquely creative and for an intelligence system unmatched by any government about conditions and crises in every part of the world.

The highest governing body of the WCC is an assembly composed of delegates appointed by the member churches and meeting once in seven years or so. The colorful gatherings, preparatory studies, intense debates, and resulting publicity make the assemblies the most visible expression of the WCC for ordinary Christians. Amsterdam in 1948, Evanston in 1954, New Delhi in 1961, Upsala in 1968, Nairobi in 1975, and Vancouver in 1983 mark milestones in the ecumenical movement. The next assembly will be convened in Australia in 1991.

Each assembly reviews the work of the WCC in the previous period and sets new priorities for the future. Worship and Bible study are at the heart of each assembly program. Five official languages (English, French, German, Russian, and Spanish) are in use and translation is provided for those who depend on other tongues. Each assembly elects from its membership a Central Committee of 150 persons to supervise the work of the council through annual meetings until the next assembly. It also elects a group of seven presidents, senior leaders representing the major families of churches and geographical regions of the world. With over 300 member churches, few churches get to have more than one person on the central committee and many have no representative at all. The presidium has a largely honorary and advisory role, but the moderator elected to chair the central committee has an influence second only to that of the general secretary.

Since the central committee is able to meet at most once a year, it chooses an executive committee of twenty persons, including the officers and the general secretary, who meet more frequently to deal with administration and to act for the central committee in matters of urgency. The central committee appoints working groups and unit committees to direct the various programs of the council and elects staff for these units on the recommendation of the general secretary. To avoid the development of an entrenched bureaucracy, staff are appointed for three-year terms and, with few exceptions, may not serve more than nine years.

The general secretary as chief executive officer and spokesperson for the WCC plays a key role in shaping its image and program. W. A. Visser t'Hooft of the Netherlands headed a small staff in Geneva during World War II and served as general secretary from 1948–1966. Other general secretaries have been Eugene Carson Blake of the United States, 1966–1972, Philip Potter of Dominica, 1972–1984, and Emilio Castro of Uruguay, since 1985.

PROGRAMS

The work of the WCC is organized under three program units, each headed by a deputy general secretary. Faith and Witness includes subunits for world mission and evangelism, the theological work of faith and order, church and society studies, and dialogue with people of living faiths.

The unit Justice and Service includes the multimillion-dollar relief program of the Commission on Inter-Church Aid, Refugee and World Service, the Commission on the Churches' Participation in Development, the Commission of the Churches on International Affairs (which among other responsibilities maintains liaison with the United Nations and its agencies), and the Christian Medical Commission and the Program to Combat Racism.

The Education and Renewal unit concentrates, though not exclusively, on the internal life of the churches with subunits devoted to education, renewal and congregational life, women in church and society, the program on theological education, and youth. Some subunits include areas of work not immediately apparent from their titles. The subunit on education, for example, includes the Office of Biblical Studies and administration of the council's program on the church and persons with disabilities.

Other administrative units that serve the life of the council as a whole come directly under the general secretary: Finance, Personnel, the Communication Department (providing not only press and information service in several languages but also audiovisual material and a wide range of periodicals and other publications), the Ecumenical Institute at Bossey, the Ecumenical Library, and the New York Office for liaison with the many member churches and supporters in North America.

Several large and conservative American Protestant churches, notably the Southern Baptist Convention and the Lutheran Church–Missouri Synod, have declined on principle to join the WCC. Some fundamentalist bodies are persistent critics. The worldwide Roman Catholic church is not a member but collaborates closely with the WCC in many individual programs. A joint working group provides continuing consultation between staff members at the Vatican and in Geneva.

A catalog of WCC publications (including official reports, periodicals, newsletters, and current study projects) is available from the Publications Office, World Council of Churches, P.O. Box 66, 1211 Geneva 20, Switzerland, or from the U.S. Office of the WCC, Room 1062, 475 Riverside Drive, New York, NY 10115. An overview of current issues, for congregational use, is found in *Vancouver Voices* by Charles H. Long, Forward Movement Publications, 412 Sycamore Street, Cincinnati, OH 45202. *See also* Councils of Churches; Ecumenical Education; Ecumenical Institutes; Mission, Education for.

C. H. Long

World Sunday School Association

See Sunday School Movement.

Worship

In the most general sense, worship may be defined as the human response of adoration, praise, and supplication to the being and mighty acts of God, usually in the context of a gathered community of faith. Worship comprehends the most intimate personal approach to God as well as the common prayer of the church. A central root meaning of the term is the ascribing of value to that which is worthy (from the Old English *weorth*, "worthy, worth," and *scipe*, "ship"). This discussion focuses primarily upon the theological and human dimensions of meaning and the forms and historic patterns of public worship found in the Christian tradition, especially in relation to the catechetical and educational tasks of the Christian churches.

General definitions of worship must admit the possibility of idolatry—the worship of false gods. Idol worship is an age-old human problem in every religious tradition and culture. This is especially true within Judaism and Christianity. Biblical traditions that call a people into covenant community with a living God also strenuously prohibit the worship of idols. Hence the first of the Ten Commandments: "You shall have no other gods before me." The worship of God sets itself in tension with basic human impulses to worship political power, money, the self, public heroes, or other finite goods. The fundamental problem of idolatry forces us to ask a normative question, "What is true and faithful worship?"

At its heart, true worship seeks what is truly holy. This quality of the divine forms and illuminates human life. Whoever seeks to live in the presence of God and in love of neighbor is drawn into worship. In the great vision of the prophet Isaiah (chap. 6), heavenly beings cry out, "holy, holy, holy" in ceaseless acknowledgment of God, and the prophetic seer immediately senses his own unworthiness. True worship of God thus involves the formation of particular dispositions, experiences, and attitudes in the worshipers that are appropriate to being in the presence of the living God. Recognizing the truth about human existence, both in our inward being and in our responsibility to care for all creation, is central to authentic encounter and communion with God. Worship occurs when God becomes a "Thou" and not simply an object of speculation for us. In this sense relationship to God is a matter of passional commitment and is not merely cognitive or rational. Yet worship does involve learning concepts and teachings as part of what it means to pray and to understand the stories and images of Scripture. To worship God is to revere and to love the divine and in the process to understand God, ourselves, and the world more deeply.

THEOLOGICAL AND HUMAN DIMENSIONS

To worship is to acknowledge the holiness, justice, and mercy of God. Yet worship also forms worshipers in and gives expression to basic human attitudes and emotions such as awe, reverence, humility, gratitude, and joy. Classic definitions of worship indicate this two-sidedness as, for example, in the phrase, "the glorification of God and the sanctification of all that is human." The activity of worship, whether alone or together, brings this mutuality of the human and the divine into focus. The reality and mystery of God is brought into relation with human inwardness as well as with our public life with others and our ethical responsibilities. Worship may be defined as the conscious and intentional act of becoming aware of the reality and presence of God by entering into special times and places of remembrance and hope. In this sense worship requires a certain discontinuity with our everydayness and our ordinary behavior. Because most human lives are spent in work, self-preoccupation, and distraction, authentic worship requires particular times, places, traditions of memory and prayer, and attentiveness to how God communicates with humankind.

Worship can be best understood as a double journey—an ongoing dialogue and communion between God and humankind. While it is true that many people worship only on certain occasions, the essence of worship in Jewish and Christian traditions is an ever-deepening response over time. The psalmist exclaims, "Seven times a day I praise thee O Lord" (Ps. 119:164). While authentic worship requires an element of discontinuity with our everyday consciousness and ways of living, it also moves toward continuity of praise, prayer, and ritual action. This is behind the meaning of Paul's admonition to present yourselves, soul and body, as "a living sacrifice" of prayer and thanksgiving to God (Rom. 12:1). Worship is both speaking and listening and a continual remembering, invoking, and hoping. This is why worship involves the disciplines of time, place, tradition, symbols, and human relationships. Scripture enjoins believers to "give thanks in all circumstances" (1 Thess. 5:18) and to "ascribe to the Lord the glory of his holy name" (Ps. 29:2).

To worship God touches upon those things essential to our humanity: memory, praise and thanksgiving, telling the truth before God and neighbor, forgiving and receiving forgiveness, feeding and being fed, being healed and reaching out to others, interceding and offering ourselves to God for the sake of others. Times, places, songs, words, and rituals that are set apart from our everyday ordinary lives thus point to the mystery of authentic worship: the ordinary becomes the bearer of the extraordinary. Our everyday acts of speaking and listening, touching, feeding, working, and resting can themselves become bearers of the holy when seen in light of their transformation in worship. This is especially prominent in the meaning of the Christian sacraments, where ordinary things such as bread, wine, water, oil, or the touch of human hands become "means of grace," the very manner of God's self-giving to us. Worship is a rehearsal of who we are to become in God.

We can certainly worship God alone, but deepening our understanding of God and God's relationship to the world is most profoundly realized only in a community of memory, suffering, and hope. In this way worship gives identity and belonging to the worshipers. To remember and to recognize the holy in our midst is dependent upon a shared common history of teaching, witness, and prayer. Such remembering overcomes the tendencies of "rugged individualism" so present in American culture. As T. S. Eliot reminds us in "Choruses from *The Rock*," we have no real life apart from life together and there is no community "not lived in praise of God."

HISTORICAL PATTERNS AND STYLES

Historical forms and patterns of public worship show an immense variety across traditions, from ecstatic dances to elaborate, often highly stylized liturgical ritual, to simple communal silence, as with the Quakers. Whether highly structured or free, the essence of worship is wholehearted acknowledgment and response to the One who has created and redeemed the world. Particular denominational traditions shape and express the faith of the community in differing ways, though all Christian patterns involve time, place, the Scriptures, symbols, a gathered assembly and the acts of proclaiming, witnessing, and receiving. Different liturgical patterns and worship forms are closely related to particular types of spirituality as well as to denominational identity.

In recent ecumenical discussions of Christian worship three fundamental types of public worship are usually mentioned: "altar-centered" or sacramental, "pulpit-centered" or proclamatory, and "waiting upon the Spirit." The first is associated with Roman Catholic, Orthodox, and Anglican traditions; the second with mainline and evangelical Protestantism; and the third with Pentecostals, certain charismatic renewal movements, and with the Quakers. While such types are by no means mutually exclusive, each worship pattern and style has a different center of gravity.

The sacramental traditions involve the reading of Scripture and preaching the word of God, but their central focus of worship is upon God's incarnational self-giving in Jesus Christ. Emphasis is upon the saving mystery of Christ's death and resurrection, which are most intensely recognized in the Holy Meal. Christ is understood to be both the one sacrificed for the salvation of the world and the one who is truly present in the words and sign-actions of the gathered church. Great stress is placed upon the continuity of the church's practice and of those authorized to celebrate the sacraments. In the more sacramentally oriented traditions, the church itself is thought of as being a sacrament to the world, extending the incarnation of Christ in the form of a community of faith, love, and service. There has been a tendency in these traditions to relegate preaching and congregational participation, except for receiving sacramental grace, to a secondary role.

In proclamation or word-oriented traditions, the sermon is regarded as central to worship; hence the leaders of worship are characteristically referred to as "preachers" or, less often, "pastors," rather than as priests. The teaching and preaching authority of the clergy is seen as that which can rightly open the Scriptures, proclaim the word, and also celebrate the sacraments. The church is in this view often regarded principally as a herald of Good News, and the community is primarily directed toward serving the world. Often in such traditions the emphasis is placed upon the "priesthood of all believers" and the function of the church is a witnessing community of the word. Here forms of worship have sometimes come, ironically, to be dominated by the preachers, while nevertheless emphasizing the people's role in hymns, responses, and the fellowship of believers.

The third type of worship, "waiting on the Spirit," covers a wide range from concentration on speaking in tongues and other congregational manifestations of being acted upon by the Holy Spirit to the Quaker meeting in which persons are moved to speak only after the "discipline" of silence and contemplative prayer. In all these, emphasis is clearly on human experience of the divine presence and on expressing what one is experiencing or discerning. The tendency in some forms of this type is toward strong discontinuity of behavior from ordinary life; worship and "being religious" are special experiences that may not relate very clearly to daily life. Black and Hispanic traditions often combine enthusiastic worship in the Spirit with vital preaching and, in some cases, with considerable formal liturgy.

The most interesting developments in the twentieth century are occurring where these three types are beginning to appreciate one another and where the laity discover aspects of their own traditions that need what has been more central in one of the others. Thus, Roman Catholicism since Vatican II (1962–1965) has recovered biblical preaching and, in some instances, has witnessed charismatic renewal flourishing alongside other forms of a renewed participation of the laity in liturgical life.

Protestant traditions have been gradually rediscovering the importance of sacramental celebration. Within the past fifteen years significant renewal within mainline Protestant churches has been related to the restoration of the classical balance between word and sacramental celebration.

In American culture within the last century, we can identify four major periods of change in the pattern and style of Protestant worship, most of which reflect changes in the surrounding shifts in American society. From the Civil War era until the turn of the century most Protestant worship was dominated by revivalism. In this period worship served the end of converting people to the faith. Sunday worship patterns focused upon preaching for a decision and inculcating a profile of expected evangelical experience. So Methodists, Baptists, Presbyterians, and others invariably concluded Sunday services of worship with a hymn of preparation, the sermon, a call to conversation or to commitment during the singing of a hymn, and a concluding prayer of blessing. The characteristic style was warm, informal, and folksy.

Shortly after the turn of the century, a marked change occurred, especially in urban settings, which James White has called the beginning of the "era of respectability." Attention was being given to more refined, aesthetic taste, and the emotional experience of revivalism was replaced by more dignified and learned preaching. Choirs began to sing Mendelssohn and classical composers, and "good taste" and the beautiful came to influence the environment of the sanctuaries. The era of respectability in Protestant worship developed in the 1940s and early 1950s into a period of searching for historical roots of liturgy. Many denominations rediscovered their Reformation roots and began to use patterns of prayer and sacramental services based on the models of the sixteenth and seventeenth centuries.

Then, in the mid 1960s churches experienced a sudden and widespread period of experimentation with nearly every aspect of worship, from new musical forms drawn from popular culture to the introduction of multimedia, drama, dance, and colloquial language. This was a period of cultural pluralism, and the sudden realization of the splintering and diversity of cultures within society is still a factor influencing the style and its counterreaction in several traditions. The hallmark words were "relevancy" and "expressive celebration." This was a time of Harvey Cox's *The Feast of Fools* and articles entitled "Liturgies When Cities Burn."

In light of these cultural and social shifts, Christian worship now faces a range of unprecedented issues for teachers, celebrants, and congregations. Significant growth in worship life in the churches in our culture today requires sustained teaching and reflection on the impact and significance of these shifts on the way we worship and our expectations. Even today many local churches exhibit all four strata within their congregations of these shifts of style and emphasis: revivalism, "good taste," historical identity and order, and relevance/experimentation.

REFORM AND RENEWAL OF WORSHIP TODAY

Such considerations of theology, human religious needs, and historical developments set the context for the task of reform and renewal in Christian worship as we move toward the twenty-first century. Reform and renewal are different, though related, tasks. Reform of the patterns and texts and music with which we worship may or may not lead to genuine renewal of worship as faithful liturgy. New music and new language do not necessarily immediately transform individual and communal lives. At the same time many of our inherited patterns and styles of worship were biblically impoverished and did not reflect an adequate understanding of the larger Christian tradition. Churches that emphasized preaching services but celebrated the Lord's Supper quarterly were not, in fact, fulfilling the Reformers' wishes—neither Luther's, Calvin's, nor Wesley's. Similarly, sacramental celebrations that were not grounded in the people's study of Scripture and in lively, biblical preaching were not adequate to the mystery of the "Word made visible" and proclaimed in Eucharist, and the "audible sacrament" of authentic preaching.

Concern for reforming our liturgical patterns that has emerged in the past twenty years, stimulated initially by the liturgical reforms of the Second Vatican Council, must now be related to the more difficult task of renewing the depth and quality of worship. This is a matter of massive education and reeducation in the heart of every denomination and every local church. Questions have been raised about the adequacy and depth of our patterns and styles of worship both from a deeper knowledge of the Jewish and Christian traditions and by the social and cultural crises of modern life—from the threat of nuclear holocaust to the disillusion of many with inherited images of church in relation to the essential questions of human existence, personal and communal. When worship becomes disconnected from the realities of life and death in our world, the question of renewal is paramount. Determining the faithfulness and adequacy of Christian worship in a time of cultural and social change is also a question about the quality and integrity of education and service and not merely about ritual or prayer.

Perhaps the most hopeful sign in our present explorations of the meaning and point of worship concerns the recovery of the "roots" of Christian worship in Scripture and the formative period of the early church. We cannot simply appeal to what the early church did as the best way for judging contemporary efforts of reform and renewal. Still, the early period serves as a reminder that, without the essentials of grounding in Scripture, the richness of the whole tradition, and the mutuality of common prayer and service to the world, Christian worship cannot be adequate to its own gospel or to "all sorts and conditions" of humanity today.

Recent discussions by theologians and historians of Christian worship have spoken of the need to understand and recover the whole "canon" of Christian worship. That is, just as there is a canon of Scripture in which the church decided what books were of primary importance to the life and faith of the church, so there is a similar canon of essential elements in Christian worship.

Four basic structures form a body of defining elements that the Christian tradition has used over the centuries. While not always understood and practiced with equal weight in each tradition, these four structures or elements are indispensable to a full and organically whole approach to worship. The four are: the rites of Christian initiation (baptism, confirmation, and the whole process leading thereto), the Lord's Supper or Eucharist, the cycles of time (feasts and seasons unfolding the story of God in Christ), and the patterns of daily prayer. In addition, we may speak of a fifth element of the canon that flows from teaching and practicing these essentials, namely, "pastoral" services of worship such as marriage and funeral rites, services of penitence and reconciliation, and various forms of prayer with the sick and the dying.

In our age of reform and renewal of Christian worship and life, the study of the whole meaning and range of Christian worship is absolutely central to growth and deeper unity among the churches. Each of the major denominational bodies and, indeed, many ethnic and Third World churches, are in the process of reappropriating the whole canon of Christian worship. At the same time, traditions are learning from each other. Each tradition has something to contribute to the others. Ignorance and intolerance of the authentic strands of Christian worship and spirituality is no longer a real option. The church ignores this canon and the diverse gifts among worshiping families at its own peril. When these are denied or neglected, as has frequently been the case in the history of Christianity, worship, theology, and spirituality all are diminished.

TRAINING FOR FULL, ACTIVE, AND MATURE PARTICIPATION

If it is true that Christian worship both forms and expresses human beings in the mystery of God in Christ, then the linkage between worship and religious education comes to central focus. Becoming a faithful person and a more mature community of faith is not a matter of gaining new information. It is a matter of formation in a whole range of capacities. Christian nurture is a gradual process of change in the heart of our personal being. Worship itself is a "school of prayer." Yet there are various levels of maturity and levels of capacity to participate in the whole range of worship.

A distinctive phrase from the *Constitution on the Sacred Liturgy* of Vatican II has been influential in much Protestant reflection on the future direction of worship: the church must teach and nurture Christians for "full, active, and mature participation" in the liturgy. The early church took the matter of formation and training for worship very seriously. The catechumenate, or preparation process for Christian initiation, was an intensive period of being formed in Scripture, in prayer, fasting, self-reflection, and in the patterns of Christian life and devotion. This was often a three-year period, as described by Hippolytus in the third century. The laity had various roles in instructing and encouraging those who were preparing for baptism. The Lenten period became a time of preparation for the whole community to participate in the great Easter celebration, thereby witnessing with the newly baptized and reaffirming their own baptismal covenant.

The current practices of easy infant baptism and the lack of intentional training period for church membership must be reevaluated and a pattern of preparation for "full, active, and mature participation" be undertaken by the whole congregation. At the same time, worship is a profoundly intergenerational experience, and the practice of infant baptism by many traditions requires that training and formation in the meaning and ways of participation in worship take seriously the various levels of human development, moral and emotional. Children are often able to respond to levels of nonverbal symbol in surprisingly strong ways. Focusing upon the wider range of visual, acoustical, and bodily forms of participation in early experiences of worship is of crucial importance to the formation of faith. Many churches have developed programs involving the whole family in common experiential learning with respect to worship and to sacramental participation. Musical training is, of course, one of the most important ways of forming younger persons in the prayer, praise, memory, and hope that constitutes the heart of Christian worship.

PASTORAL DIMENSIONS OF AUTHENTIC WORSHIP

Because Christian worship involves the whole community and the recent reforms of our patterns and styles of worship demand more thoughtful preparation of both the participants and the worship service itself, several concluding implications are in order. First, the future directions of worship will require lay participation in planning and in the various ministries within the gathered community. Education in reading and the study of Scriptures, in theology and the practice of leading prayer, of serving Communion, of sponsorship of candidates for initiation (baptism and confirmation) is part of worship renewal. Second, new catechetical structures and processes are emerging that take seriously the moral development of persons at different age levels and in different life passages. In this way, worship can be linked with the continual deepening faith life of the whole congregation without imposing a single regimented style of education. Third, the new emphasis on restoring the balance between word and sacrament and the increasingly fruitful ecumenical awareness among various churches create a need for better adult education in the history of worship and in comparative church and liturgical traditions. Finally, the future direction of Christian worship is radically dependent upon recovering the inner connection between worship and service, between love of God and love of neighbor, between prayer and work. By recovering these four aspects of the pastoral dimension of worship we may restore the ancient and venerable root meaning of liturgy as the "work of the people of God." At the same time, we may learn again what Augustine said of faithfully participating in the Eucharist, "It is your own mystery you receive." *See also* Children's Church; Choir; Choir, Children's; Church Year; Eucharist; Holidays; Holy Spirit; Hymnody, Christian; Jewish Festivals and Holidays; Lay Ministry; Lectionary; Liturgical Movement; Liturgy; Music in the Church; Prayer; Preaching; Sacraments; Sermons, Children's; Spirituality; Symbolism; Vatican II; Worship, Children's; Worship, Family.

FOR FURTHER REFERENCE

Browning, Robert L., and Roy A. Reed. *The Sacraments in Religious Education and Liturgy.* Birmingham, AL: Religious Education Press, 1985.
Burkhart, John E. *Worship.* Philadelphia: Westminster, 1982.
Hoon, Paul W. *The Integrity of Worship.* Nashville, TN: Abingdon, 1971.
Saliers, Don E. *Worship and Spirituality.* Philadelphia: Westminster, 1984.
White, James F. *The Worldliness of Worship.* New York: Oxford University Press, 1967.

D. E. Saliers

Worship, Children's

Children of all ages can worship God. They can pray, sing, listen to readings of Scripture and to preaching, offer themselves in dedication to God, and receive with thanksgiving the gifts of God through the sacraments. They participate at the level that reflects their age and development. The church usually provides worship for children in church school and families often provide informal worship at home. Churches now are making efforts to include children more fully in corporate worship and sometimes will have children leading parts of the liturgy such as songs and readings. Some churches include children for part of the service, others on specific Sundays.

NEW PERSPECTIVES

The church's perspectives on children have changed in the last two decades. Recent interpretations of the teachings of developmental psychologist Jean Piaget and social psychologist Erik Erikson have convinced teachers and leaders in the church that children do understand much of what is happening in erstwhile adult activities and do participate at levels that can be termed "mature"—levels of cognition and comprehension appropriate to the age and development of the children. Thus a seven-year-old child may participate in a corporate prayer of confession, aware of her own shortcomings and her need for forgiveness from God. This child may need help with

words like "a contrite heart," but she is capable of perceiving that she must feel sorry for what she has done to hurt others.

Along with changes in the way adults understand the issue of "readiness" in children, the church has undergone changes in its perception of the role of children in worship. There has been movement away from the notion of worship as an activity only for those reaching a certain level of intellectual and spiritual development. Worship is once again seen as an activity touching all the senses and emotions, experienced by persons at every age and level of development. Thus, even infants can meaningfully experience worship and participate with personal integrity. A child of ten years of age may have a somewhat limited ability to know what is happening when bread and wine are shared at a Eucharist, but he participates as a ten year old would, dealing with theological concepts concretely and personally. But learned and experienced adults may not understand fully what is happening in the Eucharist either, and they also respond in accordance with their own levels of development. Much mystery resides in the worship of God, and worshipers, regardless of age or background, will respond in ways that are individually appropriate and meaningful. Children as well as adults can worship meaningfully.

Furthermore, children as well as adults can contribute to the community's worship. The presence of children reminds the community of its corporate, inclusive nature—the church can hardly be the *koinonia*, the community in Christ, while excluding a whole segment of its membership, the children. Their presence enriches and helps to fulfill the community. Children usually worship with their whole persons—heart as well as head. They remind adults that they too can engage in worship with heart and soul, not just intellectually. Some Protestant services of worship are weighted toward the intellectual, culminating in a sermon aimed at a high degree of cognitive ability and implying an intellectual approach to faith. Much of this "goes over the heads" of children if they are present. When a church must consciously communicate with and engage children, its worship likely will be more active. The pace, movement, music, art, symbols, vocabulary, and length of the service will be adjusted to accommodate the abilities of the children. Adults will find that such efforts help in their own understanding and participation.

Another important motivation for involving children in worship is the expansion of the understanding of the sacraments. Communion, or the Eucharist, now is seen by many as an inclusive sacrament of community. Where children are baptized in infancy, they may be considered as members rightfully included in Communion. Members, regardless of age, have the same need for grace and the same invitation by Jesus Christ to come to the Table. The children will come and receive according to their level of development: young children will sense acceptance and belonging and may be able to respond with gratitude and trust; perhaps by age five or six, they relate the acts of breaking bread and pouring wine with Jesus, recalling his life and sacrifice; and as children grow older they understand more about love and forgiveness, dramatized and symbolized in the Eucharist, and about their own response of self-giving. As children reach adolescence they realize that the Eucharist recalls both crucifixion and resurrection and offers hope for the future.

INVOLVING CHILDREN IN WORSHIP

Many congregations desire more involvement by children and try to accomplish this by presenting a "children's sermon." While some churches conduct this with skill and dignity, others do so with no understanding of the theological, historical, and liturgical bases for worship or of the sensitivities of children. To set children apart by calling them up front and asking leading or moralistic questions to which they may respond with naively concrete answers is condescending and without theological integrity.

For children to participate it is not necessary to depart from the bounds of good theology and liturgical practice. Often it is the traditional and richly liturgical service that offers the worshipers, children and adults alike, the most drama, emotion, physical movement, involvement, and re-

sponse. There is always a need for teaching about worship but there is little need for drastic change in the service to accommodate children. As the very youngest children participate they may experience acceptance and belonging and feelings of joy, trust, and solemnity. The music, surroundings, and attitudes of the worshipers will impress the infant. Children of ages four to seven years will begin to be more comfortable with the procedures of worship and will learn when to bow in prayer, when to stand for singing and acts of offering and commitment, and when to be silent. While not understanding many of the words, these children nevertheless can join in prayers of adoration or confession with a broad sense of what is expressed. These children participate in concrete, personal ways. As children reach the age of seven to eleven years, they will understand better the overall "story" that ties together the acts of worship. In adolescence they will use their new skills of abstract conceptualization to think beyond time and space to richer understandings of how worship symbolizes relationship with God and enhances the indwelling of the Holy Spirit in the life of the worshiping community.

Children and worship bring together wonder and mystery. An age of wonder and imagination engages in an act filled with imagery and mystery. *See also* Children's Church; Koinonia; Liturgy; Sacraments; Sermons, Children's; Worship; Worship, Family.

FOR FURTHER REFERENCE

Holmes, Urban T., III. *Young Children and the Eucharist.* Rev. ed. New York: Seabury, 1982.

Ng, David, and Virginia Thomas. *Children in the Worshiping Community.* Atlanta, GA: Knox, 1981.

Sloyan, Virginia, and Gabe Huck. *Children's Liturgies.* Washington, DC: Liturgical Conference, 1970.

D. Ng

Worship, Family

Family worship comprises all forms of prayer together as a family, both at home and in other places. The religious community generally believes that corporate worship in church and synagogue, for any age person, may have little meaning if there is no dialogue with or about God in the home; that parental modeling is critical; and that early experiences with a spiritual dimension in primary relationships and family traditions—particularly within a warm and loving environment—are deep and lasting.

HISTORY AND IMPORTANCE

The significance of family worship is understood not only through a genuine doctrine of the church and the findings of the behavioral sciences, but also in the biblical mandate. For Christian and Jewish believers, instruction/worship is rooted in the Scriptures, where families (like Abraham and Sarah; and Lois, Eunice, and Timothy) are frequently the means of historical and spiritual continuity from generation to generation (Deut. 4:9–10) and the locus of the most vital spiritual communication (Deut. 6:7–9; Eph. 6:4).

In the sixteenth century, the Reformers built on that biblical family tradition. Luther's play for his children, *From Heaven on High*, based on the Christmas story in the Gospels, is an example of piety and family worship that has its variations around the crèche and Advent wreath in Christian homes throughout the world today.

Moreover, family worship is strongly implied in the convenantal content of the sacraments and confirmation liturgies. In denominations that practice infant baptism, parents and congregation make public commitments of support and nurture. Hence, the important involvement of both family and church in preparation for baptism, confirmation/commissioning, and the Lord's Supper. In families who take it all seriously, there will be prayerful response in the home.

In the prosperous 1950s, there was a strong emphasis on the family both in the culture and in the church. There was also a powerful biblical, theological, Reformation-flavored renewal emerging with the growth of the World Council of Churches and an international community of eminent theologians. It was an exciting time in some denominations for Christian educators who were called to provide the churches with theologically sound and educationally valid study resources, including materials for home use, until the movement lost momentum in the turbulent 1960s.

Today, the area of family worship is not clearly focused denominationally in mainline Protestantism. With church organizational difficulties in the 1970s and financial problems in the 1980s, production of curriculum materials on a large scale has decreased. However, with the new emerging concern in the churches for intentional ministries with families again, there may yet be a resurgent emphasis on family worship, particularly if there is also spiritual renewal.

In response to the increase in new literature on family ministries, as noted for example in the annual meetings in recent years of the Family Commission of the National Council of Churches, some denominations and local churches that take Christian nurture seriously are providing resources for families, usually separate from the regular curriculum. These are often related to the church year, especially Advent and Lent; to the sacraments—illustrated story books for children that the whole family can enjoy; or to anthologies, like Cornelia Lehn's *Peace Be with You* (Faith and Life, Newton, Kansas), about people from the early church to the present who have "loved their neighbors" in nonviolent and creative ways.

OPPORTUNITIES FOR FAMILY WORSHIP

The simplest form of family worship is the thanksgiving said before a meal. Because it connects awareness of God to the concreteness of daily food, it can be understood even by the youngest child. Beyond understanding, however, is the feeling engendered by participation in an act of worship by the whole family. This prayer may be said or sung in unison, spoken by any member of the family, or said silently (as in the Quaker tradition).

The bedtime prayer taught to children is another occasion for family worship; one or both parents teach by praying with and for the child. This is a time for quiet reassurance with thanksgiving for the day and confidence safekeeping throughout the night.

The early American Puritans had a fairly rigorous tradition of daily family prayer, but today even devout families find it difficult to maintain daily worship because of diverse schedules. In its simplest form, the blessing before a meal is augmented by Bible reading. Daily devotional manuals published by many sources provide help for adult families but there is little for families with children. If a family settles for weekly family worship, probably on Sunday evening, it might include a hymn, Scripture, brief spoken meditation, and prayer.

The Church of Jesus Christ of Latter-day Saints encourages a weekly "Family at Home" evening. On that night no congregation holds any activities and families are urged to make this the priority on their calendars. A resource book suggests themes, Scripture, discussion, worship, games, and refreshments.

Jewish families have a long tradition of Shabbat, or Sabbath observance. Before the Friday evening meal the mother lights the Sabbath candles with prayer and the father says the blessing over the cup of wine.

Some Christian families make a ceremony of setting up a manger scene on Christmas Eve, singing carols, and reading the Christmas story from the Bible. The Advent wreath with four candles, one lighted for each week of the Advent season, has recently become popular in homes and churches. The Way of the Cross is a Lenten devotion among Catholic families.

The most lasting tradition is that of the seder meal at Passover, which brings together Jewish families in a home festival that dramatically represents the deliverance from Egyptian bondage through the telling of the story, the foods eaten, and the glasses of wine taken together. The youngest child asks the question, "Why do we celebrate this night?" and the oldest member present answers. Bitter herbs and sweet foods teach through sight and taste and games enliven the evening. Through the celebration of the seder Jewish families are linked with the Jewish community around the world.

Families can also worship together to remember special events: a birthday, entering school, graduation, going away. They may plan worship for special vacation places.

Families worship together as they attend services in church or synagogue, whether these are specifically family-oriented services or not. Worship together in a family is a way by which parents share their commitment with their children, nurture their children in faith, and deepen the affectional bonds with one another. *See also* Child Development; Faith Development; Family Cluster; Family Life Education; Holidays; Jewish Festivals and Holidays; Parenting; Worship.

C. R. Ikeler

Writing

Writing as a learning exercise, that is, as a mode of grappling with events, gaining self-knowledge, clarifying concepts, and incorporating information, is a teaching method that is gaining renewed interest. The current emphasis is on the activity rather than, as it has traditionally been, on the product.

Foremost among those investigating the educational merits of writing is Janet Emig. Drawing on the work of L. S. Vygotsky, Jean Piaget, and Emil Brunner, she claims that writing is a unique way of learning since the activity constantly demands analysis and synthesis, the higher orders of the cognitive domain.

Writing can be used as soon as a child has sufficient vocabulary and manual writing skill to feel comfortable with the results. (Prior to that a teacher can write what a child dictates or a child can tape a story.) Retelling a biblical story by writing serves both to clarify the learner's understanding and to give the teacher an idea of the pupil's perspective.

With older children writing encourages interpretation: "Imagine that you were listening to Amos at Bethel. Record your response." "You were with Paul on the sea journey to Rome. Tell how you felt." Adolescents can be encouraged to write down their interpretation of a value concept or a theological understanding: "How do you think about God?" Writing down reflections on the faith journey gives adults perspective on faith and belief.

Whether individuals' writing is shared with the class or not depends on the rapport within the class and the sensitivity of the material. When a writing assignment is given, it should be made clear at the beginning whether it is for personal use or is intended for mutual sharing. In the latter case, the teacher needs to emphasize that such sharing will be voluntary. *See also* Journal Writing.

J. C. Smith

Yoga

Yoga is a spiritual path involving physical, mental, and devotional exercises intended to lead to union of the self with God (Brahman). Yoga is most closely associated with Indian religions, especially Hinduism.

According to Hindu understanding, human beings share certain basic desires for pleasure and success (fame, wealth, or power). With maturity, which may require more than one lifetime to attain, these more limited satisfactions recede in favor of community service. Eventually everyone wants the enduring satisfactions associated with religious enlightenment—eternal being, full awareness, and great joy. Yogas are paths and practices leading to spiritual discovery and release. Their purpose is to help penetrate through the ordinary preoccupations of the body, conscious mind, and subconscious to the deepest self, or soul (*atman*). When successful, the seeker experiences great joy, a liberating awareness that the deepest self is already part of the one eternal reality, Brahman.

Hinduism charts four paths to this liberating awareness. The one found most advantageous depends on one's personality type. For those people who are predominantly intellectual by nature, there is a path through knowledge (*jnana yoga*). Study of scriptures and the teaching of sages, intensive reflection, and development of the habit of always seeing oneself from afar are some of the practices of this path.

For those who live primarily from their emotions, there is the path of love (*bhakti yoga*). Based on the assumption that persons tend to become like what they love, followers of this path are encouraged to devote themselves totally to one of the incarnations of Brahman, such as Krishna or Rama. Constant repetition of the divine name and experimentation with loving God in different ways (as parent, friend, child, or lover) are additional methods of deepening devotion.

For persons who express themselves primarily in activity, there is the way of works (*karma yoga*). This way must be combined with one of the two prior paths. All work is to be done either as an expression of devotion or of duty, with no element of ego involvement or expectation of reward.

The final path involves psychological experimentation (*raja yoga*) and is intended for persons with scientific interests. Seeking to break through to a "higher consciousness," followers of this path train intensively somewhat like top athletes or musicians, following eight progressive steps. Beginning with moral restraint, the steps include postures and ways of breathing that facilitate concentration of the mind on a single object without distraction. These are preparatory to the deep meditation of the seventh step, wherein the boundary between the mind and its object of concentration dissolves—knower and known are experienced as one. In the final step (*samadi*) continued meditation gives access to an expanded awareness that self, object of concentration, nature, and Brahman are all one. Life can now be lived in the light of this liberating perception and with assurance that upon death one's soul will not be reborn but will remain a part of Brahman.

The kind of yoga best known in Western cultures is oriented toward control of the body to achieve its highest potential (*hatha yoga*). This physical type of yoga has contributed to general health in ways similar to other exercise programs, but Indian Hinduism has viewed it only as a preliminary to the spiritual disciplines described above. *See also* Hinduism; Meditation; Spirituality.

W. E. Barrick

Yom Kippur

Yom Kippur (the Day of Atonement) is the holiest day on the Jewish calendar. Jews around the world gather in synagogues for prayer, study, and deep introspection. They seek both self and communal betterment. As listed in the Hebrew Scriptures (Lev. 23:26–27), Yom Kippur is observed on the tenth day of the Jewish month of Tishri. It usually occurs anywhere from mid-September to mid-October on the Julian calendar. Jewish people are commanded, "Mark, the tenth day of this seventh month is Yom Kippur—The Day of Atonement. It shall be a sacred occasion for you. You shall practice self-denial. You shall do no work throughout that day. It is a law for all time, throughout the ages, in all your dwelling places." Since biblical times, the holy day is also known as "Shabbat Shabbaton—the Sabbath of Sabbaths."

According to tradition, services for Yom Kippur are held from one sundown to the next. In addition to the customary prayers of worship, a number of penitential prayers are included to assist self-examination. Twice during the holy day, the congregation engages in Torah study; sections from Deuteronomy 28 and Leviticus 19 are read and discussed. Jewish communities also study prophetic sections from Isaiah 58 and the book of Jonah. Several readings on Yom Kippur afternoon call forth collective memories of the ancient Temple in Jerusalem. An important aspect of Yom Kippur worship is the Yizkor (community memorial) service, which honors the memory of all deceased relatives. At the end of Yom Kippur, a *shofar* (ram's horn) is blown to signify the end of the holy day and the beginning of righteous actions based upon the prayers, meditations, and learnings of the day.

One of the most significant aspects of Yom Kippur observance comes from the biblical commandment pertaining to self-denial. Jewish people practice this ancient law in several ways. Some fast by abstaining from all food and drink. Some abstain from washing and cleaning. Some refuse to wear any form of leather on their persons. Only those who are ill, infirm, or under age thirteen are exempt from these ritual practices. Most every Jew practices at least some form of this self-denial during Yom Kippur.

The purpose of self-denial is rooted in the essence of the Yom Kippur observance. Jewish people are prompted to look deep within, and ancient rabbis surmised that one would be prevented from doing so by attending to material needs and comforts. Thus, by abstaining, Jews can focus solely upon their prayers, studies, and self-examination.

Yom Kippur services continue over a twenty-four-hour period, but there are celebrations that occur before and after the holy day. Prior to the beginning of Yom Kippur, Jews gather for festive meals and celebration, not only to physically nourish themselves for the upcoming fast, but to enjoy one another's company and affirm their Jewish identity. Similarly, a festive "break-fast" meal is served after Yom Kippur's conclusion. This meal usually comprises dairy products and fish, which are easier for the body to digest after a day without eating or drinking.

Perhaps the holiest moment of Yom Kippur occurs during the chanting of the Kol Nidre (All Vows) prayer at the beginning of the first service in the evening. The worshipers proclaim that all personal vows and oaths that have been made willingly or unwillingly, rashly or intentionally, should be rendered null and void. Subsequent to Kol Nidre, Jews are prompted to go out and apologize and seek forgiveness from others for any unrectified mistakes that may have caused harm or distress during the year.

The origins of Kol Nidre are unknown, but theories abound. One reference can be traced to the Babylonian Jewish community of the eighth century, another from twelfth-century France and Germany. A most important historical reference, usually associated with the Kol Nidre melody, relates to Jewish life during the Spanish Inquisitions. Many Jews of that era were forced to convert to Christianity under the threat of torture and death. Nevertheless, they secretly maintained their Jewish identity, customs, practices, and rituals. Although the actual source of this Spanish melody remains a matter of scholarly dispute, its spiritual impact on Jewish worship cannot be underestimated. One bit of humor underscores this impact. "Long after a person forgets the words of the rabbi," the saying goes, "a person is still humming the melody of Kol Nidre and thinking about its message."

At the conclusion of Yom Kippur, Jews share the wish to be "sealed for a blessing in God's book of life." This beautiful thought reflects the hope that the prayers, meditations, and studies of the Day of Atonement have brought the individual and the community to a higher spiritual plane. It also reflects a desire to undertake those actions that will bring peace and goodness to all the peoples of the world. Thus, Yom Kippur becomes the keynote to a new year of spiritual righteousness and human loving-kindness. *See also* Jewish Festivals and Holidays.

E. Kaplan

Young Adults

A young adult is a postadolescent person still becoming fully mature, a human being in the early period of adulthood. The period of young adulthood is still emerging as a distinctive psychosocial era in the life span. Legal demarcation by age for entry into young adulthood ranges from sixteen to twenty-one, but young adulthood most typically includes persons in their twenties—with some extension into the late teens and early thirties.

Young adults pose a particular challenge to religious communities for several reasons. First, organized religious faith communities are often oriented to traditional family life-style patterns.

Some young adults are newly married and establishing families. Many others, however, are single and not yet participating in the presumed conventional adult life patterns. And many, single or married, find their primary orientation (and sometimes all-consuming participation) in a single institution other than a traditional faith community: higher education, the military, corporations, both traditional and new religious orders, and, more than is generally recognized, prisons. Still others are wandering and wondering spirits primed for adventure either within the city or in remote, exotic lands. Some are earnest and responsible and others appear to resist adult responsibilities and commitments of any sort. Religiousness, counter-religiousness, and areligiousness—any of these may reflect the integrity of the young adult making his or her journey toward a more mature adult faith.

CHARACTERISTICS

Psychologically one becomes a young adult when the tasks of adolescence have been achieved. Thus the young adult is individuated from family of origin and has developed the capacity for critical reflection upon self and world. Young adults are capable of entering into responsible adult roles such as spouse, parent, worker, and thinker. But young adults are often yet novices or apprentices in relation to the high educational and emotional demands of a postindustrial society.

One typically becomes young adult in faith in the context of events that challenge one's most basic life assumptions. This may happen in intellectual reflection, the betrayal of a relationship, a career disappointment, a confrontation with the suffering of others, or a failure of the older adult world to provide the stability upon which young adults are still appropriately dependent. The questioning and/or collapse of earlier assumed structures of meaning, intellectual and emotional, compels young adults to seek a critically aware and informed faith. This requires a search for a faith that will meet the test of their life experience.

Thus young adulthood is characterized by a particular orientation to authority. On one hand, young adults no longer tacitly and uncritically affirm conventional assumptions and expectations—including the expectation of obedience to assumed authorities. On the other hand, young adults are still appropriately dependent upon those who appear to demonstrate competent wisdom *in terms congruent with their own experience* (which includes the young adults' emotional hungers, intellectual reflection, and observations of the world). Young adulthood is, therefore, the time of appropriate dependence upon a mentor, guru, or spiritual guide. Such mentoring influence is most significant for the formation of a mature adult faith when sponsored not by a mentoring individual alone, but by a mentoring community.

As young adults have loosened the ties with the network of belonging that earlier held the self in an uncritically defined faith, they seek a context that confirms that there will be a new "home."

This is not to say that young adults must abandon traditional faith communities. It is to say that faith communities must not only stand in continuity with young adults' past but must also meet young adults on their own horizon. Accordingly, the authority of religious life functions differently in relation to young adults than to those younger than they. Authority that functions effectively in relationship to young adults has the capacity to elicit trust, to inspire, and to share the adventure of inquiry.

Thus there are three important characteristics of young adulthood: potential, vulnerability, and ambivalence. The potential of young adults is manifest in the strength of emerging adulthood with its promise for meaningful adult vocation. Young adults' relative independence from established assumptions can enable them to serve a strategic and prophetic role in their culture. This is the era in the life span in which there is a particular capacity to yearn for the "ideal." Each young-adult generation offers the opportunity for profound renewal of human vision. At the same time, however, young adults are vulnerable to such visions and vocations as are available in their environment. Therefore, they are vulnerable to exploitation in both subtle and blatant forms (as long as the exploitation takes forms that appear to offer the promise of life in terms resonant with their experience). Young adults are, therefore, also ambivalent in relation to both self and world. In its potential for idealism, the young-adult soul tends to feel compelled to make either-or choices. The major life choices set before young adults are rarely easy to resolve in absolute ways; hence, ambivalence in regard to relationships, work, studies, and life-style is common.

RELIGIOUS EDUCATION CONSIDERATIONS

The religious education of young adults requires a willingness on the part of teachers to join them in their search for a life that is worthy of the potential of the young adult soul, accountable to its vulnerability, and respectful of its ambivalence. Effective teaching of young adults is characterized by what Parker Palmer has described as creating "a space in which obedience to truth is practiced." In such a space, young adults have access to the best of tradition, are given viable images of the future, and find opportunity to speak in their own voice—participating in the ongoing creative activity of Spirit. This space is marked by a rich blend of challenge, resources, and support. It does not presume an adulthood already achieved but unambiguously recognizes and values young adults' emerging strength.

Religious education occurs for young adults when they can both critically reflect upon and be initiated (or reinitiated) into symbols, ritual, and understanding that provides a correspondence between the inner truth of young adult feelings and the outer truth of the young adult's perceptions of the world. For many young adults this requires a religious community that exemplifies in both word and deed a clear recognition of the insights from modern science, the scope of human suffering, and the terrors as well as the possibilities of the future. Thus young adults seeking a viable lifestyle and vocation will be attracted to people, projects, and settings that invite engagement with issues that matter and that open up the imagination of the soul. But because they are still testing what society will ask, make possible, or allow and because they are yet exploring the strength of the self, their terms or forms of commitment may be relatively brief though intense. Programs such as short-term mission projects, the Peace Corps, and others have recognized the importance both of young adult formation and the capacity of young adults to give of themselves while learning to encounter and respond to the truth of others.

The young adults' capacity to be critically aware fosters a consequent "relativism" manifest in an openness to and a fascination with difference or otherness. Thus as young adults increasingly have access to a religiously pluralistic world, they will search for the holy not only in the forms of their own religious tradition, but in whatever forms present themselves as a means to a more expanded and faithful spirit. Likewise, young adults can be particularly responsive to educational experiences that seek to overcome both fear and prejudice.

Yet at the same time young adults may demonstrate a certain "overagainst" quality in relation to those who cannot share their new learning. This "overagainst" quality is a manifestation of the young adult tendency to be both fragile and fierce. Young adults are fragile in the sense that a young plant is fragile—vulnerable but full of the promise of life. Young adults are particularly vulnerable when their assumptions about how life would always be are shaken at the core and there is nothing initially to take their place. But young adults are, in any case, inevitably somewhat vulnerable as they emerge into a larger arena of responsibility for both self and world; young adults often have some sense of this fragility and earnestly search for a worthy place to stand in a relativized, dangerous, but hopeful world; therefore, young adults seek creative participation in an "ideology" grounded in a mentoring, faithful community. When the young-adult self finds such a place, the person may need to fiercely hold that which seems in fact tenuous or partial. In this sense, young adulthood is inevitably "ideological." While this may take inspiring forms, this is also a time when cruel deeds may be done in the name of highest principles. But as young adults "come to voice" and are heard, both fragility and fierceness may give way to a confident, tested, and more compassionate strength.

When young adults are in search of a fitting relationship between self and world, religion may profoundly serve to provide the mentoring community they seek. Thus when religious faith communities simply wait for young adults to return "after they have children," a primary opportunity for formative adult religious education is neglected and young adults are abandoned in their search for adult faith.

When young adults do become parents, it is, indeed, a primary moment for religious education when the new parents yearn for the very best for their infant's life. Yet while young adults will explore a religious faith community at this juncture, they will not stay "for the children" unless their own needs for ongoing faith development are honored as well. If religion fails to be an active participant in the transformation of faith in the movement from adolescence to young adulthood, not only the young adult but the religious community itself becomes diminished, failing to participate in its own renewal on behalf of the next generation. See also Adolescence; Adult Development; Faith Development; Maturation; Mentor; Psychosocial Development.

FOR FURTHER REFERENCE

Belenky, Mary, et al. Women's Ways of Knowing: The Development of Self, Voice, and Mind. New York: Basic, 1986.

Fowler, James W. Stages of Faith. San Francisco: Harper & Row, 1981.

———. Becoming Adult, Becoming Christian. San Francisc o: Harper & Row, 1984.

Gribbon, R. The Problem of Faith Development in Young Adults. Washington, DC: Alben Institute, 1977.

———. When People Seek the Church. Washington, DC: Alben Institute, 1983.

Palmer, Parker. To Know as We Are Known: A Spirituality of Education. San Francisco: Harper & Row, 1983.

Parks, Sharon. The Critical Years: The Young Adult Search for a Faith to Live By. San Francisco: Harper & Row, 1986.

S. Parks

Young Life

Young Life, a parachurch organization headquartered in Colorado Springs, Colorado, has as its purpose to introduce youth to Jesus Christ and his relevance to life today. It was founded in 1941 by Jim Rayburn, a Presbyterian minister in Texas. To accomplish its purpose, Young Life utilizes friendship evangelism, informal weekly meetings in participants' homes or community centers, and various camp programs in emphasizing ministry to the total person.

Young life operates in over three hundred urban and suburban communities in North America and in ten countries overseas. In local areas Young Life is sponsored by committees of concerned business and professional persons who volunteer service in areas of budgeting, fund-raising, and community relations. The organization's programs are handled by over four hundred full-time staff and numerous part-time student and volunteer staff persons, reaching some two hundred thousand youth yearly. Staff receive training at Young Life's institute at Colorado Springs. See also Evangelism; Youth Ministry.

R. W. Pazmiño

Young Men's Christian Association

The Young Men's Christian Association (YMCA) is a nonprofit charitable organization founded in the mid-1800s and dedicated to developing spirit, mind, and body. Although the programs offered at different YMCAs may vary, all of them in the United States are tied together by five basic goals: strengthening families, developing leadership in youth, increasing international understanding, promoting healthy life-styles, and assisting in community development.

Some two thousand YMCAs in all fifty states form one of the largest health and human services networks in the country. The Y is also one of the largest private voluntary organizations in the world, serving twenty-five million people in ninety countries. The Y is open to all people, regardless of religion, race, income, or sex. About half those served are female.

YMCAs actively promote a set of Judeo-Christian values for living. YMCAs believe that people are responsible for their own lives and actions and that they should join together in positive association with one another serving the needs of all. Ys operate on the principle that all people are children of God and worthy of respect.

YMCAs promote values through a diverse set of programs including health and fitness programs, camping, youth sports, family events, aquatics, child care, juvenile justice, health enhancement for the workplace, senior citizens activities, international education and exchange, and teen programs. Some YMCAs still offer residential and hotel facilities, though that number is decreasing. Each Y is controlled by volunteer board members from the community who make their own program, policy, and financial decisions based on the needs of that community.

The national headquarters in Chicago—called the YMCA of the U.S.A.—works closely with local Ys to discover successful program ideas at the local level and to disseminate these ideas nationally. This program discovery system has resulted in new, innovative programs. Examples, grouped under each program goal, include:

Promoting healthy life-styles

- Health enhancement programs for the workplace, where local Ys work with major corporations and insurance carriers to provide exercise, healthy back programs, stress management, and smoking cessation programs for employees
- You & Me, Baby, a prenatal and postpartum fitness program for new mothers

Strengthening the modern family

- Home Team, a program to encourage families to join with other families in the community to spend quality time with their children
- School-aged child-care programs for working parents
- Indian Guides, a parent-child activity program.

Developing leadership qualities in youth

- Employment programs that teach teens entrepreneurial as well as basic job skills
- Adventure programs to help teens learn to develop self-confidence and take risks
- Youth & Government, mock legislative assemblies where youth practice leadership roles

Increasing international understanding

- Partnerships in which a U.S. Y joins with a Y overseas to exchange staff, program ideas, and intercultural understanding
- World Service Workers, an international development that sends young people abroad for two years to work in foreign Ys

Assisting in community development

- The National YMCA Youth Program Using Minibikes (Y-NYPUM), a program to fight juvenile delinquency
- Refugee resettlement programs
- Special fitness and voluntary service programs for seniors
- Exercise and educational programs for the disabled

The YMCA was founded in 1844 in England by George Williams, a British clerk who wanted to provide young clothing store clerks with a place where they could read the Bible, relax, and find referrals for decent lodging—in other words, an alternative to the life on the streets of rapidly industrializing London. The idea spread quickly to businesses throughout Europe. It crossed the ocean in 1851 when Thomas Sullivan, a retired

sea captain who was a lay missionary, founded a YMCA in Boston. A YMCA was founded in Montreal at the same time.

Exercise and gymnastics began to appear at the American YMCA in the second half of the 1850s. The first pool opened at the Brooklyn Y in 1856. In 1891 James Naismith of YMCA-affiliated Springfield College invented a game to be played in a gym. Called basketball, the first team had nine players. Naismith simply nailed two peach baskets to the side of an elevated running track. Volleyball was invented by W. G. Morgan at the Mt. Holyoke, Massachusetts, YMCA in 1895 because he believed that basketball was too strenuous for businessmen.

The Y has had other impacts on American life. It introduced the ideas of night school and junior college and assisted in the formation of other major voluntary groups such as the Boy Scouts, Campfire, and the U.S.O. The longest continuously operating camp in the United States is Camp Dudley, which was founded in 1885 at Orange Lake near Newburgh, New Jersey. The camp has since moved to the shores of Lake Champlain in Westport, New York.

Today, the YMCA operates some 1530 gyms, 1590 pools, 1260 health and fitness centers, 2980 racquetball and handball courts, 1060 tennis courts, 520 resident camps and conference centers, and 220 residences. There are special Ys for college students, armed services Ys for military families, and transportation Ys for railroad workers. *See also* Student Christian Movement; Young Women's Christian Association.

J. Spector

Young Women's Christian Association

From two small prayer groups of women, one in Boston and the other in New York City, the Young Women's Christian Association (YWCA) of the U.S.A. was founded in 1858 and has grown to a membership of 2.5 million women. It has 450 community and student associations, with more than 21,000 staff working with 130,000 volunteer leaders.

The YWCA was born to meet the changing needs in women's lives due to the Industrial Revolution and has continued to meet their changing needs for fourteen decades. In the mid-1800s young women were leaving farms and villages to seek jobs in cities. They needed places to stay and new friends. Boarding residences were started to provide safe, clean places to live. Today women gather in support groups to cope with their problems of child abuse, single parenthood, day care, job discrimination, and fitness.

After factory women had a place to live, the YWCA saw the need for education. It offered classes for self-improvement, millinery, cooking, and health. Classes in new skills were given to help them find better jobs. Practical nursing and typing were offered by 1880. In 1870, work with college and university women was founded and continues today.

The YWCA held the first school of social work in the United States in the early 1900s. In 1976, the executive training program was developed to help women prepare for top management positions in the YWCA and business world.

It was early realized that individual education was not enough; it was important to change the laws and practices that exploited women. The YWCA struggled for reforms that would improve working conditions, child labor laws, and fair wages. The struggle continues for passage of the Equal Rights Amendment and pay equity.

Racism has been a deep concern for the YWCA. It sponsored the first interracial conference in the South in 1915. It started clubs for girls on Indian reservations. The cafeteria in the Atlanta YWCA was a first in the area to be open to blacks. Currently the YWCA, nationally, has adopted the One Imperative for Action, "to thrust our collective power toward the elimination of racism, wherever it exists and by any means necessary."

The World YWCA works with women in eighty-three countries. The YWCA of the U.S.A. is a partner in this world movement as it works in developing nations to help women combat poverty, disease, illiteracy, and discrimination.

Peace is a continuing emphasis and concern. The YWCA has been active in support of the United Nations and other peace-building efforts.

The statement of purpose of the organization declares it is a "movement rooted in the Christian faith as known in Jesus and nourished by the resources of that faith that seeks to respond to the barrier-breaking love of God in this day. The Association draws together into responsible membership, women and girls of diverse experiences and faiths, that their lives may be open to new understanding and deeper relationships, that together they may join in the struggle for peace and justice, freedom and dignity for all people."

Further information may be secured from the National Board of the YWCA of the U.S.A., 726 Broadway, New York, NY 10003. See also Student Christian Movement; Young Men's Christian Association.

E. S. Genné

Youth for Christ International

Youth for Christ International, headquartered in Wheaton, Illinois, is a parachurch organization founded in 1944 that serves youth in the United States and fifty-four foreign countries. Its mission is to participate in responsible evangelism of youth, presenting them with the person, work, and teachings of Christ and discipling them into the church. Its ministry includes crusades, conferences, camps, *Campus Life* magazine, weekly clubs at the high-school and junior-high level, and a youth guidance program for troubled youth. Youth Guidance is an outreach to delinquent and predelinquent teenagers who have been in trouble with the law or other agencies. This program concentrates on both social and spiritual needs.

Youth for Christ personnel, who number over eight hundred full-time staff, receive training at a summer institute and in year-long internship experiences. The organization's projects in foreign countries are directed by nationals and its national events attract wide participation. *See also* Evangelism; Youth Ministry.

R. W. Pazmiño

Youth Ministry

Youth ministry refers to all the activities of planning, support, and leadership within a religious community that are intended to engage and nurture youth in the outlook and priorities of that community. Formerly it was common to speak of "youth work" or "youth programming" and to assume that adults should plan activities *for* youth. The contemporary emphasis in youth ministry assumes that youth are genuine members of the religious body and, therefore, not just recipients of ministry but participants in the total congregational life and mission. A congregation implementing this point of view will think in terms of ministry *with* and *by* youth as well as *for* youth.

This newer outlook derives from four major sources, each of which sheds light on youth ministry. First, studies in the social sciences have reminded religious educators not to undervalue the benefits that result when youth participate *with* others in the full range of congregational activities. Second, ministry *by* youth is seen to be based on the New Testament pattern for ministry, which involves building up the faith community through worship, study and fellowship, and reaching outward to others through witness and service. There is increasing agreement that such ministry is not the responsibility of clergy alone but the calling of all baptized Christians, youth as well as adults. Third, there is practical evidence that youth become more involved and mature sooner if they are expected to be responsible members and leaders in congregational life. Finally, the current emphasis on ministry *with* and *by* the youth represents renewed recognition of the inadequacy of youth programs that focus almost exclusively on personal, social, and recreational interests of youth without effectively introducing the uniquely religious claims on their lives.

MODELS FROM PAST AND PRESENT

Today most Protestant, Catholic, and Jewish denominations have national agencies that oversee systematic planning, publication, and distribution of youth program ideas and materials. This has not always been the case. Beginning in 1881, Protestant youth work was pioneered by a nondenominational agency, the Christian Endeavor Society. Several decades later that agency was gradually displaced as most denominations began to develop their own youth programs. Sunday schools and youth groups operated independently until the 1940s when denominational leaders decided to provide a recommended curriculum for the Sunday schools, organize the Sunday evening groups as "youth fellowships," and integrate the planning for both.

The continuing mainstays of the youth programs—Sunday schools and youth fellowships—have overlapping purposes but different priorities. The church school is more closely controlled by adult leaders and the curriculum of the denomination. The fellowship groups give time to some of the same educational concerns but are more likely to be managed through youth officers and shaped by the concerns of the youth themselves—their relationships with peers and parents, their need to form identity, their desire for social and recreational expression, their interest in worship experience with peers, their search for opportunities to serve others, and their need for guidance in the moral decisions confronting them.

During the 1960s and 1970s, issues concerning social justice became prominent in denominational materials for youth. Discussions of race relations, the Vietnam war, and the radical changes in youth culture displaced much of the attention formerly given to more traditional forms of Christian nurture and to the ego and affiliation needs of youth. To these influences was added a clamor for more local control of church life. Under the impact of all these influences, denominational youth programs gradually lost a confident sense of direction. By the mid 1980s, efforts to rethink and reenergize youth programs were under way in several denominations.

Also worthy of note is the growing number of Christian nondenominational or parachurch groups currently involved with youth programming and publishing. Stressing evangelism with high-school students, Youth for Christ and Young Life have built popular followings. In 1986 each announced expanded commitments to work with junior-high students in response to evidence that these younger youth are now confronted with questions of sexual experimentation and drug and alcohol use. Some of the parachurch publishers of youth materials, such as Serendipity House and Youth Specialties, Inc., have demonstrated sufficient creativity and substance that their publications are widely used across denominational lines.

Youth ministry in Roman Catholic churches might be said to have lagged until 1975, when the United States Catholic Conference published "A Vision of Youth Ministry." This report's version of ministry "to, with, by and for" youth is based on Luke 24:13–35—the Emmaus road story recounting how Jesus listened to the hopes and disappointments of two disciples, instructed them, and became known to them in "the breaking of bread." One popular implementation of the vision is a thoughtful model for youth ministry that is similar to what is being done in some of the better-organized Protestant churches. It includes the following components:

1. Outreach or "ministries of welcome" to make initial contacts with young people through hosting of social events or just "hanging out" where youth gather

2. Evangelization in youth fellowship meetings that combine proclamation of the gospel through worship and study and affirmation of the youth in a loving community

3. Systematic "catechesis"—explanation of the gospel with the core group ready for deeper commitment to Christ

4. Reaching out in service

5. Ministry by youth among their peers

In Jewish programs for youth, a special role is filled by those Hebrew schools that meet two or three days a week after public school. Reform Jewish congregations often have Sunday schools, camps, etc. that resemble programs described above. However, they also seriously provide for regular regional and national meetings of youth.

LEADERSHIP

Effective youth ministry programs require lay and professional adult leaders with certain qualities: a theological grounding to give a sense of direction and purpose, an awareness of the general characteristics of youth at a given age, a love of youth and willingness to get to know them individually, and, finally, a capacity for patience and tolerance. Youth leaders need ongoing support and training. Since "burnout" in the role is common, a team approach, using pairs of adults to work with youth in different program areas, is being recommended by some as a way of making the adult roles more manageable (Holderness, *Youth Ministry*).

In summary, there is significant consensus that the gifts, interest, and responsibilities of youth need to be recognized and expressed in the whole life of the congregation. *See also* Adoles-

713

cence; Christian Endeavor Society; Lay Ministry; Ministry; Peer Ministry; Young Adults; Young Life; Youth for Christ International; Youth Service and Training Organizations.

FOR FURTHER REFERENCE

Harris, Maria. *Portrait of Youth Ministry.* New York: Paulist, 1981.
Holderness, Ginny W. *Youth Ministry: A Team Approach.* Atlanta, GA: Knox, 1981.
Parks, Sharon. *The Critical Years.* New York: Harper & Row, 1986.
Strommen, Merton P. *Five Cries of Youth.* San Francisco: Harper & Row, 1979.
Youthworker: The Contemporary Journal for Youth Ministry. A quarterly journal published by Youth Specialties, Inc., 1224 Greenfield Drive, El Cajon, California 92021.

W. E. Barrick

Youth Service and Training Organizations

In the mid-1960s, a number of organizations began to emerge to serve the needs of youth ministry within Protestant and Catholic communions by providing ecumenical resources through publications and events for both church professionals and laity, an orientation that differed from that of parachurch organizations focusing primarily on the evangelization of youth.

One of the earlier organizations to emerge was Youth Specialties founded in 1969 by Wayne Rice and Mike Yaconelli. Its publications include *Youthworker, The Wittenburg Door,* and *Youthworker Update.* Training events for volunteers and youth ministry professionals include an annual Youth Workers Convention, National Resource Seminars for Youth Workers, Grow for It Events, and specialty seminars. Youth Specialties also publishes youth ministry books with Zondervan Books.

Group Publishing was founded in 1974 by Thom Schultz, John Shaw, and Jeff Meyers. Journals for youth workers include *Group* and *Junior High Ministry.* Group publishes books and sponsors youth worker training events with an annual Youth Ministry University, National Christian Youth Congress, one-day seminars, and the National Youth Ministry Executive Summit (for national and regional denominational youth ministry executives). Both young people and adults participate in a national work camp program.

Other youth service organizations with specialized ministry programs exist to provide a wide range of educational and service opportunities for young people and youth workers. Only a sampling is possible in this context. Appalachia Service Project and Mountain T.O.P. provide home repair projects in the United States. Compassion International provides youth groups with means to study and support relief projects in the Third World. Similar approaches are taken by Church World Service and Heifer Project International. A service ministry for the handicapped is provided by Joni and Friends. Youth with a Mission and Teen Missions enable youth to travel overseas in building and service projects.

The most complete listing of these service organizations may be found in the annual editions of *Resource Directory for Youth Workers* published by Zondervan Books. *See also* Youth Ministry.

L. Keefauver

Z

Zionism

Zionism is the movement, beginning in the nineteenth century, to create a homeland for the Jewish people in the land of Israel and, since the establishment of the State of Israel in 1948, the worldwide movement that continues to support Israel in realizing the dreams of its founders.

BIBLICAL BASIS

Zionists believe that the eternal bond between the Jewish people and the land of Israel was forged at the very beginning, when God promised Abram, "I will give this land [Canaan] to your offspring" (Gen. 12:7). Some see the entire Jewish Scriptures as a cycle of gaining possession of the land, losing the land due to the failure to observe God's laws, and then regaining it (Ezra–Nehemiah). The coming of the Messiah is connected to the return of the Jews to the land of Israel (Isa. 11:12).

Despite the loss of Jewish independence in the year 70, the Jews never abandoned the land, physically or spiritually. Major works of religious literature continued to be produced in Israel in Hebrew, from the Mishnah (second century) to the main code of Jewish law, the Shulchan Aruch (sixteenth century). Judaism's main prayer (recited three times each day) includes petitions for the ingathering of Israel's exile and the rebuilding of Jerusalem. Half of the Jewish grace after meals deals with the plea that God bless the land of Israel and Jerusalem.

MODERN ZIONISM

The rise of nationalism in Europe in the nineteenth century had its impact on Jews, too. Nationalist hopes inspired many secular Jews to yearn once again for a homeland of their own. The modern Zionist movement took different forms.

Political Zionism—the need for an autonomous Jewish homeland in Israel—is most closely identified with Theodor Herzl, an assimilated Austrian Jew whose own Jewish identity was aroused by growing anti-Semitism in France and Vienna in the 1880s. He worked unceasingly until his death in 1904 to secure political recognition for a Jewish state from various world leaders. His work culminated in the first World Zionist Congress, held in Basel, Switzerland, in 1897; congresses continue to be held up to the present. Herzl's Zionist movement caught the imagination of oppressed masses of Jews in eastern Europe and around the world. In 1917, Chaim Weizman (destined to be Israel's first president), secured the Balfour Declaration from the British government (which ruled the area in place of the Turks following World War I), viewing with favor "the establishment of a Jewish national home in Palestine." This statement reinforced the World Zionist Organization, which had been created in Basel (though numerous Zionist organizations and youth movements had existed previously). Increasing Jewish immigration (about 500,000 Jews went to Israel between 1900 and 1948), the impact of the Holocaust, together with the inability of the local British authorities to govern effectively, led to a United Nations resolution in 1947 to create two independent states, one Arab, the other Jewish. When the armies of seven Arab nations ignored the resolution and invaded the Jewish sector, an independent Jewish state was declared by David Ben-Gurion on May 14, 1948. About 650,000 Jews went to the new state between 1948 and 1951.

Cultural Zionism emphasizes Israel as the cultural center of the Jewish people, radiating Jewish knowledge and creativity to the various Jewish communities around the world. The revival of Hebrew as a spoken language is an important part of this effort.

Religious Zionism has continued to grow, despite the concerns of the ultraobservant about the secular, often socialist, nature of the Zionist movement. The relationship between religious messianism and Jewish political independence continues as an unresolved question.

RECENT DEVELOPMENTS AND ISSUES

Once Israel was established, some Zionist thinkers assumed that all Jews would immediately move there. While Israel continues to be a vital refuge for Jews fleeing persecution, many Jews have remained in their countries of origin. Working out the relationship between these "diaspora" Jews—who overwhelmingly support the State of Israel—and the Jews in Israel has sometimes been complicated. For example, there are differences of opinion about the uniquely Jewish character of the state, true to prophetic values and Zionist goals. The degree to which religion should be separated from government is another aspect of this question, as is the degree to which religion should shape Israeli identity.

Zionism has also been misunderstood by those unfamiliar with its history. The spirit of nationalism that led to Israel's founding also gave rise to more than a dozen Arab states, many of them former parts of the British or French empires. Israel, as a secular democracy, offers citizenship and equal protection to people of all creeds, but it remains the sole homeland of the Jewish people. Reaching an enduring peace with all of its Arab neighbors may be Zionism's greatest challenge in the years to come. *See also* Middle East.

FOR FURTHER REFERENCE

Heschel, A. J. *Israel, Echo of Eternity*. New York: Farrar, Straus, Giroux, 1969.
Laqueur, W. A. *A History of Zionism*. New York: Holt, Rinehart, Winston, 1972.

D. A. Resnick

Zwingli, Ulrich

Ulrich Zwingli (1484–1531) was a Swiss Reformer who played a major role in advancing the Protestant Reformation even though he was often at odds with Martin Luther.

In 1525 Zwingli initiated a reform of education carried out by the authorities in the Swiss cities that joined his revolt from the Catholic church. In contrast to his own Renaissance background, Zwingli's system of education was narrow in purpose and structure. He organized basic education for children around the goals of nur-

turing the Christian soul and training preachers of the gospel.

The grammar school taught Latin and the medieval seven liberal arts along with rudimentary Greek. This provided basic literacy, including the ability to read the Bible. The second level was a school for young men of sixteen and older. Here the goal was to prepare ministers through careful study of Latin, Greek, Hebrew, and interpretation of Scripture so that they could become teachers in their congregations and communities. The strict adherence to Scripture as the subject of education was followed in the many cities influenced by Zwingli. The Reformed Church in Switzerland was the result of his work. *See also* History of Christian Education.

R. L. Harrison

Photograph Credits

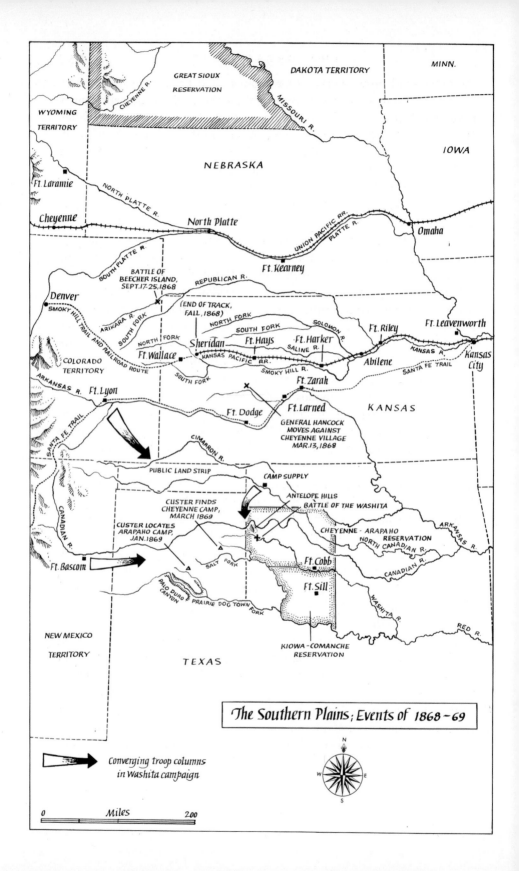

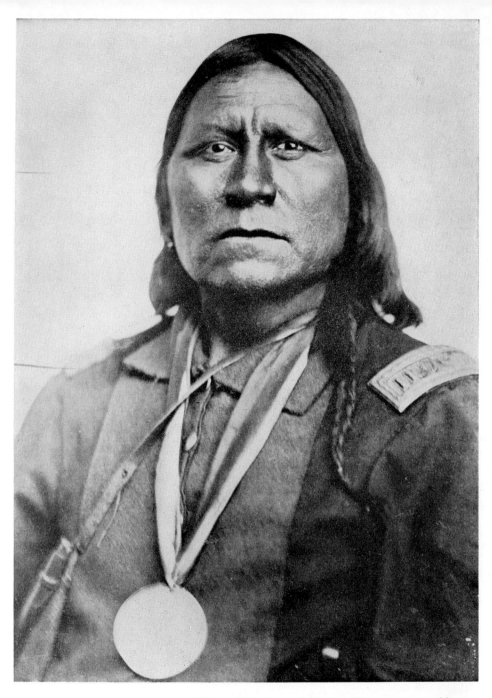

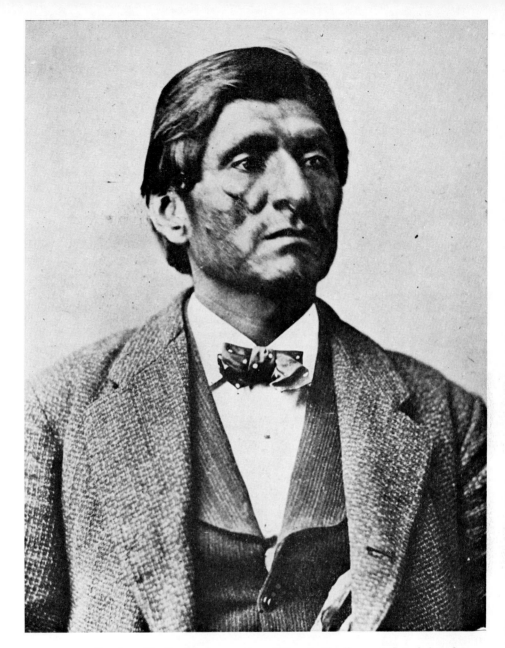

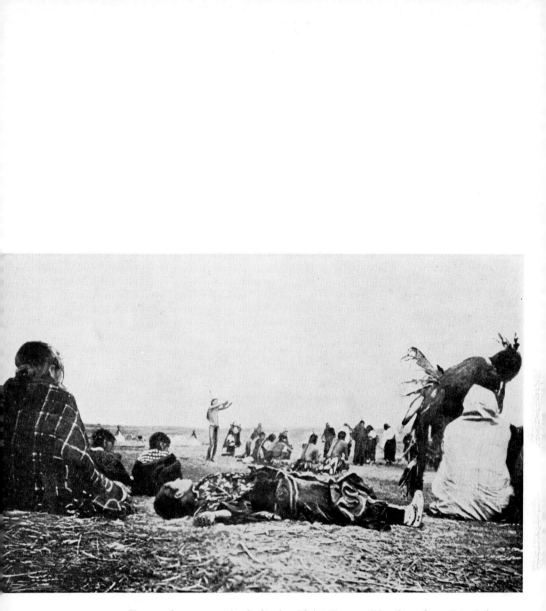

THE LONG DEATH

THE
LONG
DEATH

The Last Days
of the Plains Indian

RALPH K. ANDRIST

Maps by Rafael D. Palacios

THE MACMILLAN COMPANY, NEW YORK
COLLIER-MACMILLAN LIMITED, LONDON

11401

To Vivian—for many reasons

THE MACMILLAN COMPANY, NEW YORK

COLLIER-MACMILLAN CANADA, LTD., TORONTO, ONTARIO

Library of Congress catalog card number: 64–12545

Printed in the United States of America

MAPS BY RAFAEL D. PALACIOS

Contents

IV

Give Me Eighty Men

V

The Great Road

VI

Ten Million Dead Buffalo

VII

Diversion in the Far West

VIII

The Road to the Little Bighorn

IX

The Last Small Wars

Maps

I

As Long as the Grass Shall Grow

T HE last gunfire on the Great Plains between Indians and soldiers of the United States was exchanged on a bitterly cold day in 1890, the next to last day of the year. On that day, on Wounded Knee Creek in South Dakota, a forlorn and hungry band of Sioux, including women and children, was goaded and frightened into making a gesture of resistance to Army authority. When it was over, the Indian wars of the plains were ended, and with them the long struggle of all American Indians, from the Atlantic to the Pacific, to preserve some portion of their ancestral lands and tribal ways.

When the Civil War ended, a Union band played "Auld Lang Syne" at Appomattox, and many magnanimous words were spoken ("The men who own a horse or mule can take them home, General. They will need them to work their little farms.") But no band blared "Auld Lang Syne" into the frigid air at Wounded Knee Creek and there was no one who offered kind or noble words; when the frozen bodies were thrown into a common grave, not one of the ministers or priests who was in the area to lead the Sioux into the gentle religion considered it worth his trouble to bring God's presence to the bleak burial.

The condition of the Sioux, or of other tribes of the plains had not always been so low. Half a century earlier, the Indians had been almost sole possessors of the Great Plains. A few United States Army posts were stretched thinly along their eastern edge and a scattering of fur trading posts were lost in their enormous expanses, but these were the only permanent habitations of white men. The Santa Fe Trail cut across the southern plains, but its ruts were the only road made by wheels in the entire grasslands. No settler's fence hemmed in the smallest part of the vastness of the plains, no plow had yet cut a furrow through its hundreds of millions of acres of sod, no rancher's windmill stood anywhere against its sky. It was still a land of the Indian and the buffalo.

The entire region had been solemnly pledged to the Indians by the government in the years before 1840, to have and to hold forever. Even though the promise of the United States to Indian tribes had been proven worthless again and again, there were special circumstances that made many sincere men believe that here in the West, for the first time, an Indian treaty would actually be honored. But nothing was different. The usual encroachments by frontiersmen soon began, and steadily increased until the hardest-pressed tribes lashed back. Before long, the bright flames of open war were flickering up and down the plains, not to be completely extinguished for almost thirty years.

These Indian wars were different from the conflicts that had been waged for two centuries in the East. There were no dark ambuscades in shady forest glens but the drumming of horses' hoofs on prairie sod and battles in swirling dust under the open sky. The tribes of the plains were the first mounted warriors Americans had encountered in their westering, and the experience was to leave a profound impression on both history and legend.

The Indian of the plains has been glorified and romanticized until at last he has become *the* American Indian. In all the splendor of his eagle-feather warbonnet he sits on his horse on the bluff, watching the covered wagons roll down the valley far below; at last he raises his rifle above his head in the signal that brings a horde of whooping horsemen down on the stouthearted pioneers. The picture is seen through a pane of wavy glass, badly distorted. It is a stereotype built with the help of dime novels, nickelodeons, cliff-hanger movie serials, brewery-distributed cromolithographic fantasies of Custer's Last Stand hanging above a multitude of free-lunch counters, and similar methods of mass education.

However, while these dead warriors today ride the plains in tradition taller, swifter, and stronger than they ever did in life, they do not ride them alone. They share the sky and the horizon forever with the United States Cavalry which fought them, and by so doing made itself also a part of the legend of a world of bright and golden courage and endless space. But at the outset of this account, let there be no mistake: the wars of the plains were not clean, crisp little tableaux of cavalry with singing trumpets and snapping guidons meeting thundering charges of Sioux and Cheyenne warriors against a backdrop of grass bending in waves to the horizon and thunderheads piling up against a western sky. They were not that kind of conflict at all. As in all wars, men died unpleasantly, and often in extreme agony. Women and children suffered along with warrior and soldier, and the Army made it a part of strategy to destroy the enemy's food and possessions in order to leave him cold, hungry, and without the will to resist.

Striking at a foe by hitting his family does not quite fit in with the myth that all was bravery, sudden encounters, sharp clashes, and bright red blood—everything in primary colors. But it was effective strategy. In the end the Indian was defeated and confined to a reservation. He was no longer a hunter because the buffalo were gone; he had not learned to be a farmer. There was not much to do but sit in the sun and perhaps let a handful of dust trickle through his fingers and think how little it was to have left compared to the endless miles without a fence or a farm in the old days when the buffalo ran like a brown sea. It was too bad he did not appreciate that he would soon become a legend.

This, however, was the last scene in the long drama. There had been a time, in the years immediately following the Louisiana Purchase, when even the names of the Plains tribes were hardly known, while the possibility of fighting them seemed fantastic because no one, other than traders and trappers, had any reason to come in contact with them. Settlers had gone about as far as they could go. After two centuries, pioneers had at last come to the end of the great eastern forests, and the endless grasslands beyond stopped them as sharply as though they had come to the shore of an actual ocean. Pioneering technology, developed over more than two hundred years, depended on plenty of trees—for cabins and barns, for fences, for fuel, for a hundred other things. The sod shanty and breaking plow still lay in the future.

By 1825, it was pretty well established that the greater part of the

Louisiana Purchase was not of much account. Settlers had taken up homes wherever there were forests to be cut down (and there was enough such wooded land to produce three states—Louisiana, Missouri, and Arkansas) but the rest was largely grass and without much promise. Explorers had been even more pessimistic than the pioneers who took it as an article of faith that grassland was worthless. Lewis and Clark had seen a good bit of the plains and pronounced them "desert and barren." Zebulon Pike went across them in 1806 and made two predictions that later proved to be wildly wrong: that Pikes Peak, which he discovered, would probably never be climbed, and that most of the plains were too desert-like to be able to support a white population. He did think they had one benefit; they put a limit on the people of the United States who were "so prone to rambling and extending themselves on the frontiers . . ."

It was an 1820 pathfinder, Major Stephen Long, who summed up all the misconceptions in a phrase. He had gone up the Platte River and come back through Oklahoma on the Canadian River. He agreed with Pike that one of the few good things about the plains was that they would serve as a barrier to keep the American people from wandering too far and stretching the nation too thin. Otherwise most of it was worthless: ". . . we do not hesitate in giving the opinion that it is almost entirely unfit for cultivation, and of course uninhabitable by a people depending on agriculture for their subsistence." In fact, it was so worthless that Major Long labeled the entire Great Plains "The Great American Desert" and the name stuck. By 1825, every educated person knew that the country west of the 95th meridian was a barren wasteland, forever useless. The fable did not die easily; on the contrary it grew in later years as more and more people saw the plains for themselves and was as strong as ever between 1850 and 1860.

The plains were a long way from being a desert. The explorers were perfectly right; in the perspective of their times the plains were not suitable for cultivation, for the methods of cultivating them would not be developed for many decades. But it seems odd that any man with half an eye could have looked on the rich life of the grasslands and declared, in all seriousness, that they were a desert.

A few brief paragraphs of description of the plains are in order; this was the arena where most of the wars would be fought. Along the eastern part of this great open land of sky and grass, where rainfall was plentiful, were the true prairies, with grass taller than a man's head and

a profusion of flowers in the spring, a fertile region where the Indian tribes were corn-raising farmers who gave the lie to whites who said the land was useless for agriculture. But farther west, between the 98th and 100th meridians (a line about through the middle of the Dakotas and Kansas although it wanders somewhat) the climate becomes more arid, and the tall, lush prairie grass is replaced by short types, mainly buffalo and grama grass, only a few inches tall but very thick and supported by a sod many feet deep.

The dry, short-grass portion of the grasslands was the Great Plains proper, a land of space and sky, in places dead flat, in others gently rolling, broken occasionally in its western portions by bluffs, out-croppings and canyons, by a range of hills or a nightmare region of badlands. It was, and still is, a land of extremes of climate: burning summer heat and bitter winter cold, prolonged drought and violent thunderstorms with cloudburst rains, deadly blizzards and explosive tornadoes—and some of the most magnificent days imaginable, with an infinity of blue sky filled with smoky puffs of clouds and the grass bending and rising before a western wind exactly like slow waves on a sunny sea.

It was a land full of wild life. Bands of pronghorn antelope were an abundant commonplace; herds of elk more than fifteen hundred strong were reported. Flocks of prairie chickens were so common they were mentioned only in passing by white men early on the scene; wild tur-keys broke the branches in their evening roostings on river bottom cot-tonwoods, and the high-bounding, long-legged, long-eared jackrabbits were everywhere. Even the lowly prairie dog excited the wonder of early white men by its sheer numbers; colonies of the burrowing crea-tures covered hundreds of square miles and contained tens of millions of animals. Wolves, coyotes, the grizzly bear on the western high plains, and numerous lesser creatures were predators on this rich and varied fauna. And, surprisingly, there were great horse herds, descendants of animals escaped from the Spanish colonies in the Southwest.

But all other animals seem insignificant in numbers compared to the buffalo. They moved in herds of tens and hundreds of thousands. They covered the plains farther than a man could see. Plainsmen, finding buffalo in their way, rode all day long through grazing bison and were still in the herd when the sun went down. One man told of traveling more than a hundred miles through one herd; another estimated the size of a herd at thirty by seventy miles. Many estimates have been

The Prairies and Great Plains

0   Miles   200

MISSOURI R.
YELLOWSTONE R.
LITTLE MISSOURI R.
BLACK HILLS
CHEYENNE R.
NORTH PLATTE R.
NIOBRARA R.
SOUTH PLATTE R.
PLATTE R.
REPUBLICAN R.
SMOKY HILL R.
ARKANSAS R.
NORTH CANADIAN R.
CIMARRON R.
CANADIAN R.
STAKED PLAIN
RED R.
PECOS R.
BRAZOS R.
JAMES R.
MISSOURI R.
MINNESOTA R.
MISSISSIPPI R.
KANSAS R.
MISSOURI R.
ARKANSAS R.
RED R.
MISSISSIPPI R.

Tall-Grass Prairie
Short-Grass Region—The Great Plains
Mountains, Highlands
Woods and Forests

made of the total number of buffalo on the plains; they are so far apart as to prove only that no one really knew. But there is basis for conservatively estimating that fifteen million buffalo, at the least, were cropping the short grass of the Great Plains in the early part of the 1800's, before the great slaughter began.

And finally, there were the Plains Indians, virile peoples who had learned to come to terms with the land and had built an existence based on the horse and the buffalo. The plains had not been hard and pitiless to them. The rigors of daily life were enough to eliminate the weak and the misfits but living was pleasant enough, and there was plenty of leisure so that they were able to create, in a very few generations, the unique Plains culture which became so characteristic of all the tribes. For the Plains culture was very recent. The Indians did not obtain the horse until the Pueblo Revolt of 1680 forced the Spanish to flee and abandon their jealously guarded animals. After that, it took several generations for horses to be traded from tribe to tribe; not until almost 1800 were the northernmost tribes of the Great Plains mounted. In such a short time was the most dynamic and picturesque of modern Indian cultures created.

Nevertheless, in spite of game, grass, and Indians, it was still The Great American Desert as far as the United States was concerned. And what does a nation do with millions of acres of useless land? John C. Calhoun, Secretary of War under James Monroe, had the answer: use it as a huge Indian reservation. Make the Indians already there move over a little, transport the remaining tribes east of the Mississippi out to the plains where they would learn to hunt buffalo—and the Indian problem would be taken care of for all time.

The plan was not as callous as it might appear, because the remaining eastern tribes were in need of rescue. Government policy toward them had temporized and trimmed its sails to the winds of frontier clamor. Tribes were forced to cede land and move farther west, only to be pushed on again when the tide of settlement caught up with them. By 1825, the frontier had reached or crossed the Mississippi and there was no farther place to push the eastern Indians except out onto the open grasslands. To leave them to be surrounded by white settlers would have condemned most of them to pauperization and extinction by disease, hunger, drunkenness, and lack of purpose. Calhoun was probably completely sincere in his aims.

The first step was to get some of the western Indians to move over.

The Kansa and Osage tribes, people of the tall-grass prairies who farmed as well as hunted buffalo, agreed in 1825 to give up all their lands—present Kansas and northern Oklahoma—except for two reserves for themselves. Then government commissioners went patiently to work getting eastern tribes to agree to move into the West.

It was not a simple matter of calling out the troops and forcing Indians to move. There were certain prescribed forms to be gone through. The government had always been completely correct in its relations with Indian tribes, treating them as though they were independent nations. Under this pleasant fiction, treaties were negotiated with them and drawn up in formal language in the same form as treaties with foreign nations, and, like all treaties, had to be ratified by the Senate before becoming effective. Because Indian treaties were so negotiated, there are still defenders of the government's purity of method and purpose who will argue that the United States has never taken land from Indians without their consent. This is, with a handful of exceptions, entirely correct, but it overlooks the conditions under which consent was granted. It was given by tribes which had just been broken in wars. It was given by peoples who had been threatened or cajoled into signing, or misled about what they were agreeing to. It was often consent granted by a minority of the tribe's leaders who had been subverted or liquored up; the commissioners were never squeamish about hailing the voice of a few as the voice of all if that was the best that could be had. So, when the Indians gave up their land by their own consent, they were usually consenting with a knee in their groin.

All this was to be changed now. In the past, each time an Indian tribe had ceded its tribal grounds and accepted other lands in their place, it received the solemn assurance that the new lands were its own, to have and to hold forever—"as long as waters run and the grass shall grow" was one of the phrases the government liked to use in its treaties. Later, when the frontier had caught up with the Indians again, there was another treaty of cession to be negotiated with more promises in more poetic language. But this move, the commissioners assured the very skeptical Indians, would be absolutely the last.

The task of moving the tribes west went slowly until Andrew Jackson became President. Jackson had been a frontiersman when Tennessee was the Far West, and his first fame had come as an Indian-fighting general. His attitude toward Indians was unclouded by sentiment and was founded on the firm frontiersman's conviction that no Indian had

the slightest right that any white man was under any moral or legal obligation to respect. So, when Congress passed a bill in 1830 permitting the exchange of Indian lands east of the Mississippi for lands in the West, no crystal ball was needed to predict the results, even though there was nothing mandatory about the measure. It was, in fact, designed mainly for use against southern tribes which showed no interest in removal.

Most tribes signed removal treaties without causing difficulties. Almost all had been moved before, some of them several times, and they no longer had either the will or the ability to resist. There were a few exceptions. The Indians of New York refused to exchange their trees and lakes for grass and sky, and because no one was seriously clamoring after their small lands, they made good their refusal. The darkest tragedy of the removal was the treatment of the so-called Five Civilized Tribes in the South: the Cherokees, Creeks, Choctaws, Chickasaws, and Seminoles. The Cherokees refused to give up their reservation in Georgia which they had made into a progressive Indian state within a state (portions of the reservation extended into three neighboring states, but the heart of the Cherokee nation—and of the conflict—lay in Georgia). When a Supreme Court decision affirmed their right to the reservation, the state of Georgia ignored the ruling and, by a series of unprincipled laws, overthrew Cherokee tribal law and turned the Indian lands over to white squatters and speculators. President Jackson, when appealed to for help, blandly replied that he was helpless to force Georgia to comply with the court decision. The Creeks, Choctaws, and Chickasaws were similarly served by Mississippi and Alabama. The troop-escorted removal of the tribes was called the Trail of Tears by the Indians; several thousand died of exhaustion, hunger, and sickness on the long trip into the West.

The Seminoles alone of the Five Tribes fought removal by resort to arms. They retired to the depths of the Florida swamps, forcing the United States Army to fight a "Seminole War" lasting from 1836 to 1842. American tactics did not add many bright pages to Army annals; the most effective method used to capture Indians was to lure small groups in for a parley under the supposed sacred immunity of a flag of truce and then seize them. Seminoles were taken a few at a time and sent West—at a cost of 1,500 soldiers killed and $20,000,000. When the Army finally called off the war there were still a few hundred in the swamps but four thousand had been sent on the Trail of Tears.

The Five Civilized Tribes were given lands that make up the present state of Oklahoma excepting the Panhandle. There they quickly adjusted to new surroundings, organized their courts and governments again, and became an important factor in the Indian Country.

One flare-up of violence occurred in the north in 1832 when Black Hawk, an elderly chief of the Sauk tribe, led about four hundred warriors and a thousand women across the Mississippi to return to their lands along the Rock River in Illinois. White squatters, with military help, had forced them out the year before. This time the results were disastrous as four thousand soldiers and militia converged on the Indians and jubilantly pursued and killed women and children as well as men. Black Hawk got his band back to the Mississippi; there they were almost annihilated when a steamboat of soldiers appeared as they were trying to cross back to the west side. The soldiers lined the deck and, overcome with the joy of killing Indians, spared few. Black Hawk was taken prisoner. Never one to pass up an opportunity, the government forced the confederated Sauks and Foxes to cede a strip of land fifty miles wide on the Iowa side of the Mississippi as punishment.

By 1840, the boundary of the permanent Indian Country was complete. Starting at the edge of the Republic of Texas, it ran north along the western boundaries of Arkansas and Missouri, then east along the northern edge of Missouri to within fifty miles of the Mississippi, north through the Territory of Iowa on a line fifty miles from the Mississippi (that fifty-mile strip was the price the Sauks and Foxes had had to pay for the Black Hawk War); then to the Mississippi which it followed far up into Minnesota before cutting east across Wisconsin on an irregular line to Lake Michigan. It gave the Indians the supposedly worthless grasslands, as well as some forest land in Minnesota and Wisconsin which apparently was considered too frigid to be valuable to white men. A number of forts guarded this long line of frontier; General Edmund Gaines, commanding in the West, proposed in 1838 that the forts should all be built of stone since they were going to be permanent.

Only about twelve thousand Indians remained in the East of all the vigorous tribes that had once been there. More than ninety thousand had been carried across the Mississippi, to join, in something less than perfect amity, the almost quarter of a million already living there. It was fully believed that at last the Indian would be able to work out his own destiny, hunting buffalo and living to the sweep and rhythm

The Permanent Indian Frontier in 1840

of wind across the grass while his savage heart slowly wakened to the benisons of civilization, until one day he would put on shoes and exchange a nomad's life for regular working hours and a house with glass windows.

While the buffalo herds were expected to feed and clothe the Indians and make them self-supporting, the government was to lend a helping hand along the road to civilization by establishing schools and training the natives in farming and other arts of civilization. Congress created a Bureau of Indian Affairs in 1832 to administer these helping-hand programs and to handle relations with Indians in general; the Indian Intercourse Act of 1834, among other things, prohibited any white man from entering Indian country without a license.

The whole thing, at this remove in time, has a dreamy, never-never-land kind of quality about it, but at that time, when the future had not been revealed, it appeared to have a very attractive and compelling logic. Perhaps if they had been left alone, the Indians could have worked out their own future, although it seems very unlikely because a number of weaknesses showed up very early in the concept of the permanent Indian Country.

The planners, for one thing, had made the easy assumption that all Indians are alike, and that because a Crow or Arapaho could live off the plains in easy contentment, an Indian lately come from a life of raising corn and pumpkins and snaring rabbits and catching catfish in Indiana could immediately do the same. Many of the Easterners could not learn the high degree of horsemanship, the hunting skills, and other techniques necessary for successful buffalo hunting. On the other hand, there were enough hunters and apt learners among the immigrants to make inroads on the buffalo—or so the indigenous tribes claimed. At the same time, the Plains tribes frequently raided the cattle herds of the newcomers. There were clashes, and the United States Dragoons rode out onto the plains to show the flag and try to smooth over the difficulties.

The eastern tribes did not always fare badly in these encounters, thanks in large part to the fact that they had all been settled along the eastern edge of the Indian Country and had better access to firearms than did tribes on the more remote plains farther west. One notable fight occurred in the summer of 1854 when southern tribes of the plains met in grand council on Pawnee Fork of the Arkansas River, having decided the time had come to get rid of all eastern Indians.

The entire Kiowa and Comanche tribes were there, the Kiowa Apache, one band of Arapahoes, two of Cheyennes, and the main body of Osages. Old traders who were present estimated that there were 1,200 to 1,500 lodges, which would mean about 2,400 to 3,000 warriors.

From this camp a war party of about fifteen hundred set out to sweep the plains clear of the eastern interlopers. In eastern Kansas they got their chance when they came on a party of Sauks and Foxes with a few Potawatomies, about one hundred men in all. The Easterners took shelter in a ravine and, with their rifles, put up a fire that kept the Plains Indians from coming even close. With a few exceptions, the Plains warriors were armed with bows and arrows, deadly weapons and equal or superior to the rifles of their day at short range but use-less at a distance. In the end the chastened extermination force retired, even leaving their dead on the field, an admission of complete defeat because Plains Indians went to great risks to recover slain warriors to prevent the mutilation by the enemy which would prevent the dead heroes' entry into the spirit world as whole, vigorous fighting men.

However, antagonisms between tribes were not the greatest problems in the Indian Country. Tribes always had been fighting, and with Indian agents on hand and Army forces on the border, there was every probability that most conflicts could be nipped before they really got going. The serious threats to the security of the plains were those created by white men.

The worst assault of the white man on the integrity of the Indian was made with alcohol. The Indian Intercourse Act strictly forbade the sale of alcohol to tribesmen, but it took a strong-principled trader to resist the lure of the tremendous profits which a brisk trade in firewater brought in. It was easy to get the stuff into Indian Country because the few soldiers stretched along hundreds of miles of frontier could not possibly enforce the ban. Traders had a more or less standard formula for the near-poison they mixed up when time to do business arrived. A keg of cheap whiskey was diluted with water, a great deal of water. Pepper, and sometimes tobacco juice and other condiments, were added to give it a real bite. Despite its rather low proof, the Indians were highly susceptible to the violent mixture, probably as much because of the other horrors in it as the amount of alcohol. Profits were sky-high; the going rate for a fine buffalo robe was usually about two drinks of half a pint each. After a native had had several drinks, some traders shoved their profit margin even higher by switching to whiskey with more water in it, pretty certain the Indian no longer would notice the difference.

The results were completely predictable. During the debauch that followed, drunken rows flared into stabbings, women wailed, adulteries were committed without discretion, and initial euphoria sagged into soddenness so deep the victims lay in their own vomit. Indians who had developed a craving for alcohol awoke from such bouts with a horrible headache and nothing else, having traded away all their robes and obtained no necessities in exchange. Many traders opposed the use of alcohol as a short-sighted policy that would debauch the Indians and ruin future trade for quick present profits. But as long as some did it, all had to meet the competition.

More than alcohol, the white man's diseases so weakened the Indians that they had already partly lost the war long before any hostile shots were exchanged with the United States Army. As early as 1801, a Pawnee war party returning from New Mexico brought smallpox with them. It spread from their tribal grounds on the lower Platte all the way to Texas; some of the Plains tribes were said to have lost half their people, although there was no one to keep accurate statistics. An 1816 smallpox outbreak hit the Comanches and Kiowas on the southern plains especially hard.

The worst of the smallpox epidemics began in 1837 on the upper Missouri, the infection brought there by steamboat passengers. The Mandans, a farming people and one of the most advanced tribes of the plains, were almost wiped out; of their fifteen hundred people only thirty-one remained. Their neighbors and allies, the Arikara and Hidatsa, were cut from four thousand to about half that many. The disease spread north and west to the Crows, Assiniboines and Blackfeet; six to eight thousand of the Blackfeet were believed to have perished.

Attempts had been made to stop the spread of the epidemic by sending runners ahead with warnings, telling each camp to isolate itself, but the disease continued to spread among the wandering tribes. No one, not even the government, knew much about the tribes on the Great Plains in 1837; no one cared much. Everywhere people tried to flee the disease, abandoning tepees and the dead in them. For several years the lodges stood gaunt against the sky until the buffalo-hide covering rotted away to shreds flapping in the wind and the skeleton of poles at last settled back to earth.

The smallpox did not run its course in one summer. The Sioux escaped the worst of it, but some camps became infected, and probably four hundred Sioux died. In the spring of 1838 a war party of Pawnees took several Sioux prisoners; the captives carried the disease and an estimated two thousand Pawnees died as the sickness spread through their villages. They carried it south during the year to the Osage, who, after suffering terrible losses, in turn passed it on when some Osage visited the Kiowa and Comanche in the winter of 1839–40. The latter two tribes, when they found the smallpox was with them again, fled onto the northern Texas plains in an attempt to escape. At last the epidemic wore itself out, after taking no one knows how many lives.

Other epidemics, other diseases struck the plains. Venereal disease, that bright forerunner of culture and civilization, became common. Ailments such as measles, minor childhood upsets to the whites, were deadly to natives who had built up no immunity to them. There were many Indians killed by white men who never heard the sound of a gun.

Thus, any picture of the Indian Country as a region primeval and unreached by white men was largely illusion. The land remained untouched by a plow and unfenced, the wind blew across endless miles of grass, and the buffalo grazed in the majesty of their millions. But things had changed; nothing would ever be as it was. An additional hundred thousand Indians had been shoved, willy-nilly, onto the grasslands, to tax what had been a balanced economy. Disease had decimated some of the finest peoples of the West at a time when they would need their strength most. And liquor-bartering traders were sapping the moral fiber of large numbers of Indians.

In 1842 came the event that hurried the end of the permanent Indian Country. One hundred settlers in eighteen covered wagons took off across the plains, marking out a road that would evermore be famous as the Oregon Trail. It was not much of a showing—the grass had probably sprung back and obliterated the wheel tracks before two weeks had passed—but it was the proverbial cloud no bigger than a man's hand. The next year a thousand came, driving five thousand head of cattle with them, and from then on the trail was never empty during the traveling season.

The United States still ended at the Texas border and the crest of the Rockies, but the country laid claim, as did Great Britain, to the enormous Oregon country which extended from the Rockies to the Pacific and from the northern edge of California far up into Canada.

In 1818, the two countries had made a very sensible agreement to occupy the region jointly until they could come to an understanding on how to divide it. Nothing had been settled when word began to be passed around in the United States that the newest Promised Land was out in the Willamette Valley in the Oregon country in the very Far West—and the rush of land-hungry Americans was on again.

The Oregon Trail began at Independence, Missouri, a river port on the Missouri where the wagon trains made up and waited before they started in the spring for the grass to get green enough to feed the animals. It ran about three hundred miles northwest to the Platte River, then along the south side of that stream and of its fork, the North Platte, and finally followed the tributary Sweetwater River to South Pass where it crossed over the Continental Divide. More than half the trip, and by far the hardest part, still lay ahead, but at South Pass the trail had left the permanent Indian Country. In reaching that point, it had angled across present Kansas, Nebraska, and Wyoming, the heart of the Great Plains. It was a route almost certain to cause future troubles.

The emigration to Oregon continued and swelled, and in 1847 was joined by another migration. The Mormons, after running head-on into the harsh realities of intolerance during years of attempting to found religious communities in Missouri and Illinois, headed west for the Great Salt Lake country to have another try away from meddling neighbors. Their route started at Council Bluffs, Iowa, and followed the north side of the Platte and North Platte as far as the American Fur Company post, Fort Laramie, in eastern Wyoming; there it crossed over and joined the Oregon Trail. This was the Mormon Trail; it paralleled the Oregon Trail on the opposite site of the Platte River across most of the plains.

During these same years, political events completely changed most of the conditions on which the concept of the Indian Country had been built. Texas was annexed in 1845, the entire Oregon country south of the 49th parallel became uncontested American territory in 1846, and in 1848 the peace treaty ending the Mexican War extended the southwestern part of the country to the Pacific. The Indian Country was no longer a region out at the end of nowhere, a useful buffer between the United States and foreign nations; now it had become a barrier dividing the country. Modifications would have to be made in the pledges made to the Indian tribes. It remained to be seen whether the

United States would make those changes in good faith and with fairness to the Indians.

Gold was discovered in California in 1848; the next spring the parade of the forty-niners joined the covered wagons of the emigrants on both the Oregon and Mormon Trails. All that had gone before was nothing compared to the unending lines of wagons that moved across the plains from horizon to horizon during the traveling months of late spring and early summer. Wagon followed wagon so closely, often with the noses of horses or oxen almost against the tailgate ahead, that for miles all but the lucky earliest starters of the morning spent the day in clouds of choking dust.

The tremendous stream of westering humanity, plodding along day after day across the rutted sod, fouled the land and drove away the buffalo and other game. The way was littered with discarded tools, clothing, furniture, broken-down wagons, food of all kinds, thrown out as equipment broke down and baggage was discarded to compensate for the reduced pulling power of weakening animals. Animals gave out and died; the fresh smell of spring grass was blotted out by the corruption of rotting flesh. Hunters from the wagon trains ranged far out onto the plains after buffalo and antelope. The buffalo became nervous at the constant smell and activity of humans and began to stay well to the north and south of the Platte during the travel season; eventually they were divided completely into a northern and a southern herd.

Cholera swept along the overland trails in 1849, brought by the forty-niners and Oregon-bound emigrants, and at once spread to the Indians. To the Kiowa it was the most terrible experience of their existence, much worse than the smallpox nine years earlier. Close to half the Pawnee died; the survivors refused to bury the dead and bodies partly eaten by wolves lay within a short distance of the Pawnee Agency. The western Sioux were convinced that the disease had been deliberately introduced among them by white men in order to exterminate the Indians—to such a state had Indian trust in white motives fallen.

None of the throng of emigrants wanted anything to do with the plains. There was still the Great American Desert, an expanse to be crossed and left behind as quickly as possible. But in their crossing, they played hob with the land and the people along the way. The Pawnees, whose range centered on the Platte valley and included much of present Nebraska and a good piece of Kansas, had already been reduced to a shadow of their former powerful estate, without a shot being fired. They lived with hunger because the buffalo shunned the Platte River valley and the vicinity of the overland trails; they did not dare go out onto the plains after the herds because there was always the chance of a clash with their enemy, the Sioux, and they were too reduced in numbers to hold their own. As a result, they were reduced to begging, petty thievery, and once in a while, when conditions were right, an attack on an unprotected emigrant wagon.

The Sioux and Cheyenne farther west were not so drastically affected but they were grumbling. The emigrants took the best campsites; their hunters killed or drove away the game; there were arrogant men among them who treated the Indians in a manner calculated to cause trouble. There were even occasional young fools who tried to demonstrate what great Indian-killers they were by taking pot-shots at passing braves—fortunately without notable results in most instances. The two tribes did not resort to violence, but they did begin to demand payment for the use of the trails.

It was important to maintain a right of unobstructed passage over the Oregon Trail, to obtain treaty rights guaranteeing the free use of the road. At the same time, the government decided to make a bigger sweep than a simple right-of-passage agreement: nothing less than a fixing of limits to the territories of all the Plains Indians. Such a move, it was explained, would help reduce intertribal conflicts.

The first council—which had nothing to do with the Oregon Trail—was held on the Minnesota River, in July, 1851, at Traverse des Sioux, where the eastern Sioux Indians signed away all their lands in Iowa and Minnesota except for a twenty-mile-wide reservation along the upper Minnesota River. For this empire they were to receive $68,000 annually for fifty years. Of this amount they were immediately bilked of a fair portion by being hoodwinked into signing over their first annual payments to traders for debts they supposedly owed, totaling $210,000. The thing was a fraud; there would be other frauds and swindles so that in the end the Sioux got almost nothing while Minnesota suffered the most tragic interlude in her history.

However, the main treaty-making was on the northern plains, where the Oregon Trail passed through. There the heaviest burden of making ready for the council was borne by Thomas Fitzpatrick, known as Broken Hand to the Indians. He had been one of the greatest of the mountain men until he gave up fur trading when men began wearing high hats made of silk instead of beaver and took the rich cream from the fur business. For a period he had guided wagon trains through the mountains he had explored—he was the discoverer of South Pass, through which the Oregon Trail passed—until the government had appointed him Indian agent for the upper Platte and Arkansas in 1846. He was a good agent in a service that was becoming notorious for its bad apples, because he knew his people and had a conscience about them. Now, in 1851, he had runners all over the plains calling a council of all the tribes of the northern plains at Fort Laramie.

The result was the greatest meeting of Indians in the history of the plains; the estimates run variously between eight thousand and twelve thousand persons present. The council had been set for September 1 but the Cheyennes, Arapaho, and the Brule and Oglala bands of the Sioux were there even before July was over. Fort Laramie was now an Army post, having been purchased from the American Fur Company two years before to protect the Oregon Trail. A couple of hundred dragoons were on hand and more arrived during the council but they were there more as a symbol of the might of far-away Washington than for any practical purpose, because they could have been overwhelmed in minutes by the thousands of Indians.

The council almost did turn into war with the arrival of a Shoshone contingent, mountain tribesmen whose annual buffalo hunts out onto the plains had made them bitter enemies of the Plains tribes. As the Shoshones galloped up, magnificent horsemen led by their great chief Washakie, a Sioux whose father had been killed by a Shoshone war party, spurred his horse forward and, whooping, charged alone against the line of mounted Shoshone braves, seeking the bright answer to some private vision of glory. Washakie and his men raised their weapons, the Sioux warriors stirred to support their wild-eyed friend, but the clash that could have turned the council into a murderous melee was prevented when an interpreter raced out on his horse and threw the avenging young Sioux to the ground.

The tribal delegations continued to come in, Crows, Assiniboines, Atsinas, Arikaras, most of them with women, children, dogs, and horse herds; with a few exceptions the tribes were nomads who took everything they owned with them whenever they moved. The combined horse herds totaled many thousands and soon had the grass cropped down for acres. The camps, a forest of tepees rising thickly from acres of meadows around the fort, soon began to put forth a mighty stench until at last the harassed officers ordered that the encampment should be moved to Horse Creek, thirty-seven miles to the east.

The council was being delayed pending the arrival of wagon loads of food and gifts which were always distributed at such affairs; at last the Superintendent of Indian Affairs, David Mitchell, ordered the council to get down to business and let the gifts come when they would (it turned out that the Army, in its age-old way, had mislaid them at one of the Missouri River steamboat landings). The parley was held in a large tent, one of the most colorful such meetings ever held, with great men from great tribes sitting, rank on rank, in the full glory of their ceremonial regalia. The council lasted twenty days, being purposely drawn out to permit the Army to locate and bring the gifts.

The council had been held mainly to get the Indians' promise not to molest travelers on the Oregon Trail; this promise they gave, recognizing the right of the United States to establish the road and to build forts to protect it. Also, the commissioners got the tribes to agree to observe a general peace among themselves and to accept definite boundaries to their lands. The matter of boundaries was a difficult one. Even settled agricultural tribes have seldom agreed on the lines separating them unless it was a natural barrier such as a large river; among free-roaming Plains tribes in an open land with few natural bounds and limits, the boundaries of a tribe's land shifted with the strength of the war parties that rode along them. Nevertheless, with perseverance, the Indian leaders assembled in the tent were able to agree on definite borders for their hunting grounds.

In return for these concessions, the Indians were to be paid $50,000 a year for fifty years, the annuity to be in the form of food, various goods, and—what the wandering tribes must have agreed without enthusiasm to accept—domestic animals and agricultural implements. When the treaty came up for ratification, the Senate decided the commissioners had been too generous and reduced the term to ten years, with the possibility of extension for another five.

Thomas Fitzpatrick arranged a similar council with the Comanches and Kiowas at Fort Atkinson on the Arkansas River in present Kansas state. The two tribes, far-raiding, warlike, and closely allied, were the principal nomadic tribes of the southern plains; their main hunting range was from the Arkansas River south into the Texas Panhandle. They agreed to the right of the United States to lay out roads and to set up posts and forts to protect them—this had reference mainly to the Santa Fe Trail. They also promised not to make raids into Mexico in the future. In return, they were to receive annuities in goods worth $18,000 a year for ten years, with a five-year extension if the President in Washington decided they had merited it.

An attempt was made to get the Indians to give up their captives, but this proved impossible. Few or none of the captives wanted to leave. The tribes not only replenished their horse herds by raids into Mexico; they had kept up their own numbers in the same way. Young captive boys and girls had been accepted as full members of the tribe; the girls had grown up to be wives and mothers of Comanches and Kiowas, while some of the boys had developed into leading warriors of the tribe. Few of them, men or women, wanted to go back to being Mexicans.

The two tribes complied with the treaty quite faithfully except for the clause about raiding into Mexico. Along with this, they had a hard time accepting that New Mexico had become part of the United States, a difficulty in comprehension which caused frequent annoyance to American authorities. There was also a curious situation in regard to relations between the Comanches and Texas, although it had nothing to do with the Fort Atkinson Treaty. The Comanches, although their name has become synonymous with bloodthirstiness, actually remained at peace with the United States most of the time, but they hated Texans with a bitter hate. The Republic of Texas had followed a policy toward its Indians that made the United States appear benevolent by comparison, and the Comanches had suffered heavily. They had a special grudge as well; during a council between Texans and Comanches, a disagreement had occurred, upon which the Texans had turned on the outnumbered Indian chiefs in the room and killed them to a man. Long after the annexation, Comanches made a distinction between Americans and Texans.

The permanent Indian Country was dying fast; already the frontier that was to have divided it forever from the white man's world had bulged and given way along a great section under pressure from land-hungry settlers. The myths about the worthlessness of grasslands were evaporating; pioneers had learned that tall-grass prairie land, at least, was tremendously fertile. The Indians had been pushed off almost all the prairie land of Minnesota and Iowa—part of the original permanent Indian Country—by the weary old method of land cession treaties, and bigger things were ahead.

The government's solemn promise to most of the eastern tribes that they would not have to move again had to be broken in 1854. After long wrangling, free and pro-slavery forces had agreed to the creation of two territories on the Great Plains, but along what would be their eastern boundaries lay a solid tier of Indian reservations, most of them the homes of eastern tribes who had moved there a couple of decades before with full assurances that there would not have to be any more moves. George W. Manypenny, Commissioner of Indian Affairs and a man with a conscience, visited these tribes in 1853 to go through the dreary business of telling them that they would have to move once again. The treaties, with a few small exceptions, were signed in 1854; the tribes gave up thirteen million acres of land. Most went on small reservations elsewhere; a few remained on reserves that were a small portion of their former lands.

That same year Kansas and Nebraska Territories were organized and the permanent Indian Country came to an end. Much larger than the present states of Kansas and Nebraska, the two territories together included almost all that had remained of the Indian Country, from the southern boundary of Kansas to Canada, and from the Missouri to the Rockies. Only the land belonging to the Five Civilized Tribes in Oklahoma still remained without any organized state or territorial government. It was considered quite certain that this land, which was soon labeled the Indian Territory, was too worthless ever to be wanted by white men, and that the Indians living there could possess it indefinitely without being molested.

Thomas Fitzpatrick served as Indian agent for the upper Platte and Arkansas River country until 1854 when he died while on a trip to Washington. Only the year before he had made a final trip through his huge territory, and found that the effects of the traffic endlessly crawling westward on the Oregon Trail had been disastrous to the Indians of the area. "They are in abject want of food half the year," he wrote in his final report. "The travel upon the road drives the buffalo off or else confines them to a narrow path during the period of migration, and the different tribes are forced to contend with hostile nations in seeking support for their villages. Their women are pinched with want and their children are constantly crying with hunger. . . . Already, under pressure of such hardships they are beginning to gather around a few licensed hunters . . . acting as herdsmen, runners, and interpreters, living on their bounty; while others accept most immoral methods with their families to eke out an existence."

The year of Fitzpatrick's death, the peace between the United States and the Plains Indians was seriously broken for the first time. The event occurred four years after the great peace council of Fort Laramie and only ten miles from the spot where it had been held; the cause, as is usually the case, was trivial and in this instance was the lame cow of a Mormon emigrant. Whether the cow had strayed or been abandoned is a subject on which opinions differ. At the time, there were several thousand Arapaho, Cheyenne and Sioux camped above Fort Laramie awaiting the distribution of their annuity; a hungry young Brule Sioux came on the lame cow in the brush of the river bottom, killed her, and, with his friends, made what feasting was possible on her meager flesh.

Somehow, word of the fate of his cow got back to the owner whose wagon train was camped near the fort resting its animals and making ready for the long trip still ahead. He stormed into the fort demanding that the Army make the Indian or Indians responsible pay for the cow The Brule Sioux youth who had butchered the animal, learning that trouble was afoot, took refuge in the camp of Chief Conquering Bear whom the government had named supreme chief of the Teton Sioux.* Although the Sioux did not have such a position in their own social and political organization, the government, in its dealings with Indians, always felt a compulsion to have a top man to talk to.

Conquering Bear hurried in to Fort Laramie to take care of matters; he offered to pay $10 for the cow. The owner demanded $25. The animal was certainly not worth $25, or even $10 to its owner; there were still hundreds of miles to go over mountain, desert, and alkali flats to the Mormon country, hard enough for a whole animal to travel, and impossible for a lame one. It was said that the owner had abandoned his cow and then had showed up again when there seemed a possibility of realizing something from it. Conquering Bear stated the obvious: $25 was not only too much but beyond the resources of those who had eaten the stringy flesh of the trail-worn cow. He returned to his camp.

The United States Army has, without favoritism, included in its officer corps men ranging from geniuses down to incompetent fools lacking the slightest rudiments of judgment. Young Lieutenant Grattan

* There were three main divisions of the Sioux. The Teton Sioux were dwellers on the plains and the true nomads of the tribe; they were by far the most numerous and were further divided into the Brule, Hunkpapa, Two Kettles, Blackfeet Sioux (not to be confused with the Blackfeet proper), Sans Arcs, Miniconjou and Oglala bands. On the prairies of eastern South Dakota was the Yankton division, divided into the Yankton and Yanktonai bands, and easternmost of all were the Santee Sioux in Minnesota, whose component bands were the Sisseton, Wahpeton, Mde-wakanton and Wahpekute—who will be heard from, very vehemently, later.

who was sent out from the fort to obtain satisfaction for the dead and digested cow was one of the latter. He took a detail of thirty men and a drunken interpreter, added two cannons for extra authority, according to most reports fortified himself with whiskey against the rigors of his assignment, and marched his men off after making stirring statements about conquering or dying.

The Sioux camp contained many lodges of Brules and Oglalas and a few Miniconjous, a gathering formidable in strength but peaceful in spirit. Grattan, with no attempt at diplomacy, deployed his men, wheeled his cannon into position, and arrogantly demanded payment for the cow or surrender of the Sioux who had killed her. Conquering Bear remonstrated, an argument followed, and Grattan opened fire with his cannon, killing several Indians and mortally wounding Conquering Bear. The soldiers were set upon instantly by the shocked and infuriated Sioux; one alone escaped alive but so badly wounded that he lived only long enough to carry the story back to Fort Laramie. Knowing that retribution would be swift, the Sioux at once struck camp and headed to the northeast, taking the wounded Conquering Bear along on a horse travois. He died of his wounds and his body was placed on a scaffold, as most Plains Indians disposed of their dead, by the Niobrara River.

The killing of Grattan and his command, no matter how much it had been provoked, demanded vengeance, so the next summer Colonel William Harney with 1,300 troops marched from Fort Leavenworth to deal out summary justice. He happened on the band of Little Thunder camped at Ash Hollow on Blue Creek just off the North Platte. Little Thunder's band had had nothing to do with the attack on Grattan and his detail. They had not had anything to do with the killing of the Mormon's cow. But the United States Army subscribed to the curious theory of collective responsibility: if any band of Indians committed a crime or a depredation, any Indian who came within reach could be punished. Colonel Harney opened fire on the Sioux camp with artillery. The Indians fought back as best they could, and bravely, after recovering somewhat from the surprise, but were almost wiped out, losing 86 killed and several wounded. Many of the killed and wounded were women and children.

Harney gathered up a sad procession of captives, including the wounded, and drove them all the way to Fort Laramie. He was so elated by his victory that he had his gunners try to shoot the top off

Chimney Rock, a landmark to travelers on the Oregon Trail. The Sioux were upset and frightened by Harney's expedition, and a young Brule named Spotted Tail, along with several others, gave himself up to accept punishment for the Grattan fight. They were taken to Fort Leavenworth in chains; when Spotted Tail was released a year later he had been so impressed by the unlimited number and powers of the white man that he was thereafter convinced that it was futile to contend with them. He became one of the most ardent peace advocates among the Indians.

The Army showed an unfortunate tendency to continue Colonel Harney's tough policy. On several occasions, when young braves on the plains met detachments of cavalry on patrol, they approached after making the peace sign as they had been doing for years, only to be shot at by the troopers. After a few such incidents, the word got around, and small Indian hunting parties no longer rode up to troops to make friendly talk and beg tobacco.

The northern Cheyennes, whose roamings took them near the Oregon Trail, were the victims in several of these unprovoked shootings, and, not unreasonably, began to feel that the Army was deliberately trying to incite war. There was a considerable element among them that was all for getting the jump on the whites by attacking first and in force, while the Americans in Kansas were absorbed in the Slavery-Free Soil conflict which had the state torn and prostrate.

There were incidents; Indians attacked wagon trains and trappers, the Army administered punishment by attacking the first group of unsuspecting Indians it came across, whereupon the Indians retaliated in turn by jumping the next poorly defended wagon train they met up with. After one such chain of events in May, 1857, in which punishment always fell on innocent parties, Colonel E. V. Sumner was sent out to knock heads together and teach the northern Cheyenne some manners. Sumner trailed a large band of Indians across western Nebraska and Kansas, finally catching up with them in Kansas on the Republican River. There, but for a strange happenstance, might have begun the wars of the plains.

The American Indian was a person whose fate was determined by signs, omens, and magic. If the signs and the magic were favorable, he went into battle convinced he was invincible. If they went awry, he would often refuse even to face the enemy because he knew in advance that all was lost. This day, three hundred Cheyenne horsemen were absolutely certain of victory as they waited for Sumner to attack. Their medicine man had assured them that washing in a certain lake would make them proof against the bullets of the white soldiers, and they had washed.

But the incredible happened. Colonel Sumner ordered his men to charge with sabers, why, no one knows, for it was probably the only full-fledged saber charge ever made on the plains. To the Indians, it meant only that their bullet-proofing magic had been circumvented and all was lost in advance. They turned and ran with the cavalry in hot pursuit. They fled so fast and so far that they lost only four men (their own figures), while the soldiers lost two killed and several wounded. Sumner burned the Cheyenne village and then continued his march to further intimidate the Indians; there were no further encounters.

So, only by unlikely coincidence was a major battle avoided. The Indians became more resentful, the whites a bit more overbearing. Naked and open war was avoided for a few more years, but real peace was gone. When 1861 came, Regular Army troops were withdrawn to fight more important battles elsewhere. When the columns disappeared beyond the eastern horizon it did not mean a return to old days and old ways for the tribes of the grasslands because state and territorial militias took over, frontiersmen volunteers whose personal credos usually included a firm conviction that there were few higher achievements than killing Indians.

But the plains were vast. The conical tepees clustered tranquilly beside a hundred creeks and river campsites with the smoke from the cooking fires rising above them. The buffalo herds continued to come in numbers that shook the earth and covered its face for miles, and the white man still looked on the plains as an expanse to cross as quickly as possible. With all the changes that were being wrought, there were still things that remained comfortingly familiar, especially for peoples living well off the white man's trails.

These pleasant continuations of an older day had only a short course to run now, a couple of years for some tribes, perhaps a dozen or more for others. For each one the moment would come when the old way was irrevocably lost—and for some, that moment was already at hand.

II

Massacre in Minnesota

1. "LET THEM EAT GRASS"

IN 1862, the Sioux in Minnesota had two things to show for a little more than a half century of treaty-making with the United States: a reservation 10 miles wide and 150 miles long on the Minnesota River, and a deep and smoldering resentment over years of having been swindled.

This is not to say that the Indians were plotting an uprising of any sort. But deep frictions and hard feelings were there, and the amazing thing about Minnesota in the harvest season of 1862 is that so few people seemed to consider trouble even within the realm of possibility. It may be that there were settlers here and there who felt that it would be a good precaution to keep a rifle handy, but if such were the case, there was nothing in the events of August 18 to indicate it. When catastrophe came, no people could have been caught more completely by surprise.

There had been incidents; it was not an easy summer for the Indians. Ordinarily, the Sioux went on their annual buffalo hunt out into Dakota Territory early in July, but this year they had put it off from day to day, waiting for the arrival and distribution of their annuity, until August had arrived and they had neither buffalo meat nor the food that was part of the annuity. The annuity was paid in money, goods, and food. Only the money had not arrived; the food and goods were on hand at the two agencies on the reservation—and the sight of the filled warehouses must have been a constant irritation and temptation to the Indians. On August 4, the Sioux at Upper Agency, the westernmost of two, had finally had enough of waiting, and let grumbling turn into action. They moved against a warehouse containing food.

There were a hundred soldiers at the agency, two companies of a Minnesota volunteer regiment. Like the Indians, they had been waiting for the payment of the annuities, their job to maintain order when several thousand Sioux would be assembled in one place. The Indians acted quickly; several hundred of them ringed Lieutenant Timothy J. Sheehan's company and very effectively kept it from doing anything. At the same time, other Indians broke down the door of the warehouse and began carrying out sacks of flour. It was not a warlike move; the Indians were only after food and made no threatening gestures as they kept the soldiers aside.

However, they did not get Lieutenant Thomas Gere's company boxed in so efficiently, and Gere, only nineteen years old but a young man of mature judgment and resolution, quickly ordered a howitzer swung around and trained on the warehouse entrance. Then, as the Indians hesitated and drew back out of the field of fire, a sergeant with a squad of men took control of the door. In the meantime, Lieutenant Sheehan was arguing with the Indian agent, Major Thomas J. Galbraith (all Indian agents bore the honorific "Major"), asking him to issue the food portion of the annuity. Galbraith had the irrefutable argument of all bureaucrats, that it had never been done that way; money, food, and goods had always been issued together. Besides, he said, any concessions would make the Indians difficult to control.

After Sheehan was able to convince him that the Indians were not exactly easy to control at that moment, Galbraith had a token issue of flour and pork made, which cooled tempers for the moment. The next day a council was held with Sioux leaders; the Indians agreed to return to their villages and wait for the money if the goods and food were given them, and the agent ordered it done.

The incident at Upper Agency was a transient one, a matter of hungry people, short tempers, and bad judgment. It was dramatic, but the Sioux had older and greater resentments whose roots had grown deep and fed in a bitter soil of bad faith and broken promises during a couple of generations. Their dealings with the United States had included some very souring experiences.

To begin at the very beginning, the Minnesota Sioux were Santees, one of the three great divisions of the tribe. Once, all Sioux had lived in the lake and forest country of Minnesota until, during years of grim, no-quarter struggles in deep northern forests, they were slowly pushed onto the prairies to the south and west by the Chippewas. The Chippewas were the only people ever to defeat the Sioux decisively; they did it during years when they had the one-sided advantage of firearms.

Once out on the prairie, the Sioux obtained horses, prospered, multiplied, became the dominant tribe of the northern plains. The Teton Sioux, largest division of the tribe, moved west onto the high plains and became horse-and-buffalo nomads. The Yankton Sioux stayed farther east, with a range centering near the Missouri River in present South Dakota. Easternmost of all, the Santee Sioux remained closest to the land from which their ancestors had been expelled by the Chippewa.

The range of the Santee extended over an area that included not only the Minnesota prairies but large adjoining parts of Iowa, Wisconsin, and the Dakotas. It was not unbroken grassland, but contained numerous clumps and areas of woodland, and was rippled by many lakes and marshes. It was a rich land and a beautiful one. Settlers thought so, too, and began moving in; the government followed the frontier, as it always did, by forcing the Indians to cede the land.

In all land cession dealings, the white men were able to avoid any temptation to be honest and honorable, and carefully arranged that the Sioux came out the small end of the funnel each time with nothing left but resentment. At a treaty signed in Washington in 1837, the Sioux gave up all their lands east of the Mississippi, but the money they got in return was turned over to traders for debts supposedly owed by the Sioux. At the great council at Traverse des Sioux on the Minnesota River in 1851, the Indians signed away all the rest of their lands, more than 30,000,000 acres in Iowa, Dakota Territory, and Minnesota for $1,665,000—about a nickel an acre—keeping only a reservation extending 10 miles on each side of the general course of the Minnesota River, and from its source 150 miles downstream. There was to be a cash annuity for fifty years but those good friends of the Indians, the traders, always alert for the soft clink of coin against coin,

had arranged for the signing of separate "Traders' Papers" immediately after the treaty by which the Sioux agreed to turn over their cash
annuities for several years until more huge debts which had somehow
piled up were paid off. Long before that happened there were more
claims; the Sioux received nothing for all their lands.

Even the reservation they kept was halved in 1858 when the Senate
decreed that they should keep only the part south of the Minnesota
River, a shoestring strip 10 miles wide and 150 miles long. They were
granted compensation for the north half, but at once a swarm of white
claimants demanding pay for shadowy services descended on the
money like blowflies on a dead buffalo. The nature of the services was
never quite specified, but it ran into large amounts for some individuals. There were also traders with debts to be paid off—there were
always traders to be paid off. Once again the Sioux got little or nothing,
except another reason to feel bitter.

By 1862, the traders had been able to establish a foolproof credit
system. They sold goods to the Sioux on credit, chargeable against the
Indians' cash annuity. At annuity time, when the pay tables were set
up, the traders were on hand. As each Indian stepped forward, the
traders called out their claims and were paid. The Indian received
what was left, if any. No accounting was demanded; it seems to have
occurred to no Indian agent that it was part of his duty to his wards
to ask for one. But, to repeat, a lot of fancy work was being done with
Indians' money.

Leaders among the Sioux had a strong suspicion that there was a lot
of water in the traders' accounts, and they wanted the traders barred
from the pay tables. At the same time, they wanted to eat their cake,
too; they depended on credit, and especially so that summer, with the
buffalo hunt delayed and the annuity not yet paid. The Indians at
Upper Agency had obtained temporary relief by forcing the distribution of the food and goods, but nothing of the kind had happened at
Lower or Redwood Agency to the east. There the Indians continued
to buy on credit until the traders became worried that they might have
difficulty collecting, especially if the Sioux were successful in getting
them barred from the pay tables. Some of them went to Fort Ridgely
across the river to ask whether they could depend on the Army's help
if there were trouble. The commanding officer, Captain John Marsh,
gave them cold comfort with the tart observation that the Army was
not in the collection business.

On this, the traders immediately cut off all further credit. When protests were made that many of the Sioux would suffer actual hunger as a result, one of the traders, Andrew Myrick, retorted, "Let them eat grass."

The date was August 15, 1862. Myrick's words were repeated among the Sioux—with sullen satisfaction by the most ardently anti-white factions. However, it was going to have little effect on events. The shape of the future at that moment was in the hands of a small hunting party of Sioux who were a long distance north of the Minnesota River and the reservation, in an area known as the Big Woods. Unfortunately, the hunting was bad, and two days later the party were patting in their moccasins through the dust of a prairie road in Acton Township in Meeker County on the way home. Such hunting parties passed by often because the Indians were under no constraint to remain on their reservation, and if any settler saw it passing, he probably paid it little attention.

But this group was in a bad humor. It was returning empty-handed and it was hungry. As the men proceeded, sullen and wrangling by turns, one of them came on a nest of eggs in the tall grass by the side of the road, the gift of a hen from a farm well off the road. The finder began to gather in this godsend to hungry men, was warned by another that the eggs belonged to a white man and that taking them could cause trouble, expressed his disdain of all white men in return, and punctuated his sentiments by smashing the eggs. The disputation grew acrimonious and took a dangerous turn: from who was afraid of a white man it turned to who was afraid to kill a white man. Eventually, four young men had taunted each other into a position where it was difficult to find a middle ground between killing a white man or admitting to being a coward. The rest of the hunting party goaded them until it was even more difficult to find a line of retreat, and then went ahead, leaving the four to consider the folly of intemperate remarks.

However, they had traded dares and there was no backing down without loss of face. Probably with a hope all around that one among them would offer an honorable way out, they turned off the road into the farmyard of Robinson Jones whose house was also post office and an inn of sorts which offered rooms and meals to travelers. Jones was at home; so was his fifteen-year-old daughter and an infant son. The four Sioux were boisterous but they hesitated to consummate their purpose; Jones, on his part, had no qualms about walking out after a period of arguing with the young Indians, taking his daughter with him and leaving the Sioux in full possession of the house and the sleeping boy. He merely announced that he was going to join his wife who was visiting at the neighboring farm of Howard Baker, not much more than a stone's throw away.

In a short time the Indians followed Jones to the nearby farmyard where Mrs. Jones, Mr. and Mrs. Baker and an emigrant couple with their covered wagon were enjoying the bright Sunday weather visiting in the yard. When the four young Sioux arrived, there was probably a certain amount of fluttery excitement on the part of Mrs. Viranus Webster, the emigrant woman, but the Indians only proposed a shooting at targets, a challenge quickly accepted. The white men shot first and, without reloading, stood back to see how the young Indians would do. Here was a measure of how complacent the Minnesota settlers had become, because it is basic frontier doctrine to reload a gun at once.

The settlers had a brief moment to realize their error—or perhaps time was too short for them to comprehend what was happening. The Sioux, instead of firing at the targets, swung their guns on their hosts, and killed the three men, and Mrs. Jones and the daughter. Then, their bravado evaporating, they took horses and fled without completing the bloody and senseless deed by killing the other two women.

They had approximately forty-five miles to go to reach home, which was the village of Chief Red Middle Voice. It was after dark when they arrived, and reported to Red Middle Voice what they had done. The chief probably heard the news with some secret satisfaction. He hated the white men and he was a troublemaker—as a matter of fact, his village was made up of malcontents, dissidents, and general bad apples who had been asked to leave other villages. Red Middle Voice called in his nephew, Chief Shakopee, no lover of the settlers either, for advice. The two knew there was going to be trouble and elected without hesitation to stand behind the four young murderers. The important thing was to marshal tribal support. They sent messengers through the night to summon leading men to an immediate council at the house of Little Crow, the Sioux chief who wielded the most influence.

A brief explanation of the geography of the situation becomes almost essential at this point. The Minnesota River has its source in Big Stone Lake on the western border of the state and flows southeast for about two-thirds of its length before making a sharp elbow and running northeast till it meets the Mississippi. The Sioux reservation lay along

Scene of the 1862 Sioux Uprising

RED RIVER OF THE NORTH

DAKOTA TERRITORY

Ft. Abercrombie

L. TRAVERSE

BIG STONE L.

SIOUX RESERVATION

Camp Release

Sacred Heart Settlement

Upper Agency

YELLOW MEDICINE R.

REDWOOD R.

BATTLE OF WOOD LAKE

L. SHETEK

BIRCH COULEE
Lower Agency

Ft. Ridgely

New Ulm

South Bend

Acton P.O.

DEATH OF LITTLE CROW

Hutchinson

MINNESOTA R.

Le Sueur

St. Peter

Mankato

WINNEBAGO RESERVATION

THE BIG WOODS

Ft. Ripley

St. Cloud

MISSISSIPPI R.

St. Croix R.

WISCONSIN

St. Paul

Ft. Snelling

Shakopee

CHIPPEWA R.

MISSISSIPPI R.

DES MOINES R.

IOWA

Miles

0   100   200

the south side of the river for its first 150 miles, from Big Stone Lake almost to the village of New Ulm. About twenty-five miles upriver from the lower or southeastern end of the reservation was Lower Agency, also called Redwood Agency because the Redwood River flowed into the Minnesota nearby. Another thirty miles upriver beyond Lower Agency, and also overlooking the Minnesota, was Upper Agency —or Yellow Medicine Agency, so named from Yellow Medicine River which enters the Minnesota below the bluffs on which the Agency perched.

The agencies were busy communities with government offices and warehouses, churches and missionary schools, traders' stores, and other activities. It was not caprice, inefficiency, nor an Indian Bureau swindle that had caused two agencies to be built only thirty miles apart to serve one tribe. There were four bands of Santee Sioux, too many Indians to have their problems handled by a single agency. Upper Agency was responsible for the Wahpeton and Sisseton bands; Lower Agency took care of the problems of the Mdewakantons and Wahpekutes.

A few of the Indians had adopted permanent dwellings built by the government, either story-and-a-half brick houses or frame houses. Most still lived in tepees, tepees covered not with buffalo hide but with government-issue canvas. About a hundred families among them were doing their best to live as whites; they cut their hair short; the men wore coats and trousers; they went to school and church, farmed, and buried their dead. The majority remained Indians, wore their hair long, kept the breech clout, blanket and leggings, exposed their dead on scaffolds, and sent out war parties to fight the Chippewas to the north.

Red Middle Voice, Shakopee, Little Crow, and other Sioux who took part in the midnight council at the home of Little Crow were Mdewakantons and Wahpekutes whose villages were all in the vicinity of Lower Agency. It would have been desirable to have representatives from the Wahpetons and Sissetons but Upper Agency was thirty miles away and the matter could not wait. The council was an acrimonious one, hopelessly split on what course should be followed. Some argued persuasively—with any amount of historical precedent to back them up—that it would do no good to turn the four murderers over to the whites for punishment because all Indians would be punished indiscriminately anyway; the thing to do was to attack first. There would never be another time like the present, they said; Indians who passed

through settled country on hunting trips toward the Big Woods remarked that they saw nothing but old men, women, and children
because all the fit young men were away in the war. On the other hand,
a strong peace faction whose spokesmen included Wabasha, Wacouta,
and other respected chiefs, argued eloquently the futility of bloodshed.
Voices rose, taunts were hurled, threats made in the hot, crowded room.

Little Crow spoke last. He began by ridiculing the war faction with
its talk of killing or driving out all the whites. He had visited some of
the cities of the white men; he had seen their numbers and their power.
Crushing defeat lay at the end of the war trail. Then, when the war
leaders were shouting and threatening him, he dramatically reversed
himself to announce that, if they wanted war, he would lead them. The
meeting broke up in complete pandemonium. The news was passed to
the groups of young men who had gathered outside and there was more
whooping and shouting. Plans were made for an attack at daybreak,
August 18, only a few hours away.

Little Crow had been very much of a disappointment to his father—
also Chief Little Crow, as was his grandfather—because he had been
the Sioux equivalent of a playboy and had showed no aptitude nor
interest in leadership. Some of his tribesmen accused him of a notable
lack of enthusiasm for the hazardous little raids against the Chippewa,
preferring to spend his time bringing comfort and companionship to
wives whose men had gone after scalps. He did not extend his circle
of friends greatly by such good works, and one time, in a shooting
scrape, a bullet shattered both wrists, leaving them crooked and weakened. (He was also said to have had a double set of teeth, though how
this prodigy was arranged is not made clear.)

Then he abruptly ended his wastrel life, took four wives—sisters—
simultaneously (which was cause and which effect remains unknown),
and settled down to assume the responsibilities of leadership, which he
did with surprising vigor and ability. Of recent years he had been
gradually becoming something of a white man's Indian; he wore
trousers, lived in a wooden house, did some farming. Major Galbraith,
the Indian agent, had talked to Little Crow on the fifteenth, only two
days before the murders and had promised to build him a bigger and
better house if he would use his influence to bring the young men of
the tribe to "habits of industry and civilization." The chief had agreed
to do all he could and had picked out the site for the house. And the
day of the murders he had attended services at the Episcopal chapel

at the agency. He was not a Christian but he had been very attentive,
and the missionary priest was hopeful of making such an important
catch in his fishing for souls.

But to gain favor with whites was to lose it with a very large segment
of his own people. The Sioux began calling him a "cut-hair" and a tool
of the whites. He felt the chill breeze very keenly when, in the election
for the speakership among the Lower Indians, a position of great
prestige which he had long held, he was defeated. At the midnight
council, he had been forced to make a choice between responsible
leadership and the loss of his remaining prestige. When he found the
Sioux meant to fight regardless of his warnings, he had decided that it
was better to lead a lost cause than become a nobody.

Lower Agency was the target of the first attack. The council had
broken up very late; the chiefs had had to hurry to get their warriors
assembled and moved to the agency. There they were split up into
groups and quietly put into positions around every building where
there were white men and women. This was no war-whooping raid.

Early risers at the agency were surprised to see Indians around even
before full morning light but they were not apprehensive. The Sioux
waited until the agency began stirring; the smoke of breakfast fires
was already rising out of several chimneys before they fired their first
shot. The first victim was James Lynd, clerk in the store of trader
Andrew Myrick, who was killed as he came to the door, probably still
a little heavy with sleep. Lynd was a former state representative but
the Sioux knew him better as a man who had fathered children by
several of their daughters, and they undoubtedly put a bullet into him
with considerable satisfaction. Myrick was upstairs. He could have
had no illusions about the chances of a man who had said, "Let them
eat grass." Leaping out the window, he ran for the shelter of a clump
of brush but a bullet cut him down in flight. The Indians pulled a
handful of prairie grass and stuffed it into his dead mouth.

Another trader, François La Bathe, was killed in his store, and three
clerks were shot down in a third store. Three men in charge of the barn
left off feeding horses and walked out to see what all the shooting was
about; they were killed as they walked into the open air. Thirteen men
were killed at the agency and another ten while fleeing; no women
were slain but ten were taken captive. The Sioux could easily have
wiped out everyone if they had only kept their mind on their bloody
business but they were soon diverted by the treasures that became

available as they broke into buildings. Killing was soon almost forgotten in favor of looting while white survivors took advantage of the opportunity to escape.

No one at the agency knew the dimensions of the uprising; most were in some state of shock. But there was no doubt where the nearest chance of security lay: at Fort Ridgely across the river and downstream, about fifteen miles away. The agency stood on the prairie; from it a road led down the river bluff to the river bottoms, passed through the trees and brush and across the river, climbed the opposite bluff to the prairie again, and continued to Fort Ridgely.

The road crossed the river on a small ferry which was the bottleneck on this morning of August 18. When he might easily have escaped on one of his early crossings, the ferryman continued to ply back and forth, taking refugees across until some Sioux left off looting long enough to notice what was happening down below and put a stop to it. The ferryman, Hubert Millier but almost unknown to Minnesota history by any name other than Old Mauley, was shot and mutilated, but by then he had taken most of the refugees across. Up above, at the agency, flames were rising from burning buildings and Sioux warriors, in a delirium of excitement, were alternately war-dancing and adding to their stacks of plunder. The white women captives were not enjoying their part in the victory celebration.

2. MURDER ON THE PRAIRIE

Not all the Sioux attacked the agency. Bands were ranging the prairies, raiding the farms of settlers, and the paths of two or three of them intercepted the straggling parade of refugees on foot and in wagons and buggies on their way to Fort Ridgely. Seven more were killed during this flight. Old friendships did not necessarily mean anything. Philander Prescott was an interpreter who had lived at peace among the Sioux for forty years—since long before there had been settlers in Minnesota—and had an Indian wife; he was shot when a war party caught up with him as he headed toward the fort. On the other hand, there were instances aplenty where Sioux warriors allowed whites to escape, or gave them warning of impending attack, because of past friendship or simply "because he was a good man."

Disaster came in many ways on the prairie that day. Teen-age Mary

Schwandt worked for a man and his wife, both government school-teachers, whose home was off the agency. When word came that the Indians were killing and burning, Mary found a place in a wagon with two other young girls and three men, who headed for New Ulm. Half-way there they were cut off by a band of Indians. The men were shot at once; one of the girls, Mary Anderson, was also hit in the back when the three made a futile attempt to escape into the tall grass of a slough. The girls were taken captive, and were raped many times during the period they were held by the Sioux, even Mary Anderson, till she died of her wound and mistreatment. Indians of the plains and prairies, unlike those of the East, had no taboo about taking sexual advantage of women prisoners, and a white woman taken captive could expect the proverbial fate worse than death.

At about the same time Mary Schwandt was traveling across the prairie, her father was shingling the roof of his new house on the opposite side of the river when a party of Sioux rode up. Probably the first intimation of disaster he had was in the split second when he saw a rifle raised and aimed at him; then the gun fired and he rolled off the roof and fell to the ground. His wife, his sons aged five and seven, his married daughter and son-in-law, and the young son of a neighbor were slain before the warriors passed on to other deeds of bravery. One son, eleven, ran into some brush, escaped, and made his way to Fort Ridgely to relate the story.

There were unknown numbers of settlers who died with just as little warning as these people, as the war parties, usually in groups of about ten or twenty men, criss-crossed the prairies. The settlers made vir-tually no attempt to fight back that day; if any of them fired a gun there is no record of it. The American frontiersman of tradition, keen-eyed and ever alert, with rifle always within reach, apparently did not exist on the Minnesota prairie. The Indians had given no cause for alarm for a long time—and no one remains perpetually keyed up when no danger is in sight. Besides, many of the settlers were immigrants, chiefly German, who knew little of Indians and probably owned no guns.

Other families were wiped out, or nearly so, in the small settlement called Middle Creek where the Schwandts died. A Justina Boelter who lost her husband, father-in-law, and sister-in-law escaped into the bushes with her small child where she lived on berries and raw vege-tables which she dug up from gardens at night. She watched helplessly as the child died of starvation; finally, not knowing and not caring any longer whether Indians were around, she crawled back to her own home where she was found by soldiers nine weeks after the day of the outbreak, still alive, but just barely. Her husband, in his death throes, had inflicted one of the very few casualties on the Indians that first day of the uprising; he had almost bitten off the thumb of Cut Nose, one of the most murderous of the Sioux.

Other Indian bands south of the river rode at least as far as Milford Township in Brown County, twenty miles from the Sioux villages, where almost fifty German settlers lay dead by night, while another eight died as far away as Nicollet County on the north side of the river below Fort Ridgely, thirty miles and more east of homes of the Sioux. The Indians were ranging far.

Pillars of smoke from burning farms rose here and there against the sky, although the Sioux did not make it their common practice to fire buildings before riding on (it was commonly believed that they were saving them for their own use later). The word "massacre" has been loosely used and misused, but what occurred in Minnesota was a massacre in the true sense of the word. No one knows how many settlers were killed that first day, but it may have run into the hundreds. There were not usually witnesses left to come in and report the time and manner of their families' and friends' going.

The vanguard of the miserable parade of refugees plodding its way to Fort Ridgely reached its destination during the middle of the morning, bringing stories of terror and death that were not always coherent. Few, if any, of the survivors had a very good idea of what had happened; for most it was a nightmare alley of impressions: of hitherto friendly Sioux suddenly shooting, of seeing someone pitch and fall and struggle to rise and then go down limply with his skull crushed by a club, of running to get away.

Out of these impressions Captain John Marsh, commanding, gathered for certain only that there had been an outbreak of violence by the Sioux at Lower Agency; he erred tragically in not considering that he might have an entire war on his hands. Captain Marsh turned command of the fort over to young Lieutenant Thomas Gere, and set out at once for the agency with a force of forty-eight men, including himself and a civilian interpreter. On the way, the detachment continued to pass refugees, several of whom warned Marsh that this looked like a major outbreak and not just the actions of a few radical malcontents. Captain Marsh was a brave man, as his record at the first Battle of Bull Run proved, but he had never fought Indians. So, without hesitating, he led his command down the road onto the river bottom to the ferry, where they were hemmed in by trees and brush.

The only Indian in sight was on the other bank, a man named White Dog who worked at the agency and was considered completely civilized. Through the interpreter, he invited them to come across and assured them everything was perfectly all right. The body of Old Mauley, the ferryman, lying in sight suggested that all was not quite all right, and Marsh hesitated to put his men on the ferry. While the parleying was going on, Sioux warriors were crossing the river upstream and sneaking through the thickets; several even got into the ferryman's shack.

The ambush caught the soldiers with devastating surprise, a hail of bullets and arrows from the bushes on both sides of the river. A number of Marsh's men died in the first minute or two—several in the first volley. The Captain got the rest out of the most exposed position on the ferry landing and into grass and willows; then, looking for a way of retreat, Marsh decided that the best plan would be to cross the river well below the ferry where there appeared to be no Indians on the opposite side, and return to the north side somewhere near the fort. He attempted to find a place to ford, apparently stepped into a hole, and drowned. From then on, it was a case of every man for himself, but most of those still alive were well enough hidden in the thickets by then so that the Sioux had no great stomach for going in and routing them out. The coming of twilight enabled most to escape from their hiding places to straggle back across the prairie, the last reaching the fort well past midnight. Only twenty-three returned of the forty-eight who left in the morning.

As for the Sioux, they had lost one man at the ferry, apparently the only Indian killed anywhere in a day that saw so many whites die. The Indians were jubilant; the defeat of Marsh's force convinced them that they could handle any white soldiers without the least trouble.

The distance between Lower and Upper Agency was about thirty miles; word of the uprising crossed that distance in a matter of a few hours. The Sisseton and Wahpeton bands soon received overtures to join the war; they debated long and finally took the somewhat less than forthright position that they would not join in the fighting but would not refuse their support. It was not that they had any more love for the Americans than the Lower Sioux; they just wanted to see how things developed before going out on a limb. Many of their young men went off to join Little Crow and share the excitement and glory, but Little Crow had hoped for much more. It was the first great blow to his expectations.

Indians at Upper Agency did loot traders' stores, killing one man and mortally wounding another in the process, but there might have been an outbreak of much worse violence that would have put the Upper Sioux into the war willy-nilly, if it had not been for a Christian Indian, John Other Day. Other Day and his white wife gathered most of the whites into a brick warehouse in the evening, and he and a small group of Wahpeton friends guarded them through a tense night. At daybreak the next morning (August 19), he led sixty-two people across the Minnesota River, carrying the young and the feeble in five wagons and buggies, and after three days of travel got them safely to Hutchinson.

On Tuesday, the nineteenth, the Indians were still ranging ahead of the news that they were on the warpath. When settlers at Sacred Heart Creek settlement on the north side of the river learned that Indians had committed murders at nearby farms, thirteen families gathered, took counsel, and rejected a proposal that they make a stand at one of the farms that possessed a large and heavy log house, well suited for defense. Instead, they set out by wagon for Fort Ridgely, but were overtaken by a party of Sioux who told them that the Chippewa were on the warpath and that their only safe course was to return home under the protection of the Sioux (the Sioux included Chief Shakopee who had been the first to argue for war, and Cut Nose, he who had had his thumb almost bitten off by a dying settler the day before; the two were among the worst that the Sioux had to offer). The settlers turned around; they had guns, but they had stowed them in the bottom of one of the wagons instead of carrying them, and the Indians kept carefully between the men and the wagon. When they reached home, the Indians suddenly opened fire, killing twenty-five; all the men, and some of the women and children. The women and children not slain were taken prisoner.

One woman, Justina Kreiger, was left behind when the Sioux rode off with their captives. She had seen her husband murdered but there was no time for grief; she had waited till the Indians' attention was distracted and then pushed the eleven children in her wagon toward a roadside thicket. The escape was detected and several Indians ran up and began clubbing the running children. One of those killed was Justina's, but seven got away and eventually were saved. Mrs. Kreiger jumped from the wagon and attempted to follow the children into the bushes but a shotgun blast knocked her down and put seventeen pellets in her back. The Indians left her lying for dead and moved on, but events would prove that there was an amazing amount of life left in her body yet.

Across the prairie on this second day of the uprising, as on the first, settlers were being murdered in reprisal for all the grudges the Sioux had against the government of the United States. They died, in most cases, with the way of their going unknown because only Indians stood over the bodies, although occasionally their fate became a matter of record because one of the intended victims managed to escape and report the fate of the others. But on Tuesday, August 19, everything else that happened on the Minnesota prairie country was of minor importance to what was occurring at Fort Ridgely.

3. THE GATE TO THE VALLEY

On that second morning of the uprising, Fort Ridgely was the hope of the entire southwestern part of the state. At the same time, it was almost as vulnerable as any point within range of the Sioux horsemen. Captain Marsh had led the major part of its defending force into ambush at the ferry, and only twenty-three of his forty-eight had stumbled back. Yet those twenty-three hollow-eyed, beaten men doubled the force available to defend Ridgely. Lieutenant Tom Gere had been left in command of twenty-two men on duty and seven on the sick list. With the defeated survivors of Marsh's detachment, he had approximately fifty soldiers. He also had about two hundred refugees to take care of; they had continued to trickle in long after dark that first night of the uprising and were there to give him something to worry about when he woke up early on Tuesday morning.

On the Indians' side, Little Crow well understood the strategic value of Fort Ridgely. If it could be taken, the farms and villages of the older and more populous lower Minnesota River valley would lie open to Sioux attacks. But Little Crow could not order an attack, he could only propose one, and at the moment, the young Sioux warriors were more interested in the sport of ranging over the country, raiding and looting farms. They voted against attacking the fort.

In withholding their attack, the Indians made a priceless gift of time to the defenders. On Tuesday morning, the gate to the lower valley stood almost wide open. During the day, while Sioux warriors made raids that could have no real effect on the war, the gate slowly began to close. On Monday morning, First Lieutenant Timothy Sheehan had left Fort Ridgely with his company of the 5th Minnesota Infantry after having been on detached duty to oversee the annuity payments at Upper Agency, and was on the way back to their regular post at Fort Ripley up north in Chippewa country. The last thing Captain Marsh had done before setting out on his tragic march to the ferry was to send a messenger after Sheehan, recalling him. The messenger caught Sheehan already forty miles out, and Lieutenant Sheehan, being a soldier of decision, turned around at once and marched his company all night to reach the fort about Tuesday noon where, as senior officer, he took over command from Gere.

Lieutenant Gere had also put in a call for help. As soon as the first survivors of the ambush at the ferry came in with the story of the catastrophe, he realized this was a matter for much larger forces and higher authority. He prepared a terse report outlining what he knew of the events of the day: the attack on the agency, the killing of settlers, and the defeat of Marsh's command. This, together with a request for reinforcements without delay, was addressed to the commanding officer at Fort Snelling; the message was handed to Private William Sturgis who had saddled the best horse at the fort; Sturgis disappeared down the New Ulm Road into the darkness to begin a long and grueling ride, 125 miles in 18 hours.

Private Sturgis's message initiated large-scale operations against the Indians, but he also sent some immediate help to the garrison. As he galloped down the lower Minnesota River valley, at St. Peter his path overtook that of a group of about fifty recruits also on their way to Fort Snelling to be mustered into the Union Army. It was late at night but Sturgis was playing Paul Revere as he went through the river towns and villages, and the recruits were wide awake in a minute.

They had been signed up in an enlistment drive by Major Galbraith, the Indian agent, who had brought in about fifty boys, many of them half-breed youths who had been hanging around the agency with nothing to do. Most of them had come from Renville County which lay directly across the river from Lower Agency; Sturgis, in his few brief moments, could tell them that refugees had been coming in from that direction all during the day before he left. Galbraith himself was taking the recruits to Fort Snelling; now he scouted around, arousing the sleeping village, located fifty old Harpers Ferry muskets in storage and got them released, found powder and lead, and put his men and local volunteers to work casting bullets. After remarkably little delay, they were on their way at 4 A.M., swinging along the dusty dirt road toward Fort Ridgely where they arrived on Tuesday afternoon. The unit quickly named itself the Renville Rangers; for a while it was looked at with some suspicion because of the Sioux blood of so many of its members but all feelings of doubt disappeared as soon as the Rangers were seen in action.

There was one other small and very ironic addition to the fort's garrison that same Tuesday when a stagecoach carrying four armed guards stopped on its way to Lower Agency. When the driver and guards learned the situation, they decided to stay and help fight Indians, but first they carried a strongbox into the commanding officer's quarters for safekeeping. It contained $71,000, the annuity money then about two months overdue. Had it come only three or four days earlier it is very possible there would have been no massacre.

By Tuesday afternoon, Sheehan's refugee list had risen to about 250. Of these, some 25 men had presented themselves as ready and willing to fight. The number of soldiers under his command—using the term soldiers advisedly for some were raw recruits—had become about 180 by the time the day ended. His total force, then, was more than 200; with it Sheehan should ordinarily have been able to hold off a force of tribesmen several times his defending force.

The only flaw was that Fort Ridgely was not designed for a hard defense. It sat on the north side of the Minnesota, on the prairie but only a short distance from the bluffs that overlooked the valley. Ravines led back from the bluffs, growing smaller until they petered out in the prairie. One such ravine cut into the western edge of the fort, another ran along most of its northern side, still another lay to the east. They were filled with trees and thick brush and provided perfect cover for an enemy to approach unseen. The river bluffs, too, were wooded; at the same time they were too far from the fort to be defended and not steep enough to bother an enemy on foot. Only to the northwest was there unobstructed prairie.

Fort Ridgely in 1862

ST. PETER ROAD

TO LOWER AGENCY

RAVINE

BLUFFS

BLUFFS

LOG BUILDINGS

OFFICERS' QUARTERS

BAKERY

OFFICERS' QUARTERS

STONE BARRACKS

COMMISSARY

PARADE

OFFICERS' QUARTERS

HQ.

SURGEON

NEW ULM ROAD

STABLES

GUARD

MAGAZINES

WOOD PILES

ICE HOUSE

ROOT HOUSE

STORAGE

SUTLER

HAYSTACKS

ICE HOUSE

ROOT HOUSE

ROAD TO FERRY

The heart of the fort was its parade, a square about ninety yards on a side, about which were built the barracks, officers' quarters, commissary, headquarters, surgeon's quarters, and bake house. Scattered to the north, south, and west were various other buildings, some near, some far: stables, magazines, ice houses, warehouses, hospital, quarters for civilian employees, root house, and granary, as well as long rows of cordwood and hayricks. Where nature had not supplied cover for an enemy, these structures made up for the lack.

By Wednesday, Little Crow had assembled a large war party. The morning was spent by the Sioux warriors in working their way up the ravines that brought them close to the central quadrangle of the fort. Although four hundred or more men were involved, the operation was conducted so quietly the defenders were not aware an enemy was near till Little Crow himself appeared on horseback on the open prairie to the northwest, riding back and forth and waving a blanket as though asking for a parley.

It was purely a diversion, for suddenly some two hundred yelling warriors broke out of the ravine on the opposite side of the quadrangle. They drove in the picket line easily, gained an excellent advanced line by seizing a line of small log houses just north of the quadrangle, and at one point pierced the inner defenses at a gap between two buildings where three warriors got through before the break was closed in a bloody, snarling little fight in which the three were killed, along with one soldier killed and two wounded.

A year before, an artillery unit of the Regular Army had been stationed at Fort Ridgely but had been withdrawn for war service. It had left behind a number of guns, along with Ordnance Sergeant John Jones to look after them. Jones must have found it dull merely keeping his big guns free from rust, because he obtained permission to train some of the men of Company C of the 5th Minnesota Infantry in the handling and firing of artillery. Enough men had been given a chance at Jones's special training squad to form three gun detachments and this Wednesday, the twentieth of August, their training was being put to good use.

After the attack on the north had been repulsed, another from the south got close enough to put the gunners at an artillery piece under rifle and arrow fire. But the return fire was too hot for them and the Indians drew back, with grape shot from the cannon speeding them on their way. Five hours of almost continuous attack had accomplished nothing for the Sioux except that they had run off the fort's horses and cattle. The artillery had been a complete and unpleasant surprise to Little Crow, but he was not dismayed and made plans for a more vigorous assault the next day.

However, a very heavy rain fell that night and into the next afternoon, and the Indians did not attack. The defenders used the time to strengthen protecting works in the gaps between buildings of the quadrangle; there were very few shovels so breastworks were made of sacks of oats and cordwood. The day was not lost for Little Crow, either. All day, braves drifted in to join his forces. Many of them came from the Upper Reservation even though the Sissetons and Wahpetons continued officially neutral in the war. By Friday, as many as eight hundred warriors may have been ready for the fight, although the number was probably somewhat less.

Once again the Sioux spent the morning—Friday, the twenty-second —getting into position, working their way up the ravines and along the river bluff. At one o'clock in the afternoon they attacked, opening fire from all directions. They quickly seized the large post stables south of the quadrangle and only about eighty yards away, a protective position as good as that of the defenders. The artillery changed the odds, however; shells set the stables on fire and the Indians were driven out.

Stubbornly, the Sioux attacked here and there, probing for a weak spot, but each time were repulsed. Then they withdrew completely to regroup their forces in the shelter of a ravine to the southwest. But the charge never got organized. Two of the fort's three cannon were wheeled around to the threatened side; as the Sioux began to come out of the brushy ravines, double charges of canister exploded among them and cut them down. It took the last heart for fighting out of them; after gathering their dead and wounded they moved away, giving up all hope of taking the fort.

". . . the soldiers fought so bravely we thought there were more of them than there were . . . ," Chief Big Eagle recalled many years later. "We thought the fort was the door to the valley as far as St. Paul, and that if we got through the door nothing could stop us this side of the Mississippi. But the defenders of the fort were very brave and kept the door shut."

It had been a costly defeat for Little Crow, an estimated one hundred dead and many wounded, while the whites lost only three killed and thirteen wounded. The fort itself was stronger than ever; material damage had been limited to the burning of a few scattered buildings and the stolen horses and cattle.

However, there was more than one way to skin a cat. On the opposite side of the river from Fort Ridgely and about twenty miles downstream was New Ulm. Thirty miles farther to the southeast was Mankato, just about at the elbow where the river swings to the northeast and flows toward Fort Snelling and its meeting with the Mississippi. The northeast-flowing reach below Mankato was the lower valley on which the Sioux had their eyes fixed, a well-settled stretch with many villages and farms. Little Crow, who fancied himself a strategist, reasoned that if Fort Ridgely could not be taken, it could be by-passed if the Indians moved down the south side of the river. But first New Ulm would have to be captured to eliminate any threat in their rear.

Most of the Sioux warriors did not know whether Little Crow's strategy was sound or not. Most of them did not care one way or the other. But they were eager to strike at New Ulm where they had not been willing at first to attack Fort Ridgely. Young warriors in their teens and early twenties might not understand strategy but they could understand a village filled with more loot than they could haul away in wagons.

New Ulm was a community settled largely by Germans. It was growing rapidly, and in 1862 had a population somewhere near nine hundred. But for five days refugees had been pouring into the town until the population was more than doubled; many were wounded; many numb with grief and horror. Except for its riverfront, the town was almost without natural defenses. From the bottomlands on which it lay, the land rose in a couple of natural terraces to the prairie to the south; an attacking foe would come down from higher ground undeterred by any obstacles except those the defenders might put in its way.

On the other hand, as the Sioux moved to attack on Saturday the twenty-third, New Ulm had the powerful advantage of a determined defending force. As soon as word of the uprising reached the nearer towns of the lower valley, they sent help to New Ulm. On Tuesday, the day after the outbreak, Mankato had already sent a hundred men and a company came from South Bend. Militia units hurried out, the St. Peter Guards, the Le Sueur Tigers and others who had some small military training, along with volunteers who had nothing much except the will to help; in some instances they actually came without guns, possibly expecting—who knows—to throw rocks at the Sioux. The men from South Bend did not stay to fight, however; a rumor that the Winnebagoes in a small reservation about ten miles south of South Bend were about to go on the warpath sent them hurrying back to protect their own. The story was without foundation; the Winnebagoes had already been harried and moved about so much that all they wanted was to be left alone.

Charles Flandrau, justice of the Minnesota Supreme Court and former Indian agent among the Sioux, had been elected to command the St. Peter unit; at New Ulm he was put in top command by a vote of all officers. Popularity contests are not ordinarily the best way to ferret out military talent, but this was one case where it could have done worse. He posted his forces outside the village, making use of the protection offered by the natural embankment where the land rose from one terrace to the next. In the business district, near the river, he barricaded six blocks as an inner bastion in case a last-ditch stand became necessary, and there he put the crowd of some 1,200 refugees and noncombatants.

Flandrau's first move, though, proved to be a tactical error. He sent a group of seventy-five militia across the river by ferry to reconnoiter. The detachment was cut off by Sioux from returning by the ferry and was forced to retreat far down the river before it could find a place to recross. It did not get back to New Ulm that day at all; as a result, it missed the battle completely, thereby costing the defense about a quarter of its badly needed strength. The white forces actually taking part in the battle were about 250, the Sioux probably twice as many.

Pillars of smoke from burning farms and haystacks announced the coming of the Indians well in advance. When the Sioux forces at last appeared on the rim of the valley, it was as a great mass, but as they came down the slopes they fanned out, groups of horsemen swinging to right and left until they enveloped the entire land perimeter of the town by the time they were almost within rifle shot of the defense lines. There were an estimated five hundred of them; watching them come on in a seemingly inexorable advance was doing unpleasant things to the nerves of the defenders, so that when the warriors broke into a sweeping charge, yelling as they came, the militia broke and ran.

Once their panic had spent itself, they settled down to businesslike fighting, but the lapse had been costly, for by then they were inside the village itself, and it had become a matter of house-to-house fighting. When foes could not be driven from a house with weapons, they were burned out. Flandrau had a number of houses put to the torch even before the fighting reached them to deny their cover to the Sioux; the Indians, in their turn, started fires on the windward side of the village and burned out blocks of houses.

In the midst of a small inferno of smoke, flames, yells, curses, the crack of rifles, and the thud of arrows, the fighting went on, hardly a battle but dozens of separate deadly fights, usually for possession of strong points. A stone windmill was a prize much coveted by the Sioux but a band of militiamen inside doggedly refused to give it up. The post office, a brick building, was another fortress of the defenders that gave a good account of itself and refused to be taken. Flandrau's men were gradually constricted toward the barricaded downtown area; a large group of Sioux began gathering for a heavy assault to take the inner fortifications before the militia could get themselves sorted out and a defense organized. Flandrau, with considerable trepidation in view of the way his men had fled at the first Sioux charge of the day, ordered sixty of his men against the Sioux. It was surprise against planned surprise. Flandrau's worries about his men were baseless; they made an irresistible, cheering charge that broke and scattered the assembling Indian force.

The repulse marked the real end of the battle; thereafter the Sioux leaders were unable to exhort their men to any real effort. There was fighting till after sundown but the heart was gone from it, and some long-distance shooting the next morning, but the Sioux were finished and New Ulm was saved. The village, though, had not come off easily. Of its defenders, 26 were dead and more than 60 wounded. Only 25 of its houses stood; 190 were in ashes. Ammunition was almost gone; food was running low. The noncombatants were crowded into a small area under intolerable conditions. Flandrau took counsel with his lieutenants and decided there was no choice but to abandon the town and run whatever risks there might be in leaving the protection of its defenses.

On Monday, the children, the aged, and the wounded were put on 153 wagons, and with everyone else walking, the procession headed for Mankato, thirty miles away. The militia kept a close guard but no Indians appeared. Mankato was reached in one day; the volunteers returned to their own towns and became civilians again on the instant.

As for the Sioux, they had withdrawn to the northwest after their repulse. They did not stop at their villages around Lower Agency but had packed up their tepees and taken their captives and moved on until they were among the Wahpetons and Sissetons. It was not an admission of defeat, but they knew the white soldiers would probably soon be after them, and that it would be best to get their families and captives out of the probable area of fighting.

All the Sioux had not taken part in the attacks on Fort Ridgely and New Ulm; many groups of warriors had searched the prairies in ever-widening arcs to find farms where no warnings had reached and to intercept fleeing settlers before they could reach security. On Wednesday, the twentieth, while Fort Ridgely was undergoing its first attack, a raiding party struck the isolated settlement of Lake Shetek in the southwestern part of the state fifty miles south of Upper Agency. The settlers, after attempting to flee by wagon, ran into the tall dead grass of a dry slough where they tried to hide while the Indians on higher ground at the margin fired at leisure into every movement of the dry reeds. The Sioux treacherously shot several emerging settlers after a surrender agreement, clubbed two or three children (the women seem to have been mainly responsible for this), and took the rest of the women and children captive. Surprisingly, only fifteen were killed out of fifty members of the community, and a good number escaped—in the case of several of the men, by cowardly abandoning women and children and running.

Many remarkable things happened and prodigies were performed during the uprising; one of them during the Lake Shetek killings. A family named Eastlick suffered tragically in the episode: the husband was killed instantly, the wife, Lavina Eastlick, received four gunshot wounds and was clubbed over the head with a rifle until the stock broke; two of her children were beaten and died during the next twenty-four hours of their injuries and hunger and exposure as thundershowers beat down on the dismal scene. But two of her children escaped unscathed, and eleven-year-old Merton obeyed his mother's dying request that he take care of his eighteen-month-old brother Johnny. Somehow this young boy managed to lead and carry his baby brother for fifty miles during the next several days, finding enough berries to keep them going. Help finally came in the form of his erstwhile dying mother who had at last found new strength to rise up and start out in the direction of civilization. As she stumbled on her way she was picked up by the mail carrier, who either did not know what was happening, or took the slogan about the mail going through with more than ordinary seriousness. Mother and two small sons were reunited and won through to safety. Also saved was the Eastlick boys' Uncle Tom who had come out of the slough to attempt truce talks and had sunk back riddled with buckshot. He had bade Merton a tearful farewell but, like the boys' mother, at last had wearied of lying cold and wet, bleeding to death, and had also risen up out of the slough grass and headed eastward to safety. He survived for many garrulous, story-telling years.

There is no point in giving the complete calendar of raids and kill-ings—nor is it possible because no one knows when or how many of the settlers were slain. By the twenty-third, a week after the first attacks, a raiding party had reached almost to the Iowa border, killing thirteen at a Norwegian settlement on the Des Moines River in Jackson County. At almost the same time, and in exactly the opposite direction, the commanding officer of Fort Abercrombie on the Dakota side of the Red River of the North received news of the uprising and was advised to take appropriate action. He sent word to the scattered settlers in that far northwest area to come in to the fort. Three men in Wahpeton on the Minnesota side of the river decided to hole up in the village's primitive hotel and take their chances; they were all found dead when white men at last returned to Wahpeton. The driver of the mail coach to St. Paul got no warning; he was killed and the mail scattered over the prairie.

Fort Abercrombie was no more built as a fortification than was Fort Ridgely; it was a mere collection of buildings without any stock-ade or protective works. Its only advantage over Ridgely was that there were no ravines or other cover; an enemy had to approach in the open over flat prairie. The fort's garrison, Company D of the 5th Minnesota Infantry, was eighty-four strong; eighty refugees had crowded in with them. Captain Vander Horck, commanding, strength-ened the defenses as much as possible, using cordwood to build breast-works.

An attack by a small force of Sioux came on August 30; a much larger one on September 3 was repulsed leaving three of the defenders wounded. The Indians made their main effort on September 6, attack-ing at dawn and directing their main assault at the fort stables. The defenders had the tremendous advantage of artillery, three howitzers

—which were brutally effective on the dead-flat Red River Valley prairie where an anthill is an eminence; artillery fire broke up groups of warriors every time they attempted to assemble. Even so, one of the defenders was killed, two wounded, one of them mortally, in the days' fighting. The Sioux did not attack again but their sporadic presence in the area kept the garrison in a state of apprehension for more than a month until a relieving force finally arrived from Fort Snelling, two hundred miles away.

4. THE STATE UNDERTAKER AND HIS GRAVEDIGGERS

While these hundreds of individual dramas of violent death, terror, flight, and stout resistance were being played out on the prairie frontier, preparations were going ahead for full military action against the Indians. When Private Sturgis ended his long ride and brought the first news of the uprising to Fort Snelling, Governor Alexander Ramsey in St. Paul, a few miles away, was immediately informed. The Governor at once went out to the fort to see how many men were available (most were recruits waiting to go to join the Union army), then took the ferry across the Minnesota to the old fur trading village of Mendota to call on his personal friend and political foe, Henry Sibley, whom he immediately commissioned a colonel of militia and put in full charge of all operations against the Indians.

Sibley had been the first governor of Minnesota and Ramsey's immediate predecessor. He had been a fur trader for years, knew personally many of the leaders among the Sioux, was well acquainted with the habits of the Sioux, and had a good insight into their ways of thinking. But as far as fighting Indians was concerned, he was completely without experience.

Sibley started briskly, putting four companies of the 6th Minnesota Infantry the next morning on a steamboat which took them a little more than twenty miles up the river to Shakopee, whence they marched for two days to reach St. Peter on Friday, the same day Fort Ridgely was standing off its second attack. There was no reassurance in the stories pouring into the lower valley, with refugees hourly bringing new tales of horror which seldom suffered from understatement. Sibley became convinced the fort had fallen; he believed it highly possible that the entire Sioux nation with seven thousand warriors was moving in from the Great Plains and that fifteen hundred warriors might at that moment be waiting just over the horizon.

Men from St. Peter where he waited were even then out beyond that same horizon defending New Ulm. They had gone without asking about the number of Indians they might meet, but Sibley was not imbued with the same spirit. He sent messages back to Governor Ramsey complaining about the rifles and demanding Springfields, asking for more men, saying he needed more supplies. Ramsey sent the Springfields at once, dispatched supplies, filled six more companies of the 6th Minnesota and sent them. Sibley was carrying on a recruiting drive of his own among the excited people of the valley, enlisting militia and impressing farmers' horses and wagons into service. Finally, with a force of 1,400, including 300 of what might, with courtesy, be called cavalry, he set out for Fort Ridgely on Saturday morning, the day of New Ulm's agony.

The mounted troops pushed ahead and traveled all day and night to reach the fort where they were greeted as deliverers. Sibley and the main force showed no similar tendency to make haste. When evening forced them to make camp, they were only six miles from St. Peter, an advance so tortoiselike one wonders what the force could have been doing most of the day. It speeded up somewhat thereafter, reaching the fort a day and a half after the mounted troops.

Sibley sent the refugees back to safety in the lower valley with an escort, then cautiously reconnoitered for Indians. None appearing after three days of search, he sent a detachment of about 160 men under Major Joseph R. Brown down the road toward Lower Agency. It was accompanied by a number of civilians, most of them in the grim hope— or fear—of finding the bodies of missing relatives or friends.

The detachment moved slowly because it found sixteen bodies to bury on its way to the Agency. It camped overnight on the river bottoms; the next morning one section of it buried twenty men of Marsh's command at the ferry. In the ruins of Lower Agency, the body of trader Andrew Myrick was identified by his brother Nathan who had accompanied the detachment for just that purpose; Nathan knew precisely why his dead brother's mouth was stuffed with grass.

On the north side of the river, they came on a living being—although one so emaciated, so unkempt, so crusted with dirt and dried blood that at first they did not know whether she was white or Indian. They had chanced on Justina Kreiger, the first part of whose story has already been told, how she had been shot and left for dead when Shakopee's raiders had intercepted a band of settlers fleeing toward Fort Ridgely. Two Indians had later returned after dark to look for plunder among the bodies; one decided to take the dress from Mrs. Kreiger's body and slit it with a sweep of his knife. The blade cut a four-inch slash in her body but she did not flinch; then the Sioux changed his mind and went away. The woman survived her cruel wounds, and for twelve days had wandered on the prairie with no food except a few wild berries. She was too weak to give much information to the soldiers, so they wrapped her in blankets and laid her carefully in one of the wagons.

On their second night, they made camp on the prairie on the north side of the river near Birch Coulee, a deep, wooded ravine that runs several miles through the prairie to the river bluffs. Major Brown had been explicitly directed not to camp near timber or any uneven terrain. He should not have needed such instructions. He was married to a half-Sioux woman; he had been an Indian agent; he had lived among the Sioux most of his life. Yet, like the rankest greenhorn, he placed his camp only about 200 yards from the trees and brush of the coulee, and south of a swell in the prairie that made it impossible to see anyone approaching from the north.

The complete absence of any sign of Indians had convinced Brown and his officers that all was well. What they did not know was that a large force of Sioux led by Chiefs Mankato and Big Eagle was going down the south side of the river to pick up plunder they had left behind when they withdrew from their villages, and possibly even to have another try at New Ulm. The detachment had not seen any Indians, but the Indians had seen them and during the night had crossed the river and quietly surrounded the soldiers' camp.

The Sioux plan had been to kill the sentries noiselessly with bow and arrows, then fall on the sleeping camp and annihilate the soldiers. The scheme went awry when a sentry saw a movement in the grass in the first faint gray light and fired at it. The shot woke the camp but there was little margin against disaster for, with their original plan upset, the Sioux attacked at once. A number of soldiers were shot and killed in the first moments as they tried to shake off sleep and get their bearings in a world that was exploding in a chaos of Indian yells, gunfire, neighing horses, and soldiers' curses.

Major Brown and his officers set about rallying the men and improvising a defense. Wagons were heaved on their sides to form a barricade of sorts, all except the one in which Justina Kreiger lay. After the first overwhelming element of surprise was gone, the Sioux were checked for the moment and drew back. There is nothing more open and exposed than a piece of prairie, and the beleaguered soldiers did what they could to make it more hospitable, improvising protection with dead horses, chunks of tough sod laboriously cut out with knives, with anything, in fact, that came to hand.

The Sioux knew exactly where the defenders were. The warriors, on the other hand, could stay out of range, crawling forward through the tall grass to fire for a while and withdrawing again before the soldiers could pinpoint them. As the sun climbed higher, thirst and heat tortured the men lying on the ground inside the defense line; the Sioux, when fighting began to weary them, could go back into the shade of the trees of Birch Coulee for something to eat and perhaps a nap.

The gunfire was heard very plainly at Fort Ridgely only fifteen miles away, a distance that should have been an easy march of five hours or less. After discussing its meaning with his officers, Sibley ordered Colonel Samuel McPhail to take a strong force of 240, including artillery, to investigate. The relief force was sighted by Sioux scouts long before it reached the battlefield, and a small band of braves on horseback was sent out to meet it.

The Sioux were few, but noisy and active. They galloped about, whooping, shooting, dashing in first from one quarter and then another. Colonel McPhail halted his force and had his artillery fire a few rounds at the elusive Indians, upon which they slowly withdrew, making derisive gestures. Then the timid Colonel took up a strong defensive position and sent word back to Sibley that he was outnumbered and almost surrounded and needed help.

At Birch Coulee, the hard-pressed soldiers had heard McPhail's cannon and had taken immediate heart, but the hours passed and nothing happened except that the sun grew hotter, their thirst became fiercer, and the moans of the wounded became more urgent. McPhail was sitting and waiting for help and looking uneasily over his shoulder for Indians, while Sibley was coming to his rescue with all the precipitate speed of a glacier.

Colonel Sibley, with one thousand men and artillery, finally reached McPhail at midnight. With the hard muscle of 1,250 men and strong artillery, the combined forces might have been expected to push on with full speed. Instead, there was an unaccountable delay of three hours before anyone moved. Finally, at three o'clock in the morning, the force got under way. Birch Coulee was only three miles away; while there was little firing at that time of night, the sporadic shots could be heard very plainly at that distance and it would seem a time for haste. Yet it took until eleven o'clock—eight hours—to cover the last three miles. Then the besieging Sioux simply withdrew, and the thirty-one-hour ordeal of the detachment was ended.

Thirteen were dead, another three so badly wounded they would soon die. Forty-four were seriously wounded but would live. Among the casualties were some of the civilians who had gone along to find the bodies of relatives and friends. All who came out of the circle of makeshift defenses were dazed with fatigue and suffering from hunger and thirst. The wagon in which Justina Kreiger lay still stood upright but its wood had been literally torn to splinters in places by rifle bullets. When they looked to see what violence had been done to her body, they found not a shattered corpse but a woman very much alive. "They seemed perfectly astonished to find me alive," Mrs. Kreiger related afterward. "The blanket on which I lay wrapped in the wagon was found to have received over two hundred bullet holes in the fight." Yet not a bullet had pierced her flesh, although five had grazed her in so superficial a manner as hardly to have left a mark on the skin.

The Birch Coulee battle ended on September 2. On that same day, another force of soldiers was moving toward battle without knowing it. More than a week earlier, Governor Ramsey had answered appeals from Meeker County settlers on the edge of the Big Woods by sending a company of the 10th Minnesota Infantry, commanded by Captain Richard Strout, to protect and reassure the people there. Strout and his men had been moving through the settlements and letting themselves be seen as much as possible, to show that all was well. But all was not going to remain well; Little Crow was moving into the same area.

When Mankato and Big Eagle had started down the south side of the river, Little Crow with another band had headed northeast to raid settlements toward the Big Woods. His warriors agreed wholeheartedly with the plan for it would take them into country untouched by the war and ripe for looting. But Little Crow was still thinking in terms of grand strategy; he had no way of knowing the other Sioux force had been diverted at Birch Coulee, and he began talking about swinging behind the army in a great arc to join Mankato and Big Eagle, catching Sibley in a giant pincers movement.

His warriors wanted only the uncomplicated pleasures of raiding and plundering. If the chief was interested in strategy, he was welcome to it. When he became insistent, approximately two-thirds of them seceded from his band. The two bands went along separately, but on parallel roads that brought them into Acton Township, where the murders that had started the whole bloody string of events had occurred only a little more than two weeks before. That night they made separate camps, while not far away Captain Strout with sixty-four men was making a bivouac near Acton Post Office.

The next morning Strout set out with his company. He had been warned there were Indians in the vicinity and he had skirmishers out, so he was not caught by surprise when he ran into Little Crow's warriors. There was a brisk exchange of shots. One soldier fell mortally wounded but the Indians were beginning to give way after a short fight when the second group of Sioux came up in back of the company. Undismayed, Strout detailed men to face about and fight off the new attack. A lake lay on the company's left; the Indians extended their lines to cut off escape on the land side completely. Strout ordered a bayonet charge that opened the road, then quelled a panicky attempt by his own teamsters to abandon the company and make a frenzied dash for safety.

Captain Strout formed up his company for a fighting retreat and started down the road, holding off the outnumbering Sioux as they went. But, having been almost an exemplary leader thus far under the most difficult circumstances, Strout somehow let control of his men slip away from him. Panic began to spread; the march became a headlong and utterly disorderly flight which continued all the way to the village of Hutchinson, twenty-five miles to the southwest, with Indians riding on the flanks for miles and shooting into the terror-stricken soldiers. Three soldiers were killed during the flight, three fatally wounded, many more less seriously hurt. Nine horses were lost and most of the ammunition and rations. The dead were left where they fell. It was a disgraceful rout, especially after the brave beginning of the battle, and led to a second flight of settlers from the counties north of the Minnesota River.

After the disaster at Birch Coulee, Sibley returned to Fort Ridgely.

His lack of aggressiveness and slowness were raising a tremendous amount of criticism. Newspaper editors, sharpening their similes and metaphors in St. Paul far from any danger, called him a "snail" who "falls back on his authority and dignity and refuses to march," and the "state undertaker with his company of grave diggers." Although communications were not the best, Sibley received the papers from the state capital no more than three days late, so he knew what they were saying about him. Still he delayed, but now he had a rationale for his delay: he did not want to make any move that would endanger the lives of the prisoners in the hands of the Sioux. He carried on a form of negotiation with Little Crow by means of messages left in forked sticks thrust into the prairie; Little Crow used a half-breed prisoner who wrote a somewhat shaky English as his amanuensis. This channel of communication was also adopted by Wacouta and Wabasha, the peace chiefs who had opposed war ever since the midnight council; they put up messages asking how they could come in with their people and be sure they would not be harmed.

Negotiations were getting nowhere and the army at Fort Ridgely was beginning to suffer from slack discipline, desertions and the other ills of sitting around and doing nothing. At last, on September 18, one day short of a month from the afternoon when Governor Ramsey had made him a colonel and told him to save the state from the Sioux, Sibley led his forces out to do battle. He commanded exactly 1,619 men, a very potent force, especially since it included strong artillery units. He did suffer one major handicap, the lack of cavalry. The horsemen who had come with him to the fort had long since gone home to their own trades and businesses, leaving Sibley without any mounted troops.

The force crossed the Minnesota and moved upstream on the south side toward the Indian camps; in four days of cautious advance it traveled forty miles to Wood Lake, with the Sioux camps still twenty miles ahead. While the soldiers bivouacked near Wood Lake, the Sioux prepared their final battle, an ambush to catch the army when it took up its march again in the morning. It was a sound plan, which was simply to conceal seven hundred or eight hundred Indians in tall grass, and other cover on both sides of the trail the army column would follow. When the column was on its way and strung out over several miles, it would be attacked simultaneously from both sides and cut into disorganized fragments that could be wiped out easily.

Luck was not with the Indians—it seldom was. Among Sibley's forces was a group of real veterans, men from the 3rd Minnesota who had been taken prisoner and paroled by the Confederates, and were back in Minnesota until they could be formally exchanged and go back to fighting rebels again. In the meantime, they were lording it over the recruits in the Indian-fighting army, and this morning were about to demonstrate the possibilities of adding variety to an Army mess by foraging. A dozen of them had obtained four teams and wagons and had started across the prairie to raid the gardens of deserted Indian villages near Upper Agency. Their course took them directly toward the grassy clump where two or three Sioux were lying, waiting for the Army to get under way; the Indians had no choice except to shoot or be run over.

One of the soldiers was killed at once. His battle-wise comrades jumped out of the wagons and withdrew, firing as they went, giving the rest of the men of the 3rd time to come up and form a line of battle. The Sioux, with all hope of surprise gone, came out of hiding and moved in to attack; in turn the scrappy Renville Rangers hurried up to support a threatened flank of the veterans of the 3rd. Sibley, help-lessly watching a battle develop without having a thing to do with it, became concerned at the exposed position of the 3rd and the Renville Rangers, and two or three times sent orders for them to fall back on the main body of the Army. The cocky veterans paid no attention to him, and after a brisk battle, the Sioux gave way and ran. Just as very few of Sibley's forces had a chance to get in the fighting before it was over, so only a fraction of the Sioux were near enough to reach the battlefield. The main engagement lasted a very short time; desultory firing kept up for possibly as much as two hours on the outer fringes. This, in Minnesota history, is the Battle of Wood Lake, and Colonel Sibley was promoted to brigadier general for winning the great victory.

However, it had been a bitter fight for those who were engaged. Seven soldiers were killed or mortally wounded, another thirteen wounded. Counting the Indian casualties was, as usual, an inexact science because the Sioux carried off their dead if humanly possible, but they had been driven back so sharply that they had abandoned fourteen bodies. Chief Mankato died in the battle, although his body was carried away. Sibley was quite shocked to learn that all the Indian dead had been scalped and gave his troops a stern lecture about acting like civilized gentlemen. There was some attempt to blame it on the savage instincts of the half-breeds among the Renville Rangers, but no one was very convinced.

The Sioux now realized the hopelessness of their struggle and began a flight into Dakota Territory. Not all ran. The Wahpeton and Sisseton bands had remained officially neutral even though large numbers of their young men had joined the fighting, and most of them felt they had nothing to fear. A considerable number of the Lower Reservation Indians had also remained apart from the fighting and refused to join the exodus. There were some, too, who had fought through the uprising and believed that they were too unimportant to be noticed if they remained and kept their mouths shut.

The Sioux were camped about twenty miles above Wood Lake. A large army and a beaten foe did nothing to speed Sibley. He went into camp for another two days at Wood Lake, probably to contemplate his victory, and then took another two days to march the twenty miles to the Indian camp. His explanation for his leisurely advance was still that he did not want to endanger the lives of the captives. However, they were almost slain while he dawdled; their preservation was due in little part to his efforts.

Little Crow, making ready for the retreat west, debated the massacre of the captives as a last gesture of defiance at the soldiers closing in. Other leaders whose hands were bloodied were all for it; those whose consciences were clear were against a step that would turn the whites irrevocably against all Sioux. While the arguing went on, Chief Wabasha quietly moved his tepees next to the camp of the captives, indicating that he was taking them under his protection. Little Crow had no wish for a civil war right then; he forgot about a general killing and moved on out into Dakota. When Sibley at last appeared, deporting himself like a conqueror, as a contemporary observer described his arrival, the captives were perfectly safe in the custody of friendly chiefs and Sibley was doing his posturing principally for Sioux who had supported him from the beginning.

There were 107 white and 162 half-breed captives in the camp, which was quickly named Camp Release. Almost all were women and children; the Sioux had shown little mercy toward adult males, and none at all toward those of all-white blood. The Sioux women had made some effort to dress up the captives a little before the arrival of the soldiers but they were still a pathetic band, ragged and hungry and showing in their haunted faces the mental strain they had undergone. Some of the younger women had been badly misused; others among the captives seem to have been treated about as well as the conditions of an Indian camp at war could give them to expect. "There were some instances of stolidity among them," Sibley wrote, "but for the most part the poor creatures, relieved of the horrible suspense in which they had been left, and some of the younger women freed from the loathsome attentions to which they had been subjected by their brutal captors, were fairly overwhelmed with joy." But the attentions of the brutal captors were not universally loathsome. Sibley, writing to his wife, mentioned one married woman who had become infatuated with the Indian who had captured her. Some of the women remained with the army to be witnesses against the Sioux but the rest of the captives were sent back to Fort Ridgely and then to the settlements.

5. "HAVE MERCY UPON US, O JEHOVAH"

To Sibley, his mission from that point on was one of vengeance, the speedy hanging of many Sioux. Detachments scouted the surrounding country, bringing in Indians, until eventually they had collected about two thousand. The only flaw with plans for mass executions to make the Minnesota frontier happy was that the really big fish were far out of reach in Dakota Territory. Most of those Sibley had rounded up were there because they had no reason to run. However, he did have about four hundred who looked like prime suspects.

A court was organized which had no close counterpart in either civil or military jurisprudence; after a brief warm-up period to establish working procedures, it became so efficient that it could try and sentence a man to the gallows in as little as five minutes. It was not considered necessary to prove actual killing or other crime; taking part in a battle, or even presence at the scene of a battle were ruled to be punishable by death.

In the latter part of October, with hard frosts biting down on the prairie at night and the growing possibility that before long an early snowstorm might pin an unprepared army in an empty region, Sibley took his prisoners and his troops to Lower Agency, where the trials continued in the only building that had escaped the torches of the Sioux. The work of justice was finished in the first week in November. Almost 400 men had been tried; 306 of these were sentenced to hang for murder, rape, or, in most instances, simply for taking part in a battle. Another 16, with tempered justice, were given prison sentences for robbery.

Those who were considered free of any culpable act—approximately 1,700 and mostly women and children—were taken to Fort Snelling; the convicted men were taken in irons two days later to a prison stockade at Mankato. The first group was set upon by enraged citizens as it passed through the village of Henderson on the lower Minnesota; no Sioux raider had come within miles of Henderson, nor did it occur to the villagers that the Indians passing through were almost entirely those who had remained friendly during the uprising. The townspeople were now admirably valiant in defending their homes and one especially intrepid soul snatched an infant from its mother, fatally injuring it.

The condemned men had even worse misfortune; they passed through New Ulm on the day the bodies of those killed in the defense were being taken from temporary graves in the streets and reinterred in the cemetery. Villagers, especially the women, set upon the Sioux with everything from hot water to scissors and pitchforks. The infantry guard had to use bayonets to drive back the angry, clamoring townsfolk; several soldiers were injured along with more than a dozen of the prisoners.

Even though the nation was more concerned with the Battle of Antietam in mid-September than with an Indian uprising on an obscure frontier, there were great protests in the East at the idea of executing more than three hundred Indians. Minnesota settlers, looking over the wreckage of a very considerable portion of their state, felt no such compunction, and wanted a vengeance as ruthless as possible. There were rare exceptions, and one of the foremost was the Right Reverend Henry Whipple, Episcopal Bishop of the Missionary District of Minnesota. Bishop Whipple went to President Lincoln himself to plead the Indian's cause; the uprising, he said, was the result of years of lies, broken promises, and being shamelessly cheated and victimized. Lincoln was convinced, although Whipple was virtually ostracized in Minnesota. The Minnesota Sioux, the President decreed, had been fighting a war, and therefore those who had done nothing beyond fighting in its battles were to be treated as any other prisoners of war. The records were gone over; the work of Sibley's court collapsed. Using the new criterion, the list of condemned men was reduced to forty who had committed murder or rape. One of these was later pardoned, another died a natural death before the day of execution.

The thirty-eight were hanged at Mankato on the day after Christmas, 1862, on a single scaffold built in the form of a hollow square. They met their deaths bravely, though far from stolidly. They kept up a death chant, a monotonous "Hi-yi-yi-yi, Hi-yi-yi-yi" through most of the proceedings, and although hanging is an odious way of death to an Indian, they made no objection to the placing of the noose or other preparations until the hoods were drawn over their heads. This, though, was too ignominious for many of them; they tried to object but the traditional ritual of legal life-taking had to be gone through in its entirety.

At the last there was a great deal of weaving and twisting around among the condemned as they worked to get their tied hands in a position to grasp the hand of a neighbor in a final handclasp. For two or three seconds there was absolute silence, not only among the troops drawn up around the scaffold but also in the surrounding crowd of spectators. Then three taps on a drum, at the third the executioner cut a single large rope which sprung all traps, dropping all thirty-eight men into eternity at the same moment. It did not go entirely without a hitch. A rope broke and the body of one man, Rattling Runner, dropped heavily to the ground under the scaffold. He was quite plainly dead or dying, but a new rope was attached and his body was hoisted again, to dangle yet a while for the edification of the spectators.

The hangman was a man named William Duley who had escaped during the massacre at Lake Shetek. The bodies of three of his children were still lying on the frozen prairie—would, in fact, not be buried until the following October when a military expedition would reach the spot and gather the bleached bones—and his wife and two other children, according to somewhat unclear records, were still captives of the Sioux who had taken them on their retreat toward the Missouri River. Duley, on his day of vengeance, did not know whether they were dead or alive. He was a very willing executioner.

It was discovered afterward that one of the men put to death was the wrong one; it was possible that other mistakes had been made. Sibley's court had operated at such high speed that it had kept only scanty records; it was difficult or impossible to transliterate many Sioux names very closely into the English alphabet which lacked some of the necessary sounds—and no one had been very careful at the time anyway because it seemed silly to go to much trouble for an Indian who was being sentenced to death. However, it created problems later when it turned out that many of the Indians were not going to be dead in a hurry after all—and it was not the white jailers who paid for the inevitable mistakes that were made.

The bodies were buried in a shallow mass grave on a sandy flat by the river, but they did not rest quietly there even during the night. A number of doctors from surrounding towns had come to the hanging with something more in mind than an interest in watching human beings sent to death; after dark they dug up the bodies and drew lots to decide how they should be assigned. The doctors were interested in turning them into articulated skeletons, almost a necessity for a physician in that day of few medical schools. A skeleton was a ready reference book he could turn to for help when a balky plow horse left a farmer with a tricky fracture; it was also an important training aid because likely youths became doctors by "reading medicine" with an established physician and it had no substitute for demonstrating bone anatomy.

Among the doctors was a William W. Mayo from Le Sueur. He had been at the New Ulm battle and had attended wounded all during the uprising; in the drawing of lots he had gotten the body of Cut Nose, the same battle-shy cutthroat who had been the companion of Chief Shakopee on his raids; he had refused to flee although he well knew what would happen to him at the hands of the Americans. Two of the young men Dr. Mayo first taught anatomy with the help of the skeleton of Cut Nose were his own sons, William and Charles. Later—much later—father and sons went on to establish the Mayo Clinic at Rochester, Minnesota, which soon became world-famous. It thus becomes a matter for interesting philosophical discussion whether Cut Nose, through his bleached and wire-hung bones, had thus expiated any small part of his vast guilt.

The men who were reprieved from the gallows by Lincoln, almost 270, were still technically prisoners of war. They were kept in the Mankato prison during the winter, where they were gentle and tractable prisoners, and almost all of them became Christians. In the spring they were put on the steamboat *Favorite* and sent down the Mississippi to Rock Island, Illinois, where a prison camp for Confederate soldiers was located. As the steamboat passed the flats below Fort Snelling where their families, along with the other Sioux, brought down from the Upper Reservation, had been penned in a stockade during the winter, the prisoners aboard sang the hymn "Have Mercy Upon Us, O Jehovah."

At Rock Island, they were no trouble at all; they were soon permitted to come and go freely, and began working as farm hands and doing odd jobs in the neighborhood. At the end of three years they were allowed to join their families who in the meantime had been sent to a reservation in Dakota Territory. Their people had not had it easy since they had passed them at Mendota and saluted them with a hymn; the government had put them on a barren reservation, ignoring completely that many of the deported Sioux had had nothing to do with the uprising. The reservation had been so poor, however, that even the government had taken notice and had given them something better.

Minnesota had got rid of almost all her Sioux—and nearly with a clear conscience, because if some of them had made war, it stood to reason that all should be made to pay, even those who had remained friends of the whites during the hostilities. There were, however, about twenty-five whose services to the settlers had been so outstanding that they, with their families, were permitted to remain. Their descendants are still there, farmers in large part, most of them living around the two agencies which still are in operation, as hard-working citizens as the state could wish.

Payment of annuities to all Santee were stopped for four years, 1863–66, with no favors granted to bands that had been neutral or had aided the whites. The funds so saved were used to pay off settlers' claims for damages, although a committee set up to take a hard look at some of the claims reported that most of them had been greatly exaggerated, and also that much of the looting of abandoned houses had not been done by Sioux warriors at all but by white men willing to take advantage of another's misfortune.

Nevertheless, the uprising depopulated a large strip of frontier. An estimated 30,000 fled their homes and had retreated, some to the lower Minnesota Valley, some as far as the Mississippi, some all the way back to homes in the East, never to return. Twenty-three counties were devastated and left almost completely without humans, a region 50 by 200 miles. More than a year later no one had returned to nineteen of those counties; in the other four only a portion of the former population was cautiously returning.

No one knows how many died in the uprising. For years 737 was accepted as reasonably close to the truth; more recently experts have, by some legerdemain, counted the dead again and one says there were 644 dead, another that 490 died. The truth is, it was impossible to tell. With new families arriving daily, there was no way of knowing how many people were on the frontier when the Indians struck; there is no way of knowing how many of those who were presumed to have abandoned their farms and fled east actually were slain out on the prairie. Settlers were killed or crawled to die in lonely thickets or in the tall grass of marshes; it was a year or more before other white men returned to the vicinity and by that time what had been human was reduced to bones and tatters of cloth with grass and prairie flowers growing through them. It might be years, if ever, before a plow turned up the grass-veiled bones, and by then who could say whether it was victim of the massacre or possibly an Indian killed in a battle between Sioux and Chippewa fifty years before?

The spring following the outbreak, a punitive army headed into Dakota Territory to chastize the Sioux. It went in two columns, General Sibley leading the southern one of 3,300 men, which set out from the upper end of the former reservation, Brigadier General Alfred Sully in command of the other, with a strength of about 3,000, which headed across the prairies from up in the Red River Valley. The strategy was to catch the tribesmen in a pincers, but it was a pincers so ponderous in its closing that the nimble, fast-moving Indians, even with their families and baggage, were able to sidestep, and only a couple of inconclusive brushes occurred.

Little Crow attempted to enlist the aid of the western Sioux, but without success although the presence of the troops bumbling around west of Devil's Lake was not doing anything to calm the western bands. The Santee chief then went to Canada on the strength of a vague and pathetic legend that the British were so grateful for help given by the Sioux in the War of 1812 that they would return the favor whenever their aid was needed. The legend was tied up with a cannon supposedly captured during the war and held by the British for the Sioux, the sort of story told around tepee fires by old men until it becomes hazy and distorted. There was, of course, no cannon and no promise.

There was blood on the prairie in Minnesota again in 1863 as small bands of warriors cut in behind the punitive army and killed thirty settlers in scattered raids. One band was audacious enough to camp overnight on a hill within sight of St. Paul. Late in the summer, a farmer named Chauncey Lamson and his son came undetected on an Indian man and youth picking berries in a clearing on some brushy land, and in an unheroic engagement, shot the man from ambush. The youth escaped. The body was taken to Hutchinson four or five miles to the south, but when no one could identify it, it was thrown into the offal pit of a slaughter-house.

A month later, a sixteen-year-old Indian youth was captured. His name, he said, was Wowinapa; he was the son of Little Crow, and had been with his father when the one-time powerful chief was shot down while picking berries. Little Crow, according to his son, was not in Minnesota for revenge but only to steal a few horses. Wowinapa was permitted to join the few Sioux who were still in the state, and in time, this son of a great war chief became the man who founded the Young Men's Christian Association among the Sioux in Minnesota.

White man's justice caught up with Chief Shakopee, who had wanted war but had been interested only in murder and rapine. He was captured near the Canadian border (some accounts say he was kidnaped from Canada where he had taken refuge, others that he had been lured across the border), and brought to Fort Snelling where he was hanged late in 1865. There is a legend that, as Shakopee stood on the gallows on the river flats below the fort, the whistle of the first railroad locomotive in the valley echoed between the limestone river bluffs. Shakopee gestured. "As the Indian goes out, the white man comes in," he said. It is a fine story, very symbolic. The only thing wrong with it is that it did not happen.

or three months and started back across the plains, putting up new signs on their wagons, "Busted, by Gosh."

While the homeward parade was going on, another strike was made, and the word went out that the North Fork of Clear Creek, not Cherry Creek, was the place to find wealth beyond all dreaming. The tide reversed, another gold rush was on. And once again most of the rushers found little gold; they chased rumors up and down the flanks of the Rockies but before the summer was over, many of them were heading east once more.

The gold rushers, with all their running back and forth, had driven a trail right down the middle of the Cheyenne domain, along the Smoky Hill River midway between the Platte and the Arkansas. The buffalo avoided the long lines of men in wagons and men on foot (there were almost a hundred thousand in 1859) moving under their banner of dust, and the Indians found it difficult to live on their once-fat land.

At first the tribesmen had been friendly. Little Raven, leading chief of the Arapahoes, went into Denver when it was a new mining camp to promise the prospectors his people would remain at peace. An Arapaho camp sat near the shacks of miners; the Indian men would go out hunting or after Ute scalps while the miners went to work in the gold diggings. This friendly arrangement came to an end when a gang of miners headed for the Arapaho camp while the men were gone and raped some of the women.

Such incidents quickly dispelled early good will. After the first couple of frantic years of gold rushing, mining became a big-capital business and the surviving camps became communities where wives and school-teachers displaced most of the fancy ladies. And north and south, along the foothills, ranchers and farmers were settling in the more fertile and well-watered valleys. There was no place for the Indians on the western part of their own lands any more; they did not fit into the new scheme of things.

A government report, drawn up later when a great many were dead and beyond all caring, agreed that the use of the Smoky Hill Trail was probably based on sound legal right since the Fort Laramie Treaty had reserved the right of transit over Indian lands for travelers. But, far beyond crossing these lands, the travelers "took possession of them for the purpose of mining, and, against the protest of the Indians, founded cities, established farms, and opened roads. Before 1861 the Cheyenne and Arapaho had been driven from the mountain regions down upon the waters of the Arkansas and were becoming sullen and discontented because of this violation of their rights.

"The Indians saw their former homes and hunting grounds overrun by a greedy population thirsting for gold," the commissioners continued in their report, becoming lyrical in their indignation as they warmed to their subject. "They saw their game driven east to the plains, and soon found themselves the objects of jealousy and hatred. They too must go. The presence of the injured is too often painful to the wrong-doer, and innocence offensive to the eyes of guilt. It now becomes apparent that what had been taken by force must be retained by the ravisher, and nothing was left for the Indian but to ratify a treaty consecrating the act."

There were, as the report indicates, people who sympathized with the Indian. Unfortunately, most such were in the East where they could do little beside send up clouds of words of protest, while the frontiersmen who believed that the only good Indians were dead were right on the spot where they could put their ideas into practice. The treaty which the report mentions was signed by the two tribes at Fort Wise * on the Arkansas River on February 18, 1861. They gave up their huge range for a triangular tract lying—except for an inconsequential portion—between the Arkansas River and Big Sandy Creek which flows into the river from the northwest (the stream was almost always called simply Sand Creek, even though there is another stream of that name in Colorado; the Indian reserve was invariably designated the Sand Creek Reservation). It was a miserable piece of land, not only a patch on the former range in terms of size, but sterile, sandy and useless. It was so poor that only a few of the chiefs present at Fort Wise could be induced to sign the treaty, and some of those who did sign claimed later that they had been fast-talked into believing the agreement meant something other than what the government claimed it did.

* The person who attempts to learn more about Fort Wise may well walk into a nomenclatural ambush where he will be shot down from all sides. In 1849, William Bent, by then sole proprietor of Bent's Fort and its trading business, blew up the adobe post with gunpowder for reasons that are only poorly explained by tradition, and moved forty miles down the river where he built Bent's New Fort, a stone structure. In 1859, the government leased the New Fort, built barracks, and christened it Fort Wise in honor of the governor of Virginia. In 1861, governors of Virginia no longer being held in high esteem, the name was changed to Fort Lyon in honor of Union General Nathaniel Lyon who had been killed in battle in Missouri. To further compound confusion, high waters endangered the fort so that New Fort Lyon was built upstream in 1866, on the site where the present Fort Lyon stands today.

The Indians did not stay on the new reservation much of the time—they would have gone hungry if they had—but continued to roam freely, managing to remain peaceful even though they were being crowded more and more by the growing number of white men who traveled the plains. It was rather extraordinary, the way the two tribes continued to abide by their promises, given at Fort Laramie, to refrain from making war, especially since they—and especially the Cheyennes—were proud and warlike peoples. This is not to say that the plains were any place for a Sunday School picnic; there were plenty of young braves who were tired. of forbearance and could not always be depended on to pass by a chance-met white man without lifting his scalp if it could be accomplished without too much risk. But, with minor exceptions, they kept the peace.

Most of the exceptions, at first, were the result of actual want. By 1863, both tribes were suffering greatly from hunger, and were afflicted with a variety of diseases to which malnutrition and lowered resistance had made them easy prey. Their agent, Samuel G. Colley at Fort Lyon, had reported that winter that no buffalo were to be found within 200 miles of the reservation, and precious little game of any kind. The Indians had made a number of attacks on wagon trains, but not for scalps; they had robbed the wagons of the food and, in almost every case, left the men unharmed. Colley, with as little understanding of the desperation of hunger as of grammar, wrote in his report, "Most of the depradations committed by them are from starvation. It is hard for them to understand that they have no right to take from them that have, when in a starving condition."

Major Colley was not going to be of much help to the Indians in the days ahead, although occasionally he appeared to be stirred by a feeling of mission and responsibility. His son, Dexter, was a trader, and it was commonly believed, and fairly well established, that Major Colley diverted a good portion of annuity goods to son Dexter, who later sold them back to the Indians.

Fortunately, times improved somewhat for the tribesmen after this hunger year, although their relations with the Americans did not get better. The beginning of the incidents that led to war appears to have come April 11, 1864 when a rancher named Ripley rode into Camp Sanborn on the South Platte River trail, northeast of Denver, with an excited report that Indians had driven stock from his ranch on Bijou Creek. It is very possible they had. On the other hand, men who had been around the country said that every time a horse or cow strayed out of sight, a greenhorn lost his head and blamed it on the Indians; a few of the more cynical pointed out there was no proof Ripley ever had any stock.

The next morning, Lieutenant Dunn with forty men was sent out with orders to find and disarm the Indians and recover the stolen stock. Ripley went along as guide. The detachment eventually came on a party of Indians driving some horses Ripley claimed were his. The soldiers had no interpreter along, and Dunn was too impatient for much parleying by sign language; he demanded that the horses be handed over. The Indians willingly agreed (later, much later, after all the damage was done, a less impatient Colorado officer talked to some of the Indians involved, who said the horses were not stolen but strayed beasts they had found; this may or may not have been so), but when the Indians came up to shake the soldiers' hands, the latter began trying to snatch their weapons away. It was a foolish move. Arrows were flying in an instant; the detachment found itself involved in more than it had bargained for. Two soldiers were killed, two mortally wounded, another two less seriously hurt. Lieutenant Dunn was certain his men had killed a dozen Indians, but there was no proof that even one had died.

The Colorado authorities apparently felt that they had a small Indian war on their hands now, or at least, could build the situation up into one. There had never been any doubt about official policy; Governor John Evans had advocated war with the Plains Indians from the time he took office. A few days after Dunn's fight, Major Jacob Downing was sent to Camp Sanborn to handle Indian-fighting operations. He did not have long to wait for action; on April 18 word came that Cheyennes had driven settlers from a ranch on the South Platte. Downing took sixty men and went in hot pursuit. The only trouble was that, although the company rode more than fifty miles east along the river, it found no Cheyennes, no deserted ranch, no evicted settlers.

Having found nothing, Downing, with consummate logic, decided on a campaign to punish the Indians for their outlawry. He made a new start from Camp Sanborn with forty men, and at a place called Cedar Canyon found a Cheyenne village to punish. Then, as this fearless knight later described it: "We commenced shooting. I ordered the men to commence killing them. . . . They lost . . . some twenty-six killed and thirty wounded. . . . I burnt up their lodges and everything I could get hold of. . . . We captured about one hundred head of stock, which was distributed among the boys."

The distribution of the horses helps to explain one of the powerful forces that moved many of the "boys" to take the field against Indians, not only in Colorado but in other arenas. Such divisions of spoils often made the boys over-eager to start trouble so that there might be some tangible benefits to show for their time and trouble. The troops in Colorado during the Civil War were entirely volunteers, local boys with all the frontier contempt for the rights of the red man, and many of them hoping to reap some reward.

The scattered actions continued. Colonel John Chivington, commanding all Colorado Volunteers, had ordered Lieutenant George S. Eayre with an independent battery of artillery out early in April to pursue Indians who reportedly had stolen a couple of hundred head of cattle from a government contractor. The Indians denied the theft, but no one listened. No one knows; perhaps they took the cattle, perhaps they did not. Lieutenant Eayre with fifty-four men and two twelve-pound howitzers headed east, across the line into Kansas where he came on a village that had obviously just been abandoned by its frightened people ahead of his coming; he destroyed tremendous quantities of dried buffalo meat, powder and lead, robes, and various equipment and utensils and burned down tepees. Fifteen miles farther on he found another empty village which he treated in the same fashion.

Eayre returned to Denver to replenish his supplies, commandeered a dozen or more wagons from their astonished owners in the street, and returned to Kansas again, bearing orders, so it is claimed, to "kill Cheyennes whenever and wherever found." On May 16, about fifty miles northwest of Fort Larned on the Arkansas, he found a large camp of Cheyennes—not deserted this time. He was met by Chief Lean Bear, who rode out with his son to greet the soldiers. There are two versions of many of the episodes of this conflict; there is only one of what happened next. The soldiers let the two Indians approach, hands upraised in the universally understood peace sign until they were within point-blank range; then they were gunned down.

The results were more than Eayre had bargained for. The Cheyennes began buzzing like angry hornets around the Colorado troops, who lost four dead and three wounded in the resulting battle. Incredible as it may seem, the retreat of the soldiers was facilitated by Black Kettle, leading chief of the Cheyennes, a staunch peace man, who man-

aged to get his warriors under control enough so that Lieutenant Eayre
and his command could withdraw to Fort Larned. Eayre immediately
sent word of a great victory back to Denver; he was also asked by
higher military authority in Fort Leavenworth to the east how he happened to be so far out of his own military jurisdiction.

After Eayre's exploit, Cheyenne Dog Soldiers raided several ranches
on Walnut Creek generally north of Fort Larned. Each Plains tribe
had several military societies, partly social, partly charged with police
duties on the hunt and in various other circumstances. The Dog Society
was considered the strictest in discipline of these groups among the
Cheyennes; its members also had a reputation as young firebrands.
Yet, after spending a night raiding, the Dog Soldiers had killed only
one man. Clearly, the Cheyennes still had not quite got the hang of
fighting white men.

Lieutenant Eayre, hurrying back without his command to make his
report to Colonel Chivington in Denver, met an unlikely person on the
way: William Bent, trader, good friend of the Cheyennes. Much had
happened since that time, at the old Bent's Fort, when he had persuaded half the Cheyennes and Arapahoes to move down to the Arkansas. He had married a Cheyenne, Owl Woman, and fathered two daughters and three sons, and when his wife had died, he had married her
sister, Yellow Woman. He loved the Cheyennes, their blood was in his
wife and his own children, and now he listened as Eayre told how he
had shot down Cheyennes with no more feeling than he would have
squashed a bug.

Whatever Bent's personal feelings he must have submerged them.
Shortly thereafter, an Indian rider found him on the plains and gave
him a message from Black Kettle. The Cheyennes were upset and
worried about Eayre's attack, the chief said; they did not know why
he had done such a thing, and they would like Bent to come and talk
to them about it. Bent did. Then he went on to Fort Lyon to talk to
Colonel Chivington and tell him that the majority of the Indians still
wanted peace. The Colorado military leader replied that things were
now out of his hands and that he was without the authority to make
peace. Besides, he was not interested because now he was making war
and meant to continue.

Bent tried again. He pointed out the consequences of a general
Indian uprising. There would be attacks along the Oregon and Santa Fe
trails. With the soldiers available, it would be impossible to protect all

settlers in Kansas, Colorado, and Nebraska in Cheyenne country. Many would be killed. Chivington replied callously that he could not worry about the settlers; they would have to find ways of taking care of themselves. Bent went away half-believing he had heard wrong. The primary role of a frontier military leader was to protect the settlers; here was a military leader who was interested only in killing Indians, and the devil take the settlers.

Colonel John M. Chivington, an elder of the Methodist Church, was a huge man, over six feet tall and more than broad in proportion, weighing at least 250 pounds, little of which was fat since he was enormously barrel-chested. Chivington was a native of Ohio where he had taken up the ministry; he had preached his way westward across half a dozen states before reaching Colorado. In Denver he had been presiding elder of the First Methodist Episcopal Church in the camp, and had gone preaching in neighboring camps, where his size probably saved him much trouble in an era when a minister often had to defend his doctrine with his fists. But whatever his skills in exegesis may have been, he somehow never got even within shouting distance of the real meaning of the religion he was trying to preach, as events abundantly proved.

Chivington's reputation as a military leader, on the other hand, was built on a sound foundation of performance. When he had been offered a chaplain's commission in the 1st Colorado Volunteer Regiment, he had asked instead for a fighting commission. In the one Civil War campaign of consequence west of the Missouri, he had very competently handled volunteer troops in a manner which had contributed considerably to the decisive Union victory over Confederates attempting to invade New Mexico. His political enemies afterward claimed that his lack of interest in a peaceful settlement of the trouble with the Indians was due to his desire to add more luster to his standing as a military hero. Chivington, they said, was planning to go into politics, and in the West, about the best vote-getting record a candidate could have was a period of defending the frontier against the bloodthirsty redskins.

What Chivington and a great many like-minded Indian-fighters needed was a good atrocity to stir people up; they got it on June 11, 1864, when a settler named Ward Hungate, his wife, their four-year-old daughter and an infant child were murdered, their ranch burned, and their stock run off on Box Elder Creek only twenty miles east of

Denver. It was a vicious crime, and when the bodies, scalped, mutilated, and swollen by sun and exposure, were brought into Denver and
put on exhibit, the result was completely predictable. Four young
Arapaho warriors had carried out the senseless raid, but it was accepted
as proof that all Indians were murderers and cut-throats.

2. "KILL AND DESTROY—
WHEREVER FOUND"

Governor John Evans of Colorado Territory was beginning to sense
that the mood of the Indians was growing sullen and that big trouble
might be brewing, something beyond the ability of his own Colorado
Volunteers to handle with a few free-ranging attacks on Indian camps.
On June 24 he issued a proclamation that called on the Plains tribes
in the region to report to certain forts and to make their camps in
their vicinity to avoid "being killed by mistake." As evidence that they
were friendly, the Southern Cheyennes and Arapahoes were to go to
Fort Lyon, the Comanches and Kiowas to Fort Larned in Central
Kansas, the northern bands of the Cheyennes and Arapahoes to Camp
Collins in northeast Colorado, and all Sioux in the area were to go to
Fort Laramie. There was to be food and protection for the Indians
who showed their good will and friendliness by gathering at the forts,
harsh punishment for those who remained on the warpath.

The purpose of concentrating the friendly Indians around the forts,
he said, was so that they "should not fall victims to the impossibility
of soldiers discriminating between them and the hostile, upon whom
they must, to do any good, inflict the most severe punishment." The
proclamation was made known to the leading chiefs of the tribes with
the help of Indian agents, traders, and friendly Indians but the response
was not overwhelming. The soldiers had not been showing much interest of recent months in "discriminating between the friendly and the
hostile," and it probably seemed unwise to the Indians to concentrate
around the forts. A couple of small bands came in, but that was all.

William Bent, in the meantime, was doing his best to try to patch
up a peace, and was actually making some headway, doing the work
that should have been done by Indian agent, Major Colley. Of course,
Bent had considerable incentive. Three of his children were somewhere
in the Cheyenne camps. George and Charles were living—and would

soon be fighting—as warriors. Julia was tending a cooking pot beside a tepee; she had married a man like herself, the half-breed son of a trader married to a Cheyenne woman. William Bent had sent all his five half-breed children except Julia back to Westport (very long-since swallowed by Kansas City) to be educated, but as they grew older, these three had felt more at home with their mother's people.

Whatever his incentive, Bent worked hard. He arranged discussions at Fort Larned between the Cheyenne chiefs and the Army officers in charge—which were very nearly wrecked at the very beginning by the commanding officer, Captain Permeter, a rum-pot who antagonized the Indians by his arrogant manner. Bent, however, had smoothed things over and had moved on to expand his peace missions when a large band of Kiowas, led by Chief Satanta, had camped near the fort to hold a scalp dance.

Satanta, in the next few years, was to be one of the more troublesome antagonists of the United States government. Yet only months earlier, in April, a government physician out vaccinating the Plains tribes against smallpox had found the Kiowa a friendly people, and Satanta a hospitable host. The chief spread carpets in his lodge for his guests to sit on, and had painted boards about three feet by twenty inches, ornamented with brass tacks around the edges, on which he had his meals served. When meals were ready, he announced them by blowing on a French horn.

But Satanta was as touchy as hot gunpowder. Now, three or four months after the physician had found him such a pleasant dinner companion, the Kiowa chief and a cousin left the scalp dance and rode toward the gate of Fort Larned, for reasons now unknown. The fort command had directed that Indians not be permitted to approach within a specified distance of the fort; as often happens in such cases, no one had told the Kiowas that such a limitation existed. A sentry warned Satanta and his cousin off but they could not understand what he was trying to tell them. When he raised his gun as a warning, Satanta accepted it as a challenge and whipped two arrows which laid the sentry low (the records do not inform us whether this young man performing a simple duty died as a result). In the confusion that followed, the Kiowa ran off the post's string of horses which were grazing in a meadow well away from the fort, and hastily moved out, safe from pursuit by the horseless troopers.

The Kiowas claimed that it was the first time they had clashed with

United States troops. It would not be the last, and over the next ten
years or so, Americans who encountered Satanta were not to find him
a genial, French horn-tooting host.

Shortly after the Kiowas had run off the fort's horses, Chief Left
Hand with his band of Arapahoes came to Larned. Left Hand very
much wanted to keep the peace; he had come to offer his services to help
recapture the stolen horses. But as he rode up to the fort to give his
offer of assistance in running down Satanta's band, a very jittery sentry
guard shot at the Indians with an artillery piece. Their aim was as
shaky as their nerves and they did not come near the Arapahoes, but
Left Hand's friendliness had been shot full of holes.

In this manner, with a few incidents, Bent's attempts to bring peace
back to the plains were completely shattered.

Convinced that the whites had no desire for peace, the Indians met
in a great council on the Solomon River in Kansas to talk things over.
Present were both northern and southern divisions of the Cheyennes
and Arapahoes, as well as the bands of Sioux from the Platte River
region. The northern tribes shied away from giving any promise to
join in a general war, although the idea of raiding settlements and
wagon trains appealed greatly to the young men. They could be depended on to give substantial help when the time came.

And the time came during the first part of August, about the tenth of
the month, when war parties struck more or less simultaneously along
the entire length of the main trails. The booming stage and freight
business of Ben Holladay, transportation king of the plains, came
almost to a halt, unable to continue in the face of the mounting debit
of drivers' scalps on Cheyenne lances. The stage stations were attacked
and burned along both the Smoky Hill Trail and the northern road,
which followed the Platte River (on the Oregon Trail) to the forks of
the river, and then went along the South Platte to Denver. Isolated
farms were burned, settlers killed, small parties of emigrants on the
trails wiped out. At Plum Creek on the Platte Trail the Indians caught
a party of thirteen in ten wagons; nine were murdered, two women and
two children taken captive, the wagons looted and burned. At Ewbank
Station a family of ten was killed and mutilated. Ben Holladay's general superintendent stated that for 370 miles every ranch but one was
"deserted and property abandoned to the Indians."

Holladay was still claiming damages from the government fifteen
years after the war. In view of the magnificent deliberation with which

the Federal government operates on such matters, that in itself means nothing, but the supporting affidavits are interesting. Driver George Carlyle related how he had come on the bodies of the nine victims of the Plum Creek massacre lying amid the burned-out remains of their wagons and had interrupted his trip to help bury them; he told how every ranch between Fort Kearney on the Platte in mid-Nebraska and Julesburg on the South Platte in northeast Colorado had been abandoned—and in most cases, burnt to the ground; he described his wild flight of twenty miles, whipping up the horses on his stagecoach to stay ahead of pursuing Indians.

The Cheyennes are known in Western history as fearless foemen, but during this war they appeared to exercise caution and restraint. There were none of the headlong, reckless charges so typical of the Cheyenne in battle; they moved in small bands to attack a stage station when the chance for surprise was good, waited along the trails for wagon trains and stagecoaches, and did not move if they saw that their prospective prey was better guarded than they had planned on.

There were no really notable battles. Indians fell on the advance guard of troops moving along the Pawnee Fork of the Arkansas River west of Fort Larned and almost wiped them out; east of the fort they struck a government wagon train, killing fourteen teamsters. In all, about two hundred whites lost their lives during the summer, most of them ranchers and travelers. Denver was never in any danger for the Indians did not come within miles of it, but it had its scares—and its hysterical moments. One night, the entire population was sent racing in panic to the two sturdiest stone buildings in town when a wild-eyed horseman galloped into town with the news that the Indians were coming. The buildings were turned into forts with women and children on the second floor; at one building, two men stood ready with axes to chop away the supports of an outside stairway the moment an Indian appeared. Nothing happened; no Indians showed up anywhere near. However, if Denver did not suffer from Indians, it did have some troubles with food shortages. Most of its provisions came across the plains on Ben Holladay's wagon trains; after that route was cut food supplies dropped alarmingly. For a while flour was selling at $25 for a hundred pounds.

During this time, the Cheyennes and Arapahoes were not the only Indians making war. A number of Sioux were taking part along the Platte, while the Kiowa and Comanche were raiding in the south into

Texas, driving off hundreds of horses and mules and killing many settlers. The Comanches were taking full advantage of both sides' preoccupation with the Civil War to indulge some of their old hate of Texas and Texans.

Governor Evans, in the meantime, had been keeping the telegraph wires hot to Washington. Not one for understatement, the Governor shrilled that all tribes, from the Canadian border to Texas, had formed an alliance for war and would soon be screaming down on the whites the length of the plains. When a report was brought to him that a man and boy were said to have been killed by Indians a few days earlier south of Denver, he whipped off a message to Washington: "Extensive Indian depredations, with murder of families, occurred yesterday thirty miles south of Denver. Our lines of communication are cut. . . . Large bodies of Indians are undoubtedly near to Denver, and we are in danger of destruction both from attacks of Indians and from starvation. . . ."

However, Evans failed to move anyone in the seats of the mighty in Washington. His plea for Federal troops was answered with what amounted to "Don't you know there's a war on?" and he was no more successful in attempts to get Colorado's own 2nd Volunteer Regiment returned from Missouri where it was serving with the Union Army. He did obtain approval for raising a third regiment to serve for one hundred days only against the Indians. The Governor also issued a proclamation "authorizing all citizens . . . to go in pursuit . . . also to kill and destroy as enemies . . . wherever they may be found, all such hostile Indians."

In all the sad and brutal record of these months, almost the only voices heard were those who, like Evans, could think only in terms of "kill and destroy." It was not unique to Colorado; these were the same voices that were raised everywhere on the plains, and in all our relations with our Indians, from the Atlantic to the Pacific. But while Evans and Colonel Chivington were making plans for military action and killing, William Bent was having still another try at ending hostilities. Major Colley, who should have been trying to make contact with his Indian wards, was sitting at the agency at Fort Lyon after having done a Pontius Pilate washing of hands in a letter to the Governor in late July: "There is no dependence to be put in any of them. I have done everything in my power to keep peace. I now think a little powder and lead is the best food for them."

In late August, Bent sent a letter to the elder chiefs, proposing that they approach the white leaders with overtures for ending hostilities. Bent's plan was upheld in tribal council at which the young hotheads were voted down, and identical letters, written by Bent's son George who was in camp as a warrior, were sent to Major E. W. Wynkoop, commanding officer at Fort Lyon, and to Colley, the Indian agent.

> Cheyenne Village, August 29, 1864
>
> We received a letter from Bent wishing us to make peace. We held a council in regard to it. All came to the conclusion to make peace with you, providing you make peace with the Kioways, Comanches, Arapahoes, Apaches * and Sioux.
>
> We are going to send a message to the Kioways and to the other nations about our going to make peace with you.
>
> We heard that you have some Indian prisoners in Denver. We have seven prisoners of yours which we are willing to give up, providing you give up yours. . . . We want true news from you in return.

On receiving the letter, Major Wynkoop took 130 men and a battery of artillery and went to the Cheyenne village at Bend of Timber, 80 miles northeast of Fort Lyon. As usual, the young braves were set to make a fight of it, but the chiefs kept them under control and turned over four white children, promising to give up three more as soon as they could be brought in from other villages.

Major Edward W. Wynkoop was something of an anomaly among the Colorado military leaders. Instead of having a fixation about killing the natives, he recognized a chance to promote peace and seized it. He did not have the authority to make peace, he told the chiefs, but he would accompany a delegation of them to the big white chief, Governor Evans, to make sure that they were not harmed on the way. The chiefs, accepting his sincerity, agreed, and on September 28 a group of them, both Cheyenne and Arapaho, arrived at Camp Weld on the edge of Denver with an escort of Wynkoop's soldiers. Black Kettle, leading Cheyenne chief, was spokesman for the group.

---

* The Apaches referred to are not the Southwestern tribe of such fearsome reputation for ambush and homicide, but a separate people, the Kiowa Apaches, who were closely confederated with the Kiowas even though they spoke completely different languages. Like the real Apaches, they were members of the great Athabascan linguistic family; the two had probably come down out of the north at somewhat near the same time because their languages were still quite similar. There resemblances ceased; the Kiowa Apaches were so closely attached to the Kiowas as to be considered another band in the tribal circle while the Southwest Apaches were traditional enemies of the Kiowas.

Proofs of their sincerity, said Black Kettle opening the council, were their delivery of the prisoners and the very fact that they were there. "We have come with our eyes shut, following his handful of men, like coming through the fire," Black Kettle said, referring to the trip to Denver under Wynkoop's escort. "All we ask is that we may have peace with the whites. We want to hold you by the hand. You are our father. We have been traveling through a cloud. The sky has been dark since the war began. These braves who are with me are all willing to do what I say. We want to take good tidings home to our people, that they may sleep in peace. I want you to give all these chiefs of the soldiers here to understand that we are for peace, and that we have made peace, that we may not be mistaken by them for enemies."

Black Kettle's proffer of the peace pipe got a chilly reception. For all his screaming to Washington about the terrible threat that hung over Denver and the surrounding region, Evans was strangely reluctant when the opportunity came to remove the danger. The Governor told the chiefs it had taken them a long time to get around to talking about peace instead of coming to the forts when he had told them to; he asked them searching questions about the early incidents in the troubles without conceding that his own boys might have been at least partly at fault.

"I have learned that you understand that as the whites are at war among themselves," the Governor went on, "you think you can now drive the whites from this country; but this reliance is false. The Great Father at Washington has men enough to drive all the Indians off the plains, and whip the rebels at the same time. Now the war with the whites is nearly through, and the Great Father will not know what to do with all his soldiers, except to send them after the Indians on the plains. My proposition to the friendly Indians has gone out; I shall be glad to have them all come in under it. I have no new proposition to make."

Evans said he had no power to make a treaty now that war had begun; the chiefs would have to deal with Major General S. R. Curtis, commanding the Department of Kansas (which also included eastern Colorado), whose headquarters were in Fort Leavenworth. Evans probably did not give a great deal of thought to how a band of tepee-dwelling Indians was to get in touch with the General.

Colonel Chivington spoke last. His speech was short and simple, in a style he evidently felt befitted a blunt fighting man. Most of it, and all its meaning, was contained in a couple of sentences: "I am not a big war chief, but all the soldiers in this country are at my command. My rule of fighting white men or Indians is to fight them until they lay down their arms and submit."

The chiefs left; their interpreter afterward said that they were "perfectly contented, deeming that the matter was settled," and that their peaceful overtures had been accepted. Many young men were still out on the warpath, but there was a sharp autumn chill in the night air of the high plains that would bring them in soon. Winter was never a war season for the Plains Indians; their grass-fed ponies could run rings around the heavier grain-fed cavalry horses during the spring and summer when the grass was green and thick but they could not extract enough nourishment from frost-killed grass to carry an Indian on the strenuous riding of the warpath.

However, the authorities in Colorado had no wish to call an end to the fighting, whatever impression the chiefs may have received. They were bolstered in their decision by a telegram from General Curtis in Fort Leavenworth, which arrived shortly after the chiefs had left; "I want no peace till the Indians suffer more. . . . I fear Agent of the Interior Department will be ready to make presents too soon. . . . No peace must be made without my directions."

As a matter of fact, Governor Evans had been so interested in proceeding with the war against the Indians that the arrival of Wynkoop with the peace-minded chiefs had been a severe embarrassment. He had pleaded with Washington for help against the murdering redskins; he had depicted a scene of suffering and terror and bleeding bodies, almost with orchestral background, and now that the War Department had given permission for the raising of hundred-day troops against the Indians, he was suddenly and desperately faced with the possibility that the Indians would turn docile and eager to be friendly. It would, to put it in the most simple terms, leave him looking like a fool. He did not want to have to report back to Washington that he had let his fears run away with him and that the hundred-day soldiers, the 3rd Colorado Volunteers, had not been necessary at all. At the close of the council he had expressed his displeasure with Major Wynkoop for bringing the chiefs to Denver: "What shall I do with the third regiment if I make peace?" he asked. They were, he said, "raised to kill Indians and they must kill Indians."

Returned to his post at Fort Lyon, Wynkoop gave the Cheyennes permission to bring their camp in close to the fort, which they did. There, he said, they would be under the protection of the government and completely safe. But they were not completely safe. Governor Evans, rankling over the young major who embarrassed him by bringing the chiefs to Denver, had Wynkoop replaced by Major Scott J. Anthony, whose principles swung like an unlatched gate in the plains wind.

Anthony, in a change-of-command conference with Wynkoop and the chiefs, agreed to continue Wynkoop's permission for the Indians to camp under the protection of the fort. Then, after Wynkoop departed on November 26, the new commander became worried that he might be overstepping his authority and ordered the Indians away from Fort Lyon. They packed up their camp and moved forty miles away to set up a new camp on Sand Creek. There were no complaints; Anthony appears to have handled things in an amicable manner and, as a matter of fact, made Black Kettle a gift out of his own pocket.

3. "ALL ACQUITTED THEMSELVES WELL"

Now Colonel Chivington entered the arena, meaning to get some service out of the 3rd Regiment before its hundred-day period of enlistment drew to a close. There were still a good number of warriors out on the plains, enough to occupy this quondam man of God who had told the chiefs in Denver that his rule of war was simply to fight until his enemies laid down their arms and submitted. He chose, instead, to make his war on Indians who had already submitted.

Along with the 3rd Volunteers, Chivington also had a part of the 1st Volunteers, making a total force of perhaps 750 men. He arrived at Fort Lyon with this force on November 28, after traveling over ground covered with snow, and immediately threw pickets around the fort to prevent any news of his coming or his purpose from getting out. He conferred regarding the situation with Major Anthony, who swung with the winds of opportunity. He heartily hoped the Colonel would attack the Indians, Anthony said, and he would have done it himself if he had had troops enough.

But others at the post were not completely willing to sell principle to curry the colonel's favor. Second Lieutenant Joseph Cramer argued with Chivington that Wynkoop had promised to protect the Indians, and he felt that he and all other post officers who were serving under Wynkoop at the time were indirectly bound by the same promise. Chivington was scornful and abusive, and said, as Cramer later testified, that "he believed it to be right and honorable to use any means under God's heaven to kill Indians that would kill women and children and 'damn any man that was in sympathy with Indians,' and such men as Major Wynkoop and myself had better get out of the U. S. service."

The force was on its way again at nine o'clock that night, and rode until morning. Robert Bent, one of the half-breed sons of William Bent, was forced to go along as guide. George and Charles Bent, and Julia Bent Guerrier were all living in the camp on Sand Creek as Cheyennes. Only one of Bent's children, his oldest daughter, Mary, would miss the tragedy that was almost at hand.

Chivington's instructions to his boys were simple: "Kill and scalp all, big and little; nits make lice." Two of his officers later claimed he made a further inspirational exhortation just before the battle: "Now boys, I shan't say who you shall kill, but remember our murdered women and children."

Dawn comes late at the end of November. The first light was in the sky when the soldiers saw the Indians' pony herd, about five hundred animals, still half-shadows on the frosted grass meadow. Then the conical lodges showed up, in the creek bottom below a low bluff. The cannon were swung around and aimed while a detachment ran off the ponies to deprive the Indians of any chance of fleeing or fighting on horseback.

A woman coming out of a tepee saw the soldiers on the bluff and shouted an alarm. Black Kettle ran from his lodge shouting reassurance, and raised an American flag and a white flag on a pole. Then, in a withering blast, cannon and rifle fire swept through the camp. Few of the Cheyennes had arms or any opportunity to obtain them because the first overwhelming charges drove them away from their lodges. White Antelope, an old chief of seventy, refused to retreat, saying that it was the fault of himself and other chiefs that this was happening. He folded his arms and sang his death song, "Nothing lives long, except the earth and the mountains." Then a bullet took his life.

Here and there, braves with weapons attempted to make stands in hollows or pits in the creek bank to protect women and children. In one such defense, George Bent had his hip broken by a bullet. Black Kettle attempted to make a death stand as White Antelope had done, but his young men almost carried him from the field. His wife, however, was shot down, and passing soldiers, in a spirit of thoroughness that would have been commendable in any other cause, put seven more bullets into her. She lived, though, and recovered.

The bravery of the Cheyennes in their hopeless situation won the admiration even of their enemies. The changeable Major Anthony, who presumably was on the side of God and Elder Chivington at the moment, described it later: "I never saw more bravery displayed by any set of people on the face of the earth than by these Indians. They would charge on the whole company singly, determined to kill someone before being killed themselves."

Most of Chivington's boys, though, were too busy with homicide to pay tribute to desperate valor. At times, soldiers were firing from opposite sides of the camp so heavily as to seriously endanger each other; it is highly probable this is the way some of their casualties occurred. At least one man, however, was having no part in the fighting. Captain Silas S. Soule had remonstrated bitterly with Chivington against the attack; he made his own private protest at the camp by refusing to give his men the order to fire. It had not prevented them from going ahead on their own, but it kept a burden off Soule's conscience. The captain strode up and down amid the drifting powder smoke, an anguished witness to the massacre he refused to join.

The Colonel had told his boys to kill and scalp all, big and little. They did more than that. Some of them went into an orgy of butchery and sadism that shrunk any imagined gap between the savage redskin and the civilized white man to nothing. Read, with a bit of nausea, Robert Bent's taut description of some of the things he witnessed when he accompanied Chivington onto the field as his unwilling guide:

> I saw five squaws under a bank. When troops came up to them they ran out and showed their persons to let the soldiers know they were squaws and begged for mercy but the soldiers shot them all. I saw one squaw lying on a bank whose leg had been broken by a shell. A soldier came up to her with drawn saber. She raised her arm to protect herself when he struck, breaking her arm; she rolled over and raised her other arm when he struck, breaking it; then he left without killing her. . . . Some thirty or forty squaws, collected in a hole for protection . . . sent out a little girl about six years old with a white flag on a stick. She was shot and killed. . . . I saw one squaw cut open with an unborn child lying by her side. I saw the body of White Antelope with the privates

cut off, and I heard a soldier say he was going to make a tobacco pouch out of them. I saw one squaw whose privates had been cut out. . . . I saw a little girl who had been hid in the sand. Two soldiers drew their pistols and shot her, and then pulled her out of the sand by the arm. I saw quite a number of infants in arms killed by their mothers. . . .

Young Bent's vignettes of horror should not be discounted on the grounds that he was half-Cheyenne and hence probably biased. On the contrary, his account is restrained in contrast to those given later by some of Chivington's own boys.

The slaughter went on into the afternoon; by that time the Indians had been pursued several miles. After making a halfhearted search for the main camp of Arapahoes along the Arkansas so he could treat them as he had the Cheyennes, Colonel Chivington led his victory-flushed heroes back to Denver. He had sent a conqueror's exultant report on ahead, direct from the smoking field of battle: "I at daylight this morning attacked a Cheyenne village of . . . from nine hundred to a thousand warriors. We killed . . . between four and five hundred. All did nobly." The Colonel's figures were blown full of air. There were not nine hundred to a thousand warriors in the camp; there were not that many persons all told; best estimates seem to be about seven hundred in the camp, of whom about two hundred were men. No one knows how many were killed. Estimates range from 150 to 500. George Bent, who lay in the camp with a broken hip and was the only one who stayed around long enough to make a thorough count, said that 163 were slain, of whom 110 were women and children. The boys also took 2 men, 3 women, and 4 children captive, but one of the men was shot later.

Chivington and the boys were received in Denver as heroes and saviors of the frontier. ("All acquitted themselves well," said the Denver *News*. "Colorado soldiers have again covered themselves with glory.") They appeared between acts of a performance at the theater, receiving great applause as they exhibited dozens of Indian scalps, with running commentary. The captured children were exhibited like monkeys in a zoo for a time until the government obtained their release.

The Sand Creek massacre brought a bloody reaction from the infuriated Indians, who, except for a few holdouts, had given up the warpath at the time Chivington went out after his cheap glory. During the summer, the older chiefs of the tribe had tried to restore peace even after the shooting had begun. It was mainly the young braves, hot of blood, short on judgment, and eager for a reputation, who did most of the raiding. But after the massacre, things were different. Everyone, old chiefs, young braves, squaws, were united in a single wish for revenge.

As usual, the wrong people suffered. Wagon trains along the Platte and Smoky Hill trails were attacked again, and whatever settlers had been missed during the summer were burned out and slain. Julesburg on the South Platte had not been touched during the summer raids; now it was twice attacked and pillaged. The Sioux were riding with the Cheyenne in the north; in the south the Comanche and Kiowa were striking into Texas again, farther and bolder than before, even to the vicinity of Austin and San Antonio, desolating the northern Texas settlements, with victims left unburied and nothing but chimneys to mark where farms had been.

The worst fury of the Indian attacks was abated by the fact that they came in winter. The dry grass did not give the Indian ponies the stamina needed for sustained action. Nor were there emigrant trains on the trails at that time of year; the only thing that jolted over the frozen ruts were wagon supply trains and stagecoaches. On the other hand, it was extremely unusual for Plains Indians to make war at all in winter; that they did is a measure of their bitter hate after Sand Creek.

After troops had tried fruitlessly to run the war parties down, it was decided to starve the Indians out by burning off all grazing for their horses and driving out the game in the region. Fires were started at intervals in the dry grass along many miles of the south bank of the Platte River. Swept south by the wind, the individual fires spread, joined, moved on in a solid wall of flame. Wherever a river barred the way, sparks blew across in a hundred places to start new blazes that joined again to make a solid front of destroying prairie fire. Not until they reached the northern Panhandle of Texas did the last flames flicker out. It must have killed a frightful number of wild animals and birds, but it did not bother the Indians because they had already felt the pinch of hunger and had gone north, across the Platte River up into the Powder River country. It was a country teeming with game— the Sioux would soon be fighting to keep Americans out of it—and a hospitable refuge for the war-weary Cheyennes.

Brigadier General Patrick E. Connor, a man with a great reputation because of a victory over Bannocks and Shoshones in 1863, was sent up after them when summer came to teach them a lesson. Commanding 800 soldiers and 100 Pawnee scouts, Connor made great preparations for wiping out all resistance. After organizing his expedition into three columns to squeeze the Cheyennes and their allies between them, he issued orders as explicit as those of Chivington: "You will not receive overtures of peace or submission from Indians, but will attack and kill every male Indian over twelve years of age."

There was a to-do back East when General Connor's order became known among Indian sympathizers, and the Army was not happy about it, but there had been no need to worry unduly. Two of the Indian-killing columns went badly astray and lost most of their horses to Indian attacks; they ran out of rations, and finally wandered in on foot, hungry and lucky to have made it at all. The third column, personally led by Connor, fared better; it destroyed an Arapaho camp, but it was a very small result for a large effort. General Connor was sacked at the close of the campaign.

Colonel Chivington did not take part in the campaigns against the Indians after the Sand Creek massacre. Denver had treated him as a hero, but Denver was a frontier town; elsewhere, and particularly in the East, there was revulsion at the great and glorious victory on Sand Creek. Chivington soon resigned his commission to avoid a court-martial.

A military commission investigated. Of the 33 witnesses who testified, 14 supported Chivington, 17 condemned him. Most of those who spoke had been present at the massacre; a majority of those who spoke against him had been his own boys. The Colonel and the Colorado authorities took the position that the Indians at Sand Creek were still at war, no matter what Major Wynkoop might have told them, and the expedition against them was a punitive one to teach them a lesson. If they were peaceful, asked someone, why did they have those pits under the creek banks into which some of them crawled when the soldiers started shooting at them?

But the voices which damned Chivington and gave evidence of the peaceable actions of the Indians were more numerous and convincing. Even Major Colley spoke out. Colley had given no evidence of great intellectuality, but it took no genius to understand the situation in the terms he reduced it to: peace was when you have no war. And from the time Major Wynkoop had first gone out to talk to the Cheyennes

and recover the white captives from them until the time Colonel
Chivington had arrived at Fort Lyon there had not been any Indian
depredation of any kind within two hundred miles of the post. To
Colley, that had not looked like Indians very actively at war. Everyone at the fort, he testified, civilians and officers alike, had pleaded
with the Colonel not to go out and stir things up and start the war all
over. But the hundred-day Indian-fighting regiment had to be justified
—and Chivington had to brighten his own reputation in preparation
for his coming political career.

The great amount of testimony was concerned with the manner in
which Indians died. The statement of Robert Bent has already been
quoted; it is not necessary to add a mass of testimony in the same
vein. One of the most bitter witnesses against the Colonel was Captain
Silas Soule, he who had refused to order his men to fire on Black
Kettle's camp. Feeling ran high; Soule was several times shot at from
ambush in Denver. He ignored these omens of a short life and was
married on April 1. On the twenty-third he was called down in the
street in Western frontier fashion; both men fired; both were hit. Soule
died, but the other man was only wounded and skipped the country.
Picked up soon after in New Mexico and brought back, he was found
dead of poisoning while waiting a hearing, presumably a suicide.
though there is no good explanation why.

The nation-wide uproar led Congress to have its own look at the
massacre and its causes. An investigating committee of three came
to Fort Lyon in August, 1865 and plowed somewhat different ground
than had been turned up by the military hearing. Kit Carson, as
famous and as fair an Indian-fighter as the country had, was called as
an expert witness. He was asked what he thought of Chivington's
campaign. He replied succinctly that the Colonel and his boys were
cowards and dogs.

Congress made reparations to the widows and orphans of those
killed at Sand Creek (a not too meaningful recompense since most
of the dead were women and children). But these small steps could
not undo the harm. The Commissioner of Indian Affairs, having worked
with the magnificent leisureliness of all government bodies, published
its own report on Chivington's victory four years later, and concluded
that it had been an expensive adventure:

> No one will be astonished that a war ensued which cost the govern-
> ment $30,000,000 and carried conflagration and death to the border

settlements. During the summer of 1865 no less than 8,000 troops were withdrawn from the effective force engaged in suppressing the rebellion to meet this Indian war. The result of the year's campaign . . . was useless and expensive. Fifteen or twenty Indians had been killed at an expense of more than a million dollars apiece, while hundreds of our soldiers had lost their lives. Many of our border settlers had been butchered and much property destroyed.

Major Colley had given his opinion when the congressional committee had come to Fort Lyon, and it had been both sententious and banal. "My opinion," said he, "is that white men and wild Indians cannot live in the same country at peace." Colley, in his attempt to be trenchant, had said a great deal, much more than he meant. Either the government had to give the Indians a place where they could live as "wild" Indians, keeping their own customs and ways, apart from all white men, or else the Indians had to begin to adapt themselves to the white man's way of living. The first way had failed tragically. William Bent and Kit Carson were eloquent advocates of the second course when they served on the commission which attempted to work out another treaty with the Cheyennes and Arapahoes in October of 1865. The war had simply burned itself out. The southern divisions of the two tribes had drifted back from the Powder River country; there had been a few minor raids, but it was like a wet firecracker fizzling out. The tribes wanted an end to fighting.

The council was held near the present site of Wichita. Both Bent and Carson talked in terms of supplying the Indians with farming implements, seed, training in agriculture, schools. Some of the more far-seeing Cheyenne chiefs had discussed the possibility of becoming a farming tribe again, as their tradition told them they had been in the past. It was obvious to them, as it was to Bent and Carson, that nothing but hunger could lie ahead for a buffalo-hunting people in a land where the buffalo were disappearing.

But the government commissioners, after agreeing in principle with Bent and Carson, provided no implements, no seeds, no schools. The Cheyennes and Arapahoes were forced to give up even their barren Sand Creek reservation; they, as well as the Kiowa and Comanche agreed to move south of the Arkansas. But the new reservations were drawn so clumsily, part of the Kiowa and Comanche reserve even on Texas land which the government had no legal right to use for reservations, that the Senate refused to ratify the agreements. As a result, the tribes roamed the southern plains for two years without a square inch of land they could call their own.

William Bent's two sons who had been Cheyenne warriors during the raiding and fighting continued to live as tribesmen. Both had been in Black Kettle's camp at the time of the massacre, when George had had his hip broken by a soldier's bullet. But it was Charles who reverted completely to his Cheyenne blood, and even beyond, demonstrating a savagery that the Dog Soldiers he led could not match. No cruelty against whites was too much for him; in a raid on a station on the Smoky Hill road, he and his fellow warriors captured two of the men there by drawing them out of their defenses by guile and false promises; then, in full sight of the remaining beleaguered station workers, he fed the flames of his measureless hate by staking one of the prisoners out on the ground, cutting out his tongue, building a fire on his stomach, and performing other abominations. His savageries became so inhuman that his father disowned him, a compliment that was returned with interest; once he came back to the ranch to shoot his father from ambush but luckily chose a time when the elder Bent was away. He was one of the worst the plains had known; it was good riddance for all when he was badly hurt in a fight with Pawnees in 1868, caught malaria when in a weakened condition, and died.

George Bent, the second brother, also continued to live as a Cheyenne. He had as much reason to go savage as Charles, but, although he went on the warpath with the Cheyennes after the massacre, the same fierce hate was not there. He continued to ride to the ranch occasionally to see his father, his brother Robert, and sister Mary, and when the tribes were called together in 1867 for the Treaty of Medicine Lodge, George was one of those who helped bring them in.

And John Chivington—what became of him? The ex-colonel found his reputation as an Indian-killing hero not completely an asset, even in tough, frontier Colorado. His political enemies accused him of deliberately stirring up trouble in order to make a name for himself; there were some citizens, even on the frontier, who remembered the blood-drenched camp on Sand Creek and agreed with Kit Carson that a man who would serve even an Indian like that was a dog and a coward. Chivington finally went back to his native Ohio where he did enter politics at last, running for minor offices with less than spectacular success.

IV

Give Me Eighty Men

1. JOHN BOZEMAN'S ROAD

WHEN the Civil War ended, Major General William Tecumseh Sherman, hero of Atlanta and the Great March, stood only a step below Ulysses S. Grant in the estimation of a jubilant Union. He was in the fortunate position of being pretty much able to pick his next duty assignment, and, having no stomach for policing the beaten South, he asked for, and in September, 1865, was given command of the Military Division of the Mississippi.

The Division of the Mississippi included the territory from Canada to Texas and from the Mississippi River to the Rockies, plus the Department of the Ohio which was composed of the states north of the Ohio River. Within a year, however, the states north of the Ohio would be detached to make it an entirely trans-Mississippi command, its name would be changed to the Division of the Missouri, and with few changes thereafter, it would administer the Army's complex affairs over the vast plains, involving thousands of men in isolated wind-swept and sun-baked posts spread thinly over endless miles of grasslands, until the Indians were finally beaten to their knees.

The face Sherman turned to the world was not a warm one. It was gnarled as a chunk of applewood, and somehow suggestive, with beard and hair awry, of an indignant rooster that had been tumbled about by a Kansas windstorm. He was a man without the faintest germinal stirrings of tact. When he stopped at Colorado Springs during his first inspection tour of his command and the citizens of the town asked for protection against the Indians, he replied, with full sarcasm, that he was sure it would be a good thing if there were an Army post in the vicinity to provide a market at high prices for farmers' grain, hay, and other products. During the same tour, a petition was handed him at Pueblo, Colorado, likewise begging protection from murdering redskins. Sherman scanned it briefly, then remarked that more men had signed the petition than he had as garrisons at most of the Army posts in the area.

On the other hand, very many Westerners were opposed to the return of the Army and the replacement of local volunteers by regulars. Some of the more bloodthirsty among them were calling for a bounty on Indian scalps—$100 was a popular figure—which, they said, would be incentive enough for the local boys to go out and exterminate the Indians without any help from the Army. The Regular Army, in the days ahead, would commit savagely brutal acts against Indians—and not all of them because it was carrying out orders and helpless to do otherwise—but, by and large, it fought as part of a job that had to be done and not from hate.

Sherman replaced volunteers with regulars as rapidly as possible, and thereafter refused to authorize any territorial government to form its own volunteer units except under strict control by the United States Army, which would mean Army pay, food, and allowances. The Westerners did not want to play soldier that badly; they complained bitterly, but volunteer units were formed in only one or two special instances.

For some time, Sherman's main concern was going to be the protection of communications lines, a task that promised to be a large one with the means at hand and the tribes in an ugly temper. There were the three transplains roads to be kept open at all costs: the Santa Fe Trail, the Oregon Trail, and the Smoky Hill Trail. There was the Missouri River which provided access by steamboat—still mainly for traders—into the northern plains and foothills; it was not yet a major concern. There was the military telegraph crossing the plains along the line of the Platte River to Fort Laramie with various branches (for some reason, the Indians did not bother the telegraph line as much as they might have; either they did not realize how much trouble they could cause with almost no effort or, as some theories had it, they held the message-carrying wire in superstitious awe).

Sherman would, in a very short time, have to be providing protection for railroad construction crews. The Union Pacific had pushed ten or twelve miles west from Omaha in the fall of 1865 when Sherman took over his western command, its destination an eventual meeting with the Central Pacific working east from California. Across the plains the Union Pacific would follow the north side of the Platte, the opposite side from the Oregon Trail, which would then soon pass into oblivion. That same fall, the Kansas Pacific had also laid down its first dozen miles of track westward from Kansas City, on a route that would follow the general line of the Smoky Hill Trail to Denver. The Army would have a heavy responsibility during the building if the Indians continued hostile; once they were completed, the railroads would make it possible to shift troops rapidly over long distances and would hasten the pacification of the Plains tribes.

One other major road lay in Indian country and under the probable danger of Indian attack: the Bozeman Trail. It was a new road, cutting off from the Oregon Trail west of Fort Laramie and running north and west into Montana Territory; its importance resulted entirely from the accident that intrepid prospectors, risking lives and scalps, had found gold in the Rocky Mountains in Montana.

The Bozeman Trail was not only particularly vulnerable to Indian attack, it was an invitation to trouble because it ran through the choicest of all the hunting lands of the Sioux nation, and the Sioux resented its existence. For that reason, forts were being established along the road during 1866, and General Sherman himself made the trip in May out to old Fort Kearney in Nebraska Territory on the Oregon Trail to wish Godspeed to an expedition just setting out to establish Army authority.

General Sherman had been working for several months to acquaint himself with the problems of his sprawling command. There must have been some things he missed, or else he would not have permitted this expedition to take wives and children. Not only permitted, but assured the colonel in command that he saw no prospect of danger to the women and children. Whatever his sources of intelligence, they were badly misinformed about conditions on the Bozeman Trail.

The Bozeman Trail, 1866–68, and its Forts

Colonel Henry B. Carrington was in command of the expedition, which was composed of the 2nd Battalion of the 18th U. S. Infantry, about 700 men. The battalion was driving a herd of a thousand cattle, and had a train of 226 mule-drawn wagons with baggage and stores, as well as a number of Army ambulances carrying a couple of dozen women and children (the ambulance was a high-wheeled, covered wagon; it became a popular vehicle for personal transportation on the plains because it was the only wagon with springs that were at all effective). Several officers with families brought a cow, chickens, and similar impedimenta indicating they had every hope of living a reasonably well-ordered home life in the wildnerness. The expedition even included a twenty-five piece regimental band, which tootled as the long column left the sagging old fort behind.

The Bozeman Trail, whither Colonel Carrington and his expedition were heading, was the creature of one John M. Bozeman, who came from Colorado to the new gold fields centering around Virginia City in Montana in 1862. The fields had been reached either from Fort Hall in Idaho on the Oregon Trail, or from Fort Benton, the ordinary head of navigation on the Missouri. Either way was difficult, hazardous, and roundabout. Bozeman set himself the task of finding a route that would connect directly with the Oregon Trail and would be suitable for freighting in supplies to the gold fields by wagon.

He and a companion named Jacobs found the answer to the problem when they discovered a pass that took them from Virginia City and the mining country into the valley of the east-flowing Yellowstone. Their trail then continued east till it cleared the north spur of the Big Horn Mountains, when it turned southeasterly to skirt the east flank of the mountains. It struck the North Platte and the Oregon Trail at a point about seventy miles west of Fort Laramie. The Sioux caught them before they had quite finished their free-lance survey, and took their weapons, horses, and even clothes. With fine forebearance, the Indians refrained from physically harming the two men—although turning them loose on the high plains naked with winter coming on was not precisely an act of mercy. Nevertheless, they made it safely through to settlements on the Platte River.

The next spring, Bozeman undertook to lead freighters with a pack train back along his new trail to the Montana camps. Sioux warriors met them before they had made a good beginning; placed themselves athwart their path, and motioned them to go back. They had no choice, but once out of sight of the Sioux, they doubled back, and made it through to the mining country by traveling during the night and hiding by day. The road was so practicable and so profitable for men willing to put up with hardships and risk life and scalp that wagon and pack trains were soon traveling over it, making up in sufficient strength to discourage Indian attacks, though never enough to guarantee safety.

Inevitably, an anguished cry for government protection echoed back across the plains into the halls of Congress; as a result an act was passed to create certain federal roads in several parts of the western territories, one of these being the Bozeman Trail. The act put the Army squarely into the business of protecting the Bozeman Trail (it was often called the Powder River Trail because it cut across the upper waters of that river).

So far, the Army had not been able to do much. When Brigadier General Patrick Connor made his ill-fated expedition into the Powder River country in pursuit of the Cheyennes and their allies to punish them for their depredations following the Sand Creek massacre, one thing he accomplished was to build a fort where the Bozeman Trail crossed the main branch of the Powder River. It was called Fort Connor at first—until the War Department put an end to the practice, commanding officers showed a shameless lack of modesty by naming forts and posts after themselves—but it was changed to Fort Reno the next year, 1866. Establishing the fort was a small accomplishment; the section of the Trail north of Fort Reno was the part the Sioux were most concerned about, and they were beginning to make travel on that section hazardous indeed.

The Sioux—particularly the Oglala and Miniconjou bands—had dug in their heels and were prepared to make a last-ditch fight for their hunting grounds in the Powder River region through which the road passed. Here the Great Plains become broken and uneven and finally splinter against the Big Horn Mountains. It was a beautiful land, with slope after slope covered with meadows of excellent grass. Trout-filled streams of clear snow-water flowed out of the mountains, through valleys wooded with aspen, willow, cottonwood and chokecherry. Raspberries, cherries, strawberries, currants, and plums grew in meadow and underbrush. Nearer the flanks of the mountains were forests of pine, fir, and spruce.

Buffalo, elk, and antelope grazed on the open grasslands, deer abounded in the breaks, and there was an abundance of bear, sage hens, rabbits, and lesser game. The animals were so abundant and so well-fed that hunting was easy, and the Sioux, understandably, did not want it despoiled as they had seen other hunting grounds ruined when white men had driven their roads through them.

Having arrogantly moved to take control of the road at the time of General Connor's expedition and been badly set back, the government now attempted a belated diplomatic approach to the matter. Chiefs of the western bands of the Sioux were called to a council at Fort Laramie in June, to meet with a commission sent by the Indian Bureau. The government showed rare timing in its council; the negotiations had no more than got a good start when Colonel Carrington and his column arrived at Laramie with a rattling and creaking of wagons, the bawling of their beef herd, and making no secret that they were on their way to establish forts to keep the Bozeman Trail open.

There was an angry outcry from the assembled chiefs, who very understandably considered it bad faith that the government had sent a powerful force of soldiers to take possession of the trail at the same time it was negotiating with the Indians for permission to use it. "Great Father sends us presents and wants new road," Chief Red Cloud of the Oglala Sioux said during the stormy council that followed Carrington's arrival, "but White Chief goes with soldiers to steal road before Indian says yes or no."

Most of the chiefs stalked out. Red Cloud was adamantly opposed to the Bozeman Trail, so was Young-Man-Afraid-of-His-Horses, another Oglala chief. Spotted Tail of the Brule argued for a peaceful settlement, as he had on every question since he had gone to prison at Fort Leavenworth as a belated victim of the affair of the Mormon's cow. During his prison year, Spotted Tail had become convinced that the number and strength of the Americans was endless; it had taken the heart out of him so that ever since, he had felt it was folly to oppose an irresistible force. Red Cloud and Young-Man-Afraid-of-His-Horses disappeared from Fort Laramie with the Oglalas; Spotted Tail and a few of the old chiefs remained to sign a treaty which meant very little as far as guaranteeing the security of the Bozeman Trail was concerned.

Colonel Carrington pressed on, still following the Platte and the Oregon Trail. Jim Bridger, one of the great mountain men but growing creaky now, was guide for the expedition. He was beginning to warn of the need for caution, although not suggesting that any special danger existed. About seventy miles west of Fort Laramie, the column abandoned the Oregon Trail and struck off northward, for here the Bozeman Trail began. For the 2nd Battalion of the 18th Infantry, the road was going to lead straight to tragedy.

2. FORT PHILIP KEARNY

Five days of hard travel brought the column to Fort Reno. The post was located where the Bozeman Trail crossed the Powder River, a few buildings of logs with roofs of dirt. Two companies of low-morale volunteer troops garrisoned the place, wondering, until Carrington's arrival, whether they were ever going to be relieved.

No Indians had been seen between the Platte River and Fort Reno although Jim Bridger had insisted that they were watching the column. He was proved right the evening of the day of arrival at Fort Reno when braves swooped down and ran off horses of the post sutler who had grown complacent and kept a very loose watch on his animals. There had been no Indians attacks on the post before, he said plaintively.

The volunteers were relieved and sent back toward civilization, Carrington left one of his eight companies to garrison and rebuild the post, and the column headed up the trail again on July 9 after a two-week stay. Five days and sixty-five miles later Carrington selected a site for a second fort, where the road crossed a tributary of the Powder River named Big Piney Fork. The location was a level, grassy shelf of land in the fork of Big Piney Creek and a branch called Little Piney. Tents were pitched and the force lived under canvas for the time being. Five or six miles up Big Piney, one of the most crucial of the expedition's operations got under way as quickly as possible: sawing lumber for the buildings of the new post.

Establishing a self-contained fort on virgin land involved more than putting up a barracks with a stockade around it. There were perhaps two dozen buildings, such diverse structures as officers' quarters, hospital, workshops for blacksmiths, carpenters, and other mechanics, guardhouse, and bakery. Carrington did not forget a bandstand, out there in hostile Indian country. These structures were surrounded by a palisade of posts, eight feet high and sharpened at the top, enclosing a space 400 by 400 feet. Stables and certain other less important buildings, as well as haystacks and woodpiles, lay in an area outside the stockade; an extension of the stockade was later built to enclose them but it was not a part of the fort to be defended to the last ditch.

The post was named Fort Philip Kearny, in honor of Major General Philip Kearny of the Union Army who was killed in action in Virginia in 1862.* Only two days after it was laid out, the Sioux made their first attack, stampeding and making off with 175 horses and mules, and killing two soldiers and wounding three in the chase that followed. Almost at the same time, Indians attacked parties of emigrants and soldiers between Forts Reno and Kearny, making travel between the two strongholds extremely risky. From that time on, Fort Phil Kearny could look for an attack of some kind at almost any time: a foray against the stock, an attack on the wagon trains bringing timber from the woods, occasionally a solitary exploit as when a brave under a wolf skin crawled near enough at night to shoot a sentry. The Indians made raids, attacks or threats near the fort fifty-one times in five months; they undoubtedly had the post under constant watch.

On August 3, Captain Nathaniel C. Kenney with two companies of infantry was sent to establish a third fort where the road crossed the Bighorn River, about ninety miles to the northwest. The new post, which would be named Fort C. F. Smith, was placed just about at the point where the Bozeman Trail cleared the northern spurs of the Big Horns and swung almost due west. It was in Montana Territory; Forts Reno and Kearny were in present Wyoming, though then in Dakota Territory. Approximately 280 miles still lay between Fort Smith and Virginia City but it was mainly through the lands of the Crow Indians who had elected friendship with the Americans long before and had never seriously departed from their resolve. Even so, there were still dangers; the next year, 1867, John Bozeman was killed on his own trail while on his way from Virginia City to Fort Smith, not by Sioux or Crows, but by a band of marauding Blackfeet.

All the lush and beautiful hunting grounds east of the Big Horns

* The post, except in official correspondence, was usually called Fort Phil Kearny. There was, for some reason, an irresistible compulsion to insert an additional "e" in the name and make it "Kearney." That had happened to Fort Kearney on the Oregon Trail in Nebraska, named after Stephen Watts Kearny, Mexican War commander and uncle of Philip Kearny. Even officers stationed at Fort Kearney insisted on putting the unnecessary "e" in the name until at last the War Department surrendered and made it Fort Kearney. Officers at Fort Phil Kearny more often than not did the same thing and wrote it "Fort Philip Kearney" in official correspondence.

that Red Cloud and his Sioux were so vehemently determined to keep free of white men had been dominated by the Crows not long before. Then for several years the Crows had been outclassed in the endless wars of raid and counterraid that went on between them and the Sioux, and had been pushed out of most of the prized Powder River country. In 1866, however, Red Cloud had been careful to protect his flank by arranging a truce with the Crows so that the full Sioux strength could be turned against the Americans.

Operations went on at a feverish pace at all three forts to get them in shape before winter. Besides constructing buildings, the garrisons had to pile up mountains of cordwood for fuel against a winter when the land would be locked by deep snow and cold far below zero; tremendous amounts of hay for horses and cattle had to be put up. The Sioux made regular attacks on the wood-cutting and haying details, especially at Fort Kearny, where several men were killed. Indians had run off a large part of the Kearny horses and mules, which had been in short supply even at the beginning, while by the end of September only one hundred of the seven hundred beef cattle brought with the column remained.

Despite Sioux activity, emigrant trains continued to pass at intervals over the Bozeman Trail. Carrington was shocked by the lackadaisical way in which travelers took heed of warnings of the Indian threat and by their slipshod precautions against surprise attack. However, he was not able to wet-nurse them, and went no further than setting up the rule that travelers would not be permitted to proceed on the road unless they had at least forty able-bodied men in their company. Now and then there were desertions from the fort, enlisted men either bored by the tedium of post life or lured by gold in Montana to the point that the desire to get out was stronger than the remembrance of the smell of blood on the bodies of comrades they had seen brought in, mutilated and scalped, after an Indian attack. It was very seldom that anyone knew whether they made it through to the mining camps or not.

For the women and children, life in Kearny had been circumscribed by the walls of the stockade since very soon after arrival. Margaret Carrington had taken seriously General Sherman's advice at Fort Kearney on the Platte that the women of the expedition should keep diaries. At first her entries had been expansive with descriptions of the sun on the Big Horns, of the immensity of a sky full of stars in the clear mountain air. Very shortly she was writing more like a prisoner;

there were twelve women and eleven children at the fort, and with Indian attack always imminent, they seldom saw the world except over the top of an eight-foot palisade.

Early in November, a company of cavalry, long overdue, arrived at Fort Kearny. Colonel Carrington had been badly hampered in his pursuit of Indian raiders because he had had to depend on mounted infantry, men not trained to fight from the back of a horse. The company comprised sixty-three men under Lieutenant Horatio S. Bingham. Traveling with the company were Captain James Powell and Captain William J. Fetterman, both of whom were destined to command in important battles against the Indians.

Captain Fetterman was no stranger to the 2nd Battalion of the 18th Regiment, for he had fought with it through the war where he had achieved a splendid combat record, winning the brevet rank of lieutenant colonel for battlefield valor. He was a type that occurred frequently in the Indian-fighting Army—and often did not last very long at the trade. It was a type that was arrogant, contemptuous of Indians and their fighting ability, usually excessively brave, a braggart, and loud talker. Lieutenant Grattan, he whose Indian-fighting career had begun and ended at the Battle of the Mormon's Cow near Fort Laramie in 1854, was one such. George Armstrong Custer, whose story is yet to be told, was another, albeit a more complex character. And Captain Fetterman fell into the classic pattern.

He immediately became a divisive influence. Carrington had operated cautiously, letting the Indians come to him and fighting only a defensive war. It was a strategy forced on him. Until Bingham arrived with his company, there had been no cavalry, and even the use of mounted infantry had been hampered because horses and mules were in poor condition since there were too few and they were being worked too hard. Many rifles were in bad condition; ammunition was in short supply. Moreover, he had had to use his men for building the fort and getting ready for winter because cold weather, if they were not prepared, would be more deadly than Indians.

Fetterman, however, was not interested in practical considerations. He was a fire-eater who talked always of attacking; he belittled Carrington for treating the fighting abilities of the Indians with so much respect. Inevitably, the officers and many of the enlisted men drew up sides.

Henry Carrington had recruited and organized the 18th Regiment in Ohio early in the war and became its Colonel. It was only a nominal command, for he was kept in the North against his will all during the war doing various administrative work while the regiment was fighting. Now that the war was over, he was at a distinct disadvantage in the unhealthy rivalry with Fetterman for influence; the captain had served in the war with several of the other officers of the 2nd Battalion and could pluck the chords of comradeship and shared perils.

"Give me eighty men and I would ride through the whole Sioux nation," was one of Fetterman's boasts. Possibly if he had been able to travel forty or fifty miles north he might have changed his mind. Crow Indians reported that the hostile camps were lined for forty miles along the Tongue River. Other bands had rallied to the Oglalas and Miniconjous who had been the original opposition: Hunkpapas, many young Brules from the band of the peaceable Spotted Tail, and Santees exiled from Minnesota, as well as northern Cheyennes and Arapahoes. When the battalion had first arrived, the Cheyennes had professed neutrality, but the taunts of the Sioux, along with the disinclination of soldiers to draw any distinction between friendly and unfriendly Indians, swung them into the hostile alliance. According to the Crows, there were perhaps four thousand warriors in the enemy camp as mid-December neared.

3. "UNDER NO CIRCUMSTANCES PURSUE OVER LODGE TRAIL RIDGE"

The Bozeman Trail ran in a northwesterly direction past Fort Phil Kearny. It crossed Little Piney Creek, passed on the northeastern side of the fort, forded Big Piney Creek, and then disappeared from sight of the post behind a long hill known as Lodge Trail Ridge. Behind the far end of Lodge Trail Ridge a spur ridge extended from it; the road ran along this spur somewhat below its crest for more than a mile until the spur ridge ended and the road dropped down to cross a small stream then known as Peno Creek.

The road passed on the north side of Lodge Trail Ridge; Big Piney Creek lay on the south side of the ridge. South of the creek again was another ridge, which Carrington had named Sullivant Hills in honor of his wife's maiden name, and south once more of Sullivant Hills was the wood road from the fort to the "pineries" of timber about six miles away. The wood road, Sullivant Hills, Big Piney Creek, Lodge Trail Ridge, and the section of the Bozeman Trail on the opposite side of the ridge were all very nearly parallel; it was the habit of the Indians to come over the ridge, cross the creek and, passing over the Sullivant Hills, swoop down on the wood trains, attempting to take them by surprise.

Colonel Carrington had devised tactics for meeting such threats. On a high point near the fort, Pilot Hill, a lookout station was manned whenever wood trains were out; from it the wood road could be kept under observation and the fort informed, by a system of flag signals, of the number and direction of approaching Indians and of actual attack on the wood trains. Frequent drill had reduced the time needed to get a relief force on its way from the fort to a wagon train under attack. Finally, a discipline was worked out for the wood trains themselves that made them invulnerable except to a very large force: they traveled in large trains of about thirty or forty wagons with well-armed escorts, moving along in double lines in such a way that they could form a defensive corral almost on the instant. Lives hung on the perfection of such specialized skills.

On December 6, a party of Sioux made one of their many attacks on a wood train. Colonel Carrington ordered Captain Fetterman to take a cavalry company and a force of mounted infantry down the wood road to relieve the besieged wood train while he took another force and came up behind the Sullivant Hills in an attempt to cut off the warriors. But everything went wrong. The Colonel had taken along one squad of cavalry; its young lieutenant, George Grummond, dashed ahead against orders in his excitement and escaped being cut to pieces in an ambush only by the speed of his horse and some lucky strokes of his saber. Not so fortunate was Lieutenant Bingham who had commanded the cavalry under Captain Fetterman; when the Sioux had broken off their attack on the wagon train he had led a pursuit over the Sullivant Hills, across Big Piney Creek and up Lodge Trail Ridge where he had also spurred ahead of his men and into an ambush. His body, when found, had more than fifty arrows in it. An enlisted man had died in the same ambush; several men had been wounded during the fighting.

Nothing of what had happened during the brief engagement had escaped the Indians. Again and again during the summer they had noted each change in the habits and routine of the post, each bit of careless procedure, and wherever possible they had taken advantage of it. The growing number of graves in the cemetery above the fort was an indicator of their skill in utilizing each lapse in the defense's vigilance.

And now Red Cloud and other leading chiefs were convinced, from the lack of skill, discipline—and even common sense—with which the soldiers had fought that day that they had found a way to defeat them. The whites had been led into ambushes so easily—why not a great ambush into which a considerable part of the fort's strength could be drawn and cut to bits?

A plan was carefully worked out to decoy troops into ambush by an attack on the wood train, and was even rehearsed so that excitable young warriors would not spring the trap prematurely if only a hand-ful of soldiers came into the ambush instead of the large force for which it was being baited. Ten warriors—two Cheyennes, two Arapa-hoes, six Sioux—were carefully selected for the honor of acting as the main decoys. The place selected for the ambush was the section of the Bozeman Trail that ran along the spur ridge behind Lodge Trail Ridge. Here the warriors picked out their places of concealment among boul-ders and in high grass on both sides of the road.

On December 19 the Indians attacked. Colonel Carrington sent Captain James W. Powell out to relieve the wagon train, giving him explicit orders not to pursue across Lodge Trail Ridge. Powell, the most cautious of Carrington's officers, refused to let any of his men be drawn out of formation by the decoys, and turned back as ordered when he reached the top of the ridge. The Indians' ruse had failed, but they would try again.

However, the next day the wood train went unmolested to the pineries and returned without an Indian being seen. During the night a snow had fallen; the impossibility of putting fifteen hundred or two thousand warriors into hiding without leaving a web of tracks that would have blared the secret to the world undoubtedly explained why the Indians remained in camp.

In the meantime, Captain Fetterman had made up his mind to settle the whole Indian business, once and for all. That evening he came to Colonel Carrington, and in all seriousness asked to be permitted to put into action his frequent boast that he could ride through the entire Sioux nation, except that now he was proposing to do it with a hundred men instead of eighty. He was accompanied by Captain Frederick H.

Brown, regimental quartermaster, who agreed completely with Fetterman that the only way to whip Indians was to go out after them, and damn the odds, because everyone knew a good white man could whip a room full of Indians. Brown was being detached from Fort Kearny and wanted a last chance at the Indians.

What the two officers proposed was an attack on the camp on Tongue River. Fifty civilian employees at the fort, they said, had agreed to join fifty mounted soldiers in an expedition to wipe out the Sioux villages. The request was so preposterous it had the ring of lunacy. The tepees lay for perhaps as much as forty miles along the Tongue River; merely to ride through them would take hours. And if there were four thousand warriors there, as Crow Indians had reported to old Jim Bridger, then the odds would be forty to one.

Carrington possibly may have wished he could have sent Fetterman against the Indian camps and so have gotten rid of him for good. Instead, he denied permission for the mad scheme, pleading that the fort had neither the men nor the horses to spare from its regular duties and commitments.

On the twenty-first, the Indians tried again. And now events were beginning to move forward, with the inexorable purpose of a Greek tragedy, to give Captain Fetterman his eighty men and his chance to ride against the Sioux. The snow had melted off during the day the Indians waited; if they had delayed one more day their chance would have been gone for the year because the load of logs to be brought back on the twenty-first was to be the last of the season. Carrington had provided a strong guard for this last logging party; escort, wood-cutters, and teamsters together formed an armed force of more than eighty men. It left the fort a short time after ten o'clock; about eleven the lookout on Pilot Hill signaled that the train was under attack.

Bugles sounded and men assembled on the parade in quick time. Captain Powell was given command of the relief column by Colonel Carrington who had been pleased with the way Powell had handled the situation two days before. But Captain Fetterman, reporting with his company, came over to Carrington and demanded that he be given command of the entire force since he outranked Powell. The Army being what it is, the Colonel had no choice but to acquiesce, although he admitted later that he had not been happy about the change.

In Fetterman's infantry company were forty-eight enlisted men. Second Lieutenant George W. Grummond commanded the cavalry

Fort Philip Kearny
and the scene of the Fetterman Fight, Dec. 21, 1866.

company; he and his twenty-seven men increased to a grand total of seventy-six the men under Fetterman's command. One almost hesitates to continue the enumeration; it seems too contrived, too much like bad melodrama. But Captain Brown rode up on a borrowed horse, seizing his last possible opportunity to kill another Indian before leaving Fort Kearny—and Fetterman had seventy-seven.

While last-minute inspections of arms and equipment were being made, Private Maddeon, armorer for the regiment, repairer of small arms, appeared with a rifle in hand and asked Colonel Carrington for permission to join the relief force. Maddeon, as an artificer who spent all his time within the fort with the garrison, probably had his own private dreams of glory; he wanted to be able to write the folks back home at least once that he had shot at an Indian. Carrington granted permission, and Fetterman now had seventy-eight men.

Now, also asking for permission to accompany the force, came two civilian employees at the fort, James Wheatley and Isaac Fisher, and permission was granted. The two would not be excess baggage or mere sight-seers; both were Civil War veterans and both carried sixteen-shot Henry rifles, whereas the infantrymen still were armed with single-shot muzzle-loaders.

Fetterman now had his eighty men, and on the other side of Lodge Trail Ridge lay, not the entire Sioux nation, but enough of it for a substantial beginning.

Colonel Carrington's orders to Fetterman were explicit: "Support the wood train. Relieve it and report to me. Do not engage or pursue Indians at its expense. Under no circumstances pursue over Lodge Trail Ridge."

Fetterman moved out with his company, but Carrington sent his adjutant across the parade to stop him at the gate to repeat the Colonel's orders. Carrington had his misgivings about the young fire-eater with his contempt of Indians; he wanted to leave no room for misunderstanding.

After the infantry had departed, a roll call and inspection showed the cavalry company ready in all respects—carbines in good condition, each man with full ammunition box—and after Lieutenant Grummond had been ordered to report to Captain Fetterman, the company set out after the slower-moving infantry. Colonel Carrington was not quite finished; he stopped Grummond at the gate, and once again repeated his admonition: under no circumstances was he to cross Lodge Trail

Ridge. It is hard to see how he could have made it any more emphatic.

The first part of Fetterman's progress could be watched from the fort. Instead of following the wagon road, which ran along the south side of Sullivant Hills, directly to the wood train, he took his force around on the north side of the hills, apparently meaning to cut off the retreat of the Indians attacking the train and to catch them from the rear. It was perfectly sound strategy, and was no cause for worry as long as Captain Fetterman obeyed his basic orders.

Colonel Carrington had his attention diverted from the relief force by four or five Indians who came out of the brush on the far side of Big Piney near the Bozeman Trail ford. The Colonel ordered a couple of canister shot from one of the howitzers fired at them; one warrior was knocked off his horse and the hail of balls brought about thirty more boiling out of the woods and sent them away up the road at full gallop.

When Carrington turned back toward the relief force, Fetterman's command had disappeared from sight behind the Sullivant Hills. It occurred to the Colonel that the party had no surgeon, and he sent the assistant post surgeon, C. M. Hines, with an escort of four men, to join up with Fetterman. Hines left; soon after, the lookout on Pilot Hill reported that the Indians had broken off the attack and the wood train was proceeding on its way.

It was then about 11:30 A.M. Surgeon Hines came galloping back about noon, and reported to the commanding officer that he had not seen a sign of Fetterman's command, and that he had not been able to look further because Lodge Trail Ridge and the valley of Big Piney below was alive with hundreds of Indians. While Carrington was trying to digest this news, the sound of rifle fire was plainly heard at the fort; it came from the northwest, the direction of Peno Creek, which flowed near, then crossed, the Bozeman Trail.

Carrington recognized from the intensity of the firing that something important was afoot. He immediately ordered Captain Tenedor Ten Eyck to take a force to the relief of Fetterman, and had a column of fifty-four officers and men, with an ambulance and wagons, on its way in little more than fifteen minutes. Ten Eyck took his force down the road at double time while the Colonel immediately set about putting a column of reinforcements together, and soon sent forty more men, with extra ammunition, to follow and join Captain Ten Eyck.

Captain Ten Eyck did not go straight down the road. He followed it over the Big Piney ford and for a short distance thereafter, then bore off to the right onto a ridge that paralleled the road and over-looked it. He reached the high point of the ridge just about the time the last sounds of gunfire died out, at about 12:45 P.M. The shooting had lasted approximately forty-five minutes.

There was no possibility whatever at that moment that Captain Ten Eyck could have led his command down from the ridge toward the road and Peno Creek to learn what might have happened to Fetter-man. There were hundreds of Indians on the road below him; as soon as his force appeared many of them moved to the base of the ridge and began hurling taunts, calling on the soldiers to come down and fight. Despite their enormous superiority in numbers, they made no move to attack—this is one of the mysteries of the Indian character, why, when they held an overwhelming advantage, they did not make the most of it. They apparently had to celebrate and digest one triumph before moving on to another. Beyond the warriors below the ridge were others moving off up the valley; the soldiers on the ridge gasped at the num-ber of them, more Indians than they had ever seen before, two thou-sand, they guessed.

But the mass of Indians was thinning out as they streamed west on their ponies, and those immediately below the ridge gradually left off their demonstrations and joined in the withdrawal. Captain Ten Eyck and the men in his detachment had been straining their eyes for some sign of Captain Fetterman's force. Now, as the Indians below joined the great throng riding away through the valley, it became easier to make out objects on the road; a private was the first to sight the bodies of soldiers, and all dead.

Dark comes early on December 21, the time of the shortest day of the year, and it was dusk as Captain Ten Eyck led his force cautiously down from the ridge onto the road, where the shape of disaster became very clear. The bodies that had been sighted from the ridge lay near a scattering of great boulders. Most were stripped naked, scalped, and mutilated. Among them were the bodies of Captains Fetterman and Brown, bullet wounds with powder burns on temples; every indica-tion was that they had shot each other to prevent being captured.

Ten Eyck had the dead loaded into his wagons and ambulances; the bodies were beginning to freeze and retained the same attitudes in the wagons they had had on the ground, resulting in horrible grotes-queries. Forty-nine were piled aboard the vehicles "like you see hogs brought to market," the surgeon afterward recalled. There was no time to search for more; it was growing dark—and besides, nerves were probably overwrought more than anyone cared to admit.

In the meantime, Colonel Carrington had felt the great hand of doom closing in on the fort during the afternoon. Captain Ten Eyck had taken a mounted courier with him when he left; as soon as he reached the crest of the ridge and found an estimated two thousand warriors in the valley below, he sent word back to the fort, with the ominous detail that Fetterman's force was nowhere in sight.

Colonel Carrington had been alerted for bad news since the rifle firing at noon; the message sent back by Ten Eyck left little doubt that something very serious had happened to Captain Fetterman. And if there were as many Indians as Captain Ten Eyck reported, or even a half or a quarter as many, they might well ride in and take the fort without serious trouble, because it was an empty shell at the moment. Captain Fetterman had taken eighty men; some fifty soldiers, as well as thirty civilians, were with the wood train; ninety-four soldiers were out with Ten Eyck. Only about one hundred and twenty remained in the fort.

Carrington released all men under arrest, armed civilian employees, and manned the stockade to repel attack. A courier was sent to recall the logging party at once; on its arrival at the fort the force manning the stockade was strengthened. And so apprehension and fear were at their height and everyone on the post rushed out on hearing the sound of the wagons, Ten Eyck's returning force. The gates swung open. The early winter darkness was deep enough to hide some details as the wagons with their gruesome freight swung across the parade like a line of butcher's carts, but not nearly dark enough to blot out all the horrid truth of heaped-up bodies, bloody and maimed, with arms and legs reaching out in grotesque postures.

That night Fort Philip Kearny slept on its arms, when it slept at all.

How had this situation come about? What had happened to Captain Fetterman and his eighty, from the time they disappeared behind Sullivant Hills until, only about two hours later, their mutilated bodies were first sighted beside the Bozeman Trail, far across Lodge Trail Ridge?

The story of Captain Fetterman's defeat can never be known in all its details, but deduction and the stories told, usually many years later, by warriors who had taken part have left little mystery about the battle. After the relief force had come around Sullivant Hills, the decoys had broken off their attack on the wagon train and rode across the hills to intercept Fetterman and draw him up Lodge Trail Ridge. They retreated slowly, taunting, yelping, making obscene gestures, dashing away when the infantry raised rifles on the order to fire.

The decoys reached the crest of the ridge and continued down the other side, but Fetterman stopped when he reached the top. His orders had been unequivocal: "Under no circumstances pursue over Lodge Trail Ridge." He despised Carrington's caution, and he probably cursed him as he sat looking down the slope where the decoys were jeering and waving blankets to try to frighten the cavalrymen's horses. It must have been particularly galling for the captain, who held the fighting qualities of Indians in low esteem.

On their part, the Indians became fearful as the soldiers paused that the plan would fail, as it had two days before when the careful Captain Powell had turned back after reaching the top of the ridge. They redoubled their efforts; one of the Cheyenne decoys drove his horse in so close to the troops that, to the Indians hidden along the road below, he seemed to be actually among the troops. At just about this time, the small party of Indians which had just been fired on by a howitzer from the fort came riding down the Bozeman Trail and joined the decoys. The taunts of the decoys, the arrival of more Indians to kill— it was a combination Fetterman was unable to resist. He gave the order, and the force moved over the crest and down onto the Bozeman Trail in pursuit.

Lieutenant Grummond had almost lost his life two weeks earlier in an ambush when he had dashed heedlessly ahead of the rest of his force. This day he was doing the same thing, probably whooping just as joyfully, as his cavalry pulled ahead of the infantry, while both cavalry and infantry began to string out. The force was losing some of the characteristics of a disciplined military unit and was starting to act a little like a crew of schoolboys racing to see who would be first in the water.

Very soon the strung-out force was on the stretch of road atop the spur ridge, completely within the ambush area, while the decoys had reached the end of the ridge and had clattered on down the road, across Peno Creek. There half of them swung off the road to the left, half to the right, and circled in returning arcs back to the road again. The maneuver was the signal for the springing of the trap. On the instant, hundreds of Indians sprang out of high grass and from behind rocks; other hundreds spurred on horseback from concealment behind rock ledges at the side of the ridge. Only a small portion of the warriors carried guns, but the lack placed them at little disadvantage under the conditions of the fighting. The main superiority of the Springfield muzzle-loaders of the infantry over Indian bows and arrows, was in range—and range was of no importance here where the enemy was usually less than a stone's throw away. Arrows were as accurate as the muzzle-loaders, as deadly, and could be fired many times as rapidly.

Lieutenant Grummond, in the van with his cavalry, held most of his men together for a period and made a courageous fight, apparently trying to cut their way back to rejoin the infantry. Grummond was killed in the attempt; his body was found on the road. Indian accounts say that the pony soldiers became panicky when their chief fell, and retreated in confusion to higher ground at the west side of the road. The road ran somewhat below the high point of the backbone of the ridge at this point, and it was up toward the imagined greater security of the higher land at the peak of the ridge that the cavalrymen worked their way after Lieutenant Grummond was killed.

In the meantime, the two civilians, Wheatley and Fisher, were causing more trouble for the Indians than any other two men in the force. Both were war veterans of considerable combat experience, not the type to panic in a tight spot, and each carried a nice, deadly sixteen-shot Henry rifle. It was, as a matter of fact, mainly to try out their new rifles that they had come along this day—and the guns were getting a real test. The pair found shelter behind some large boulders and were joined by several of the more experienced of Fetterman's infantrymen, also veterans. The latter were armed with Springfield muzzle-loaders, but the Civil War had shown that muzzle-loaders, handled by men to whom the complicated sequence of loading, ramming home, aiming, firing, and all the rest had become second nature, could be a deadly weapon.

Now, as the Indians came in yelling, Wheatley and Fisher coolly knocked them off—twenty, thirty, no one knows how many were piled in the circle around them—with the infantrymen's steady shooting adding to the total. Eventually, of course, it had to end. Ammunition ran short; the warriors finally overwhelmed them as the whites died defending themselves with clubbed rifles and knives.

The main body of the infantry had been rallied by Captain Fetter-

Fort Kearney, Nebraska, in 1860. This major Army post was built in 1848 to protect travelers on the Oregon Trail. Its buildings were not so trim as this contemporary sketch makes them appear; with lumber scarce and expensive, many structures were made largely of cottonwood logs and sod, and soon sagged into a dilapidated condition. (Courtesy of The Bettmann Archive)

William Bent, "trader, good friend to the Cheyennes; . . . their blood was in his wife and his five children." No one worked harder to prevent the Cheyenne War of 1864, but it was not a propitious season for a man of good will. (Courtesy of the Library of the State Historical Society of Colorado)

Colonel John M. Chivington, commander of Colorado militia and perpetrator of one of the most infamous massacres of Indians by whites in frontier history. "My rule of fighting white men or Indians is to fight them until they lay down their arms and submit," he told a group of chiefs— then fell on them after they had submitted completely. (Courtesy of the Library of the State Historical Society of Colorado)

James W. Lynd, clerk at a trader's store and probably the first victim of the Minnesota Sioux uprising. "Lynd was a former state representative, but the Sioux knew him better as a man who had fathered children by several of their daughters." (Courtesy of Whitney's Gallery, St. Paul, Minn.)

Little Crow, or the Hawk That Hunts Walking, chief leader of the massacre of whites in Minnesota in 1862. "When he found the Sioux meant to fight regardless of his warnings, he decided that it was better to lead a lost cause than become a nobody." (Courtesy of the Bureau of American Ethnology, Smithsonian Institution)

Lieutenant Colonel George A. Custer, his Indian scouts, and a mere two of the forty hounds he brought to the Northern Pacific surveying expedition on the Yellowstone in 1873. The Indian pointing to the map is the Arikara Bloody Knife, Custer's favorite, who was killed beside Major Reno at the Little Bighorn. (Courtesy of The Bettmann Archive)

Henry H. Sibley, in charge of all military operations against the Sioux during the uprising in Minnesota. He was a former governor; he had been a fur trader for years; he was well acquainted with the Sioux and their ways. "But, as far as fighting Indians was concerned, he was completely without experience." (Courtesy of the Minnesota Historical Society)

Lieutenant Timothy Sheehan was in command of Fort Ridgely during the early days of the Minnesota uprising, and led the spirited defense that stopped the Sioux advance. "The soldiers fought so bravely we thought there were more of them than there were," a Sioux warrior said. (Courtesy of the Minnesota Historical Society)

General Alfred Sully's force at Fort Berthold, Dakota Territory, in 1864. The long (1863–65) and fumbling campaign to punish the Santee Sioux for the Minnesota uprising also succeeded in upsetting the western Sioux. (Courtesy of the Minnesota Historical Society)

Refugees from the Sioux in Minnesota. "Twenty-three counties were
devastated and left almost completely without humans, a region 50
by 200 miles." (Courtesy of the Minnesota Historical Society)

Two Moons, Cheyenne chief. Friendly up to the time his camp was attacked without provocation, he thereafter became an implacable foe of the Army, and led his people against Custer at the Little Bighorn. (Courtesy of the Museum of the American Indian, Heye Foundation)

man—under difficulties without doubt, because it must have been almost impossible to make his orders heard amid the high-pitched yelping of the Indians—who tried to move his men forward to join up with the cavalry to close the fatal gap which had developed during the pursuit. Then (and the reader recognizes that this account of the sequence of events is laced with surmise, albeit surmise based on historical evidence) Grummond died and the cavalry took its own course toward higher ground, while Fetterman led his men off the road to a group of large boulders that offered good cover.

There, among the rocks, they held out for a while, perhaps ten or fifteen minutes, while they mechanically dropped cartridges in muzzles, rammed them home, and fired, again and again. Not all among the constant flights of arrows splintered on the rocks; some found flesh and defenders died or dropped mortally wounded, although probably more than one soldier, hurt and hampered by the feathered shaft that had suddenly appeared in his body, broke off the projecting portion and so was able to continue fighting a short while longer.

But the tide of Indians clamoring to get at the knot of soldiers was impossible to resist. The streams of arrows were so heavy and continuous they endangered the warriors who came between and over the boulders, performing feats of reckless bravery; many died, but they quickly overwhelmed the defenders in a melee of hand-to-hand fighting of clubs, hatchets, and lances against clubbed rifles and bayonets.

Captain Fetterman died there among the boulders, and with him his good friend Captain Frederick Brown who had got exactly what he was hoping for: one last chance at the Indians before he was transferred out of Fort Phil Kearny. With the Indians closing in, and facing the possibility of capture and torture, they had saved the traditional last bullet for themselves. Then they probably put their pistols at each other's temples, and counting in unison, "One! Two! THREE!" their fingers tightened on the triggers at the same instant. Their bodies were found together; there were smoke burns around the bullet holes in the temples.

A few of the surviving infantrymen had escaped from the tightening ring of warriors and had run up the ridge to where the cavalrymen still held out, the only survivors now, although it is doubtful whether more than fifteen or twenty minutes had passed since the force had had its first horrified shock on seeing grass and rocks come alive with yelling Indians beyond counting. The cavalrymen owed their longer survival simply to the circumstance that the Indians had not given them their full attention yet—few carbine shells and no bodies marked their first position part way up the slope. They had then climbed higher, at last reaching the top of the ridge, where they took up a position among rocks. They were there when the full fury of the attack struck them.

The soldiers had an advantage of higher position; they had good cover among the boulders and their carbines gave them heavy fire-power, and for a while they held the oncoming warriors to a standstill. Then Indian lookouts reported more soldiers coming from the fort—it was Ten Eyck's column—and the attack was redoubled. Indians swarmed among the rocks faster than they could be killed, shooting arrows, clubbing, thrusting lances. One of those who died here was Adolph Metzger, bugler, an old cavalryman since long before the Civil War. It was appropriate that his only weapon at the last should have been his bugle; with everything else gone he used it as a club until it was beaten completely out of shape. One of the men who later helped bring in the dead said that Metzger's body alone was not mutilated in any way, but had been covered with a buffalo robe. (A number had crosses slashed on breast or back, the Indian mark of recognition of a brave man. They did not sell their lives cheaply.)

After Captain Ten Eyck had come back with his wagonloads of dead, Carrington was certain a massive assault was about to break on the fort. Such was his mood of pessimism now that he not only strengthened the defenses of the fort in every way possible but made preparations for catastrophe. He had a barricade of upturned wagons placed around the underground powder magazine which was located in one corner of the parade. The women and children of the post were to enter the magazine in case of attack; if driven from the stockade, the defenders would retire within the barricade for a desperate final defense; if the fight were being lost at the barricade, Colonel Carrington would touch off a powder train leading to the ammunition storage and women, children, soldiers, and a great many exulting Indians would go to Glory together.

That same black evening he wrote out his report of the battle, with a plea for reinforcements and handed it to a civilian employee of the post, John (Portugee) Phillips, who had volunteered to try to take it through to Fort Laramie, 236 miles away. The weather was bitter, there was every sign that a blizzard was about to break over the Big

Horns. Between Indians and weather, Phillips appeared to have only the slightest chance of getting through. But, mounted on a thorough-bred belonging to Colonel Carrington, the best mount in the fort, he set out after dark.

The snow came, pushed by high winds; the temperature fell far below zero. Phillips reached Horseshoe Station, the end of the military tele-graph forty miles west of Fort Laramie, at ten o'clock on Christmas morning. Then, having had the operator send his messages, he refused to take any chances that they might not get through, and rode on the remaining forty miles to deliver them in person. It was well he did; the message from Horseshoe Station had been badly garbled and the post commandant at Fort Laramie refused to credit them. Phillips ar-rived at eleven o'clock at night just four days after leaving Fort Kearny; the post was holding its Christmas ball when, garbed in buf-falo-skin clothing from hat to boots, caked with ice, and plastered with snow, almost too exhausted to walk, he stalked like some monstrous specter through the holiday crowd. He was a long time recovering from exhaustion and frostbite, while Carrington's thoroughbred had run its heart out on the long trip and died soon after.

At Fort Philip Kearny, Carrington had turned his attention to the immediate problems of defense as soon as he heard the hootbeats of Portugee Phillips's horse receding down the trail. He got no sleep that night, and early the next day set out with eighty men to recover the bodies of the remaining thirty-two victims. The most elaborate pre-cautions were taken to guard against another surprise attack, but, although Carrington did not know it, the Indians had departed, leaving only a few scouts who lingered on for a few days more to report on activities around the fort.

Most of the remaining bodies were found at the top of the ridge where the cavalrymen had died. Lieutenant Grummond's body was found by the road; so were those of Wheatley, Fisher, and the few veteran infantrymen who had made a stand with them. The Henry repeating rifles of Wheatley and Fisher had plainly done great slaugh-ter; Colonel Carrington counted sixty-five pools of frozen blood sur-rounding their position, marking spots where dead or badly injured Indians had lain. The warriors, in retaliation, had shot arrows into Fisher after they had stripped off his clothes; 105 of them bristled from his corpse. (The Indians had treated a number of bodies in this man-ner; perhaps they had been men in whom some breath of life still flickered after they had been stripped and scalped.) There were no warrior dead; the Indians had followed their usual custom of taking their slain with them.

Threatening skies were bringing dusk on even earlier than it otherwise would have been at this time of short days, and it was long after dark before the grisly search was concluded and the wagons had returned to the fort. That same night a blizzard struck, driving the temperature to twenty degrees below zero, and piling in great quantities of snow.

The next five days were spent in preparing the bodies for burial, building coffins, and in digging graves in the frozen ground of the snow-swept cemetery. Although a large crew of men aided the medical officers, they needed two days to get the bodies ready. The official report prepared by Carrington two weeks after the disaster explains why this grim task was so difficult: "I give you some of the facts as to my men, whose bodies I found just at dark, . . . Eyes torn out and laid on rocks; noses cut off; ears cut off; chins hewn off; teeth chopped out; joints of fingers, brains taken out and placed on rocks with other members of the body; entrails taken out and exposed; hands cut off; feet cut off; arms taken out from sockets; . . ." (The gruesome catalogue continues to a length it is not necessary to pursue.) *

The burial took place on the day after Christmas. Red Cloud had done quite well in his war to keep the Americans from taking over the Big Horn country. Since Colonel Carrington had come out with such bright hopes to build his fort by Big Piney Creek, 154 soldiers and civilians had been killed on the Bozeman Trail. More than half had died in a single action, the one that within days would begin to be called the "Fetterman Massacre." It was no massacre, it was a battle in which the military had been outwitted and hopelessly outnumbered, and one of the two battles in American history in which there was not a single American survivor (or one of three, if you choose to think of

---

* Such mutilations, barbaric and horrible as they are, were not inspired by savage blood lust but had their basis in Indian religious beliefs. Men enter the afterworld, the Plains Indians believed, in the same form they held immediately after death. It was only common sense, then, to make sure that an enemy should be sightless in the hereafter, or without hands to hold a warclub, or perhaps with teeth knocked out so that he could not enjoy roast buffalo and the other good things of the shadow world.

The other side of the coin was the supreme risks warriors would take to recover the body of one of their own dead; they were thereby saving a comrade from the mutilations by the enemy which would have crippled him in the spirit world.

the defenders of the Alamo as Americans. The other no-survivor battle
was nine years in the future but only about seventy miles distant; many
of the same warriors who ambushed Fetterman's command would be
present at the Little Bighorn).

It is not known whether Red Cloud himself was even present at the
greatest triumph of his nation's arms. In later years he claimed that
he personally led the fight, but others who fought there say the chief
was elsewhere that day. However, the great Oglala chief, Hump, was
present and very probably was the leading chief. As for Indian casualties, the accounts given by the natives varied so widely as to be meaningless. One set the figure at only fourteen dead, another made it fifty
or sixty, others agreed that about sixty were killed and at least a hundred of the wounded were so badly hurt that they died later.

When word of the disaster reached Colonel Carrington's immediate
superior, Brigadier General Philip St. George Cooke, commanding the
Department of the Platte (Iowa, Nebraska, and most of Wyoming),
that crusty old Indian campaigner at once ordered reinforcements sent
from Fort Laramie; Lieutenant Colonel (Brevet Brigadier General)
Henry W. Wessells who had been post commander at Fort Reno since
November was ordered to assume command of the reinforcements on
their arrival at Fort Reno and bring them on to Fort Kearny where he
would relieve his commanding officer, Colonel Carrington, assuming
command of all three forts.

As a matter of fact, the move was more complex than that. The Army
was increasing its forces on the frontier, and the 2nd Battalion of the
18th Infantry was being expanded into a new regiment, the 27th
Infantry. Carrington was still Colonel of the 18th Regiment whose 1st
and 3rd Battalions had been serving elsewhere on the frontier while he
was at Kearny, and a new 2nd Battalion was to be organized, but he
deeply resented the way Cooke had ordered his relief, before getting
his full report, as though to place the onus of Fetterman's defeat on
him. However, it was a game others could play; Sherman had not been
happy with Cooke as one of his departmental commanders; he considered the general, whose Indian-fighting career went back to the Black
Hawk War of 1832, to be too old and inflexible. Soon after Cooke
relieved Carrington, Sherman removed Cooke.

Carrington left Fort Philip Kearny on January 23 with an escort
of sixty men, taking with him all women and children. The snow was
deep, the temperature got as low as forty below zero, and by the time

the sixty-five miles to Fort Reno had been traversed, two of the cavalry escorts had frozen their legs so badly they had to be amputated. Women and children rode in covered wagons made as cold-proof as possible and provided with small stoves; even so, the temperature within the wagons often stood well below zero. The trip in the jolting wagon was a special torture to the widow of Lieutenant Grummond whose pregnancy was far along. One wagon carried the pine coffin with her husband's body; she had prevailed on the Colonel to let her take it back for burial in Tennessee.

4. A STATE OF SIEGE

Sherman (now Lieutenant General Sherman) had undoubtedly learned a great deal about the Plains tribes and their temper since the May day when he had said, at old Fort Kearney, that he did not see any danger ahead for the women and children accompanying Colonel Carrington to the Bozeman Trail. But he still had not learned enough to prepare him for the news he had received just after Christmas. "I do not understand how the massacre of Colonel Fetterman's party could have been so complete. . . . We must act with vindictive earnestness against the Sioux, even to their extermination, men, women and children. Nothing else will reach the root of this case."

One of the most frequently used words in Sherman's vocabulary would be "extermination." For the world of William Tecumseh Sherman was black and white. It was a world in which orders were given and obeyed—and in the West it was for the Army to command and the red man to do the obeying. Sherman was fairly representative of the military attitude—and an excellent argument against returning the Indian Service to the military, as the Army had been demanding ever since 1849 when it had been given to the Interior Department.

However, that is not the same as saying that the Interior Department was doing an ideal job with the Indian Service—far from it. The Fetterman disaster brought the old controversy between the two services to a high pitch again. The arrangement between the two was custom-built for trouble: the civilian Bureau of Indian Affairs handled all relations with the natives until trouble broke out and it became necessary to apply force; then it called on the Army to take over. The Army claimed that the Bureau mishandled affairs until events got out of hand and then had to call in the military to put its mistakes right, a chore that cost human lives.

Another favorite Army charge was that the Indian Service supplied the warriors with guns and ammunition (or, what amounted to the same thing, permitted traders to supply firearms), often more modern than the Army issue, which were then turned against Army troops; the Bureau replied that whatever guns the Indians got they desperately needed for hunting game which was getting scarcer all the time. (The truth lay somewhere between. The number of firearms furnished to Indians, and their superiority over those used by the Army has been grossly exaggerated; the legend of heroic soldiers with muzzle-loaders fighting off superbly armed Indians was developed mainly on the verandas of Old Soldiers' Homes. Throughout the plains wars the bow and arrow remained the predominant Indian weapon—at the Fetterman fight, which set off the squabble, there were very few Indian guns of any kind.)

The Bureau had its own list of complaints against the Army; its outstanding one was, in blunt terms, that the Army was brutal in its treatment of Indians. However, while the Bureau talked about its own humanitarian objectives, the tribes had not exactly thrived under the guardianship of a long series of corrupt, indifferent or stupid officials, from Commissioner on down to agent.

The nation, though, was wearied for the moment of the endless wrangling between Army and Indian Bureau. Rather strangely, the news from Fort Kearny had not given rise to a call for revenge, but instead had sent the country into one of its rare moods of introspection and soul-searching about its treatment of its Indians. An investigation was made of the entire Indian policy and the obvious was discovered: a great deal of trouble was caused by the split authority between Interior Department and War Department. Even more at fault, said the report, was the constant violation by white men of rights which the government had solemnly guaranteed to the Indians, very often with the Army protecting the whites while they did the violating.

As a result, Congress passed a bill in March, 1867, to establish peace with the tribes, and to settle the Indian problem with justice and without interference by the War Department. However, in spite of all good intentions about preventing War Department interference, military influence was going to make itself felt, for of the seven Peace

Commissioners to be appointed to talk with the Indians, three were to be generals. One of them would be Sherman.

Sherman had spent a frustrating winter. First had come the unnerving news of the catastrophe on the Bozeman Trail. Then, in January, he received reports that Indians in Kansas and Colorado were getting guns and ammunition from traders, although he had issued an order in June which permitted only authorized persons to sell arms to the natives. He hit the ceiling when he discovered that the Indian Bureau had, on its own, given such authorization to all traders, and ordered General Winfield Hancock to put a stop to the trade.

But the most irritating of all to him was a persistent rumor that Fort C. F. Smith, most remote of the three on the Bozeman Trail, had been taken by the Indians and destroyed, with its entire garrison killed or tortured to death. Like all rumors, it sifted through his fingers when he tried to get hold of it; one person responsible for disseminating it, he did learn through devious channels, was the wife of some officer in his own Omaha headquarters. If that were true, it was fortunate for the lady that the commanding general could not pinpoint the source—by discovering her identity.

While the rumors spread hundreds of miles away, things were not going well on the Bozeman Trail itself. Lieutenant Colonel Wessells had stepped into a post where food supplies were limited, during an exceptionally cold winter that exhausted firewood supplies long before spring came. Hay and other feed for horses and mules ran out and the starving beasts were fed cottonwood branches. Clothing was inadequate; scurvy from improper food became prevalent; morale dropped low, and as soon as the snow went, the Sioux were back. Communications were maintained during the winter, though with great difficulty, from the outside world with Fort Reno and Fort Kearny, but Fort C. F. Smith to the north had dropped from the earth since before Fetterman and his force were wiped out. When a detail finally got through from Fort Kearny in March, 1867, half-expecting to find everyone dead, they discovered that Fort Smith had actually come through the winter in better shape than they had, without scurvy, thanks to the antiscorbutic properties of a good supply of potatoes and cabbage which had been purchased from the Montana mining towns in the fall.

The return of spring brought no lessening of the isolation of the three forts because the returning Indians held the road in as tight a grip as the winter ever had. During the next months the three posts lived in a virtual state of siege; only well-armed Army supply convoys traveled the road between them, and that only rarely. Attacks were frequent, especially on Kearny, which, in the center of the Sioux hunting lands, was the main focus of their hate. Then, at the beginning of August, the Indians struck in heavy force at Forts Smith and Kearny.

On August 1, Red Cloud sent something over five hundred warriors, mostly Cheyennes, against Fort Smith. There they found and attacked a haymaking detail at work in a meadow of tall grass about three miles northeast of the fort where a stream called Warrior Creek emptied into the Big Horn River. There were six civilians in the haymaking crew, guarded by nineteen soldiers. The detail did not ordinarily return to the fort at night but kept its mules and made its own camp within a corral of logs. The corral was hardly a fort but it gave good protection because the lowest log rested directly on the ground, a good gun rest for a prone man and a stopper for arrows and bullets.

Small bands of Indians had made hit-and-run raids from time to time and had been fought off from the corral, but the haymakers lashing their mowing machine teams to a gallop to reach cover in the corral this morning had never seen anything like the hundreds of warriors who suddenly appeared. All took cover behind the bottom log and began firing—all, that is, except Second Lieutenant Sigmund Sternberg who commanded the guard. He said he believed a soldier should fight standing up. It was a noble-sounding idea but it had one weakness; he was killed very soon by a bullet through the head.

The natives were unable to pierce the defenses in several hours of fighting. Twice they tried to overwhelm the defenders by their traditional tactic of riding back and forth close to the corral, clinging to the off-side of their ponies by a leg hooked over the back, and shooting under the neck. Several attempts were made to set fire to dry grass near the corral and to hay inside it, and a final charge was made by warriors on foot but was driven off. After this last repulse, the Indians withdrew, except for a few snipers who lingered for a time.

Three of the defenders were killed, three injured. The success of the small force in the corral against such heavy odds was almost entirely a matter of firepower. Only a week earlier, Springfield rifles modified to make them breech-loaders had arrived at the fort. They were a much faster weapon than the old muzzle-loaders; although still single-shot weapons, the empty cartridge could be ejected and a new one slapped in the breech in a moment—and almost without taking the sights off a target, something decidedly not possible with a muzzle-loader.

Although the fort was the primary objective of the attack, the Indians never got close to it. Nor, as a matter of fact, did the commanding officer show any eagerness to get close to the Indians. As soon as he was informed that an attack was under way, he closed the gates and confined all hands to the fort, and refused permission to an officer who wanted to take a relief column to the beleaguered corral. The commander, Lieutenant Colonel L. P. Bradley, appears to have been haunted by the fear of another Fetterman episode. Only after a messenger from the corral informed him that the war party had gone did he send help.

The day after the fight at Fort Smith—which, not too surprisingly, has become known as the Hayfield Fight—Chief Red Cloud himself appeared near Fort Philip Kearny with an estimated 1,500 or more warriors. Woodcutting operations were going on at the pineries just as they had been the year before when Captain Fetterman was decoyed to his death. However, this year the woodcutting crews and their guards, like the haymakers at Fort Smith, camped near their work in order to save time getting started in the morning.

The woodcutters' camp was located about six miles from the fort and a very short distance from the scene of logging operations, on an area of open, grassy land. An oval enclosure had been laid out with fourteen wagon boxes set on the ground; the wheels and bases were being used to haul wood. Ordinarily, the enclosure was a corral for horses and mules at night. But ready boxes of ammunition were provided at intervals inside the enclosure, and miscellaneous objects, as ox-yokes, logs, sacks of grain, bags of the ever-present Army beans, and the like were at hand, ready to come to the defense of white civilization if needed. They would be needed this second of August, 1867.

About seven o'clock in the morning, hundreds of Indians appeared over the hills north of the wagon box corral. By that time, a wagon train of cordwood was heading for the fort and a string of empty wagons from the fort was nearing the pineries. There was confusion and bravery and lost opportunity before affairs took definite shape. A party of warriors ran off the mule herd of the woodcutters, isolated pickets and mule herders fought their way to the corral and had a dozen hairbreadth escapes. The wagon train from the fort was unable to reach the corral and battled its way all the way back to the fort, bearing the alarm.

There were thirty-two men in the enclosure, four of them civilians. In command was Captain James W. Powell, an old Fort Kearny hand, who had arrived on the same day Captain Fetterman had. It was Powell, careful and given to exemplary obedience of orders, who had been ordered to relieve the wood train on the day when Fetterman had pulled his rank and taken command—with results the whole country knew.

In the situation in which he now found himself, all Powell could do was look around the enclosure, make sure his men were all posted where they could hurt the enemy without exposing themselves too much, and let it go at that. Powell, apparently, was not given to inspirational exhortations; he is reported to have sent his men into battle with a simple, "Men, here they come! Take your places and shoot to kill."

The wagon boxes with their thin sides were no protection against bullets but they did hide the man inside from view; they were possibly not even much protection against arrows since Indians sometimes had the disconcerting habit of getting behind a defense by arcing their arrows into the air in a high, plunging fire which came down almost vertically. The boxes were very like the familiar old covered-wagon type but no canvas was drawn over the wooden roof bows. Loopholes had been bored in the outer sides of the boxes for just such a situation as this, and the piles of oxen yokes, sacks of corn, a barrel of salt, and similar breastworks between the wagon boxes provided good firing positions.

The attacking Sioux—there seems to have been few or no Cheyennes and Arapahoes in this war party—were also provided with shelter on one side because the level, grassy shelf on which the wagon-box corral stood ended about a hundred yards away where it dropped away to the valley of Big Piney Creek. The drop-off gave cover to Sioux snipers.

The first attack was made by a large group of mounted warriors (five hundred, Captain Powell estimated) riding hidden behind their ponies and coming close to the corral. The Sioux tactics were spectacular, with the pounding of hundreds of hoofs, the shrill yelling of warriors, the surge of galloping ponies only half-seen through a pall of dust, and all too often the headlong dive and rolling somersault of a badly hit horse and rider.

However, the warriors had not planned to ride back and forth indefinitely, like ducks in a shooting gallery. They knew from experience that after the first blast of fire from the corral there should be a pause while the defenders reloaded; they were ready to thunder in and overwhelm the men inside the ring of wagon boxes the instant the fire diminished. But the pause never came; the cracking of rifles went on at a tempo far greater than the number of beleaguered whites warranted, while the number of dead and wounded Indians and horses on the grassy plain mounted into the dozens. At last the bewildered Sioux ended their assault.

The Indians' perplexity at the heavy rifle fire was understandable. Fort Kearny, like Fort Smith, had very recently received modified breech-loading Springfields to replace the old muzzle-loaders. The mounted warriors had planned to make their final assault while the defenders' rifles were empty after the first volley and the soldiers were going through the complicated loading procedure with the ramrods. But there had been no break in the murderous fire.

With several other chiefs, Red Cloud sat on his horse on a rise of ground, making no move to interfere or direct the attack until it ground to a halt. Then a council of war was held, in which an attack on foot was decided on, to come from the north, where the sharp slope down to the creek valley would provide cover for such an assault. Indians with guns—probably most of them the firearms gathered up after the Fetterman battle—had been stationed behind the rim of this drop-off during the fight, keeping the corral under fire. Their aim had been effective; they had killed an officer and two enlisted men, all three shot through the head. From the same protected position, flights of fire arrows had arced into the corral, starting hay to blazing and setting smoldering fires among accumulated dry horse and mule dung which sent up choking clouds of smoke. The fires did no damage but they were an acute discomfort.

Now, behind the same rim the attack on foot was organized. There was a small ravine in the plain; hundreds of warriors, almost naked, moved from behind the drop-off up this ravine, taking advantage of the cover it gave till they were forced to cross the open plain toward the corral. They came on in a compact wedge while the defenders fired rapidly and accurately, but with mounting panic as the seemingly irresistible tide moved down on them. But, at the last moment, the Sioux broke and ran, leaving a few of their dead within five feet of the wagon boxes.

It was, at the same time, a telling demonstration of one of the weaknesses of the Plains Indian as a military man. He seldom had the ability to improvise tactics, especially consecutive tactics. When the foot attack was so near to succeeding, a small amount of support would probably have carried it through. The defense had concentrated almost all its strength against the courageous men attacking over the open plain; the south side of the corral was almost unprotected and could have been carried by a sudden and determined assault. Yet hundreds of mounted braves remained aloof, merely interested spectators. Nor apparently did Red Cloud make any attempt to intervene.

With the smashing of the foot attack, the heart went out of the Sioux. Sniping continued from behind the rim of the drop-off, but the Indians gave most of their attention to rescuing their wounded and recovering the bodies of their dead, something in which they often took risks greater than in the battle itself.

Shortly after noon a relief party armed with a howitzer arrived from the fort and the Indians withdrew far enough to be out of range of the big gun. The corral was evacuated at once and the return to the fort made with no attempt at harassment by the Sioux. The siege had lasted probably five hours but only three of the defenders were killed and two wounded, resisting possibly fifteen hundred Indians (Captain Powell estimated three thousand, but this figure is hard to swallow). How many men the Sioux lost is a matter of guesswork for the estimates run all the way from six killed to more than a thousand. Both extremes are completely ridiculous. Captain Powell estimated sixty killed and a hundred and twenty badly wounded, a figure probably bearing some approximate relation to the truth. Years later Red Cloud said he lost the flower of his men in the fighting.

The two defeats suffered by the Indians on the Bozeman Trail had not affected the resolves made earlier in the year in the East to work out a solution to the Indian problem which would recognize and honor the just claims of the tribes. The seven-member Peace Commission to treat with the Indians was appointed in August, not long after the Hayfield and Wagon-Box Fights. General Sherman was one of the three military men. (Another was General Harney, who had attacked an innocent Brule village long ago as retribution for the Mormon's cow affair and so became one of the first Indian fighters on the plains.) N. G. Taylor, Commissioner of Indian Affairs was a member, so was Senator John B. Henderson of Missouri, Chairman of the Senate Committee on Indian Affairs, and two prominent private citizens completed the group.

After a 1,300-mile steamboat trip to talk to tribes on the Missouri River, the Commission next went by train to North Platte, Nebraska, in mid-September for a meeting with a delegation of Oglala and Brule Sioux. At the council, the Indians complained about the way the whites were ruining the hunting along the Smoky Hill Road in Kansas and Colorado and along the Bozeman Trail; the whites, they said, would have to get out of those regions. Sherman answered that both roads were necessary to the white man and would have to stay. Then he went on to describe how well tribes like the Cherokees and Potawatomies had done farming their own lands, and suggested that the Sioux pick themselves a nice reservation before the good land was all gone. Having left these thoughts, and promising to be back in November, the Commission moved on to negotiate with the Southern tribes.

On November 6 they were back at North Platte, but only a single chief, Swift Bear of the Brule Sioux, was there of a dozen or more important leaders who had been present in September. Even Spotted Tail, the great lover of peace, did not show up the second time.

They moved on to Fort Laramie. Messengers had been sent up into the Powder River country asking Red Cloud and other chiefs to meet them at the fort for a council, but on their arrival they found no one. The chiefs had had the delicate courtesy to send a message saying they were too busy to appear just then. General Harney and another two of the commissioners considered this a piece of insolence which a white man should not have to take from one with red skin, and they asked Sherman how many troops would be required to whip the Powder River Sioux thoroughly.

However, there was no talk in the Bozeman Trail forts about thrashing the Sioux. The men there could see the snow whitening the Big Horns, and they damned the portent of the skin of ice that edged the streams in the morning. Those who had spent the previous frigid and hunger-stalked winter in the forts did not welcome another season there. But, though they would stay on, the jig was up with the forts. The day Sherman was asked how many soldiers it would take to whip the Powder River Sioux, he knew, no matter what answer he gave to the question, that the Sioux had won and that peace overtures had been approved.

For already in October, the quartermaster at Fort Kearny, Captain

Dandy, had met with Sioux, Cheyenne, and Arapaho chiefs on a meadow about a quarter mile from the fort for the first talks between the government and the Indians on the matter of abandoning the Bozeman Trail and the three forts. Red Cloud was not present.

The next spring the Peace Commissioners returned to Fort Laramie and on April 29, 1868, signed a treaty with leaders of the Brule, Oglala, Miniconjou, and Yanktonais bands of the Sioux and of the northern Arapaho. The tribes agreed to accept reservations, and all of the present state of South Dakota west of the Missouri River was set aside as Indian reservation land. The tribes also insisted on their right to hunt buffalo on lands north of the North Platte and on the Republican River, and the treaty guaranteed them this right "so long as buffalo may range there in numbers sufficient to justify the chase."

Sherman was not present at the signing, but he objected to the buffalo clause and later wrote to General Philip Sheridan that the best thing that could be done would be to invite all the sportsmen of England and America to a great buffalo shoot. For, he said, until the Indians were out from between the great transplains roads the danger of collisions would remain.

Red Cloud did not appear for the signing and would not accept the treaty—or any treaty—as long as the Bozeman Trail and the forts remained. And even though Oglala and Miniconjou chiefs had touched the pen at Fort Laramie, probably the greater part of the two bands were still sitting it out with Red Cloud.

Sherman had already made up his mind that the road would be given up. (The advance of the railroad made it possible to use a road into Montana farther west, he said, a statement that seems to have a little of the flavor of sour grapes.) The actual order for abandonment was given on May 19 by Major General Christopher C. Augur, commanding the Department of the Platte, and in August the soldiers marched out and left what had not been consumed or hauled away during the summer. Fort C. F. Smith was first, then Fort Philip Kearny, and finally Fort Reno. Before August was over there was nothing left except the dead in the post cemeteries (a numerous company), they and some heaps of ashes because the jubilant Indians had burned each fort almost before the departing rearguard of the garrison had disappeared over the first ridge.

At last, on November 6, Red Cloud came to Fort Laramie to sign a treaty. He was the first and only Indian leader in the West to win a war with the United States. He had fought for two years to preserve the beautiful hunting lands of the Sioux and now the soldiers were gone. The Bozeman Trail was empty. The forts were destroyed. And in the treaty, the government agreed that the Big Horn country would be considered as unceded Indian territory, forbidden to whites, where the Sioux and their Cheyenne and Arapaho allies were to have full and unrestricted rights to hunt.

Red Cloud promised not to make war again, and he kept his promise, through a period of great turbulence for the Sioux nation. Some among his people questioned his motives and many were deeply puzzled by his decision to walk a road of peace, but no one accused him of being a coward because Red Cloud had counted eighty coups, that is, he had performed eighty feats of valor meriting special recognition. Have nothing to do with white men, he told his people, and added cynical advice on how to become wealthy like the white men: "You must begin anew and put away the wisdom of your fathers. You must lay up food and forget the hungry. When your house is built, your store-room filled, then look around for a neighbor whom you can take advantage of and seize all he has."

Red Cloud could afford the luxury of being cynical. He had done about as well as any Indian ever had.

V

The Great Road

---

1. GENERAL HANCOCK'S WAR

I N his annual report to the Secretary of War early in November, 1866, General Sherman had stated that the Sioux would have to be kept north of the Platte River, west of the Missouri, and east of the Bozeman Trail (here Sherman proposed but Red Cloud disposed), while the Arapaho, Cheyenne, Comanche, and Kiowa should be kept south of the Arkansas River and east of Fort Union, New Mexico. "This," he wrote, "would leave for our people exclusively the use of the wide belt, east and west, between the Platte and the Arkansas, in which lie the two great railroads, and over which pass the bulk of travel to the mountain territories."

There is in Sherman's report a quaint echo of the Great American Desert, a survival of the idea that the plains were only an expanse to be crossed in moving from East to West. Actually, settlers were becoming interested in them. The Homestead Act of 1862 offered land to men and women for no other coin than the courage to farm it, and pioneers were already seeking their dream in a sod shanty and a horizon over which nothing much appeared but clouds. (Sherman, who thought in military terms, was not in sympathy with these early settlers; he believed it would be better if they abandoned their exposed positions and gave the Army a more compact perimeter to defend.)

Settlement was bringing a profound change to the plains but it tended to be a gradual one; a few sod-busters today, a couple tomorrow and half a dozen the next day, and almost without anyone quite realizing it was going on, a dozen townships had been settled. On the other hand, there was nothing gradual about the changes being wrought by the railroads. To the Army, they meant a change in both logistics and tactics. They were making it possible to abandon many small Army posts and garrisons scattered throughout Indian country. Sherman pointed out that it would be far easier to bring detachments out onto the plains by railroad in the spring and let the soldiers live under canvas during the summer and fall than to try to maintain them on the plains the year around.

Indian war parties very seldom operated in winter, anyway, while for the soldiers, there was something less than complete comfort in spending the cold months on the plains in buildings of sod or cottonwood logs, most of them none too airtight and miserably uncomfortable when the wind blew across the plains and the thermometer registered far below zero.

The two railroads left much of the plains unaffected, and garrisons in scores of posts were still condemned to frostbite, boredom, and other hazards of winter station on the frontier, but where the lines reached, winter soldiering was changed drastically and made a less irksome occupation. By the end of the summer of 1866, the Union Pacific had built some 200 miles west of Omaha; the Kansas Pacific was about 125 miles west of Kansas City.

To the military, to promoters, to settlers, to land speculators, to the great heterogeneous collection of humans that makes up an advancing frontier, the railroads were the ultimate herald of advancing civilization. To the Indians, the building of the iron road was little less than catastrophic. Great crews of white men came to lay the rails, and soldiers protected the builders. Noisy locomotives and trains frightened the game. Professional hunters shot thousands of buffalo to keep the cook cars supplied with the mountains of meat needed to feed an army of railroad builders. It was not a good year for Indians on the middle plains.

There was no warfare, but there was no peace, either. Red Cloud was fighting to close the Bozeman Trail and the Sioux were edgy as a result; the Cheyennes were still smoldering over the Sand Creek Massacre. It was not surprising that Indian resentment broke out now and again in the killing of a surveying party, or a sudden attack on a grading or track-laying crew. All that was needed to break a good number of eggs was for some clumsy-footed fool to walk through the scene at this point. And just such a person was on hand: Major General Winfield Scott Hancock, commander of the Department of the Missouri.*

General Hancock was one of those men who capped grandeur with anticlimax. He had been one of the greatest of the great during the war, a general with a record surpassed by very few. A Beau Brummel among officers, the rare type who was cheered by the ranks when he rode by, he fought with distinction all through the war with the Army of the Potomac, but the moment when the rays of true glory shone down came on the third day at Gettysburg. He commanded the II Corps on Cemetery Ridge; he exposed himself to the enemy's fire to inspire his men, and went down at the last, grievously wounded after repulsing the supreme Confederate effort known ever after as Pickett's Charge.

Things were different out on the plains. It was hot, dusty, and barren, or else cold and windy—no place for a Beau Brummel to appear at his best. However, a man of action could operate in this kind of country—even if he did not know exactly what he was doing—and Hancock decided on a great spring campaign against the Arapahoes and Cheyennes. It was about as ill-conceived an idea as one can look for. The Indians in his department were not at war. A campaign could only antagonize them. All indications are that he merely meant to go out and swagger around a bit, daring the natives to fight.

Or, as he put it in a letter to the Indian agent at Fort Larned, his campaign was only to awe the Indians and to impress them with the might of the white man. He was not looking for war, he said, but added rather ominously that he would not avoid it. The agent had begged him not to send a military expedition into the plains because the memory of Sand Creek was still fresh in the minds of the Cheyennes, even in this spring of 1867, and they would be certain that armed forces would

* Not to be confused with the Division of the Missouri, of which it was a part. The Department of the Missouri included Kansas, Missouri, eastern Colorado, and northeastern New Mexico. The Division of the Missouri, Sherman's over-all command, was divided into five departments at that time, although there were adjustments in later years.

be approaching only for another massacre attempt. Sherman, of course, had approved the campaign and so deserves part of the blame, but it is doubtful that he anticipated Hancock's arrogance and ineptitude in carrying out his plans.

"No insolence will be tolerated from any bands of Indians whom we may encounter," Hancock wrote. "We wish to show them that the government is ready and able to punish them if they are hostile, although it may not be disposed to invite war." The general sounded like a man determined to start trouble through sheer stupidity.

The Indian agent at Fort Larned was Colonel Edward W. Wynkoop, the same who, then a major, had been commanding officer of Fort Lyon, and after bringing the Cheyenne chiefs to Denver to see the governor and Colonel Chivington, had promised them security if they camped near the fort. Perhaps he carried a sense of guilt over his unwitting part in leading Black Kettle's Cheyennes into a slaughter trap and felt he could atone for it by serving them; whatever the reason, he was now agent for the Southern Cheyennes and Arapahoes. He had been patiently working to regain their confidence and to get them to congregate closer to Fort Larned. Now Hancock was about to upset the entire applecart.

General Hancock set out from Fort Leavenworth late in March loaded for bear, with a column that included six companies of infantry, a battery of light artillery and—how to state the incredible as simple fact?—a train whose freight included pontoons for bridging the ankle-deep rivers of western Kansas. At Fort Riley, Fort Harker, and Fort Larned the column was joined by companies of the 7th Cavalry until at last the expedition was 1,400 strong. The colonel designated to lead the newly-formed 7th Cavalry not having arrived, its acting commander was George Armstrong Custer, who held a brevet rank of major general but at the moment was only a lieutenant colonel in the Regular Army.

At Larned, Colonel Wynkoop once more tried to make Hancock see sense. There was a camp of Cheyennes with some Sioux on the Pawnee River about forty miles west of the fort. They would become frightened and take it as a warlike move if the soldiers moved on them, warned Wynkoop. They would run away, he said, but they would retaliate on the first stage station they came to. Hancock complied with Wynkoop's warnings to the degree that he remained at Fort Larned and summoned the chiefs to a council. Then, after the chiefs had shown up, and Hancock had falsely accused them of having white prisoners, he marched anyway.

A delegation of chiefs and warriors met the advancing column and asked Hancock not to bring his soldiers near the camp because the women and children were frightened. He would have to bring his soldiers closer, the general insisted, but he would see that none of them approached the lodges. There is no way of knowing whether it was complete pigheadedness that drove this man on, or whether he had some obscure end in mind, possibly to force the Indians into an overt hostile move.

The state of mind of the natives by this time must have bordered on panic. At midnight, Hancock ordered Custer to surround the camp —for what reason, it is again difficult to guess. However, it is not difficult to imagine what would have happened had the cavalry surrounded the camp before the Indians discovered it. The Cheyennes, on finding themselves encircled, would beyond a doubt have decided on the instant that they were about to be killed as they had been at Sand Creek. They would have tried to fight their way out without stopping to make inquiries, and then there would have been a massacre. It is difficult to believe Hancock could have been so obtuse as to have thought anything else could have happened. On the other hand, it is not easy to understand many things Hancock did during the entire misbegotten campaign.

In any event, the tragedy never occurred. The nervous Indians had quietly abandoned their camp as soon as darkness fell; Custer's men carefully surrounded a camp which the gray morning light revealed to be absolutely deserted. General Hancock was enraged at this perfidy and ordered the cavalry out in pursuit. It was a hopeless quest. Even under the best of conditions, cavalry stood little chance of catching the Indians during the summer months when the light ponies of the warriors could run rings around the heavier government horses. And Custer was not operating under the best of conditions. He knew next to nothing about fighting Indians at that stage in his career, while the 7th Cavalry was a new regiment whose men, for the most part, were not much past the stage of raw recruits. Whenever Custer came on a good, strong trail, it had a maddening way of dividing and dividing again, until soon he found himself following the tracks of only three or four horses.

In the meantime, the angry Cheyennes, convinced that they had barely escaped another massacre, had attacked and burned several stage stations, just as Colonel Wynkoop had warned they would. Hancock thereupon set fire to the deserted Cheyenne village—it was about the only thing he could do in his frustration—and took most of his infantry and his pontoons and headed back toward Fort Leavenworth by easy stages, leaving Custer and the 7th to carry on. The government shortly thereafter declared the Cheyennes, Arapahoes, and the Sioux south of the Platte to be at war with the United States, all in all a very good showing for Hancock's little expedition to awe the Indians and impress them with the white man's might.

As for Custer, while he was accomplishing little, he was trying hard. He was pushing his men beyond the point of endurance for many of them; had they been old campaigners it would have been a rigorous and exhausting period of soldiering, but his men were far from seasoned. As a result, many had deserted, most were exhausted and saddle-sore. George Custer was not a man who wearied like ordinary mortals; he had no understanding of physical frailties or any sympathy for them. A strict disciplinarian (for everyone but himself), his answer when his men began to complain was to give them a stronger dose of the same medicine.

The matter came to a small climax one midday early in June when the regiment had halted for a rest. Twelve men—seven mounted, five on foot—decided during the stop to desert, and, with no show of stealth, simply left camp, their destination the Platte River not many miles away. It was one thing to desert, it was quite another to walk out in broad daylight in such a manner that it was tantamount to thumbing noses at the commanding officer. Colonel Custer, losing both his temper and his head, shrilled an order to the officer of the day to go after the deserters and to "bring none in alive." Two officers took up the chase. The mounted men escaped easily, but three of those on foot were shot, of whom one died several weeks later. Two avoided injury by pretending to be dead.

This was the great General George Armstrong Custer, the man turned legend, who in popular fancy stands with the great ones—Lewis and Clark, Kit Carson, the Pony Express Riders, Buffalo Bill, Wyatt Earp—as openers of the West. But an order, in rage, to shoot a dozen soldiers was not the act of a great man, nor even that of an officer of average competence and self-control. Did the god have feet of clay? Does the legend, after all, mask a man who was no more than other men?

It is difficult to find a starting place for describing Custer. Those who have already formed opinions about the man have done so with such vehemence that it is hard to believe that the two sides are talking about the same person. To one group, he remains the brave and gallant soldier and peerless Indian fighter who died heroically and gloriously battling against hopeless odds; to the other he was a big-mouthed braggart and incompetent who blundered away the lives of more than two hundred men by rushing joyfully into a deadly situation without taking the simplest precautions demanded by military prudence. On one point all agree: Custer was a man of supreme physical courage who apparently did not know what it was to feel fear. Beyond that, there is agreement on very little.

Custer graduated at the bottom of his class at West Point, in large part for demerits received for what his admirers like to describe as "boyish pranks and escapades," although a good part of his bad record was the result of slovenly habits. This last was highly ironic because no officer would demand more later from his men in the way of snap and polish and taut discipline than he. He received his commission just in time to get into the First Battle of Bull Run.

He had a dash about him and a vivaciousness, to say nothing of his courage, which could not help but attract the attention of his superiors, and he received choice assignments for such a very young officer. He had a superb confidence that fortune was always working for him; "Custer's luck," he called this continual smile of the gods, and for a number of years it appeared that he was right and that it actually existed. As it turned out, "Custer's luck" was not an inexhaustible commodity.

Some points in his career remain hazy. He was, for instance, jumped all the way from first lieutenant to brigadier general after having played only minor parts in engagements where he performed in no manner worthy of such recognition. Even Custer's luck could not explain such a promotion; it seems possible that political influence was also involved. In any event, at twenty-three, he was (and still is) the youngest man ever to have held the rank of brigadier general in the United States Army; two years later he was breveted major general and so became the youngest ever in that rank—with the single exception of the Marquis de Lafayette during the Revolution.

He was a flamboyant leader. He designed his own uniform which consisted of a wide-brimmed hat, trousers with a double stripe running down the seam, a sailor's wide-collared shirt, a red cravat, and on the sleeves of his jacket an intricate arabesque of interlacing loops of gold braid. Add to this the golden hair grown long and lying in ringlets on his shoulders and the man becomes rather overpowering in his gaudiness and glitter.

However, these were personal things; the important thing in a soldier is whether he can fight. General Custer could fight all right, but there was a great deal of question about his competence as a commander. During the war, he two or three times showed a disconcerting habit of forgetting his main responsibility to go whooping off after some side issue that was more exciting—as the time he entered a Virginia town and spied a Confederate locomotive and cars about to make their escape; he left his command to take care of itself and made a wild dash to capture the train. Such actions can turn disastrous, and it was perhaps only Custer's luck that saved him each time.

Because of his impulsiveness, he was not a good tactician. His joy was leading a cavalry charge, saber swinging, yellow hair streaming in the wind, the field behind him thundering with hundreds of men and horses answering to his command. He had not enough patience for the careful reconnoitering, the consideration of alternatives, the working out of plans that make a good commanding officer.

Custer had been a teetotaler since the day when, a young and arrogant lieutenant home on furlough, he had been staggering under more than he could carry and had met Elizabeth Bacon. Miss Bacon, the future Mrs. Custer, was not amused; young Custer took the pledge and never drank again. He appeared not to know the meaning of weariness; he could spend a day campaigning on the plains that exhausted the men with him, and then come back to his tent and spend most of the night writing a long letter to Mrs. Custer. On occasion, if no operations were scheduled for the next day, he would be up early and out on an all-day hunt after getting only one or two hours of sleep. He seemed completely unable to understand that his men could not do likewise; the result was over-strict discipline—and a "bring-none-back alive" incident. Add miscellany on Custer: he carried hound dogs with him, sometimes as many as two or three dozen, and let them share his tent and—within capacity—his bed.

The preceding, and all other facts about Custer, add up to a man of supreme courage and boundless energy who had retained the enthusiasm of a youth at the cost of never quite attaining the judgment of a man. His inability to accept the harsh restraints of discipline had shown itself on occasion during the war; now it came to the surface once again when he received orders from General Hancock to move farther west and make his base at Fort Wallace.

Fort Wallace was on the Smoky Hill River in western Kansas, almost at the Colorado border; Custer arrived there on July 14. His orders directed that "The cavalry will be kept constantly engaged." He had also been ordered to leave wives of officers behind—the danger from Indians was too great. So, while Custer was now at Fort Wallace, Elizabeth Custer languished at Fort Riley far to the east. However, Custer also languished. It is difficult to say whether he felt an overpowering love for his wife, or whether he needed her to feed his ego; he showed her the gallantries of true love but at the same time ruthlessly and selfishly demanded that she devote all her time, attention, and solicitude to him.

There was cholera, always a dreaded disease, at Fort Wallace, although apparently nowhere near epidemic proportions. There was also word that the disease had struck Fort Hays to the east—and furthermore, that it had hit Fort Riley, way back where Elizabeth Custer was. There was no telegraph to Fort Wallace, no way for Custer to pin down the rumors. He took the direct method, exactly what he had ordered twelve men shot for doing a little more than a month earlier. He deserted his command. On the fifteenth, the day after he arrived at Fort Wallace, he left the post.

However, a commanding officer has ways of doing such things so that, if black cannot be made to appear white, it can usually be given a gray tinge. Custer selected the seventy-five horses of his command that looked the least exhausted, took men to mount them as an escort, selected three officers, including his brother Tom (General Custer was a strong believer in nepotism; the 7th Cavalry would collect several family members as time passed), and set out along the Smoky Hill Trail headed east.

An explanation was needed for such an unusual procedure; Custer's was that he was going to Fort Hays to pick up a load of important supplies. It was a weak explanation; a commanding officer of a regiment leaves the procurement of supplies to his quartermaster and busies himself with other matters. On the other hand, it was about as good a reason as Custer could have come up with; there are not many ways a commanding officer can justify leaving his post.

Near Downers Station, an important stage stop garrisoned by troops, the rear of the detachment was hit by Indians and two soldiers killed. Custer had been pursuing Indians for weeks, and pushing his men beyond their endurance in doing so; now, with a fresh trail and real reason to seek revenge, he merely gave the command to march on. He made no attempt to pursue the Indians, or even to bury the dead; he ordered the captain in command of the infantry detachment at Downers Station to take care of that small chore.

The detachment reached Fort Hays, 150 miles from Fort Wallace, in fifty-five hours. Only six of those fifty-five had been wasted on rest. His escort had almost given out by now, so he left it, and rode on with brother Tom, another officer, and two orderlies. The ride had been costly, if he had been interested: twenty of his escort had had their bellies full of that particular kind of soldiering and deserted on the way.

Custer, the obsessed, pushed on, covering the next sixty miles to Fort Harker in less than twelve hours. Fort Harker was the end of the rails for the Kansas Pacific Railroad just then; Custer took the train on to Fort Riley for a reunion with his wife which lasted one night. The next morning he received peremptory orders to return at once to his command. About a week later he was placed under arrest and, beginning in mid-September, he went on trial before a court-martial at Fort Leavenworth on seven charges, among them deserting his command, having ordered the shooting of deserting men, damaging horses belonging to the government during his dash to his wife's arms, failing to pursue Indians who attacked his escort, and not recovering the bodies of his men who were killed by Indians.

Custer's luck ran thin; he was found guilty on all charges and was suspended from his rank and his command for one year. Or possibly Custer's luck ran strong; a string of charges like that would have gotten many men cashiered from the service permanently.

General Hancock also disappeared from the plains. Sherman brought Major General Philip Sheridan up from Texas where his over-harsh handling of the occupation had created angry protest and sullen resistance, and put him in command of the Department of the Platte. General Hancock, in return, was made military governor of Texas and Louisiana but was not much of a success because he did not have the heart for the stern measures sometimes required of him in dealing with the beaten South. Hancock, it would seem, found it easier to be stern with red men.

2. "WE ARE BEYOND ALL HUMAN AID"

The year previous to Hancock's war, the government had prepared the way for the concentration of Indians on (supposedly) worthless reservations by a completely shameless swindle. After their removal from the southeastern states along the Trail of Tears, the Five Civilized Tribes had started anew in the territory given them, the present state of Oklahoma, and had once again established their separate nations. When the war came, they were caught in a cruel dilemma. They were occupied by the Confederacy; many of their citizens owned slaves. However, most of the Indians tried to remain neutral, and many actually fled north where some of the men joined the Union forces.

Nevertheless, it was a golden opportunity, not the kind to pass up lightly, so the government charged the Five Tribes with treason for aiding and abetting the Southern cause and forced them to give up half their territory. How little the government was really concerned about treason, and how much about the land, may be detected in the fact that the lighest punishment fell on the Choctaws and Chickasaws who had contributed most to the Southern fight. The tribes received compensation of a sort for part of the land; the most unconscionable robbery was that of the Seminoles who were given fifteen cents an acre for their lands and then forced to buy a smaller reservation at fifty cents an acre. The Indians were forced, in almost all cases, to leave their farms, mills, roads, and other improvements to start over again. By the end of 1866 the job was completed and the western half of their former lands was empty. The entire Oklahoma area was named Indian Territory; it was firmly believed that this was land that would be worthless to white men and could be held by the Indians forever. O! oft-heard words!

The next year, agents of the Indian Bureau began another round of uprooting tribes. The Osage, Oto, and Kansa nations, once-proud peoples of the prairie lands, were moved onto small reservations in Indian Territory, and so were the sad remnants of the eastern tribes, so often moved by now that most of their members had lost all tribal traditions. Then, in October came the Peace Commissioners, except for General Sherman who had been called to Washington, to meet with the

Comanches, Kiowas, and Southern Cheyennes and Arapahoes on Medicine Lodge Creek in Kansas. This, it should be remembered, was the year when American consciences had begun to bother, and Congress had ordered that peace with justice should be made with the Indian tribes.

It is interesting that the Commissioners had had no trouble making contact with the tribes during the summer in preparation for the council, even though they were at war, particularly the Cheyennes. The Indian concept of war was more flexible than that of his white antagonist. Now, as the council opened, there were between two and three thousand Indians from the four tribes present. The horse herds grazed over hundreds of acres; the conical lodges ranged on and on; the camp was noisy and busy, and from its activities rose a thin haze of dust that blended with the autumn haze hanging over the prairies. And, as the council drew on day after day, the typical odorousness of an Indian camp ripened and grew stronger.

Applying the new concepts of understanding between the two races and justice toward the Indian, the Commissioners used a combination of bribes and threats, cajolery and coercion to get the tribes to accept reservations in Indian Territory. The great and tempestuous Satanta, he who formerly announced dinner with a French horn, wanted no part of settling down and acting like poor imitations of white men: "I love the land and the buffalo and will not part with it," he said. "I want the children raised as I was. I don't want to settle. I love to roam over the prairies. A long time ago this land belonged to our fathers, but when I go up the river I see the camps of the soldiers on its banks. These soldiers cut down my timber; they kill my buffalo; and when I see that it feels as if my heart would burst with sorrow."

Although Satanta was opposed to the treaty, he nevertheless signed, and promised to abide by it. The Comanches and Kiowas signed a treaty on October 21, the Cheyennes and Arapahoes approved theirs a week later, October 28. The Comanches and Kiowas were given a reservation in western Indian Territory between the Red and Washita rivers; the Cheyennes and Arapahoes accepted one of about three million acres just to the north of them, a tract so arid that the streams dried in the summer. The treaties also included promises of food, clothing, and other supplies (a promise which would be kept only sporadically), and of seeds, farming implements, and instruction in agriculture, something the tribes wanted no part of yet. The council ended with the opening of a mountain of boxes filled with gifts: blankets, clothing, food, guns, ammunition, hunting knives.

The Commissioners moved on to treat with other tribes. The Crows agreed to a reservation on the upper Yellowstone, the Colorado Utes accepted a large reservation in the western part of the state, the Shoshone and Bannock gave up their lands in Wyoming and Idaho except for two reservations in those states. The Commissioners split into two groups to talk to the Navajos, the Snakes, the Southern Shoshones and various other tribes. And, as already related, they got the Sioux and northern Cheyennes to accept reservations in western South Dakota. Only Red Cloud and the Powder River Sioux still had not signed a treaty, but it was by then certain they would, for the Bozeman Trail forts were being abandoned. Sherman therefore issued an order on August 10, 1868, to his departmental commanders to bring the Indians in to their assigned reservations. Avoid force, Sherman directed; use only persuasion.

Sherman was concerned almost entirely with the Sioux and with the four Southern tribes; they had been involved in most of the fighting and presented the only potential source of future fighting on the plains. Unfortunately, many Indians were not in a mood to be persuaded to move onto the reservations. A good number, like the redoubtable Satanta, had not approved them from the beginning. Others, during the long winter months in the tepees, had decided that the treaties had been sold to them by misrepresentation.

For the Southern tribes, one of the main causes of growing Indian resentment was the continued wanton slaughter of buffalo. Hunters who took only the tongue and left the rest to rot had been bad enough, but there were many soldiers among them who killed for no other reason than to watch the shaggy beasts go down. Passengers on the Kansas Pacific Railroad kept their guns with them, and when the train ran through a herd of buffalo—a frequent occurrence—everyone grabbed his rifle and banged away rapidly and at random, shooting into the herd with no concern that many more animals were crippled than were killed. The dead buffalo were left where they fell until there were thousands of carcasses along the right of way in all stages of putrefaction, creating a stench that was carried for miles by the prairie wind. In 1868 the Kansas Pacific began boosting its revenue by selling round-trip tickets to sportsmen from Leavenworth to the shooting grounds where the hunters could kill their animals with a little more finesse—

though not much more—than shooting them from a moving railroad coach.

The accumulated resentments of the natives broke out into open warfare in the middle of August, just a few days after Sherman had issued his orders for Indians to be brought onto the reservations. Cheyenne and Arapaho war parties rode north and began attacking settlers between the Solomon and Saline rivers in northwestern Kansas, killing 117, taking seven women captive, burning buildings. Sheridan reported that the Indians were committing acts more bloody even than the newspapers reported; the order came back from Omaha to herd the Indians south of the Kansas line into Indian Territory at once, killing all who resisted.

But Sheridan was in no shape to do much herding. He had about 2,600 men under his command, about evenly divided between cavalry and infantry. However, most of these were committed as garrisons at military posts, for escort duties, as railroad guards, and for other irreducible chores. As a result, he could send only about eight hundred men into the field, and he estimated that the two tribes had six thousand warriors against him, each supplied with two to ten extra horses. It was a gross over-estimate—there were probably nearer two thousand warriors—but the difference was only one of degree for he was outnumbered either way.

To compensate for his shortage of troops, Sheridan attempted the expedient of using civilians. Late in August of 1868, he ordered Major George A. Forsyth of the 9th U. S. Cavalry, his war-time aide-de-camp, to hire "fifty first-class hardy frontiersmen, to be used as scouts against the hostile Indians, to be commanded by yourself." The theory was fine, but even in those days the West had already developed its legends, and one of them was that it was peopled with hardy frontiersmen, dead shots and skilled in fighting Indians, waiting for a call to action. There was that kind of man, but he was not usually unemployed. What Forsyth got in his recruiting among the civilian hangers-on around Forts Harker and Hays were a lot of young drifters who would turn their hand to anything, including stage-coach robbery, that meant a meal and a dollar. The surprising thing was that he got so many good men.

First Lieutenant Frederick H. Beecher of the 3rd U. S. Infantry was made second in command; he had served long enough on the plains to understand the special problems of soldiering on the great empty grasslands. A Dr. John Mooers had signed on as surgeon, and Abner Grover, an Indian scout of considerable reputation, was guide.

Major Forsyth led his command westward from Fort Hays, scouting without success for signs of Indians, and a week later brought his men into Fort Wallace. There he got a fresh report: a Cheyenne war party had attacked a wagon train a few miles to the east, near Sheridan, the boom town and work camp, long since disappeared, which marked the temporary end of the tracks of the Kansas Pacific. He set out at once, picked up the trail, and refused to be discouraged when it thinned out as the Indians followed their usual tactic of splitting up to throw off any pursuit. The Major had never fought Indians but he was a good officer who had learned all he could by listening to experienced Indian fighters; as a result, he was traveling light, with only a week's rations, no tents, and a train of four mules that carried little in their packs besides extra ammunition.

Gradually the trail grew stronger and included the drag marks of many travois poles, proof positive that they were following not merely a party of raiding warriors but a large camp on the move. Some of Forsyth's hardy frontiersmen were all for calling an end to the whole thing and finding a party of Indians more manageable in size. Forsyth refused such counsel; their assignment was to find and fight Indians, he said, and that was what they were about to do. It was strange how men new to Indian fighting could approach the subject from completely different directions and end up in much the same place. Captain Fetterman, arrogant and contemptuous of the fighting ability of Indians, had been certain that he could ride through the Sioux nation with eighty men. Major Forsyth, who had carefully learned all he could about Indian-fighting by talking to old hands, was nevertheless going ahead as though fifty-one men could whip any number of warriors. Either way there were possibilities for trouble.

The command had followed the trail of the Indians along the upper Republican River and then up one of its tributaries, the Arickaree River, into northwestern Kansas and just across the border into Colorado. There, on the evening of September 16, the force made camp on the Arickaree where it flowed through a shallow basin with good grass for the horses. The stream itself had only a few inches of water running in its bed; the only feature of the site worth noting at the moment was a low island about 20 yards wide and perhaps 100 long in the center of the creek opposite the camp, a place only a little higher than the

creek bed (on these plains, nothing was very much higher than anything else), covered with brush, and dignified by a lone cottonwood
tree at its lower end. Grover, the party's Indian scout, marked the island
as the one place suitable for a stand in case of attack, not because he
especially anticipated an attack, but because such things were his
business.

Forsyth had come closer to the Indians than he realized; he had
camped ten or twelve miles downstream from a very large village of
Sioux and northern Cheyennes with a few northern Arapahoes (the
tribes north of the Platte had not been able to resist the opportunity to
get in their licks against the whites). Indian scouts had sighted his
force, lost it, and then found it again in time to bring a dawn attack
screaming up the sandy bed of the creek.

Forsyth was up and awake and talking to his sentry when the first
Indians appeared, whooping and yelping. There was no total surprise
in this attack. Forsyth and the sentry yelled an alarm; thanks to their
good field of view they saw the enemy coming far enough away so that
Forsyth had time to get his men and their horses onto the island. Then
the yelling, pounding tide swept by, throwing up a cloud of mud, gravel
and spray from the shallow stream, and the battle was joined.

Forsyth's command was well armed, with seven-shot Spencer carbines as well as Army revolvers, and they met the onrushing Indians
with a very considerable amount of metal, working their weapons as
fast as they could fire. The island was so low that the red horsemen
could have ridden over it without difficulty, and they apparently
planned to do so, but the heavy fire discouraged all but a few so that
they split and thundered by on both sides. Two or three did gallop
straight down the length of the island, through the scrub brush and
among the scouts.

The Indians made two or three of their typical horseback attacks,
riding past the island hidden behind the off-side of their horses. More
damage, however, was done by natives who took up positions on the
banks of the creek behind bushes and tall grass and shot arrows or
guns from there. Forsyth ordered his men to dig pits for protection; in
the soft sand they were able to scoop out shallow entrenchments with
knives, cups, metal plates, or anything else at hand. It was during the
first part of the attack, before they had dug in, that the scouts suffered
most of their casualties. Major Forsyth was hit in his upper right leg
by a bullet; a few minutes later a bullet broke his other leg. A third

bullet grazed his skull, producing a slight depressed fracture that caused him terrible pain but did not quite put him out of action. Dr. Mooers, the surgeon, was hit in the head and from that time on was unconscious, although it was four long days before he drew his last breath. Lieutenant Beecher, the second in command, was mortally wounded. One man recalled—it was years later when memories sometimes play tricks—that Forsyth, after his skull had been broken, had cried out, "We are beyond all human aid, and if God does not help us, there is none for us."

All the horses were killed within the first hour. When night fell, the scouts counted three dead, two mortally wounded, another seventeen wounded in various degrees. The Indians appear to have had rather few losses, considering that there were probably somewhere between seven hundred and a thousand of them involved, and that they exposed themselves in several charges to the rapid-firing carbines of the scouts. They suffered one grievous loss in the death of their leader, Roman Nose. The great Cheyenne leader—no chief, but the bravest of the brave in war—was helped along in his valor, as so many Indians were, by the knowledge that great magic protected him from harm as he performed incredible feats of daring in battle.

Such magic was a powerful, but also a fragile thing, and Roman Nose's special medicine was rendered impotent if his food touched iron after being cooked. Visiting at the lodge of a Sioux chief just before the battle, he was served food which his host's wife had lifted from the cooking pot with an iron fork. He had eaten before he discovered the lapse; there was no time to go through the elaborate ceremony of purification necessary to renew his power.

Roman Nose remained out of the battle at the outset, but eventually he gave in to the entreaties of his men who were certain they could prevail if only he would lead them. The Cheyenne leader, knowing he was a doomed man, took his men on the next thundering charge and —just as any writer of melodrama would have had it—he was hit and fell from his horse, dead.

Superstitions of this sort made the Indian an erratic fighting man. He lived surrounded by strange powers to help or harm, and if his magic were vitiated, he might as well go home—and usually did— giving up the battle or the war. On the other hand, when the omens were right, he was prone to take unnecessary risks in the assurance that he was invulnerable.

However, at this moment it did not appear that the Indians would have to take many risks. If they were willing to wait a short while they could take the island with very little cost to themselves. When night came, Major Forsyth, still in command although in agonizing pain from his three wounds, told his men that their one chance of coming out alive lay in getting aid, and asked for volunteers to try to get through to Fort Wallace, 125 miles away. Pierre Trudeau, a man on the distant side of middle age, and Jack Stilwell, a nineteen-year-old, but both skilled scouts, agreed to try, and slipped away in the middle of the night.

The detachment deepened its defense works, collected a supply of meat from the dead horses, and dug a well so they could have water without having to expose themselves by crawling down to the shallow flow in the creek. When morning came, the Indians made a few horse-back charges, but without any great enthusiasm because the scouts were putting up a great volume of fire from their defenses. Thereupon the Sioux and Cheyennes dug their own rifle pits on the banks and settled down to a siege.

Firing went on into the third day, but now both sides were too well protected for any decision to be reached in that manner. Only one scout was wounded, but otherwise the plight of the defenders was turning desperate. The dead horses were beginning to stink, and the meat salvaged from them had likewise gone rotten. Some of the wounded were in extreme pain. That night, two more volunteers were sent to try to make it to Fort Wallace, for there was no way of knowing whether Trudeau and Stilwell had succeeded.

The Indians did not fire at the island on the fourth day. Once again they were demonstrating the inability of the Plains Indian to carry on a prolonged siege. Their tradition of battle was a tradition of action. The coming of the horse had not only turned the Plains Indians into buffalo-hunting nomads, it had also given them the instrument and the leisure to turn war into a great game—which is exactly what it was, a dangerous game, but still a game, with very formalized rules. For example, under those rules, no special honor accrued to the warrior who killed an enemy, but a man was acclaimed for "counting coup" on a dead enemy, that is, being the first to touch his body after he was slain, or for touching a live enemy. There were, of course, also wars fought with deadly purpose—to defend a hunting range from encroachment or the current conflicts to preserve something from the rapacious white

men—but even then the Plains Indian could not bring the deadly implacability of purpose to his fighting that the Americans did. To him,
battle was motion and excitement, the thunder of hoofs over the grass.
There was no prestige, no glory, no coups to be counted in defeating a
foe by starving him.

So, on the fourth day, the Sioux and Cheyenne warriors began moving away. On the island, Dr. Mooers, unconscious since he was shot
in the head early on the first day, at last quietly died. Forsyth, suffering agonies from one of his legs, took his razor and cut out the bullet
himself. All food was gone; a coyote that ventured too close and some
wild plums did not go far among forty-six men. The stench from the
putrefying horses had become almost unbearable.

An occasional Indian was seen on the fifth day, but there were none
at all after that. However, the detachment could not move out of its
defenses, because there was no way of knowing whether the enemy
lingered nearby; and even if the enemy was gone, they could get nowhere without food, without horses, and burdened with injured men.

On the morning of the ninth day, help at last arrived, the 10th U. S.
Cavalry, a Negro regiment.* Trudeau and Stilwell had made it through
to Fort Wallace. The first night they had walked backward in their
stocking feet so that if Indians saw their tracks they would think they
were made by moccasin feet going in the opposite direction. Thereafter
they were unable to wear their boots because their feet were in such
bad condition from cactus spines, so they wound strips of blanket
around their feet and kept going. On the evening of the third day they
reached a station called Cheyenne Wells on the stage road and waited
for the stage coach which took them the rest of the way in comparative
comfort; they arrived at Fort Wallace the next night.

The 10th Cavalry had been sent to the rescue at once; on the way
it met the other two scouts who had also made it safely through the
Indian lines. Five scouts were dead, including one who died of an
emergency amputation of his leg, performed immediately on the arrival
of the rescue force. Eighteen lay wounded amid the maggot-swarming

* There were two such mounted regiments, recruited when the Regular Army was
increased in size in 1866: the 9th Cavalry, Major Forsyth's regiment from which he
was on detached duty at the time of the fight, and the 10th Cavalry. They were
officered by whites but all enlisted men were Negroes; the 9th, especially, was a
crack outfit, although both had excellent records. The colored troopers were called
"buffalo soldiers" by the Indians from a fancied resemblance of their hair to that
on the head of a buffalo.

carcasses of half a hundred dead horses. All were suffering from extreme exhaustion.

Forsyth survived his wounds, although there were two years of pain before his legs were whole again. The head wound caused him headaches the rest of his life but he remained in the Army—he was breveted brigadier general for bravery in the battle—and would command in another famous engagement, though not so creditably, many years later.

The fight on the Arickaree River was called the Battle of Beecher Island (so named from the young lieutenant who, with the other four dead, was buried there), and the site is still known as Beecher Island.

Buried just as surely as the dead from the battle were Sheridan's plans to use "first-class, hardy frontiersmen" to fight Indians. After Forsyth's last-ditch stand, no more was heard about the scheme.

3. CUSTER'S FIRST STAND

Sherman took a simple and direct view of the situation on the plains. "We have now selected and provided reservations for all, off the great road," he said in September of 1868. "All who cling to their old hunting grounds are hostile and will remain so till killed off."

In a letter to his brother John, a United States Senator from Ohio, he was even more blunt, and would have had the Indian sympathizers of the East screaming for his hide if they had read it: "The more we can kill this year, the less will have to be killed the next war, for the more I see of these Indians the more convinced I am that all have to be killed or maintained as a species of pauper. Their attempts at civilization are simply ridiculous."

When the Peace Commission met in Chicago to tie up loose ends after finishing their year of treaty-making, five of the seven members agreed with Sherman that now the Indians should be given the stark choice of going on reservations or being killed. As Sherman argued, the natives had been given liberal treaties and large reservations in perpetuity, and still they were fighting. What more did they want? There is something almost quaint in the hurt indignation of the Commissioners over the refusal of the Indians to accept the latest treaties gratefully and at face value. The Plains tribes had signed other treaties and had been given other lands in perpetuity—for as long as waters run and the grass shall grow. Every other promise had been cynically broken. It occurred to many other officers fighting the Indians, but apparently never to William Tecumseh Sherman, that there came a time when Indians decided that the only way to keep anything was to fight for it.

It was a fight in which they could look for very little sympathy or understanding where it would do any good. General Grant was in Chicago and backed Sherman completely. It was absolutely necessary to protect emigrants on the plains, he said, "even if the extermination of every Indian tribe was necessary to secure such a result." Grant, as commanding general of the Army, was Sherman's superior; he was also Republican candidate for the Presidency and there seemed little doubt he would be successful in the election less than a month ahead.

With a clear go-ahead from above, Sheridan planned a campaign to drive the four warring Southern tribes back onto their Indian Territory reservations. He was outnumbered and he could not hope to match the warriors on the plains where their fast, light ponies could hit and run and be miles away before his cavalry could reach the scene. It was getting late in the season, however, and he decided on a winter campaign, a completely unorthodox kind of Indian fighting.

Jim Bridger, erstwhile mountain man, guide to emigrant trains, and lately scout at unhappy Fort Phil Kearny, was asked for expert advice and threw cold water on the scheme. So did other men who knew the plains and the Indians. But Sheridan's arguments made sense. In winter the Indians went into permanent camps; they could not flee very far nor fight very effectively with no feed for their ponies except the withered remnants of plains grass. Their villages could be destroyed and they could be beaten or starved into submission. It was a concept very familiar to the general who had gone through the Shenandoah Valley in 1864, turning it into a burned-out desert "so that crows flying over it . . . have to carry their provender with them." The phrase had been Grant's but Sheridan had done the work. Now he was going to try it out in Indian fighting.

The winter camps of the four tribes were believed to be concentrated just west of the Texas Panhandle, and probably along the Washita River. General Sheridan's strategy was one of which he was fond: three converging columns to sweep up and crush between them any Indians who might be out in the field. One was to come down from Fort Lyon in southeastern Colorado and march toward the Antelope Hills in northwestern Indian Territory. A second was to originate at Fort

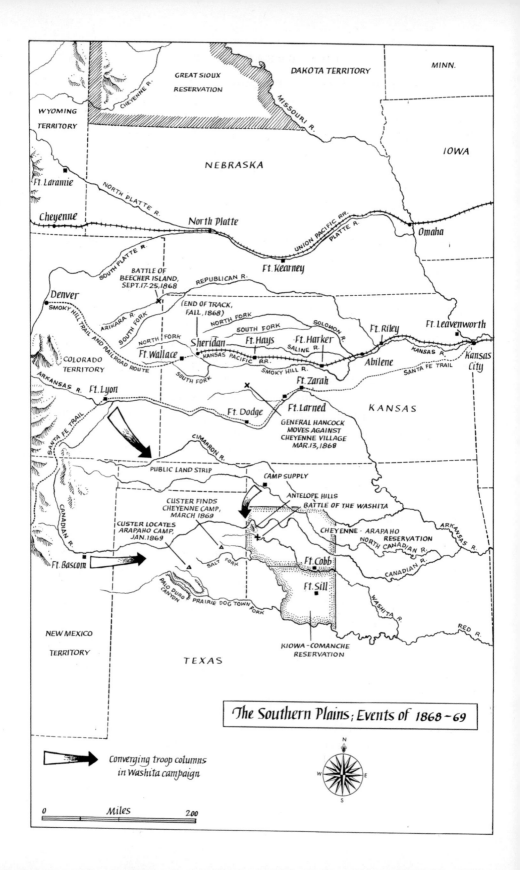

MINN.

GREAT SIOUX
RESERVATION

DAKOTA TERRITORY

CHEYENNE R.

MISSOURI R.

IOWA

WYOMING
TERRITORY

NEBRASKA

Ft. Laramie

NORTH PLATTE R.

Cheyenne

North Platte

UNION PACIFIC RR.

PLATTE R.

Omaha

Ft. Kearney

SOUTH PLATTE R.

BATTLE OF
BEECHER ISLAND,
SEPT. 17-25, 1868

REPUBLICAN R.

Denver

SMOKY HILL TRAIL AND RAILROAD ROUTE

(END OF TRACK,
FALL, 1868)

ARIKARA R.

SOUTH FORK

NORTH FORK

NORTH FORK

SOUTH FORK

SOLOMON R.

Ft. Riley

Ft. Leavenworth

COLORADO
TERRITORY

Ft. Wallace

Sheridan

Ft. Hays

Ft. Harker

SALINE R.

KANSAS PACIFIC R.R.

Abilene

KANSAS R.

Kansas
City

SOUTH FORK

SMOKY HILL R.

SANTA FE TRAIL

ARKANSAS R.

Ft. Lyon

Ft. Zarah

Ft. Dodge

Ft. Larned

KANSAS

SANTA FE TRAIL

CIMARRON R.

GENERAL HANCOCK
MOVES AGAINST
CHEYENNE VILLAGE
MAR. 13, 1868

PUBLIC LAND STRIP

CAMP SUPPLY

ANTELOPE HILLS

CUSTER FINDS
CHEYENNE CAMP,
MARCH 1869

BATTLE OF THE WASHITA

CANADIAN R.

CUSTER LOCATES
ARAPAHO CAMP,
JAN. 1869

CHEYENNE - ARAPAHO
RESERVATION

NORTH CANADIAN R.

ARKANSAS R.

Ft. Bascom

SALT FORK

Ft. Cobb

CANADIAN R.

WASHITA R.

PALO DURO CANYON

PRAIRIE DOG TOWN FORK

Ft. Sill

RED R.

NEW MEXICO

TERRITORY

KIOWA - COMANCHE
RESERVATION

TEXAS

The Southern Plains; Events of 1868~69

Converging troop columns
in Washita campaign

N
W   E
S

0   Miles   200

Bascom in New Mexico and follow the Canadian River across the Texas Panhandle. The third and main column was to operate from a base established north of the Antelope Hills by an advance element. The base was named Camp Supply; its location is well commemorated today by the community of Fort Supply, Oklahoma. The main force operating out of Camp Supply was to consist of the 7th Cavalry with eleven companies, five companies of infantry, a train of 450 wagons, and the 19th Kansas Volunteer Cavalry, commanded by Colonel S. J. Crawford, such a fire-snorting believer in the benefits to be gained by killing Indians that he had resigned as Governor of Kansas to head the regiment. The Kansas regiment was one of the few formed after Sherman had laid down his firm rule that any volunteer units would serve under firm Army control, with Army pay and allowances. Sherman authorized the unit because of the frequent Indian attacks on railroad construction crews in Kansas.

Sheridan may have been a bit nervous about his decision to conduct the first winter campaign against Plains Indians. "I deemed it best to go in person, as the campaign was an experimental one—campaigns at such a season having been deemed impracticable and reckless by old and experienced frontiersmen," he wrote, "and I did not like to expose the troops to great hazards without being present myself to judge of their hardships and privations." He took the Kansas Pacific as far as Fort Hays in central Kansas, then, with an escort, traveled south for six days to Camp Supply. During the first two days, the weather was mixed rain and snow, so wet and windy it was impossible to make a fire, but nothing other than personal discomfort marred the trip.

Even in Indian country, the Army remained the Army; officers observed protocol and made their courtesy calls on their newly-arrived commanding officer. There was even a concert by the 7th Cavalry band, blaring away in the snow that had begun falling just after Sheridan's arrival.

Back in command of the 7th Cavalry was Lieutenant Colonel George Armstrong Custer (but still entitled to be addressed as "General" by virtue of his brevet rank). Custer would never achieve full command of the 7th but it made little difference, for the colonel of the regiment, for various shadowy reasons, never appeared on the scene. Custer had returned after completing his year of penance, more like a hero than a man who had been punished. General Sheridan sent a telegram to Custer at his home in Michigan:

Fort Hays, Kansas, September 24, 1868

General G. A. Custer, Monroe, Michigan

Generals Sherman, Sully, and myself, and nearly all the officers of your regiment, have asked for you, and I hope the applications will be successful. Can you come at once? Eleven companies of your regiment will move about the first of October against the hostile Indians, from Medicine Lodge Creek toward the Wichita Mountains.

P. H. Sheridan, Major General Commanding

Custer arrived six days later, to be told by Sheridan that the General relied completely on him and would allow him to act on his own judgment on the coming campaign. It was more an expression of Sheridan's confidence in Custer than the carte blanche it appeared, but it was still a hearty welcome home. Custer had served under Sheridan in the Shenandoah Valley, and in the fighting from Petersburg to Appomattox when his division had played a large part in blocking the retreat of the Confederate Army. His dashing type of leadership had appealed to Sheridan—at least the part visible to him—because he had been that kind of commander himself: everywhere on a foam-flecked horse, urging on the faltering, shoring up a threatened breach in the lines, riding from Winchester twenty miles away.

Custer immediately took up the work of fashioning the 7th into a unit. It had never fought together as a regiment before; now he worked to give it that all-important element called *esprit*. One of his devices was to "color the horses," a cavalry term meaning to give each company horses of the same color. Another was to reward the forty best marksmen of the regiment by making them an elite unit which rode separate from the rest of the regiment and was excused from guard and picket duty. Of such details are military morale built. It is worth noting that the officer who had driven men to desertion a year earlier was now giving them pride of company and regiment.

Sheridan waited two days for the Kansas Volunteers; when they failed to arrive he decided to go ahead without them. On the morning of November 23, the 7th rose to a cold three o'clock reveille, with the snow a foot deep and still falling. Three hours later the column set out, its band playing the 7th's regimental song, "Garry Owen," a tune that sounds vaguely as though it would be more at home on bagpipes, and with words about carousing through the streets of Limerick, breaking down doors, beating up the bailiff, and other delinquencies.

Custer's orders from Sheridan were to go south to the low range called Antelope Hills, then head toward the Washita River. Any warriors not killed in battle were to be hanged; all women and children were to be taken prisoner; all villages destroyed, and all ponies killed. These were brutally explicit orders. Sherman could lose his temper and talk about extermination; Sheridan could coldly put extermination into effect.

General Sherman's own policy was rather high-handed; he had personally declared that the portion of the Medicine Lodge Treaty which permitted the Indians to hunt buffalo anywhere south of the Arkansas River was abrogated; he had ordered all four tribes to concentrate around Fort Cobb on the Washita River, and had declared that any bands which did not comply would be considered outlaws. Thus, Sheridan's orders to kill and hang were not directed against tribes which had made war the past summer, but against any which Custer happened to find camping off the reservation. The Comanches and Kiowas had had almost nothing to do with the fighting in Kansas (though they had raided south in their continuing war with Texas), and a number of Cheyenne and Arapaho bands had remained aloof from the fighting. However, the Army subscribed to the genial theory that one Indian was as good as another for purposes of punishment, and neither Sherman nor Sheridan was going to change the system.

On the twenty-eighth, Major Joel Elliott, who had commanded the 7th during Custer's year of suspension, found the trail of a large band of Indians while scouting along the Canadian River near where it crossed the Texas border. When Custer was informed, he sent word back to Elliott to keep on the trail, detailed about eighty men to guard the wagon train, made each man leave his overcoat with the wagons and take on a small pack of hard biscuit and coffee for himself and grain for his horse, and set out with the main part of the regiment to catch up with Major Elliott.

It was long after dark before they came up with Elliott, who had stopped because his Osage Indian trailers were certain an Indian village was only a short distance ahead. The advance was resumed, very cautiously, with the Osages well in advance till about 1:30 A.M., when the trailers reported a village among the trees lining the Washita River. Custer turned the regiment about, eight hundred men moving as quietly as possible and trying to muffle the creaking of saddles and gear, and withdrew to a safer distance, where he divided the command into four columns which circled to take up positions at separate points around the village. After a long wait through the bitter night, during which the men were forbidden even to stamp their feet, the trumpet sounded the charge at dawn, the band swung into "Garry Owen," and the regiment closed in, cheering and shooting, from four sides.

The village was that of the Cheyenne chief, Black Kettle, who must have sprung awake to the sound of the attack convinced that a nightmare was repeating itself; it was his band that had been camped at Sand Creek. This time Black Kettle had come to the end of his trail and died trying to defend his camp. Although caught completely off-guard, the Cheyennes recovered quickly and began a spirited return fire. Many of them jumped into the icy, waist-deep waters of the Washita and used the banks as breastworks. Others took advantage of trees, hollows, and other protection. Captain Louis Hamilton was killed at the beginning of the action; Lieutenant Tom Custer, who suffered a minor wound, was one of two officers and a dozen enlisted men hurt during the fight.

Women and young boys took part in the desperate fighting, but the odds were too great and the surprise too overwhelming for the Cheyennes ever to have had a chance. Even so, Indian resistance continued on the edge of the camp through mid-morning. Major Joel Elliott took a detachment of nineteen men in pursuit of a group of Indians and disappeared behind a rise of ground; gunfire was heard indicating that he had caught up with his quarry. There were a white woman and boy in the camp as captives; they were slain by Indian women to prevent their rescue.

As soon as resistance had been beaten down, the regiment set about the methodical destruction of the camp—there were forty-seven Cheyenne lodges, two Arapaho and two Sioux. Custer, in his report made out later, gives a very complete inventory of all that was destroyed, so precise, in fact, that one wonders how the regiment found time to count everything in the confusion and excitement. Some of the items he listed were: 1,100 buffalo robes, 4,000 arrows, 500 pounds of powder, 1,000 pounds of lead, tons of dried meat, 875 ponies. The lodges and the combustible materials were put to the torch; the rest was thrown into the river.

The work of destruction went on now at an increasingly frantic pace. The number of Indians on higher ground overlooking the village had been steadily increasing, and Custer learned the reason from cap-

tive squaws: Black Kettle's village was only the first in a series of
Cheyenne, Arapaho, Comanche, and Kiowa winter camps along the
Washita. Little fault can be found with the way Colonel Custer organized and carried out the attack on Black Kettle's village. However, as
a regimental commander, he had other responsibilities besides yip-
yipping at the head of a charge, and one was to reconnoiter his ground.
For several hours during the night he had kept his command, including
white and Indian scouts, standing around idle waiting for dawn, when
a short scout up and down the river, no more than a mile, would have
revealed the situation. Custer was prone to overlook the duller details
of command. The lapse was not a costly one this time, however, for
the Indians were still overawed and outnumbered and made no real
effort to attack.

Over a considerable period of time, shots were heard in the distance,
plainly from the guns of Major Elliott and his detachment who were
somewhere engaged with Indians. The fact was duly reported to the
commanding officer several times, but Custer made no move either to
send a strong detachment out, or to move to the rescue with the entire
regiment. He later explained that, among other reasons that would have
made it dangerous to have gone in search of Elliott was a shortage of
ammunition—yet at the time his men were engaged in shooting 875
captured Indian ponies. No one ever accused Custer of cowardice;
the abandonment of Elliott and his men remains unexplained. But from
that day on, there were officers and men in the 7th Cavalry who no
longer trusted their commanding officer completely, or felt that they
could depend on him in time of real trouble.

It was getting late in the afternoon; the men were feeling the cold
without their overcoats, and the Indians from other camps were still
gathering. To disengage himself, Custer marched the regiment, band
playing (sometimes it seems that the real heroes of the 7th were its
band), straight down the valley toward the other camps. The surprised
warriors withdrew before the advance; then Custer countermarched
back through the destroyed village, leaving the Indian warriors well
behind him. At two o'clock in the morning he deemed it safe to make
camp for a few hours, then continued on to join up with the wagon
train.

Custer sent scouts ahead to announce the victory to General Sheridan, and to say that he would like to pass in review before the commanding general when the 7th arrived at Camp Supply. With his flair

for the flamboyant gesture, he turned the review into a small Roman triumph. The Osage guides, in bright clothing and paint, carrying fresh scalps on lances and firing their rifles into the air, led off the procession. The white scouts came next, followed by the band playing the inevitable "Garry Owen," then Colonel Custer and his staff, next the captured women and children, then the sharpshooters' corps, and finally the regiment, company by company. Sheridan was well-pleased both with the review and the results of the campaign.

Colonel Custer's official report claimed 103 warriors killed, a figure considered completely ridiculous by many plainsmen for a camp of fifty-one lodges, for it was ordinarily reckoned as a rule of thumb that there were two warriors to a lodge, and there was not any doubt that a great many warriors escaped. On the other hand, his report said nothing at all about women and young boys being slain, although an unknown number were—in some cases, at least, in pure self-defense by soldiers who were being fired on by women or boys. The 7th lost two officers and nineteen men killed, three officers and eleven men wounded.

There had never been any real doubt about the fate of Major Elliott and his detachment, but any small uncertainty was removed when Sheridan moved on farther into Indian Territory on December 11, nine days after Custer's triumphal return to Camp Supply, and passed within eight miles of the devastated village. With Custer and an escort, he visited the site. It was a shambles in the literal meaning of the word. The smell of smoke and death hung over everything. Thirty bodies still lay amid the charred debris, and the frozen carcasses of almost a thousand horses lay over a large area. Some distance away the bodies of Elliott and his command were found, stripped naked and mutilated.

The punitive force continued on toward Fort Cobb, in the northern part of the Comanche and Kiowa reservation. The Comanches were now assumed to be at peace again, but the Kiowas were fleeing in panic before the avenging columns of Sheridan and his long-haired cavalryman. General W. B. Hazen, commanding at Fort Cobb, finally halted the nemesis with a dispatch to Sheridan. All Kiowas south of the point the expedition had reached were friendly, wrote General Hazen, and had not been on the warpath that season.

Sheridan and Custer were not happy at being stopped, but Hazen spoke in a loud voice that could not be ignored: he was Sherman's own appointee, and he was not a typical Indian agent of the kind the military scorned so much, but an Army man who was performing this duty while he recovered from a wound—a wound received fighting Indians.

A number of Kiowa chiefs, including Satanta and Lone Wolf, the head chief, accompanied the courier who brought General Hazen's message, and the disgruntled Sheridan made one belligerent gesture still possible: he had the two chiefs seized and brought in to Fort Cobb as prisoners. There was, apparently, a bitter quarrel between Sheridan and Custer on the one hand, who claimed at first that Satanta and Lone Wolf had been at the Washita fight, and General Hazen, on the other, who quickly set them straight by informing them that the two chiefs had slept in his tent during the night that had ended in the massacre, well over a hundred miles away. But if Sheridan could not hang the Kiowa chiefs for being present at the Washita, he could use them as hostages; he announced that he would hang them unless all Kiowas still at large came to Fort Cobb within two days. Runners were sent out to find and inform the scattered bands of the danger to the chiefs; all hurried to the fort within the time specified, and Satanta and Lone Wolf were set free.

The Cheyennes and Arapahoes had also fled, but they had no one to stand up to General Sheridan and insist on fair treatment for them. Their agent was a mere colonel, and he had resigned—and well he might, for he had proven to be extremely bad luck for his charges. He was the unhappy Colonel E. W. Wynkoop. Through no fault of his own he had played a part in the massacre of Black Kettle's band at Sand Creek; three years later, in spite of all he could do, he had been involved in General Hancock's clumsy blundering which had destroyed a Cheyenne camp and started a war. Once again he had tried, only to have his work shattered again in the moment when the 7th Cavalry swept down on a sleeping Cheyenne camp to the unearthly blare of "Garry Owen."

Wynkoop had resigned because his life, he said, would no longer be worth anything among the Cheyennes; after the three episodes they would be convinced he had been deliberately betraying them and would kill him for revenge at the first opportunity. He insisted that Black Kettle, despite all his reasons to be bitter, had not joined in the summer's hostilities, but had continued to work for peace.

On the other hand, defenders of the night attack pointed to the captive white woman and boy in the camp who were ruthlessly murdered when the soldiers attacked, as well as to scalps of whites and to various other proofs of depredations. There is no way of knowing where the truth lies. It was perfectly possible, in a society as individualistic as that of the Plains tribes, that Black Kettle's village contained several young braves just back from a summer on the warpath even though the leading chief of the band deplored war and had kept most of his men at peace.

General Sherman completely backed up his two officers in the field. He wrote to Sheridan on December 23, saying that the captives, stolen horses, and other trophies found in the village proved it to be a war camp: "I am well satisfied with Custer's attack, and would not have wept if he had served Satanta and Bull Bear's band in the same style. I want you to go ahead; kill and punish the hostile, rescue the captive white women and children, capture and destroy the ponies, lances, carbines &c &c of the Cheyennes, Arapahoes and Kiowas; mark out the spots where they must stay, and then systematize the whole (friendly and hostile) into camps with a view to economical support until we can try to get them to be self-supporting like the Cherokees and Choctaws."

At the same time, there was a roar of criticism in the East when the news of the attack became known there. The so-called humanitarians were soon referring to the Washita attack as another Sand Creek Massacre. Possibly some echo of this criticism came back to Sheridan and Custer, or perhaps it was the result of their confrontation with General Hazen, but the two men ignored Sherman's sanguinary exhortation to go out and kill more Indians. They also lost their own former fervor to do the same thing, decided the tribes had learned their lesson, and set about bringing the Arapahoes and Cheyennes onto the reservation. Custer, against Sheridan's better judgment, went out in mid-January with his forty sharpshooters, a few scouts, and a pack train of mules with supplies. His object was to talk rather than bludgeon the tribes into submission.

It was a new role for the cavalry commander. So far his concept of dealing with Indians had been to kill them; now he was going to be forced to rely on diplomacy. From warrior he had become peacemaker. And he carried out this difficult assignment in a manner greatly to his credit.

The fleeing tribes had gone west, toward the upper Red River. The camp of the Arapahoes was located first, on Mulberry Creek in the Texas Panhandle. Custer went through the long business of sitting with the chiefs in council and convincing them they should go onto the reservations. Patience won out; they gave their promise that they would go back, following their leading chief, Little Raven.

The small detachment went on. Their mounts gave out; they ate horse meat and continued on foot but still no sign of Cheyennes. At last Custer gave the order to return to Fort Sill, a new post which the expedition had built during January and February to replace Fort Cobb; it was south of Cobb and just about in the center of the Kiowa-Comanche reservation. After Custer's return, Sheridan at last headed back toward Fort Hays, turning operations over to Custer.

The cavalry commander went out into the field again, but this time with the entire 7th Cavalry and the 19th Kansas Volunteer Cavalry. The Kansas regiment, however, was mounted on shank's mare. It had finally turned up at Camp Supply, a week too late to take part in the Washita raid because it had become lost in the snow that was falling at the time; it had wandered around for days and had lost 700 horses from exhaustion and exposure. The event gave considerable satisfaction to Sherman who considered that it vindicated him in his continuing opposition to those who argued that state militia could do as good a job of policing the frontier as the Regular Army. As the force moved out on March 2, the Kansans were getting a taste of soldiering at its toughest.

At last, after many days of searching, the column's Osage trackers found a trail where two or three Cheyennes had traveled, then one where twenty or thirty had passed with lodges and families, but the scratch marks of the travois poles had grown faint because the winter wind had sifted dust into them for two weeks. By that time a third of the 7th had lost its horses and the men were trudging along on foot like the Kansans. Custer stayed doggedly with the old trail; at last it brought them to the Cheyenne camp.

Because he was riding well ahead of his command, and because he was George Armstrong Custer, he rode with a single orderly down into the broad valley, making the sign of friendship. The Colonel began a long council with his unhappy hosts, while the soldiers on the edge of the village and the Cheyennes quietly jockeyed for position. Custer had three warriors seized as hostages to force the Indians to give up two white women captives believed to be hidden somewhere in the camp; he threatened a hanging the next sunset unless the women were produced. The bluff worked and the captives were released, whereupon

Custer did a double cross and announced that he was still keeping his three hostages and would not turn them loose until all Indians were back on the reservation.

There was no way the Indians could be made to go in then, late in March, with the grass still sere and useless to feed their ponies. Custer accepted the pledge of the Cheyennes that they would come in as soon as the grass turned green enough for traveling—always remembering that he held three of their leading warriors, Dull Knife, Big Head, and Fat Bear, to make sure they complied. The force started toward home; both Arapahoes and Cheyennes did come to the reservation later by themselves. Custer had accomplished his difficult task without firing a shot.

The 7th and the Kansas Volunteers moved north across the plains where the iron-hard grip of winter had been broken and the buffalo wallows were filled with wind-rippled water left by melting snow. They reached Fort Hays on April 7, but Custer's great and good sponsor was not there to welcome him. On his way back from Fort Sill to Fort Hays, General Sheridan had been met by a courier bringing him the message that he had been promoted to the command of the Division of the Missouri. Grant had just been inaugurated President; Sherman had succeeded to the post of commanding general of the Army vacated by Grant; Sheridan had moved up into Sherman's former command.

They were not changes that promised much comfort to the Indians.

VI

Ten Million Dead Buffalo

---

1. PHILANTHROPISTS AND WARRIORS

THE Indian Service had, almost from its beginning, been notorious for inefficiency and corruption. From time to time, attempts had been made at reform, but they had always foundered on the inertia of established bureaucracy and the opposition of too many men reluctant to give up a lovely opportunity to put some of the public money into their own pockets.

On his inauguration in 1869, Ulysses S. Grant became the latest person to attempt some reform of the Indian Service. His program was a simple one; it aimed only to improve the caliber of the men serving as Indian agents. The means which were to be used to accomplish this laudable and long-overdue reform appear quaintly naïve to a more skeptical generation; religious denominations were to be asked to submit lists of nominees, and from these lists Indian agents were to be appointed. The plan soon became known as the "Quaker Policy" because the Society of Friends took over responsibility for the first two agencies; surprisingly, it worked well enough to produce a definite improvement over several years in the general quality of men serving as agents, although it was not able to produce miracles.

An honest man who became an Indian agent could expect little more than that virtue would be its own reward, for the pay was pitifully meager, and living conditions could seldom be called luxurious. Political patronage-seekers clamored after agency posts only because there were so many attractive ways of diverting a steady stream of Indian Bureau money into their own pockets, but an honest man who planned to live on his salary would not eat very high on the hog.

To the extent that the Quaker Policy replaced corrupt and indifferent agents with honest men honestly concerned for the welfare of the Indians under their charge, it was a success. However, corruption in the Indian Service was not limited to the agencies. At times it reached the Commissioner of Indian Affairs in Washington himself, and extended on down to agents and sub-agents in the most remote posts.

Frauds were perpetrated and funds misappropriated, often with complete indifference to public opinion. In 1867, Congress made an investigation of Indian policy and a subsequent report was prepared by the Commissioner of Indian Affairs. The following excerpt describes the activities, not of a mere agent, but of the superintendent for the entire Territory of Idaho:

> The credit of the Indian Department is utterly destroyed, and the tribe is greatly disaffected toward the government, . . . Mr. O'Neill, who is the only Indian agent within the territory, is utterly powerless to remedy the evils. The regulations of the department require him to conduct his correspondence through the Superintendent of Indian Affairs for his district. "Caleb Lyon of Lyondale," who is governor and ex-officio superintendent of Indian Affairs, has not been heard of in Idaho since last spring.
>
> His absence from his post, however, seems to entail no embarrassment on the management of Indian affairs. When present, he conducted them with an ignorance unparalleled, and a disregard of the rights and wants of the Indians, and of the laws regulating intercourse with them, deserving of the severest rebuke. . . .
>
> I have examined invoices and purchases made by the department or its agents in eastern cities, where the prices charged were from fifty to one hundred percent above the market value of good articles. Upon examination of the goods, I have found them, as a general thing, worthless and deficient in quality. "Steel spades" made of sheet iron; "chopping axes" which were purely cast iron; "best brogans" with paper soles;

"blankets" made of shoddy and glue which came to shreds the first time they were wet. . . . Many articles were purchased which would be utterly worthless to the Indian . . . ; in one case forty dozen pairs of elastic garters were sent to a tribe in which there was not a single pair of stockings.

There is no record that "Caleb Lyon of Lyondale" suffered even a mild chastisement for his gross abuse of his office. But the corrosion had eaten into much higher places. It was somewhat ironic that Grant, who was going to clean up the Indian Service by starting at the ground floor and getting honest agents, should before his term ended have both his Secretary of the Interior and Secretary of War forced out of office because of corruption in connection with Indian affairs.

Along with his Quaker Policy, Grant turned a hospitable ear to those who advocated a peaceful approach to relations with the Indians. A special committee of philanthropists (the word "philanthropist" acquired a special connotation during this era and came to mean a person interested in the welfare of the Indians) had been appointed to advise the government on Indian policy; this Board of Peace Commissioners had prominent supporters who could marshal powerful political forces if necessary, and was able to make its weight felt in Indian matters. But the great, onrushing current of events was too powerful for such a group to stem or divert.

For, when it came down to it, no Board of Peace Commissioners or any other organization of Eastern philanthropists, no Quaker Policy or other reform on the agencies was going to save the Indian as long as he stood in the way of Western pioneers. Indian sympathizers might improve his condition while he was on a reservation, but nothing was going to protect him when settlers decided they wanted the reservation itself.

To Westerners, of course, any hint of softness in Indian policy was idiocy. Strong voices among them were still insisting that the best way to solve the whole Indian problem would be to put an attractive bounty on scalps. Far too many rapacious, land-hungry whites considered Indians little more than annoying vermin, to be got rid of without inhibitions as to methods. When the Nez Percés demanded that treaty terms be enforced to evict whites who were squatting on their reservation lands, a Boise, Idaho, editor wrote indignantly against such presumption, and proposed that a shipment of blankets infected with smallpox be obtained. The good citizens of Idaho would see, he said, that they were distributed among the Nez Percés where they would do the most good.

A fight occurred between Indians and frontiersmen at a Montana trading post shortly after Grant's pro-Indian policy became known and cursed in the West. Several warrior dead were left behind, and the victorious defenders demonstrated their sentiments, if not their superiority to the barbaric red man, by cutting off the heads of the slain enemy, pickling the ears in whiskey (for reasons not made clear), and boiling the flesh from the skulls. The bleached skulls were then inscribed with what the Montanans considered apt, and probably hilarious, sentiments: "I am on the Reservation at Last," "Let Harper's Tell of My Virtues," and "Horace Greeley Knows I'm Out." (*Harper's* Magazine and Greeley's New York *Tribune* gave sympathetic treatment to the Indian and his problems.) There was also a more cryptic legend; "A good-looking half-breed, the son of a very distinguished Peace Commissioner," which appears to be a sly reference to some imagined miscegenation.

So much for philanthropy and understanding as far as the West was concerned, and so much for the Peace Commission. All the humanitarians back East would do the Indian very little good because the Westerners were going to continue to play the tune he would have to dance to.

While Sherman was disgruntled with the administration's Indian policy, he soon had worse worries. Grant's first Secretary of War remained in office only a few months, and was succeeded by William W. Belknap, who very shortly began to operate as though William Tecumseh Sherman, commander of the Army, did not exist. Belknap had served in the Western armies during the war, much of the time under Sherman's command. He had been an excellent officer and had been promoted to brigadier general by war's end. Hence, frustration during his military career could not have moved him to act as he did.

Whatever the cause, he not only acted as War Secretary but also as commanding general, handling even such minor details as the appointment of commanders of minor Western posts. Sherman tried to get Grant to intercede and straighten out the lines of authority but his old commanding officer was much surrounded now by prosperous-appearing men with diamond stickpins. He was always glad to reminisce with Sherman about old times at Shiloh or in front of Vicksburg, but on the Belknap matter he said he was sure things would work out but that it wouldn't be right for him to go over his Secretary's head. Sherman, a mere figurehead, was reduced to useless shuffling of papers on his desk, and finally moved his headquarters from Washington to St. Louis.

The beginning of Grant's term was a time of comparative peace on the plains, a lull of two or three years before the final series of wars. There was no complete tranquillity. Skirmishes occurred here and there; settlers were occasionally killed; cavalry patrols traded long-distance shots with bands of Indians. One small campaign was carried out, beginning late in 1869, when the 2nd Cavalry, commanded by Colonel E. M. Baker, took out after the Piegans, one of the three bands of Blackfeet, in Montana. Miners and settlers had been complaining; General Sheridan decided that a winter campaign was the best way to teach the natives to behave.

Baker and his cavalry found and struck a Piegan camp in January, killing 173, burning forty-one lodges. Almost immediately, curiously conflicting stories of the attack—it was not a battle; only one soldier was killed—began to be heard. The Peace Commission sent a man to investigate; he was told by an agent for the Blackfeet that 140 of the dead had been women and children; 18 were old men, and only 15 were men of fighting age. The agent, a Lieutenant Pease, was an Army man and hardly a hostile witness.

Colonel Baker denied that it was so; 120 of the 173 had been vigorous warriors. He deeply regretted that 53 women and children had died; every effort had been made to spare them during the battle but it was not always possible due to the fierceness of the fighting (witness that one dead cavalryman). General Sherman came to the support of Baker: "Did we cease to throw shells into Vicksburg or Atlanta because women or children were there?"

One additional but very important fact came to light. The Army refused ever to admit its truth, but it explains why the cavalry was able to take an Indian camp so completely by surprise that only one soldier was killed. It turned out that this was a friendly camp whose people had no idea they were to be attacked until it was too late to defend themselves.

On the southern plains, Sheridan's and Custer's campaign had driven the Southern tribes onto their reservations, but the Indians were showing no real inclination to settle down and become farmers. For one thing, the people themselves were not yet ready to give up their free ways; farming was women's work, hunting was for men. For another, the government was not doing much to help them make the transition. Agents more often than not promoted their own welfare more vigorously than they did the good of the Indians. Instruction in the crafts of civilization was lacking; much of the land was unfit for farming; and annuities were so often late in arriving or insufficient in amount that the tribes were forced to continue their buffalo-hunting ways in order to keep from going hungry.

The Kiowa and Comanche were the most intractable of the four tribes, at least at the outset. They continued to raid into Texas, killing people, running off stock, destroying property. The Kiowas committed acts of calculated insolence. Once they even attacked the Kiowa-Comanche agency at Fort Sill, drove off the agency cattle, killed and wounded several employees, and then challenged the soldiers at the adjacent Army post to come out and fight. In these displays of high spirits the two tribes were egged on by the Kwahadi Comanche, the fiercest band of the Comanches, who had never signed a treaty, and who roamed the Staked Plain of northwestern Texas and eastern New Mexico, the inhospitable high plains rising toward the Rockies. The taunts of the Kwahadi helped to keep their already high-strung reservation brothers stirred up, and the result was constant trouble. The situation became so bad that in 1870 (only a year after Custer and Sheridan had supposedly beaten and cowed the Southern tribes!) the Indian Commissioner proposed that a line of military reservations be established along the southern border of the Kiowa-Comanche reservation as a barrier to raiding into Texas, and that the two tribes be placed under military control until they had learned how to behave.

In May, 1871, General Sherman went to have a personal look at the situation—and narrowly missed becoming a casualty himself in another instance of Kiowa truculence and insolence. A band of 100 to 150 Kiowas, led by Chiefs Satanta, Satank, Big Tree and Eagle Heart, attacked a train of ten wagons of grain, about seventeen miles from Fort Richardson in north-central Texas and headed for the fort. If they had happened along about three hours earlier, they would have caught much bigger game: Sherman with a small escort had passed down the same trail on his way to Fort Richardson. As it was, the marauding warriors killed the wagonmaster and five teamsters; five teamsters escaped to the fort where Sherman heard the story and reacted in a characteristic way. He ordered the colonel in command to take 150

The Great Plains in 1870
Showing railroads, trails, strategic Army posts and the general ranges of the most important Indian tribes

APPROXIMATE RANGE
OF NORTHERN BUFFALO
HERD IN 1870

CHIPPEWAS

MILK R.

MISSOURI R.

MONTANA TERRITORY

BLACKFEET

Ft. Buford

YELLOWSTONE R.

DAKOTA
TERRITORY

MINNESOTA

CROWS

BIG HORN R.

POWDER R.

SIOUX

GREAT SIOUX
RESERVATION

BIG HORN MTS.

WYOMING TERRITORY

MISSISSIPPI R.

SHOSHONES

S I O U X

MISSOURI R.

N. PLATTE R.

UNION PACIFIC RR.

Ft. Laramie

NEBRASKA

IOWA

UTAH
TERR.

Cheyenne

North Platte

UNION PACIFIC RR.

PLATTE R.

Omaha

GREEN R.

S. PLATTE R.

REPUBLICAN R.

Ft. Leavenworth

Denver

KANSAS PACIFIC RR.

Ft. Wallace

Ft.
Hays

Ft.
Harker

KANSAS R.

Ft.
Riley

Kansas
City

UTES

COLORADO R.

COLORADO
TERRITORY

SMOKY HILL R.

Ft. Lyon

Ft. Larned

SANTA FE TRAIL

Ft. Dodge

KANSAS

SANTA FE TRAIL

CHEYENNES AND ARAPAHOES

PUBLIC LAND

ARKANSAS R.

Santa Fe

COMANCHES AND KIOWAS

INDIAN TERRITORY
(HOME OF 20 TRIBES IN 1870)

NEW MEXICO
TERRITORY

Ft. Sill

PECOS R.

RIO GRANDE

RED R.

TEXAS

APPROXIMATE RANGE
OF SOUTHERN BUFFALO
HERD IN 1870

0   Miles   300

cavalrymen and thirty days' rations and to keep after the raiders until he had hunted them down. He was to report to Sherman at Fort Sill on the Kiowa-Comanche reservation, four days' travel to the north.

The cavalry detail found nothing. Heavy rain washed out the trail of the raiders, and the colonel arrived at Fort Sill several days later to report failure. By that time, Satanta, Satank (the names mean, respectively, White Bear and Sitting Bear), and their fellows had already arrived at the Fort Sill agency (it was common practice to have an Indian agency adjacent to a military post). The agent, Lawrie Tatum, had admitted that the Comanches and Kiowas were no longer under his control and that without military restraint there was no way to keep them from leaving the reservation on raids. It was an admission that gave Sherman considerable secret satisfaction, although personally he respected Tatum as "a good honest man," for in his sight it proved once again that, while the Indian Bureau might feed and supply the natives, it was powerless to make them behave.

The raiders had come to the agency because it was the time for the regular issue of allotments. Tatum called the chiefs into his office and asked them if they knew anything of an attack on a wagon train in Texas. With no attempt to dissemble, Satanta replied that he had been the leader. In fact, he said, if any other Indian claimed the honor of having led that party, he would be lying, because he, Satanta, deserved all credit for it.

It could not have been put more plainly, nor much more arrogantly. Agent Tatum sent a message to the commandant of the Fort Sill military post, asking that the chiefs be arrested. Eagle Heart saw what was happening and fled, but the rest were captured, and Satanta, Satank, and Big Tree, with Sherman's full approval, were ordered to be sent to Jacksboro, Texas, the town immediately adjoining Fort Richardson, there to stand trial for murdering the teamsters.

Satanta was then past sixty. He was an unreconstructed savage who had remained true to the way of life into which he had been born, and he had lived a life more complete than most men even dream of, whatever their color. He had achieved his first fame as a warrior but had solidified his reputation through his ability in council and in diplomacy. He was one of the most skilled orators of the southern plains, and white Commissioners who had been sent to treat with the Southern tribes, as at the Medicine Lodge Council, found it difficult to answer his simple but incisive arguments. He had won from his people not only their respect but also a certain affection, and had been leading chief of the Kiowas for several years.

Satank, on the other hand, was quite generally feared and disliked in the tribe, because he was believed to possess magical powers and because of a vindictive nature. He was chief of the Kaitsenko, a Kiowa military society, and somewhat of a distinctive figure because, unlike most Indians, he cultivated a mustache and beard—a bit scraggly, perhaps, but very definite. A year before his arrest, his son, also named Satank, had been killed in a raid into Texas. Old Satank, with friends, went down and recovered the bones, which he wrapped in several fine blankets and put on the back of a led horse. After the old chief returned home, he had a tepee set up with a raised platform inside, on which he placed the blanket-wrapped bones that had been his son. Then he went out through the camp issuing an invitation to a feast, "My son calls you to eat." Thereafter, the bundle of bones was always on a platform in camp and on a led horse when the chief moved. He acted always as though his son were only sleeping.

For the trip to Jacksboro, Satanta and Big Tree were carried in one wagon, and Satank in another. A guard rode in the wagon with Satank, others were with the other two chiefs, and a squadron of cavalry and several Tonkawa Indian scouts rode beside the wagons. The small procession had not passed much beyond the gates of Fort Sill before Satank called to the other two Kiowas that he was a chief and warrior and too old to be treated as a child. Pointing to a tree where the road dipped to cross a small stream about a mile south of the fort, he announced, "I shall never go beyond that tree."

Although he spoke loudly, no one but the other two chiefs understood him; the post commander, in his wisdom, had neglected to send along an interpreter with three such important prisoners. He sang the death song of the Kaitsenko:

> O Sun, you remain forever, but we Kaitsenko must die.
> O Earth, you remain forever, but we Kaitsenko must die.

When the song was ended, he removed his manacles by wringing them off over his hands, at the cost of considerable skin and flesh and a great deal of pain. Then, suddenly producing a butcher knife which he had somehow secreted about his person, he attacked the soldier guard in his wagon, severely wounding that worthy. (Many Kiowas, who had long been convinced that Satank had occult powers, were ever after certain that he had swallowed the knife and disgorged it when it was needed.) He was struggling to get a shell into the chamber of the guard's rifle—not with any thought of escaping but only hoping to kill another American before he died—when the cavalry guard around the wagon recovered from its surprise and knocked him down with several shots. He lived for twenty minutes or so, in great agony, but without a groan or complaint.

Satanta and Big Tree made no move to court death or seek freedom, and arrived in chains, in due time, in Jacksboro. They were found guilty—a verdict it is hard to quarrel with—after a surprisingly fair trial, and were sentenced to die by hanging. There was an immediate and loud outcry among the pro-Indian groups in the East who considered the sentence too harsh and an incitement to Kiowa reprisals. Texans demanded that the sentence be carried out, but the philanthropists brought their influence to bear on the President, and Grant, who had seldom been able to resist pressure applied by prominent men, interceded strongly with Governor Davis of Texas. That bedeviled gentleman, pulled from several directions, succumbed to the political leverage applied by the President. Satanta and Big Tree were sent to the Texas State Prison for life.

Only it was not for life, or anything near it. The two chiefs had hardly been well established in prison before the philanthropists— "Lo! the Poor Indian advocates" they were often called in derision by Westerners—were calling for their release. Their continued imprisonment would only make the wild tribes more excited and unruly, it was claimed. Secretary of the Interior Columbus Delano appealed to Governor Davis to pardon the chiefs. Texans brought their own alarmed pressure to bear on the unhappy governor, and the state's legislature passed a joint resolution, without a single no-vote, asking Davis not to release the pair from prison.

Satanta and Big Tree were not important enough, in themselves, to cause such a ruction across the country. They merely provided a focus about which opposing forces could polarize: the philanthropists of the East, whose grandfathers had taken the land from the Indians so long ago that now they could afford the luxury of consciences; and the settlers of the West, who were still grabbing and finding the Indian a dangerous nuisance. But because the chiefs were such a focus, the big guns on both sides continued to roar. And once again, Governor Davis gave way to the Easterners rather than his own people, and freed the two. Whereupon William Tecumseh Sherman, who could become more indignant than anyone else, sat down and, pen jabbing the paper, shot off a short but hot letter to the Texas governor:

> I believe in making a tour of your frontier, with a small escort, I ran the risk of my life, and I said to the military commander what I now say to hat I will not again voluntarily assume that risk in the interest of frontier, that I believe Satanta and Big Tree will have their revenge, if they have not already had it, and that if they are to have scalps, that yours is the first that should be taken.

The two chiefs were released in October, 1873. Almost immediately Texas newspapers were trumpeting loudly that they were leading raids again. A Quaker, Thomas Battey, who spent eight months or so among the Kiowa as a schoolteacher without accomplishing a thing except to establish very friendly relations with the Indians, wrote, "To my certain knowledge the latter [Big Tree] was at home, sick in his lodge, and the former [Satanta] enjoying, after two years' confinement in prison, the pleasures of the buffalo chase, on territory assigned for the purpose." Innocent or guilty, the two were going to be blamed for anything that happened from then on.

As a matter of fact, there was a sharp increase in the amount of raiding and the depredations not only by the Kiowas but by other Indians, particularly the Comanches, whose hate for Texas had not cooled with passing years. Some of it may have resulted from exuberance over release of the chiefs, who very possibly took part in it after Big Tree recovered his health and Satanta had had his fill of hunting buffalo. But the trouble on the southern plains had larger dimensions than the influence of a pair of impetuous chiefs on a tribe with a flair for homicide. The Indians were increasingly restive and resentful for a number of reasons, large among them the old matter of broken promises in regard to annuities, because food and goods arrived late, or in insufficient quantities, or sometimes not at all.

These things were serious enough, but they were not the main cause of the deep anger that was beginning to burn in the Southern tribes in 1873. White hunters were carrying out an unceasing mass slaughter of the buffalo herds; the plains people saw their way of living threatened as nothing that had happened so far had threatened it.

2. THE TIME OF THE HIDE HUNTERS

By the Medicine Lodge Treaty of 1867, the Cheyennes, Arapahoes, Comanches, and Kiowas, "as well as such other bands as might be located there," i.e., in Indian Territory, had been granted the right to hunt not only in the Territory, but also north into Kansas as far as the Arkansas River "so long as the buffalo may range thereon, in such numbers as to justify the chase." There, and out west of their reservations into the empty Texas Panhandle they continued to hunt, and there were buffalo in plenty for them. Now, only five years or so after the treaty, all that was coming to an end.

For years, the buffalo herds had been under heavy pressure, and had been decreasing in numbers. Many men had a part in their dwindling: meat-suppliers for railroad work gangs, so-called sportsmen, killers for commercial butcher firms, wanton killers who shot into herds for no reason other than the momentary excitement of seeing one of the great beasts stagger and drop. The Indians did their part; they were not the great conservationists they are made out to have been, and did a great deal of wasteful killing. Many early travelers tell of Indians killing buffalo for nothing but the tongue, and the maneuver of stampeding a buffalo herd over a cliff, when one was handy, killing far more animals than could possibly be used, was standard practice. A band of Western Cree in Canada so thoroughly wiped out the buffalo in their area by driving them over cliffs that they were forced to move to new hunting grounds; they chose the buffalo range of the Blackfeet who were thereafter their bitter enemies.

A special condition that did not help the survival of the herds in the slightest was the highly superior meat of the cows. Hunters who took the animals for food and not for sport killed the females almost exclusively until some herds that had been heavily hunted had three or four times as many bulls as cows.*

---

* Elizabeth Bacon Custer survived her husband by almost fifty-seven years, and spent every one of them glorifying his memory. Among other things, she wrote three books which, while giving valuable insights into Colonel Custer's character through her ingenuous revelations of his foibles, at the same time offer some of the purest moonshine in attempting to prove that the heroically dead love of her life was all that was brave, gentle, and noble. Witness this passage from *Following the Guidon,* relative to hunting buffalo:

. . . I hardly need say how careful the officers were not to shoot the cows. The reverence for motherhood is an instinct that is seldom absent from edu-

For these several reasons, the great buffalo herds were doomed to be eventually wiped out. Indeed, it was almost necessary that they should be, because great buffalo herds were not compatible with cities, farms, and railroads.

But there was still plenty of time, and plenty of land that no one would want for two or three generations, where small buffalo herds could graze and grow fat. Then, in 1871, a small technological development wrote the death sentence to the millions of bison still roaming the plains. A method of tanning buffalo hide to produce excellent leather was developed.

Until that time, buffalo skins had been used almost entirely with hair on, as sleigh and carriage robes, overcoats, cold-weather gauntlets, and the like. The tanning process was a painstaking one that had been left entirely to Indian women, and inroads on the herds for robes had not been catastrophically heavy. A small amount of leather had been made from hides but it was too soft for other than a few limited uses, as in belt drives for machinery. Then, in 1871, a young Vermonter named John Mooar, who had a wood-cutting contract at Fort Hays, became interested in buffalo hides. A friend, who hunted buffalo to supply meat for the post commissary, threw away the skins, and probably young Mooar's frugal New England soul was repelled by the waste. He and the hunter, James White, put together a bale of about fifty skins which they sent to Mooar's brother Wright in New York; Wright sold them to a tannery willing to experiment, and out of the tanning vats came a superior leather, suitable for shoes, saddles, upholstery, harness, or anything else cowhide had been used for until then. An order for three thousand buffalo hides at $3.50 each went to John Mooar and James White, and the rush for buffalo hides was on.

Dodge City, Kansas, became the outfitting point and market center for hide hunters by the pure coincidence that the rails of the Atchison, Topeka & Santa Fe had reached that point when the great new bonanza developed. The first passenger train rolled into Dodge City in 1872; it was held up several miles outside the raw new settlement by a buffalo herd said to be three miles long and two miles wide. The men in the train spent the waiting period happily shooting into the massed beasts, killing some, wounding and crippling many more, and starting small

cated men. Besides, I know too many instances in proof of the poet's words, "the bravest are the tenderest." Our officers taught the coarsest soldier, in time, to regard maternity as something sacred.

stampedes in which the herd trampled the injured members. When the track was finally cleared and the train puffed on, about 500 buffalo were left behind, thoroughly and uselessly dead.

It was not for long that trains were so inconvenienced, or passengers given a chance to enjoy such artlessly cruel slaughter. For when that first train arrived in Dodge City in 1872, the booming of the hide-hunters' guns was just getting under way in earnest—and very soon there were not enough buffalo along the rails to hold up a train. In the spring of 1872, a good bull hide was bringing $3.50 in Dodge City. It was a magnet too strong to resist. Every sod-shanty settler who had not made a crop, every drifter between jobs, every man looking for the pot of gold at the end of the Western rainbow, got himself a Sharps 50-caliber rifle, a supply of ammunition, a wagon and mule team or ox-haul to take out the hides he expected to get, and then set out to make his stake, sometimes alone, more often with a partner or two. The next year, 1873, was a panic year, and the stream of hopeful hide-men became a flood, each man expecting to recoup his blasted personal fortunes with a few loads of buffalo hides.

The inevitable happened. By September, 1873, the buyers in Dodge City were picking and choosing, and hides were worth only 80¢ to $1.50. A few months later, during the winter of 1874, bull hides were bringing only one dollar, cows sixty cents, a calf hide but forty cents.

There is something terribly wrong in the spectacle of a magnificent brute of a buffalo, which had withstood blizzards and bitter cold, drought and dust, heat and windstorm, at last sinking to earth to give up a hide worth a mere dollar—and a dollar which the hide-man as like as not spent on cheap whiskey or the charms of a dance-hall girl reduced to accepting the buffalo skinner trade. The picture is even more depressing when it is considered that during the first year or two only about one out of three or four buffaloes killed supplied a usable hide. So many inept amateurs were in the field that the majority of hides were lost by being ruined through clumsy skinning, or by spoilage through poor drying or by failure to protect against insect damage.

The hide hunter played his part in the opening of the West, just as definitely as did the mountain man, the sod-buster, and the cowtown marshal. But he was perhaps the most unattractive harbinger of civilization the frontier has known—and the frontier has not been famous for men and women sleeked down and smelling of cologne. "The great American buffalo hunter, fearless as a Bayard, unsavory as a skunk!"

Colonel Richard I. Dodge, commandant at Fort Dodge, saluted them. Over weeks and months of skinning buffalo, a hide man's clothing became impregnated with grease and tallow and liberally encrusted with blood. Since neither facilities nor his inclinations were conducive to frequent baths or laundry, he quickly became very gamey, not a good man to share a warm room with.

Hide outfits ranged in size from the loner, who preferred to do his own shooting and skinning, to large outfits which would establish a camp on the plains and then fan out for the day's shooting in units of a killer and three or four skinners. Once it was systematized, the killing of buffalo for hides was a pathetically businesslike operation in which the beast had not the slightest chance. The killer, having located a small herd, crept as close as possible on the leeward side of them, usually managing to get within about 300 to 400 yards before the sentinels became uneasy. Then the hunter settled down on the ground with his canteen, a supply of cartridges, and often an extra rifle, for a gun became overheated with continuous shooting.

By always selecting as his target the most uneasy buffalo, or the one that was starting to lead the herd away, the hunter could keep the stupid beasts completely bewildered while one after another of them staggered and went down. A skilled shooter, wise to the ways of buffalo, could often get nearly a hundred animals from a single stand without moving, and on several occasions hunters brought down more than a hundred. One man got 204 from a single stand, but this seems clearly a prodigy in a class by itself—although the same hunter, a Frank Nixon, also claimed to have killed 120 buffalo in forty minutes on one occasion, one every twenty seconds! Otherwise, the highest claim seems to be 121 from a stand, a very impressive bit of murder. Another mighty slayer of buffalo, one Orlando A. Bond, averaged 97 a day during two months in the fall of 1876 (no time off for Sunday devotions), a total of 5,855 animals. Bond kept five skinners busy at their greasy and bloody trade during this time; he suffered a just retribution by going deaf from the constant roar of his own rifle.

There was nowhere for the buffalo to go. An English sportsman, William Blackmore, traveled thirty to forty miles along the north bank of the Arkansas River east of Fort Dodge in the fall of 1873; he wrote: "There was a continual line of putrescent carcasses so that the air was rendered pestilential and offensive to the last degree. The hunters had formed a line of camps along the banks of the river and had shot down the buffaloes, night and morning, as they came to drink. I counted sixty-seven carcasses in one spot covering four acres."

The Indians came to bear the hide men a bitter hate which led to attacks on the hide camps and on skinners at work on the plains. The attacks became more frequent as the buffalo killers worked their way nearer to Indian Territory and to the Texas Panhandle. It did not take them long to get there. A number of outfits were on the Cimarron River at the southern edge of Kansas in 1873, and there was talk of pushing south to the Canadian River. The rights of the tribes to hunt in Kansas south of the Arkansas were just about a thing of the past, because in another year, at the most, the buffalo would not "range thereon, in such numbers as to justify the chase." What was of more concern to the Indians was the southwestward drive of the hide men. The remaining hunting ground of the tribes was in the Texas Panhandle, and the hunters were coming dangerously close.

Hide men were a tough lot. Some of them had already slipped across into the Texas Panhandle to look at the situation, and had come back with wildly enthusiastic reports of the great herds of buffalo roaming there. Parts of Kansas that had been carpeted with grazing buffalo a season ago were now great expanses of bones.* When a drought hit eastern Kansas very hard in 1873, the government sent soldiers to the rich bison grounds of the Republican River valley in western Kansas to shoot buffalo and ship back the meat for the relief of the striken settlers; the Army hunters found only a few forlorn buffalo amid uncountable stinking carcasses and half-bared bones left by the hide men.

With such a situation, the hide hunters were becoming worried, and the Texas reports had the same effect on them that news of a new gold strike would have on a prospector working a failing vein. However, the Panhandle was dominated by Indians, and white hunters were forbidden to enter it. Wright Mooar and another leading hide man, John Webb, went to Fort Dodge to talk to the commandant there, Colonel Richard Irving Dodge, to try to sound him out on what the Army's attitude

* For many settlers on land where the hide men had been active, buffalo bones were their first "cash crop," the one thing that carried them through the first lean years. They gathered the bones and sold them at the nearest railroad station, whence they were shipped to fertilizer plants for phosphates and to sugar refineries for carbon. Huge ricks of bones were piled along railroad sidings (one 12 ft. high, almost 12 ft. wide at the base, and ½ mile long was reported at Granada, Colorado), entire freight trains sometimes carried nothing but bones, and the Santa Fe alone hauled seven million tons of them in 1874, one year in a sad commerce that continued for many seasons.

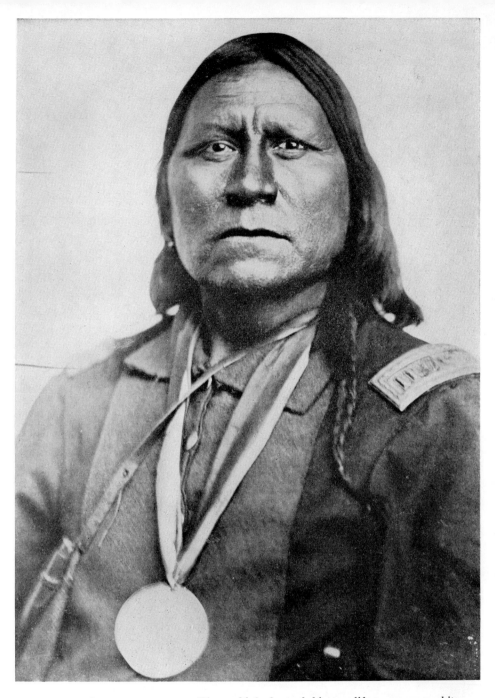

Satanta, tempestuous Kiowa chief who took his own life to escape a white man's prison. "I don't want to settle. I love to roam over the prairie. . . . These soldiers cut down my timber, they kill my buffalo, and when I see that it feels as if my heart would burst with sorrow." (Courtesy of the Bureau of American Ethnology, Smithsonian Institution)

Scarface Charlie, Modoc warrior. Although Charlie wanted to bring the Modoc War to an end, it was he who led the deadliest ambush of the entire conflict. (Courtesy of the Bureau of American Ethnology, Smithsonian Institution)

Sitting Bull, perhaps not the greatest, but certainly the most famous Sioux leader during a tragic period. The photo shows him in 1885 when he was just past fifty years of age; he was an embittered man, a prophet whose visions had been replaced by memories of past glories. (Courtesy of the Smithsonian Institution)

Chief Joseph, Nez Percé leader, won the deep respect of everyone but the bureaucrats. Said an officer who had once fought him, "I think that in his long career, Joseph cannot accuse the Government of the United States of one single act of justice." (Courtesy of the Bureau of American Ethnology, Smithsonian Institution)

Quanah Parker, Comanche warrior, was given his un-Indian last name because his mother had been a white captive. From chief of the most untamed Comanche band, he changed to become a leader in walking the white man's road when he realized the old days were forever gone. (Courtesy of the Bureau of American Ethnology, Smithsonian Institution)

Satank, a noted Kiowa warrior and chief—and one of the few Indians who cultivated a mustache. His own people feared and disliked him; he was believed to possess magical powers which he used for vengeful purposes. (Courtesy of the Bureau of American Ethnology, Smithsonian Institution)

Captain Jack, leader of the Modoc Indians in their long resistance to outnumbering Army forces. He asked for a reservation only six miles square; he got a noose and six feet of ground. (Courtesy of the Bureau of American Ethnology, Smithsonian Institution)

Gall, famed Hunkpapa Sioux warrior. His greatest hour came on the Little Bighorn when he was leading chief of the force that wiped out Custer's battalion. (Courtesy of the Bureau of American Ethnology, Smithsonian Institution)

Looking Glass, considered by some to be the greatest of all Nez Percé chiefs. He fought through the long retreat only to die by a chance bullet in the closing moments before the surrender. (Courtesy of the Bureau of American Ethnology, Smithsonian Institution)

Issuing rations to Sitting Bull's band at Fort Randall, Dakota Territory, in 1882. The band had returned from Canada the year before, and its members were still being treated as prisoners. The man in the foreground is apparently merely curious about the photographer. (Courtesy of the Bureau of American Ethnology, Smithsonian Institution)

Wood gatherers, women of Sitting Bull's band in 1882. The tepees indicate the destitute condition of the band on its return from Canada; all are of government canvas rather than the Indians' own buffalo hide. (Courtesy of the Bureau of American Ethnology, Smithsonian Institution)

Unconscious—an episode in the Ghost Dance. "As they danced to bring the new day nearer, the excess of their emotions sent many of them into trances in which they saw visions. . . ." (Courtesy of the Bureau of American Ethnology, Smithsonian Institution)

Aftermath of a massacre: collecting the Indian dead at Wounded Knee on New Year's Day, 1891. "A blizzard had swept over the Dakotas after the massacre, and the bodies were found partially covered with snow and frozen into the attitudes of violent death." (Courtesy of the Bureau of American Ethnology, Smithsonian Institution)

Gathering up the Dead at the Battle Field at Wounded Knee S.D.
Copy Righted by the North Western Photo Co.
Jan 17 1891 Chadron Neb

The slain Sioux Chief Big Foot lies at Wounded Knee like a man still struggling to rise. The "battlefield" was plainly tidied up before this picture was taken, for most of his band died with Big Foot under the rifles and cannon of the 7th Cavalry, and the area of greatest slaughter was immediately around where the sick chief was killed. (Courtesy of the Bureau of American Ethnology, Smithsonian Institution)

might be if they hunted into northern Texas. They found Dodge affable and full of questions about their business and its problems, but he volunteered no answer to their oblique questions. At last they were forced to ask him point-blank what the government might do if they crossed into Texas.

"Boys," said the Colonel, "if I were a buffalo hunter, I would hunt where the buffalo are."

So much for the protection the Indians could expect in preserving their hunting grounds. Dodge's slightly veiled proposal to the hide men to move across into the Panhandle was a deliberate invitation to trouble with the Indians, and he was not so naïve as not to have known it. However, he was not speaking carelessly and expressing only his own views; Sherman, Sheridan, and other (but not all) Army officers had taken the position that the quickest way to tame the roving Indians and keep them on the reservations would be to hurry up the extermination of the buffalo.

Mooar and a number of like-minded hide men did not care whose policy it was; it was sufficient that the Army would not cause trouble. When the plains dried out sufficiently the next spring—1874—to take the weight of the big hide wagons, the hunters left Dodge City and splashed across the Arkansas, heading south for Texas. The caravan, however, was not composed entirely of hide men. During the winter it had occurred to a trader named A. C. Myers that the Panhandle is a long way from Dodge City, and that a man on the grounds with guns, ammunition, and a hundred other things to sell would have the perfect market with no competition. Moreover, he would be able to buy the choice hides before the Dodge City traders ever saw them. Myers laid in a stock of goods and made ready. A blacksmith, Tom O'Keefe, was won over by the same logic of big demand and no competition and put his tools and forge in a wagon. A gentleman named Jim Hanrahan decided to operate a saloon at the post. Some time after the first contingent had left, another trader and hide buyer, Charles Rath, followed with a large stock of goods, and William Olds and his wife came to open a restaurant.

The post was built on the Canadian River in what is now Hutchinson County, Texas. Although it consisted of several structures of sod and small logs with a horse corral, it became known as Adobe Walls because it was located only about a mile from the remnants of an old adobe trading post built by the Bents in the long ago and soon abandoned, possibly in 1844. (There had been a battle at Adobe Walls in 1864 when Kit Carson had destroyed a Kiowa camp, and then had been lucky to escape with almost a full skin when the Indians had recovered from their surprise and had driven him into retreat.) A log-and-sod shanty is no palace but, compared to what the hide men were used to, it was high living—and at how many other camps was there a saloon at the end of the hard day?

The hunters and skinners fanned out from the post in the morning and came back at night if at all possible because these plains were not friendly. Indians hung around out of sight, waiting a chance to steal in, and two or three isolated parties lost lives and scalps. An attack on the post itself was inevitable, but when it did come, it had something of the accidental about it. In May, 1874, the Comanches were in a high state of excitement, not only because of the buffalo hunters and lagging annuity payments, but because they had come off second best in fighting with a small tribe called the Tonkawas during recent raids into Texas and had lost several men. The Tonkawas were the remnants of a tribe that had once been of much more consequence, but they had not lost their fighting spirit, as the Comanches had discovered. They were thoroughly hated by other tribes. For one thing, they had sold out completely to the white man, and served him as scouts on campaigns against any and all other Indians. Worse yet, they were, or had been, cannibals.

In the Comanche lodges, wives, sisters, and mothers of warriors slain by the despised Tonkawas wailed, blackened their faces, tore their flesh and otherwise mourned after their fashion, and called for revenge. And, contrary to the popular misconception of the Indian woman as a creature completely subservient to her man, she could bring to bear taunts and pleadings to which he was no more resistant than any tamed and civilized male today.

While the tribe was in a state of excitement and indecision over both the Tonkawas and the post at Adobe Walls, a young man named Isatai came forth from the untamed Kwahadi Comanche proclaiming himself a great medicine man. He could bring the dead back to life, said Isatai, and cure all diseases. He had been taken into the spirit world many times by the Father of all Indians, who had given him control over wind and rain, thunder and lightning, heat and drought, and other meteorological phenomena, which he could send down on the world as he pleased. He could protect his friends against the guns of the whites so that enemy bullets would fall harmless at point-blank range, and he could supply them with all the ammunition they needed by producing it in unlimited quantities from his stomach.

Now, they were rather strong claims which, if he could support them, would make Isatai a valuable man to have about. It would seem that someone of a skeptical turn of mind would have called on him for a demonstration, perhaps to reanimate a dead person, or bring on a rain out of a clear sky. Such are the capabilities of humans to delude themselves that the medicine man did not even have to face challenges. Many members of the tribe stepped forward to testify that they had personally witnessed these marvels; some had seen him rise into the sky to talk with the Spirit and later descend again; there were others who had watched in wonder as he produced almost a wagon load of cartridges from his stomach. After such testimonials, no Comanche dared question further, and many of the Cheyennes and Kiowas were convinced.

With the supernatural powers of Isatai on its side, the tribe began seriously to plan an expedition to take revenge on the Tonkawas. In May, the young medicine man called a meeting of the entire tribe where Elk Creek joins the Red River. So great was his reputation by then that all bands of the Comanche nation showed up, the first time in the memory of the oldest men that the entire tribe had met in council. Moreover, most of the Cheyennes were present, and part of the Kiowas. The Arapahoes, though, had had an end of fighting; they were doing their best to follow the white man's road.

Isatai told them that he had had another meeting with the Great Father, who had sent down orders with him that they should exact vengeance for their fellow warriors who had been killed by the Tonkawas. But there had been too much talking beforehand; word of the threat against the Tonkawas had reached the commanding officer of Fort Griffin (not far north of today's Abilene, Texas) near where the Tonkawas lived, and he had gathered the threatened tribe in under the fort's protection. The news reached back to the war party on Elk Creek before it had started out, but with war spirit at a high pitch, it was easy to change plans to an attack on the hide hunters at Adobe Walls instead.

However, enthusiasm for fighting white men was not what it had been a few years before, in spite of the bitterness the Indians felt. More and more, the thoughtful among them were coming to see that they never won, no matter how much right was on their side; in the end the soldiers always came to punish them. A number of the Comanche, including one entire band, the Penateka, were unhappy with the decision to attack Adobe Walls. Tonkawa scouts and cannibals were one thing; white men were something completely different.

The war leaders had anticipated that there might be some faint hearts, and had announced that they would prevent anyone from leaving before the attack was over, even if they had to kill all their horses to do so. They were determined this attack was not going to be ruined, as the one on the Tonkawas had been, by word getting out to the prospective victims. Nevertheless, many Comanches did manage to slip away, although the Cheyennes present remained resolute, and so, apparently, did the small group of Kiowa who were there.

As the planners had feared, the secret did get out. Traders were told of the council, apparently by Comanches who had stolen away from it, and they carried the word to Adobe Walls. But at that outpost of trade and meager comfort, the news was kept within a very elite circle: the Mooar brothers, the two traders, Myers and Rath, and saloonkeeper Hanrahan. These gentlemen considered the possibility that word of the impending attack might send all the hide men running back to Dodge City, leaving the post undefended, then decided to keep quiet. After all, they had a big investment to think about.

The warning of the approaching attack had come on June 18, and it had even had a date on it: June 27 appeared, from all signs, to be the most likely day. Indian raids increased. A pair of hunters were killed, then two more, and one day a raiding party followed the Mooars to the trading post from the prairie. The Mooars' nerve broke a couple of days before the day predicted for the attack. They loaded the big hide wagons, and in the morning headed the six-horse teams north toward Kansas and safety. They had been on the trail only a few hours when Myers and Rath, on horseback, caught up with them; the traders had succumbed to their own cases of cold feet.

Only saloonkeeper Jim Hanrahan was left of those who knew the secret—for some reason blacksmith O'Keefe, though also a founder of the trading post, had never been told of the warning. Even when the evening of the twenty-sixth came, he was reluctant to tell the men; if they waited up in the middle of the night for an Indian assault that never came (first morning gray was a favorite time for Indian attacks), he would be the butt of their heavy-handed humor. After all, the attack might not come on the twenty-seventh—or on any other day. On the other hand, he could not leave them—and himself—to be killed in their beds if it did come. Hanrahan's way out of the dilemma was ingenious. In the middle of the night he fired a pistol into the air, shouting that the ridgepole was breaking. Three or four men were sleeping in the saloon under the heavy sod roof supported by the threatened ridgepole; they were out in a hurry, and other men awakened by the commotion also appeared. It was warm weather and men were sleeping outdoors as well as in the buildings. No one questioned that the sharp report that had wakened them was the sound of wood cracking.

Someone found a pole suitable for propping the ridgepole even though it showed no signs of sagging or cracking, and Hanrahan served up free drinks to everyone to keep them awake. Several men decided that, since they were up, they might as well get an early start. It must then have been about three o'clock and the first hint of gray showing in the eastern sky, as two hunters walked out of the saloon, one to get things ready in the wagon, the other to bring the horses from the corral.

The two men saw the long line of Indians thundering out of the darkness at almost the same instant. Billy Dixon, at the wagon, had his buffalo gun with him, and got off one shot before he took to his heels and ran to the saloon. Billy Ogg, at the corral, had no weapon; when he saw the mass of Indians riding straight for him he did what any rational person would do and ran at top speed, also to the saloon. Then the roar and thunder of hoofs was around the buildings of the post, mounted Indians pounded on doors and windows, and the fight was on.

The supreme leader of the war party was the leading chief of the Kwahadi Comanche, a man named Quanah whom the whites, however, always called Quanah Parker because his mother had been a white woman, Cynthia Ann Parker, who had been captured by the Comanche when a young girl. Isatai had worked his medicine beforehand to assure success in the fight: all warriors had been bullet-proofed, and incantations had been performed so that the men at the post would be deep in sleep and all doors open. Isatai rode stark naked except for a little cap of sagebrush stems; it was all an essential part of his medicine. The picture is ludicrous; it is also pathetic, for by such forlorn and futile means the Plains people hoped to overcome the men who were ravaging the last of their buffalo country.

Two brothers, Ike and Shorty Shadler, haulers of freight, achieved their small immortality in Western history by being killed in the first charge, probably without quite realizing what was happening. They had arrived from Dodge City with a load of supplies only the day before, and had immediately reloaded with hides and were sleeping in their wagons, ready to start back as soon as daylight came. It never dawned for them; the wave of Indians engulfed their wagons and the brothers were killed and scalped.

There were left twenty-seven defenders, one a woman, forted up in three buildings, against an unknown number of Indians, probably somewhere between five and seven hundred. The first charge carried the warriors right up to the buildings, where they battered away at doors and windows, getting one partially open before being driven away. The defenders, as they overcame their first surprise and became organized, finally forced the Indians to retreat.

That was the only dangerous assault. There were some weaker charges later in the day, but the warriors seemed more interested in trying to recover some of their dead than in anything else. The heart had gone out of them with the discovery that Isatai was a false prophet, one more disappointment on a long trail of broken hopes. Isatai himself sat on his horse apart and did not enter the battle in spite of taunts which rose to loud jeers when his horse, in spite of a complete covering of bullet-proofing paint, was shot from under him.

A third white man was killed early in the day when the warriors were still dashing in close, but they soon stopping taking chances. The defenders were well protected and a number of them were equipped with rifles of tremendous power and range and were dead shots at long range. The warriors established a siege but it was not a very tight one, for hunters who had been out on the plains made their way in to the post, and a messenger was sent for help to Dodge City. Rescue forces, one of buffalo men from Dodge City, the other a cavalry detachment, set out for Adobe Walls. The Indians, as always, soon wearied of siege and drifted away. On or about the first of July, one warrior appeared about a mile away. Billy Dixon, who had sighted the first morning charge of the Indians, carefully rested his Sharps 50-caliber on a support, allowed for windage and extreme range, and pressed off his shot. The Indian brave tumbled from his horse. It was a shot that awed even the buffalo men, who always referred to it as

Dixon's mile shot, although measurement showed it to be 1,538 yards, a stone's throw scant of a mile, close enough for all but quibblers.

The defenders suffered their fourth and final casualty on July 2 when a party of Indians was reported on the plains and William Olds, the man who, with his wife, had come to Adobe Walls to start a restaurant, started up a ladder to the lookout post that had been established on the roof of one of the buildings. He was careless; the trigger of his rifle caught in something, and the gun went off. The charge caught him in the head and he tumbled down at the feet of his wife.

Soon after, the decision was made to abandon the post and leave the country. The hunters with their hides, O'Keefe with his blacksmith tools, Hanrahan with his liquor and his dreams of a nice profit, all went back to Dodge City. Behind them, drying on the pickets of the corral, they left the heads of twelve warriors, dead Indians the war party had not been able to recover. In August, almost two months later, Colonel Nelson Miles passed that way with troops and found the heads still on the posts, looking across the plains with hollow-socketed, lipless grins.

3. THE RED RIVER WAR—1874–75

The anger of the Indians following the Adobe Walls attack had spread to encompass all whites. More and more warriors were riding off the reservation, once again filled with the old dreams and illusions that the warpath was a road filled with glory. Raiding parties struck far from home, into Kansas, Colorado, New Mexico, as well as Texas, killing perhaps eighty persons. Most of the attacks were cruel and senseless ones, on white men who had nothing to do with killing the buffalo or with repressing the Indians, chance-met men whose only fault was that they were white. For instance, there was Patrick Hennessey who, with three other men, was taking a small wagon train of supplies from Wichita, Kansas, to the Wichita agency at Anadarko in Indian Territory when they were attacked by Cheyennes at a spot now commemorated by the town of Hennessey, Oklahoma. They were not enemies of the Indians; in fact, at that moment they were hauling food meant for red men, but they were nevertheless killed and scalped. Hennessey suffered death by torture on a pile of burning grain taken from the wagons, but it was not the Cheyennes who did the torturing. Several Osages, members of a tribe that had been walking the white man's road for years, came along during the attack. They took charge of poor Hennessey, and put him to death with savage cruelty. There were, apparently, deep resentments even in tribes which had been assumed to be completely tamed.

There was no unanimity in this last journey down the warpath. Whirlwind, an important chief of the Cheyennes, came in to the Cheyenne-Arapaho agency at Darlington with his followers and settled down, refusing to have anything to do with the conflict that was breeding, and two or three other bands of Cheyennes joined them, although in general the Cheyennes were to be the staunchest fighters in the days ahead. The Arapahoes, after fighting white men for many years as loyal allies of the Cheyennes, at last decided that they had had enough of being whipped and bloodied. They remained completely friendly, and moved in to the Darlington agency where they furnished a police force that stood guard every night till all danger was past.

Neither did the other two tribes show any singleness of purpose about making war. Probably as many as three-quarters of the Kiowas (including the entire Kiowa Apache band which refused to join in any more fighting) declared themselves friendly. Early in July, after the tribe's annual religious convocation, the Sun Dance, most of the Kiowa, except for a minority under Chiefs Lone Wolf and Swan, had come in to their agency at Fort Sill to declare themselves for peace, and had been duly enrolled as friendly and directed to camp near the fort. A large number of Comanches had also come in and been enrolled, and were also told to set up their tepees in the friendly camp. Any Indian who came in later would not only have to give up his arms but would have to convince the agent that he had not committed any warlike acts.

On July 21, the order came from Sheridan's headquarters to carry out active military operations to punish the hostiles, even to pursuing them onto the reservations. General Pope, in command of the department, at once began organizing troops for a vigorous campaign.

Every Indian conflict seems to have some blunder or stupidity that makes it worse than it need be, and this was no exception. In late August, before there had been any important contact between warriors and soldiers, a number of Comanches of the Nokoni band came in to the Wichita agency at Anadarko to surrender. The agency served the Wichitas, Caddoes, Delawares and Pawnees, and on this day, because it was ration day, a large number of Comanches and Kiowas were also present. So, too, was the commanding officer and a detachment of troops from Fort Sill, some thirty miles to the south, come to keep order during the distribution of rations.

The agent explained to the surrendering Nokoni Comanches that they would have to give up their weapons, and this they readily agreed to. A number of guns had been given up when the question arose as to whether bows and arrows would have to be surrendered too. Apparently there was no rancor in the dispute, and a messenger was sent to the commanding officer to obtain his interpretation. While his return was awaited, the Nokoni chief—his name was Red Food—gave a whoop. Afterward, the Comanches insisted the chief was merely calling to another chief; the military insisted it was a warwhoop and a signal for an attack, something that seems unlikely because Red Food would hardly have waited until many of his men had given up their guns before calling for action. No one ever learned from Red Food what he meant for the result of his whoop was disastrous to him; he was immediately shot down by soldiers.

Infuriated Indians began shooting at soldiers. The fighting spread, although it was only Kiowas and Comanches who became involved; the other tribes had lost their taste for combat long since. Warriors burned the agency school and several houses belonging to friendly Indians, looted a store, killed four civilians and wounded several soldiers. Not all took part in the fighting; many fled, but others continued the attack the next day before finally giving up the attempt to capture the agency. Some of those who had run from the fighting returned to Fort Sill where they had been enrolled as friendlies before going to Anadarko without permission; they had been innocent bystanders and were permitted to return without reprisals. But most of those who had been present, even though they had been friendly and had avoided the fighting, kept going right out into the Panhandle to join the hostiles already there. The quickness of the military to shoot first and ask later was going to cost a number of lives.

Satanta and Big Tree, a year out of prison now, were caught up in the separation of the sheep from the goats, the friendlies from the hostiles. They, with their followers, had enrolled as friendlies at Fort Sill but the monotony of sitting in a camp while things were happening was too much for them. They left without permission and rode out along the upper Washita before eventually returning, not to Fort Sill but to the Cheyenne agency at Darlington. They did not like their own agency, they explained. There was no proof that they had taken part in hostilities while away, but with their reputations, and the truculent history of the tribe, it was assumed that they must have. They were treated as surrendered prisoners of war, their horses and weapons taken from them, and the entire band sent back to Fort Sill. Satanta, whom the military looked on as a hostage for the good behavior of all Kiowas, was sent back to prison in Texas for breaking his parole.

In the meantime, military operations were underway against the Indians on the Texas plains. Five columns, some three thousand troops in all, converged on the plains of the Panhandle, from Fort Griffin and Fort Concho to the south in Texas, from Fort Supply to the northeast and Fort Sill to the east, both in Indian Territory, and from Fort Union in New Mexico. The five columns operated more or less independently, with the sole mission of pursuing Indians, but Colonel Nelson A. Miles (brevet brigadier general) was in overall command. Miles personally commanded the force coming from Fort Supply, and had one of the first brushes with the Indians when he encountered them near the head of the Washita and drove them west in a running battle. A few days later, a strong hostile force attacked his wagon train. The wagons immediately went into corral and fought off the Indians—one of those scenes so dear to early motion picture makers, wagons drawn up in an oval with defenders firing through wheel spokes at circling warriors—until relief came after several days. The force moving from Fort Union also had a hard fight with Indians before finally defeating them.

But these Indians were not out on the plains for the purpose of fighting soldiers. Most of them wanted only to get away from them, the farther the better, and to return to an old way of life. Most of the places where they had roamed so freely within the memory of men still young and vigorous were shut out to them. The empty grasslands that had once seemed to go on forever, beyond where the sky bent down to meet the horizon, were no longer empty. Settlers and ranchers had moved into the most attractive stream valleys, and plumes of smoke and crawling strings of railroad cars moved across the once magnificently empty horizon. Even the buffalo were gone from the old places, slain by men who did nothing else but kill them from morning till night. But out on the Panhandle the old way remained, where there was still space and buffalo—if only white men could be kept out.

This northwest corner of Texas is more than an expanse of flat grassland; it has complexities that made the war against the Indians more mid-November a message to "ease down on the parties hostile at present," came from none other than William Tecumseh Sherman, that apostle of the heavy hand and spokesman for extermination.

An unusual engagement took place early in November when Lieutenant Frank Baldwin of the 5th Infantry was convoying a train of twenty-three empty wagons drawn by six-mule teams from the Red River to a supply camp on the Washita. He had with him a company of cavalry, one of infantry, and a howitzer, a force strong enough for protection against most attacks that might be expected. When the detachment reached a stream named McClellan Creek, it was met by its scouts who had come hurrying back with the information that the camp of Cheyenne chief Grey Beard was just ahead.

Lieutenant Baldwin was too near the camp to turn around and retreat, because if he were discovered and attacked while withdrawing he would be caught at an absolute disadvantage. On the other hand, even if he could commit every soldier to battle, his small detachment would still be greatly outnumbered by the Cheyenne warriors—and it would be impossible to send his entire force into action because it was necessary to leave a substantial detail at the rear to guard the wagons. Tossed between the horns of this dilemma, Baldwin found a third way out. He put his twenty-three wagons and his howitzer into line abreast, loaded the infantry into the wagons, and put the cavalry on the two flanks. Then, with the trumpet sounding the charge, the whole fantastic line of battle swept over a rise in ground and bore down into sight of the startled Cheyennes in their camp, with teamsters and infantrymen yelling, and cavalrymen whooping and shooting as soon as they got within range.

Audacity paid off. The terrified Indians did not stop to assess the force bearing down on them, but turned and ran, abandoning the camp and everything in it to Baldwin's onrushing line of battle. The Cheyenne warriors paused only once to give battle, and then just long enough to hold the Army forces while women, children, and old people got away. At last, after a pursuit of a dozen miles or so, the last Indian warriors faded away into the plains.

In the abandoned camp, Lieutenant Baldwin found two very small white captives, Adelaide and Julia German. The German family homestead on Smoky Hill River in Kansas had been attacked in September by a wide-ranging band of Cheyennes who had killed parents, a son and one daughter, and had taken four other daughters captive.

The two small girls had been separated from their older sisters at the time of their capture and had not seen them since.

The war went on through the winter, until the last important group of reservation Indians still at large were Cheyennes. Their breaking point under the constant harrying and driving came in March, when their leading chief, Stone Calf, came in with the entire part of the tribe still at large. In surrendering, they gave up the two older German girls, aged fifteen and seventeen, who, for half a year had, as the journals of the period would put it, "suffered all the unspeakable horrors of Indian captivity." Those horrors were very real. A woman could usually expect to find herself traded from brave to brave, and her lot was not at all mitigated by the jealousy of wives whose beds she temporarily usurped and who took every opportunity to cuff the captive about and load her down with onerous tasks. In his treatment of women captives, the best that could be said of the Plains Indian is that he was not a whit worse than his white brother.

Colonel Nelson Miles later became guardian of the four German girls. They were installed in a comfortable home at Fort Leavenworth, and to assure their support, Congress authorized that an amount sufficient to take care of them be withheld from the annuities of the Cheyennes.

As the Cheyennes came into their agency at Darlington after their surrender, they were disarmed and their horses were taken from them. But they gave up mostly bows and arrows; there was enough guile left in them that they had hidden most of their firearms before they came in to the agency. Physically, they had resisted until they had nothing left to fight with. Their agent wrote:

> A more wretched and poverty-stricken community than these people presented after they were placed in the prison camp it would be difficult to imagine. Bereft of lodges and the most ordinary cooking apparatus; with no ponies nor other means of transportation for food or water; half starved and with scarcely anything that could be called clothing, they were truly objects of pity; and for the first time the Cheyenne seemed to realize the power of the government and their own inability to cope successfully therewith.

However, events soon proved that there was still fire in the Cheyennes. In its constant and usually clumsy and heavy-handed attempts to devise ways to keep the tribes under control, the military had come up with a new dodge at the close of this, the Red River War. It had been decided that the best way to render the tribes incapable of making war again would be to strip them of their leadership, to select the men most responsible for the war, and send them into exile. The Cheyennes were required to provide thirty-three; two more came from the Arapaho, but for other crimes since that tribe had remained aloof from the conflict.

The selection of the Cheyenne prisoners to be exiled was done at Darlington agency on April 6, with the two older German girls present to help in picking out culprits who should be sent away. But by the end of the day the task was still far from complete; only fourteen men had been selected, and one woman, whom the German girls had spotted in the crowd of onlooking women and children and recognized as having taken part in the murder of their family. But the officer in command, Lieutenant Colonel Thomas H. Neill, decided to call a halt to the chore for the time being, and, in order that no unfinished business would appear on the record, he ordered that eighteen men be arbitrarily taken from the line to complete the required quota of thirty-three. Naming the men to be exiled, he said, would be continued later; then the unhappy eighteen would be replaced by men identified as deserving punishment.

Colonel Neill, what with this and that, did not get around to resuming the selection; other matters kept coming up, until finally he decided one Indian was as good as another and concluded to let things stand. On April 9, the thirty-three prisoners, including the unlucky eighteen, were brought out to have balls and chains fastened on their legs. As the warriors were led, one by one, to the blacksmith to have shackles riveted on, Cheyenne women taunted their men for submitting tamely to being fettered like animals. One young warrior, the possessor of many coups, Black Horse by name, was stung by the scorn of the women enough to knock the blacksmith aside and attempt to get away. A volley from the soldier guards caught him, but their aim was not the best; Black Horse was seriously but far from fatally injured. The Cheyennes began an attack on the guard with bows and arrows, and even with a few guns that had somehow appeared from concealment, and then, while military reinforcements were being sent for from Fort Reno (built the previous year, 1874) only two miles away, the Indians hurriedly fled to sandhills on the opposite side of the North Canadian River where they had hidden most of their firearms when they had come in to the agency and surrendered.

There was a sharp fight, with several killed on each side. The Army forces brought up Gatling guns; the Indians, already destitute after their long resistance on the Texas plains, fought off the troops till dark when they fled—men, women, and children—once again. Colonel Neill reported that about 2 5 0 warriors, with their families, left the agency. Many of them soon surrendered again but a small band headed for Dakota country. Traveling across the plains was not what it had been a few years ago—or for that matter, even a year ago, things changed that fast. The buffalo were virtually gone in Kansas—wiped out by the hide hunters; there were ranchers and farmers to avoid; telegraphs reported the movement of a band of Indians far ahead of them.

Lieutenant Austin Henley with a detachment of the 6th Cavalry and about twenty-five buffalo hunters attacked the fugitive Indians while they were camped on the Sappa River in northwestern Kansas. There, in a murderous onslaught with annihilation as its purpose, the soldiers and hunters disregarded Indian attempts to surrender, shot down every person capable of defending himself, and then dragged wounded women and infants from pits under the river bank and clubbed them to death. Some escaped, and with others who had not been at the Sappa camp, eventually found haven with their brothers, the Northern Cheyennes.

The Sappa River afterwards was a bitter name to the Cheyennes, a Sand Creek on a smaller scale. The Army never boasted about it either. Lieutenant Henley's official report said that nineteen men and eight women and children had been killed, but only after the Indians had refused to surrender. Two soldiers were killed in the line of duty. There was no mention of buffalo hunters. However, it was impossible to keep rumor down, and some of the buffalo men claimed that the number of dead Indians was around a hundred—some said more, some less—and that most of them were women and children. It was not an engagement the Army was especially proud of.

The naming of the thirty-three most guilty Cheyenne leaders for exile never was resumed. Those already selected (except for Black Horse who had broken away and precipitated the entire flight), together with the eighteen poor devils who had been grabbed at random to fill out the quota, were sent to ancient Fort Marion in Florida.

There were still a number of Comanches out, most of them Kwahadis who had never submitted to the government and had never been on a reservation. Although the band had taken a leading part in the attack on the trading post at Adobe Walls, it had spent most of its time during the war far out on the Staked Plain. It was a vast country and a miserable one for an army to operate in. At one time, Colonel Miles' command became so tortured by thirst while operating on these plains that men opened their own veins to get blood to relieve their thirst. This was the home of the Kwahadi Comanches, men made lean and tough from living on the stark, high plains. The Army was never able to bring them to bay; the best it could do was to keep them on the move so constantly that they had difficulty hunting, and wore out or lost much of their camp equipment.

Colonel Miles at last gained by diplomacy what he was not able to get by force of arms, sending scouts out to treat with the Comanches and argue the case of peace on the reservation as against war and privation for themselves and their families. In April, almost two hundred came in and gave themselves up. Another message sent out with an experienced plainsman reached Quanah Parker, leading chief of the Kwahadis, who was himself becoming convinced that remaining at war was slow suicide. He led his band in to Fort Sill, arriving there on June 2. They turned over their weapons and 1,500 horses and mules, an indication that they were not destitute. Actually, while their equipment was shabby, they had lost very few men in fighting, and only about twenty had been captured; all the rest had surrendered voluntarily.

With the Comanches—and the Kiowas—a surrender was a surrender; there was no burying of weapons to be used in another outbreak. Both tribes were required to send their leaders responsible for the outbreak off to exile as the Cheyennes had, and nine Comanches and twenty-six Kiowas were selected. The list of Kiowas selected to go was a joke to almost everyone except those whose names were on the list. The chore of making the selection was turned over to Chief Kicking Bird, who had long been the leader of the peace faction among the Kiowas. He picked half a dozen chiefs who had been notorious in the fighting, but for the rest he shielded his friends by naming men of no importance, many of them Mexicans who had been captured and made members of the tribe.

The prisoners joined the Cheyennes in Florida at Fort Marion. Their captivity was not onerous. There was no close confinement; the prisoners were merely kept under a general surveillance. They were released in May, 1878, after three years. Even so, it had not been an easy exile. The strange climate and separation from friends and families caused many to sicken and die.

Eastern philanthropists took a great deal of interest in the prisoners while they were there, and tried to give them a smattering of white man's civilization and a large dollop of Christianity, it being considered a truism that no Indian could accomplish anything worthwhile without first becoming a Christian. Some of the younger men were persuaded to remain on when the rest were permitted to return, some in private homes, some in the Normal Institute at Hampton, Virginia, a Negro school which became an Indian school as more young tribesmen were brought in. The experiment was considered so successful that a year later, in 1879, the famous Indian school at Carlisle, Pennsylvania, was started to carry on the work permanently.

And what of the one other warrior who was put in prison during those times? Satanta remained in the Texas penitentiary; no one came this time with an offer of amnesty. His first imprisonment of two years he had borne with equanimity, but after he was sent back in 1874, he was an embittered old man who argued that many others were much more guilty than he, and that he had, in fact, kept his parole and had not turned his weapons against the white man again. In 1878, finding imprisonment too much to bear after a lifetime of roaming the plains, he leapt to his death from an unbarred upper window.

Oddly, it was Quanah Parker, chief of the Kwahadi Comanche, the most completely untamed of all Indian bands until the Red River War, who was one of those best able to adjust to changing times. Once he became convinced that it was hopeless for Indians to attempt any longer to resist the advance of the white man's civilization, he became a progressive, counseling his people always to walk in the white man's road. It was popular to explain Quanah's progressiveness in terms of his "superior" white blood. This was poppycock. His mother may have been white but Quanah was pure Indian in culture, and he thought as an Indian.

There were, alas, limits to Quanah Parker's ability to abandon the comfortable old ways. He had, because of his prominence, been appointed a judge on a Court of Indian Offenses, one of the bodies set up at agencies to help the agents administer their Indian charges. The courts heard complaints against Indians who the agents felt were not making proper speed toward civilization—and many agents, with a

Caucasian myopia, considered the persistence of tribal dances, the activities of medicine men, even some Indian ways of dressing and wearing the hair, as prima facie evidence of savagery still unshed. Bigamy, of course, was a sure sign of a savage. Eventually the agent got around to inquiring into Quanah Parker's own household arrangements. He discovered five wives, living contentedly but unprogressively together.

This is ahead of the story, however. The trouble had started because the Indians had tried to protect their buffalo from the hide hunters, and in the end the buffalo were killed anyway. With the Indians driven back onto the reservations, and the Army completely happy to have the buffalo wiped out, the hide hunters had nothing to fear. Charles Rath, who had helped to set up the trading post at Adobe Walls, and Bob Wright, of a large and prosperous hide-buying outfit, established a post in the Panhandle on Sweetwater Creek. The enterprise prospered; a mushroom settlement grew up that not only supplied the necessary supplies to hunters but had three saloons and a dance hall that catered to the redolent skinners' primitive vices while two restaurants took care of their more conventional appetites.

The great Texas herd began to melt away under the deep booming of the Sharps Fifties. It did not take long; in the spring of 1878 the hide hunters looked about, incredulous, to discover that there was not going to be any buffalo hunting on the southern plains that year. Six years it had taken to wipe out the millions of bison that had ranged from northern Kansas southward into Texas and New Mexico. The mighty brown sea had turned into a nightmare of rotting, putrid carcasses, and at last into a vista of white bones. A few buffalo survived here and there in the isolation of the Staked Plain after the hunters had gone away to wipe out the northern herd. But these few were fair game to every roving cowboy and homesteader; what was apparently the last band, fifty-two in number, was killed by a hunting party in 1887.

So, from the close of the Red River War in 1875, no free Indians roamed anywhere on the southern plains. The magnificent horse-and-buffalo days were over forever south of the Platte River, in the land that had once seemed so measureless. And that same year when the end of freedom came for the Southern tribes, events were closing in on the Northern peoples to deprive them of what remained of the old ways.

VII

Diversion in the Far West

1. HOW TO START A SMALL WAR

WHILE events were leading toward war on the southern plains, the Army found itself involved in another Indian war in a very unexpected quarter, a flare-up of fire in old ashes far from the Great Plains. It should have been the most inconsequential of skirmishes, the United States against half a hundred warriors on the California-Oregon border. Instead, it turned into the most costly Indian war the Army had ever fought, considering the number involved. It was also, beyond doubt, one of the most humiliating.

As a general thing, the Indians of the Far West had not put up a very effective resistance to the settlers and prospectors who shoved them aside (there were notable exceptions), and the Indians of California were among the most vulnerable of all. It was their misfortune that they belonged to a hodge-podge of tribes, were poor, lacked the social organization to combine for defense, and were low in warlike spirit to begin with. It was their calamitous misfortune that they stood in the path of the gold rush, and that the gold-hunters included a high proportion of "hard cases": thieves, jailbirds, cutthroats, and assorted gallows bait.

In no other part of the United States were the Indians so barbarously treated and so wantonly murdered. There were an estimated 100,000 of them in California in 1848, the year it was annexed and gold was discovered. By 1859, there were only 30,000 left, a considerable accomplishment in only eleven years, and by the end of the century a scant 15,000. Indians were ruthlessly driven from their tribal grounds—and when they did attempt to resist by attacking isolated miners, the prospectors hunted down all natives in the area in the same joyous fashion they would have gone after jackrabbits. Women were brutalized by gang rapes; men were captured like animals and forced to do field labor, kidnaped children were treated as slaves.

Thus did the gentle and enlightening hand of white civilization touch and raise up the Indians of California. But not quite all the natives were so docile and easily victimized, and among the exceptions were the Modocs. The tribe lived in the area close around Tule Lake, a large shallow, reedy body of water astride the California-Oregon border (today most of it is drained) in a region whose terrain varied widely within short distances: lakes, small mountain peaks, areas of grassland, and, bordering the south shore of the lake, an area of strange and fantastic ancient lava outflows which today is set aside as Lava Beds National Monument. From the Tule Lake center the Modocs ranged over a radius of fifty miles or so in all directions in their hunting, and were not noticeably hospitable to white men who trespassed on their preserve. The South Emigrant Road, an alternate route for the western end of the Oregon Trail, skirted the eastern shore of Tule Lake, and the Modocs frequently hid among the jumbled boulders at the spot and ambushed wagon trains.

When prospectors made their way up the wild valleys of the Northern California rivers, the Modocs attacked them just as they had the emigrants, but the miners fought back a great deal more roughly. By fortunate happenstance, no gold was found near the heart of the Modoc range, or the tribe might have suffered near-annihilation like so many others. Instead, a mutual accommodation developed between miners and Indians. The Modocs became frequent and welcome visitors in Yreka, about sixty miles from Tule Lake; they liked the excitement of the busy, noisy mining camp, and in return they peddled their women to the miners, who provided an active market for such rental merchandise.

This last was one of the less endearing traits of the Modocs. When they began trading with other tribes early in the century, they made themselves brokers in female flesh because they had nothing to offer in the way of handiwork, pelts, feathers, or the other ordinary commodities. They brought girls and young women to the annual trade meetings, where the Northern tribes eagerly purchased the unhappy slaves for concubines. So, when they turned their women over to the miners, it was sanctioned by old custom and was not a depravity forced on them by white men.

While the miners and the Modocs worked out a fairly amicable relationship, the same was not so true of ranchers who began settling around Tule Lake, particularly to the north of it in Oregon. There, on a stream called Lost River which flowed into the lake, the villages of the Modocs were centered, close by lands the settlers were finding desirable. In such situations, the Indian was always the one who had to move out of the way, so in 1864 a treaty was negotiated whereby the Modocs moved to a large reservation whose nearest boundary lay about twenty-five miles to the north. The Klamaths, who outnumbered the Modocs about two to one, shared the reservation. The two tribes were much alike in language and customs, but that was the only way in which there was any closeness between them. The Klamaths were well pleased with the reservation since it was part of their original tribal range; the Modocs, to whom it was alien ground, were said to have signed the treaty very reluctantly.

Things did not go well for the Modocs on the reservation. This was partly due to an overbearing and bullying attitude of the Klamaths, partly to a struggle for leadership between two Modoc chiefs, Old Schonchin and one whose Indian name was Kientpoos but who was never called anything other than Captain Jack by the whites. Schonchin was more amenable to the direction of the agency officials and received their support; Captain Jack, nobody's man but his own, got fed up with things after a year and led his followers back to Lost River, declaring that his signature on the treaty had not meant a thing.

During the year the Modocs had been gone, more settlers had moved onto their old lands near Lost River and Tule Lake, and the return of Captain Jack and his band, about 175, caused a small panic. An appeal to the government to force the Indians back on their reservation got nowhere. The Army was busy with other concerns, and the Indian Bureau was pretty much indifferent. In four years, only twice did any Indian Bureau officials come to try to talk Captain Jack into returning; after a year, a subagent managed to make the fifty-mile trip from the agency, and after still another year, the Indian Superintendent for Oregon got around to calling. Jack was polite but adamant. In fact, he was so opposed to having anything to do with the reservation that when the first annuities came in 1867, he refused to accept them if it meant coming to the agency to collect them.

Four years after Captain Jack and his band had bolted the reservation, things were no more settled than the day they had left. His band lived in their villages near the mouth of Lost River, they hunted, the young men and women went in to Yreka for excitement, and they caused little or no trouble. But their presence was becoming intolerable to the ranchers in the vicinity, and it was unfinished business to the Indian Office. Then, in 1869, Grant became President and appointed a man named Alfred B. Meacham Indian Superintendent for Oregon. Meacham's immediate qualification was that he was a Republican faithful who had worked hard for Grant's election, but he had more pertinent qualities which showed up after he had been appointed. When he was young he had helped in the unhappy removal of the Sauk and Fox tribe from Iowa, but his real knowledge of Indians came from carefully observing them in the West and from a sincere interest.

Meacham was appalled at the conditions he found on the Klamath reservation, and set about putting them right. Gambling, polygamy, and all forms of slave-holding were forbidden, and he directed that any white man living on a reservation with an Indian woman should either marry her or give her up, a directive aimed not only at occasional traders but at widespread concubinage practiced by Army officers who purchased Indian girls to relieve some of the tedium of frontier duty.

Meacham also began a campaign against the ancient shamanistic or witch doctor practices of the Indians. This was not a bit of smug Christian superiority; shamanism had caused all manner of trouble and mischief and had frequently led to ritualistic murders. The campaign was quickly successful; when Indian agents ignored witchcraft countermeasures by the shamans and nothing happened to them, the prestige of the medicine men quickly declined.

After getting affairs in order around the state, Meacham at last went to see Captain Jack in December of 1869. He had asked the chief for a meeting and Jack had agreed, on the condition that the Superintendent would come to him. When he arrived, Meacham was accompanied not only by the agent from the reservation, but also by Old Schonchin, a small detachment of soldiers, and various auxiliaries.

The talks at Captain Jack's camp went on for two days. At the end of that time, Jack had agreed to try reservation life again, provided he could select the section on which his band would be settled. Actually, the decision was not all that simple. Curly Headed Doctor, the shaman with Jack's band, had spoken up to damn all white men and vehemently oppose any return. The Doctor, of course, had a big personal stake in the matter; he was a man of importance and influence at Lost River but he would not stand so tall on the reservation where Meacham's campaign against the shamans had had considerable success. At one point, Curly Headed Doctor made such inflammatory remarks that it appeared as though the Modocs were about to kill the white negotiators; at the critical moment, the detachment of soldiers which had been camped outside the village suddenly appeared and scattered the threatening Indians.

Jack brought his band back to the reservation, and Meacham did his best to see that things worked out this time. He arranged a ceremony of reconciliation between Jack and the Klamath chief, and tried to fill it with symbolisms of a new beginning between the two tribes. Jack appears to have tried sincerely to get along, but the Klamaths again took advantage of their superiority in numbers and their proprietary feelings about the reservation. They demanded that the Modocs turn over to them, as tribute, part of the wood they cut for their wickiups or shelters; they beat and taunted the women when they went to gather wild grain at the lake, and harassed the men when they went fishing.

Meacham had tried, but he was Superintendent for the entire state and could not remain to oversee events on one reservation. That was the responsibility of the agent, but that gentleman's attitude toward his job was that the less he had to do with Indians, the better. When Captain Jack went to complain about the way his people were being treated, he got neither help nor sympathy. Not only that, the agent cut off all rations to the tribe in April of 1870; the Modocs, he said, could go out and find their own food.

Whereupon, that same month, Captain Jack led his band back to Lost River again, loudly swearing for a second time not to have anything to do with the reservation. This time not only his own band went with him, but so many of Old Schonchin's band that the latter had to follow along or be a chief without anyone to lead. After a short time, though, the old chief and some of his people returned, and most of his band gradually trickled back to join him. Then, and only then, a solution to the problem came to the obtuse and slow-moving minds of the Indian Office bureaucracy. Schonchin and his people were given their own agency at Yainax, about thirty-five miles from the one the Modocs had formerly shared with the troublesome Klamaths. The answer was so simple, so effective—and it had taken so long to occur to anyone. A little sooner, and it would have prevented Captain Jack from going back to Lost River—and made the coming war unnecessary.

The reception of Captain Jack's band at Lost River was somewhat less than overwhelmingly cordial. More white settlers had come into the Tule Lake country, certain that the Modocs, at last, were gone for good. But Jack's band settled down again on Lost River, and there, overlooking the reedy waters of the shallow lake to the south, they built once again their lodges of earth and timber, odd, rounded structures entered by ladders through holes in the roofs.

The Lost River Modocs got along in relative peace with the ranchers, but the ranchers were not happy with the relationship. Indians often walked into ranchers' homes without warning and demanded to be fed; they flopped down on beds, or otherwise made nuisances of themselves, and frightened settlers' wives. They turned their horses loose into pastures, until some ranchers paid an annual tribute as the simplest way to be rid of this kind of harassment.

Jack refused to listen to further talk about returning to the reservation; twice was more than enough. His counterproposal was clear and uncomplicated. The Lost River country was the old land of his people, and he claimed he had never agreed to the 1864 treaty by which it had been given up. He was perfectly willing, however, to accept a reservation, provided it was on Lost River at the head of Tule Lake; he demanded a tract six miles square. Meacham supported it as a fair claim, even though there were several ranches on the proposed reserve. No one else, however, had a good word to say for the plan.

So once again time passed without decision, but a resolution of the problem could not be delayed much longer. The country was still sparsely settled, but there were by now enough ranchers to make themselves heard, and they were clamoring for protection. The military was not able to do much at the moment—far-Western posts had been stripped to send men to Arizona to fight Apaches—but the Army warned the Indian Bureau that something was going to have to be done, and soon, about Captain Jack's band. At last, in 1872, the Indian Bureau acted. A new superintendent, T. B. Odeneal, had replaced Meacham who had been sympathetic to Jack; in the summer he received orders to take Captain Jack's band to rejoin the rest of the Modocs at Yainax agency on the reservation, "peaceably if you can, forcibly if you must."

Odeneal sent one last mission to Captain Jack to ask him to come in to talk things over. His emissaries, a pioneer rancher named Ivan Applegate and another man, not only received a refusal from Jack but had the very harrowing experience of listening helplessly while the chief argued with firebrands who were all for killing the two whites and starting a war then and there.

When the pair returned to report their failure and the manner of it, Odeneal was highly upset by the talk of war by the Modocs, and went at once to Fort Klamath on the reservation to ask Major Green, the commanding officer, for troops to use against Jack's Indians. And for some unexplained reason, Green immediately complied with this request from a civilian, without first obtaining approval from his superiors (General E. R. S. Canby, commanding the Department of the Columbia, had specifically asked to be advised before soldiers were used against the Modocs). Major Green ordered Captain James Jackson to take Company B of the 1st Cavalry to Lost River, "to arrest Jack, Black Jim, and Scarfaced Charley by the next morning." (With few exceptions, the whites knew these Modocs only by nicknames they themselves had given them. A very few, like Old Schonchin, were known by transliterations of their Modoc names; none by translations of their Indian names into the Yellow Horses, Standing Bears, Great Hawks, and the like so familiar in other tribes.)

Within a short time, Captain Jackson was on his way with some forty officers and men, a small pack train, and five packers. On the way they were joined by about fifteen ranchers. It was November 28 —a freezing rain was falling that turned worse as gray day turned into night, until soon it was freezing on men and horses. Captain Jack's village was on the west side of Lost River almost at its mouth on Tule

Lake. Directly on the opposite bank was the village of Hooker Jim, a subchief of Jack's band.

Captain Jackson asked the ranchers to remain on the opposite bank near Hooker Jim's village in case there was trouble and they were needed in that quarter. Then he led his detachment into Captain Jack's village, at about seven in the morning. But there was no surprise. A man crossing the river in a canoe after a night of gambling in Hooker Jim's village saw the soldiers and gave the alarm, so that when the troopers rode up, Captain Jack and several other Indians were there to receive them. While Captain Jackson (those two names are confusing!) parleyed and tried to plan his next move, the Indians hurried into the wickiups to grab weapons. Jackson's planned arrest was turning into a very tense situation.

On the other side of the river, the ranchers, waiting outside Hooker Jim's village, could see nothing through the grayness and sleet, and assumed from the absence of gunfire that all had gone well. They therefore went on into the village, only to find it wide-awake and perfectly aware that something was happening across the river. Seventeen fully armed men faced them suspiciously as they rode in.

A small spark would have been enough to set off such an explosive situation, and the Indians provided a bonfire. Scarfaced Charley, one of the three who was to have been arrested, suddenly pointed his rifle at Lieutenant Boutelle, Jackson's second in command. Boutelle in quick self-defense took a snap shot with his pistol that missed Charley but threw his aim off enough that he only grazed the lieutenant's arm. The two shots set off a general fusillade of rifles and shooting of arrows among Indians on both sides of the river.

In Hooker Jim's camp, the ranchers ran ingloriously, although a few fired their weapons as they fled, and one of these wild shots, a blast from a double-barreled shotgun, wounded a woman and killed the baby in her arms. Two ranchers who ran in the wrong direction were killed. In Jack's camp, the soldiers did a great deal of shooting but their aim was far from spectacular, and casualties were about even: one killed on each side, seven soldiers wounded, and probably about the same number of Indians.

And so the Modoc war was on. The engagement lasted no more than five minutes at the most. The Indian warriors fled through the sagebrush, sending back a few shots at the soldiers who briefly attempted a pursuit. Captain Jackson ordered the village burned, and women and old men were told to leave the camp. They did so in canoes, taking the wounded with them and paddling across Tule Lake, more than ten miles, where they were almost swamped when the wind caught them on the shallow, choppy lake. All, however, made it safely to the south shore.

The warriors went on foot to join up with their families. Captain Jack and his men, on the west side of Lost River, had only to go down the west side of Tule Lake, through an uninhabited region. Hooker Jim and his men, on the other side of the stream, went around the lake in the opposite direction, not only a much longer trip but one that took them through a number of ranches on the north side of the lake. Thirteen unsuspecting men, most of them caught at work away from their homes, were killed, but no attempt was made to harm women. Scarfaced Charley, on the other hand, traveling separately with several other men, met several ranchers who did not know that trouble was afoot; he told each of them to get on home because he did not want his friends to be hurt.

One other small band of Modocs was caught, quite unhappily, by the course of events. About ten miles east of Tule Lake a small stream called Hot Creek flowed through sagebrush and rock outcrops to Lower Klamath Lake. In the vicinity of the creek lived a small body of Indians who had left the reservation with Captain Jack but had built their wickiups well apart, a good twenty miles from the rest of the band. They also had ranchers for neighbors, but these were California ranchers, who, at least in this particular instance, seemed to be a more easygoing lot than those on the Oregon side of the line.

When word of the fighting at Jack's village reached the Hot Creek Modocs, they wanted nothing at all to do with it. They went to a rancher in the area, John Fairchild, for help, and Fairchild suggested that the best thing for them to do would be to get back on the reservation as soon as possible. Not only that, he offered to escort them there, enlisted the help of another rancher, a man named Dorris, also trusted by the Indians, and the two started north with their charges.

The news of their coming preceded them and in Linkville (today's Klamath Falls, Oregon) the usual crowd of loud-talkers congregated, found courage in bottles, and agreed that "something ought to be done." A small group started out to take the Indians, but the two ranchers had been forewarned, and, with the help of three or four other ranchers with level heads, were able to talk the small mob out of its purpose. The brave Indian fighters were cooling off, anyhow, as the cheap courage they had taken aboard in a Linkville saloon wore off in the chilly night air, and they gave up their purpose rather meekly.

One fool, though, was not content to let it drop at that point. While the talking was going on, he sidled up to the Modocs, to assure them, in lurid detail, that many other whites were lying in ambush on the road ahead and that they were certain to be killed if they went any further. Fairchild and Dorris could not convince the terrified Indians that they had been lied to. They ran away, and hurried straightway to join forces with Captain Jack. There were about forty-five of them, of whom at least fourteen were warriors. This may not seem like a large number, but it becomes large when it is considered that the total number of Jack's warriors never was much higher than fifty. From that point on, the Hot Creekers formed an intensely prowar faction, absolutely opposed to all proposals to negotiate or surrender. The war would have been much shorter and less costly if they had been taken back to the reservation without interference.

2. "TREACHERY IS INHERENT IN THE INDIAN CHARACTER"

The problem had grown beyond Captain Jackson and his forty horsemen, nor was it any longer in the hands of Major Green, commanding at Fort Klamath, who had sent Jackson to arrest Captain Jack. Jurisdiction had moved to a higher military level, and Lieutenant Colonel Frank Wheaton, commanding the District of the Lakes, with headquarters at Camp Warner about one hundred miles east of Fort Klamath, assumed control.

From Camp Warner he sent two companies of the 1st Cavalry, commanded by Captains David Perry and R. F. Bernard, to join Captain Jackson's Company B of the same regiment, already on hand. Two companies of the 21st Infantry, under Major E. C. Mason, were sent from Vancouver by boat, railroad, and overland under their own foot-power during a week of rain which turned the roads to mud of such depth and adhesiveness that wagons had almost to be lifted at times to move them forward.

Having obtained all the men immediately available, Colonel Wheaton then went to the scene of action to take personal command for a sharp and decisive campaign. However, he took his time preparing his forces so that when he did attack, his victory would be overwhelming. The Governor of Oregon issued a statewide call for volunteers to reinforce the Army, and sixty-five patriots hastened to defend the state against the Indian menace. An Oregon rancher did slightly better sticking to his own neighborhood; he signed up sixty-eight volunteers in the vicinity of Klamath Lake—but most of these were Klamath Indians from the reservation. California ranchers Fairchild and Dorris also raised a group of about thirty volunteers to act as scouts because no one else knew the California terrain in which the campaign was developing.

There would be no cavalry charges, or lines of men advancing with bayonets over grassy fields in this fighting. The region in which Captain Jack and his followers were making their defense was—and is—called the Lava Beds. They began at the south shore of Tule Lake and extended about twelve miles southward, in a belt perhaps ten miles wide. The surface of this region is a weird jumble of cracks, chasms, caves, ridges, and pits, the result of a series of outpourings of lava in relatively recent geological times. More than one person, attempting to describe it, has summed it up by saying it looks like a sponge.

The Modocs were holed up in a small portion of the beds, an area which quickly came to be called the Stronghold; it fronted on the lake and was perhaps half a mile long and a third as wide. Large cracks in the lava rock up to ten feet or more deep provided perfect trenches. Where there were gaps, the defenders piled up rocks, leaving loopholes. The Indians lived quite comfortably, making their homes in the large pits common throughout the Lava Beds. These pits in places have overhanging walls, and under the overhangs the Indians found quite snug shelters, often hanging skins or blankets in front for added warmth and privacy. Within this fortress, Captain Jack had approximately 165 people, of whom about fifty were fighting men.

Wheaton's job was to pry this small kernel of Indians out of an enormously tough shell. They could not be shot out because they could not be seen, and their protection against rifle fire and even artillery was almost perfect. They could not be starved out because there was plenty of game and water in the Lava Beds. The one remaining alternative was direct attack.

It was, however, the Modocs who drew first blood. The progress of a wagon train of rifle ammunition had been watched by the Indians as it came down the east side of the lake and approached the Army camp on December 2 1. When it was less than a mile from the camp, a raiding party dashed out of the protection of the lava outcrops and struck the train. So certain had the military been that the Indians would not venture beyond the safety of the lava flows that only five soldiers had been sent out to meet the train and escort it back. The surprise attack killed two of the escort and five horses; the remaining three soldiers and the teamsters fled. The ammunition was saved only by a quick-thinking lieutenant who charged out with half a dozen men whose horses happened to be saddled and drove off the raiders. This skirmish, the Battle of Land's Ranch, was the first of many incidents that soon filled the soldiers with an unreasoning fear of the Modocs.

Christmas, 1 8 7 2, passed miserably, with the men cold, bored, and, worst 'of all, without their holiday whiskey. But Lieutenant Colonel Wheaton continued to ready his big offensive, which was at last set for January 1 7. He had three hundred men, and he confidently assured his superiors that it would soon be over.

His strategy was basically simple—at least, on paper. Two independent forces drawn up in line of battle were to attack the Stronghold from east and from west. Their northern flanks were to be on the lake; as the northern sections of the two lines of battle struck Indian resistance and slowed down, the unopposed southern sections would continue ahead, pivoting as they went, until east and west forces met and the Indians were completely enclosed, with troops on three sides and the lake on the north. Then the forces would drive north, pushing the Modocs toward the lake. In analogy, it was to be very much like a pair of outstretched arms enfolding, drawing in and crushing an object. There was the slight modification that the right arm was going to be considerably longer and stronger.

On the west side, where the advance was to begin, was a long north-and-south ridge, rising gently from the west, but falling in a steep bluff on the side facing the Lava Beds. Army forces moved onto the ridge on the afternoon of the sixteenth, advancing slowly through a heavy fog. There were a few Modocs around; the Indians were good soldiers and had sentries out on the ridge. They upset the advancing soldiers by pinging rifle bullets around them, but it was impossible to hit anything in the fog and they soon withdrew down the bluffs and took up positions nearer the Stronghold.

The handful of California volunteer scouts, twenty-four of them, held the extreme left flank, next to the lake. Next were two companies of the 21st Infantry, commanded by Major E. C. Mason, which were expected to provide the heavy muscle of the attack. To the right of the infantry were the Oregon volunteers, about seventy-five men, and after them, on the extreme right flank, was Captain David Perry's company of cavalry, dismounted, which was to take part in the great pivoting movement, like a huge gate swinging shut to trap the Modocs.

On the other side of the Lava Beds, the cavalry companies of Captain James Jackson and Captain C. F. Bernard, formed the eastern force, with the latter as force commander. On the sixteenth, Jackson took his men on a reconnaissance and got too near the Stronghold; four soldiers were wounded and the Modocs were alerted that the attack was going to come from the east as well as the west.

The infantry battalion built sagebrush fires atop the ridge to keep off some of the bitter chill during the long evening and short night. In the Stronghold, the Modocs were making their own preparations for the battle. A great burden of responsibility fell on the shaman, Curly Headed Doctor, who had given full assurances that his magic would provide complete protection against the white soldiers. He had spent days braiding tule rushes from the lake into a rope several thousand feet long which was laid around the entire perimeter of the Stronghold; it was impregnated with magic powers which made it impossible for any white soldier to cross it. Now, with battle imminent, the Doctor erected a medicine pole which was nothing more than a limb from a small tree hung with assorted bits of fur, feathers, and other materia medica of his calling. All night long the Indians danced around a fire, which did nothing to soothe the edgy nerves of the white soldiers who could hear snatches of the chanting of the warriors floating eerily through the black night.

Bugles sounded reveille at four o'clock, but few of the men had been sleeping because of the cold and nervousness. It was six o'clock before the ranks had gotten their blood circulating enough to scramble down the bluffs and form up. On the opposite side of the Lava Beds, in the east force, preparations were simpler because there were no bluffs to negotiate, but there was no noticeably higher degree of dash and élan.

Dawn still had not come when three howitzer shots signaled that the battle was on. On the command to advance, the troops moved ahead, banging away blindly and uselessly into the fog and dark as they went. It was typical of the lack of battle discipline which was to mark this undistinguished army. The Modocs were still a mile away; even in good visibility the chances of hitting any of them would have been almost precisely zero. The advance was never rapid, and it became even less so when the Indians began shooting back, so that the second mile required six hours to cover, even though no one had yet been hit.

The pivoting movement that was to swing Captain Perry's dismounted cavalry across the south of the Stronghold and drive the Indians into the lake never got started. The group of Oregon volunteers who held the position between the infantry and the cavalry lost interest in fighting Indians early in the day, although they had suffered nothing but fright. They simply turned around and got out of the engagement, and absolutely refused to go back. A large gap was left between the cavalry and the infantry; before it could be patched and the pivoting movement attempted, there were other things to worry about.

On the east side, the might of the United States Army was not being displayed any more shiningly. Bernard's forces moved forward slowly and carefully for a short distance until they reached a long but not too spectacular fissure; this, they decided, was impassable, and lay there all the rest of the day. A few of the more intrepid souls raised themselves at intervals to send a rifle bullet at random toward the west but most of these shots arced across and struck among the positions of the western force.

In the meantime, the artillerymen stood idle by their howitzers on the west bluffs. It was impossible to give any support; the fog hung on long after daylight came—and even with the best of visibility it would have been difficult to determine where the position of friend and where that of foe.

Colonel Wheaton made a late attempt to salvage something from the mess, which was growing worse by the moment, by massing the western force, dismounted cavalry and infantry, near the lake front and driving along the shore to join up with Captain Bernard's apathetic forces on the east. Major John Green (he who had triggered the war by sending out a force to arrest Captain Jack at Lost River), who was field commander for the west forces, won himself a Congressional Medal of Honor by jumping up on the rocks in full view of the Indians and loudly damning his men for arrant cowards while Modoc bullets pinged around him. It inspired some of the men, and they moved past the point of danger to effect a junction with Bernard's men, who, however, remained completely unstirred by the event.

The winter twilight was beginning to fall, and Wheaton decided it was time to call an end to the fighting before it turned into a complete debacle. He called for a general withdrawal—although most of the men had already anticipated him in that—and the hundred or so who could be considered still in action fell back. It was no army that retired, but a frightened, beaten mass of men who wanted no more of fighting these terrifying Indians (most of them had not seen a Modoc). Many had thrown away rifles and knapsacks in their hurry to escape.

But there was further panic and humiliation for them—for those, at least, of the west force. When they reached the bottom of the bluff, they were halted by the rumor that Modocs had somehow gained command of the top. And so they huddled in fear until around two in the morning when finally someone, brave or skeptical, climbed to the top and found no Indians, and the retreat was resumed.

To cap the tribulations of this inept force, no one had considered the possibility that there might be wounded, and so there were no stretchers. Those unfortunate enough to be hurt were carried in blankets, and were bumped against the ground and rocks in the dark. One man had been killed and five wounded among the west forces, while on the east side one had been killed and eight wounded.

In the Indian camp, Curly Headed Doctor could claim complete effectiveness for his medicine. Not one soldier had crossed the rope of braided tule rushes surrounding the Stronghold. Not one Modoc had been killed or injured in the fighting. The shaman had powerful magic, stronger than anything the white man could bring against him.

The Indians showed continuing audacity against a force that outnumbered them six to one. To the west, a good ten miles outside the security of the Stronghold, a small scouting party sent a few bullets down toward the Army camp from a peak overlooking it and caused a near-panic. On the opposite side of the Lava Beds, when Captain Bernard drew his forces back a few days later, Modocs attacked the wagons hauling his grain, driving off the escort and burning wagons and grain. And way around on the north side of Tule Lake, several doughty Oregon volunteers were attacked by a far-ranging band of Modocs. The volunteers, who had retreated and refused to fight in the attack on the Stronghold, now began to desert and go home.

A defeat so humiliating immediately became the concern of Colonel Wheaton's superior, who had given the colonel a free hand on Wheaton's assurance that his one offensive would crush Modoc resistance.

General E. R. S. Canby, commanding the Department of the Columbia, which included roughly what is now called the Pacific Northwest, was an able officer with a long and distinguished record. It is an interesting measure of the speed with which the West changed that the first duty assignment of Canby, a young lieutenant just out of West Point in 1839, had been to help in the removal of the Seminole Indians from Florida to the permanent Indian Country, the land that was to belong to the red men forever. Now, little more than thirty years later, the permanent Indian Country was long forgotten, and Canby, still only a vigorous fifty-five years old, was concerned with a war against an Indian band in a region that had not even been part of the country when he had taken his oath to defend the Constitution.

The first thing Canby did was to remove Lieutenant Colonel Wheaton from command and replace him with Colonel Alvin C. Gillem. It was hardly an inspired beginning because Gillem was thoroughly disliked and distrusted by other officers who knew him; they believed that he had received undeserved promotions through friendship with President Johnson. Canby also kept shipping more men to the scene of action, until there were almost seven hundred of them ready for action. And finally, he came to see for himself just what the situation was.

Gillem was in San Francisco; storms delayed him for some time from assuming his command, and by the time he did, the situation had been lifted out of the purely military realm. Alfred B. Meacham, the former Indian Superintendent for Oregon, was in Washington to take part in the quadrennial ritual known as casting the electoral vote, and one day was discussing the Modoc war with other Oregonians in the capital. Someone advanced the sound but usually ignored proposition that talking is better than fighting, and suggested that a peace conference would be worth trying. The idea grew, was approved by Secretary of the Interior Delano, and a Peace Commission was eventually appointed, headed by Meacham, who immediately threw some sand into the wheels of good will by objecting loudly to the other Commissioners. Changes were made; the final commission which satisfied Meacham consisted of himself, rancher Jesse Applegate from the Modoc country, and Samuel Case of the Indian Bureau.

War weariness was beginning to affect Captain Jack during this same period. He sent word to rancher John Fairchild that he would like to end the war, and he and Scarfaced Charley, who emerges as his chief supporter and right-hand man, started to leave the Stronghold

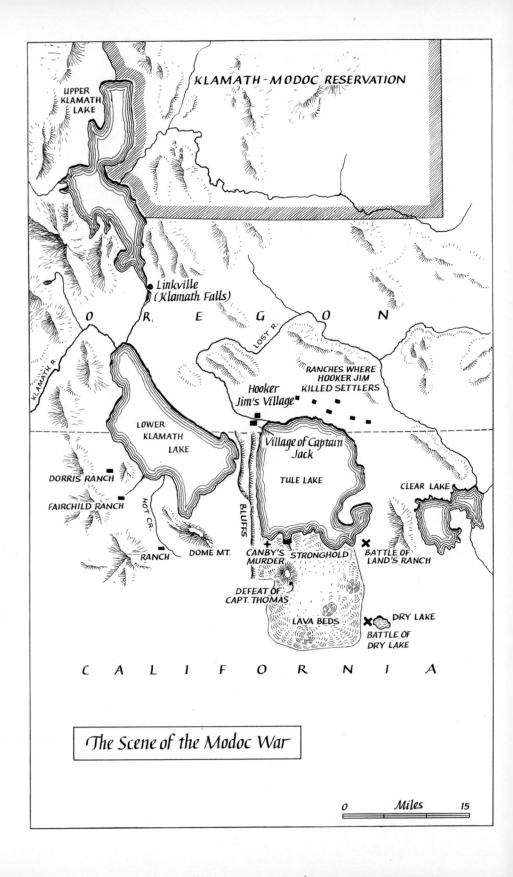

KLAMATH-MODOC RESERVATION

UPPER KLAMATH LAKE

Linkville (Klamath Falls)

O R E G O N

LOST R.

KLAMATH R.

RANCHES WHERE HOOKER JIM KILLED SETTLERS

Hooker Jim's Village

LOWER KLAMATH LAKE

Village of Captain Jack

DORRIS RANCH

TULE LAKE

CLEAR LAKE

FAIRCHILD RANCH

HOT CR.

BLUFFS

RANCH

DOME MT.

CANBY'S MURDER

STRONGHOLD

BATTLE OF LAND'S RANCH

DEFEAT OF CAPT. THOMAS

LAVA BEDS

DRY LAKE

BATTLE OF DRY LAKE

C A L I F O R N I A

The Scene of the Modoc War

0   Miles   15

to confer with Fairchild. They were intercepted by Curly Headed Doctor and Shacknasty Jim, one of the Hot Creek band and now red-hot for continuing the war. There was a violent quarrel; Jack and Charley were told that if they left they must expect to be killed if they ever returned. They stayed, but the quarrel went on all night.

Beginning February 20, the Peace Commission conducted its tortuous and frustrating negotiations with the Indians. The initial contact was made by a couple of Modoc women, wives of white men. The Modocs wanted men; men were sent. Captain Jack announced that he was willing to negotiate but that he did not like anything about the present Peace Commission; two men he knew in the mining town of Yreka, one a judge of Superior Court, the other a lawyer, were appointed to the Commission on his insistence.

As the negotiations went on, several of the Modoc warriors came into the Army camp two or three times (a strange Indian war, this one!) and vague suggestions of willingness to surrender were made by the Indians but faded away before they could be examined. The currents of optimism that floated periodically through the Peace Commission affected General Canby at one time so much that he sent a glowing telegram to General Sherman, saying that everything had been settled peaceably.

But nothing had been settled. One day Jack seemed eager for a settlement; the next he would be cooled off again. The state of Oregon was busily creating a major obstruction by insisting that the Modocs would have to stand trial for the murder of the ranchers by Hooker Jim's band at the beginning of the trouble, and since one of Jack's bedrock demands was a small reservation on Lost River in Oregon, a basic bargaining point was lost. The Army could only insist that the Modocs be sent to Indian Territory where they had no immediate enemies.

Captain Jack did not appear during any of the meetings, nor did any of the other Modoc leaders surrender. After almost two months even the sanguine General Canby decided that patience was ceasing to be a virtue. He directed Colonel Gillem to begin moving his forces closer to the Stronghold to put the Modocs under greater pressure. Although seven hundred soldiers were supposedly ringing them, the Indians had been undergoing the loosest of sieges. They had not only been moving through the Lava Beds outside the limits of the Stronghold, but on one occasion Hooker Jim and four companions had made a trip all the way to the reservation to visit friends and relatives there, and the Army command had known nothing of it until later.

At one time, this easy ability of the Modoc warriors to move about brought a face-to-face meeting between Captain Jack and Canby. While the troops were being shifted, the General and Colonel Gillem, with another officer, were riding along the top of the bluffs from which the abortive January offensive had been made when two Indians came to the foot of the bluff below them, and shouted that they did not want to fight any more. It turned out that one of the two was Scarfaced Charley, and that Captain Jack was back in the rocks with several other men, one of them John Schonchin, brother of the chief of the reservation Modocs and second in command to Jack. Charley proposed that the three officers come without their weapons and meet Jack, John Schonchin and a third Indian, also unarmed, and that the six should talk openly and unafraid.

Canby and Gillem agreed at once, but things did not come off quite as Scarfaced Charley had outlined. Instead of John Schonchin, Jack was accompanied by his nemesis, Curly Haired Doctor—and the Doctor carried weapons. Three other Indians appeared, all armed, to join the group. But no threatening moves were made, although the Modocs could easily have killed the three officers. Captain Jack repeated his demand for a reservation on Lost River, and Canby promised only that if the Modocs surrendered they would be given many gifts and would be treated fairly. It was about all he could offer; he had been given very little latitude for bargaining.

The Army squeezed a little closer to the Stronghold on the east side of the Lava Beds, and considerably nearer on the west side, where Colonel Gillem established his headquarters camp at the foot of the bluffs on April 1. The next day Jack sent word he was willing to meet the Peace Commissioners halfway between the Stronghold and Gillem's camp, and another series of inconclusive talks began.

The composition of the Peace Commission had changed. Three of the members had resigned in frustration over the vacillating actions of the Indians. Meacham alone remained, but his place as head of the group had been taken by General Canby. The other two new members were L. S. Dyar, subagent at the Klamath agency, and the Reverend Eleasar Thomas, a middle-aged Methodist minister from a small California town. Thomas' presence on the Commission was just one of the many improbabilities of this wholly improbable war; he was a completely unworldly gentleman and entirely incapable of comprehending what went on in the minds of the men he was dealing with. Two other members made up the Commission group: the interpreters, Frank Riddle and his Modoc wife, Winema, who was generally known as Tobey.

When the Army forces moved closer to the Stronghold, Jack became worried. He asked to see Canby again, but nothing came out of several new meetings. Jack repeated that he wanted his Lost River reservation; he wanted the soldiers to go home; he wanted a promise that there would be no punishment of Hooker Jim and his men for killing the ranchers. And Canby, with his limited bargaining power, could only offer the Modocs fair treatment by the Army if they surrendered.

As for that, Captain Jack's bargaining position was just about as circumscribed as Canby's. The war party was not only in the majority, its leader exerted the influence that goes with absolutely unspotted success. Curly Headed Doctor could point out that his medicine had kept the band off the reservation for several years, and now had enabled them to whip a much larger Army force without losing a man (the one killed in the fighting at the village on Lost River apparently did not count). Nothing succeeds like success, so when Tobey Riddle was sent to the Stronghold to say that anyone who wanted to surrender would be given protection against those who wished to remain, Captain Jack and eleven others were the only ones out of fifty-odd men who wanted to quit. The usual quarrel arose between Jack and Curly Headed Doctor, and their respective followers. Those who wanted to surrender were told bluntly that they would be killed if they tried to leave. When Tobey left this scene of discord, one of Jack's followers took her aside and warned her that she and the white Commissioners should not come to another meeting because plans for violence against the Commissioners were afoot.

On April 10, the Indians sent four men to Gillem's camp to say they would like another peace talk the next day, Good Friday. And that night, around the band's council fire deep in one of the pits in the lava rock, the leaders of the war party made ready either to force Jack out as chief or to make him take an unequivocal position in favor of continuing the war through to its end.

At the council, Jack presented his position: he was in favor of ending the war and going back to the reservation. The strength of the

Army would win in the end, Jack said, all the Doctor's magic notwith-
standing. But the war party speakers argued that they could and
should win the war in one stroke by killing the leaders of the whites,
and especially the top Army leader, General Canby. The next day
would be the best time.

At this, Captain Jack rose again. There would be no murders, he
said. As chief, he absolutely forbade anything of the kind. The war
party leaders were expecting this and were prepared for it. As Jack
was warming to his theme, several men seized him and pinioned his
arms while others put a woman's shawl and headcovering on him, jeer-
ing, "Woman! Coward!" and similar taunts.

What appears a malicious but puerile prank was deadly serious in
purpose. If Jack could be made to look ridiculous before his entire
band, the war party could oust him and put in one of their own men as
chief. They did not get Jack out, but they did just as well. Jack pulled
himself free, and shouted that if they wanted to murder the Commissioners that badly, he was the man to see that it was done. Moreover,
he went on, he was demanding for himself the right to kill General
Canby.

Plans were made. Two men, Barncho and Slolux, who otherwise
would have gone through the war unnoted—so obscure the whites had
not even hung nicknames on them—were to go to the rocks near the
conference site (a tent had been set up by the military for use in bad
weather) before daylight and hide with a supply of rifles ready for
distribution at the critical moment. Each Modoc was assigned a Commissioner as his victim. It was agreed that Frank and Tobey Riddle
were not to be harmed.

In the white camp, grapevine warnings had made a number of people
very unhappy about the coming meeting. Meacham and Indian agent
Dyar caught the pungent smell of danger so sharply that they slipped
derringers into their pockets although weapons were forbidden at the
peace talks. Tobey Riddle was ready for anything; she had been
warned, and she was a Modoc, with a better understanding than anyone else of what was going on in the minds of the people in the Lava
Beds. Her attempts to warn General Canby had fallen on unhearing
ears; he seems to have approached the Good Friday meeting without
hesitancy or even the slightest precaution, a strangely trusting attitude
in a man who had dealt with many enemies, white and red. As for the
Reverend Mr. Thomas, he lived in a world apart, and had greeted the

news that the Modocs wanted another conference as a sign that they
had seen the light of Christianity.

Two of the Modocs who had gone to Gillem's camp the day before
to request the peace conference, Boston Charley and Bogus Charley,
had spent the night there. Now they accompanied the Peace Commissioners as they rode to the meeting in no man's land, and both were
carrying rifles, despite the prohibition. Canby appeared not to notice.
At the tent they met Captain Jack, John Schonchin, Hooker Jim,
Ellen's Man, whose short, fat figure belied his toughness, Black Jim,
and Shacknasty Jim.

The conference started with a rehashing of the old proposals, but
the only ones who were really interested were Canby and Thomas.
Meacham had hung his jacket on his saddle horn; Hooker Jim walked
over and put it on as though he were trying it for fit. "You think me
look like old man Meacham?" he asked. Meacham, trying to make
light of an incident which had ominous undertones, for he suspected
that Jim very soon expected to be owning his jacket, held out his hat.
"Better take my hat, too." "I will by and by," Hooker Jim said coolly.
"Don't hurry, old man."

After some speech-making on both sides, Captain Jack suddenly
dropped the play-acting and gave the signal that brought Barncho and
Slolux out of their hiding place with guns for everyone. At the same
time, Jack pulled out a pistol he had concealed under his coat and shot
Canby under the eye at point-blank range. Although it was a mortal
wound, some residue of strength in his dying body enabled the General to leap to his feet and run for more than a hundred feet before
he fell to the ground, where Ellen's Man shot him again with a rifle
and Jack came up and stabbed him.

Thomas was shot by Boston Charley. When the minister collapsed
and begged the Modoc not to shoot again because he was going to die
anyway, Charley sneered. "Why don't you turn the bullets?" he asked.
"Isn't your magic strong enough?"

Meacham had been poised for trouble, and began running the instant things started happening, reaching for his derringer as he did so.
John Schonchin had been assigned to kill him, but the sight of the
little pistol made him pause and very probably saved Meacham's life
by giving him a chance to get out of point-blank range. He stumbled,
and bullets clipped off part of his ear and grazed his forehead, leaving
him unconscious. Shacknasty Jim, coming up, assumed he was dead

and did not give the *coup de grâce,* but slashed at one side of his head and was considering how best to take the scalp of a man nearly bald when Tobey diverted him by shouting that the soldiers were coming.

Dyar, also, had been ready for trouble and ran, turning long enough to wave his derringer at Hooker Jim who was pursuing. Jim turned and fled, while Dyar kept running, unharmed. Frank Riddle also ran toward the camp; Tobey threw herself on the ground to avoid bullets and remained where she was.

While this was happening, three Indians—Miller's Charley, Curly Headed Jack (not Doctor) and one other—approached the Army camp on the opposite side of the Lava Beds and told the sentry they wanted to talk to the top man in command. The sentry called the Officer of the Day, Lieutenant William Sherwood, along with another lieutenant who understood the lingua franca of the northwest tribes. The three Modocs attempted to draw the officers away from the protection of the sentry, but when the officers became suspicious, the Indians dropped their pretense and started to shoot. Sherwood was hit so badly he died three days later; the other man ducked and dodged with bullets ricocheting off the rocks around him and escaped.

For all their elaborate preparations and their advantages in weapons and surprise, the Modocs had done rather poorly: only three slain, counting Lieutenant Sherwood. The body of Brigadier General E. R. S. Canby, lying stripped of clothing (Captain Jack wore his uniform in later fighting), however, represented an accomplishment unique in all the long annals of Indian warfare: he was the only general ever killed by Indians.

Tobey, going to Meacham after the Modocs had fled, saw or felt no stirring and was certain that he, too, was dead. His face was covered with blood from the gashes in his scalp and from his clipped ear, but a party of soldiers soon came hurrying up and the surgeon with them found life. Not only life but spirit. As the surgeon tried to force brandy into the wounded man's mouth, Meacham clenched his teeth and turned away his head, murmuring that he was a temperance man; he had taken the pledge. Pledge or no, they got some brandy into him, and carried him back to camp where he soon recovered.

The news of the murders reached the country almost immediately. Newspaper correspondents, chronically bored because of the lack of news while the inconclusive peace talks had dragged on, raced to be the first to Yreka to get the story on the telegraph wires to their papers.

The news shocked the country; a great body of sympathy had developed for the Modocs in their stand of a few against so many, but now it was suddenly wiped out and the old cry of "murdering redskins" was heard again. President Grant demanded action, and Sherman sent a message with a familiar phrase to the Lava Beds, "You will be fully justified in their utter extermination." When asked whether this was not an act of treachery without equal, Sherman shook his head as he considered the unlimited capacity for perfidy of the American Indian. "No, sir. Treachery is inherent in the Indian character. I know of a case where the Indians murdered the man who not two hours before had given them food and clothing."

While the murders were acts of the most unjustifiable treachery, they were the result of a very definite if crude logic. The Modoc concept of social organization still had hardly risen beyond the tribe and the war party, and they naïvely believed that if they killed the leaders of the army besieging them, then the leaderless soldiers would lose heart and go home. They had not the slightest understanding that the United States could replace a dozen officers like General Canby and hardly notice the difference.

3. THE TIME OF RETRIBUTION

The great punishment to be meted out to the Modocs was delayed several days while a few details were cleaned up. Colonel Gillem retained immediate command of the forces on the scene, but General Canby had to be replaced. Sherman selected General Jefferson C. Davis, an officer with a fine record, who considered his name an undeserved slap by fortune at a man who had served the Union well and faithfully.

The advance started on Tuesday, April 15, five days after the murders. There was no bluff to climb down this time; the west force was camped in front of it and a great deal closer to the Stronghold than it had been in the January disaster. But it soon became clear that neither the long wait, nor a great increase in numbers, had instilled any new valor into these soldiers. The advance was so slow that it was almost two hours before the troops got close enough to the Stronghold for the Modocs to open fire on them, and then virtually all motion ceased. The strategy of this battle was to be almost exactly the same as that of the first encounter; the right wing of the western force was to pivot and swing like a gate, linking up with the east forces and then driving north either to wipe out the Indians or force them into the lake.

The army by now had five infantry companies, four companies of cavalry, four batteries of artillery, and seventy-two Indian scouts, a total of about a thousand men. There were about four hundred men in the right wing of the west force which was to accomplish the pivoting movement. From their own half hundred the Modocs sent eight snipers out to oppose and stop the maneuver. And stop it they did, completely and quickly; the first bullets that whined off the rocks sent all four hundred soldiers crouching low for protection. Officers tried to urge their men on; they would get a few crawling unhappily forward in one place but when they turned elsewhere to get a few more moving, the first ones would snuggle down into the protecting rocks again. At the end of six hours, the gallant four hundred had gone ahead approximately half a mile and had not even seen any of the eight Indians who were still sniping and keeping the fear of God and Modocs in them.

The attack on the east side, in the meantime, was doing even less to exact vengeance for Canby's murder. The artillery there had commenced the action with a bombardment of the Stronghold, but the howitzers had been located so far back that most of the shells did not even reach the Modoc positions. Captain Mason, commanding the east forces, directly disregarded orders by making almost no attempt to move his men up toward the Stronghold. It was almost certainly an act coolly calculated to embarrass Gillem. Mason, along with several other officers, disliked and resented Gillem intensely, but permitting personal feelings to guide decisions on the field of battle was so contrary to all military regulations as well as traditions that it is surprising Gillem did not call for a court-martial later.

Almost nothing had been accomplished by the attackers by nightfall. During the night, the howitzers lobbed shells from both sides into the Stronghold at intervals, and while the chance of any shell making a hit amid the labyrinth of fissures and pits was exceedingly slight, the explosions kept the Indians on edge. So they crept as close as possible to the Army lines where no shells were falling, and the opposing forces spent the night in a pastime of soldiers from time immemorial, shouting obscene insults back and forth.

The soldiers had lost three killed and half a dozen wounded for all their extreme caution. The Modocs, as usual, had not lost a man or had one hurt, and the magic tule rope around the Stronghold had not been crossed. Curly Headed Doctor's prestige was higher than ever— but its hours were numbered.

On the second day of fighting, April 16, the pivoting wing, the gate that was to swing around in the rear of the Modocs, showed even less spirit than it had the day before. Then, at least, the officers had tried to exhort their faint-hearted legions into advancing against the eight Modocs who opposed them. But this day even the officers showed no enthusiasm, and were willing to let a creeping advance lose its small momentum without making any attempt to keep it going; they reported back that the ground was impossible to move across, and soon ordered their men to retreat.

On the other hand, at the northern end of the lines the Army forces showed a surprising amount of spirit—reluctant and snail-like, perhaps, by most standards, but a display of something approaching fighting spirit for this sad army. From east and west the two forces advanced along the lake shore, and the remarkable thing is that they had been expressly ordered *not* to move forward across the lake front. Major Green from the west, and Captain Mason, immovable the day before, from the east, pushed their forces until they joined up, cutting the Modocs off from the lake.

The very opposite of the planned strategy had been accomplished. Instead of being hemmed in by a force to the south and driven toward the lake, the way south into the labyrinthine jumble of the rest of the Lava Beds stood open while a line of soldiers was cutting the Modocs off from the lake front and the water of Tule Lake. However, the action of Green and Mason had one unexpected result. In the movement of their men, the tule rope had been crossed. The Stronghold was not absolutely impregnable, then, as their shaman had assured the Modocs again and again.

That night, Indian morale suffered a second blow. A man had attempted to remove the fuse from a dud howitzer shell with his teeth; when the smoke cleared, his head was gone and so was the rest of Curly Headed Doctor's prestige. Within less than twenty-four hours, both the things he had repeatedly promised would never happen had occurred. The Stronghold had been violated, and a Modoc had been killed by a soldier's weapon. The Doctor's medicine was no good, after all.

Jack had regained complete leadership of his band again; it was a somewhat shaken group, although on the basis of past experience the Modocs were convinced they were more than a match for the Army, magic or no. With the water of the lake no longer available, Captain Jack ordered an immediate withdrawal from the Stronghold. A rear-guard kept up a busy sniping to give an appearance of normal activity; when it, too, withdrew to the south and things became unnaturally quiet, the troops cautiously moved in to investigate. They found one old, wounded man who was promptly killed and scalped; in the zeal for souvenirs his scalp was divided into half a dozen or more pieces and even his eyebrows taken.

The Modocs were now at large in the jumbled expanse of the Lava Beds where they had good prospects of playing hide-and-seek indefinitely with the Army. The beds extended for about a dozen miles south from the lake and were about ten miles wide. The terrain was far from being a uniform expanse of sharp, black volcanic clinkers. There were buttes where lava had thrust through breaks in the rock below and flowed upward to harden into rounded hills; there were long ridges; there were caves and mounds and depressions; there were loose rocks which had broken off larger lava masses. And between the lava outcroppings were expanses of ground almost level, where the stony earth supported sagebrush, mahogany bushes, and bunch grass. There was plenty of game to provision the Modocs, and there was water in a number of caves in the lava, either in pools or frozen into ice.

Gillem set about the tedious task of trying to locate and pin down the Modocs. Two or three times a few of them were sighted, but they disappeared and it was useless to attempt to follow them in the chaotic lava formations. It occurred to Gillem that the answer to his problem might be to establish himself boldly within the Lava Beds by emplacing artillery on commanding positions where it could control large areas in all directions and be always ready to fire on any Indians who showed themselves. To put the idea to the test, he sent Captain Evan Thomas, an artillery officer, with a strong sixty-four-man party composed of two artillery batteries and an infantry company to take a howitzer to the top of a lava butte about four miles south of headquarters camp. Thomas and two or three of his officers had fine Civil War records but they were lacking in the much more pertinent experience of Indian-fighting.

The march was made along the western edge of the Lava Beds, over fairly level ground. The force moved slowly; the men would have moved more slowly yet, or not at all, had they known that a band of Modoc warriors in the lava formations only about half a mile away was not only observing them but was traveling on a slowly converging course.

When it became obvious to the Indians that the column was headed for the butte, Scarfaced Charley, their leader, hurried his men on ahead to post them at the top of the butte and along both sides of the path the column would have to take to reach the top. It was a deadly ambush, and Captain Thomas was taking no precautions against being caught in such a trap. At first he had flankers out, and a skirmish line in front, but the nervous soldiers kept drawing in toward the column, and the inexperienced officers, not realizing the importance of such precautions in Indian country, soon gave up attempts to keep the men out.

When the column was on the butte and well within the trap, the Modocs opened fire. The soldiers responded as they always had to Indian bullets; they became panic-stricken and ran. Captain Thomas Wright, commanding the infantry company, attempted a charge with his men to allow the rest of the column to escape, but as soon as the infantrymen came under fire, they, too, turned tail and joined the general wild flight. Wright was killed, and the last semblance of organization among the infantry vanished; they fled in sheer animal terror, some of them making the four-mile trip over rocky ground back to headquarters camp in less than an hour.

A young lieutenant named Cranston had attempted to rally some of the men to make a stand; when he called for volunteers only five men stood by him—and when the gallant and forlorn six came out of the shelter of desert shrubs to try to help stem the rout, they were killed almost on the spot. Captain Thomas got a group of about twenty men into a rocky hollow but it was no shelter because Modocs on the ridge above were able to shoot down into them with the greatest ease. Thomas and most of the men with him were slain by midafternoon when the firing stopped unexpectedly and Scarfaced Charley called, "All you fellows that ain't dead had better go home. We don't want to kill you all in one day."

Back at headquarters, they were aware that Wright's column had had some sort of brush with the Modocs. A signal tower had been erected on high ground near the camp for communication with the east force; it also served as an excellent lookout, and from it the column was in sight of observers with glasses a good part of the time. When gunfire was heard and running men were seen, a watching officer interpreted it as a retreat in good order. Even when the first of the fleeing men reached camp early in the afternoon, still too incoherent from terror to explain what had happened, Gillem was not worried because he knew Captain Thomas would outnumber any band of Modocs that might oppose him, and he was sure Thomas could take care of himself (it is hard to say whence such confidence came, in view of the fighting record of men and officers to that time). Not till late afternoon did he order a relief column out, and for this delay he was relieved of his command almost immediately.

The relief column—and this could almost have been predicted in advance with this unhappy, maladroit army—got lost in the dark and had to make a bivouac of sorts for the night, and when it did reach the scene of the disaster in the morning, it was discovered that no one had thought of sending doctors along to care for the wounded. The relief force found a grim scene: twenty-three dead. Nineteen had been wounded; some had made it back to camp but many still lay on the battlefield. The Modocs, as usual, had not lost a man. And, as usual, the Indians had acquired stores of rifles, ammunition, and other supplies. They made no attempt to attack the rescue forces but perched on the ridges watching from a distance, making the soldiers very nervous.

Captain Jack, however, was having serious problems, and the most critical of them was the matter of water. The Lava Beds are dotted with caves into which water slowly percolates through the porous volcanic rock and collects, sometimes as pools of water but more often frozen into great ice masses which do not melt during the summer. The Modocs chopped out chunks of the ice and melted it for use, but there were about 165 of them, men, women, and children, and they could use all the ice in a cave in a short time. Then it was necessary to move on to another source of water. Since it took the caves months to replenish themselves by seepage, and most of that during the winter rainy months, the field of maneuver of the Modocs was being gradually compressed. But against the spiritless army they had been fighting, there was still plenty of water and game to enable them to hold out for a long time yet.

General Jefferson Davis had relieved Colonel Gillem and sent him back to San Francisco (this inconsequential war against half a hundred perverse Indians was costing military reputations as well as lives), and having personally assumed command, he pondered ways of putting some fighting spirit into this craven group that called itself an army. It was made up, much of it, of immigrants who had enlisted without the faintest stirring of patriotism but only because it offered three meals a day, a bed of sorts, and a few dollars to spend on pay day. It was a refuge, too, for ne'er-do-wells, who, in the Far West of 1873, hardly expected to be called on to fight Indians in dead earnest. And, without doubt, there were a good many young men who had enlisted with every expectation of being good soldiers but had been infected with the atmosphere of fear that had come to permeate an entire army of a thousand men that outnumbered its enemy twenty to one.

Davis's eye fell on Captain H. C. Hasbrouck and his company of cavalry, who had reported for duty after Thomas had been killed and his command cut to pieces; the smell of confidence was still strong about Hasbrouck and his men, and their morale was high. General Davis determined to make use of their rare quality before they, too, had been tainted by the unreasoning fear of the Modocs and the defeatism that obsessed everyone else in the camp. He sent Hasbrouck and his horsemen out after Modocs, giving him as support a battery of artillery and two companies of cavalry which had shown no talent for fighting in the past. A detachment of Indian scouts completed the column.

Hasbrouck's column went down the east side of the Lava Beds where the Modocs had last been reported as having been seen, and after an uneventful march, bivouacked by a body of mud called Dry Lake, while the artillery made its separate camp about a mile away. The Modocs, of course, had been observing every move and had decided that the Army forces were in an ideal spot for a surprise attack. By striking from the right direction they could stampede the soldiers —who had never yet failed to run when properly frightened—into a choice of running into the mud of the lake or toward the Modocs.

The attack came at daybreak. Its initial effect was just what the Modocs had anticipated. The soldiers were befuddled with sleep and unable at first to get their bearings and comprehend what was happening. Two were killed at once, and several wounded. There was a general flight from the attacking Indians which was halted, as the Modoc leaders had foreseen, by the mud of the lake, and there many of the soldiers huddled, numbed by fear and lack of direction. But

Captain Hasbrouck was a different kettle of fish; he at once began setting things to rights, bellowing commands and sorting order out of chaos. He sent one of his officers to the artillery camp a mile away for help, hurried others down to the lake shore to rally the men cowering there. The Modocs were pressing ahead, exploiting what they had come to expect as the typical panic of white soldiers caught unawares, when they, in their turn, were taken by surprise. The frightened soldiers on the lake front had rallied under their officers' exhortations, and were pushing ahead in a skirmish line, firing briskly as they came. The Indians were not prepared for such a turn of events, and in their turn began to retreat, a withdrawal that was greatly hastened when one warrior fell badly wounded and the Army's Indian scouts began firing on the Modocs from the rear.

The Modocs abandoned the field completely. On the face of it, they had not come out too badly. The Army had lost three soldiers and two Indian scouts killed and half a dozen soldiers and two scouts wounded while the Modoc losses had been only one man mortally wounded. But the Modocs had, for some curious reason, loaded their most important supplies on pack horses and had brought them close to the field of action. Twenty-four loaded pack horses were captured; they carried much of the Modocs' ammunition as well as other supplies. Previously, battlefields had been sources of supply to the Indians; now they suddenly found themselves facing scarcity.

The biggest failing of the Modoc band was that it could not stand adversity. There were too many factions and too much antagonism. The man wounded in the battle at Dry Lake was Ellen's Man who died a few hours later; he had been one of the murderers of General Canby, and he was one of the Hot Creek band who had been such vehement supporters of Curly Headed Doctor in the days when a tule rope promised perpetual security. Now that the war they had wanted so much was turning sour on them, the Hot Creek group tried to make Jack the scapegoat. Ellen's Man was dead, they charged, because Jack had deliberately put him in a dangerous position where he would be likely to be hit. There was a violent quarrel, and the Hot Creek band, along with Hooker Jim and Curly Headed Doctor—fourteen warriors and their families—departed the Lava Beds entirely, going about forty miles to the northwest.

The shape and tide of the war changed with surprising swiftness. The victory had performed the near-miracle of raising the morale of the spiritless troops who had been frightened for half a year by the mere mention of Modocs. Now the soldiers hunted for Indians as though they wanted to find them, and for ten days Captain Hasbrouck led a column of some three hundred men, trying to corner Captain Jack who now had only thirty-three warriors and was hampered by women and children.

But it was the Hot Creek band who surrendered first. They returned to the area, apparently out of pure curiosity to see what had been going on in their absence. Once there, however, they decided to give themselves up, and went to rancher Fairchild, the same man they had gone to for help when they had first tried to avoid the war. And having surrendered, they were eager to play the part of Judas. Four of them, Bogus Charley, Steamboat Frank, Hooker Jim, and Shacknasty Jim, offered to act as guides in helping the Army find Captain Jack. General Davis, quite certain the dispirited quartet would not betray his trust, sent them out to try to talk Jack into coming in. They found him well to the east of the Lava Beds and advised him to give himself up; after all, they said, they had been treated very well. Jack responded with justifiable anger; the men standing before him had opposed him several times when he had wanted to surrender; they had forced him to agree to the murder of the Peace Commissioners by the business of the women's clothes; three of them, in fact, had had a hand in the actual killing. Now they had earned forgiveness from the white men by offering to bring him in. Jack well knew that he could not, in his turn, buy his way out by offering to betray someone else. He told his erstwhile comrades-in-arms to go to hell.

But his followers gradually gave up as hunger, the fatigue of constant flight, and just plain hopelessness overcame them. Soldiers at last caught up with Jack himself. There was no drama; he was in a position where he could have slipped away and remained free for at least a while longer, or he could have put up a fight. He did neither, but capitulated, explaining matter-of-factly that his legs had given out. That day, June 1, 1873, the Modoc war came to an end, although a few other Indians came in later.

Four Modocs never did make it. They had given themselves up to that good friend of the Modocs, rancher Fairchild, who was bringing them in in a wagon when he was stopped by a band of Oregonians. Fairchild was forced to get down from the wagon; then the men fired into the four Indians from a few feet away, killing all four and wounding a woman, although this last was apparently by mistake. The Modocs were small fry; their names, Little John, Mooch, Pony, and Tee-hee Jack, are not otherwise mentioned in accounts of the war. The Oregonians who made this late contribution toward winning the war were never known and General Davis made no effort to find out who they were; very possibly some of them were among the heroes who had deserted rather than face these same Modocs when they were armed.

Davis believed, along with the rest of the Army, that hard and immediate punishment of the Modocs was necessary to deter other Indians from flouting white authority, and he planned to hang a number of the leaders as soon as preparations could be made. However, in this case the matter was too important to be left to the discretion of a commander in the field. The Modoc war had been thoroughly covered by newspaper correspondents on the scene, and the public was well acquainted with the situation and the principal figures involved. A number of summary executions would raise a storm of protests among the philanthropists and Indian sympathizers in the East.

So, while Davis fumed and the state of Oregon screamed for blood, the War Department put its legal experts to work determining the questions of law involved. Their findings were that since the Modocs were not citizens of the United States they could not be punished for violating the laws of either the nation or the state of Oregon. There was something grotesquely comic in this solemn performance; for almost a hundred years the United States and the several states had been chastising Indians for all manner of crimes and misdemeanors, including that of trying to protect rights that had been guaranteed to them, and now it was ruling that they could not legally be punished. However, having erected this wall which apparently protected the Modocs against retribution, the devious legal mind then had to find a way through it so that they could be punished, all orderly and according to law. While the Indians could not be brought to trial for anything not considered a crime under their own law, the opinion continued, treachery, by almost universal custom, was considered an act punishable by death. And so, very neatly, the way was left open to try the Indians for the murder of the unsuspecting ranchers at the outset of the conflict, but, more important, to exact retribution for the one dramatically barbaric episode of the war, the murder of the Peace Commissioners.

The Indians were taken north to Fort Klamath and put in a stockade which had been built to receive them. There were forty-four men and one hundred and eleven women and children; these and the half dozen men who had been lynched or otherwise killed were the mighty band that had stood off an army of the United States, numbering about one thousand men during the last half of the war, for half a year. Curly Headed Jack, one of the three who had killed Lieutenant Sherwood on the east side of the Lava Beds, grabbed the gun away from a guard and shot himself because he was certain that he would hang. Otherwise, all who had any connection with the murders were present when the trial began on July 1.

Hooker Jim, Shacknasty Jim, and Bogus Charley had hands as bloody as anyone, but the grateful Army granted them amnesty for betraying Captain Jack after they had surrendered. Hooker Jim's former band was put on trial for the murder of ranchers at the very outset of the war, but the only persons who had witnessed any of the killings were the wives of two of the victims, and on the stand they could not positively identify a single one of the murderers. The case was dropped.

That left six men who could not sidestep approaching doom. The names by which the white men called them were Captain Jack, Schonchin John, Boston Charley, Black Jim, Slolux, and Barncho, and the charge against them was murdering General Canby and the Reverend Eleasar Thomas. The entire trial lasted ten days, and was no more than an approximation of a trial under American law. The Indians had no defense counsel, and they did not understand enough English to know what was going on during most of the trial. Barncho was so indifferent that he slept on the floor under a table much of the time. At the same time, the court went out of its way to bring in any evidence that might have any bearing on the case, even when it meant departing from its own procedures to do so.

Even so, the results were foregone, and all six were sentenced to be hanged on October 3. But there was a wide demand that Slolux and Barncho be shown clemency; they were very young, said their pleaders, and were nothing but tools in the hands of the other men in the killings. The conduct of Barncho in the courtroom indicated that he did not understand or did not care that his life was at stake. In any event, President Grant did commute the sentences of the two to life imprisonment a month before the execution, but from an apparent belief that there was a redemptive power in looking close-on into the face of death, he specified that the two were not to know that they had been spared until they reached the foot of the gallows.

So, on the day of execution, the six men, sitting on four coffins, were driven to the gallows. It was not until the other four were led up the stairs to the nooses and they were left behind that Barncho and Slolux realized that they were being spared.

The rest of the band were put aboard train and taken to Indian Territory, to be settled before the end of November in the extreme northeastern corner of that dumping ground for unwanted Indians. Malaria got in its work, and the band dwindled to about one-third of its original number within the next thirty years. There was never any more sign of fight in them; they sent their children to school, did some farming, and adjusted well to a settled life.

In 1909, the government at last permitted any who wished to do so to go back to the reservation. As for Barncho and Slolux, the authorities had long since decided they were no longer menaces. They were sent to Alcatraz Island to serve life sentences, but were set free after only five years.

VIII

The Road to
the Little Bighorn

1. THE TECHNIQUES OF TREATY-BREAKING

T
HE Modoc War was fought in 1873, the Red River War in 1874-75. During all of those years, the government of the United States, to oblige various of its sovereign citizens, was moving with a sureness born of long practice down the path to another Indian war, another broken treaty, and still another land grab. The Sioux and their Northern Cheyenne allies were to be the victims and the battlefields would be on the northern plains and foothills.

At Fort Laramie in 1868, it will be recalled, most of the Sioux and Northern Cheyenne and Arapaho bands signed a treaty by which they accepted as a reservation that great segment of Dakota Territory which now comprises all of South Dakota west of the Missouri River. The Oglala chief, Red Cloud, refused to accept this Great Sioux Reservation, however, until he had forced the United States to abandon the Bozeman Trail and to agree that the game-rich Powder River country belonged to the Sioux, and was absolutely forbidden to white men. This has been related in detail earlier; now it becomes the beginning of a new episode.

After Red Cloud won his war with the United States, he promised never to fight again, settled down near an agency, and took up the responsibilities of a reservation chief. But when he moved with his band to the reservation, there were many who remained behind. It was not to become tame Indians in the end that they had closed the white man's Bozeman Trail and burned the forts, the recalcitrants said. They had fought to remain free—and remain free they would, living in the old way by hunting the buffalo, and not by waiting for Washington to send food in sacks and boxes.

Their victory over the United States had given these "wild" Indians delusions of invincibility; they were certain they could drive out any future force the Army might send against them. As for Red Cloud, he had lost their respect because of what they considered his surrender to the white man. The Indians who had refused to sign a treaty included notable men: Sitting Bull, medicine man and oracle, whose name is probably the best-remembered of any Indian who ever lived; Crazy Horse, a leader whose genius for handling even the individualistic red warriors earns him the right to be named among the great American cavalry leaders of whatever color; Gall, the serious-minded Hunkpapa who would be leading chief at the battle of the Little Big-horn; Two Moon of the Cheyennes, Crow King, Hump, Spotted Eagle, and others.

The nontreaty Indians remained in the Powder River country, which was "unceded Indian territory" according to the treaty. And there they were perfectly content to live, setting up their lodges in the valleys of the clear rivers, hunting the buffalo and lesser game, holding back the calendar and living in the past while everything in the outer world was changing. However, if that was what they wanted, they appeared to be perfectly within their rights in trying to protect here, in the shadow of the Big Horn Mountains, a last remnant of a way of life that had once been as normal on the western prairies and the Great Plains as the rise and fall of the grass before the wind.

But change was closing in on them. White civilization began moving with its heavy tread through the remaining untouched portion of the northern plains when the Northern Pacific Railroad, building west from Duluth toward the Pacific, sent its survey crews ahead across the plains. The portion of the route laid out through Dakota Territory did no violence to treaty agreements; it ran due west through present North Dakota, well north of the Great Sioux Reservation, and while news that a railroad was to come through the buffalo range caused some consternation to the reservation Indians, the white man was completely within his treaty rights in laying his tracks there. It was hardly possible to keep the entire northern plains an unspoiled buffalo range.

But quite another matter was the section of the railroad's line through Montana. The survey line, after crossing from Dakota into Montana, struck the Yellowstone River valley which it then followed as the only practical route toward a pass through the mountains. A preliminary survey had been made by Colonel D. S. Stanley in 1872, on the basis of which it had been decided that the tracks should be laid on the south side of the river—and the south side was Indian country.

Although the Fort Laramie treaty completely neglected to define the northern limit of the unceded land, there was not any doubt where it lay. The Sioux had taken the region as far as the Yellowstone River from the Crows by conquest more than a generation before, and had held it firmly ever since. They were completely in control of everything south of the river, so the government sent two Commissioners to negotiate with them for a right-of-way for the railroad. They were completely unsuccessful. The chiefs announced, without discussion, that they wanted no railroad or other work of the white man anywhere on their last hunting range.

The Commissioners returned and duly reported failure. They also suggested that the hostiles probably had neither sufficient ammunition nor other resources to prevent the building of the railroad. The Army moved fast. The two Commissioners had had their futile talks with the Sioux on May 9, 1873; on June 20 a military expedition, to act as escort for surveyors laying out the railroad line in the Yellowstone valley, set out from Fort Rice on the Missouri. There was more than one way to amend a treaty.

The column was a powerful one: 19 companies of infantry, 10 of cavalry, a couple of artillery pieces, and the inevitable wagon train and beef herd, in all more than 1,500 soldiers and some 350 teamsters, herders and other auxiliaries, and a couple of dozen Arikara scouts. Colonel (brevet Brigadier General) D. S. Stanley, wartime commander of cavalry in the Army of the Cumberland, was in command.

The ten cavalry companies with the expedition were the 7th Regiment, and commanding them again was Lieutenant Colonel (brevet Major General) George Armstrong Custer. Since 1870, the 7th had been split up and sent into the South, a company here, another there, to keep order during the lawless times of the Ku Klux Klan. In the

First Violations of the Sioux Treaty

spring of 1873 it was brought together again to serve on the plains. Custer had arrived at Yankton with his wife and his usual mountain of impedimenta, including his pack of hounds which on this trip had numbered forty dogs. His luck held; the colonel of the 7th was S. D. Sturgis, who had replaced the never-present Colonel A. J. Smith only shortly before the regiment had been broken up and sent south. Now, when it was together again and about to see action, Sturgis was detached and assigned to staff duty in St. Paul, leaving Custer once again in complete command. Ten companies were with the Yellowstone expedition; the remaining two, under Major Marcus Reno, had been detailed for duty as escorts to surveyors running the U. S.–Canadian boundary.

General Stanley was not favorably impressed with his young subordinate. In a letter to his wife he expressed his opinion that Custer was a "coldblooded, untruthful and unprincipled man. He is universally despised by all the officers of his regiment, excepting his relatives and one or two sycophants. He . . . carries an old negro woman and a cast-iron cooking stove and delays the march often by his extensive packing up in the morning. As I said, I will try but am not sure I can avoid trouble with him."

A few days later, Custer, trying how far he could take the bit in his own teeth, was brought up short. Stanley wrote to his wife:

> I had a little flurry with Custer as I told you I probably would. We were separate four miles and I intended him to assist in getting the train over the Muddy River. Without consulting me, he marched off 15 miles, coolly sending me a note to send him forage and rations. I sent after him, ordered him to halt where he was, to unload his wagons and send for his own rations and forage and never presume to make another movement without orders.
>
> I knew from the start it would have to be done. . . . He was just gradually assuming command and now he knows he has a commanding officer who will not tolerate his arrogance.

Colonel Stanley had no more trouble with Custer during the rest of the mission. The survey was carried out; there were several brisk clashes with the nontreaty Sioux and Cheyennes with dead and wounded on both sides, but considering the size of the forces on both sides that might have been involved, the campaign was completed with a rather small amount of fighting.

The crisis that actual construction of the railroad through the Yellowstone valley would have caused was averted when the Panic of 1873 stopped the rails on the east bank of the Missouri. The rough, raw frontier town of Bismarck grew up at the railhead; across the river and three or four miles down stream, the Army built a new post, Fort Abraham Lincoln; and there the 7th Cavalry was stationed, with its commanding officer also commandant of the fort.

Although the Northern Pacific had halted, it would not be forever, and General Sheridan, looking over his maps in his Chicago headquarters, contemplated the need for another fort to guard the line when building should begin again. Between Fort Abraham Lincoln and Fort Ellis far across Montana near Bozeman, there was nothing. It was a mighty big gap, and Sheridan decided that the Black Hills would be an ideal spot for his new fort: central location, lumber, water, firewood, all the other advantages.

There was only one thing wrong with the location: it was in the Great Sioux Reservation, Indian land, pure and simple. However, Sheridan cared less than a snap of his fingers for any rights of Indians, and he directed Colonel Custer to make a reconnaissance of the Black Hills to determine the best site for such a post. The move would be a brutal smashing of the Fort Laramie treaty—but then, General Philip Sheridan had often operated in a brutal manner.

The Black Hills were more than just a portion of the Sioux reservation. They were charged with a deep and mystical meaning for the Indians, for this was a sacred place, a spot where spirits dwelt. Here, in geological ages past, a section of the earth's crust, some 40 by 120 miles in extent, was lifted upward. It stands like an island amid the monotonous plains, a range of small mountains, split with shadowed canyons, dramatic with rock formations, cool with the shade of pine trees, watered with frequent streams. Even the climate is different in this place; the rains fall more abundantly while around the plains are dry and alkaline.

Custer led his exploration force out of Fort Lincoln on July 2, 1874. Besides ten companies of the 7th Cavalry (the remaining two were still guarding the surveyors marking out the U.S.–Canadian border), there were two companies of infantry, three Gatling guns, an artillery piece, Indian scouts, and the usual wagon train and complement of civilian auxiliaries. Lieutenant Colonel George A. Forsyth was on Custer's staff during the expedition, the same Forsyth who had been in command during the desperate fight at Beecher's Island six years earlier. Events would so order themselves that one day he would be Colonel of the 7th and would command it during its last and least praiseworthy action against Indians.

Besides exploring the area for possible sites for a fort, the expedition also included several scientists among whom geologists were prominent. There was no secret that the column also meant to look into the truth of persistent rumors that there was gold in the hills.

The expedition was out and back in somewhat less than two months, after a trip that often took on the aspects of a big picnic. There was no opposition from the Indians. Most of them did not even know what was happening until it was all over. By then their last hope of keeping the Black Hills was doomed, for the expedition had found gold. Not, it is true, gold in the quantities proclaimed by Custer, who announced that there were veins of gold-bearing quartz on the side of almost every hill, and that it had been found among the roots of the grass. He was so eager to trumpet these exaggerated accounts to the world without delay that he sent his scout, Lonesome Charley Reynolds, on a dangerous trip south across Indian country to Fort Laramie and the nearest telegraph. As a result, the country was burning with gold fever by the time the column returned, and no one listened to the protests of the expedition geologists that Custer's stories were extravagant and premature. As a matter of fact, prospectors were already entering the Black Hills before the column had reached Fort Abraham Lincoln. A few were killed by the angry Sioux, but many made it before winter closed down on the plains.

Having opened the door, the Army made ineffectual attempts to close it. Sherman announced that any white men who entered the reservation would be driven out at gunpoint, if necessary. It was all right for people on the frontier to complain about the Indians breaking the law, he observed, but they did not seem to see anything at all unjust about their going onto Indian land and grabbing it. He ordered officers in the area to arrest all civilians entering the reservation and to destroy their guns, transportation, and other property. (One almost has the feeling that Sherman would have liked to have threatened to exterminate them.) Not many officers carried out these stringent provisions; most were satisfied merely to escort prospectors off the reservation and there turn them over to the nearest civil authority—who, without exception, turned them loose for another try at slipping into the gold fields.

By the middle of 1875, there were hundreds of men panning for gold in the midst of the Black Hills.

The government could not keep its own citizens out of the Sioux lands, any more than it had been able to keep them out of any other Indian treaty land, in spite of solemn pledges, since the time when the land just across the Appalachians was the West. It was now up to the Indian Bureau to find some way to legalize this latest trespass. The government wanted the Black Hills and was willing to buy them—if the price was right, of course—and so it brought the leading treaty chiefs to Washington and there threatened and cajoled them. But the chiefs steadfastly refused to make a decision without talking things over with their people back home, and the frustrated government finally sent them home, promising it would take up the matter again very soon.

During that same summer, a geological party went into the Black Hills with an Army escort. Since the government was offering to buy the region from the Sioux, it wanted to see whether it really was worth anything, or whether the gold discoveries announced with such flourishes of trumpets by Custer were anything more than superficial indications which would soon be exhausted. The resulting report was more than satisfactory. In September, Commissioners arrived at the Red Cloud Agency to discuss revising the Fort Laramie treaty *—specifically, they wanted the Sioux to sell the Black Hills. Senator William Allison of Iowa was chairman; the Commission included other members of Congress and Major General Alfred Terry, commanding the Department of the Dakota. It was a distinguished group, but the Indians received it with no songs of welcome.

On the contrary, the Commissioners came close to being the central figures in a massacre during the first hours after their arrival. Bellicose Indians among the many hundreds present suddenly surrounded them with leveled guns; one of them, Little Big Man, called to his followers that this was as good a time as any to begin a war. Bloodshed was averted, but only narrowly, partly by the coolness of two cavalry offi-

* Actually, there was no writing of treaties with Indian tribes after 1871, when the entire ridiculous pretense that tribes were sovereignties was abolished. It would be pleasant to be able to report that the change was made because common sense prevailed, but such was not the case. The House of Representatives had long complained that the Senate had too big a hand in Indian affairs, for under the Constitution only the Senate approved treaties. So, in 1871 the treaty fiction was ended, and relations with tribes were conducted by "agreements" which required the approval of both Senate and House. The practical difference was small.

cers who formed their commands into line of battle with carbines at the ready, and waited impassively and motionless, ready to charge the instant a hostile move was made, partly by the imperturbability of Spotted Tail, the Brule peace chief, who bluffed the war party by offering them a fight then and there if that was what they wanted.

What composure remained to the Commissioners must have been shaken when they sat in council later to discuss the purchase of the Black Hills and heard Red Cloud calmly propose that $600,000,000 seemed like a fair price for a region that meant so much to the red man, and appeared to mean even more to the white. When they had recovered their decimal points, they suggested that $6,000,000 would be a reasonable offer, and there the matter was left. The Commissioners apparently had no heart for haggling after their chilling experience and soon left. "The Commission were the gladdest people to get away from that part of the country that had ever visited there," General George Crook, who knew more about fighting than grammar, wrote. "They didn't recover their courage until they got the Missouri River between them."

Unfortunately for the Sioux, the discomfited Commissioners represented considerable influence in the government. They had been frightened and embarrassed, and their report reflected their resentment. It was necessary to teach the Indians a lesson, they said, for the Sioux had made no attempt to abide by the 1868 treaty—they had made no move to learn farming, for instance—and all in all, these people on the northern plains were never going to become civilized unless the government got very stern with them and taught them a lesson. The report did not put it in exactly these words, but the tenor was unmistakable.

The government soon moved to bring the Indians to heel. In early November, the Commissioner of Indian Affairs issued an ultimatum that all Indians must come onto the reservation and report to their agencies at once. The order was both impossible to comply with and a flagrant violation of the Fort Laramie treaty. It was a violation because the bands not on the Great Sioux Reservation were nevertheless on Indian land when they were on the unceded territory, and nothing in the Laramie agreement gave the government any right to restrict the Indians' use of that territory. It was impossible to comply with because agents were not able even to get word to all of their charges in the winter-locked country by January 31, and it was even less possible for the bands to make it back to the agencies. As for the nontreaty bands of Crazy Horse, Sitting Bull, and Gall, it is doubtful if they even knew an order had been issued.

Winter is a gaunt and skeletal season on the northern plains. The cold is unbelievably brutal, especially when driven by the wind that blows unchecked over the flatlands. To the Plains Indians, it was a season for sitting around the fire in tight-laced tepees, in the shelter of stream valley bluffs. Even if an Indian band were foolhardy enough to expose children and infants to the hardships of a long trip during the dead of winter, its ponies would probably not be up to the task on the meager desiccated grass they could graze where the harsh wind had swept the ground free of snow.

The January 31 deadline came; one small band had come in and that was all. The Indian Bureau turned the matter over to the Army; the Indians still off the reservation were now assumed to be in a state of war against the government. General Sheridan made plans to smash the hostiles. The government had its war, one of the most cynically contrived in all the long history of Indian wars, for at no point had the Sioux or Cheyenne given the slightest provocation.

Sheridan, planning his strategy, decided to use one of his favorite concepts, three converging columns. Major General Alfred Terry, commanding the Department of Dakota with headquarters in St. Paul, was to lead one column of about 1,000 men west from Fort Abraham Lincoln to the Yellowstone. Brigadier General George Crook, commanding the Department of the Platte, was to move from the North Platte River northward through the Powder River country to the Yellowstone River. And finally, Colonel John Gibbon would command a third column of about 450, moving eastward along the Yellowstone from Fort Ellis in Montana Territory. The three would meet somewhere in the vicinity of the junction of the Bighorn and the Yellowstone Rivers, driving the hostiles into a surround until they had no choice but to surrender or be annihilated.

There were estimated to be about 1,000 warriors in the Powder River country—one or two officers thought there might even be as many as 1,500. When the true size of the Indian forces would be learned, it would be one of the rudest shocks ever suffered by American arms.

General Crook was the first to move when he marched up into the unceded Indian territory—the government had knocked that phrase to bits!—in March. Crook had been transferred the year before to command of the Department of the Platte from command of the Department of Arizona where he had succeeded in getting the Apaches under control without excessive cost in lives or loss of honor to either side. On graduating from West Point in 1852, Crook had been assigned to fighting Indians in California, and had spent his entire career since on the Indian frontier except for the Civil War interlude. General Sherman was to call him the greatest Indian fighter and manager the United States ever had. The Sioux, however, were not going to add greatly to the brightness of that reputation during the next few months.

George Crook was a man of somewhat startling personal appearance because his beard parted naturally and was forked; he braided the two sides to keep them under control during the rigors of a campaign. He was a rather prickly character; his standards of conduct, both for himself and for others, were high, so that his comments on many of the prominent personalities of his times were caustic, and his evaluations of them often more critical and severe than those since made by history. Sheridan, for one, he held in very low esteem; he believed that the General built his reputation largely by assuming credit for the accomplishments of others (including those of Crook).

Crook left Fort Fetterman on the North Platte on March 1, on what he planned should be mainly a scouting trip "to get some idea of the country and the difficulties to be overcome in a summer campaign." Fort Fetterman had been built in 1867 on the south side of the river at approximately the point where the old Bozeman Trail had cut north; now the column pushed up the abandoned trail. The force consisted of ten companies * of cavalry (five each from the 2nd and 3rd Regiments) and two companies of the 4th Infantry.

During the first days, the column marched in beautiful sunny weather; then, about 125 miles north of the fort it had just made camp at sunrise after an all-night march, when a blizzard struck, with snow and harsh winds so blinding it was impossible to see more than a few yards, and temperatures that dropped steadily. After waiting in vain a day for the weather to improve, the column pushed on. It had left its wagon train encamped a day's march behind, and the rations it now carried were too limited to permit it to wait longer for better weather. The march north was continued, to the Tongue River and down that

---

* "Company" was still used in 1876, and for some time after, as the name of the cavalry as well as the infantry unit of organization next smaller than a regiment. It was replaced by "troop" in cavalry parlance during the next decade or so.

Bighorn Campaign of 1876:
Strategy and Principal Movements

stream to within less than a hundred miles of the Yellowstone; then, no signs of Indians having been found, the force cut east to the Powder River. For the first few days after the blizzard the cold was so intense that the thermometer often would not register—and mercury does not freeze until −38° F.

On the Powder, the tracks of two ponies were found and back-tracked to the village from which they had come. It was a camp set under a high bluff by the river. Colonel J. J. Reynolds, who with three companies of cavalry had followed the pony tracks, had come out on the bluffs almost immediately above the unsuspecting village just about at daybreak·on March 17. Reynolds gave the order to attack at once, and the horsemen scrambled down the steep slopes and fell on the sleep-befuddled Indians. What the Army did not know until afterward—and never was concerned about—was that this was a camp of friendly Northern Cheyennes of Chief Two Moon who had concluded, on learning that soldiers were moving into the country, that it would be best to go back to the reservation. With the Cheyennes were some Sioux who had also decided to return to their agency.

"The army," Custer wrote in his book, *My Life on the Plains,* "is the Indian's best friend." The Indian could do without such friends. The Army on the Indian frontier could fight wars but—except under rare leaders—it had seldom shown much talent for preventing them. The tools of its trade were the sword and the cannon, and it instinctively fell back on them when confronted by a problem. Army officers complained that the civilian Indian Bureau, through ineptness and corruption, created situations which the military had to put to rights, often at great cost and hardship. But, on a good many occasions, it had created its own situations of crisis, perhaps by retaliating against one band for depredations committed by another, perhaps, as here, by the stupidity of ruling that every Indian found in the region was, *ipso facto,* an enemy.

There was no doubt that Two Moon was friendly up to the time the yelling troopers fell on the camp that February morning. For that, we have the authority of young Lieutenant Sibley of Crook's staff who was a keen observer of all that occurred during the campaign. The chief and his Cheyennes would thereafter be implacable enemies of the Army, and four months later, on the heights above the Little Bighorn, would extract some small revenge for Reynolds' attack.

As a matter of fact, they did not wait that long. The cavalry swept through the camp, driving out the Indians and seizing many of their ponies as well as all their other belongings. But Cheyenne and Sioux warriors quickly rallied, and moved up to occupy the bluffs from which the soldiers had just attacked. There they held the advantage of position, and swooped down, putting up an intense rifle and arrow fire. Panic overtook the troops who retreated precipitously, leaving their dead behind, and there were dark whispers among the men that a wounded soldier had been abandoned. Even to leave dead was serious enough in view of the importance which the Indians place on the capture of bodies of enemies; to give up a wounded man was unthinkable.

The Indian pursuit of the cavalry continued until the next morning; the warriors recovered many of their ponies. General Crook himself retrieved something from the defeat by overtaking a party of Indians returning to camp and taking from them the ponies they were driving, but it was small consolation. The expedition returned to Fort Fetterman, where Crook brought charges against Colonel Reynolds and two captains as a result of the rout. The court-martial was an acrimonious one, with the three officers making counteraccusations, but all three were found guilty, two of them of neglect of duty, the third of the lesser charge of conduct to the prejudice of good order and military discipline. Colonel Reynolds, who received the sternest sentence, was suspended from command for one year.

It was not, from any point of view, a spectacular beginning to the great offensive against the so-called hostiles. Crook's setback had elated the tribesmen, and filled them with confidence. Agency Indians customarily moved out into the Powder River country in spring to hunt until cold weather drove them in again; this year the flow was greater than ever. A patriotic fervor was sweeping through the northern people moving them to cast their lot with Crazy Horse, Sitting Bull, and other nontreaty leaders who, after trying to avoid the white man, were now preparing to defend their land against him.

2. WHOM THE GODS WOULD DESTROY

The three-pronged campaign had been planned for early spring, sometime in April, if possible, as soon as the ground had dried out enough to bear up under the sharp edges of iron wagon tires, and the buffalo grass had turned green and was tall enough to supply grazing for horses, mules, and beef herds. But April came and went, and the great expedition was still immobilized, for reasons rather complicated but ultimately amounting to nothing more obscure than the indiscretion of a single man. That man was George Armstrong Custer.

To begin with, Custer was to have led the eastern column from Fort Abraham Lincoln. General Terry, as commander of the entire Department of Dakota with both the Fort Lincoln force and Colonel Gibbon's column under his overall command, did not think it wise to tie himself too closely to either. Hence he had selected Custer, an officer experienced in Indian fighting, to command the column from the east.

However, as the time for taking the field arrived, the commanding officer of the 7th Cavalry and commander-designate of the Fort Lincoln column was in Washington, frantically trying to extricate himself from webs of his own weaving.

The previous fall, when cold winds had brought a season of routine campaigning on the plains to an end, the acting colonel of the 7th Cavalry and his lady had left the West behind for a three-month leave in New York. The couple had a pleasant and exciting time, and at the end of the three months, Custer requested, and was granted, an extension of two months. Then, the pleasures of the big city still not having palled as the extension drew to a close, he asked for still more time. By then he had had five months away from his post.

It was then getting near to March, and, one would think, time for Custer to be giving thought to returning to make plans for the summer campaign and to start honing a sharp edge on his command. But if he was willing to let his staff in Dakota handle all preparations until it was time for him to lead the column out onto the plains, Secretary of War Belknap had other ideas. The Secretary denied Custer's latest request for more leave.

If the refusal had come from any other man, the Colonel might have taken it philosophically and been thankful for the long vacation he had already had. But, since the rejection had come from Secretary Belknap, Custer did take it personally, very much so. He was a man who often lost his temper but he harbored almost no lasting animosities, so far as is known. Even within his own regiment he showed no special aptitude for holding grudges against the officers in the anti-Custer group. The one virulent hatred of his life was William Worth Belknap.

The feud, whose violence appears to have been almost entirely on Custer's side, seems to have arisen over the matter of the sutler at Fort

Abraham Lincoln. By way of explanation, a sutler was a civilian who was granted the concession to operate what in a later day would be called a post exchange; he sold shoelaces, canned oysters, needles and thread, licorice root, chewing tobacco, and the hundred other articles that soldiers far from the nearest town could not possibly get otherwise. It was, as might be expected, a lucrative business because there was no competition.

Formerly, post commandants had appointed and removed sutlers, but Belknap had transferred this power to the Secretary of War in 1870 on his assumption of one-man rule over the Army. When soldiers at Fort Abraham Lincoln complained about the high prices at the sutler's store, Custer could do nothing about the store itself. However, he did circumvent the sutler completely by having company officers go in to Bismarck, only three or four miles away, to make purchases for the enlisted men.

The idea was ingenious, but a lieutenant colonel should not have expected to win a battle with the Secretary of War. The sutler appealed to Belknap, who immediately ordered Custer to cease and desist in his attempts to interfere with the sutler's business. The rebuff came when Custer was already in short temper from having his active body and expansive spirit shut up within the limited confines of a northern plains post in winter. Perhaps at any other time, when he was busy, he would have forgotten it in a few days; now he had plenty of time to brood, and out of his dark musings grew a violent hate of Secretary Belknap.

A little later, Custer had an opportunity to show his contempt for the Secretary of War. Belknap, on an inspection trip through the West in the summer of 1875, had included Fort Abraham Lincoln on his itinerary. It was the most elementary military courtesy for the post commandant to meet the Secretary of War at the border of the reservation. Custer, with a fine instinct for self-destruction, waited in his headquarters for Belknap to come to him. When the sutler sent over a gift of champagne to be drunk at the meeting of the two men, Custer sent it back.

Thus, it may have been with a certain smug satisfaction that Belknap refused the leave extension—or very possibly, he thought nothing further than that it was time for Custer to get back to the duties the government was paying him to perform. All this has appeared to be far away, not only in distance but in relevance, from the Sioux and

Cheyenne Indians and the coming campaign. Custer, with some help from fate, would soon begin drawing the elements closer together.

Before the Custers had left New York to return to Dakota Territory, disaster struck Secretary Belknap. Grant's administration was collapsing under its dull weight of corruption as the extent of malfeasance, abuse of public trust, and stealing of public money began to come to light. Secretary of the Interior Delano had resigned some months earlier because of huge frauds in connection with Indian Bureau funds; now, on March 2, Belknap suddenly resigned when a House investigating committee discovered that he was involved in the selling of sutlers' concessions at Army posts and voted impeachment proceedings.

Custer, going ahead with his packing, seems to have heard of the fall of his enemy with satisfaction, but he could not resist a possible chance to kick Belknap when he was down. He sent off word to a Congressman acquaintance saying that he stood ready to tell all he knew about Belknap's part in many murky transactions involving Army posts on the frontier. Then, having set this time bomb which would hurt no one but himself, he and Elizabeth Custer ("Libbie," he called her) left on the steam cars for Bismarck.

The train stalled in deep drifts some forty or fifty miles short of Bismarck, but brother Tom came through from the fort in a bobsled, to rescue the Custers and three new hounds the Colonel had bought in the East. The homecoming was a brief one. They had been at Fort Lincoln only about a week when, on March 15, Custer received a summons to come to Washington and tell the House committee all about Belknap's questionable activities in the frontier posts, as he had offered to do.

Custer at first naïvely proposed to answer by mail a list of written questions sent him by the committee, but he quickly learned that Congress was not so easily put off. He went to Washington where, in the witness chair, he proved to know absolutely nothing. His every charge, every accusation was pure hearsay, rumor, gossip, a story heard at third-hand from dubious sources. Under the questioning of the committee members, all of his promised revelations turned out to have no more substance than an old woman's tittle-tattle. Custer became increasingly reckless as his stories of scandal in high places fizzled like wet squibs. His tactics in battle had always been to attack, and he could not suppress the instinct to do so now. In his wide and sweeping accusations, he included Orvil Grant, the President's brother, as one of those who had been involved in chicanery in the West, and he even hinted that the President himself had adjusted the boundary of the Great Sioux Reservation for the benefit of certain parties. His statements could not have been better calculated to put his neck in a noose.

Time was passing. General Terry had planned to start Custer and his column from Fort Lincoln about April 1; now April was almost over and Terry could not wait forever. Custer, in Washington, was becoming frantic with worry that he would miss the big show against the Sioux, and was sending plaintive telegrams from time to time asking advice and help of Terry and Sheridan. Then, on April 28, Sheridan telegraphed Terry that it was time to pick someone else to lead the column, and, after some discussion, it was decided that Terry himself would take command.

The decision to replace Custer did not spring from the brain of General Sheridan; it had originated as high in the chain of command as it was possible to go. Sheridan was merely forwarding orders he had received from Sherman (now reinstated in Washington that Belknap was gone), who in turn had received them from Secretary of War Alphonso Taft, who had had them from the President of the United States himself. Ordinarily, Grant would not have concerned himself with a relatively minor matter of who should command a force in a Western military department, but Custer had been more rash than he knew when he included the President's own family in his accusations.

Custer was at last released by the House committee, which told him he was free to go. However, Sherman advised him to see the President before he started for the West, so he presented himself at the White House on Monday morning, May 1, at ten o'clock, and sent in his card. He was still there at three in the afternoon when the President's secretary came out to tell him there was no point in waiting any longer because Grant would not see him. Custer then wrote a primly formal note saying he regretted any offense he might have given the President, but that it had been unintentional, etc., left the message, and departed. He appears to have blithely assumed that he had now completely taken care of Sherman's suggestion that he see the President. Military protocol required that he should call on Sherman himself before departing. He did call at the General's office once during the afternoon, and at his hotel twice during the early evening, but Sherman had not yet returned from a trip. And the cavalry officer, who should have known better, decided he had also discharged this obligation, and entrained for Dakota Territory.

At Chicago, Custer had changed trains and was waiting to start for St. Paul when an aide of General Sheridan located him. Sheridan had received a telegram from General Sherman, ". . . He was not justified in leaving without seeing the President and myself. Please intercept him and await further orders; meanwhile let the expedition proceed without him."

Custer sent a long and bewildered telegram back to Sherman, explaining about the hours spent waiting to see the President, and about his attempts to see Sherman. Perhaps this was all that was expected of him, that he abase himself. Sherman responded by directing that Custer be permitted to proceed to Terry's headquarters in St. Paul.

There is an element almost of Greek tragedy in the way this man, who had been a favored son of the gods, was being made their jest now. No matter how he tried to extricate himself from the trap he had built with his own indiscreetness, he only succeeded in embroiling himself still deeper. Nothing could have been more tragic for him, to whom campaigning on the Great Plains had become not only a professional assignment but a glorious and intoxicating way of life, than to be left behind by the greatest of all the expeditions against the Indians. Yet by this time Custer the confident, flamboyant egotist had been reduced to such a state of abject humbleness that he sent a telegram to Washington asking only that he be permitted to proceed on to Fort Abraham Lincoln, to join his wife rather than being required to remain in St. Paul during the campaign.

On May 5, General Terry received orders from Sherman: "Have just come from the President who orders that General Custer be allowed to rejoin his post, to remain there on duty, but not to accompany the expedition supposed to be on the point of starting against the hostile Indians under General Terry." During the war, the implacability of Grant had worn the Confederate armies down to bare bones; it now appeared that Custer was the hapless victim of that same stubborn character trait that refused to let an antagonist go until he had been crushed.

Missing the campaign would have been a personal tragedy to Custer, but one possible avenue of appeal still remained open to him, General Alfred Terry, his immediate superior. When his train reached St. Paul, he humiliated himself once more and begged Terry to be permitted to accompany his regiment on the campaign.

General Terry was no tough, hard-bitten officer, but a rather gentle man who looked as though he would be more at home in a scholar's study than at the head of troops. A lawyer at the outbreak of the Civil War, he had volunteered and quickly found himself in a colonel's uniform. In that day of regiments manned and officered entirely by volunteers, it was not at all unusual to find lawyers with no military training becoming colonels, especially if they had helped recruit the regiment. But Terry had had the feel of the business; he fought from First Bull Run to the storming of Fort Fisher on the North Carolina coast where, as a major general, he was in command. After the war, he decided to remain in the Army. His brilliant conduct of the Fort Fisher operation had caught the eye of Sherman so that, when the latter was organizing his Division of the Missouri after the war, he reached out without hesitation for Terry to command the Department of Dakota.

It would have been easy for many commanding officers to have turned Colonel Custer aside. After all, the President himself had ordered that the cavalry officer who talked too much about things of which he knew nothing should remain at Fort Abraham Lincoln. It was not that easy for the kindly Terry. As he explained long afterward to friends, "Custer, . . . with tears in his eyes, begged my aid. How could I resist it?"

The thing was done in formal military fashion. Custer, under Terry's eye, composed a letter to Grant, asking that he be permitted to serve with his regiment even though he was not to command the expedition. "I appeal to you as a soldier to spare me the humiliation of seeing my regiment march to meet the enemy and I not to share its dangers."

Terry added his endorsement in forwarding the letter: he had no desire to question the orders of the President, but if it were possible to modify those orders, Custer's services would be very valuable.

General Philip Sheridan was next in the chain of command. There had been another day when Custer had been under a cloud and suspended from duty, and Sheridan had intervened to bring him back to the plains. He had been Sheridan's protégé and darling then and for years was the cavalryman who struck some responsive chord in the General who saw only the dash and courage and never the shortcomings. But, at last, Sheridan was becoming bored with this perennial seeker after glory, now in his thirty-seventh year, whose ideas of leadership and responsibility were not much advanced from what they had been a dozen years earlier, and still found their highest expression in whooping at the head of a charge. Sheridan's thin endorsement did not advance Custer's cause:

> I am sorry Lieutenant Colonel Custer did not manifest as much interest in staying at his post to organize and get ready his regiment and the expedition as he now does to accompany it. On a previous occasion in eighteen sixty-eight I asked executive clemency for Colonel Custer to enable him to accompany his regiment against the Indians, and I sincerely hope that if granted this time it may have sufficient effect to prevent him from again attempting to throw discredit upon his profession and his brother officers.

The next morning Terry got an answer from Sherman. No one knows what occurred, whether Grant decided that he had inflicted enough punishment on Custer, whether Sherman prevailed on the President to modify his stand, or whether Grant was influenced by the outcry in the Democratic newspapers that he was ruining Custer's career solely because of his petty vengefulness. Whatever the reason, the cigar-smoking man in the White House relented; Custer could go if Terry wanted him.

"Advise Custer to be prudent, not to take along any newspaper men, who always make mischief, and to abstain from personalities in the future," Sherman added soberly in his telegram sending along the good news for Custer. Sherman's advice was ignored by Custer. When the 7th Cavalry headed west, it was accompanied by newspaper correspondent Mark Kellogg who died at the Little Bighorn.

Custer was given the good news at Terry's headquarters. There is no record of his reactions, but certainly he must have profusely thanked Terry, who alone was making it possible for him to take part in the war against the Sioux. Yet, after leaving General Terry's headquarters to walk to his hotel he met an acquaintance, Colonel Ludlow, and informed him that he was now back in command of the 7th Cavalry. Custer, in obvious high spirits after the news he had just received, added that at the first opportunity during the campaign he was going to "cut loose from General Terry during the summer," that during operations two years earlier along the Yellowstone he had "got away with Stanley and would be able to swing clear of Terry." Aside from Custer's faulty memory of how he had been able to get away from Stanley in 1874, the episode indicates an ultimate in ingratitude, that within the hour after learning that his command had been restored, Custer should be openly planning to flaunt the authority of the one man responsible for getting it returned to him.

And so at last the campaign was underway, the greatest combination of forces ever sent out to do battle with Indians. General Terry's column was the first to march. It departed from Fort Abraham Lincoln on the morning of May 17. Reveille had been at three, and the column, 1,207 strong, swung out at Terry's signal at five o'clock, through wisps of cold fog which still clung to the ground. While the infantry and the train headed directly from the encampment area down the road that mounted the river bluff and headed west, Colonel Custer led the 7th Cavalry through the fort and across the parade so that wives and their men might see each other briefly once again. Then the regimental band tootled away at the inevitable "Garry Owen," and then the almost equally inevitable "The Girl I Left Behind Me." The last company passed out of the fort; the music dwindled in the distance, and the regiment passed over the edge of the bluff and was gone.

However, rank has its privileges, and Elizabeth Custer did not flutter her handkerchief in farewell that morning but rode along with her husband, to remain with him through the first night's bivouac and return the next morning with the regiment's paymaster. The presence of the paymaster on the first day's march had not caused any great rejoicing. Custer had arbitrarily held out the pay of the enlisted men even though it was overdue because, as self-appointed guardian of his men's morals, he had wanted to keep their pockets empty until they were a full day's march from the fleshpots of Bismarck. He undoubtedly prevented some morning-after headaches, but the episode did not increase his popularity. Later, some of the money was found blowing among the litter of the Little Bighorn battlefield.

The main strength of Terry's column was the 7th Cavalry. As late as the middle of February, the General had been pleading for the return of three companies that had been sent back to the South on duty; they had finally been transferred back and all twelve companies were now present. In addition to the cavalry, there were three companies of infantry, a special infantry detachment with a battery of three Gatling guns, forty-five Indian scouts, and 190 civilians: teamsters, guides, packers, herders, blacksmiths, interpreters, wheelwrights, and all the rest of the varied crew of craftsmen and specialized talents needed to keep an army operating on the frontier. Among these civilians was Boston, youngest of the Custer brothers, signed on as a forage master and hoping the dry plains air would help a bronchial condition, and nephew Armstrong ("Autie") Reed, seventeen, carried on the roster as a herder but really his uncle's guest on a glorious outing.

The column moved almost due westward, along the route followed by the Northern Pacific today, but then only a survey line, until it reached the Yellowstone River. It was to push up the Yellowstone until it met the column of Colonel John Gibbon moving downriver. The forces would be supplied by a Missouri River steamboat, the *Far West*.

Affairs went almost exactly as they had been outlined in the Plan of Operations, and the two forces met near the mouth of Rosebud Creek, whose waters flow into the Yellowstone from the Powder River country to the south. There was no sign or word of General Crook who was somewhere to the south, presumably driving the Indians toward the forces on the Yellowstone. As a matter of fact, Crook's course had brought him against the Indians, but he was doing very little driving.

3. "COME ON, DAKOTAS, IT'S A GOOD DAY TO DIE"

As he had in March, Crook moved north in May from Fort Fetterman, following the empty Bozeman Trail. At the site of Fort Reno, he found little to indicate that this had once been a busy Army outpost; in their eagerness to wipe out all vestiges of military occupation, the Indians had razed even the cemetery so that not a headboard remained standing. Fort Philip Kearny, which Colonel Carrington had built up from nothing, had returned to nothing, and those who had ridden out to die with Captain Fetterman lay in graves no longer marked.

Crook led a powerful force: five companies of the 2nd Cavalry, ten of the 3rd Cavalry, two of the 4th Infantry, and three companies of the 9th Infantry, totaling about 1,050 officers and men. There were also the usual civilian teamsters, packers, and other auxiliaries. Crow Indian scouts, 180 of them, arrived to join the force on June 14 when it was camped north of the site of Fort Kearny, at the junction of the two branches of Goose Creek. Two hours later, 86 Shoshones followed them. Crook drew up this troops in a regimental front on the flat now covered by the northern end of the city of Sheridan, Wyoming; holding his forces in formation he welcomed his red allies and then treated them to a feast.

Several streams flow northward to join the Yellowstone through the country where the nontreaty Indians ranged. The most important ones, from west to east, are Rosebud Creek, Tongue River, and Powder River. Of them all, the Powder River is the longest and has the most extensive set of tributaries, and for that reason gave its name to the entire region. Another stream to the west of these, the Bighorn River, had its own importance. Its upper waters lay west of the Big Horn Mountains, in Crow Indian territory, but its lower course to the Yellowstone was the boundary between the unceded Sioux territory and the Crow lands to the west. It had a tributary, the Little Bighorn, which came in through the unceded country from a southeasterly direction to join it. The Little Bighorn would acquire some considerable fame in the weeks immediately ahead.

Scouts brought in word that the Sioux were probably on Rosebud Creek to the north, and Crook at once began making ready. His wagon train was left behind with the civilians and a small infantry guard in camp; supplies were stripped to a minimum and put on pack mules. To make for greater speed, the infantrymen were also mounted on mules, although the gain was not as much as it might have been because many of the unhappy fellows knew almost nothing about riding. It would seem that it might have been advantageous to have given them some training before the eve of battle—but the Army has always been the Army. On the morning of June 16, almost 1,300 men, including the Indian scouts, rode out to meet the Sioux.

The hostile Indians were completely aware of what Crook was doing, for their scouts watched all his movements. They were optimistic about their prospects in battle, because only a week earlier they had held a Sun Dance in which Sitting Bull, after permitting fifty pieces of flesh to be cut from his arms and chest and undergoing other tests of fortitude, had had a vision of soldiers falling into the Indian camp. It was interpreted as a clear omen that the soldiers would be defeated, and the warriors consequently were eager for battle. So eager, in fact, that a large force of Sioux and Cheyennes traveled during the night of the sixteenth to come to grips with the Army forces. That same night, Crook's column had made its camp in a wide, grassy spot in the valley of the Rosebud in southern Montana, sleeping on the ground in the open

The Bighorn Campaign
Troop Movements of Northern Forces
to Noon, June 25, 1876

MONTANA TERRITORY

YELLOWSTONE R.

O'FALLON'S CR.

CONFERENCE
ON FAR WEST
JUNE 21

GIBBON

TERRY-CUSTER

TULLOCK'S CR.

TONGUE R.

PUMPKIN CR.

MIZPAH CR.

POWDER R.

NOON
JUNE 25

CUSTER

RENO'S SCOUT

WOLF MTS.

ROSEBUD CR.

NOON
JUNE 25

SIOUX
CAMP

LITTLE POWDER R.

BIGHORN R.

CROOK'S
DEFEAT
JUNE 17

ROUTE ORDERED
BY GEN. TERRY

BIG HORN MTS.

CROOK'S
CAMP

POWDER R.

N
W   E
S

WYOMING TERRITORY

0   Miles   50

because tents had been left behind with the wagons. When morning came, the hostile force was only five miles away.

When the column set out after breakfast, the Indian scouts were very reluctant to lead the way. The day before, they had been full of braggadocio about what they would do to any Sioux or Cheyennes they met; now they had to be prodded into going out to scout ahead of the troops. They did not have far to look; very shortly there was gunfire ahead and a number of the scouts came galloping back, shouting that there were many Sioux in front. In a matter of minutes, a great force of Sioux and Cheyennes swept into sight and made a spirited full-scale assault on the column, and the battle was joined.

There is no way of knowing exactly what the numerical odds were in the battle. General Cook had almost 1,300 men. The Army account credited the Indians with 1,500 warriors in the battle, and another figure, obtained in part from Indians who took part in the fight, says that Chief Crazy Horse led about 1,000 warriors into combat and was reinforced with several hundred more during the course of the fighting. It would seem that the two sides were fairly evenly matched as far as numbers were concerned.

Crook took some of the infantry onto a bluff which they held while he looked over the lay of the land from his vantage point. He decided to charge the Indians and sent for the cavalry, but in his absence two companies of his mounted troops had been sent to a high hill on the opposite side of the creek, and the rest had disappeared somewhere off in the other direction. There they were attacked so hard and so continuously that they had to take up defensive positions on the edge of a bluff.

There is no point in trying to describe the battle in terms of lines and positions. General Crook did his best at first to form a line of battle according to conventional Civil War doctrine, but his attempts to recall the main body of cavalry, out on his left and out of sight, produced no results for more than two hours. When the cavalry at last was able to join up with him, the Indians were no longer assaulting his front, and opportunities for an attack were gone.

It had been a mad, swirling fight, actually three battles within one, as the Sioux and Cheyennes kept up a constant pressure on the troops, riding among them, and at some points splitting them into small groups of a few men and engaging in hand-to-hand fighting. There was an incongruous element in the scene: wild plums and crabapples were in full bloom and their petals, shaken loose by the pounding passage of hundreds of horsemen, drifted constantly down, while their fragrance found its way even to men enveloped in dust and powder smoke.

Crazy Horse, the Oglala chief, was in the forefront of the fighting, exhorting his warriors to greater feats with his famous war-cry, "Come on, Dakotas,* it's a good day to die." At one point, when the Sioux started to fall back in the beginning of a retreat, Crazy Horse, with several other chiefs, rode among them, encouraging and heartening them, and they returned to the battle. Neither side would have to walk with heads bent in shame later, for bravery was in the air. At one point, the Crow and Shoshone scouts engaged in savage hand-to-hand combat with a group of Sioux while nearby soldiers had to hold their fire and watch because it was next to impossible to distinguish the copper skin of ally from that of foe in the whirling melee.

For the Army force, there would have been no chance to extricate itself, no opportunity to withdraw from the battle if it had so attempted. If the troops had panicked or broken anywhere along the line, the result would have been annihilation. The Sioux were carrying the fight to the soldiers in a very un-Indian manner; usually they were no desperate threat to resolute men who maintained a stout defense. But eventually the individualistic nature of the Sioux and Cheyenne warriors began to assert itself. Early in the afternoon they started to break off fighting and to drift away. It was not that they had at last become intimidated by the forces opposed to them; theirs was a simpler motive. One of the warriors explained it later, "They were tired and hungry, so they went home."

As the enemy began to withdraw, General Crook made a last attempt to achieve a decisive victory. His white scouts had told him that there was a large Sioux village about eight miles down the Rosebud. He had, in fact, been making ready to move on it in the morning when Crazy

---

* "Dakota," meaning "allies," is the Sioux's own name for themselves. The more common "Sioux" is an etymological monstrosity, the truncation of Nadouessioux, which in turn is a French form of the Chippewa Nadoue-is-iw, meaning little snake, and hence, enemy, the Chippewa appellation for their foes, the Dakotas (the Iroquois of the East were the big snakes). Although whites also used the word Dakota quite frequently, Sioux was by far the most common term, and for the sake of consistency has been used exclusively in this book.

The picture might be muddied by adding that Crazy Horse did not say "Dakota." The Sioux nation was a large one, and had three distinct dialects. The Santee Sioux of the eastern prairies, the Yanktons, and the western Teton Sioux, respectively called themselves Dakotas, Nakotas and Lakotas. So, Crazy Horse on the Rosebud: "Come on, Lakotas, it's a good day to die."

Horse caught him first and gave him something more substantial to cope with than a village whose inhabitants would have included a large proportion of women, children, and old men. Now, at midday, he sent Captain Anson Mills with eight companies of cavalry sweeping down the valley to overwhelm the village lying ahead.

But after the force was on its way, Crook looked more carefully at the valley of Rosebud Creek lying before him. It was narrow and quite steep and hemmed in, and everything considered, it would be an ideal place for an enemy force to ambush Mills's detachment. The General thereupon sent his aide with a single orderly dashing down the valley after Mills, who was finally overtaken after a chase of several miles. Mills sensibly led his command up out of the valley and back to the main force on higher ground. The move very possibly did save him from an ambush. At the same time, it enabled him to catch some of the Sioux from the rear as he circled behind them on his return. One thing it did not do was save a Sioux village from destruction, because Crook's scouts had been wrong and the village Mills had been hurrying to attack did not exist.

That night Crook camped where he had the night before, near the spot where the battle had begun. The dead were buried in the dark, and all traces of the graves obliterated. The next morning the bruised column retraced its way the forty miles to the camp on Goose Creek. Crook's official report claimed victory: "My troops beat these Indians on a field of their own choosing and drove them in utter rout from it, as far as the proper care of my wounded and prudence would justify." But Sheridan observed that if it was a victory, it was one without results since Crook had not followed it up. As a matter of fact, Crook in his own heart considered it a defeat, too, and it rankled all his life as the one real licking he had received at the hands of Indians. He insisted ever after that if the battle had gone as he had planned, if his orders had been obeyed and the cavalry had come up when he had summoned it, the Indians would have been defeated—and how many other commanders have made the same lament!

But there was more to it than that. The Army forces had fought well and there had been no serious mistakes in tactics. Crook failed to recognize that he had been up against something new in Indian warfare. These warriors had fought with a purpose and maintained a constant pressure completely different from their charge-and-run-away tactics of the past. It appeared that a new spirit was animating them, causing them to submerge, at last, their self-defeating individualism in common effort for the good of all. Unfortunately, the hour was very late and the red men had already lost too many wars.

While Crook lay glumly in camp awaiting reinforcements, the Sioux and Cheyennes filled the countryside about, harassing his force in every possible way. They set fire to the grass, tried to run off the horse and mule herds, shot at small details whose duties took them away from the camp, even came close enough to fire into the camp at long range. Crook's force remained completely immobilized for more than a month.

4. "NOW, CUSTER, DON'T BE GREEDY"

During the time General Crook had been moving toward his battle on the Rosebud, the combined forces of Terry and Gibbon were going ahead with operations. A supply base had been established on the Yellowstone at the mouth of the Powder River, and was provisioned by the Missouri River steamboat, *Far West*. It was the opinion of most officers that the hostiles would be found on either Rosebud Creek or the lower Bighorn River, and so it was decided that the logical first step in the campaign was to look into the possibility that they might instead be on either the Tongue or Powder River.

Major Marcus A. Reno, second in command of the 7th Cavalry, was sent with six companies of the regiment on an eight-day scout. His orders were to go up the Powder River to its head, cross over to the upper Tongue, and return down that stream to the Yellowstone. Major Reno for some reason chose to disobey his orders. Instead of returning down the Tongue River, he led his command across the valley of the Tongue and on to Rosebud Creek, which he reached on June 17, the same day Crook was being turned back by Crazy Horse forty miles to the south. However, Reno had no way of knowing of Crook's nearness, and turned north, following the Rosebud back to the Yellowstone. Terry had wanted to stay clear of the Rosebud for the time being for fear the Sioux might be alerted, but Reno saw no Indians. However, he did find the trail of many Indians, but he had not followed it to learn where it led.

General Terry was now almost certain that the Sioux had crossed over from the Rosebud to the stream known as the Little Bighorn, a tributary of the Bighorn River. His strategy, in that case, was obvious to him: he would send Gibbon up the Bighorn and the Little Bighorn while Custer and the 7th Cavalry circled around and came down the Little Bighorn from the south; the hostiles would be caught between the two forces. Gibbon's column started on its way at midday on June 21 from the camp opposite the mouth of the Rosebud, headed up the Yellowstone for the mouth of the Bighorn River fifty miles away. Colonel Gibbon and his cavalry commander, Major James Brisbin, remained behind for a council of war; they, with General Terry, would travel on the *Far West* to catch up with the column.

Terry outlined his strategy at a meeting with Custer, Gibbon, and Brisbin on board the *Far West* on the evening of the twenty-first, as the stern-wheeler lay tied up at the bank near the mouth of the Rosebud with the current of the Yellowstone gurgling past her hull. Custer was to proceed up the Rosebud with his regiment till he found the trail Reno had discovered a few days earlier. If he found that the trail turned west and led across the divide toward the Little Bighorn, "as it appears to be almost certain that it will be found," he was not to follow it but to continue south up the Rosebud, even well beyond the headwaters of that stream, before swinging west to the Little Bighorn and down that stream toward the north again.

In his entire movement, Custer was to travel at a rate of speed which would bring him, as nearly as he could estimate it, to the valley of the Little Bighorn from the south at the same time Gibbon was entering it from the north, so that any hostiles present would be caught between the two columns and forced to surrender or be defeated in battle. General Terry laid off Custer's estimated daily marches on the map with compasses to make sure the plan was feasible.

Custer was also ordered to scout the upper waters of a stream called Tullock's Creek which flows from southeast to northwest into the Bighorn; Gibbon's scouts would examine the lower part of the stream. Crow Indian scouts had suggested that the hostile camp might possibly be on this stream. In order to learn the result of Custer's examination of Tullock's Creek as quickly as possible, General Terry sent one of his own scouts, George Hernandeen, along with the 7th Cavalry; he was to bring the news across country when the time came.

Custer had boasted long and often that the 7th Cavalry was capable of whipping any and all Indians on the plains. The other officers at the meeting were apparently not quite so sanguine about the invincibility of the regiment and its leader. Terry suggested to Custer that it might be wise to strengthen his column, at the expense of Gibbon's, by attaching Major Brisbin's cavalry to the 7th Regiment for the operation. Custer demurred; the 7th was such a closely knit outfit that reinforcements in the form of a strange unit would add nothing to its strength. It was then proposed that the 7th Cavalry be given more firepower by sending along with it the column's three Gatling guns. Again Custer objected. The guns would "embarrass" him; the regiment would be more than strong enough without them.

After the conference on the steamboat, Custer went ashore and called a meeting of his officers. The other officers remained aboard the *Far West,* which would soon be taking them upstream to rejoin Gibbon's column. Terry suggested to Brisbin, who was leaning over the rail and looking glumly into the river water coiling by, that he did not seem to have much faith in Colonel Custer. None at all, Brisbin replied, none at all.

The 7th left about noon on June 22. A review had been ordered by Custer, with General Terry, Colonel Gibbon, and Major Brisbin (Brisbin and Gibbon both held brevet ranks as generals) as reviewing officers, with Custer beside them, presenting his beloved regiment. Custer was on a sorrel horse named Vic; he wore a fringed buckskin suit in the best Western style with a double-breasted blouse with military buttons, and a light-gray, low-crowned hat with broad brim.

A shrill of the massed trumpets of the entire regiment announced the beginning of the review, with Major Reno leading the march-by. (The notes of "Garry Owen" were missing; the band as well as Custer's hounds were being left behind.) Custer sat proudly observing what he had wrought. However, his pleasure was diluted somewhat when the pack train went by. The regiment was leaving its wagons behind and it was rusty at the business of lashing on a pack saddle, consequently some of the results left a bit to be desired. Terry was a kindly man and his criticisms were gentle, but Custer flushed.

The last of the regiment passed, the dust settled, and Terry conferred briefly with Custer. Then the two shook hands, and Terry said, "God bless you." The colonel reined his horse around, ready to spur off and gallop to the head of the regiment. Colonel Gibbon called to him, "Now, Custer, don't be greedy. Wait for us." It was not a jocular remark; sharp-nosed, dour John Gibbon was not a man given to badinage, and certainly not at this moment when he was griped by an intestinal upset. Gibbon, who had been campaigning on the plains when Custer was still playing marbles, well knew the reputation of the cavalry leader for impetuousness and made his admonition, as he said afterward, in the hope that it might restrain the colonel of the 7th.

"Now, Custer, don't be greedy. Wait for us," Gibbon had called, and Custer turned in his saddle, waved gaily, and replied, "No, I won't." And with this cryptic reply, he galloped off.

The regiment continued its march through the twenty-third and twenty-fourth. It mustered about six hundred men, and had with it forty-four Crow and Arikara scouts, and twenty civilian guides, packers and interpreters. Boston Custer and nephew Autie Reed were present; Custer had had them transferred from the quartermaster department so they would not miss the fun. The trail that Reno had found was located and the regiment continued along it, passing through abandoned campsites that indicated a large number of hostiles had been there. The regiment traveled carefully, trying to raise as little dust as possible, with bugle calls forbidden. It had gone into camp on the evening of June 24 under a steep bluff when the scouts came back to report that the trail left the valley of the Rosebud just ahead and, as had been expected, went west across the divide into the valley of the Little Bighorn.

Custer supporters have defended their hero ever since 1876 against the charge that he willfully disobeyed orders. If he was not willful, he was decidedly contemptuous and highhanded in his disregard of the plan of operations that had been outlined on board the *Far West* and which, as written orders, he carried in his pocket.

Those orders, for one thing, directed him very explicitly to "thoroughly examine the upper part of Tullock's Creek" and to try to send a scout through to Gibbon's column with information on the result. He completely ignored Tullock's Creek; no orders were given to his chief of scouts to send men to look it over, and the white scout, George Hernandeen, whom Terry had sent with Custer specifically to carry word of the result to Gibbon's column, continued along with the regiment. That there were no Indians on Tullock's Creek is beside the point; it was a willful—call it a cavalier—disregard of orders. And it probably had its effect on events, because General Terry held Gibbon's column at the mouth of Tullock's Creek for more than a day, awaiting the arrival of the message from Custer which never came. If there had not been this delay, subsequent events might well have been somewhat different.

Now, after the scouts brought back word that the trail led over the divide into the valley of the Little Bighorn, Custer once again ignored his orders. Those orders were clear and unequivocal: "Should [the trail] be found, as it appears to be almost certain that it will be found, to turn toward the Little Big Horn he [General Terry] thinks that you should still proceed southward, perhaps as far as the head-waters of the Tongue, and then turn toward the Little Big Horn, . . ." Nothing could be clearer—and do not be misled by that "he thinks"; when a superior officer "thinks" or "suggests" or "believes," it is still an order. Nevertheless, Custer called his officers together in the dark and outlined a completely different plan of operation to them. During the night, they would follow the trail across the divide, a low range called the Wolf Mountains then and the Rosebud Mountains today. When daylight came, the regiment would remain concealed in the wooded and rocky high country, and would lie low all day (June 25) while the scouts located the hostile camp, and would then strike at dawn on the twenty-sixth.

The weary regiment was routed out, and the march resumed, with nothing but the stars for light, and they provided little illumination when the trail passed down deep ravines or under trees. Troopers gave their horses their heads and dozed intermittently at first, but confusion spread and soon there was no napping as the regiment, in single file, resorted to a clanking of tin cups to maintain contact through the complexity of ridges and ravines. Colonel Custer, the tireless, himself admitted the futility of the night march at last, and called an end to it about 2 A.M., when the regiment settled down for some rest.

The scouts had continued on ahead, and by daybreak had climbed to a high point on the divide between the Rosebud and the Little Bighorn known as the Crow's Nest. Lieutenant Charles A. Varnum, chief of scouts, had gone with the Crow scouts to the top of the peak, which overlooked the valley of the Little Bighorn for many miles. The Crows explained that their warriors used the high point when they were out to steal horses from the Sioux because from it the early daylight revealed the smoke of the morning cooking fires of any camp in the valley. This morning, as dawn spread over the valley, the Little Bighorn was so far away that it was revealed only by the trees and bushes along its banks outlining its course, merely a dark line meandering through the dusty wrinkled plain. But the sharp eyes of the Indians and of the two guides, Charley Reynolds and the half-breed Mitch

Bouyer, saw something in addition, the indefinable stirring of a dark spot by the river that their trained eyes told them was an immense herd of ponies, and along the river they were able to identify, even at that distance, a very large Indian camp.

They tried to point out the hostile camp to Lieutenant Varnum. "Look for worms," they told him, but strain his eyes as hard as he would, he could not make out any of the pulsing movement that marked the slow milling of the pony herd, much less the village itself. He had ridden for seventy hours without sleep, and, as Varnum admitted afterward, his eyes were sore and not much good for long distance. He wrote a message to the commanding officer, reporting what he had seen and been told; while he awaited for the dispatch to be taken back, he noted that the smoke rising from the regiment's camp-fires could be seen without trouble ten miles away. The Crow scouts were very angry that Custer would even have allowed fires at such a time and place.

The regiment concealed itself in a ravine about three miles short of the Crow's Nest while Custer rode on ahead to have a look for himself at the Sioux village. Although he climbed the Crow's Nest and used glasses, he was unable to make out any pony herd or village, for by that time the sun had come over the hills and cast an obscuring haze over the valley. He returned and told his officers he did not think there was any hostile camp there.

During the confused night march, one of the mule packs had become loose, and a sack and a box of hardtack had dropped off. As soon as the disappearance was discovered, a sergeant was sent back to recover the lost articles. He found them several miles back—but he also found several Sioux warriors sitting around, examining the contents of the sack. The Indians rode off when they saw the sergeant, but later, several more were observed watching the regiment. If surprise were planned, it was too late.

Custer decided to attack at once. The Army command was convinced that the Indians would attempt to run if confronted by a military force of any competence. In accord with this belief, Custer now made ready to pursue and bring the hostiles to battle before they could escape. However, by his self-willed action, he was going into action a day earlier than General Terry's plan called for—which meant he would fight without Gibbon's support. The cost of Custer's disregard of his orders was going to be high—very high—and the bill was coming due very soon.

Giving up all further attempts at concealment, Custer led the regiment from the ravine to the divide where the land sloped down into the valley of the Little Bighorn and there, a few minutes after noon, he halted and made his dispositions for action. The usual division of the regiment into battalions had been abolished during the march, and company commanders had answered directly to the commanding officer. Now Colonel Custer drew a short way apart with his adjutant, Lieutenant William W. Cooke, whose Canadian birth and imposing side whiskers had led Custer to dub him "The Queen's Own." With Cooke making notations in his memorandum book, Custer quickly divided the regiment into battalions.

One battalion, composed of Companies H, K, and D, was commanded by Captain Frederick Benteen, commander of H Company and senior captain of the regiment. A second battalion, also three companies strong—A, G, and M—was given to Major Reno, the only field officer, other than Custer, in the regiment. Five companies Custer retained under his personal command: Company C, his own brother, Captain Thomas Custer commanding; Company L of his brother-in-law, Lieutenant James Calhoun; and, to complete the list, for these units and their commanders would very soon achieve immortality, Companies E, F, and I, led by Lieutenant Algernon Smith, Captain George W. Yates, and Captain Miles W. Keogh. The one remaining unit, B Company, was detailed to guard the pack train, and each of the other companies was required to provide six privates and one noncom to lead the pack mules.

It took less than ten minutes to complete this task. The regiment stood at the small upper waters of a stream since named Reno Creek, which flows pretty much due west into the Little Bighorn about a dozen miles, as the crow flies, from where the regiment paused. The land between was furrowed and broken, cut by ravines and creeks, and wrinkled by hillocks and ridges, for this is country where the last fringes of the Great Plains are breaking against the mountains.

Colonel Custer ordered Captain Benteen with his three companies, about 125 men, to proceed to the southwest, angling away to the left from the line of march of the rest of the regiment which would follow the creek to the river. Benteen was to investigate some bluffs three or four miles away, then go on to the first valley beyond, attacking any Indians he might find, and report back to the commanding officer. Benteen signaled his command forward and almost immediately disappeared from sight because of the uneven ground. But in the next few minutes messengers were twice sent after him to amplify his orders: if he found no Indians in the first valley, he was to go on until he found a second one, and then a third.

Custer and Reno continued on their way toward the river, Reno and his battalion on the left or south bank of the creek, Custer and the other five companies on the opposite side, the pack train trailing behind. Their course was taking them, without their knowing it yet, almost directly toward the camp that had been sighted by the scouts from the Crow's Nest at daybreak; the creek emptied into the Little Bighorn only two or three miles below the lower end of the hostile camp. And the scouts had been right, it was a big camp.

It was, in fact, without doubt the largest Indian encampment that has ever assembled on the western plains. Plains Indians seldom gathered in great numbers because their huge pony herds quickly ate off the grass over a large area, while supplying game for the humans quickly hunted out the region for miles around the camp. But these were extraordinary times. Crazy Horse and his warriors had thrown Crook back only a few days earlier, and were still elated and ready to fight any other force the Army might send against them. Thousands of Indians had left the agencies, determined to fight after having seen their protests against the rape of the Black Hills ignored. All had joined together, ready for any soldiers who might come, and certain they could whip them. It was perhaps the last time in American history that a force of Indians stood ready to meet the United States Army with confidence of winning.

The camp lay on the west side of the river; from northernmost to southernmost tepee was probably three miles and in places it was half a mile wide. There were some 1,500 lodges, and many wickiups or temporary brush shelters. At the north lay the camp circle of the Cheyennes; the Hunkpapas of Gall, Crow King, and Sitting Bull had set up their tepees at the most southerly end of the great camp. Between the two were camp circles of other bands of the Sioux nation: Miniconjous under Chief Hump, Sans Arcs led by Chief Spotted Eagle, Oglallas under the great Crazy Horse and Low Dog and Big Road, and smaller contingents of Blackfeet Sioux, Two Kettles, Yanktons, Santees who had not forgotten their war in Minnesota, and even a few lodges of Arapahoes. There were, by the best later estimates, between twelve and fifteen thousand Indians in the encampment, of whom at least four and possibly five thousand were warriors.

As the regiment, less the three companies Benteen had led off into the broken badlands, and the lagging guard of the pack train, proceeded along the creek, it came to a solitary tepee, standing among circles of yellow grass left by the lodges of a village only recently moved. Inside, on a low scaffolding, was the body of a Sioux warrior, presumably one who had died in the battle with Crook—although Custer's force had no inkling of Crook's setback. The Arikara scouts set the tepee afire with considerable glee.

During this time, something else was discovered that interested Custer much more, a heavy cloud of dust about five miles away, on the other side of the Little Bighorn, and a short way downstream, the sign of a Sioux village with its pony herd, or possibly of fleeing Sioux. The general conviction that the Indians would flee when opposition appeared now seemed well-founded, for a civilian interpreter, Frank Girard, sitting his horse on a higher knoll apart from the regiment, called, "Here are your Indians—running like devils." Girard had sighted about forty warriors in the direction of the river and running away.

Custer at once ordered the Indian scouts in pursuit but they refused, even when the commander ordered them to turn in their horses and rifles in an effort to shame them. He then gave an order to Cooke which the adjutant rode over and transmitted to Reno, "General Custer directs that you take as fast a gait as you deem prudent, and charge afterward, and you will be supported by the whole outfit." A considerable number of men heard the order given, and although they disagreed afterward on whether Cooke had said "charge the village," or "charge the Indians," or "make for the dust," or some other wording, all were unanimous in agreeing that he had said that Reno's battalion would be "supported by the whole outfit." And with this attack order, the most famous Indian battle of the West was under way.

5. "FOR GOD'S SAKE, BENTEEN, HELP ME. I'VE LOST HALF MY MEN"

A brief look at Custer's troop dispositions may be helpful. The commander of the 7th Cavalry Regiment had not only put himself in a position where he would have to fight the hostiles alone (a situation he probably did not regret because there would be no sharing of glory for the victory he was certain he would win), but he was entering battle with a tactical ineptitude that would have been inexcusable in the most junior of his officers. He was completely aware that a very large hostile force was somewhere near at hand: his scouts had seen a large camp from the Crow's Nest and he himself had followed the trail beaten by many Indians across the divide into this valley. Yet, in the face of this evidence that he would soon be engaged in battle with a strong enemy, he had done what was almost militarily indefensible under all but exceptional circumstances: he had split his forces.

And he had split them not once, but into four parts. Under his own command, in five companies, he had about 225 men. Major Reno had 112 soldiers, augmented by about 25 Indian scouts, 3 white scouts, and a Negro interpreter. Benteen had about 125 men, and 130 soldiers—the escort company and men detailed from other companies to lead pack mules—were with the pack train. Moreover, not the slightest provision was made for coordination between these four elements. At the moment Reno was ordered into action, Benteen was ten or a dozen miles away to the southwest, and getting further away all the time on orders to scout one valley after another for Indians. The pack train, with most of the ammunition that would be needed in a heavy engagement, was several miles behind the rest of the force. No plan of battle existed to tie these scattered forces together, no instructions had been communicated by the commanding officer to the commanders of the several units except the vague one to Reno: ". . . charge afterward, and you will be supported by the whole outfit." Luck alone could prevent trouble if the regiment ran into determined resistance when it was in such poor disposition. But Custer had depended too much on luck, and the lady was not riding at his elbow this day.

Major Reno and his battalion had about three miles to go to the Little Bighorn; they reached and crossed it about 2:30 P.M. The ad-

BATTLEFIELD
INDIAN CAMP
BATTLE
BATTLE
RENO CR.
NORTH FORK
LITTLE BIGHORN R.
DEAD INDIAN TEPEE
CUSTER
PACK TRAIN
RENO
SOUTH FORK
BENTEEN
WOLF MTS.

CUSTER DIVIDES THE REGIMENT INTO BATTALIONS NOON, JUNE 25

N
W   E
S

The Battle of the Little Bighorn
Custer Divides his Forces

Miles
0   1   2   3   4   5

jutant, Cooke, and Captain Keogh, Commander of I Company, had ridden along to see the battalion safely across the river; then they turned back, apparently still convinced that the running Indians sighted by Girard indicated that the Sioux were in panicky flight. However, as they rode back, Girard came galloping after them, to inform them that the Indians were not fleeing but were coming out to meet Reno. Presumably, they carried the message to Custer, whose tactics were accordingly modified.

After fording the Little Bighorn, Reno formed his command in line of battle with Lieutenant Varnum and the Indian scouts, and Companies A and M in line, and Company G in reserve. In this formation they trotted down the valley, and for the first time actually saw tepees, but a jutting point of cottonwoods and dust clouds hid all but a few lodges and gave them only the slightest idea of what they were getting into. As they came within two miles of the camp, Reno called Company G up into the line, and then, going into a gallop, the battalion swept on to hit the village.

It never reached the camp. Ahead, hundreds of mounted warriors were half-revealed, then hidden again, in the thick dust clouds they were deliberately raising to screen their movements by riding furiously back and forth. At the same time, the Indian scouts, most of them Arikaras, panicked and fled, leaving Reno's left flank unprotected. Appalled at the mass of warriors ahead, Reno halted his force, and as he searched his mind for the right decision in a confused and perilous moment, a large group of Sioux came out of a ravine and moved against his exposed left flank. He looked around for the support that had been promised by Custer, but there was no sign of help. He had perhaps 115 men against a thousand or more. To attempt to continue the advance into the village would have meant certain annihilation, so he took the one alternative and ordered his command to dismount and fight on foot. Horse-holders led the mounts to the protection of the woods behind the battalion, which formed a line of battle with its right flank resting on the river and its left stretching toward the low hills. There, against fearful odds, it took up its fight.

The warriors opposing Reno's men were almost entirely Hunkpapas, the tribe of Gall and Sitting Bull, Crow King and Black Moon, and the smaller band of Blackfeet Sioux, since it was against the upper end of the camp where the two bands had their camp circles that Reno's charge had been directed. Indians charged and darted away and drove in again, out of the obscuring cloud of dust, putting irresistible pressure against the thin line of troops. Sioux were working their way around the left flank of the dismounted line and appearing in its rear, and Reno, fearful that they would accomplish their favorite trick of stampeding his horses, sent Company G back to the timber to guard the mounts. The two companies remaining, A and M, had to spread out to fill the gap, but there just was not enough substance to take up the slack. The left flank was pushed back, and the Sioux galloped around in force to the battalion's rear.

Up to this point the battalion had lost no men, thanks to the common Indian failing of being more interested in shooting rapidly than accurately (two unhappy troopers were carried into the Sioux lines by their frantic and ungovernable horses on the first charge but miraculously escaped, though wounded). On the other hand, the soldiers were not inflicting much damage, either. The 7th Cavalry, despite its reputation as the *ne plus ultra* of Indian-fighting regiments, was not drawn to a sharp edge when it started the campaign. Its ranks were filled with recruits who were now in their first battle. For thirty to forty percent of the men in the companies, this was their first service. A sergeant in Company A of Reno's battalion later testified that about a third of his company, and about half of G Company, were recruits. "The new men had had very little training," he said; "they were very poor horsemen and would fire at random. They were brave enough, but they had not had the time nor opportunity to make soldiers. Some were not fit to take into action." But, fit or not, these men were courageously but futilely banging away, firing as fast as they could but with little attempt to aim while their limited supply of ammunition dwindled rapidly.

Major Reno recognized that his position was rapidly becoming impossible to hold. Behind him, in the timber where he had sent the horses, the terrain offered better possibilities for defense. He ordered a change of front and the battalion wheeled backward on its right flank as a hinge. Now the line stretched across the neck of a loop in the river, so that both flanks rested on the stream. The fight went on from the new position for another half hour or so, but the improvement was only temporary. Undergrowth was heavy, making it difficult to maintain contact between men. Sioux warriors were infiltrating the lines, and, like woodland Indians, were firing from behind trees and bushes from all sides and the rear. Both men and horses were now being struck by bullets. Reno saw that his position once again had become untenable, and gave the order to stand to horses.

The command was not given by trumpet, and in the noise and confusion, only those near heard the major. Although the order was passed on, it never reached some of the men. Those who had heard formed up in a clearing, and Reno gave the order to mount. Sioux were bursting through the woods into the clearing; at that instant, a bullet caught the scout, Bloody Knife. The Arikara, Custer's favorite scout, had stood firm when the rest of the Indian scouts with the battalion had melted away, and had continued to fight alongside Reno. The bullet that killed him hit him in the head, spattering blood and brains in the Major's face. At almost the same instant a soldier was hit and fell from the saddle with a loud cry. The events were momentarily too much for Reno, his mind stretched taut by the demands of leadership and decision-making in a situation that had worsened every moment since he had first led his command against the village. He barked out the order to dismount, recovered himself and gave the order to mount again, and led the column out into the open where it formed up hastily. Then, with Major Reno leading, the column forced its way through the mass of Indians and headed for the ford it had crossed an hour—and a lifetime—ago.

Losses had been heavy. Seventeen living were left behind when the battalion withdrew, besides several dead; two of the seventeen died very shortly as they tried to catch the fleeing column. Lieutenant Donald McIntosh, commander of G Company, had delayed to rally his men, many of whom had not heard the order to withdraw; consequently, he left the woods in the rear of the column and was surrounded and cut down. Guide Charley Reynolds also made a run to catch the battalion and fell from his horse with a bullet in his chest—Lonesome Charley Reynolds, the shy, soft-spoken scout who did the seemingly impossible so often that he had become almost a legendary figure even while still alive.

Lieutenant Varnum, lagging behind at the beginning, spurred his horse to the head of the column, shouting, "For God's sake, men, don't run; we've got to go back and save the wounded." The voice that replied beside him was that of Reno, "Sir, I am in command here."

The Sioux were pressing so hard the retreat was turning into a rout. Moreover, the hundreds of Sioux racing along beside the column were all on its right side, exerting pressure that was pushing it inexorably toward the river. It was impossible for the battalion to regain the ford by which it had crossed over, and so it made a crossing about a mile farther downstream. The bank at the point was about six feet high; most of the horses hesitated until forced over by the press of those coming behind. Then, as men and animals floundered in the water, Sioux on the banks fired down on them, not just from one side but from both. A number of good men died at the crossing, some help-lessly, some bravely firing at the overwhelming mass of Indians.

The east bank which they had just gained rose to hills 200 to 300 feet above the river, and on a high point the survivors were organized by Reno, as best he could, for defense. About half the battalion were casualties, killed, wounded, or left behind in the woods. The men were confused, dispirited, their ammunition was almost gone, and they could undoubtedly have been overwhelmed by a determined assault. However, the Indian attack was unaccountably slackening off to almost nothing; all but a few of the enemy warriors had streamed away, their interest attracted by something else. What it was Reno's men could not see.

It was then about four o'clock in the afternoon. While Reno had been fighting his desperate battle, Captain Benteen had been carrying out his reconnaissance of the country south of the creek and the trail the rest of the regiment had followed. He had scouted the bluffs Custer had been interested in, sending an officer to their tops a number of times, and personally investigating them for several miles. His orders had called for him to go on to the first valley, then, if he found no Indians, to continue on to the second, and then the third valley. But after riding a dozen miles, he had not even found a first valley.

The terrain was a jumble of hills, ravines, gullies, bluffs, and bad-lands in general. Benteen was convinced that no Indians were going to be found in such country; he was equally convinced that a battle would take place and that he could be of use only by returning to the regiment. He directed a change in course, and the three companies angled back, striking the trail after having traveled fifteen miles on the fruitless scout. He was, Benteen admitted afterward, technically violating his orders, but he felt he might have gone on for twenty-five miles without ever finding any valley, and certainly no Indians.

The battalion stopped to water horses at a marshy place at the junction of Reno Creek and its south fork, and had just started on when the pack train, lagging far behind the main section of the regiment, came down the trail. The thirsty mules broke from control and, braying loudly, rushed into the morass where they immediately became mired. Benteen's column left them thus, with packers and troopers assigned to pack-train duty cursing and trying to get things straightened out again. Several miles on, the battalion passed the dead man's tepee which had been set afire earlier by the Indian scouts, and two miles beyond, Sergeant Daniel Kanipe of Captain Tom Custer's Company C galloped up. "We've got 'em, boys," he announced in high humor, and told Captain Benteen that he had been sent by Colonel Custer to direct that the ammunition packs be hurried as fast as possible because Custer was preparing to go into action against a large Indian village. Benteen sent him back to the pack train in the rear, and had proceeded another mile or so when a second messenger came up on a bleeding and exhausted horse.

Benteen knew him well; he was John Martin, trumpeter for his own Company H, who had been detailed that day for duty as Custer's orderly trumpeter. Martin had been Giovanni Martini when he had come to America only a year before; he had not been with the 7th Cavalry long and his English was poor, but he was excited and elated as he handed Captain Benteen a hastily scrawled message: "Benteen— Come on. Big village. Be quick. Bring packs. W. W. Cooke P.S. Bring pacs."

Custer had given the order which his adjutant, Cooke, had then written on a page of his notebook, Martin said. On his way back, Sioux had fired at him and had hit his horse which was bleeding badly, but Martin said that Custer was attacking the village and that on his dash he had seen Reno fighting down in the valley. There was no doubt about it, the happy trumpeter said, the Indians were "skedaddling."

Martin also offered the information that he had passed Boston Custer galloping to join the force Martin had just left. Boston had gone to the pack train for some reason and was hurrying to rejoin the fated battalion in order not to miss any of the excitement.

There was nothing more to be done about the ammunition packs; Sergeant Kanipe had already gone back with word to hurry them up as much as possible. Benteen moved forward faster now. The sound of guns reached him very plainly in a few minutes; very shortly he arrived on ground overlooking the river, just in time to see great numbers of mounted Sioux riding down and killing the last stragglers from

Reno's column, those unfortunates who had somehow become un-horsed and were making a forlorn and desperate attempt to fight through to the river. Appalled by the sight, the column moved forward cautiously until it met several of the regiment's Crow scouts who pointed out the hill where Reno was preparing to make a final stand.

Benteen led the command to the hill at a trot. Reno, a pistol in his hand, greatly agitated, greeted him. "For God's sake, Benteen, halt your command and help me. I've lost half my men." The command dismounted, and Captain Benteen immediately began disposing his men for a more effective defense.

Reno was badly unnerved, overwrought, and discouraged, as were most of his men at the moment. It would be unfair to judge Major Reno solely on his actions since the moment a Sioux bullet had split the skull of Bloody Knife and spattered him with its contents. The major had an excellent Civil War record and had been breveted for gallantry in action. But there was not much doubt about it, for the moment, Reno was only half a man. Captain Benteen took over the defense and, for all practical purposes, was in command during the next hours.

Benteen was a superb officer, brave, cool in action, with the natural instincts of leadership. His hair was pure white, and his pictures show a man with a rubicund and rather friendly face, giving him more than a little of the appearance of a clean-shaven Santa Claus. Most of his officers and men found him friendly and fair, but on infrequent occasions he went on long drinking bouts during which he became irascible and gave way to violent temper outbursts. He despised Custer and had ever since the day he reported for duty with the 7th and, according to his story, had to spend two or three hours listening to his commanding officer boast tediously and shamelessly of his many past exploits. Benteen's dislike had deepened into hate when Custer had failed to make any attempt to find the missing Major Joel Elliott and his detachment during the Washita attack. He had written an anonymous letter to a newspaper about the abandonment of Elliott and his men, and then admitted his authorship and faced down Custer when the latter had called a meeting of his officers to promise to horsewhip the letter writer if he found out who he was. Benteen always referred to Custer's book, *My Life On the Plains* as "My Lie on the Plains." Yet there is no evidence that he let his personal feelings interfere with his duty as a soldier—and he was a good soldier.

When they had ridden off just before Benteen's column had arrived, the Sioux had left only a few warriors to keep up a long-range fire at the beleaguered soldiers. An officer made a dash back to the pack train on the freshest horse available, to have the ammunition mules brought up as quickly as possible, and to hurry the rest of the train and its protecting cavalrymen as well. Custer's whereabouts were a mystery, except that he was somewhere north of them, on the east side of the Little Bighorn. They heard gunfire, very heavy, indicating that hard fighting was underway. It was without doubt that gunfire and fighting that had been the magnet that had drawn away the hundreds of warriors who had been attacking Reno. Captain Thomas B. Weir, commanding Company D of Benteen's battalion, became impatient when Reno made no move to go out to support Custer, wherever he might be, and finally, without orders, rode with his company about a mile to the north, to a high hill (now called Weir Point). Benteen followed with three companies to give support. From the hill they could see, about four miles north, a mighty cloud of dust and smoke, and many Indians, some of whom appeared to be shooting at the ground. The scene did not quite connect into a meaningful picture in the minds of the beholders on the hill.

Reno waited for the pack train to come up; then, his ammunition replenished, he began moving the rest of the force up to Weir Point. The difficulties were tremendous, especially moving the wounded. And in the meantime, the Indians had looked up at Weir Point and seen the blue uniforms atop it, and had begun racing to attack. The leading companies were soon engaged, and Reno and Benteen quickly decided that their original position was superior. A withdrawal under fire was completed just before the full force of the attack struck.

The assault was furious, and did not slacken until darkness fell. Then the warriors withdrew, leaving a number of the defenders dead or wounded. All during the night the soldiers, about three hundred strong, worked to dig defenses, employing knives, mess plates, and any other makeshift that came to hand, for they had only three spades and two axes. Saddles and anything else that would stop a bullet were piled as breastworks. The hill was well suited for defense because its top had a saucer-shaped depression; there the animals were picketed and the surgeon established his hospital. It was a busy night for him, too.

All during the night, as they made ready for the inevitable morning attack, the men on the hill could look across the river toward the village where a mighty victory celebration went on. Great fires burned, drums throbbed, and the elated warriors yelped and chanted as they danced. Several times, sentries were alerted by someone approaching through the dark, but each time it turned out to be survivors of the debacle across the river who had been left in the woods when they had failed to hear Reno's command to mount. Fifteen had hidden successfully and most came in that night, a few not until the next day.

Dawn comes early on June 26, just past the shortest night of the year, and the immense world of sky over the Little Bighorn valley was getting gray at 2:45 A.M. when the first Indian rifle cracked and opened a fusillade that thereafter continued hour after hour without letup. There was no noisy and aimless answering fire from the hill; fire control was being rigidly enforced and most of the time only a few crackshots were permitted to shoot at the Indians.

On all sides except the east the hill fell away sharply; on that quarter natural defenses were weak and a maze of gullies and hillocks gave natural cover to attacking warriors. Captain Benteen had chosen to defend this vulnerable spot on which the Sioux were concentrating their fire and were working nearer through the abundant cover afforded by the terrain. He went to Reno for reinforcements; during his absence an especially bold warrior dashed in and counted coup by touching the body of a dead cavalryman. Such were the opportunities for concealment afforded by the broken nature of the ground. Benteen put into practice the old adage about the best defense, and ordered his men to charge the Indians. They scattered the Sioux in front of their position, and returned without a single casualty.

Benteen urged Reno to order a general charge on the Indians to clear them from positions they were gradually pushing closer to the entrenchments. Reno agreed and led the charge, four companies strong, which went down the western slope of the hill whooping and cheering, scattering warriors who were gathering for their own assault. The cavalrymen returned to their defenses completely untouched; they had forced the Sioux and Cheyenne back and rendered them considerably more cautious.

Thereafter, the warriors kept up a more or less token fire. Thirst became the great enemy on the hill; for the wounded, water was becoming a matter of life or death. Volunteers crawled down to the river with canteens, kettles, and other vessels while sharpshooters stood up to keep under cover any Indian who tried to interfere with the operation.

Soon after midday (June 26) the pressure began to ease. Down in the Indian camp, scouts came in with news that led to earnest conferences among the chiefs, and then to the dismantling of tepees and preparations for moving. The besieged men on the hill realized only that something was going on among the Indians; they had no way of knowing that the enemy was beginning to withdraw because scouts had reported the approach of Colonel Gibbon and his column.

Late in the afternoon, the grass in the valley was set afire, and behind the rising clouds of smoke the Indians began moving out, possessions packed on ponies, tepees rolled up and lashed to travois, thousands of men, women, and children on horseback, and additional thousands upon thousands of ponies. Officers watched in awe from the hill. It was no straggling, savage rabble but a precision movement. Each of the bands moved as a unit, and the soldiers on the hill compared the river of horses and humans to a cavalry division on the march. By dark, the last of the encampment had disappeared from sight, headed in the direction of the Big Horn Mountains.

The band on the hill buried their dead (there is no agreement on how many died on the hill and in each phase of the fighting, but the total losses of Reno and Benteen in the two days of fighting were somewhere between forty and fifty killed and at least fifty wounded), and moved their position somewhat to be nearer the river and its water, and to get away from the stench of dead horses. With the Indians gone, several men still hiding in the woods rejoined their comrades. The main subject of conversation was the whereabouts of Custer, and there was widespread cursing of the commanding officer because it was almost universally believed that he had deserted them to go off on some chase of his own. No one suspected that there might be a much more calamitous reason for his disappearance.

6. A VICTORY TOO COMPLETE

That same night, June 26, Terry and Gibbon were camped about nine miles away, down the Little Bighorn. During the day, Lieutenant James Bradley, in charge of Gibbon's Indian scouts, reported back to the column that his men had come on Crow Indians up ahead who had been scouts with Custer's regiment; they told a story of a great battle in which the pony soldiers had all been killed. No one believed the story in its entirety, but it was accepted that hard fighting must have taken place, and Gibbon had pushed his infantry as fast as possible during the rest of the afternoon and long into the lingering June twilight.

The next morning at daybreak they took up the march and soon closed the remaining nine miles. The approaching column was sighted from afar by Reno's men, who were unable to make out whether it was soldiers, or Indians returning, but as it neared, it became identifiable as an Army column. Lieutenants Hare and Wallace were sent out to cross the river and learn who was approaching. When they discovered General Terry riding with Gibbon at the head of the column, they galloped up to the general, reined in their horses, saluted, and both spoke at once, "Where is Custer?"

Terry did not know the answer, but it came a short time later when he and Gibbon, and their staffs were standing on the hill talking to Major Reno and his officers. Lieutenant Bradley rode up; with his scouts he had been working through the hills on the east side of the river and had sighted objects that shone white in the distance. Approaching, they had been horrified to find that they were naked human bodies, lying among the carcasses of many horses. Bradley had counted 197 dead.

The annihilation of Custer and the five doomed companies has woven its spell ever since, not only for its drama and tragedy but for the element of mystery. More than two hundred rode out, and not one came back to tell what happened. The Indians who fought that day told their stories only long afterward and reluctantly—and they could not throw any light on what went on in the minds and hearts of the commander of the 7th Cavalry and his men. There is much that is unknown and unknowable, a situation that is a rich seedbed for the growth of legend. But there is no deep enigma about the general path that led the five companies to death and immortality. It is mainly in details of the picture that the mystery lies and will remain forever.

After having sent Reno to attack the lower end of the huge Indian camp, Custer followed him for a short distance, apparently meaning to support him as he had promised. But then he turned off the trail and went north, more or less parallel to the river. He seems to have changed his mind about supporting Reno when Captains Cooke and

Keogh returned from seeing Reno to the river and brought word that the Indians were not fleeing, as he had thought, but were attacking. Then, beyond any doubt, Custer made the decision to attack the Indian camp in its flank—probably at its lower end to nip the enemy between his force and Reno's.

Custer had known that Reno was desperately engaged and needed help. During the first ten minutes of Reno's fight, when he had halted his charge in the face of the hundreds of warriors confronting him and had dismounted his men, Lieutenant Varnum had somehow found a moment in the chaos of combat to raise his eyes to the river bluffs opposite, about half a mile away. It was a brief glimpse—he was too occupied for much gazing—but he saw, clear and unmistakable, Company E of Custer's column. He sighted only a portion of it through a break in the bluffs, but there had been no doubt. How could he be sure at that distance it was E Company? Because of Custer's custom of coloring the horses; Company E was the Gray Horse Company. If Varnum saw Custer, Custer saw Reno under attack.

Custer had become completely aware that a large village lay across the river. He had sent Sergeant Kanipe back to hurry up the ammunition supplies in the pack train for the battle he was preparing, and then, for a better look, rode to the top of a high hill. With him were not only his adjutant, Cooke, and Trumpeter John Martin of H Company, his orderly trumpeter, but also brother Tom, commander of Company C, and nephew Autie Reed (the Custers were together whenever possible).

Even though the trees hid much of the camp, it stretched some three miles long, and he could not have escaped an impression of its great size. But size did not faze Custer; he dangerously underrated the fighting ability of the Indians, and at the same time, had convinced himself that the 7th Cavalry was invincible—at least, when it was under his leadership. The camp half a mile or so across the river and below represented no possibility of defeat but another step on the ladder to fame.

There were few signs of activity in the camp: women here and there tended cooking fires, children played their games among the tepees; a few dogs slept in the sun. Custer spurred his horse down the hill and rejoined his command with the jubilant announcement that the Indians had been caught napping. The command took on new life and galloped ahead—still north and parallel to the river—for about another mile before Custer called Martin to him. "Orderly, I want you to take a message to Captain Benteen," the colonel said, as nearly as his order can be reconstructed, for Martin's command of English was poor. "Ride as fast as you can and tell him to hurry. Tell him it's a big village, and I want him to be quick and bring the ammunition packs."

At this point, Lieutenant Cooke, recognizing the danger of Martin misunderstanding the message, halted the trumpeter before he could gallop away and wrote down on a page of his memorandum book the message which Martin later handed to Benteen: "Benteen—Come on. Big village. Be quick. Brink packs. W. W. Cooke. P. S. Bring pacs." Martin was the last survivor of the 7th Cavalry to see Custer alive.

From that point on, everything must be pieced together from circumstantial evidence and what light the Sioux and Cheyenne threw on the event long afterward. There is no way of knowing whether he meant to strike the village in the flank and was thrown back by the sudden attack of Indian forces, or whether he was planning to cross the river and hit the lower end of the camp, where the Cheyenne tepees stood. Whatever his plans, they go no further, for the somnolent camp had been an illusion, and soon after Martin had left, a mass of yelling warriors pounded over the rise from the river and struck like a thunderbolt.

Custer got the battalion on a ridge, the first one of any size back of the river. His five companies, about 225 cavalrymen and several civilians (no one, not even the Army's own records, can say for certain exactly how many men were there), stretched along a front of about three-quarters of a mile. The first mass of warriors had struck from the southwest; they were led by the great and dour Hunkpapa chief, Gall, and had just turned from throwing back Reno's attack to meet this new threat. Gall's men hit Lieutenant Calhoun's Company L at the southern end of the line first and then swept on to Keogh's I Company; these two units were simply overwhelmed by superior numbers and wiped out where they stood, so that bodies of officers and men lay in platoon formation as they had died.

The ordered line of battle was knocked apart as new hundreds upon hundreds of warriors, Crazy Horse's Oglalas and the Cheyennes of Two Moon came in a solid mass from the northwest after fording the river at the lower end of the camp. The bodies of the officers and men of the remaining three companies were found grouped more or less by

CRAZY HORSE AND TWO MOON

COL. CUSTER
CO. C · CO. F, YATES
T. CUSTER
· CO. I, KEOGH
· CO. L, CALHOUN
CO. E, SMITH

ATTEMPT TO CROSS
AT MIDDLE FORD ?

N

W   E

S

GALL

INDIAN CAMP

WEIR POINT

RENO'S 1ST POSITION

2ND POSITION

RENO'S RETREAT

APPROXIMATE ROUTE OF CUSTER

RENO'S ADVANCE

LITTLE BIGHORN R.

BENTEEN

RENO CR.

The Battle of the Little Bighorn
"Custer's Last Stand"

Miles

0   1   2

companies, but beyond that there was no semblance of formation, indicating that the field had been broken up into a swirling, milling nightmare of dust, smoke, yells, and curses in which war had often been reduced to its most elemental form of one man against another in hand-to-hand combat.

The battle was fought on foot by the cavalry and by most of the Indians because of the rough terrain with its hills and gullies. Some of the cavalry horses had been shot and used as breastworks but the Indians had stampeded most of them; many of the men were firing from prone positions to present as poor a target as possible, but their situation was hopeless with bullets and arrows coming from rear as well as front. And the hopeless odds kept increasing as Sioux warriors who had been fighting Reno kept streaming across the river.

George Armstrong Custer, who had dreamed of leading the 7th Cavalry to new glory for it and for himself, was at the northernmost point on the ridge. His adjutant Cooke was near him, and so were Boston Custer, who had hoped to cure a bronchial condition in the West, and nephew Autie Reed, who was being shown the fun and excitement of Indian-fighting. Also at the last were his brother Tom, Lieutenant Smith, and Captain Yates, with almost half a hundred enlisted men, who had rallied to their commander.

There were fifty-one of them in the little knot of men standing by Custer, a little cluster of frantically fighting men that dissolved and grew smaller almost by the minute. Custer did not stand to the last with revolver in one hand, saber in the other, long golden locks streaming in the smoky air, as decades of saloon art have portrayed. The revolver was almost certainly in his hand, but the cavalry carried no sabers in 1876, and just before leaving Fort Abraham Lincoln, Custer had had the horse clippers run over his head, shearing his hair almost to the skull.

There, on the ridge, Custer's luck, which its possessor had had in such abundance and had so badly abused, at last choked off. A bullet took Custer in the temple, another in his breast. Either would have been fatal.

The Indians stripped off his clothing and left him naked, but they did not scalp him. In the afternoon, Lieutenant Bradley, who had discovered the battlefield, led Captain Benteen and two other officers of the regiment back to the field to identify the body of Custer. They found him lying in an attitude of perfect composure, with a look of repose on his face as though he were asleep rather than having ended his life at the height of violence. After they had left, Bradley asked the three officers if they had noted Custer's death wounds; the wounds, though in plain sight, were so inconspicuous that none of the three could say where Custer had been shot.

Later, when the story reached the outside world and rumors began to multiply, among the most persistent were accounts of horrible mutilations of those who had fallen by the Little Bighorn. Lieutenant Bradley, who had some knowledge of this macabre subject, felt called upon to put the record straight in a letter to the Helena, Montana, *Herald* about a month after the battle. Wrote Bradley, in part: "Of the 206 bodies buried in the field, there were very few that I did not see, and beyond scalping, in possibly a majority of cases, there was little mutilation. Many of the bodies were not even scalped, and in the comparatively few cases of disfiguration, it appeared to me the result rather of a blow with a knife, hatchet, or war club to finish a wounded man, than a deliberate mutilation." *

The only bodies that had suffered deliberate mutilation were those of Major Reno's men who had fallen near the village and had been set upon by the women and children. Scalping, yes, but even that was not universal, as Lieutenant Bradley pointed out. Most of the dead had been stripped of their clothing, but not all. The dead were buried in shallow graves where they had fallen. The difficulties of identifying naked bodies were great, especially after they had lain in the hot sun for two days, and eighteen were unaccountably missing: four officers and fourteen men as near as it was possible to tell. Their bodies were never found—but not one of them ever turned up alive. The Indians removed their own dead, as usual. Estimates of their losses range widely, but they appear to have come off rather lightly.

One living being, and one alone, was found on the field of battle. Comanche, the horse of Captain Myles Keogh, commanding officer of Company I, was grievously and almost mortally hurt with seven

* A favorite story was that Captain Thomas Custer had had his heart cut out by a Sioux named Rain-in-the-Face; this tale gained credibility because it was told by Rain-in-the-Face himself, who bore a special grudge against Tom Custer because the latter had once arrested him on Colonel Custer's arbitrary orders in a rather involved matter arising from the Yellowstone Expedition of 1873. Rain-in-the-Face was a big-mouth and a brag-hard; Lieutenant Bradley, in the same letter quoted above, denies the truth of his account of the removal of Captain Custer's heart. Yet Elizabeth Custer later presented the story to the world as the unvarnished truth in *Boots and Saddles,* and biographers of Custer are presenting the limp and tired story even today.

wounds in its body but it was still alive and strong enough to be led some twenty miles to where the Little Bighorn joined the Bighorn River. The *Far West* had been able to follow Terry and Gibbon that far, and the horse was put aboard, with the wounded from Reno's command. Comanche survived his wounds and was, by regimental order, placed on the retired list; no one was ever permitted to ride or work the animal. The horse was led in all 7th Cavalry reviews and parades, and died, full of years, at Fort Riley, Kansas, at the age of thirty.

The *Far West* had to wait at the mouth of the Bighorn to ferry the troops over to the north bank of the Yellowstone; then it set out down the Yellowstone to the Missouri and on to Fort Abraham Lincoln under forced draft with its load of wounded and its heavy cargo of news. The 700-mile trip was made in fifty-four hours, a record never again equaled. Captain Marsh, skipper of the sternwheeler, paused at Fort Buford on the Missouri long enough to take aboard a large amount of crape with which he draped his boat, and thus appropriately dressed out in keeping with her doleful mission, the *Far West* swung into the Fort Lincoln landing at 11 P.M. on July 5.

The telegraph operator at Bismarck, J. M. Carnahan, spent twenty-two hours without relief sending the basic dispatch of the disaster, and then settled down for another sixty hours without rest, with his finger on the key tapping out dispatches for newspaper correspondents. The country was quick to condemn one side or the other. Grant said that Custer had sacrificed his men. Terry and his staff had no doubts that the tragedy had occurred because Custer had disobeyed orders, and Terry said so in a confidential report. With characteristic dislike of saying anything derogatory about a man, he prepared another report for release to the public which made no mention of disobedience, but an enterprising newspaperman posing as a War Department messenger got the confidential report from General Sherman and printed it in full. On the other hand, very soon Reno and Benteen were being accused of pusillanimous conduct, and in some quarters, of deliberate refusal to support Custer because of their personal dislike of the man.

As the accusations continued over the months, Reno demanded a court of inquiry, which finally met in January of 1879, and after two months of intensive hearings, returned its findings which, while hardly acclaiming Reno as a hero, did absolve him of cowardice. It had also been the opinion of virtually every surviving officer of the regiment that if Reno had not retreated when he did, the battalion would have been wiped out. The enlisted men of the regiment gave their own vote of confidence: nine days after the battle a petition signed by 236 who had fought under Reno and Benteen was submitted to the President; it asked that Reno be promoted to lieutenant colonel of the regiment, and that Benteen be promoted to major to fill Reno's position. The men said in their petition that the two officers, "by their bravery, coolness and decision . . . saved the lives of every man now living of the 7th Cavalry who participated in the battle . . ." The petition, of course, was not acted upon. General Sherman returned it with the explanation that promotion in the United States Army depended on seniority, not heroism.

The disaster (Custer's Massacre, it inevitably became, although it was no massacre but a battle in which Army troops were outguessed and outnumbered) profoundly shocked the nation. When Captain Judd Fetterman had led his command into an ambush and got it annihilated in much the same fashion, the national mood had been one of soul-searching amid a widespread feeling that greedy white men had been largely to blame for driving the Indian to defend his dwindling heritage. There was little such feeling after the battle of the Little Bighorn. The news reached the country on July 6, in the midst of the celebration of the nation's centennial, and it was a harsh discord amid all the patriotic rodomontade about past glories and the predictions of limitless bright futures. It was unthinkable that a people so favored by destiny should be thus humiliated by savages. The Sioux and Cheyenne had made two serious mistakes: they had won far too overwhelmingly, and they had won at the worst possible moment.

General Sheridan combed his command for troops to reinforce both Terry and Crook. General Crook had waited in his camp on Goose Creek ever since June 19 following his defeat at the Battle of the Rosebud. He at last set out on August 5 marching north down Rosebud Creek again, his force enlarged to 2,100 men, including 225 Shoshone and 25 Ute scouts. Among the white guides was none other than Buffalo Bill Cody, gathering publicity between theatrical engagements.

Three days later, General Terry with a force of 1,600 left the Yellowstone and started up Rosebud Creek. It was expected that these two mighty forces would catch the overconfident Sioux between them and grind him to powder. Instead, they came together in a great cloud of dust and confusion without having sighted a hostile Indian.

The campaign was almost equally sterile of results during the rest of the summer. After a couple of weeks during which their commands operated more or less together, Crook and Terry separated again. General Terry went back to the Yellowstone and worked toward the east where he accomplished nothing. Crook also headed east, but farther south than the ground covered by Terry. He was a great believer in cutting loose from hampering wagon trains and depending on pack mules and what his men could carry in their saddle bags. This time he cut it too fine, and the rations his column carried gave out completely; the journey became known as the "horse-meat march." As cavalry horses gave out, they became food for the column; it was a choice between that and starvation. The weather added to the misery with rain pouring down most of the time, and great portions of the route were through difficult badlands. Men who had struggled to the limit of endurance sat down and broke into tears because of their inability to continue—but all somehow found the strength to go on.

Crook's course took him more or less directly east into present North Dakota till he was due north of the Black Hills; then he headed directly south. At a place called Slim Buttes in northwestern South Dakota, just north of the Black Hills, the column found and attacked the village of Chief American Horse, which they captured. The Sioux defenders sent an urgent appeal for help to Crazy Horse a few miles away, but reinforcements reached the attacking Army force at about the same time more Sioux warriors arrived, and the troops remained in possession of the village.

This was the only victory of the entire expedition, indeed, the only passage at arms with the Indians since Custer's defeat. Several men on each side were killed, including American Horse himself, and the village was destroyed, but the mountain had labored to bring forth a mouse. The Indian Wars produced certain statistics: one was that it cost the government $1,000,000 to kill an Indian; another, that the cost of keeping a regiment fed, clothed, and otherwise maintained on the plains for a year was $2,000,000. These figures should be highly suspect—they are too nicely rounded, for one thing—but they do indicate that fighting Indians was no bargain basement matter. The campaign of Crook and Terry proved that fact; the government had spent many millions of dollars to kill several warriors and burn a number of tepees and buffalo robes at Slim Buttes.

Sheridan disbanded the Bighorn and Yellowstone Expedition and

The Yellowstone Expedition, 1876
General Crook's activities; alone and in concert with
General Terry following the defeat of Custer

MILK R.

MISSOURI R.

MISSOURI R.

MONTANA TERRITORY

YELLOWSTONE R.

MISSOURI R.

LITTLE MISSOURI R.

TERRY

CROOK

Ft. Abraham
Lincoln

Bismarck

HEART R.

DAKOTA

TERRY'S
CAMP

CROOK
AND TERRY
SEPARATE,
AUG. 25

CANNONBALL R.

YELLOWSTONE R.

TERRY
AND CROOK
JOIN FORCES,
AUG. 10

BIGHORN R.

LITTLE BIGHORN R.

ROSEBUD CR.

TONGUE R.

POWDER R.

NORTH FORK

TERRITORY

SOUTH FORK

GRAND R.

MISSOURI R.

SLIM BUTTES BATTLE,
SEPT. 9

MOREAU R.

CROOK LEAVES
CAMP, AUG. 5

BELLE FOURCHE R.

BLACK HILLS

Deadwood
SEPT. 13

Rapid City

CHEYENNE R.

BIG HORN MTS.

POWDER R.

CHEYENNE R.

WHITE R.

WYOMING TERRITORY

Ft. Fetterman

NIOBRARA R.

N

NEBRASKA

Ft. Laramie

NORTH PLATTE R.

W   E

NORTH PLATTE R.

S

0   Miles   100

IX

The Last Small Wars

1. "I LOVE THAT LAND MORE THAN ALL THE REST OF THE WORLD"

THE company guidons still snapped in the wind when cavalry patrols passed on the plains just as they had for years, but there was a difference. The patrols no longer really expected trouble. There would be no ambush ahead; there was no chance that they would come on the burned wagons and the scalped bodies of a party of emigrants. Their main call to action was likely to be a request from an Indian agent to round up and escort back a few tribesmen who had wandered off the reservation. The Army on the plains had changed from fighting force into jail warden.

Custody of the Sioux had been returned to the Indian Bureau again, now that the war was over, and the Army had relinquished control. But the military was always close at hand. There were Army posts on almost all the reservations, most of them nearly within shouting distance of the agency and ready for any trouble. The chances of further trouble would appear remote, but while most tribes now settled down to empty and frequently hungry existences, a few last flickering fires of resistance born of desperation were to break out during the next several years. Then, and only then, would it all be over, and the white man would at last have conquered and caged every Indian, from sea to shining sea.

The year after the Little Bighorn, it was the turn of the Nez Percés —or rather, a band of nontreaty Nez Percés—to face the United States Army. The Army never fought a more unjust war, nor did it ever oppose so superior a type of Indian foe. If any people deserved well of the United States, they did, and in the end they got less than nothing.

The Nez Percés are a people of the Pacific Northwest, who originally lived in the region where Washington, Oregon, and Idaho meet, in the valley of the Clearwater River and in part of the valleys of the Salmon and Snake. It was—and is—a magnificent country of deep canyons, ridges, evergreen forests, and grassy meadows carpeted in season with flowers of many colors and kinds. They had lived here for hundreds of years, hunters of deer, bear, mountain sheep, and lesser game, eaters of salmon which the rivers supplied bountifully, dwellers in semipermanent lodges. Then about 1760 they acquired the horse, and it worked the same revolution in their lives as it had with so many other tribes. They became superb horsemen, and were deeply influenced by the horse-and-buffalo culture of the Plains, to the extent that they actually became buffalo Indians to a degree, crossing the Continental Divide and traveling three or four hundred miles to the nearest buffalo ranges in Montana on hunting trips. They adopted the tepee and a seminomadic way of life, and many other attributes of the Plains people, although in other ways retaining their old culture.

Lewis and Clark came through Nez Percé lands in 1805 on their famous trip to the Pacific, and again on their return when they stopped with the tribe for several weeks while waiting for the snow to melt in the mountain passes. The Nez Percés were hospitable hosts, and it continued to be their claim through succeeding decades and increasing provocations that they had never killed a white man.

At the Council of Walla Walla in 1855, when treaties were made restricting the tribes of the region to reservations, the Nez Percés managed to retain about half the country they claimed, partly because no one was yet interested in such wild and remote country, partly because the government wanted the backing of the powerful Nez Percés in negotiating with other tribes. White indifference to the country disappeared when prospectors came looking for gold, and the

Indians, after turning them back for a time, were at last persuaded to let the gold-hunters in—under proper restrictions, of course.

There is no point in detailing the betrayal of the Nez Percés once the whites had an entering wedge. The prospectors spread beyond the limits set for them; settlers followed although it had been a clearly stated part of the agreement that no farmers should enter the Nez Percé lands; Indian fences were torn down, their pastures taken over and they were driven off lands they were farming. When the Nez Percés demanded that the government enforce the 1855 treaty, there was a cry of outrage at such impertinence. The government did at last intervene in 1863 to set things right—which it accomplished by a new treaty taking away three-quarters of the Nez Percé lands. The remaining reservation lay entirely in Idaho on the Clearwater River; the lands in Washington and Oregon were outside the reduced reserve. Despite gaining so much land, however, whites only increased their depredations against what remained.

Two-thirds of the chiefs present at the council had refused to sign the treaty, saying there was no point in a new agreement when the government had not honored or enforced the old one. One of the nontreaty chiefs was known as Joseph, a name he had taken long ago when he had become a Christian. A good and long-time friend of the whites, he now tore up his New Testament and swore to have nothing more to do with white men in whom no trust could be placed. Joseph and his band were more fortunate than many of the nontreaty Nez Percés who were living on land where they were now being pushed around by settlers, because Joseph's home was in the country of the Wallowa River in the northeastern corner of Oregon, a region no white man had yet become interested in. The band was still living there in peace in 1871 when Joseph, very old, died, leaving two sons, Ollikut, a great athlete and warrior, and Hinmaton-yalatkit (Thunder-Rolling-in-the-Mountains), better known as Young Joseph. Young Joseph, the elder son, became Chief Joseph on his father's death. "I buried him in that beautiful valley of the winding waters," Joseph later said. "I love that land more than all the rest of the world."

Love it he might, but keep it he could not. The time came, as inevitably it would, when settlers began moving into the area. They and state officials set up the familiar anguished cries for soldiers to come and take Joseph's band away to the reservation. For a time the Federal government resisted the pressure and set aside part of the Wallowa country as a reserve for "roaming Nez Percés" by presidential order in 1873, but minds were changed two years later and the entire region thrown open to homesteaders.

Chief Joseph, however, continued to maintain that the land belonged to him and his people. His father had not given it up, neither had he parted with it. Old Joseph, in his last days, had told him never to sell the land. "This country holds your father's body," he told his son. "Never sell the bones of your father and mother."

A five-man commission was sent to talk to Chief Joseph. Two members were Army officers, three civilians. One of the officers, whom the Nez Percés were to have considerable to do with very soon, was Major General Oliver O. Howard, who had lost his right arm at Fair Oaks in the early part of the war, and had commanded a wing of Sherman's army during the March to the Sea during the last part. Howard was a man of pinch-nosed religiousness. During the war he liked to bring cheer to the boys in the hospitals by appearing among them on Sundays to distribute religious tracts, homilies, and fruit. He was much interested in helping the recently freed Negroes (he was instrumental in founding Howard University for Negroes) but his heart did not go out in a like manner to the Indian in his time of trouble.

Joseph made the commissioners uneasy. He was a man of quiet dignity and commanding presence. He was confident, calm, intelligent, capable of expressing himself with a logic the five white men found difficult to answer. Moreover, he nettled them because there was no trace of obsequiousness in his manner. He acted with the quiet assurance that he was the equal of the white men to whom he was talking— and as every Indian ought to be taught, no red man was the equal of any white. He denied the commissioners' contention that the Wallowa country had been signed away by the Nez Percés in the Lapwai Treaty in 1863. His father had not signed the treaty, said Joseph, and the Wallowa belonged to his father. "If we ever owned the land we own it still, for we have never sold it," Chief Joseph said. "In the treaty councils, the commissioners have claimed that our country has been sold to the government. Suppose a white man should come to me and say, 'Joseph, I like your horses, and I want to buy them.' I say to him, 'No, my horses suit me, I will not sell them.' Then he goes to my neighbor and says to him, 'Joseph has some good horses. I want to buy them but he refuses to sell.' My neighbor answers, 'Pay me the money and I will sell you Joseph's horses.' The white man returns to me and says, 'Joseph, I have bought your horses and you must let me have them.' If we sold our lands to the government, that is the way they were bought."

But in spite of Joseph's logic—or perhaps because of it, for the commissioners resented being put on the defensive by an untutored savage —the five whites decided that Joseph's band should be removed to the Lapwai reservation, by force if necessary, and there receive about sixty plots of twenty acres each (they had about a million acres in the Wallowa country). Just about six months earlier, the other officer on the commission, Major H. C. Wood, had made another investigation of the Wallowa question and had decided that the right was all on Joseph's side, and General Howard had rendered a similar opinion. The truth and right could vary from month to month where Indian policy was involved.

Joseph bowed to the inevitable. He selected land on the reservation on May 15, 1877, and then was given one month by General Howard to bring his band in. Joseph asked for more time. The stock was foaling and calving at that season; the animals were still scattered in dozens of secret valleys and it would take time to round them up. Even more serious, the Snake River, which the band would have to cross—women, infants, aged—was half a mile wide and raging with melt waters. One month, Howard repeated. If the band delayed one day beyond that time—only one day—the troops would be there to drive them in.

The band was in no position to resist—it had only 55 men of fighting age—and the thing was somehow accomplished. Stock was rounded up, although hundreds of head were missed in the haste, and the crossing of the Snake was made without loss of human life, with the very young and the very old of the band towed on rafts through the swift, wide current. More livestock was lost when several hundred head were swept away in the river, and white settlers hanging around the edge of the band like jackals were able to cut out and stampede a large number of horses.

After the crossing, the band stopped to camp for the ten days or so still remaining before they had to come on the reservation. Other non-treaty bands, likewise ordered to settle down, joined them, and the encampment became a lively and cheerful place, considering the circumstances. But some tempers were thin. During a parade two days before the deadline date, someone became irritated by the antics of a young man named Wahlitits who was clowning on a horse, and made a waspish comment to the effect that he had not been such a big man when it had come to avenging his father's murder two years before.

Wahlitits's father had died at the hands of a white man who had squatted on his land while he had been away; when the Nez Percé had returned and protested, the white man shot him. The dying man made his son promise not to take revenge, but now, burning from the taunt made at the parade, Wahlitits set out the next day with a cousin and another youth to take belated vengeance. They were unable to find the guilty man but they killed four others, at least two of whom well deserved it. They returned to camp, recruited another fifteen or twenty firebrands, and set out on a carnival of raiding and murder. With the help of liquor which they found and dipped into heavily, they killed fifteen more white men, plundered homes, and assaulted women.

The Nez Percés had always claimed they had never killed a white man, but now they had done in a good number of them, and rather messily, in a few hours. The encampment was shocked at the news, and broke up rapidly as families left to disassociate themselves from the murderers. Many went south, to the canyon of White Bird Creek, a stream emptying into the Salmon River. Joseph had been away from the encampment when the raids had taken place, but he knew that neither that circumstance, nor that none of the murderers were members of his band, was likely to be taken into consideration when retribution was dealt out. He stayed for two days with his wife who had just given birth to a daughter, then the three joined the others at White Bird Canyon.

General Howard, at Lapwai on the reservation, got the news on June 15, and at once sent Captain David Perry with two companies of the 1st Cavalry after the Indians. On the way Perry was joined by eleven volunteers, to give him a total of about 110 men. As the force neared the Indian camp at White Bird Canyon, the Nez Percés sent several men with a flag of truce to meet it, but they were fired on. The Indians were outnumbered; they had only about sixty to sixty-five men, some of them old, some still in sorry condition from too much stolen whiskey the night before, about a third armed with bows and arrows, many of the rest with old muzzle-loaders. But fighting a battle which they improvised as they proceeded, they routed the troops, cut them into sections, pinned one group of nineteen men against a rocky wall and wiped them out, and killed thirty-four and wounded four, while suffering only two wounded themselves.

The Indians picked up sixty-three badly needed rifles and large amounts of ammunition from the battlefield. They behaved in a very un-Indianlike manner by leaving the bodies of the enemy unmutilated, unscalped, and completely clothed.

General Howard moved more cautiously now. He called in more men from posts throughout the entire Pacific Northwest while reserves were brought in from as far as Atlanta, Georgia, to stand by in case the war spread. The Nez Percés picked up some strength, too. Two competent warriors, Five Wounds and Rainbow, returning from a buffalo hunt in Montana, met the fugitives and joined them with their small bands. General Howard, through a stupid act, gave them more recruits. A prominent chief named Looking Glass was camped on the reservation with his band, completely divorced from all the violence that had been occurring. Nevertheless, when wild-eyed settlers brought stories that Looking Glass was preparing to join the hostiles, Howard, without investigating, sent a Captain Whipple with two companies of cavalry against Looking Glass's village. Nor did he direct Whipple to investigate before he took action, so Whipple did not hesitate to launch an attack when he found a peaceful camp. Only three or four Indians were killed in what was a completely treacherous attack, but the village was destroyed. The infuriated Indians thereupon left the reservation and set out to join the hostile force.

While Captain Whipple was making his ill-advised raid on Looking Glass's camp, General Howard had been decoyed across the swollen Salmon River and led on a chase through the rugged, almost trackless country south of that river. Then the Indians doubled back, leaving Howard to flounder about in the wilderness. The Nez Percés headed north to a new camping place on the Clearwater River at the mouth of Cottonwood Creek, annihilating on the way a reconnoitering party of ten men sent out by Captain Whipple. At the Clearwater camp, they were joined by Looking Glass and his still-angry band, giving them just under 200 men, and about 450 women and children.

By July 11, General Howard, with his army reinforced and increased to 400 soldiers and 180 scouts, teamsters, and packers, had caught up with the hostile band, who were still camped on the Clearwater, and took them completely by surprise by opening fire from the bluff across the river with a howitzer and two Gatling guns. However, before Howard could get his attack underway, Toohoolhoolzote, chief of one of the nontreaty bands, an elderly man but a noted warrior, dashed across the river and up the bluffs with only twenty-four men to hold the soldiers off until reinforcements could follow and swing around Howard's flanks and rear.

In spite of a numerical advantage of six to one, and despite his possession of artillery, the chagrined General Howard soon found himself completely surrounded and besieged, with his forces drawn up in a hollow square. For more than a day, the Indians kept up the close siege, sometimes coming near enough for hand-to-hand fighting. Then, tiring of the battle, they broke it off, after first giving the camp plenty of time to move on. They had lost four killed and six wounded, the Army thirteen killed and twenty-three wounded.

After traveling a safe distance to the east, the Nez Percés camped to take stock of their situation and decide their future course. They had fought their battle on the Clearwater as five separate bands, each under its own chief (Ollikut, Joseph's brother, had led the Wallowa band), and with no clear idea of what they were fighting for except to defend themselves. Now it was decided that the only course open to them was to leave Idaho Territory and go east across the mountains. There they could join their friends, the Crows, on the buffalo plains in Montana. Chief Joseph objected; he wanted to continue to fight for his beautiful land, to the death if need be, but he was overruled. The Nez Percés, in their naïveté, believed that their fight was only with General Howard, and that if they crossed the mountains beyond his jurisdiction there would be nothing more to fear. Looking Glass was named war chief for the united band, and the march began, over the difficult Lolo Trail across the high Bitterroot Mountains. Besides its aged and infirm, its children and infants, its sick and wounded who had to be carried through, the band was driving a herd of two to three thousand horses. Yet they made it, through a trail so blocked by jack-straw tangles of fallen trees and boulders that Howard's forces, following behind, had to be preceded by a crew of forty axmen.

The band passed over the high point of the Bitterroots and were moving down its eastern slope into Montana when they found their way blocked by hastily built fortifications manned by about thirty-five regular Army infantrymen and some two hundred volunteers, under the command of Captain Charles C. Rawn. Chief Joseph, Looking Glass, and old Chief White Bird rode forward to parley. They explained that

Chief Joseph's Retreat

they had no quarrel with anyone but General Howard and would harm no one if permitted to pass. The volunteers knew the Nez Percés well and favorably from their buffalo-hunting trips. They decided that, since they were there only to defend their homes from Indians, and since their homes needed no defending from these Indians, they might as well go home. Most of them did; only thirty volunteers remained with Rawn and his regulars.

The unhappy Captain Rawn had been ordered by Howard to hold the Indians but he could do little with his depleted forces. The Indians swung wide around the end of the fortifications, and Rawn wisely refrained from opening fire on them. The defense works were promptly dubbed Fort Fizzle by the public.

The band moved on to Stevensville where supplies were replenished, not by looting and pillage, but by decorous purchase in the town's stores. These strange Indians, who could easily have taken anything they wanted, quietly paid with gold and currency for their sugar, coffee, and tobacco, and at prices which the merchants had raised sky-high for the occasion. There was, however, no buying of liquor because the chiefs had told the town fathers to have all supplies locked up till the band had moved on.

Now they turned south, following the Bitterroot River to its head, then crossed the Continental Divide and passed into the Big Hole Valley just south of it, where at last they set up their tepees for a long rest and to repair some of the ravages of the hard trip. They were sure they were in friendly country now, with nothing to fear. But Colonel John Gibbon had come by forced marches from Fort Shaw on the Sun River, gathering men from other posts as he came, and at dawn on August 9, he attacked the sleeping camp with approximately two hundred men. There was no warning. The shot that killed a solitary horse herder came almost at the same instant as the crash of rifle fire into the lodges and the whoops of charging soldiers. Women were shot without hesitation; children were gunned down; even babies had their heads crushed with a kick or a clubbed rifle. Such, at least, is the testimony of an officer who took part in the campaign.

But despite the overwhelming surprise of the attack, some of the Indians recovered and began to fight back, rallied by doughty old White Bird. One sharp stroke of luck fell their way; the lieutenant commanding Gibbon's left wing was killed, and as the leaderless troops lost purpose, the Indians opposing them organized a counterattack that continued until it had rolled up Gibbon's entire force, which was now giving too much of its attention to plundering. The marksmanship of the Nez Percés was taking a heavy toll (their accurate shooting, unusual among Indians, was remarked in every engagement). Gibbon was soon on the defensive and besieged; Chief Joseph had taken charge of getting the camp packed up and moving, and the weary, never-ending flight was on again.

When a detachment of soldiers attempted to set up a howitzer, a handful of Indians drove them off, seized the cannon, and, since they did not know how to use the weapon, wrecked it. Gibbon, running out of food, water, and ammunition, was saved only by the arrival of General Howard. He had lost thirty-three dead and thirty-eight wounded, including himself. He claimed the Indians lost eighty-nine, and this appears to be correct, or very nearly so, but most of those dead were women, children, and aged. The Nez Percés later said that only twelve warriors died, but they included some of the best, among them Rainbow and Five Wounds.

The Nez Percés buried their dead before withdrawing; Howard permitted his Bannock Indian scouts to dig up the bodies to scalp and mutilate them. This barbarism, coming on top of the savage slaughter of noncombatants, shocked the Nez Percés, who had been fighting by all the rules of so-called civilized warfare. Howard became the most despised man in the world as far as they were concerned, not completely logically, for it was Colonel Gibbon who had been guilty of killing the women and children.

Looking Glass was displaced as war leader because he had let the camp be taken by surprise, his place taken by a chief named Lean Elk who had recently joined the band; he had been buffalo hunting and was camped in the Bitterroot valley with half a dozen lodges when the fugitives came by shortly after the affair of Fort Fizzle. But the stories going out to the country—and the public was by now intensely interested in what was occurring—all credited Chief Joseph with the military leadership of the band. General Howard, recalling Joseph's astuteness in council and his leadership in peace, assumed that he was continuing to guide the Nez Percés in battle. So the legend arose of a rude military genius in the northern mountains, a redskinned Napoleon, maneuvering his outnumbered warriors so skilfully as to confound, confuse, and defeat, time and again, the trained troops of the United States.

The truth is somewhat less exciting. Joseph was not a war chief, and although he took part in the fighting once or twice, he usually took charge of the camp to see that it was struck, packed for traveling, and on its way, with women and children taken care of. It was an important and necessary function and not to be denigrated—most tribes had peace chiefs and war chiefs—but it lays to rest the myth of the master tactician in moccasins. The Nez Percé victories were due, not to any unusual brilliance in battle, but to a combination of bravery, determination, and the rare ability to stand fast when caught off-balance and then recover and take the initiative. That, along with overconfidence and some fortuitous (for the Nez Percés) mistakes on the part of their white foes.

The fleeing band paralleled the general line of the Continental Divide, which swung in a great arc toward the east. General Howard was pushing them hard. To slow him up and give the fugitives some respite, a group of warriors, whose leaders included Ollikut, made a raid on the night of August 20 on the horse and mule herd of Howard's column at a place called Camas Meadows. The Army camp was alerted by an alarm in time to save its cavalry mounts but the mules were run off, and Howard was held up several days while he gathered new pack animals in settlements in the surrounding regions.

The fugitives passed on into Yellowstone Park, then only five years old but already attracting a considerable number of hardy tourists. They barely missed one party containing General William Tecumseh Sherman, but swept up another, shooting and almost fatally wounding one man. The timely arrival of Lean Elk saved the rest of the party from injury and the women from molestation (the young Nez Percés had become much less forbearing toward whites since the affair at Big Hole).

The flight continued, through Yellowstone Park and the northwestern corner of Wyoming; then the Indians swung northward where more trouble awaited. Part of the 7th Cavalry, commanded by Colonel Samuel Sturgis (who had been on detached duty when almost half the regiment died at the Little Bighorn), tried to head them off, but the Nez Percé band found its way through mountainous country which had been considered impassable for men with horses and came out behind Sturgis on Clarks Fork of the Yellowstone River.

The decision was made to continue the weary journey on to Canada. They had discovered that there was to be no haven among the Crows as they had planned. The embarrassed Crows had explained to Looking Glass and other emissaries who had gone to them that they were not only at peace with the whites but were working for them as scouts. However, when Army commanders in the area shortly afterward tried to enlist them as scouts against the Nez Percés, an unusual number of them proved to be busy elsewhere. Those who did agree to serve showed an amazing ineptness.

Sturgis and his companies of the 7th picked up the trail again, and caught up with their quarry, after a pursuit of perhaps seventy-five miles, at Canyon Creek, a small tributary of the Yellowstone, not far west of the present site of Billings, Montana. The attacking cavalry was stopped by warriors protected behind rocks and ravines while the rest of the band retreated up the creek canyon; then the Indians fought a rear-guard action as they retreated. By nightfall Sturgis, with four dead and a number of wounded, gave up the chase; no Nez Percé was known to have been killed although at least three had been wounded.

The band, exhausted, slowed down now that pursuit appeared to have been left behind. Their course took them north across Montana, as far as a low range called the Bear Paw Mountains which rose from the plains in the northern part of the Territory. There, only thirty miles from the Canadian border, the fugitive band made camp to rest and to hunt and lay in a supply of dried meat and buffalo skins against the coming winter.

Once again they had reckoned without the telegraph. Colonel Nelson E. Miles was hurrying up from Fort Keogh on the Yellowstone with six hundred men: parts of the 2nd and 7th Cavalry and the mounted 5th Infantry, along with a considerable number of Cheyenne warriors. Another day and the Nez Percés would probably have made it to Canada, for most of the pack animals already had their burdens lashed on and the band was making ready to move again when Miles's scouts sighted their lodges on the morning of the last day of September.

Colonel Miles ordered an immediate attack, hoping to smash the Nez Percés with a single charge. But he had begun the charge a good four miles away, and the Indians had that much warning; old White Bird quickly posted his men in front of the camp, and as the onrushing battle line of troops came within range, it met a withering fire which killed two officers and twenty-two men, and injured another four officers and thirty-eight men. The charge stopped as though it had been poleaxed, and the men took shelter behind rocks and in gullies. But they did not retreat; the camp remained under fire.

White Bird had only 120 men against Miles's six hundred; the 2nd Cavalry which formed Miles's right wing extended so far beyond the Nez Percé defenses that it met no opposition and swept on toward the horse herd, most of which it captured. The pack horses, standing ready to go, had been started on their way by women and children as soon as the troops were seen approaching; about fifty warriors went along and beat off attempts of the cavalry to pursue and capture the pack train. When the soldiers gave up the pursuit, many of the warriors turned back, too, and slipped into the camp.

Two brave leaders, Chief Toohoolhoolzote and Ollikut, were among the good men who died in the first confused fighting. Chief Joseph and his twelve-year-old daughter had been with the horse herd when the attack came. He told the girl to catch a horse and join those who were cut off from the camp. Then he galloped his horse through the line of soldiers, unharmed, though his horse was wounded and his clothes pierced many times. His wife met him at the entrance of his lodge and handed him his rifle. "Here is your gun. Fight."

The battle quickly settled down to a siege. The next morning, October 1, heavy snow fell and the storm continued for two days; although it added to the discomfort of both sides, it brought fighting almost to a halt. Colonel Miles, attempting to win by deception, tricked Joseph into his camp with a white flag on the pretense of wanting to negotiate, and then seized the chief. The Indians countered by capturing an officer; an exchange of prisoners restored the situation as it had been.

On October 4, General Howard arrived with more troops, making the situation of the Nez Percés hopeless. Negotiations were begun through two treaty Nez Percés who had come with Howard as interpreters. The few remaining chiefs were told that Howard would treat the band with honor if they surrendered, and would send them back to the Lapwai reservation in the spring, when the mountains were clear of snow again. Looking Glass and White Bird wanted to fight on, but Chief Joseph insisted that they must make their decision for the freezing women and children crouching in the pits that had been dug for shelter from Miles's howitzer.

Just as the council broke up, brave Looking Glass fell dead, struck in the head by a chance bullet. For four months, and over a trail 1,300 miles long, the Nez Percé band had fought and fled, to be caught only thirty miles from freedom. A short distance still remained for Chief Joseph to travel, the ride from the camp to the hill where General Howard and Colonel Miles were waiting, but for him it would be the longest part of the journey. He had already sent his message of surrender ahead with Captain John, one of the Nez Percé interpreters, who had carried it to General Howard and repeated it with tears in his eyes: *

> Tell General Howard I know his heart. What he told me before I have in my heart. I am tired of fighting. Our chiefs are killed. Looking Glass is dead. Toohoolhoolzote is dead. The old men are all dead. It is the young men who say yes and no. He who led the young men [Ollikut] is dead. It is cold and we have no blankets. The little children are freezing to death. My people, some of them, have run away to the hills, and have no blankets, no food; no one knows where they are—perhaps freezing to death. I want to have time to look for my children and see how many I can find. Maybe I shall find them among the dead. Hear me, my chiefs, I am tired; my heart is sick and sad. From where the sun now stands, I will fight no more forever.

About two hours later, Joseph rode over, with several of his men walking beside him. He dismounted and handed his rifle to Howard, who motioned that he should give it to Colonel Miles. Thereafter, he was treated as a prisoner of war.

Chief White Bird escaped to Canada that night with a handful of followers. A number of those who had gotten away on the first day also made it to safety across the border, but some had been killed by hostile Assiniboines and Hidatsas. A few more than 400 were captured of about 650 who had started on the long trip; probably close to 200 died during the flight or on the plains. But Joseph's fears that his own children might be dead were groundless; of his six children, only the baby born on the eve of the long journey remained with him at the time of the surrender, but all were later found safe.

* There are two versions of the manner in which the famous message was delivered. The one given here was contained in the *Report of the Secretary of War, 1877*, and would appear to have the ring of authenticity. Another and more dramatic description of the event later became current: it had the saddened Joseph making his speech directly to General Howard and Colonel Miles. This version also seems made of sound metal since it was the story recounted by Charles E. S. Wood, who, as Lieutenant Wood, had been General Howard's aide and was present at the surrender. However, when he wrote of the event he had become a professional author, and probably was tampering with history to increase the dramatic effect.

The captives were taken to Fort Keogh, a logical place to hold them until they could be returned to Idaho in the spring. But soon an order came from General Sheridan to send them to Fort Abraham Lincoln. It would be too expensive, he said, to maintain them at Fort Keogh through the winter. Colonel Miles, after making a futile protest, put most of his prisoners on flatboats to make the long trip down the Yellowstone and Missouri without military guard or escort except for one enlisted man on each boat. The able-bodied men and some of the women marched overland with Miles and his troops. All arrived safely.

When Miles arrived in Bismarck with the overland contingent of Nez Percés, a remarkable thing occurred. Bismarck, it will be remembered, was still a frontier community, and most of its people were convinced of the basic rightness of Sheridan's dictum, "The only good Indian is a dead Indian." * Not only that, it was at Fort Abraham Lincoln, near Bismarck, that the 7th Cavalry had been stationed. Many of the townspeople had had friends who had died only a year before with Custer.

Bismarck would, in short, seem an unwise place to bring a group of Indians who had lately been at war with the Army. But as the column rode through the main street, with Chief Joseph on horseback beside Colonel Miles and the rest of the Nez Percé following, enclosed by a protecting square of soldiers, crowds of townspeople surged out into the street, and against the cordon of troops. However, there was no hate and no violence intended; they carried food, and broke through the square of troops to give it to the Indians. Only when the people had exhausted all their gifts was the column able to proceed on to Fort Lincoln.

Two days later an even more remarkable event occurred. The good ladies of Bismarck were hostesses at a dinner at which Chief Joseph and the other chiefs were guests of honor. But these were the only two bright spots in their treatment by white people since their war began, and would be just about the last. Two days after the dinner, they were on a train, headed for Fort Leavenworth, with Indian Territory as their eventual destination. Colonel Miles and General Howard protested this

---

* Sheridan appears not to have made his deathless remark in quite these words. At Fort Cobb in Indian Territory, in January, 1869 during the Washita campaign, a Comanche named Turtle Dove introduced himself to Sheridan, adding, "Me good Indian." "The only good Indians I know are dead," the General graciously replied, according to the man who overheard and recorded the exchange. The quotation was revised into the more serviceable one the world knows.

betrayal of the promises made by Howard to the Nez Percés at the time of the surrender, but the higher powers in Washington felt under no kind of obligation to honor the promises. General Sherman, while refraining from talking about extermination in this case, announced that the Nez Percés must be suitably punished to discourage other tribes who might feel moved to defend their rights.

The Nez Percés were settled in a low, malarial part of Indian Territory, especially deadly to these highland people whose resistance to disease had been lowered by their recent hardships and suffering. Within a few months, more than a quarter of them were dead. They got along fairly well after they became somewhat acclimated to their new surroundings, and even prospered in a small way through their skill at stock raising, but they remained hopelessly homesick for their mountains. Strong public sentiment had been aroused by their magnificent retreat and by the way they conducted themselves during it, and the public was not permitted to forget their story. Colonel Miles (brigadier general after 1880), a firm friend of Joseph since the end of the war, regularly recommended that the Nez Percés be permitted to return.

A few widows and orphans were allowed to go to the Lapwai reservation in 1882, and the rest were sent north three years later. Slightly more than half went to Lapwai; the rest, among them Joseph, were for some reason sent to the Colville reservation in northern Washington to live among the several small tribes there. None of Joseph's six children returned north with him; he had buried them, one by one, in alien soil, victims of the climate and disease of the south.

Chief Joseph, during the rest of his life, asked to be permitted to returned to the Wallowa country, of which he had said, "I love that land more than all the rest of the world." But where the rest of the country had come to admire Joseph, the ranchers in his former home opposed his return, and the government supinely gave in to their wishes. Joseph died, still grieving for his lost country, in 1904. Charles Erskine Wood, aide to General Howard during the Nez Percé War, wrote what might be Joseph's epitaph: "I think that, in his long career, Joseph cannot accuse the Government of the United States of one single act of justice."

2. "A NUMBER OF INSUBORDINATE, CUNNING, TREACHEROUS INDIANS"

The Bannocks of southeastern Idaho went on the warpath, briefly and futilely, in 1878, the year after the Nez Percé lunge toward freedom. Their bill of particulars is long but the cause of their hopeless uprising can be reduced to three words: they were hungry.

During the great period of treaty making on the plains and in the mountains in 1867 and 1868, the Bannocks accepted a reservation on the upper Snake River, being careful to reserve all rights to an area called Camas Prairie. The camas is a plant of the lily family which covers entire meadows with its blue flowers in spring; its onion-shaped root-bulb, when baked, formed an important part of the diet of the Bannocks as it did of most of the tribes of the Pacific Northwest. The Camas Prairie was an especially extensive and prolific source of this foodstuff.

After the treaty was signed and the Bannocks had moved onto the reservation in 1868, the usual things happened. The government was late with the annuities it had promised, and when it did send them, the amounts were less than had been agreed on in the treaty. To keep from starving, the Bannocks went after buffalo. They were part-time horse-and-buffalo Indians, and at one time bison had ranged as far west as the headwaters of the Snake in their own country, but now the buffalo ranges were farther away each year, and it required some nine months for a hunting expedition to cross the mountains to the plains and return. Nevertheless, it was a choice between that or going hungry, and even their agent encouraged the hunts because with part of the tribe gone, the food annuities went further among those who remained on the reservation.

Even so, it was not enough. Food was so scarce one year that the agent reported that the people came begging because their children were crying for something to eat. Under these circumstances, the food supplied by the camas roots became even more important than usual, but white settlers were encroaching more and more on the Camas Prairie, using it not only to pasture horses and cattle, but as a feeding ground for large herds of swine which uprooted and destroyed the camas plants.

Trouble came in the spring of 1878. The Bannocks had been on very short rations because there had been no buffalo hunt the previous winter; like all other tribes in the region they had been ordered to stay on their reservation of fear they might join the hostile Nez Percés. The food rations were stretched thin to go around. Then, when spring came and the tribe moved to Camas Prairie, they found settlers there herding their hogs and cattle, as they had done for several years. Only this time, Chief Buffalo Horn, who had led the Bannock scouts against Chief Joseph's Nez Percés, had had enough of it. He ordered the herders off Bannock land. Before they could get off, two were shot and wounded by a pair of irresponsible young Indians.

The war that followed was confused, but was uniformly disastrous to Bannock arms. Some of the tribe returned at once to the agency to remain clear of the conflict; the rest headed west and north, hoping to enlist the Paiutes, Umatillas and other tribes of the region in the conflict. No one joined them; on the contrary, the Umatillas offered their services to the Army. The Bannocks, defeated and their leaders killed, turned east, and in small groups tried to find refuge among friendly tribes. A few got as far as Wyoming Territory across the Continental Divide, where they were attacked by Colonel Miles, and a number were killed when a cannon was turned on their lodges; others were slain when an Army unit ignored their attempts to surrender and met them with heavy gunfire.

The war was over by October. Nine soldiers and thirty-one civilians were listed by the Army as having been killed. Seventy-eight Bannocks were reported to have died, but it was probably more because the Indians had undoubtedly carried off many of their dead and wounded whom the Army knew nothing of. There was no talk by Sherman either of extermination or of removal to Indian Territory. The principal punishment was to keep the captured Bannocks, about six hundred, at Fort Simcoe, Washington, for periods up to two years before permitting them to return to their own agency.

General George Crook had been on the Bannock reservation a year before the outbreak, and to enlighten his professional colleagues about the situation, wrote an article which appeared (in the *Army and Navy Journal,* June 29, 1878) shortly after the start of the trouble:

. . . I was up there last spring, and found them in a desperate condition. I telegraphed, and the agent telegraphed for supplies, but word came that no appropriation had been made. They have never been half supplied.

The agent has sent them off for half a year to enable them to pick up something to live on, but there is nothing for them in that country. The buffalo is all gone, . . . and there aren't enough jackrabbits to catch. What are they to do?

Starvation is staring them in the face, and if they wait much longer, they will not be able to fight. They understand the situation, and fully appreciate what is before them.

The encroachments upon the Camas' prairies was the cause of the trouble. These prairies are the last source of subsistence. . . . I do not wonder, and you will not either that when these Indians see their wives and children starving, and their last sources of supplies cut off, they go to war. And then we are sent out to kill them. It is an outrage.

The last of the Bannock hostiles had not yet surrendered before there was new trouble, this time on the Great Plains again. At the close of the Sioux War, the defeated Cheyenne band of Chief Dull Knife, as well as a smaller number of other surrendered Cheyennes, had been sent south to join their southern kinsmen on the Cheyenne-Arapaho reservation in Indian Territory. The Indians had been misled about what they would find in the south, and about how they would be treated when they got there. Dull Knife claimed he had been promised that they could return north if they did not like their new home, and it is very probable, in view of the usual practices of government commissioners, that such assurances were given with no intention of abiding by them.

The Cheyennes did not like their new home. They suffered from malaria and other illnesses. They were hungry most of the time because the Indian Bureau did not send the food that had been promised— their agent said he received rations enough to feed them only nine months of the year—and there were no buffalo to hunt as there were on the northern plains. Perhaps hardest of all to bear, they were acutely homesick.

By 1878, after a year and a half in the south, they had had all they could stand, and a band of them, under the leadership of Dull Knife and a warrior chief, Little Wolf, decided to go home. Little Wolf had told the agent that they were not going to remain; the agent called troops from near-by Fort Reno, and a cordon was placed around the

Cheyenne camp. Yet one September morning, daylight revealed to the guard that the tepees were empty.

Flight across the plains was not the same matter of escape through empty distance it had been ten years earlier. Three railroads now cut across from east to west, lines along which troops could be moved rapidly. Telegraph lines had proliferated. Ranchers and homesteaders were numerous, and every one of them was ready to report the passage of a band of Indians. It would be next to impossible to get through without being seen and pursued.

There were very nearly three hundred Indians in the band when it started north. Perhaps seventy were warriors, the rest were women, children, and old men—although it was a very old man who did not fight when the time came. Many were without horses. But they trudged on north, skillfully hiding their trail where a white man would consider it impossible to do so, turning at bay to fight when troops caught up with them. They fought four battles of importance, beating off troops and suffering only six killed; their wounded the medicine men treated, often with results that made Army surgeons shake their heads in wonderment later.

They tried to avoid contact with homesteaders and ranchers, but they needed horses and they needed meat, and usually there was no other source than the horses and cattle of whites. Sometimes the owners tried to stop Indians from making off with their animals; then there were exchanges of gunfire, and white men were killed—and the Western newspapers spread stories of great massacre and bloodshed. It was an unhappy situation for both Indians and settlers.

General Sheridan's entire Division of the Missouri hastily mobilized its manpower to block the northward march of the Cheyennes. Nevertheless, the Indians crossed the Atchison, Topeka & Santa Fe, they crossed the Kansas Pacific, and at last they passed over the Union Pacific, where troops were spread out in a great net to snare them, but were unable to prevent them from slipping through.

After crossing the Union Pacific, the Cheyennes split into two groups, both heading into the sand hills of northwestern Nebraska. One band, under Little Wolf, settled down to winter on a stream called the Lost Chokecherry. The others, led by Dull Knife, were moving through a heavy snowstorm near Camp Robinson in the extreme northwestern corner of the state when they suddenly found horsemen looming up

Flight of the Cheyennes

MISSOURI R.

MONTANA TERRITORY

YELLOWSTONE R.

BAND IS BROUGHT TO FORT KEOGH NEAR JUNCTION OF TONGUE WITH YELLOWSTONE

Bismarck

NORTHERN PACIFIC RR.

Ft. Abraham Lincoln

Ft. Keogh

CANNONBALL R.

MINNESOTA

LITTLE WOLF'S BAND IS CAPTURED BY U.S. TROOPS

SIOUX RESERVATION

DAKOTA TERRITORY

WYOMING TERR.

BELLE FOURCHE R.

CHEYENNE R.

THE LAST OF THE ESCAPING CHEYENNES ARE BROUGHT TO BAY AND KILLED OR CAPTURED

WHITE R.

Pine Ridge Agency

MISSOURI R.

CAPTIVITY AND ESCAPE FROM CAMP ROBINSON

Camp Robinson

NIOBRARA R.

IOWA

Ft. Laramie

DULL KNIFE'S BAND CAPTURED BY ARMY FORCES

NORTH PLATTE R.

LITTLE WOLF TAKES HIS BAND THROUGH THE WINTER ON LOST CHOKECHERRY CREEK

THE BANDS OF DULL KNIFE AND LITTLE WOLF SEPARATE

NEBRASKA

Omaha

SOUTH PLATTE R.

UNION PACIFIC RR.

PLATTE R.

MISSOURI R.

Denver

Ft. Kearney

REPUBLICAN R.

KANSAS PACIFIC RR.

COLORADO

Ft. Wallace

Ft. Hays

SOLOMON R.

Ft. Riley

Ft. Leavenworth

Topeka

MISSOURI

KANSAS R.

Kansas City

Pueblo

SMOKY HILL R.

ATCHISON, TOPEKA AND SANTA FE RR.

Ft. Larned

Ft. Lyon

ARKANSAS R.

KANSAS

Dodge City

PUBLIC LAND

NORTH CANADIAN R.

INDIAN TERRITORY

CIMARRON R.

ARKANSAS R.

CANADIAN R.

Ft. Reno

TEXAS

CHEYENNE-ARAPAHO RESERVATION

Ft. Sill

0 Miles 200

out of the whiteness ahead. They had run into two companies of the 3rd Cavalry by pure chance in the obscuring snow; the soldiers were as surprised as they were, and Captain J. B. Johnson, commanding, was happy to see Dull Knife raise a white flag rather than prepare to fight.

During the next two days, as Johnson parleyed with Dull Knife and his chiefs about what should be done with them, the military forces were gradually increased. The Indians had been certain that now they were so near their old hunting grounds, they would be permitted to remain, and the situation became tense when Johnson indicated that it was not quite as simple as that. At last, faced with overwhelming Army strength that now included artillery, the Indians were induced to give up their weapons and to move on to Camp Robinson. They gave up only their oldest guns, however; the best ones were secretly taken apart and hidden under the women's clothing.

At Camp Robinson they were quartered in an empty barracks. They had wanted to join the Sioux on Pine Ridge agency (the former Red Cloud agency), just across the Dakota border not far to the northeast, but the Army decided otherwise. For a time, their captivity was a light burden. They were allowed to roam in the near vicinity of the fort, hunting grouse, rabbits, and such other small game on the river bottoms as they could bring down with bow and arrow, which they were permitted to use. The main restriction was that they all must be in the barracks each night; their future liberties would depend on observing that rule.

But, although they had been treated with kindness, the sword hung over their heads. They knew that someone in Washington was making up his mind what should be done with them, and they were afraid of being sent back to Indian Territory. They knew only that they did not want to go back to the empty land in the south. "We will not go there to live," Dull Knife said. "That is not a healthful country, and if we should stay there we would all die. We do not wish to go back there and we will not go. You may kill me here, but you cannot make me go back."

After two months, the easy-going captivity came to a sudden end. When the prisoners were first brought to Camp Robinson, and before they had been counted, one woman escaped and joined the Sioux on Pine Ridge agency. In time, her lorn husband, a warrior named Bull Hump, found the separation too much to bear, and went off to the agency to see his wife. He was found and brought back within a few days, but as a consequence, all the prisoners lost their privileges of moving freely around the post, and henceforth were locked in the barracks.

In the meantime, the Cheyennes had become the focus of attention of do-gooders, of Indian-haters, of people sincerely concerned with helping the Indians, of revenge-seekers, of a host of the other types who appeared from all directions whenever Indians became involved in controversy. The magnificent flight of the Nez Percés was only a year past, and the public had become more acutely aware of the injustices being done to Indians. Not all the voices raised in defense of the Cheyennes and their right to remain in the North spoke with Eastern accents. Even the editor of the Omaha *Herald,* in the frontier state where the Cheyennes were at that moment imprisoned and where Indians were not loved, appealed to the Indian Bureau not to take the plucky little band back south. For, said Editor Miller, it would mean hauling them back trussed up like cattle. "It means starvation for them. I implore you for justice and humanity to those wronged red men. Let them stay in their own country."

There were, of course, other voices. Kansas authorities were demanding the surrender of the Cheyenne men, to stand trial for the murder of ranchers and homesteaders. And Lieutenant General Philip Henry Sheridan, deploring the tears shed for the Cheyennes, was certain that unless they were severely disciplined, all Indians would break loose from every restraint. "The condition of these Indians is pitiable but it is my opinion that unless they are sent back to where they came from, the whole reservation system will receive a shock which will endanger its stability."

At Camp Robinson, the temperature dropped lower and lower: to zero, to ten below, to as low as forty below zero. There are degrees of cold that one who has not experienced them cannot quite imagine; they are not merely uncomfortable but dangerous and potentially deadly to those not properly protected. While the cold hung so deep, the long-expected word came through; the Cheyennes were to be sent back to Indian Territory, and immediately.

The order came as no surprise because it had long been more than rumor that the Indians would be returned. It was the impossibly bad timing of the move that upset the military authorities. General Crook, commanding the Department of the Platte in which Camp Robinson was located, telegraphed the Indian Bureau to send a man to take charge of the move. If the Indian Bureau was going to insist on moving the Cheyennes in the iron-hard depths of winter, Crook felt it should assume the responsibility. The Cheyennes themselves, who had already sensed that they were going to be shipped back south, were told definitely and finally, on January 3, 1879, that they would have to get ready to move. Their answer, as it had always been, was that they would not go back to Indian Territory; they would prefer to have the soldiers kill them than to die slowly in the south.

Captain Henry W. Wessells, Jr., commanding officer of the post, went in to the prison barracks with an ultimatum: agree to go south or go cold and hungry. Once again they gave the same answer, that they would rather die than return to Indian Territory. They were given no more food or firewood. They bundled up in their ragged blankets and kept tiny fires going by burning the crude furniture; the few scraps of food they had saved were carefully doled out to the children.

A few days later, Wessells gave the screws another turn by ordering water withheld, even drinking water. He offered to take care of the women and children if they would come out, but the Cheyennes disdained even to answer. To quench their thirst somewhat, they scraped the thick frost from the windows. At that time there were 149 Cheyennes in the barracks, less than a third of them males between the ages of eleven and eighty.

On January 9, Captain Wessells called Dull Knife and two other chiefs, Old Crow and Wild Hog, to a council. Only the latter two came; the Cheyennes would not let Dull Knife out of the barracks for fear of treachery. Their suspicions were completely justified; after trying to get a surrender agreement out of Old Crow and Wild Hog and receiving only a scornful reply, Wessells had the two chiefs seized and put in irons. An alarm reached the prisoners in the barracks, who at once prepared to defend themselves against an expected assault by troops. The rifles were taken out from hiding places under floor boards, and men without guns armed themselves with the women's household knives with their worn-down blades, and even with pieces of board for clubs. With such weapons, they stood ready to resist Army rifles.

The attack did not come, nor had Captain Wessells any intention of attempting to drive the Cheyennes out by force. He was so confident that his campaign to starve and freeze the Indians out was going to succeed that he was perfectly content to wait. In his assurance, it did not occur to him that hungry, desperate people might be driven to extreme measures. The Cheyennes had been forced to just such extreme. They had decided that same day that it was far preferable to die like free people in the open air than miserably like caged beasts.

About ten o'clock that night, they made their desperate try for freedom. Warriors of the Dog Society leapt from the windows first to shoot the sentries and cover the escape, deliberately giving up their lives to delay the first pursuit and give the others a few minutes start. Wessell's refusal to believe that the imprisoned, hungry Indians could be dangerous also gave them a few minutes; he had declined to post any extra guard in spite of the trouble of the afternoon, although other, less sanguine officers sat up waiting for the disturbance they were afraid would come. But there were no enlisted men waiting at the ready, and some of them actually set out in pursuit in their underwear, even though the temperature was far below zero. They suffered acutely before they were ordered back to camp for warm clothing.

The Indians headed for the bluffs some two miles distant from the post, leaving the way strewn with their dead and wounded. When warriors fell, women and young boys picked up their guns and tried to fight on. A lieutenant stumbled into a pit and found himself with two Indians who set upon him with knives. Despite a bright full moon, it was not possible to make out much in the hollow except that he was in mortal danger; he shot the Indians with his pistol and then found they were both women. There were, without doubt, instances of the indiscriminate killing of men, women, and children that had been such a common feature of Army attacks on Indians, but they appear not to have been so much in evidence during these bloody minutes. Perhaps it was that the sympathies of the soldiers had been with the Cheyennes in their simple, understandable pleas not to be sent back south. In any event, attempts were made to obtain surrenders where possible, and wounded were brought in to the post hospital.

Most of the crimes against the wounded seem to have been the work of the traders and other civilians at the post who soon arrived with wagons and followed the path of the flight, clearly marked by dark bundles easily visible against the moonlit snow. The dead they stripped of their garments and sometimes scalped; there were dark indications that more than one dead person had been only wounded when these body-robbers came on him.

The mass of the Cheyennes reached the bluffs at last, at a point they had noted at some time in the past; it was an inconspicuous break in the cliffs which provided a way to the top for people on foot. There was no other way up anywhere in the vicinity, and for men on horseback it was necessary to travel six miles to find a way to the top. The pursuit had to be given up for the night; the Cheyennes had gained that much time—at a terrible cost.

By daylight, some thirty dead Indians had been brought into the camp, and perhaps thirty-five wounded, along with a number of uninjured prisoners. More dead were found after it became light, and more living, too, who were killed, or wounded, or surrendered half-frozen and filled with the hopelessness of resistance. Warriors had to be shot out of caves; elsewhere, women gave up, saying there had been enough killing.

The main body of the escaped Cheyennes, after gaining the top of the bluff, had pushed on westward during the night and next morning, covering an unbelievable seventeen miles in the bitter cold, hungry and weak as they were, some of them carrying children, some of them wounded. Then, when troops from the post did catch up with them, they did the completely unexpected: they circled about and lay in ambush for the column. Two soldiers were shot down and several horses; the Cheyennes were in a strong position on a timbered hill and could not be dislodged by an attack. At night, Captain Wessells left a line of decoy fires around the Cheyenne position and took his troops back to Camp Robinson, because so sure had he been that he would bring the Indians back at heel that he had come without camp equipment or rations. The Cheyennes were not fooled by the decoy fires; that night they cut up the dead cavalry horses and had their first food in days, then moved on.

The cavalry column picked up their trail again the next day, and found and besieged them, only to have them slip away again at night. This went on day after day, the intrepid little band always managing to find a position virtually impregnable to direct attack before their pursuers caught up with them, and always gliding like ghosts through the Army picket lines at night. But time after time there was a price to pay: a man or woman killed here, another there, someone wounded. And constant hunger and cold, the cold that could freeze fingers and toes, hands and feet, of those whose necessary errands or carelessness exposed them to it.

At last, on January 21, twelve days after the breakout, the end came.

The band, now shrunken to thirty-one persons, was brought to bay about forty-five miles west of Camp Robinson, near the head of War Bonnet Creek. They took shelter in a washout in the bluffs, digging in deeper for better protection. Wessels, greatly reinforced on this last day, carefully surrounded the pits before calling on the Indians to surrender.

He was answered by a scattering fire, and the death chants of the Cheyennes.

He ordered an attack on the Indian positions. The soldiers charged to the edge of the pits; only the exhaustion of the Cheyenne's ammunition saved the lives of many soldiers, so closely were they grouped as they fired down into the holes. As they sprang back to reload, three men leaped out of the defenses and charged the troops—three against three hundred. Two were armed with knives, the third with an empty pistol. They were dropped in their tracks.

The soldiers fired another volley into the heap of dead and dying in the defense pits, and then it was over. Seventeen men were dead; one still lived, but only for a matter of a few hundred heart-beats. Six women and children were dead, another woman dying. All but two of the remaining seven women and children were badly wounded but would live.

These were the people who had wanted only to go home.

Dull Knife had been much sought by questing troops, who neither found his body nor were able to get any information about him from those who were captured. In the flight, he and his wife, his son and his son's wife, a young child and a youth, had become separated from the main party. They had hidden in a cave for a number of days, almost starving, until it was safe for them to strike north for Pine Ridge agency, living on rose hips, roots, and moccasins tops as they traveled. At the agency they were taken in by a half-breed interpreter and cared for until the day when it was no longer necessary to hide.

At Camp Robinson, the inevitable court of inquiry had convened to sift through events. There were a number of loose ends still dangling. What had happened to Dull Knife? Where was Little Wolf and his band? What was to be done with these people now—those who remained? What about the continuing demands from Kansas that the men be returned there to stand trial for murder? The Army was not happy; the affair had been handled very messily, which is to say it had been done with too much publicity. Indignation was nationwide; protests against military brutality came from everywhere. The figures were damning: 149 had broken out of the barracks; now only 78 were known to be alive, and many of these were wounded, crippled with frozen hands or feet, or sick. Sherman's brittle temper cracked when a newsman asked him, soon after the escape from the barracks, for more details on the massacre. "Massacre!" the prickly General snapped. "Why do you call it a massacre? A number of insubordinate, cunning, treacherous Indians."

But the voices of national conscience, already raised against the treatment of the Nez Percés, now moved even the ponderous bureaucracy of the Indian Office—to a degree. It was ruled that women, children, and a few badly crippled men could go to live among the Oglala Sioux on the Pine Ridge agency. They were loaded into wagons and taken north, fifty-eight of them, arriving at last without hindrance in the northern country to which they had set out when they left Indian Territory—but arriving as widows, orphans, and cripples.

Seven men of the band—all who appeared whole enough to stand trial—were taken to Kansas, along with their families. Defense funds poured in from across the country; lawyers offered their services without cost. But the case against the seven never went to a jury; it was soon dismissed by the court for lack of evidence. Nevertheless, they were sent on south to Indian Territory with their families, but the voices of indignation found them out even there, and the Indian Bureau soon permitted them to go north again.

While the prisoners at Camp Robinson were going through their time of trouble, Little Wolf and his band remained in their winter camp on the stream named the Lost Chokecherry in Nebraska's Sand Hills. They had settled in for the winter shortly after they split away from Dull Knife's band, and had spent the cold months in all the careful concealment of hunted animals, livings in pits in the stream bank, keeping their fires small and burning only fuel that would send up no smoke, always staying to the windswept ridges when they hunted or scouted—to avoid leaving tracks in the snow—and somehow the troops endlessly patrolling the great reaches of prairie never came upon them.

In March, they started on their way again, and on the twenty-fifth of the month, when they were just west of the headwaters of the Little Missouri River in the extreme southeastern corner of Montana Territory, the band, 112 strong, met strong cavalry forces under Lieutenant

W. P. Clark. It was not a surprise meeting; Northern Cheyennes living in the region had met Little Wolf and told him that Army forces were in the vicinity. The Cheyenne leader placed his people on a strong defensive position; then, when the cavalry forces appeared, he went out alone to talk to Lieutenant Clark, an old friend for whom he had scouted two years earlier, and an officer the Indians trusted completely. Clark could promise him only that he would do all he could to see that they were permitted to remain in the north—and for a mere lieutenant, that would be nothing, because even generals had not been able to keep promises made to Indians.

But Little Wolf accepted his assurance for want of anything better. He and his people rode along with the cavalry to Fort Keogh, where the Tongue River empties into the Yellowstone, and when they arrived there was no locking them up in barracks. They were back in the Powder River country where they wanted to be, and such was the public temper after what had happened to Dull Knife's band that not the Indian Bureau, nor Sherman nor Sheridan spoke of returning them to Indian Territory. They were permitted to remain where they were; later, the Tongue River Reservation was established for all Northern Cheyennes, to include portions of the valleys of both the Tongue and Rosebud. Here Dull Knife and most of the battered survivors of his band eventually came, and here were gathered the Northern Cheyennes who had never been sent south.

It was not, however, quite as they had dreamed it. Very soon the buffalo were gone in the North, too, and the Cheyennes found themselves not only idle and purposeless a good part of the time, but sometimes hungry when the government annuities failed to arrive. But that was the way it was with all Indians now, and if nothing else, they were home.

3. GHOST DANCE AND GATLING GUNS

And still the unnecessary and bloody little wars continued. In 1878, Nathan Meeker, a single-minded and arbitrary man, was appointed agent for the White River Utes, one of the three bands of a tribe whose reservation covered most of western Colorado. Meeker, a theorizer on agricultural subjects, looked on his position as an ideal opportunity to put some of his ideas into action, and he immediately proceeded to do so, attempting in the process to turn the Utes from hunters into farmers almost in a matter of weeks.

As Meeker became more and more demanding and high-handed, the Indians became more resentful. The explosion came in September 1879 when, after long and shrill demands, Meeker prevailed upon his superiors to have troops sent in for his protection. The Utes took the arrival of soldiers as a declaration of war, ambushing and besieging the column and killing eleven. At the same time, the agency was destroyed; Meeker and nine other white employees were slain, and Meeker's wife and daughter, and the wife of another employe were taken captive and handed around among the Indian men for a number of days until released.

The war, if such it can be called, was over as quickly as it had started, and Meeker's dreams and ambitions had been wrecked and his life taken by his own stubborn refusal to understand the customs and point of view of the Indians. But for Governor Frederick Pitkin of Colorado, the war was an unqualified success. He had been trying with indifferent success for some time to work up convincing atrocity cases against the Utes as an excuse to take their lands from them; now at last he had something spectacular to work with. He made the most of it.

"My idea is that, unless removed by the government, they must necessarily be exterminated," a reporter for the New York *Tribune* quoted Pitkin. "I could raise 25,000 men to protect the settlers in twenty-four hours. The State would be willing to settle the Indian problem at its own expense. The advantages that would accrue from the throwing open of twelve million acres of land to miners and settlers would more than compensate all the expenses incurred."

The attitude of the frontier toward the Indian could not have been stated much more cynically: land was everything; the rights of Indians nothing. There is no way of knowing how much of what Pitkin was saying was bluster and bluff, but the Federal government, probably remembering when Colonel Chivington led other Coloradans to do some exterminating, took no chances. The Utes were removed from the state, their great reservation turned over to white settlers. It made no difference that only one of the three bands of Utes had been involved in the affair, and only part of that band. All were moved to Utah, to share the reservation of the Uintah Utes there, each family on an individual piece of land. A portion of the southern band was permitted to remain on a small reserve in the southwestern part of Colorado, on arid land no white man could possibly want; they were granted this special favor because of the pleading of their chief, Ouray, who had always jumped through hoops for the white men.

That was almost the end of the Indian wars, but not quite. In the spring of 1885, a small group of Chiricahua Apaches, the stubbornest fighters of all, fled from their reservation under the leadership of their renegade chief, Geronimo, and disappeared into the almost trackless mountains of Arizona and Mexico. General Crook, who knew the Apaches as no other white man did (and who was convinced that every one of their outbreaks could be laid to white harassment, cupidity, and larceny), persuaded most of the hostiles to surrender after a strenuous ten-month campaign. Then he resigned as commander of the Department of Arizona in vigorous protest because President Cleveland and the commander of the Army, General Sheridan (he had succeeded Sherman in 1883), repudiated the surrender terms Crook had granted and, in a shameless breach of faith, had the Apaches sent to Florida for imprisonment for an indefinite period.

General Nelson Miles replaced Crook. There were only thirty-three Apaches still at large, and thirteen of them were women, but Miles chased them futilely for more than five months; he finally caught them only by adapting Crook's strategy and sending a couple of Apache scouts into the mountain to find and parley with them. Because Geronimo and his ragged handful of followers were weary and tired of fleeing, they agreed to give themselves up.

Less than three dozen Apaches had been hostile when General Miles induced them to surrender, yet the government gathered up the entire Chiricahua band, 498 in number, and sent them into captivity in Florida. These were people who had remained at peace when a minority of the band had followed Geronimo into the mountains. Among them were the scouts who had fought so hard for General Crook; their number included even the two scouts who had risked their lives at General Miles's request to go into the mountains to establish contact with Geronimo. All were sent into exile, and treated in no way different from those who had actually been hostile.

For those interested, it may be noted that the Chiricahuas never did return to their native Arizona. Many friends—chief among them General Crook until he died in 1890—worked for them, while they sickened and died in the lowland climate. In 1894 they were at last sent to Fort Sill in Oklahoma Territory, but not till 1913 was the unjust sentence of exile completely lifted. Even then, those who wished to return to the Southwest (many had farms in Oklahoma by then and remained there) were permitted only to join the Mescalero Apaches on their reservation in New Mexico; they were not allowed to go back to Arizona.

But that is looking ahead; no Indian in the years around 1880 knew what was going to happen to the Chiricahua Apaches forty years hence, and no one cared. They had their own troubles of the moment. Civilization was blotting out the last remnants of the old ways of life everywhere in the West, and in few places more thoroughly than on the Great Plains. There were still great spaces where a man could raise his eyes and still see nothing but grass and horizon—there are even today, although one must search well to find them—but with each passing year the open plain was giving way to cattle herds, sod shanties, plowed fields, and the sky-pointing towers of windmills.

Nothing did more to break up the open character of the plains than barbed wire. Fencing had been one of the unsolvable problems of living in a treeless country until Joseph F. Glidden of De Kalb, Illinois, devised a wire fence with barbs for use around his own farm. It worked so well he started a small factory in 1874 with five boys stringing barbs on wires; by 1880 he had a huge factory in De Kalb with 202 machines turning out 600 miles of fencing every ten hours. As fast as it was produced, this barbed wire was being strung over land where herds of buffalo had grazed less than ten years before.

The semblance of the old plains disappeared last in the North. Even while homesteaders were laying up blocks of sod to make their shanties in Kansas and Nebraska, and the cattlemen were fencing off the high plains with barbed wire, the Sioux were still hunting buffalo in the Dakotas and Montana. The last of the southern herd had been killed in Texas in 1878, except for a few scattered buffalo it did not pay the hide hunters to go after. The next spring the professionals moved up north with their hide wagons and their Sharp Fifties and commenced the final slaughter.

The last remnant of the great, brown living blanket that had once grazed the plains from Canada to Texas was now concentrated in Montana, and, to a lesser extent, in northwestern Dakota Territory. And there the professional hunters went to work with a skill that had been drawn fine with several years of practice. The grass to the north of the herd was burned over to discourage the beasts from migrating northward into Canada. The buffalo, surrounded on all sides, were helpless before the hunters, whose equipment now included telescopic sights. A hunter could lie, with his gun on a good rest, and wipe out a small herd from a distance; all he had to do was to keep knocking down the animal that became nervous and tried to lead the herd away.

The northern herd was much smaller than the huge masses of buffalo that had ranged in the south. It melted away under the guns of experts who seldom wasted a shot or spoiled a hide; the clumsy amateurs of the early days in Kansas who wasted more than they marketed were missing. "I saw buffaloes lying dead on the prairie so thick that one could hardly see the ground," a hunter described the scene created by the industrious killers along the Little Missouri in the winter of 1881–82. "A man could have walked for twenty miles upon their carcasses."

By the end of 1883 about all that did remain were the carcasses. The incessant shooting had driven the animals out of their normal migrating pattern, and a herd of about ten thousand wandered eastward across Dakota where the hunters made short work of most of them. But a thousand or more evaded the hunters, and were located by the Sioux. Sitting Bull led his band out from Standing Rock agency to hunt the buffalo as they had in days past. They found the herd about midway between Bismarck and the Black Hills, and in two days of hunting in October, wiped it out to the last animal. It was the last time a band of Indians ever rode out to hunt buffalo.

It was also just about the last time anyone hunted buffalo. The season was very nearly over at the time of Sitting Bull's hunt, and after the hide men had outfitted and gone out at the beginning of the next season, their first impression was that the buffalo had wandered farther from their accustomed range than usual. It was only after they had searched as far west as the Rockies, among the stinking carcasses and bones that marked their deeds of prowess of former years, and had found no buffalo, that it came to them that the Great Slaughter was over. No hides came off the plains in 1884; the carcasses disintegrated, and for years homesteaders earned an extra dollar now and then by gathering bones and hauling them to the nearest railroad station.

There had been a time when it was an article of faith that the civilizing of the Plains Indians would follow close on the annihilation of the buffalo—and a civilized Indian was universally understood to mean one who had given up everything of his own culture and had become an imitation white man. Once the buffalo were gone, it had been believed, the Indian would be forced to give up his roaming ways and settle down to feed and clothe himself by the sweat of his brow as a farmer, a herdsman, or a laborer. There were a couple of things wrong with this theory. One was that the former nomadic tribes had no experience in farming, and although the government promised implements, seeds, and instruction every time a treaty was made, it produced precious little that was tangible.

What was even more to the point was that almost all tribes, former farming peoples from the east and from the tall-grass prairie as well as the one-time horse-and-buffalo tribes, had been put on land that could by no means be called the best. Dohesan, a Kiowa chief, remarked acidly that if the President was so eager to have Indians raise corn, he should have given them land that would grow corn.

But even yet the land greed of the settlers was not satisfied. The biggest prize remaining was Indian Territory, the last piece of the old and forgotten permanent Indian Country. In the beginning, it had been the land of the Five Civilized Tribes until the government had taken the western half away from them on the thin pretext that it was punishing them for treason during the Civil War; the vacated western part was used as a dumping ground for unwanted tribes that were in the way of the tide of settlement elsewhere. All this has been detailed in earlier pages. However, after the other tribes had been brought in, a large tract of land in the center of Indian Territory remained empty. These "Unassigned Lands" began to be irresistible to settlers as early as 1879, and organizations of land-seekers, who came to be called "Boomers," persistently moved in and were ejected by troops. When they transferred their efforts to Washington and began speaking the loud, clear language of votes, Congress listened and soon opened the Unassigned Lands to white settlement. The result was one of the most fantastic episodes in American history, when a pistol shot at high noon on April 22, 1889 set off tens of thousands of men and a good number of women from the Kansas border by wagon, horseback, railroad train (a line ran south through the lands), and even on foot to stake out claims.

Before night, the entire Unassigned Lands, almost two million acres, had been claimed and entire cities had been platted. Once the camel's head was in the tent, the rest of the beast quickly followed. The next year, the entire western half of Indian Territory, along with the Panhandle to the west, which was part of no state or territory, was organized into the Territory of Oklahoma. The Indian reservations were sold during the next several years and the land opened to settlers some of it by land rushes, some by lotteries. The eastern half of the former Indian Territory, the lands of the Five Civilized Tribes, continued to bear the old name for a few years more. Then the tribes, although they were operating as strong, effective nations with their laws and governments, were coerced into giving up their free existence. The result was the extinguishment of the last part of Indian Territory, which was merged with Oklahoma Territory.

But this, again, is moving ahead of the story. A great deal of other Indian land was taken in smaller bites, a nibbling away by "adjusting" reservation boundaries. Scores of such changes were made during the decade of the 1880's by simple presidential decree. Some of these adjustments, let the truth be said, were for increased efficiency in administration and two or three did correct minor injustices, but most of them seemed to end up leaving the Indians with less territory, or edging them onto land that was more rocky, sandy, or hilly.

There were few ways in which these were good years for Indians. Hunger was often with them; deprived of most ways of obtaining their own food, they had to depend overmuch on the annuities that were usually late in arriving and short in amount. Children were often virtually kidnaped to be sent away to boarding school, or sometimes rations were withheld from parents who refused to let their youngsters be taken. Disease was prevalent, fostered by malnutrition and exposure. Even the fact of being an Indian was a cause for shame as both agents and missionaries often tried to root out symbols of the old culture: tribal dances, Indian clothing, even the traditional way the men wore their hair.

In a time of misery and hopelessness, people who can see no way out of their troubles and woes are prone to look to some higher power for help, and the voice that now spoke to the unhappy Indians came from Nevada, from a messiah named Wovoka. This young man—he was about thirty-five—was a Paiute; he had never been outside the narrow limits of mountain-girt Mason Valley (about fifty miles southeast of Reno). When his father died when he was a young boy, he had been taken in by the family of a rancher named Dave Wilson, and so had come to be called Jack Wilson by all the whites in the valley (he had, several years before becoming famous, adopted the name of his grandfather, Kwohitsauq or "Big Rumbling Belly," which is undoubtedly a perfectly good Paiute name, but mercifully did not replace his boyhood name, Wovoka or "Cutter," in general use).

Wovoka received his inspiration from on high in 1888 during an eclipse which occurred while he was ill with a severe fever. The event, which he considered supernatural—"the sun died"—had a powerful effect on a mind disordered by fever. He was taken up into heaven where he not only saw God in a long white robe but all the people who had died in the past, now forever young and happy and engaged in their old sports and pursuits. God directed Wovoka to go back and teach his people to put aside war and love each other, and that they must also live in peace with the white men.

But the heart of the revelations was that the earth was to be regenerated and returned to the Indians, including all the dead of the past who would come back in all the beauty and strength of their youth. The Indians were given a special ceremonial dance, which required five successive nights to complete; the oftener they performed the dance, the more they would hasten the coming of the millennial future.

Wovoka, whose beliefs were a strange blend of Indian religion and the Christian theology he had learned from the Wilson family, apparently never claimed to be other than a prophet, although he had received certain small powers from God, such as songs by which he could produce fog, snow, a shower or a hard rain, or sunshine (once he had offered, for an annual fee, to keep Nevada supplied with rain but was ignored, a short-sighted act by a state which can use a great deal more precipitation). But rain-making and such were minor matters; it was the vision of the return of the Indians' old days of glory that won him his following as soon as he began preaching his doctrine. His own people, the Paiutes, danced, and soon Paiutes went out as missionaries to spread the new gospel to the tribes beyond the mountain valleys.

And the tribes, in their unhappiness, listened eagerly, because here was exactly what they wanted to hear. The Arapahoes and Cheyennes, both northern and southern, the Bannocks, Sioux, Shoshones, Utes and other tribes sent delegates to talk to the messiah; they returned full of wonders to start the dance—which the whites had named the Ghost

Dance because it was to help bring back the dead—among their own tribesmen.

The Ghost Dance religion spread over most of the West, with the exception of the Columbia River country and much of the Southwest. Each tribe practiced it with its own variations, just as there are differences of liturgy among Christian denominations, but all believed in the same basic thing: the world made young again and returned to the Indians, with the dead come back to enjoy the good life. As they danced to bring the new day nearer, the excess of their emotions sent many of them into trances in which they saw visions—and this appears to be much of the hold it had over many of them, almost like a narcotic—and from their visions they built most of the simple, chanting songs which they used in subsequent dances. They are songs without much meaning today, but others are still all too clear, as when the Arapaho dancers sang:

> My Father, have pity on me!
> I have nothing to eat,
> I am dying of thirst—
> Everything is gone!

White people anywhere in the vicinity of Indian reservations became nervous at the activity and chanting and interpreted it as a war dance, but the usual talk of troops and protection usually disappeared rather quickly when investigation showed how little the white community had to worry about. The Ghost Dance was no war dance; the full participation of women should have indicated that to the most suspicious white observer. After all, why should they fight when the world was going to become theirs only for believing and dancing—and in as short a time as a year or two, according to Wovoka?

There was one place where the Ghost Dance did take on a slight martial note. Among the Sioux, where the new religion happened to coincide with a number of causes of unrest, "Ghost shirts" magically impervious to white men's bullets were worn, at first only in the dance, but later beneath the outer garments at other times.

The catalogue of misery and despair of the Sioux had grown very long by 1890. There was of course, the passing of the buffalo and the growing scarcity of deer and other game which deprived them of food and clothing, and except for what the poor land of their reservation would produce, put them at the mercy of government annuities. Then,

The Sioux Reservations in 1890–91
At the time of the Ghost Dance Troubles

NORTH DAKOTA

MONTANA

MISSOURI R.

LITTLE MISSOURI R.

LITTLE MISSOURI R.

CEDAR CR.

CANNONBALL R.

STANDING ROCK
RESERVATION

Standing Rock Agency
Ft. Yates

N. D.
S. D.

CAMP OF SITTING BULL

GRAND R.

CAMP OF GALL

45°30'

FLIGHT OF THE
FUGITIVES

MOREAU R.

CHEYENNE RIVER
RESERVATION

SOUTH DAKOTA

Ft. Meade

BELLE FOURCHE R.

CAMP OF HUMP

Cheyenne River Agency
Ft. Sully

Ft. Bennett

Pierre

CROW CREEK
RESERVATION

CAMP OF BIG FOOT

FLIGHT OF
BIG FOOT'S BAND

LOWER BRULE
RESERVATION

BLACK HILLS

ELK CR.

SPRING CR.

Rapid City

CHEYENNE R.

Ft. Lookout

Ft. Thompson

CHEYENNE R.

WHITE R.

MISSOURI R.

BADLANDS

CAPTURED BY TROOPS

PINE RIDGE
RESERVATION

ROSEBUD
RESERVATION

WOUNDED KNEE CR.

WOUNDED KNEE
MASSACRE

Rosebud Agency

WYOMING

Pine Ridge Agency

NIOBRARA R.

NORTH PLATTE R.

N
W E
S

Miles
0   100

103°   101°   99°

only the year before, they had been separated from more of their land. About one-third of the Great Sioux Reservation had been lost when the Black Hills and adjacent regions were taken from the Indians during the Sioux War. A few years later, settlers in the Black Hills were demanding a corridor to eastern Dakota so they would not have to cross the reservation. They finally got their passage in 1889; it carved out the heart of the remaining reservation, cutting it in two and taking half its area, an opening sixty miles wide—no danger of rubbing elbows against Indian land on either side as they went down that alleyway. The remaining land was divided into five reservations.

The Sioux had been assured they would continue to receive the same rations after giving up so much of their lands, but immediately after the agreement had been approved, Congress cut the beef ration by 2,000,000 pounds at Rosebud Reservation, by 1,000,000 pounds at Pine Ridge, and by lesser amounts at the other three reservations. When the agent at Pine Ridge informed the Indian Bureau in April, 1890 that the monthly beef issue was only 205,000 pounds when agreements with the Sioux called for 470,400, he received the helpful answer that it was better to give half rations all year than to give three-quarters or full rations for a few months and none for the rest of the year. However, this was one case where the Indian Office was not much to blame. The fault rested with Congress which then, as ever, economized in the wrong places.

In both 1889 and 1890, severe outbreaks of measles, influenza, and whooping cough caused many deaths. Agency physicians blamed the high death rate on the poor physical condition of the Indians due to hunger. Whatever the cause, it greatly increased the mood of gloom and hopelessness affecting the Sioux. So did poor harvests and drought.

Into this unhappy situation, in March of 1890, came a group of returning Sioux who had been sent the previous autumn to visit the messiah and learn about the new religion. The stories they brought back were wonderful indeed. Wovoka had come to earth in a cloud of smoke to talk to them, and had shown them nail marks on his hands and feet; the very next spring he was going to wipe out the white men for being so wicked to him at his first coming to earth. When they were returning home, they had come on an encampment of the dead of their tribe and had visited with old friends for some time. On continuing their journey, they found a herd of buffalo (these buffalo had apparently returned from the dead for the occasion, too), and had killed one and feasted on its meat; head, hoofs, and tail were left lying as Wovoka had instructed them, and as they walked off, had reassembled into a new buffalo. This appears to be the most outrageous kind of fabrication, but many visitors to Wovoka came back with tales no less fantastic; apparently in their extremely suggestible state of mind the difference between reality and illusion all but disappeared.

The delegates made their report at Pine Ridge agency and a council was called to discuss these marvels, but the agent, Colonel Gallagher, arrested three of the delegates and threw them in jail for two days. This attempt to nip the Ghost Dance before it got started failed because very shortly another delegate, Kicking Bear, arrived after having tarried on the trip home to visit the Northern Arapahoes on their reservation in Wyoming, and now brought the exhilarating information that the Arapahoes had not only taken up the dance but were able to see and talk to dead family and friends during their trances.

The story produced wild excitement. Red Cloud announced that he was accepting the new religion. The famed chief was considerably older than when he had closed the Bozeman Trail, but his leadership was still accepted by most of the six thousand Oglalas on Pine Ridge Reservation. The first dance was begun a few miles from the agency, with some of the returned delegates serving as priests and leaders.

But while the Ghost Dance religion was promising a glorious hereafter, the present was looking more and more grim. Agent Gallagher, who had earlier written the Indian Bureau that his charges at Pine Ridge were getting less than half the beef they were supposed to, was writing more letters as the summer wore on, reporting that the Indians were suffering from hunger. The Bureau received warnings from other sources as well that the Sioux were becoming increasingly restive, but no more food arrived, and in the summer the Pine Ridge Indians rebelled and refused to accept the half-ration. They eventually took it—they had not much choice—but Gallagher decided his job was a hopeless one and resigned.

He was replaced in early October by one D. F. Royer. Few men less qualified have held the post, even in a service known for the general sorry level of its appointees. He was described as "destitute of any of those qualities by which he could justly lay claim to the position—experience, force of character, courage and sound judgment." The Indians quickly took his measure and dubbed him Lakota Kokipa-Koshkala, "Young-man-afraid-of-the-Sioux." From the first he had no control over his Indians; before he had been there a week he had stood by helplessly while a handful of them had released a prisoner from the jail. Before two weeks were up he was reporting that more than half his six thousand Indians were dancing, and that he was afraid troops would be needed because the situation was entirely beyond the control of the Indian police at his disposal.

The Sioux were dancing at the other four reservations, too, but the agents there, better endowed than Royer with judgment and courage, remained calm and tried to stop the dancing, though with only partial success. The fervor with which the Sioux were accepting the Ghost Dance religion was a measure of their need of it.

Agent Royer became more and more frightened by the strange chanting and dancing going on a few miles from his agency. He wrote to the Indian Bureau on October 30, saying that the situation could be saved only by the arrival of six hundred or seven hundred troops; within a week he was sending daily telegrams asking for permission to come to Washington to explain, but was told that the place of an agent during a crisis was at his post. At last, on November 15, he was directed to report the situation to the commander of Fort Robinson in northern Nebraska, the nearest Army post. Royer, by now in a state of near-panic, had sent off a message saying that the Sioux were wild and out of their heads, and that at least a thousand soldiers were needed to cope with the situation. But Royer was not speaking completely from hysteria, for the agent at adjoining Rosebud Reservation reported that his Indians were so engrossed in their dancing as to be beyond the control of himself and his police.

The old formality was observed, of transferring jurisdiction over the Sioux from the Interior to the War Department. The Army at once began moving units into the region, most of them into the area around the Pine Ridge agency, until within a matter of days it had almost three thousand men in the field. On the appearance of the troops, a large number of the Sioux, almost two thousand, living on Pine Ridge and Rosebud reservations fled to an area called the Bad Lands on the western edge of Pine Ridge, a place of hills, canyons, and weirdly eroded tablelands which provided a hiding place where an army might not find them. Within a short time, as more refugees joined them, their numbers increased to at least three thousand. The escaped Indians, some of them rebellious but most only frightened, were declared to be hostiles, although the last thing most of them wanted was to engage in hostilities with Army forces. The movement to the Bad Lands had been almost entirely a stampede caused by panic at the appearance of the soldiers.

Things became quieter on the reservations with so many troops around. Most of the Ghost Dancing ended or was reduced to a much smaller scale; the main centers where it continued were at the camp of Sitting Bull on Grand River in Standing Rock reservation, northern-most of the five reserves, and at the camp of a chief named Big Foot on the Cheyenne River. The Indian Bureau, feeling that it should get some use out of all the troops on hand, asked its agents to submit lists of trouble-makers who should be arrested and removed, with the help of the military if necessary. Among them, four of the agents produced a total of about fifteen names. The fifth agent was Royer; all by him-self he came up with a list of sixty-four which was a "conservative estimate" and to which no one paid any attention.

As it turned out, most of the men honored by being included on the list were in the Bad Lands at the moment, but the one considered the most potentially dangerous of them all, Sitting Bull, was within easy reach. There is not much doubt that the great medicine man was a center of mischief during most of the time since he had reached the agreement with the government that had let him return from Canada in 1881. Except for joining Buffalo Bill Cody's Wild West show for a season and touring the country, he had remained on or near the reser-vation, brooding on the past and feeding his hate of white men. Toward the last he refused even to come in to the agency. He was a matter of concern to the authorities because he was a rallying point for all con-servative and dissident elements among the Sioux. When the Army took control of the Sioux reservations, it moved quickly to arrest the famous medicine man, and as its deputy it called on William F. Cody. It was believed that Cody had a great deal of influence over Sitting Bull, supposedly the result of friendship engendered by shared experi-ences in show business, and he was given authority to reach surrender terms with the Sioux leader or, failing that, to arrest him and bring him in by force. Cody arrived at Fort Yates on November 28, but the scheme was called off when Agent James McLaughlin of Standing Rock heard of it and urgently protested.

Wait until the weather got colder, said McLaughlin. Then Sitting Bull and his band would not be so likely to bolt and join the hostiles in the Bad Lands. McLaughlin also felt that the arrest should be made by his own Indian police, who were trained, dependable men, and not as liable to arouse opposition as white soldiers. The agent got his way; the arrest was deferred until December 12 when orders came to Colonel Drum commanding Fort Yates to make arrangements with McLaughlin to take Sitting Bull in. The two decided to arrest the famous chief on the twentieth, when most of the Indians would be at the agency collecting their annuities and Sitting Bull would have few potential defenders.

But on the afternoon of the fourteenth, a messenger came from the Indian school near Sitting Bull's camp, saying that Sitting Bull had just received an invitation to come to Pine Ridge because God was about to appear there. The medicine man was even then making preparations for the trip, the informant said.

It was then sundown, but McLaughlin and Colonel Drum made plans to arrest Sitting Bull the next morning. The agent already had police watching the Sioux leader's camp; more were assembled by hard-riding couriers until forty-three men, under the command of Lieutenant Bull Head, approached the camp at daybreak. Two troops of cavalry, about one hundred men, with a Hotchkiss gun (a rapid-fire gun that shot two-inch explosive shells), rode more than thirty miles from the fort during the night to be within supporting distance of the police.

Indian police had been first authorized by Congress in 1878, and eventually they were used on a majority of reservations, although to varying extents. Those on the Sioux reservation were, in general, well-trained men with excellent morale. But Agent McLaughlin had miscalculated in thinking that an arrest by them would be less offensive to Sitting Bull than one by white soldiers. For the police represented the most progressive element among the Sioux, those who had accepted the white man's way completely. Sitting Bull and those around him were the most conservative element; the medicine man himself was an apostle of the good old days and looked with scorn on all Indians who cooperated with the white authorities.

At dawn on December 15, these two opposed forces confronted each other. The police surrounded Sitting Bull's house; then Lieutenant Bull Head and several others entered to find the prophet asleep on the floor. When he was awakened and told he was a prisoner, Sitting Bull agreed rather mildly to go with them to the agency, but as his followers began to gather outside, calling on him to resist, he started to berate the police for breaking into his house and waking him. When his seventeen-year-old son, Crow Foot, taunted him as a coward, he abruptly refused to go, and called on his people to rescue him.

By that time, the police outside had been backed up against the house wall by more than a hundred threatening men, and as Sitting Bull was brought outside and the police attempted to clear a path, one of the followers shot Bull Head in the side. The police lieutenant was walking beside Sitting Bull; as he sagged, mortally wounded, he turned and shot the Sioux Chief in the side as another policeman, Red Tomahawk, behind Sitting Bull, shot the leader through the head. The entire situation exploded into a deadly, close-quarter combat, in which the training of the police more than made up for the difference in numbers. They drove their attackers off and held the house until the cavalry came up to their relief about two hours later.

Six policemen were killed or fatally wounded, while their assailants lost eight, including Sitting Bull and his son, Crow Foot. Sitting Bull died in his fifty-sixth year, a great man, not only a valiant fighting leader, but a famous prophet and medicine man. In the end, however, the gift of prophesy faded; during his last years his visions were increasingly of the past.

Next after Sitting Bull, the most dangerous leader among the Sioux outside the Bad Lands was assumed to be a chief named Hump, head of a band of about four hundred, whose camp was on the Cheyenne River. Dancing had been going on at his camp on the Cheyenne River for several weeks, and civil authorities considered him so sullen and hostile that it would probably be dangerous for anyone even to attempt to talk to him. To cope with this problem, the Army had a Captain E. P. Ewers transferred from Texas because Ewers had been in charge of Hump and his band in former years and had gained their confidence.

Captain Ewers cheerfully disregarded the dark warnings and left Fort Bennett on the Missouri with a lieutenant as his only companion. They rode sixty miles west on the plains, where they were met by Hump who had heard Ewers was coming; the chief greeted the captain like the old friend he was. When it was explained to the Sioux chief that the military authorities would like to have him take his people to Fort Bennett to get them away from hostile Indians who were causing trouble, Hump immediately answered that he would do anything that General Miles wanted. He not only brought his band to the fort, but at once enlisted as a scout and did valuable service for the

Army in getting fugitives from Sitting Bull's band to surrender rather than join the hostiles in the Bad Lands. The case of Hump was a classic example of how little the so-called Indian experts often really knew about their Indians, and of how much could be accomplished by a man the Indians had learned to trust.

With Sitting Bull dead, and Hump on the side of the angels, Chief Big Foot was next on the list of supposed trouble-makers. The chief and his village on the Cheyenne River were being watched by Lieutenant Colonel E. V. Sumner with one troop of the 8th Cavalry. Big Foot had voluntarily assured Sumner that he meant no trouble and was not going to run away. The relationship between chief and officer appears to have been relaxed and friendly. When Big Foot came in mid-December to bid good-bye because he and his people were going to the agency for their annuities, Sumner did not send an escort, and when orders came a day later from General Miles's headquarters to arrest Big Foot, he demurred. Big Foot was keeping his warriors under control, he reported, and if he were arrested and taken away from them, trouble might occur. Besides, he could always arrest the chief on his return from the agency if it still seemed advisable.

But very shortly afterward, Sumner received word that Big Foot's band had camped and had been joined by some refugees from the camp of the late Sitting Bull. He immediately set out in pursuit but had traveled no more than a dozen miles or so when Big Foot met him and informed him that he was still friendly. Then why, asked Sumner, had he taken in these other people, knowing they were refugees from their own reservation (there appear to have been thirty-eight of these dangerous characters). Because, replied the chief, they had come to his people tired, hungry, footsore, and almost naked; they were his brothers and his relatives, and he had given them shelter and food; no one with any feelings could have done any less.

It was a good answer, and it is hard to understand why Sumner did not accept it at face value. On the contrary, he now considered Big Foot's and his band as having had outlawed themselves. They were brought back to their village, and Big Foot was informed that he and his people would be taken under escort to the agency the next day. The chief not only protested the removal because he had done nothing wrong, but added that there would be trouble forcing the women and children away from the camp again because they had suffered from hunger and cold during the previous few days when they were traveling.

But Colonel Sumner was adamant. And since it was fairly plain that he was going to have to use some force, he sent out a call for additional units of the regiment. Word that more troops were on the way was carried to the Indians, and that evening Sumner was informed that the entire band had fled, and were headed in the general direction of the Bad Lands, probably meaning to join the hostiles already there.

Except for the few military units engaged in controlling potential trouble-makers in the north, the great body of troops was operating against the Indians in the Bad Lands. Almost three thousand of them were there, under the immediate command of General John R. Brooke, although General Miles was in over-all command. It was the general strategy of the two men to avoid bloodshed if at all possible, and Brooke had thrown a strong wall of troops to the north and west of the hostiles' stronghold. With these he maintained a steady pressure which gradually forced the Indians toward the east and Pine Ridge agency.

Most of the Indians were weary and cold and ready to give up anyway; some of them never had had any real chip on their shoulder but had fled only from fear. Along with military pressure, General Brooke got word to the Indians that he would protect their rights as far as he was able, and this helped swing the balance toward surrender, even though the Sioux had scant faith left in the government. The hostiles began moving in, and on December 27, the entire body left the Bad Lands to go to the agency. There had not been a single battle except for a fight between hostiles and Cheyenne scouts; the only engagements between troops and Sioux were two or three very minor skirmishes. But the book had not yet been closed on the uprising, if such it can be called.

Big Foot and his people, fleeing south, had nothing on their minds except to get away from soldiers. They passed very near several ranches without committing any depredations, and once went directly through a pasture without taking even one of the horses or cattle there. At the edge of the Bad Lands, they sent scouts to make contact with the Indians camped in the stronghold, but no answers were received to their signals for the hostiles had already gone and were on their way to the agency. It was then, on December 28, as the band was proceeding along the edge of the Bad Lands, that it was intercepted by

Major S. M. Whitside with four troops of the 7th Cavalry, about two hundred men.

Big Foot was ill, too sick with pneumonia to ride on a horse, and was being carried on a travois. He got to his feet, had a white flag raised, and asked for a parley. Whitside refused, insisting on nothing other than unconditional surrender, and the Sioux chief, with only about one hundred cold and hungry warriors, was in no position to resist even if he had been of a mind to. The band was conducted by the cavalry to a place called Wounded Knee which was only a post office and a few scattered Indian houses near Wounded Knee Creek. There they went into camp as directed by Major Whitside, while the cavalry set up its tents nearby.

General Brooke, when informed of the capture, sent Colonel George A. Forsyth, commander of the 7th Cavalry, with four more troops of the regiment to reinforce the guard around the Sioux. A company of scouts also joined the guard, and a battery of four Hotchkiss guns, making a total of 470 men to keep a watch over about 340 Indians, of whom only 106 were warriors.

Forsyth provided a tent warmed with a camp stove for the sick Big Foot and sent his own regimental surgeon to attend the chief, set a strong cordon of troops around the Indian camp, and made plans to disarm the Sioux in the morning. It was General Miles's intention either to return the band to their own reservation, or possibly to remove them entirely from the country for a while until the excitement had died down a bit—he had not yet made up his mind which.

Colonel Forsyth, whom the combined workings of promotion, rotation of duty, and happenstance had brought to command of the 7th Cavalry, was the same man who had been in command during the epic defense at Beecher Island twenty-two years earlier. There had been a great deal of campaigning on the plains for him in the years since; after the next morning it was always to be a debatable question whether he had grown as much in judgment during that time as he had accumulated years of experience. Note, too, that a number of the 7th's company commanders—among them Captains Wallace, Varnum, Moylan, Edgerly, and Godfrey—were men who had stood on the hill with Reno and Benteen at the Little Bighorn to beat back the Sioux charges, and a desire for revenge may still have smoldered in some of them.

The next morning, December 29, Forsyth made ready to disarm the Sioux. Their lodges had been set up on a flat piece of ground a short

Wounded Knee
DEC. 29, 1890

The disposition of the 7th Cavalry around the camp of Big Foot's band at the beginning of the massacre

INDIAN HOUSE

WOUNDED KNEE CREEK

INDIAN HOUSE

INDIAN HOUSE AND WOUNDED KNEE P.O.

4 HOTCHKISS GUNS

"B" DISMOUNTED

TROOPS "A" AND "I", 76 MEN, DISMOUNTED, RINGING CAMP.

COUNCIL RING

"K" DISMOUNTED

SIOUX CAMP

PONIES

TROOP "G", MOUNTED

DRY RAVINE

SCOUTS

INDIAN

TROOP "D", MOUNTED

TROOP "C", MOUNTED

ABOUT 80 MEN AND OFFICERS TOTAL, BOTH TROOPS.

distance west of Wounded Knee Creek, which there flows approximately north. Just south of the tepees, a dry ravine running from west to east opens into the creek; to the north of the camp was a slight hill on which the four Hotchkiss guns were posted, and trained directly on the camp. On all sides of the camp, soldiers were stationed, both mounted and on foot. The Sioux had hoisted a white flag in the center of their camp as an indication of their peaceful intentions and a guarantee of safety.

At about eight o'clock the warriors came out of their lodges and sat on the ground in a semicircle. They were instructed to go, about a score at a time, into their tepees, and return with their weapons. The first twenty went, and came back with only two guns. The officers conferred. It was plain that this method was not going to produce the guns. Troops stationed by the council ring were ordered to move up to within ten yards of the seated warriors, and other enlisted men were detailed to search the tepees. It is exactly at this point that the situation began to get out of hand—and it is hard not to blame Forsyth, who approved the action, for letting it get out of control.

The soldiers acted like bully-boys, overturning beds and other lodge furnishings, shoving aside the women who protested loudly and tried to bar their way. The Sioux men were becoming greatly agitated at the sounds of strife from their tepees and the voices of their women, especially since they did not know what was going on. Most of them had knives under their blankets, and were approaching a state of mind when they were ready to use them. In the midst of this tense situation, a medicine man, Yellow Bird, walked about, blowing an eagle-bone whistle, and calling on the men to resist because, as he reminded them, they were invulnerable to bullets because of the Ghost shirts they wore. The officers did not understand Sioux; the dangerous trend of Yellow Bird's exhortations passed them by.

The search was completed and produced about forty guns, most of them antiquated and worn pieces. But one weapon they did not find, for the good reason that it was being carried under his blanket by a young Indian, name unknown but probably Black Fox, who was described by a Sioux witness to the event, later testifying in Washington, as "a crazy man, a young man of very bad influence and in fact a nobody, . . ." But for a brief moment he was a very important somebody as he pulled out the gun and fired into the line of soldiers, killing one of them.

Bibliography

Athearn, Robert G., *William Tecumseh Sherman and the Settlement of the West*, Norman, Okla., 1956.

Beal, Merrill D., *"I Will Fight No More Forever,"* Seattle, 1963.

Billington, Ray Allen, *Westward Expansion*, New York, 1949.

Bourke, Captain John G., *On the Border with Crook*, New York, 1892.

Brady, Cyrus T., *Indian Fights and Fighters*, New York, 1904.

Brown, Dee, *Fort Phil Kearny*, New York, 1962.

Bryant, Charles S., and Abel B. Murch, *A History of the Great Massacre by the Sioux Indians in Minnesota*, Cincinnati, 1864.

Carrington, Margaret I., *Absaraka, Land of the Crows*, Philadelphia, 1868.

Clapesattle, Helen, *The Doctors Mayo*, Minneapolis, 1941.

Clark, Dan Elbert, *The West in American History*, New York, 1937.

Crook, General George, *His Autobiography*, as edited and annotated by Martin F. Schmitt, Norman, Okla., 1960.

Custer, George A., *My Life on the Plains*, New York, 1876.

Custer, Elizabeth Bacon, *Boots and Saddles*, New York, 1885.

———, *Following the Guidon*, New York, 1890.

———, *Tenting on the Plains*, New York, 1887.

Ellison, R. S., "John 'Portugee' Phillips and His Famous Ride," *Old Travois Trails*, Vol. II, No. 1, 1941.

Emmett, Robert, *The Last War Trail: The Utes and the Settlement of Colorado*, Norman, Okla., 1954.

Finerty, John F., *War Path and Bivouac, or the Conquest of the Sioux*, Chicago, 1890.

Folwell, William W., *A History of Minnesota* (Vol. 2), St. Paul, 1924.

Freeman, Winfield, "The Battle of the Arickaree," *Kansas Historical Collections*, Vol. VI, pp. 346–67.

Gard, Wayne, *The Great Buffalo Hunt*, New York, 1959.

Godfrey, General Edward S., "Custer's Last Battle," *Century* Magazine, Vol. XLIII, January, 1892.

Graham, Colonel W. A., *The Story of the Little Big Horn*, 5th edition, New York, 1962.

Grinnell, George B., *The Cheyenne Indians*, New Haven, 1924.

——, *The Fighting Cheyennes*, New York, 1915.

Guthrie, John, "The Fetterman Massacre," *Annals of Wyoming*, Vol. 9, 1932.

Hagan, William T., *American Indians*, Chicago, 1961.

Haines, Francis, *The Nez Percés*, Norman, Okla., 1955.

Heard, Isaac V., *History of the Sioux War and Massacres of 1862 and 1863*, New York, 1864.

Hebard, Grace R., and E. A. Brininstool, *The Bozeman Trail* (2 vols.), Cleveland, 1922.

Hodge, Frederick Webb (editor), *Handbook of the American Indians North of Mexico*, American Bureau of Ethnology, Smithsonian Institute, Washington, D.C., 1912.

Hoig, Stan, *The Sand Creek Massacre*, Norman, Okla., 1961.

Jones, Evan, *The Minnesota*, New York, 1962.

Josephy, Alvin M., Jr., *The Patriot Chiefs*, New York, 1961.

Knight, Oliver, *Following the Indian Wars*, Norman, Okla., 1960.

Lavender, David, *Bent's Fort*, New York, 1954.

Lowie, Robert H., *Indians of the Plains*, Garden City, N.Y., 1963.

McConkey, Harriet E., *Dakota War Whoop*, St. Paul, 1864.

McLaughlin, James, *My Friend the Indian*, New York, 1926.

Madsen, Brigham D., *The Bannock of Idaho*, Caldwell, Idaho, 1958.

Meacham, Alfred B., *The Tragedy of the Lava Beds*, Washington, D.C., 1883.

Mellor, William J., "The Military Investigation of Colonel John M. Chivington Following the San Creek Massacre," *The Chronicles of Oklahoma*, Vol. XVI, No. 4, December 1938.

Miles, General Nelson A., *Personal Recollections and Observations*, Chicago, 1897.

Mooney, James, *Calendar History of the Kiowa Indians*, 17th Annual Report (1895–96), Part 1, Bureau of American Ethnology, Smithsonian Institute, Washington, D.C., 1898.

——, *The Ghost Dance Religion and the Sioux Outbreak of 1890*, 14th Annual Report (1892–93), Part 2, Bureau of American Ethnology, Smithsonian Institute, Washington, D.C., 1895.

Murray, Keith A., *The Modocs and Their War*, Norman, Okla., 1959.

Payne, Davis P., *Captain Jack, Modoc Renegade*, Portland, Ore., 1938.

Paxson, Frederic L., *History of the American Frontier*, Boston, 1924.

——, *The Last American Frontier*, New York, 1910.

Richardson, R. N., and C. C. Rister, *The Greater Southwest*, Glendale, Calif., 1934.

Riegel, R. E., *America Moves West*, New York, 1947.

Rister, Carl C., *Border Command: General Phil Sheridan in the West*, Norman, Okla., 1944.

——, *Border Captives*, Norman, Okla., 1940.

Royce, Charles C., *Indian Land Cessions in the United States*, 18th Annual Report

(1896–97), Part 2, Bureau of American Ethnology, Smithsonian Institute, Washington, D.C., 1899.

Sandoz, Mari, *Cheyenne Autumn*, New York, 1953.

Satterlee, M. P., *A Detailed Account of the Massacre in 1862*, Minneapolis, 1923.

Seymour, Flora W., *Indian Agents of the Old Frontier*, New York, 1941.

Van de Water, Frederic F., *Glory-Hunter: A Life of General Custer*, New York, 1934.

Vestal, Stanley, *Sitting Bull*, Boston, 1932.

Webb, Walter P., *The Great Plains*, Boston, 1936.

Wheeler, Colonel Homer, *Buffalo Days*, Indianapolis, 1925.

Wyman, Walker D., *The Wild Horse of the West*, Lincoln, Neb., 1945.

Index

Index